HANDBOOK
of
PSYCHOLOGY

HANDBOOK
of
PSYCHOLOGY

VOLUME 11
FORENSIC PSYCHOLOGY

Alan M. Goldstein

Volume Editor

Irving B. Weiner

Editor-in-Chief

John Wiley & Sons, Inc.

Library of Congress Cataloging-in-Publication Data:

Handbook of psychology / Irving B. Weiner, editor-in-chief.
     p.   cm.
    Includes bibliographical references and indexes.
    Contents: v. 1. History of psychology / edited by Donald K. Freedheim — v. 2. Research methods in psychology / edited by John A. Schinka, Wayne F. Velicer — v. 3. Biological psychology / edited by Michela Gallagher, Randy J. Nelson — v. 4. Experimental psychology / edited by Alice F. Healy, Robert W. Proctor — v. 5. Personality and social psychology / edited by Theodore Millon, Melvin J. Lerner — v. 6. Developmental psychology / edited by Richard M. Lerner, M. Ann Easterbrooks, Jayanthi Mistry — v. 7. Educational psychology / edited by William M. Reynolds, Gloria E. Miller — v. 8. Clinical psychology / edited by George Stricker, Thomas A. Widiger — v. 9. Health psychology / edited by Arthur M. Nezu, Christine Maguth Nezu, Pamela A. Geller — v. 10. Assessment psychology / edited by John R. Graham, Jack A. Naglieri — v. 11. Forensic psychology / edited by Alan M. Goldstein — v. 12. Industrial and organizational psychology / edited by Walter C. Borman, Daniel R. Ilgen, Richard J. Klimoski.
    ISBN 0-471-17669-9 (set) — ISBN 0-471-38320-1 (cloth : alk. paper : v. 1)
— ISBN 0-471-38513-1 (cloth : alk. paper : v. 2) — ISBN 0-471-38403-8 (cloth : alk. paper : v. 3)
— ISBN 0-471-39262-6 (cloth : alk. paper : v. 4) — ISBN 0-471-38404-6 (cloth : alk. paper : v. 5)
— ISBN 0-471-38405-4 (cloth : alk. paper : v. 6) — ISBN 0-471-38406-2 (cloth : alk. paper : v. 7)
— ISBN 0-471-39263-4 (cloth : alk. paper : v. 8) — ISBN 0-471-38514-X (cloth : alk. paper : v. 9)
— ISBN 0-471-38407-0 (cloth : alk. paper : v. 10) — ISBN 0-471-38321-X (cloth : alk. paper : v. 11)
— ISBN 0-471-38408-9 (cloth : alk. paper : v. 12)
    1. Psychology. I. Weiner, Irving B.

BF121.H1955 2003
150—dc21

2002066380

Printed in the United States of America.

10 9 8 7 6 5 4 3 2 1

Editorial Board

To the three most important people in my life:
Paula, Naomi, and Marion.
Each day you bring joy to my life and to those whose lives you touch.

Handbook of Psychology **Preface**

Psychology at the beginning of the twenty-first century has become a highly diverse field of scientific study and applied technology. Psychologists commonly regard their discipline as the science of behavior, and the American Psychological Association has formally designated 2000 to 2010 as the "Decade of Behavior." The pursuits of behavioral scientists range from the natural sciences to the social sciences and embrace a wide variety of objects of investigation. Some psychologists have more in common with biologists than with most other psychologists, and some have more in common with sociologists than with most of their psychological colleagues. Some psychologists are interested primarily in the behavior of animals, some in the behavior of people, and others in the behavior of organizations. These and other dimensions of difference among psychological scientists are matched by equal if not greater heterogeneity among psychological practitioners, who currently apply a vast array of methods in many different settings to achieve highly varied purposes.

Psychology has been rich in comprehensive encyclopedias and in handbooks devoted to specific topics in the field. However, there has not previously been any single handbook designed to cover the broad scope of psychological science and practice. The present 12-volume *Handbook of Psychology* was conceived to occupy this place in the literature. Leading national and international scholars and practitioners have collaborated to produce 297 authoritative and detailed chapters covering all fundamental facets of the discipline, and the *Handbook* has been organized to capture the breadth and diversity of psychology and to encompass interests and concerns shared by psychologists in all branches of the field.

Two unifying threads run through the science of behavior. The first is a common history rooted in conceptual and empirical approaches to understanding the nature of behavior. The specific histories of all specialty areas in psychology trace their origins to the formulations of the classical philosophers and the methodology of the early experimentalists, and appreciation for the historical evolution of psychology in all of its variations transcends individual identities as being one kind of psychologist or another. Accordingly, Volume 1 in the *Handbook* is devoted to the history of psychology as it emerged in many areas of scientific study and applied technology.

A second unifying thread in psychology is a commitment to the development and utilization of research methods suitable for collecting and analyzing behavioral data. With attention both to specific procedures and their application in particular settings, Volume 2 addresses research methods in psychology.

Volumes 3 through 7 of the *Handbook* present the substantive content of psychological knowledge in five broad areas of study: biological psychology (Volume 3), experimental psychology (Volume 4), personality and social psychology (Volume 5), developmental psychology (Volume 6), and educational psychology (Volume 7). Volumes 8 through 12 address the application of psychological knowledge in five broad areas of professional practice: clinical psychology (Volume 8), health psychology (Volume 9), assessment psychology (Volume 10), forensic psychology (Volume 11), and industrial and organizational psychology (Volume 12). Each of these volumes reviews what is currently known in these areas of study and application and identifies pertinent sources of information in the literature. Each discusses unresolved issues and unanswered questions and proposes future directions in conceptualization, research, and practice. Each of the volumes also reflects the investment of scientific psychologists in practical applications of their findings and the attention of applied psychologists to the scientific basis of their methods.

The *Handbook of Psychology* was prepared for the purpose of educating and informing readers about the present state of psychological knowledge and about anticipated advances in behavioral science research and practice. With this purpose in mind, the individual *Handbook* volumes address the needs and interests of three groups. First, for graduate students in behavioral science, the volumes provide advanced instruction in the basic concepts and methods that define the fields they cover, together with a review of current knowledge, core literature, and likely future developments. Second, in addition to serving as graduate textbooks, the volumes offer professional psychologists an opportunity to read and contemplate the views of distinguished colleagues concerning the central thrusts of research and leading edges of practice in their respective fields. Third, for psychologists seeking to become conversant with fields outside their own specialty and for persons outside of psychology seeking information about psychological matters, the *Handbook* volumes serve as a reference source for expanding their knowledge and directing them to additional sources in the literature.

The preparation of this *Handbook* was made possible by the diligence and scholarly sophistication of the 25 volume editors and co-editors who constituted the Editorial Board. As Editor-in-Chief, I want to thank each of them for the pleasure of their collaboration in this project. I compliment them for having recruited an outstanding cast of contributors to their volumes and then working closely with these authors to achieve chapters that will stand each in their own right as valuable contributions to the literature. I would like finally to express my appreciation to the editorial staff of John Wiley and Sons for the opportunity to share in the development of this project and its pursuit to fruition, most particularly to Jennifer Simon, Senior Editor, and her two assistants, Mary Porterfield and Isabel Pratt. Without Jennifer's vision of the *Handbook* and her keen judgment and unflagging support in producing it, the occasion to write this preface would not have arrived.

IRVING B. WEINER
Tampa, Florida

Volume Preface

When first asked by Irving Weiner, Editor-in-Chief of the *Handbook of Psychology,* to serve as editor of the Forensic Psychology volume, I was somewhat hesitant to do so. The task seemed enormous: selecting topics and authors, meeting deadlines, and assembling a volume that speaks in "one voice," a book that reads as more than a hodgepodge of separate manuscripts housed in a single binding.

It was my experience as chair of the Continuing Education Program of the American Academy of Forensic Psychology that persuaded me to participate in this project. To paraphrase Will Rogers, I've never met a forensic psychologist I didn't like. Workshop leaders have always generously shared their knowledge with tremendous enthusiasm and communicated complex information so that others could understand and apply what they had learned. This group of forensic psychologists would serve as the core team of authors, allowing this volume to hit the road running.

Each person asked to participate in this volume agreed to do so without hesitation. Everyone generously gave of their time, their expertise, and most important, did so with enthusiasm. Each contributor recognized the potential significance of this book, a volume that would reflect the state of the art as we begin the twenty-first century. It is hoped this book will be valuable to psychology graduate students as well as to psychologists who already work in forensic psychology areas or who seek to do so.

Topics were chosen to reflect the scope of forensic psychology practice and research. This volume is organized so that those with little or no prior knowledge and experience can develop an understanding of the unique nature of the field. It includes chapters focusing on the nature of the field: what forensic psychologists do, ethical conflicts they encounter, and the field's special methodology, such as the use of third-party information and the assessment of malingering and deception. The nature of expert witness testimony is reviewed, along with the limits imposed on such testimony. A wide range of civil and criminal psycholegal issues is addressed. Chapters focus on topics such as eyewitness memory, jury selection, screening for high-risk occupations, sexual offenders, battered women, those with violent attachments (e.g., stalkers), and risk assessment of those about whom there are questions of potential future acts of violence.

This volume also considers emerging directions in forensic psychology, including therapeutic jurisprudence and the application of forensic psychology to public policy and the law.

Each chapter reviews the professional literature relevant to its topic. Major ethical conflicts and their potential resolutions are presented; where appropriate, authors have discussed statutes and landmark case law and have described practical implications of conducting forensic evaluations. Appropriate forensic assessment methodology, including the use of traditional psychological techniques, specialized forensic assessment instruments, and forensically relevant instruments, is reviewed. When appropriate, chapters discuss the nature of written reports and expert testimony. Future trends in each area of forensic practice are predicted.

Authors for each chapter were selected because of their reputations as experts in their specific subfield. Those readers familiar with forensic psychology research, attendees of continuing professional education programs, and those experienced in forensic practice will, most likely, recognize the names of the authors included in this volume. All bring to their topic a vast array of knowledge and experience typically acquired through their own research and research conducted by their graduate students or postdoctoral fellows. Most authors' expertise has been recognized by awards from national professional organizations. Many are authors of their own texts and serve as editors or on editorial boards of the major journals in the field.

I gratefully acknowledge the major contribution each author has made in preparing this volume. Each has not only written or coauthored the most up-to-date, inclusive treatment of the subject matter, but has done so with a sense of dedication, professionalism, and enthusiasm that has made the job of editor almost unnecessary. Not a single chapter arrived past the deadline (although one or two made it a close finish!). No one complained (at least to my face) about my "subtle" e-mail reminders about deadlines, sent on an all-too-frequent basis. Many of the authors started out as personal friends and, despite my calls and e-mails, remain so today. Others, whose names I knew only through their publications and reputations, I now count as friends. I am grateful to each for producing a work in which we all can take pride. Thank you for being such flexible, professional, wonderful people.

I am appreciative to Irving Weiner, Editor-in-Chief, for inviting me to serve as editor of this volume and for his suggestions and support. He allowed me free rein to choose authors and topics, and he always presented comments and suggestions as guidance, with options to accept or reject. He embodies the concept of academic freedom. Jennifer Simon, Senior Editor at John Wiley and Sons, was most helpful in guiding this book to completion. There was not a question she could not answer nor a request she could not fulfill, and I am most appreciative.

My involvement in the field of forensic psychology dates back approximately 30 years. During that time, I have learned much from lawyers with whom I have worked and from numerous forensic psychologists—attendees of AAFP workshops and presenters, most of whom are diplomates in Forensic Psychology of the American Board of Professional Psychology. In particular, I would like to thank attorneys Jean Barrett, Jim Kervick, Jean Mettler, Arlene Popkin, and David Ruhnke for educating me about the law and for never causing ethical crises to arise. I will always be indebted to a number of psychologists for sharing with me, when I was relatively new to the field, their knowledge, encouragement, enthusiasm for forensic psychology, and their sense of ethics: Curt Barrett, Chuck Ewing, Tom Grisso, Kirk Heilbrun, Paul Lipsitt, Bob Meyer, Richard Rogers, David Shapiro, and Herb Weissman. There is no question in my mind that forensic psychologists such as these are among the most giving, open, communicative professionals that exist.

No list of acknowledgments would be complete without expressing my eternal gratitude to Paula Goldstein, my wife, for her patience in dealing with me (before, during, and after I edited this book) and for her reviews of many chapters and her outstanding suggestions. To my daughter (and forensic psychologist), Naomi Goldstein, thank you for the many hours when you set aside your own work to review those chapters I wrote or coauthored, editing the editor. Not a single recommendation was ignored and each chapter is infinitely better as a result. To Marion Goldstein, your creativity, perspective, and recommendations were, as always, invaluable.

ALAN M. GOLDSTEIN, PhD
Hartsdale, New York

Contents

PART SIX
FORENSIC ASSESSMENT OF SPECIAL POPULATIONS

PART SEVEN
EMERGING DIRECTIONS

Contributors

Nancy Lynn Baker, PhD, ABPP
Diplomate in Forensic Psychology
Independent Practice
El Granada, California

Curtis L. Barrett, PhD, ABPP
Diplomate in Forensic Psychology
University of Louisville School of Medicine
Louisville, Kentucky

Scott D. Bender, PhD
University of North Texas
Denton, Texas

Randy Borum, PsyD, ABPP
Diplomate in Forensic Psychology
University of South Florida
Tampa, Florida

Jacqueline K. Buffington-Vollum, MA
Sam Houston State University
Huntsville, Texas

Mary Alice Conroy, PhD, ABPP
Diplomate in Forensic Psychology
Sam Houston State University
Huntsville, Texas

Mark D. Cunningham, PhD, ABPP
Diplomate in Forensic Psychology
Independent Practice
Abilene, Texas

Brian L. Cutler, PhD
University of North Carolina, Charlotte
Charlotte, North Carolina

Susan Daicoff, MS, JD, LLM
Florida Coastal School of Law
Jacksonville, Florida

Deborah M. DeBow, JD
Private Practice of Law
Rancho Santa Fe, California

Jason J. Dickinson, MA
Florida International University
Miami, Florida

Eric Y. Drogin, JD, PhD, ABPP
Diplomate in Forensic Psychology
University of Louisville School of Medicine
Louisville, Kentucky

John F. Edens, PhD
Sam Houston State University
Huntsville, Texas

Charles Patrick Ewing, JD, PhD, ABPP
Diplomate in Forensic Psychology
State University of New York at Buffalo, School of Law
Buffalo, New York

Diane R. Follingstad, PhD, ABPP
Diplomate in Forensic Psychology
University of South Carolina
Columbia, South Carolina

William E. Foote, PhD, ABPP
Diplomate in Forensic Psychology
University of New Mexico School of Law
Albuquerque, New Mexico

Alan M. Goldstein, PhD, ABPP
Diplomate in Forensic Psychology
John Jay College of Criminal Justice, CUNY
New York, New York

Naomi E. Goldstein, PhD
MCP Drexel University
Philadelphia, Pennsylvania

Stuart A. Greenberg, PhD, ABPP
Diplomate in Forensic Psychology
University of Washington
Seattle, Washington

Thomas Grisso, PhD, ABPP
Diplomate in Forensic Psychology
University of Massachusetts Medical Center
Worcester, Massachusetts

Stephen D. Hart, PhD
Simon Fraser University
Burnaby, British Columbia

Kirk Heilbrun, PhD, ABPP
Diplomate in Forensic and Clinical Psychology
Drexel University
Philadelphia, Pennsylvania

James F. Hemphill, PhD
Simon Fraser University
Burnaby, British Columbia

Margaret Bull Kovera, PhD
Florida International University
Miami, Florida

Daniel A. Krauss, JD, PhD
Claremont McKenna College
Claremont, California

Kathryn Kuehnle, PhD
University of South Florida
Tampa, Florida

Elizabeth F. Loftus, PhD
University of Washington
Seattle, Washington

J. Reid Meloy, PhD, ABPP
Diplomate in Forensic Psychology
University of California, San Diego
San Diego, California

John Monahan, PhD, ABPP
Diplomate in Forensic Psychology
University of Virginia
Charlottesville, Virginia

Stephen J. Morse, JD, PhD, ABPP
Diplomate in Forensic Psychology
University of Pennsylvania Law School
Philadelphia, Pennsylvania

Lois B. Oberlander, PhD, ABPP
Diplomate in Forensic Psychology
Harvard Medical School
Boston, Massachusetts

Randy K. Otto, PhD, ABPP
Diplomate in Forensic Psychology
University of South Florida
Tampa, Florida

Ira K. Packer, PhD, ABPP
Diplomate in Forensic Psychology
University of Massachusetts Medical School
Worcester, Massachusetts

Kim Picarello, MA
Drexel University
Philadelphia, Pennsylvania

Michelle Rand, MPA
University of South Florida
Tampa, Florida

Richard Rogers, PhD, ABPP
Diplomate in Forensic Psychology
University of North Texas
Denton, Texas

Bruce D. Sales, PhD, JD
University of Arizona
Tucson, Arizona

David L. Shapiro, PhD, ABPP
Diplomate in Forensic Psychology
Nova Southeastern University
Ft. Lauderdale, Florida

Sandra L. Shullman, PhD
Executive Development Group
Columbus, Ohio

Steven N. Sparta, PhD, ABPP
Diplomate in Forensic and Clinical Psychology
University of California at San Diego School of Medicine
San Diego, California

Kathleen Powers Stafford, PhD, ABPP
Diplomate in Forensic Psychology
Psycho-Diagnostic Clinic
Akron, Ohio

John Super, PhD, ABPP
Diplomate in Forensic Psychology
Manatee County Sheriff's Office
Bradenton, Florida

Melba J. T. Vasquez, PhD, ABPP
Diplomate in Clinical Psychology
Anderson House at Heritage Square
Austin, Texas

Janet Warren, DSW
University of Virginia
Charlottesville, Virginia

Herbert N. Weissman, PhD, ABPP
Diplomate in Forensic and Clinical Psychology
University of California San Diego School of Medicine
San Diego, California

Gary L. Wells, PhD
Iowa State University
Ames, Iowa

David B. Wexler, JD
University of Arizona College of Law
Tucson, Arizona

PART ONE
NATURE OF THE FIELD

CHAPTER 1

Overview of Forensic Psychology

ALAN M. GOLDSTEIN

Forensic psychology has received considerable attention from the public and media during the past decade, thanks, in large part, to books and films such as *Silence of the Lambs* and assorted television series and made-for-TV movies. A commonly asked question of forensic psychologists is "How do I become a profiler?", replacing, for better or worse, "So, you dissect dead people?" In fact, forensic psychologists have no contact with corpses (leaving that to forensic pathologists, forensic scientists, and forensic anthropologists). And some definitions of the field do not consider criminal profiling to be part of forensic psychology.

This book is intended to present the most up-to-date description of the field of forensic psychology. The chapters represent contemporary topics and areas of investigation in this exciting, rapidly expanding field. Forensic psychology's roots date back to 1908, predating the public's awareness of the field. As is explained in the chapter by Ira Packer and Randy Borum, although Münsterberg (1908) proposed various roles for psychologists as experts in court, it was not until the 1970s that efforts began to more formally define the field, to recommend qualifications for those practicing in this area, and to develop guidelines for both ethics and training.

SELECTION OF TOPICS

Topics were selected to reflect forensic psychology's applicability to both the civil and criminal justice systems. This volume is organized into sections, grouping topics with common themes. The reader will first develop an understanding of the nature of the field—*what* it is and *why* it is different from other areas of specialization—and, next, *how* forensic psychologists gather information: the methods they use to conduct assessments.

Not all psychologists testify in court about a specific individual (e.g., a plaintiff in a personal injury suit or a defendant in an insanity case). Some serve as consultants to law enforcement agencies evaluating police applicants, to attorneys as jury selection specialists, or testify as experts to educate juries about specific topics, such as accuracy of eyewitness memories. A section of this volume focuses on these "specialized" roles.

Two sections address topics involving a range of civil and criminal forensic assessments, including child custody, personal injury, trial competence, and criminal responsibility. Another section comprises chapters involving the forensic assessment of special groups or populations, such as sexual predators and battered women. The final section consists of

3

chapters exploring future directions of the field, such as its application to public policy formation.

Although this volume may serve as a text on forensic psychology, chapters were written to stand on their own. Each reviews the professional literature relevant to the topic. Ethics and case law are explained, and, when appropriate to the topic, current assessment methodology is described. Chapters reflect the current state of the field. The volume should serve the novice as well as the experienced forensic psychologist as an indicator of the state of the field at the start of the twenty-first century.

DEFINITION OF FORENSIC PSYCHOLOGY

The word *forensic,* derived from the Latin, *forensis,* means "forum," the place where trials were conducted in Roman times. The current use of forensic denotes a relationship between one professional field, such as medicine, pathology, chemistry, anthropology, or psychology, with the adversarial legal system.

Many definitions of forensic psychology exist. The "Specialty Guidelines for Forensic Psychologists" (Committee on Ethical Guidelines for Forensic Psychologists, 1991), a set of ethical guideposts for those working in the field, defines forensic psychology as a field that covers "all forms of professional conduct when acting, with definable foreknowledge, as a psychological expert on explicitly psychological issues in direct assistance to the courts, parties to legal proceedings, correctional and forensic mental health facilities, and administrative, judicial, and legislative agencies acting in a judicial capacity" (p. 657).

Forensic psychology is a specialty recognized by the American Board of Professional Psychology (ABPP). ABPP defines the field in their written material as "The application of the science and profession of law to questions and issues relating to psychology and the legal system." In the "Petition for the Recognition of a Specialty in Professional Psychology" prepared by Kirk Heilbrun, Ph.D. (2000), on behalf of the America Board of Forensic Psychology (the forensic Specialty Board of ABPP) and the American Psychology—Law Society (Division 41 of the American Psychological Association), it is defined as "the professional practice by psychologists within the areas of clinical psychology, counseling psychology, neuropsychology, and school psychology, when they are engaged regularly as experts and represent themselves as such, in an activity primarily intended to provide professional psychological expertise to the judicial system" (p. 6).

The editor of this volume considers forensic psychology to be a field that involves the application of psychological research, theory, practice, and traditional and specialized methodology (e.g., interviewing, psychological testing, forensic assessment, and forensically relevant instruments) to provide information relevant to a legal question. The goal of forensic psychology as an area of *practice* is to generate products (information in the form of a report or testimony) to provide to consumers (e.g., judges, jurors, attorneys, hiring law enforcement agencies) information with which they may not otherwise be familiar to assist them in decision making related to a law or statute (administrative, civil, or criminal). As an area of *research,* its goal is to design, conduct, and interpret empirical studies, the purpose of which is to investigate groups of individuals or areas of concern or relevance to the legal system. Numerous other definitions exist (Bartol & Bartol, 1999; Hess & Weiner, 1999; and see the chapter by Packer and Borum, and the chapter by Ewing in this volume, and the chapter by Brigham and Grisso in Volume 1. For a discussion on how judges, prosecutors, and defense attorneys view mental health testimony see Redding, Floyd, and Hawk (2001)).

DIFFERENCES BETWEEN CLINICAL AND FORENSIC PSYCHOLOGY

The fields of psychology and law are concerned with and focus on understanding and evaluating human behavior. The law exists to regulate human conduct; for this reason, psychologists are invited to participate in the civil and criminal justice systems. Because psychology is involved in studying behavior, in certain legal cases, findings and insights may assist the judge or jury in deliberations and decision making. However, there are significant differences between psychologists working in traditional settings and those conducting forensic assessments for the courts. Goldstein (1996) has summarized some of these significant differences. Greenberg and Gould (2001) considers role boundaries and standards of expertise of treating and expert witnesses in child custody cases.

Roles

The major role of psychologists working in clinical settings, whether as psychotherapists or as psychological evaluators, is to help the *client*. What is learned about the patient is used to benefit the patient in terms of personal growth and support. However, in forensic psychology, the role of the expert is significantly different. Forensic psychologists are charged with using the results of their assessment to help or educate the *court,* without regard to the potential benefits to the examinee.

Diagnoses

In clinical psychology, psychiatric diagnosis serves a major function in treatment strategy. In addition, a diagnosis, based on criteria described in the *Diagnostic and Statistical Manual of Mental Disorders,* fourth edition (*DSM-IV*) or *IV-Text Revision* (*DSM-IV-TR;* American Psychiatric Association, 2000), is required for patients to receive insurance reimbursement. In forensic psychology, the role of psychiatric diagnosis is generally less critical an issue. Diagnoses are *not* required in many legal issues (e.g., child custody, *Miranda* rights waivers, personal injury). Although insanity statutes require a diagnosis as a prerequisite for its consideration by a jury, the psychiatric diagnosis does not, per se, define insanity. Rather, in forensic psychology, "diagnoses" are based on statutes, which define the relevant behaviors of concern to the court and, therefore, become the focus of the evaluation. For example, the question of a defendant's ability to validly waive *Miranda* rights is defined as being able to do so knowingly, intelligently, and voluntarily—in legal, not psychological, terms. The job of the forensic psychologist is to operationalize or translate the legal terms into psychological concepts, which can be objectively evaluated (Grisso, 1986).

Conceptualization of Human Behavior

During Introduction to Psychology, college students are taught that behavior falls on a continuum. The normal distribution curve is the statistical and visual representation of the orientation of psychologists: Behavior is complex and cannot be readily categorized into discrete groups (e.g., intellectually gifted versus mentally retarded; normal versus psychotic). Unfortunately, the legal system most often considers behavior to be dichotomous. Typically, it requires the trier of fact to classify people and behavior into one of two categories (e.g., guilty versus not guilty; sane versus insane; liable versus not liable). With the exception of awarding monetary damages and instructing jurors to consider lesser charges in criminal proceedings, gradients rarely exist in the justice system. Ethical conflicts arise when those who view behavior as falling on a continuum are expected to sort individuals into discrete categories.

Product of the Professional Relationship

Clinical psychologists conducting traditional assessments seek to explain the client's behavior. The underlying focus of the written report is typically cognitive functioning and psychodynamics. In forensic psychology, explanations of behavior and level of intelligence are generally irrelevant. Such explanations may be accurate, but they do not respond to the specific legal issue or question. To be valuable, forensic reports should address psycholegal behaviors, rather than focusing on explanations, psychodynamics, IQ, or "excuses" for conduct.

Trust of the Client's Responses

Rarely do clinical psychologists question the truthfulness or motivation behind a patient's statements or test responses. Inaccuracies are typically attributable to a lack of insight rather than a conscious effort to deceive. However, in forensic assessments, the motivation to consciously distort, deceive, or respond defensively is readily apparent. Consequently, forensic psychologists cannot take the word of the client unquestioningly. All information must be corroborated by seeking consistency across multiple sources of information (e.g., interview of third parties, review of documents). In addition, tests that objectively evaluate test-taking attitude are available to address the validity of claims of cognitive impairment and mental illness.

Temporal Focus of the Evaluation

Most clinical assessments are *present*-oriented; that is, they focus on the client's state at the time of testing (e.g., his or her psychodynamics, level of intellectual function). Some forensic assessments have at least part of their focus on the present (e.g., which parent is best suited to address the current needs of the child), but most address either exclusively or partially *past* or *future* behavior. For example, insanity assessments focus on the defendant's state of mind at the time a crime occurred: days, weeks, months, or years before. In personal injury cases, the court is interested in not only the plaintiff's current impairments, but also in what he or she was like before the injury, whether there was a connection between the alleged wrong and the damage, and the prognosis for restoration to the preincident state. Even in child custody assessments, developmental changes attributable to age require the evaluator to assess the parents' ability to best serve that child's interests.

Level of Proof

Because psychology is a science, the level of proof is based on the normal distribution. Empirical studies must demonstrate statistical significance to be considered interpretable; this level is typically set at the .05 level of probability. That is, the investigator must be 95% certain that the results of the study are attributable to the variables under investigation rather than to chance. In court, various standards of proof exist (e.g., beyond a reasonable doubt, clear and convincing evidence, preponderance of the evidence), the level dependent on the legal issue in question and which side bears the burden of proof. However, as expert witnesses, forensic psychologists typically are asked whether they were able to reach an opinion "to a reasonable degree of psychological certainty." This level does not refer to the .05 level of statistical significance, nor does it relate to other legal levels of proof. Rather, it refers to the data on which the opinion is based: Can the expert describe the reasons for his or her opinion based on all the information considered, and, at the same time, can he or she explain why alternative opinions (such as malingering) can be ruled out?

Professional Accountability

The "Ethical Principles and Code of Conduct" govern the professional activities of psychologists (American Psychological Association [APA], 1992). As such, psychologists are answerable to their professional organization (as well as to state boards in which they hold licenses) for complaints of unethical conduct. However, relative to the number of psychologists who are members of the APA, complaints are few. Without implying misconduct on the part of large numbers of psychologists, psychotherapy is conducted behind closed doors with only the patient as witness. In traditional testing situations, the client is evaluated and a report is sent to the referring party. Because that party made the referral, a sense of trust in the psychologist's competence exists; few people look over the psychologist's shoulder. However, in forensic psychology, reports and testimony are carefully examined, dissected by opposing counsel, and subjected to close, probing cross-examination. Transcripts of the testimony are prepared. If an attorney, judge, opposing expert, or party in the litigation believes, justly or unjustly, that misconduct has occurred, an ethics complaint may result. Forensic psychologists are responsible not only to their profession, but, in some ways, they are answerable to all parties involved in the legal system, suggesting the need for a conservative approach to those issues and conflicts that arise in the legal arena.

Who Is the Client?

In clinical psychology, the client is readily identifiable: The person to whom professional services are offered is the client, the one owed the legal duty, the one to whom privilege belongs. In contrast, in the judicial system, forensic psychologists serve multiple clients. In his landmark book, *Who Is the Client?,* Monahan (1980) confronted a fundamental

difference between forensic practice and clinical practice. He argued that the expert serves not only the person being evaluated, but many others as well. Because of the nature of the assessment, the nature of the oath (to tell the whole truth and nothing but the truth), and APA ethical principles, clients include the retaining attorney, the consumer of the product (e.g., the judge and jury), and those potentially affected by the expert's opinion: society as a whole.

Other Noteworthy Differences

Greenberg and Shuman (1997) discussed several other irreconcilable differences between clinical and forensic evaluations. They described differences in the *cognitive set* of the clinical psychologist and the forensic expert. Clinical psychologists approach clients with supportive, empathic orientations; the unique requirements of forensic assessments necessitate detached, neutral, and objective approaches. In terms of the amount of *structure and control* in the relationship, patient-structured relationships have relatively less structure than forensic examiner-examinee relationships.

These fundamental differences shape and determine the approach of forensic psychologists to conducting assessments, their methodology, and the structure of their opinions and testimony. Only by recognizing and addressing these major differences can forensic psychologists function in an effective, ethical manner.

A BRIEF HISTORY OF FORENSIC PSYCHOLOGY

Hugo Münsterberg, a student of Wilhelm Wundt and a professor at Harvard University, is generally credited with founding the field of forensic psychology. His landmark textbook, *On the Witness Stand* (1908), comprised nine chapters arguing for the involvement of psychologists in a number of aspects of the legal system. Relying, in part, on his own experience as an expert witness, Münsterberg considered such topics as memories of witnesses, crime detection, untrue confessions, hypnosis and crime, and crime prevention. He found it "astonishing that the work of justice is ever carried out in the courts without ever consulting the psychologist" (p. 194). Despite his importance in addressing psycholegal issues, his 269-page book lacks any references. According to Bartol and Bartol (1999), "His claims were often exaggerated . . . and his proposals were rarely empirically based" (p. 6). At the turn of the twentieth century, psychology was in its infancy, lacking a sufficient scientific foundation to support the admissibility of expert testimony. Despite Münsterberg's impassioned pleas for psychology's involvement in the legal system, his suggestions were largely ignored. However, he generated interest in the possibility that, some day, psychology might make contributions to the judicial system.

A law professor, John H. Wigmore, was familiar with Münsterberg's text. As a leading scholar on the law of evidence, he wrote a satirical article, published in the *Illinois Law Review* (Wigmore, 1909), mocking the value of psychology to the legal system. Wigmore's criticisms of Münsterberg's somewhat grandiose views of psychology's relationship to the law delayed the growth of the field for approximately 20 years.

As psychology continued to develop as a science based on empirical studies, the judicial system slowly began to use the services of psychologists in court. However, because they lacked a medical degree, psychologists' qualifications were, at times, questioned. In 1962, the D.C. Circuit Court of Appeals held in *Jenkins v. United States* that psychologists could provide expert opinions in court regarding mental illness at the time a defendant committed a crime. In the opinion, Judge David Bazelon reviewed the training and qualifications of psychologists. Writing for the majority, he indicated that experts on mental disease could not be limited to physicians, but rather, such factors as training, skills, and knowledge should serve as the basis on which experts were qualified. Consequently, psychologists were accepted by courts as experts on a wide range of legal issues.

In 1954, the U.S. Supreme Court, in *Brown v. the Board of Education,* held that school segregation was illegal, in violation of the 14th Amendment. In this case, an appendix prepared by three psychologists, Kenneth B. Clark, Isider Chein, and Stuart Cook, was included with the plaintiff's brief. Social science research, including the psychological effects of segregation on the self-image of children, was cited in 35 footnotes (Brigham & Grisso, 2002). Points raised in this appendix and in a subsequent response to the Court were cited in the opinion, representing the application of psychological research to appeals court decisions.

In 2000, a petition was submitted to the APA in support of recognition of forensic psychology as a specialty in professional psychology. In August 2001, APA's Counsel of Representatives formally approved forensic psychology as an area of specialization within the field of psychology. With this recognition, the number of graduate programs and postdoctoral fellowships are likely to increase, and the demand for forensic psychologists in a wide range of research, academic, and practice settings should intensify. (The origins of forensic psychology are addressed in the chapter by Ewing of this volume and in greater detail in the chapter by Brigham and Grisso in Volume 1. In addition, Bartol & Bartol, 1999, provide a detailed history of the development of the field).

ORGANIZATION OF THIS VOLUME

The Nature of the Field

Forensic psychology is unique. By its very nature, it must respond to questions of a legal nature, requiring not only an understanding of how the legal system operates but also a working familiarity with relevant statutes and case law.

At the turn of the twenty-first century, no one in the United States had earned a doctoral degree in forensic psychology (in Canada, Simon Fraser University comes closest to this qualification, with a degree in clinical psychology with a specialty in either forensic research or forensic practice). Consequently, those practicing in the field are, for the most part, clinical, counseling, or neuropsychologists with little or no formal graduate school education in forensic psycholegal issues nor in the specialized methodology required to conduct valid assessments. In most states, licenses to practice psychology are generic in nature; only a few states have specialty certification for forensic practitioners. Those identifying themselves as forensic psychologists do so on the basis of their personal, somewhat subjective belief that they possess the background, experience, skills, training, and knowledge that legally qualify them to make this claim. The only credentialing organization recognized by the APA for inclusion in its Directory as specialists are those holding the Diplomate in Forensic Psychology from the American Board of Professional Psychology, approximately 200 individuals nationwide. How are experts to be validly identified in this specialized area of practice?

The issue of professional training and qualifications is a critical one for the field, and it should be equally significant to judges who are in the position of declaring a psychologist an expert for the purposes of offering testimony. What should be included in the graduate training of those intending to enter forensic practice? At the postdoctoral level, what should be required as part of the training fellowship? How can those from traditional psychology doctoral programs "retool" to develop the knowledge and skills expected of experts in the field?

The APA's (1992) "Ethical Principles and Code of Conduct for Psychologists" is written in somewhat general terms because it is intended to apply to *all* areas of psychology. Yet, the conflicts and issues that develop when attempting to practice ethically and objectively in the legal arena, a system of advocacy, readily become apparent. Where do forensic psychologists find guidance and direction working in this unique area of practice?

Forensic assessments are conducted for a purpose. Although many, if not most, cases in both civil and criminal court do not go to trial, forensic experts must anticipate that their work will require court testimony (forensic reports frequently contribute to pretrial settlements in civil suits and in plea bargains in criminal cases). How can forensic psychologists offer expert testimony that is objective, data-based, and effective? How can they know the legal limits of their intended testimony?

In this section, forensic training and practice, the relationship among professional ethics, professional competence, and effectiveness, and the nature of expert testimony are examined. Authors argue for specialized training, skills, and knowledge, consider unusual ethical dilemmas and their resolutions, and discuss methods of conveying complex information to laypeople in an effective, objective fashion while conforming to the requirements and expectations of the legal system.

Forensic Training and Practice

Although the origins of forensic psychology date back approximately 100 years to the publication of *On the Witness Stand* (Münsterberg, 1908), attempts to define and establish the field as a specialty area of practice began in the 1970s. The APA established a division devoted to Forensic Psychology (American Psychology-Law Society). The ABPP recognized the field as a Specialty Board, certifying, as Diplomates in Forensic Psychology, those licensed psychologists demonstrating expertise through peer review of written work samples and oral examinations. The field has its own set of ethical guidelines, the "Specialty Guidelines for Forensic Psychologists" (Committee on Ethical Guidelines for Forensic Psychologists, 1991), and the "Ethical Principles of Psychologists and Code of Conduct" (APA, 1992) contains a section devoted to forensic psychology. Books and journals, both nationally and internationally, abound. Most recently, the American Board of Forensic Psychology (a specialty board of ABPP) and the American Psychology-Law Society submitted to the APA a petition for the recognition of forensic psychology as a specialty in professional psychology. Consequently, the issue of professional training is a critical one for this rapidly expanding field.

In the chapter by Ira Packer and Randy Borum, the historical development of forensic psychology is briefly described. They review the roles of social, developmental, cognitive, and clinical psychologists in the field and consider areas of focus, subspecialization, and psycholegal issues addressed by forensic psychologists (most of the topics are covered in detail in this volume). They describe graduate training in the field, doctoral programs, and joint degree programs (those that award the Ph.D. or Psy.D. and the J.D.). Packer and Borum discuss levels of training, internships, postdoctoral programs, and the nature and goals of continuing professional education, including those offered by such organizations as the APA and the American Academy of Forensic Psychology. They include a list of relevant case law for Diplomates in Forensic Psychology and discuss models for future training in the field.

Ethical Principles and Professional Competencies in Forensic Practice

Because of its uniqueness, perhaps no area of psychological practice receives more scrutiny than does forensic psychology. Reports and testimony focusing on the opinions reached by the expert are open to both criticism and formal cross-examination. The findings of forensic assessments often have profound effects on the lives of litigants, whether used to award or deny a parent custody of a child, to determine a financial verdict in a personal injury suit, or to deprive a defendant of his or her freedom. Forensic psychologists are expected to possess specialized knowledge of statutes and case law, familiarity with rules of evidence, and experience in administering forensic assessment and forensically relevant instruments, as well as traditional clinical psychological tests. The "Ethical Principles of Psychologists and Code of Conduct" (APA, 1992) is meant to apply to *all* areas of professional psychological activity. Because of the conflicts between the demands of the legal system and the "Ethical Principles," forensic experts continually face conflicts and challenges in attempting to satisfy the needs of the court and the ethics of their profession.

Herbert Weissman and Deborah DeBow discuss professional standards implicit in the competent professional practice of forensic psychology. They contend that *legal* competence is addressed through the application of *ethical* professional competency. In conforming one's practice to the APA's "Ethical Principles" and the "Specialty Guidelines for Forensic Psychologists" (Committee on Ethical Guidelines for Forensic Psychologists, 1991), professional competence is enhanced. They describe impediments and influences that impact ethical conduct, many of which derive from conflicts inherent in the relationship between psychology and the law. Weissman and DeBow offer ways to mediate such conflicts.

The Nature of Expert Testimony

Forensic psychologists typically conduct evaluations with the expectation that findings will be presented in the courtroom as expert witness testimony. Whereas witnesses of fact (lay witnesses) may testify only to knowledge they have acquired firsthand through the senses (generally, what they have seen and heard), experts offer testimony about their thoughts (including inductive and deductive reasoning) and can offer opinions based on hearsay testimony. Since the landmark decision in *Jenkins v. U.S.* (1962), qualified psychologists have been permitted to offer expert witness testimony on a wide range of psycholegal issues in both civil and criminal courts.

Charles Patrick Ewing examines the history of expert testimony. He reviews the general legal rules that govern expert witness testimony, including the Federal Rules of Evidence. Ewing explains statutes and case law that determine who qualifies as an expert, the admissibility of topics for expert testimony, and the limitations placed on expert witness testimony. Selected practical aspects of the process of providing effective, ethical expert testimony are described, focusing on specific types of expert testimony, cross-examination, and the issue of immunity of experts from civil liability.

Approaches to Forensic Assessment

In clinical psychological evaluations, with few exceptions, the psychologist interviews the person being evaluated and then administers a battery of tests appropriate to the referral question. Data are analyzed and a report is prepared. Typically, no other information is considered. The assumption is made, for the most part correctly so, that the examinee has been truthful during the interview and candid in answering test questions, that no conscious attempts were made to look better or worse than the actual clinical picture. In forensic psychology, however, there is an obvious motivation to consciously present a distorted picture for an obvious, identifiable, secondary gain. In the civil setting, parents seeking custody may attempt to look more virtuous than they actually are, and plaintiffs in a personal injury suit may distort responses to appear more damaged than is the case. In criminal cases, defendants may choose to present a picture of being more emotionally disturbed than is justified to avoid trial, criminal culpability, or a sentence of death.

Chapters in this section address ways of increasing the objectivity and validity of opinions on psycholegal issues. The need to consider corroborative information by way of third-party interviews and review of written records is explored. Using psychopathy as a model, the ways in which the use of reliable, objective measures of relevant psycholegal behavior and familiarity with the professional literature serve to increase the validity of forensic evaluations is detailed. In addition, because the cornerstone of any forensic assessment is the evaluation of malingering, exaggeration, and defensiveness, relevant research and the use of measures designed to provide information on this topic are described.

The Use of Third-Party Information in Forensic Assessment

A forensic psychologist conducting a psycholegal evaluation, whether in a civil or criminal context, must obtain information from those *directly* involved in the legal case (i.e., the plaintiff or respondent in a civil lawsuit; the parents, children, and others when custody is an issue; the defendant in a criminal case). However, such sources of information are "interested parties," biased at best and, possibly, providing false or selective information because of malingering (simulation or dissimulation) and defensiveness. For this reason, experts must consider data provided by independent sources, *third-party information,* to corroborate data obtained from the interested party through interviews and psychological testing. Sources for third-party information include others knowledgeable about the party involved in the suit or the events related to the case, and documents and records that may relate to statements made by the individual or that may provide additional information helpful in forming an opinion.

Kirk Heilbrun, Janet Warren, and Kim Picarello examine the relevance of third-party information in the forensic assessment process, describing its importance in forensic evaluations. They present research on this method, including a review of empirical studies on the use and value of third-party information. Relevant law and ethical standards related to these independent sources of data are explained. Heilbrun, Warren, and Picarello review the practice literature regarding the use of such data in terms of standards of practice, and they describe the process by which experts obtain, apply, and communicate third-party information in forensic assessments.

Forensic and Clinical Issues in the Assessment of Psychopathy

Forensic assessments frequently incorporate traditional psychological tests, as well as instruments designed to provide data relevant to specific psycholegal questions. In the field of psychopathy, a specific form of personality disorder, we have witnessed the development of such specialized methodology during the past two decades (Hare, 1996). The presence or absence of psychopathy is relevant to a number of civil (e.g., civil commitment) and criminal contexts (e.g., probation and parole, detention under violent offender statutes, and death penalty cases; Hart, 2001). The reliable and valid assessment of psychopathy is, therefore, critical to issues of freedom and, in some cases, to decisions regarding life and death.

James Hemphill and Stephen Hart describe the nature of psychopathy, identifying its distinction from antisocial, psychopathic, dissocial, and sociopathic personality disorders in their chapter of this volume. Current conceptualizations of psychopathy, including symptom patterns, are reviewed. As part of the overall evaluation strategy, Hemphill and Hart present assessment methodology, focusing on the Psychopathy Checklist-Revised (Hare, 1980, 1991). They consider questions, conflicts, and legal issues arising when forensic psychologists assess psychopathy, and they report the occurrence of psychopathy in juveniles and among various cultural groups. Priorities for future research on this critical topic are suggested.

Evaluation of Malingering and Deception

Evaluators in a forensic context cannot accept unquestioningly a respondent's answers as a valid or optimal representation of mental state. The motivation to respond in a self-serving fashion for secondary gain is readily apparent (e.g., financial reward in a personal injury case; custody of a child in a custody dispute; the assumption, often incorrect, of a shorter period of restricted freedom in an insanity case). Consequently, forensic experts must consider the possibility that the examinee may have attempted to distort test results because of malingering, exaggeration, and defensiveness. Neither rare nor very common in forensic evaluations, malingering is estimated to occur in 15% to 17% of forensic cases (Rogers, Salekin, Sewell, Goldstein, & Leonard, 1998; Rogers, Sewell, & Goldstein, 1994).

In the chapter by Richard Rogers and Scott Bender of this volume, they present an overview of conceptual issues and response styles related to malingering and defensiveness. They describe explanatory models of why individuals may attempt to portray psychological and physical impairments, and they examine major empirical issues and false assumptions frequently made about malingering. Rogers and Bender review detection strategies designed to identify response styles, including the use of both traditional and forensically relevant instruments, such as the Structured Interview of Reported Symptoms (Rogers, Bagby, & Dickens, 1992) and the Validity Indicator Profile (Fredrick, 1997).

Special Topics in Forensic Psychology

At times, forensic psychologists are retained as consultants. They are asked to assess job applicants or current employees or to assist as expert witnesses testifying about specific *topics* or areas of specialized research, rather than about specific *people*. These roles, though somewhat different from those of traditional experts expected to provide information relevant to specific individuals in courts of law, nonetheless require knowledge about the relevant professional literature, case law, and the legal system.

In this section, three topics are considered, representative of roles of the psychologist as consultant and as expert witness on specific areas of research. Law enforcement and other agencies employing those in high-risk occupations frequently retain psychologists as consultants. Experts on a specific area or topic of research may be consulted and asked to serve as expert witnesses to review, for a jury, research related to such topics as eyewitness memories for people and events. Still other experts are retained as jury consultants, advising lawyers about which potential jurors might be most open to the arguments and evidence likely to be raised during trial.

Forensic Assessment for High-Risk Occupations

In recent years, there has been a significant increase in requests to evaluate job applicants and current employees in law enforcement and other high-risk positions (Inwald & Resko, 1995). Forensic psychologists prescreen applicants for these occupations to assess their psychological suitability for high-risk jobs. In addition, referrals are made to conduct fitness-for-duty evaluations when questions have been raised about a current employee's ability to perform the full duties associated with his or her position (and, in many cases, to carry firearms). The methodology used in these evaluations applies not only to law enforcement personnel, but also to corrections officers, security officers, firefighters, airline pilots, and nuclear power plant operators (Rigaud & Flynn, 1995).

Randy Borum, John Super, and Michelle Rand examine representative ethical issues confronting those performing such assessments in a chapter of this volume. They discuss legal issues regarding the right to conduct evaluations for high-risk occupations and cite case law supporting its role in the employment process. From a practice perspective, Borum, Super, and Rand review job-related abilities, assessment methodology, and suitability analysis. The primary focus of this chapter is on preemployment screenings and fitness-for-duty evaluations.

Eyewitness Memory for People and Events

In a criminal trial, attempts are made, through the introduction of evidence, to reconstruct what occurred at the moment of the crime. In addition to physical evidence (e.g., fingerprints, tire tracks, DNA), eyewitnesses to the crime (including the victim) may be called on to testify about memories of what they saw. However, for a number of reasons, memories may become contaminated, lost, or destroyed, resulting in well-intentioned, but nonetheless inaccurate testimony. The consequences for the defendant and society may be significant. Mistakes in eyewitness identification account for more convictions of innocent defendants (exonerated by DNA evidence) than all other factors combined (Scheck, Neufeld, & Dwyer, 2000; Wells et al., 1998).

Gary Wells and Elizabeth Loftus argue for a scientific model to collect, analyze, and interpret eyewitness evidence in a chapter of this volume. The scientific literature and theory on eyewitness memory for events is reviewed, and they examine factors that may impact accuracy. The literature on eyewitness memory for people, focusing on the ability of eyewitnesses to identify suspects from lineups, is detailed, and those factors that may impair this ability are discussed. Scientific procedures for lineups are suggested to reduce these factors demonstrated to increase error rate. Wells and Loftus present a case to illustrate major points raised in their chapter.

Voir Dire and Jury Selection

The jury is the hallmark of a democratic system of justice. Decision making as to guilt or innocence in a criminal case and for or against a plaintiff in a civil case is placed in the hands of ordinary citizens, expected to consider evidence in an objective, unbiased fashion. However, it has long been recognized that potential jurors bring into the courtroom their prior experiences, attitudes, biases, and personality characteristics, factors that may interfere with the impartial outcome of a trial. The process of voir dire (to speak the truth), mandated both by federal and state statutes, is designed to uncover biases that might interfere with the objective weighing of evidence. Who is on the jury is critical, therefore, for both sides in a trial.

Margaret Bull Kovera, Jason Dickinson, and Brian Cutler describe the process of voir dire, as well as the system developed to challenge potential jurors, in this volume. They review the traditional methods of jury selection, typically relying on conjecture, the use of stereotypes, body language, and anecdotal strategies to predict inclinations favorable toward a specific verdict. They contrast this approach with scientific jury selection, developed by Schulman, Shaver, Colman, Emrich, and Christie (1973). This approach relies on demographics, personality traits, and attitudes and their relationship to trial outcome. Kovera, Dickinson, and Cutler explain the limitations of research on jury selection and suggest directions for future research in this area.

Civil Forensic Psychology

The judicial system operates on the premise that those who have committed a wrong should be punished. This holds true in both the *civil* and the *criminal* justice systems. Whereas the criminal justice system may punish those found guilty of a crime by depriving them of freedom, those found responsible for committing a wrong from which a damage resulted may be punished by having to pay a monetary award to the injured party. In a civil case of child custody, the parent deemed more likely to fulfill the best interests and needs of the child is awarded custody, and the other parent may be permitted only limited or supervised visitation or no contact at all.

In this section, a range of topics related to forensic assessments in the civil arena is considered. Each specialized area of practice requires knowledge of the relevant statutes and case law, familiarity with the professional literature, and an awareness of the forensic assessment methodology available to address the specific type of civil psycholegal issue in question.

Authors consider child custody assessments, personal injury evaluations related to both childhood trauma and breach of duty, and discrimination evaluations based on claims of harassment, sexual harassment, hostile work environment, retaliation, physical and emotional disability, learning disability, and substance abuse. In addition, substituted judgments involving such matters as living wills, health care surrogacies, and right to refuse treatment are discussed. For each civil issue, statutes, case law, ethical considerations, and assessment methodology are reviewed.

Child Custody Evaluation

The assessment of child custody is one of the most complex, challenging, and professionally risky areas of forensic evaluation. The vast majority of other types of forensic referrals address relatively specific, well-formulated psycholegal issues. Often, assessments involve evaluating only one person (e.g., a personal injury litigant, a defendant for whom trial competence is an issue, a victim of rape), but custody assessments require assessing multiple parties, each individually and in various combinations (e.g., each child, each parent, child and stepparents, child and stepsiblings). The standard "best interests of the child" is somewhat more complex and vague than other psycholegal criteria, requiring a multifocused approach to the overall assessment process (e.g., mental heath of each parent, needs of the child, attitudes, interests of the parents). Because the stakes are high in a custody case, at least one parent is apt to be angry or resentful of the outcome; consequently, ethics complaints against forensic psychologists involved in this area of assessment are more frequent than in any other facet of consultation (APA Ethics Committee, 2001).

In the chapter by Randy Otto, Jacqueline Buffington, and John Edens in this volume, they review judges' and attorneys' perceptions of the value of child custody assessments. They describe the legal standards for the determination of custody in the United States and review child custody evaluation guidelines developed by professional organizations. The evaluation process is described, including the value and use of traditional psychological tests and forensic assessment instruments available for this purpose. Otto, Buffington, and Edens discuss research related to child custody evaluations and decision making, including the effects of divorce on children. The nature of reports and testimony is considered as well.

The Assessment of Childhood Trauma

During the past two decades, mental health professionals and attorneys increasingly have focused attention on the causes and effects of traumatic stress on children. Trauma has been associated with a number of psychological responses, including posttraumatic stress disorder (Pynoos, Steinberg, & Goenjian, 1996). Claims of emotional damage or injury from childhood trauma may be relevant in a number of legal contexts, including personal injury, child custody, special education eligibility, and delinquency cases.

In Steven Sparta's chapter, he examines the definitions and categories of childhood trauma, as well as the determents of traumatic affects. The concept of trauma is discussed from a developmental perspective. He presents a number of psycholegal contexts in which trauma may be the proximate cause of a claimed injury or damage. Sparta reviews assessment strategies to evaluate these questions, including interviews with children and specific tests that are appropriate for this special population.

Personal Injury Examinations in Torts for Emotional Distress

The law typically allows those who believe they have been physically or emotionally harmed to bring suit, in civil court, against those they believe damaged them. To prevail in a personal injury law suit, the plaintiff usually must demonstrate that there has been a breach of a legal duty owed by the defendant to the plaintiff and that the plaintiff has been proximately harmed by that tort or wrong (Greenberg & Shuman, 1999). The plaintiff must demonstrate a relationship between the wrong and the damage, such that the damage would not have occurred but for what the defendant did: the concept of proximate cause.

Stuart Greenberg explains the legal framework of personal injury cases, the law of torts, placing it in historical perspective. He examines the role of the forensic psychologist in such cases, including assessing the plaintiff's functioning before the harm; the extent of distress caused to the plaintiff; the extent of impairments and injuries to the plaintiff's functioning; the likely cause of each impairment or injury; and the prognosis and steps necessary to restore the plaintiff's preincident level of functioning. Greenberg reviews the rules of civil procedure on both federal and state levels. Methodology for conducting personal injury evaluations is described. He discusses depositions and report writing in personal injury cases, as well as expert witness testimony. He presents a mock transcript, highlighting how the neutral, objective expert can offer effective, ethical testimony and advocate for his or her opinion.

Assessing Employment Discrimination and Harassment

Title VII of the 1964 Civil Rights Act made it illegal to discriminate against others based on race, sex, religion, or national origin. Forensic psychologists may be called on to evaluate claims of alleged discrimination and harassment involving a range of issues. Questions asked of experts include: Did harassment or discrimination occur, and if so, why? Was it welcomed or unwelcome, voluntary or coerced? Could there have been misinterpretation? Was there harm? and What were the effects of this tort?

Melba Vasquez, Nancy Lynn Baker, and Sandra Shullman present the legal bases underlying these claims in their chapter. Forms of legal discrimination, including harassment, sexual harassment (heterosexual and same-sex), hostile environment, and retaliation are considered. The professional literature on sexual and racial discrimination is reviewed. The roles of the forensic psychologist are described, and specialized methodology addressing issues of employment discrimination and harassment are reviewed. Vasquez, Baker, and Shullman discuss the future directions of this area of forensic practice.

Forensic Evaluation in Americans with Disability Act Cases

Whereas the Civil Rights Act of 1964 banned discrimination on the basis of race, sex, religion, and national origin, it was not until the Americans with Disabilities Act of 1990 (ADA) that discrimination against those with physical and mental disabilities was prohibited. Designed to help those with disabilities achieve full functioning in the workplace, this legislation outlawed discrimination on the basis of disability for hiring, training, compensation, and benefits (Bell, 1997). In addition, it became illegal to employ tests or other non-job-related criteria that would result in screening out those with disabilities if they might otherwise be "reasonably accommodated." The ADA also prevented retaliation against those who filed claims under this Act.

In William Foote's chapter, he examines the issue of disability in the workplace and how the ADA fits with existing disability systems. He details the impact of discrimination on the basis of disability and focuses on mental disabilities, learning disabilities, and substance abuse disorders. Foote presents methodologies to evaluate claims of disability related to both the assessment of damages and failure to provide reasonable accommodations. He explores the topics of disparate treatment and disparate impact assessments, reprisals for pursuing claims, and disability harassment and hostile work environments for those with disabilities.

Substituted Judgment

Questions may arise regarding a person's ability to make informed, reasoned judgments in his or her best interests and that accurately reflect the individual's intentions. Situations in which this issue may arise include decisions involving the abilities to consent or refuse medical or psychiatric treatment, execute a will, and prepare a health care proxy. The concept of substituted judgment involves the replacement of an individual's judgment with that of a substitute: another person or agency. Substitutions may involve *prior* judgments made by the individual (advanced directives), *present* judgments, or *future* judgments. Forensic psychologists may be called on to offer opinions about decisions to be made or already made by individuals, alive or deceased.

Eric Drogin and Curtis Barrett describe the role of the forensic psychologist in the assessment of psycholegal issues related to substituted judgment. They review the legal and historical background for evaluating past, present, and future substituted judgment. Drogin and Barrett explain substitutions for prior judgments, including living wills, health care surrogacies, and durable powers of attorney. The right to refuse or consent to treatment, the informed consent doctrine, and affirmations of an individual's autonomy to make decisions regarding present concerns are examined. They discuss decisions related to guardianships and conservatorships. A range of forensic assessment instruments developed for conducting these forensic evaluations is described.

Criminal Forensic Psychology

In the forensic criminal arena, issues related to legal competencies are the focus of most requests for forensic psychological assessments. The 5th, 6th, 8th, and 14th Amendments are guaranteed, even to those accused of horrific crimes. In recent years, considerable attention has been given to crimes committed by juveniles. Depending on the state, juveniles of a specified age, having been charged with a predetermined specific crime, may be transferred to adult court, where adult penalties are imposed. Consequently, juveniles, despite their age and immaturity, are expected to be as competent as adults in understanding their rights and must be afforded the same constitutional protections as adults. (Some states allow appropriate developmental immaturity as a basis for incompetence.)

Issues related to the comprehension of the rights to remain silent, to avoid making incriminating statements, and to be represented by an attorney serve as the basis for assessments of a defendant's ability to make a valid waiver of *Miranda* rights. Defendants are entitled to be represented by an attorney in court, and such representation includes the ability to assist the attorney in defense strategy, to communicate rationally with the attorney, and to understand courtroom procedures. This requirement may result in questions regarding the ability of a defendant to be competent to stand trial. To be convicted of a crime, it must be established that, not only did the defendant commit the criminal act, but, at the time of the offense, he or she possessed the required mental state or *mens rea* necessary to be held culpable. Assessment of criminal responsibility represents a major area in which forensic psychologists may be asked to provide information to the court on matters of mental or emotional culpability, such as insanity or extreme mental or emotional disturbance. When a defendant has been found guilty of a capital offense, a sentencing phase of the trial is held. The jury is asked to decide whether he or she should be executed. Forensic psychologists may be retained to evaluate the defendant in terms of the presence or absence of aggravating and mitigating factors in capital cases. When accusations of child sexual abuse are made without physical supportive evidence or third-party witnesses, questions may be raised about the validity of the child's report.

In this section, forensic evaluations focusing on a number of criminal psycholegal issues are reviewed. Waiver of youths to adult court, competence of children to waive *Miranda* rights, and the competence of youths to stand trial are examined. In addition, the assessment of violence risk in juvenile offenders is discussed. The ability to make a knowing, intelligent, voluntary waiver of *Miranda* rights and issues and assessment methodology related to confessions that may be untruthful are detailed in a chapter in this section. Evaluations of fitness to stand trial and restoration of trial competence are the focus of another chapter. Legal issues and evaluation methodology related to criminal culpability is discussed, and sentencing in capital cases is presented. This section concludes with a chapter focusing on evaluating allegations of child sexual abuse.

Forensic Evaluation in Delinquency Cases

The first juvenile court was established in Chicago in 1899, acknowledging, in part, that juveniles were not miniature adults, and that because of immaturity associated with age, their misguided "transgressions" should not be viewed nor treated as crimes. The goal of juvenile court—rehabilitation rather than punishment—was significantly different from that of adult court. However, the U.S. Supreme Court acknowledged in 1967 (*In re Gault*) that because juveniles are deprived of their freedom when placed in a youth facility, they are entitled to most of the constitutional protections afforded adults. It was recognized that youths may not be competent in a number of legal domains because of their immaturity. However, the courts tended to avoid addressing these issues because juveniles were not to be punished but, rather, rehabilitated. The 1990s appear to have brought these issues to a head. Juveniles currently arrested and charged with crimes may be exposed to a very different system of justice, one in which adult penalties apply. Attorneys representing juveniles can no longer look the other way, expecting the youth to receive help if sentenced. Instead, attorneys are obligated to ensure that their young clients are, in fact, competent to waive their *Miranda* rights and stand trial and meet all of the psycholegal competencies legally required of adults.

Thomas Grisso argues that the knowledge base and the development of forensic assessment instruments to evaluate the psycholegal competence of juveniles have lagged behind the development of other areas of forensic knowledge and practice. He presents a history of the juvenile justice system and describes general methods for evaluating juveniles, including personality and problem scales developed for delinquency cases. Legal standards and specialized assessment methodology needed to evaluate waivers to adult criminal court, competence to waive *Miranda* rights, and competence to stand trial are explained. Grisso reviews the current state of knowledge regarding the assessment of violent juvenile offenders and recidivism, and discusses actuarial methods, base rates, and methods and instruments. He concludes with a consideration of future advancements in forensic assessment in delinquency cases.

Competence to Confess: Evaluating the Validity of Miranda Rights Waivers and Trustworthiness of Confessions

Confessions to crimes are valuable commodities, which, once introduced to a judge or jury, are exceedingly difficult for defense lawyers to overcome. Unchallenged, inculpatory statements are devastating, typically taken as a clear sign of the defendant's guilt. In *Miranda v. Arizona* (1966) the U.S. Supreme Court held that the process of interrogation is hidden from public scrutiny. Suspects are often frightened, and investigators are equipped with a range of interrogation strategies designed to take advantage of the suspect's weaknesses. To level the playing field, the Court required interrogators to administer the *Miranda* warnings to those placed under arrest or made to believe they are not free to leave. In *Dickerson v. United States* (2000), the Court ruled that the *Miranda* warnings had become so deeply ingrained in our culture that they could neither be revoked nor could Congress override them by legislation. In *Crane v. Kentucky* (1986), the Court opined that a defendant has the right to introduce evidence to a jury that a confession found to have been legally obtained through a valid waiver of *Miranda* rights may, nonetheless, not be trustworthy.

Lois Oberlander, Naomi Goldstein, and Alan Goldstein examine case law regarding the ability to waive *Miranda* rights and the validity of confessions. They describe research relevant to child, adolescent, and adult *Miranda* rights comprehension, and the relationship between understanding these rights and IQ, academic achievement, reading ability, familiarity with the criminal justice system, race, and socioeconomic status. Forensic assessment instruments developed to objectively evaluate the ability of an individual to make a knowing, intelligent waiver are reviewed, and the use of traditional clinical tests as an adjunct in the evaluative process is described. Oberlander, Goldstein, and Goldstein explore the literature on false confessions: the significance of inculpatory statements; frequency of false confessions; and why some defendants may provide a false confession. The authors present methodology for evaluating those factors that may contribute to inculpatory statements that may not be truthful.

Assessment of Competence to Stand Trial

A defendant in a criminal case must be more than just a physical presence in the courtroom; he or she must be competent to stand trial, a two-pronged standard delineated by the U.S. Supreme Court in *Dusky v. U.S.* (1960). According to *Dusky*, fitness for trial is based on whether a defendant "has sufficient present ability to consult with his attorney with a reasonable degree of rational understanding—and whether he has a rational as well as factual understanding of the proceedings against him." Fitness-for-trial assessments are the most common of all criminal evaluations, court-ordered in 2% to 8% of all felony cases (Hoge, Bonnie, Poythress, & Monahan, 1992).

Kathleen Powers Stafford reviews the legal framework of trial competence, placing it in historical perspective in her chapter of this volume. She describes the variables relevant to trial competence that are reported in the empirical literature. She examines the methodological approaches to assess competence to stand trial, including the use of forensic assessment instruments designed expressly for this purpose. Stafford considers trial competence with special populations: those with psychosis, the mentally retarded, and those with severe hearing and communication impairments. Dispositional issues, including prediction of competence restoration, treatment of incompetent defendants, and permanent incompetence, are considered.

Evaluation of Criminal Responsibility

Perhaps no other area of forensic assessment engenders more attention and, at the same time, feelings of hostility and resentment than evaluations focusing on issues of criminal responsibility. The trial of John W. Hinkley for the attempted murder of President Reagan and his acquittal by reason of insanity (*U.S. v. Hinkley,* 1982) fanned the flames of the perceived injustices resulting from insanity defenses. However, public perceptions differ significantly from reality in terms of the frequency of insanity defenses, their rate of success, and what ultimately happens to those acquitted by reason of insanity. The evaluation of a defendant's mental state at the time of an offense is central to the issue of criminal culpability and, hence, punishment. These assessments require the "reconstruction" of a prior mental state to assist the trier of fact in rendering a decision of legal responsibility.

Alan Goldstein, Stephen Morse, and David Shapiro explain the basic doctrines of criminal liability. They focus on mental state issues relevant to culpability, including negation of *mens rea,* provocation and passion, extreme mental or emotional disturbance, voluntary and involuntary intoxication, imperfect self-defense, and duress. The authors review the history of the insanity defense, including its development, changes, and recent reforms. Ethical issues and conflicts that arise in conducting these assessments are explored. Goldstein, Morse, and Shapiro describe the methodology necessary to evaluate a defendant's prior mental state. Two

cases involving insanity and extreme emotional disturbance defenses are presented and discussed.

Sentencing Determinations in Capital Cases

Unlike any other form of punishment, the death penalty is the ultimate, irrevocable sanction. The U.S. Supreme Court held that death penalty statutes must not be "capricious" and that specific guidelines are required to avoid the "uncontrolled discretion" of judges and juries, whereby "People live or die, dependant on the whim of 1 man or 12" (*Furman v. Georgia,* 1972). Similarly, the Court rejected North Carolina's statute making all first-degree murder convictions punishable by death (*Woodson v. North Carolina,* 1976), reasoning that each case must be individualized. In *Gregg v. Georgia* (1976), the Court accepted as constitutional that state's requirement that at least one aggravating factor must be established during a separate sentencing phase of a capital trial before a defendant could be sentenced to death. The defense was permitted to introduce mitigating facts or circumstances for the jury or judge to weigh against the aggravating factor or factors before the death penalty could be imposed. Because sentencing must be individualized, the defense is permitted to introduce *any* aspect of the defendant's character or record and *any* circumstances of the offense in mitigation (*Lockett v. Ohio,* 1978).

Mark Cunningham and Alan Goldstein describe the nature and structure of capital trials and the data regarding the administration of the death penalty. They examine landmark U.S. Supreme Court decisions related to capital punishment, and they address ethical issues regarding the role of the psychologist in sentencing evaluations and in assessments addressing competence to be executed. The authors discuss methodology in conducting capital evaluations, including assessment parameters. Cunningham and Goldstein focus on violence risk assessment in death penalty cases and detail common errors in such evaluations. They also discuss issues related to base rates, risk management, and group statistical data. Two capital case assessments are presented to illustrate teaching witness and evaluating witness testimony. The role of forensic psychologists is discussed in postconviction and *habeas* relief cases and in assessing competence to waive appeals and competence to be executed.

Child Sexual Abuse Evaluations

When allegations are made involving sexual abuse of a child, the victim is, typically, the only witness to the crime. Usually, medical evidence is absent; behavioral symptoms, if present, may be attributable to factors other than or in addition to the claimed abuse; and admissions of culpability by the alleged perpetrators are rare (Myers, 1998). There is considerable controversy in the academic and practice community about the frequency of false reports of abuse, attributable to distortions of memory and suggestibility of the child. However, there is agreement that any mental health professional retained to evaluate claims of child sexual abuse must be familiar with relevant statutes and case law, the professional literature on child development, and potential behavioral manifestations of child sexual abuse. In addition, the evaluator must be well versed in the specialized methodology required to conduct such evaluations. To address issues raised by these complex and emotionally charged cases, Kuehnle (1998) proposed a scientific-practitioner model of assessment.

Kathryn Kuehnle describes this model for assessing child sexual abuse, a model based on the empirically established relationship between science and the child's behavior. She reviews the data on the prevalence of child sexual abuse and those factors demonstrated to increase children's vulnerability to the risk of sexual abuse. Symptom patterns associated with child sexual abuse are examined. In addition, Kuehnle reviews the literature on factors that may distort valid recall and reporting of the event in question: childhood memory and suggestibility. She considers the interview process with children who may have been victims of sexual abuse and describes a range of tools and instruments that may assist in the assessment procedure. She also explores relevant legal issues in relationship to these topics.

Forensic Assessment of Special Populations

At times, forensic psychological evaluations focus on legally relevant issues as well as identifying and making predictions about "special populations," or those identified in the professional literature as belonging to a unique category. Recently enacted sexual violent predator statutes have given rise to requests to evaluate those convicted of violent sexual crimes who have fulfilled their prison sentence. Such individuals can be transferred to civil commitment status if they meet criteria defined by each state. Assessments may be requested to evaluate the risk of future sexual offending of those belonging to this special group. Similarly, battered women have been singled out as a special category. Admissible in most states, battered women's syndrome may be introduced to explain a defendant's mental state if charged with the murder or assault of her batterer.

Those who have developed violent attachments, including pathologies of bonding, represent still another special population. Such individuals are at increased risk for violent behaviors directed against those with whom they have relationships,

whether real or imagined. Forensic experts may be consulted in such cases, not only for forensic assessments focusing on acts of violence *previously* committed, but also regarding *potential* actions by those who have committed acts of violence against others. In a number of psycholegal areas (e.g., civil commitment, child custody, presentencing reports, probation and parole, death penalty cases) violence risk assessment is a crucial process.

In this section, chapters focus on conducting assessments with those belonging to identifiable, special populations. Authors address legal, ethical, and assessment methodology necessary to evaluate violent sexual predators, battered women, those with a history of violent attachments, such as stalkers and those engaging in interpartner violence, and risk assessment. The limits of such assessments for expert testimony are described.

Evaluation of Sex Offenders

With the exception of drug offenders, during the 1990s the sex offender population has increased faster than any other group of violent criminals (La Fond, 1998). The nature of these crimes, especially those against children, drew the attention and ire of the public, legislators, and courts. Many states passed both civil and criminal legislation requiring mandatory, lengthy sentences for sex-related crimes and, in some states, lifelong probation. For sex offenders who have completed their prison sentence and been released, requirements may include registration as a sex offender with local police authorities, notification to neighbors that a sex offender has moved into their community, and the possibility of civil commitment following the expiration of their prison term (Bumby & Maddox, 1999). The decision of the U.S. Supreme Court in *Kansas v. Hendricks* (1997) stated that the civil commitment of sex offenders deemed at risk for recidivism after completion of their prison term violated neither the double jeopardy nor *ex post facto* clauses of the Constitution. This decision further encouraged states to enact sexual predator statutes.

Mary Alice Conroy describes the impact of this legislation on forensic practice in her chapter in this volume. She reviews sex offender legislation (including sexual violent predator statutes) and evaluations in legal and historical contexts, and considers issues related to evaluating the sex offender's mental state and assessing the risk for recidivism. Both clinical and actuarial predictions are explained and the use and abuse of "profiles" are reviewed. Conroy examines forensic assessment instruments that have been developed to evaluate future risk of offending. In addition, she reviews specialized treatment modalities important to risk management with this special population. Included in this chapter are sections addressing the evaluation of minorities (women, juveniles, and ethnic minorities), as well as ethical concerns and expert testimony.

Battered Woman Syndrome in Courts: Issues and Applications

A battered woman who assaults or kills her partner or spouse may be charged with a criminal offense. Frequently, there is little or no *physical* evidence that the woman was in imminent danger, nor had she memorialized her prior battering in hospital records or by confiding in friends or family. Conceptualized and labeled by Lenore Walker (1979, 1984), battered woman syndrome (BWS) may represent a defense against such charges. BWS represents an attempt to establish that the woman's actions at the time of the crime were motivated by self-defense. In fact, BWS is the predominant method of defending battered women who have assaulted or killed their batterers, and it is the most successful syndrome testimony in terms of acceptance in court (Downs, 1996).

In the chapter by Diane Follingstad, she argues that Walker's initial conceptualization of BWS and its dynamics have shaped the criteria by which judges determine its admissibility and that provide the "scientific evidence" that informed appellate court review about this syndrome. Based on the scientific literature, Follingstad concludes that there are serious problems with the validity and applicability of BWS to legal cases. She reviews the history and uses of BWS in court, including major legal issues and case law focusing on those decisions addressing the admissibility of testimony on this issue. She describes difficulties with syndrome evidence in general, and with BWS in particular, questioning whether BWS is an actual syndrome. The relevance of BWS in other cases involving allegations, such as fraud, drug running, child abuse, child homicide, divorce, and custody, is examined. Follingstad describes methodology for assessing battered women's legal cases and suggests future directions for defending battered women without relying on BWS, while still using data *about* battered women as an organizing principle in their defense.

Pathologies of Attachment, Violence, and Criminality

Interpersonal violence most frequently occurs between those who know one another. However, rates are still higher for a subcategory of people: those who are attached or bonded to one another. Meloy (1992) described the nature of these "violent attachments," identifying a group of individuals at risk for acts of violence against those with whom they have intense or sexual relationships.

J. Reid Meloy focuses on the relationship among attachment, violence, and criminality. He reviews the origins of attachment theory and considers the psychobiology of attachment. Meloy places pathologies of attachment in historical perspective and describes the relationship between this attachment and interpartner violence. He suggests new avenues of forensic psychological research, including stalking behavior, which he has described as an old behavior but a new crime (Meloy, 1999).

Violence Risk Assessment

Despite the U.S. Supreme Court's decision in *Barefoot v. Estelle* (1983) that clinical predictions of violence could *not* be made with an acceptable degree of reliability, the Court indicated that to prevent such testimony was "like asking us to disinvent the wheel." In both the civil and criminal legal systems, courts frequently consider risk of future violence in the decision-making process. Questions regarding orders of protection, involuntary commitment, parental child abuse, transfers of juveniles to adult court, sex offenders transferred to civil commitment status, and mitigation and aggravation in death penalty cases are but a few of the areas relying on violence risk assessment.

John Monahan describes the relevance of violence risk assessment to the legal system and how such evidence is legally evaluated. He contrasts clinical and actuarial risk assessment and then reviews instruments developed specifically to evaluate risk of violence. He summarizes those risk factors found to be related to the occurrence of violence as identified in the MacArthur Violence Risk Assessment Study (Monahan et al., 2001; Steadman et al., 2000). Monahan addresses the issue of the relationship between clinical and actuarial risk assessment in formulating opinions and explains how such opinions should be communicated.

Emerging Directions

Forensic psychologists and attorneys are beginning to recognize the potential influence that forensic psychological research and practice could have on public policy and the law. In the final section of this volume, the interdependence between psychology and law is explored. Psychologists are encouraged to take a more active role in familiarizing themselves with case law and the legal system and improving the quality of services they offer to the law. They are urged to advise legislators about what psychologists can and cannot validly assess and to attempt to influence legislation and public policy.

In addition, it is recognized that the law, public policy, and psychology have a direct impact on those they serve and affect. Legal decision making may have a profound influence on the mental health of all parties in civil and criminal litigation. The final chapter in this volume describes ways in which forensic psychology can encourage judges and attorneys to promote the emotional well-being of parties in legal cases while minimizing the law's negative effects on overall psychological functioning.

Forensic Psychology's Interdependence with Law and Policy

There are a number of roles for forensic psychologists (i.e., consultant, testifying about a specific individual or topic, providing legislative testimony), each involving knowledge of the law and the ability to apply it. Consequently, forensic psychologists must possess knowledge of the appropriate statutes, case law, and policies to effectively practice and conduct relevant research. They must understand the explicit wording of the law and be aware of the subtle shifts in legal language that occur regularly.

Daniel Krauss and Bruce Sales explore the interdependent relationship between forensic practice and research and law and policy. They examine problems arising when nomolithic data are used to address idiographic questions. Using two common areas of forensic practice and research, forensic evaluations and testimony, the authors demonstrate the impact of law and policy on the field of forensic psychology. The ability of forensic psychologists to influence lawmakers and shape public policy is still in its infancy. Although *Brown v. the Board of Education* (1954) involved the application of social psychology research to public policy, few examples exist that so clearly demonstrate the relevance of psychological research to the law. Krauss and Sales argue that because legislators frequently assume, often incorrectly, that psychologists can provide information of direct relevance to a legal question, forensic psychologists should have a greater sense of involvement in the formation of laws and policies. The authors provide guideposts for improving the quality of forensic services to the law, consider issues related to evidentiary reliability and relevance, and describe other criteria addressed by *Daubert v. Merrell Dow Pharmaceuticals, Inc.* (1993).

Therapeutic Jurisprudence

The emerging field of therapeutic jurisprudence (TJ) represents another point at which law, public policy, and psychology (and the social sciences in general) intersect. TJ recognizes that, intentionally or unintentionally, the law af-

fects the mental health and functioning of those whom it impacts (Stolle, Wexler, Winick, & Dauer, 1997). As defined by Slobogin (1995), TJ uses the social sciences to "study the extent to which a legal rule or practice promotes the psychological and physical well-being of the people it affects" (p. 767). TJ represents a more humane, therapeutic approach to the legal system, the goal of which is to maximize the positive or therapeutic consequences of laws and their administration while minimizing the negative or antitherapeutic consequences. TJ evaluates the behavior of those involved in the legal system: attorneys; judges, probation officers, and law enforcement officers.

The chapter authored by Susan Daicoff and David Wexler in this volume, considers the law from a therapeutic perspective, focusing on criminal, personal injury, employment, and family law. They discuss the concepts of "therapeutic lawyering" and "therapeutic judging," and they examine the ways laws may be altered, administered, or applied to increase their positive therapeutic consequences. Daicoff and Wexler consider ethical and philosophical issues involved in the TJ approach to the law and discuss future trends in this emerging field.

SUMMARY

Although the roots of forensic psychology date back to the early 1900s, marked by the publication of *On the Witness Stand* (Münsterberg, 1908), it required almost two decades for the field to demonstrate the empirical basis necessary to qualify as evidentiary expert testimony. Both state and federal courts now generally accept the application of forensic psychology theory, research, and methodology to a wide range of civil and criminal legal questions. Programs offering doctorates in forensic psychology have been established, and postdoctoral fellowships, although limited in number, are available. Continuing professional education programs, presented by APA-approved sponsors, designed to provide the skills, training, and knowledge required of experts in court, are readily available. Most recently, the APA approved forensic psychology as a specialty within the field of psychology—a landmark recognition of its current status.

It is hoped that graduate students and mental health professionals reading this book will develop an appreciation for the field as a whole, recognizing its uniqueness, its complexity, and the need for specialized training and knowledge. In addition, each chapter should serve as a reference source on a specific topic, reviewing the state of the art in the early twenty-first century.

REFERENCES

Americans with Disabilities Act of 1990, 42 U.S.C.A. 12101 *et seq.*

American Psychiatric Association. (2000). *Diagnostic and statistical manual of mental disorders* (4th ed., text rev.). Washington, DC: Author.

American Psychological Association. (1992). Ethical principles of psychologists and code of conduct. *American Psychologist, 47,* 1597–1611.

American Psychological Ethics Committee. (2001). Reprint of the Ethics Committee, 2000. *American Psychologist, 56,* 680–688.

Barefoot v. Estelle, 463 U.S. 880 (1983).

Bartol, C. R., & Bartol, A. M. (1999). History of forensic psychology. In A. K. Hess & I. B. Weiner (Eds.), *The handbook of forensic psychology* (2nd ed., pp. 3–23). New York: Wiley.

Bell, C. (1997). The Americans with Disabilities Act, mental disabilities and work. In R. J. Bonnie & J. Monahan (Eds.), *Mental disorder, mental disability and the law* (pp. 203–219). Chicago: University of Chicago Press.

Brown v. Board of Education of Topeka, 74 S. Ct. 686 (1954).

Bumby, K. M., & Maddox, M. C. (1999). Judges' knowledge about sexual offenders, difficulties presiding over sexual offender cases, and opinions on sentencing, treatment, and legislation. *Sexual Abuse: A Journal of Research and Treatment, 11,* 305–315.

Committee on Ethical Guidelines for Forensic Psychologists. (1991). Specialty guidelines for forensic psychologists. *Law and Human Behavior, 15,* 655–665.

Crane v. Kentucky, 106 S. Ct. 2142 (1986).

Daubert v. Merrell Dow Pharmaceuticals, Inc., 509 U.S. 579, 113 S. Ct. 2786 (1993).

Dickerson v. U.S., 166 F.3d 667 (2000).

Downs, D. A. (1996). More than victims: *Battered women, the syndrome society, and the law.* Chicago: University of Chicago Press.

Dusky v. U.S., 362 U.S. 402, 80 S. Ct. 788 (1960).

Fredrick, R. I. (1997). *The Validity Indicator Profile.* Minneapolis, MN: National Computer Systems.

Furman v. Georgia, 408 U.S. 238 (1972).

Goldstein, A. M. (1996). *An introduction to forensic psychology practice.* Continuing education workshop sponsored by the American Psychological Association, Toronto, Ontario, Canada, August 22, 1996.

Greenberg, L. R., & Gould, J. W. (2001). The treating expert: A hybrid role with firm boundaries. *Professional Psychology: Research and Practice, 32,* 469–478.

Greenberg, S. A., & Shuman, D. W. (1997). Irreconcilable conflict between therapeutic and forensic roles. *Professional Psychology Research and Practice, 28,* 50–57.

Greenberg, S. A., & Shuman, D. W. (1999). *Personal injury examination: The application of psychology to the law of torts.* Unpublished manuscript.

Gregg v. Georgia, 428 U.S. 153 (1976).

Grisso, T. (1986). *Evaluating competencies: Forensic assessments and instruments.* New York: Plenum Press.

Hare, R. D. (1980). A research scale for the assessment of psychopathy in criminal populations. *Personality and Individual Differences, 1,* 111–119.

Hare, R. D. (1991). *Manual for the Revised Psychopathy Checklist.* Toronto, Ontario, Canada: Multi-Health Systems.

Hare, R. D. (1996). Psychopathy: A clinical construct whose time has come. *Criminal Justice and Behavior, 23,* 25–54.

Hart, S. D. (2001). Forensic issues. In W. J. Livesley (Ed.), *Handbook of personality disorders: Theory, research, and treatment* (pp. 555–569). New York: Guilford Press.

Heilbrun, K. S. (2000, July 20). *Petition for the recognition of a specialty in professional psychology.* Submitted on behalf of the American Board of Forensic Psychology and the American Psychology–Law Society to the American Psychological Association.

Hess, A. K., & Weiner, I. B. (Eds.). (1999). *The handbook of forensic psychology* (2nd ed.). New York: Wiley.

Hoge, S. K., Bonnie, R. J., Poythress, N., & Monahan, J. (1992). Attorney-client decision-making in criminal cases: Client competence and participation as perceived by their attorneys. *Behavioral Sciences and the Law, 10,* 385–394.

In re Gault, 387 U.S. 1 (1967).

Inwald, R., & Resko, J. (1995). Pre-employment screening for public safety personnel. In L. VandeCreek & S. Knapp (Eds.), *Innovations in clinical practice: A sourcebook* (Vol. 14, pp. 365–382). Sarasota, FL: Professional Resource Exchange.

Jenkins v. United States, 307 F.2d 637 (U.S. App, D.C., 1962).

Kansas v. Hendricks, 117 S. Ct. 2072 (1997).

Kuehnle, K. (1998). Child sexual abuse evaluations: The scientist-practitioner model. *Behavioral Sciences and the Law, 16,* 5–20.

La Fond, J. Q. (1998). The cost of enacting a sexual predator law. *Psychology, Public Policy and the Law, 4,* 468–504.

Lockett v. Ohio, 438 U.S. 586, 604 (1978).

Meloy, J. R. (1992). *Violent attachments.* Northvale, NJ: Aronson.

Meloy, J. R. (1999). Stalking: An old behavior, a new crime. *Psychiatric Clinics North America, 22,* 85–99.

Miranda v. Arizona, 384 U.S. 436 (1966).

Monahan, J. (Ed.). (1980). *Who is the client? The ethics of psychological intervention in the criminal justice system.* Washington, DC: American Psychological Association.

Monahan, J., Steadman, H., Silver, E., Appelbaum, A., Robbins, P., Mulvey, E., et al. (2001). *Rethinking risk assessment: The MacArthur Study of Mental Disorder and Violence.* New York: Oxford University Press.

Münsterberg, H. (1908). *On the witness stand.* New York: Doubleday.

Myers, J. E. B. (1998). *Legal issues in child abuse and neglect* (2nd ed.). Newbury Park, CA: Sage.

Pynoos, R. S., Steinberg, A. M., & Goenjian, A. (1996). Traumatic stress in childhood and adolescence: Recent developments and current controversies. In B. A. van der Kolk, A. C. McFarlane, & L. Weisaeth (Eds.), *Traumatic stress: The effects of overwhelming experience on mind, body and society* (pp. 331–358). New York: Guilford Press.

Redding, R. E., Floyd, M. Y., & Hawk, G. L. (2001). What judges think about one testimony of mental health experts: A survey of the courts and bar. *Behavioral Sciences and the Law, 19,* 583–594.

Rigaud, M., & Flynn, C. (1995). Fitness for duty evaluation (FFD) in industrial and military workers. *Psychiatric Annals, 25,* 315–323.

Rogers, R., Bagby, R. M., & Dickens, S. E. (1992). *Structured Interview of Reported Symptoms (SIRS) and professional manual.* Odessa, FL: Psychological Assessment Resources.

Rogers, R., Salekin, R. T., Sewell, K. W., Goldstein, A. M., & Leonard, K. (1998). A comparison of forensic and nonforensic malingerers: A prototypical analysis of explanatory models. *Law and Human Behavior, 22,* 353–367.

Rogers, R., Sewell, K. W., & Goldstein, A. M. (1994). Explanatory models of malingering: A prototypical analysis. *Law and Human Behavior, 18,* 543–552.

Scheck, B., Neufeld, P., & Dwyer, J. (2000). *Actual innocence.* New York: Cambridge University Press.

Schulman, J., Shaver, P., Colman, R., Emrich, B., & Christie, R. (1973, May). Recipe for a jury. *Psychology Today,* 37–84.

Slobogin, C. (1995). Therapeutic jurisprudence: Five dilemmas to ponder. *Psychology, Public Policy, and Law, 1,* 193–219.

Steadman, H., Silver, E., Monahan, J., Appelbaum, A., Robbins, P., Mulvey, E., et al. (2000). A classification tree approach to the development of actuarial violence risk assessment tools. *Law and Human Behavior, 24,* 83–100.

Stolle, D. P., Wexler, D. B., Winick, B. J., & Dauer, E. A. (1997). Integrating preventive law and therapeutic jurisprudence: A law and psychology based approach to lawyering. *California West Law Review, 34–1,* 15–51. (Reprinted from *Practicing therapeutic jurisprudence: Law as a helping profession,* pp. 5–44, by D. P. Stolle, D. B. Wexler, & B. J. Winick, Eds., Durham: Carolina Academic Press)

United States v. John Hinkley, 525 F. Supp. 1342 (D.D.C. 1982).

Walker, L. E. (1979). *The battered woman.* New York: Harper & Row.

Walker, L. E. (1984). *The battered woman syndrome.* New York: Springer.

Wells, G. L., Small, M., Penrod, S., Malpass, R. S., Fulero, S. M., & Brimacombe, C. A. (1998). Eyewitness identification procedures: Recommendations for lineups and photospreads. *Law and Human Behavior, 22,* 603–647.

Wigmore, J. H. (1909). Professor Münsterberg and the psychology of testimony: Being a report of the case of *Cokestone v. Münsterberg. Illinois Law Review, 3,* 399–445.

Woodson v. North Carolina, 428 U.S. 280, 305 (1976).

CHAPTER 2

Forensic Training and Practice

IRA K. PACKER AND RANDY BORUM

At the beginning of the twenty-first century, the field of forensic psychology is now sufficiently mature to be considered a well-defined area of specialization. Psychological historians often trace the intellectual origins of the discipline of psychology and law to Hugo Münsterberg's publication of *On the Witness Stand* in 1908. However, coordinated and formalized attempts to define and establish an area of forensically specialized professional practice only began to gain momentum in the 1970s.

The first landmark in that era was the founding of the American Psychology-Law Society, and its subsequent recognition as a division of the American Psychological Association (Division 41). Since then, the field of psychology and law has witnessed the formal recognition of forensic psychology as a practice specialty by the American Board of Professional Psychology (ABPP); the development of "Specialty Guidelines for Forensic Psychologists" (Committee on Ethical Guidelines for Forensic Psychologists, 1991); the addition of a section on "Forensic Activities" (Section 7) within the American Psychological Association's Ethical Principles and Code of Conduct for Psychologists (American Psychological Association [APA], 1992); the emergence of over a dozen professional journals and hundreds of books, published nationally and internationally, focusing on forensic mental health issues (Borum & Otto, 2000); and growth in the membership of the American Psychology-Law Society to 2,500, approximately 85% of whom identify themselves as forensic clinicians (Grisso, 1991).

The publication in 1980 of the edited book, *Who Is the Client?* (Monahan, 1980), was significant in laying out the contours of the field of forensic psychology and differentiating it from therapeutic practice in clinical psychology. It highlighted the notion that the practice of forensic psychology requires a specialized orientation and mind-set and cannot simply be considered a subcategory of clinical psychology. It represented an early attempt to clarify the boundary issues and role definitions inherent in forensic psychological practice.

Most significantly, in 2001, the APA formally recognized forensic psychology as a specialty within psychology. This designation signifies that a substantial body of professional literature and specialized knowledge exists that distinguishes forensic psychology from other specialties. Furthermore, it reflects the development of specific educational programs throughout all levels of training, from undergraduate through graduate and postdoctoral levels as well as continuing education for practitioners.

As the field first began to emerge, the term forensic psychology was used broadly to include the many streams of research and practice at the intersection of psychology and law. More recently, attempts have been made to refine and delineate the parameters of how the specialty should be defined. At a practical level, the Committee on Ethical Guidelines for Forensic Psychologists (1991) suggested that, for purposes of applying the "Specialty Guidelines for Forensic Psychologists," the definition should apply to "psychologists, within any subdiscipline of psychology (e.g., clinical, developmental, social, experimental) when they are engaged regularly as experts and represent themselves, as such, in an activity primarily intended to provide professional psychological expertise to the judicial system" (p. 656). With a somewhat broader view, Hess (1999) describes forensic psychology as having three aspects: "(1) the application of basic psychological processes to legal questions; (2) research on legal issues, such as the definition of privacy or how juries make decisions; and (3) knowledge of legal issues" (p. 24).

These definitions are sufficiently specific to designate specialists and an area of specialization, but remain sufficiently broad so that they may include psychologists whose specialties are more clinically oriented (e.g., clinical, counseling, school), as well as those that are primarily experimental (e.g., social, cognitive, developmental). Although there is broad recognition of the common substrates and basic concepts that characterize the discipline (Bersoff et al., 1997), a recent trend has emerged to distinguish the labels applied to the clinical and experimental facets of the field. The term forensic psychology is becoming more readily associated with applications of clinical specialties to the law (also sometimes referred to as clinical-forensic psychology), and the term legal psychology is being used to refer to the application of other areas of psychology to the law (Bersoff et al., 1997; Careers and Training Committee, 1998). Indeed, the definition of forensic psychology that was submitted to the APA as part of the application for recognition as a specialty is as follows

> For the purposes of this application, forensic psychology will be defined as the professional practice by psychologists within the areas of clinical psychology, counseling psychology, neuropsychology, and school psychology, when they are engaged regularly as experts and represent themselves as such, in an activity primarily intended to provide professional psychological expertise to the judicial system. (Petition for the Recognition of a Specialty in Professional Psychology: Forensic Psychology, 2000, p. 1)

To maintain clarity in this chapter and within the field, we also use this definition when referring to forensic psychology.

TRAINING AND PRACTICE

Specialists in legal psychology are represented predominantly from three areas: social, developmental, and cognitive psychology. *Social psychologists* with this specialty often conduct research and consult with attorneys and courts regarding issues such as jury selection (e.g., Johnson & Haney, 1994), credibility of witnesses, (Bank & Poythress, 1982), and influences on jury decision making (Bornstein, 1999). Research and practice often focus on identifying and understanding group processes that affect jury deliberation and decision making (see chapter by Kovera, Dickinson, & Cutler in this volume). In addition to studying the behavior of actors in the legal system, the system itself may be viewed as an institution whose processes can be subjected to social psychological analysis, studying, for example, the relative values of the adversary system versus mediation and arbitration. Social psychological paradigms, theories, and research methods also can be applied to legally relevant social issues such as the impact of race and gender on decision making in the criminal justice system (e.g., Sweeney & Haney, 1992) or the perception of what constitutes sexual harassment (e.g., Hurt, Wiener, Russell, & Mannen, 1999; see the chapter by Vasquez, Baker, & Shullman in this volume).

Developmental psychologists specializing in legal psychology often conduct legally relevant consultations and perform research on issues related to children and adolescents in the legal system. Substantive issues of interest often include the accuracy and suggestibility of children's testimony (e.g., Ceci & Bruck, 1995), ability of adolescents to make legally relevant decisions and to comprehend their rights (e.g., Grisso, 2000), and the impact of divorce, separation, and varying custody arrangements on children's development (e.g., Wallerstein & Lewis, 1998; see the chapter by Otto, Buffington-Vollum, & Edens in this volume). A major field of inquiry has focused on whether, and under what circumstances, the testimony of child witnesses should be considered to be credible. This has been a particularly important area in light of some highly publicized cases of elaborate child abuse rings, such as the McMartin case in California and the Fells Acre case in Massachusetts. Studies within this legal psychology specialty have focused, for example, on the effects of age and types of questioning (e.g., direct versus open-ended) on accuracy and suggestibility (e.g., Saywitz, Goodman, Nicholas, & Moan, 1991; see the chapter by Kuehnle in this volume). Other researchers have focused on the impact of compelling children who were allegedly abused to testify directly at the trial of their abuser (e.g., Goodman, Levine, Melton, & Ogden, 1991). This body of research led to the submission of an amicus brief to the Supreme Court by the APA in the case of *Maryland v. Craig* (1990).

Cognitive psychologists specializing in legal psychology are often involved in extrapolating research on perception and memory to legally relevant issues. Several topics have received a great deal of attention, including eyewitness identification (e.g., Wells, 1978), accuracy of witness memory (e.g., Loftus & Davies, 1984), issues related to "recovered memories" (e.g., Alpert, Brown, & Courtois, 1998; Ornstein, Ceci, & Loftus, 1998), and people's ability to detect lying or deception (e.g., Zaparniuk, Yuille, & Taylor, 1995).

As is true for psychologists in all subdisciplines of legal psychology, specialists are well-grounded in general theory and research, then apply these concepts and knowledge to questions that may be relevant to the law or legal system. For example, empirical research regarding factors that affect memory—including stress, cross-racial identification, and decay of memory—all have implications for the criminal justice system. One of the most significant contributions of cognitive psychology to the legal system has been in the area of eyewitness identification. Wells et al. (1998) published a set of recommendations and guidelines for lineups, incorporating theory about the impact of relative judgment (i.e., eyewitnesses tend to identify the person from the lineup who most resembles the culprit, *relative* to the other members of the lineup, even when the suspect is absent) with experimental studies on lineups (i.e., incorporating empirical findings about factors that influence the validity of an identification) and scientific logic (i.e., treating a lineup as an experiment, thereby requiring removal of confounding and influencing variables and requiring that the experimenter, that is, the person conducting the lineup, be blind to the true identity of the suspect). Findings and recommendations from this white paper were incorporated into official policy by the U.S. Department of Justice and have made a significant contribution to the conduct of law enforcement lineups and the evaluation of their validity.

The *clinical* application of mental health issues to the law occurs in both criminal and civil contexts. In the criminal law, the most common issues involve assessments of cognitive and psychological status and the relevance of that status to specially defined legal questions, such as competency to stand trial, criminal responsibility, amenability to treatment, and violence risk (see chapters by Stafford; Goldstein, Morse, & Shapiro; Cunningham & Goldstein; and Monahan in this volume). In civil areas, referral questions may also revolve around issues of cognitive and psychological status, but the specific legal question or relevant functional capacity may be somewhat different (e.g., testamentary capacity, need for guardianship, need for involuntary psychiatric hospitalization, psychological damages resulting from the act of another, worker's compensation suits; see the chapter by Greenberg in this volume). Similarly, forensic psychological consultation is often sought in family law matters, such as child custody, visitation, and termination of parental rights (see the chapter by Otto, Buffington-Vollum, & Edens in this volume).

Although clinical forensic practice is most often associated with evaluations and expert witness testimony (see Table 2.1 for a list of sample areas of forensic practice), forensic psychologists also may provide specialized treatment services. Treatment to populations involved with the legal system is certainly provided by a broad range of psychologists (e.g., correctional psychologists providing treatment to inmates, clinical psychologists working with divorced or divorcing

TABLE 2.1   Sample Areas of Forensic Psychological Practice

Criminal
Competence to waive Miranda rights.
Competence to stand trial.
Criminal responsibility (insanity defense).
Diminished capacity.
Aid in sentencing.
Competency of a witness.
Risk assessment (e.g., for discharge from hospitals, parole, or probation).
Juvenile's amenability to treatment.
Juvenile transfer or waiver (i.e., of jurisdiction from juvenile to adult court).

Civil
Civil commitment.
Appointment of guardian.
Personal injury.
Worker's compensation.
Testamentary capacity (i.e., ability to competently compose a will).
Eligibility for disability.
Eligibility for special education.
Fitness for duty (e.g., police, firefighter).
Child custody.
Termination of parental rights.
Parental visitation rights.

families). What characterizes forensic treatment is the application to specific psycholegal issues. For instance, forensic psychologists may provide treatment to defendants adjudicated incompetent to stand trial, with the aim of restoring these individuals to competency. In this case, the psychologist applies not only general clinical treatment principles but must focus the treatment on issues that are specific to the legal context.

An area that is in particular demand at present involves violence risk assessment. Forensic psychologists provide valuable expertise to other practitioners, agencies, and the legal system regarding assessing risk of violence. This involves not only providing risk assessments, but also consulting on the appropriate use of specialized tests and actuarial instruments. With increasing public concern about school shootings, workplace violence, and sex offending, there is increasing demand for clarity about the reliability, validity, and generalizability of proposed instruments (McNeil et al., in press; Otto, 2000; Otto, Borum, & Hart, 2001).

As is evident from this discussion, the practice of forensic psychology spans a wide range of populations, including young children, adolescents, families, the elderly, people with severe mental illness, and criminal offenders. Accordingly, with regard to training, a forensic specialist should begin with a strong foundation of general clinical training and skill development. Although forensic training involves specialized knowledge and skills (described next), these specialized applications require a foundation of clinical competence in understanding psychopathology, assessment, interviewing, conceptualization, and other general clinical skills. This is analogous to the sequence for legal psychologists, who first must be well grounded in their subdiscipline, and then subsequently apply concepts and knowledge to the legal area of specialization.

One who engages in the practice of forensic psychology, however, may not necessarily have competence or expertise with all populations and in all areas of forensic practice. For example, psychologists who have been trained primarily to work with children, adolescents, and families may then learn to apply their knowledge in child custody cases but may not necessarily have the requisite background to assess testamentary capacity in mentally ill adults. In some instances, though, the population may be more specific to the forensic arena; one obvious example of this is forensic work with adult criminal offenders. Unless a psychologist has trained in a correctional or forensic setting, for example, he or she may not be familiar with, or competent to assess, defendants who are psychopathic. Therefore, training in forensic psychology needs to focus both on understanding the appropriate clinical population as well as gaining the specialized legal knowledge and skills in forensic methodology.

GRADUATE TRAINING IN FORENSIC PSYCHOLOGY

Models of Training

As noted above, appropriate training for forensic psychologists involves developing core competencies in applied psychology (e.g., clinical psychology), augmented by specialized didactic courses in areas of law and forensic psychology, specialized assessment techniques, and opportunities to apply these skills and knowledge under supervision in clinical settings. In the current state of affairs, it is difficult to find a direct path to such coherent training. Rather, there are a number of programs that are available at each level of education for those interested.

The American Psychology-Law Society (AP-LS) has identified, as of 1998, 19 accredited doctoral degree programs in psychology that offer specialized training in psychology and law. One of the major ways to classify these programs is according to the type of academic training

TABLE 2.2   Doctoral Programs in Forensic Psychology

University of Alabama, Tuscaloosa
University of British Columbia, Vancouver
California School of Professional Psychology, Fresno
Long Island University, Brooklyn, New York
Queen's University, Kingston, Ontario
Sam Houston State University, Huntsville, Texas
Simon Fraser University, Burnaby, British Columbia

TABLE 2.3   Doctoral Programs in Legal Psychology

Florida International University, North Miami
University of Illinois at Chicago
University of Kansas, Lawrence
University of Nevada–Reno
Simon Fraser University, Burnaby, British Columbia
University of Texas at El Paso
University of Virginia, Charlottesville

offered in the two disciplines. Many of these programs offer a terminal doctoral degree in psychology (typically a Ph.D. or Psy.D.), with a specialization, concentration, specialty "track," or minor in forensic psychology or law and psychology. The specialized concentration typically requires two or more forensic courses and often some forensically relevant clinical experience. AP-LS has identified seven graduate programs that offer specialty training in clinical-forensic psychology (see Table 2.2). Many other universities offer informal opportunities, such as individual courses in forensic psychology or practicum placements in correctional or forensic settings. More recently, some programs have begun to offer a doctoral degree specifically in forensic psychology or forensic clinical psychology, although the long-term viability or advisability of such specialized degrees remains an open question. Eight programs have been identified that offer specialty training in legal psychology (see Table 2.3).

Another model of training is the joint degree program (see Table 2.4), in which students take all coursework in psychology required for the doctoral degree (Ph.D. or Psy.D.) and all coursework in law (from an affiliated law school) required to earn a professional law degree (J.D.). Two key issues are relevant to determining the appropriateness of a joint degree model for a psychologist who aspires primarily to be a forensic practitioner. The first is whether there is a significant incremental advantage in gaining a complete professional legal education, if one intends only to practice psychology. The answer here mainly depends on what the student hopes to achieve by attaining a dual degree. If one is attracted by the process of legal education or has a particular affinity for studying the law, then the joint degree should be considered, whether any concrete advantages would accrue to one's clinical practice. If, on the other hand, one seeks the added

TABLE 2.4   Joint Degree Programs

University of Arizona, Tucson: J.D.-Ph.D.
MCP Hahnemann University/Villanova College of Law, Philadelphia, Pennsylvania: Ph.D.-J.D.
University of Nebraska, Lincoln: J.D.-Ph.D.
Pacific Graduate School of Psychology, Palo Alto, California: Ph.D.-J.D.
Stanford University, Stanford, California: Ph.D.-J.D.
Widener University, Chester, Pennsylvania: Psy.D.-J.D.

degree solely to enhance professional "credibility" in clinical forensic practice, then one may be disappointed to discover its lack of significance to judges and attorneys in most circumstances. If one does decide to pursue both degrees, the second issue is whether there is any incremental advantage in obtaining these degrees from a joint degree program, as opposed to independently obtaining the degrees from separate programs. Even programs that consider themselves to be joint degree programs differ substantially in the level of integration that occurs with the psychological and legal aspects of training.

Some commentators have expressed concern that the graduates of joint degree programs are perceived as neither psychologists nor lawyers (Melton, Huss, & Tomkins, 1999) and that practical opportunities to integrate the two disciplines may be limited. Accordingly, some would argue that this type of program may not be well suited for most students who are interested primarily in clinical forensic psychology careers, and that time spent in law school may detract from time available to further one's clinical training. This joint degree model may be more useful for those interested in other career tracks, such as public policy development or social science research in the legal arena. The opportunity to be educated in both disciplines may provide graduates with skills that those with single degrees may not possess. That is the hope and expectation of these programs. To date, however, the validity of this expectation is unknown.

Levels of Training

In 1995, 48 leading scholars, educators, and clinicians in the field of psychology and law were invited to the National Invitational Conference on Education and Training in Law and Psychology at Villanova Law School, chaired by Donald Bersoff, J.D., Ph.D. This conference, known as the Villanova Conference, produced recommendations about all levels of training in legal and forensic psychology.

Participants at the Villanova Conference recommended that graduate training programs in forensic psychology could offer any of three levels of training. The first level is referred to as the entry level: the legally informed clinician. The primary objective for this level of training is to develop a working knowledge of legal issues relevant to professional psychological practice (e.g., confidentiality, privilege, third-party reporting, responding to subpoenas). The impetus for this proposal was a recognition that forensic issues have now permeated many traditional clinical practices, and *all* clinicians, not only those who specialize in forensic psychology, need to be aware of certain aspects of the law that may impact on their practice. It was proposed that a substantial proportion of this legally relevant information could be incorporated into existing courses, such as ethics, assessment, and clinical practice, although it is possible that an added overview course on mental health law would be beneficial. Many states now require, in addition to the National Licensing Examination, that psychologists pass a state jurisprudence examination focusing on state/provincial laws relevant to psychological practice to be licensed in that jurisdiction. Table 2.5 poses some examples of legally relevant situations that a clinical psychologist may encounter.

The second level of training is referred to as the proficiency level. The primary objective of this level of training is to establish forensic competence in one or more circumscribed areas related to some other major clinical specialty with which the psychologist has primary identification and expertise (e.g., a general child psychologist who performs custody evaluations as a secondary part of practice or a psychologist with expertise in trauma who performs personal injury evaluations). This would be appropriate for clinicians who do not specialize in forensic psychology but wish to do some forensic work in a limited area of practice. The requirements for training at this level would be more extensive than those for the legally informed clinician, and would likely include the necessity of one or more formal academic courses on forensic issues as well as some exposure to supervised clinical work in forensic settings.

The third level, specialty level, is oriented toward the training of psychologists whose professional activities focus primarily on the provision of services to courts, attorneys, law enforcement, or corrections, and whose main specialty identification is in forensic psychology. Training for this level of specialization involves intensive didactic and supervised practical experience. It includes in-depth study of case law

TABLE 2.5 Sample Forensic Issues for Clinicians

1. You have been providing psychotherapy services to a 16-year-old girl. After several months, her mother calls you and asks that the records be released to her. The girl does not want her mother to have the information. Should you release the information to the mother?

2. A mother brings her 10-year-old son in for treatment. You provide therapy to both of them for a period of several months. The mother then asks if you would testify at her upcoming divorce hearing that she should be awarded custody of her son. Should you agree to testify?

3. You receive a subpoena from an attorney of a psychiatrist who is being sued by your client for malpractice. The subpoena is for records of your client's treatment with you. Should you provide the records?

4. Your psychotherapy client informs you that he is the one who set fire to a house a year ago, in which two people died. The police have yet to solve the case. Do you report this information to the police?

5. A father who has visitation rights but not legal custody brings his daughter in for an initial psychological evaluation, expressing concern that she has been sexually abused by his ex-wife's new boyfriend. How should you proceed?

and significant clinical experience with different forensic populations and types of evaluations. Ultimately, a postdoctoral fellowship in forensic psychology and the attainment of board certification status in forensic psychology by the ABPP will likely be considered the hallmarks of the forensically specialized psychologist.

Graduate Training in Legal Psychology

Training for legal psychology typically occurs at the graduate level. Most training occurs in traditional academic departments with a faculty member who is interested in the application of research to issues of relevance to the law and legal system. A few departments have now developed minors in psychology and law, providing more specific knowledge in this area. Students are required to combine knowledge of psychology with an understanding of the legal system to appreciate how the former can impact the latter. The purpose of such programs is to educate future scholars to apply the principles, methodologies, and substantive knowledge of the social sciences to legal problems. Recommendations from the Villanova Conference suggest that, in addition to the core curriculum in psychology, students wishing to specialize in legal psychology should also obtain legal knowledge, including an understanding of legal processes, evidence, sources of law, and substantive law (i.e., basics of criminal and civil law). This knowledge may be obtained in law-related courses in a university curriculum or in special courses at law schools. In addition, it was recommended that the curriculum include courses on substantive legal psychology, including research (as noted above) and relevant case law and statutes.

Internships

The internship is typically structured as one year of full-time supervised clinical practice, and is most often initiated by students in a professional psychological specialty (e.g., clinical, counseling, school) during the final year of graduate training and before conferral of the doctoral degree. As with graduate training, it is generally recommended that students use the internship year to refine a solid foundation of clinical skills. In addition, it presents an opportunity to begin or enhance one's specialized forensic experiences. As it is advantageous to the intern to be exposed to a variety of clinical populations to aid in development of basic diagnostic and treatment skills that subsequently can be applied to forensic issues, most internships, even those in correctional settings, are not (and arguably should never be) completely "specialized." Some sites do, however, offer an opportunity to concentrate one's activities in forensic practice. According to a survey of APA-approved

internship sites conducted in 1997 (Bersoff et al., 1997), among those sites that purported to offer forensic placements (of which there was a return rate of 31%), only 38 indicated that they offered "major" forensic rotations, where interns spend 50% of their time in forensic placements. Many of these settings also offer some form of forensic seminar or didactic training.

Postdoctoral Training in Forensic Psychology

The postdoctoral fellowship is emerging in professional psychology as the benchmark of specialized training. Fellowships in forensic psychology, however, have been fairly slow to develop. There are currently 11 identified postdoctoral programs in forensic psychology (see Table 2.6), most of which accept only one or two Fellows each year. Most of these programs offer clinical placements that focus on criminal forensic assessment, particularly in the public sector and mostly with adults, although some programs (e.g., Massachusetts General Hospital and University of Massachusetts Medical School) also offer specialty training in juvenile forensic psychology. Because there are currently so few fellowship opportunities available, it is realistic to expect these programs to focus on developing leaders in the field, and it is premature to expect completion of a postdoctoral fellowship as a prerequisite for forensic practice.

In addition, because opportunities for graduate and internship training in forensic psychology often are limited, postdoctoral programs are, in some circumstances, the forum for basic forensic training. An example of the didactic curriculum from one such program is listed in Table 2.7. This curriculum begins with a basic orientation to the law and forensic concepts, such as competency to stand trial and criminal responsibility, and proceeds to cover a broad range of criminal and civil areas. The basic text for the course (Melton, Petrila, Poythress, & Slobogin, 1997) is one that would be considered appropriate for graduate-level courses in a more coordinated

---

TABLE 2.6 Postdoctoral Programs in Forensic Psychology

Center for Forensic Psychiatry, Ypsilanti, Michigan
Federal Bureau of Prisons, Springfield, Missouri
Federal Medical Center, Rochester, Minnesota
Florida State Hospital, Chattahoochee
Kirby Forensic Psychiatric Center, New York, New York
Massachusetts General Hospital, Juvenile Track, Boston
Patton State Hospital, Highland, California
St. Louis Hospital, St. Louis, Missouri
University of Massachusetts Medical School (Adult and Juvenile), Worcester
University of Southern California–Los Angeles
Western State Hospital, Tacoma, Washington

TABLE 2.7   Sample Curriculum for a Postdoctoral Fellowship in Forensic Psychology

Orientation to the Field of Psychology and Law.
Basic Introduction to Legal Principles.
Introduction to Finding and Understanding Case Law.
Review of Mental Health Statutes.
Mandated Reporting Requirements; Duty to Protect.
Confidentiality and Privilege.
Ethical Issues for Forensic Psychologists.
Psychological Testing for Forensic Issues: special considerations.
Introduction to Competence to Stand Trial (CST) Evaluations.
Advanced Issues in CST: decisional competence/restoration to competence.
Introduction to Criminal Responsibility.
Advanced Issues in Criminal Responsibility: diminished capacity/
   dispositional issues.
Malingering.
Use of Violence Risk Assessment Instruments.
Violence Risk Assessment: clinical issues.
Assessment of Sex Offenders.
Neuropsychological Issues in Forensic Evaluations.
Substance Abuse and Criminal Forensic Evaluations.
Psychopharmacology and Medication Issues in Forensic Evaluations.
Civil Competence (to consent to treatment, to care for self/property).
Civil Commitment.
Issues in Guardianship, Conservatorship, and Testamentary Capacity.
Personal Injury and Workers' Compensation.
Disability Evaluations.
Introduction to the Juvenile Court System and Juvenile Statutes.
Juvenile Forensic Evaluations.
Child Welfare and Child Custody Evaluations.
Expert Witness Testimony.

Source: Adapted from the University of Massachusetts Medical School Program.

and integrated training environment. Because this is a postdoctoral seminar, the textbook is supplemented by articles and books focusing on recent developments in the field and more advanced areas of inquiry. In addition, the curriculum includes a Landmark Cases Seminar, addressing the basic and fundamental cases in mental health law (e.g., *Carter v. General Motors,* 1961; *Dusky v. U.S.,* 1960; *Jones v. U.S.,* 1983; *Painter v. Bannister,* 1966), but also includes more recent cases with more complex issues (e.g., *Foucha v. Louisiana,* 1992; *Godinez v. Moran,* 1993; *Troxel v. Granville,* 2000). In this manner, several levels of training are combined into one postdoctoral year.

Continuing Education

Because the emergence of formal academic training in forensic psychology is fairly recent, many practicing psychologists have not had easy access to specialty training at the graduate or postdoctoral fellowship level. Thus, for many, the opportunity to develop new knowledge and skills is obtained through continuing education (CE). These programs are directed toward licensed professional psychologists who are seeking

to expand their practice by developing at least a proficiency in one or more areas of forensic psychology.

Participants at the Villanova Conference identified five goals of CE in forensic psychology: (a) improve standards of forensic practice and ethical decision making, (b) improve and update knowledge in specific content areas, (c) provide paths for the improvement of forensic skills, (d) provide opportunities for interdisciplinary interchange, and (e) stimulate research and the dissemination of new knowledge (Bersoff et al., 1997). They concluded, however, that many existing programs were not meeting all these requirements due to several factors, including inadequate quality control over presentations and presenters, failure to bridge the gap between research and practice, lack of accessibility, lack of standards to measure workshop success, and lack of clarity about the preexisting level of knowledge and experience that the audience may possess. This last point is especially significant given the wide range of individuals who may attend a forensic CE offering: very experienced forensic psychologists, those who have had some formal training in forensic psychology, those who have learned on the job, and those who have very little or no exposure to forensic concepts and practice.

A series of recommendations to address these problems and improve CE in forensic psychology emerged from the Villanova Conference: (a) delineating CE offerings into three identified levels: basic, specialty, and advanced; (b) considering credentialing of CE sponsors for forensic education (in addition to basic APA credentialing); (c) attracting a more diverse group of presenters (in terms of ethnic and gender composition) and addressing ethnic, cultural, gender, and linguistic differences directly in workshops; (d) developing alternatives to the one-day didactic workshop format, including summer institutes that would include supervised practical experience; and (e) making CE activities more multidisciplinary and interactive.

Some of these recommendations have already been incorporated into forensic CE training. For example, in 1999, the APA and American Bar Association sponsored several joint educational activities, including a three-day conference entitled Psychological Expertise and Criminal Justice. In addition, the American Academy of Forensic Psychology, perhaps the foremost forensic CE provider, has recently begun to offer four-day intensive training workshops in forensic psychology, divided into two tracks: beginner and advanced. Models for incorporating direct clinical experience into CE activities have not yet been successfully developed. Integrating this component of training poses a significant challenge because most training models involve direct supervised experience over a sustained period of time, as is the case with graduate school practica, internships, postdoctoral fellowships, and on-the-job training.

Certification and Credentialing

In 1978, the American Board of Forensic Psychology (ABFP) was formed for the purpose of credentialing and certifying forensic psychologists who were practicing at an advanced level of competence. This level of board certification, known as the forensic diplomate, was never intended to certify those at a basic or journeyman level of competence, but rather to designate only advanced practitioners. In 1985, ABFP joined the ABPP, becoming one of its Specialty Boards. Since then, the diplomate in forensic psychology has been awarded by ABPP through a process developed and implemented by ABFP.

Currently, applicants for board certification through ABFP/ABPP must be licensed psychologists who have at least five years of experience performing forensic work, including a minimum of 1,000 hours of forensic work over that period. In addition, applicants must have obtained at least 100 hours of specialized training in forensic psychology, which includes direct clinical supervision and/or didactic training (e.g., CE activities). This requirement of 100 hours of specialized training is deliberately modest, in recognition of the current state of affairs in which access to such training is limited. The application is reviewed by ABPP and ABFP to determine whether the basic requirements have been met, and, with the applicant's consent, an inquiry is sent to the appropriate state licensing board and state psychological association to verify that there are no outstanding ethical complaints against the psychologist. If there is an outstanding complaint, the certification process is placed on hold pending resolution of that matter. If there is a record of disciplinary action, the particular issue and circumstances will be considered in the decision of whether to accept the application.

Once an applicant has been determined by the board to meet the basic requirements, he or she must submit two work samples for review by a panel of forensic diplomates. The two samples must represent two *different* areas of forensic practice (e.g., competence to stand trial and personal injury; child custody and waiver of juvenile to adult court). This reflects the requirement that the diplomate have breadth of knowledge within the forensic field. A psychologist who is extremely skilled in performing child custody evaluations but does no other forensic work, for example, would not be a candidate for the forensic diploma. This in no way reflects on the quality of the individual psychologist, but rather is a function of the current standard for the diplomate, which requires breadth as well as depth of knowledge. The work samples are not simply examples of forensic reports. Rather, the applicant is expected to go beyond the report and demonstrate understanding of the clinical, ethical, and legal issues involved in performing those types of evaluations. For instance, the applicant may explain the rationale for the particular approaches taken to assess the psycholegal issue.

If both work samples are deemed acceptable as a result of this peer review, the applicant is required to participate in a three-hour oral examination (with three forensic diplomate examiners), the purpose of which is to examine further the candidate's knowledge and practice in forensic psychology, using the work samples as a starting point. The candidate is examined to determine if he or she practices ethically, demonstrates an ability to practice at a high level of competence, understands relevant psycholegal principles, and can apply psychological expertise to the legal issues. Furthermore, in keeping with the concept outlined above of having a broad knowledge of the field, the candidate is expected to be familiar with other areas of forensic practice in addition to those in which he or she practices. The level of knowledge in these other areas is not expected to be as high as in the areas of direct practice, although some basic familiarity with the major issues and case law is required. In this regard, forensic psychologists are expected to have knowledge of legal cases that impact on forensic and mental health practice, but are not expected to engage in exegetic legal case analysis. Candidates are provided with a list of cases that are considered important for forensic practitioners to be familiar with. They are informed that this list is not exhaustive, as the law is continually evolving. The list is updated every few years to incorporate new case law; Table 2.8 contains a sample of the case law included in the current list. In recognition of the complexity of forensic practice, applicants are provided with multiple opportunities to be examined. If a work sample is considered unsatisfactory, the applicant is provided with explicit feedback and invited to present another sample to be reviewed. Similarly, if the applicant does not pass the oral examination, he or she is afforded the opportunity to submit another set of work samples, which, if approved, will serve as the basis for a second oral examination.

The multi-stage certification process provides an opportunity for applicants to demonstrate their basic understanding of forensic psychological principles, knowledge of the psychological literature and relevant case law, ethical practice, and quality of forensic work. Given these requirements, it is perhaps not surprising that as of the time this book went to press, there were only 200 forensic psychology diplomates in the United States. It is important to keep in mind that the diplomate process is a voluntary system (i.e., there is no expectation that a psychologist obtain the diplomate to practice in the forensic arena or to qualify as an expert witness). As the field develops, though, there may be changes in the meaning of the diplomate, or the field may develop more basic levels of certification.

TABLE 2.8   Sample of Recommended Case Law for the Forensic Diplomate (ABPP)

Confidentiality and Duty to Protect
——— *In re Lifschutz,* 467 P.2d 557 (1970)
——— *Jaffee v. Redmond,* 518 U.S. 1 (1996)
——— *Tarasoff v. Board of Regents,* 551 P.2d 334 (1976)
——— *McIntosh v. Milano,* 403 A.2d 500 (1979)
——— *Jablonski v. U.S.,* 712 F.2d 391(1983)
——— *Lipari v. Sears,* 497 F. Supp. 185 (1980)
——— *Peck v. Addison County Counseling Service,* 499 A.2d 422 (1985)

Experts and Evidence
——— Federal Rules of Evidence (701–705)
——— *Frye v. United States,* 293 F. 1013 (1923)
——— *Daubert v. Merrell Dow Pharmaceuticals, Inc.,* 509 U.S. 579 (1993)
——— *Kumho Tire v. Carmichael,* 526 U.S. 137 (1999)
——— *Jenkins v. United States,* 307 F.2d 637 (1962)

Civil Commitment and Involuntary Treatment
——— *Rennie v. Klein,* 720 F.2d 266 (1983)
——— *Rivers v. Katz,* 495 NE 2d 337 (1986)
——— *Rogers v. Okin,* 638 F. Supp. 934 (1986)
——— *Washington v. Harper,* 494 U.S. 210 (1990)
——— *Riggins v. Nevada,* 504 U.S. 127 (1992)

Competence to Stand Trial
——— *Jackson v. Indiana,* 406 U.S. 715 (1972)
——— *Dusky v. U.S.,* 362 U.S. 402 (1960)
——— *Drope v. Missouri,* 410 U.S. 162 (1975)
——— *Wilson v. U.S.,* 391 F. 2d 460 (1968)
——— *Colorado v. Connelly,* 479 U.S. 157 (1986)
——— *Godinez v. Moran,* 509 U.S. 389 (1993)
——— *Frendak v. U.S.,* 408 A.2d 364 (1975)

Criminal Responsibility
——— *Durham v. U.S.,* 214 F.2d 862 (1954)
——— *U.S. v. Brawner,* 471 F.2d 969 (1972)
——— *Jones v. U.S.,* 463 U.S. 354 (1983)
——— *Foucha v. Louisiana,* 504 U.S. 71 (1992)
——— *Ake v. Oklahoma,* 470 U.S. 68 (1985)
——— *Shannon v. U.S.,* 512 U.S. 573 (1994)

Child Custody
——— *Painter v. Bannister,* 140 NW 2d 152 (1966)
——— *Santosky v. Kramer,* 455 U.S. 745 (1982)
——— *Troxel v. Granville,* 530 U.S. 57 (2000)

Juvenile Justice
——— *Kent v. U.S.,* 383 U.S. 541 (1966)
——— *In re Gault,* 387 U.S. 1 (1967)
——— *Parham v. J.R.,* 442 U.S. 584 (1979)
——— *Fare v. Michael C.,* 442 U.S. 707 (1979)

Tort Law and Workers Compensation
——— *Dillon v. Legg,* 441 P.2d 912 (1968)
——— *Carter v. General Motors,* 106 NW 2d 105 (1961)
——— *Molien v. Kaiser Foundation Hospital,* 27 Cal 3d 916 (1980)
——— *Griggs v. Duke Power Co.,* 401 U.S. 424 (1971)
——— *Harris v. Forklift Systems,* 510 U.S. 17 (1993)

Prediction of Dangerousness and Sex Offender Commitment
——— *Estelle v. Smith,* 451 U.S. 454 (1981)
——— *Barefoot v. Estelle,* 463 U.S. 880 (1983)
——— *Kansas v. Hendricks,* 117 S. Ct. 2072 (1997)

The rigor and reputation of the ABPP forensic diplomate status has become more significant recently, as other entities have begun awarding their own forensic credentials, creating some confusion among consumers of forensic services. Some of these organizations purport to offer "board certification" or specialty credentials in forensic practice without credential verification, peer review of work samples, or formal examination in substantive specialty content (Hansen, 2000; Otto, 1999). This obviously creates the potential for the emergence of a new cadre of clinicians foraging in a new area, with certifications and credentials that may exceed their demonstrated competence (MacDonald, 1999). Golding (1999) has summarized the distinctions between the ABPP diplomate and alternative certifications, including recommending cross-examination techniques to highlight the limitations of these alternatives. He specifically recommends focusing on whether alternative certifications include "grandparenting" clauses (i.e., awarding certification with a waiver of requirements) and whether they require work sample review, oral examination, and specific training and supervision.

Although the APA does not award certifications and diplomates and does not officially endorse *any* of the credentialing organizations, it is noteworthy that the ABPP diplomate is the only one recognized by APA in terms of allowing this designation to be included as part of a member's credentials in the APA directory. (A special exception exists for one diplomate in hypnosis.) Similarly, the National Register of Health Services Providers recognizes the ABPP diplomate for listing in its registry. At present, psychologists may claim board certification status based on credentials from any number of private organizations. As the field of forensic psychology continues to grow and psychologists claim "board certification" status on voir dire in court, courts will be searching for guidance regarding the meaning and value of reputed certification. In this context, the importance of psychology's developing professional standards for use of the terms board certification and diplomate will increase.

Models for the Future

As is evident from the above review, training in forensic psychology is available at all levels of education, but there is as yet no formalized track for comprehensive training. Our expectation is that with the recognition of forensic psychology as a specialty by APA, the field can move to develop a more integrated approach to training. Although clinicians could still be conceptualized as working at either the proficiency level (having some expertise in one or more specified forensic areas) or specialists (having more in-depth and broader expertise), these differences likely would emerge not at the graduate level, but perhaps after licensure.

Recognition as a specialty will likely lead to increased opportunities for developing skills at different levels of training. An important caveat is that forensic specialization should not come at the expense of a broad-based clinical education. Taking the long view, forensic training would be conceptualized as occurring from graduate school through internship through postdoctoral training. Therefore, graduate programs would be able to focus on developing basic clinical skills and knowledge in addition to providing specialty courses and some forensic experiences. For example, graduate programs with faculty specializing in forensic psychology could offer basic forensic didactic courses and provide opportunities for supervised clinical experience with populations and activities relevant to forensic work (e.g., correctional settings, families involved in divorce). In the didactic courses, graduate students would be exposed to fundamentals of law and be introduced to forensic psychological issues. The training would educate students about some of the basic differences between law and psychology, including the principle of the adversarial system of law versus the scientific approach in psychology; legal assumptions of free will versus psychological principles of determinism; and legal categorization (e.g., guilty/not guilty, proximate cause) versus psychology's focus on complex interactions.

In addition, graduate training would help students to identify and navigate differences between clinical and forensic approaches (Greenberg & Shuman, 1997), including identifying the actual client (the individual versus the court); relationship to client (supportive, helping versus objective, perhaps even confrontational); the goal of the relationship (helpful versus evaluative); sources of data (client's perspective versus collateral data); and use of therapeutic alliance versus critical judgment. Ethics courses, which are now part of the standard graduate curriculum, could be expanded to include a section on the "Specialty Guidelines for Forensic Psychologists" (Committee on Ethical Guidelines for Forensic Psychologists, 1991). Although these guidelines need to be a part of all levels of training for forensic psychologists, they should be introduced formally at the graduate level.

Another major component of forensic training at the graduate level would involve learning specialized assessment techniques. Students should be trained on some basic forensic instruments, such as the Psychopathy Checklist-Revised (Hare, 1991), the Structured Interview of Reported Symptoms (Rogers, 1992), and the HCR-20 (Webster, Douglas, Eaves, & Hart, 1997). They should become familiar with basic issues in the field, such as construction of actuarial instruments (e.g., the Violent Recidivism Assessment Guide; Harris, Rice, & Quinsey, 1993) as well as conceptual issues related to the application of clinical instruments, such as the Minnesota Multiphasic Personality Inventory 2, in forensic settings (e.g., Lees-Haley, 1997; Megargee, Mercer, & Carbonell, 1999).

Doctoral students should be familiar with the applications of such instruments to specific psycholegal issues; how to incorporate such instruments as part of a comprehensive evaluation; and generalizability of the instruments across different populations (e.g., applicability to both sexes, different racial groups, subpopulations of forensic groups).

As noted previously, forensic psychology, although centered largely on assessment and evaluation, also contains a treatment component. Psychological interventions with forensic populations require focus on ameliorating the deficits specific to the functional legal capacities required. This includes treatment for restoration to competence to stand trial, treatment to reduce risk of violent behavior in insanity acquittees as well as inmates, probationers, and parolees, and conciliation/mediation approaches in child custody litigation. These concepts should be addressed at the graduate level.

At the internship level, trainees should be afforded more opportunities to apply their clinical skills with forensic populations and begin to perform some forensic evaluations under supervision. Again, however, we caution against becoming too specialized or narrowly focused at this stage of training. The internship year provides the best opportunity for sustained clinical training, and it is important that basic clinical skills be obtained prior to applying them to the forensic arena. Otto, Heilbrun, and Grisso (1990) emphasize the importance of the internship for the development of clinical skills; they discuss the advantages and disadvantages of the specialist model (focusing clinical training almost exclusively in a forensic setting) versus the generalist-specialist model, which provides some forensic experience in a general clinical internship. The disadvantage of the former is that interns may become too narrowly focused early in their careers and may not obtain a sufficiently broad range of experiences. The disadvantage of the latter is that it may not provide adequate opportunity to develop the requisite forensic skills. Currently, with the dearth of postdoctoral fellowship opportunities, this is indeed a dilemma. However, as more postdoctoral programs emerge, it may no longer be necessary to obtain the depth of forensic training during the internship year because such training would more appropriately be obtained during a fellowship. In this model, the postdoctoral fellowship would become a more basic requirement for specialization. Rather than an opportunity to train only the leaders in the field, opportunities would expand considerably so that many more psychologists could obtain a full year of intensive, supervised forensic experience. During this year, they would obtain advanced knowledge from seminars in forensic practice and the law.

Continuing professional education activities would provide opportunities for trained forensic psychologists to keep up to date on new developments, research, and instruments. Also, because the field is so broad, it would provide opportunities for forensic psychologists to branch out from their current areas of expertise to other areas in which they are clinically qualified (e.g., moving from criminal forensic work to personal injury work). It is likely that CE activities would continue to serve as a major source of education for those who have some training in forensic psychology at the graduate level, but who choose not to become specialists. For these individuals, the types of models suggested by the Villanova Conference (i.e., more intensive trainings, including both didactic and experiential components) would be most appropriate.

Finally, with regard to professional credentialing, as the field develops with more formal training, there may be pressure to develop certification at the journeyman level, in addition to the current certification of only highly advanced practitioners. This could be accomplished in several ways. For example, the current diplomate could be modified to include individuals with only one area of expertise, rather than at least two. However, there are significant drawbacks to such a change. The current system recognizes individuals who develop a broad-based and scholarly approach to the forensic practice; the expectation of both breadth and depth of knowledge encourages immersion in the forensic arena and the development of a range of skills, which can be applied flexibly as new legal doctrines are developed and as our clinical knowledge expands. Abandonment of this requirement would substantially lower the standard.

Another approach, following the model developed by the APA, is to recognize, within the specialty of forensic psychology, *proficiencies* in specific areas. A proficiency is a circumscribed area of expertise within a broader specialty; for example, one might be proficient in performing specific types of evaluations in criminal, child custody, or personal injury cases. A model would have to be developed to certify proficiencies in one of these subspecialties within forensic psychology. This would attest that the individual has mastered the skills and knowledge necessary to practice competently in that area. This level of recognition likely would come earlier in the career than the current diplomate, and individuals might develop more than one proficiency. The diplomate still would be reserved for generalists who have demonstrated expertise and knowledge across domains.

CONCLUSION

The field of forensic psychology is continuing to develop. It is evolving from a stage of growth marked by a spurt of academic, clinical, and research activity into a more mature field that has begun to set and develop standards for training and practice.

Although recent research indicates improvement in quality of forensic reports over the past 20 years (Nicholson & Norwood, 2000), there is still a great deal of variability in the quality of these reports, across criminal as well as civil areas. A major factor contributing to this variability is the lack of consistent training. However, we are now at the point of having a clearer understanding of normative practice and standards that we expect will result in agreement about core models of training, spanning the range from graduate school, through internship, postdoctoral fellowship, and continuing professional education. The efforts of the American Psychology-Law Society and the ABFP to define and articulate the specialty of forensic psychology are likely to bear fruit in terms of improving the training and educational opportunities available and, ultimately, in leading to improvement in forensic psychological practice.

REFERENCES

American Psychological Association. (1992). Ethical principles of psychologists and code of conduct. *American Psychologist, 47,* 1597–1611.

Bank, S., & Poythress, N. (1982). Elements of persuasion in expert testimony. *Journal of Psychiatry and Law, 10,* 173–204.

Bersoff, D. N., Goodman-Delahunty, J., Grisso, T., Hans, V. P., Poythress, N. G., & Roesch, R. G. (1997). Training in law and psychology: Models from the Villanova conference. *American Psychologist, 52,* 1301–1310.

Bornstein, B. H. (1999). The ecological validity of jury simulations: Is the jury still out? *Law and Human Behavior, 23,* 75–91.

Borum, R., & Otto, R. (2000). Advances in forensic assessment and treatment: An overview and introduction to the special issue. *Law and Human Behavior, 24,* 1–8.

Careers and Training Committee. (1998). Careers and training in psychology and law. *American Psychology-Law Society.*

Carter v. General Motors, 106 N.W.2d 205 (1961).

Ceci, S. J., & Bruck, M. (1995). *Jeopardy in the courtroom: A scientific analysis of children's testimony.* Washington, DC: American Psychological Association.

Committee on Ethical Guidelines for Forensic Psychologists. (1991). Specialty guidelines for forensic psychologists. *Law and Human Behavior, 15,* 655–665.

Dusky v. United States, 362 U.S. 402 (1960).

Foucha v. Louisiana, 504 U.S. 71 (1992).

Godinez v. Moran, 509 U.S. 389 (1993).

Goodman, G. S., Levine, M., Melton, G. B., & Ogden, D. W. (1991). Child witnesses and the confrontation clause: The American Psychological Association brief in *Maryland v. Craig. Law and Human Behavior, 15,* 13–29.

Greenberg, S. A., & Shuman, D. W. (1997). Irreconcilable conflict between therapeutic and forensic roles. *Professional Psychology: Research and Practice, 28,* 50–57.

Grisso, T. (2000). What we know about youths' capacities as trial defendants. In T. Grisso & R. G. Schwartz (Eds.), *Youth on trial: A developmental perspective on juvenile justice* (pp. 139–171). Chicago: University of Chicago Press.

Grisso, T. (1991). A developmental history of the American Psychology Law Society. *Law and Human Behavior, 15,* 213–231.

Hansen, M. (2000). Expertise to go. *ABA Journal, 86,* 44–52.

Hare, R. D. (1991). *Manual for the Hare Psychopathy Checklist–Revised.* Toronto, Ontario, Canada: Multi-Health Systems.

Harris, G. T., Rice, M. E., & Quinsey, V. L. (1993). Violent recidivism of mentally disordered offenders: The development of a statistical prediction instrument. *Criminal Justice and Behavior, 20,* 315–335.

Hess, A. K. (1999). Defining forensic psychology. In A. K. Hess & I. B. Weiner (Eds.), *Handbook of forensic psychology* (pp. 24–47). New York: Wiley.

Hurt, L., Wiener, R. L., Russell, B. L., & Mannen, R. K. (1999). Gender differences in evaluating social-sexual conduct in the workplace. *Behavioral Sciences and the Law, 17,* 413–433.

Johnson, C., & Haney, C. (1994). Felony voir dire: An exploratory study of its content and effect. *Law and Human Behavior, 18,* 487–506.

Jones v. U.S., 463 U.S. 354 (1983).

Lees-Haley, P. R. (1997). MMPI-2 base rates for 492 personal injury plaintiffs: Implications and challenges for forensic assessment. *Journal of Clinical Psychology, 53,* 745–755.

Loftus, E. F., & Davies, G. M. (1984). Distortions in the memory of children. *Journal of Social Issues, 40,* 51–67.

MacDonald, E. (1999, February 8). The making of an expert witness: It's in the credentials. *Wall Street Journal,* p. B1.

Maryland v. Craig, 497 U.S. 836 (1990).

McNeil, D., Borum, R., Douglas, K., Hart, S., Lyon, D., Sullivan, L., et al. (in press). Risk Assessment. In J. Ogloff (Ed.), *Psychology and law: Reviewing the discipline.* New York: Plenum Press.

Megargee, E. I., Mercer, S. J., & Carbonell, J. L. (1999). MMPI-2 with male and female state and federal prison inmates. *Psychological Assessment, 11,* 177–185.

Melton, G. B., Huss, M. T., & Tomkins, A. J. (1999). Training in forensic psychology and the law. In A. K. Hess & I. B. Weiner (Eds.), *Handbook of forensic psychology* (pp. 24–47). New York: Wiley.

Melton, G. B., Petrila, J., Poythress, N. G., & Slobogin, C. (1997). *Psychological evaluations for the courts: A handbook for mental health professionals and lawyers.* New York: Guilford Press.

Münsterberg, H. (1908). *On the witness stand: Essays on psychology and crime.* New York: Clark, Boardman.

Nicholson, R. A., & Norwood, S. (2000). The quality of forensic psychological assessments, reports, and testimony: Acknowledging the gap between promise and practice. *Law and Human Behavior, 24,* 9–44.

Ornstein, P. A., Ceci, S. J., & Loftus, E. F. (1998). More on the repressed memory debate: A reply to Alpert, Brown, and Courtois. *Psychology, Public Policy, and Law, 4,* 1068–1078.

Otto, R. K. (1999). Message from the president. *Bulletin of the American Academy of Forensic Psychology, 20,* 11.

Otto, R. (2000). Assessing and managing violence risk in outpatient settings. *Journal of Clinical Psychology, 56,* 1239–1262.

Otto, R., Borum, R., & Hart, S. (2001). *Professional issues in the use of actuarial instruments in sexually violent predator evaluations.* Manuscript submitted for publication.

Otto, R. K., Heilbrun, K., & Grisso, T. (1990). Training and credentialing in forensic psychology. *Behavioral Sciences and the Law, 8,* 217–231.

Painter v. Bannister, 140 N.W. 2d 152 (1966).

Petition for the recognition of a specialty in professional psychology: Forensic psychology. (2000). Submitted by Division 41 of the American Psychological Association and the American Board of Forensic Psychology.

Rogers, R. (1992). *Structured Interview of Reported Symptoms.* Odessa, FL: Psychological Assessment Resources.

Saywitz, K. J., Goodman, G. S., Nicholas, E., & Moan, S. F. (1991). Children's memories of a physical examination involving genital touch: Implications for reports of child sexual abuse. *Journal of Consulting and Clinical Psychology, 59,* 682–691.

Sweeney, L. T., & Haney, C. (1992). The influence of race on sentencing: A meta-analytic review of experimental studies. *Behavioral Sciences and the Law, 10,* 179–195.

Troxel v. Granville, 530 U.S. 57 (2000).

Wallerstein, J. S., & Lewis, J. (1998).The long-term impact of divorce on children: A first report from a 25-year study. *Family and Conciliation Courts Review, 36,* 368–383.

Webster, C. D., Douglas, K. S., Eaves, D., & Hart, S. D. (1997). *HCR-20: Assesing risk for violence, Version 2.* British Columbia: Simon Fraser University.

Wells, G. L. (1978). Applied eyewitness testimony research: System variables and estimator variables. *Journal of Personality and Social Psychology, 36,* 1546–1557.

Wells, G. L., Small, M., Penrod, S. J., Malpass, R. S., Fulero, S. M., & Brimacombe, C. A. E. (1998). Eyewitness identification procedures: Recommendations for line-ups and photospreads. *Law and Human Behavior, 22,* 603–647.

Zaparniuk, J., Yuille, J. C., & Taylor, S. (1995). Assessing the credibility of true and false statements. *International Journal of Law and Psychiatry, 18,* 343–352.

CHAPTER 3

Ethical Principles and Professional Competencies

HERBERT N. WEISSMAN AND DEBORAH M. DeBOW

This chapter addresses professional standards implicit in competent forensic practice, thus ethical professional competencies. It is through the application of such competencies that legal issues are coherently addressed. Ethical professional competencies are reflected in knowledge of both psychological concepts and legal constructs and in the skillful construction of methodologies that bridge the two in the service of answering legal questions fairly and honestly in each area of the psycholegal domain. Expert opinions can thereby meet criteria for relevancy and admissibility in both psychology and the law.

Also addressed are impediments to sound practice and the influences that can interfere with ethical conduct. Such impediments and influences can be internally mediated and/or externally caused and result from ignorance, naïveté, cynicism, avarice, and/or inadequate moral-ethical development. These influences often derive from the adversary process implicit in the legal system and the medicolegal context in which forensic psychologists work. It is a system and a context in which the expert is pulled, via persuasion and other means, to adopt the perspective and the position of the retaining party. Pressures take the form of subtle and overt influences on the expert (whether court-appointed or retained) to vary from the role of neutral, objective examiner. These influences then potentially can become expressed unconsciously and/or consciously in biased methodologies, as reflected in slanted choice of clinical-forensic methods; selective scrutiny of data; biased reportage of data; omission of Axis I or Axis II findings; ignoring personal strengths, resiliencies, or vulnerabilities; omitting information on credibility; and ignoring dynamics of deception.

Adoption of an advocacy position is suitable for and required of attorneys, but the opposite is true for experts who must remain disinterested third parties. Understanding of and adherence to codes of ethics and professional guidelines, coupled with adequate personal boundaries and self-awareness, can serve as both guides and buffers against improper influences in the medicolegal context, a context that is known for its adversarial pressures. Although disinterested in the outcome, the expert is, of course, interested in the data, findings, and formulations that undergird his or her opinions that are supported vigorously in reports and in testimony. The challenge for the forensic expert is "to do the right thing" and "to be a straight shooter" despite pulls and pressures to veer off course. Staying on course can enable the expert to enjoy a long and productive career in a most rewarding and intellectually complex and challenging field.

UNIQUENESS OF FORENSIC PRACTICE

The uniqueness of forensic work calls for similarly unique ethical/professional principles, guidelines, case law, and research, usually separate and apart from those relevant in other areas of psychological practice. In forensic psychology, the past two decades have seen a burgeoning conceptual and empirical literature with a growing acceptance of forensic psychology's participation in legal contexts. In the past decade, specialized forensic ethical codes and guidelines have emerged that build on the foundations already in place with such documents as the American Psychological Association's

(APA) "Ethical Principles of Psychologists and Code of Conduct," whose 1992 revision includes a set of ethical principles at Section 7 that is devoted specifically to "Forensic Activities." The most comprehensive and widely accepted set of forensic standards was developed and published in 1991 by the Committee on Ethical Guidelines for Forensic Psychologists, a committee of APA's Division 41, the American Psychology-Law Society, in collaboration with the American Academy of Forensic Psychology. Entitled "Specialty Guidelines for Forensic Psychologists" (Committee on Ethical Guidelines for Forensic Psychologists, 1991), it was years in the making and provides essential guidance for practicing in the field of forensic psychology. Much attention will be devoted in this chapter to this document and also one promulgated by the Committee on Professional Practice and Standards of APA's Board of Professional Affairs, "Guidelines for Child Custody Evaluations in Divorce Proceedings" (APA, 1994). There is also a proposed revision of APA's "Ethical Principles of Psychologists and Code of Conduct," to be published in 2002, reviewed later in this chapter. These documents provide the parameters of sound forensic practice.

Despite the availability of numerous sets of rules and guidelines, the parameters of sound practice in child custody and personal injury areas of civil litigation are fraught with subjectivity and ambiguity. Child custody cases, relative to all other areas of forensic practice, yield the greatest number of ethics complaints lodged against psychologists with state and provincial psychology boards and with the APA's Ethics Committee (Kirkland & Kirkland, 2001). The tort liability system in which personal injury evaluations take place is psycholegally complex and is governed more by case law than statutory law. Emphasis in this chapter is on these two areas of the civil litigation domain in which psycholegal evaluations are being requested in increasing numbers.

PROFESSIONAL/ETHICAL STANDARDS AND IMPEDIMENTS TO THEIR IMPLEMENTATION

Misunderstandings and Assumptions

There are many potential misunderstandings based on erroneous assumptions found in the interface between psychology and law. One or more of these can find their way into one's practice and lead inadvertently to ethical breaches.

The Beg Ignorance Argument

It is mistaken to assume that it is acceptable to be ignorant of specialized psycholegal knowledge bases. The long and rather tortuous history of the psychology-law interface makes it clear that ignorance has never been acceptable. It is a history characterized by marked fluctuations in the regard with which the courts have held the role of the expert and in the value placed on scientific evidence. It is a history of tensions between needs and expectations of the courts for assistance in understanding and adjudicating very difficult and vexing human problems, balanced against the scientific knowledge base of a young science that was limited in the assistance it could provide the courts.

Early scholarly debates between Harvard Psychology Professor Hugo Münsterberg (1908) and University of Illinois Law Professor John Wigmore (1909) foreshadowed these historical tensions in their arguments on evidence and rules governing the admissibility of evidence. Professor Münsterberg's essays overzealously promoted the value of what psychology could reliably offer at the time. Because of this, he drew the attention and criticism of Professor Wigmore, who forcefully argued that the absence of published scientific evidence rendered psychology not ready for the law. Wigmore's rebuke had a chilling effect for a quarter century as regards involvements between psychology and law (Blau, 1984).

Professor Lewis Terman of Stanford University's Psychology Department picked up the debate in 1931, addressing Münsterberg's exuberance and Wigmore's critique. He placed in perspective psychology's potential for ethical professional contributions to the law. He emphasized that psychology's value would derive from its growing scientific foundation (Terman, 1931), which would ensure greater reliability in court testimony. Not long after this, Wigmore (1940), in the most definitive work on evidence at the time, opined that "the Courts are ready to learn and to use, whenever the psychologists produce it, any method which the latter themselves are agreed is sound, accurate and practical. . . . Whenever the Psychologist is ready for the Courts, the Courts are ready for him" (pp. 367–368).

Both fields have done much to enhance readiness and thus to benefit the legal process. Psychology has established increasingly sound conceptual and empirical scientific bases. The law has established sophisticated rules for the admissibility of scientific evidence. The current contours of the debate carry distinct echoes of Wigmore's lamentations over and Terman's cautious optimism for what psychology could ethically and competently offer the courts.

The U.S. Supreme Court decisions are on point. They echo Wigmore's injunctions by demanding sophisticated experts. The most significant cases are *Frye v. U.S.* (1923), and *Daubert v. Merrell Dow Pharmaceuticals* (1993). Under *Frye's* "general acceptance" standard, if a method, test, concept, or diagnosis has not achieved general acceptance within the professional-scientific community in which the testifying expert holds membership, then evidence based on such methods, tests, concepts, or diagnoses would not be admissible. In *Daubert,* the Court accepted the case for the purpose of resolving whether the appropriate legal standard concerning the admissibility of scientific evidence in federal courts is (a) *Frye's* general acceptance standard or (b) an admissibility standard derived from the Federal Rules of Evidence (FRE; 1975). The *Daubert* Court decided in favor of the FRE 403 and 702 standards of relevance, reliability, and the legal sufficiency of the proffered evidence (Goodman-Delahunty, 1997).

Further elaboration and clarification of the revised admissibility standard are found in U.S. Supreme Court decisions subsequent to *Daubert,* namely, *General Electric v. Joiner* (1997) and *Kumho v. Carmichael* (1999), and ultimately in the newly revised FRE 702. The impact of *Daubert* has yet to be fully felt or determined. Some judges, given more latitude as gatekeepers by *Daubert* and FRE 702 than they have had before, may opt to become more lenient rather than more strict in their scrutiny of expert testimony for its admissibility (Weiner, 2001). Applying the same rules, other judges may opt to examine closely the expert's qualifications as well as case-specific empirical literature underlying the expert's methodology and opinions. These evidentiary rules are concluded in a later section (see also Chapter 4 for further discussion).

In state jurisdictions, there are case and statutory laws permitting psychologists to testify, and rules that govern admissibility of scientific evidence similar to the above described federal laws. Beyond each state's laws and the federal rules for accepting expert testimony in court proceedings, there is now a sound body of research-based knowledge in general experimental and forensic psychology. Münsterberg, Terman, and Wigmore would be impressed by the relevancy and significance of such knowledge to the courts. However, the prospective expert has the duty to be aware of and to stay current with such knowledge and the rules germane to the jurisdiction of his or her practice. "Ethical Principles of Psychologists and Code of Conduct" (APA, 1992) specifically states that "psychologists base their forensic work on appropriate knowledge of and competence in the areas underlying such work" (Standard 7.01). Further, the "Specialty Guidelines for Forensic Psychologists" (Committee on Ethical Guidelines for Forensic Psychologists, 1991) states, "Forensic psychologists are responsible for a fundamental and reasonable level of knowledge and understanding of the legal and professional standards that govern their participation as experts in legal proceedings" (p. 658).

Ignorance thus can no longer legitimately be claimed as justification for insufficient preparation at any level of expert involvement in legal matters. The courts will not permit it; the information is readily available; and ethical duties prohibit begging ignorance on matters that are legitimately within the expert's purview. Provided that an individual expert's competence can be established, there is now wide acceptance of psychological testimony in state and federal courts.

Advocacy: Gamesmanship

There is an accompanying issue based on a rather pernicious underlying assumption, which is governed more by cynicism than ignorance. It has to do with an unfortunate myth of "gamesmanship" perpetuated by some celebrated cases in the media, to wit, that the adversary system somehow is a "game," a game that lawyers play and that experts can join. Examples of "playing the game" include such practices as formulating biased methodologies that favor one side over the other, failing to disclose findings in an objective and balanced manner, conducting interviews and framing questions to fulfill advocacy agendas, and promoting positions in affidavits or rendering opinions in reports and when testifying that lack adequate basis. Such conduct leads to advocacy by experts and other unethical, unprofessional, and sometimes illegal or extralegal activities and involvements, which ultimately serves to injure parties, compromise justice, and ruin professional reputations.

There are numerous specific rules prohibiting experts from participating in this kind of advocacy and bias. Principle 7.04 of "Ethical Principles of Psychologists and Code of Conduct" states, "(a) In forensic testimony and reports, psychologists testify truthfully, honestly, and candidly and, consistent with applicable legal procedures, describe fairly the bases for their testimony and conclusions [and] (b) Whenever necessary to avoid misleading, psychologists acknowledge the limits of their data or conclusions" (APA, 1992). "Specialty Guidelines for Forensic Psychologists" Section VI.C states:

> In providing forensic psychological services, forensic psychologists take special care to avoid undue influence upon their methods, procedures, and products, such as might emanate from the party to a legal proceeding by financial compensation or other gains. As an expert conducting an evaluation, treatment, consultation, or scholarly/empirical investigation, the forensic psychologist maintains professional integrity by examining the issue at hand from all reasonable perspectives, actively seeking information that will differentially test plausible rival hypotheses. (Committee on Ethical Guidelines for Forensic Psychologists, 1991, p. 661)

An expert joining an attorney's "legal team" of other experts and attorneys, rather than maintaining neutrality, objectivity, and suitable boundaries, is an example of proscribed behavior.

Advocacy: Promoting Personal Agendas and Political Positions

Another mistaken approach to forensic work builds on flawed logic and is driven by the dynamics of advocacy. It is not born strictly of ignorance but rather of an idealistic desire to promote a social, political, or economic cause (e.g., regarding capital punishment, child interests, elder rights, feminism, gender equity). Adherents of this approach believe that the ends justify the means, so do not hesitate to conduct biased child custody evaluations with methodologies that are calculated to favor one party over the other; or to omit reporting potentially exculpatory data and findings (evidence that clears or tends to clear from blame) in a criminal evaluation; or to ignore providing a balanced portrayal of personal strengths as well as vulnerabilities and Axis I and Axis II disorders when testifying in personal injury, fitness-to-work, and disability evaluations.

The way to protect against bias is to adopt an attitude of neutrality, taking an objective, scientific hypothesis-testing approach to psychological evaluations and to the reporting of findings and data emanating from clinical-forensic assessments. This implies reliance on and knowledge of legal standards and legal test questions in each area of the forensic domain in which the expert is involved, as well as adherence to professional standards. When working in the legal system, one must adhere to the rules of the system and its case and statutory law. When one encounters conflicts between one's professional ethical constraints on the one side, and rules or laws on the other, such conflicts must be addressed and resolved before proceeding. In situations where the expert does not agree with prevailing laws (e.g., joint custody, death penalty), it is best not to accept referrals of such cases.

Relevant to the matter of remaining neutral are several specialty guidelines. Specifically, Guideline III.E. (Competence), states:

> Forensic psychologists recognize that their own personal values, moral beliefs, or personal and professional relationships with parties to a legal proceeding may interfere with their ability to practice competently. Under such circumstances, forensic psychologists are obligated to decline participation or to limit their assistance in a manner consistent with professional obligations. (Committee on Ethical Guidelines, 1991, p. 658)

Further, the courtroom is not the place for the forensic expert to attempt to influence public policy. For this, there are more suitable forums, such as professional associations and legislatures.

Lack of Specialized Forensic Training

A variant of the "beg ignorance" argument is the argument that a solid background of preparation as a clinical psychologist and competent clinical skills are all that is necessary and sufficient for the psychologist who accepts forensic-clinical referrals. This is a severely mistaken assumption. Whereas competent clinical work is necessary, it is by no means sufficient. A *clinical* diagnostic evaluation is not a *forensic* diagnostic evaluation.

The psychology-law literature and professional standards of practice make it clear that, to perform ethical and professionally competent work, the practitioner must know the elements of the *legal standards,* hearsay rules, and other criteria for admissibility of evidence. This information, in conjunction with *psychological standards,* defines the parameters of everything one does in the psycholegal context, from framing questions in a psychological evaluation to providing opinions in expert testimony. One cannot conduct a competent child custody evaluation without knowing the best interest standard and without awareness of controlling child custody case law and statutory decisions within one's own jurisdiction. One cannot conduct a competent personal injury assessment in a medicolegal civil context without knowing issues of causation and the causal nexus of impairment. In personal injury evaluations, a good therapeutic clinician can provide differential diagnostic and treatment implications but may fail to address credibility/deception, causation, or prognosis. And one cannot conduct a competent criminal evaluation without knowing the different legal standards involved when evaluating defendants for competency to stand trial, insanity, or other diminished responsibility defenses. Being a good clinician may enable one to provide a very accurate diagnosis of a criminal defendant's current condition but to completely fail to address mental state at the time of the offense. Specialty Guideline III.A. requires: "Forensic psychologists provide services only in areas of psychology in which they have specialized knowledge, skill, experience, and education" (Committee on Ethical Guidelines for Forensic Psychologists, 1991, p. 658).

Erroneous Assumptions Regarding Relationship with Retaining Attorney

A classic misunderstanding held by many mental health professionals is that the retaining attorney can and will provide requisite psycholegal information and accurate advice on legal, ethical, and professional issues that arise in a case.

There are two flaws here. First, the attorney is required to be an advocate for his or her client, not for the expert. Thus, he or she is not obligated to inform or protect the expert (unless it aids the client). Although it is unusual for experts to hire their own attorney to accompany them to depositions and to other legal forums, it may be advisable on occasion. Forensic experts usually have an attorney knowledgeable in mental health law on retainer or otherwise available to provide legal advice and counsel.

The second flaw is believing that most attorneys are sufficiently knowledgeable about mental health law in general or about the ethical and legal burdens that control the expert's specialty in particular to provide accurate advice.

Assumed Similarities among Jurisdictions

Mistakes can be made when applying psychology in legal contexts due to errors of assumed similarity. Jurisdictional differences can be critical in a case, influencing everything from criteria applied to the admissibility of evidence to standards of proof. Differences of this kind do not occur in the sciences, where, by convention, there are uniform standards (rather than regional differences) for testing hypotheses and evaluating data. The burden thus remains with the forensic practitioner both to be aware of requisite ethical, legal, and professional jurisdictional obligations (e.g., by reviewing original sources of regulatory, case, and statutory laws) and to implement them. There is an implied prior duty to have acquired specialized forensic education; there is an accompanying duty on accepting a case to know or to learn the pertinent issues/laws.

Interdisciplinary Misunderstandings Regarding Standards of Proof

Standards of proof differ in psychology and law, which can cause serious interdisciplinary misunderstandings. For example, the confidence limits in the behavioral sciences are set at higher levels (i.e., alpha levels of .05 or .01) than those inherent in certain legal probative standards (i.e., alpha level of .51 in most civil areas). This difference potentially affects whether a piece of evidence is interpreted by the expert as "significant" or not. Thus, in civil cases where the preponderance of evidence standard implies confidence limits with a probability greater than .51 that Event A would have constituted a substantial factor in causing Effect B, "more likely than not" is acceptable. Weissman (1985) points out:

> Ambiguity and conflict may enter when the expert while testifying is asked by the examining attorney whether a given event

(legally relevant behavior) had been viewed as a significant factor in the formulation of his/her opinion about plaintiff's mental/emotional condition. . . . The expert will likely respond here from a frame of reference that implies $p \geq .95$ (95% certainty) in contrast to the attorney's frame of evidentiary reference that implies $p \geq .51$ (51% certainty). (p. 141)

The presence of any "significance" in the causal relationship at issue may well be denied by the psychologist for reasons that are unclear to the attorney and court.

It is important to note that experts, seeking to establish scientific bases for their opinions, would of course use scientifically sound tools and data that rest on the higher standards of proof typical of the behavioral sciences (.95 or .99). It is in the formulation of the expert's opinions in the medicolegal context that lower standards of proof in selective areas of the law (i.e., civil may be involved).

The requisite standard to which the expert is held in formulating opinions is generally referred to as the reasonable medical/scientific certainty standard. This standard must have been met for each expert opinion being offered. This standard does not imply absolute certainty, nor does it permit conjecture or speculation, but rather a reasonable probability and degree of certainty. The credibility and probative value of expert testimony are assisted further by identifying and discussing alternative hypotheses for one's data. The reasonable medical/scientific certainty standard is enhanced further by expert testimony that expresses the degree of conviction attached to different opinions with well-reasoned bases for opinions proffered.

Assumptions Regarding the Economics of Private Practice

The aims of psychology are very different from aims implicit in the law—other than earning a living. Psychology seeks truth through hypothesis testing and impartial weighing of findings, whereas the law seeks just resolution of problems via advocacy and strategies calculated to win, even if this may involve suppressing information/evidence "in the interest of justice." Both psychiatry and the psychology guidelines prohibit forensic examiners from contracting to provide services on a contingency-fee basis (Melton, Petrila, Poythress, & Slobogin, 1997). Providing services on a contingency-fee or other lien basis, in which the outcome of the case determines whether the expert will be paid, promotes biased expert testimony. The expert's mantra becomes "We will win," obliterating any neutrality. Such arrangements are proscribed because they constitute a conflict of interest or the appearance of a conflict of interest because the expert's side of the case must prevail to receive compensation for services rendered (Committee on Ethical Guidelines for Forensic Psychologists, 1991).

Even with a typical fee-for-service contract, practitioners may feel that if they do not yield to persuasive pressures, they will not be successful in the future in receiving more referrals. This mentality deserves empathy but is erroneous, at least in the long term. The moral pivot for practitioners of a scholarly profession with a service ethic is found in upholding professional standards that protect parties and that honor the scientific and knowledge bases of the field. It is not found in advocacy, nor in commercialism. The most suitable role for the expert remains that of a disinterested third party assisting the trier of fact as a scientist and educator. The expert can build a solid reputation as a rigorous professional whose opinions the courts can rely on ("a straight shooter") by adhering to standards in both psychology and law.

The issue of morality or personal ethics involves the quality of one's own moral development coupled with knowledge of ethical requirements and motivation to do the right thing. The increased availability of knowledge bases and of rules and guidelines has increased the likelihood that the majority of experts will adhere to them the majority of the time. Some will do so because they know that documents containing ethical codes, legal rules, and professional standards that are available to them are equally accessible to attorneys and judges. Most will do so because it is the right thing to do. A few may or may not do so, depending on changing external contingencies.

Research from classic studies by Hartshorne and May (1928) and from a line of research on moral development and moral reasoning by Kohlberg (1976) and Kohlberg, Levine, and Hewer (1983) is also relevant to the matter of understanding reasons for substandard performance despite abundant sources of knowledge. Addressing the generality or specificity of honesty, Hartshorne and May studied consistency of children in different situations involving telling the truth. They found that honest-dishonest behavior varied as a function of situational influences and of the motivations and constraints involved.

Moral reasoning, according to Kohlberg (1976), evolves over a successive series of stages, with each stage representing a qualitatively different organization and pattern of maturational thought from the preceding one. There are three levels of moral reasoning, in Kohlberg's view: the preconventional, the conventional, and the postconventional. In *preconventional* reasoning, rules and social expectations are not yet internalized; thus, externally mediated consequences of one's actions determine judgments of actions. In *conventional* reasoning, internalization of others' rules and expectations has taken place, and ethical/moral decisions are made on the basis of whether approval is anticipated for conforming to others' perceived expectations and for obeying authority. In contrast, the professional person idealistically is one who has attained the *postconventional* level of ethical reasoning, exhibiting relative autonomy from others' expectations and making decisions in terms of self-chosen principles and constraints implicit in ethical codes.

Information derived from these studies indicates that with maturational development there can be expected greater degrees of stability, consistency, and reliability of moral-ethical judgments. Thus, despite situational influences implicit in the adversary system, an expert's motivation to do the right thing, coupled with a reasonable degree of character development, plus knowledge of professional constraints, can assist in staying the course. Specialized education and training is critical here. Ethical professional competencies serve as a buffer or defense against undue influence and protect against slipping down Kohlberg's hierarchy on entering the forensic domain.

Violations of Boundaries and Roles

There are critical decisions to be made from the very inception of a referral, beginning with the expert's judgment of the referring attorney's skills, attitudes, and ability to understand psychological findings, and "the degree to which the attorney is interested in finding the answer to a question versus merely wanting to hire an expert who will support the case, often termed a 'hired gun'" (Hess, 1998, p. 110). Such early discussions enable experts to determine whether the case-related issues and tasks called for are within their scope of competency, whether time frames are congenial, and whether the role(s) requested (i.e., consultation or expert) are suitable as well as suitably defined.

It is a mistake to assume that one can serve a case in the dual capacity of both expert and consultant. Hess (1998) points out that whereas the expert and consultant roles fall on a continuum and the "expert typically serves to some minimal extent as a consultant," there are nonetheless significant differences between the roles (p. 111). On the respective ends of the continuum are the "expert," whose commitment is to finding and expressing the truth, versus the "consultant," whose commitment is to assisting attorneys in their preparation of cases for litigation and helping attorneys understand psychological evidence. The two roles can be oppositional to one another. Saks (1990) addresses role conflicts and ethical dilemmas that can emerge in the course of involvement as a consultant or an expert in a case. He points out that the law cannot be relied on because it is not very clear in its definitions or its expectations. The burden to ensure clarity again falls on the expert.

Another mistaken assumption is that it is permissible to serve both as therapist and expert in a given case. Doing so can constitute serious role and ethical conflicts. Through the presentation of 10 principles, Greenberg and Shuman (1997) argue that serving both as therapist to a patient and as the patient's expert in a legal matter constitutes an impermissible dual relationship. Serving both roles threatens the efficacy of psychotherapy and also threatens the accuracy of judicial determinations. The patient's therapist serving also as expert (e.g., in a personal injury case) cannot overcome advocacy bias or the appearance of such bias. There can be no independent or unbiased investigation by a psychotherapist into factual bases of the patient's allegations and complaints or critical analysis of deception. Instead, there typically is uncritical reliance on the patient's subjective report, which perforce is taken at face value. The 10 principles are found in Table 3.1.

Greenberg and Shuman (1997) make it clear "that the logic, the legal basis, and the rules governing the privilege that applies to care providers are substantially different from those that apply to forensic evaluators" (p. 52). Because of this, the duty to inform forensic examinees of the lack of privilege and the intended use of the examination product is embodied in case law (*Estelle v. Smith,* 1981) and in "Specialty Guidelines for Forensic Psychologists" (Committee on Ethical Guidelines for Forensic Psychologists, 1991). The latter states:

> Forensic psychologists have an obligation to ensure that prospective clients are informed of their legal rights with respect to the anticipated forensic service, of the purposes of any evaluation, of the nature of procedures to be employed, of the intended uses of any product of their services, and of the party who has employed the forensic psychologist. (p. 659)

Ethical principles and forensic specialty guidelines substantiate Greenberg and Shuman's (1997) argument against such dual relationships. One provision (Guideline IV.D.1.) states: "Forensic psychologists avoid providing professional services to parties in a legal proceeding with whom they have personal or professional relationships that are inconsistent with the anticipated relationship" (Committee on Ethical Guidelines for Forensic Psychologists, 1991, p. 659). Prohibition against combining roles of therapist and expert is also found in the APA's (1994) "Guidelines for Conducting Child Custody Evaluations." It is stated at Guideline II.7: "The psychologist avoids multiple relationships," such as "conducting a child custody evaluation in a case in which the psychologist served in a therapeutic role for the child or his or her immediate family or has had other involvement that may compromise the psychologist's objectivity" (p. 678).

TABLE 3.1   Ten Differences between Therapeutic and Forensic Relationships

	Care Provision	Forensic Evaluation
1. Whose client is patient/litigant?	The mental health practitioner.	The attorney.
2. The relational privilege that governs disclosure in each relationship.	Therapist-patient privilege.	Attorney-client and attorney work-product privilege.
3. The cognitive set and evaluative attitude of each expert.	Supportive, accepting, empathic.	Neutral, objective, detached.
4. The differing areas of competency of each expert.	Therapy techniques for treatment of the impairment.	Forensic evaluation techniques relevant to the legal claim.
5. The nature of the hypotheses tested by each expert.	Diagnostic criteria for the purpose of therapy.	Psycholegal criteria for the purpose of legal adjudication.
6. The scrutiny applied to the information used in the process and the role of historical truth.	Mostly based on information from the person being treated, with little scrutiny of that information by the therapist.	Litigant information supplemented with that of collateral sources and scrutinized by the evaluator and the court.
7. The amount and control of structure in each relationship.	Patient-structured and relatively less structured than forensic evaluation.	Evaluator-structured and relatively more structured than therapy.
8. The nature and degree of "adversarialness" in each relationship.	A helping relationship; rarely adversarial.	An evaluative relationship; frequently adversarial.
9. The goal of the professional in each relationship.	Therapist attempts to benefit the patient by working within the therapeutic relationship.	Evaluator advocates for the results and implications of the evaluation for the benefit of the court.
10. The impact on each relationship of critical judgment by the expert.	The basis of the relationship is the therapeutic alliance, and critical judgment is likely to impair that alliance.	The basis of the relationship is evaluative, and critical judgment is unlikely to cause serious emotional harm.

Source: Adapted with permission from S. A. Greenberg and D. W. Shuman (1997). Irreconcilable conflict between therapeutic and forensic roles. *Professional Psychology: Research and Practice, 28*(1), 50–57. Copyright ©1997 by the American Psychological Association.

Guideline II.7 distinguishes serving as a fact (percipient) witness concerning treatment of the child, which is permissible, provided that the psychologist "is aware of the limitations and possible biases inherent in such a role and the possible impact on the ongoing therapeutic relationship" (p. 678). Further, "Although the court may require the psychologist to testify as a fact witness regarding factual information he or she became aware of in a professional relationship with a client, that psychologist should generally decline the role of an expert witness who gives a professional opinion regarding custody and visitation issues . . . unless ordered by the court" (p. 678).

Misunderstanding of Privacy Issues: Confidentiality and Privilege

Confidentiality is the duty owed the client, whereas *privilege* is the legal right held by the client, as a function of statute (in most states) or common law, with certain exceptions (mandatory reporting, express or implicit waiver, duty to protect, duty to warn; Golding, 1996). The increasing complexity of the legal requirements imposed on psychologists regarding the reporting of information has resulted in more emphasis on issues of privacy and privilege. Canter, Bennett, Jones, and Nagy (1994) define privacy as generally referring to "the right of individuals not to have their physical person or mental or emotional process invaded or shared without their consent," whereas "confidentiality means that nonpublic information about a person will not be disclosed without consent or special legal authorization" (p. 105). Further, "Except in special circumstances (e.g., lawsuits, mandatory reporting laws), psychologists are required by the Ethics Code and by law to maintain the confidentiality of communications shared with them. . . . The recipients of psychological services retain the right to release the confidential information in most situations" (p. 105).

The forensic setting severely limits the protections of confidentiality. For this reason, limitations on confidentiality are disclosed from the outset to persons being evaluated. Ethical Principle 5.01 states:

> (a) Psychologists discuss with persons and organizations with whom they establish a scientific or professional relationship (including, to the extent feasible, minors and their legal representatives) (1) the relevant limitations on confidentiality . . . and (2) the foreseeable uses of the information generated through their services. (b) Unless it is not feasible or is contraindicated, the discussion of confidentiality occurs at the outset of the relationship and thereafter as new circumstances may warrant. (c) Permission for electronic recording of interviews is secured from clients and patients. (APA, 1992, 5.01)

Best practice in forensic settings is to provide written waivers as to specific persons, timeframes, and purposes.

Ethical Principle 5.03 emphasizes: "In order to minimize intrusions on privacy, psychologists include in written and oral reports, consultations, and the like, only information germane to the purpose for which the communication is made" (APA, 1992, 5.03). Principle 5.05 states: "Psychologists disclose confidential information without the consent of the individual only as mandated by law, or where permitted by law for a valid purpose" (5.05).

In legal contexts where information is obtained on litigants through psychological assessment, there are conditions under which confidentiality is waived for purposes of the litigation, such as when a patient or litigant has voluntarily placed his or her mental state in issue (Stromberg, 1993). Melton et al. (1997) discuss further limitations to confidentiality in the forensic context. They point out that in the purely evaluative relationship, privileges designed to protect psychologist-patient disclosures, for instance, are irrelevant: "The clinician-patient privileges do not apply when the clinician-'patient' relationship is a creature of the court; as is the case with court-ordered evaluations" (pp. 77–78). Further, "The law takes the position that, for purposes of evidence law, the evaluator's client is the party that requests the evaluation, not the person being evaluated" (p. 78).

However, there are two situations commonly encountered by forensic examiners where confidential information remains protected despite the psychologist-patient privilege having been waived (Melton et al., 1997). The first is the attorney work-product privilege, which protects communications between attorney and client and may, under this same privilege, protect communications between the client's expert and attorney, at least until such time as the expert is disclosed as an expert witness. The second situation pertains to raw test data, which also may not be directly discoverable. The APA's (1992) Ethics Code prohibits "releasing raw test results or raw data to persons . . . who are not qualified to use such information" (2.02). It also requires psychologists to "make reasonable efforts to maintain the integrity and security of tests and other assessment techniques consistent with law" (2.10).

The concepts of confidentiality, privilege, and privacy are very broad and very complex. Psychologists must turn to primary sources in their own jurisdiction for guidance in how these concepts specifically apply to a particular case.

Mistaken Assumptions in Failing to Regard Uniqueness of Psycholegal Assessment Methodologies

Operations attached to formulating assessment methodologies when doing forensic work can be very different from those involved in nonforensic contexts. There is a considerable amount of guidance available for constructing methodologies that meet criteria in both psychology and law (Grisso, 1986; Melton et al., 1997; Meyer, 1995; Weissman, 1985, 1990, 1991a).

Documentation

Meyer (1995) advises keeping meticulous notes. Specifically, he advises recording both the overall impressions of the person being evaluated (i.e., mental status examination) and the circumstances of the interviewing and testing at the time of the evaluation. This can be particularly important in highly contentious cases, and also where there is a long interval between conducting the evaluation and providing testimony. Reconstruction of contingencies of the assessment process can be difficult with the passage of time, yet very important in litigation or when facing standard of care challenges. In this context, it is relevant to note the importance of observing guidelines for record keeping. Guidelines promulgated by the APA's (1993) Board of Professional Affairs represent *general* guidelines, whereas the "Specialty Guidelines for Forensic Psychologists" (Committee on Ethical Guidelines for Forensic Psychologists, 1991) provide *specific* forensic guidelines. They underscore the importance of maintaining the highest level of documentation and record keeping. Guideline VI.B of "Specialty Guidelines for Forensic Psychologists" states:

> Forensic psychologists have an obligation to document and be prepared to make available, subject to court order or the rules of evidence, all data that form the basis for their evidence or services. The standard to be applied to such documentation or recording *anticipates* that the detail and quality of such documentation will be subject to reasonable judicial scrutiny; this standard is higher than the normative standard for general clinical practice. When forensic psychologists conduct an examination or engage in the treatment of a party to a legal proceeding, with foreknowledge that their professional services will be used in an adjudicative forum, they incur a special responsibility to provide the best documentation possible under the circumstances.
>
> 1. Documentation of the data upon which one's evidence is based is subject to the normal rules of discovery, disclosure, confidentiality, and privilege that operate in the jurisdiction in which the data were obtained. Forensic psychologists have an obligation to be aware of those rules and to regulate their conduct in accordance with them.
>
> 2. The duties and obligations of forensic psychologists with respect to documentation of data that form the basis for their evidence apply from the moment they know or have a reasonable basis for knowing that their data and evidence derived from it are likely to enter into legally relevant decisions. (p. 661)

Structure

Assessment methodologies used in conducting psycholegal evaluations have historically ranged in the degree of structure that examiners have applied to conducting them. Standardized interview protocols and objective testing measures have the greatest likelihood of meeting evidentiary standards in both psychology and law. They are more likely to yield valid findings that are trustworthy and specifically address pertinent legal standards. The greater degree of structure inherent in an evaluation, the greater the probability that the findings derived therefrom will be reliable and valid (Dawes, 1989). Well-structured and psychologically relevant assessment methodologies can enhance one's assistance to the court. They also can serve as a buffer against adversarial and interprofessional pressures, which protects the examiner from potential standard of care challenges. For example, in child custody evaluations, each parent is interviewed and tested in the same manner to elicit information addressing the elements of the best interest standard (parental competencies). A model to explicate this process is presented later in this chapter.

Methodologies are designed to enhance (a) fairness and objectivity as to the issues; (b) impartiality as to roles and responsibilities; (c) comprehensiveness as to data sources; (d) comparability in type and length of interviews and assessment methods in cases involving multiple litigants (i.e., reasonably parallel format); (e) reliability and validity of findings through relevant standardized, professionally recognized assessment measures and interview and observation protocols that are as structured as is feasible; and (f) independence and neutrality by staying well bounded within predefined professional roles.

Data Sources

In psycholegal contexts, sources of information (data sources) are more extensive than in traditional clinical contexts. Clinical contexts assume honesty by the patient and typically involve only differential diagnosis and treatment. Forensic contexts have a broader range of goals and are governed not only by the rules and ethics of psychology, but also by the rules and ethics of the legal profession.

Forensic goals require answering psycholegal questions (in addition to clinical questions) often involving causation, apportionment, prognosis, residual impairment, responsibility, and credibility. Ethical evaluations call on the expert to use multisource, multimodal methodologies for the task of answering such complex psycholegal questions as are involved in determining child custody, criminal responsibility, risk assessment, factors of causation, and disability. Multiple data sources are necessary for corroborating findings, for ascertaining genuineness and substantiality of allegations, and for testing alternative hypotheses. Confidence in one's findings and the probative value of one's opinions are thereby enhanced.

Data sources typically include (a) case-oriented, clinical diagnostic and psychosocial/biohistorical interviewing; (b) mental status examination; (c) standardized psychological testing; (d) record review (pre- and postincident medical, mental health, academic, employment); (e) contacts with relevant collateral sources (e.g., significant others, parents, teachers, physicians, therapists, coworkers); (f) case-specific empirical data, including base rates if available and relevant, and theoretical concepts; and (g) case and statutory law. Depending on the area of psycholegal involvement and other contingencies, there may be fewer relevant sources or additional sources to consider. Certainly, such decisions must be made on a case-by-case basis.

In child custody evaluations, for instance, additional data sources include: (a) clinical child custody-oriented mental status and psychosocial interviews, including relevant history of the parties and of the minor children; (b) psychological testing of the parties and of the minor children; (c) assessment/observation of the interaction between respective parties and the minor children; (d) assessment of significant others; and (e) contacts with relevant collaterals (APA, 1994).

Case Examples and Discussion

A Case Example: Child Custody

The following case illustration contains *multiple* examples of violations of both professional standards and ethical practice, including role boundary violations and violations of privacy, privilege, and confidentiality. It also illustrates problems inherent in yielding unduly to adversarial influences, using biased methodologies, and being dishonest in reporting findings. The best interests of the children were ignored and subverted.

Anatomy of Co-option. In this case study, Parties A and B had stipulated, through their attorneys, to joint legal custody. A mediator (mental health professional) was then appointed for the sole purpose of establishing a parenting plan. The young children were in counseling with another mental health professional for the sole purpose of ameliorating dissolution and transitional discomfiture. Then, Party A changed counsel, retaining Attorney A just prior to the first session scheduled with the mediator.

Attorney A had a master plan, one calculated to win custody for Client A (using property and other issues as leverage) by creating a custody dispute where there previously had not been one. This began with Attorney A insisting that the mediator and the children's therapist formally assert their need for psychological testing to complete their work. They did so, even though their work (establishing a parenting plan in the context of stipulated joint custody) did not require this, and neither child custody nor fitness were at issue.

In so doing, the mental health professionals yielded to undue influence. Failing to recognize standards of care in child custody matters, they continued to embark on a course of conduct that would violate privileges, constitute conflicts of interest, and compromise the welfare of the parties and the best interests of the children.

Events unfolded in the following sequence. The designated mediator sought to meet with the parties, but failed in this effort because Attorney A instructed Client A *not* to attend joint mediation sessions. *The mediator* (a) failed to inform counsel that mediation was not going forward; (b) failed to respond to Attorney B's request for information as to status of mediation; (c) initiated instead an individual psychotherapeutic relationship with Client A; (d) clinically supervised the children's therapist concerning the children's treatment; (e) met repeatedly with the psychological examiner about the case, and had multiple contacts with collateral sources without specific authorizations to do so; (f) ultimately rendered diagnoses of both parties, despite the fact that doing so was outside the scope of this professional's licensure; (g) made child custody recommendations, despite not having examined anyone and not having conducted a formal child custody evaluation; and (h) took no notes and recorded nothing.

The children's therapist (a) met with the children in individual treatment while under the supervision of the "designated mediator" (Party A's therapist); (b) failed to respond to Attorney B's request for clarification of purposes of treatment; (c) took no notes; (d) ultimately rendered diagnoses of adult parties, despite the fact that rendering formal diagnoses was outside the scope of this professional's licensure; (e) made custody recommendations without having examined the parents or their interaction with the children, and despite not having conducted a formal child custody evaluation; and (f) met repeatedly with the psychological examiner about the case, and had multiple contacts with collaterals absent specific authorizations to do so.

Both the designated mediator and the children's therapist, in response to Attorney A's insistence, formally requested that a psychological child custody examination be conducted for purposes ostensibly of advancing goals of mediation, identifying the psychological examiner promoted by Attorney A.

The examiner (a) met with Attorney A on multiple occasions prior to, during, and after the examination, never with Attorney B; (b) received and reviewed multiple sets of records provided by Attorney A, none from Attorney B; (c) failed to respond to Attorney B's request for clarification of purposes and procedures of the psychological examination; (d) failed to examine respective parent-child interactions; (e) had multiple contacts with the designated mediator (Client A's therapist), children's therapist, and collaterals without specific authorizations permitting such contacts; (f) claimed independent status as an examiner although communicated only with Attorney A, and thereafter sought to prevent an independent evaluation of the parties and minor children; (g) diagnosed the children as acutely disturbed and suicidal due to Party B, despite multiple sources of information indicating otherwise, including school records and the examiner's own assessment findings; (h) diagnosed Client B as severely disturbed and of imminent danger to the children despite the fact that all test findings (Minnesota Multiphasic Personality Inventory [MMPI-2]; Butcher, Dahlstrom, Graham, Tellegen, & Kaemmer, 1989; Millon Clinical Multiaxial Inventory [MCMI-II]; Millon, 1987; Rorschach, 1989) placed this party entirely within normal limits and positive on indices of parental competency, which the examiner claimed were "classic test misses"; (i) interviewed about nonlegally relevant material disproportionately more than about legally relevant material in child custody; (j) conducted a nonparallel examination, seeking an abundant and disproportionate amount of negative information about Party B from Party A and by seeking biohistorical information only from Party B; (k) failed to inquire about Party A's background, despite the importance of doing so in child custody examinations, and despite extremely elevated validity indices on objective personality tests; and (l) ultimately filed a report on the basis of the foregoing, resulting in an ex parte hearing that removed the children from Party B's home, placing sole custody with Party A, and monitored, limited visitation with Party B.

When Attorney B sought to petition the court to permit an independent child custody evaluation because of problems inherent in the first one, the psychological examiner participated in attempts to deny presentation of evidence contrary to his own position, this time by preparing (with Attorney A) a declaration to prevent a new evaluation, asserting that the stress associated with yet another evaluation would adversely impact the children's best interests.

A court trial one year later resulted in the children being returned to Party B with a finding that Party B was not personality disordered, was otherwise within normal limits, and was positive on indices of parental competency. The psychologist lost his license following a complaint filed with APA's Ethics Committee.

The APA's (1994) "Guidelines for Child Custody Evaluations in Divorce Proceedings," if adhered to, should prevent such violations. The standards and guidelines inform not only the mental health community of what constitutes acceptable practice in the field, they inform the trier of fact (typically, judges in child custody determinations) and attorneys. Armed with these professionally ratified standards that are readily accessible, attorneys are enabled to frame meaningful and incisive questions based on them.

Child custody evaluations are emotionally laden and involve vulnerable children and parents whose resources, emotionally and financially, may be exhausted. These evaluations carry disproportionate risk to the examiner of licensure complaints. The "Guidelines for Child Custody Evaluations in Divorce Proceedings" (APA, 1994) provides specific and also general guidelines for conducting ethical evaluations. The three specific (orienting) guidelines from this document are as follows:

1. The primary purpose of the evaluation is to assess the best psychological interests of the child.
2. The child's (rather than the parents') interests and well-being are paramount.
3. The focus of the evaluation is on parenting capacity, the psychological and developmental needs of the child, and the resulting fit. . . . This involves (a) an assessment of the adult's capacities for parenting, including whatever knowledge, attributes, skills, and abilities, or lack thereof, are present; (b) an assessment of the psychological functioning and developmental needs of each child and of the wishes of each child where appropriate; and (c) an assessment of the functional ability of each parent to meet these needs, including an evaluation of the interaction between each adult and child. (p. 678)

Experts may wish to rely on the model presented in Table 3.2, which facilitates *ethical* and *competent* evaluations. It was developed by the first author (Weissman), following Grisso's (1986) seminal work on evaluating competencies. This model helps identify the salient functional parenting abilities that derive from legal constructs and psychological concepts. It thus guides data to be gathered and findings to be reported, consistent with legal relevance. In this model, A pertains to *legal constructs* in child custody, B to *psychological* constructs useful to the task of comprehending legally relevant behaviors, and C bridges the two. Referring to functional abilities in parental competencies, C defines psycholegal concepts capable of being evaluated (using clinical and forensic assessment instruments). The model contains a nonexhaustive list of a dozen or so

TABLE 3.2   Child Custody Evaluation Model

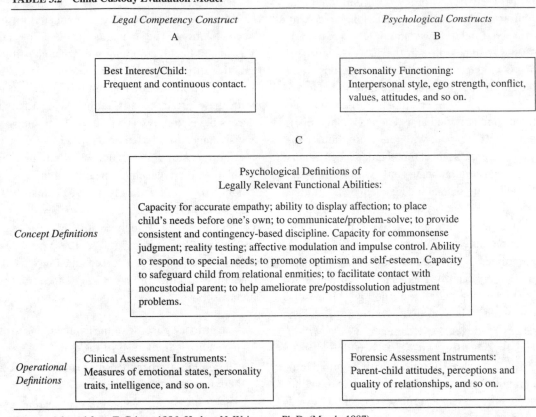

Source: Adapted from T. Grisso, 1986; Herbert N. Weissman, Ph.D. (March, 1997).

concept definitions of functional abilities that an examiner might assess in a given child custody case.

The use of psycholegally coherent models such as these increases the likelihood that methodologies derived therefrom will fulfill requirements for *competent* forensic practice as well as requirements for *ethical* forensic practice. A central theme of this chapter is that there is an essential correspondence between competent conduct and ethical conduct. In practice, one cannot exist without the other. Thus, formulating competent assessment methodologies (i.e., coherent, psycholegally relevant, balanced, comprehensive) is requisite to conducting ethical evaluations.

A Case Example: Personal Injury

Another example of the usefulness of this model is found in the personal injury context, illustrated first by a case example and then by a conceptual framework for evaluating personal injury cases (see Table 3.3).

In an employment discrimination case involving wrongful discharge secondary to whistle-blowing, the physician plaintiff had been the quality assurance director for a large HMO. Following "constructive discharge," she sued for pecuniary damages (lost wages, reduced career options) but not for emotional distress-type damages.

The defense, nonetheless, sought to have a psychiatrist conduct an independent medical examination (IME), which required petitioning the court because plaintiff counsel refused to stipulate to an IME where no medical or emotional damages were being claimed. Defense won its IME petition on the basis of the defense psychiatrist "diagnosing" the plaintiff as "severely personality disordered" with marked borderline and narcissistic features. The psychiatrist had reviewed only two data sources: memoranda that the plaintiff had written several years earlier in the employment context, and a diary that the plaintiff had written 20 years earlier, at age 15.

A defense IME was performed by a second psychiatrist, whose diagnostic opinions, not surprisingly, were identical to those of the first psychiatrist, this time on the basis of the above data sources plus record review, collateral contacts, a mental status examination, as well as results from the MMPI-2 and MCMI-III. The second psychiatrist had stated that the

TABLE 3.3   **Personal Injury Evaluation Model**

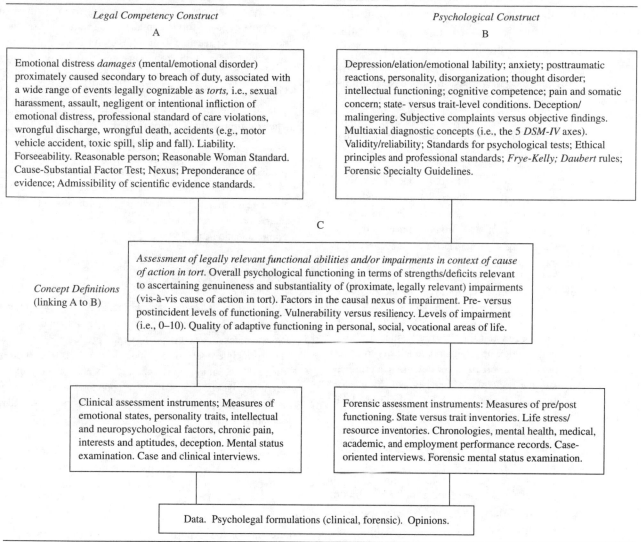

Legal Competency Construct

A

Emotional distress *damages* (mental/emotional disorder) proximately caused secondary to breach of duty, associated with a wide range of events legally cognizable as *torts,* i.e., sexual harassment, assault, negligent or intentional infliction of emotional distress, professional standard of care violations, wrongful discharge, wrongful death, accidents (e.g., motor vehicle accident, toxic spill, slip and fall). Liability. Forseeability. Reasonable person; Reasonable Woman Standard. Cause-Substantial Factor Test; Nexus; Preponderance of evidence; Admissibility of scientific evidence standards.

Psychological Construct

B

Depression/elation/emotional lability; anxiety; posttraumatic reactions, personality, disorganization; thought disorder; intellectual functioning; cognitive competence; pain and somatic concern; state- versus trait-level conditions. Deception/ malingering. Subjective complaints versus objective findings. Multiaxial diagnostic concepts (i.e., the 5 *DSM-IV* axes). Validity/reliability; Standards for psychological tests; Ethical principles and professional standards; *Frye-Kelly; Daubert* rules; Forensic Specialty Guidelines.

C

Concept Definitions
(linking A to B)

Assessment of legally relevant functional abilities and/or impairments in context of cause of action in tort. Overall psychological functioning in terms of strengths/deficits relevant to ascertaining genuineness and substantiality of (proximate, legally relevant) impairments (vis-à-vis cause of action in tort). Factors in the causal nexus of impairment. Pre- versus postincident levels of functioning. Vulnerability versus resiliency. Levels of impairment (i.e., 0–10). Quality of adaptive functioning in personal, social, vocational areas of life.

Clinical assessment instruments; Measures of emotional states, personality traits, intellectual and neuropsychological factors, chronic pain, interests and aptitudes, deception. Mental status examination. Case and clinical interviews.

Forensic assessment instruments: Measures of pre/post functioning. State versus trait inventories. Life stress/ resource inventories. Chronologies, mental health, medical, academic, and employment performance records. Case-oriented interviews. Forensic mental status examination.

Data. Psycholegal formulations (clinical, forensic). Opinions.

Source: Adapted from T. Grisso, 1986; © H. N. Weissman, Ph.D. (February, 1998).

plaintiff's severe Axis II pathology (which he opined had caused her to become a whistle-blower because of hostility and personal instability and maladjustment) was due to anger at management (observed in memoranda). He argued that her recent angry behavior corresponded to anger many years earlier toward her father (diary). Further, he based his diagnosis of Axis II pathology on collateral contacts, which consisted of a subset of defense-selected interested parties rather than a balanced set of collateral sources. A critical review of findings, however, revealed all objective data to be entirely within normal limits, based on data from the mental status examination, MMPI-2, and MCMI-III.

Disappointed because all objective findings were within normal limits, defense counsel sought to dismiss the psychiatrist (who had performed the IME) and successfully substituted a third psychiatrist (reporting that the prior one had taken ill) and retained a clinical psychologist who would perform a wide range of cognitive and personality assessment measures. All objective measures again yielded findings within normal limits, yet both the psychiatrist and the psychologist concluded that the plaintiff was severely personality disordered, borderline, narcissistic, and now also antisocial. They opined that the plaintiff had successfully "tricked" the tests, which required them to rely not on standardized, objective test data but instead on such subjective and biased sources as memos, an adolescent's diary, and statements by highly selected collaterals. All examiners had accepted their respective referrals on a contingency-payment basis.

This example, which actually occurred, is nonetheless a caricature of the unfortunate games, tricks, and manipulations that can result from ill-conceived and regrettable collusions between legal and mental health professionals. There are many violations of APA ethical principles and "Specialty Guidelines for Forensic Psychologists" in this case example that are useful to reference.

The preamble to the "Ethical Principles of Psychologists and Code of Conduct" (APA, 1992), states as "its primary goal"

> the welfare and protection of the individuals and groups with whom psychologists work. It is the individual responsibility of each psychologist to aspire to the highest possible standards of conduct. Psychologists respect and protect human and civil rights, and do not knowingly participate in or condone unfair discriminatory practices. (p. 3)

Psychiatry guidelines (*Ethical Guidelines for the Practice of Forensic Psychiatry*) carry similar language:

> The forensic psychiatrist functions as an expert within the legal process. . . . Although he may be retained by one party to a dispute in a civil matter or the prosecution or defense in a criminal matter, he adheres to the principles of honesty and striving for objectivity. His clinical evaluations and the application of the data obtained to the legal criteria are performed in the spirit of such honesty and striving for objectivity. . . . His opinion reflects this honesty and striving for objectivity. (American Academy of Psychiatry and the Law, 1993, p. 329)

Practitioners in the case example on personal injury made use of uncorroborated, third-party material. "Specialty Guidelines for Forensic Psychologists" cautions against doing so. Guideline VI.F. states:

> Forensic psychologists are aware that hearsay exceptions and other rules governing expert testimony place a special ethical burden upon them. When hearsay or otherwise inadmissible evidence forms the basis of their opinion, evidence, or professional product, they seek to minimize sole reliance upon such evidence. Where circumstances reasonably permit, forensic psychologists seek to obtain independent and personal verification of data relied upon as part of their professional services to the court or to a party to a legal proceeding. (Committee on Ethical Guidelines for Forensic Psychologists, 1991, p. 662)

Specialty Guideline VI.H prohibits use by experts of inadequate information. It states:

> Forensic psychologists avoid giving written or oral evidence about the psychological characteristics of particular individuals when they have not had an opportunity to conduct an examination of the individual adequate to the scope of the statements, opinions, or conclusions to be issued. Forensic psychologists make every reasonable effort to conduct such examinations. When it is not possible or feasible to do so, they make clear the impact of such limitations on the reliability and validity of their professional products, evidence, or testimony. (Committee on Ethical Guidelines for Forensic Psychologists, 1991, p. 663)

Further on this point (Guideline VII.A):

> Forensic psychologists make reasonable efforts to ensure that the products of their services, as well as their own public statements and professional testimony, are communicated in ways that will promote understanding and avoid deception, given the particular characteristics, roles, and abilities of various recipients of the communications. (p. 663)

Finally, Guideline VII.D states:

> When testifying, forensic psychologists have an obligation to all parties to a legal proceeding to present their findings, conclusions, evidence, or other professional products in a fair manner. This principle does not preclude forceful representation of the data and reasoning upon which a conclusion or professional product is based. It does, however, preclude an attempt, whether active or passive, to engage in partisan distortion or misrepresentation.
>
> Forensic psychologists do not, by either commission or omission, participate in a misrepresentation of their evidence, nor do they participate in partisan attempts to avoid, deny, or subvert the presentation of evidence contrary to their own position. (p. 664)

Clear bias of the experts in the case example was no doubt promoted by their financial interest in the outcome (see discussion on prohibition of contingency-fee contacts at II.A.8).

The framework presented in Table 3.3 illustrates the essential correspondence between psycholegally sound methodologies and ethically sound forensic professional practice in the personal injury context. Implicit in this conceptual framework is the goal of answering legal questions by constructing methodologies that bridge legal competency constructs (A) and psychological constructs (B). The results are the comprehensive assessment of legally relevant functional abilities and/or impairments (C) using general clinical as well as specialized forensic assessment instruments. Concept definitions (C) uniquely pertain in this case to causes of action in tort in which the comparison of pre- and postincident functioning is central to ascertaining whether or not "damages" resulted proximately from the instant incident.

UNDERSTANDING ADMISSIBILITY OF EVIDENCE AND ETHICS OF FORENSIC PRACTICE

Having discussed erroneous assumptions and misunderstandings in the first portion of this chapter, the emphasis now turns to elements of ethically competent practice in forensic psychology. Rules both in psychology and law that help define and control admissible evidence are discussed. Information is presented on admissibility of evidence in law and on assessment methodologies in psychology. Such information increases the likelihood that psychological findings can be relied on as scientific evidence by the courts and that they conform to ethical standards.

The central issue here revolves around evidence: how it is gathered and how it is presented. Unless ethical principles and specialized forensic guidelines are used in designing unbiased assessment methodologies, the findings that ultimately result cannot be reliable. Any opinions based on biased sets of findings would themselves be flawed and also would fail to meet the evidentiary criteria in law for admissibility of scientific evidence as specified in FRE 702.

FRE 702 was modified as of December 1, 2000, for use by the federal courts. The new version supersedes prior case law as to the specific issues FRE 702 addresses. It continues to be subject to interpretation and modification by case law published after December 1, 2000. FRE now reads as follows:

If the scientific, technical, or other specialized knowledge will assist the trier of fact to understand the evidence or to determine a fact in issue, a witness qualified as an expert by knowledge, skill, experience, training, or education, may testify thereto in the form of an opinion or otherwise, if (1) the testimony is based upon sufficient facts or data; (2) the testimony is the product of reliable principles and methods; and (3) the witness has applied the principles and methods reliably to the facts of the case. (O'Connor & Krauss, 2001, p. 4)

Although not bound by FRE 702, state courts often model their own rules for admitting expert testimony on this rule. Experts must be aware of rules in their jurisdiction and subsequent case law that may interpret and modify the local rules and the FRE.

Noteworthy here are the *legal gatekeeping controls* historically articulated in *Daubert* and its progeny and now applied in the new FRE 702. A major purpose of the rule is to prevent unqualified experts from testifying in the courtroom on the basis of irrelevant or inadequate evidence.

Noteworthy also are the corresponding *psychological gatekeeping controls* articulated in psychology's ethical principles (APA, 1992) and forensic guidelines (Committee on Ethical Guidelines for Forensic Psychologists, 1991). For example,

"Ethical Principles of Psychologists and Code of Conduct" (APA, 1992) states: "Psychologists provide services, teach, and conduct research only within the boundaries of their competence, based on their education, training, supervised experience, or appropriate professional experience" (1.04) and do so "only in the context of a defined professional or scientific relationship or role" (1.03). Also, they must "rely on scientifically and professionally derived knowledge when making scientific or professional judgments or when engaging in scholarly or professional endeavors" (1.06).

Further, "Psychologists' forensic assessments, recommendations, and reports are based on information and techniques . . . sufficient to provide appropriate substantiation for their findings" (7.02). "Psychologists who develop, administer, score, interpret, or use psychological assessment techniques, interviews, tests, or instruments do so in a manner and for purposes that are appropriate in light of the research on or evidence of the usefulness and proper application of the techniques" (2.02).

"Specialty Guidelines for Forensic Psychologists" (Committee on Ethical Guidelines for Forensic Psychologists, 1991) are consistent with principles articulated in APA's "Ethical Principles of Psychologists and Code of Conduct" and provide further refinement consistent with legal gatekeeping controls: "Forensic psychologists are responsible for a fundamental and reasonable level of knowledge and understanding of the legal and professional standards that govern their participation as experts in legal proceedings" (p. 658).

Further:

Because of their special status as persons qualified as experts to the court, forensic psychologists have an obligation to maintain current knowledge of scientific, professional and legal developments within their area of claimed competence. They are obligated also to use that knowledge, *consistent with accepted clinical and scientific standards,* in selecting data collection methods and procedures for an evaluation, treatment, consultation or scholarly/empirical investigation. (p. 661; emphasis added)

In doing so, "the forensic psychologist maintains professional integrity by examining the issue at hand from all reasonable perspectives, actively seeking information that will differentially test plausible rival hypotheses" (p. 661). Additional parallels between legal and psychological gatekeeper controls are found in Forensic Specialty Guideline VII.F., which explicitly defines forensic experts' role as providing assistance to "the trier of fact to understand the evidence or to determine a fact in issue . . . and to explain the relationship between their expert testimony and the legal issues and facts of an instant case" (p. 665).

When discussing evidence in a legal setting, "forensic psychologists avoid offering information from their investigations or evaluations that does not bear directly upon the legal purpose of their professional services and that is not critical as support for their product, evidence or testimony, except where such disclosure is required by law" (Committee on Ethical Guidelines for Forensic Psychologists, 1991, p. 662). This guideline, like the others, is critical to protecting the legal rights of litigants and defendants. It encourages competent practice by underscoring the importance of designing sound methodologies that go to the legal issues in a case, by seeking to answer relevant legal questions directly and coherently, rather than indirectly and diffusely.

There is an additional benefit to be derived by staying focused on the issues in a case. Report writing, often considered a daunting task, can become more reasonable because the data-gathering stage (assessment) is more efficiently connected to the information-disseminating stage (report writing). By recognizing the essential correspondence between competent clinical-forensic methodologies of assessment and ethical practice, the expert can meet the mandates of the courts regarding admissibility.

IMPLICATIONS AND APPLICATIONS

Ideally, there would be a close and smooth correspondence between psycholegal rules (e.g., principles, codes, guidelines) and their application, ensuring ethically competent professional conduct. As is the case with societal rules of normative conduct, for which the correspondence between the actual and the expected is less than perfect, so too is the case with professional rules. There is also a significant difference, however, between what is expected of the reasonable citizen versus the reasonable professional. Professional covenants require more disciplined commitments to upholding ethical competencies and to safeguarding individual rights and legal justice. Furthermore, there are legal and fiduciary responsibilities to honor, whose breach or violation can have obvious and serious consequences at numerous levels.

Legal objections to the scientific reliability of psychological testimony are less frequent, but tensions remain, as does skepticism regarding the value of what psychology has to offer the courts. As discussed earlier, both psychology and law have taken important steps by establishing ethical guidelines, codes of conduct, and rules that govern the admissibility of evidence. Credible and probative forensic work requires understanding these rules and the motivation to adhere to them. It also requires knowing how to apply the rules in a manner that assists the court by addressing relevant legal questions

with methods, concepts, and diagnoses that have a scientific foundation and enjoy general acceptance in psychology.

This is the reason for using well-standardized assessment measures whose psychometric properties are known versus untested assessment devices created in a local clinic or laboratory whose properties are unknown. The former are more likely to have gained general acceptance among clinical-forensic psychologists, to be reliable, to have known error rates, and to assist the court in answering relevant psycholegal questions (*Daubert v. Merrell Dow Pharmaceuticals,* 1993; FRE, 1975, p. 702; *Frye v. United States,* 1923). This same logic applies to the choice of diagnostic concepts for describing mental disorders. Specifically, it is the *Diagnostic and Statistical Manual of Mental Disorders (DSM-IV)* that is the authoritative source that has achieved general acceptance in the scientific and professional community (American Psychiatric Association, 1994) and must be used in the legal setting.

For example, there is *less* tendency to misapply the overly used posttraumatic stress disorder diagnosis when appropriate models are applied to the assessment of emotional complaints secondary to allegations of stress and trauma. This is an example of the role competent, ethically based methodologies can play in helping the mental health expert resist undue influence by attorneys who have come to prefer this diagnosis above all others when representing plaintiffs in personal injury litigation. The reason attorneys prefer the posttraumatic stress disorder diagnosis may have nothing to do with the merits of the case. Rather, it rests on the belief that both liability and damages are implicit within the very definition of the disorder, thus implying known causation. Many cases fail, on critical legal scrutiny (i.e., cross-examination), to meet the criteria for this disorder. The retained psychologist will be subjected to ethical, professional, and legal challenges by misapplying the posttraumatic stress disorder diagnosis when the evidentiary bases are deficient.

Concepts drawn from legal rules and psychological principles define broad competency-based methodologies. These have a greater likelihood of yielding reliable and replicable findings that the court can rely on as trustworthy evidence, and they stand up to critical scrutiny and to ethical and professional standard of care challenges. At each stage of the process, the same logic applies, as we have already seen: (a) by choosing standardized, proven clinical-forensic methods versus untested devices; (b) by rigorous application of the *DSM-IV*'s multiaxial diagnostic system versus alternative nonconsensual approaches; (c) by using conceptually and empirically grounded methodological approaches for assessing parental competencies, or criminal responsibility; and (d) by determining proximate versus alternative factors of causation, rather than accepting parties' complaints, excuses, or allegations at face value.

A relevant example of a conceptually grounded and empirically sound framework that would qualify under legal rules (i.e., FRE, state court rules of evidence, other statutes, case law) and under psychological rules (i.e., ethical principles, forensic guidelines) is the biopsychosocial frame of reference that has achieved general acceptance in psychology as a useful principle for analyzing and formulating interactive bases of causative events. This framework can be useful in elucidating specific factors, for example, those factors responsible for a defendant's mental state at the time of committing a criminal act, or responsible for causing a plaintiff's acute low-back pain to convert into chronic low-back pain. A psycholegal formulation that involves multiple interactive causative factors (i.e., biopsychosocial) versus a formulation that involves merely a single explanatory factor is more likely to have gained general acceptance in the scientific community, to have acquired a greater scientific basis, and to be more capable of providing reliable and probative bases for psycholegal opinions.

In a case in which the biopsychosocial framework was applied, the expert found that low-back pain persisted more than six months after the occurrence of a soft tissue back injury (thus, chronic versus acute). The expert explained that at a biological level, records indicated the presence of a preexisting degenerative spine disease process and an absence of evidence of acute trauma. At the psychological level, there was a somatoform propensity; at the psychosocial level, there was an incentive structure that favored disability over health. Thus, the injury resulted proximately in brief acute pain in a person biologically vulnerable to suffering such pain on the basis of preexisting susceptibility. Subjective complaints and pain behaviors significantly exceeded objective findings, and there was no evidence found for organic medical factors responsible for protracted pain complaints. A preexisting tendency to internalize negative affects (depression, anger, distress) and to convert intense affective states into somatic complaints suggested a strong somatoform component. There was further evidence for psychosocial factors serving to protract pain complaints and disability status, such as pending litigation/compensation, avoidance of onerous tasks at work, and opportunity to spend time at home with family. Dynamics of deception and malingering were examined. Whereas there was abundant evidence showing exaggeration of symptoms along with rationalization of their cause and displacement of responsibility for their remedy and remediation, these dynamics were operating mostly at unconscious and involuntary levels.

On cross-examination, opposing counsel sought to disassemble the multifactorial biopsychosocial formulation by asking the expert to offer opinions on the basis of alternative hypothetical scenarios in which each factor was selectively eliminated. For example, what would be the degree of disability/residual damage if evidence for the biological vulnerability factor were removed, if evidence for a somatoform (psychological) factor were eliminated, or if the factor of protracted litigation (psychosocial) did not exist? The expert responded by asserting that to offer separate opinions about a disorder that is multifaceted and interactive both in its causation and in its effects would misrepresent the evidence and therefore would be a disservice to the court. Further, to offer opinions on the basis of separate versus interactive factors would violate FRE 702 for the admissibility of scientific evidence. Such an approach would also distort the application of the generally accepted biopsychological model and its scientific foundations. It would thus fail to assist the court's efforts at just decision making.

Another time-tested, useful, and relevant multifactorial conceptual framework is the scientist-professional model. Kuehnle (1998) effectively applies it to the examination of child sexual abuse allegations. According to Kuehnle, this dual model's value to the court rests on (a) its reliance on empirically derived evidence; (b) base rates of behavior for distinguishing differences between nonsexually abused and sexually abused children; (c) measurement instruments with proven sensitivity and specificity; and (d) safeguards to avoid mistaken cause-effect relationships between a child's responses (e.g., symptoms, figure drawings, reactions to anatomically detailed dolls), and the occurrence of an event (e.g., sexual abuse). Comprehensive understanding of the impact of child sexual abuse requires elucidation of a complex matrix of interacting biopsychosocial factors, including (a) biological risk factors; (b) chronological age and developmental stage; (c) competency/credibility; (d) personality characteristics; (e) interpretation of the event by the child; (f) degree of parental support received; (g) nature of the abuse; and (h) litigation pressures on children susceptible to influence (Kendall-Tackert, Williams, & Finkelhor, 1993; Weissman, 1991b).

Kuehnle (1998), based on extensive review of the child sexual abuse literature, supports the point that with complex psychological evaluations such as these, simple univariate methodologies/analyses do not provide reliable information. She writes that, "while there is no simple test, marker, or mathematical equation for determining whether a child has experienced sexual abuse, the empirical data, historical information, test results, and children's statements must all be evaluated against a complex matrix of interrelated factors" (p. 18). Doing so increases the likelihood that an ethically competent psychological evaluation will have been conducted.

Ethically sound forensic practice considers rival hypotheses to avoid hindsight and other biases. By way of illustration, testing rival hypotheses in a personal injury case involves considering the differential impact on the plaintiff's damages of the role of (a) preexisting factors, (b) coexisting factors, (c) protracted litigation, (d) the dynamics of deception, and (e) chronic, preexisting underlying disorders. The expert should be aware that the same clinical picture could be present even in the absence of proximate (personal injury) factors of causation. If findings from one's comprehensive evaluation yield evidence indicating that proximate factors, all or in part, are the most compelling, one needs to address possible alternative causes. The expert would explain that alternative causes of the plaintiff's mental/emotional impairments were evaluated as well as alleged proximate factors of causation, to ascertain genuineness and substantiality of each factor in the causal nexus of the plaintiff's impairment. On considering the respective impact of each in the plaintiff's damages, a confluence of evidence indicates, for example, that only proximate factors were substantial enough to be responsible for the plaintiff's damages. The expert would offer these opinions on the basis of reasonable medical/scientific certainty. If there is evidence pointing to substantial impact by other factors as well, then the differential contribution to the plaintiff's disorder that these respective factors constituted would also be described.

Take, for example, a case in which a plaintiff fell from a second-story window on his head at age 5 years. The plaintiff sustained multiple skull fractures and a severe cerebral concussion. Now age 19, he filed a lawsuit for damages against the apartment house owner on the liability theory that if the window frames and screens had been more secure, they would not have broken on impact by a young child's playful behavior. Proximate factors involved skull fractures, cerebral concussion, and learning disabilities (reading and information processing) throughout his school career (from ages 5 through 19). Alternative factors of causation involved preexisting history (prior to age 5) of verbal slowness, family history of verbal slowness, bilingualism, parental discord and divorce, and multiple academic and residential changes. A confluence of evidence (based on site of impact on the head, nature of physical injuries, type and quality of learning disabilities) pointed to proximate factors (the fall) constituting the substantial factor. There was evidence as well for the role of preexisting and coexisting influences, which in this case represented mitigating elements.

A final example of relevant application of legal and psychological rules and gatekeeping controls is drawn from medicolegal cases involving the assessment of alleged psychological trauma. In such cases, multifactorial concepts, including the biopsychosocial framework, find greatest acceptance and reliable scientific foundation for analyzing the multiple dimensions associated with psychological trauma. A multifactorial methodology involves analyzing and assessing details of (a) the *event* itself; (b) the *person* who is impacted by the event, using biopsychosocial logic; and (c) the extended *context* in which the event takes place (Briere, 1997; Pynoos, Steinberg, & Goenjian, 1996; van der Kolk, McFarlane, & Weisaeth, 1996). Deception is assessed as well because of the subjectivity commonly associated with self-reports of psychological trauma (Lees-Haley, 1997; Resnick, 1995; Rogers, 1997; Simon, 1995). It would be inadequate to assess only one or another of the factors (i.e., person, event) and to then render a diagnosis and offer opinions based on the plaintiff's subjective self-report. Doing so would violate gatekeeping controls in both psychology and law. By contrast, ethically competent professional practices fulfill time-honored criteria and provide the court with reliable evidence on which it can safely rely.

ETHICS AT THE INTERFACE OF PSYCHOLOGY AND LAW

What is the suitable role for the psychologist when serving in the capacity of forensic expert? The role is a multifaceted one, due to (a) often unclear perceptions and expectations between lawyer and expert, as discussed above; (b) the economics of independent practice where fee-for-service is involved; and (c) conflicts associated with role boundaries that, from the outset of a case, may be ambiguous and then shift or change over the course of the relationship. The difference between the goals and aims of psychology and those of law adds to communication difficulties. Marked differences in terms of art and frames of reference between psychology and law can add additional layers of misunderstanding and disappointment. The psychologist, needing to practice ethically and professionally, must exercise judgment in choosing cases.

From the attorney's point of view as an advocate, stakes can be enormous at many levels, including professional liability, financial risk, and significant fiduciary responsibility. Further, there can be responsibility for defending life and liberty, protecting victims' rights, obtaining damages for wrongs, or seeking custody visitation in a child's best interests. The attorney often believes that choice of an expert can make the difference between winning and losing a case. So the process of applying criteria to selecting experts becomes a high-risk and complex dynamic. The balance is a delicate one in which the attorney wants to retain a competent expert that he or she can work with, who has solid credentials, and who the judge and/or jury will find credible, understandable, and likeable. Attorneys are deserving of empathy for the enormous burden they must carry as an advocate.

The expert is equally deserving of empathy for efforts to strive for professional objectivity and technical independence. The attorney needs to feel comfortable with an expert who, from the outset, must be capable of clearly communicating the scope of his or her practice, areas of expertise, methodologies of assessment, and general philosophy and points of view about the psycholegal areas involved in the case at hand. The attorney needs to know in advance about potential conflicts of interest that may compromise an expert's usefulness, as well as the values and biases of the expert that might influence opinions. In this context, (a) ethical and standard of care concerns should be addressed; (b) role definitions, role boundaries, and scope of the assignment should be defined; and (c) professional fees should be clarified. Once these matters are addressed, the elements should be incorporated into a written contract to avoid later misunderstandings.

Communication between attorney and expert is critical. For example, the expert needs to inquire about receiving medical and legal records and to request clarification of the legal standards pertinent to the case at hand. The expert also needs to inform the attorney of his or her findings, thus enabling use of those findings by the attorney in efforts to settle or to try the case.

Serious problems can result when either the expert or the attorney "blind-sides" the other. Examples include an attorney failing to provide full sets of records the expert needs to rely on for competent formulation of opinions and provision of testimony; by a psychologist misleading the attorney about the psychological merits of a case; and by an expert misrepresenting or failing to be clear about how far he or she is able to go in the opinions he or she will be offering. The more that can be addressed and clarified early in the process of being retained, the less room for misunderstandings at later stages of the process. This translates into the expert providing sound opinions supported only by sound data and reasoning. This approach is both more professionally comfortable as well as ethical.

Given the complexities and all the cautionary reminders, experts can potentially become overly cautious and thus rendered ineffectual by being unable or unwilling to express conviction in their findings. The "Specialty Guidelines for Forensic Psychologists" (at VII.D) make it clear that experts have the right, and even the obligation, to testify with an appropriate degree of conviction regarding their findings and opinions. While underscoring the expert's obligation to pre-

sent findings, conclusions, and evidence in a fair manner, the Guidelines also state: "This principle does not preclude forceful representation of the data and reasoning upon which a conclusion or professional product is based" (Committee on Ethical Guidelines for Forensic Psychologists, 1991, p. 664).

FUTURE DIRECTIONS

The APA's Ethics Committee has its Ethics Code Task Force currently drafting a proposed revision to the 1992 Ethics Code. The draft is scheduled to be submitted to APA's Council of Representatives for review and action in 2002 (APA, 2001).

Of particular relevance here is the section entitled "Forensic Activities," which differs from the 1992 version in some respects. The proposed revision to the former Principle 7 carries similar language as regards prior relationships and clarification of role. Its new section on forensic competence is similar to the former section on professionalism, the latter emphasizing the importance of possessing a reasonable level of knowledge of both psychological *and* legal bases of forensic activities. Also proposed is a new section on informed consent for forensic services, which highlights the requirements that consent, to be legitimately obtained, must have been truly informed. This reflects a refreshing emphasis on (a) candor as to methods and procedures; (b) transparency as to purposes and intended uses of results; and (c) the limits of confidentiality that may exist.

There is a continuing trend toward developing specialized sets of guidelines in respective areas of the psycholegal domain. As we have seen, "Specialized Guidelines for Forensic Psychologists" was published in 1991 (Committee on Ethical Guidelines for Forensic Psychologists, 1991), followed soon thereafter by child custody guidelines (APA, 1994), and then by guidelines for psychological evaluations in child protection matters (APA Committee on Professional Practice and Standards, 1998). The APA's (1992) "Ethical Principles" carries a separate section devoted to forensic activities, which also will be included in its projected revision for 2002.

New specialized sets of guidelines should articulate ethically competent methodologies that coherently bridge psychological and legal concepts to enhance the reliability and validity of resulting findings. The 1994 child custody document attempts to accomplish this by enunciating the parameters and components of ethical child custody evaluations. Future specialized sets of guidelines should include explication of legal controls drawn from Federal Rules of Evidence and from case and statutory law. Competency-based ethics guidelines serve to facilitate training in forensic practice.

Ethical behavior in the individual, although subserved by personal motivations and characterological features, nonetheless can be understood as a set of learnable functional skills. When properly implemented (e.g., in the formulation of assessment methodologies that address psycholegal issues and protect rights and privileges of all the parties to a legal action), these ethical skills constitute an essential component of competent forensic practice.

REFERENCES

American Psychiatric Association. (1994). *Diagnostic and statistical manual of mental disorders* (4th ed.). Washington, DC: Author.

American Psychological Association. (2001). Ethical principles of psychologists and code of conduct: Draft for comment. *A.P.A. Instructor, 32,* 77–89.

American Psychological Association. (1994). Guidelines for child custody evaluations in divorce proceedings. *American Psychologist, 49,* 677–680.

American Psychological Association. (1993). Record keeping guidelines. *American Psychologist, 48,* 984–986.

American Psychological Association. (1992). Ethical principles of psychologists and code of conduct. *American Psychologist, 47,* 1597–1611.

American Psychological Association Committee on Professional Practice and Standards. (1998). *Guidelines for psychological evaluations in child protection matters.* Washington DC: American Psychological Association.

Blau, T. H. (1984). *The psychologist as expert witness.* New York: Wiley.

Briere, J. (1997). *Psychological assessment of adult posttraumatic states.* Washington, DC: American Psychological Association.

Butcher, J. N., Dahlstrom, W. B., Graham, J. R., Tellegen, A., & Kaemmer, B. (1989). *Minnesota Multiphasic Personality Inventory (MMPI-2). Manual for administration and scoring.* Minneapolis: University of Minnesota Press.

Canter, M. B., Bennett, B. E., Jones, S. E., & Nagy, T. F. (1994). *Ethics for psychologists: A commentary on the APA ethics code.* Washington, DC: American Psychological Association.

Committee on Ethical Guidelines for Forensic Psychologists. (1991). Specialty guidelines for forensic psychologists. *Law and Human Behavior, 15,* 655–665.

Daubert v. Merrell Dow Pharmaceuticals, Inc., U.S. 113 S. Ct. 2786 (1993).

Dawes, R. M. (1989). Experience and validity of clinical judgment: The illusory correlation. *Behavioral Sciences and the Law, 7,* 457–467.

Estelle v. Smith, 451 U.S. 454 (1981).

Ethical Guidelines for the Practice of Forensic Psychiatry. (1993). AAPL Guidelines, in AAPL Membership Directory, XI-XIV.

Federal Rules of Evidence for United States Courts and Magistrates. (1975). St. Paul, MN: West.

Frye v. United States, 293 F. 1013, 1014 (D.C. Cir 1923).

General Electric v. Joiner, 118 S. Ct. 512 (1997).

Golding, S. (1996). *American Academy for Forensic Psychology, Workshop Syllabus,* p. 38.

Goodman-Delahunty, J. (1997). Forensic psychological expertise in the wake of *Daubert. Law and Human Behavior, 21,* 121–140.

Greenberg, S. A., & Shuman, D. W. (1997). Irreconcilable conflict between therapeutic and forensic roles. *Professional Psychology: Research and Practice, 28,* 50–57.

Grisso, T. (1986). *Evaluating competencies: Forensic assessments and instruments.* New York: Plenum Press.

Hartshorne, H., & May, M. A. (1928). *Studies in the nature of character: Studies in deceit* (Vol. 1). New York: Macmillan.

Hess, A. K. (1998). Accepting forensic case referrals: Ethical and professional considerations. *Professional Psychology: Research and Practice, 29,* 109–114.

Kendall-Tackert, K. A., Williams, L. M., & Finkelhor, D. (1993). Impact of sexual abuse on children: A review and synthesis of recent empirical studies. *Psychological Bulletin, 113*(1), 164–180.

Kirkland, K., & Kirkland, K. L. (2001). Frequency of child custody evaluation complaints and related disciplinary action: A survey of the association of state and provincial psychology boards. *Professional Psychology: Research and Practice, 32,* 171–174.

Kohlberg, L. (1976). Moral stages and moralization: The cognitive-developmental approach. In T. Lickona (Ed.), *Moral development and behavior: Theory, research and social issues.* New York: Holt, Rinehart and Winston.

Kohlberg, L., Levine, C., & Hewer, A. (1983). *Moral stages: A current formulation and a response to critics.* Basel, Switzerland: Karger.

Kuehnle, K. (1998). Child sexual abuse evaluations: The scientist-practitioner model. *Behavioral Sciences and the Law, 16,* 5–20.

Kumho Tire Company Ltd. et al. v. Carmichael et al., 526 U.S. 137 (1999).

Lees-Haley, P. R. (1997). MMPI-2 base rates for 492 personal injury plaintiffs: Implications and challenges for forensic assessment. *Journal of Clinical Psychology, 53,* 745–755.

Melton, G. B., Petrila, J., Poythress, N. G., & Slobogin, C. (1997). *Psychological evaluations for the courts: A handbook for mental health professionals and lawyers* (2nd ed.). New York: Guilford Press.

Meyer, R. G. (1995). *Preparation for licensing and board certification examinations in psychology* (2nd ed.). New York: Brunner/Mazel.

Millon, T. (1987). *Manual for the Millon Clinical Multiaxial Inventory-II* (MCMI-II) (2nd ed.). Minneapolis: National Computer Systems.

Münsterberg, H. (1908). *On the witness stand.* New York: Doubleday.

O'Connor, M., & Krauss, D. (2001). Legal update. *American Psychology-Law Society News, 21*(1), 1–18.

Pynoos, R. S., Steinberg, A. M., & Goenjian, A. (1996). Traumatic stress in childhood and adolescence: Recent developments and current controversies. In B. A. van der Kolk, A. C. McFarlane, & L. Weisaeth (Eds.), *Traumatic stress: The effects of overwhelming experience on mind, body and society* (pp. 331–358). New York: Guilford Press.

Resnick, P. J. (1995). Guidelines for the evaluation of malingering in posttraumatic stress disorder. In R. I. Simon (Ed.), *Posttraumatic stress disorder in litigation: Guidelines for forensic assessment.* Washington, DC: American Psychiatric Association.

Rogers, R. (Ed.). (1997). *Clinical assessment of malingering and deception* (2nd ed.). New York: Guilford Press.

Rorschach, H. (1942). *Psychodiagnostics: A diagnostic test based on perception.* Bern, Switzerland: Hans Huber. (Original work published in 1921).

Saks, M. J. (1990). Expert witnesses, nonexpert witnesses and nonwitness experts. *Law and Human Behavior, 14,* 291–313.

Simon, R. I. (Ed.). (1995). *Posttraumatic stress disorder in litigation: Guidelines for forensic assessment.* Washington, DC: American Psychiatric Press, Inc.

Stromberg, C. (1993). The psychologist's legal update. *National Register of Health Service Providers in Psychology, No. 1.*

Terman, L. M. (1931). Psychology and the law. *Los Angeles Bar Association Bulletin, 6,* 142–153.

van der Kolk, B. A., McFarlane, A. C., & Weisaeth, L. (Eds.). (1996). *Traumatic stress: The effects of overwhelming experience on mind, body, and society.* New York: Guilford Press.

Weissman, H. N. (1985). Psycholegal standards and the role of psychological assessment in personal injury litigation. *Behavioral Sciences and the Law, 3,* 135–147.

Weissman, H. N. (1990). Distortions and deceptions in self presentation: Effects of protracted litigation on personal injury cases. *Behavioral Sciences and the Law, 8,* 67–74.

Weissman, H. N. (1991a). Child custody evaluations: Fair and unfair professional practices. *Behavioral Sciences and the Law, 9,* 469–476.

Weissman, H. N. (1991b). Forensic psychological examination of the child witness in cases of alleged sexual abuse. *American Journal of Orthopsychiatry, 61*(1), 48–58.

Wigmore, J. H. (1909). Professor Münsterberg and the psychology of testimony. *Illinois Law Review, 3,* 399–445.

Wigmore, J. H. (1940). *Evidence in trials at common law* (3rd ed.). Boston: Little, Brown.

CHAPTER 4

Expert Testimony: Law and Practice

CHARLES PATRICK EWING

A major aspect of the practice of forensic psychology involves providing expert testimony in trials, hearings, and administrative proceedings. As is clear from many of the other chapters in this volume, today, expert testimony is heard from psychologists on a host of issues, including, but far from limited to, child custody, personal injury, disability, substituted judgment, competency to waive rights, competency to stand trial, insanity, and diminished capacity.

This chapter briefly examines the history of expert testimony by psychologists, explains the general legal rules governing expert testimony, and then details selected practical aspects of the current process of giving such testimony, with specific emphasis on the types of expert testimony given by forensic psychologists and related mental health professionals.

THE HISTORICAL ROOTS OF MODERN EXPERT TESTIMONY

Expert testimony that today would be regarded as within the province of forensic psychology was given in U.S. courts as early as 1846 (see, e.g., Gravitz, 1995). But modern-day expert testimony by forensic psychologists and other psychological experts probably owes its birth most clearly to Hugo Münsterberg, a Harvard University professor, experimental psychologist, and contemporary of Freud and Watson. In 1908, Münsterberg published the first textbook of forensic psychology. In his now classic *On the Witness Stand,* a collection of chapters in which he recounted many of his

own pioneering experiences as an expert witness in a number of celebrated trials, Professor Münsterberg asserted that the legal process would be well served by greater use of psychological principles and expertise.

Clearly anticipating the development of what is now known as forensic psychology, Münsterberg (1908) made numerous optimistic claims for psychology's value to the courts and to the legal system as a whole. For example, in describing an instrument he and his psychological colleagues used to measure minute time intervals, he wrote that "the chronoscope of the modern psychologist has become, and will become more and more, for the student of crime, what the microscope is for the student of disease" (p. 77). Münsterberg also wrote that the psychology of associations (the relationships among thoughts and other mental processes) "has become, indeed, a magnifying-glass for the most subtle mental mechanism, and by it the secrets of the criminal mind may be unveiled" (p. 108).

While praising his own discipline, Münsterberg (1908) harshly criticized the legal system for failing to rely more heavily on the developing science of psychology. He noted, for example, that "while the court makes the fullest use of all the modern scientific methods when for instance a drop of dried blood is to be examined in a murder case, the same court is completely satisfied with the most unscientific and haphazard methods of common prejudice and ignorance when a mental product . . . is to be examined" (pp. 44–45). Münsterberg found it "astonishing that the work of justice is ever carried out in the courts without ever consulting the psychologist . . ." (p. 194).

Given the existing state of psychology as a science and profession in the early twentieth century, Münsterberg's claims for the benefits of psychology in the courtroom were undoubtedly premature, if not grandiose. Thus, not surprisingly, his words clearly irritated judges, lawyers, and legal scholars, many of whom complained—and not without good cause—that psychology had yet to develop the data and methods needed to back up his claims.

In a scathing, satirical law review article published in 1909 in the Illinois Law Review, Professor John Henry Wigmore, the leading evidence law scholar of the day, described an imaginary legal proceeding in which a jury examined Münsterberg's assertions about the value of psychology to the legal system. Wigmore's fictional trial took place on April 1, 1909 (April Fool's Day) in the Superior Court of Wundt County, a jurisdiction undoubtedly named for Wilhelm Wundt, the father of experimental psychology. Münsterberg's views were advanced by an attorney named X. Perry Ment and almost instantly rejected by the jury. In Professor Wigmore's caricature, Münsterberg is ridiculed as the author of "The Psychology of the Wastebasket" (a study relating personality characteristics to "the number of times the letter M occurred on the scraps thrown into the basket"), "Studies in Domestic Psy-collar-gy," and "The Psychology of the Collar Button (the results of over 9000 observations of the behavior of the ordinary collar button)" (p. 402). In Wigmore's fictional cross-examination of the "defendant," the examining attorney caustically derides Münsterberg's unduly optimistic view of psychology and his unwarranted criticism of the legal system. After reviewing the works of other psychologists less positive than Münsterberg about what psychology could offer the courts, the plaintiff's attorney asks the psychologist-defendant the following long-winded but telling question:

> Now then, professor, I want you to be good enough to explain to this jury how anyone could have predicted . . . that precisely you would commit the whimsical mistake of bearing testimony against our innocent profession . . . for neglecting to use new and "exact" methods which were and still are so little "exact" and so incapable of forensic use that even their well-wishers confess that thousands of experiments and years of research will be required before they will be practicable, if ever? (p. 414)

To this, as well as to the succeeding barrage of tough questions, the humiliated "Münsterberg" has "no answer."

Though Wigmore's biting parody was widely read, well received by judges and lawyers, and probably reflected the sentiments of most knowledgeable legal professionals and scholars of the day, it was Münsterberg who really had the last laugh.

By 1923, when a second edition of Münsterberg's book was published, it included a foreword by Attorney Charles S. Whitman. Former Governor of New York, past District Attorney of New York County, and a man of unquestionable stature in the American legal community, Whitman described Münsterberg's treatise as "an instructive exposition of what may be termed 'legal psychology' " (p. xii). Noting that the articles in the book had initially been published 14 years earlier, Whitman concluded that "they have lost none of their timeliness, interest or helpfulness [and] contain lessons in experimental psychology which are invaluable to any one interested in the administration of justice" (p. xii).

Münsterberg was a psychologist trying to educate the legal system regarding psychology. The next major influence in the history of forensic psychology came not from psychology but from within the legal establishment.

American legal theory, from the mid-eighteenth century through the dawn of the twentieth, largely accepted without question the conception of law as "a set of rules deduced by logic from eternal principles" (Aichele, 1990, p. 23). Oliver Wendell Holmes (1881), who once wrote "The life of the law has not been logic; it has been experience" (p. 1), joined several other prominent jurists and legal scholars in challenging this conception as early as the late nineteenth century. But it was not until the early twentieth century that legal scholars began to consider empirically testing the many behavioral assumptions and propositions of law.

Early in the century, Roscoe Pound, the Harvard Law School Dean, armed with both a law degree and a Ph.D. in botany, helped establish what would come to be called "sociological jurisprudence." In 1910, Pound urged those in the legal profession to "look to economics and sociology and philosophy, and cease to assume that jurisprudence is self-sufficient" (pp. 35–36).

Still, Pound and other early adherents to sociological jurisprudence were essentially jurists and legal philosophers. It was not until the 1920s and 1930s that there developed what has come to be called a school of legal realism. The legal realists, a group of law professors at a handful of elite Eastern law schools, not only attacked traditional legal theory and emphasized the social and political functions of the law, but attempted to impose both an objectivity and an empiricism on the study of law.

Most significantly, many of the legal realists not only saw principles of law as essentially psychological but believed that legal assumptions could and should be tested empirically in keeping with the then infantile but rapidly developing techniques of psychology and the other behavioral sciences. That attitude is perhaps nowhere better or more strongly captured than in a 1935 book, *Law and the Lawyers,* written by

Edward Stevens Robinson, a psychologist who was then on both the psychology and law faculties at Yale University.

Robinson's (1935) book, which the author proudly presented as "part of the realistic movement in American jurisprudence," begins with this sentence: "This book attempts to show that jurisprudence is certain to become one of the family of social sciences—that all of its fundamental concepts will have to be brought in line with psychological knowledge" (p. v). Later in the volume, Robinson wrote, "The law is concerned with the regulation, mitigation and composition of human disputes. The fundamental stuff with which it deals is therefore psychological" (p. 72). Then, almost echoing Münsterberg, Robinson took the legal system to task for its reliance on theories and assumptions that cannot withstand the empirical scrutiny of psychology and the other social sciences:

> Of all the social studies jurisprudence has collected perhaps the largest assortment of theories which, though obviously in disagreement with the facts, are said to be convenient. Falsifications of history, economics, and sociology as well as psychology, are the devices by means of which juristic thought simplifies a baffling world. (p. 73)

The promise of legal realism was never fully met, and the pronouncements of Robinson, like those of Münsterberg before him, were greeted with grave skepticism by many jurists and legal scholars. Still, it must be acknowledged that the realist movement of the 1920s and 1930s set the stage for much of the modern interface between law and psychology and helped pave the way for forensic psychology by framing many legal issues as concerns that psychologists would later be well equipped to address. Certainly, the early jury studies and other pioneering psycholegal research on issues such as eyewitness testimony were stimulated in large measure by the critiques of the realists and their successors.

Until the advent of the field of clinical psychology, psychological contributions to the legal system came mostly in the form of research, consultation, and occasional expert testimony on issues related to memory, perception, intellect, and other cognitive issues. However, even once clinical psychology was clearly established as a recognized profession and psychological specialization, psychologists rarely were involved in the kinds of legal issues that are the bread and butter of today's forensic psychologists. Until as recently as the early 1960s, forensic issues such as insanity, competence to stand trial, psychological injury, and other major psycholegal concerns were defined by the courts as almost exclusively the province of psychiatrists. The role played by psychologists in the legal system was similar to what it was in the mental health field more generally: Psychologists were regarded as adjuncts to the dominant profession of psychiatry.

That role was well described in 1955 by Guttmacher and Weihofen, two psychiatrists who wrote the classic text, *Psychiatry and The Law.* According to Guttmacher and Weihofen: "The clinical psychologists are those most frequently confused with psychiatrists, and understandably so. They have special training in evaluating the intelligence and personality structure of healthy and mentally disordered individuals" (p. 9). These authors then went on to explain how and why clinical psychologists were already becoming "dissatisfied with mere testing" and were clamoring for a larger professional role "under the guidance of the psychiatrist" (p. 9). To their credit, Guttmacher and Weihofen seemed open to the thought of clinical psychologists playing an expanded role in the evaluation and treatment of cases involving legal issues. Their colleagues in the American Psychiatric Association, however, were not so open-minded.

In the watershed case of *Jenkins v. United States,* decided by the D.C. Circuit Court of Appeals in 1962, the issue was whether a clinical psychologist could give expert testimony that a criminal defendant had a mental disease when he committed the crimes charged. Three highly qualified Ph.D. clinical psychologists had so testified, but the trial court had instructed the jury to totally disregard their testimony because they were not physicians.

On appeal of the defendant's conviction, both the American Psychiatric Association and the American Psychological Association weighed in with *amicus* briefs. The Psychological Association argued that clinical psychologists were professionally qualified to diagnose mental illness and should not be barred from presenting testimony regarding such a diagnosis (American Psychological Association, 1962). In its *amicus* brief, the Psychiatric Association repeatedly emphasized that, although they might be good testers, psychologists were not medical doctors, functioned merely as assistants to psychiatrists, and did not qualify as experts in the diagnosis or treatment of mental illness (American Psychiatric Association, 1962).

A ruling in favor of the psychiatrists' position would undoubtedly have been a serious setback to the development of the barely emerging field of forensic psychology. Fortunately for this nascent profession, the court held in favor of psychology and against psychiatry. Writing for the majority of the court, Judge David Bazelon recounted the extensive training and qualifications of Ph.D. clinical psychologists and held that such psychologists were not, as a matter of law, precluded from testifying in court regarding mental illness simply because they were not medical doctors.

Although the *Jenkins* case is now a mere footnote—if it is mentioned at all—in most law and psychology texts, its importance to the history of forensic psychology cannot be underestimated. While this decision dealt solely with the admissibility of forensic psychological testimony regarding criminal responsibility, it opened the courtroom doors for psychologists more generally and helped pave the way for modern rules that clearly permit psychologists to provide expert testimony on a host of issues.

THE LAW OF EXPERT TESTIMONY

Expert testimony in all courts is generally governed by well-defined rules of evidence. Many jurisdictions have formal codes of evidence. California and the federal system are two notable examples. The California evidence rules are contained in the California Evidence Code, and the rules for the federal courts can be found in the Federal Rules of Evidence. The Federal Rules of Evidence govern the admissibility of expert testimony in the federal courts of the United States, regardless of their location, and have served as a model for many state evidence codes. In some states, such as New York, for example, there is no code of evidence; in those states, the rules of evidence, including those governing expert testimony, are embodied in case law (the published decisions of the state's appellate courts).

Whether found in codes or cases, the rules of evidence always provide the legal structure for expert testimony. That structure obviously varies somewhat among jurisdictions. To simplify matters, this chapter relies heavily on the Federal Rules of Evidence and the California Code of Evidence. Thus, readers must bear in mind that the rules discussed below may not be those governing testimony in their particular states. Any doubt about local rules should always be resolved by seeking the advice of legal counsel.

In most courts of law, the rules of evidence permit witnesses to testify only to that which they have personally perceived (i.e., seen, heard, touched, tasted, or smelled). Witnesses are generally limited to testifying regarding facts about which they have firsthand knowledge and are generally barred from offering opinions or conclusions. For example, under Federal Rule of Evidence 701:

> If the witness is not testifying as an expert, the witness' testimony in the form of opinions or inferences is limited to those opinions or inferences which are (a) rationally based on the perception of the witness and (b) helpful to a clear understanding of the witness' testimony or the determination of a fact in issue.

Perhaps foremost among several exceptions to this "no opinion" rule is that permitting certain specially qualified witnesses to state opinions and/or conclusions in their testimony. In all jurisdictions, witnesses recognized by the courts as "experts" are generally allowed to testify not only to facts and perceptions but to opinions and conclusions.

Who Is an Expert?

Who are these "experts" granted this exception to the general "no opinion" rule that governs lay witnesses, and why are these witnesses allowed this exceptional latitude in their testimony?

The rules in most American courts set a fairly low standard in determining who qualifies as an expert witness. Under California Evidence Code Section 720, for example, "A person is qualified to testify as an expert if he has special knowledge, skill, experience, training or education sufficient to qualify him as an expert on the subject to which his testimony relates." Under Federal Rule of Evidence 702, "If scientific, technical, or other specialized knowledge will assist the trier of fact to understand the evidence or to determine a fact in issue, a witness qualified as an expert by knowledge, skill, experience, training or education, may testify thereto in the form of an opinion or otherwise." As explained by the Advisory Committee of Congress, which enacted this federal standard:

> The rule is broadly phrased. The fields of knowledge which may be drawn upon are not limited merely to the "scientific" or "technical" but extend to all "specialized" knowledge. Similarly, the expert is viewed, not in a narrow sense, but as a person qualified by "knowledge, skill, experience, training or education." Thus, within the scope of the rule are not only experts in the strictest sense of the word, e.g., physicians, physicists, and architects, but also the large group sometimes called "skilled" witnesses, such as bankers or landowners testifying to land values. (*Federal Rules of Evidence Handbook, 2000–2001 Ed.,* 2000, p. 104)

Whether a witness has the necessary knowledge, skill, experience, training, or education to testify as an expert is generally left to the sound discretion of the trial judge. As a rule, before being recognized by the court as an expert, unless there is no objection, the party calling the witness to testify will have to present the witness's qualifications. California Evidence Code Section 720 provides, for example: "Against the objection of a party, such special knowledge, skill, experience, training or education must be shown before the witness may testify as an expert."

Courts are generally lenient in determining whether a witness qualifies as an expert. Indeed, the Advisory Committee to the U.S. Congress, which recently amended Federal Rule of Evidence 702, specifically noted:

Nothing in this amendment is intended to suggest that experience alone—or experience in conjunction with other knowledge, skill, training or education—may not provide a sufficient foundation for expert testimony. To the contrary, the text of Rule 702 expressly contemplates that an expert may be qualified on the basis of experience. In certain fields, experience is the predominant, if not sole, basis for a great deal of reliable expert testimony.

Why a Special Rule for Experts?

The rule allowing expert witnesses to offer opinions and conclusions stemmed initially from the concern that some issues of fact were too complex, difficult, or technical for lay jurors to resolve without assistance from witnesses allowed to state opinions or conclusions. Indeed, the common law standard for expert testimony was, and remains in some jurisdictions, that such testimony be concerned with subject matter or issues "beyond the ken" (i.e., outside the understanding) of the average lay juror. Under that standard, the role of the expert was to provide the jury with guidance in the form of an opinion or conclusion.

Gradually, this common law rule has given way, in the federal courts and many others, to a "helpfulness" standard. As the Advisory Committee of Congress, which enacted the Federal Rules of Evidence, has explained:

Whether the situation is a proper one for the use of expert testimony is to be determined on the basis of assisting the trier. "There is no more certain test for determining when experts may be used than the common sense inquiry whether the untrained layman would be qualified to determine intelligently and to the best possible degree the particular issue without enlightenment from those having a specialized understanding of the subject involved in the dispute." When opinions are excluded, it is because they are unhelpful and therefore superfluous and a waste of time. (*Federal Rules of Evidence Handbook, 2000–2001 Ed.,* 2000, p. 104)

Proper Subjects for Expert Testimony

On what subjects may a witness offer expert testimony? Most expert testimony, particularly that given by forensic psychologists and those in related professions, rests at least partially on science. From 1923 to 1993 in the federal courts, the admissibility of scientifically based expert testimony was controlled by the *Frye* test. This test was first enunciated in *Frye v. United States* (1923), a District of Columbia Court of Appeals decision on the admissibility of evidence derived from an early version of the polygraph. In *Frye,* the court established a general acceptance test for scientific testimony:

Just when a scientific principle or discovery crosses the line between the experimental and demonstrable stages is difficult to define. Somewhere in this twilight zone the evidential force of the principle must be recognized, and while courts will go a long way in admitting expert testimony deduced from a well recognized scientific principle or discovery, the thing from which the deduction is made must be sufficiently established to have gained general acceptance in the particular field in which it belongs. (p. 1014)

In *Frye,* the court essentially held that to be admissible, expert testimony must be based on generally accepted scientific theories and methods. Thus, for example, expert testimony would be inadmissible as a matter of law unless the judge concluded that the majority of experts in the relevant scientific discipline subscribed to the theory and/or methods on which the testimony was based.

Although the *Frye* test remains the standard in some state courts to this day, in federal courts, its use came to an end in 1993, when the U.S. Supreme Court rendered its decision in *Daubert v. Merrell Dow Pharmaceuticals.* In *Daubert,* the Court held that expert testimony in the federal courts is governed by Federal Rule of Evidence 702, which the Court said superseded *Frye* when adopted in 1975. According to the court, the Federal Rules of Evidence require the judge to determine whether proffered scientific evidence is "relevant," "reliable," and likely to assist the trier of fact (as required by Federal Rule of Evidence 702).

To meet those criteria, the Court said, testimony must be "grounded in the methods and procedures of science" and "scientifically valid." The Court held that although such testimony need not be "certain," it must have "a valid scientific connection to the pertinent inquiry" or issue at stake in the trial. Offering some "general observations" to trial courts that would be called on to serve as "gatekeepers" under this new rule, the Court suggested that trial judges may, but are not required to, consider the following factors in deciding whether to admit expert testimony with a purportedly scientific basis:

1. Whether the principles and methodology underlying the testimony have been or can be tested.
2. Whether they have been subjected to peer review and publication.

3. Whether the known or potential error rate is acceptable.

4. Whether the underlying principles have gained general acceptance in the scientific community.

Although the fourth of these *Daubert* criteria clearly echoes the *Frye* test, neither that standard nor any of the three others is by itself a necessary or sufficient basis for admitting scientifically based expert testimony. Indeed, none of these suggested criteria is, in itself, dispositive. Instead, as the *Daubert* Court noted:

> The inquiry envisioned by Rule 702 is, we emphasize, a flexible one. Its overarching subject is the scientific validity—and thus the evidentiary relevance and reliability—of the principles that underlie a proposed submission. The focus, of course, must be solely on principles and methodology, not on the conclusions that they generate. (1993, pp. 594–595)

The flexibility of the determination, as well as the broad discretion of the judge in deciding whether to admit expert testimony, was reinforced by the U.S. Supreme Court in two important decisions that followed *Daubert.*

In *General Electric Co. v. Joiner* (1997), the Court held that a trial judge's decision to allow or reject expert testimony under Rule 702 may not be overturned on appeal unless the judge's ruling constituted a clear abuse of discretion—a very difficult standard to meet. More recently, in *Kumho Tire Co. v. Carmichael* (1999), the Supreme Court held:

> *Daubert*'s general holding—setting forth the trial judge's general "gatekeeping" obligation—applies not only to testimony based on "scientific" knowledge, but also to testimony based on "technical" and "other specialized knowledge." We also conclude that a trial court *may* consider one or more of the more specific factors that *Daubert* mentioned when doing so will help determine that testimony's reliability. But, as the court stated in *Daubert,* the test of reliability is "flexible," and *Daubert*'s list of specific factors neither necessarily nor exclusively applies to all experts or in every case. Rather the law grants a district court the same broad latitude when it decides *how* to determine reliability as it enjoys in respect to its ultimate reliability determination. (p. 142)

In a passage from the *Kumho* decision perhaps most relevant to the expert testimony of forensic psychologists, whose testimony is often based on a combination of science and professional experience, the Court reemphasized "the importance of *Daubert*'s gatekeeping requirement":

> The objective of that requirement is to ensure the reliability of and relevancy of expert testimony. It is to make certain that an

expert, whether basing testimony upon professional studies or personal experience, employs in the courtroom the same level of intellectual rigor that characterizes the practice of an expert in the relevant field. (1999, p. 152)

Other Limitations on Expert Testimony

In addition to the rules above, expert testimony is also governed by several other general legal doctrines.

Notice and Discovery Requirements

In virtually all instances, applicable law requires that the giving of expert testimony be preceded by some sort of notice to opposing parties and, in many instances, the opportunity for opposing parties to discover the substance if not the basis of the proposed testimony. These requirements vary from state to state. Prior to presenting expert testimony, a litigant must notify opposing counsel of the intent to do so and usually specify the name of the expert who will testify. Additionally, opposing counsel virtually always will be entitled to be informed in advance of the substance of the proposed expert testimony. Depending on the nature of the case and the jurisdiction's discovery rules, such advance notice may require nothing more than a brief written notice. However, in many cases, especially civil matters, would-be expert witnesses may be required, prior to trial testimony, to respond to questions posed by opposing counsel. Generally, such examination before trial is done in the form of a deposition, a procedure in which opposing counsel has the opportunity to question the proposed expert witness directly, under oath, and with the questions and answers recorded verbatim.

Sworn Testimony

Any testimony, including expert testimony, whether given at trial or deposition, regardless of jurisdiction, virtually always will have to be given under oath or affirmation. Generally, there is no prescribed language for an oath or affirmation; the witness must simply promise to tell the truth. Bibles often are used and the name of God sometimes invoked, but neither is required. For example, as Federal Rule of Evidence 603 commands: "Before testifying, every witness shall be required to declare that the witness will testify truthfully, by oath or affirmation administered in a form calculated to awaken the witness' conscience and impress the witness' mind with the duty to do so."

Cross-Examination

The law in every jurisdiction provides for what is called the order of examination. Witnesses, including experts, first are questioned by the attorney who calls them to testify; they then are subject to questioning, known as cross-examination, by opposing counsel. Cross-examination is always limited to the scope of the questions asked on direct examination, but the issue of scope is often liberally interpreted. Consequently, experts may expect to be cross-examined about any issue related to their direct testimony.

Federal Rule of Evidence 611(b) states, for example, "Cross-examination should be limited to the subject matter of the direct examination and matters affecting the credibility of the witness. The court may, in the exercise of discretion, permit inquiry into additional matters as if on direct examination." That last phrase, "as if on direct examination," is significant for reasons to be explained shortly.

After cross-examination, there may be redirect examination, that is, questioning again by the attorney who called the witness. Redirect is limited to the scope of the preceding cross-examination; that is, attorneys may not use redirect to simply ask questions they have forgotten or failed to ask on direct examination.

After redirect examination, there may be further recross, more redirect, more recross, and so on, until the attorneys have exhausted their questions. Sometimes, the questioning will go back and forth for several rounds, each successive round of questions becoming shorter because of the scope requirement. Once the attorneys have completed their questioning, the witness is generally excused. It should be noted, however, that in most jurisdictions, judges also have the prerogative to question witnesses. Though rare, when judicial questioning of a witness occurs, it opens up at least the possibility of more redirect and cross-examination by the attorneys.

In addition to specifying the order of examination of witnesses, the rules of most courts dictate what type of questioning is allowed on cross-examination as opposed to direct examination. In both the federal and state courts, leading questions, those essentially calling for a yes or no answer, are generally prohibited on direct examination but allowed on cross-examination. An exception, at least in federal courts, occurs when, for example, Federal Rule of Evidence 611(b) permits cross-examination to deal with matters other than those dealt with during direct examination. Recall that, according to 611(b), in that case, the questioning will proceed "as if on direct examination." That means without leading questions.

Voir Dire

A final aspect of questioning related to cross-examination is the process of voir dire. Generally, experts are questioned about their credentials by the attorney who calls them to testify. These questions serve two purposes, one practical, the other legal. As a practical matter, these questions on direct examination are used to enhance the expert's credibility in the eyes of the trier of fact. More important, as a legal matter, the questions are aimed at qualifying the witness as an expert, so that he or she may offer opinion testimony.

To prevent a witness from giving expert testimony before opposing counsel has the chance to question the witness regarding his or her credentials, the law in most jurisdictions provides for voir dire. Voir dire is an opportunity for opposing counsel to interrupt the direct examination and essentially cross-examine the witness regarding his or her qualifications as an expert. If questions on voir dire raise sufficient doubt as to the basis for the witness's claimed expertise, the judge has the discretion to refuse to allow the witness to offer expert testimony.

Proper Basis for Expert Opinion

Traditionally, American courts required that expert opinions be based on facts in evidence (i.e., evidence that has previously been introduced and admitted at trial). In practice, of course, few expert witnesses, particularly forensic psychological experts, base their opinions on any such artificially limited realm of data. Recognizing that experts often rely on data that has not been, indeed, may never be admitted in court, the modern trend has been toward a more liberal rule allowing experts to rely on facts or data of the sort normally relied on in their field of expertise, whether or not those facts or data are admissible in court. This modern approach is reflected most clearly in Federal Rule of Evidence 703:

> The facts or data in the particular case upon which an expert bases an opinion or inference may be those perceived by or made known to the expert at or before the hearing. If of a type reasonably relied upon by experts in the particular field in forming opinions or inferences upon the subject, the facts or data need not be admissible in evidence in order for the opinion or inference to be admitted.

Disclosing Basis for Opinion

Most rules of evidence, whether statutory or common law, require experts to specify the bases for their opinions. Interestingly, however, many jurisdictions leave that option to the cross-examining attorney. In these jurisdictions, which include the federal courts and those in California, an expert is not required to state the basis for his or her opinion unless asked to do so on cross-examination. Under Federal Rule of Evidence 705, "The expert may testify in terms of opinion or inference and give reasons therefor without first testifying to the underlying facts or data, unless the court requires otherwise. The expert may in any event be required to disclose the underlying facts or data on cross-examination." Pursuant to California Code of Evidence Section 721(a)(3), an expert witness may be "fully cross-examined as to . . . the matter upon which his or her opinion is based and the reasons for his or her opinion."

There remains, however, the problem of what to do with facts or data that underlie an expert's opinion but are not themselves admissible. To allow an expert to reveal otherwise inadmissible facts or data to the trier of fact, it has been argued, is to circumvent the general rules of evidence and to allow a litigant to use an expert witness as a conduit of information that may be untrustworthy and/or otherwise barred from consideration. One remedy has been to instruct the trier of fact that the data or "facts" in question are not to be regarded as factual, but only as part of the basis for the expert's opinion. Although that approach remains valid in some jurisdictions, the modern trend, as reflected in Federal Rule of Evidence 703, is not to allow an expert to testify to inadmissible facts or data unless the judge determines that "their probative value in assisting the jury to evaluate the expert's opinion substantially outweighs their prejudicial effect."

Ultimate Issue Rule

Traditionally, until mid-twentieth century, courts generally proscribed expert opinions that went to what the courts called the ultimate issue: the specific question before the trier of fact. These proscriptions were based on the argument that experts who testified to the ultimate question were invading the province of, or usurping the function of, the trier of fact. That reasoning has now been largely rejected and most jurisdictions allow ultimate opinion testimony.

This modern trend was reflected fully in the Federal Rules of Evidence until 1984, when Congress amended Federal Rule of Evidence 704, adding subdivision (b):

> (a) Except as provided in subdivision (b), testimony in the form of an opinion or inference otherwise admissible is not objectionable because it embraces an ultimate issue to be decided by the trier of fact. (b) No expert witness testifying with respect to the mental state or condition of a defendant in a criminal case may state an opinion or inference as to whether the defendant did or did not have the mental state or condition constituting an element

of the crime charged or of a defense thereto. Such ultimate issues are matters for the trier of fact alone.

EFFECTIVE PRACTICE OF EXPERT TESTIMONY

In keeping with the various rules of evidence, expert testimony generally follows a fairly predictable pattern. Understanding this pattern and its dynamics enables forensic psychologists and related professionals to better prepare and deliver their testimony.

Expert Qualifications

As noted earlier, expert witnesses must be qualified by knowledge, skill, experience, training, or education, yet courts have wide discretion and are often lenient in qualifying witnesses as experts. In practice, opposing attorneys sometimes stipulate to a witness's qualifications, thus obviating the legal need for any extensive recitation of qualifications. Even then, however, as a practical matter, it is often important for the witness to present his or her credentials so that they are heard by the trier of fact, who will be judging not only the content of the expert testimony but the credibility of the individual giving that testimony.

Thus, even when a judge readily agrees to qualify a witness as an expert or the opposing attorney agrees to stipulate that the witness is an expert, it is ordinarily preferable to present the witness's full qualifications on direct examination. The nature of the case as well as the actual qualifications of the witness generally dictate precisely what questions are asked, but as a general matter, forensic psychological experts should be asked many of the following questions:

What is your profession?

What is your current employment?

What positions have your held previously?

Do you specialize in any particular areas of psychology?

What has been your experience in these areas of professional practice?

Describe your education.

Are you licensed?

When were you first licensed?

What does it mean to be a licensed psychologist?

Are you board certified?

When did you become board certified?

What does board certification mean?

By what process did you become board certified?

Are you a member or fellow of any professional organizations?

Have you published any books, papers, or articles?

Do you hold any editorial positions?

Have you conducted any independent research in the field of psychology?

Have you received any grants to support your research?

Have you received any awards or honors in the field of psychology?

Have you previously qualified as an expert witness?

In what courts?

On what subject matter?

The witness should be well aware of what questions are to be asked in the qualification process and prepared to answer them fully and, of course, truthfully. This is not a time for modesty; neither is it a time for exaggeration. The witness should anticipate that his or her qualifications may be questioned if not challenged on voir dire.

Most aspects of qualification are straightforward. One that has begun to cause problems in many proceedings, however, is the issue of board certification. With rare exceptions, there is no explicit requirement in any court that a witness be board certified (or have any other particular credential) to offer expert testimony. However, because some psychologists, including forensic psychologists, are in fact board certified by the American Board of Professional Psychology (and its affiliated boards, including the American Board of Forensic Psychology), many psychologists who have not been so certified recently have begun to seek certification from so-called vanity boards. These vanity boards, for the most part, have few if any real standards and lack the rigorous evaluative procedures of the American Board of Professional Psychology and its affiliated boards. In some cases, little more than a check or credit card payment is required for "certification" by these boards. Witnesses who attempt to present themselves as board certified when all they possess are certificates from one or more of these vanity boards increasingly are finding themselves embarrassed by effective voir dire and/or cross-examination aimed at revealing the process by which they became "board certified."

Discrediting the Expert

Expert witnesses are occasionally discredited on the basis of their credentials, or lack thereof. More commonly, their credibility is attacked on the basis of bias or conflict of interests. These attacks are most frequently based on two concerns: the expert's fee and any other relationship the expert may have with one or more of the parties.

The fee issue is a simple one. Most expert witnesses are compensated for their professional time. Clearly, being compensated for the time preparing for and delivering expert testimony is no bar to that testimony. However, courts almost invariably allow cross-examination of an expert to include questions about his or her fee in the matter. Indeed, in some jurisdictions, this issue is made explicit in the rules of evidence. For example, California Evidence Code Section 722(b) provides: "The compensation and expenses paid to an expert witness by the party calling him is a proper subject of inquiry by any adverse party as relevant to the credibility of the witness and the weight of his testimony."

The more difficult issue arises when the witness has a relationship—other than that of expert witness—with one or more of the parties. Perhaps the most common conflict of this sort occurs when a psychologist (or other mental health professional) is called on to serve as an expert witness with regard to a patient or client he or she has been treating. There is significant ethical debate as to the propriety of the treating professional assuming the role of expert in such a case, but courts are rarely bothered by such apparent conflicts. Instead of seeing such conflicts as a bar to expert testimony, courts generally regard them as fodder for cross-examination and issues to be considered by the trier of fact in judging the expert's credibility.

As an example of how extreme a conflict of interest would have to be before a court would view it as a bar to expert testimony, consider the decision of a federal court in Illinois. In *Baskerville v. Culligan* (1994), the plaintiff in a sex discrimination case sought to present expert testimony regarding her "psychological condition, treatment, and prognosis." The proposed expert witness was not only the plaintiff's treating psychologist but also her sister. The defendant argued that the psychologist's expert testimony should be disallowed because it "would violate the American Psychology Association [*sic*] ('APA')'s ethical code" because under "APA's code of ethical principles, psychologists must refrain 'from entering into [a] personal, scientific, professional, financial, or other relationship . . . if it appears likely that such a relationship reasonably might impair the psychologist's objectivity'" (pp. 9–10). The defendant also argued that the court should preclude this expert testimony "to preserve the public confidence in the fairness and integrity of the judicial proceedings" (p. 10). The court disagreed:

> If at trial the court determines that Dr. Bell may testify as an expert, the court would not be sponsoring her testimony or vouching for its objectivity. Rather, it would be the jury's function to assess the credibility of Dr. Bell's opinions and to determine the weight to be given her testimony. Culligan shows that Dr. Bell's professional relationship with Baskerville is unorthodox and raises serious questions regarding Dr. Bell's objectivity. However, these are appropriate subjects for Culligan's cross-examination of Dr. Bell. The testimony is not excluded. (pp. 10–11)

Impeaching the Expert

Like all witnesses, experts are subject to impeachment on cross-examination. The most common and often most effective form of impeachment is that using prior inconsistent statement (i.e., statements previously made by an expert that conflict with statements made in his or her current testimony). Experts are particularly vulnerable to this kind of impeachment for two reasons. First, their testimony in prior cases has been recorded and is a matter of public record available to opposing attorneys. Second, many experts have published books and articles in which they have made known their positions on various issues related to their professions.

Clearly, an expert's previous testimony and writings may be used to impeach him or her, but they are not the only sources of ammunition available to opposing attorneys. Another important impeachment technique often used with expert witnesses is the so-called learned treatise method. The learned treatise method involves confronting expert witnesses on cross-examination with authoritative published works that contradict or otherwise tend to undermine their opinions. For example, a psychologist who has testified to an interpretation of a certain psychological test result might be confronted with one or more books or articles indicating that such a result should lead to an interpretation other than that reached by the psychologist. Traditionally, learned treatises used in such a fashion must either have been relied on in formulating the expert's opinion or acknowledged by the expert as authoritative.

Modern evidence law, however, is much less restrictive. The California Evidence Code, for example, specifies three instances in which a learned treatise may be used in cross-examining an expert witness. Rule 721(b) states:

> If a witness testifying as an expert testifies in the form of an opinion, he or she may not be cross-examined in regard to the content or tenor of any scientific, technical, or professional text, treatise, journal, or similar publication unless any of the following occurs: (1) The witness referred to, considered, or relied upon such publication in arriving at or forming his or her opinion. (2) The publication has been admitted in evidence. (3) The publication has been established as a reliable authority by the testimony of the witness or by other expert testimony or by judicial notice.

Expert Witness Immunity

In most jurisdictions, it has long been the law that a witness in a judicial proceeding may not be subjected to civil liability for the content of his or her testimony. This privilege, which pertains to all witnesses, including experts, has generally protected any other communications preliminary to a proposed judicial proceeding in which the witness may anticipate testifying, if those communications have some relation to the proceeding.

Recently, however, several cases have cast doubt on what was once considered an absolute privilege, at least as that privilege is applicable to expert witnesses. The first of these cases involved a psychologist who was disciplined by a state licensing board on the basis of work he performed as an expert witness in child custody cases.

In *Deatherage v. State of Washington Examining Board of Psychology* (1997a, 1997b), the licensing board brought disciplinary proceedings against a psychologist, alleging that he "failed to meet professional ethical standards in work that formed the basis of his expert testimony in several child custody suits" (1997a, p. 1269) by his "failure to qualify statements, his mischaracterization of statements, his failure to verify information, and his interpretation of test data" (1997b, p. 829). After a hearing, the board found the psychologist "had committed misconduct . . . and suspended his license for 10 years" (p. 829).

The psychologist then sought judicial review of the board's decision, claiming that witness immunity prevented the board from disciplining him on the basis of his testimony in the child custody cases in question. The Supreme Court of Washington concluded that the doctrine of witness immunity could not be used as a defense in a state licensing board's professional disciplinary proceeding.

More recently, courts in two other states, Connecticut and Louisiana, have considered placing additional limitations on the doctrine of absolute immunity for expert witnesses. Most previous cases dealt with the question of whether an expert could be sued by an opposing party for testimony or other pretrial involvement in litigation against that party. These cases dealt with whether litigants may sue their own expert witnesses for malpractice in trial preparation or testimony. This question, which has important implications for all expert witnesses, was answered differently by two trial courts.

In *Pollock v. Panjabi* (2000), a Connecticut Superior Court denied a motion to dismiss a lawsuit against a medical biomechanics expert. This expert had been retained by the quadriplegic plaintiff in a police brutality suit to help determine the cause of the plaintiff's paralysis. The expert concluded that a police officer's wrestling hold on the plaintiff was the cause of the paralyzing injury. Three times, however, a trial court barred the expert from testifying, finding that he had based his expert opinion in part on improperly conducted analyses. Despite winning a $783,000 judgment against the police department, the injured plaintiff filed a breach of contract lawsuit, alleging that the expert improperly conducted the tests he had been hired to perform. In allowing the lawsuit to continue, the Connecticut judge ruled that the point of contention was not the expert's testimony but his alleged failure to meet his contractual obligation to provide scientifically supportable conclusions.

In *Marrogi v. Howard* (2000), the defendants were experts in medical billing retained by a physician to assist in his lawsuit against a former employer. The physician, who claimed he had been underpaid by the employer, retained the defendants to analyze billing records and testify on his behalf. When the physician's lawsuit against the employer was dismissed, he blamed the experts, alleging that the dismissal was the result of their "substandard expert performance" (p. 2). In dismissing the physician's lawsuit against the experts, a U.S. District Court cited "a line of Louisiana cases that uniformly recognize absolute immunity to witnesses in judicial or quasi-judicial proceedings" (p. 7).

Although the issue has rarely been litigated in the past, a small number of courts have ruled, as the court did in *Pollock v. Panjabi,* to allow lawsuits to be brought against expert witnesses by the litigants who hired them. Others, however, have refused to so limit the doctrine of expert immunity and have dismissed similar lawsuits.

For example, *in Murphy v. A. A. Mathews* (1992), the plaintiff hired the defendant engineering firm to investigate and provide testimony about the plaintiff's claims for additional compensation in an arbitration proceeding. Following the testimony, Murphy sued, "alleging that Mathews was negligent in its performance of professional services involving the preparation and documentation of [the plaintiff's] claims" and that, as a result, the plaintiff "was unable to support its claims for all of the additional compensation" (p. 672). The Missouri Supreme Court ultimately sided with the plaintiff, holding that "witness immunity does not bar suit if the professional is negligent in providing the agreed services" (p. 672). As the court explained:

> Witness immunity is an exception to the general rules of liability. It should not be extended unless its underlying policies require it be so. In Missouri, this immunity generally has been restricted to defamation, defamation-type, or retaliatory cases against adverse witnesses. This narrow restriction is consistent with the historical development of immunity. . . . While witness immunity might properly be expanded in other circumstances, we do not believe that immunity was meant to or should apply to bar a suit against a privately retained professional who negligently provides litigation support services. (p. 680)

In a similar lawsuit, however, the Supreme Court of the State of Washington reached the opposite conclusion. In *Bruce v. Byrne-Stevens & Associates* (1989), that court held that witness immunity applies not only to an expert's testimony but to actions taken by the expert in preparation for testimony. Acknowledging some merit to the plaintiff's claim that "the threat of liability would encourage experts to be more careful, resulting in more accurate, reliable testimony" (p. 670), the court offered two justifications for refusing to exempt experts from the traditional witness immunity rule:

> First, unless expert witnesses are entitled to immunity, there will be a loss of objectivity in expert testimony generally. The threat of civil liability based on an inadequate final result in litigation would encourage experts to assert the most extreme position favorable to the party for whom they testify. . . . Second, imposing civil liability on expert witnesses would discourage anyone who is not a full-time professional expert witness from testifying. Only professional witnesses will be in a position to carry insurance to guard against such liability. The threat of liability would discourage the 1-time expert—the university professor, for example—from testifying. Such 1-time experts, however, can ordinarily be expected to approach their duty to the court with great objectivity and professionalism. (p. 670)

SUMMARY

The law governing expert testimony changed significantly over the last decade of the twentieth century (see, e.g., *Daubert v. Merrell Dow Pharmaceuticals,* 1993; revised Federal Rule of Evidence 702, *Deatherage v. State of Washington Examining Board of Psychology,* 1997a, 1997b; *Kumho Tire Co. v. Carmichael,* 1999; *Pollock v. Panjabi,* 2000), and exert testimony by psychologists and other mental health professionals remains controversial. However, nearly a century after Münsterberg published his groundbreaking treatise *On the Witness Stand,* and four decades after a federal court's watershed decision in *Jenkins v. United States,* the role of forensic psychology in the American courtroom remains not only secure but, in many realms, indispensable.

REFERENCES

Aichele, G. J. (1990). *Legal realism and twentieth-century American jurisprudence: The changing consensus.* New York: Garland Press.

American Psychiatric Association. (1962). Brief *Amicus Curiae, Jenkins v. United States* (U.S. App., D.C. Circuit, 1962).

American Psychological Association. (1962). Brief *Amicus Curiae, Jenkins v. United States* (U.S. Court of App., D.C. Circuit, 1962).

Baskerville v. Culligan International Company, 1994 U.S. Dist. LEXIS 5296 (1994).

Bruce et al. v. Byrne-Stevens & Associates Engineers, Inc. et al., 776 P.2d 666 (Washington, 1989).

Daubert v. Merrell Dow Pharmaceuticals, 509 U.S. 579 (1993).

Deatherage v. State of Washington Examining Board of Psychology, 932 P.2d 1267 (Washington, 1997a).

Deatherage v. State of Washington Examining Board of Psychology, 943 P.2d 662 (Washington, 1997b).

Federal Rules of Evidence Handbook 2000–2001. (2000). Cincinnati, OH: Anderson.

Frye v. United States, 293 F. 1013 (D.C. Cir. 1923).

General Electric Company et al. v. Joiner *et ux.,* 522 U.S. 136 (1997).

Guttmacher, M. S., & Weihofen, H. (1952). *Psychiatry and the law.* New York: Norton.

Gravitz, M. A. (1995). First admission (1846) of hypnotic testimony in court. *American Journal of Clinical Hypnosis, 37,* 326–330.

Holmes, O. W. (1881). *The common law.* London: Macmillan.

Jenkins v. United States, 307 F.2d 637 (U.S. App. D.C., 1962).

Kumho Tire Company Ltd. et al. v. Carmichael et al., 526 U.S. 137 (1999).

Marrogi v. Howard et al., 2000 U.S. Dist. LEXIS 8525 (2000).

Münsterberg, H. (1908). *On the witness stand: Essays on psychology and crime.* New York: Clark, Boardman.

Münsterberg, H. (with Whitman, C. S.). (1923). *On the witness stand: Essays on psychology and crime* (2nd ed.). New York: Clark, Boardman.

Murphy v. A. A. Mathews, 841 S.W.2d 671 (Mo. 1992).

Pollock v. Panjabi, 47 Conn. Supp. 179, 781 A.2d 518 (Superior Court, Conn., 2000).

Pound, R. (1910). Law in books and law in action. *American Law Review, 12,* 44–46.

Robinson, E. S. (1935). *Law and the lawyers.* New York: Macmillan.

Wigmore, J. H. (1909). Professor Münsterberg and the psychology of testimony: Being a report of the case of *Cokestone v. Münsterberg. Illinois Law Review, 3,* 399–445.

PART TWO

APPROACHES TO FORENSIC ASSESSMENT

CHAPTER 5

Third Party Information in Forensic Assessment

KIRK HEILBRUN, JANET WARREN, AND KIM PICARELLO

The contributions of the mental health professions and behavioral and medical sciences to legal decision making have expanded and matured significantly during the past two decades. Such contributions have been documented by a variety of scholars and commentators during the past several years (e.g., Greenberg & Brodsky, in press; Grisso, 1998; Heilbrun, in press; Melton, Petrila, Poythress, & Slobogin, 1997; Roesch, Hart, & Ogloff, 1999; Rogers, 1997). Despite important conceptual and empirical advances, however, there are a number of areas in which there remains a gap between the practice and the promise of forensic mental health assessment (FMHA; Nicholson & Norwood, 2000).

The present chapter addresses one such area: third party information (TPI) as it is applied to and informs FMHA. For present purposes, we define third party information as any information that is not obtained directly from the party being evaluated as part of criminal adjudication or civil litigation. There are two primary sources of such TPI: documents and interviews with collateral informants. Such collateral interviews are considered broadly to include unstructured, semistructured, and structured questioning. These may encompass standard measures designed for observations by third parties (e.g., the Child Behavior Checklist [CBCL], Achenbach, 1991), address a case-specific set of questions designed to elicit observations regarding a particular individual

(Heilbrun, 1992), or offer a number of broader observations regarding the history, symptoms, or functional behavior of a particular plaintiff or defendant as it informs the legal standard being explored.

In this chapter, we address a number of areas relevant to the use of TPI in FMHA. First, we describe the particular importance of TPI in forensic assessment. In the next four sections of the chapter, we address the relevant research, law, ethical standards, and practice literature in this area. We follow with sections devoted to obtaining TPI, applying it (both through evaluating its accuracy and integrating it with other data), and communicating it in reports and testimony. Finally, we offer concluding comments about the current state of the art and science in this area, and offer suggestions for improvement that encompass both areas for additional research and broad guidelines for practice.

IMPORTANCE OF THIRD PARTY INFORMATION IN FORENSIC ASSESSMENT

An important assumption underlying mental health evaluation of various kinds is the notion that information about an individual is best obtained directly from that individual. This is particularly true for assessment that is done for diagnosis as well as for treatment planning, which we call "therapeutic" assessment. With some noteworthy exceptions, encompassing cases in which the individual being evaluated is too young or impaired to function as an accurate informant, an important expectation in such therapeutic evaluation is that information will be obtained directly from that individual. For the most part, it is reasonable to expect that individuals who are consulting a mental health professional in the beginning of a treatment process will attempt to provide accurate information that will facilitate effective treatment. The confidentiality surrounding the therapeutic relationship strengthens the expectation that the patient can provide important, highly personal information without concern that this communication will be harmful.

However, there are a number of important differences between therapeutic and forensic assessment. These differences have been described by a number of individuals (e.g., Greenberg & Brodsky, in press; Heilbrun, in press; Melton et al., 1997) and are summarized in Table 5.1. Each of these underscores the importance of broadening the scope of the evaluation beyond the individual and his or her self-report. As summarized in Table 5.1, the goal of the forensic evaluation is to inform some aspect of criminal adjudication or civil litigation. It is ultimately oriented to enhancing fairness and justice, rather than specifically helping a particular individual. As such, it requires verifying the information that is collected and synthesized into an opinion by the evaluating expert. In this framework, the defendant/plaintiff is only one of many potential sources. As many forensic questions also involve retrospective inquiries that examine behavior and events that have occurred months and years earlier, sources of information that were obtained closer to the time in question may help to reconstruct the event more clearly and accurately.

For present purposes, we focus on the differences described in the final five areas of Table 5.1: data sources, response style of examinee, clarification of reasoning and limits on knowledge, the nature of the written report, and the expectation of testimony. The sources of data used in both kinds of evaluation are comparable, with the exception of "observations made by others" and "relevant legal documents" that are described as part of forensic assessment. Why this difference?

One reason is summarized under "response style" in Table 5.1: Such response style is "not assumed to be reliable" in forensic assessment. Response style has been described as including four particular styles: (a) *reliable/honest* (a genuine attempt is made to be accurate; factual inaccuracies result from poor understanding or misperception); (b) *malingering* (conscious fabrication or gross exaggeration of psychological and/or physical symptoms, understandable in light of the individual's *circumstances* and not attributable merely to the desire to assume the patient role, as in factitious disorder); (c) *defensive* (conscious denial or gross minimization of psychological and/or physical symptoms, as distinguished from ego defenses, which involve intrapsychic processes that distort perception); and (d) *irrelevant* (failure to become engaged in the evaluation; responses are not necessarily relevant to questions and may be random; Rogers, 1984, 1997; see

TABLE 5.1   Differences between Treatment and Forensic Roles for Mental Health

	Therapeutic	Forensic
Purpose	Diagnose and treat symptoms of illness.	Assist decision maker or attorney.
Examiner-examinee relationship	Helping role.	Objective or quasi-objective stance.
Notification of purpose	Implicit assumptions about purpose shared by doctor and patient. Formal, explicit notification typically not done.	Assumptions about purpose not necessarily shared. Formal and explicit notification.
Who is being served	Individual patient.	Variable; may be court, attorney, and client.
Nature of standard being considered	Medical, psychiatric, psychological.	Medical, psychiatric, psychological, and legal.
Data sources	Self-report, psychological testing, behavioral assessment, medical procedures.	Self-report, psychological testing, behavioral assessment, medical procedures, observations made by others, relevant legal documents.
Response style of examinee	Assumed to be reliable.	Not assumed to be reliable.
Clarification of reasoning and limits on knowledge	Optional.	Very important.
Written report	Brief, conclusory note.	Lengthy and detailed; documents findings, reasoning, and conclusions.
Court testimony	Not expected.	Expected.

Source: Heilbrun, 2001. Reprinted with permission from Kluwer Academic/Plenum.

also the chapter by Rogers & Bender in this volume, on malingering and dissimulation). Two additional categories of response seem relevant to forensic assessment. The first we term *uncooperative,* in which the individual responds minimally or not at all to assessment questions. We call the second additional response style *impaired;* it involves experiencing communication deficits resulting from young age, thought and speech disorganization, intellectual deficits, and/or memory problems. If the individual being evaluated responds in any style other than honest, the information being provided may be inaccurate or incomplete, and other sources of information—from third parties and documents—can help to provide a more accurate picture.

An important part of FMHA involves forming and testing hypotheses about an individual's motivations and capacities (Greenberg & Brodsky, in press; Heilbrun, in press). TPI can be used both to help develop possible explanations in these areas and to test hypotheses that have already been developed. In this process, the forensic clinician functions more as an objective truth seeker (comparable to an investigative journalist; see Levine, 1980) than as a therapeutic change agent who seeks, and accepts, a more subjective view of the individual's reality. In this kind of inquiry, the forensic clinician strives to develop and describe a comprehensive outline of an event and its relevant features. Like the gradual unfolding of an image in a developing photograph, an event takes shape as information from various sources depicts an increasingly detailed outline. This type of broad-based exploration is most typical in capital mitigation cases (in the criminal context) and in personal injury cases (in civil litigation). It is developed through contact with a variety of individuals and reviews of third party sources into a framework of explanation and description.

Consistent development of a multimethod approach to information collection and consistency assessment also provides the evaluator with a logical framework for the formulation of opinions. It addresses the concern that criminal defendants will minimize the degree of their culpability and civil litigants will exaggerate the extent of their distress and impairment. Through the information and observations obtained from diverse sources, the forensic evaluator is able to present an opinion that is logical and minimizes jargon. The consumer of the report is provided an opportunity to consider the various sources contributing to the findings and to evaluate the reasoning used in reaching a particular conclusion.

FMHA has the potential to be used as evidence in litigation every time one is conducted. Legal decision making is better informed when there is explicit clarification of the reasoning and limits on knowledge that are part of FMHA. Such clarification is facilitated by citing both the different sources of information that are used in FMHA and the consistency of results across sources. TPI includes material that is specific to the case being litigated and, therefore, particularly relevant. It can potentially increase the accuracy of findings and conclusions through its integration with other sources of data, as part of a multitrait, multimethod approach to FMHA. It also invariably increases the face validity of FMHA, one of the most important forms of validity in legal decision making (Grisso, 1986). TPI can enhance communication with judges and attorneys regarding such assessment. The perception that individuals selectively exaggerate or minimize certain kinds of information about themselves to avoid negative consequences is accurate in some cases, but it is difficult to refute effectively without TPI when it does *not* apply. Outlining the various sources of information that were requested and obtained (or withheld) also provides a strong basis for responding to attorneys on cross-examination by countering the implication that the evaluator was biased, naïve, or seriously limited in the information that he or she considered and integrated into the findings. Finally, the use of TPI may help the evaluator distinguish between deliberate distortion and genuine memory loss by serving as a source of prompts or cues that can facilitate recall in cases of genuine amnesia (Schacter, 1986).

TPI is essential when using some of the more recently developed tools that are particularly applicable in forensic contexts, such as the Psychopathy Checklist-Revised (PCL-R; Hare, 1991). Incorporating TPI when using such tools is important to protect against deception by the individual being evaluated; there is some evidence that lying is not accurately detected by mental health professionals and other professional groups (Ekman & O'Sullivan, 1991). It should be noted that the Ekman and O'Sullivan research has somewhat limited applicability to FMHA interviewing, however. These investigators showed participants brief video vignettes of individuals, some of whom had been instructed to lie about their feelings and others to describe their feelings accurately, and asked participants to use cues such as facial expression and voice tone in judging who was lying. This can be contrasted with typical FMHA procedures, in which the evaluator has the opportunity to review TPI and conduct a detailed interview and relevant testing. Comparing the consistency of results from different sources, the evaluator can then ask clarifying follow-up questions. It would be fairest to say, therefore, that Ekman and O'Sullivan have demonstrated that stylistic cues observed from brief contact cannot be interpreted very accurately in deciding who is being deceptive, but the use of longer exposure and substantive questioning is more likely to allow the evaluator to determine (at least) that the individual being evaluated is providing information that is inconsistent with multiple other sources. The need for integrating information from third party sources is so important that evaluation using the PCL-R, for example, can be conducted using file information only but not using self-report alone (Hare, 1991).

Finally, the use of TPI can facilitate the effective communication of results in FMHA. Most often, such communication occurs in a written report; in a minority of cases, testimony in a deposition, hearing, or trial may supplement the report. These observations suggest that TPI is one of the most essential components of a high-quality forensic assessment, enhancing the integrity of the process, the impartiality of the evaluator, and the weight given the results by the trier of fact. In the remainder of this chapter, we describe in more detail the applications of TPI to FMHA.

RELEVANT RESEARCH ON THIRD PARTY INFORMATION

In this section, we review research in two areas. First, we describe empirical studies that address how TPI is used in criminal and civil FMHA, or how mental health professionals value its use. Second, we address the use of TPI in the assessment of various kinds of psychopathology (e.g., substance abuse, psychopathy, dementia, personality characteristics) and behavior (e.g., violence) to provide a basis for considering its applicability to forensic issues. As will become clear from this review, research on the application of TPI in forensic contexts is in its infancy. It is our view that operationalization, standardization, and quantification (Grisso, 1986) are important elements of any mental health assessment domain; the review of how TPI is used in related areas should make it clearer how such goals can be promoted.

Empirical Studies on the Use and Valuation of Third Party Information in Forensic Assessment

According to a recent review of forensic assessment (Nicholson & Norwood, 2000), there have been six empirical studies describing the characteristics of criminal FMHA reports: Heilbrun and Collins, 1995 (Florida); Heilbrun, Rosenfeld, Warren, and Collins, 1994 (Virginia and Florida); Nicholson, LaFortune, Norwood, and Roach, 1995 (Oklahoma); Otto, Barnes, and Jacobson, 1996 (Florida); Robbins, Walters, and Herbert, 1997 (New Jersey and Nebraska); and Skeem, Golding, Cohn, and Berge, 1998 (Utah). Although each study encompasses a broader range of variables applicable to FMHA, all except Robbins et al., specifically describe different aspects of FMHA. These are summarized in Table 5.2. As may be seen, there is a wide range of findings regarding how various aspects of TPI are applied in forensic evaluation reports. Because the evaluations studied in each of

TABLE 5.2   Use of Third Party Information in Criminal Forensic Reports

Type of Information	State				
	FL	FL	OK	VA	UT
Review of records					
Arrest/offense report	96/49	40	Nr[a]	65	68/87
Prior mental health	86/40	37	0/4	37	35/50
Victim or witness	—	1–2[b]	NR	NR	18/36
Current jail	NR	24	1/13	NR	NR
Prior criminal justice	NR	8	1/<1	8	NR
Collateral interviews					
Attorneys	NR	8	0/5	NR	9
Hospital staff	70/4	0	NR	NR	NR
Jail personnel	1/17	14–19[c]	0/4	NR	7
Relative	NR	9	0/9	NR	22

Note: Studies providing these data were, from left to right by state, Heilbrun & Collins (1995), Otto et al. (1996), Nicholson et al. (1995), Heilbrun et al. (1994), and Skeem et al. (1998). Although Robbins et al. (1997) reported findings for the citation of "any" third party information in their sample of forensic reports, they did not report findings for specific types of third party information. Hence, Robbins et al. is not included in the table. Studies in Florida sampled community-based reports for incompetent/insane defendants only. Multiple values reported for the first Florida, Oklahoma, and Utah studies reflect findings for hospital- and community-based evaluations, respectively. NR indicates that the information was not reported in the study.
[a]In Oklahoma, an information sheet, which lists the charge and provides basic data regarding the alleged offense (e.g., approximate time, location, witnesses), typically accompanies the court order for pretrial competence assessment. Examiners presumably review this information, although they rarely cite it in reports submitted to the court.
[b]The reported percentage reflects citation of interviews with victims or other witnesses, rather than review of statements by victims or witnesses. Because such statements often are incorporated into or appended to arrest reports in Florida (R. Otto, personal communication, March 29, 1999), the percentage of criminal forensic reports using this type of third party information is probably comparable to that listed for arrest report (i.e., about 40%).
[c]Findings were reported separately for medical staff and detention officers. The reported values reflect minimum and maximum percentages.
Source: Nicholson and Norwood (2000). Reprinted with permission from Kluwer Academic/Plenum.

these reports focused on the legal questions of competence to stand trial, and some on sanity at the time of the offense, it is not surprising that the majority of the reports in three studies (Heilbrun & Collins, 1995; Heilbrun et al., 1994; Skeem et al., 1998) cited having reviewing the arrest report as part of the evaluation. However, other documents were reviewed far less frequently, judging from what was cited in the reports or reported by the evaluators. Records of prior mental health evaluation and treatment, for example, were cited as being reviewed in fewer than half the cases in a number of samples (Heilbrun & Collins, 1995 [community sample]; Heilbrun et al., 1994; Nicholson et al., 1995; Otto et al., 1996; Skeem et al., 1998 [hospital sample]). Other records were reviewed even less frequently. Collateral interviews were conducted with other hospital staff members by 70% of the hospital evaluators in one study (Heilbrun & Collins, 1995), but apparently very rarely conducted in other samples. With the exception of the arrest report, therefore, it appears that both relevant records and collateral interviews are infrequently used in criminal FMHA.

This finding contrasts sharply with the value placed on TPI by mental health professionals who specialize in forensic work. Borum and Grisso (1996) surveyed forensic psychologists and forensic psychiatrists regarding their views on appropriate content for criminal forensic reports on competence to stand trial (N = 102 respondents) and criminal responsibility (N = 96 respondents). Participants were asked to rate various report components as "essential," "recommended," "optional," or "contraindicated." For evaluations of competence to stand trial, the investigators asked participants to rate the value of two elements of TPI: mental health records and police information. Mental health records were rated as extremely important (93% of psychologists and 82% of psychiatrists rated this element as either essential or recommended). Police information was valued somewhat lower, with 57% of psychiatrists and 44% of psychologists describing it as essential or recommended. These elements of TPI were seen as even more important in criminal responsibility reports. A total of 100% of psychologists and 98% of psychiatrists rated mental health records as essential or recommended, and 98% of psychiatrists and 94% of psychologists described police information as essential or recommended. An additional element for criminal responsibility (a collateral description of the circumstances of the alleged offense) was also rated as quite valuable, with 96% of psychologists and 93% of psychiatrists rating it as essential or recommended.

Three surveys addressing the use of TPI (and other procedures) in child custody evaluation have been conducted. It is worth noting that each of the six studies cited earlier in the area of criminal forensic assessment involved a review of the actual work product—the report—with the exception of the Virginia sample from one study (Heilbrun et al., 1994), which used a database composed of questions about the evaluation answered by evaluators when they submitted a form requesting payment. By contrast, each of the following studies surveyed mental health professionals regarding their practice in child custody: Ackerman and Ackerman (1997); Keilin and Bloom (1986); and LaFortune (1997). It is unclear whether comparable results would be obtained using the two different methods—reviewing reports and surveying evaluators—on the same sample, as there apparently have been no studies using both to facilitate such a comparison. There is potential for error using either method. Some evaluators may review material but not cite it in their reports; although this would be problematic for other reasons, the review of such a report would mistakenly conclude that TPI

was not used at all. (This problem may be resolved conceptually if the forensic report itself, rather than the forensic evaluation, is viewed as the unit of analysis. Certainly, the legal consumer is better informed by research focusing on what is actually used, rather than what may have occurred.) There is even greater potential for factual error in surveys, however, as evaluators asked to rate the frequency with which a certain kind of TPI is used may be grossly inaccurate—unless the TPI is used routinely, or never. While forensic report review seems more likely to be factually accurate, the survey approach ought to yield results that are more generalizable, if the percentage of those responding is reasonably high.

In the first study, a total of 302 psychologists, psychiatrists, and master's-level practitioners were surveyed, with usable responses received from 27% (N = 82), with another 13% (N = 39) declining to participate and 23% (N = 69) excluded due to lack of experience with child custody (Keilin & Bloom, 1986). Only one element that is clearly within the scope of this chapter was described; 48.8% of those responding indicated that they spent an average of 1.32 hours per evaluation on "conversations with significant others (friends and relatives)."

The second study (Ackerman & Ackerman, 1997) updated much of the Keilin and Bloom (1986) material a decade later. However, the Ackermans provided more detail about the particular categories of TPI in child custody evaluation. Surveying 800 doctoral-level psychologists in the United States, they received usable responses from 25% (N = 201). Overall means for time spent in various components of child custody evaluation were calculated for the following TPI areas: "reviewing materials" (M = 2.6 hours), "collateral contacts" (referring to interviews with teachers, therapists, and the like; M = 1.6 hours), and "interviewing significant others" (i.e., those who live in the children's home; M = 1.6 hours). (Clarification of the distinction cited in this chapter between "collateral contacts" and "interviews with significant others" in the Ackerman and Ackerman [1997] study was obtained from the senior author; Marc J. Ackerman, personal communication, December 5, 2000.) The mean number of hours for the entire evaluation was reported as 21.1, suggesting that TPI collection was responsible for a substantial part of the total mean time involved in performing child custody evaluations. A small number of respondents in this study (3% to 4%) also reported that they sometimes administered measures using third party informants, such as the CBCL (Achenbach, 1991; Achenbach & Edelbrock, 1983).

Finally, a third survey (LaFortune, 1997) was sent to 268 mental health professionals from Georgia, Nebraska, New York, North Carolina, and Oklahoma who indicated a competence in conducting child custody evaluations. LaFortune received responses from 53% (N = 141), a higher response rate than either of the two studies just described. A total of 90% of respondents were licensed psychologists who had completed a median of 24.5 child custody evaluations. Consistent with the findings of Ackerman and Ackerman (1997), she reported that respondents "often" interviewed significant others and reviewed school records as part of evaluation.

Third Party Information in Measuring Violence and Psychopathology

Judging from the limited available data, it would appear that both record review and collateral interviews are used and cited more often in FMHA today than they were 10 to 15 years ago. This is consistent with a research trend in several different areas during this period. Research on the risk of violent behavior, for example, increasingly uses the report of a designated collateral observer as a dependent variable, particularly when combined with self-report and records of arrest and hospitalization, to address the question of the nature and frequency of violent behavior during a designated outcome period. In a detailed conceptual discussion of such violence research, Mulvey and Lidz (1993) identified a number of sources of information relevant to violence measurement. These sources include police and court records, treatment records, unit incidence and seclusion reports, collateral interviews, and direct interviews with the individual being assessed. It is noteworthy that each of these sources, with the exception of the last, would be considered TPI within the definition used in this chapter.

The use of collateral sources such as these has become a standard part of violence research during the past decade. Both self-report and collateral observer report were employed in a large-scale study on the contribution of clinical judgment to accuracy in risk assessment (Lidz, Mulvey, & Gardner, 1993; Newhill, Mulvey, & Lidz, 1995), involving a six-month follow-up on 357 patients treated in a psychiatric emergency room and assessed by clinicians to be violent, and 357 controls (assessed by clinicians not to be violent). Participant groups were matched for age, race, and sex. The investigators reported that violence (defined as touching another person with aggressive intent, or threatening with a weapon in hand) occurred in 36% of controls and 53% of the violence-concern group. This overall rate of violence is higher than reported in most previous studies; one possible explanation for this higher rate is the more sensitive measurement of violence that is possible through the systematic incorporation of collateral information.

This approach to measuring violence by combining self-report with collateral report and official records has been used in other recent studies as well (e.g., Steadman et al., 1998; Swanson, Borum, Swartz, & Hiday, 1999). The latter investigation, funded by the John D. and Catherine T. MacArthur Foundation, comes as close to a state-of-the-art study of violence prediction as can be achieved presently. It included 1,136 male and female patients with mental disorders between the ages of 18 and 40, monitored for violence toward others every 10 weeks during the first year following discharge from psychiatric hospitalization; these results were compared with violence toward others by a comparison group (N = 519) randomly sampled from the same census tracts as the discharged patient group. Outcome behavior was measured at two levels of seriousness: *violence* (battery resulting in physical injury, sexual assaults, and threats with a weapon) and *other aggressive acts* (battery that did not result in a physical injury). Information sources included self-report (every 10 weeks); collateral report of an individual designated in the beginning of the study by the participant, chosen because of anticipated reasonably frequent opportunity for observation (every 10 weeks); and agency records (arrest and hospitalization). The investigators reported a significant addition of self-report and collateral report to the identified frequency of violence and other aggressive acts beyond the frequency reflected in official records. More specifically, the overall frequency of violence reflected by agency records was 4.5% over a one-year period; the addition of self- and collateral report increased this frequency to 27.5%. The increase for other aggressive acts was even greater: from 8.8% (reflected by agency records) to 56.1% (reflected by any of the three sources). These findings offer tangible evidence of the impact of collateral sources of information on increasing the sensitivity and accuracy of measuring violent behavior.

The accurate measurement of psychopathy has been greatly facilitated by the development of the Psychopathy Checklist, its revised version, the PCL-R (Hare, 1991), and its screening version (PCL-SV; Hart, Cox, & Hare, 1995). (For an extensive discussion of psychopathy, see the chapter by Hemphill & Hart in this volume.) The standard administration of the PCL-R incorporates two major sources of information: self-report on a semistructured interview and a review of existing records (Hare, 1991). (Much of the validation work on the PCL-R has been performed with individuals in correctional and secure forensic settings, for whom there is typically a detailed institutional record that includes social, vocational, criminal, medical, and mental health histories.) It is possible to deviate from the standard procedure by using a "file only" rating based on only collateral information, which can be done "if there is sufficient high-quality information available" (Hare, 1991, p. 6; see also

Wong, 1988). However, Hare clearly cautions against making PCL-R ratings under any circumstances in the absence of "adequate collateral information" (p. 6). While the Screening Version of the PCL-R requires somewhat less collateral information (Hart et al., 1995) and functions as an effective short form of the PCL-R (Cooke, Michie, Hart, & Hare, 1999), the principle remains the same: the PCL-SV items cannot be scored without the incorporation of relevant collateral information.

The role of TPI in evaluating other forms of psychopathology has also been addressed. The assessment of Alzheimer's disease and related dementias was addressed by a group (CPG 19) developing clinical practice guidelines on the recognition and initial assessment of Alzheimer's disease and related dementias (Costa et al., 1996; Somerfield & Costa, 1999). Using meta-analysis of existing measures, they identified the Functional Activities Questionnaire (FAQ; Pfeffer, 1995) as the best discriminator between demented and nondemented groups, with an effect size of 2.46 (which corresponds to sensitivity and specificity in the range of 85% to 90%; Hasselblad & Hedges, 1995). The FAQ, an informant-based structured measure of functional performance, has the collateral observer rate the performance of the target person on 10 complex, higher-order functional activities, such as writing checks and preparing a balanced meal. On the basis of the meta-analysis, the CPG 19 panel recommended using the FAQ in the initial assessment of dementia, in conjunction with noting patients' signs and symptoms and evaluating their performance on mental status examinations.

Additional research using TPI to assess older participants has investigated disagreement between self- and collateral report on the Geriatric Depression Scale (GDS; Burke et al., 1998). A total of 198 participants with possible or probable Alzheimer's disease and 64 cognitively intact participants completed the 30-item GDS; the collateral version of the GDS was completed by an observer who knew the participant. A noteworthy difference was found in the reporting of depressive symptoms by the participants, when contrasted with the same kinds of symptoms reported by collateral observers; the investigators suggested that both "level of insight" and degree of physical illness in those with Alzheimer's significantly influenced this difference. Collateral observers consistently reported more depressive symptoms experienced by participants than were reported by the participants themselves, particularly those participants with limited awareness of their cognitive impairment.

The application of TPI has also been considered in the assessment of substance abuse and other kinds of addictive behavior. Several studies have suggested that, at least when there is little motivation for participants to exaggerate or minimize their reports of alcohol use, there is good agreement between self- and collateral reports, or self-report actually yields more detailed (and presumably more accurate) information. For example, among patients who have been diagnosed with bipolar disorder and substance abuse, a total of 132 instances of collateral description of substance use uncovered only three instances in which collateral informants described substance abuse for patients who denied it and who had negative urine screens (Weiss, Greenfield, Griffin, Najavits, & Fucito, 2000). In participants who were tracked for alcohol consumption and smoking during pregnancy, there was strong agreement between self- and collateral report on smoking, but poorer agreement on alcohol consumption, with participants describing more drinking than collaterals (Chang, Goetz, Wilkins-Haug, & Berman, 1999). Participants responding to standard questions about drinking in another study (Chermack, Singer, & Beresford, 1998) yielded results showing that participants generally reported more drinking consequences than collaterals, although participant and collateral reports of the participant's alcohol consumption did not differ significantly. It is noteworthy, however, that none of these studies addressed circumstances that are typical in forensic assessment. An individual may stand to gain or lose a great deal through litigation, and therefore may be more inclined to respond to the *litigation-induced* incentive to distort the accuracy of self-reported symptoms or patterns of behavior.

Finally, we located one interesting study that may have implications on rating accuracy based on how long and how well a collateral observer has known the individual being rated, and what is being rated. Personality characteristics of 177 participants in four groups of varying length and depth of relationships were assessed using the Eysenck Personality Inventory (EPI; Udofia, Etuk, & John, 1996). Participants themselves completed the EPI, which was also completed by either a friend or a spouse. Results suggested that third parties who had known the participants for more than three years were able to give a more accurate account of variables such as introversion and extroversion. The lowest levels of agreement between self- and collateral accounts were for the neuroticism dimension of the EPI. These findings would support the commonsense notion that an observer who has known the participant longer and has experienced more opportunity to observe the individual under a variety of circumstances would provide more accurate information about the participant's behavior. They might also suggest that ratings dependent on inferences about internal experience will be less accurate than those that can be operationalized by the straightforward observation of behavior.

RELEVANT LAW ON THIRD PARTY INFORMATION

We were not able to locate specific appellate cases involving TPI in FMHA. As a result, our comments in this section focus on the admissibility of TPI under the two standards for admitting expert evidence that currently exist in the United States: *Frye* and *Daubert*. Under *Frye v. United States* (1923), the standard for admissibility of expert evidence is given in terms of "general acceptance":

> Just when a scientific principle or discovery crosses the line between the experimental and demonstrable stages is difficult to define. Somewhere in this twilight zone the evidential force of the principle must be recognized, and while courts will go a long way in admitting expert testimony deduced from a well-recognized scientific principle or discovery, the thing from which the deduction is made must be sufficiently established to have gained general acceptance in the particular field in which it belongs. (p. 1014)

Under *Daubert v. Merrell Dow Pharmaceuticals* (1993), the standard for admissibility of expert scientific evidence was expanded to include the following criteria: (a) The proposition to which the evidence pertains is testable; (b) it has been tested; (c) the technique used to test it has a known error rate; (d) there are accepted standards for operation of the technique; and (e) the evidence has been subjected to peer review and publication (Giannelli & Imwinkelried, 1993).

Although *Daubert* was a case in which the nature of the expert evidence was clearly scientific, and the question has been raised as to whether FMHA might more appropriately be considered "technical" or "other specialized knowledge" under Federal Rule of Evidence 702, it has also become clear that a *Daubert*-type analysis can be applied to the admissibility of any expert evidence (*Kumho Tire Company, Ltd. v. Carmichael,* 1999; for a more extensive discussion, see the chapter by Weismann & Debow in this volume).

Under *Frye,* there seems to be no real question that TPI should be admissible as part of FMHA. It is consistently described as a generally accepted, important part of forensic assessment, as will be discussed in more detail later in this chapter and summarized in Appendix A (Greenberg & Brodsky, in press). The empirical evidence shows that record review is probably used more than collateral interviews, but that both are applied in both criminal and civil forensic evaluations. Moreover, if there is a trend to be identified from research in this area, it would involve the increasing identification of TPI as a distinct source of information in FMHA and the more frequent application of such information in this context.

In *Daubert* jurisdictions, the issue becomes more complex. There are two distinct ways in which TPI can be used in forensic assessment: as a primary measure of relevant capacities, and as a secondary source of information to "check" the accuracy of more primary measures. It seems clear that using relevant records and collateral interviews to assess the consistency of conclusions drawn from interview and testing data could very well enhance the accuracy of such interview and testing data; in this single case, it provides one kind of a "test" described among the *Daubert* criteria. Moreover, using TPI in this way is consistent with how it is applied in research on various aspects of psychopathology and behavior, as discussed earlier.

However, employing TPI as a primary measure of relevant capacities could be more problematic under *Daubert*. There are existing behavioral science data for using TPI in this way for some measures (e.g., a "file only" Psychopathy Checklist, a teacher version of the Child Behavior Checklist). Without the research available to support such application, however, the use of TPI as a primary source of information in FMHA (particularly without other sources of information, such as personal interview and possibly testing) could potentially be challenged and excluded under *Daubert*.

Heilbrun (in press) observed that there are competing considerations in the law on the potential application of TPI. There is the prospect that forensic assessment may be more relevant and more reliable when TPI is integrated, which is certainly a desirable combination of goals that could enhance both the admissibility of forensic evidence and the credibility with which it is regarded by the legal decision maker. (For an example of a deposition arguing for the use of TPI in a single case, see Appendix A.)

However, there are legally limiting considerations in the application of TPI as well. Some sources of TPI described in this chapter might be challenged as hearsay on the grounds that they constitute out-of-court statements being presented to prove the truth of the in-court statement, and hence inadmissible. Under Federal Rule of Evidence 703, it is not necessary for facts or underlying data to be admissible if they are of a kind "reasonably relied on by experts . . . in forming opinions or inferences upon the subject."

States are not consistent on this point, however; some have evidentiary rules similar to Rule 703, while others (see, e.g., *Mayer v. Baiser,* 1986) require that expert testimony use only sources of information that would be independently admissible (Melton et al., 1997). In some cases, therefore, in a jurisdiction with the latter kind of requirement, it seems possible that certain TPI or its content could be ruled inadmissible, and the entire forensic assessment (if it had relied significantly on this TPI) also held inadmissible. As

Melton et al. noted, however, this is not likely to happen often. Rather than considering the admissibility of each source of data, the trial court typically may rule on the admissibility of the forensic assessment more broadly. It would be extremely labor-intensive to do otherwise, and (at least judging from appellate case law) does not seem to occur often. A review of appellate cases citing FMHA and *Daubert* (1993) suggests that specific sources of data in FMHA are rarely singled out for admissibility scrutiny, and none of them (in the 276 appellate cases cited) used *Daubert* as grounds for admitting or excluding document review or collateral interviews (Heilbrun, 1996). We also note that two of the present authors (Heilbrun and Warren) have collectively performed or supervised approximately 3,000 forensic mental health assessments in the past 20 years and testified about 250 times. Neither of us has ever had a court exclude TPI from testimony or, to our knowledge, from a report that has been admitted into evidence in a hearing or trial. We are aware of one instance involving a colleague (which occurred almost 15 years ago) in which the mental health history obtained in part from a third party source was excluded as hearsay. It was reasoned that the defense had failed to provide the proper foundation for the relevance of history to diagnosis, and had not established the relevance of TPI to forensic assessment.

RELEVANT ETHICS ON USING THIRD PARTY INFORMATION

There are four sources of ethics authority that are particularly relevant in FMHA: the American Psychological Association's (APA) "Ethical Principles of Psychologists and Code of Conduct" (1992), the "Specialty Guidelines for Forensic Psychologists" (Committee on Ethical Guidelines for Forensic Psychologists, 1991), *The Principles of Medical Ethics with Annotations Especially Applicable to Psychiatry* (American Psychiatric Association, 1998), and the *Ethical Guidelines for the Practice of Forensic Psychiatry* (American Academy of Psychiatry and the Law [AAPL], 1995). These four have been cited in a broad discussion of the principles of FMHA (Heilbrun, in press) and are commonly cited in the psychological and psychiatric literature on forensic assessment. The APA Ethics Code notes that the interpretation of assessment results by psychologists involves a consideration of the various "characteristics of the person being assessed that might . . . reduce the accuracy of their interpretations. They indicate any significant reservations they have about the accuracy or limitations of their interpretations" (1992, p. 1603). TPI, in the form of both records and

collateral interviews, could affect the accuracy of the findings in FMHA and the nature of the reservations about such findings.

The use of TPI in FMHA is approached somewhat differently in the "Specialty Guidelines for Forensic Psychologists" (Committee on Ethical Guidelines for Forensic Psychologists, 1991). An important aspect of forensic assessment described in the Specialty Guidelines involves "differentially test[ing] rival hypotheses" (p. 661), such as whether symptoms of psychopathology are genuine, factual information is accurate, and legally relevant capacities are presented in a way that describes their potential well. TPI can help to formulate relevant hypotheses and to test them.

Although the *Principles of Medical Ethics with Annotations Especially Applicable to Psychiatry* (American Psychiatric Association, 1998) does not contain language that helps to weigh the use of TPI in a forensic assessment context, the *Ethical Guidelines for the Practice of Forensic Psychiatry* (AAPL, 1995) also considers the potential contribution of TPI to both enhancing the accuracy of observations and facilitating the reasoning about their meaning:

> Practicing forensic psychiatrists enhance the honesty and objectivity of their work by basing their forensic opinions, forensic reports and forensic testimony on all the data available to them. They communicate the honesty of their work and efforts to attain objectivity, and the soundness of their clinical opinion by distinguishing, to the extent possible, between verified and unverified information as well as between clinical "facts," "inferences," and "impressions." (1995, p. 3)

This is another way of considering the applicability of TPI. One way of distinguishing between verified and unverified information is to describe the extent to which data that are consistent across interview, medical tests, and TPI are reasonably consistent in pointing toward the same conclusion. When they are not, the *Ethical Guidelines for the Practice of Forensic Psychiatry* suggests that they might be described using cautionary language such as partially verified impressions or other ways of communicating the absence of strong or consistent findings.

RELEVANT PRACTICE LITERATURE ON THIRD PARTY INFORMATION

There is some inconsistency in the extent to which empirical research and legal and ethical authorities address the use of TPI in forensic assessment. There is greater consistency, however, in the relevant literature on standards of practice. Recent texts (e.g., Appelbaum & Gutheil, 1991; Greenberg &

Brodsky, in press; Heilbrun, in press; Melton et al., 1997) on forensic assessment have devoted significant space to TPI. We review this material in this section.

One of the most important reasons to obtain TPI involves the need to verify the accuracy of symptoms and behavior reported by the individual being evaluated. Melton et al. (1997) observed:

> Obtaining information contradicting the client's version of events is probably the most accurate means of detecting fabrication and may be the only viable one with clients who sabotage interview and testing efforts. (pp. 57–58)

A second important reason involves hypothesis formation and testing in FMHA. In discussing the use of psychological testing in forensic assessment, Heilbrun (1992) observed:

> Because of premium on the accuracy of information provided to the factfinder, the results of psychological tests should not be used in isolation from history, medical findings, and observations of behavior made by others. This point has been made emphatically by Matarazzo (1990) in his discussion of forensic assessment of neuropsychological issues involved in personal injury and child custody litigation. It has also been made by others. . . . Impressions from psychological testing in the forensic context should most appropriately be treated as hypotheses subject to verification through history, medical tests, and third-party observations . . . [this can] significantly reduce . . . problems in relevance and accuracy. (p. 263)

Using TPI for either or both of these reasons is widely cited by a number of commentators. The diagnosis of dissociative disorders in forensic contexts, for example, should not be made in the absence of collateral data from records and third party interviews (Coons, 1989). Clinicians' accurate detection of deception through clinical judgment alone is not supported by the research (Faust, 1995), although it is apparently not significantly worse than in other professional groups (Ekman & O'Sullivan, 1991), so collateral information is important to supplement interview and testing impressions regarding symptoms, history, and behavior. A review of instruments used by clinical neuropsychologists to detect malingering suggested no consistent support for any tool (Frazen, Iverson, & McCracken, 1990). Although this has improved somewhat in the 10 years since Frazen published this review (see, e.g., Frederick, 1997; McCann, 1998; Rogers, 1997), it still appears advisable to incorporate TPI into the assessment of response style.

The use of TPI can also be viewed through the comments of those addressing FMHA in different areas. It has been encouraged in employment discrimination cases (Goodman-Delahunty & Foote, 1995), personal injury litigation (Borum, Otto, & Golding, 1993; Greenberg & Brodsky, in press; Melton et al., 1997; Resnick, 1995), child custody evaluation (Ackerman, 1999; Otto, Edens, & Barcus, 2000), and civil commitment of sexual offenders (Hoberman, 1999). The incorporation of TPI into criminal FMHA generally has been a recognized practice for years (Melton et al., 1997; Shapiro, 1984), and it has recently been concluded (through a review of the relevant empirical, legal, ethical, and standard of practice literature) that the use of TPI is a broad principle with application to FMHA generally (Heilbrun, in press). An example of a sample affidavit summarizing the support for using one kind of TPI (collateral interviews) in FMHA is provided by Greenberg and Brodsky (in press) and reprinted in Appendix A.

OBTAINING THIRD PARTY INFORMATION

There are a variety of potential sources of TPI in forensic assessment. In this section, we offer a description of a number of such sources. We also address questions related to how such information is obtained (e.g., in person versus by telephone). Finally, we comment on the nature of TPI needed for specific measures that were designed to use TPI, and how the collection of TPI can be structured very specifically to meet the demands of a particular case.

Sources of Third Party Information

As summarized in Table 5.3, the two broad categories of TPI—collateral interviews and records—may vary considerably in their relevance and availability in a particular case. This list is clearly not exhaustive. The collection of TPI must be guided to some extent by case-specific questions, and will thus be somewhat different in each case. TPI collection also should facilitate hypothesis formulation and testing, which should not be completed until the needed TPI is obtained.

The individuals who have had the greatest degree of contact with the person being evaluated are potentially the most valuable collateral informants. These are described in the first section of Table 5.3, under "Personal Contact." In approximate order of exposure, these include spouses or partners, roommates, family members, employers and coworkers, neighbors, and other collateral observers. The importance of each of these sources depends on the nature of the case and the evaluative questions that are raised. For example, if a defendant is charged with a sex crime or a capital case that involves a rape/murder, the wife or consensual partner of the defendant will be an important source of information

TABLE 5.3   Sources of Third Party Information in Forensic Assessment

Interviews

Personal Contact
  Spouses or partners.
  Roommates.
  Family members.
  Employers, supervisors, and fellow workers.
  Neighbors.
  Other collateral observers with familiarity with litigant.
  Victims.

Professional Contact
  Police.
  Jail staff.
    Nurses.
    Officers.
    Social workers.
    Consultants.
  Community case managers.
  Probation/parole officers.
  Emergency room, psychiatric hospital, or correctional facility staff.
  Teachers.
  Medical and mental health professionals who previously have been involved in assessing or treating the individual being evaluated.

Documents

Personal Documentation
  Statements.
    Litigants.
    Victims.
    Witnesses.
  Letters, journals, diaries.

Professional Documentation
  Transcripts of previous hearings, depositions.
  Previous FMHA reports.
  Police reports.
  Crime scene evidence.
  Autopsy reports.
  Presentence investigations.
  Probation and parole records.
  Jail and prison records.
  Juvenile placement records.
  Mental health records.
  Medical records.
  Criminal and juvenile history records.
  School records.
  Employment and personnel records.
  Military records.
  Department of Social Service records.
  Financial records.

regarding the sexual interests and preferences of the particular individual being evaluated. Alternatively, if the issue involves some type of workplace allegation or incident, fellow employees might be central to determining the patterns of a particular individual's relationships and performance in the work setting. In cases in which there is a viable insanity defense, family members often are valuable adjuncts in documenting a history of mental illness and possible patterns of noncompliance with medication.

In determining which individuals will be contacted, it is important to be sensitive to the potential biases of each third party. In the majority of instances, those individuals who know a defendant or plaintiff well are generally interested in talking to the evaluator and in ensuring that their input will be identified and considered. There is, however, still significant potential for distortion in this type of report. Due to their proximity to a person or an event, many respondents will be interested in convincing the evaluator of the guilt, innocence, or incapacity of a particular individual in the criminal context or in maximizing or minimizing the distress a person is experiencing or the degree of responsibility a particular person had for making a certain decision in the civil context. These biases must be anticipated and neutralized as much as possible by informed interviewing and the consideration of interview data from individuals with varying perspectives and interests. Respondents might also be suggestible, uninformed, lacking in specific knowledge, or unable to recall important information. In addition, there may be a particular focus on a specific time in the past (e.g., around the time of the alleged offense) or the present. Collateral observers may have been familiar with the individual for most of his or her life, but unable to provide specific information about the particular time in question. All of these problems must be considered and the information obtained weighed accordingly. The assessment of influences that have the potential to affect the accuracy of third party interviewees is addressed later in this section.

The next group of collateral observers are those who have had professional contact with the individual being evaluated. Similar considerations apply. The greater the exposure, particularly during relevant periods, the more valuable may be the information obtained from a collateral interview. The simultaneous consideration, however, is whether the collateral interviewee experiences the problems described in the previous paragraph. Those whose contact with the individual was professional may be less inclined to be uncooperative (assuming appropriate authorization has been obtained) and offer greater specific expertise (e.g., treating therapists would be expected to be familiar with various levels of psychopathology; arresting officers should have some training and experience observing the impact of substance abuse on behavior). Problems with memory can sometimes be improved through referral to documentation, which is more likely to be present in a professional context.

It is important when determining which collateral interviews will be conducted that professional status not be used to prioritize the importance of various respondents. Trained mental health professionals may have useful information to provide regarding diagnosis and treatment, but observations derived from health care providers who have more sustained day-to-day contact with an individual or law enforcement officers who have conducted thorough investigations of a certain crime series may prove to be more relevant in some cases. For example, orderlies, cafeteria staff, physical therapists, home help assistants, and others in similar roles may have important observations, particularly in cases of malingered psychosis and exaggerated claims of psychic distress and impairment. In other instances, skilled police investigators may describe commonalties across a series of offenses that is clearly inconsistent with an impulsive, unplanned offense. The importance of any professional source thus arises from the collateral's proximity to certain behavior rather than the source's professional status.

TPI personal documentation in Table 5.3, such as statements made by litigants, witnesses, or alleged victims, has the advantage of already existing in written form and, in many instances, being available to both sides through reciprocal discovery. Often, however, such documents provide only limited information relevant to the questions being assessed by the forensic clinician. A review of all available documents prior to scheduling collateral interviews can be advantageous for several reasons, therefore. First, the information available in collateral documents can provide a context for the interviews and help shape the questioning. Second, and more specifically, when a collateral interviewee has difficulty recalling an event, the forensic clinician can use third party documents to provide details that might help to facilitate such recall. Of course, the forensic clinician doing this must be extremely careful to avoid providing information that might affect the nature of the interviewee's description of "sensitive" information; generally, such memory prompts should be entirely limited to nonsensitive details such as date, time, location, and the like. (Sensitive information refers to information that is directly relevant to the forensic capacities being evaluated, and usually includes thoughts, feelings, behavior, and skills. Nonsensitive information can typically be distinguished when there is a focus on a particular event or time period; nonsensitive details in such cases include date, time, location, and activities unrelated to the legally relevant events or forensic capacities being assessed.) Third, when information provided by collateral informants is not consistent with that contained in third party records, the forensic clinician can attempt to clarify the reasons for such inconsistency. It is particularly important to determine whether such inconsistency seems to result from recall problems or bias.

In certain cases, it is important to review personal documentation that has been created by the defendant or plaintiff. Personal diaries can contain information about events that can be highly relevant to criminal adjudication or civil litigation. Collections have been found to be of central importance in the investigation and evaluations of certain types of repetitive sex offenders (Warren, Hazelwood, & Dietz, 1996). In cases of alleged serial murder, videotapes, photographs, and pornographic drawings have been located by police investigators and can be used by the forensic evaluator to assess sexual preferences, relevant interactions between coperpetrators, and commonalities in the preparation for and perpetration of particular crimes. Letters between spouses or romantic partners can be important in determining the nature of the relationship and any particular events that may have preceded the violent behavior. Moreover, office notations or reading material can be relevant in assessing the risk and needs of particular individuals in a workplace violence context.

Professional documentation can be considered on two levels. As sources of behavioral observations, such documents can be quite valuable, particularly when they are detailed in their description of relevant behavior. However, professional documents sometimes reflect the conclusions of the writer in the very areas being evaluated in the present FMHA. Forensic clinicians are responsible for drawing their own conclusions and should not be overly influenced by conclusions drawn by other professionals. Unless there is some reason to regard observations by other professionals as inaccurate, it is reasonable to accept such observations. However, conclusions (such as those regarding diagnosis or specific forensic capacities) should *not* be accepted as accurate, although they should be recorded as documented in the records.

TPI documentation can provide valuable information in both criminal and civil cases when unusual defenses or issues are raised. For example, it was once not uncommon for criminal defendants who were Vietnam veterans to report that they committed a certain offense while experiencing flashbacks related to Post Traumatic Stress Disorder (PTSD). In some such cases, while the individual's presentation was quite credible, it was determined through collateral sources that they had never actually served in Vietnam or had served in a capacity in which they were not exposed to combat. Without confirmation of significant trauma, either through military records or third party interview, the viability of a PTSD diagnosis and the associated defense in such cases was greatly diminished.

How to Obtain Third Party Information

An important question in obtaining collateral interviews is whether such interviews should be conducted in person, over the telephone, or through written questions submitted through an attorney, through the mail, or even via e-mail. There is virtually no research guidance to assist in answering any of these questions, so our comments are largely limited to our perceptions regarding the advantages and disadvantages of these different approaches.

One recent study suggests that telephone interviews are comparable to face-to-face interviews in the quality of the information obtained regarding diagnostic information (Rohde, Lewinsohn, & Seeley, 1997). A total of 60 adults were interviewed in person and by telephone concerning Axis I disorders, and another 60 adults were interviewed twice regarding Axis II disorders. Agreement between telephone and in-person interviews was contrasted with interrater agreement, obtained through a second rating of the original interview. The following kappa (chance-corrected agreement) values were obtained between face-to-face and telephone interviews: anxiety disorders (.84), substance use disorders (.73), alcohol use disorders (.70), and major depressive disorder (.67). A lower kappa was observed for adjustment disorder with depressed mood (.31). Judging from these very limited data, it is possible to achieve comparable results when asking structured questions by telephone or in person. The disadvantage of using telephone interviewing involves losing access to cues obtained from observing the individual who responded, although auditory cues would still be available. Our view is that whatever slight advantage may be lost in the telephone interview would be outweighed by the facilitation of ease of access and greater mutual convenience for both interviewee and forensic clinician. It is always possible to schedule an in-person interview for a longer or less structured interview, at the discretion of the forensic clinician, or to schedule such an interview at the preference of the collateral individual being interviewed.

Conducting a third party interview in written form, whether through mail or e-mail, presents a different context. The advantages of structured interviewing are retained—specific, preplanned questions are asked—but all prospects for follow-up questioning based on substance of response or visual or auditory cues provided by the interviewee are sacrificed. This format might remain useful when trying to confirm or disconfirm previously developed material, but would be less helpful when exploring or trying to develop newer material.

Specific Measures Using Third Party Information

There are two kinds of measures that deserve mention for their incorporation of TPI. Some established psychological tests, such as the CBCL (Achenbach, 1991) and the PCL-R (Hare, 1991), have been designed and validated using the observations of collaterals such as parents and teachers (CBCL) or existing records in the form of a prison or hospital file

(PCL-R). The application of TPI with these respective measures is guided by the questions that are asked and the administration instructions contained in their manuals. These are examples of how structured use of TPI can not only be included as a valuable source of input, but can also fill a particular niche. In the case of the PCL-R, record-based TPI must be incorporated to ensure that deception in self-report does not unduly influence the ratings that are assigned. Teachers and parents who serve as informants on the CBCL have the advantage of presumably greater accuracy in some cases than children, for whom developmental immaturity might interfere with accurate self-reporting.

A second approach to collecting TPI involves providing structure that is tailored to a specific case. In one such case (see Heilbrun, 1990), a defendant in an inpatient forensic setting whom we suspected of malingering was entirely uncooperative with any attempts to evaluate him. Because he consistently refused to meet with an evaluator, we tried to obtain extensive behavioral observation data on him by developing a "checklist" consisting of every symptom he had ever reported to a hospital staff member or attributed to him in evaluation reports written prior to his hospitalization. We attempted to translate each symptom into the observable behavior that would be expected from someone who genuinely experienced such a symptom; for example, an individual who was hearing voices might appear distracted or talk to himself. When we had reduced this list to a total of 20 items, we asked a ward staff member from day shift (7:00 to 3:00) and another from evening shift (3:00 to 11:00) to indicate yes or no on each item, reflecting whether the behavior had been observed at any time during the eight-hour shift. Over the course of 400 ratings (each over an eight-hour shift, for a total of 3,200 hours of observation time), "no symptom was observed in more than 2% of the rating periods and many were not reported at all" (p. 194). Although it would have been useful to incorporate self-report and testing data into this evaluation, this approach demonstrates how collateral observers can be used in a specific way, performing observations that have been carefully structured, to yield data that were useful in considering the question of whether his reported symptoms were genuine.

COLLECTING AND APPLYING THIRD PARTY INFORMATION

In some important respects, the forensic clinician is like an investigative journalist. The use of multiple sources, the assessment of consistency across sources, and the attribution of information to source are all shared methods of gathering and interpreting relevant information (Levine, 1980; Melton et al., 1997). In this section, we offer some specific comments about how TPI can be collected and applied in FMHA, focusing particularly on collateral interviewing.

We address two considerations in collecting and applying TPI from collateral interviews. The first concerns individuals who are reluctant to participate in such an interview. The second broad area involves influences that can limit the accuracy of information obtained through collateral interviews: bias, lack of specific expertise, suggestibility, and memory loss (see Table 5.4).

Individuals who are asked to participate in FMHA by providing collateral information may be reluctant or simply unwilling to do so. Such unwillingness to participate should be respected. However, there are instances in which an individual's reluctance to participate may change when further information is provided. This information should be provided in the form of a notification of purpose, which should address the following: (a) the names of relevant individuals, including

the forensic clinician, the individual(s) being evaluated, and the attorney representing that individual; (b) the voluntary nature of participation in the collateral interview; (c) a description of the legal question(s) that triggered the evaluation; (d) who requested the forensic clinician's involvement (typically, the prosecution or defense attorney in criminal cases, defense or plaintiff's attorney in civil cases, or the court in either); (e) the purpose(s) for which the evaluation could be used; (f) how the information collected in this information will be used, including citation of the name of the interviewee in the report and testimony, and attribution of the information obtained in the interview specifically to its source; and (g) an offer to answer any questions that the individual may have before he or she decides whether to participate. This notification should allow the individual to make an informed choice about participation, and may facilitate involvement when reluctance is based on general apprehension about the legal process. More specific concerns may not be overcome, however. For individuals who are concerned

TABLE 5.4   Problems Limiting Collateral Interview Accuracy and Suggested Strategies for Problem Management

Problem	Problem Description	Suggested Strategy
Reluctance to participate	• Apprehensive about process. • Concerned about personal consequences of participating. • Unwilling to have information attributed.	• Notification of purpose and limits of confidentiality. • Informed about voluntary nature of participation. • Informed that unattributed information cannot be used.
Bias	• Lack of impartiality. • Strong positive or negative feelings about the litigant. • Preference for outcome.	• Consider potential bias from the beginning. • May be assessed near the end of the interview with question such as "What do you think should happen with _____?" • Third party information should be obtained from multiple sources, particularly when bias is suspected. • Conclusions should be developed from trends rather than single-source observations.
Lack of specific expertise	• Interviewee is without training or experience in specific area (e.g., psychopathology, substance abuse). • May not detect subtle indicators of disorder or capacity being assessed.	• Initial questions should elicit broad observations (What did the defendant say? do? act like?). • Later questions should focus on specific, preselected observations of symptoms and behavior (Did the individual show X? act like Y?). • No questions should elicit conclusions (Was she psychotic?).
Suggestibility	• May be prone to influence from leading questions.	• Initial questions should elicit broad observations (What did the defendant say? do? act like?). • Later questions should focus on specific, preselected observations of symptoms and behavior (Did the individual show X? act like Y?). • Allows comparison between uncontaminated description (given with little guidance from the interviewer) and specific but possibly less impartial version given when asked about specific relevant areas.
Memory loss	• May have difficulty remembering relevant details if saw individual only once. • Influences such as stress, different race of observer and individual, gun focus, and others factors interfering with eyewitness identification may operate.	• Beginning with general questions and moving to more specific areas. • Providing nonsensitive memory aids, such as date and location.

about the perceived consequences to them or those close to them, this notification may be less than reassuring. Some individuals may express a willingness to provide information on "background," with the assumption that they would not be identified as the source. This is not possible, however, as the forensic clinician is ethically obligated to identify the respective sources of data used in FMHA.

The second broad area concerns attributes of those interviewed that might yield inaccurate information. Many individuals who might be interviewed as part of FMHA are not impartial; they may have strong feelings about the individual being evaluated and an associated wish for a certain kind of outcome to the litigation. Potential bias must be considered a possibility for every collateral observer interviewed. Part of our recommended approach to managing the influence of bias would be carried out in the course of FMHA for a number of reasons: multiple sources should be used and conclusions should be developed based on trends across sources rather than from a single observation.

Professional expertise is usually not present in those who are interviewed as collaterals in FMHA. Because the forensic clinician should be seeking observations, not conclusions, from collateral interviewees, this is less of a problem than it might appear. The questioning should begin by eliciting broad observations and subsequently move to more specific areas when the general observations have been completed. More specific areas can be preselected by the forensic clinician for relevance and importance and the questions asked in a way that calls for behavioral observations and does not presuppose expertise.

The same approach to questioning (initially broad, subsequently more specific) is useful to prevent the interview itself from giving the interviewee suggestions about what is being sought. Caution should be used with information provided by a collateral interviewee who does not describe noteworthy aspects of, for example, mental health symptomatology during a broad description of the litigant, but responds affirmatively to questions about whether a number of specific symptoms have been observed. The greater this discrepancy, we suggest, the more the information should be scrutinized for consistency with that provided by other sources.

Finally, there is the very real problem of difficulty remembering what occurred at a specific time (for collateral interviewees who see the litigant frequently) or recalling what occurred in cases in which the interviewee was the victim or witness of an alleged offense. Influences such as extreme stress and weapon focus, for example, can further limit the accuracy of an account that may have already been based on fairly brief observation (Tooley, Brigham, Maass, & Bothwell, 1987). We recommend providing nonsensitive but relevant details (e.g., date, location), particularly for interviewees who often see the litigant, to facilitate a more focused account. However, we must emphasize the extreme importance of not providing details that could affect the interviewee's account of legally relevant behavior or capacities.

COMMUNICATING THIRD PARTY INFORMATION

There are two primary ways to communicate TPI in FMHA: in reports and in testimony. We offer comments on each. Each FMHA report should contain a specific, comprehensive listing of the sources of information used in the evaluation. Such a listing is particularly important because of the recommended approach to writing an FMHA report, with all factual information attributed to its source(s). Some form of organization of the source listing can be very useful, particularly in cases that have a large number of documents to be reviewed. Because each source citation should include the name of the source, its author, and its date, the sources could be organized alphabetically, by date, or by broader section, with subsequent organization within the section.

When reviewing third party documents, it is useful to identify the source and content by date. If this is done during the review process, it greatly facilitates writing the report in terms of the sequence of events as documented by third party records. A summary of each event can be recorded in the report and will automatically be placed in the order in which it has occurred. It is a straightforward task to transfer material to specific sections of the report once this is accomplished.

Many times, information from different third party sources is inconsistent. Such inconsistent material should be cited fully in the text, perhaps with language pointing out the inconsistency (e.g., "James and his mother both indicated that he has been arrested once for trespassing; by contrast, his juvenile arrest history reflected two arrests: one for trespassing and the second for possession with intent to distribute"). The meaning of all material, including that which is inconsistent with other sources, should be reflected in a formulation of findings (whether this is a separate section or integrated with other sections), but this meaning should not be addressed while describing the results of each source of TPI.

Some of the organizational aspects of TPI communication in reports are useful for testimony. When multiple sources are listed in a way that allows quick location of a specific source, and when all information is attributed by source, it facilitates providing testimony that is precise and efficient. The attribution of "truth" or "validity" to a given source can be problematic in forensic contexts, for two reasons. First, it is ultimately the job of the trier of fact to determine what is true in a legal case. Second, it is typically not feasible to systematically assess the accuracy of one's findings in a given case. Thus, we prefer to speak about sources being "inconsistent" or "consistent" rather than indicating that one source "verifies" or "confirms" what another has indicated. Finally, being comprehensive and using multiple sources of information to support findings are very important in both testimony and report writing. Critical thinking, which should be reflected in the writing of the report, may be demonstrated in other ways (such as in response to hypothetical questions) during testimony.

Finally, it is important to document all attempts to obtain TPI, whether successful or not. Whatever format is used to identify the respondents and sources of information that were received, a similar format should be used to reference information or collateral interviews that an unsuccessful attempt was made to obtain. For example, if an evaluator attempts to obtain a police report but this document is not provided, this should be noted and referenced by time and date in the sources of information. If a particular collateral respondent declines to participate in an interview, this should be similarly noted. This type of record encourages the evaluator to contact all relevant sources without predicting who will and will not participate. By noting these failed efforts or contacts in the report, the forensic clinician demonstrates the effort that was made to obtain comprehensive, relevant TPI.

CONCLUSION

There have been some important advances in the conceptual consideration of using TPI in FMHA during the past decade. Unfortunately, research in this area has lagged behind practice. In some respects, the application of TPI may remain something of an art, similar to that seen in investigative journalism. In other ways, however, the behavioral and medical sciences have important contributions to make in documenting the use, structuring the applications, and validating the approaches used in collecting and applying TPI. We hope this chapter both promotes needed research and contributes to better practice in this area. We also expect that the appropriate use of TPI in forensic assessment will improve the actual and perceived quality of the evaluations and testimony provided to the courts. On that basis, we strongly encourage the use of TPI as forensic clinicians address the diverse aspects of human nature that are seen in this area of practice.

REFERENCES

Achenbach, T. (1991). *Manual for the Child Behavior Checklist/4–18 and 1991 profile.* Burlington: University of Vermont Department of Psychiatry.

Achenbach, T. M., & Edelbrock, C. (1983). *Manual for the Child Behavior Checklist and Revised Child Behavior Profile.* Burlington: University of Vermont, Department of Psychiatry.

Ackerman, M. (1999). *Essentials of forensic psychological assessment.* New York: Wiley.

Ackerman, M. J., & Ackerman, M. C. (1997). Custody evaluation practices: A survey of experienced professionals (revisited). *Professional Psychology: Research and Practice, 28,* 137–145.

American Academy of Psychiatry and the Law. (1995). *Ethical guidelines for the practice of forensic psychiatry.* Bloomfield, CT: Author.

American Psychiatric Association. (1998). *The principles of medical ethics with annotations especially applicable to psychiatry.* Washington, DC: Author.

American Psychological Association. (1992). Ethical principles of psychologists and code of conduct. *American Psychologist, 47,* 1597–1611.

Appelbaum, K. (1990). Criminal defendants who desire punishment. *Bulletin of the American Academy of Psychiatry and the Law, 18,* 385–391.

Appelbaum, P., & Gutheil, T. (1991). *Clinical handbook of psychiatry and the law* (2nd ed.). Baltimore: Williams & Wilkins.

Borum, R., & Grisso, T. (1996). Establishing standards for criminal forensic reports: An empirical analysis. *Bulletin of the American Academy of Psychiatry and the Law, 24,* 297–317.

Borum, R., Otto, R., & Golding, S. (1993). Improving clinical judgment and decision making in forensic evaluation. *Journal of Psychiatry and Law, 21,* 35–76.

Burke, W., Roccaforte, W., Wengel, S., McArthur-Miller, D., Folks, D., & Potter, J. (1998). Disagreement in the reporting of depressive symptoms between patients with dementia of the Alzheimer type and their collateral sources. *American Journal of Geriatric Psychiatry, 6,* 308–319.

Chang, G., Goetz, M., Wilkins-Haug, L., & Berman, S. (1999). Prenatal alcohol consumption: Self versus collateral report. *Journal of Substance Abuse Treatment, 17,* 85–89.

Chermack, S., Singer, K., & Beresford, T. (1998). Screening for alcoholism among medical inpatients: How important is corroboration of patient self-report? *Alcoholism: Clinical and Experimental Research, 22,* 1393–1398.

Committee on Ethical Guidelines for Forensic Psychologists. (1991). Specialty guidelines for forensic psychologists. *Law and Human Behavior, 15,* 655–665.

Cooke, D., Michie, C., Hart, S., & Hare, R. (1999). Evaluating the screening version of the Hare Psychopathy Checklist–Revised

(PCL:SV): An item response theory analysis. *Psychological Assessment, 11,* 3–13.

Coons, P. (1989). Iatrogenic factors in the misdiagnosis of multiple personality disorder. *Dissociation: Progress in the dissociative disorders, 2,* 70–76.

Costa, P., Williams, T., Somerfield, M., et al. (1996, November). *Recognition and initial assessment of Alzheimer's disease and related dementias* (Clinical Practice Guideline No. 19, AHCPR Publication No. 97–0702). Rockville, MD: U.S. Department of Health and Human Services.

Daubert v. Merrell Dow Pharmaceuticals, 113 S. Ct. 2786 (1993).

Ekman, P., & O'Sullivan, M. (1991). Who can catch a liar? *American Psychologist, 46,* 913–920.

Faust, D. (1995). The detection of deception. *Neurological Clinics, 13,* 255–265.

Frazen, M., Iverson, G., & McCracken, L. (1990). The detection of malingering in neuropsychological assessment. *Neuropsychology Review, 1,* 247–279.

Frederick, R. (1997). *Validity Indicator Profile manual.* Minneapolis, MN: National Computer Systems.

Frye v. United States, 293 F. 1013 (D.C. Cir 1923).

Goodman-Delahunty, J., & Foote, W. (1995). Compensation for pain, suffering, and other psychological injuries: The impact of Daubert on employment discrimination claims. *Behavioral Sciences and the Law, 13,* 183–206.

Greenberg, S., & Brodsky, S. (in press). *The civil practice of forensic psychology: Torts of emotional distress.* Washington, DC: American Psychological Association.

Grisso, T. (1986). *Evaluating competencies: Forensic assessments and instruments.* New York: Plenum Press.

Grisso, T. (1998). *Forensic evaluation of juveniles.* Sarasota, FL: Professional Resource Press.

Hare, R. D. (1991). *Manual for the Revised Psychopathy Checklist.* Toronto, Ontario, Canada: Multi-Health Systems.

Hart, S., Cox, D., & Hare, R. (1995). *The Hare Psychopathy Checklist: Screening version.* Toronto, Ontario, Canada: Multi-Health Systems.

Hasselblad, V., & Hedges, L. (1995). Meta-analysis of screening and diagnostic tests. *Psychological Bulletin, 177,* 167–178.

Heilbrun, K. (1988, March). *Third party information in forensic assessment: Much needed, sometimes collected, poorly guided.* Presented at the American Psychology-Law Society/Division 41 mid-year conference, Miami, FL.

Heilbrun, K. (1990). Response style, situation, third party information, and competency to stand trial: Scientific issues in practice. *Law and Human Behavior, 14,* 193–196.

Heilbrun, K. (1992). The role of psychological testing in forensic assessment. *Law and Human Behavior, 16,* 257–272.

Heilbrun, K. (1996, March). *Daubert and forensic mental health assessment: Use and implications.* Presented at the biennial

conference of the American Psychology-Law Society/Division 41, Hilton Head, SC.

Heilbrun, K. (in press). *Principles of forensic mental health assessment.* New York: Plenum Press.

Heilbrun, K., & Collins, S. (1995). Evaluations of trial competency and mental state at the time of the offense: Report characteristics. *Professional Psychology: Research and Practice, 26,* 61–67.

Heilbrun, K., Rosenfeld, B., Warren, J., & Collins, S. (1994). The use of third party information in forensic assessments. *Bulletin of the American Academy of Psychiatry and the Law, 22,* 399–406.

Hoberman, H. (1999). The forensic evaluation of sex offenders in civil commitment proceedings. In A. Schlank & F. Cohen (Eds.), *The sexual predator* (pp. 7-1–7-41). Kingston, NJ: Civic Research Institute.

Keilin, W., & Bloom, L. (1986). Child custody evaluation practices: A survey of experienced professionals. *Professional Psychology: Research and Practice, 17,* 338–346.

Kumho Tire Company, Ltd. v. Carmichael, 526 U.S. 137 (1999).

LaFortune, K. (1997). *An investigation of mental health and legal professionals' activities, beliefs, and experiences in domestic court: An interdisciplinary survey.* Unpublished doctoral dissertation, University of Tulsa, OK.

Levine, M. (1980). Investigative reporting as a research method: An analysis of Bernstein and Woodward's *All the President's Men.* *American Psychologist, 35,* 626–638.

Lidz, C. W., Mulvey, E. P., & Gardner, W. (1993). The accuracy of predictions of violence to others. *Journal of the American Medical Association, 269,* 1007–1011.

Matarazzo, J. D. (1990). Psychological assessment versus psychological testing: Validation from Binet to the school, clinic, and courtroom. *American Psychologist, 45,* 999–1017.

Mayer v. Baiser, 497 N. E.2d 827 (1986).

McCann, J. (1998). *Malingering and deception in adolescents.* Washington, DC: American Psychological Association.

Melton, G., Petrila, J., Poythress, N., & Slobogin, C. (1997). *Psychological evaluations for the courts: A handbook for mental health professionals and lawyers* (2nd ed.). New York: Guilford Press.

Mulvey, E., & Lidz, C. (1993). Measuring patient violence in dangerousness research. *Law and Human Behavior, 17,* 277–288.

Newhill, C., Mulvey, E., & Lidz, C. (1995). Characteristics of violence in the community by female patients seen in a psychiatric emergency service. *Psychiatric Services, 46,* 785–795.

Nicholson, R., LaFortune, K., Norwood, S., & Roach, R. (1995, August). *Quality of pretrial competency evaluations in Oklahoma: Report content and consumer satisfaction.* Presented at the annual convention of the American Psychological Association, New York.

Nicholson, R., & Norwood, S. (2000). The quality of forensic psychological assessments, reports, and testimony: Acknowledging the gap between promise and practice. *Law and Human Behavior, 24,* 9–44.

Otto, R., Barnes, G., & Jacobson, K. (1996, March). *The content and quality of criminal forensic evaluations in Florida.* Presented at the biennial meeting of the American Psychology-Law Society, Hilton Head, SC.

Otto, R., Edens, J., & Barcus, E. (2000). The use of psychological testing in child custody evaluations. *Family and Conciliation Courts Review, 38,* 312–340.

Pfeffer, R. (1995). A social function measure in the staging and study of dementia. In M. Bergener, J. Brocklehurst, & S. Finkel (Eds.), *Aging, health, and healing* (pp. 459–475). New York: Springer.

Resnick, P. (1995). Malingering. *Mental and emotional injuries in employment litigation.* Washington, DC: Bureau of National Affairs.

Robbins, E., Waters, J., & Herbert, P. (1997). Competency to stand trial evaluations: A study of actual practice in two states. *Journal of the American Academy of Psychiatry and Law, 25,* 469–483.

Roesch, R., Hart, S., & Ogloff, J. (Eds.). (1999). *Psychology and law: The state of the discipline.* New York: Kluwer Academic/ Plenum.

Rogers, R. (1984). Towards an empirical model of malingering and deception. *Behavioral Sciences and the Law, 2,* 93–112.

Rogers, R. (Ed.). (1997). *Clinical assessment of malingering and deception* (2nd ed.). New York: Guilford Press.

Rohde, P., Lewinsohn, P., & Seeley, J. (1997). Comparability of telephone and face-to-face interviews in assessing Axis I and II Disorders. *American Journal of Psychiatry, 154,* 1593–1598.

Schacter, D. (1986). Amnesia and crime: How much do we really know? *American Psychologist, 41,* 287–295.

Shapiro, D. (1984). *Psychological evaluation and expert testimony: A practical guide for forensic work.* New York: Van Nostrand-Reinhold.

Shapiro, D. (1991). *Forensic psychological assessment: An integrative approach.* Boston: Allyn & Bacon.

Skeem, J., Golding, S., Cohn, N., & Berge, G. (1998). The logic and reliability of evaluations of competence to stand trial. *Law and Human Behavior, 22,* 519–547.

Somerfield, M., & Costa, P. (1999). Toward more evidence-based guidelines for psychology. *American Psychologist, 54,* 1131–1132.

Steadman, H. J., Mulvey, E., Monahan, J., Robbins, P., Appelbaum, P., Grisso, T., et al. (1998). Violence by people discharged from acute psychiatric inpatient facilities and by others in the same neighborhoods. *Archives of General Psychiatry, 55,* 1–9.

Swanson, J., Borum, R., Swartz, M., & Hiday, V. (1999). Violent behavior preceding hospitalization among persons with severe mental illness. *Law and Human Behavior, 23,* 185–204.

Tooley, V., Brigham, J., Maass, A., & Bothwell, R. (1987). Facial recognition: Weapon effect and attentional focus. *Journal of Applied Social Psychology, 17,* 845–859.

Udofia, O., Etuk, L., & John, M. (1996). Personality assessment through third party interview: How valid? *Journal of Psychology in Africa, South of the Sahara, the Caribbean and Afro Latin American, 1,* 1–11.

Warren, J., Hazelwood, R., & Dietz, P. (1996). The sexually sadistic serial killer. *Journal of Forensic Sciences, 41,* 970–974.

Weiss, R., Greenfield, S., Griffin, M., Najavits, L., & Fucito, L. (2000). The use of collateral reports for patients with Bipolar and substance use disorders. *American Journal of Drug and Alcohol Abuse, 26,* 369–378.

Wong, S. (1988). Is Hare's Psychopathy Checklist reliable without the interview? *Psychological Reports, 62,* 931–934.

CHAPTER 6

Forensic and Clinical Issues in the Assessment of Psychopathy

JAMES F. HEMPHILL AND STEPHEN D. HART

Psychopathy—also known as psychopathic, antisocial, or dissocial personality disorder—has been the focus of intensive research investigations for the past two decades (Hare, 1996). A large body of research has examined the assessment of the disorder, evaluated different etiological models, described its patterns of comorbidity with other mental disorders, and investigated its association with antisocial behavior (Cooke, Forth, & Hare, 1998; Hare, Cooke, & Hart, 1999). An important factor in the growth of interest concerning psychopathy was the development of the original and revised versions of the Psychopathy Checklist (PCL and PCL-R; Hare, 1980, 1991). Unless otherwise stated, the term PCL will be used to refer to both psychological instruments because findings obtained from the original PCL and the PCL-R are generalizable to the other version (see Hare, 1991, p. 4).

Research using these tests has revealed clear associations between psychopathy and criminal behavior, especially specific forms of interpersonal violence, in a variety of populations (Hart & Hare, 1997). Psychopathy now is recognized as a critical factor in risk assessment (Hart, 1998) and can affect decisions involving civil commitment, parole from prison, access to treatment, detention under dangerous offender legislation, and even capital sentencing (Hart, 2001; Lyon & Ogloff, 2000; Zinger & Forth, 1998). Accordingly, the assessment of psychopathy is a fundamental skill for clinical-forensic psychologists.

This chapter begins with a discussion of the nature of psychopathy, focusing on current clinical conceptualizations of the disorder. The second section reviews the most commonly used methods for assessing psychopathy, focusing on the PCL-R. The third section identifies important professional and clinical issues that practitioners should keep in mind when assessing psychopathy. The fourth section examines practice recommendations concerning the assessment of psychopathy in clinical-forensic settings. The chapter concludes with a discussion of issues that are priorities for future research.

THE NATURE OF PSYCHOPATHY

Clinical Features

Psychopathy is a specific form of personality disorder. Like all personality disorders, it is characterized by a disturbance in relating to one's self, others, and the environment. It is chronic in nature, typically is evident in childhood or adolescence, and persists into middle or late adulthood (American Psychiatric Association, 1980, 1987, 1994; World Health Organization, 1992).

Symptoms of personality disorders are rigid, inflexible, and maladaptive personality traits: tendencies to act, think, perceive, and feel in certain ways that are stable across time, across situations, and in interactions with different people. What distinguishes psychopathy from other personality disorders is the specific symptom pattern, detailed in now classic works by Arieti (1963), Cleckley (1941), Karpman (1961), and McCord and McCord (1964). Interpersonally, psychopathic individuals are arrogant, superficial, deceitful, and manipulative. Affectively, their emotions are shallow and labile; they are unable to form strong emotional bonds with others and are lacking in empathy, anxiety, and guilt. Behaviorally, they are irresponsible, impulsive, sensation seeking, and prone to delinquency and criminality.

Diagnostic Issues

Laypeople sometimes conclude that psychopathy does not exist, confused by the fact that it is not listed in the fourth edition of the *Diagnostic and Statistical Manual of Mental Disorders* (*DSM-IV;* American Psychiatric Association, 1994) or the 10th edition of the *International Classification of Diseases* (*ICD-10;* World Health Organization, 1992). This is, of course, incorrect. As noted previously, at a conceptual or linguistic level, psychopathic personality disorder is synonymous with antisocial, dissocial, and sociopathic personality disorder; they are simply different terms for the same disorder (this is explicitly recognized in the *DSM-IV;* see American Psychiatric Association, 1994; p. 646). Numerous other terms have been used to refer to the same disorder, and Werlinder (1978, Appendix) has identified more than 175 of them. So, psychopathy *is* listed in the *DSM-IV,* where it is referred to as antisocial personality disorder, and in the *ICD-10,* where it is referred to as dissocial personality disorder.

At an operational level, it must be emphasized that various diagnostic criteria sets for psychopathic, antisocial, dissocial, and sociopathic personality disorder definitely are *not* equivalent. Perhaps the biggest difference is that diagnostic criteria

TABLE 6.1   *ICD-10* Criteria for Dissocial Personality Disorder

A. Callous unconcern for the feelings of others and lack of the capacity for empathy.
B. Gross and persistent attitude of irresponsibility and disregard for social norms, rules, and obligations.
C. Incapacity to maintain enduring relationships.
D. Very low tolerance to frustration and a low threshold for discharge of aggression, including violence.
E. Incapacity to experience guilt and to profit from experience, particularly punishment.
F. Marked proneness to blame others or to offer plausible rationalizations for the behavior bringing the subject into conflict with society.
G. Persistent irritability.

Source: Adapted from World Health Organization (1992). *International Classification of Diseases* (10th ed.). Geneva, Switzerland: Author.

for psychopathic or dissocial personality disorder typically include a broad range of interpersonal, affective, and behavioral symptoms (e.g., Cleckley, 1941; Hare, 1980, 1991; Hart, Cox, & Hare, 1995; World Health Organization, 1992). As an example, Table 6.1 summarizes the *ICD-10* diagnostic criteria for dissocial personality disorder. In contrast, diagnostic criteria for antisocial or sociopathic personality disorder tend to focus more narrowly on overt delinquent and criminal behavior (e.g., American Psychiatric Association, 1980, 1987, 1994; Feighner et al., 1972; Robins, 1966). As an example, Table 6.2 summarizes the *DSM-IV* criteria for antisocial personality disorder. The differences between these two diagnostic traditions are discussed at length elsewhere (Cunningham & Reidy, 1998; Hare, Hart, & Harpur, 1991; Hart & Hare, 1997; Lilienfeld, 1994; Widiger & Corbitt, 1995). Perhaps the most

TABLE 6.2   *DSM-IV* Criteria for Antisocial Personality Disorder

A. Antisocial behavior since age 15, as indicated by three or more of the following:

1. Repeated criminal acts.	5. Recklessness.
2. Deceitfulness.	6. Irresponsibility.
3. Impulsivity.	7. Lacks remorse.
4. Irritability and aggressiveness.	

B. Current age at least 18.

C. Conduct disorder before age 15, as indicated by clinically significant impairment in social, academic, or occupational functioning resulting from three or more of the following:

1. Bullied.	9. Destroyed property.
2. Fought.	10. Break and enter.
3. Used weapons.	11. Lied.
4. Cruel to people.	12. Stole.
5. Cruel to animals.	13. Stayed out late (before age 13).
6. Robbed.	
7. Forced sex on others.	14. Ran away from home.
8. Set fires.	15. Truant.

D. Occurrence of antisocial behavior not exclusively during the course of Schizophrenia or manic episodes.

Source: Adapted from American Psychiatric Association (1994). *Diagnostic and Statistical Manual of Mental Disorders* (4th ed.). Washington, DC: Author.

important consequence of the focus on delinquent and criminal behavior in diagnostic criteria sets for antisocial or sociopathic personality disorder is that they lack specificity (i.e., misconduct can be a manifestation of other forms of disorders as well), and this can lead to overdiagnosis in forensic settings and underdiagnosis in other settings. (This point is discussed explicitly in the *DSM-IV;* see American Psychiatric Association, 1994, p. 647; see also Hare, 1983, 1985; Hare et al., 1991; Widiger & Corbitt, 1995.)

Assessment Issues

The nature of assessment procedures should reflect the decision-making purpose for which the assessments will be used and the nature of the disorder being assessed. Such "goodness-of-fit" has been referred to as *method-function match* and *method-mode match,* respectively (Haynes, Richard, & Kubany, 1995).

Clinical or expert ratings of psychopathy have a better goodness-of-fit than other assessment methods when used in forensic decision making, as they permit the integration of diverse sources of information. The use of self-report methods (e.g., questionnaires, structured diagnostic interviews) or projective methods to assess psychopathy is potentially problematic, unless findings are subsequently confirmed through a review of information from other sources, such as collateral informants and official records.

Method-Function Match

Assessment procedures for psychopathy should take into account the special needs and requirements of forensic decision making. These have been discussed at length by others, both generally (e.g., Committee on Ethical Guidelines for Forensic Psychologists, 1991; Heilbrun, 1992; Melton, Petrila, Poythress, & Slobogin, 1997) and with respect to the assessment of personality disorders (e.g., Hart, 2001). One important legal issue is that assessment procedures should not rely unduly on uncorroborated statements made by the person being evaluated.

Three practical issues should also be kept in mind. First, assessment procedures should require minimal levels of cooperation. Contextual pressures encourage response distortion, particularly minimization and denial of psychopathic symptomatology. Acute and chronic mental disorders are common in forensic settings and it is not always possible to obtain informed consent from the individuals being assessed.

Of course, in cases where informed consent cannot be obtained from individuals to be assessed because they lack the mental capacity, clinicians may be legally and/or ethically required to obtain informed consent from substitute decision makers. In other cases, individuals who have the mental capacity to consent may refuse for a variety of reasons to participate in the clinical assessments. Individuals who refuse to participate in the assessments but who will nonetheless be assessed from collateral information should be told of this so that they can be informed of the assessment procedures before they refuse to participate. Informed consent requires that potential participants be informed of the nature and purpose of the assessment, the risks and benefits associated with participating and not participating in the assessment, the alternatives available to them, and who has access to the assessment findings (Ogloff, 1995).

Although clinicians typically should obtain informed consent from the persons being assessed, informed consent is not always legally required (e.g., in some court-ordered assessments or reviews of correctional files; see Ogloff, 1995; Schuller & Ogloff, 2001, pp. 19–20). Second, assessment procedures for psychopathy should require minimal levels of insight. Almost by definition, people suffering from personality disorders do not have sufficient insight into the impact of their behavior on others. This is particularly true for psychopathic individuals, whose symptoms may include affective deficits, including a severe lack of empathy. Third, assessment procedures for psychopathy should require minimal literacy skills. Forensic populations are characterized by low levels of educational achievement and a high prevalence of deficits in intellectual and neuropsychological functioning (e.g., Wilson & Herrnstein, 1985). Assessment procedures that rely on reading ability or require sustained attention are problematic for this reason.

Method-Mode Match

There are at least four important features of psychopathy that should be taken into account when assessing the disorder (Hart et al., 1995). First, psychopathy is associated with symptoms that fall into three distinct domains: interpersonal, affective, and behavioral (Cooke & Michie, 2001; Hare, 1991). A corollary of this is that assessment procedures sample systematically and comprehensively from these symptom domains, ideally providing separate measures of each. Second, psychopathy as a personality disorder is assumed to be reasonably stable throughout adulthood. One corollary of this assumption is that assessment procedures for psychopathy should have moderate to high temporal stability (i.e., test-retest reliability), even over lengthy periods of time. Another corollary is that assessment procedures for psychopathy should not be sensitive to the affective state of persons being evaluated (i.e., their mood at the time of assessment). Third, an important symptom of psychopathy is deceitfulness. A corollary of this is that assessment procedures for psychopathy should evaluate the extent to which a person characteristically lies and manipulates. Another is that procedures should attempt to minimize the extent to which deceitfulness interferes with the assessment of other psychopathic symptomatology. Fourth, psychopathy is associated with delinquency and criminality. There is, however, lack of consensus regarding the nature of this association. According to some, delinquency and criminality are a primary symptom of psychopathy; to others, they are an important secondary symptom or associated feature—perhaps even a consequence—of the disorder. Regardless, a corollary is that assessment procedures should be useful for making distinctions among offenders or patients in forensic settings; another is that assessment procedures should be related systematically to, but be distinct from, measures of criminality and delinquency.

REVIEW OF ASSESSMENT PROCEDURES

In this section, we review some commonly used procedures for the clinical-forensic assessment of psychopathy in adults. The procedures we discuss fall into three general categories: structured diagnostic interviews, self-report questionnaires and inventories, and expert rating scales. A comprehensive review of these procedures is beyond the scope of this chapter. These and other assessment methods are elaborated in detail in Volume 10 (*Assessment Psychology*) of this *Handbook*. The goal in the present discussion is to highlight their important strengths and weaknesses in light of the assessment issues discussed previously.

Structured Diagnostic Interviews

These procedures use interview schedules to gather information from the person being evaluated to make a diagnosis according to fixed and explicit criteria (e.g., Rogers, 1995). Commonly used structured diagnostic interviews for the assessment of psychopathy include the Structured Clinical Interview for *DSM-IV*, Axis II (SCID-II; First et al., 1995) and the International Personality Disorder Examination (IPDE; Loranger et al., 1994).

Structured Clinical Interview for DSM-IV

As its name implies, this interview was intended to assist in the diagnosis of *DSM-IV* personality disorders, including antisocial personality disorder. The SCID-II is intended to be administered by trained and experienced clinicians. The interview schedule contains a series of questions designed to tap each symptom of the various personality disorders. The questions are phrased so that they encourage respondents to acknowledge relatively minor adjustment problems; accordingly, clinicians ask the standard questions and, if the person admits to problems, they are free to probe or ask follow-up questions to confirm the presence and severity of symptoms. Consistent with this approach, evaluators can administer a self-report questionnaire to the person before the interview and then probe only those areas in which the person admits problems. Clinicians are expected to be familiar with the person's psychiatric history in advance, which assists in the differential diagnosis of *DSM-IV* Axis I and II disorders. It is possible, although not a requirement, to incorporate collateral information in a SCID-II assessment.

The SCID-II does not yield scores per se. Severity ratings for individual symptoms are used to diagnose the presence or absence of each personality disorder and can also be used to create symptom counts for each disorder. Including time spent taking a psychosocial history, overviewing mental disorder, and administering the self-report screening questionnaire, a SCID-II assessment requires approximately two to three hours to complete.

International Personality Disorder Examination

The IPDE was designed to permit the diagnosis of both *DSM-IV* and *ICD-10* personality disorders, including *DSM-IV* antisocial and *ICD-10* dissocial personality disorder. The IPDE is intended to be administered by trained and experienced clinicians. The interview schedule contains a series of general questions, organized thematically, that are designed to tap symptoms of the various personality disorders. Clinicians ask the standard questions and must follow up with a series of probes to confirm the presence and severity of symptoms. Each question is posed to every respondent. Prior to the interview proper, clinicians obtain an overview of the respondent's psychosocial history. The format of the IPDE encourages clinicians to incorporate collateral information in their symptom ratings. The IPDE severity ratings for individual symptoms can be used to diagnose the presence or absence of each personality disorder and to create symptom counts and dimensional ratings for each disorder.

Commentary

With respect to the assessment issues discussed previously, it is obvious that structured diagnostic interviews rely heavily on statements made by the respondent. This is particularly true for SCID-II assessments that use the self-report questionnaire as a screen. It is possible, though, to corroborate the respondent's statements by incorporating a review of collateral information in the assessment.

Structured diagnostic interviews require cooperation by the respondent. Most respondents who consent to undergo assessments are willing and able to answer questions about their psychosocial history. It is impossible to complete such interviews when the person refuses consent. Administration of a structured diagnostic interview requires relatively little insight on the part of the respondent. The ability of interviewers to ask extensive probe or follow-up questions to determine the severity of symptoms minimizes the chances that clinicians will overidentify individuals who satisfy the criteria. A greater concern is the possibility of failing to correctly identify individuals who satisfy the criteria due to simple denial of symptomatology, especially when the SCID-II self-report questionnaire is used as a screen. Review of collateral information can help to avoid this problem. Administration of a structured diagnostic interview does not require much in the way of literacy or intellectual ability on the part of the respondent (except for the self-report questionnaire of the SCID-II). A strength of the interviews is that administration can be spread across several sessions in cases where the respondent's attention or concentration is impaired without affecting the validity of the assessment results.

The content of structured diagnostic interviews is limited in the same way as the diagnostic criteria sets they are trying to evaluate. As measures of the *DSM-IV* antisocial personality disorder criteria and *ICD-10* dissocial personality disorder, for example, the SCID-II and IPDE fail to comprehensively assess many of the characteristics of psychopathy that clinicians and laypersons find central to the disorder (e.g., Davies & Feldman, 1981; Hare et al., 1991; Rogers, Dion, & Lynett, 1992; Rogers, Duncan, Lynett, & Sewell, 1994; Tennent, Tennent, Prins, & Bedford, 1990; Widiger & Corbitt, 1993). In particular, as measures of *DSM-IV* criteria, the SCID-II and IPDE underemphasize interpersonal characteristics such as manipulativeness and egocentricity and affective characteristics such as callousness and lack of empathy. As a measure of *ICD-10* criteria, the IPDE neglects characteristics of self-absorption, grandiosity, and smooth interpersonal style that is characterized by deceit, manipulation, and pathological lying. Neither the SCID-II nor the IPDE yields separate scores or indices for the individual symptom clusters, although both yield some kind of dimensional score related to global psychopathic symptomatology.

An important strength of diagnoses made using the SCID-II and IPDE is that they have adequate reliability, including test-retest reliability, and there is no indication that they are unduly influenced by mood at the time of assessment (e.g., First et al., 1995; Loranger et al., 1994). The SCID-II/ *DSM-IV* criteria include an item related to deceitfulness, but the IPDE/*ICD-10* criteria do not. SCID-II and IPDE assessments may be susceptible to response distortions on the part of the person being evaluated, especially when the self-report questionnaire is used as a preinterview screen in the case of the SCID-II. This susceptibility can be minimized, however, through the systematic integration of collateral information in the assessment process.

Finally, there is relatively little information concerning the association between criminality and SCID-II/*DSM-IV* or IPDE/*ICD-10* diagnoses. As noted previously, the *DSM-IV* criteria for antisocial personality disorder have been criticized for their lack of specificity in forensic settings. Epidemiological research in correctional and forensic psychiatric facilities using criteria on which the *DSM-IV* criteria were based indicates that a very high proportion of offenders and patients, typically between 50% and 80%, fulfill the criteria for antisocial personality disorder (e.g., Hare, 1983; Robins, Tipp, & Przybeck, 1991). Consequently, it is not possible to differentiate meaningfully among offenders or patients with respect to psychopathy in forensic settings using the SCID-II or IPDE. There is no systematic evidence that either diagnosis has prognostic significance with respect to future criminality or violence.

Self-Report Questionnaires and Inventories

These procedures require the person being evaluated to respond to a series of specific questions using a fixed response format. Usually, they are administered in written form, although it is possible in many cases to administer them orally or by means of audiocassettes. Commonly used questionnaires and inventories for the assessment of psychopathy include the second edition of the Minnesota Multiphasic Personality Inventory (MMPI-2; Butcher, Dahlstrom, Graham, Tellgen, & Kaemmer, 1989), the third edition of the Millon Clinical Multiaxial Inventory (MCMI-III; Millon, Davis, & Millon, 1997), and the Personality Assessment Inventory (PAI; Morey, 1991). Several promising questionnaires specifically designed to assess psychopathy have been developed (e.g., Blackburn & Fawcett, 1999; Gustaffson & Ritzer, 1995; Hare, 1985; Levenson, Kiehl, & Fitzpatrick, 1995; Lilienfeld & Andrews, 1996), but they are not reviewed here because they are not extensively used in clinical-forensic contexts. Some evidence suggests that, among forensic samples, self-report measures of psychopathy are not related to measures of physical violence (e.g., Edens, Poythress, & Lilienfeld, 1999) and crime severity (e.g., Rogers, Gillis, & Dickens, 1989).

Minnesota Multiphasic Personality Inventory

The MMPI-2 is a multiscale self-report inventory intended to be a broad-band measure of personality and psychopathology. All 567 items on the MMPI-2 are declarative statements phrased in the first person singular. Respondents are asked to indicate whether the statements are true or false, or mostly true or false, as applied to them. The MMPI-2 takes approximately 1 to 1.5 hours to complete (see Pope, Butcher, & Seelen, 1993, p. 14), and according to the MMPI-2 manual, requires "an eighth grade reading level to comprehend the content of all the MMPI-2 items and to respond to them appropriately" (Butcher et al., 1989, p. 14; see also p. 1). The MMPI-2 has been translated into a variety of languages, and norms are available for large, representative samples of community residents.

Two clinical scales from the MMPI-2—the Psychopathic Deviate (*Pd*) scale and the Hypomania (*Ma*) scale—have been used singly and in combination to assess characteristics of psychopathy. The MMPI-2 has a number of validity scales, in addition to the clinical scales, that are relevant for conducting clinical-forensic assessments. Scores on the Variable Response Inconsistency Scale (VRIN) and True Response Inconsistency Scale (TRIN) validity scales, for example, become elevated when many pairs of items similar in content are answered inconsistently. The *L*, *F*, and *K* validity scales are also useful for assessing protocol credibility and response bias in forensic contexts (Pope et al., 1993). Items were selected for most MMPI-2 clinical scales by statistically contrasting for each item the response rate from a clinical group of interest with the response rate from a comparison group or groups (Hathaway & McKinley, 1940). The clinical group that was used to construct the original MMPI *Pd* scale was composed of adolescents, most of whom were females with a long history of minor delinquency, diagnosed as "psychopathic personality, asocial and amoral type." McKinley and Hathaway (1944) acknowledge that "no major criminal types" (p. 167) were involved in the construction of the MMPI *Pd* scale. It should be recognized that, in addition to characteristics of clinical interest, this empirical approach to scale construction selects items that reflect sample characteristics such as socioeconomic background and education (Wiggins, 1973).

Millon Clinical Multiaxial Inventory

The MCMI-III is a multiscale self-report inventory intended "to provide information to clinicians . . . who must make assessments and treatment decisions about individuals with emotional and interpersonal difficulties" (Millon et al., 1997, p. 5). It was constructed using a combination of rational/theoretical and empirical approaches. The MCMI-III contains 175 items, all declarative statements phrased in the first person singular. Respondents are asked to rate the degree to which they agree with the statements using a true/false response format. Administration of the MCMI-III takes approximately 30 minutes, and self-administration requires at least an eighth-grade reading ability.

The items form a number of overlapping scales and indices. Four scales are used to assess response styles that may potentially invalidate MCMI-III profiles: the Validity Index (Scale V), which measures "bizarre or highly improbable" (p. 118) responses; the Disclosure Index (Scale X), which measures the tendency to provide self-revealing or secretive responses; the Desirability Index (Scale Y), which measures the tendency to provide overly favorable responses; and the Debasement Index (Scale Z), which measures the tendency to overreport personal difficulties. Scales 6A and 6B were designed to assess, respectively, antisocial personality disorder and sadistic (or aggressive) personality disorder. Norms for the MCMI-III were derived from a large sample of people assessed or treated in a wide range of inpatient and outpatient mental health settings. Norms for community residents are not available.

Personality Assessment Inventory

The PAI is a multiscale self-report inventory intended to measure "critical clinical variables" (Morey, 1991, p. 1). It comprises 344 items, all declarative statements phrased in the first person singular. Respondents are asked to rate the degree to which the statements are true of them on a 4-point scale (1 = very true, 2 = mainly true, 3 = slightly true, 4 = false). Administration of the PAI takes approximately one hour. Self-administration requires approximately grade 4 reading ability; a Spanish translation is available. The items form a number of nonoverlapping scales, including 4 to assess response bias, 11 to assess clinical syndromes, 5 to assess treatment-related characteristics, and 2 to assess interpersonal style. Norms for the PAI were based on a large, representative sample of community residents and supplemented with norms from clinical settings.

One scale, Antisocial Features (ANT), was designed to assess "personality and behavioral features relevant to the constructs of antisocial personality and psychopathy" (Morey, 1991, p. 18). Three subscales measure distinct facets of psychopathic symptomatology. Antisocial Behaviors (ANT-A) taps a history of conduct problems and criminality. Egocentricity (ANT-E) measures self-centered, callous, and remorseless behavior, or "the pathological egocentricity and narcissism often thought to lie at the core of this disorder" (p. 72). Stimulus Seeking (ANT-S) reflects "a tendency to seek thrills and excitement and low boredom tolerance" (p. 72).

Commentary

Self-reports, by definition, rely only on statements made by the respondent. There is no opportunity to use collateral information to corroborate the respondent's statements when scoring self-reports.

Self-reports require considerable cooperation. Respondents who consent must be willing and able to answer a large number of specific questions, some of which may strike them as odd or irrelevant to the assessment. Administration of self-reports requires some, albeit limited, insight on the part of the respondent. This is particularly true for self-report tests that include items that tap interpersonal and affective symptoms, which are less concrete and specific than items that tap behavioral symptoms. Administration (especially self-administration) of self-report measures requires substantially intact literacy or intellectual ability on the part of the respondent. Self-report measures vary according to recommended minimum level of reading ability (e.g., fourth grade for the PAI, eighth grade for the MMPI-2) and to the degree of sustained attention (e.g., 175 items on the MCMI-III, 567 items on the MMPI-2) necessary to complete them.

The content of self-reports typically is restricted, focusing primarily on behavioral features of psychopathy. The exception is the PAI ANT scale, which contains multiple subscales to assess various symptom domains. Some self-reports, in particular, the MMPI-2 *Pd* scale, contain items whose content seems either irrelevant to or negatively associated with psychopathy. Self-report scales have temporal stability that ranges from adequate to impressive. From data presented in the test manuals, however, it appears that scores on psychopathy-related scales often are moderately or moderately-to-highly correlated with scales of negative affect on the same inventory. This raises the possibility that observed temporal unreliability on the psychopathy scales is the result of contamination by mood state at the time of assessment rather than true fluctuations in psychopathic symptomatology.

Most self-reports contain questions related to deceitfulness, although they may be quite simplistic in nature (e.g., "As a teenager, did you lie a lot?"). Many self-reports, including all those reviewed here, contain scales or indices to evaluate response distortion. Such scales evaluate only the most common forms of response distortion, such as malingering of general psychopathology or unduly positive self-presentation; they do not evaluate more specific or sophisticated distortion,

such as malingering of specific mental disorder or minimization of responsibility for antisocial behavior. Furthermore, self-reports may be unable to control for the impact of response distortion on the assessment of psychopathy. As a consequence, evaluators may be able to determine that respondents were engaging in response distortion, but are unable to use this information to assist in their assessment of psychopathy.

The MMPI-2, MCMI-III, and PAI were *not* designed for use in forensic settings, but correctional norms of some type either exist or are in development for all three inventories. There is not a large and systematic literature involving self-report measures that has consistently found associations with antisocial, criminal, and violent behaviors among offenders or patients in forensic settings. Despite this, some research concerning the validity of self-report measures has accumulated in forensic samples (e.g., Bayer, Bonta, & Motiuk, 1985; Hart, Forth, & Hare, 1991; Salekin, Rogers, & Sewell, 1997). For example, Edens and colleagues (Edens, Hart, Johnson, Johnson, & Olver, 2000) examined the correlation between ANT total scores on the PAI and total scores on the PCL-R and the PCL-SV in two different forensic samples. Even though the correlations were among the highest found in a clinical setting between a self-report measure of psychopathy and the PCL (i.e., $r = .54$ with the PCL-SV; $r = .40$ with the PCL-R), diagnostic agreement was only low to moderate. Similarly, Hart and colleagues (1991) examined the correlation between total scores on Scale 6A of the MCMI-II (Millon, 1987) and total scores on the PCL-R in a large sample of offenders. Again, even though the correlation was high ($r = .45$), diagnostic agreement between the measures was low ($\kappa < .25$).

Expert Rating Scales

These procedures are multi-item rating scales. Trained observers rate the severity of symptoms based on all available clinical data (e.g., interview with the respondent, review of case history information, interviews with collateral informants). The PCL and PCL-R fall into this category, as does the Screening Version of the PCL-R (PCL-SV; Hart et al., 1995).

Revised Psychopathy Checklist

The original PCL (Hare, 1980) was a 22-item rating scale, later revised and shortened to 20 items (PCL-R; Hare, 1991). The PCL-R was designed for use in adult male forensic populations, with some items being scored entirely or primarily on the basis of criminal records. Items are scored on a 3-point

TABLE 6.3   Items and Factors in the Hare Psychopathy Checklist-Revised

		Factor Solutions	
Item	Description	Two[a]	Three[b]
1.	Glibness/superficial charm.	1	Interpersonal.
2.	Grandiose sense of self worth.	1	Interpersonal.
3.	Need for stimulation/proneness to boredom.	2	Behavioral.
4.	Pathological lying.	1	Interpersonal.
5.	Conning/manipulative.	1	Interpersonal.
6.	Lack of remorse or guilt.	1	Affective.
7.	Shallow affect.	1	Affective.
8.	Callous/lack of empathy.	1	Affective.
9.	Parasitic lifestyle.	2	Behavioral.
10.	Poor behavioral controls.	2	—
11.	Promiscuous sexual behavior.	—	—
12.	Early behavioral problems.	2	—
13.	Lack of realistic, long-term goals.	2	Behavioral.
14.	Impulsivity.	2	Behavioral.
15.	Irresponsibility.	2	Behavioral.
16.	Failure to accept responsibility for own actions.	1	Affective.
17.	Many short-term marital relationships.	—	—
18.	Juvenile delinquency.	2	—
19.	Revocation of conditional release.	2	—
20.	Criminal versatility.	—	—

Note: — = item does not load on any factor.
[a]See Hare et al. (1990).
[b]See Cooke & Michie (2001).
Source: Adapted from Hare (1991).

scale (0 = item doesn't apply; 1 = item applies somewhat; 2 = item definitely applies). Table 6.3 lists the PCL-R items, which are defined in detail in the test manual. Total scores can range from 0 to 40; scores of 30 or higher are considered diagnostic of psychopathy. Earlier analyses identified two factors underlying the PCL-R items, one reflecting interpersonal and affective features, and the other reflecting impulsive and antisocial behavior (Hare et al., 1990). More recent research using confirmatory factor analysis has identified distinct interpersonal, affective, and behavioral factors whose measurement is uncontaminated by items reflecting antisocial behavior (Cooke & Michie, 2001). There are now hundreds of published articles reporting research using the PCL-R, ranging from basic research on etiology to applied research examining the use of the test in violence risk assessment (for a summary, see Cooke et al., 1998). Psychometric analyses based on classical test theory and item response theory indicate that the PCL-R has excellent psychometric properties (Cooke & Michie, 1997; Hare et al., 1990).

Normative data presented in the PCL-R manual (Hare, 1991) comprise ratings from seven samples of offenders ($N = 1,192$) and four samples of forensic patients ($N = 440$), all adult men (age 16 or older) from institutions in Canada, the United States, and the United Kingdom. Translations of the PCL-R into more than a dozen languages are completed or

in progress, and research supports its cross-cultural validity (Cooke & Michie, 1999; Hare, Clarke, Grann, & Thornton, 2000). Conducting a psychosocial history interview and reviewing case history information to facilitate scoring of the PCL-R typically requires at least 90 to 120 minutes; however, if the PCL-R is added to a standard assessment battery, which typically includes an interview and review of case history, completion may require 10 or 15 minutes. Although it is standard clinical practice to complete the PCL-R from both interview and collateral file information, it is possible to complete without an interview if extensive collateral information of high quality is available (see Hare, 1991, p. 6). File-only ratings are sometimes conducted if the person refuses or is unable to consent and if all appropriate ethical and legal requirements have been satisfied. When individuals refuse to be interviewed for court-mandated assessments but nonetheless are assessed exclusively from collateral file information, they should be told of this in advance of the assessments. This procedure allows individuals to be fully informed when they refuse to participate in clinical interviews.

Psychopathy Checklist-Screening Version

The PCL-SV is a 12-item scale derived from the PCL-R. It was designed for use in adult populations, regardless of gender, psychiatric status, or criminal history. Table 6.4 lists the PCL-SV items, which are defined in detail in the test manual. Scoring of the PCL-SV requires less information, and less detailed information, than does the PCL-R; further, the PCL-SV can be scored even when the person does not have a criminal record or when the complete record is not available. Items are scored on the same 3-point scale used for the PCL-R. Total scores can range from 0 to 24; scores of 12 or higher indicate "possible psychopathy," and scores of 18 or higher indicate "definite psychopathy." Psychometric analyses indicate that the PCL-SV has excellent structural properties and is strongly related to the PCL-R (Cooke, Michie, Hart, & Hare, 1999; Hart et al., 1995). Also, the PCL-SV has a factor structure strongly parallel to that of the PCL-R (Cooke & Michie, 2001).

Normative data presented in the PCL-SV manual comprise ratings from numerous samples of male and female

TABLE 6.4   PCL-SV Criteria for Psychopathy

Part 1	Part 2
1. Superficial.	7. Impulsive.
2. Grandiose.	8. Poor behavioral controls.
3. Deceitful.	9. Lacks goals.
4. Lacks remorse.	10. Irresponsible.
5. Lacks empathy.	11. Adolescent antisocial behavior.
6. Doesn't accept responsibility.	12. Adult antisocial behavior.

Source: Adapted from Hart et al. (1995).

offenders, forensic psychiatric patients, civil psychiatric patients, and university students. Translations of the PCL-SV into several languages are completed or in progress. Conducting a psychosocial history interview and reviewing case history information to facilitate scoring of the PCL-SV typically takes at least 60 to 90 minutes; however, if it is added to a standard assessment battery, which typically includes an interview and review of case history, completion may require 5 or 10 minutes. As with the PCL-R, it is possible to complete the PCL-SV without an interview, provided that all ethical and legal requirements have been satisfied.

Commentary

Expert rating scales do not rely heavily on uncorroborated statements made by the respondent. Indeed, under some conditions, it is possible to score the PCL-R and PCL-SV without conducting an interview.

Expert rating scales require relatively little cooperation. Most respondents who consent to undergo assessment are willing and able to answer questions about their psychosocial history. Administration of expert rating scales requires relatively little insight on the part of the respondent. Heavy reliance on collateral information and the ability of interviewers to ask extensive probe or follow-up questions to determine the severity of symptoms minimize the chances that clinicians will over- or underidentify individuals who satisfy the criteria. Administration of expert rating scales does not require much in the way of literacy or intellectual ability on the part of the respondent. A strength of the interviews is that, in cases where the respondent's attention or concentration is impaired, administration can be spread across several sessions without affecting the validity of the assessment results.

Expert rating scales have good coverage of all symptom domains of psychopathy. They can be used to obtain separate scores or indices for symptom clusters, as well as dimensional and categorical scores related to global psychopathic symptomatology. Expert rating scales have reliability that is adequate or better, including test-retest reliability, and there has been no indication that they are unduly influenced by mood at the time of assessment (e.g., Cooke & Michie, 1997; Cooke et al., 1999; Hare, 1991; Hare et al., 1990; Hart et al., 1995). The PCL-R and PCL-SV contain items directly related to deceitfulness. Their susceptibility to response distortion is minimal as a result of the systematic integration of collateral information in the assessment process. Finally, there is good information concerning the association between criminality and expert ratings scales. The PCL-R and PCL-SV can be used to make meaningful distinctions among people, even in samples of serious and persistent offenders. In samples in which the prevalence of antisocial personality disorder

according to *DSM-III* or *DSM-III-R* criteria is between 50% and 80%, the prevalence of psychopathy according to PCL-R criteria is approximately 20% to 25% (Hare, 1991). Also, there is a large body of research indicating that psychopathy is a robust risk factor for criminality and violence (Hart, 1998; Hart & Hare, 1997; Hemphill, Hare, & Wong, 1998; Salekin, Rogers, & Sewell, 1996).

IMPORTANT ISSUES

Psychopathy as a Legal Concept

The term psychopathy has been used throughout this chapter to refer to a psychological, not a legal, concept (Lyon & Ogloff, 2000; Ogloff & Lyon, 1998). This distinction is important because, although the term psychopathy may be used in a variety of legal statutes (e.g., in "sexual psychopath" legislation), these statutes often define and use the term in a manner that bears little relationship to the concept discussed here. Simply diagnosing someone as a "psychopath" does not necessarily mean that the person will satisfy the legal criteria for psychopathy or that the diagnosis will be relevant for the purposes of the assessment (Hart, 2001). It is therefore important that clinicians first identify the purpose of the assessment; that they be familiar with the relevant law, legal issues, and legal standards for the task at hand; and that they determine whether—and if so, how—an assessment of psychopathy is relevant to the legal issue or issues. Ogloff and Lyon have stated: "In many cases the precise 'label' given to a defendant is irrelevant because it is the person's behavior and cognitive processes and their implications for the specific legal issues in question that is critical for the law" (p. 411). Put another way, diagnoses of psychopathy typically are not relevant to the law, but a consideration of the cognitive and behavioral processes of psychopaths that bear on the legal issues are.

Psychopathy in Childhood and Adolescence

For most people, the major features of personality, normal or abnormal, are evident in childhood or adolescence. This is as true for traits related to psychopathy as it is for those related to other personality disorders. Indeed, there has been some research on psychopathy-related traits in childhood and adolescence (e.g., Barry et al., 2000; Forth, Hart, & Hare, 1990; Lynam, 1997), sometimes using measures derived from or inspired by the PCL. It is important to recognize that there is no clear consensus among developmental psychopathologists that personality disorder in general, or psychopathy in particular, exists in childhood or adolescence (see Edens, Skeem,

Cruise, & Cauffman, 2001; Vincent & Hart, in press). First, it has been argued that one's "true" personality does not crystallize or stabilize for some years after the maturational changes (both biological and social) that follow puberty. Second, even if personality disorder does exist in childhood or adolescence, it will not be manifested as it is in adulthood. For example, it is not until late adolescence or early adulthood that people enter into important social roles and obligations, such as employment, marital relationships, and parenthood, and have the opportunity to succeed or fail in them. Similarly, how would one assess a symptom such as "glibness and superficial charm" among children? Third, it is difficult to determine the extent to which a personality feature is traitlike—that is, stable across time and contexts—in people who are still young.

Research to date has confirmed that it is possible to assess psychopathy-related traits in childhood and adolescence with adequate interrater reliability, and that the associations among these traits may have important parallels to those observed in adults; the psychopathy-related traits are also associated with antisocial behavior in ways parallel to that found in adults (for a review, see Forth & Burke, 1998). So, there are reasonable grounds to suspect that we can assess something in childhood or adolescence that looks, at least superficially, similar to psychopathy in adulthood. We cannot, however, confirm this suspicion absent a clear demonstration from longitudinal research that the traits persist into adulthood. It may be that psychopathy-related traits disappear by adulthood as a result of maturation or other factors, and it is also possible that these traits emerge in early adulthood for some individuals. There is simply no good evidence that we are able to identify "psychopathic children" or "fledgling psychopaths" (see Lynam, 1996).

It is critical to continue research in this area. If it turns out that we are able to identify children or adolescents on a developmental trajectory toward adult psychopathy, then perhaps it will be possible to develop early intervention programs that prevent or reduce symptomology (e.g., Frick & Ellis, 1999; Gresham, Lane, & Lambros, 2000). Investigators should keep in mind, however, potential ethical problems (e.g., Edens et al., 2001; Ogloff & Lyon, 1998). The procedures for assessing psychopathy among children have received little validation among independent investigators.

Psychopathy and Violence Risk

The association between psychopathy and criminal behavior, as well as the appropriate use of psychopathy in violence risk assessments, has been discussed at length elsewhere (Hart, 1998; Hart & Hare, 1997; Hemphill, Hare, & Wong, 1998; Salekin et al., 1996). Here, we remind readers that

psychopathy may be sufficient in some cases to conclude that an individual is at high risk for future violence, but it is never a necessary factor. That is, there are many ways that someone can be at high risk for violence that are unrelated to psychopathy (Hart, 1998). This is especially true when examining risk for specific forms of violence, such as spousal assault, stalking, and sexual violence, where violence may be related more to disturbances of normal attachment processes rather than the pathological lack of attachment associated with psychopathy.

It is also important to note that there is no good scientific evidence (contrary to some claims; e.g., Harris, Rice, & Quinsey, 1993) that diagnoses or traits of psychopathy, including scores on the PCL-R, can be used either on their own or in combination with other variables to estimate the absolute likelihood of future violence for a given individual with any reasonable degree of scientific or professional certainty. This is particularly important given the practice of some professionals to use diagnoses of psychopathy or antisocial personality disorder to support the conclusion that an individual is "more likely than not" (i.e., more than 50% likely) to commit acts of future violence or sexual violence. In some jurisdictions, such a conclusion can be used to justify indeterminate civil commitment as a sexual predator (e.g., Janus, 2000) or even capital punishment (Cunningham & Reidy, 1998, 1999). Such a practice is simply unfounded and unethical at the present time.

Precision of Measurement

All diagnoses and test scores are imprecise, that is, associated with measurement error. For example, with respect to the PCL-R, the standard error of measurement (SEM) is a statistical index of the extent to which raters would be expected to disagree concerning a particular individual's score. The SEM on the PCL-R is approximately 3.25 points (see Hare, 1991, p. 36). This means that when two reasonably competent raters conduct independent assessments of the same people at around the same time, we expect that in approximately 68% of cases their scores will be within 3 points of each other (i.e., 1 SEM), and in approximately 95% of cases their scores will be within 6 points (i.e., 1.96 SEM). Factors such as the lack of an interview, inadequate collateral information, and even poor training of evaluators may increase measurement error.

The important point here is that psychologists should qualify their conclusions in light of measurement error. For example, the cutoff for diagnosing psychopathy on the PCL-R is 30 and higher (Hare, 1991, p. 17). When an individual's total score on the PCL-R is, say, 31 or 28, then the evaluator should be careful in any report to admit that there is some possibility that other competent evaluators might disagree about the individual's diagnosis (Salekin et al., 1996).

Because of the uncertainty associated with categorical diagnoses, evaluators should consider interpreting PCL-R scores dimensionally, that is, by characterizing the individual's trait strength relative to some comparison group.

Association among Assessment Procedures

Even though we have emphasized throughout this chapter the conceptual differences among criteria sets for assessing psychopathy, readers should keep in mind that the empirical associations between them are nonetheless quite strong. The correlations between PCL-R Total scores and antisocial personality disorder diagnoses or symptom counts typically are large in magnitude (approximately $r = .55$ to $.65$), and diagnostic agreement between the procedures typically is fair to good, even in forensic settings (e.g., Hare, 1980, 1985; Widiger et al., 1996). However, the disorders have different prevalence rates. According to *DSM* criteria, anywhere between 50% and 80% of offenders and forensic patients are diagnosed with antisocial personality disorder, whereas only approximately 15% to 30% of the same people meet the PCL-R criteria for psychopathy (Cunningham & Reidy, 1998; Hare, 1983, 1985; Hare et al., 1990; Robins et al., 1991). Another important finding is that the link between psychopathy and antisocial personality disorder is asymmetric. Most people (approximately 90%) diagnosed as psychopaths by PCL criteria meet the criteria for antisocial personality disorder, whereas a minority (approximately 30%) of those with antisocial personality disorder meet PCL criteria for psychopathy (e.g., Hart & Hare, 1989).

Several studies have found low to moderate correlations (typically between $r = .30$ and $r = .45$) between PCL diagnoses and popular self-report measures of psychopathy (e.g., Cooney, Kadden, & Litt, 1990; Hare, 1985, 1991; Hart et al., 1991). These results are not simply the result of method variance, as the correlations among self-reports are as low as the correlations between self-reports and clinical diagnoses. Further, self-report scales of psychopathy tend to be biased in their assessment of psychopathy, correlating more highly with social deviance aspects of psychopathy (as measured by Factor 2 of the PCL) than with the interpersonal and affective features (as measured by Factor 1; e.g., Harpur, Hare, & Hakstian, 1989; Hart et al., 1991). This may reflect a bias in the content of self-reports, as suggested above, but may also represent a tendency for psychopaths to be poor observers or reporters of their interpersonal and emotional styles.

Psychopathy among Various Cultural Groups

Until recently, there has been little systematic and sustained research examining the influence of race and culture on the reliability, validity, and psychometric properties of the PCL (see also Cunningham & Reidy, 1998). Kosson, Smith, and Newman (1990) conducted one of the earliest studies examining the influence of race on PCL scores. These authors, who used the original 22-item version and not the 20-item version of the PCL currently in use, concluded that "the overall pattern of results [among African American and White offenders] contains more parallels than disparities" (p. 257). There were some differences between African Americans and Whites, however. Compared with Whites, African Americans obtained PCL scores that were on average 2.3 points higher and displayed smaller corrected item-to-total correlations for 2 of the 22 items (Previous diagnosis as a psychopath [or similar], Pathological lying and deception), and the congruence coefficient between African Americans and Whites was low for PCL Factor 1, suggesting the factor structure found among samples of White male offenders (Harpur, Hakstian, & Hare, 1988) did not parallel those found in their sample. Despite these differences, readers should recognize that Kosson et al. could not rule out the influence of rater bias on their results because all of their raters were White. Further, the authors had a reasonably small sample (i.e., $n = 124$) of African American offenders with which to make psychometric comparisons.

More recently, researchers have been using item response theory (IRT) analyses to investigate the psychometric properties of the PCL (e.g., Cooke & Michie, 1997). IRT is a statistical procedure for examining psychometric properties of test items that theoretically results in analyses independent of the particular items administered and samples studied (Henard, 2000). Cooke et al. (1999) outline a number of important advantages of IRT analyses, and Cooke (1996) argues that IRT approaches are particularly well suited for conducting cross-cultural research with the PCL. Cooke, Kosson, and Michie (2001) applied IRT analyses to a sample of White and African American adult male inmates. They concluded that, although 5 of the 20 PCL-R items had significant differences in item performance between the African American and the White offenders, these differences were small in magnitude and tended to cancel each other out when PCL items were summed together to form total scores. Cooke et al. also conducted confirmatory factor analyses and failed to find the difference in factor structure between African Americans and Whites reported earlier by Kosson et al. (1990). Taken together, these authors concluded that there are few differences between African American and White offenders in terms of item functioning and that the PCL-R has similar psychometric properties among both African American offenders and White offenders. Of course, in addition to these psychometric analyses of PCL items, validation studies need to be done to establish the clinical utility of the PCL among a variety of cultural groups. Recent research concerning recidivism among African American offenders yields findings that are similar to those among White offenders. That is, inmates with high PCL scores are convicted at higher and faster rates than are inmates with low PCL scores, and these results are particularly marked for violent offences (Hemphill, Newman, & Hare, 2001).

RECOMMENDATIONS FOR PRACTICE

In this section, we identify a number of issues that arise as part of the clinical-forensic assessment of psychopathy and make recommendations for dealing with them. Some of the points raised are relevant to the clinical-forensic assessment of *all* personality disorders (e.g., Hart, 2001); others are unique to psychopathy (e.g., Hare, 1998). Note that some sections below have been adapted or excerpted from Hart (2001).

Failure to Use Accepted Assessment Procedures

Because forensic mental health testimony can have significant impact on individual and collective freedoms, the standards of practice in forensic psychology must be higher than in regular clinical practice. One common mistake in clinical-forensic practice is the failure to use, or the misuse of, accepted assessment procedures. Forensic psychologists who testify about the assessment of psychopathy should expect to be confronted with opinions from other experts or with authoritative treatises regarding recommended practice. For example, it would be easy for a competent lawyer to attack the credibility of an expert who assessed psychopathy in a criminal defendant relying solely on self-report inventories. There are at least three concerns here. One is that a clinical interview is the basic method for assessing *any* form of mental disorder, and triers of fact may be justifiably concerned by diagnoses that are not based on standard procedures. The second is that, arguably, self-report inventories constitute a series of uncorroborated statements made by the accused.

Some investigators argue, because of the way the MMPI/MMPI-2 was constructed (i.e., items were selected if they statistically differentiated clinical from comparison groups), that independent corroboration of responses is irrelevant to the interpretive significance of MMPI/MMPI-2 scale elevations. It should be emphasized, however, that it is impossible to know whether items included in each clinical scale were statistically selected because they reflect characteristics of clinical interest or instead reflect sample characteristics largely irrelevant to clinical interpretation (e.g., see Wiggins, 1973). Further, items that are purportedly "subtle" in content (i.e., that reliably differentiate clinical from comparison groups but that do not clearly reflect characteristics of the clinical group of interest) may be less clinically discriminating, and hence clinically useful, than items that are "obvious" in content (i.e., that clearly reflect characteristics of the clinical group of interest; for a discussion, see Graham, 1999, pp. 186–187). Taken together, these findings suggest that independent corroboration of responses may be clinically important when interpreting the meaning of MMPI/MMPI-2 scales, particularly in forensic settings.

The scales designed to detect response distortion incorporated in most self-report inventories do not obviate this fact. Finally, there is no body of research supporting the concurrent validity of self-report inventories with respect to clinical diagnoses of psychopathy in forensic settings. The little evidence that does exist suggests their concurrent validity is moderate at best (e.g., Edens et al., 2000; Hare, 1991; Hart et al., 1991).

Improper Reliance on Scientific Literature

Forensic psychologists should make clear when their testimony is based on established scientific principles and findings and when it is based on professional experience. Unfortunately, it is common for psychologists to fail to cite, or to cite improperly, relevant scientific literature when forming their opinions. For example, the consistent body of literature that supports the use of psychopathy assessments as a reliable indicator of a variety of antisocial, criminal, and violent behaviors is based on research conducted using the PCL (Hart & Hare, 1997; Hemphill, Hare, et al., 1998; Salekin et al., 1996). It is therefore inappropriate to cite research based on the PCL to support a professional opinion in which the patient was assessed using some other measure or set of diagnostic criteria (Hare, 1998). Findings generated from PCL assessments may not generalize to other assessment procedures, and a lack of generalizability from the PCL to other procedures seems likely given the low to moderate correspondence among different measures of psychopathy.

Training

Psychopathy assessments involve considerable clinical judgment. To adequately rate most PCL items, clinicians typically must conduct a comprehensive interview, review extensive collateral information, consider behaviors across time and multiple domains, assess the credibility of and differentially weigh many sources of information, reconcile discrepancies, and arrive at a single score. Adequate training and experience concerning the proper use of the PCL is essential for clinicians who conduct forensic assessments.

Although this point seems obvious, particularly in forensic contexts, where important clinical decisions are made and lives may be greatly affected, Hare (1998) has amply documented a number of egregious examples concerning the misuse of the PCL. It is important to recognize that clinicians who wish to refer to the large body of empirical literature concerning the PCL to support their decision to use this instrument must complete the PCL in a manner consistent with the way in which the reliability and validity information was obtained. Clinicians who fail to adhere to the scoring procedures outlined in the respective manuals or who routinely obtain scores that are markedly inconsistent with those obtained by experienced raters may be subject to ethical complaints and professional liability. Given that the PCL is a psychological test, users should be careful to use and interpret the instrument for the purposes for which it was intended and validated (American Educational Research Association, American Psychological Association, & National Council on Measurement in Education, 1999). This means that test users constantly need to keep apprised of recent developments, research studies, and the appropriate uses of the PCL.

Consider Other Assessment Findings

Psychopathy is only one factor, albeit an important one, that is often considered when conducting a comprehensive forensic assessment. In addition to interpreting the meaning of PCL ratings, decision-makers routinely should consider other psychological test scores and collateral information from a broad range of sources. Inmates, correctional employees, and parole board members sometimes comment on the heavy weight that is attached to PCL scores when clinical decisions are made. The practice of giving excessive weight in clinical decision-making contexts to PCL scores may be undesirable and concerning if it is widespread.

It is true that the PCL is among the most robust measures currently available in the area of risk assessment of violence and that it consistently emerges among the strongest risk variables in recidivism studies conducted in a variety of forensic (e.g., Harris et al., 1993) and civil psychiatric (Steadman et al., 2000) settings. Hart (1998) has even argued that "psychopathy is such a robust and important risk factor for violence that failure to consider it may constitute professional negligence" (p. 133). Nonetheless, to make decisions based solely on PCL scores sometimes can lead to misleading conclusions because, although high scores on the PCL are associated with high risk to violently reoffend, low scores on the PCL are not necessarily associated with low risk to violently reoffend. It is not uncommon for some groups of sexual offenders who might be at high risk to reoffend to receive PCL scores and prevalence rates that are substantially lower than those typically found among normative samples of adult male offenders. Porter et al. (2000), for example, found that 6.3% of extrafamilial child molesters received PCL-R scores $\geq$ 30. This percentage contrasts with 22.9% of a normative sample of male prison inmates (Hare, 1991), 35.9% of rapists, and 64% of mixed rapists and child molesters (Porter et al., 2000). Despite having PCL scores that are low on average, many child molesters still pose a significant risk of sexual recidivism decades after release (Rice & Harris, 1997). To summarize, we argue that clinicians who conduct risk assessments and other types of forensic assessments should routinely administer the PCL but should not uncritically rely solely on PCL scores to guide their decision making.

Categorical versus Dimensional Models of Personality Disorder

There is considerable debate in the scientific literature concerning the appropriateness of categorical versus dimensional models of personality disorder (Widiger & Sanderson, 1995), including psychopathy (e.g., Harris, Rice, & Quinsey, 1994; Lilienfeld, 1994; Rogers & Dion, 1991). To summarize, the categorical model assumes that personality disorder symptomatology can be defined in terms of a small number of "types" that are more or less independent of each other. Each type is characterized by a specific set of symptoms, and people with a given type of personality disorder are assumed to be a relatively homogeneous group. Both the *DSM-IV* and the *ICD-10* rely on a categorical model for the diagnosis of personality disorder. In contrast, the dimensional model assumes that personality disorder symptomatology can be well described in terms of relative standing on a small number of global traits. The PCL-R and related tests are based on the dimensional model.

Forensic psychologists should be prepared to acknowledge both the strengths and the limitations of the measurement models on which their assessments of psychopathy are based and the consequent impact on their opinions. The categorical model is commonly used in clinical practice and has been a focus of considerable research. This widespread acceptance is compelling to laypeople when they attempt to judge the credibility of a professional opinion, even if it is considered weak evidence of credibility in the scientific community. As a consequence, forensic psychologists whose opinions regarding psychopathy are based solely on dimensional models should be prepared to defend their "unusual" practice by outlining the clear advantages of the dimensional approach.

The High Prevalence of Personality Disorder

Regardless of whether forensic psychologists adopt a categorical or a dimensional model, their assessments are complicated by the high prevalence of personality disorders in forensic settings. According to epidemiological research, between 50% and 80% of all incarcerated adult offenders meet the diagnostic criteria for antisocial personality disorder (Hare, 1983; Robins et al., 1991); if one considers *all* the personality disorders contained in the *DSM-IV* or *ICD-10,* the prevalence rate may be as high as 90% (Neighbors, 1987). Even using the more conservative PCL-R criteria, the prevalence of psychopathy averages approximately 15% in forensic psychiatric patients and approximately 25% in offenders (Hare, 1991). Of course, from the dimensional perspective, things are even worse. Every offender has traits of personality disorder; the only question is, How severe are the traits?

Triers of fact may be unaware that personality disorder is pandemic in forensic settings and place undue weight on or draw unwarranted conclusions from the diagnosis. Accordingly, forensic psychologists should attempt to provide a context for diagnoses of psychopathy in three ways. First, they should explicitly acknowledge its high prevalence (e.g., "Mr. X meets the *DSM-IV* diagnostic criteria for antisocial personality disorder, which is found in approximately 50% to 80% of all incarcerated adult offenders"). Second, they should characterize it in terms of relative severity (e.g., "My assessment of Mr. X using the PCL-R indicates that he has traits of psychopathic personality disorder much higher than those found in healthy adults, but only average in severity relative to incarcerated adult male offenders"). Third, they should explain what they believe to be its legal relevance in the case at hand (e.g., "In my opinion, Mr. X poses a high risk for future sexual violence relative to other sexual offenders that is due at least in part to a mental disorder, specifically, a severe antisocial personality disorder characterized by extreme impulsivity and lack of empathy"). This last point is discussed in more detail later in this chapter.

Complexity of Personality Disorder Symptomatology

It is difficult to describe in simple terms a person's functioning with respect to a domain as broad as personality. Forensic psychologists who rely on categorical models are forced to grapple with the issue of comorbidity (Zimmerman, 1994). Research indicates that people who meet the diagnostic criteria for a given *DSM-IV* or *ICD-10* personality disorder also typically meet the criteria for two or three other personality disorders (e.g., Stuart et al., 1998). Even people with the same personality disorder diagnosis vary considerably with respect to the number and severity of symptoms they exhibit. Psychologists who rely on dimensional models are no better off, as the same level of trait severity can be manifested at the behavioral level in many different ways. Regardless of which model they use, psychologists must rely on information provided by the patient or from other sources to reach a judgment regarding the presence or absence of symptomatology, a judgment that is inherently subjective.

Forensic psychologists should be prepared to admit—without making a personal apology for the limitations of scientific knowledge—that assessing personality can be a messy business; the types or dimensions used in assessment are somewhat fuzzy and imprecise concepts. Of course, this does not necessarily render invalid the inferences psychologists can draw from the assessment of psychopathy. Also, it should be remembered that acknowledging the limitations of one's opinions might help to establish the credibility of those opinions in the eyes of the triers of fact.

Comorbidity with Acute Mental Disorder

In forensic settings, personality disorder frequently is comorbid with acute mental disorders such as substance use, mood, and anxiety disorders (more generally, Trestman, 2000; with respect to psychopathy, e.g., Hart & Hare, 1989; Hemphill, Hart, & Hare, 1994). Acute mental disorders can complicate the assessment of personality disorder, leading to uncertain or even incorrect inferences about personality (e.g., poverty of affect in a person with schizophrenia mimicking the shallow emotion often associated with psychopathy). Also, the existence of acute mental disorder can be obscured by comorbid personality disorder. If the acute mental disorder has an impact on psychological functioning or behavior that is independent of but mistakenly attributed to personality disorder, the evaluator may reach inaccurate conclusions regarding the severity and forensic relevance of the personality disorder.

Forensic psychologists should conduct comprehensive assessments of acute mental disorder before making diagnoses of psychopathy. They should also clearly indicate the existence of any acute mental disorder and discuss the extent to which it may have influenced any opinions related to psychopathy.

Causal Role of Psychopathy

An evaluator's opinion that a person suffers from psychopathy is, in itself, not of much interest in forensic decision making. In the law, personality disorder generally is relevant only if the evaluator's opinion is that it *causes,* at least in part, some impairment of competency or elevated risk for criminality and violence *for this individual* (i.e., the psychologist establishes a "causal nexus"). The unwarranted assumption of causality may render an opinion inadmissible because it is deemed to be irrelevant, not probative, or more prejudicial than probative.

Forensic psychologists should make explicit their opinions regarding the causal role played by psychopathy with respect to the relevant legal issue, whether impairment or risk. They also should acknowledge that such opinions are, ultimately, professional rather than scientific in nature, that is, based on inference and speculation, not on the direct application of scientific principles or findings.

The Diagnostic Significance of Antisocial Behavior

A history of antisocial behavior may be of considerable diagnostic significance in civil psychiatric settings, where only a minority of patients has been charged with or convicted of criminal offenses. In the *DSM-IV*, the diagnostic criteria for antisocial personality disorder are based largely on such a history. Obviously, antisocial behavior is of little diagnostic significance in many forensic settings, in which virtually everyone has arrest records (American Psychiatric Association, 1994).

Forensic psychologists should be careful not to overemphasize antisocial behavior, especially isolated criminal acts, when diagnosing psychopathy. By definition, personality disorders should be manifested across various domains of psychosocial functioning, across time, and across important personal relationships (American Psychiatric Association, 1994; World Health Organization, 1992). A person who engages in antisocial behavior only of a specific type, only against a specific person, or only at specific times may not suffer from a personality disorder at all. For example, consider a 50-year-old man who suffers from a sexual deviation and exposes his genitals to teenage girls in public places several times per year, but who is otherwise well adjusted (i.e., has a relatively stable marriage, holds a steady job, has good peer relationships). In this case, the sexual deviation accounts for the patient's antisocial behavior; there is no need to infer the presence of psychopathy or even traits of psychopathy. Other mental disorders commonly associated with specific patterns of antisocial behavior include impulse control disorders such as kleptomania (stealing) and pyromania (fire-setting).

Recommendations

Following is a list of specific recommendations for practice regarding the clinical-forensic assessment of psychopathy. The recommendations are intended to improve the usefulness of expert testimony by clarifying the foundation of professional opinions, increasing the richness of information provided to decision makers, and facilitating discussion of the limitations of the testimony.

- Psychopathy should be assessed using methods that integrate information obtained from collateral sources with (whenever possible) information from direct interviews; methods based solely on oral or written self-report should not be used.
- Psychopathy should be assessed using methods that provide dimensional information regarding symptoms and/or symptom dimensions (e.g., severity ratings and symptom counts), either in addition to or instead of categorical diagnoses made according to established or accepted criteria.
- When communicating their opinions, psychologists should acknowledge the limitations of the assessment methods they used and the information on which the assessment was based and discuss the likely impact of these limitations on their conclusions.
- Psychologists should conduct comprehensive assessments of acute mental disorder before making diagnoses of psychopathy.
- Psychologists should provide a context for their assessment of psychopathy by discussing its prevalence in forensic settings.
- When communicating their opinions, psychologists should outline the (putative) causal connection between psychopathic symptomatology and any legally relevant impairment from which the person suffers or risk the person presents.
- Psychologists should avoid overestimating the significance of antisocial behavior in the assessment of psychopathy.

AREAS FOR FUTURE RESEARCH

Despite the popularity of the PCL in forensic settings and the large body of rapidly accumulating research supporting its reliability and validity, there are some important areas that have been inadequately studied. Here, we consider some areas that we believe are research priorities. In addition to these areas, researchers should continue to examine the reliability and validity of the PCL in a variety of contexts, samples, and cultural groups.

Examine Stability of PCL Scores

As discussed previously, psychopathy is presumed to be first evident early in life and to remain stable across the lifespan. A corollary of this is that PCL scores should demonstrate high test-retest reliability across time. Another is that individuals identified with psychopathic characteristics early in life should be the same individuals as those identified with psychopathic characteristics later in life. This line of research is important for both conceptual and practical reasons. From a conceptual perspective, the stability of PCL scores supports the view that psychopathy reflects a stable constellation of personality and behavioral characteristics. The PCL is expected to display high test-retest reliability because of the emphasis during assessment on lifetime functioning across many domains of functioning. From a practical perspective, the stability of PCL scores allows practitioners to use the PCL as an important clinical construct relevant to a broad range of clinical tasks that require stability of scores. The clinical application of the PCL for conducting risk assessment, for example, assumes that PCL scores are reasonably stable across time; if the scores were not stable, the PCL would not be expected to accurately identify individuals at risk for committing future antisocial and violent behaviors. The stability of the PCL is suggested by the finding that it consistently is among the most powerful risk factors for antisocial and violent behavior (Harris et al., 1993; Steadman et al., 2000), and that the PCL is still a potent predictor of future criminal behavior with follow-up periods that exceed a decade (e.g., Hemphill, Templeman, Wong, & Hare, 1998; Rice, Harris, & Cormier, 1992).

With few exceptions, surprisingly little research has been conducted to examine the test-retest stability of PCL scores. Schroeder, Schroeder, and Hare (1983), who conducted the first study of this type, obtained a generalizability coefficient of .89. Their sample was composed of 42 inmates who had each been assessed on the original 22-item PCL and then reassessed on the same instrument approximately 10 months later. Test-retest reliability of PCL-R scores at one month have been $r \geq .85$ among male methadone patients (Alterman, Cacciola, & Rutherford, 1993) and $r = .79$ among female methadone patients (Rutherford, Cacciola, Alterman, & McKay, 1996). Of course, PCL-R scores conceptually should be stable for periods of time, with long intervals between the first and second set of assessments. Rutherford, Cacciola, Alterman, McKay, and Cook (1999) conducted a study with a test-retest interval of two years, and these researchers again found that the PCL-R demonstrated reasonably high test-retest reliability among male and female methadone patients. Nonetheless, these studies conducted with methadone patients should be replicated in forensic samples with long test-retest intervals to establish the stability of PCL-R scores over time, because the psychometric properties of PCL-R scores among substance-dependent patients may differ in important ways from the psychometric properties of PCL-R scores typically found among forensic samples (e.g., Darke, Kaye, Finlay-Jones, & Hall, 1998; McDermott et al., 2000).

Examine Incremental Validity

It is often useful in applied settings to examine the unique and shared contributions that psychopathy and other variables make to the clinical task at hand. Sechrest (1963) has argued that "validity must be claimed for a test in terms of some *increment* in predictive efficiency over the information otherwise easily and cheaply available" (p. 154; emphasis in original). In the area of risk assessment, for example, researchers would examine not only predictive validity coefficients between the PCL and recidivism, but also the additional contribution, if any, that the PCL makes to the prediction of recidivism beyond that offered by other variables.

Hemphill, Hare, and Wong (1998) reviewed the evidence concerning the incremental predictive validity of the PCL and other sets of variables with respect to recidivism. They conducted a series of statistical analyses across studies to test the incremental predictive validity of the PCL with these other sets of variables, and they concluded that the PCL contributed unique information to the prediction of recidivism beyond that offered by key criminal history and demographic variables and by personality disorder diagnoses; the reverse was not true. PCL scores also were as strongly correlated with general recidivism as were actuarial risk scales designed specifically to predict reoffending, but PCL scores were more strongly correlated with violent recidivism than were these same actuarial risk scales. Researchers might extend this body of research by routinely testing the incremental validity of the PCL with variables that are theoretically relevant or practically related to the task at hand. By amassing a literature that examines the incremental validity of different measures, clinicians will be in a better position to identify the unique and shared contributions of different measures and to select measures that each contribute unique information to the clinical task.

Study Clinical Settings

Practicing clinicians do not always score and use the PCL and PCL-SV according to the procedures outlined in the test manual (Hare, 1991; Hart et al., 1995). For example, despite Hare's (1998) cautions that "the PCL-R does not provide an appropriate index of change . . . at least not over periods of less than 10 years or so" (p. 116), we have found that some clinicians consider the PCL to be a dynamic measure whose scores are sensitive to short-term psychotherapeutic interventions. This misuse of the PCL-R reflects a poor understanding of a basic scoring rule clearly described in the administration section of the test manual (e.g., see Hare, 1991, p. 6), namely, that the PCL-R items should be rated on the basis of the person's *lifetime* functioning.

Given that PCL assessments can have considerable impact on the lives of those assessed, it is important to determine whether clinicians or raters are using the PCL consistent with the manner in which it was validated. Do raters in clinical practice have the requisite training, experience, and education? Do they obtain scores similar to those of experienced raters? Audits of clinical files would be useful for investigating the accuracy of ratings in clinical practice. Absolute (and not simply relative) scores obtained on the PCL are of particular interest in clinical settings, where diagnoses often form the basis of important clinical decisions. In this regard, it would be instructive to determine what specific cutpoints, if any, are used in clinical practice; how clinicians interpret PCL scores; whether psychopathy is viewed as a mitigating or an exacerbating factor, or as a treatable or an untreatable condition; the extent to which clinicians separately consider and differentially interpret PCL factor scores; and so forth.

Another issue concerning the assessment of psychopathy that is important in clinical practice but that has received little research attention is the ability of those being evaluated to intentionally influence or manipulate their PCL scores. The impetus to present oneself in a particular way would seem to be considerable in forensic contexts. The public has easy access via popular books (e.g., Hare, 1993) to detailed accounts of the procedures used to assess psychopathy and to descriptions of the key symptoms of psychopathy substantively similar to the criteria outlined in the PCL-R manual. Given that PCL assessments are based on lifetime functioning and rely heavily on collateral sources, it seems unlikely that PCL scores could be markedly distorted. Research might nonetheless clarify the parameters under which PCL scores could be distorted (e.g., when collateral information is limited) and the PCL items most susceptible to distortion.

Evaluate Treatment Efficacy

It makes good sense to believe that psychopaths will change little as a consequence of treatment or other interventions (at least, not in the short term). Psychopaths, by definition, experience little remorse or guilt that might propel them into treatment. They are not motivated to actively participate in treatment once enrolled because they see little wrong with themselves, they lack insight and do not recognize the adverse impact that their behaviors have on others, and they habitually lie and manipulate others. These characteristics are generally the antithesis of those that have been found to be important for effecting positive therapeutic change.

Many readers may be surprised, therefore, to learn that virtually no methodologically sound treatment study has been conducted evaluating the treatment efficacy of a contemporary treatment program for psychopaths. Most of the evidence concerning poor treatment outcomes ascribed to criminal psychopaths is based on anecdotal case studies or weak research designs (e.g., see Dolan & Coid, 1993; Hemphill & Hart, in press; Wong & Elek, 1989; Wong & Hare, in press). Perhaps the most methodologically rigorous and oft-cited research study to date concerning the efficacy of treatment for psychopaths was conducted by Rice et al. (1992). These authors concluded that treated psychopaths were more violent than were untreated psychopaths during a 10.5-year follow-up. It is important to recognize that this treatment program, although considered innovative in the late 1960s and 1970s, is a nontraditional treatment program that "would not meet current ethical standards" (Harris, Rice, & Cormier, 1991; p. 628).

Research that evaluates the efficacy of treatment among psychopaths and that addresses a number of basic methodological concerns is clearly a priority. Methodologically superior studies would include large groups of clearly defined psychopaths who have received well-established treatments that have been delivered consistently and evaluated systematically across long follow-up periods using several measures of treatment outcome. Although research methodologies have improved greatly across time (e.g., Hare et al., 2000; Hobson, Shine, & Roberts, 2000; Seto & Barbaree, 1999), there is still considerable room for improvement concerning studies that examine the efficacy of treatment among offenders in general and among psychopaths in particular.

SUMMARY

The procedures for assessing psychopathy can be grouped into three broad categories: structured diagnostic interviews; self-report questionnaires and inventories; and expert rating scales. This chapter critically examined each of these three broad procedures while keeping in mind the unique assessment issues with respect to forensic contexts and psychopathy assessments. Expert rating systems are considered superior to the other two categories for assessing psychopathy. A variety of professional and clinical issues that clinicians should keep in mind when conducting psychopathy assessments were discussed, as were practical recommendations for dealing with many of these issues. The chapter concluded with an examination of inadequately studied areas concerning psychopathy that should be a focus of future research.

REFERENCES

American Educational Research Association, American Psychological Association, & National Council on Measurement in Education. (1999). *Standards for educational and psychological testing*. Washington, DC: American Educational Research Association.

American Psychiatric Association. (1980). *Diagnostic and statistical manual of mental disorders* (3rd ed.). Washington, DC: Author.

American Psychiatric Association. (1987). *Diagnostic and statistical manual of mental disorders* (3rd ed., rev.). Washington, DC: Author.

American Psychiatric Association. (1994). *Diagnostic and statistical manual of mental disorders* (4th ed.). Washington, DC: Author.

Arieti, S. (1963). Psychopathic personality: Some views on its psychopathology and psychodynamics. *Comprehensive Psychiatry, 4,* 301–312.

Barry, C. T., Frick, P. J., DeShazo, T. M., McCoy, M. G., Ellis, M., & Loney, B. R. (2000). The importance of callous-unemotional traits for extending the concept of psychopathy to children. *Journal of Abnormal Psychology, 109,* 335–340.

Bayer, B. M., Bonta, J. L., & Motiuk, L. L. (1985). The Pd subscales: An empirical evaluation. *Journal of Clinical Psychology, 41,* 780–788.

Blackburn, R., & Fawcett, D. (1999). The Antisocial Personality Questionnaire: An inventory for assessing personality deviation in offender populations. *European Journal of Psychological Assessment, 15,* 14–24.

Butcher, J. N., Dahlstrom, L., Graham, J. R., Tellgen, A., & Kaemmer, B. (1989). *Minnesota Multiphasic Personality Inventory–2.* Minneapolis: University of Minnesota Press.

Cleckley, H. (1941). *The mask of sanity.* St. Louis, MO: Mosby.

Committee on Ethical Guidelines for Forensic Psychologists. (1991). Specialty guidelines for forensic psychologists. *Law and Human Behavior, 15,* 655–665.

Cooke, D. J. (1996). Psychopathic personality in different cultures: What do we know? What do we need to find out? *Journal of Personality Disorders, 10,* 23–40.

Cooke, D. J., Forth, A. E., & Hare, R. D. (Eds.). (1998). *Psychopathy: Theory, research, and implications for society.* Dordrecht, The Netherlands: Kluwer Press.

Cooke, D. J., Kosson, D. S., & Michie, C. (2001). *Psychopathy and ethnicity: Structural, item and test generalizability of the Psychopathy Checklist–Revised in Caucasian and African-American participants.* Manuscript in preparation.

Cooke, D. J., & Michie, C. (1997). An item response theory analysis of the Hare Psychopathy Checklist–Revised. *Psychological Assessment, 9,* 3–14.

Cooke, D. J., & Michie, C. (1999). Psychopathy across cultures: Scotland and North America compared. *Journal of Abnormal Psychology, 108,* 58–68.

Cooke, D. J., & Michie, C. (2001). Refining the construct of psychopathy: Toward a hierarchical model. *Psychological Assessment, 13,* 171–188.

Cooke, D. J., Michie, C., Hart, S. D., & Hare, R. D. (1999). Evaluating the screening version of the Hare Psychopathy Checklist–Revised (PCL:SV): An item response theory analysis. *Psychological Assessment, 11,* 3–13.

Cooney, N. L., Kadden, R. M., & Litt, M. D. (1990). A comparison of methods for assessing sociopathy in male and female alcoholics. *Journal of Studies on Alcohol, 51,* 42–48.

Cunningham, M. D., & Reidy, T. J. (1998). Antisocial personality disorder and psychopathy: Diagnostic dilemmas in classifying patterns of antisocial behavior in sentencing evaluations. *Behavioral Sciences and the Law, 16,* 333–351.

Cunningham, M. D., & Reidy, T. J. (1999). Don't confuse me with the facts: Common errors in violence risk assessment at capital sentencing. *Criminal Justice and Behavior, 26,* 20–43.

Darke, S., Kaye, S., Finlay-Jones, R., & Hall, W. (1998). Factor structure of psychopathy among methadone maintenance patients. *Journal of Personality Disorders, 12,* 162–171.

Davies, W., & Feldman, P. (1981). The diagnosis of psychopathy by forensic specialists. *British Journal of Psychiatry, 138,* 329–331.

Dolan, B., & Coid, J. (1993). *Psychopathic and antisocial personality disorders: Treatment and research issues.* London: Gaskell.

Edens, J. F., Hart, S. D., Johnson, D. W., Johnson, J. K., & Olver, M. E. (2000). Use of the Personality Assessment Inventory to assess psychopathy in offender populations. *Psychological Assessment, 12,* 132–139.

Edens, J. F., Poythress, N. G., & Lilienfeld, S. O. (1999). Identifying inmates at risk for disciplinary infractions: A comparison of two measures of psychopathy. *Behavioral Sciences and the Law, 17,* 435–443.

Edens, J. F., Skeem, J. L., Cruise, K. R., & Cauffman, E. (2001). Assessment of "juvenile psychopathy" and its association with violence: A critical review. *Behavioral Sciences and the Law, 19,* 53–80.

Feighner, J. P., Robins, E., Guze, S. B., Woodruff, R. A., Winokur, G., & Munoz, R. (1972). Diagnostic criteria for use in psychiatric research. *Archives of General Psychiatry, 26,* 57–63.

First, M. B., Spitzer, R. L., Gibbon, M., Williams, J. B. W., Davies, M., Borus, J., et al. (1995). The Structured Clinical Interview for *DSM-III-R* personality disorders (SCID-II) II: Multi-site test-retest reliability study. *Journal of Personality Disorders, 9,* 92–104.

Forth, A. E., & Burke, H. C. (1998). Psychopathy in adolescence: Assessment, violence, and developmental precursors. In D. J. Cooke, A. E. Forth, & R. D. Hare (Eds.), *Psychopathy: Theory, research, and implications for society* (pp. 205–229). Dordrecht, The Netherlands: Kluwer Press.

Forth, A. E., Hart, S. D., & Hare, R. D. (1990). Assessment of psychopathy in male young offenders. *Psychological Assessment: A Journal of Consulting and Clinical Psychology, 2,* 342–344.

Frick, P. J., & Ellis, M. (1999). Callous-unemotional traits and subtypes of conduct disorder. *Clinical Child and Family Psychology Review, 2,* 149–168.

Graham, J. R. (1999). *MMPI-2: Assessing personality and psychopathology* (3rd ed.). New York: Oxford University Press.

Gresham, F. M., Lane, K. L., & Lambros, K. M. (2000). Comorbidity of conduct problems and ADHD: Identification of fledgling psychopaths. *Journal of Emotional and Behavioral Disorders, 8,* 83–93.

Gustaffson, S. B., & Ritzer, D. R. (1995). The dark side of normal: A psychopathy-linked pattern called aberrant self-promotion. *European Journal of Personality, 9,* 1–37.

Hare, R. D. (1980). A research scale for the assessment of psychopathy in criminal populations. *Personality and Individual Differences, 1,* 111–119.

Hare, R. D. (1983). Diagnosis of antisocial personality disorder in two prison populations. *American Journal of Psychiatry, 140,* 887–890.

Hare, R. D. (1985). A comparison of procedures for the assessment of psychopathy. *Journal of Consulting and Clinical Psychology, 53,* 7–16.

Hare, R. D. (1991). *The Hare Psychopathy Checklist–Revised.* Toronto, Ontario, Canada: Multi-Health Systems.

Hare, R. D. (1993). *Without conscience: The disturbing world of the psychopaths among us.* New York: Pocket Books.

Hare, R. D. (1996). Psychopathy: A clinical construct whose time has come. *Criminal Justice and Behavior, 23,* 25–54.

Hare, R. D. (1998). The Hare PCL-R: Some issues concerning its use and misuse. *Legal and Criminological Psychology, 3,* 99–119.

Hare, R. D., Clark, D., Grann, M., & Thornton, D. (2000). Psychopathy and the predictive validity of the PCL-R: An international perspective. *Behavioral Sciences and the Law, 18,* 623–645.

Hare, R. D., Cooke, D. J., & Hart, S. D. (1999). Psychopathy and sadistic personality disorder. In T. Millon, P. H. Blaney, & R. D. Davis (Eds.), *Oxford textbook of psychopathology* (pp. 555–584). Oxford, England: Oxford University Press.

Hare, R. D., Harpur, T. J., Hakstian, A. R., Forth, A. E., Hart, S. D., & Newman, J. P. (1990). The Revised Psychopathy Checklist: Reliability and factor structure. *Psychological Assessment: A Journal of Consulting and Clinical Psychology, 2,* 338–341.

Hare, R. D., Hart, S. D., & Harpur, T. J. (1991). Psychopathy and the DSM-IV criteria for antisocial personality disorder. *Journal of Abnormal Psychology, 100,* 391–398.

Harpur, T. J., Hakstian, R. A., & Hare, R. D. (1988). Factor structure of the Psychopathy Checklist. *Journal of Consulting and Clinical Psychology, 56,* 741–747.

Harpur, T. J., Hare, R. D., & Hakstian, R. A. (1989). Two-factor conceptualization of psychopathy: Construct validity and assessment implications. *Psychological Assessment: A Journal of Consulting and Clinical Psychology, 1,* 6–17.

Harris, G. T., Rice, M. E., & Cormier, C. A. (1991). Psychopathy and violent recidivism. *Law and Human Behavior, 15,* 625–637.

Harris, G. T., Rice, M. E., & Quinsey, V. L. (1993). Violent recidivism of mentally disordered offenders: The development of a statistical prediction instrument. *Criminal Justice and Behavior, 20,* 315–335.

Harris, G. T., Rice, M. E., & Quinsey, V. L. (1994). Psychopathy as a taxon: Evidence that psychopaths are a discrete class. *Journal of Consulting and Clinical Psychology, 62,* 387–397.

Hart, S. D. (1998). The role of psychopathy in assessing risk for violence: Conceptual and methodological issues. *Legal and Criminological Psychology, 3,* 121–137.

Hart, S. D. (2001). Forensic issues. In W. J. Livesley (Ed.), *Handbook of personality disorders: Theory, research, and treatment* (pp. 555–569). New York: Guilford Press.

Hart, S. D., Cox, D. N., & Hare, R. D. (1995). *Manual for the Hare Psychopathy Checklist–Revised: Screening version (PCL:SV).* Toronto, Ontario, Canada: Multi-Health Systems.

Hart, S. D., Forth, A. E., & Hare, R. D. (1991). The MCMI-II as a measure of psychopathy. *Journal of Personality Disorders, 5,* 318–327.

Hart, S. D., & Hare, R. D. (1989). Discriminant validity of the Psychopathy Checklist in a forensic psychiatric population. *Psychological Assessment: A Journal of Consulting and Clinical Psychology, 1,* 211–218.

Hart, S. D., & Hare, R. D. (1997). Psychopathy: Assessment and association with criminal conduct. In D. M. Stoff, J. Breiling, & J. D. Maser (Eds.), *Handbook of antisocial behavior* (pp. 22–35). New York: Wiley.

Hathaway, S. R., & McKinley, J. C. (1940). A multiphasic personality schedule (Minnesota). I: Construction of the schedule. *Journal of Psychology, 10,* 249–254.

Haynes, S. N., Richard, D. C. S., & Kubany, E. S. (1995). Content validity in psychological assessment: A functional approach to concepts and methods. *Psychological Assessment, 7,* 238–247.

Heilbrun, K. (1992). The role of psychological testing in forensic assessment. *Law and Human Behavior, 16,* 257–272.

Hemphill, J. F., Hare, R. D., & Wong, S. (1998). Psychopathy and recidivism: A review. *Legal and Criminological Psychology, 3,* 139–170.

Hemphill, J. F. & Hart, S. D. (in press). Motivating the unmotivated: Psychopathy, treatment, and change. In M. McMurran (Ed.), *Motivating offenders to change: A guide to enhancing engagement in therapy.* Chichester, England: Wiley.

Hemphill, J. F., Hart, S. D., & Hare, R. D. (1994). Psychopathy and substance use. *Journal of Personality Disorders, 8,* 169–180.

Hemphill, J. F., Newman, J. P., & Hare, R. D. (2001, April). *Psychopathy and recidivism among Black and White adult male offenders.* Paper presented at the International Association of Forensic Mental Health Services, Vancouver, British Columbia, Canada.

Hemphill, J. F., Templeman, R., Wong, S., & Hare, R. D. (1998). Psychopathy and crime: Recidivism and criminal careers. In D. J. Cooke, A. E. Forth, & R. D. Hare (Eds.), *Psychopathy: Theory, research and implications for society* (pp. 375–399). Dordrecht, The Netherlands: Kluwer Press.

Henard, D. H. (2000). Item response theory. In L. G. Grimm & P. R. Yarnold (Eds.), *Reading and understanding more multivariate statistics* (pp. 67–97). Washington, DC: American Psychological Association.

Hobson, J., Shine, J., & Roberts, R. (2000). How do psychopaths behave in a prison therapeutic community? *Psychology, Crime and Law, 6,* 139–154.

Janus, E. S. (2000). Sexual predator commitment laws: Lessons for law and the behavioral sciences. *Behavioral Sciences and the Law, 18,* 5–21.

Karpman, B. (1961). The structure of neuroses: With special differentials between neurosis, psychosis, homosexuality, alcoholism, psychopathy and criminality. *Archives of Criminal Psychodynamics, 4,* 599–646.

Kosson, D. S., Smith, S. S., & Newman, J. P. (1990). Evaluation of the construct validity of psychopathy in Black and White male inmates: Three preliminary studies. *Journal of Abnormal Psychology, 99,* 250–259.

Levenson, M. R., Kiehl, K. A., & Fitzpatrick, C. M. (1995). Assessing psychopathic attributes in a non-institutionalized population. *Journal of Personality and Social Psychology, 68,* 151–158.

Lilienfeld, S. O. (1994). Conceptual problems in the assessment of psychopathy. *Clinical Psychology Review, 14,* 17–38.

Lilienfeld, S. O., & Andrews, B. P. (1996). Development and preliminary validation of a self report measure of psychopathic personality traits in noncriminal populations. *Journal of Personality Assessment, 66,* 488–524.

Loranger, A. W., Sartorius, N., Andreoli, A., Berger, P., Buchheim, P., Channabasavanna, S. M., et al. (1994). The International Personality Disorder Examination: The World Health Organization/Alcohol, Drug Abuse, and Mental Health Administration international pilot study of personality disorders. *Archives of General Psychiatry, 51,* 215–224.

Lynam, D. R. (1996). Early identification of chronic offenders: Who is the fledgling psychopath? *Psychological Bulletin, 120,* 209–234.

Lynam, D. R. (1997). Pursuing the psychopath: Capturing the fledgling psychopath in a nomological net. *Journal of Abnormal Behavior, 106,* 425–438.

Lyon, D. R., & Ogloff, J. R. P. (2000). Legal and ethical issues in psychopathy assessment. In C. B. Gacono (Ed.), *The clinical and forensic assessment of psychopathy: A practitioner's guide* (pp. 139–173). Mahwah, NJ: Erlbaum.

McCord, W., & McCord, J. (1964). *The psychopath: An essay on the criminal mind.* Princeton, NJ: Van Nostrand.

McDermott, P. A., Alterman, A. I., Cacciola, J. S., Rutherford, M. J., Newman, J. P., & Mulholland, E. M. (2000). Generality of Psychopathy Checklist–Revised factors over prisoners and substance-dependent patients. *Journal of Consulting and Clinical Psychology, 68,* 181–186.

McKinley, J. C., & Hathaway, S. R. (1944). The Minnesota Multiphasic Personality Inventory V: Hysteria, hypomania, and psychopathic deviate. *Journal of Applied Psychology, 28,* 153–174.

Melton, G. B., Petrila, J., Poythress, N. G., & Slobogin, C. (1997). *Psychological evaluations for the courts: A handbook for mental health professionals and lawyers* (2nd ed.). New York: Guilford Press.

Millon, T. (1987). *Millon Clinical Multiaxial Inventory. II: Manual.* Minneapolis, MN: National Computer Systems.

Millon, T., Davis, R., & Millon, C. (1997). *Millon Clinical Multiaxial Inventory–III (MCMI-III) manual* (2nd ed.). Minneapolis, MN: National Computer Systems.

Morey, L. C. (1991). *The Personality Assessment Inventory professional manual.* Odessa, FL: Psychological Assessment Resources.

Neighbors, H. (1987). The prevalence of mental disorder in Michigan prisons. *DIS Newsletter, 4,* 8–11.

Ogloff, J. R. P. (1995). Navigating the quagmire: Legal and ethical considerations. In D. G. Martin & A. D. Moore (Eds.), *First steps in the art of intervention: A guidebook for trainees in the helping professions* (pp. 347–376). Pacific Grove, CA: Brooks/Cole.

Ogloff, J. R. P., & Lyon, D. R. (1998). Legal issues associated with the concept of psychopathy. In D. J. Cooke, A. E. Forth, & R. D. Hare (Eds.), *Psychopathy: Theory, research, and implications for society* (pp. 401–422). Dordrecht, The Netherlands: Kluwer Press.

Pope, K. S., Butcher, J. N., & Seelen, J. (1993). *The MMPI, MMPI-2, and MMPI-A in court: A practical guide for expert witnesses and attorneys.* Washington, DC: American Psychological Association.

Porter, S., Fairweather, D., Drugge, J., Hervé, H., Birt, A., & Boer, D. P. (2000). Profiles of psychopathy in incarcerated sexual offenders. *Criminal Justice and Behavior, 27,* 216–233.

Rice, M. E., & Harris, G. T. (1997). Cross-validation and extension of the Violence Risk Appraisal Guide for child molesters and rapists. *Law and Human Behavior, 21,* 231–241.

Rice, M. E., Harris, G. T., & Cormier, C. A. (1992). An evaluation of a maximum security therapeutic community for psychopaths and other mentally disordered offenders. *Law and Human Behavior, 16,* 399–412.

Robins, L. N. (1966). *Deviant children grown up: A sociological and psychiatric study of sociopathic personality.* Baltimore: Williams & Wilkins.

Robins, L. N., Tipp, J., & Przybeck, T. (1991). Antisocial personality. In L. N. Robins & D. Regier (Eds.), *Psychiatric disorders in America: The Epidemiologic Catchment Area study* (pp. 258–290). New York: Free Press.

Rogers, R. (1995). *Diagnostic and structured interviewing: A handbook for psychologists.* Odessa, FL: Psychological Assessment Resources.

Rogers, R., & Dion, K. (1991). Rethinking the *DSM-III-R* diagnosis of antisocial personality disorder. *Bulletin of the American Academy of Psychiatry and Law, 19,* 21–31.

Rogers, R., Dion, K. L., & Lynett, E. (1992). Diagnostic validity of antisocial personality disorder: A prototypical analysis. *Law and Human Behavior, 16,* 677–689.

Rogers, R., Duncan, J. C., Lynett, E., & Sewell, K. W. (1994). Prototypical analysis of antisocial personality disorder: *DSM-IV* and beyond. *Law and Human Behavior, 18,* 471–484.

Rogers, R., Gillis, J. R., & Dickens, S. E. (1989). A research note on the MMPI Pd scale and sociopathy. *International Journal of Offender Therapy and Comparative Criminology, 33,* 21–25.

Rutherford, M. J., Cacciola, J. S., Alterman, A. I., & McKay, J. R. (1996). Reliability and validity of the Revised Psychopathy Checklist in women methadone patients. *Assessment, 3,* 145–156.

Rutherford, M., Cacciola, J. S., Alterman, A. I., McKay, J. R., & Cook, T. G. (1999). The 2-year test-retest reliability of the Psychopathy Checklist–Revised in methadone patients. *Assessment, 6,* 285–291.

Salekin, R., Rogers, R., & Sewell, K. (1996). A review and meta-analysis of the Psychopathy Checklist and Psychopathy Checklist–Revised: Predictive validity of dangerousness. *Clinical Psychology: Science and Practice, 3,* 203–215.

Salekin, R. T., Rogers, R., & Sewell, K. W. (1997). Construct validity of psychopathy in a female offender sample: A multitrait-multimethod evaluation. *Journal of Abnormal Psychology, 106,* 576–585.

Schroeder, M. L., Schroeder, K. G., & Hare, R. D. (1983). Generalizability of a checklist for assessment of psychopathy. *Journal of Consulting and Clinical Psychology, 51,* 511–516.

Schuller, R. A., & Ogloff, J. R. P. (2001). An introduction to psychology and law. In R. A. Schuller & J. R. P. Ogloff (Eds.), *Introduction to psychology and law: Canadian perspectives* (pp. 3–28). Toronto, Ontario, Canada: University of Toronto Press.

Sechrest, L. (1963). Incremental validity: A recommendation. *Educational and Psychological Measurement, 23,* 153–158.

Seto, M. C., & Barbaree, H. E. (1999). Psychopathy, treatment behavior, and sex offender recidivism. *Journal of Interpersonal Violence, 14,* 1235–1248.

Steadman, H. J., Silver, E., Monahan, J., Appelbaum, P. S., Robbins, P. C., Mulvey, E. P., et al. (2000). A classification tree approach to the development of actuarial violence risk assessment tools. *Law and Human Behavior, 24,* 83–100.

Stuart, S., Pfhol, B., Battaglia, M., Bellodi, L., Grove, W., & Cadoret, R. (1998). The co-occurrence of *DSM-III-R* personality disorders. *Journal of Personality Disorders, 12,* 302–315.

Tennent, G., Tennent, D., Prins, H., & Bedford, A. (1990). Psychopathic disorder: A useful clinical concept? *Medicine, Science, and the Law, 30,* 39–44.

Trestman, R. L. (2000). Behind bars: Personality disorders. *Journal of the American Academy of Psychiatry and the Law, 28,* 232–235.

Vincent, G., & Hart, S. D. (in press). Psychopathy in adolescents. In R. R. Corrado, R. Roesch, S. D. Hart, & J. Gierowski, J. (Eds.), *Multi-problem violent youth: A foundation for comparative research on needs, interventions, and outcomes.* Amsterdam: IOS Press.

Werlinder, H. (1978). *Psychopathy: A history of the concepts. Analysis of the origin and development of a family of concepts in psychopathology.* Doctoral dissertation, Institute of Education, Uppsala University, Sweden.

Widiger, T. A., Cadoret, R., Hare, R. D., Robins, L., Rutherford, M., Zanarini, M., et al. (1996). *DSM-IV* antisocial personality disorder field trial. *Journal of Abnormal Psychology, 105,* 3–16.

Widiger, T. A., & Corbitt, E. M. (1993). Antisocial personality disorder: Proposals for *DSM-IV. Journal of Personality Disorders, 7,* 63–77.

Widiger, T. A., & Corbitt, E. M. (1995). Antisocial personality disorder in *DSM-IV.* In J. Livesley (Ed.), *DSM-IV personality disorders* (pp. 127–134). New York: Guilford Press.

Widiger, T. A., & Sanderson, C. J. (1995). Toward a dimensional model of personality disorders. In W. J. Livesley (Ed.), *The DSM-IV personality disorders* (pp. 433–458). New York: Guilford Press.

Wiggins, J. S. (1973). *Personality and prediction: Principles of personality assessment.* Reading, MA: Addison-Wesley.

Wilson, J. Q., & Herrnstein, R. J. (1985). *Crime and human nature.* New York: Touchstone.

Wong, S., & Elek, D. (1989). *The treatment of psychopathy: A review.* Unpublished manuscript.

Wong, S., & Hare, R. D. (in press). *Program guidelines for the institutional treatment of violent psychopaths.* Toronto, Ontario, Canada: Multi-Health Systems.

World Health Organization. (1992). *ICD-10: International statistical classification of diseases and related health problems* (10th rev.). Geneva, Switzerland: Author.

Zimmerman, M. (1994). Diagnosing personality disorders: A review of issues and research methods. *Archives of General Psychiatry, 51,* 225–245.

Zinger, I., & Forth, A. (1998). Psychopathy and Canadian criminal proceedings: The potential for human rights abuses. *Canadian Journal of Criminology, 40,* 237–276.

CHAPTER 7

Evaluation of Malingering and Deception

RICHARD ROGERS AND SCOTT D. BENDER

CONCEPTUAL ISSUES

The validity of most psychological measures is predicated on the cardinal assumption that evaluatees are responding in a forthright manner and putting forth a sincere effort. Is this assumption warranted in forensic practice? External influences on self-reporting and effort may include the adversarial effects of litigation and pressures exerted by interested others, such as attorneys and family members. Internal influences may include (a) reactions to questioned credibility, (b) stigmatization of mental disorders or disability status, (c) effects of a genuine disorder, or (d) efforts to obtain undeserved benefits. Forensic psychologists tend to focus on the last as it relates to malingering and de-emphasize other internal and external influences.

Forensic psychologists may wish to address openly internal and external influences that potentially arise from their evaluations. As part of the informed consent process, they may choose to ask evaluatees about their understanding of the purposes of the evaluation and what they have been told about the evaluation by others. Disclosures from the forensic psychologist about the purpose of the evaluation and his or her role may allay some concerns about partiality. Especially in civil cases, an unhurried and respectful discussion of the evaluation, its purpose, and parameters is needed to address strong negative reactions regarding perceived coercion (e.g., "I had to come") or questioned legitimacy (e.g., "You think I am making this up").

Tests of cognitive abilities and achievement are premised on optimal effort by evaluatees. Less than optimal effort may vitiate the accuracy of test results and lead to concerns about deliberate underperformance. A largely neglected consideration is the effect of genuine disorders on test performance. For example, major depression may reduce performance on cognitive tasks that require sustained attention and concentration. Forensic psychologists are cautioned against facile and unwarranted assumptions that suboptimal efforts are always equated with malingering.

This section provides an overview of response styles with a summary of accepted terminology. Three general perspectives of malingering are explicated. Explanatory models are reviewed with a discussion of inferred motivations for why persons engage in malingering and defensiveness. In addition, misassumptions about response styles are examined in the context of forensic evaluations.

Definitions of Response Styles

Rogers (1997) summarized the basic terminology used to describe response styles. Basic definitions are provided with several updated references:

- *Malingering* (American Psychiatric Association, 2000) is the deliberate fabrication or gross exaggeration of psychological or physical symptoms for the fulfillment of an external goal.

- *Defensiveness* is the polar opposite of malingering; it is the deliberate denial or gross minimization of symptoms in the service of an external goal.

- *Irrelevant responding* is a disengagement from the assessment process typically reflected in inconsistent responding that is unrelated to the specific content (e.g., not reading test items).

- *Feigning* is the deliberate fabrication or gross exaggeration of psychological or physical symptoms (Rogers & Vitacco, in press) without any assumptions about its goals. Available tests typically assess feigning, because they are unable to evaluate supposed goals required for the classification of malingering or the diagnosis of factitious disorders.

- *Secondary gain* is an imprecise clinical term that should be avoided in forensic evaluations (Rogers & Reinhardt, 1998). In nonforensic settings, the term is used to describe the perpetuation and possible augmentation of symptoms based on *unintentional* responses to internal (i.e., psychodynamic models) or external (i.e., behavioral-medicine models) forces.

- *Suboptimal effort* (also called "incomplete effort") is a descriptive inference that maximum performance was not achieved. Suboptimal effort may be the result of internal states (e.g., fatigue or frustration) or comorbidity (e.g., depression subsequent to a head injury). Only when suboptimal effort is extreme in its presentation should feigning be considered, although internal states and comorbidity must still be addressed.

- *Dissimulation* is a general term to describe an inaccurate portrayal of symptoms and associated features. It is typically used when more precise terms (e.g., malingering and defensiveness) are inapplicable.

Perspectives of Malingering in the Forensic Context

A heuristic typology is proposed to explain differences in how forensic psychologists approach the evaluation of response styles. Three main perspectives are identified: intuitional, standard, and specialized. These perspectives are considered in the context of malingering.

The *intuitional* perspective presupposes that malingering and other response styles will be recognizable based on clinical acumen without the need for empirically validated strategies, scales, and indicators. Despite its lack of empirical validation, we suspect that the intuitional perspective is widespread in forensic practice. A key example is found with competency to stand trial evaluations. Despite nearly three decades of research on competency evaluations (Rogers, 2001), malingering and related response styles have been virtually ignored. Even the most recent and best-funded competency measure, MacArthur Competency Assessment Tool–Criminal Adjudication (Poythress et al., 1999), implicitly adopted an intuitional perspective for malingering. While acknowledging that response styles may confound competency evaluations, no indices of any kind are provided (see Poythress et al., 1999, p. 5).

The *standard* perspective routinely evaluates malingering and defensiveness on the basis of traditional tests and measures. The advantages of this approach are twofold: (a) highly efficient use of customary measures for dual purposes (e.g., psychopathology and feigning), and (b) application of empirically tested strategies. The major shortcoming of the standard perspective is that traditional testing lacks the diagnostic utility for making clinical determinations. The most common examples of the standard perspective involve multiscale inventories (e.g., the Minnesota Multiphasic Personality Inventory 2 [MMPI-2; Butcher, Williams, Graham, Tellegen, & Kaemmer, 1989]) and intelligence testing (i.e., predominantly the Wechsler Adult Intelligence Scale–Revised [WAIS-R; Weschler, 1981] rather than WAIS-III; Weschler, 1997).

The *specialized* perspective supplements traditional testing with measures that are specifically designed for the assessment of response styles. Common forensic examples include the Structured Interview of Reported Symptoms (SIRS; Rogers, Bagby, & Dickens, 1992) for feigned mental disorders and the Portland Digit Recognition Test (PDRT; Binder & Willis, 1991) for feigned cognitive impairment. Despite the additional expenditure time, the specialized perspective is generally superior to the standard perspective in its classificatory accuracy. The specialized perspective is recommended as the necessary model for the determination of feigning in both clinical and forensic practice.

Explanatory Models of Malingering

When conducting evaluations and rendering conclusions, forensic psychologists are likely to be influenced by explanatory models of malingering. Explanatory models attempt to explain *why* individuals strive to malinger psychological and physical impairment. Rogers (1990a, 1990b) outlined three explanatory models of malingering: pathogenic, criminological, and adaptational. Several prototypical analyses (Rogers, Sewell, & Goldstein, 1994; Rogers, Salekin, Sewell, Goldstein, & Leonard, 1998) provide general support for these explanatory models as distinct explanations for malingering. A synopsis of the three explanatory models of malingering is provided.

The *pathogenic model* assumes that the underlying motivation is an ineffective attempt to control the symptoms and clinical presentation of a chronic and progressive mental disorder. With increased impairment, intentionally produced symptoms become gradually less deliberate, until they are involuntary and unintended. The pathogenic model predicts that feigning is an ineffectual attempt at adjustment that eventually is resolved by the patient's further deterioration.

The *criminological model* is championed by the *Diagnostic and Statistical Manual of Mental Disorders* (*DSM-IV-TR*; American Psychiatric Association, 2000); it assumes that the primary motivation is characterological. Namely, antisocial persons faced with legal difficulties will attempt to garner unwarranted advantages either in circumstances (e.g., a hospital rather than a prison) or material gain (e.g., financial settlement). Antisocial persons are presumed to be generally deceptive. With malingering viewed as a variant of deception, the criminological model predicts an intermittent use of malingering based on situational opportunities.

The *adaptational model* assumes that the person perceives the circumstances as adversarial and considers malingering to be a feasible alternative. This model avoids the monistic notions of "mad" (pathogenic) or "bad" (criminological) and views malingering in terms of a cost-benefit analysis. The adaptational model views malingering as a situational response based on an appraisal of alternatives.

Rogers, Salekin, et al. (1998) found that the pathogenic model was low in prototypicality for both males and females in forensic evaluations. In contrast, both the adaptational and criminological models achieved moderately high prototypical ratings for forensic cases. A potential danger of the criminological model is that forensic psychologists may attempt to use this explanatory model as a detection model.

The *DSM-IV-TR* indices only raise the suspicion of malingering; they do not constitute formal criteria for the classification of malingering. Even for suspicions of malingering, these indices (i.e., antisocial personality disorder, medicolegal evaluation, uncooperativeness, and results inconsistent with objective findings) falter on both conceptual and empirical grounds. Rogers (1997) provides a conceptual analysis of their major shortcomings. Even in defending the *DSM-IV-TR* indices, LoPiccolo, Goodkin, and Baldewicz (1999) conceded most of these shortcomings. Empirically, *DSM-IV-TR* indices fail entirely even for screening purposes. Their use in a criminal forensic setting resulted in a false-positive rate of approximately 80% (Rogers, 1990a).

Explanatory Models of Defensiveness

Rogers and Dickey (1991) proposed that explanatory models of defensiveness could be extrapolated from the malingering literature, at least in the case of sex offenders. The pathogenic model is the least persuasive; psychodynamic formulations have suggested that loss of ego functions may result in unconscious denial. More persuasive explanations were the criminological and adaptational models, suggesting that denial and gross minimization might result from either a general criminal orientation or an attempt to cope with highly adversarial circumstances. As noted by Rogers and Dickey, sex offenders often are placed in an irresolvable bind: Honesty, disclosing the true extent of their paraphilac behavior, is likely to result in negative sanctions based on the extent of criminal activity; defensiveness, grossly minimizing the true extent of their paraphilac behavior, is likely to result in negative sanctions because nondisclosure is viewed as a barrier to treatment.

Sewell and Salekin (1997) expanded on Rogers and Dickey's (1991) framework and proposed a socioevaluative model of defensiveness. For offenders, especially sex offenders, evaluations are consistently linked with punishment and ostracism. The socioevaluative model posits that evaluatees react to the likely threat of a negative outcome and attempt to protect themselves. The socioevaluative model is similar to the adaptational model in its appraisal of a highly adversarial context. It is distinguished from the adaptational model in its generalized reaction. Even when "there is nothing to lose," the socioevaluative model predicts a generalized response of defensiveness based on past learning.

Under the rubric of cognitive distortions, the notion of self-deception has been considered, especially with sex offenders. According to Vanhouche and Vertommen (1999), cognitive distortions involve "learned assumptions" and "sets of beliefs and attitudes" (p. 164) that serve in the denial and minimization of criminal behavior. In the course of the evaluation, denials of responsibility may be influenced by "self-deceptive" beliefs (e.g., educative goals of incest). However, such denials are unlikely to explain the overall defensiveness expressed by many offenders.

The understanding of defensiveness in forensic practice is constrained by the focus on sex offenders. Although extrapolations to other forensic populations are possible, explanatory models of defensiveness remain in their initial stages of development and validation.

Misassumptions about Malingering and Dissimulation

Forensic psychologists are not immune to common misassumptions about malingering and other response styles.

Moreover, forensic psychologists must be prepared to address erroneous assumptions made by others in the legal system. Five key misassumptions, common to forensic practice, are outlined:

- *Malingering is very rare*. Equating infrequency with inconsequentiality, some clinicians neglect the evaluation of malingering except in very obvious cases. Estimates (Rogers et al., 1994, 1996) based on more than 500 forensic experts suggest that malingering is not rare, but likely occurs in 15% to 17% of forensic cases.

- *Malingering is very common*. Fueled by fears of fraud and injustice, certain attorneys (e.g., defense counsel in civil litigation and prosecutors in criminal matters) suspect that malingering and dissimulation are very prevalent. Despite speculation that the majority of forensic evaluatees may be malingering, the best estimates (Rogers et al., 1994, 1996) indicate this is not the case.

- *Malingering occurs at a predictable rate*. If stable base rates could be achieved, the classification of malingering and other response styles could be improved. In a desire to improve classification, clinicians often ignore the fact that malingering does not occur at predictable rates. The best available data (Rogers et al., 1996) found highly variable rates ($SD = 14.44$). Even within the same setting, rates are likely to vary markedly based on referral issues (see Rogers & Salekin, 1998).

- *Malingering is most likely to occur in persons with antisocial personality disorder (APD)*. Psychopaths and persons with APD likely engage in deception (Rogers & Cruise, 2000), but no data indicate an increased likelihood for malingering in forensic settings. This unsupported assumption likely is based on a methodological artifact: Because most forensic studies are conducted in *criminal* settings, the facile connection between malingering and APD is understandable.

- *Malingering and mental disorders are mutually exclusive*. Neither malingering nor mental disorders offer any natural immunity to the other. Some individuals with valid psychopathology "gild the lily" by adding feigned symptoms. Most clinicians are willing to acknowledge the co-occurrence of malingering and mental disorders; however, many forensic reports do not address the mental disorders after malingering has been determined.

Applications to Forensic Practice

Determinations of malingering often supersede all other clinical issues. When a forensic psychologist concludes that a person is malingering, this opinion is likely to invalidate all claims by that person, destroying his or her credibility. Because of its overshadowing importance, forensic psychologists carry a further responsibility to ensure the accuracy of their conclusions with respect to malingering. We recommend that the classification of malingering should never rely on a single indicator. In addition to confirmation by multiple sources, forensic psychologists should systematically exclude alternative explanations (e.g., factitious disorders or irrelevant responding) in their determinations of malingering. To avoid misclassifications based solely on idiosyncratic data, Rogers and Shuman (2000) put forth the following forensic guideline: *No determination of malingering should rest solely on traditional interviews*.

The classification of malingering often appears dispositive of the verdict. Given this observation, what are the responsibilities of a forensic psychologist who believes that another expert's conclusions about the presence of malingering were inaccurate? That psychologist bears the onerous responsibility of comprehensively evaluating the issue of malingering. If the data continue to support his or her conclusion (i.e., the absence of malingering), then great care must be taken to marshal this evidence in a manner to convince the trier of fact. In general, forensic psychologists should assume an uneven playing field, with a much heavier burden of disproving than proving malingering.

In sentencing and postverdict criminal evaluations, defensiveness is often the preeminent issue. Courts and other adjudicative bodies are concerned that dangerous persons not be released prematurely based on minimization of their psychological impairment. Forensic psychologists must exercise a rigorous standard in conducting these evaluations, comparable to malingering determinations.

EMPIRICAL ISSUES

The clinical assessment of response styles rests solidly on their validation. As demonstrated in this section, *no single research design is sufficient to validate measures of response style*. With respect to preparing for testimony, Rogers (1997) provided a thorough review of these research designs. The purpose of this section is to provide forensic psychologists with a brief summary of research designs and their relevance to the assessment of response styles.

Basic Designs

Three designs predominate the validation of clinical measures for the evaluation of malingering and defensiveness.

Simulation Design

Simulation studies use an analog design in which participants are randomly assigned to simulator and control conditions. For feigning studies, the addition of a clinical comparison sample is essential; otherwise, researchers cannot ascertain whether differences are attributable to feigning or to genuine disorders. With appropriate debriefing, the simulation design excels at internal validity but has limited external validity.

Known-Groups Comparison

Known-groups studies are conducted with independently classified malingerers who are compared with genuine patients. The challenge is the identification of actual malingerers in sufficient numbers for research. The known-groups comparison excels at external validity but has limited internal validity.

Differential Prevalence Comparison

Differential prevalence studies assume that certain groups will have a higher prevalence of a specific response style (e.g., forensic patients for feigning and job applicants for defensiveness). Group differences have little practical significance without knowing what is the proportion of dissimulation in different groups, or whether deviant scores represent dissimulation. Differential prevalence comparison fails to establish internal validity and has limited external validity.

Bootstrapping Comparisons

A fourth design, bootstrapping comparisons, recently has been observed in studies of feigned cognitive impairment. Persons identified by deviant scores on other measures of feigning are compared to those without these deviant scores. The key issue with bootstrapping comparisons is the selection of measures with nearly perfect specificity, so that the "feigning" group does not contain genuine patients. Experimental rigor can be increased through the classification based on several measures representing different detection strategies.

The best validation for measures of response styles is a combination of studies representing simulation design and known-groups comparisons. This combination maximizes both internal (simulation design) and external (known-groups comparison) validity. Forensic psychologists should take particular care to select measures with known-groups comparisons, because these studies are frequently omitted from the test validation.

Incremental Validity

Psychologists often believe that a convergence of findings across different measures contributes to incremental validity. As a counterposition, Sechrest (1963) demonstrated in his seminal article that the single best measure often is not improved by adding additional measures. As a forensic example, Kurtz and Meyer (1994) found that the SIRS was more accurate for the classification of feigning than either the MMPI-2 alone or the combination of the SIRS/MMPI-2. Forensic psychologists must decide whether to use the single best measure or a convergence of measures in establishing classificatory accuracy for response styles.

We recommend that forensic psychologists employ multiple indices from different measures when malingering is suspected. Because the determination of malingering carries such grave consequences, its assessment should be comprehensive. The results should be analyzed on two parameters: domain and detection strategies. Feigning can be divided into at least three broad domains (i.e., mental disorders, cognitive impairment, and medical illness) that differ substantially in clinical presentation. For each domain, detection strategies can be identified for the clinical classification of malingering; these detection strategies vary in the extent of their validation and accuracy of classification. To facilitate this analysis, subsequent sections of this chapter address domains and their respective detection strategies. Clinicians must be ready to grapple with both convergent and divergent results.

What about *convergent* results? With consistent results from well-validated strategies derived from dissimilar measures, forensic psychologists likely will have confidence in their conclusions about response styles. Such confidence should not be confused with increased accuracy (i.e., incremental validity); unless empirically demonstrated, psychologists cannot conclude a higher level of accuracy.

What about *generally* consistent results? The most common finding in forensic evaluations is that most of the indicators agree; however, one or more indices of response styles do not fit with the other indicators. One temptation is to ignore or explain away the discrepant findings. A more prudent course is to evaluate the results, taking into account the accuracy of the measures and the validity of the detection strategies. For example, a "nonfeigning" classification on the SIRS has an excellent positive predictive power that is likely to outweigh a more nebulous elevation on an MMPI-2 validity scale. In addition, some detection strategies (e.g., symptom validity testing) are much more robust than others (e.g., forced choice testing); their comparative validity can be taken into account in making determinations.

What about *inconsistent* findings? The first possibility is that the results are domain-specific. For example, an evaluatee with major depression (a mental disorder domain) may feign problems with attention, concentration, and immediate memory (a cognitive impairment domain) in the context of a disability evaluation. Sometimes, these cases can be resolved based on the accuracy of measures and relative validity of detection strategies. In other cases, the only logical decision is that the results are inconclusive.

Forensic psychologists should be aware that some clinicians adopt a "fall-through-the-ice" mentality: Any failure (e.g., an indicator of feigning) is viewed as decisive evidence of a pervasive response style. Like falling through the ice, the results are immediately catastrophic and summarily generalized. This mentality is empirically unwarranted and is probably more illuminating about the clinician than the evaluatee.

MALINGERING OF MENTAL DISORDERS

Detection Strategies

Rogers (1997) and Rogers and Vitacco (in press) provide extensive descriptions of detection strategies for feigned mental disorders. The purpose of this section is to highlight these primary strategies. These strategies are important for understanding how scales and specific indicators are utilized in the assessment of malingering. Using detection strategies, a conceptually based approach combines theory and empiricism. It offers judges and juries more than simply numbers and cut scores; it supplies the underlying logic and rationale for how the scales were constructed and the classification was reached.

A distillation of eight detection strategies for feigned psychopathology is enumerated:

1. *Rare Symptoms*. Items in this strategy are very infrequently endorsed by clinical populations. Malingerers often are unaware that certain symptoms are infrequently experienced. Rare symptoms represent one of the most robust detection strategies.

2. *Improbable Symptoms*. A minority of malingerers report or endorse symptoms that have a fantastic or preposterous quality. When a pattern of improbable symptoms is endorsed, the credibility of the evaluatee's reporting is brought into question.

3. *Symptom Combinations*. Many symptoms commonly occur alone but rarely are paired together (e.g., grandiosity and increased sleep). To foil this strategy, malingerers

would need to have a sophisticated understanding of psychopathology.

4. *Symptom Severity*. Even severely impaired patients experience only a discrete number of symptoms as "unbearable." Malingerers often are unable to estimate which symptoms and how many symptoms should have extreme severity.

5. *Indiscriminant Symptom Endorsement*. When asked about a broad array of psychological symptoms, some malingerers do not respond selectively but endorse a large proportion of symptoms.

6. *Obvious versus Subtle Symptoms*. Malingerers tend to endorse a high proportion of obvious symptoms (i.e., clearly indicative of a mental disorder). Obvious symptoms are either considered alone or in relation to subtle symptoms (i.e., "everyday" problems, not necessarily indicative of a mental disorder). When compared to genuine patients, malingerers often report a higher proportion of obvious symptoms.

7. *Erroneous Stereotypes*. Many persons have misconceptions about symptoms associated with mental disorders. When displaying erroneous stereotypes, persons feigning mental disorders can sometimes be detected.

8. *Reported versus Observed Symptoms*. Marked discrepancies between the person's own account and clinical observations appear useful in the detection of malingerers when standardized measures are used. The risk of this approach is that many genuine patients lack insight about their psychopathology.

These eight detection strategies account for most of the systematic approaches to feigned mental disorders and constitute the framework for the evaluation of malingered symptomatology. Several additional strategies have been explored. Morel (1998) used forced-choice testing (see section on Malingering and Cognitive Impairment) to test for feigned posttraumatic stress disorder; the bogus effects of emotional numbing were evaluated in a two-choice paradigm. Wildman and Wildman (1999) explored whether malingerers might be detected by their overly virtuous self-descriptions.

Featured Measures

A single chapter cannot comprehensively review the broad array of psychological measures adapted or developed for the assessment of feigned mental disorders. Therefore, this section addresses three featured measures that have been extensively validated. Featured measures include two multiscale inventories and one structured interview.

As a general caution, forensic psychologists should closely inspect test manuals and validation studies prior to using any test for feigned mental disorders. For example, we have observed numerous forensic reports attempting to use the Millon Clinical Multiaxial Inventory III (MCMI-III; Millon, 1994; Millon, Davis, & Millon, 1997) to assess feigning. Is this use warranted based on a careful examination of the MCMI-III's validation? The answer is clearly negative. For example, the debasement index is promoted as a fake-bad scale for detecting persons attempting to appear psychologically impaired. Close inspection reveals the following: (a) both the 1994 and 1997 MCMI-III test manuals neglected the validation of the MCMI-III debasement index; (b) the MCMI-III debasement index appears confounded by psychopathology (i.e., 9 clinical scales correlate $\geq .75$ in the normative sample); and (c) extrapolations from MCMI-II research would be inappropriate because only 19 of 46 (41.3%) MCMI-II items were retained on the MCMI-III debasement index. More than five years after the MCMI-III's publication, research (Daubert & Metzler, 2000; Thomas-Peter, Jones, Campbell, & Oliver, 2000) is now beginning to emerge on the debasement index and feigning; more extensive research is needed before its use in forensic evaluations. Importantly, validational problems are *not* limited to the MCMI-III; forensic psychologists are urged to scrutinize closely the validation of all response style measures.

Minnesota Multiphasic Personality Inventory-2

A large array of validity indices has been developed to evaluate whether MMPI-2 protocols have been feigned. Table 7.1 provides a summary of indices for the detection of both feigning and defensiveness. Summary data include the range of cut scores, available data on effect sizes, and a brief description of scale development.

Forensic psychologists are likely to be in a quandary about which MMPI-2 indices should be employed for the evaluation of malingering. Standard MMPI-2 texts provide conflicting conclusions. Championing the traditionalist model, Butcher and Williams (1992) advocated the use of the F and Fb scales, virtually ignoring specialized scales for feigning. Graham (2000) also emphasized the use of traditional MMPI-2 indicators. However, he endorsed one specialized indicator (Fp) and discommended the use of other specialized indices. In stark contrast, Greene (1997, 2000) embraces a comprehensive model, with the use of both traditional and specialized indices of malingering. Both models are critically evaluated in subsequent sections.

The *traditionalist model* of malingering, beyond history and convention, has several advantages that must be considered. In an MMPI-2 meta-analysis, Rogers, Sewell, and Salekin (1994) found the F and Fb had several of the largest effect sizes (2.56 and 1.85, respectively) for feigning when compared to clinical

TABLE 7.1   Description of MMPI-2 Validity Indices for Feigning and Defensiveness

| Scale Items | Cut Scores | Effect Sizes[a] | | | Scale Development |
		r^a	Feigning	Defensive	
Feigning Indices[b]					
F	60	8–30	1.00	2.56	Infrequency in normative samples.
Fb	40	9–25	.86	1.85	Infrequency in normative samples.
Fp	27	NA	.75	NA	Infrequency in inpatient samples.
Dsr2	32	13–28	.61[c]	1.54	Stereotypes of mental disorders.
FBS	43	NA	NA	NA	Rational: personal injury claims.
LW	107	40–67	.84	1.38	Rational: urgent clinical issues.
O-S	NA[d]	74–190	.81	2.30	Rational: obvious versus subtle symptoms.
Defensiveness Indices[e]					
L	15	6–9	.43	.94	Rational: borrowed from earlier scales.
K	30	17–22	1.00	.90	Empirical: $\geq 30\%$ for defensive patients.
Mp	34	16–20	.48[f]	1.42	Empirical: identify best impression.
Wsd	33	21–23	.28	1.60	Empirical: socially desirable items.
Esd	39	35–36	.76	.67	Rational: socially desirable items.
S	52	NA	.88	NA	Differential prevalence with pilots.[g]

Note: NA = not available.
[a]Correlations are reported in Greene (2000) for clinical samples between (a) feigning indices and Scale F and (b) defensiveness indices and Scale K.
[b]Effect sizes and range of cut scores reported in MMPI-2 meta-analyses of feigning (Rogers, Sewell, & Salekin, 1994).
[c]Dsr2 is not reported in Greene (2000); this estimate is based on the original 58-item Ds2 from which the Dsr2 was extracted.
[d]Uses T-score transformations of subscales.
[e]Effect sizes and range of cut scores reported by Baer, Wetter, and Berry (1992). Please note that this meta-analysis is based on the original MMPI and should be viewed only as a general benchmark for MMPI-2 performance.
[f]Based on slightly modified Od scale.
[g]Pilot applicants were assumed to have a high proportion of defensive persons; they were compared to a normative sample.

populations. Other research (Bagby, Buis, & Nicholson, 1995; Timbrook, Graham, Keiller, & Watts, 1993) has used hierarchical multiple regression to evaluate whether the use of additional validity indices would add incremental validity (i.e., account for more of the variance). These studies concluded that the F scale alone appeared to be the most predictive of malingering. A final advantage of the traditionalist model is its simplicity; forensic psychologists do not have to explain to the courts potentially conflicting MMPI-2 data.

The traditionalist model also has significant limitations in the evaluation of feigning. Its primary constraints are outlined:

- Both F and Fb are based on the same strategy (rare symptoms); this overreliance on a single strategy is a weakness of the traditionalist model. This shortcoming is accentuated by the flawed development of both F and Fb scales. Items on both were selected if they were infrequently endorsed by normative (nonclinical) samples. The critical comparison between genuine and bogus disorders was omitted. The fact that patients with genuine disorders often have marked F and Fb elevations is directly attributable to its flawed development.

- Studies indicating that specialized MMPI-2 indices do not add incremental validity to scale F have serious methodological constraints. Because of unaddressed issues with multicolinearity (e.g., 25% of items on F also appear on O-S), results likely are skewed toward nonsignificance. Also, forensic psychologists are primarily interested in whether the use of specialized indices improves accuracy of classification for feigning and genuine disorders. This matter was left unaddressed by these multiple regression studies.

The *comprehensive model* provides, in unambiguous cases, an array of empirically validated strategies for the classification of feigned and genuine disorders. Forensic psychologists can present data to the court based on multiple detection strategies: (a) rare symptoms (i.e., F, Fb, and Fp); (b) erroneous stereotypes (i.e., Dsr2); (c) overendorsement of obvious symptoms (i.e., O-S); and (d) indiscriminant endorsement of severe symptoms (i.e., LW). Convergent data from multiple strategies are often compelling, especially because they minimize the limitations found with any particular scale, such as multiple interpretations for marked elevations on the F scale.

The challenges of the comprehensive MMPI-2 model are how to understand discordant data and how to explain apparent discrepancies to the court. Validity indices on forensic protocols sometimes range from low to marginally elevated to extremely elevated. Occasionally, the pattern of scores is clearly understandable in light of other clinical data. In many cases, the range of validity indices presents a conundrum to forensic psychologists, who must explain their uncertainties to the court.

The incremental validity of MMPI-2 indices remains unresolved. Forensic psychologists will opt for either the simple traditionalist model or the more complex comprehensive model. They must weigh the risks of overlooking valuable data (traditionalist model) against the possibilities of unexplainable discrepancies (comprehensive model). For either choice, forensic psychologists must have a clearly articulated rationale.

For clinicians seeking guidance with this decision, one recommended course of action is a two-phase approach. Consistent with the traditionalist model, the first phase comprises standard indicators, which are routinely evaluated in all forensic cases. When standard indicators are marginally or markedly elevated, the second phase consists of 3 to 4 specialized indices, which likely include the Fp, Dsr2, LW, and O-S. In marginal cases, a second phase may resolve ambiguities. In marked cases, additional data are sought to confirm or disconfirm the initial findings.

Forensic psychologists should be aware of *common MMPI-2 missteps*. An important responsibility of forensic psychologists is to evaluate the conclusions drawn by other clinicians from test data, including the MMPI-2. A careful scrutiny of MMPI-2 reports reveals three common missteps in using the MMPI-2 for the assessment of feigning:

- *Inconsistent Profiles*. A random or otherwise inconsistent profile is likely to have extreme elevations of MMPI-2 feigning indices. Although malingerers may deliberately respond inconsistently, psychologists generally cannot rule out other common reasons for inconsistent profiles, including a haphazard completion of the answer sheet without carefully reading the test items. The very rare exception occurs when the MMPI-2 feigning indices are consistently above chance endorsement (e.g., raw F = 40).

- *Incompatible Profiles*. Clinicians sometimes observe that an MMPI-2 profile is incompatible with other documented findings and erroneously conclude that the client is feigning. This grave error is based on the misassumption that certain profiles or scale elevations are nearly always linked with certain diagnoses or symptoms. The simplest rebuttal of this error is that a within normal limits (WNL) profile with *no* clinical elevations is the most common profile among inpatients and outpatients (Greene, 2000).

- *Validity Scale Configurations*. Historically, the relative elevation of scale F in relationship to scales L and K was interpreted as indicative of feigning. The validity of this interpretation has not been established. Interestingly, Greene (2000) suggested that this configuration is desirable for psychological intervention.

Personality Assessment Inventory

The PAI now rivals the MMPI-2 as a multiscale inventory for the evaluation of malingering and other response styles. Although more malingering studies have been conducted with the MMPI-2, the PAI has several important advantages:

- The PAI validity scales are nonoverlapping. In contrast, specific MMPI-2 validity scales overlap with each other and with clinical scales, thereby confounding their interpretation and classificatory utility.

- The PAI validity scales typically use a standardized cut score for feigning. In contrast, MMPI-2 validity scales utilize a broad range of cut scores. This range diminishes the effectiveness of the MMPI-2's classification of feigned and nonfeigned profiles.

- The PAI validity indices were tested with both simulation and known-groups designs. In contrast, the MMPI-2 validity scales have very limited testing with actual cases of suspected malingerers.

Three PAI indices are used to evaluate feigning. The standard indicator, NIM scale (>11), is based on items infrequently endorsed by normative and patient samples. More recently, Morey (1996) developed the Malingering index (≥5), composed of eight configural rules using PAI scales and subscales. Finally, Rogers, Sewell, Morey, and Ustad (1996) cross-validated a discriminant function, which was derived from 20 loadings on PAI scales and subscales. Primary references for the feigning on the PAI include a recent review by Morey and the known-groups comparison by Rogers, Sewell, Cruise, Wang, and Ustad (1998).

The following guidelines are based on a synthesis of data from simulation research and known-group designs. In forensic evaluations, the guidelines are provided:

- *Rule out Feigning.* A NIM score <77T (raw score ≤8) indicates a low probability that the evaluatee is feigning.

- *Screen for Feigning.* Marked elevations on NIM (77T to 109T) indicate the need to evaluate thoroughly issues of feigning. Forensic psychologists should examine the PAI Malingering index and specialized measures (e.g., the SIRS) for the assessment of feigning.

- *Likely Feigning.* Extreme elevations on NIM (>110T) or the Malingering index (≥5) indicates a strong likelihood of feigning.

The PAI should not be used as the primary measure to evaluate feigning, although low scores may be effective at eliminating cases unlikely to be malingering. For "likely feigning," the strengths of extreme elevations are twofold:

(a) a very low proportion of false-positives (NIM = .02; Malingering index = .01), and (b) high (NIM, PPP = .82) to very high (Malingering index, PPP = .92) classifications when these cut scores are met. The problem is that relatively few feigners achieve such extreme elevations; the sensitivity estimates are .10 and .09, respectively. Therefore, these extreme scores are likely to miss 9 out of 10 feigners.

The PAI discriminant function is not recommended for forensic evaluations. Although highly effective in clinical evaluations, its accuracy was substantially diminished when applied to forensic patients in a known-groups comparison. Its sensitivity plummets from .84 to .51, and its specificity declines from .89 to .72. Even in clinical settings, psychologists are cautioned to inspect the PAI clinical profile before using the discriminant function. A case has been identified in which all the clinical scales were unelevated and the individual was not feigning, despite a positive finding on the discriminant function.

Structured Interview of Reported Symptoms

The SIRS is a structured interview for the systematic assessment of feigned mental disorders. Rogers, Bagby, and Dickens (1992) outline its general validation; forensic psychologists may wish to consult Rogers (2001) for the most recent update of SIRS validity studies. Unlike the MMPI-2 and PAI, the SIRS was developed specifically for the assessment of feigning and related response styles. This focus has resulted in extensive research for both the development of strategy-based scales and their clinical implementation.

The SIRS's primary scales employ all detection strategies described previously, with the exception of "erroneous stereotypes." Persons feigning mental disorders typically are classified based on three or more scales in the probable feigning range. Less frequently, feigners will have extreme elevations (i.e., definite feigning range) on one or more primary scales. Forensic psychologists classify SIRS profiles into one of three general categories: feigning, indeterminate, and nonfeigning.

The principal features of the SIRS are summarized:

- *Validation.* The SIRS has been extensively validated not only by its developers but also by independent researchers (see Rogers, 2001; Rogers et al., 1992). Importantly, the SIRS combines both simulation design and known-groups comparisons to optimize its validation. The SIRS has also been validated with clinical, forensic, and correctional populations.

- *Clinical Applications.* A major emphasis on the SIRS is the individual classification of evaluatees with respect to response styles. To reduce misclassifications, an indeterminate category was implemented for marginal cases. In the classification of feigners, the positive predictive power is very high to minimize misclassifications. Classification rules are also available for nonfeigning profiles.

• *Coaching.* A particular concern of forensic evaluators is whether evaluatees are coached by others or otherwise "educated" about a response style measure and its scales. Coaching participants on the SIRS strategies does reduce elevations; however, most participants still have marked elevations on the SIRS primary scales.

• *Generalizability.* Available research (see Rogers, 2001) indicates that the SIRS appears to function equally well across gender, ethnicities commonly encountered in forensic settings, and type of setting.

An important caution is that the SIRS has not been validated for repeat administrations, especially across brief intervals. We have observed several forensic cases in which an expert, apparently dissatisfied with the results from an earlier expert, readministered the SIRS. One grave concern is whether the evaluatee had access to the results of the previous report (written or oral) or reasonably inferred this feedback from general comments made by his or her attorney. This type of specific feedback on past SIRS performance may invalidate subsequent administrations.

In summary, the SIRS is probably the best-validated measure for the assessment of feigned mental disorders. In forensic cases in which malingering is suspected, the SIRS should be a standard component of the assessment. Given the accuracy of its individual classifications, results of the SIRS should be weighted heavily when discrepancies occur in the assessment of malingering.

DEFENSIVENESS AND MENTAL DISORDERS

Overview

Defensiveness, involving the denial and minimizing of mental disorders, is often cast into a secondary role in forensic evaluations. Cases of potential malingering take center stage because of concerns within the criminal justice system that criminal defendants may evade their punishments or that civil litigants may reap undeserved rewards. Less attention is paid to defensive clients who may be deliberately underreporting their symptomatology, possibly motivated by the stigmatization of mental illness. As an extreme example, some criminal defendants would rather face the death penalty than admit that they are mentally disordered.

Methods of assessing defensiveness in forensic evaluations are not nearly as well developed as those for malingering.

Three major reasons contribute to our limited knowledge of defensiveness:

• Defensiveness is difficult to assess because clients simply deny or minimize their symptomatology.

• Defensiveness is often difficult to distinguish from "lack of insight." Many chronic patients, especially those with psychotic disorders, do not recognize their symptoms and therefore do not report them.

• Defensiveness has been largely neglected by recent forensic research.

This section focuses on two measures that have been used with varying degrees of success in the assessment of defensiveness. These measures consist of the MMPI-2 and Paulhus Deception Scales (PDS; Paulhus, 1998).

Minnesota Multiphasic Personality Inventory

The MMPI-2 has two traditional scales and a handful of specialized scales for the evaluation of defensiveness (Baer, Wetter, & Berry, 1992). Beyond the traditional scales (L and K), this review focuses on two highly effective specialized scales (Wsd and Mp) as well as a recently developed and highly touted scale (S). Table 7.1 summarizes the pertinent information about these five scales.

Baer et al. (1992) conducted a meta-analysis on 25 studies with a first-rate review of defensiveness on the original MMPI. As an important and unexpected finding, Baer and her colleagues found that Wiggins' Social Desirability (Wsd) scale and the Positive Malingering scale (Mp) outperformed the traditional defensiveness scales, L and K. More recent MMPI-2 studies have highlighted the importance of specialized scales in the determination of defensiveness. Key findings are summarized:

• Baer, Wetter, and Berry (1995) found that traditional scales are vulnerable to coaching; tips on how to avoid detection foiled scales L and K (i.e., negligible effect sizes of $-.06$ and $-.04$, respectively). In contrast, Wsd produced a moderate effect size with coaching (.86).

• Studies have indicated that specialized indices of defensiveness add incremental validity. Specialized indices include Wsd, S, Edwards Social Desirability (Esd), and Other Deception (Od), which add incremental validity to the traditional scales (Baer, Wetter, Nichols, Greene, & Berry, 1995; Bagby et al., 1997). As a concrete example, Baer et al. (1995) found that a discriminant function based on scales L and K produced a 78% classification, while the addition of Wsd and S improved this classification to 90%.

A critical issue for forensic psychologists is whether MMPI-2 indices are effective in forensic cases in which defensiveness is likely to occur. Bagby, Nicholson, Buis, Radovanovic, and Fidler (1999) addressed this issue indirectly by comparing the clinical profiles of defensive and nondefensive parents in custody and access evaluations. Using a variation of standard indicators (i.e., L − K), they found virtually no difference between defensive and nondefensive profiles (*M* effect size = 0.00). With specialized indices (Wsd and S), very modest effect sizes were found (*M* effect size = .17). The use of single cut scores may have modest utility when most parents are engaging in some level of defensiveness (i.e., overall *M* elevations for clinical scales = 51.2). Alternative explanations are that most parents in child custody litigation do not have psychological impairment, or their psychological impairment is not captured by the MMPI-2.

The basic recommendation for forensic practice is that psychologists routinely score Wsd in all cases. In addition to robust effect sizes, the Wsd has two major advantages: it is less vulnerable to coaching than other indices, and it has a narrow range of cut scores. Other specialized indices (S and Mp) are likely to be used selectively in cases where defensiveness is suspected.

Paulhus Deception Scales

Paulhus (1998) developed the PDS, composed of two scales for measuring defensiveness. The purpose of each scale is examined in detail.

The Impression Management (IM) scale is intended to measure deliberate efforts at social desirability, although the scale correlates moderately with personality traits of conscientiousness and agreeableness. Under "high-demand" circumstances, scores on the IM scale tend to increase. Complicating the interpretation of the IM scale is the finding that highly religious persons tend to have very high scores (see Paulhus, 1998, p. 9, note 1); the question remains whether religious persons deliberately engaged in social desirability or the IM scale is confounded by devout beliefs.

The Self-Deceptive Enhancement scale (SDE) is intended to measure "an unconscious favorability bias closely related to narcissism" (Paulhus, 1998, p. 9). High SDE scores are associated with self-described personal adjustment; observers vary in their descriptions from confident and well-adjusted to arrogant and domineering. Perhaps the most controversial part of the SDE scale is its designation of an "unconscious" bias. Some forensic psychologists are likely to be unwilling to adopt the PDS's explicit psychoanalytic framework. Moreover, the admissibility of expert evidence following *Daubert* must take into account the falsifiability of scale interpretations, a

formidable challenge for the unconscious formulation for the SDE scale. Although the test manual reports factor analytic results supporting two dimensions, it does not provide evidence that the second dimension was unconscious. In citing his earlier research, this factor was described as a portrayal of "exaggerated mental control or dogmatic overconfidence" (Paulhus, 1998, p. 23). This description leaves open the question of unconscious motivation.

Results of Pebles and Moore (1998) further question the validity of the SDE scale. When simply asked to "make a good impression," participants easily doubled their scores on SDE from 5.5 to 11.6. The ability of uncoached participants to achieve an extreme elevation (T score = 85) casts doubt on the SDE as an *unconscious* measure of self-deception.

Salekin (2000) provided a useful summary of the PDS in relation to forensic practice. He observed problems in understanding the SDE scale in relation to psychopathy (e.g., grandiosity and superficial charm) and narcissism. He also noted the absence of cross-validated cutting scores and the lack of research with clinical-forensic samples. Amplifying on this latter point, an inspection of the test manual suggests that the PDS validation does not include any identified clinical sample; instead, Paulhus (1998) relied on general population, college students, prison entrants, and military recruits. Without formal comparisons to Axis I and Axis II disorders, forensic psychologists have no way of knowing whether scale elevations signify defensiveness or simply reflect a normative pattern in patient populations.

FEIGNED COGNITIVE IMPAIRMENT

Feigned cognitive impairment shares a similar definition and concomitant goals with other types of malingering. However, it differs fundamentally from the malingering of mental disorders in two crucial ways: tasks required of the malingerer and detection strategies. As observed by Rogers and Vitacco (in press), the principal task for feigned cognitive impairment is "effortful failure." In other words, would-be malingerers must convince the examiner that their efforts to succeed are sincere and that their ostensible impairments are genuine. Effortful failure is strikingly different from fabrication of symptoms and associated features typically required for feigned mental disorders. Because of these differences, forensic psychologists must use detection strategies that focus specifically on cognitive feigning. As a concrete example, strategies such as "rare symptoms" make little conceptual sense for the detection of purported deficits on the WAIS-III. Therefore, detection strategies specific to feigned cognitive impairment must be considered.

The definition of malingering does not change, despite differences in presentation and detection strategies. *The malingering of cognitive impairment must involve the gross exaggeration or fabrication of intellectual and neuropsychological deficits for an external goal.* This point must be emphasized. Many studies have attempted to substitute other terms, such as "incomplete effort," "suboptimal effort," and "poor motivation." These terms cannot be equated with either feigning or malingering.

Most clients are *required* to participate in forensic evaluations. The level of perceived coercion is likely to vary widely by circumstances of the evaluation and the individual characteristics of the clients. The far-reaching implications of these evaluations are not overlooked. For instance, the client's financial well-being is often at stake in civil proceedings. Although generally adequate, forensic evaluations do not represent the optimal conditions for the assessment of cognitive functioning. To expect clients to put forth optimal efforts under suboptimal conditions appears naïve.

The concept of "poor motivation" is both imprecise and inferential. What are the standards for judging certain motivation as "poor," "adequate," or "good"? The simple designation of poor motivation may have devastating consequences for a client. The process of assessing gradations of motivation is poorly understood and highly inferential. Forensic psychologists will want to avoid this level of imprecision and the potential ethical concerns of drawing unwarranted conclusions.

An important distinction must be drawn. Forensic psychologists certainly encounter clients who put forth an incomplete or suboptimal effort. The reasons for this suboptimal effort are typically unknown but may include (a) decreased interest and effort as a result of genuine cognitive impairment; (b) decreased interest and effort as a result of a comorbid condition (e.g., depression secondary to head injury); (c) expectations of failure based on recent performance; (d) stress and preoccupation with the potential consequences of the evaluation (e.g., loss of disability income); (e) reaction to inferences from the examiner's questions that the impairment is trivial; and (f) attempts to feign cognitive impairment. Psychologists must address these six reasons for suboptimal effort. Two types of conclusions are possible:

1. In a minority of cases, forensic psychologists may feel confident that they are able to address effectively each of these reasons for suboptimal effort. In very rare cases, they may have sufficient data to conclude that the suboptimal effort was a result of feigning and systematically rule out other explanations.

2. In most cases, forensic psychologists lack the data to address systematically the various reasons for suboptimal effort.

How should forensic psychologists describe suboptimal effort in the great majority of cases in which feigning cannot be isolated as the predominant reason? To avoid any serious misunderstandings, we recommend that forensic psychologists employ two safeguards: address the possible reasons for suboptimal effort, and proactively clarify the lack of known relationship between this diminished effort and feigning. An example of this recommendation is provided for a female client evaluated following a motor vehicle accident: "The client did not appear to put forth her best possible effort during several tests of her cognitive ability. Reasons for this could include cognitive and emotional impairment as a result of her car accident, her expectations of failure, stresses related to the evaluation, or deliberate attempts to appear more impaired. These test findings cannot be used to establish feigning or any other reason for suboptimal effort."

Evaluations of feigned cognitive deficits pose several important ethical issues for forensic psychologists. Because many cognitive feigning measures are single-purpose scales (i.e., only intended for dissimulation), what type of informed consent is required ethically? Youngjohn, Lees-Haley, and Binder (1999) argue that informing clients about cognitive feigning measures may reduce their effectiveness; instead, they advocate instructing clients to put forth maximum effort. Although maintaining the effectiveness of cognitive feigning measures is a laudable goal, it should not be achieved via the neglect of informed consent. In describing the nature of psychological services (American Psychological Association, 1992, Ethical Standard 1.07a), a basic obligation occurs to describe their broad objectives, including response styles. This obligation can be satisfied by a general statement at the onset of the evaluation; this statement may also serve a beneficial purpose in diminishing the likelihood of malingering (Johnson & Lesniak-Karpiak, 1997). A second ethical issue is posed by deliberate misrepresentations to the evaluatee. For example, the Rey 15-item test (see Lezak, 1995) is sometimes intentionally misdescribed as a "difficult" memory task, when this is known to be inaccurate. Forensic psychologists should categorically avoid any misrepresentations to persons being evaluated.

The next section outlines the detection strategies for feigned cognitive impairment. It summarizes the recent literature on the effectiveness of specific strategies and presents an overview of specific measures.

Detection Strategies

Rogers, Harrell, and Liff (1993) identified six basic detection strategies for feigned cognitive impairment. These strategies have been augmented by forced-choice testing and reaction time (Rogers & Vitacco, in press) and pairwise comparisons of comparable items (Frederick, 1997). In general, detection strategies can be grouped into two domains: detection by *excessive impairment* and detection by *unexpected patterns*. Examples of excessive impairment are failures on very easy items (i.e., floor effect) and failures below chance on forced-choice formats (i.e., symptom validity testing or SVT). Examples of unexpected patterns include similar performance on easy and difficult items (i.e., performance curve) and unexpected answers on forced-choice formats (i.e., magnitude of error). In general, detection strategies using unexpected patterns are less transparent than excessive impairment and likely to be robust indicators of feigning.

Three common detection strategies are subsumed within the "excessive impairment" domain, with feigned performance overreaching the level of impairment typically found in brain-injured patients. These strategies include floor effect, SVT, and forced-choice testing (FCT). Table 7.2 summarizes these detection strategies and provides representative examples of the sample cognitive measures.

TABLE 7.2   Detection Strategies on Feigned Cognitive Impairment: Measures and Validation

Strategy	Scale	Clinical Usefulness
Floor effect	Rey 15-Item	Many studies found good specificity but modest sensitivity; it is limited by varying cut scores and possible false-positives with specific conditions.
Floor effect	TOMM	Several studies found high classification rates; it is not tested with comorbid mental disorders.
Floor effect	HDMT	Guilmette, Hart, & Giuliano (1993) found that lower than 90% correct yielded high classifications; it needs cross-validation.
Floor effect	Digit Span	Two studies found cut score <7 had good specificity but modest sensitivity; research has relied on differential prevalence design.
Floor effect	LMT	Inman et al. (1998) reported 3 studies supporting the use of the LMT as a screen.
Perfor. Curve	TONI-S	Frederick & Foster (1991) found very positive results when restricted to higher scores; it is limited by the small number of memory-impaired patients and needs replication.
Perfor. Curve	Ravens-S	Gudjonsson & Shackleton (1986) found moderately high classification rates; it was partially replicated by McKinzey, Podd, Krehbiel, Mensch, & Trombka (1997).
Perfor. Curve	DCT	Several studies yield moderately high classifications, but studies use different cut scores.
Perfor. Curve	LNNB-S	McKinzey et al. (1997) found high rates on cross-validation; it appears clinically useful for LNNB administrations.
Mag. of Error	WMS-R-S	Martin, Franzen, & Orey (1998) found moderately high classification; it needs replication.
Atypical	WAIS-R-S	Mittenberg, Theroux-Fichera, Zielinski, & Heilbronner (1995) found moderate classification but with a substantial false-positive rate.
Atypical	CVLT-S	Sweet et al. (2000) found moderately high classification but did not report sensitivity or specificity estimates.
Atypical	WMS-R-S	Mittenberg, Azrin, Millsaps, & Heilbronner (1993) found high classification; it has been replicated (Iverson, Slick, & Franzen, 2000).
Sequelae	NSI	Ridenour, McCoy, & Dean (1998) provide promising data on the overall level of reported symptoms to identify simulators; it needs replication with a range of neuropsychological conditions.
SVT	PDRT	Several studies found superb specificity but poor sensitivity.
SVT	HDMT	Several studies found superb specificity but poor sensitivity.
SVT	TONI-S	Frederick & Foster (1991) found superb specificity but poor sensitivity.
SVT	TOMM	Several studies found superb specificity but poor sensitivity.
FCT	PDRT	Moderate classification; research is limited by differential prevalence design and lack of studies on comorbidity.
FCT	HDMT	Guilmette et al. (1993) used performance below 75% correct to achieve a high classification; it needs replication with large samples and evaluation of comorbidity.
FCT	21-Item Memory	Highly variable classification rates were found across studies.
FCT	"b" Test	Boone et al. (2000) found promising data; it needs replication.
FCT	WMT	Iverson, Green, & Gervais (1999) summarize past research that shows promise as a screen.
Consistency	TONI-S	Frederick & Foster (1991) found this useful in conjunction with other strategies.
Time	PDRT-C	Rose, Hall, & Szalda-Petree (1995) found shorter response times for simulators than brain-injured patients; it needs replication.
Time	TOMM	Rees, Tombaugh, Gansler, & Moczynski (1998) found longer response times for simulators than brain-injured patients; it needs replication.

Note: TOMM = Test of Memory Malingering (Tombaugh, 1996); HDMT = Hiscock Digit Memory Test (Hiscock & Hiscock, 1989); LMT = Learning Memory Test (Inman et al., 1998); Digit Span = sum of raw scores for highest number forward plus highest number backward; Perfor. Curve = Performance Curve; TONI-S = specially scored Test of Nonverbal Intelligence (Frederick & Foster, 1991); Ravens-S = specially scored Ravens Standard Matrices (Raven, 1981); DCT = Dot Counting Test (Lezak, 1995); LNNB-S = specially scored Luria-Nebraska Neuropsychological Battery (Golden, Purisch, & Hammeke, 1985); Mag. of Error = Magnitude of Error; WMS-R-S = specially scored Wechsler Memory Scales–Revised subtests (Wechsler, 1987); Atypical = Atypical Presentation; WAIS-R-S = specially scored Wechsler Adult Intelligence Scale-Revised (Wechsler, 1981); CVLT-S = specially scored California Verbal Learning Test (Delis, Kramer, Kaplan, & Ober, 1987); Sequelae = psychological sequelae; NSI = Neuropsychological Symptom Inventory (Rattan, Dean, & Rattan, 1989); SVT = symptom validity testing; PDRT = Portland Digit Recognition Test (Binder, 1992); consistency = consistency across parallel items; WMT = Word Memory Test (Green, Astner, & Allen, 1996); Time = response time; PDRT-C = computerized version of the PDRT.

Floor effect strategy is based on the notion that malingerers have difficulty distinguishing which cognitive abilities are unlikely to be compromised in patients with genuine neuropsychological impairment. This strategy was first promulgated by Andre Rey in the 1940s (see Lezak, 1995) in devising a cognitive task (Rey 15-item memory test) that appears moderately complex (recall of 15 separate items) but is actually simple (items are organized into easy-to-remember sequences). As operationalized, the floor effect strategy typically uses a very simple recall and recognition task that can be successfully completed by most (≥90%) cognitively impaired persons. For example, most patients with genuine cognitive impairment are able to achieve a 90% accuracy on the second trial of the Test of Memory Malingering (TOMM; Tombaugh, 1996). The majority of simulators do not recognize the simplicity of the memory task, especially when given repeated trials.

The floor effect strategy has become a popular detection method for cognitive feigning (see Table 7.2). Despite its intuitive appeal, forensic psychologists should be cautious in applying the floor effect strategy for two reasons. First, the range of genuine cognitive impairments militates against the selection of items that work equally well for all cognitive deficits. For example, the second trial of the TOMM appears to be highly effective with brain injury cases (false-positives = 2.2%) but not with dementia (false-positives = 27.0%). Second, evaluatees can be easily coached to foil the floor effect.

Symptom validity testing (SVT) examines an improbable failure rate based on statistical probability. First championed by Brady and Lind (1961), most SVT methods have a two-choice format; even persons with total incapacity should not score significantly below chance. The SVT strategy has been used by numerous cognitive measures, typically in combination with other strategies. Because the SVT takes into account total incapacity, this strategy tends to be effective only with extreme forms of malingering. Generally successful in less than one-third of simulating cases, the SVT is unique among detection strategies in ruling out other reasons for poor performance. The only logical reason for below-chance performance is the recognition of the correct response and subsequent selection of the incorrect response. Forensic psychologists can be very confident in their conclusions about cognitive feigning when performance on SVT is significantly below chance.

Memory complaints in forensic cases are sometimes focused on personal recollections (e.g., amnesia for the offense). Frederick, Carter, and Powel (1995) proposed that SVT could be used to address purported amnesia by constructing two-choice alternatives for the events in question. Care must be taken to develop equally plausible alternatives (Denney, 1996;

Frederick & Denney, 1998) and to test these alternatives on naïve persons to ensure that they have an equal likelihood of being selected. For example, a question about the victim's hair color may elicit "brown" more often than "blond" responses based on reasonable inferences about the prevalence of different hair colors (see Rogers & Shuman, 2000).

Forced-choice testing (FCT) is simply lower-than-expected performance based on normative data. Unlike other detection strategies, FCT does not apply a logical principle (e.g., floor effect) or mathematical probability (e.g., SVT). It simply evaluates group differences and attempts to establish an optimum cut score. FCT appears to have been introduced because SVT yielded only modest sensitivity rates (Binder & Willis, 1991). Without extensive samples of cognitively impaired individuals, including those with comorbid mental disorders (e.g., major depression or substance abuse), the false-positive rates of FCT cannot be established. Forensic psychologists must be careful to distinguish between FCT (questionable specificity) and SVT (very high specificity) in drawing their conclusions.

The second domain for cognitive feigning is "unexpected patterns" that capitalize on unlikely responses to specific items or sets of items. Detection strategies include magnitude of error, performance curve, and consistency across parallel items. Methods using these strategies are summarized in Table 7.2.

Magnitude of error (MOE) evaluates the degree of inaccuracy for incorrect responses. Especially in multiple-choice formats, incorrect responses can be grouped into "expected" and "unexpected" categories by inspecting patients with genuine cognitive impairment. A reasonable assumption is that most malingerers focus on *what* items to answer incorrectly, rather than *how* to answer items incorrectly. Extrapolating from case reports, Rogers et al. (1993) formally identify this strategy. Martin, Franzen, and Orey (1998) designed a multiple-choice format for Visual Reproduction and Logical Memory subtests of the WMS-R (Wechsler, 1987). They found MOE was highly effective at identifying simulators who endorsed a high proportion of unexpected errors. Bender (2000) found the MOE to be the most effective strategy for identifying simulators, even when simulators were warned about MOE.

Performance curve is based on the thesis that malingerers do not take into account item difficulty in choosing which items to fail. First identified by Goldstein (1945), performance curve compares the proportion of correct items across different gradations of item difficulty. When plotted on a graph, genuine patients and controls typically evidence a negative curve with lower performance on more difficult items. In contrast, some malingerers exhibit flat or even positive curves. This strategy appears to be moderately effective across different measures, including Raven standard progressive matrices (Gudjonsson & Shackleton, 1986; McKinzey, Podd, Krehbiel, & Raven, 1999), the Dot Counting Test (DCT; Binks, Gouvier, & Waters, 1997), and the Luria-Nebraska Neuropsychological Battery (LNNB; McKinzey, et al., 1997). In addition, several versions of the performance curve are central to the Validity Indicator Profile (VIP; Frederick, 1997). In summary, performance curve strategy appears to be robust, with consistent, positive findings across different measures.

Atypical presentation was traditionally considered an unstandardized evaluation of symptoms that did not make "neuropsychological sense" (Rogers et al., 1993). However, more recent studies have examined disparate findings that rarely occur in patients with genuine cognitive impairment. For example, bona fide patients generally score higher on the WMS-R Attention/Concentration index than the General Memory index, whereas simulators tend to manifest the opposite pattern (Mittenberg, Azrin, Millsaps, & Heilbronner, 1993; Iverson et al., 2000). Atypical presentation has also been applied to the WAIS-R in the Vocabulary and Digit Span difference. Mittenberg, Theroux-Fichera, Zielinski, and Heilbronner (1995) found that a discriminant function accurately identified 70.5% of the participants, although the false-positive rate was unacceptably high (36.8%) for forensic use. Descriptive data from disability evaluations cast further doubt on Vocabulary-Digit Span difference. Contrary to predictions, Williams and Carlin (1999) found that claimants with atypical presentations had significantly *higher* IQ scores than those with expected presentations. Finally, research on the California Verbal Learning Test (CVLT; Delis, Kramer, Kaplan, & Ober, 1987) indicated that simulators evidence atypical performance on both recognition and recall (Sweet et al., 2000; Trueblood & Schmidt, 1993).

Psychological sequelae is a variation of atypical performance that extends beyond cognitive abilities. Rogers et al. (1993) noted that simulators sometimes report symptoms of a mental disorder (Miller & Cartlidge, 1972) or physical complaints that are not typically found with genuine patients. For example, Heaton, Smith, Lehman, and Vogt (1978) found that simulators of head injury commonly reported elevations on six MMPI clinical scales. One limitation to this strategy is that nonprofessionals appear to have an intuitive understanding of concomitant symptoms for common conditions, such as mild brain injury (Lees-Haley & Dunn, 1994) and postconcussion syndrome (Mittenberg, D'Attilio, Gage, & Bass, 1990). However, promising work by Ridenour, McCoy, and Dean (1998) suggests that evaluatees can be presented with a wide array of neuropsychological symptoms, with simulators potentially

identifiable by the range and severity of reported symptoms. This strategy requires further evaluation before clinical implementation.

To evaluate *consistency across comparable items,* Frederick and Foster (1991) proposed a consistency ratio for examining performance across items of equal difficulty. Frederick (1997) elaborated on this approach in his development of the VIP. This strategy is difficult to implement because clinicians need items that have been rigorously tested across diverse clinical samples to ensure comparability in item difficulty. Especially for crystallized intelligence, cognitive abilities (e.g., vocabulary) may be highly variable in genuine patients. As an important caveat, consistency across parallel items should be not confused with consistency of test results. Many genuine patients produce anomalous results on neuropsychological testing. By themselves, inconsistent test results are not helpful to the classification of malingering.

Response time measures the average time to complete test items. Research is mixed on whether simulators take more time (Rees et al., 1998) or less time (Rose et al., 1995) than patients with compromised cognitive functioning. For practical purposes, response time is typically limited to computer administrations. At present, response time is not recommended as a general detection strategy.

Guidelines for the Classification

Forensic psychologists involved in neuropsychological cases are faced with several daunting tasks. The first task is a thorough understanding of detection strategies for feigned cognitive impairment and the available measures employing these strategies. Although not exhaustive, Table 7.2 summarizes most of the cognitive feigning measures reported in the clinical literature. In malingering cases, forensic psychologists bear the onerous responsibility of knowing the range of cognitive feigning measures, their detection strategies, and their general utility. Table 7.2 provides a useful starting point in developing this expertise.

The second task for forensic psychologists is the selection of detection strategies and cognitive feigning measures for suspected malingering cases. Psychologists will likely be influenced by the clinical presentation in their selection of strategies and methods. Two issues must be considered:

- *Purported Deficit.* Does the measure address the supposed impairment? Reported problems with analytic thinking are unlikely to be addressed by simple tests of memory recognition.
- *Detection Strategy.* Do the selected measures represent different selection strategies? As a general rule, detection

strategies should represent both the excessive impairment (floor effect and SVT) and the unexpected pattern (MOE and performance curve) domains.

Slick, Sherman, and Iverson (1999) propounded stringent standards for definite and probable malingering of cognitive impairment. For *definite* malingering, they proposed that only below-chance performance on SVT accompanied by external incentives would be sufficient for this determination. For *probable* malingering, they proposed at least two of the following: (a) indicators of feigning on one or more well-validated measures of feigned cognitive impairment; (b) discrepancies between test data and known patterns of brain functioning; (c) discrepancy between test data and observed behavior within a specific domain on two or more neuropsychological tests; (d) discrepancy between test data and reliable collateral reports; and (e) discrepancy between test data and documented background history. Alternatively, they proposed only one of the above plus discrepancies with self-reported symptoms or history. For *possible* malingering, proposed criteria include any major discrepancy between self-reported symptoms and other data (history, patterns of brain functioning, behavioral observations, or collateral information) or exaggerated/fabricated responses on tests of psychological impairment, such as the MMPI-2.

Slick et al. (1999) should be applauded for their efforts to systematize the classification of malingered cognitive impairment. However, this model has substantial limitations for forensic practice. Three major constraints are outlined:

1. Definite malingering is too narrowly construed. Exclusive reliance on SVT would exclude the great majority of malingerers that are not feigning extreme impairment. We propose that definite malingering include either SVT or multiple indicators of feigning (including detection strategies from the unexpected patterns domain), plus marked discrepancies between test performance and collateral data.

2. Probable malingering is too broadly construed. Forensic psychologists should be aware that distinctions between probable and definite malingering may not have any differential effect on the legal outcome. Therefore, great care must be exercised in establishing probable malingering in forensic cases. A major difficulty with the Slick et al. model is that the determination of probable malingering can be rendered without the objective application of systematic decision rules. Discrepancies in self-reporting and collateral sources can be explained without invoking the concept of malingering. We propose that "probable malingering" be invoked only when multiple indices of

feigned cognitive impairment are present in addition to marked discrepancies.

3. Possible malingering should not be used in forensic cases. Most complex forensic cases have some discrepancies in test data and subsequent reports. As an analogue, forensic psychologists often reach different conclusions about complex neuropsychological cases based largely on the same data. Test and collateral findings might be viewed as "discrepant" based on the propensities of a particular neuropsychologist rather than the response style of the evaluatee. Terms such as "inconsistent presentation" can be used without the pejorative effects intrinsic to the term "malingering."

Featured Measures

Three measures of feigned cognitive impairment from a broad array of potential measures are summarized: PDRT, VIP, and TOMM. They were selected based on their availability and substantial validation.

Portland Digit Recognition Test

Binder and Willis (1991) developed the PDRT as a 72-item digit recognition test of motivation and effort. A five-digit number is presented and followed by a distractor (i.e., counting backwards). Increasing intervals are included to increase the apparent difficulty of the task. The client is asked to choose the previously presented string of digits from two choices. The two-choice format allows the assessment of below-chance performance (i.e., SVT). Alternatively, the client's performance is compared to expected accuracy of cognitively impaired patients (i.e., FCT).

Binder (1993) investigated the SVT in a differential prevalence design. He found that none of the nonforensic patients with moderate to severe head injuries scored below chance. In contrast, 17% of the forensic sample with only mild head injuries scored below chance. He concluded that the SVT is an effective detection strategy, and financial incentives explained the differences in performance. In the same research, Binder also used an FCT with a cut score of <39 (no more than 54.2% correct) to distinguish patients with "unambiguous brain dysfunctions" from simulators. This research did not appear to take into account either comorbid conditions (e.g., depression) or the effects of stress and preoccupation with the potential consequences of the evaluation.

Variations of the PDRT include abbreviated and computerized versions. Discontinuation rules can be employed when an individual performs well on the first 18 or 36 items, thereby shortening the administration time. A modification of the computer administration allows for an examination of unusual response times. Rose et al. (1995) found higher reaction times in patients than in simulators on the PDRT. They concluded that the patients required more time to process the material due to cognitive slowing associated with head injury. Alternatively, the simulators may have underestimated the impact brain injury has on processing speed and failed to slow their responses accordingly.

The PDRT is appropriate for use in forensic contexts when employed to evaluate SVT via below-chance performances. When used appropriately, SVT virtually eliminates false-positives, making below-chance performances highly indicative of feigning. However, this strategy has only modest sensitivity, meaning that most feigners are not identified by SVT on the PDRT. Forensic psychologists are likely to be divided on the usefulness of the FCT with the PDRT, even as a screen for feigning. Without ruling out other explanations (e.g., comorbidity), the relationship between unexpectedly poor performance and potential feigning has not been fully evaluated. Finally, the RT strategy has not been sufficiently validated as to warrant its forensic application.

Validity Indicator Profile

The VIP (Frederick, 1997) employs a two-choice format for the assessment of suboptimal effort on two subtests addressing verbal and nonverbal abilities. The VIP is distinguished from other cognitive measures by its use of multiple strategies focused predominantly on unexpected patterns. The strategies include three estimates of response consistency and five estimates of performance curve. Because of the high intercorrelations for response consistency (M $r = .81$), forensic psychologists may be concerned whether they are discrete or largely redundant scales. Estimates of SVT are also possible, although not employed as a primary strategy.

The VIP classifies profiles as either "valid" or "invalid" rather than feigning *per se*. Invalid profiles are sorted into three categories (Frederick, 1997, p. 2): (a) "careless" (poor effort but motivated to do well); (b) "irrelevant" (intention to perform poorly but not a sustained effort); and (c) "malingered" (intention to perform poorly with a sustained effort). Using the broad categories of valid and invalid, the classification rates are moderately high. The VIP nonverbal subtest has a sensitivity rate of 73.5% and a specificity rate of 85.7%. The VIP verbal test has a sensitivity rate of 67.3% and a specificity rate of 83.1%.

The VIP is best conceptualized as a measure of *suboptimal effort* rather than feigning. Very few simulators and suspected malingerers are correctly classified in the "malingering"

category. Specific estimates of malingering classifications are provided:

- *Nonverbal subtest.* 3 of 52 (5.8%) simulators and 1 of 49 (2.0%) suspected malingerers were classified correctly in the malingering category (Frederick, 1997, p. 28, Table 8). The combined accuracy is 4/101 or 4.0%.

- *Verbal subtest.* 4 of 52 (7.7%) simulators and 1 of 49 (2.0%) suspected malingerers were classified correctly in the malingering category (Frederick, 1997, p. 29, Table 9). The combined accuracy is 5/101 or 5.0%.

- *Combined subtests.* The classification integrating both tests for malingering is not reported but should not exceed 9.0%. An extrapolation from Table 12 (p. 29), summarizing the concordance for invalid subtests, yields 6.2% as an approximate estimate.

These estimates derived from the VIP test manual do not support its use for the classification of malingering or feigning. As a measure of suboptimal effort, should forensic psychologists conclude that "invalid" profiles are likely the result of feigning? Substantial percentages of brain-injured patients have "invalid" results on the nonverbal (26.2%) and verbal (36.1%) subtests. Depending on the prevalence rate for feigned cognitive impairment, invalid profiles may be found at comparable rates between brain-injured patients with no apparent motivation to feign, and simulators and suspected malingerers.

The VIP should not be used clinically with two groups manifesting cognitive impairment, namely, those with mental retardation or learning disabilities. As noted by Frederick (1997), the VIP should not be used to evaluate patients with mental retardation (i.e., operationalized as Shipley IQs ≤75). Almost all (95.0%) of these participants produced invalid profiles. Psychologists are cautioned not to use educational attainment as an indirect measure of mental retardation; approximately two-thirds (67.5%) had at least a high school education. In addition, persons with learning disabilities were systematically excluded from the cross-validation phase and are not included in the classification tables.

In summary, the VIP is an ambitious effort to evaluate response styles through the use of multiple detection strategies and the evaluation of both nonverbal and verbal abilities. The most judicious use of the VIP is the assessment of suboptimal effort. Forensic psychologists should be careful not to equate suboptimal effort with deception or fraud. Depending on base rates, invalid VIPs may be just as likely to represent genuine impairment as any form of dissimulation. In rare cases where the VIP designates a protocol as "malingering," it is likely to be the result of feigning (found in seven cases) or possibly random responding (found in two cases).

Test of Memory Malingering

The TOMM (Tombaugh, 1996, 1997) is a two-alternative memory recognition task composed of 50 line drawings. Presented in two trials, the optimum cut score (45 or 90% correct) occurs in Trial 2. Scores at or above the cut score correctly classified 95% of nondemented patients; scores below the cut score identified 100% of the simulators. A small number of patients in a differential prevalence design had average scores substantially below the cut score ($M = 32.8$). In addition to the floor effect, the TOMM also uses SVT, which apparently has a low detection rate for feigners (Rees et al., 1998).

Several cautions apply to the use of the TOMM in forensic practice. First, the TOMM appears to produce much lower results when applied to patients in litigation or those seeking disability (Tombaugh, 1996). Although some litigating patients are malingering, the differential prevalence design leaves questions unanswered about its applicability to forensic cases. As noted by Smith (1998), the directions for the cognitively impaired group differed substantially from the standard TOMM instructions. In its validation, cognitively impaired participants were (a) verbally redirected to the task, (b) focused on both alternatives with expanded instructions, and (c) selectively re-instructed about the task (patients with dementia). This focusing and prompting may have artificially inflated TOMM scores for those with genuine cognitive impairment. The real danger is that the standard instructions may substantially increase false-positives, wrongly classifying genuine patients as feigners.

SUMMARY

Forensic psychologists are faced with formidable challenges in the assessment of malingering and defensiveness. As noted in this chapter, many clinicians and attorneys have misunderstandings and misassumptions about response styles. Forensic psychologists must be able to address these inaccuracies, including the potential misuse of *DSM-IV* indices. Clinically, they develop expertise through the knowledge of detection strategies and their application to psychological measures. Although faced with a daunting number of response style measures, they select empirically validated scales that are domain-specific (e.g., feigned psychopathology versus feigned cognitive impairment) and relevant to the immediate case. Forensic psychologists carefully integrate multiple sources of data, consistent with established detection strategies, in rendering their opinions on response styles to the courts.

Enduring challenges remain for forensic research on response styles. The next century should bring additional detection strategies that are rigorously tested by both simulation designs and known-groups comparisons. For cognitive assessment in particular, detection strategies need to be both expanded to cover diverse neurocognitive abilities and refined to improve clinical classification. From a forensic-psychological perspective, the standardized assessment of feigned medical conditions remains a vast, uncharted territory that requires both sophisticated conceptualization and sound empiricism.

REFERENCES

American Psychiatric Association. (2000). *Diagnostic and statistical manual of mental disorders* (4th ed., text rev.). Washington, DC: Author.

American Psychological Association. (1992). Ethical principles of psychologists and code of conduct. *American Psychologist, 47,* 1597–1611.

Baer, R. A., Wetter, M. W., & Berry, D. T. R. (1992). Detection of underreporting of psychopathology on the MMPI: A meta-analysis. *Clinical Psychology Review, 12,* 509–525.

Baer, R. A., Wetter, M. W., & Berry, D. T. R. (1995). Effects of information about validity scales on underreporting of symptoms on the MMPI-2: An analogue investigation. *Assessment, 2,* 189–200.

Baer, R. A., Wetter, M. W., Nichols, D. S., Greene, R., & Berry, D. T. R. (1995). Sensitivity of MMPI-2 validity scales to underreporting of symptoms. *Psychological Assessment, 7,* 419–423.

Bagby, R. M., Buis, T. E., & Nicholson, R. A. (1995). Relative effectiveness of the standard validity scales in detecting fake-good and fake-bad responding: Replication and extension. *Psychological Assessment, 7,* 84–92.

Bagby, R. M., Nicholson, R. A., Buis, T., Radovanovic, H., & Fidler, B. J. (1999). Defensive responding on the MMPI-2 in family custody and access evaluations. *Psychological Assessment, 11,* 24–28.

Bagby, R. M., Rogers, R., Nicholson, R. A., Buis, T., Seeman, M. V., & Rector, N. A. (1997). Effectiveness of the MMPI-2 validity indicators in the detection of defensive responding in clinical and nonclinical samples. *Psychological Assessment, 9,* 406–413.

Bender, S. D. (2000). *Strategic detection of cognitive feigning: Preliminary support for the TOCA.* Unpublished doctoral dissertation, University of North Texas, Denton.

Binder, L. M. (1992). *Portland Digit Recognition Test.* Unpublished test, Department of Veteran Affairs Medical Center, Portland, OR.

Binder, L. M. (1993). Assessment of malingering after mild head trauma with the Portland Digit Recognition Test. *Journal of Clinical and Experimental Neuropsychology, 15,* 170–182.

Binder, L. M., & Willis, S. C. (1991). Assessment of motivation after financially compensable minor head trauma. *Psychological Assessment: A Journal of Consulting and Clinical Psychology, 3,* 175–181.

Binks, P. G., Gouvier, W. D., & Waters, W. F. (1997). Malingering detection with the Dot Counting Test. *Archives of Clinical Neuropsychology, 12,* 41–46.

Boone, K. B., Lu, P., Sherman, D., Palmer, B., Back, C., Shamieh, E., et al. (2000). Validation of a new technique to detect malingering of cognitive symptoms: The b Test. *Archives of Clinical Neuropsychology, 15,* 227–241.

Brady, J., & Lind, D. (1961). Experimental analysis of hysterical blindness. *Archives of General Psychiatry, 4,* 331–339.

Butcher, J. N., Williams, C. L., Graham, J. R., Tellegen, A., & Kaemmer, B. (1989). *MMPI-2: Manual for administration and scoring.* Minneapolis: University of Minnesota Press.

Daubert, S. D., & Metzler, A. E. (2000). The detection of fake-bad and fake-good responding on the Millon Clinical Multiaxial Inventory III. *Psychological Assessment, 12,* 418–424.

Delis, D. C., Kramer, J. H., Kaplan, E., & Ober, B. (1987). *California Verbal Learning Test–Adult version.* San Antonio, TX: Psychological Corporation.

Denney, R. L. (1996). Symptom validity testing of remote memory in a criminal forensic setting. *Archives of Clinical Neuropsychology, 11,* 589–603.

Frederick, R. I. (1997). *The Validity Indicator Profile.* Minneapolis, MN: National Computer Systems.

Frederick, R. I., Carter, M., & Powel, J. (1995). Adapting symptom validity testing to evaluate suspicious complaints of amnesia in medicolegal evaluations. *Bulletin of the American Academy of Psychiatry and the Law, 23,* 231–237.

Frederick, F. I., & Denney, R. L. (1998). Minding your *p*s and *q*s when using forced-choice recognition tests. *Clinical Neuropsychologist, 12,* 193–205.

Frederick, R. I., & Foster, H. G. (1991). Multiple measures of malingering on a forced-choice test of cognitive ability. *Psychological Assessment: A Journal of Clinical and Consulting Psychology, 3,* 596–602.

Golden, C. J., Purisch, A. D., & Hammeke, T. A. (1985). *The Luria-Nebraska battery manual.* Palo Alto, CA: Western Psychological Services.

Goldstein, H. (1945). A malingering key for mental tests. *Psychological Bulletin, 42,* 104–118.

Green, P., Astner, K., & Allen, L. M., III. (1996). *The Word Memory Test: A manual for oral and computer-administered forms.* Durham, NC: CogniSyst Inc.

Greene, R. L. (1997). Assessment of malingering and defensiveness on multiscale inventories. In R. Rogers (Ed.), *Clinical assessment of malingering and deception* (2nd ed., pp. 169–207). New York: Guilford Press.

Greene, R. L. (2000). *The MMPI-2/MMPI: An interpretive manual.* Boston: Allyn & Bacon.

Gudjonsson, G. H., & Shackleton, H. (1986). The pattern of scores on Raven's Matrices during "faking bad" and "non faking" performance. *British Journal of Clinical Psychology, 25,* 35–41.

Guilmette, T. J., Hart, K. J., & Giuliano, A. J. (1993). Malingering detection: The use of a forced-choice method in identifying organic versus simulated memory impairment. *Clinical Neuropsychologist, 7,* 59–69.

Heaton, R. K., Smith, H. H., Lehman, R. A., & Vogt, A. T. (1978). Prospects for faking believable deficits on neuropsychological testing. *Journal of Consulting and Clinical Psychology, 46,* 892–900.

Hiscock, C. K., & Hiscock, M. (1989). Refining the forced-choice method for the detection of malingering. *Journal of Clinical and Experimental Neuropsychology, 11,* 967–974.

Inman, T. H., Vickery, C. D., Berry, D. T. R., Lamb, D. G., Edwards, C. L., & Smith, G. T. (1998). Development and initial validation of a new procedure for evaluating adequacy of effort given during a neuropsychological testing: The Letter Memory Test. *Psychological Assessment, 10,* 128–139.

Iverson, G. L., Green, P., & Gervais, R. (1999). Using the Word Memory Test to detect biased responding in head injury litigation. *Journal of Cognitive Rehabilitation, 17,* 4–8.

Iverson, G. L., Slick, D. J., & Franzen, M. D. (2000). Evaluation of a WMS-R malingering index in a non-litigating clinical sample. *Journal of Clinical and Experimental Neuropsychology, 22,* 191–197.

Johnson, J. L., & Lesniak-Karpiak, K. (1997). The effect of warning on malingering on memory and motor tasks in college samples. *Archives of Clinical Neuropsychology, 12,* 231–238.

Kurtz, R., & Meyer, R. G. (1994, March). *Vulnerability of the MMPI-2, M Test, and SIRS to different strategies of malingering psychosis.* Paper presented at the American Psychology-Law Society, Santa Fe, NM.

Lees-Haley, P. R., & Dunn, J. T. (1994). The ability of naïve subjects to report symptoms of mild brain injury, posttraumatic stress disorder, major depression, and generalized anxiety disorder. *Journal of Clinical Psychology, 50,* 252–256.

Lezak, M. D. (1995). *Neuropsychological assessment* (3rd ed.). New York: Oxford.

LoPiccolo, C. J., Goodkin, K., & Baldewicz, T. T. (1999). Current issues in the diagnosis and management of malingering. *Annals of Medicine, 31,* 166–174.

Martin, R. C., Franzen, M. D., & Orey, S. (1998). Magnitude of error as a strategy to detect feigned memory impairment. *Clinical Neuropsychologist, 12,* 84–91.

McKinzey, R. M., Podd, M. H., Krehbiel, M., Mensch, A., & Trombka, C. (1997). Detection of malingering on the Luria-Nebraska Neuropsychological Battery: An initial and cross-validation. *Archives of Clinical Neuropsychology, 12,* 505–512.

McKinzey, R. M., Podd, M. H., Krehbiel, M., & Raven, J. (1999). Detection of malingering on Raven's standard progressive matrices: A cross-validation. *British Journal of Clinical Psychology, 38,* 435–439.

Miller, H., & Cartlidge, N. (1972). Simulation and malingering after injuries to the brain and spinal cord. *Lancet, 1,* 580–586.

Millon, T. (1994). *The Millon Clinical Multiaxial Inventory-III manual.* Minneapolis, MN: National Computer Systems.

Millon, T., Davis, R., & Millon, C. (1997). *The Millon Clinical Multiaxial Inventory-III manual* (2nd ed.). Minneapolis, MN: National Computer Systems.

Mittenberg, W., Azrin, R., Millsaps, C., & Heilbronner, R. (1993). Identification of malingered head injury on the Wechsler Memory Scale–Revised. *Psychological Assessment, 5,* 34–40.

Mittenberg, W., D'Attilio, J., Gage, R., & Bass, A. (1990, February). *Malingered symptoms following mild head trauma: The post-concussion syndrome.* Paper presented at the 18th meeting of the International Neuropsychological Society, Orlando, FL.

Mittenberg, W., Theroux-Fichera, S., Zielinski, R., & Heilbronner, R. (1995). Identification of malingered head injury on the Wechsler Adult Intelligence Scale–Revised. *Professional Psychology: Research and Practice, 26*(5), 491–498.

Morel, K. R. (1998). Development and preliminary validation of a forced-choice test of response bias for posttraumatic stress disorder. *Journal of Personality Assessment, 70,* 299–314.

Morey, L. C. (1996). *An interpretive guide to the Personality Assessment Inventory (PAI).* Tampa, FL: Psychological Assessment Resources.

Paulhus, D. L. (1998). Paulhus Deception Scales (PDS): *The Balanced Inventory of Desirable Responding-7.* North Tonawanda, NY: Multi-Health Systems.

Pebbles, J., & Moore, R. J. (1998). Detecting socially desirable responding with the Personality Assessment Inventory: The positive impression management and the defensiveness index. *Journal of Clinical Psychology, 54,* 621–628.

Poythress, N. G., Nicholson, R., Otto, R. K., Edens, J. F., Bonnie, R. J., Monahan, J., et al. (1999). *Professional manual for the MacArthur Competence Assessment Tool-Criminal Adjudication.* Odessa, FL: Psychological Assessment Resources.

Rattan, G., Dean, R. S., & Rattan, A. I. (1989). *Neuropsychological Symptom Inventory.* Muncie, IN: Author.

Raven, J. C. (1981). *Manual for Raven's Progressive Matrices and Mill Hill Vocabulary Scales.* London: H. K. Lewis.

Rees, L. M., Tombaugh, T. N., Gansler, D. A., & Moczynski, N. P. (1998). Five validation experiments with the Test of Memory Malingering. *Psychological Assessment, 10,* 10–20.

Ridenour, T. A., McCoy, K. D., & Dean, R. S. (1998). Discriminant function analysis of malingerers' and neurological headache patients' self reports of neuropsychological symptoms. *Archives of General Neuropsychology, 13,* 561–567.

Rogers, R. (1990a). Development of a new classificatory model of malingering. *Bulletin of the American Academy of Psychiatry and Law, 18,* 323–333.

Rogers, R. (1990b). Models of feigned mental illness. *Professional Psychology: Research and Practice, 21,* 182–188.

Rogers, R. (Ed.). (1997). *Clinical assessment of malingering and deception* (2nd ed.). New York: Guilford Press.

Rogers, R. (2001). *Handbook of diagnostic and structured interviewing.* New York: Guilford Press.

Rogers, R., Bagby, R. M., & Dickens, S. E. (1992). *Structured Interview of Reported Symptoms (SIRS) and professional manual.* Odessa, FL: Psychological Assessment Resources.

Rogers, R., & Cruise, K. R. (2000). Malingering and deception among psychopaths. In C. B. Gacono (Ed.), *The clinical and forensic assessment of psychopathy: A practitioner's guide* (pp. 269–284). New York: LEA.

Rogers, R., & Dickey, R. (1991). Denial and minimization among sex offenders: A review of competing models of deception. *Annals of Sex Research, 4,* 49–63.

Rogers, R., Harrell, E. H., & Liff, C. D. (1993). Feigning neuropsychological impairment: A critical review of methodological and clinical considerations. *Clinical Psychology Review, 13,* 255–274.

Rogers, R., & Reinhardt, V. (1998). Conceptualization and assessment of secondary gain. In G. P. Koocher, J. C. Norcross, & S. S. Hill, III (Eds.), *Psychologist's desk reference* (pp. 57–62). New York: Oxford University Press.

Rogers, R., & Salekin, R. T. (1998). Beguiled by Bayes: A re-analysis of Mossman and Hart's estimates of malingering. *Behavioral Sciences and the Law, 16,* 147–153.

Rogers, R., Salekin, R. T., Sewell, K. W., Goldstein, A. M., & Leonard, K. (1998). A comparison of forensic and nonforensic malingerers: A prototypical analysis of explanatory models. *Law and Human Behavior, 22,* 353–367.

Rogers, R., Sewell, K. W., Cruise, K. R., Wang, E. W., & Ustad, K. L. (1998). The PAI and feigning: A cautionary note on its use in forensic-correctional settings. *Assessment, 5,* 399–405.

Rogers, R., Sewell, K. W., & Goldstein, A. M. (1994). Explanatory models of malingering: A prototypical analysis. *Law and Human Behavior, 18,* 543–552.

Rogers, R., Sewell, K. W., Morey, L. C., & Ustad, K. L. (1996). Detection of feigned mental disorders on the Personality Assessment Inventory: A discriminant analysis. *Journal of Personality Assessment, 67,* 629–640.

Rogers, R., Sewell, K. W., & Salekin, R. (1994). A meta-analysis of malingering on the MMPI-2. *Assessment, 1,* 227–237.

Rogers, R., & Shuman, D. W. (2000). *Conducting insanity evaluations.* New York: Guilford Press.

Rogers, R., & Vitacco, M. J. (in press). Predictors of adolescent psychopathy: The role of impulsivity, hyperactivity, and sensation seeking. In B. Van Dorsten (Ed.), *Forensic psychology: From classroom to courtroom.* Boston: Kluwer Academic/Plenum.

Rose, F. E., Hall, S., & Szalda-Petree, A. D. (1995). Portland Digit Recognition Test–computerized: Measuring response latency improves the detection of malingering. *Clinical Neuropsychologist, 9,* 124–134.

Salekin, R. T. (2000). Test review: The Paulhus Deception Scales. *American Psychology-Law Society News, 20,* 8–11.

Sechrest, L. (1963). Incremental validity: A recommendation. *Educational and Psychological Measurement, 23,* 153–158.

Sewell, K. W., & Salekin, R. T. (1997). Understanding and detecting dissimulation in sex offenders. In R. Rogers (Ed.), *Clinical assessment of malingering and deception* (2nd ed., pp. 328–350). New York: Guilford Press.

Slick, D. J., Sherman, E. M. S., & Iverson, G. L. (1999). Diagnostic criteria for malingered neurocognitive dysfunction: Proposed standards for clinical practice and research. *Clinical Neuropsychologist, 13,* 545–561.

Smith, G. P. (1998). Test review: The Test of Memory Malingering. *American Psychology-Law Society News, 18,* 16–18, 29–30.

Sweet, J. J., Wolfe, P., Sattlberger, E., Numan, B., Rosenfeld, J. P., Clingerman, S., et al. (2000). Further investigation of traumatic brain injury versus insufficient effort with the California Verbal Learning Test. *Archives of Clinical Neuropsychology, 15,* 105–113.

Thomas-Peter, B. A., Jones, J., Campbell, S., & Oliver, C. (2000). Debasement and faking bad on the Millon Clinical Multiaxial Inventory-III: An examination of characteristics, circumstances and motives of forensic patients. *Legal and Criminological Psychology, 5,* 71–81.

Timbrook, R. E., Graham, J. R., Keiller, S. W., & Watts, D. (1993). Comparison of the Wiener-Harmon subtle-obvious scales and the standard validity scales in detecting valid and invalid MMPI-2 profiles. *Psychological Assessment, 5,* 53–61.

Tombaugh, T. N. (1996). *TOMM: The Test of Memory Malingering.* North Tonawanda, NY: Multi-Health Systems.

Tombaugh, T. N. (1997). The Test of Memory Malingering (TOMM): Normative data from cognitively intact and cognitively impaired individuals. *Psychological Assessment, 9,* 260–268.

Trueblood, W., & Schmidt, M. (1993). Malingering and other validity considerations in the neuropsychological evaluation of mild head injury. *Journal of Clinical and Experimental Neuropsychology, 15,* 578–590.

Vanhouche, W., & Vertommen, H. (1999). Assessing cognitive distortions in sex offenders: A review of commonly used versus recently developed instruments. *Psychologica Belgica, 39,* 163–187.

Wechsler, D. (1981). *Weschler Adult Intelligence Scale–Revised.* San Antonio: Psychological Corporation.

Wechsler, D. (1987). *Wechsler Memory Scale–Revised manual.* San Antonio, TX: Psychological Corporation.

Wechsler, D. (1997). *Weschler Adult Intelligence Scale–Third edition.* San Antonio, TX: Psychological Corporation.

Wildman, R. W., & Wildman, R. W., Jr. (1999). The detection of malingering. *Psychological Reports, 84,* 386–388.

Williams, R. W., & Carlin, M. (1999). Malingering on the WAIS-R among disability claimants and applicants for vocational assistance. *American Journal of Forensic Psychology, 17,* 35–45.

Youngjohn, J. R., Lees-Haley, P. R., & Binder, L. M. (1999). Comment: Warning malingerers produces more sophisticated malingering. *Archives of Clinical Neuropsychology, 14,* 511–515.

PART THREE

SPECIAL TOPICS IN FORENSIC PSYCHOLOGY

CHAPTER 8

Forensic Assessment for High-Risk Occupations

RANDY BORUM, JOHN SUPER, AND MICHELLE RAND

In recent years, psychologists have been increasingly active in conducting assessments for candidates and incumbent employees in law enforcement and other "high-risk" occupations (Blau, 1994; Inwald & Resko, 1995). A mid-1980s survey indicated that there has been substantial growth in the use of psychological services in law enforcement. More than 75% of responding agencies reported a need for psychologists to assist in recruit screening and evaluating candidates for promotion, and 67% of respondents reported a need for psychological evaluations for suspended and problem officers (Delprino & Bahn, 1988). These represent the two primary types of occupational assessments requested for high-risk occupations: preemployment screening, an assessment of an applicant's psychological suitability for prospective employment, and "fitness for duty" evaluation, an assessment that typically occurs after an employee has engaged in some behavior or communication that has raised concern about his or her psychological suitability to perform job duties or about risk of harm to self or others in the workplace. These evaluations are considered forensic because they address and inform a legally relevant issue of psychological suitability for a sensitive position.

In this chapter, we first review ethical issues in conducting high-risk occupational assessments generally, then discuss legal and practice issues in preemployment psychological screening and fitness-for-duty evaluations specifically. Although most of the current literature and practice guidelines are focused on assessments for law enforcement personnel, many of the same issues apply to other high-risk occupations that affect public safety, including correctional officers, security officers, firefighters, air traffic controllers, airline pilots, and nuclear power plant operators (Rigaud & Flynn, 1995).

ETHICAL ISSUES IN HIGH-RISK OCCUPATIONAL ASSESSMENTS

There are two primary sources of authority for psychologists in understanding the ethical contours of conducting high-risk occupational assessments: the American Psychological Association's (APA) "Ethical Principles of Psychologists and Code of Conduct" (hereinafter, APA Ethics Code, APA, 1992), and "The Specialty Guidelines for Forensic Psychologists" adopted by the American Psychology-Law Society and the American Academy of Forensic Psychology (hereinafter, Specialty Guidelines; Committee on Ethical Guidelines for Forensic Psychologists, 1991). We consider below several key ethical issues drawn from these sources.

Competence

Preemployment psychological screenings and fitness-for-duty evaluations for public safety and other high-risk occupations are specialized forensic assessments. Psychologists cannot reasonably assume that they are qualified to conduct these assessments based solely on their knowledge of testing and clinical competence to conduct general psychological assessments. At a minimum, the psychologist should have some understanding of and experience working with public safety (or high-risk occupation) personnel, familiarity with the essential job functions of the relevant position, a knowledge of the scientific and professional literature on testing and screening for high-risk occupations, a clear understanding of the unique roles and limits of confidentiality and privilege, and a fundamental grounding in the state and federal legal issues that affect these evaluations (Super, 1997a, 1997b; see also Specialty Guidelines, Section III; IACP, 1998).

Practicing only within one's sphere of competence is, of course, a basic tenet of psychological practice. Indeed, Principle A of the APA Ethics Code directs: "Psychologists strive to maintain high standards of competence in their work. They provide only those services and use only those techniques for which they are qualified by education, training, or experience" (APA, 1992, p. 1599). This is reiterated in Standard 1.04 (a): "Psychologists provide services, teach and conduct research only within the boundaries of their competence, based on their education, training, supervised experience or appropriate professional experience" (p. 1600). Section III(a) of the Specialty Guidelines similarly addresses this issue as it applies specifically to forensic practice: "Forensic psychologists provide services only in areas of psychology in which they have specialized knowledge, skill, experience, and education."

Role Definition

One of the most vexing ethical issues for psychologists conducting psychological assessments for high-risk occupations is in defining and navigating roles (Super, 1997a, 1997b). Typically, when an individual meets with a mental health professional, he or she reasonably expects that the information exchanged will be confidential and will not be disclosed to third parties. This is *not* the case in preemployment or fitness-for-duty assessments. The applicant is not a patient and the evaluating psychologist should not promise confidentiality or offer or attempt counseling. The psychologist's primary client in these evaluations is the hiring or employing agency, not the individual applicant/employee. The examinee should be notified of this fact before the evaluation begins, and

reminded that the purpose of the evaluation is only to gather information about his or her psychological suitability for employment and not to provide treatment or therapeutic services. Standard 1.21 of the APA Ethics Code underscores this recommendation:

> When a psychologist agrees to provide services to a person or entity at the request of a third party, the psychologist clarifies to the extent feasible, at the outset of the service, the nature of the relationship with each party. This clarification includes the role of psychologist (such as therapist, organizational consultant, diagnostician, or expert witness), the probable uses of the services provided or the information obtained, and the fact that there may be limits to confidentiality. (APA, 1992, p. 1602)

The Specialty Guidelines cover extensively the issue of relationships and role definition in forensic assessments. Section IV advocates that the psychologist obtain informed consent, to include providing reasonable notice of legal rights pertaining to the service, purpose of the evaluation, procedures to be employed, intended uses of any product of the services, and the identity of the party who has employed the psychologist.

Confidentiality and Access to Results

In preemployment and psychological fitness-for-duty assessments, the psychologist owes a primary duty of confidentiality to the hiring agency as the client of record. Certainly, the psychologist should respect the privacy of the examinee and not report information that is sensitive but unrelated to employment suitability (Super, 1997a, 1997b). Nor should he or she reveal other information gathered in the assessment beyond what is necessary to support the opinion about psychological/emotional fitness. Standard 5.03 (a) of the APA Ethics Code states: "In order to minimize intrusions of privacy, psychologists include in written and oral reports, consultations, and the like, only information germane to the purpose for which the communication is made" (APA, 1992, p. 1606). A corresponding section of the Specialty Guidelines directs: "In situations where the right of the client or party to confidentiality is limited, the forensic psychologist makes every effort to maintain confidentiality with regard to any information that does not bear directly upon the legal purpose of the evaluation" (V.C). Nevertheless, conventional stipulations of confidentiality do not apply and, because there is no "doctor-patient" relationship, statutory provisions of privilege may similarly be inapplicable.

One of the greatest areas of contention concerns the examinee's access to the results or report of the evaluation. Although psychologists typically have an obligation to provide feedback to an individual who has been evaluated, this is not mandated and may be contraindicated for preemployment and fitness-for-duty assessments (Janik, 1994a, 1994b). It is necessary, however, for the psychologist to notify the examinee at the outset of the evaluation that no feedback or interpretation will be provided. Standard 2.09 of the APA Ethics Code stipulates:

> Unless the nature of the relationship is clearly explained to the person being assessed in advance and precludes provision of an explanation of results (such as in some organizational consulting, preemployment or security screenings, and forensic evaluations), psychologists ensure that an explanation of the results is provided using language that is reasonably understandable to the person assessed or to another legally authorized person on behalf of the client. (APA, 1992, p. 1604)

If an examinee does request evaluation results, information can be provided only with consent of the agency as holder of confidentiality. If feedback is given (with agency consent), the examinee should be informed that evaluation results apply only to his or her suitability for the position and may not relate to his or her mental health or adjustment in other areas.

In *Roulette v. Department of Central Management Services* (1987), an applicant who was not selected for employment as a police officer filed a request under the Freedom of Information Act to obtain the psychologist's preemployment evaluation report. The circuit court ordered the psychologist to provide the report; however, he did not comply and was found in contempt of court. The appellate court reversed the decision, holding that the "information was exempt from disclosure under Freedom of Information Act exemptions for examination data, information relating to internal personnel rules and practices, and trade secrets and commercial or financial information" (p. 60). Similar court rulings have been applied limiting an employee's access to results of fitness-for-duty assessments (Super, 1997a).

PREEMPLOYMENT SCREENING

Most major law enforcement agencies currently have comprehensive, multistage selection systems that include psychological screenings as one component of the program. Indeed, this component of the screening process has been widely advocated (National Advisory Commission on Criminal Justice Standards and Goals: Police, 1967; Milton, Halleck, Lardner, & Albrecht, 1977) and is mandated by the Commission on Accreditation for Law Enforcement Agencies (CALEA) for police and sheriff's departments seeking accreditation.

Although preemployment psychological screening does not guarantee the identification of all applicants who may have or subsequently develop psychological problems that could interfere with job performance, it may provide relevant information to hiring agencies about candidates who may be at higher risk. For example, personnel interviews, written tests, and careful background investigation may reveal characteristics, such as a history of impulsive or aggressive behavior or poor emotional control, that suggest the applicant could have a greater than average propensity to show an inappropriate response in a stressful use-of-force encounter (Stock, Borum, & Baltzley, 1996, 1999). Indeed, courts have ruled that police agencies have a right to conduct psychological evaluations (*McCabe v. Hoberman,* 1969; *Conte v. Horcher,* 1977) and that they may be held liable for the actions of employees who were not properly screened or evaluated (*Bonsignore v. City of New York,* 1982).

Legal Issues

Although the existence and application of statutes and case law pertaining to high-risk occupational evaluations vary by state, there are several key principles and provisions that should be familiar to any psychologist who conducts these assessments (Flanagan, 1995; Ostrov, 1995). In addition, however, psychologists should be aware of the law and how it is applied in the jurisdiction in which they practice (Super, 1997b).

One of the most significant and far-reaching legal provisions affecting these assessments is The Americans with Disabilities Act of 1990 (ADA, 1991), a federal statute enacted to prevent discrimination in employment and related activities based on an applicant's physical or mental disability. For purposes of the statute, disability is defined by the existence of "(A) physical or mental impairment that substantially limits one or more of the major life activities of such individual; (B) a record of such impairment; or (C) being regarded as having such an impairment." (For a complete discussion on the ADA and related legal issues, see the chapter by Foote in this volume.)

The ADA has affected whether and when hiring agencies, and psychologists contracted by those agencies, may inquire about an applicant's disability, including psychological, mental, or emotional impairment (Rubin, 1994). ADA interpretive guidelines promulgated by the Equal Employment Opportunity Commission (EEOC) state that "an employer cannot inquire as to whether an individual has a disability at the pre-offer stage of the selection process." Prior to enactment of the ADA, preemployment psychological evaluations often were conducted near the beginning of the hiring process. Because the purpose of these assessments is to identify psychological and behavioral problems that could negatively affect job performance, the examiner typically conducts an inquiry into psychological symptoms and areas of possible mental impairment, using certain psychological tests that identify psychopathology. Accordingly, the ADA views this inquiry as "medical" in nature and prohibits such an examination until *after* a candidate has been given a conditional offer of employment by the hiring agency. Even then, the inquiry about disability must be based on factors that are job-related and consistent with business necessity (Ostrov, 1995; Rubin, 1994).

EEOC Guidelines provide that "An employer is permitted to require post-offer medical examinations before the employee actually starts working . . . those employees who meet the employer's physical and psychological criteria for the job, with or without reasonable accommodation, will be qualified to receive a confirmed offer of employment to begin working" (Interpretative Guidelines Section 12630.14(b)). Thus, the examining psychologist should be reasonably assured by the hiring agency that candidates referred for screening have been given a conditional offer before conducting any inquiry that might otherwise be proscribed. Some psychologists have expressed concern that this process shifts undue weight to the psychological screening within the overall selection process. If a candidate presents with a conditional offer of employment, indicating that the agency believes he or she is otherwise qualified to be hired, but receives a less than suitable rating from the evaluator, it may create an appearance that the psychological assessment was the "cause" for disqualification or a decision not to hire.

Just as the ADA was enacted to prevent discrimination in employment based on disability, the most recent version of the Civil Rights Act (CRA, 1991) was adopted to prevent discrimination based on gender, race, or creed. This law has several important implications for psychologists who conduct preemployment psychological screenings (Rubin, 1995), but one of the most practical is that it prohibits using differential cutting scores on job-related tests based on a candidate's gender or race. Certain psychological tests, such as the Minnesota Multiphasic Personality Inventory (MMPI/MMPI-2), typically use different normative comparisons based on gender for determining a respondent's T-score. It has been argued that this practice would violate CRA requirements (Inwald, 1994). It is easily remediated by using combined norms, but the psychologist must be aware of the issue to make such a correction.

Courts have generally supported the right of public safety agencies to require a psychological examination as part of its selection procedure. In *McKenna v. Fargo* (1978), several ap-

plicants for the position of firefighter with Jersey City, New Jersey, challenged, as a violation of their civil rights, the city's requirement that they undergo psychological testing to determine their ability to withstand the psychological pressures inherent in the job. The district judge denied the claim, ruling that "the interest of the City in screening out applicants who would not be able to handle the psychological pressures of the job was sufficient to justify the intrusion into the privacy of the applicant" (p. 1355).

Municipalities may even be held liable if employees are not screened for emotional fitness and later engage in negligent behavior or misconduct on the job (Super, 1999). Under the doctrine of *respondeat superior,* sometimes referred to as vicarious liability, employers may be responsible for the acts of their employees when such acts are performed in the line of duty. Indeed, in *Monell v. Department of Social Services* (1978), the U.S. Supreme Court ruled specifically that municipalities and administrators could be held liable for behavior of subordinates if the subordinate employees were negligently supervised, trained, or selected.

The applicant's right to privacy, however, may carry different weight for security officers than for public safety officers. In *Soroka v. Dayton Hudson Corporation* (1991), applicants for security officer positions in Target department stores brought suit against the parent company, Dayton Hudson Corporation, for its policy of administering preemployment psychological testing, claiming that the tests included objectionable items that unduly invaded their privacy. At the time, Target used a test that combined items from the MMPI and the California Psychological Inventory (CPI) to screen prospective applicants for store security positions. The court agreed that the testing did invade the applicants' privacy, and distinguished the use of these tests for screening public safety versus store security personnel:

> Both of these tests [MMPI and CPI] have been used to screen out emotionally unfit applicants for public safety positions such as police officers, correctional officers, pilots, air traffic controllers, and nuclear power plant operators. We view the duties and responsibilities of these public safety personnel to be substantially different from those of store security officers. (p. 79)

Practice Issues

The current prevailing practice is to use psychological assessments to "screen out" applicants who may be at increased risk for job-related behavioral problems or who might pose a substantial risk to public safety as a result of psychological or behavioral problems (Janik, 1994a, 1994b). Although psychologists have conducted these evaluations since at least the early 1900s, it has only been recently that professional guidelines have been available to bring some uniformity and accountability to the assessment process. Perhaps the most widely used and accepted of these practice guidelines are the "Preemployment Psychological Evaluation Guidelines" developed and adopted by the Police Psychological Services Section of the International Association of Chiefs of Police (hereinafter, IACP Preemployment Guidelines; IACP, 1998). The principles contained in this document are consistent with CALEA standards and with best practices in the specialty of police psychology. It is reasonable and recommended for a law enforcement agency to require its evaluators to conduct their assessments in accordance with these guidelines.

Identifying Job-Related Abilities

The first step in conducting a preemployment assessment is to establish and understand the psychological requirements for the position. According to the ADA, a candidate must be able to perform the essential functions of the job with or without reasonable accommodation; therefore, the examiner must know the nature of those functions and the capacities required to perform them under job-related conditions. The most precise source of information on job requirements is a job task analysis, which many public safety agencies and other employers already have conducted. This analysis should distinguish essential functions and critical job tasks from other work functions and identify the knowledge, skills, abilities, and other characteristics necessary for the position.

The IACP Guidelines direct that "data on attributes considered most important for effective performance in a particular position should be obtained from job analysis, interview, surveys, or other appropriate sources" (Preemployment Guideline #4; IACP, 1998). These identified factors should guide the selection of instrumentation and help to focus areas of inquiry during a personnel interview.

Obtaining Consent

As noted previously, the examining psychologist has an ethical obligation to obtain informed consent from the candidate prior to the evaluation. This requires that the examiner provide information about the nature and purpose of the evaluation, the psychologist's role, and any limits on confidentiality and privilege, including who will have access to the report. Typically, this disclosure includes notice that the examiner is a licensed psychologist and that the hiring agency has requested an assessment of psychological suitability for the position as part of the selection process. It is important to clarify that

although the candidate will be the subject of the assessment, the hiring agency is the designated client; that examiner's only role will be as an evaluator; and that there is no treatment relationship; therefore, psychologist-patient privilege will not apply. Additionally, the candidate should be informed that, based on findings from the assessment, the examiner will send a report to the hiring agency, and, to that extent, the content of the interviews, testing, and observations will not be confidential or privileged. (In practice, however, the evaluator should attempt to maintain the confidentiality of sensitive, nonrelevant information about the applicant.) The candidate should also be informed that he or she may refuse to participate in the examination or to answer any specific questions, but that such refusals will be noted in the report.

To document this disclosure appropriately, it is recommended that the notification be done verbally and in writing. The examiner should consider using an informed consent form for preemployment evaluations where candidates acknowledge their understanding of each point. The notification and consent procedure is particularly important in these assessments because the roles, relationships, and contours of confidentiality are atypical for psychologist-examinee interactions. In particular, it may be difficult for candidates to understand that they are not the designated client, and that they may not be permitted access to the report, except through consent of the hiring agency.

Assessment Methods

Current practice standards, including the IACP Preemployment Guidelines, suggest that preemployment psychological screenings should include psychological testing and a job-related interview. Decisions regarding which tests to use will, of course, be affected by where the assessment is occurring in the overall selection process. Because the ADA prohibits any "medical inquiry" prior to a conditional offer of employment, no tests that assess or aid in the diagnosis or appraisal of psychopathology may be used at that time. Most law enforcement agencies have adapted to this requirement by positioning the psychological evaluation at the postoffer stage. This allows the examiner to use assessment methods and ask questions that will help screen for psychological problems, while maintaining compliance with provisions of the ADA.

In national- and state-level documents that make recommendations about test selection and use in these assessments, two suggestions consistently emerge: that instruments should be objective rather than projective, and that validation research should exist to support the test's use in preemployment screening (IACP Preemployment Guidelines, 1998; Hargrave & Berner, 1984).

In the early 1990s, Scrivner (1994) conducted a survey of 65 experienced, practicing police psychologists, 45 of whom conducted preemployment screenings. Among those who conducted these assessments, almost all used psychological testing (96%) and clinical interviews (91%). A much smaller proportion used supplemental or alternative protocols such as risk assessment models (22%), situational tests (15%), or job simulations (4%) (Scrivner, 1994). Only a few tests were used regularly, including the MMPI/MMPI-2 (91%), the CPI (54%), Sixteen Personality Factors Questionnaire (16PF)/Clinical Analysis Questionnaire (28%), Sentence Completion Form (20%), and the Inwald Personality Inventory (15%; Scrivner, 1994).

The frequent use of the MMPI-2 is not surprising, as it is also one of the most widely used tests in clinical psychological assessment. Prior research has examined the relationship between MMPI scales and various criteria of police academy and job performance. Several studies have found significant relationships between certain scale scores from the original MMPI and criterion measures of academy attrition (Hargrave & Berner, 1984), disciplinary action (Hiatt & Hargrave, 1988a; Weiss, Johnson, Serafino, & Serafino, 2001), length of time on the job (Saxe & Reiser, 1976), performance ratings from supervisors (Hiatt & Hargrave, 1988b; Weiss et al., 2001), and even promotion (Peterson & Strider, 1968).

Two newer trends in testing for high-risk occupations, however, are worth noting. The first is the development of the Personality Assessment Inventory (PAI; Morey, 1991). Like the MMPI-2, the PAI is a broad-based measure of psychopathology and clinical syndromes in adults. However, it offers some distinct advantages over other instruments: It is shorter (344 items versus 567 items on the MMPI-2); it has easier readability (Schinka & Borum, 1993); and its item content is more straightforward and is unlikely to be viewed as intrusive or offensive. Recent data, using a sample of over 3,000 law enforcement applicants, showed that PAI scales had higher correlations than MMPI-2 scales with applicants' reported problem behavior (e.g., anger control problems and illicit drug use) and psychological suitability ratings (Roberts, 1997). Normative PAI data for more than 17,000 public safety applicants are available as part of a specialized Police and Public Safety Report developed by the test publisher (Roberts, Thompson, & Johnson, 1999). The PAI may not be as widely used as the MMPI-2, but there clearly is a strong conceptual and empirical rationale to support its use in public safety preemployment screenings.

The second major development is a series of instruments from Hilson Research that are designed and validated specifically for use in high-risk occupational screenings and assessments (Inwald, in press). The oldest and most established of these is the Inwald Personality Inventory (IPI), a 310-item true-false instrument that goes beyond traditional assessment of psychopathology to include scales that measure other behavioral and interpersonal factors relevant to high-risk personnel selection decisions (Inwald, Knatz, & Shusman, 1982). Factors such as rigidity (Reiser & Geiger, 1984), suspiciousness, authority problems (Lawrence, 1984), past work and legal history, and status of current relationships (Johnson, 1984) have a demonstrated relationship to applicant suitability and subsequent job-related success. The IPI measures these dimensions in addition to some common clinical syndromes. Based on existing research, predictions derived from Fisher discriminant function equations are provided on the IPI reports predicting the likelihood of absence, lateness, disciplinary action, and termination of the applicant within the first year of employment.

A number of predictive validity studies have found significant relationships between IPI scales and subsequent academy and on-the-job performance criteria, including termination, lateness, absence, disciplinary action, injuries, leadership potential, supervisor's ratings, and overall performance (Inwald, 1988; Inwald & Shusman, 1984; Scogin, Schumacher, Howland, & McGee, 1989; Shusman, Inwald, & Knatz, 1987). Some research suggests that IPI variables predict job-related criteria better than MMPI variables (Inwald, 1988; Inwald & Shusman, 1984; Shusman, Inwald, & Knatz, 1987), and that the two instruments are not measuring the same factors. In fact, a redundancy analysis of the IPI and MMPI has indicated an overlap in variance of only about 20% (Shusman, 1987). Although much of the early research on the IPI was conducted by investigators from Hilson Research,

> an independent meta-analysis was conducted using IPI studies available as of 1991 (Ones, Viswesvaran, Schmidt, & Schultz, 1992). This analysis resulted in an estimated criterion-related validity of the IPI for predicting job performance in general of .37, with the standard deviation of the true validity at .07, indicating that this validity applies across situations in organizations. (Inwald, in press)

Although psychological testing is an important component of a preemployment psychological screening, it is generally not a sufficient basis to render an opinion about a candidate's psychological suitability. IACP Preemployment Guidelines direct that "individual, face-to-face interviews with candidates should be conducted before a final psychological report is submitted" (Guideline #12). It is also recommended that this interview take place *after* the examining psychologist has reviewed the results of the psychological testing, so that any concerns raised by these results can be explored or clarified with the candidate. The content of the

TABLE 8.1   Preemployment Psychological Interview Areas of Inquiry

- Family history
  - Where born and raised.
  - Siblings.
  - Mother: status and background.
  - Father: status and background.
  - Home problems, abuse/neglect, fighting.
  - Marital status and history.
  - Children.
- School history
  - High school attended and graduated.
  - Grade average, failures.
  - Learning problems, special placements.
  - Sports and club participation.
  - School discipline.
  - College education.
- Work history
  - Military; branch.
    - Type of discharge.
    - Military occupational specialty.
    - Rank at discharge, time of enlistment.
    - Disciplinary actions.
  - Work history
    - Past employers, position, time employed.
    - Reasons for leaving past positions.
    - Work-related disciplinary actions.
    - Work performance.
    - Conflicts with supervisors or coworkers.
- Behavioral history
  - Juvenile law enforcement contact/arrest.
  - Adult law enforcement contact/arrest.
  - Other legal system involvement.
  - Physical fights as an adult.
  - Moving violations and motor vehicle accidents.
  - Mental health treatment or problems that needed treatment.
  - Substance use treatment or problems that needed treatment.
  - Alcohol consumption.
  - Illicit drug use/experimentation.
  - Medical problems.
- Job-Specific
  - Reason for seeking position.
  - Best qualities.
  - Worst qualities.
  - Perception of job and role.
- Possible job-related scenarios

interview typically covers relevant historical and background information. The interview should follow a semi-structured format to ensure that all relevant areas are covered. Common areas of inquiry for a preemployment psychological interview are shown in Table 8.1.

Suitability Analysis

Once the relevant information has been collected through testing and interviews, the key to determining a candidate's psychological suitability is to assess the degree of "fit" between his or her capacities and the requirements of the position (Grisso, 1986). If there are indications from test results, history, or interview of psychological or behavioral problems,

the expert must assess the extent to which those problems would interfere with the applicant's ability to safely perform the essential functions of the position under job-related conditions. For example, disturbances in thinking could impair one's perceptions or judgment under pressure, severe disturbances in mood could affect behavioral controls or reaction speed, and problems with impulsivity or anger management could increase the risk of inappropriate aggression. Ratings of psychological suitability are typically offered in at least three categories, rather than simply as a yes or no decision.

Although these ratings often are not operationally defined in practice, this specification is helpful for heuristic purposes, for increasing the consistency of judgments across candidates, and for enhancing the clarity of the rating to the hiring agency. Provided below is one example of how these levels might be defined:

- *Suitable.* No indications of significant psychopathology or severe behavioral problems/patterns that would negatively affect job performance. Few or no areas of concern were noted. Any moderate or marked elevations or critical items on psychological testing have been examined in the context of the face-to-face interview, and are not believed to indicate significant psychopathology or behavioral problems.

- *Marginally Suitable.* No indications of significant psychopathology, although some symptom patterns or behavioral traits may exceed normal limits. One or more significant areas of concern were noted; however, either (a) the evidence for the problem, (b) the type of problem, or (c) the level of severity of the problem is currently insufficient to justify the applicant's exclusion. Some moderate or marked elevations or critical items on psychological testing may exist, which, on follow-up, either suggested mild-moderate potential for job-related difficulties or that the applicant was not able to satisfactorily explain.

- *Unsuitable.* Well-supported indications of significant psychopathology or potential for severe behavioral problems that could negatively affect job performance. Multiple areas of concern may be present, or the type or severity of the problem suggests a substantial potential for job-related difficulties. Moderate or marked elevations or critical items on psychological testing are believed to reflect potential psychological or behavioral problems that could negatively affect job performance.

Communicating Results

Preemployment psychological reports vary widely in format, content, and length. A psychologist may even have a different report format for different agencies, depending on their needs and preferences. In general, however, the screening report will contain identifying information for the candidate (e.g., name, age, race, date of birth, position sought), a listing of the sources of information used in the assessment (e.g., list of tests, interview), a statement describing the consent procedure, background/historical information, behavioral and mental status observations, test results, and conclusions. In the conclusion section, the psychologist assigns the suitability rating and provides a summary of the key information and analysis that supports that opinion, but should avoid using clinical diagnoses or psychiatric labels (IACP Preemployment Guideline #16).

FITNESS-FOR-DUTY EVALUATIONS

Whereas preemployment psychological evaluations are intended to screen out candidates who may be psychologically unsuitable *before* they are hired, psychological fitness-for-duty evaluations (FFDEs) are indicated for incumbent employees whose communication, behavior, or performance raises a specter of concern about safety or about behavioral or psychological problems that might significantly interfere with job performance (Stone, 1995, 2000). Thus, there are two primary circumstances that might cause an agency to refer an employee for an FFDE:

1. When there is reasonable cause to suspect that an employee may pose a significant risk of harm to self or others in the workplace.
2. When there is reasonable cause to suspect that the employee may have a psychological, psychiatric, or substance use disorder, or psychological/psychiatric symptoms that significantly interfere with his or her ability to perform the essential functions of the position.

Concerns about an employee's risk of harm or excessive force may be handled in accordance with agency policies relating to use of force, threats, harassment, or violence. Behaviors that raise concerns about serious harm and violate policy may not always result in an FFDE. If the employee is to be terminated, however, an assessment or consultation in these circumstances may be useful to help assess the degree of risk inherent in the termination. Concerns about psychological or psychiatric impairment may result from observation or credible evidence that a disturbance in the employee's behavior, thinking, mood, perception, orientation, or memory may be interfering with his or her ability to perform the essential functions of the position or assigned duties.

Stone (1990), an experienced police psychologist, analyzed the reasons for FFDE referrals in his own practice over a 10-year period. The most frequently cited causes were suspected psychopathology (26%), excessive force issues (19%), substance abuse (15%), repeated poor judgment (13%), domestic violence (9%). This distribution may not be representative of all FFDEs nationally, but it does give some indication of common reasons for referral by public safety agencies.

Agencies that hire employees for high-risk occupations should have policies in place addressing the substantive and procedural issues involved in FFDE referrals (Ostrov, Nowicki, & Beazley, 1987; Saxe-Clifford, 1986). These policies should be developed and implemented before an employee-related crisis occurs. In the sections below, we describe several key legal and practice issues in FFD assessments.

Legal Issues

As previously noted, psychologists should be aware of the relevant law and how it is applied in the jurisdiction in which they practice; however, it is instructive to consider the manner in which legal disputes regarding FFDEs have been resolved by other courts. Federal statutes, such as the ADA and CRA, are also relevant to FFDEs, but because they were addressed in the section on preemployment evaluations, the information will not be repeated (Flanagan, 1995; Ostrov, 1995).

The most fundamental legal issue in FFDEs is whether the hiring agency has a right to require an employee to submit to a psychological evaluation to assess his or her continued psychological suitability or fitness for employment. The landmark case in this area is *Conte v. Horcher* (1977), a case in which a police lieutenant brought suit against the chief of police for ordering him to undergo a psychiatric evaluation, claiming that the mandate was inappropriate and unlawful. The court ruled that the police chief had not only the authority to order the evaluation, but also an obligation to do so if the facts warranted concern about an officer's psychological suitability:

> It is the duty of the police chief to maintain a capable and efficient force. An examination, either physical or mental, enables the chief to ascertain the qualifications of a person to perform particular duties or to fill a particular position. (p. 569)

This supports the rulings of other courts that agencies employing high-risk personnel, particularly law enforcement officers, should have official policies and procedures in place for monitoring the psychological fitness of employees, including mandated assessment referrals where appropriate (*Bonsignore v. City of New York*, 1982).

A second legal issue pertains to the question of who is permitted to be present during the evaluation itself. In *Vinson v. The Superior Court of Alameda County* (1987), an employee argued that mandating a psychiatric evaluation violated her right to privacy, but that if she was to be compelled to submit, she should be allowed to have her attorney present with her during the examination. The court denied this request:

> We were skeptical that a lawyer, unschooled in the ways of the mental health profession, would be able to discern the psychiatric relevance of the questions. And the examiner should have the freedom to probe deeply into the plaintiff's psyche without interference by a third party. (p. 412)

In response, Vinson argued that the presence of counsel would provide her with comfort and support in an adversarial setting. The court responded:

> An examinee could view almost any examination of this sort, even by her own expert, as somewhat hostile. Whatever comfort her attorney's hand-holding might afford was substantially outweighed by the distraction and potential disruption caused by the presence of a third person . . . we concluded counsel's presence was not necessary. (p. 412)

Another key issue at the confluence of ethics and law is whether an employee has a reasonable expectation of privacy or confidentiality when mandated to undergo a psychological FFDE. In the matter of *David v. Christian* (1987), the central issue was whether the examinee or the agency mandating the assessment held the privilege of confidentiality. The petitioning police officer was discharged from employment after undergoing a psychiatric evaluation. The petitioner then claimed that confidentiality was abrogated when the report of his FFD Evaluation was released to his superiors. The court ruled:

> The employee counseling unit's confidentiality requirement only attached where counseling was for the purpose of remedying personal employment problems. Here, the psychiatric report was sought exclusively by the petitioner's superiors in order to determine whether the petitioner's condition warranted his termination. (p. 826)

The courts appear to acknowledge the distinction between circumstances in which an employee voluntarily contacts a mental health professional and enters into a treatment relationship (and thereby holds the privilege of confidentiality) and those in a mandatory FFDE, where the referring agency holds the right of confidentiality.

A similar, but more complex set of facts occurred in *Redmond v. City of Overland Park* (1987), a case involving the confidentiality of information and the balance between an employee's right to privacy and the agency's need to ensure the continued psychological fitness of its employees. Ms. Redmond was a probationary police officer with the City of Overland Park from December 1984 to May 1985. During this time, she engaged in behaviors that resulted in the request for an evaluation to assess her mental fitness. Mental health professionals were contacted and conducted an initial interview; however, they apparently did not have her sign a form on which she acknowledged that results would be reported back to the agency. Redmond sought legal counsel, alleging that police officials and the consulting mental health professionals disclosed private information about her. On review, the court found that these mental health professionals did not render "any professional opinion or diagnosis of the plaintiff's condition or her ability to function as a police officer" (p. 482). The initial mental health consultants withdrew from the case. Subsequently, other mental health consultants were asked to provide a mental evaluation of Redmond, and had her sign an appropriate informed consent and release of information. The court found:

> Clearly, any disclosures made on or after April 22, 1985 [the date of the signed consent] are not protected since plaintiff signed a release allowing the Mission Psychology Group to disclose records and information regarding the plaintiff to the Department. (pp. 482–483)

Regarding the balance between the rights of the employee and those of the department, the court concluded:

> The court must weigh the Department's legitimate interest in determining the plaintiff's fitness to serve as a police officer and the plaintiff's narrow interest in preventing disclosure of the personal information. The court finds that overwhelming evidence has been presented which shows that the municipality's interest in insuring that the plaintiff was capable of performing her duties substantially outweighed the privacy interest the plaintiff had in the information in question. (p. 484)

To summarize, trends in case law seem to suggest the following:

- Police chiefs have a right, and an affirmative obligation, to mandate their employees to undergo an FFDE if their mental health or emotional stability is called into question.
- Individuals who are mandated to undergo an FFDE do not have a legal right to have counsel present during interviews or testing sessions.
- A law enforcement agency's responsibility to ensure the psychological fitness of its officers outweighs the right to

privacy of an individual officer whose mental fitness may be in question.

Practice Issues

Psychological FFDEs tend to be more extensive and more complex than preemployment screenings, although many of the fundamental practice issues are quite similar. The ultimate question is whether the examinee has a psychological or behavioral problem that would significantly interfere with his or her ability to perform the essential functions of the position or pose a direct risk of harm in the workplace. The Police Psychological Services Section of the IACP, the authors of the IACP Preemployment Guidelines, have recently approved a set of guidelines for psychologists who conduct FFDEs (hereinafter, IACP FFDE Guidelines; IACP, 1998). As with the Preemployment Guidelines, the principles are consistent with CALEA standards and with best practices in the specialty of police psychology. They should guide the expectations of examiners, examinees, and agencies.

Identifying Job-Related Abilities

As with preemployment evaluations, the examiner should identify the psychological requirements for the position, and analyze the capacities required to perform the essential functions under job-related conditions (Stone, 1990). Job descriptions and job task analyses are critical sources of information. Trompetter (1998) suggests several psychological domains that he believes are essential for effective functioning as a law enforcement officer and that should be assessed during an FFDE (see Table 8.2).

TABLE 8.2   Psychological Domains for Effective Functioning as a Law Enforcement Officer

- Emotional control/anger management.
- Stress and threat tolerance.
- Acceptance of criticism.
- Impulse/risk control.
- Positive attitude.
- Assertiveness/tenacity.
- Command presence/persuasiveness.
- Integrity.
- Dependability/reliability.
- Initiative/achievement motivation.
- Conformance to rules and regulations.
- Adaptability/flexibility.
- Vigilance/attention to detail.
- Interpersonal sensitivity.
- Social concern.
- Teamwork.
- Practical intelligence/decision-making ability.
- Objectivity/tolerance.

Source: Trompetter (1998).

Even if the psychologist is generally familiar with the job or knows specific abilities identified from other agencies, it is often helpful to obtain a job description from the specific requesting agency to ensure that one is providing the most precise assessment of fit between the examinee's condition and the agency's requirements.

Obtaining Consent

The process of obtaining consent for a psychological FFDE is nearly identical to that described for preemployment screenings. Indeed, the IACP FFDE Guidelines state: "No FFDE should be conducted without either the officer's informed written consent or a reasonable alternative" (Guideline #6). The provision for a reasonable alternative is included to address situations in which the examinee may decline to sign a notice of consent. In such cases, the psychologist could choose not to proceed, could refer the matter back to the agency for resolution, or could proceed with a written notice of the provisions of the assessment that is signed by a third party and/or recorded on audio- or videotape. Regardless, it will be necessary for the examiner to disclose information about the nature and purpose of the evaluation, the psychologist's role, the designation of the agency as the client of the consultation, and any limits on confidentiality and privilege, including who will have access to the report. Again, the examinee may be informed that he or she may refuse to participate in the examination or to answer any specific questions, but should be notified that such refusals will be included in the report to the agency.

Assessment Methods

The IACP FFDE Guidelines recommend a multimethod approach to the psychological FFDE, which typically includes the following:

1. Review of requested background information.
2. Psychological testing using objective, validated tests appropriate to the referral question.
3. Face-to-face comprehensive clinical interview that includes a mental status examination.
4. A biopsychosocial history.
5. Third-party collateral interviews with relevant individuals, if deemed necessary and appropriate by the examiner.
6. Referral to and/or consultation with a specialist if the presenting problem goes beyond the expertise of the evaluator. (Guideline #7)

One of the major differences in the assessment methods between preemployment screenings and FFDEs is the nature and degree of reliance on records and collateral information. IACP FFDE Guidelines suggest that, to assess an officer's patterns of behavior, it is usually helpful for the psychologist to review background information such as "performance evaluations, commendations, testimonials, internal affair's investigations, preemployment psychological screening, formal citizen/public complaints, use-of-force incidents, officer-involved shootings, civil claims, disciplinary actions, incident reports of any triggering events, [and] medical/psychological treatment records" (Guideline #5). To ensure a fair and balanced process, it may also be probative for the expert to ask the examinee if there are specific individuals he or she thinks should be interviewed or documents that should be reviewed as part of the evaluation.

The extent to which a psychologist chooses to use psychological testing in an FFDE may depend on the facts of the case and the circumstances precipitating the referral. Typically, it will be helpful to have at least one broad-based measure of psychopathology such as the PAI or the MMPI-2 because there is often an implicit or explicit predicate question about the presence of a psychological disorder. Testing, in this circumstance, provides an efficient way to gather information across multiple symptom areas and to screen for indications of significant problems that may occur even if there is no history of prior treatment. Including in one's test battery an inventory that assesses normal dimensions of personality, such as the NEO-Personality Inventory-Revised (NEO-PI-R), the CPI, or the 16PF, may help to reveal strengths that can lend balance to the evaluation, or may suggest personality traits that may be problematic, inflexible, or maladaptive, even if there are not clear indications of a formal personality disorder.

If the psychologist selects a battery with more than one test, the objective should be to maximize convergent and discriminant validity while minimizing measurement redundancy (Borum, Otto, & Golding, 1993). A psychologist does not want to simply select multiple measures of the same construct or constructs, all of which are highly correlated with each other. Rather, it is helpful to achieve a sufficiently broad sample of behavioral domains and to examine areas of convergence across assessment methods. Inwald (in press) notes: "The best predictors of job behavior are past indications/admissions of similar behavior in similar situations. When compared with predictions based on psychopathology, predictions based on behavioral admissions are consistently better." Following the assertion of Hogan, Hogan, and Roberts (1996) that "most performance criteria are best predicted by a combination of scales," Inwald currently advocates a six-test battery of Hilson Instruments for FFDEs: the

Hilson Career Satisfaction Index (Inwald, 1989), Inwald Survey 5 (Inwald, 1992), Hilson Safety/Security Risk Inventory (Inwald, 1995), Inwald Survey 2 (Inwald, Resko, & Favuzza, 1996b), Hilson Life Adjustment Profile (Inwald, Resko, & Favuzza, 1996a), and the Hilson Personnel Profile/Success Quotient (Inwald & Brobst, 1988). The advantage of this approach is that the measures are research-based and cover a broad range of relevant behaviors with comparative data available for incumbent employees in high-risk occupations, and for persons undergoing mandatory evaluations. The potential disadvantage is that many of the instruments contain items derived from the same large item pool, so that without results of a formal redundancy analysis, it is difficult to determine how independent each of these measures are from each other. Moreover, the degree of incremental validity associated with using each of the six tests in the battery has not, to our knowledge, been systematically evaluated or reported.

Fitness Analysis

As with preemployment assessments, the psychologist must evaluate the degree of fit between the employee's current capacities or impairments and the essential requirements of the position (Grisso, 1986; Stone, 1995). The assessment can be done by (a) determining if there are psychological or behavioral problems, and if so, evaluating their potential impact on the employee's ability to perform the functions of the job; and (b) determining if there are any significant impairments in the employee's ability to perform essential job functions, and if so, evaluating their cause. If impairments are caused by a mental or emotional disorder, the psychologist must then assess whether the condition is remediable and whether the nature and degree of impairment is sufficient to justify a designation of being unfit for duty. If impairment is sufficiently severe that the employee is unfit for duty and the condition causing that impairment is not reasonably remediable, the employee would generally be considered permanently unfit for duty. If the condition is treatable, however, the examiner should recommend a course of intervention most likely to remediate it and specify the conditions necessary for restoring the employee to work status.

Based on this analysis, a determination is typically made that the employee meets one of four conditions:

1. *Fit for duty.* The employee does not have a psychological or behavioral disorder that causes substantial impairment in his or her ability to perform the requirements of the job or that poses a direct threat of foreseeable harm in the workplace.

2. *Fit for duty with mandatory treatment.* The employee does not pose a direct threat of foreseeable harm in the workplace. Some psychological or behavioral condition exists that may negatively affect job functioning, but the nature or severity is not sufficient to classify the employee as being unfit for duty. The condition is remediable within a reasonable time frame with appropriate treatment. Specific treatment recommendations are provided, and the employee should be directed to adhere to the treatment plan as a condition of continued employment with the agency. Reasonable accommodations (e.g., light duty assignment) may be suggested as an interim or ongoing measure.

3. *Temporarily unfit for duty, mandatory treatment.* The employee has a psychological or behavioral disorder that causes substantial impairment in his or her ability to perform the requirements of the job or that poses a direct threat of foreseeable harm in the workplace. The nature or severity of the condition and/or the attendant impairment is sufficient to classify the employee as being unfit for duty; however, the condition is likely remediable within a reasonable time frame with appropriate treatment. Specific treatment recommendations are provided, and the employee should be directed to adhere to the treatment plan as a condition of continued employment with the agency or eligibility to return to work.

4. *Permanently unfit for duty.* The employee has a psychological or behavioral disorder that causes substantial impairment in his or her ability to perform the requirements of the job or that poses a direct threat of foreseeable harm in the workplace. The nature or severity of the condition and/or the attendant impairment is sufficient to classify the employee as being unfit for duty, and the condition causing the impairment is judged not to be remediable within a reasonable period of time.

There are two circumstances where the fitness determination requires some special consideration: those involving officers involved in a duty-related shooting and those that are reassessments after being found temporarily unfit or being assigned to light duty. Taking a life in the line of duty and witnessing the violent death of a partner are among the most stressful critical incidents experienced by law enforcement officers (Sewell, 1983). Although these events are unquestionably traumatic, the range of individual reactions varies widely. Many will cope well with no apparent difficulty; some will initially experience some transient symptoms of anxiety or distress but quickly regain equilibrium. Others, however, will be severely and profoundly affected in a way that could interfere with their ability to perform their peace officer functions. The evaluating psychologist should understand the typical phases of posttraumatic

reactions and consider the appraisal of fitness in light of the nature and severity of the reactive symptoms and length of time that has elapsed since the incident. Officers who initially show no reaction may subsequently develop problems, and some officers who initially have problems find that they resolve quickly. The examiner must seek information about whether the involved officer has experienced any changes in thinking, mood, or behavior after the incident. In addition to assessing usual symptoms of posttraumatic stress disorder, depression, and anxiety, the psychologist should specifically probe and consider a possible heightened sense of danger, excessive reactivity, anger, dissociative and intrusive experiences, substance abuse problems, and suicidal thoughts (Solomon & Horn, 1986). The job-related abilities are the same as for any other FFDE, but it is useful to consider how any adjustment difficulties may interfere with those essential functions. If there is significant potential for impairment in job-related abilities, as in other FFDEs, the assessor must then consider the prospect for remediation through treatment.

If an officer has been found temporarily unfit or otherwise temporarily relieved of full duty for psychological reasons, typically, an FFDE will be requested at some point to assess his or her capacity to return to work. The nature of the evaluation and analysis is not substantially different than in other types of FFDE referrals; the key distinction is the appraisal of what has happened since the declaration of unfitness and what changes have occurred in the symptoms or impairments that initially caused concern. In this way, the reassessment is somewhat more focused, but certainly no less challenging. Reliance on third-party information is critical to gauge any changes in thinking, mood, or behavior that may be observable by others and to assess the extent to which they are consistent with the officer's self-report. If the officer has been referred for treatment, the evaluator ordinarily should contact the treatment provider to request records (with written consent of the officer) and to gather, preferably through discussion, relevant information about specific symptoms or behaviors of concern. The treating professional may also have relevant data and opinions about the officer's prognosis. When consulting a treating professional, however, the FFDE examiner must always consider that the provider has a primary alliance with the officer, and that the applicability of any information must be considered in light of the known distinctions between therapeutic and forensic roles.

SUMMARY

Psychologists have been involved in conducting assessments for applicants and incumbents in high-risk occupations for many years; however, only recently have professional practice guidelines begun to emerge that provide accountability and consistency to the evaluation process based on professional consensus about best practices. Psychologists who are asked to conduct preemployment screenings or FFDEs must first consider whether they have the necessary base of specialized knowledge and skill to be ethically competent to conduct such an assessment. If so, they will have to carefully navigate the complex contours of defining roles and clarifying limits of confidentiality, so that the applicant or employee can make an informed decision about participation. The evaluations should then be conducted in accordance with existing guidelines (IACP, 1998) and reported clearly to the intended audience. Clearer expectations about who should conduct forensic assessments for high-risk occupations and how they should appropriately be conducted should result in higher-quality evaluations and a fairer process for agencies, applicants, and employees.

REFERENCES

Americans with Disabilities Act of 1990, 42 U.S.C.A. 12101 *et seq.*

American Psychological Association. (1992). Ethical principles of psychologists and code of conduct. *American Psychologist, 47,* 1597–1611.

Blau, T. H. (1994). *Psychological services for law enforcement.* New York: Wiley.

Bonsignore v. City of New York, 683 F.2d 635 (1982).

Borum, R., Otto, R., & Golding, S. (1993). Improving clinical judgment and decision making in forensic evaluation. *Journal of Psychiatry and Law, 21,* 35–76.

Civil Rights Act of 1991, 42 U.S.C. § 1981, *et seq.*

Committee on Ethical Guidelines for Forensic Psychologists. (1991). Specialty guidelines for forensic psychologists. *Law and Human Behavior, 15,* 655–665.

Conte v. Horcher, 365 N.E.2d 567 (1977).

David v. Christian, 520 N.Y.S.2d 827 (A.D. 2 Dept. 1987).

Delprino, R., & Bahn, C. (1988). National survey of the extent and nature of psychological services in police departments. *Professional Psychology: Research and Practice, 19,* 421–425.

EEOC Equal Employment Opportunity for Individuals with Disabilities, Final Rule, 55(44) Fed. Reg. (1991).

Flanagan, C. (1995). Legal issues regarding police psychology. In M. Kurke & E. Scrivner (Eds.), *Police psychology into the 21st century* (pp. 93–107). Hillsdale, NJ: Erlbaum.

Grisso, T. (1986). *Evaluating competencies: Forensic assessments and instruments.* New York: Plenum Press.

Hargrave, G., & Berner, J. (1984). *POST psychological screening manual.* Sacramento: California Commission on Police Officer Standards.

Hiatt, D., & Hargrave, G. (1988a). MMPI profiles of problem peace officers. *Journal of Personality Assessment, 52,* 722–731.

Hiatt, D., & Hargrave, G. (1988b). Predicting police performance problems with psychological screening. *Journal of Police Science and Administration, 16,* 122–125.

Hogan, R., Hogan, J., & Roberts, B. (1996). Personality questions and employment decisions: Questions and answers. *American Psychologist, 51,* 469–477.

IACP Police Psychological Services Section. (1998a). *Fitness-for-duty evaluation guidelines.* Alexandria, VA: Author.

IACP Police Psychological Services Section. (1998b). *Pre-employment psychological evaluation guidelines.* Alexandria, VA: Author.

Inwald, R. (1988). Five-year follow-up study of departmental termination as predicted by 16 pre-employment psychological indicators. *Journal of Applied Psychology, 73,* 703–710.

Inwald, R. (1989). *HCSI technical manual.* Kew Gardens, NY: Hilson Research, Inc.

Inwald, R. (1992). *IS5 Technical manual.* Kew Gardens, NY: Hilson Research, Inc.

Inwald, R. (1994). *Hilson Job Analysis Questionnaire Technical manual.* New York: Hilson Research.

Inwald, R. (1995). *Hilson Safety/Security Risk Inventory technical manual.* Kew Gardens, NY: Hilson Research, Inc.

Inwald, R. (in press). The Hilson Research Inventories: Development and rationale. In *Handbook of adult personality inventories.* New York: Plenum Press.

Inwald, R., & Brobst, K. (1988). *Hilson Personnel Profile/Success Quotient technical manual.* Kew Gardens, NY: Hilson Research, Inc.

Inwald, R., Knatz, H., & Shusman, E. (1982). *Inwald Personality Inventory manual.* New York: Hilson Research.

Inwald, R., & Resko, J. (1995). Pre-employment screening for public safety personnel. In L. VandeCreek & S. Knapp (Eds.), *Innovations in clinical practice: A source book* (Vol. 14, pp. 365–382). Sarasota, FL: Professional Resource Press/Professional Resource Exchange.

Inwald, R., Resko, J., & Favuzza, V. (1996a). *Hilson Life Adjustment Profile (HLAP) technical manual.* Kew Gardens, NY: Hilson Research, Inc.

Inwald, R., Resko, J., & Favuzza, V. (1996b). *Inwald Survey2 (IS2) & Inwald Survey8 (IS8) technical manual.* Kew Gardens, NY: Hilson Research, Inc.

Inwald, R., & Shusman, E. (1984). The IPI and MMPI as predictors of academy performance for police recruits. *Journal of Police Science and Administration, 12,* 1–11.

Janik, J. (1994a). Consideration in administering psychological pre-selection procedures to law enforcement applicants. *Journal of Police and Criminal Psychology, 10,* 24–32.

Janik, J. (1994b). Why psychological screening of police candidates is necessary: The history and rationale. *Journal of Police and Criminal Psychology, 10,* 18–23.

Johnson, E. (1984). Problems in assessing police and firefighter candidates. *Journal of Police Science and Administration, 12,* 404–406.

Lawrence, R. (1984). Police stress and personality factors: A conceptual model. *Journal of Criminal Justice, 12,* 247–263.

McCabe v. Hoberman, 33 A.D.2d 547 (1st Dept. 1969).

McKenna v. Fargo, 451 F. Supp. 1355 (1978).

Milton, C., Halleck, J., Lardner, J., & Albrecht, G. (1977). *Police use of deadly force.* Washington, DC: Police Foundation.

Monell v. Department of Social Services, 436 J.S. 658, 98 S. Ct. 2018 (1978).

Morey, L. (1991). *The Personality Assessment Inventory (PAI) professional manual.* Odessa, FL: Psychological Assessment Resources.

National Advisory Commission on Criminal Justice Standards and Goals: Police. (1967). Washington, DC: U.S. Government Printing Office.

Ones, D., Viswesvaran, C., Schmidt, F., & Schultz, S. (1992). *Meta-analysis results for criterion-related validity of the Inwald Personality Inventory.* Unpublished study, University of Iowa, Department of Management and Organizations.

Ostrov, E. (1995). Legal, psychological, and ethical issues in police-related forensic psychology evaluations. In M. Kurke & E. Scrivner (Eds.), *Police psychology into the 21st century* (pp. 133–145). Hillsdale, NJ: Erlbaum.

Ostrov, E., Nowicki, D., & Beazley, J. (1987, February). Mandatory police evaluations: The Chicago model. *Police Chief, 54,* 30–35.

Peterson, M., & Strider, F. (1968). *Psychiatric screening of policemen.* Paper presented at the Midwest divisional meeting of the American Psychiatric Association, Chicago.

Redmond v. City of Overland Park, 672 F. Supp. 473 (D. Kan. 1987).

Reiser, M., & Geiger, S. (1984). Police officer as victim. *Professional Psychology Research and Practice, 15,* 315–323.

Rigaud, M., & Flynn, C. (1995). Fitness for duty (FFD) evaluation in industrial and military workers. *Psychiatric Annals, 25,* 246–250.

Roberts, M. (1997, August). *The role of the PAI Law Enforcement, Corrections, and Public Safety Selection Report in the applicant screening process.* Paper presented at the annual meeting of the American Psychological Association, Chicago.

Roberts, M., Thompson, J., & Johnson, M. (1999). *PAI Law Enforcement, Corrections, and Public Safety Selection Report module.* Odessa, FL: Psychological Assessment Resources.

Roulette v. Department of Central Management Services, 490 N.E.2d 60, (Ill. App. 1 Dist. 1987).

Rubin, P. (1994). The Americans with Disabilities Act and criminal justice: Hiring new employees. In *Research in action.* Washington, DC: National Institute of Justice.

Rubin, P. (1995). Civil rights and criminal justice: Employment discrimination overview. In *Research in action.* Washington, DC: National Institute of Justice.

Saxe, S., & Reiser, M. (1976). A comparison of three police applicant groups using the MMPI. *Journal of Police Science and Administration, 4,* 419–425.

Saxe-Clifford, S. (1986, February). The fitness for duty evaluation: Establishing policy. *Police Chief,* 38–39.

Schinka, J., & Borum, R. (1993). Readability of adult psychopathology inventories. *Psychological Assessment, 5,* 384–386.

Scogin, F., Schumacher, J., Howland, K., & McGee, J. (1989). *The predictive validity of psychological testing and peer evaluations in law enforcement settings.* Paper presented at the 97th American Psychological Association Convention, New Orleans, LA.

Scrivner, E. (1994, April). *The role of police psychology in controlling excessive force.* Washington, DC: National Institute of Justice.

Sewell, J. (1983). The development of a critical life events scale for law enforcement. *Journal of Police Science and Administration, 11,* 109–116.

Shusman, E. (1987). A redundancy analysis for the Inwald Personality Inventory and the MMPI. *Journal of Personality Assessment, 51,* 433–440.

Shusman, E., Inwald, R., & Knatz, H. (1987). A cross-validation study of police recruit performance as predicted by the IPI and MMPI. *Journal of Police Science and Administration, 15,* 162–169.

Solomon, R., & Horn, J. (1986). Post-shooting traumatic reaction: A pilot study. In J. Reese & H. Goldstein (Eds.), *Psychological services for law enforcement* (pp. 383–393). Washington, DC: U.S. Government Printing Office.

Soroka v. Dayton Hudson Corporation, Cal. Rptr. 2d 77 (Cal. App. 1 Dist, 1991).

Specialty Guidelines for Forensic Psychologists. (1991). *Law and Human Behavior, 15,* 655–665.

Stock, H., Borum, R., & Baltzley, D. (1996). Police use of deadly force. In H. V. Hall (Ed.), *Lethal violence 2000: Fatal domestic, acquaintance, and stranger aggression* (pp. 635–662). Kameula, HI: Pacific Institute for the Study of Conflict and Aggression.

Stock, H., Borum, R., & Baltzley, D. (1999). Police use of deadly force. In H. V. Hall & L. Whitaker (Eds.), *Collective violence: Effective strategies for assessing and interviewing in fatal group and institutional aggression* (pp. 391–417). Boca Raton, FL: CRC Press.

Stone, A. (1990). Psychological fitness for duty evaluations. *Police Chief, 52,* 39–53.

Stone, A. (1995). Law enforcement psychological fitness for duty: Clinical issues. In M. Kurke & E. Scrivner (Eds.), *Police psychology into the 21st century* (pp. 109–131). Hillsdale, NJ: Erlbaum.

Stone, A. (2000). *Fitness for duty: Principles, methods, and legal issues.* Boca Raton, FL: CRC Press.

Super, J. (1999). Forensic psychology and law enforcement. In A. Hess & I. Weiner (Eds.), *The handbook of forensic psychology* (2nd ed., pp. 409–439). New York: Wiley.

Super, J. (1997a). Legal and ethical aspects of pre-employment psychological evaluations. *Journal of Police and Criminal Psychology, 12,* 1–6.

Super, J. (1997b). Select legal and ethical aspects of fitness for duty evaluations. *Journal of Criminal Justice, 25,* 223–229.

Trompetter, P. (1998, October). Fitness-for-duty evaluations: What agencies can expect. *Police Chief, 60,* 97–105.

Vinson v. The Superior Court of Alameda County, 740 P.2d 404 (Cal. 1987).

Weiss, W., Johnson, J., Serafino, G., & Serafino, A. (2001). Three-year follow-up of the performance of a class of state police academy graduates using the MMPI-2. *Journal of Police and Criminal Psychology, 16,* 51–55.

CHAPTER 9

Eyewitness Memory for People and Events

GARY L. WELLS AND ELIZABETH F. LOFTUS

A criminal trial is, among other things, an attempt to reconstruct a past event to aid the trier of fact in determining what happened. Physical trace evidence, such as fingerprints, fibers, or blood, are often used to assist this reconstruction because, when properly collected and analyzed, trace evidence can help determine the nature of the events and the identity of the perpetrator. Eyewitness evidence can be likened to other forms of trace evidence (Wells, 1995). In effect, a criminal event involving an eyewitness leaves a trace in the brain of the eyewitness. The "memory as trace evidence" metaphor has rich implications. Like physical evidence, memory trace evidence can be contaminated, lost, destroyed, or otherwise made to produce results that can lead to an incorrect reconstruction of the event in question. Like physical trace evidence, the manner in which memory trace evidence is collected can have important consequences for the accuracy of the results.

The criminal justice system, however, has treated memory traces very differently from physical trace evidence. The collection of physical trace evidence is relatively well prescribed according to protocols that have a scientific foundation, grounded in what experts have suggested are the optimal ways to avoid contamination (Technical Working Group on Crime Scene Investigations, 1999). Police protocols for the collection, preservation, and interpretation of physical evidence are dictated largely by forensic scientists, and the practice of physical evidence collection and examination has tried to borrow as much as possible from science. Eyewitness evidence, on the other hand, is typically collected by nonspecialists who have little or no training in human memory.

Police protocols for collecting, preserving, and interpreting eyewitness evidence have not integrated the results of research conducted by memory experts. Hence, science has not been the backbone of police procedures for collecting, preserving, and interpreting eyewitness evidence. Whereas the justice system's analysis of physical evidence, especially biological traces, has advanced rapidly in the past decade, the analysis of eyewitness evidence has languished.

We believe that this gap is due in large part to the failure of the justice system to embrace the scientific model for eyewitness evidence while accepting the scientific model for physical evidence. Perhaps it is no surprise, therefore, that mistaken eyewitnesses account for more convictions of innocent persons than all other causes combined and that it has been scientific analysis of biological evidence (forensic DNA) that has proven that these eyewitnesses were in error (Scheck, Neufeld, & Dwyer, 2000; Wells, Small, Penrod, Malpass, Fulero, & Brimacombe, 1998).

The idea of using a scientific model to collect, analyze, and interpret eyewitness evidence is readily apparent in the case of both memory for events and memory for people. Consider, for example, how social scientists collect data from people. In surveys about past events, great care is taken in constructing questions because of clear evidence that people's reports are influenced by how the questions are worded (Loftus, Fienberg, & Tanur, 1985; Loftus, Smith, Klinger, & Fiedler, 1992). Scientific approaches to minimizing and detecting response biases and demand characteristics in surveys represent solid models for how law enforcement might go about the process of questioning eyewitnesses. In the case of eyewitness identification, the "lineup as experiment" analogy is a rich scientific model that law enforcement could follow (see Wells & Luus, 1990). According to this analogy, police conducting a lineup are like experimenters conducting research. Police have a hypothesis (that the suspect is the culprit); they create a design to test the hypothesis (embed the suspect among fillers); they provide instructions (e.g., "Don't guess. The culprit might or might not be in the lineup."); they collect responses (e.g., selection, certainty); and they interpret the results. The same factors that can make the results of a scientific experiment uninterpretable can make the results of a lineup uninterpretable (e.g., confoundings, biased instructions, experimenter expectancy effects, selective recording of results).

The failure of the criminal justice system to adopt a scientific model for memory trace evidence while embracing such a model for physical trace evidence is perhaps attributable to several related factors. We note, for instance, that eyewitness evidence was a staple in criminal investigations long before any scientific studies of eyewitnesses were conducted. The most scientific analyses of physical evidence (such as forensic DNA), on the other hand, were developed by scientists first and adopted by crime investigators later. Had the lineup been invented by scientists before it was ever used by the criminal justice system, law enforcement would be following a scientific protocol. This protocol would involve mock witness pretesting of fillers, double-blind testing procedures, carefully worded instructions, convergent measures, videotaping, careful documentation of records, and an interpretational framework for the identification responses.

The failure of the criminal justice system to adopt a scientific model for eyewitness evidence may also be attributable to the criminal justice system not having a focused theory of memory. In fact, the justice system as a whole might have no theory at all and its members may be operating under several theories. Implicitly, however, it appears that the justice system is assuming that stored information remains largely unchanged as a function of postevent information and is relatively impervious to suggestion, and that memory failures are primarily failures to retrieve information. In fact, however, memory reports are readily influenced by postevent information, are very susceptible to suggestion, and can err in numerous ways, including memory reports of entire events that were never witnessed (Loftus, 1996).

In this chapter, we review major developments in the scientific literature on eyewitness evidence. There are two main sections to this review. First, we review research and theory on eyewitness memory for events. The primary lesson of the memory for events research is that memory for events is malleable. The process of recollection is reconstructive, and sources of information that are used to reconstruct are not only from the event itself but also from postevent information gleaned in various ways after the event has occurred. In some cases, mere imagination can have the power to make people believe that they witnessed or experienced an event that did not happen. The second main section reviews work on eyewitness memory for people, especially the ability of eyewitnesses to identify culprits from lineups. The primary lesson of the eyewitness identification work is that mistaken identification rates can be very high under certain conditions and many of these conditions could actually be avoided by the use of more scientific procedures for lineups.

Before we begin our review, we describe a case that we believe illustrates many of the points that are central to this chapter.

THE MISIDENTIFICATION OF THOMAS BREWSTER

It was December 14, 1984. Terry Arendt and Sherrie Gillaspey were parked in a remote area of Shasta County, California. Terry and Sherrie were friends, not lovers, and were enjoying each other's company when a car drove by three times. After the third time, a bullet went through the driver's side window, killing Terry. A male approached the car and forced Gillaspey a short distance from the car, where he sexually assaulted her. The killer then left. A few days later, Gillaspey worked with a sketch artist to develop a likeness of the killer. Thomas E. Brewster, a lifelong resident of the area, bore a resemblance to the sketch and thereby became a suspect in the killing.

On December 19, 1984, Gillaspey was shown a photo lineup with Brewster's photo in it. She could not make a positive identification. One day later, Gillaspey was shown a live lineup in which Brewster appeared. Again, Gillaspey could not make a positive identification. Brewster was not arrested. Nearly four years later, in August 1988, detectives again showed Gillaspey a photo lineup with Brewster's picture in it. Once again she could not make a positive identification.

In 1995, 11 years after the murder, two new detectives were assigned to the case. These detectives brought photos and, after interviewing her with the photos, she signed a statement saying that Brewster was the killer. Six days later, she identified Brewster from a live lineup. The prosecutor decided to seek the death penalty and the trial did not commence until 1997 (*California v. Brewster*, 1997). Motions to suppress the identification were denied. After the trial had begun, a criminalist found a semen stain on the blouse that Gillaspey wore that evening and the stain was tested for DNA. The trial was in progress and Gillaspey was still on the stand after having positively identified Brewster in court when the DNA test results came in. Brewster was not the killer. Gillaspey was carefully debriefed and all charges against Brewster were dismissed.

At least 80 people have been released from prison in recent years after DNA proved that they had been mistakenly identified by eyewitnesses (Scheck et al., 2000; Wells et al., 1998). In many cases, there were multiple witnesses who misidentified the person, many were sentenced to death, and they served an average of about eight years before being freed based on the DNA tests. Although DNA tests eventually saved these individuals from the mistaken eyewitness identification problem, DNA can be used to exonerate only a small fraction of people from mistaken identification. Forensic DNA tests cannot prevent wrongful convictions in most eyewitness cases because the biological traces needed for DNA tests are not left behind by perpetrators in the vast majority of crimes. Most murders and nearly all robberies, drive-by shootings, burglaries, hit-and-run offenses, and other common crimes leave no biological trace evidence that can be clearly linked to the perpetrator or that can be used to exonerate an innocent person. It is no coincidence that nearly all of the DNA exoneration cases are cases involving sexual assault. Sexual assaults commonly have biological evidence (semen) that is unambiguously linked to the perpetrator, whereas most other cases do not.

The Brewster case is somewhat unique in one respect; the new detectives who took over the case (13 years after the murder) taperecorded their interview with Gillaspey. We think it is important to print excerpts from that interview because they illustrate some of the dynamics of the eyewitness problem. Keep in mind that the victim-witness, Gillaspey, had already viewed either photos or live lineups containing Brewster at least four times before the new detectives interviewed her in 1995. She had never made a positive identification of Brewster despite these numerous attempts prior to the 1995 interview.

The interview itself is quite long, so we reprint only a small portion here. A full transcript of the taped interview was entered into evidence at a hearing on a motion to suppress the identification and can be obtained from the first author on request. Most of the interview involves Gillaspey recalling the events of the night of the murder. At some point, however, the detectives decided to show her a photospread that included yet another photo of Brewster. In the following transcript quotes from the tape, D1 is the first detective, D2 the second detective, and SG is the witness, Sherrie Gillaspey:

SG: Who is this guy? (apparently pointing to the photo of Brewster).

D1: Why do you ask me that?

SG: I don't know, he looks familiar but (unintelligible).

D1: Have you seen him before?

The conversation turned to a discussion of whether she could recognize the voice of the perpetrator. The detectives then turned the conversation back to the photos.

D1: And what photograph are you talking about?

SG: Number three.

D1: And that individual looks familiar to you, you don't know in what respect?

SG: Nobody else here does, all I know is he does for some reason.

D1: Well, let's go through a process of elimination. Is he somebody that you went to school with?

SG: Huh uh.

D1: Is he somebody who works in a store where you shop?

SG: No.

D1: Is he somebody you bought a car from?

SG: No.

D1: Is he an old schoolteacher?

SG: Nope.

D1: Is he an old boyfriend?

SG: No.

D1: He work in a service station?

SG: No, no.

D1: Is he somebody that has hit on you?

It is important to note that these detectives were fully aware that Sherrie Gillaspey had been shown photos of Brewster and had viewed him in a live lineup at various times over the prior 13 years. Not once, however, did they ever ask if he looked familiar because he was the same person that other detectives had shown her previously. The interview continued:

D1: Could he be the guy that assaulted Terry and you that night?

SG: It's possible. I mean, I would really like to hear, I would really like to hear him talk.

D1: Well, I can arrange that.

Gillaspey had already heard his voice in the 1985 lineup. Again, however, the detectives offered no information to her about that fact. Instead, the discussion turned to signing a statement. She was asked to indicate number three on the statement form and to write in the comments section.

> SG: So, what do you want me to put, just write . . .
>
> BM: Well, let's think about that for a minute. . . . One of the things that I, that I probably rely on more than anything else is body language . . . and emotional reaction. I think it's safe to say that you went to number three just like that.
>
> SG: Uh huh, totally, yeah.
>
> D1: And my next question is you became flushed. Why did you do that?
>
> SG: I don't know, well immediately, immediately in my mind, you know, in my mind thinks, is that the person, you know, kind of . . .
>
> D1: That's the answer I'm looking for. Could that be the guy that did all this?
>
> SG: Yeah.

Notice how the detective tells Gillaspey what her emotional reaction was and interprets her body language. Then, when she says something that agrees with the detective's suspicions about the guilt of Brewster, he tells her that was the answer he was looking for. The interview continues.

> D1: Then what, see what, what I have to worry about now is if in fact you do come back over and we conduct a physical lineup and you identify this individual as absolutely unequivocally, without a doubt the guy that was there . . .
>
> SG: Uh huh.
>
> D1: Then obviously the next thing that happens is somewhere down the line we have to think about what happens in court. And we don't want to taint that with some, with a comment that you might inadvertently make on the back of that card.

The taped interview then ended. Six days later, Gillaspey picked Brewster from a live lineup and was absolutely positive of her identification.

The Brewster case illustrates much of what concerns scientific psychologists about eyewitness testimony. First, it illustrates what seems to be a general misunderstanding about the nature of human memory, namely, that memory might get better (or at least not deteriorate) with time. Gillaspey had already viewed a photo of Brewster a mere five days after the incident and viewed him again in a live lineup that included Brewster a mere six days after the incident. In neither case could she identify Brewster. And yet, police, the

prosecutor, and the judge were willing to accept her identification of Brewster over 3,850 days later.

Second, this case illustrates the detective's lack of understanding of the processes and the power of suggestive procedures in shaping an eyewitness's recollections. Presenting Brewster, both in photos and live, to the eyewitness several times over an 11-year period is not the only suggestive aspect of the case. The key interview in 1995, as noted in the transcript, included the detective interpreting the eyewitness's behavior for her ("you went to number three just like that . . . you became flushed"). It included a suggestive prediction regarding how she might behave in the subsequent live lineup ("we conduct a physical lineup and you identify this individual as absolutely unequivocally, without a doubt the guy that was there"), and suggestions that she not say anything in her photo-identification card that would not play well later in court.

Third, this case illustrates a problem of source monitoring. Gillaspey seemed to be unaware that Brewster's familiarity was the result of her being exposed to him after the murder rather than his being the person she saw on the night of the murder. Fourth, this case illustrates how the certainty of an eyewitness is not only a poor indicator of whether the witness is accurate (Gillaspey was positive at trial even though she had mistakenly identified the defendant), but also how certainty is a product of variables other than the memory of the eyewitness.

Finally, this case illustrates how the justice system fails to take advantage of what is known about human memory and social influence to develop appropriate safeguards against mistaken identification. There was a detailed and reasonable motion to suppress the eyewitness identification evidence. The suppression motion was denied in the Brewster case, as it is rather routinely in nearly all cases, even though the identification procedures were highly suggestive (Loftus & Doyle, 1997/2000). As previously stated, we believe that some members of the justice system seem to operate under a theory of memory that does not give much credence to the idea that postevent information can account for serious mistakes by eyewitnesses.

MEMORY FOR EVENTS

As the Brewster case suggests, postevent viewings of a suspect's likeness, either by photograph or in person, can help to make someone look familiar later. That enhanced familiarity can lead to a false identification of the suspect as the person who committed the crime. But decades of research has shown that postevent information, particularly when it is misleading, can also alter recollections of other details about key events. A typical finding is that after receiving new information that is misleading in some way, people make errors when they report what they saw. The new, postevent information is often incorporated into the recollection, supplementing or altering it, sometimes in dramatic ways.

Misinformation Effects

Current research showing how memory can become skewed when people assimilate new data uses a three-part procedure. Experimental witnesses first see a complex event, such as a simulated violent crime or an automobile accident. Subsequently, half of the witnesses receive new misleading information about the event. The other half do not get any misinformation. Finally, all witnesses attempt to recall the original event. In a typical example of a study using this paradigm, witnesses saw a simulated traffic accident. They then received written information about the accident, but some people were misled about what they saw. A stop sign, for instance, was referred to as a yield sign. When asked whether they originally saw a stop or a yield sign, those given the phony information tended to adopt it as their memory; they said they saw a yield sign (see Loftus, Coan, & Pickerell, 1979/1996, for a review of this study and similar research). In these and many other experiments, people who had not received the misleading information provided much more accurate memories. In some experiments, the deficits in memory performance following receipt of misinformation have been dramatic, with performance differences as large as 30% or 40% (Belli, 1993; McCloskey & Zaragoza, 1985).

This degree of distorted reporting has been found in scores of studies, involving a wide variety of procedures. People have recalled nonexistent broken glass and tape recorders, a clean-shaven man as having a mustache, straight hair as curly, stop signs as yield signs, hammers as screwdrivers, and even something as large and conspicuous as a barn in a bucolic scene that contained no buildings at all. In short, misleading postevent information can alter a person's recollection in a powerful, and often predictable, manner. The change in report arising after receipt of misinformation is often referred to as the "misinformation effect" (Loftus & Hoffman, 1989).

Planting False Childhood Memories

During the last decade of the twentieth century, eyewitness researchers took things a step further; they turned their attention to the question: Just how far can we go with people in terms of distorting their memories with suggestion and misinformation? Rather than merely adding a detail to a previously acquired memory or tinkering with a detail here and there, they studied whether suggestive procedures can create entirely false memories for the past. Researchers devised procedures that could make people believe and remember that earlier in life they had been hospitalized when they had not (Hyman, Husband, & Billings, 1995), that they had been lost and frightened in a mall when they had not (Loftus et al., 1996), that they had been victims of vicious animal attacks as children even though they had not been (Porter, 1998; Porter, Yuille, & Lehman, 1999), and even that they had witnessed demonic possession when they were very young (Giuliana, Mazzoni, Loftus, & Kirsch, 2001). This line of false memory research shows that it is indeed possible to create quite complex, elaborate, and "confident" false memories in the minds of research participants.

To see how false memories of events can be created, we describe one method in some detail: planting a childhood memory for something that never happened. One goal of the research was to find a method for planting a memory that, if the event had actually occurred, would have been at least mildly traumatic. But the experience should not, of course, be so upsetting to the person that it would be unethical to create a false memory about it.

Loftus and colleagues settled on the idea of trying to plant a very specific memory of being a 5-year-old lost in a shopping mall, being frightened, crying, and ultimately rescued by an elderly person and reunited with the rest of the family (see Loftus & Ketcham, 1994, for a description of the origin of the idea, and Loftus et al., 1996, for more details on this research). Here is how it was done: The participants, all adults, were asked to try to remember childhood events that were supplied by their mother, father, older sibling, or other close relative. Three of the events were true, and one was the research-crafted false event about getting lost in a shopping mall, department store, or other public place. In phase 1, participants completed a booklet containing four one-paragraph stories about events from their childhood provided by their relative. Three events actually happened, and the fourth, always in the third position, was false.

The false event was constructed from information provided by a relative of the participant who gave the researchers details about a plausible shopping trip. The relative told the researchers (a) where the family would have shopped when the participant was about five years old; (b) which members of the family usually went along on shopping trips; (c) what kinds of stores might have attracted the participant's interest; and (d) verification that the participant had not been lost in a mall around the age of 5. This information was then used to craft the false event. The false events always included the following elements about the participant: (a) lost for an extended period of time; (b) crying; (c) lost in a mall or large department store at about the age of 5; (d) found and aided by an elderly woman; and (e) reunited with the family.

Participants read what their relative had told us about each event, and then completed the booklets by writing what they remembered about each event. If they did not remember the event, they were told to write "I do not remember this." When the booklets were returned, participants were called and two interviews were scheduled. These occurred approximately one to two weeks apart. Participants were told that the researchers were interested in examining how much detail they could remember and how their memories compared with those of their relative. The event paragraphs were not read to them verbatim, but rather bits of information were provided as retrieval cues. When participants had recalled as much as possible, they were asked to rate the clarity of their memory for the event on a scale of 1 to 10, with 1 being not clear at all and 10 being extremely clear.

In all, participants remembered something about 68% of the true events that they were asked about. This figure did not change from the initial report through the two follow-up interviews. The rate of "remembering" the false event was lower, at about 25%. Statistically, there were some differences between the true memories and the false ones: More words were used to describe the true memories, and the true memories were rated as being somewhat more clear. But with many of the participants, if an onlooker were to watch the participant describe an experience, it would be difficult indeed to tell whether the report was of a true or a false memory.

Other investigators used a similar procedure to plant false memories of even more unusual events. In one study, college students were asked to recall actual events that had been reported by their parents and one experimenter-crafted false event (Hyman et al., 1995). The false event was an overnight hospitalization for a high fever with a possible ear infection, or a nonexistent birthday party with pizza and a clown. Parents confirmed that neither of these events had happened, yet participants were told that they had experienced one of the false events at about the age of 5.

Participants tried to recall childhood experiences that they thought had been supplied by their parents, in the belief that the experimenters were interested in how people remember shared experiences differently. All events, both the true ones and the false one, were first cued with an event title (family vacation, overnight hospitalization) and an age. Hyman et al. (1995) found that participants remembered approximately 80% of the true events. As for the false event, by the end of the second interview, 20% of the participants had remem-

bered all or part of this creation. In a separate study, Hyman and collaborators created even more unlikely false memories, such as attending a wedding reception and accidentally spilling a punch bowl on the parents of the bride or having to evacuate a grocery store when the overhead sprinkler systems erroneously activated. This time, approximately 25% accepted all or part of the false memory by the end of the third interview (see Hyman & Billings, 1998; Hyman & Pentland, 1996).

A recent doctoral dissertation project also succeeded in planting false memories via suggestion that ostensibly came from relatives of the participants. This research planted memories not only for getting lost and having undergone serious medical procedures, but also for serious animal attacks, serious indoor accidents, and serious outdoor accidents, events that would have been traumatic had they actually occurred (Porter, 1998; Porter et al., 1999). These investigators reported that just over 25% of their participants created a rather complete false memory, and another 30% created a partial memory. Clearly, these methods are capable of inducing false memories in a sizable percentage of people.

Like Hyman and Billings (1998), Porter et al. (1999) found that the participants who were most susceptible to memory implantation were those who scored high on the Dissociative Experiences Scale, a self-report measure of the extent to which participants experience lapses in memory and perception in their everyday life. As Loftus and colleagues had found (e.g., Loftus et al., 1996), these investigators also found that participants gave higher ratings of vividness or clarity when relating a real memory as opposed to an implanted one. Interestingly, the real memories related by the participants did not contain more details than the planted memories.

In remarking about their findings, Porter and colleagues (1999) were particularly impressed that fully 20% of created memories were given with the highest possible confidence rating. At the end of their study, over 33% of the participants who had created a false memory were willing to wager money that the false event occurred. Moreover, the investigators reported that at the time the participants were debriefed, most of them appeared to be "genuinely astonished" when told about the parental reports and the fact that their memories were false. Many appeared amused and wanted to talk more with the researchers about the process of memory creation, in some instances, even requesting literature in the area of research. These features of the reaction help convince the researchers that the participants had in fact recalled the false event, as opposed to responding to demand characteristics of the study. It seems evident from these findings that participants are actually "remembering" these false experiences, in the sense that they have a genuine recollective feeling about the experiences.

Imagination and Memory

It should be kept in mind that these studies used a rather strong form of suggestion in which a source with some prestige suggested that an event had occurred in the past. However, such heavy-handed methods are not needed to get people to increase their confidence that they had experiences in the past that they probably did not experience. Inducing people to imagine that they have had an experience can influence people to recall having had such an experience.

To explore what happens to memory when people imagine events that did not occur, Garry, Manning, Loftus, and Sherman (1996) used a three-stage procedure. Participants were first asked about 40 possible events from their childhood and indicated the likelihood that these events happened to them on a scale of responses ranging from definitely did not happen to definitely did happen. Two weeks later, the participants were asked to imagine that they had experienced some of these events. The events included falling and breaking a window with their hand, getting in trouble for calling 911, finding a $10 bill in a parking lot, or being pulled out of the water by a lifeguard. Different participants were asked to imagine different events.

Consider a typical one-minute imagination exercise, one in which participants imagined breaking a window with their hand. They were told to picture that it was after school and they were playing in the house when they heard a strange noise outside. They were told to imagine themselves running toward the window, tripping, falling, reaching out, and breaking a window with their hand. While imagining the scene, the participants were asked several questions, such as "What did you trip on?" and "How did you feel?" After imagining several situations, the participants again, sometime later, were given the list of 40 childhood events to respond to.

Comparing the responses to the two questionnaires about possible childhood experiences, it was found that a one-minute act of imagination led a significant minority of participants to indicate that an event was more likely to have happened after previously identifying it as unlikely to have occurred. In the broken window scenario, 24% of the participants who imagined the event showed an increase in confidence that the event had actually occurred. For those participants who did not imagine breaking the window, 12% showed a corresponding increase. In the "got in trouble for calling 911" scenario, 20% of the participants who imagined the event showed an increase in confidence that the event had occurred when they were children. For those participants who

did not imagine getting in trouble for calling 911, only 11% showed a corresponding increase.

Numerous other investigators have used imagination to alter people's beliefs about their past. Imagination can make people believe that they have had experiences in the distant past (Heaps & Nash, 1999; Paddock, Joseph, Chan, Terranova, Maning, & Loftus, 1998), but it also can make people believe that they have had experiences in the recent past (Goff & Roediger, 1998; Thomas & Loftus, 2001).

Other Suggestive Procedures

The power of suggestion to create false beliefs and false memories has now been shown repeatedly. Suggestive dream interpretation has led people to believe that they were lost for an extended period of time, or that they faced a great danger from which they were rescued (Mazzoni & Loftus, 1998). Reading suggestive stories and getting false feedback about one's fears has led people to believe that they witnessed demonic possession in the past or that they nearly swallowed an object and choked (Mazzoni et al., 2001). Suggestive false feedback about one's visual-motor skills has led people to believe that they could remember experiences from the day after birth (DuBreuil, Garry, & Loftus, 1998; Spanos, Burgess, Burgess, Samuels, & Blois, 1999). These findings should give pause to investigators and others who think that they are extracting recalcitrant, accurate memories from witnesses and suspects by using techniques that resemble the ones that psychologists have studied. The danger lies in planting the seed of suggestion that then takes root and grows into a mighty false memory that has the power to convict an innocent person.

MEMORY FOR PEOPLE

An eyewitness's identification of a particular person as the one who committed a crime is a powerful form of evidence. An eyewitness who says "That's the man I saw pull the trigger" is providing direct evidence of guilt. Even fingerprints are not direct evidence of guilt because they indicate only that a given person touched a given surface, and there might have been many innocent ways to have touched the surface. Hence, although most evidence in courts of law is circumstantial, eyewitness identification evidence is *direct* evidence of guilt.

Eyewitness researchers' concern about the accuracy of eyewitness identification evidence is grounded in two broad observations. First, eyewitness experiments involving staged crimes show that rates of mistaken identification can be very high under certain conditions (Wells, 1993). These conditions are often represented in real-life cases. Second, real-world cases in which people have been convicted of crimes that they did not commit show that mistaken identification was the primary evidence leading to their conviction (Huff, Rattner, & Sagarin, 1986; Scheck et al., 2000; Wells et al., 1998).

Variables Affecting Identification Accuracy

How do mistaken identifications happen? Like most important phenomena, the causes are many. The scientific approach to studying the causes of mistaken identification has generally been to isolate suspected variables in controlled experiments. The list of variables that have been shown to affect rates of mistaken identification is rather large. One common approach to organizing the findings has been to categorize the variables into witness characteristics (e.g., sex, intelligence), characteristics of the witnessed event (e.g., exposure duration, presence of a weapon), postevent variables (e.g., suggestions from other witnesses, exposure to a sketch), characteristics of the identification task (e.g., structure of the lineup, instructions to witnesses prior to viewing the lineup), and postidentification events (e.g., feedback to the eyewitness regarding the identification). We refer to this as the chronological approach because the categories are ordered in the temporal sequence in which they unfold. Another way to organize these variables is according to whether they are controllable by the criminal justice system in actual cases (e.g., the structure of a lineup) or are not controllable in real cases (e.g., exposure duration), which is known as the system-variable versus estimator-variable distinction (Wells, 1978).

More recently, Wells and Olson (2001) suggested yet another distinction among eyewitness identification variables: between suspect-bias variables and general impairment variables. A suspect-bias variable is one that can account for why an eyewitness, when presented with a lineup, specifically selected the innocent suspect rather than one of the fillers in the lineup (or simply saying "I don't know" or "None of these people"). A general impairment variable, on the other hand, cannot account for which person the suspect picked, but can account only for poor eyewitness performance more generally. Consider, for instance, the other–race effect: There is now rather good evidence that people have more difficulty identifying persons of another race than their own race (see meta-analysis by Meisner & Brigham, 2001). The other-race effect is a general impairment variable in the sense that it cannot account for why the witness would select the suspect in the lineup rather than one of the fillers in the lineup. (This example assumes, of course, that all members of the lineup are of the same race, a race different from that of the eyewitness.)

On the other hand, consider the problem of structurally biased lineups. In a structurally biased lineup, the suspect fits the description that the eyewitness had given of the culprit, whereas the fillers (known innocents, distractors, or foils) do not fit that description. Structural lineup bias is a suspect-bias variable rather than a general impairment variable because it can account for why the eyewitness selected the suspect rather than selecting some other lineup member.

Table 9.1 lists a large number of variables known to affect the accuracy of eyewitness identification. The list is not exhaustive, but it represents the variables that have been studied most often. Each variable is then categorized according to each of the three types of categorization. The last column of Table 9.1 lists one representative publication dealing with each variable. We recommend a meta-analysis by Shapiro and Penrod (1986), which included most of these variables, for information on estimates of effect size, a standardized statistical estimate of the impact that one variable has on another variable. Effect sizes are often used to compare the relative impact of one variable versus some other variable. We caution readers, however, against inferring too much from effect size estimates. Effect sizes are very sensitive to the particular operationalizations that are used in manipulating each of the variables.

It is apparent from Table 9.1 that chronological categorization and system versus estimator categorization are related. This is because system variables do not normally come into play until after the crime event has occurred. The general impairment versus suspect-bias variables distinction, on the other hand, is not restricted to any particular chronological frame. In addition, the general impairment and suspect-bias variables can be either system or estimator variables. Finally, note that a few variables are not restricted to a single category. One variable is the period of time between the event and the person's recollection, sometimes referred to as retention interval. Retention interval is commonly construed as an estimator variable. However, there are times when the justice system has some control over the retention interval, such as when investigators show eyewitnesses a lineup that could have been conducted at an earlier point in time. Also, exposure to mugshots might normally be considered a general impairment variable because it generally interferes with the witness's ability to keep the perpetrator's face in mind later, when viewing the lineup. At other times, however, exposure to mugshots could be a specific-suspect-bias variable if it makes an innocent suspect seem familiar because he or she was seen in the set of mugshots.

Each of the three ways of categorizing eyewitness identification variables has a different utility. The chronological categorization assists in developing a temporal understanding

TABLE 9.1 Eyewitness Identification Variables and Their Categories

Variable	Chronological Category	System versus Estimator Category	General Impairment versus Suspect-Bias Category	Example Citation
Sex of witness	WC	E	GI	
Intelligence of witness	WC	E	GI	Brown, Deffenbacher, & Sturgill, 1977
Age of witness	WC	E	GI	Chance & Goldstein, 1984
Face recognition skills	WC	E	GI	Woodhead, Baddeley, & Simmonds, 1979
Personality	WC	E	GI	Hosch & Platz, 1984
Alcohol	WC	E	GI	Yuille & Tollestrup, 1990
Prior exposure/source confusion/bystander	WC	E	SB	Read, 1994
View	EC	E	GI	Lindsay, Wells, & Rumpel, 1987
Disguise of perpetrator	EC	E	GI/SB	Cutler, Penrod, & Martens, 1981
Exposure time	EC	E	GI	Ellis, Davies, & Shepherd, 1977
Same versus other-race identification	EC	E	GI	Anthony, Cooper, & Mullen, 1992
Stress	EC	E	GI	Christianson, 1992
Weapon	EC	E	GI	Steblay, 1992
Retention interval	PE	E/S	GI	Krafka & Penrod, 1985
Interpolated mugshots	PE	S	GI/SB	Brigham & Cairns, 1988
Overheard descriptions	PE	S	SB	Loftus & Greene, 1980
Prelineup instructions	ID	S	GI	Steblay, 1997
Structure of lineup/fillers	ID	S	SB	Wells, Rydell, & Seelau, 1993
Simultaneous/sequential procedure	ID	S	GI	Lindsay & Wells, 1985
Suggestive behaviors during lineup	ID	S	SB	Phillips, McAuliff, Kovera, & Cutler, 1999
Postidentification feedback	PI	S	SB	Wells & Bradfield, 1998

Note: WC = witness characteristics, EC = event characteristics, PE = postevent factors, ID = identification test variables, PI = postidentification variables, S = system variable, E = estimator variable, GI = general impairment variable, SB = suspect-bias variable.

of the order in which these variables come into play in the witnessing experience. The system versus estimator categorization is useful for developing methods for increasing the accuracy of eyewitness identification evidence via system-variable recommendations to the justice system. The general impairment versus suspect-bias categorization is relevant to understanding how jurors might reason about eyewitness identification in a given case.

The relevance of the general impairment versus suspect-bias distinction to jurors' judgments of eyewitness identification evidence requires more explanation. Consider a case in which it is argued to the jury that the eyewitness had a very poor view of the perpetrator, was of a different race than the perpetrator, and did not view a lineup until two months after the crime. Wells and Olson (2001) argue that these variables might not matter much to the jury when they deliberate because they fail to explain why the eyewitness picked the suspect out of the lineup and did not pick a filler. If the other-race effect made the lineup members "all look alike," then how was the witness able to pick out the suspect? The problem with general impairment variables is that they tend to beg the question for the jury as to why the eyewitness picked the suspect instead of one of the fillers. Suspect-bias variables, on the other hand, tend to answer that question. A structurally

biased lineup, for instance, serves to explain why the eyewitness preferred the suspect rather than one of the fillers. Hence, the general impairment versus suspect-bias variable distinction may be very useful in terms of understanding why some variables might be more important to juries than others in terms of their willingness to accept identification testimony.

The Process of Lineup Identification

One of the simplest and most useful ideas in understanding mistaken identifications from lineups is the *relative judgment conceptualization*. According to this conceptualization, eyewitnesses tend to identify the person from a lineup who most closely resembles the eyewitness's memory of the perpetrator *relative* to the other members of the lineup (Wells, 1984). This process of identification works reasonably well as long as the actual perpetrator is in the lineup. When the perpetrator is not in the lineup, however, there is still someone who looks more like the perpetrator than do the other lineup members, and eyewitnesses have a propensity to identify that person.

There are several reliable phenomena that support the relative judgment conceptualization. For example, failure to give explicit instructions to the eyewitness that emphasize that the perpetrator might *not* be in the lineup leads eyewitnesses to pick someone from the lineup at very high rates regardless of whether the perpetrator is present (Malpass & Devine, 1981). Even with these instructions, eyewitnesses tend to use relative judgments. For example, removing the perpetrator from a lineup without replacement leads most eyewitnesses who otherwise would have selected the perpetrator to instead select the "next best" person in the lineup rather than indicate that the perpetrator is not there (Wells, 1993). In addition, eyewitnesses who report that they used a relative comparison process (e.g., "I compared number three to number two") or an elimination process (e.g., "I knew it wasn't number one") are more likely to have made a mistaken identification than are those who report that the face "just popped out" (Dunning & Stern, 1994). This makes sense to the extent that the relative judgment process is an effortful, deliberate elimination strategy whereas absolute judgments are automatic, rapid, true recognition responses.

Perhaps the best evidence that relative judgments are involved in mistaken identification comes from research on simultaneous versus sequential presentation procedures for identifications. Simultaneous lineups are ones in which all members of the lineup are shown to the eyewitness at one time, whereas a sequential procedure involves showing the eyewitness one lineup member at a time and forcing the eyewitness to make a recognition decision (yes or no) before viewing the next lineup member. The sequential procedure prevents relative judgments because, even though the eyewitness can compare the lineup member being viewed to those who have already been shown, the eyewitness cannot be sure what the next lineup member looks like. As a result, the sequential procedure forces eyewitnesses to use a more "absolute" criterion for making an identification. Compared to the simultaneous procedure, the sequential procedure produces fewer mistaken identifications in lineups that do not contain the actual perpetrator, but it does not significantly impair eyewitnesses' abilities to identify the perpetrator in perpetrator-present lineups (Cutler & Penrod, 1988; Lindsay, Lea, & Fulford, 1991; Lindsay & Wells, 1985).

CONCLUSIONS AND PROSPECTUS

We began this chapter with a metaphor in which human memory is likened to trace evidence. Although the legal system shows considerable concern and exercises caution to avoid contaminating physical traces at a crime scene (e.g., blood, fibers), similar cautions tend not to be exercised in avoiding the contamination of human memory in eyewitnesses. We have described research showing how suggestive questioning

and suggestive lineup procedures can have immense effects on the testimony of eyewitnesses. Memories for events that never occurred are readily confused with memories for actual events, and mistaken eyewitness identifications are readily confused with accurate eyewitness identifications. Although there has been some recent success in getting the criminal justice system to make use of psychological science in its procedures for collecting eyewitness evidence (see Wells, Malpass, et al., 2000), there remains a large gap between what psychological science advises for collecting eyewitness evidence and actual practices of criminal investigators.

Future research needs to address this gap between psychological science and the practices of the legal system with regard to eyewitness memory. To some extent, this might be facilitated by research directed at the question of what theories the criminal justice system is using in collecting eyewitness evidence. Undoubtedly, these theories are more implicit than explicit, so it is unlikely that one can simply ask criminal justice actors to articulate their theories about memory. However, we believe that an understanding of these implicit theories can tell us something about how to better communicate our findings to those in the criminal justice system with a somewhat better chance to actually affect how the justice system thinks about and manages the collection of eyewitness evidence.

REFERENCES

Anthony, T., Cooper, C., & Mullen, B. (1992). Cross-racial facial identification: A social-cognitive integration. *Personality and Social Psychology Bulletin, 18,* 296–301.

Belli, R. F. (1993). Failure of interpolated tests in inducing memory impairment with final modified tests: Evidence unfavorable to the blocking hypothesis. *American Journal of Psychology, 106,* 407–427.

Brigham, J. C., & Cairns, D. L. (1988). The effect of mugshot inspections on eyewitness identification accuracy. *Journal of Applied Social Psychology, 18,* 1394–1410.

Brown, E., Deffenbacher, K., & Sturgill, W. (1977). Memory for faces and the circumstances of the encounter. *Journal of Applied Psychology, 62,* 311–318.

California v. Brewster, 95 F 8703 (1997).

Chance, J. E., & Goldstein, A. G. (1984). Face recognition memory: Implications for children's eyewitness testimony. *Journal of Social Issues, 40,* 69–85.

Christianson, S. A. (1992). Emotional stress and eyewitness memory: A critical review. *Psychological Bulletin, 112,* 284–309.

Cutler, B. L., & Penrod, S. D. (1988). Improving the reliability of eyewitness identification: Lineup construction and presentation. *Journal of Applied Psychology, 73,* 281–290.

Cutler, B. L., Penrod, S. D., & Martens, T. K. (1987). The reliability of eyewitness identification: The role of system and estimator variables. *Law and Human Behavior, 11,* 233–258.

DuBreuil, S. C., Garry, M., & Loftus, E. F. (1998). Tales from the crib: Age regression and the creation of unlikely memories. In S. J. Lynn & K. M. McConkey (Eds.), *Truth in memory* (pp. 137–160). New York: Guilford Press.

Dunning, D., & Stern, L. B. (1994). Distinguishing accurate from inaccurate identifications via inquiries about decision processes. *Journal of Personality and Social Psychology, 67,* 818–835.

Ellis, H. D., Davies, G. M., & Shepherd, J. W. (1977). Experimental studies of face identification. *Journal of Criminal Defense, 3,* 219–234.

Garry, M., Manning, C., Loftus, E. F., & Sherman, S. J. (1996). Imagination inflation: Imagining a childhood event inflates confidence that it occurred. *Psychonomic Bulletin and Review, 3,* 208–214.

Giuliana, A. L., Mazzoni, G. A. L., Loftus, E. F., & Kirsch, I. (2001). Changing beliefs about implausible autobiographical events: A little plausibility goes a long way. *Journal of Experimental Psychology: Applied, 7,* 51–59.

Goff, L. M., & Roediger, H. L. (1998). Imagination inflation for action events. *Memory and Cognition, 26,* 20–33.

Heaps, C., & Nash, M. (1999). Individual differences in imagination inflation. *Psychonomic Bulletin and Review, 6,* 313–318.

Hosch, H. M., & Platz, S. J. (1984). Self-monitoring and eyewitness accuracy. *Personality and Social Psychology Bulletin, 10,* 283–289.

Huff, R., Rattner, A., & Sagarin, E. (1986). Guilty until proven innocent. *Crime and Delinquency, 32,* 518–544.

Hyman, I. E., & Billings, F. J. (1998). Individual differences and the creation of false childhood memories. *Memory, 6,* 1–20.

Hyman, I. E., Husband, T. H., & Billings, F. J. (1995). False memories of childhood experiences. *Applied Cognitive Psychology, 9,* 181–197.

Hyman, I. E., & Pentland, J. (1996). The role of mental imagery in the creation of false childhood memories. *Journal of Memory and Language, 35,* 101–117.

Krafka, C., & Penrod, S. (1985). Reinstatement of context in a field experiment on eyewitness identification. *Journal of Personality and Social Psychology, 49,* 58–69.

Lindsay, R. C. L., Lea, J. A., & Fulford, J. A. (1991). Sequential lineup presentation: Technique matters. *Journal of Applied Psychology, 76,* 741–745.

Lindsay, R. C. L., & Wells, G. L. (1985). Improving eyewitness identification from lineups: Simultaneous versus sequential lineup presentations. *Journal of Applied Psychology, 70,* 556–564.

Lindsay, R. C. L., Wells, G. L., & Rumpel, C. (1981). Can people detect eyewitness identification accuracy within and between situations? *Journal of Applied Psychology, 66,* 79–89.

Loftus, E. F. (1996). *Eyewitness testimony* (2nd ed.). Cambridge, MA: Harvard University Press.

Loftus, E. F., Coan, J. A., & Pickrell, J. E. (1996). Manufacturing false memories using bits of reality. In L. M. Reder (Ed.), *Implicit memory and metacognition* (pp. 195–220). Hillsdale, NJ: Erlbaum. (Original work published 1979)

Loftus, E. F., & Doyle, J. M. (1997). *Eyewitness testimony: Civil and criminal* (3rd ed., Supp. 2000). Charlottesville, VA: LEXIS Law Press.

Loftus, E. F., Fienberg, S. E., & Tanur, J. M. (1985). Cognitive psychology meets the national survey. *American Psychologist, 40,* 175–180.

Loftus, E. F., & Greene, E. (1980). Warning: Even memory for faces may be contagious. *Law and Human Behavior, 4,* 323–334.

Loftus, E. F., & Hoffman, H. G. (1989). Misinformation and memory: The creation of memory. *Journal of Experimental Psychology: General, 118,* 100–104.

Loftus, E. F., & Ketcham, K. (1994). *The myth of repressed memory.* New York: St. Martin's Press.

Loftus, E. F., Smith, K., Klinger, M., & Fiedler, J. (1992). Memory and mismemory for health events. In J. M. Tanur (Ed.), *Questions about questions: Inquiries into the cognitive bases of surveys* (pp. 102–137). New York: Russell Sage.

Malpass, R. S., & Devine, P. G. (1981). Eyewitness identification: Lineup instructions and the absence of the offender. *Journal of Applied Psychology, 66,* 482–489.

Mazzoni, G. A. L., & Loftus, E. F. (1998). Dreaming, believing, and remembering. In J. DeRivera & T. R. Sarbin (Eds.), *Believed-in imaginings* (pp. 145–156). Washington, DC: American Psychological Association.

McCloskey, M., & Zaragoza, M. (1985). Misleading postevent information and memory for events: Arguments and evidence against memory-impairment hypotheses. *Journal of Experimental Psychology: General, 114,* 1–16.

Meisner, C., & Brigham, J. C. (2001). Twenty years of investigating the own-race bias in memory for faces: A meta-analytic review. *Psychology, Public Policy, and Law, 7,* 3–35.

Paddock, J. R., Joseph, A. L., Chan, F. M., Terranova, S., Manning, C., & Loftus, E. F. (1998). When guided visualization procedures may backfire: Imagination inflation and predicting individual differences in suggestibility [Special issue]. *Applied Cognitive Psychology, 12,* S63–S75.

Phillips, M. R., McAuliff, B. D., Kovera, M. B., & Cutler, B. L. (1999). Double-blind photoarray administration as a safeguard against investigator bias. *Journal of Applied Psychology, 84,* 940–951.

Porter, S. (1998). *An architectural mind: The nature of real, created, and fabricated memories of emotional childhood events.* Doctoral dissertation, University of British Columbia, Vancouver, Canada.

Porter, S., Yuille, J. C., & Lehman, D. R. (1999). The nature of real, implanted, and fabricated memories for emotional childhood events. *Law and Human Behavior, 23,* 517–538.

Read, J. D. (1994). Understanding bystander misidentifications: The role of familiarity and contextual knowledge. In D. F. Ross, J. D. Read, & M. P. Toglia (Eds.), *Adult eyewitness testimony: Current trends and developments* (pp. 56–79). New York: Cambridge University Press.

Scheck, B., Neufeld, P., & Dwyer, J. (2000). *Actual innocence.* New York: Random House.

Shapiro, P. N., & Penrod, S. (1986). Meta-analysis of racial identification studies. *Psychological Bulletin, 100,* 139–156.

Spanos, N. P., Burgess, C. A., Burgess, M. F., Samuels, C., & Blois, W. O. (1999). Creating false memories of infancy with hypnotic and non-hypnotic procedures. *Applied Cognitive Psychology, 13,* 201–218.

Steblay, N. M. (1992). A meta-analytic review of the weapon focus effect. *Law and Human Behavior, 16,* 413–424.

Steblay, N. M. (1997). Social influence in eyewitness recall: A meta-analytic review of lineup instruction effects. *Law and Human Behavior, 21,* 283–298.

Technical Working Group on Crime Scene Investigations. (1999). *Crime scene investigations: A guide for law enforcement.* Washington, DC: United States Department of Justice, Office of Justice Programs.

Technical Working Group for Eyewitness Evidence. (1999). *Eyewitness evidence: A guide for law enforcement.* Washington, DC: United States Department of Justice, Office of Justice Programs.

Thomas, A., & Loftus, E. F. (2001). Unpublished manuscript, University of Washington, Seattle.

Wells, G. L. (1978). Applied eyewitness testimony research: System variables and estimator variables. *Journal of Personality and Social Psychology, 36,* 1546–1557.

Wells, G. L. (1984). The psychology of lineup identifications. *Journal of Applied Social Psychology, 14,* 89–103.

Wells, G. L. (1993). What do we know about eyewitness identification? *American Psychologist, 48,* 553–571.

Wells, G. L. (1995). Scientific study of witness memory: Implications for public and legal policy. *Psychology, Public Policy, and Law, 1,* 726–731.

Wells, G. L., & Bradfield, A. L. (1998). Good, you identified the suspect: Feedback to eyewitnesses distorts their reports of the witnessing experience. *Journal of Applied Psychology, 83,* 360–376.

Wells, G. L., & Luus, E. (1990). Police lineups as experiments: Social methodology as a framework for properly-conducted lineups. *Personality and Social Psychology Bulletin, 16,* 106–117.

Wells, G. L., Malpass, R. S., Lindsay, R. C. L., Fisher, R. P., Turtle, J. W., & Fulero, S. (2000). From the lab to the police station: A successful application of eyewitness research. *American Psychologist, 55,* 581–598.

Wells, G. L., & Olson, E. A. (2001). The other-race effect in eyewitness identification: What do we do about it? *Psychology, Public Policy, and Law, 7,* 230–246.

Wells, G. L., Rydell, S. M., & Seelau, E. P. (1993). On the selection of distractors for eyewitness lineups. *Journal of Applied Psychology, 78,* 835–844.

Wells, G. L., Small, M., Penrod, S., Malpass, R. S., Fulero, S. M., & Brimacombe, C. A. E. (1998). Eyewitness identification procedures: Recommendations for lineups and photospreads. *Law and Human Behavior, 22,* 603–647.

Woodhead, M. M., Baddeley, A. D., & Simmonds, D. C. (1979). On training people to recognize faces. *Ergonomics, 22,* 333–343.

Yuille, J. C., & Tollestrup, P. A. (1990). Some effects of alcohol on eyewitness memory. *Journal of Applied Psychology, 75,* 268–273.

CHAPTER 10

Voir Dire and Jury Selection

MARGARET BULL KOVERA, JASON J. DICKINSON, AND BRIAN L. CUTLER

The jury is widely regarded as the zenith of American juris-prudence: the marquee of justice designed to protect the innocent and lay blame to the guilty. But more than that, the jury is perhaps the only mechanism of democracy that so decisively places decision-making responsibilities in the hands of the people. Those people are jurors, and, as we shall see, the methods used to select these individuals is often the source of considerable debate between and among psycholegal researchers and legal practitioners. In this chapter, we describe the procedure, voir dire, through which regular citizens are chosen to serve on juries. We also review the research, examining the efficacy of traditional attorney-conducted jury selection. We contrast traditional methods of jury selection with one of the many services provided by trial consultants: scientific jury selection. Scientific jury selection relies on community surveys to identify demographic, personality, or attitudinal correlates of potential jurors' inclinations to vote guilty or not guilty in a particular case. Finally, we note the limitations of the extant research on jury selection and, based on relevant social psychological research on attitude-behavior relationships, suggest avenues for future research on voir dire and jury selection.

VOIR DIRE

Voir dire (from the French, *to speak the truth*) is a pretrial legal proceeding, mandated by federal or state statute, in which a petit jury (as opposed to a grand jury) is assembled to hear a civil or criminal trial. During voir dire, the judge and/or the attorneys (i.e., the prosecution and the defense in criminal cases, the lawyers representing the plaintiff and the defendant in civil cases) formally examine groups of prospective jurors, known as the venire. Attorneys may use the voir dire process to accomplish a variety of goals. Some attorneys advocate using voir dire as an opportunity to ingratiate themselves with the jury (e.g., Levine, 2001; Liotti & Cole, 2000; Weaver, 1993). Others argue that voir dire is a time to educate the jury about case-relevant law or the central issues in the case (e.g., Herman, 1997; McNulty, 2000). Whatever other purposes voir dire serves, its primary purpose is to provide a forum in which attorneys attempt to uncover any bias that jurors have that might prevent them from weighing the evidence fairly and arriving at an appropriate verdict (McCarter, 1999).

Voir dire is used in both criminal and civil trials. In a criminal case, because the state bears the burden of proof, the prosecution typically begins the examination, followed by the defense; in a civil case, the plaintiff's attorney usually begins the questioning. When a case is tried in federal court, however, it is very likely that the judge will ask most, if not all, of the questions of the venire. The length of voir dire may range from several hours in the typical case to several months. However, a protracted voir dire is relatively rare and is typically reserved for cases that are exceedingly complex or involve a high degree of pretrial publicity. Depending on the nature of the case, a venire person typically will be asked an array of questions, including questions designed to elicit basic demographic information, knowledge about the case, and perhaps case-specific attitudes.

When the examination is finished, the venire often is excused from the courtroom so that the attorneys may openly scrutinize the jurors and their responses to these questions. If the venire is not excused, the attorneys approach the bench and quietly convene with the judge so as not to offend any of the panel members. It is at this time that the jury is assembled. There are two mechanisms through which jurors can be excluded from a jury. Attorneys may make a motion that particular jurors should be excused because they exhibited clear bias that would prejudice their evaluation of the evidence. This motion is known as a challenge for cause. Attorneys may also remove a juror by exercising one of their peremptory challenges, which allows them to exclude a juror without stating the cause for the exclusion. After all of the challenges have been made and ruled, the surviving venire persons are then sworn into service as jurors. The individuals who are not retained for service are excused and may later be summoned to participate in a different voir dire for another trial. Because attorneys are concerned with striking prospective jurors rather than retaining them, voir dire is best characterized as a process of elimination rather than a process of selection (Elwork, Sales, & Suggs, 1981; Middendorf & Luginbuhl, 1995). That is, attorneys challenge the suitability of jurors for jury service rather than choosing those jurors they would most like to see seated on the jury.

Challenging Potential Jurors

Challenges for cause may be granted if, during voir dire, a venire person is found to hold overt prejudice, is in disagreement with fundamental principles of due process, or fails to meet minimum state eligibility for jury service. Challenges for cause are unlimited in number and, like all motions, are either granted or denied by the judge. However, if a venire person admits to holding prejudice, the judge can, and often does, ask if that individual is willing and able to set aside that bias and render a fair verdict (Berry, 1997; McElhaney, 2000). If the venire person reports that bias can be set aside, he or she often is retained for service. Challenges for cause granted are rarely; however, the venire person may still be removed through the exercise of a peremptory challenge.

Peremptory challenges refer to the removal of a venire person from the panel for no avowed reason. That is, attorneys exercise peremptory challenges at their discretion, "for any tactical reasons they desire" (Suggs & Sales, 1981, p. 246).

Peremptory challenges serve several functions (Babcock, 1972). For example, trial participants may be more satisfied with the outcome of the trial if they help to select the people who will decide the outcome. Moreover, peremptory challenges allow attorneys to eliminate jurors who may be reluctant to admit their bias and to excuse jurors that attorneys may have offended during intrusive questioning.

Unlike challenges for cause, the number of peremptory challenges allotted varies with the jurisdiction in which a case is being tried, as dictated by state or federal statute. For example, in Florida and Missouri civil trials, both defendant and plaintiff are allotted three peremptory challenges; in Michigan civil trials, they are allotted two. Depending on state law, judges may be free to grant additional peremptory challenges as they see fit. For example, in a case surrounded by intense pretrial publicity, a judge may decide that additional challenges are warranted to ensure that an impartial jury is seated. Thus, the number of peremptory challenges available to counsel is limited but routinely increases with the severity of the crime (Elwork et al., 1981). Moreover, our justice system is designed to protect the criminal defendant through mechanisms such as the presumption of the defendant's innocence and placing a high burden of proof on the prosecution. Therefore, the criminal defense is typically granted at least as many and sometimes more peremptory challenges than the prosecution. For example, in Michigan in noncapital criminal trials, defendant and plaintiff are granted 5 peremptory challenges; however, in a capital trial, the defendant is granted 20 peremptory challenges and the prosecution is granted 15.

In practice, attorneys exercise peremptory challenges for a variety of reasons. Even if a venire person may not be removed for cause, he or she may be rejected based on personal characteristics, perceived attitudes, occupational status, or other dispositions that are thought to be unfavorable to an attorney's case. There are some limitations to the use of peremptory challenges. Attorneys are prohibited from striking members of cognizable groups (i.e., an easily identifiable segment of the community). In 1986, the U.S. Supreme Court ruled that race could not constitute the sole criterion for exercising a peremptory challenge in criminal trials (*Batson v. Kentucky*, 1986). Courts have ruled that peremptory challenges may not be used to exclude jurors in civil cases because of their race (*Powers v. Ohio*, 1991). The U.S. Supreme Court has extended this protection to preclude the use of peremptory challenges based solely on gender (*J.E.B. v. Alabama, ex rel T.B.*, 1994). Although these rulings were intended to protect the integrity of the jury, it is widely acknowledged that attorneys who rationalize or fabricate alternative reasons for striking a prospective juror can circumvent the law. Thus, it is unclear to what extent these rulings have been effective (Golash, 1992; Rose, 1999).

Extended versus Minimal Voir Dire

As can be seen from this brief discussion, voir dire provides the procedural dimensions for the application of jury selection. It should be noted that judges wield sweeping discretionary power in deciding how voir dire is conducted in their courtrooms; consequently, the scope of voir dire is likely to vary widely across jurisdictions. Moran, Cutler, and Loftus (1990) argued that when the judge conducts the voir dire with limited or no participation from counsel (i.e., "minimal" voir dire), attorneys are deprived of the information they need to intelligently exercise their challenges. They further argued that only by granting counsel generous time and latitude in their questioning (i.e., "extended" voir dire) will they be able to identify potentially biased individuals.

To provide empirical evidence for their argument, Moran et al. (1990) used the results of surveys to contrast the predictive validity of the information that normally would be gained from a minimal voir dire with the information that would be gathered during an extended voir dire. In one of these surveys, participants read a case summary of a drug-related prosecution and subsequently responded to measures of defendant culpability, case-specific attitudes, attitudes toward the legal system, and demographic information. To simulate a minimal voir dire, the authors assessed the relationship between defendant culpability ratings and survey items that attorneys would normally gather from that type of examination (e.g., age, gender, education, marital status, and occupation). The authors also assessed the relationship between the same defendant culpability ratings and the information that attorneys could obtain in an extended voir dire (e.g., attitudinal dispositions in addition to demographic information). The results from this investigation demonstrate the superiority of extended voir dire, with its predictors accounting for 31% of the variance in the final culpability rating and the predictors in the minimal voir dire accounting for only 8% of the variance.

Nietzel and colleagues have provided strong empirical evidence that an extended voir dire is essential in guiding the use of not only peremptory challenges, but challenges for cause as well (Nietzel & Dillehay, 1982; Nietzel, Dillehay, & Himelein, 1987). Their field investigations of voir dire in death penalty cases found that in those trials in which the judge allowed the attorneys to conduct a thorough voir dire examination, attorneys successfully exercised a significantly greater number of challenges for cause. As is apparent from these studies, the way the judge conducts the voir dire bears directly on the ability of attorneys to obtain information from jurors that will help them predict juror verdicts.

These investigations highlight another critical point: Judges, attorneys, and trial consultants often hold different ideas as to what voir dire should accomplish (Johnson & Haney, 1994). Judges favor a minimal voir dire primarily because of the time and money consumed by an extended examination. Attorneys view an extended voir dire not only as an opportunity to question the panel thoroughly (probative voir dire), but also as a chance to ingratiate themselves with the venire, begin arguing their case, and "inoculate" prospective jurors from damaging evidence forthcoming (didactic voir dire). For the trial consultant, an extended voir dire is almost a necessity. Consultants may collect data from a community survey that indicates which attitudinal dispositions are most predictive of a verdict. Without extended voir dire, the consultant will not have the relevant information about jurors' attitudes to accurately predict which jurors will be likely to vote in favor of the consultant's client. Thus, there are inherent differences in the way that judges and advocates view voir dire. For the presiding judge, the goal of voir dire is to seat a legally qualified jury; for the advocate, it is to select a jury that is favorable to one's case, or at the very least, one that will hear the evidence objectively.

The Social Psychology of Voir Dire

As can be seen, voir dire entails an exceedingly complex social interaction, the premise of which rests on the assumption that venire persons will be honest and forthcoming in revealing some of their most personally held attitudes, beliefs, and biases. Jury selection will be as successful as the voir dire is effective. In other words, irrespective of how the voir dire is conducted, be it minimal or extended, there is a positive relationship between the forthrightness of the venire and the efficacy of jury selection (assuming that the jury selection method is valid and is executed competently). For this reason, a small but notable body of literature has analyzed the features of voir dire that can either foster or discourage potential jurors' self-disclosure.

Several system variables (i.e., aspects of the voir dire that are under direct control of the judicial system) may moderate the completeness of self-disclosure: (a) who conducts the voir dire, (b) how the voir dire is conducted, and (c) the environment in which voir dire takes place. Drawing on established social psychological research, Suggs and Sales (1981) surmised that voir dire would be most effective when conducted by attorneys because the differential status between judge and venire person may lead to socially desirable responses. In other words, because potential jurors recognize that the judge is in a position of authority, they may wish to provide desirable answers to his questions. Furthermore, because previous research has demonstrated that individuals volunteer more information in the absence of a group, they asserted that voir dire would be most effective when panel members are questioned individually as opposed to collectively. Finally, they argued that the physical dimensions and characteristics of the courtroom (e.g., the proximity between the venire, attorneys, and judge) might inhibit self-disclosure. Particular aspects of the courtroom, such as the judge's elevated bench and black robe, for example, are thought to impart cues to the panel as to what constitutes an acceptable response. For example, it may be difficult for venire persons to report to a judge that they would be unable to set aside their biases as the judge is requesting because of the judge's elevated stature and authority.

Marshall and Smith (1986) have expanded on this social psychological analysis of voir dire by comparing the voir dire process to the procedures of a psychological experiment. These researchers reason that because voir dire, like an experiment, requires individuals to undergo intense examination, certain psychological factors that have been shown to operate during an experiment will be present during the examination. These factors are collectively known as experimental artifacts (Rosenthal & Rosnow, 1969). In the context of voir dire, two artifacts in particular are thought to exert a detrimental effect on self-disclosure: evaluation anxiety and demand characteristics.

According to Rosenberg (1969), evaluation anxiety is "an active, anxiety-toned concern that [the participant] win a positive evaluation from the experimenter, or at least that [the participant] provide no grounds for a negative one" (p. 281). During voir dire, prospective jurors may experience nervousness, embarrassment, or apprehension when they realize that the judge and attorneys possess the power to determine if they are fit to serve on the jury or when they acknowledge the grave responsibility of their duty. To help alleviate their anxiety, prospective jurors may respond in less truthful but socially desirable ways to garner a favorable evaluation from the judge. This process would lead jurors to report that they could set aside their predispositions and biases when evaluating the trial evidence even if they truly believe that it would be difficult or impossible to do so.

Demand characteristics also may influence venire persons' responses during voir dire. Defined as "the totality of cues which convey an experimental hypothesis to the subject" (Orne, 1962, p. 779), demand characteristics include a wide range of situational factors, such as the formality of the court proceedings, the presence of a bailiff, the number of attorneys present, and the physical characteristics of the courtroom. One particularly salient demand characteristic thought to operate during voir dire is that of expectancy effects. Expectancy effects lead experimenters to engage in verbal or nonverbal behaviors that indicate to the subject what the experimenter is looking for or is hoping to find. Some judges, for example, are notorious for quizzing the venire using a demanding and impatient demeanor. There is convincing evidence that judges' nonverbal behaviors influence jurors' verdicts (Halverson, Hallahan, Hart, & Rosenthal, 1997; Hart, 1995). In voir dire, expectancy effects may occur when prospective jurors receive verbal or nonverbal cues from judges and/or attorneys, inadvertently guiding them to respond in a socially desirable manner (see LeVan, 1984).

In an effort to determine what influence these factors exert on self-disclosure, Marshall and Smith (1986) posed questions to ex-jurors regarding their general feelings and attitudes toward their jury selection experience. Results from this study revealed that those jurors reporting high levels of evaluation anxiety during voir dire were significantly less likely to provide honest answers than those who did not. Furthermore, measures of expectancy effects were found to be a marginally significant predictor of honesty during voir dire, whereas other demand characteristics were found to exert no effect. Although there clearly are limitations to the retrospective methodology used in this study, the findings suggest that evaluation anxiety and experimenter expectancy effects may increase the social desirability and decrease the honesty of jurors' responses to questions during voir dire.

Jones (1987) used an experimental methodology to test the hypothesis that an attorney-conducted examination will be more effective at eliciting candid responses from the venire than would an examination conducted by a judge, as usually occurs in federal court. Jones reasoned that demand characteristics emitted from the judge, relative to those emitted by attorneys, would significantly inhibit self-disclosure. Jones had jury eligible citizens participate in a mock voir dire conducted by attorneys or a judge who used either a personal or formal demeanor (thus exerting some control over the demand characteristics emitted by both parties). Participants in each condition completed a legal attitudes questionnaire and a measure of public self-awareness prior to their examination. With the voir dire then underway, the judge or attorneys posed several questions to individual panel members that they were required to publicly answer. At this point, the examination was interrupted and participants again completed the measures of legal attitudes and public self-awareness.

From first to second administration of these measures, those individuals undergoing judge-directed voir dire changed their responses at a rate nearly twice that of those undergoing an attorney-conducted examination, irrespective of whether the judge behaved in a personal or formal manner. Furthermore, participants' change scores were significantly greater when the attorneys conducted themselves with a formal rather than a personable demeanor. These results suggest that voir dire will be more effective (i.e., will yield more information) when attorneys are permitted to examine the venire, especially when they use a personable demeanor to establish rapport. These results also demonstrate that the demand characteristics emitted by the judge significantly inhibit self-disclosure and that changes in the judge's demeanor do not moderate this effect.

Middendorf and Luginbuhl (1995) further examined the influence of different styles of voir dire used by attorneys on self-disclosure during voir dire. Specifically, they studied whether jurors responded differently when attorneys used a directive style relying on closed questions (e.g., "Do you understand that it is not an admission of guilt if the defendant does not testify on his behalf?") versus a nondirective style relying on open-ended questions (e.g., "What would it mean to you if the defendant did not testify on his behalf?"). Those individuals examined with the directive style endorsed guarantees of due process to a greater degree than those examined with the nondirective style of voir dire. Participants in this latter condition also rated their own examination as more positive than did those in the direct condition, reporting that they felt more comfortable being asked and answering questions. These findings provide additional evidence that a more personable interrogation style allows attorneys to establish rapport with jurors and allows jurors the opportunity to provide honest answers and more information that will be useful to attorneys during jury selection.

To summarize, it should be clear that voir dire and jury selection are linked inexorably. Voir dire provides the procedural framework for jury selection; however, through statute, case law, and judicial discretion, this forum is likely to vary widely across jurisdictions. Consequently, practitioners of jury selection will have to steer their selection strategies though the procedural avenues provided them. The success of these selection strategies, however valid, is limited by the accuracy and trustworthiness of the information obtained during voir dire. Although some trial strategists suggest that conducting voir dire using a questionnaire rather than an oral exchange will promote self-disclosure and truthfulness (Berry, 1997; Speckart & McLennan, 1999), we know of no empirical study that directly addresses this hypothesis. However, the psychological evidence does suggest that maximal information will be obtained through attorney-conducted, nondirective voir dire. Mindful that ability of attorneys and

trial consultants to select a favorable jury is constrained by the validity of the information obtained during voir dire, we now turn our attention exclusively to jury selection, beginning with a discussion of some of the traditional methods used to select the jury.

TRADITIONAL JURY SELECTION

A distinction was previously drawn between voir dire and jury selection, the former referring to a pretrial legal proceeding and the latter referring to the execution of that procedure. At this point, we draw an additional distinction between traditional and scientific jury selection. When we speak of traditional jury selection, we are broadly referring to any strategy that has traditionally been used by attorneys to identify jurors who are favorable (or unfavorable) to their case. The hallmark of these traditional strategies is that they are based on attorneys' intuition, implicit stereotypes, and expectancies. Scientific jury selection, in contrast, refers to the application of social science methodology to the selection of jurors.

Stereotypes and Implicit Theories of Personality and Attitudes

Traditional approaches are most readily associated with attorneys' time-honored stratagem of selecting jurors by way of superstition, stereotypes, body language, implicit theories of attitude and personality, or other strategies that attorneys have developed through trial experience (Fulero & Penrod, 1990b). Evidence for this assertion comes directly from popular guides to trial tactics, literature published by attorneys, and handbooks of jury selection. According to Fulero and Penrod's compendium of jury selection folklore, some attorneys advise that women should be avoided as jurors in criminal prosecutions but are desirable in civil suits. Others argue that female jurors are advantageous in criminal cases unless the defendant is an attractive woman. Some advocates believe that wealthy individuals are conviction-prone unless trying a white-collar crime. Poor jurors may be advantageous for a civil defense because they are not used to the idea of large sums of money and are thus likely to deliver smaller rewards. Others believe that poor jurors should be avoided because they are bitter about their indigent status and are therefore likely to deliver exorbitant rewards—the "Robin Hood" effect. The similarity-leniency hypothesis may lead attorneys to select jurors who are similar to their client because of their presumed empathy for similar individuals (Blue, 1991; Kerr, Hymes, Anderson, & Weathers, 1995). In contrast, the black sheep hypothesis may lead attorneys to reject jurors who are similar to their clients, strategizing that people may want to punish in-group members who reflect poorly on their group (Marques, Abrams, Paez, & Martinez-Taboada, 1998). From these examples, it is clear that attorneys' common sense may lead to contradictory hypotheses about which potential jurors would be most helpful or most harmful to have on the jury.

Beliefs about Nonverbal Communication

In addition to the use of stereotypes and implicit personality theories, attorneys may rely on potential jurors' nonverbal communication to select a jury (e.g., Dimitrius & Mazzarella, 1999; Starr & McCormick, 2000). For example, Starr and McCormick suggest that a trial consultant should scrutinize potential jurors' clothing for hints about their ideology (e.g., antiestablishment) or personality. By examining potential jurors' posture, their willingness to express their opinions, and the amount of space they occupy in the courtroom, Starr and McCormick argue, attorneys can identify which potential jurors are likely to be influential during deliberations. Some critics will undoubtedly contend that any individual who has participated in selecting a jury will immediately recognize the value of analyzing the venire's verbal and nonverbal behavior. Unfortunately, many of the tactics recommended by trial manuals are inconsistent. Some practitioners, for example, argue that attorneys should accept a smiling juror; others suggest striking those who smile (Bodin, 1954; Darrow, 1936; Harrington & Dempsey, 1969). Some practitioners argue that nonverbal behaviors such as pupil dilation, rising voice pitch, response latency, and fidgeting indicate that a prospective juror is providing deceptive responses (Blue, 1991). Although we are not necessarily arguing with the usefulness of nonverbal behavior for the identification of favorable jurors, we are aware of no attempts to empirically validate the efficacy of such techniques in the context of legal decision making.

Effectiveness of Traditional Jury Selection

Nevertheless, any assertion that traditional methods of jury selection are ineffective at identifying desirable jurors must be tempered with empirical observation. Zeisel and Diamond (1978) conducted one of the first studies to evaluate the efficacy of attorney selection methods by "back-engineering" 12 federal juries. These researchers asked panel members removed through peremptory challenges to hear cases not as jurors but as observers, and to render a verdict at the trial's conclusion. Coupled with posttrial interviews with the actual jurors, this method allowed Zeisel and

Diamond to compare seated juries' verdicts with the verdicts that would have been rendered had juries been seated without exercising peremptory challenges. The results from this field investigation demonstrated that in a few cases, the use of peremptory challenges does significantly influence the trial's outcome. Overall, however, the results suggest that attorneys are not very accurate at predicting jurors' decisions. An additional study compared the verdicts rendered by 10 actual juries, 10 juries whose members were randomly chosen from the venire, and 10 juries composed of challenged jurors (Diamond & Zeisel, 1974). This study found that actual juries were less likely to convict than randomly chosen juries or challenged juries and that defense and prosecuting attorneys were rather effective in eliminating jurors who would likely vote against their side. Although there were several limitations to these studies that preclude a definitive conclusion about attorneys' ability to identify favorable jurors (e.g., the reconstructed jury did not deliberate; the decisions made by actual juries were the only decisions with consequences), they stand as classic investigations into the efficacy of jury selection.

In another effort to evaluate attorney's jury selection performance, Olczak, Kaplan, and Penrod (1991) conducted a series of studies to examine attorneys' lay strategies for judging jurors. In the first of these studies, attorneys read various juror profiles and reported which characteristics and information they typically would seek during voir dire. These participants then read one of two transcripts from a felony trial and rated the jurors on their perceived bias toward the defendant and a variety of personality traits (e.g., leniency, intelligence, attractiveness). Attorneys generally relied on a very small number of demographic and personality dimensions when making inferences about prospective jurors, suggesting that attorneys use rather unsophisticated stereotypes and strategies in making their decisions. These researchers, using a similar methodology, also compared the performance of college students relative to that of attorneys, finding that both groups engaged in similar, unsophisticated strategies in judging prospective jurors. Finally, Olczak et al. had law students and attorneys read a description of a manslaughter prosecution and subsequently rate the desirability of mock jurors who had previously rendered a verdict in the case. The results from this investigation coincide with their earlier findings, reporting that law students and attorneys performed comparably, with both groups judging mock jurors who had previously voted for conviction as more desirable from a defense perspective.

In the most recent investigation of the effectiveness of traditional jury selection, Johnson and Haney (1994) studied the voir dire process in four felony trials. These researchers measured potential jurors' criminal justice attitudes with questions from the Legal Attitudes Questionnaire (Boehm, 1968). To examine the effectiveness of attorney-conducted jury selection, they compared the criminal justice attitudes of jurors who were retained, jurors who were excused by the prosecution, and those who were excused by the defense. Moreover, they compared the collective attitudes of retained juries with the attitudes of juries who would have been seated if the first 12 jurors had been chosen or if jurors had been randomly chosen to serve. As seen in the earlier studies conducted by Diamond and Zeisel (1974) and Zeisel and Diamond (1978), prosecutors effectively used their peremptory challenges to eliminate more prodefense jurors and defense attorneys effectively used their challenges to eliminate more proprosecution jurors. The attitudes of the seated jurors were no different, however, from the attitudes of a randomly chosen group of 12 jurors or the first 12 jurors called for service. Thus, although attorneys could identify the most biased jurors in the venire, the removal of these jurors did not alter the attitudinal composition of the resulting jury.

To summarize, traditional approaches to jury selection generally involve conjecture, the use of stereotypes, and anecdotal strategies in choosing juries. Laboratory and field investigations designed to assess the validity of such tactics have largely reached the consensus that their predictive strength is near chance level (Fulero & Penrod, 1990a, 1990b; Olczak et al., 1991; Zeisel & Diamond, 1978). Considering the current controversy surrounding scientific jury selection (Strier, 1999) and the claims of those trial consultants said to have predicted the behavior of thousands of jurors (Dimitrius & Mazzarella, 1999), investigations of traditional jury selection are surprisingly rare.

Further research on traditional jury selection strategy is needed for several reasons. First, these tactics will undoubtedly continue to play a prominent role in contemporary jury selection, especially for those attorneys who believe scientific jury selection is a sham or whose clients cannot afford the services of a trial consultant. Second, these strategies are likely to be dynamic; that is, they are apt to change to coincide with the natural evolution of judicial philosophy and procedure. Third, it is an inevitable fact that intuition, heuristics, and stereotypes play a critical role in our everyday decision making; it would thus be shortsighted to expect an individual to engage in such a complex task while ignoring his or her instinct. Finally, in the trial consulting industry, jury selection is often practiced with a blend of both traditional and scientific methodologies. Future research would do well to determine how these approaches interact to produce the hybrid of jury selection procedures that contemporary researchers have overlooked.

SCIENTIFIC JURY SELECTION

The conception of scientific jury selection is usually credited to Jay Schulman and his colleagues (see Schulman, Shaver, Colman, Emrich, & Christie, 1973). In 1972, the "Harrisburg Seven," a group of antiwar activists, were indicted by the federal government on, among other things, charges of conspiracy to kidnap then presidential advisor Henry Kissinger. Schulman and his colleagues, who were sympathetic to the antiwar movement, initially attempted to establish that the venire drawn for the trial was not representative of the Harrisburg community at large. Schulman supervised an army of volunteers who conducted nearly 1,000 telephone surveys. The demographic data collected from these surveys revealed that the Harrisburg community was younger (and presumably less conservative) than the venire chosen for the trial. The judge ruled that a new venire should be chosen.

Convinced of the utility of the community survey, Schulman and his team conducted a more penetrating survey designed to assess the community's sentiments about the case. Approximately 250 of the original survey participants were contacted and solicited to volunteer information on a range of demographic and attitudinal questions. Respondents were asked about the quantity of their media contact, their knowledge of the case and the defendants, their attitudes toward the Vietnam War, and their trust in government. Based on the observed relationships between such measures and participants' knowledge and attitudes regarding the defendants, Schulman's team was able to construct a profile of the ideal juror that would guide the exercise of peremptory challenges.

After each day of the voir dire (which lasted three weeks), the defense team would confer to rate each venire person on a 1-to-5 scale to determine which individuals should be challenged. Although the rating system proved efficient, there were 15 individuals with marginal ratings (i.e., scores of 3) of which 5 had to be chosen. Furthermore, the dynamics of potential panel compositions had to be considered (i.e., who would likely be elected the jury foreperson). The final decisions were made by combining information from the survey data and subjective impressions of the individuals themselves. As Schulman et al. (1973) later noted: "The main use of surveys is to sort out types of people, not to pick out individuals, which was the issue at hand. The great danger and temptation was to use the survey results to select jurors mechanically" (p. 44). The prototypical juror that eventually emerged for the defense was a female Democrat with a white-collar or skilled blue-collar occupation and with no particular religious preference. Understandably, the ideal juror would also sympathize with the defendant's antiwar sentiment. When the jury was selected, it consisted of nine females and three males. The case eventually ended in a mistrial because the jury could not reach a unanimous verdict. The case was not retried.

Though a mistrial was clearly a victory for the defense, what is the verdict for scientific jury selection? Did the survey give the defense a significant advantage? Did it win the case? The answers to these questions remain elusive. Indeed, even a broad generalization of the survey's contribution to the verdict is difficult, if not impossible to estimate because, in addition to the survey data, the defense used a combination of subjective impressions, hearsay, and conjecture to select the jury. Furthermore, Schulman's team acknowledged that several extraneous factors likely contributed to the mistrial, including the leverage granted to the defense during voir dire, the sequestration of the jury, and the nature of the case itself.

This issue raises a serious concern that still resonates in the practice of jury selection today. There is no way of determining the precise contribution of scientific jury selection to a trial's outcome in any particular case. Unlike an experiment, no objective standard exists to which its efficacy can be compared. Every trial presents a unique blend of circumstance, evidence, and personalities that cannot be replicated in the field or in the laboratory. Furthermore, as Zeisel and Diamond (1978) noted, there is no way to determine how excused venire persons would have voted in deliberations because they have been removed from the trial process. Nevertheless, Schulman et al.'s methods helped to inspire not only a multimillion-dollar trial consulting industry but also a generation of psycholegal research surrounding the jury.

The Practice of Scientific Jury Selection

The tenets of scientific jury selection rest on the assumption that a person's individual differences and attitudes will predict how he or she will evaluate a given case. Through identification of correlates of verdict inclinations, scientific jury selection attempts to identify which characteristics will be associated with a favorable (or unfavorable) case evaluation, and generalize these relationships to the selection of jurors. The question remains: Does scientific jury selection work, and if so, to what degree? Unfortunately, the inherent difficulties involved in validating scientific jury selection in the field, as discussed previously, do not yield easily to laboratory investigations either. This fact, however, has not precluded research into the validity of the scientific approach.

The community survey remains the primary tool of jury selection practitioners because it has proved to be the most efficient means for collecting and weighing community sentiment surrounding a trial. The typical jury selection survey is tailored around the case in question and comprises the following five components: (a) a synopsis of the case (including a summary of the evidence) and questions designed to assess, (b) case-specific attitudes, (c) attitudes toward the legal system in general, (d) defendant culpability, and (e) basic demographic information. The survey is randomly administered, often by telephone, to jury-eligible individuals in the community in which the trial is to take place. The respondents hear the case summary and then respond to the attitudinal, culpability, and demographic measures. The data from these surveys are analyzed to identify possible relationships between the various measures and culpability ratings. The results from such a survey, for example, might reveal that lower-income individuals are statistically more likely to acquit the defendant, or that individuals with prior military service are likely to convict. Based on the survey results, and assuming that the presiding judge grants sufficient leeway for questioning, counsel may then probe for more specific demographic characteristics and attitudinal dispositions that have been found to statistically predict culpability. In the following sections, we review the research addressing whether particular demographic variables, personality traits, and attitudes are predictive of defendant culpability.

Demographic Predictors of Verdict

The possibility that demographic variables may predict a verdict must be attractive to attorneys, as many of these variables (e.g., gender, socioeconomic status, occupation) are either easily observable or obtainable even in the minimal voir dires conducted in federal courts. Unfortunately, several studies suggest that demographic characteristics are only weakly related to verdict and that the utility of these variables may be case-specific. In at least one study, juror age, gender, marital status, and occupation were unrelated to damage awards (Goodman, Loftus, & Greene, 1990). Other studies suggest that jurors who have higher incomes, more prestigious occupations, or higher educational levels are more likely to convict than are jurors with a lower socioeconomic status (Adler, 1973; Simon, 1967).

Using race to predict juror verdicts has proved complicated. Early research suggested that Black mock jurors were more likely to acquit defendants using an insanity defense than were White mock jurors (Simon, 1967). More recently, race affected community perceptions of O. J. Simpson's guilt in the death of his ex-wife (Brigham & Wasserman, 1999). Before the trial, after the conclusion of the evidence presentation phase, and after the actual jury had returned a verdict, Blacks were less likely to believe that Simpson murdered his ex-wife than were Whites. There is some evidence, however, that upper-middle-class Black jurors may be more punitive than Whites toward other Blacks, especially toward those who commit violent crimes that would reflect poorly on the Black community (Nietzel & Dillehay, 1986).

Although the Simpson trial featured evidence about domestic violence, gender did not influence participants' beliefs about his guilt (Brigham & Wasserman, 1999). In contrast, gender has proven to be a reliable predictor of verdict in many types of trials. Women are more likely to convict child sexual abuse defendants than are men (Bottoms & Goodman, 1994; Kovera, Gresham, Borgida, Gray, & Regan, 1997; Kovera, Levy, Borgida, & Penrod, 1994). Women are more likely than men to convict in rape cases (Brekke & Borgida, 1988). Finally, women are more likely to find defendants liable for sexual harassment (Kovera, McAuliff, & Hebert, 1999). Women are not always more punitive than are men; several studies show that women are less likely than men to convict battered women for murdering their partners (Schuller, 1992; Schuller & Hastings, 1996). Thus, gender appears to predict verdicts in cases that involve issues such as rape, domestic violence, and sexual harassment, issues on which men's and women's attitudes often differ. There is little evidence to suggest that gender is a reliable predictor of verdict in other types of cases.

Demographic information may provide useful data for practitioners of scientific jury selection when demographics are related to case-relevant attitudes, especially in cases in which the voir dire is limited in scope and unable to assess these attitudes directly. Death penalty attitudes are an example of a case-specific attitude that may be indirectly assessed using demographic characteristics. Community surveys (Fitzgerald & Ellsworth, 1984; Haney, Hurtado, & Vega, 1994) and surveys of impaneled felony jurors (Moran & Comfort, 1986) found that Whites, Republicans, and men were more likely to report pro-death penalty attitudes than were Blacks, Democrats, and women. These death penalty attitudes predicted verdicts in trial simulations of death penalty cases (Cowan, Thompson, & Ellsworth, 1984). Death penalty attitudes also predicted verdicts in actual cases, irrespective of whether they were capital or noncapital cases (Moran & Comfort, 1986). Similarly, education predicts antilibertarian attitudes, and jurors with antilibertarian attitudes are more likely to convict than those who do not hold antilibertarian attitudes (Moran et al., 1990).

Although demographic characteristics may have limited ability to predict verdict across a wide variety of cases, some characteristics may be useful to trial consultants for another reason. They may help to predict which jurors will be influential during jury deliberations. For example, men are generally more influential than women during deliberations. Men speak more frequently during deliberations than do women (James, 1959). Jurors also select men as the foreperson more frequently than they select women (Dillehay & Nietzel, 1985; Strodtbeck, James, & Hawkins, 1957). Similarly, jurors are more likely to elect a foreperson with high socioeconomic status than with low status (Strodtbeck et al., 1957). Thus, trial consultants can maximize the likelihood that a particular viewpoint will be expressed during deliberation if they ensure that an upper-income male who holds that viewpoint is seated on the jury.

Thus, there is evidence that some demographic characteristics may predict juror verdict in at least some types of cases; however, there is little evidence that any one demographic variable will prove useful in selecting jurors in a wide variety of cases. In federal courts or other contexts in which more detailed questions are prohibited, demographic characteristics may serve as a successful proxy for the measurement of case-specific attitudes that may be related to verdict. Although the power of juror demographics to predict verdicts appears to be limited, demographics may be more useful in anticipating those jurors who are likely to dominate the deliberation process.

Personality Traits as Predictors of Verdict

If trial consultants or attorneys have the opportunity to gather more information than mere demographic characteristics during voir dire, some collect information about personality traits, with the hope of using this information to predict juror behavior. The research on the relationship of personality characteristics to juror verdict, not unlike the research examining the relationship between demographic characteristics and verdict, suggests that the relationship between these two sets of variables is weak and inconsistent at best. Jurors who have an internal locus of control or a strong sense of personal responsibility are more likely to hold a defendant responsible for his or her actions, especially when the evidence is weak (Phares & Wilson, 1972). This trait may also be important for predicting juror behavior in civil cases; jurors with a keen sense of personal responsibility may hold plaintiffs responsible for their own injury if they contributed in any way to that injury (Hans, 1992). Research on another personality trait, belief in a just world, also produces inconsistent findings. People with a strong belief that bad things happen to bad people may either ascribe responsibility to victims for their plight or may be punitive toward defendants (Gerbasi, Zuckerman, & Reis, 1977; Moran & Comfort, 1982).

Authoritarianism has proven to be the most useful personality trait for identifying jurors' verdict inclinations across a broad spectrum of cases. The construct of authoritarianism was originally developed in the context of a research program on the nature of prejudice (Adorno, Frenkel-Brunswik, Levinson, & Sanford, 1950). People with an authoritarian personality are more likely to endorse conventional values, respect authority, and act punitively toward people who defy authority or conventional norms. Other researchers have developed measures of authoritarian beliefs that are specifically relevant to the legal system, including the Legal Attitudes Questionnaire (LAQ; Boehm, 1968), the revised LAQ (Kravitz, Cutler, & Brock, 1993), and the original Juror Bias Scale (Kassin & Wrightsman, 1983) and revised version of this instrument (Myers & Lecci, 1998).

A meta-analysis of the studies using authoritarianism as a predictor of juror verdict revealed that authoritarian participants are more likely to vote for conviction, especially when measured by the more specifically focused legal authoritarianism measures (Narby, Cutler, & Moran, 1993). Authoritarian jurors are more likely to recommend harsh sentences than are nonauthoritarian jurors (Bray & Noble, 1978). However, there are some situations that may lead authoritarian jurors to be less punitive, such as when the defendant is an authority figure (Nietzel & Dillehay, 1986). Despite this contradictory data, the findings supporting the predictive validity of authoritarianism are impressively consistent, given the inconsistency found using other personality predictors of verdict.

Attitudinal Predictors of Verdict

Both demographic characteristics and personality traits provide jury consultants with global information about jurors' attitudinal beliefs and verdict inclinations. Attitudinal measures, especially those that are tailored to assess beliefs that are specifically relevant to the case being tried, may provide more detailed and case-relevant information about jurors' predispositions to vote in a particular way. Attitudes toward tort reform reliably predicted verdict inclination in one civil and three criminal trial scenarios. Individuals favoring tort reform were more likely to side with the prosecution in a criminal trial and with the defense in a civil trial (Moran, Cutler, & De Lisa, 1994). Similarly, survey research indicates that attitudes toward psychiatrists predict community members' verdict inclinations in insanity defense cases (Cutler, Moran, & Narby, 1992), and attitudes toward drugs predict community members' perceptions of defendant culpability in drug cases (Moran et al., 1990).

Unfortunately, how these attitudinal predictors would have fared had the survey respondents rendered verdicts is not known. Some research, as previously mentioned, has addressed this issue by presenting participants with the opportunity to hear evidence before rendering an opinion about the

guilt of a defendant. The results from these studies are mixed. In a study designed to identify predictors of damage awards in civil litigation, individuals awaiting jury service read the case facts in one of three civil suits (Goodman et al., 1990). In each case, the defendant had previously been found negligent in the course of a civil suit and jurors were asked to award damages in the case. Although demographic information did not significantly predict the magnitude of damage awards, attitudes toward tort reform and monetary damages did. Unfortunately, the attitudinal data were collected *after* the presentation of the case facts. Thus, it is unclear whether jurors' attitudes toward tort reform influenced their verdicts, or their responses to the attitudinal measure provided a way for jurors to justify their verdicts.

One study that measured jurors' case-relevant attitudes *before* they watched a simulated trial found a much weaker relationship between case-specific attitudes and verdict (Narby & Cutler, 1994). These researchers carefully constructed a scale to assess attitudes toward eyewitnesses using both undergraduate and jury-eligible respondents from the community. After ensuring that the scale produced reliable and internally consistent measurement of eyewitness attitudes, it was administered to participants before they watched a robbery trial simulation in which eyewitness identification evidence was presented. Juror attitudes toward eyewitnesses did not predict verdict. These results cast doubt on the notion that those selecting juries can accurately predict juror verdict even from case-specific attitudes. These findings are especially troublesome because the attitudinal measure used in this study had psychometric properties (i.e., it was internally consistent and reliable) that increase its predictive power, and trial consultants undoubtedly assess attitudes using less reliable measures.

Data that are more encouraging about the predictive validity of attitudinal measures come from research conducted on impaneled jurors. Moran and Comfort (1986) asked formerly impaneled jurors to report whether they had voted to convict the defendant in the case they had heard. These researchers correlated this self-reported verdict with respondents' attitudes toward the death penalty. Generally, jurors who have pro-death penalty attitudes were more likely to vote for conviction, irrespective of whether they were deciding capital cases for which the death penalty is an option.

Taken together, these handful of studies suggest that attitudes, especially when they are case-relevant, may provide some information about how a particular juror is likely to vote during jury deliberations. Much of the research that clearly supports this proposition, however, comes from studies in which potential jurors do not hear trial evidence before reporting their verdict inclination. Few studies examine whether these case-specific attitudes remain predictive of verdict after the presentation of trial evidence. Even so, because traditional methods of jury selection appear to operate at chance level (i.e., 50% accuracy), any additional variance in verdict inclinations that could be explained by attitudinal or demographic predictors would bolster an attorney's ability to select favorable jurors (e.g., Moran et al., 1994; Penrod, 1990). If an attitudinal disposition accounted for 10% of the variance in defendant culpability in a community survey, for example, this finding would boost an attorney's probability of identifying a favorable juror from 50% to 60%.

Comparison of Traditional and Scientific Jury Selection Techniques

Most investigations of scientific jury selection have used one of two methodologies. Some studies are designed to establish the statistical relationships among demographics, attitudes, and verdict inclination. Other investigations extend this approach by testing the predictive strength of these variables in trial simulations. Although there are strengths and limitations to each of these approaches, studies of the last that include a behavioral criterion (e.g., verdict) will obviously be more powerful at detecting the influence of scientific jury selection on a trial's outcome (e.g., Horowitz, 1980; Narby & Cutler, 1994). However, even if it were confirmed that the scientific approach is effective at identifying favorable (or unfavorable) jurors, such a finding would not necessarily establish that these methods are more effective than traditional approaches. To justify the expense associated with scientific jury selection, more studies are needed that directly compare the efficacy of scientific and traditional techniques in an experimental framework.

To our knowledge, only one study has attempted this type of comparison. In this study, law students were trained in the use of either traditional or scientific selection methods, and their ability to predict mock jurors' verdicts in four simulated trials was evaluated (Horowitz, 1980). The results from this investigation were mixed. Although scientific jury selection was found to be superior in two cases involving a court martial and drug prosecution, traditional methods were found to be more effective at predicting verdict propensity in a mock murder trial. The results from the third trial, a drunk driving prosecution, found no significant difference between the two strategies. In light of these findings, Horowitz concluded that the scientific approach to jury selection was not superior to traditional techniques, especially when the relationships between predictors and verdict are weak. Unfortunately, there are severe limitations to this investigation that preclude any definitive conclusion about the efficacy of scientific jury

selection. As Horowitz concedes, a law student hastily trained in the craft of jury selection carries weak external validity to practice in the field. Moreover, the small number of juries examined makes the detection of any differences between traditional and scientific selection procedures difficult at best. Nevertheless, this investigation remains the sole study to compare experimentally the validity of scientific jury selection with traditional approaches.

Does the Jury Selection Process Produce Better Juror Decisions?

Most scientific jury selection research has focused on identifying variables that will help attorneys and consultants identify biased jurors. Why is the identification of biased jurors important? For advocates, the identification and elimination of jurors who are biased against their side will help them win cases. However, one of the main assumptions underlying jury selection is that prejudice will prevent jurors from appropriately weighing evidence. Researchers have operationalized the efficacy of jury selection, either traditional or scientific, as the elimination of jurors with bias. Perhaps efficacy should be operationalized as an increase in jurors' ability to recognize variations in the quality or the strength of the evidence presented.

Few studies have explored whether jury selection results in better decisions, although some studies have provided data that can inform the debate. Research on felony voir dire suggests that a jury chosen using traditional methods is similar in composition to a jury that is randomly selected from the pool or a jury composed of the first 12 jurors called to service (Johnson & Haney, 1994). Given that the bias of jurors selected through traditional methods did not differ from juries seated using other methods, it is unlikely that traditional methods of jury selection will improve jury decisions. Although it does not alter the fundamental composition of the jury, perhaps there are other ways in which voir dire might improve juror decisions. For example, a nondirective voir dire might be used to educate jurors about due process and presumption of innocence, thereby improving jurors' understanding and application of the law (Middendorf & Luginbuhl, 1995).

There has been little research on whether the voir dire process influences the quality of juror decisions. What research exists suggests that the process of voir dire may do little to improve juror decisions. Pretrial publicity continues to influence juror judgments inappropriately, whether they are exposed to an extended voir dire in which the defense attorney reminds jurors to ignore pretrial publicity or a minimal voir dire (Dexter, Cutler, & Moran, 1992). Thus, exposure to an extended voir dire does not eliminate prejudicial bias. There is some evidence that the voir dire process may actually increase juror bias in some cases. Specifically, jurors who watched a voir dire conducted for a capital case in which jurors were questioned about their death penalty attitudes were more likely to convict a defendant and were more likely to impose the death penalty than were jurors who were not exposed to a death-qualifying voir dire (Haney, 1984). Thus, there is little evidence that the voir dire process itself improves decision making. It is still possible that the removal of extremely biased jurors may result in a jury that is better able to attend to variations in evidence quality; however, there is no research addressing this point.

DIRECTIONS FOR FUTURE RESEARCH

Primarily, previous jury selection research has concentrated on examining questions about the effectiveness of jury selection rather than on the process of voir dire. Moreover, most of this research has focused on a rather simple question: Do attitudes or traits predict juror judgments? Although research on these issues has continued at a slow pace over the past decade, little has been learned. True, researchers have identified a few more situations in which case-specific attitudes predict verdict; however, there have been no major advances in our understanding of jury selection and voir dire in the past decade. It is our position that the atheoretical nature of the research on jury selection and the simplicity of the questions asked by researchers led to the stagnation of this line of research.

A similar stagnation occurred in the social psychological study of attitudes and behavior and the studies examining the links between traits and behavior in the 1960s. In both research traditions, researchers had been asking questions that are very similar to those being asked by the majority of researchers examining jury selection today. In the latter part of that decade, both attitude (Wicker, 1969) and personality (Mischel, 1968) scholars noted that across a number of studies, attitudes and traits rarely account for more than 10% of the variance in people's behavior. Similar reviews of the jury selection literature have reached a similar conclusion: Dispositional predictors account for only a small portion of the variance in jurors' verdicts (Wrightsman, Nietzel, & Fortune, 1998). Attitudinal research in social psychology moved forward only when researchers began to ask new questions about the relationship among attitudes, traits, and behaviors. Similarly, jury selection research may move past its current plateau only if jury selection researchers begin to ask new and different questions about the relationship between juror characteristics and verdicts. A consideration of the social psychological research on attitudes and behavior may provide some clues about which avenues of study will prove most successful.

For example, social psychologists responded to the criticism of the weak correlation between attitudes and behavior by investigating whether there are moderators of the attitude-behavior relationship (Kraus, 1995). That is, were there certain types of people, certain situations, or certain measurement techniques that exhibit stronger attitude-behavior relationships? Both social psychologists (Fishbein & Ajzen, 1975) and personality psychologists (Epstein, 1983) noted that attitudes and traits are very general constructs that are unlikely to correlate with specific behaviors because of their different levels of measurement. Fishbein and Ajzen (1975) argued that attitudes and behaviors must be measured with a similar level of specificity if we are to expect strong correlations between the two constructs. Psycholegal researchers have addressed these measurement issues in the study of jury selection, noting that case-specific attitudes are more predictive of verdict (i.e., a very specific behavior) than are general demographics or attitudes (Moran et al., 1994).

Although social psychologists have spent several decades examining the moderating role of situations and individual differences in the attitude-behavior relationship, jury selection researchers have not yet explored the situational and dispositional variables that may moderate the attitude-verdict relationship. For example, situationally induced self-awareness has been shown to strengthen the attitude-behavior relationship (Carver, 1975; Duval & Wicklund, 1972). Although the traditional social psychological manipulation of self-awareness (i.e., the presence or absence of a mirror when participants' attitudes and behavior are measured) is not likely to be a factor in jury decision making, other situational factors may increase jurors' self-awareness. Perhaps cameras in the courtroom will strengthen the relationship between jurors' attitudes and their verdicts. Similarly, individual rather than group questioning in voir dire may cause potential jurors to be more self-aware of their attitudinal positions.

It is even more likely that potential jurors' individual differences may help attorneys and consultants to identify jurors who are likely to have strong attitude-behavior relations. People who express confidence in their attitudes are more likely to act on those attitudes than those who do not (Fazio & Zanna, 1978). In contrast, people who are dispositionally motivated to look to the situation for cues about how to behave (e.g., high self-monitors) typically have weaker attitude-behavior correlations than do people who look inward for guidance (e.g., low self-monitors; Snyder, 1974). People who are low in public self-consciousness or high in private self-consciousness may also be more likely to act based on their attitudinal predispositions (Fenigstein, Scheier, & Buss, 1975). Finally, attitudes formed through direct experience tend to exert greater influence on behavior (Fazio & Zanna, 1978; Regan & Fazio, 1977). Perhaps future research will discover that these moderator variables apply to the attitude-verdict relationship as well.

More recently, attitudinal researchers have begun to look beyond moderators of the attitude-behavior relationship to the underlying psychological mechanisms that explain how attitudes guide behavior (Fazio, 1990). One of the primary mechanisms identified to date is attitude accessibility, or the ease with which an attitude is activated from memory on observation of an attitude object. Whether attitudes are chronically accessible or made accessible due to situational factors, attitudes that readily come to mind are more likely to predict behavior than attitudes that are less easily accessed in memory (Fazio, Chen, McDonel, & Sherman, 1982; Fazio & Williams, 1986). Attorneys and consultants may use jurors' response latency to attitudinal measures as a rough index of attitude accessibility. Attorneys also may wish to increase the accessibility of a set of favorable attitudes through repeated attitudinal references in their opening and closing arguments, as has been suggested by one set of trial consultants (Starr & McCormick, 2000), or by encouraging jurors to repeatedly express the favorable attitudes during voir dire (Schuette & Fazio, 1995). Whether these moderators and mediators of the attitude-behavior relationship also apply to the attitude-verdict relationship is a question that requires further empirical study to answer.

REFERENCES

Adler, F. (1973). Socioeconomic factors influencing jury verdicts. *New York University Review of Law and Social Change, 3,* 1–10.

Adorno, T., Frenkel-Brunswik, E., Levinson, D., & Sanford, N. (1950). *The authoritarian personality.* New York: Harper.

Babcock, B. A. (1972). Voir dire: Preserving "its wonderful power." *Stanford Law Review, 27,* 545–565.

Batson v. Kentucky, 106 S. Ct. 1712 (1986).

Berry, A. T. (1997). Selecting jurors. *Litigation, 24,* 8–12, 62.

Blue, L. A. (1991). Jury selection in a civil case. *Trial Lawyers Quarterly, 21,* 11–25.

Bodin, H. S. (1954). *Selecting a jury.* New York: Practicing Law Institute.

Boehm, V. (1968). Mr. Prejudice, Miss Sympathy, and the authoritarian personality: An application of psychological measuring techniques to the problem of jury bias. *Wisconsin Law Review,* 734–750.

Bottoms, B. L., & Goodman, G. S. (1994). Perceptions of children's credibility in sexual assault cases. *Journal of Applied Social Psychology, 24,* 702–732.

Bray, R. M., & Noble, A. M. (1978). Authoritarianism and decisions of mock juries: Evidence of jury bias and group polarization. *Journal of Personality and Social Psychology, 36,* 1424–1430.

Brekke, N., & Borgida, E. (1988). Expert psychological testimony in rape trials: A social-cognitive analysis. *Journal of Personality and Social Psychology, 55,* 372–386.

Brigham, J. C., & Wasserman, A. W. (1999). The impact of race, racial attitude, and gender on reactions to the criminal trial of O. J. Simpson. *Journal of Applied Social Psychology, 29,* 1333–1370.

Carver, C. S. (1975). Physical aggression as a function of objective self-awareness and attitudes toward punishment. *Journal of Experimental Social Psychology, 11,* 510–519.

Cowan, C. L., Thompson, W. C., & Ellsworth, P. C. (1984). The effects of death qualification on jurors' predisposition to convict and on the quality of deliberation. *Law and Human Behavior, 8,* 53–79.

Cutler, B. L., Moran, G. P., & Narby, D. J. (1992). Jury selection in insanity defense cases. *Journal of Research in Personality, 26,* 165–182.

Darrow, C. (1936, May). Attorney for the defense. *Esquire, 36–37,* 211–213.

Dexter, H. R., Cutler, B. L., & Moran, G. (1992). A test of voir dire as a remedy for the prejudicial effects of pretrial publicity. *Journal of Applied Social Psychology, 22,* 819–832.

Diamond, S. S., & Zeisel, H. (1974). A courtroom experiment on juror selection and decision-making. *Personality and Social Psychology Bulletin, 1,* 276–277.

Dillehay, R. C., & Nietzel, M. T. (1985). Juror experience and jury verdicts. *Law and Human Behavior, 9,* 179–191.

Dimitrius, J., & Mazzarella, M. (1999). *Reading people: How to understand people and predict their behavior-anytime, anyplace.* New York: Ballantine Books.

Duval, S., & Wicklund, R. A. (1972). *A theory of objective self-awareness.* New York: Academic Press.

Elwork, A., Sales, B. D., & Suggs, D. (1981). The trial: A research review. In B. D. Sales (Ed.), *The trial process* (pp. 1–68). New York: Plenum Press.

Epstein, S. (1983). Aggregation and beyond: Some basic issues on the prediction of behavior. *Journal of Personality, 51,* 360–392.

Fazio, R. H. (1990). Multiple processes by which attitudes guide behavior: The MODE model as an integrative framework. In M. P. Zanna (Ed.), *Advances in experimental social psychology* (Vol. 23, pp. 75–109). New York: Academic Press.

Fazio, R. H., Chen, J., McDonel, E. C., & Sherman, S. J. (1982). Attitude accessibility, attitude-behavior consistency, and the strength of the object-evaluation association. *Journal of Experimental Social Psychology, 18,* 339–357.

Fazio, R. H., & Williams, C. J. (1986). Attitude accessibility as a moderator of the attitude-perception and attitude-behavior relations: An investigation of the 1984 presidential election. *Journal of Personality and Social Psychology, 51,* 505–514.

Fazio, R. H., & Zanna, M. P. (1978). Attitudinal qualities relating to the strength of the attitude-behavior relationship. *Journal of Experimental Social Psychology, 14,* 398–408.

Fenigstein, A., Scheier, M. F., & Buss, A. H. (1975). Public and private self-consciousness: Assessment and theory. *Journal of Consulting and Clinical Psychology, 43,* 522–527.

Fishbein, M., & Ajzen, I. (1975). *Belief, attitude, intention, and behavior: An introduction to theory and research.* Reading, MA: Addison-Wesley.

Fitzgerald, R., & Ellsworth, P. C. (1984). Due process vs. crime control. *Law and Human Behavior, 8,* 31–51.

Fulero, S. M., & Penrod, S. D. (1990a). Attorney jury selection folklore: What do they think and how can psychologists help? *Forensic Reports, 3,* 233–259.

Fulero, S. M., & Penrod, S. D. (1990b). The myths and realities of attorney jury selection folklore and scientific jury selection: What works? *Ohio Northern University Law Review, 17,* 229–253.

Gerbasi, K. C., Zuckerman, M., & Reis, H. T. (1977). Justice needs a new blindfold: A review of mock jury research. *Psychological Bulletin, 84,* 323–345.

Golash, D. (1992). Race, fairness, and jury selection. *Behavioral Sciences and the Law, 10,* 155–177.

Goodman, J., Loftus, E. F., & Greene, E. (1990). Matters of money: Voir dire in civil cases. *Forensic Reports, 3,* 303–329.

Halverson, A. M., Hallahan, M., Hart, A. J., & Rosenthal, R. (1997). Reducing the biasing effects of judges' nonverbal behavior with simplified jury instruction. *Journal of Applied Psychology, 82,* 590–598.

Haney, C. (1984). On the selection of capital juries: The biasing effects of the death-qualification process. *Law and Human Behavior, 8,* 121–132.

Haney, C., Hurtado, A., & Vega, L. (1994). "Modern" death qualification: New data on its biasing effects. *Law and Human Behavior, 18,* 619–633.

Hans, V. P. (1992). Judgments of justice. *Psychological Science, 3,* 218–220.

Harrington, D. C., & Dempsey, J. (1969). Psychological factors in jury selection. *Tennessee Law review, 37,* 173–178.

Hart, A. J. (1995). Naturally occurring expectation effects. *Journal of Personality and Social Psychology, 68,* 109–115.

Herman, R. M. (1997). Jury selection. *Trial, 33,* 60–63.

Horowitz, I. A. (1980). Juror selection: A comparison of two methods in several criminal trials. *Journal of Applied Social Psychology, 10,* 86–99.

James, R. (1959). Status and competence of juries. *American Journal of Sociology, 64,* 563–570.

J.E.B. v. Alabama *ex rel.* T.B., 114 S. Ct. 1419, 62 U.S.L.W. 4219 (1994).

Johnson, C., & Haney, C. (1994). Felony voir dire: An exploratory study of its content and effect. *Law and Human Behavior, 18,* 487–506.

Jones, S. E. (1987). Judge- versus attorney-conducted voir dire: An empirical investigation or juror candor. *Law and Human Behavior, 11,* 131–146.

Kassin, S. M., & Wrightsman, L. S. (1983). The construction and validation of a juror bias scale. *Journal of Research in Personality, 17,* 423–442.

Kerr, N. L., Hymes, R. W., Anderson, A. B., & Weathers, J. E. (1995). Defendant-juror similarity and mock juror judgments. *Law and Human Behavior, 19,* 545–567.

Kovera, M. B., Gresham, A. W., Borgida, E., Gray, E., & Regan, P. C. (1997). Does expert testimony inform or influence juror decision-making? A social cognitive analysis. *Journal of Applied Psychology, 82,* 178–191.

Kovera, M. B., Levy, R. J., Borgida, E., & Penrod, S. D. (1994). Expert witnesses in child sexual abuse cases: Effects of expert testimony and cross-examination. *Law and Human Behavior, 18,* 653–674.

Kovera, M. B., McAuliff, B. D., & Hebert, K. S. (1999). Reasoning about scientific evidence: Effects of juror gender and evidence quality on juror decisions in a hostile work environment case. *Journal of Applied Psychology, 84,* 362–375.

Kraus, S. J. (1995). Attitudes and the prediction of behavior: A meta-analysis of the empirical literature. *Personality and Social Psychology Bulletin, 21,* 58–75.

Kravitz, D. A., Cutler, B. L., & Brock, P. (1993). Reliability and validity of the original and revised Legal Attitudes Questionnaire. *Law and Human Behavior, 17,* 661–667.

LeVan, E. A. (1984). Nonverbal communication in the courtroom: Attorney beware. *Law and Psychology Review, 8,* 83–104.

Levine, M. (2001). Persuasion in advocacy: Conditioning the jury in voir dire and opening statement. *Trial Lawyers Quarterly, 30,* 141–146.

Liotti, T. F., & Cole, A. H. (2000). Quick voir dire: Making the most of 15 minutes. *Journal of the New York State Bar Association, 72*(7), 39–42.

Marques, J. M., Abrams, D., Paez, D., & Martinez-Taboada, C. (1998). The role of categorization and in-group norms in judgments of groups and their members. *Journal of Personality and Social Psychology, 75,* 976–988.

Marshall, L. L., & Smith, A. (1986). The effects of demand characteristics, evaluation anxiety, and expectancy effects on juror honesty during voir dire. *Journal of Psychology, 120,* 205–217.

McCarter, W. D. (1999). Juror nondisclosure. *Journal of the Missouri Bar, 55,* 214–220.

McElhaney, J. W. (2000). Picking a jury: Who are you taking to? *Tennessee Law Review, 67,* 517–522.

McNulty, M. J. (2000). Practical tips for effective voir dire. *Louisiana Bar Journal, 48,* 110–114.

Middendorf, K., & Luginbuhl, J. (1995). The value of a nondirective voir dire style in jury selection. *Criminal Justice and Behavior, 22,* 129–151.

Mischel, W. (1968). *Personality and assessment.* New York: Wiley.

Moran, G., & Comfort, J. C. (1982). Scientific juror selection: Sex as a moderator of demographic and personality predictors of impaneled felony juror behavior. *Journal of Personality and Social Psychology, 43,* 1052–1063.

Moran, G., & Comfort, J. C. (1986). Neither "tentative" nor "fragmentary": Verdict preference of impaneled felony jurors as a function of attitude toward capital punishment. *Journal of Applied Psychology, 71,* 146–155.

Moran, G., Cutler, B. L., & De Lisa, A. (1994). Attitudes toward tort reform, scientific jury selection, and juror bias: Verdict inclination in criminal and civil trials. *Law and Psychology Review, 18,* 309–328.

Moran, G., Cutler, B. L., & Loftus, E. F. (1990). Jury selection in major controlled substance trials: The need for extended voir dire. *Forensic Reports, 3,* 331–348.

Myers, B., & Lecci, L. (1998). Revising the factor structure of the Juror Bias Scale: A method for the empirical evaluation of theoretical constructs. *Law and Human Behavior, 22,* 239–256.

Narby, D. J., & Cutler, B. L. (1994). Effectiveness of voir dire as a safeguard in eyewitness cases. *Journal of Applied Psychology, 79,* 724–729.

Narby, D. J., Cutler, B. L., & Moran, G. (1993). A meta-analysis of the association between authoritarianism and jurors' perceptions of defendant culpability. *Journal of Applied Psychology, 78,* 34–42.

Nietzel, M. T., & Dillehay, R. C. (1982). The effects of variations in voir dire procedures in capital murder trials. *Law and Human Behavior, 6,* 1–13.

Nietzel, M. T., & Dillehay, R. C. (1986). *Psychological consultation in the courtroom.* New York: Pergamon Press.

Nietzel, M. T., Dillehay, R. C., & Himelein, M. J. (1987). Effects of voir dire variations in capital trials: A replication and extension. *Behavioral Sciences and the Law, 5,* 467–477.

Olczak, P. V., Kaplan, M. F., & Penrod, S. (1991). Attorney's lay psychology and its effectiveness in selecting jurors: Three empirical studies. *Journal of Social Behavior and Personality, 6,* 431–452.

Orne, M. T. (1962). On the social psychology of the psychological experiment: With particular reference to demand characteristics and their implications. *American Psychologist, 17,* 776–783.

Penrod, S. D. (1990). Predictors of jury decision making in criminal and civil cases: A field experiment. *Forensic Reports, 3,* 261–277.

Phares, E. J., & Wilson, K. G. (1972). Responsibility attribution: Role of outcome severity, situational ambiguity, and internal-external control. *Journal of Personality, 40,* 392–406.

Powers v. Ohio, 449 U.S. 400 (1991).

Regan, D. R., & Fzaio, R. (1977). On the consistency between attitudes and behavior: Look to the method of attitude formation. *Journal of Personality and Social Psychology, 13,* 28–45.

Rose, M. R. (1999). The peremptory challenge accused of race or gender discrimination? Some data from one county. *Law and Human Behavior, 23,* 695–702.

Rosenberg, M. J. (1969). The conditions and consequences of evaluation apprehension. In R. Rosenthal & R. Rosnow (Eds.), *Artifact and behavioral research* (pp. 279–349). New York: Academic Press.

Rosenthal, R., & Rosnow, R. (Eds.). (1969). *Artifact and behavioral research.* New York: Academic Press.

Schuette, R. A., & Fazio, R. H. (1995). Attitude accessibility and motivation as determinants of biased processing: A test of the MODE model. *Personality and Social Psychology Bulletin, 21,* 704–710.

Schuller, R. A. (1992). The impact of battered woman syndrome evidence on jury decision processes. *Law and Human Behavior, 16,* 597–620.

Schuller, R. A., & Hastings, P. A. (1996). Trials of battered women who kill: The impact of alternative forms of expert evidence. *Law and Human Behavior, 20,* 167–187.

Schulman, J., Shaver, P., Colman, R., Emrich, B., & Christie, R. (1973, May). Recipe for a jury. *Psychology Today,* 37–84.

Simon, R. J. (1967). *The jury and the defense of insanity.* Boston: Little, Brown.

Snyder, M. (1974). The self-monitoring of expressive behavior. *Journal of Personality and Social Psychology, 30,* 526–537.

Speckart, G. R., & McLennan, L. G. (1999, January). How to tap the potential of the juror questionnaire. *Practical Litigator,* 49–51.

Starr, V. H., & McCormick, M. (2000). *Jury selection* (3rd ed.). New York: Aspen.

Strier, F. (1999). Whither trial consulting? Issues and projections. *Law and Human Behavior, 23,* 93–115.

Strodtbeck, F., James, R., & Hawkins, C. (1957). Social status in jury deliberations. *American Sociological Review, 22,* 713–718.

Suggs, D., & Sales, B. D. (1981). Juror self-disclosure in the voir dire: A social science analysis. *Indiana Law Journal, 56,* 245–271.

Weaver, D. (1993). Voir dire: Bonding with the jury. *Trial Lawyers Quarterly, 23,* 28–33.

Wicker, A. W. (1969). Attitudes versus actions: The relationship of verbal and overt behavioral responses to attitude objects. *Journal of Social Issues, 25,* 41–78.

Wrightsman, L. S., Nietzel, M. T., & Fortune, W. H. (1998). *Psychology and the legal system* (4th ed.). Pacific Grove, CA: Brooks/Cole.

Zeisel, H., & Diamond, S. S. (1978). The effect of peremptory challenges on jury and verdict: An experiment in a federal district court. *Stanford Law Review, 30,* 491–531.

PART FOUR

CIVIL FORENSIC PSYCHOLOGY

CHAPTER 11

Child Custody Evaluation

RANDY K. OTTO, JACQUELINE K. BUFFINGTON-VOLLUM, AND JOHN F. EDENS

Child custody evaluations may be the most complex, difficult, and challenging of all forensic evaluations (Otto, 2000; Otto, Edens, & Barcus, 2000a). In contrast to the majority of forensic evaluations, in which the mental health professional assesses one person with respect to a specific psycholegal ability or capacity (e.g., a criminal defendant's capacity to stand trial; a personal injury litigant's emotional adjustment and functioning pre- and postaccident; a potential witness's capacity to testify), child custody assessments involve evaluation of numerous parties with respect to multiple issues or capacities. The child custody evaluator must assess, at a minimum, the two parents contesting custody and their child or children. (Although some custody evaluations may involve one child and others may involve multiple children, we use the term children throughout the chapter for the sake of consistency.) Often, there are significant others involved and evaluation of them is required (e.g., potential stepparents, potential stepsiblings). Opinions offered by these expert evaluators then go to inform the legal decision-maker's judgments about the physical custody or placement of the children (i.e., physical or residential custody) as well as who will be involved in making important life decisions for the children (i.e., legal or decision-making custody).

What makes evaluation of these multiple parties particularly difficult is the expansive and far-ranging nature of the task. Child custody evaluators must assess the examinees with respect to a variety of behaviors, capacities, interests, and needs. This stands in stark contrast to the more narrow questions that need to be answered in many other forensic evaluations. To further complicate the evaluation task, all of the parties involved may offer their own perspectives on events and issues of relevance, and many may have an investment in a particular outcome. Finally, given the stakes involved (i.e., residential placement of the children and decision-making authority for them), emotions in cases of contested custody run high.

After discussing the family bar's perception of mental health professionals' involvement in cases of contested custody, we provide a brief overview of contemporary child custody law in the United States. Adopting Grisso's (1986) model of forensic evaluation, we believe it necessary to identify first the law that controls child custody decision making so that the psycholegal contours and factors that must be evaluated can be identified. We follow this with a discussion of child custody evaluation guidelines that have been promulgated by various authorities, as they provide some direction with respect to establishing a standard of care. After reviewing the custody evaluation process, we discuss the research most relevant to child custody evaluation and decision making.

LANDSCAPE OF CHILD CUSTODY EVALUATION TODAY

An important starting point is a consideration of the frequency with which the courts must make decisions about custody and placement of children. Although seemingly straightforward, this is more difficult to determine than it appears. First, there is no uniform formula used to derive a "divorce rate," making interpretation and comparison of data difficult. The percentage of marriages that end in divorce for some cohorts in the United States, however, may be as high as 40%, and the rate of divorce has increased dramatically over the past 40 years, the divorce rate in the United States approximately doubled between 1960 and the end of the twentieth century (Hughes, 1996). Although the above statistics may be debated, what remains clear is that a substantial number of marriages end in divorce, a fair number of which have produced children (e.g., anywhere between 36% and 48% of married couples who divorce report having children in the family below the age of 18; Clark, 1995). Thus, family courts may be faced with issues of child custody in a large number of cases.

But even with a high divorce rate among couples with children, the courts do not need to make decisions about child custody if the parties agree about what would be in the best interests of the children. Contrary to common perceptions about divorcing parents fighting over their children, in the majority of cases, they do not litigate issues of custody. Maccoby and Mnookin (1988), in a study of California divorces, reported that 70% of divorcing parents had reached an agreement about the custody of their children. Similarly, McIntosh and Prinz (1993) reported that in only 14% of the 603 family divorce files they reviewed in a metropolitan South Carolina county was custody of the children disputed; agreements presumably were reached in over 85% of the cases. Although this indicates that child custody evaluations are not common, the current divorce rate in this country suggests that significant numbers of child custody evaluations are being conducted for the courts.

Of course, the above findings do not necessarily mean that the majority of parents agree about what is in their children's best interests regarding matters of custody, only that they choose not to litigate such issues. Weitzman (1985) reported that 57% of the fathers she interviewed retrospectively that they had wanted physical custody of their children. Only 33% of this group reported that they mentioned this to their wife, and only 13% reported that they sought custody in the divorce petition. Similarly, about one-third of the fathers in Maccoby and Mnookin's (1988) study reported that they

would have liked to have been the primary residential parent, yet more than 50% of them reported not seeking custody.

Consistent with the above, contemporary research suggests that, despite changing conceptions about parenting and sex roles, mothers almost always become the primary parent subsequent to divorce. Although there is some variation as a function of children's age and sex, according to U.S. Census data, 84% or more of children live primarily with their mother postdivorce (U.S. Bureau of the Census, 1989). Whether this reflects that mothers remain the primary parents and caretakers of children despite changes in societal attitudes and thinking, that fathers perceive the legal system as biased toward women with respect to issues of custody and thus do not seek custody, or that the courts are truly biased with respect to issues of custody remains to be determined.

The Family Bar's Perception of Mental Health Professionals in Cases of Contested Custody

> Once the report comes out in your client's favor all you have to do is convince the court that this evaluator is truly an expert whose recommendations must be followed or the well-being of the client will be imperiled. Then again, if the evaluation is against your client, it is all psychobabble, erroneous data, and dangerous conclusions and clearly the court should not abdicate its responsibility to do what is right for the children because of the temptation to follow the specific recommendations of this charlatan. (Oddenino, 1994, in an article written for attorneys about how to use custody evaluations to their clients' advantage)

Although mental health professionals are involved in contested custody cases with some frequency, a separate question is how valuable attorneys and judges find their input. There is a small body of research that indicates that judges and attorneys consider the input and opinions of mental health professionals cautiously in cases of contested custody and they look to other sources of information to inform their decisions (Otto, Edens, & Barcus, 2000a).

In a survey of 57 judges and 23 trial commissioners involved in family law cases, although custody evaluations were frequently cited as an efficient means of collecting information about the family, "professional advice" ranked twelfth on a list of 20 potential custody decision-making criteria (Settle & Lowery, 1982). Similarly, in interviews with 13 family law judges presiding on the west coast of Florida, Kuehnle and Weiner (2000) reported that one of the most valued aspects of child custody evaluations was the independent information-gathering function that the experts served.

In a study of Virginia judges conducted by Melton, Weithorn, and Slobogin (1985), mental health testimony was endorsed as no more than occasionally useful in cases of contested custody. Felner, Rowlison, Farber, Primavera, and Bishop (1987) reported that only 20% of the attorneys and 2% of the judges they surveyed identified the recommendations of a mental health professional as one of the five most critical pieces of information in terms of custody decision making. In a survey examining the value that family law judges placed on different sources of information when making decisions about custody and placement of children, the expert opinions of mental health professionals were rated as less significant than the testimony of the parties and of the children themselves (Reidy, Silver, & Carlson, 1989). Thus, mental health professionals should enter the arena cautiously and with the understanding that although attorneys and judges may value their input, they are not beholden to it.

LAW OF CHILD CUSTODY

Legal Standards

The starting point for child custody evaluations, as is the case with any forensic evaluation (Grisso, 1986), is the law. Because decisions about children, their best interests, and their custody and placement are ultimately legal issues that are to be decided by legal decision makers (judges in most jurisdictions, but juries in others, e.g., Texas), psychologists and other mental health professionals who conduct custody evaluations must know the law on which legal decision makers base their opinions. Only by knowing the law can mental health professionals assess those factors with which the court is most concerned.

According to Common Law, children were considered chattel. In cases of divorce, like all chattel, their ownership and custody reverted to the father (Wyer, Gaylord, & Grove, 1987). The late nineteenth century, however, saw the development of the "tender years" doctrine, which held that mothers were considered uniquely qualified or better able to contribute to a child's development. Thus, the law presumed that children's best interests would be served by placement with their mother after divorce (Wyer et al., 1987). This presumption, of course, could be overcome in particular cases (e.g., by showing that the mother was unfit in some way).

The tender years doctrine controlled custody decision making until the 1960s, when significant changes in family law occurred. With shifting conceptualizations of sex roles and movement to a "no fault" divorce law, sexist presumptions of parental capacity were challenged. Because mothers were no longer considered better able than fathers to provide for their children's development solely as a function of their sex, the tender years doctrine was abandoned for the "best interests of the child" standard, which has been adopted by all U.S. jurisdictions (Rohman, Sales, & Lou, 1987).

Put most simply, the best interests standard dictates that decisions about custody and placement of children should be made in their best interests, as opposed to independent interests that the parents or others may have. Anything more than a superficial analysis, of course, makes clear that the best interests standard provides the legal decision maker and custody evaluator with little direction regarding how a child's interests are to be determined or what factors are to be considered (Gould, 1998). As a result, the majority of states have attempted to operationalize and define the best interests standard legislatively. Michigan's 1970 Child Custody Act (see Table 11.1) has served as a model for many state legislatures in their attempts to identify factors that the legal decision maker and custody evaluator are to consider with respect to determining the child's best interests.

Child custody evaluators are provided with considerable guidance and direction by Michigan's custody law and corresponding laws in other jurisdictions. A review of the Michigan law reveals that both psychological (e.g., "the mental . . . health of the competing parties; capacity and

---

TABLE 11.1 Michigan Child Custody Statute

Michigan's child custody statute directs that custody evaluations are to be made "in the best interests of the children" and are to be based on:

- The love, affection, and other emotional ties existing between the parties involved and the child.
- The capacity and disposition of the parties involved to give the child love, affection, and guidance and continuation of educating and raising the child in his or her religion or creed, if any.
- The capacity and disposition of the parties involved to provide the child with food, clothing, medical care, or other remedial care recognized and permitted under the laws of this state in lieu of medical care, and other material needs.
- The length of time the child has lived in a stable, satisfactory environment and the desirability of maintaining continuity.
- The permanence, as a family unit, of the existing or proposed custodial home.
- The moral fitness of the parties involved.
- The mental and physical health of the parties involved.
- The home, school, and community record of the child.
- The reasonable preferences of the child, if the court deems the child to be of sufficient age to express preference.
- The willingness and ability of each of the parents to facilitate and encourage a close and continuing parent-child relationship between the child and the other parent.
- Any other factor considered by the court to be relevant to a particular child custody dispute.

Source: Michigan Child Custody Act of 1970, 1993 amended.

TABLE 11.2   Consensus Child Custody Decision-Making Criteria

Included below are criteria appearing consistently in states' custody statutes.
Children:
    Age and sex.
    Adjustment to current and prior environments, including the length of
        time in each.
    History of child abuse/victimization.
    Educational needs.
    Special mental health or medical care.
    Wishes or desires regarding placement, if of sufficient age.
    Separation of siblings.
Parents:
    History of spouse abuse.
    Economic status and stability.
    Wishes and desires regarding placement and custody.
    Mental and physical health.
    Substance abuse.
    Level of hostility.
    Flexibility.
    Parenting skills.
    Caretaking involvement before and after separation.
    Likelihood that parent would remove children from the jurisdiction.
    Likelihood that parent would alienate the affections of the children.
Other Factors:
    Religion.
    Prior custody determinations.
    Agreements between the parents.

Source: Adapted from Schutz et al. (1989).

disposition of the competing parties to provide love, affection, guidance, continuance of education, and continued religious education" and nonpsychological factors (e.g., "moral fitness of the competing parties") are to be considered by the court, as well as case-specific factors not anticipated by the legislature (i.e., "any other issues considered by the court to be relevant to a particular child custody suit"). Although how the child's best interests are operationalized varies from state to state, Schutz, Dixon, Lindenberger, and Ruther (1989) found significant consistencies in their review of state custody statutes (see Table 11.2). Of course, the child custody examiner must be familiar with the specific law in the jurisdiction in which he or she practices.

Although the legislatures' attempts to operationalize the best interests standards provide custody evaluators and legal decision makers with some direction, *how* decisions are to be made remains unclear. Perhaps most significant is that the relative importance of the statutorily identified factors, or the weight they are to be given when considering custody and placement of children, go unstated. This probably reflects an acknowledgment by legal and mental health professionals alike that questions of custody and what is in the best interests of children may vary dramatically from case to case.

Another important legal issue central to the custody decision-making process is the definition of and distinction

between different types of custody (Schutz et al., 1989). More specifically, state law typically makes reference to and distinguishes between decision-making authority for the children (referred to as legal custody or parental responsibility in some jurisdictions) and the issue of physical placement or residence of the children (referred to as residential or physical custody in some jurisdictions). The courts, therefore, must make rulings not only about the living arrangements and visitation schedule for the children postdivorce, but also about who will be involved in making decisions about them. The court also can mix these decisions. For example, it is not uncommon for courts to grant one parent physical custody of the children (with regular visitation) and both parents legal decision-making authority for the children (i.e., joint legal custody).

Legal Presumptions

Not only does the law in a specific jurisdiction identify on which factors decisions about placement and custody of a child should be based, but the law also reflects many presumptions about custody and placement of children. These legal presumptions identify what the law assumes to be in the best interests of children in cases of contested custody. These presumptions, however, can be overcome or abandoned in a particular case with a showing of cause.

Sex and Parenting Capacity

The legal presumption that women are better able to meet the needs of children (i.e., the tender years doctrine) has been abandoned essentially by all jurisdictions and replaced by the best interests of the child standard (Schutz et al., 1989; see above for further discussion). Thus, judges are to make no presumptions about parenting ability and sex. However, many in the field offer anecdotal accounts of mental health professionals and members of the bar who, although they acknowledge that the best interests standard controls, act as if the tender years doctrine remains in place, at least insofar as they appear to hold personal beliefs that women, as a function of being women, are better parents than men. Moreover, data indicating that the large majority of children reside primarily with their mother postdivorce (U.S. Bureau of the Census, 1989; see above for further discussion) also raise questions about whether societal attitudes, behavior, and roles are congruent with legal presumptions.

Custody Arrangements

In some jurisdictions, legal presumptions are in place regarding what kinds of custody arrangements are in the best interests of children. This is important for the child custody examiner to realize because the legal presumptions for the varying types of custody may differ. For example, some state laws presume that it is in the best interests of children to have one primary residence rather than live equal or essentially equal periods of time with each parent. In contrast, with respect to the issue of parental responsibility or legal custody, some state laws direct that it is in children's best interests to have both parents involved in making decisions about them (e.g., regarding their education, religious training, health care needs; Florida Statutes 61.13(2)(b)2, 2000). Although any legal presumptions can be overcome, it is important that child custody examiners be aware of the legal presumptions in their jurisdiction because they serve as starting points from which the legal decision maker will consider a particular case.

Placement of Siblings

The law in many jurisdictions makes reference to how decisions regarding placement of siblings should be made. For example, in some states, it is presumed that it is in the best interests of siblings to live in the same household, as opposed to splitting siblings between parents in a Solomon-like solution. Thus, in cases of disputed custody, the legal decision maker is likely to start from this perspective, but a decision that "splits" siblings may follow if the decision maker is convinced in a particular case that placement of the siblings in different households would be in their best interests.

Sexual Orientation

There is less consistency regarding how states treat parents' sexual orientation as it relates to the children's best interests and decision making regarding custody. Perhaps just as important as the formal law is the attitude of judges and attorneys who are involved in child custody cases. It will be important, of course, for the examiner to be familiar with the legal presumption regarding parents' sexual orientation and describe for the court how the child might be affected by each parent's sexual orientation, as well as the literature regarding sexual orientation and parenting (see, e.g., American Psychological Association, 1995; Falk, 1989; Patterson, 1995).

CHILD CUSTODY EVALUATION PRACTICE GUIDELINES AND STANDARDS

As described above, the mental health professional's child custody evaluation will, in part, be informed by the law controlling child custody decision making in the jurisdiction in which he or she practices. The child custody evaluation process, however, is also shaped by relevant practice guidelines and standards. To date, three national organizations have promulgated custody evaluation guidelines, all of which attempt to identify a standard for child custody evaluation and provide the examiner with some direction regarding evaluation process. Although some state psychological associations have developed child custody evaluation guidelines, we do not discuss them here.

Guidelines for Child Custody Evaluations in Divorce Proceedings (American Psychological Association [APA], 1994)

In 1994, APA published guidelines for psychologists conducting child custody evaluations that focus less on the substantive nature of such evaluations and more on the format and process of the evaluation (e.g., the goal of the evaluation; the role and orientation of the examiner; the competence and ability of the examiner; and procedural matters related to confidentiality, informed consent, record keeping, financial arrangements, and use and interpretation of data). It is difficult to disagree with any of the guidelines adopted by the APA. As such, the guidelines are not objectionable, but they do not provide much direction in terms of the substantive areas of inquiry. Because of their basic nature, failure to perform one's duties in a manner consistent with the guidelines is quite likely to constitute substandard practice.

Model Standards of Practice for Child Custody Evaluations (Association of Family and Conciliation Courts [AFCC], undated)

The AFCC is an interdisciplinary group of attorneys, judges, and mental health professionals interested in matters of family law and child custody. Although psychologists who are not AFCC members cannot necessarily be held to the organization's standards, psychologists conducting child custody evaluations should, nonetheless, be familiar with them.

Like the APA evaluation guidelines, the AFCC guidelines offer direction to the evaluator regarding role definition, structuring the evaluation process, and competence. They are, however, more substantive than the APA guidelines in that they identify areas of inquiry in the evaluation process (e.g., quality of the relationships between parents and child; quality of the relationships between parents; domestic violence history; psychological adjustment of parents). As such, the AFCC guidelines provide more direction to the custody evaluator, as they focus not only on the process of the evaluation but also on its substance.

Practice Parameters of Child Custody Evaluation (American Academy of Child and Adolescent Psychiatry [AACAP], 1997)

The most recently developed custody evaluation guidelines were developed by the AACAP. These AACAP guidelines include sections devoted to both the process and substance of the evaluation and are the most detailed of any that currently exist. Not only do the guidelines identify areas of inquiry for the examiner to address, they also identify evaluation techniques and discuss some special topics (e.g., parents' sexual orientation; grandparents' rights; child sexual abuse allegations; reproductive technology issues).

Although the guidelines are informative and provide the examiner with considerable direction, they suffer from numerous shortcomings. They are overly broad in some sections (e.g., offering generic recommendations about report writing) and overly detailed in others (e.g., offering suggestions about how examiners should dress and present themselves when appearing in court). The AACAP guidelines also offer poor practice recommendations in relation to some issues. For example, it is recommended that examiners refuse to listen to tape recordings, whereas no such prohibition is offered for similar kinds of materials (e.g., videos, journals, other documents that may be produced by the parties). Although examiners should be sensitive to evidentiary issues when considering what types of third-party information they review (see below for further discussion), a wholesale recommendation against reviewing one type of information that may be of value in some cases while failing to identify limitations of or problems with similar types of information reveals a weakness of the AACAP guidelines. Finally, some sections appear to be shaped more by guild concerns than matters related to professional practice. For example, the AACAP guidelines describe psychological testing as of little help in custody evaluations, in part, because parental psychopathology is not the primary issue before the decision maker and introduction of psychological test data results in a "battle of the experts." Although there is some basis for the discussion of the limitations of psychological testing, singling out such data as the only type of information that may be interpreted differently by opposing experts is, at the very least, unusual and demonstrates that such publications are, to some extent, political documents. Moreover, the naïveté of the apparent assumption that all psychological tests are pathology-focused also reveals a limitation of the guidelines.

THE CHILD CUSTODY EVALUATION PROCESS

As described above, child custody evaluations are involved and time-intensive procedures. Ackerman and Ackerman (1997) surveyed 200 psychologists who conducted custody evaluations on a regular basis. The mean length of time per evaluation was reported to be 26.4 hours, including such activities as administering psychological tests (a mean of 5.2 hours per evaluation), interviewing parents (4.7 hours per evaluation), interviewing children (2.7 hours per evaluation), interviewing significant others (1.6 hours per evaluation), reviewing records (2.6 hours per evaluation), report writing (5.3 hours per evaluation), and testifying (2.2 hours per evaluation). Similarly, Bow and Francella (2001) performed a national survey of 198 psychologists and found highly consistent results. In general, the time spent per evaluation was quite similar, but the distribution of time spent per *method of assessment* varied somewhat (e.g., time spent interviewing parents increased to more than 7.0 hours and report writing increased to 7.3 hours per evaluation).

That custody evaluations are intensive should not be surprising when the task is considered in some detail. Jameson, Ehrenberg, and Hunter (1997) surveyed 78 psychologists in western Canada who conducted child custody evaluations and had them rate the significance of 60 custody decision-making criteria culled from legal and psychological authorities. A factor analysis of the psychologists' responses revealed three major factors around which decisions regarding custody hinge in the opinions of psychologists: interpersonal relationships (including both parent-child relationships and parent-parent relationships); the parents' understanding of and sensitivity to the children and their needs; and the parents' ability to meet their children's needs as determined by their emotional stability, history of parenting, and parenting skills and knowledge. Thus, in a custody evaluation, it is the examiner's responsibility to describe for the court the children, their adjustment and needs; the parents (and potentially others, such as stepparents), their adjustment, their parenting abilities, and their understanding of and relationships with their children; and the likely outcomes of proposed custody arrangements (for a discussion of whether psychologists should offer an "ultimate opinion" on custody, see Martindale & Otto, 2000; for a discussion of this issue more generally, see Melton, Petrila, Poythress, & Slobogin, 1997). Moreover, the custody examiner must access any and all information relevant to understanding these issues.

Appointment, Notification, and Consent

Although it is not a violation of any ethics code or custody guidelines to conduct a custody evaluation while retained by one party (i.e., either the mother or father), it is agreed generally that child custody evaluations ideally are performed when all parties agree on the examiner and have him or her appointed by the court to conduct the evaluation (Ackerman & Ackerman, 1997; Gould, 1998; Martindale & Otto, 2000; Otto, 2000; Stahl, 1994). In contrast to each party retaining an expert to conduct an independent evaluation, court appointment of one expert reduces overall costs and time of the evaluation process and minimizes opportunity for bias and forensic identification (see Otto, 1989, or Zusman & Simon, 1983, for further discussion of this issue). Court appointment also increases the parties' comfort with the evaluation process and reinforces the perception that the examiner is an impartial expert. Moreover, in some jurisdictions, court appointment may afford the custody examiner some protection from malpractice claims.

Except in the case of *pro se* litigants, examiners should have preliminary discussions regarding the case with the attorney representing each party (see Table 11.3). The examiner should make clear to the attorneys his or her qualifications, evaluation process, fees and payment procedures, and requirements for court appointment. Ideally, the examiner will have a model appointment order from which the attorneys can draft an order for the judge to review and sign.

Once appointed by the court, the examiner should seek from the attorneys any third-party information that they believe is relevant to the issues in the case. This may include legal documents (e.g., court orders and injunctions related to the case; arrest reports; depositions of knowledgeable persons, including the parties); financial documents; and mental health, medical, school, and employment records. Although opinion varies regarding whether it is best to review such records prior to or after interviewing the parties, all agree that access to third-party information is crucial in such cases (also see following).

TABLE 11.3   Appointment, Notification, and Consent

Preliminary Issues
   Except in pro se cases, have preliminary discussions with attorneys
     representing the parties.
   Make qualifications and evaluation approach known to all parties.
   Seek appointment via court order.
   Provide a model or draft order to the attorneys for review.
Postcourt Appointment
   Request relevant third-party documents from the parties.
   Notify parents of:
     Role.
     Nontherapeutic nature of contact.
     Absence of confidentiality and privilege.
     Fees and costs.
     What the evaluation will entail.
     Length of time the evaluation will take.
   Notify children of nature and purpose of the evaluation using
     age-appropriate language and concepts.

The final preliminary task is to inform the parents about the evaluation process—a particularly important aspect of the evaluation that unfortunately is neglected by many evaluators. The parents should be informed about the examiner's role, the nontherapeutic nature of their contact with the examiner, the absence of confidentiality and privilege, fees and likely costs of the evaluation, the nature of the evaluation process (i.e., the extent of interviewing and testing that may be required), how long it will take to complete the evaluation, and how feedback will be provided (e.g., in the form of a report and/or testimony). Of course, any questions the parents have should be answered. Taking the time to fully inform parents about the evaluation process may increase their participation and cooperation because they will know what is expected of them. Parents who express concern about or refuse to comply with some aspects of the evaluation after discussion with the examiner should be directed to their attorneys because it is the examiner, not the parties or their representatives, who ultimately decides the shape and direction the evaluation takes.

Examiners also should consider obtaining assent from the children who are to be evaluated. In language they can understand, children should be informed about the examiner's role, the purpose of the evaluation, and how the information will be used.

The Clinical Evaluation

As described above, the custody examiner will assess various issues with a particular family, and this requires a far-ranging inquiry and assessment of each parent, the children, informed third parties and, in some cases, significant others (e.g., potential stepparents, potential stepsiblings, grandparents). Information is gained via clinical interviews with the parties, interviewing of informed third parties (e.g., teachers, babysitters, neighbors), and administration of psychological tests (see Tables 11.4 and 11.5).

Evaluation of the Parents

With each parent, examiners may consider starting with an abbreviated social history. In addition to providing some information that may be of relevance to the court, starting the discussion by obtaining information that is likely to be less threatening may help in establishing rapport and alleviating the parties' anxiety. Factors addressed in the social history that may be of relevance include educational history (e.g., history of poor academic achievement, which may indicate that the parent will have difficulty assisting the child in meeting academic goals); employment history (e.g., involvement in a career that has limited or may interfere with the

TABLE 11.4 Clinical Inquiry in Child Custody Evaluation: Parents

Social history:
  Family history.
  Educational and occupational history.
  Medical history.
  Mental health and substance use history.
  Legal history.
Parent's description of marital relationship and family structure.
Parent's attitude and concerns regarding the other parent, his or her access to the children, nature of visitation, etc.:
  Discussion with children about the separation and divorce.
  Parent's communications with the children about the other parent.
  Evidenced hostility.
  Ability and willingness to foster the other parent's contact with the children.
Parent's goals for visitation and decision making should he or she be awarded primary residence.
Parent's prior and current relationship with the children and responsibility for care taking:
  Reaction to pregnancy and childbirth, and impact of these on relationship and functioning outside the family.
  Early caretaking.
  Current caretaking.
  Punishment/discipline.
  Leisure and social activities.
  Interactional style.
  Allegations of abuse/neglect.
Parent's prior, current, and anticipated living and working arrangements:
  Who is living in the home.
  Significant others.
  Daycare, baby-sitting.
  Schools and school districts.
Parent's emotional functioning and mental health:
  Prior or current substance abuse/dependence and treatment.
  Prior or current mental health problems and treatment.
  Emotional response to the divorce.

parent's ability to parent the children); medical history (e.g., health conditions that limit parenting ability); and mental health history (e.g., psychiatric conditions that may impact a parent's ability to parent).

The development and progression of the marital relationship should receive considerable attention. For purposes of organizing this inquiry, it may be most helpful to conceptual-

TABLE 11.5 Clinical Inquiry in Child Custody Evaluation: Children

Child's attitude and preference regarding parents, current living arrangement, visitation, and future placement.
Child's depictions and conceptualization of relationship with each parent:
  Punishment/discipline.
  Leisure and social activities.
  Interactional style.
  Allegations of abuse/neglect.
Child's emotional functioning and mental health:
  Prior or current substance abuse/dependence and treatment.
  Prior or current mental health problems and treatment.
  Emotional or behavioral responses (i.e., problem behaviors) to the separation/divorce.
Child's prior and current social, academic, and vocational functioning.

ize three phases of the marital relationship: (a) the period the couple was together but without children; (b) the phase during which the couple was together and caring for the children; and (c) the period postseparation. By focusing on the time when the marriage presumably was more harmonious and the couple was focused on caring for the children, the examiner can begin to understand the parenting abilities, parenting histories, behavioral patterns, and emotional functioning of each party. The separation period may be seen as an interim "pilot" phase during which each parent begins to anticipate and adjust to a new life (e.g., as a stay-at-home mother returns to the conventional workforce and attempts to meet the responsibilities of parenting, or as a parent who historically worked 80 hours per week attempts to restructure a work schedule that allows assumption of more parental responsibility). How the parents interact with each other regarding issues of parenting, visitation, and blameworthiness for the divorce during the separation period will provide some insight into how they might be expected to act around these issues in the future. Custody examiners should keep in mind, however, that they are assessing the parties at one of the most emotionally taxing phases of their lives, and their adjustment at the time of the evaluation may not reflect what their adjustment will be over time (Schutz et al., 1989).

Crucial to interviewing the parents is assessing their relationships with their children. It is important that the parents describe for the examiner their perceptions of their children, both in terms of their response to the separation and impending divorce, as well as over time and in more general terms. How each parent perceives the children and their needs, and how they have attempted to meet those needs, both in the past and during the separation process, is germane to understanding how the parents may interact with their children postdivorce. Observation of parent-child interactions often provides insight into the nature of their relationships, the parent's feelings about the child, the parent's knowledge of and ability to interact with the child, and the child's feelings about the parent (see below).

The examiner should obtain from each party a rich description of the custody arrangement he or she proposes. First, the examiner should gain a comprehensive understanding of the school or day care arrangements, the place of residence, baby-sitting arrangements, and work schedules that are included in each parent's proposal. The examiner must then assess how similar this is to what has occurred in the past (either during the course of the marriage or following separation), whether the parent has had to make any changes to accommodate such arrangements during the separation period, and whether he or she will be able to make changes subsequent to the divorce. For example, although a neurosurgeon may propose that he will cut back his 80-hour work week to 30 hours to be awarded primary residential placement, a failure on his part to make necessary changes related to his work schedule and residence (or a failure to consider factors such as the fact that placement with him will require a change in the children's school or day care) is problematic.

In addition to requesting relevant third-party information from each attorney, the examiner also should make this offer/request to each parent. In addition to potentially providing the examiner with valuable sources of third-party information of which the attorney may be unaware (e.g., records, informants), this practice allows each parent to be fully heard. Of course, examiners must employ their professional judgment and discretion in some circumstances (Gould, 1998) and ultimately decide what sources of information they will consider (e.g., when presented with potentially inadmissible evidence; when provided a list of third-party contacts whose reported opinions are irrelevant to the issues in the case).

Finally, the examiner should ensure that the parties have an opportunity to identify issues that they believe to be of importance, including concerns they may have about the other parent. In response, each parent should be confronted with and provided an opportunity to respond to concerns or allegations that were made about him or her by the spouse or others.

Evaluation of the Children

The nature and extent of interactions with children vary considerably depending on their age. With younger children (infants through 3 years), the examiner may simply choose to observe parent-child interactions (see below). With older children (ages 4 to 11), the interview primarily will be aimed at understanding their adjustment and "world" both prior and subsequent to their parents' separation. Children 11 and older should be able to provide an accurate depiction of their life and preferences, and also provide information helpful to understanding the family and their parents.

Regardless of their age, the examiner should focus on learning more about the children (pre- and postseparation) in three separate but related areas: (a) their relationships and interactions with parents, (b) their emotional and behavioral adjustment and functioning, and (c) their involvement and adjustment to outside activities, including school and after-school activities. As the examiner understands the child, he or she can then draw some conclusions regarding the parents' understanding of their children's needs, and their abilities to meet those needs. Moreover, in addition to providing important information regarding their own adjustment and their relationships with their parents, even young children can

sometimes provide information that helps the examiner better understand the parents and their interactions with their children (Gould, 1998).

Opinions vary regarding the appropriateness of asking children their preferences regarding custody (Rohman et al., 1987; Stahl, 1994), but there is near unanimous agreement that younger children should not be asked such questions. A recommended alternative is to query the children regarding the good things and bad things about time with each parent, although this too may have implications for younger children, particularly when queried postinterview by an over-interested parent.

An overriding concern among custody evaluators is that of rehearsed children who have been prepared by a parent to offer a particular storyline. Any time a child volunteers a preference regarding a living arrangement, more important than knowing the child's stated preference is knowing and understanding the underlying reasoning. Careful questioning of younger children may reveal preparation or rehearsed answers (e.g., "Is there anything that your mom or dad told you it was really important to let me know?"). Perhaps most important for the examiner to know and communicate to the child is that, absent unusual conditions (i.e., local legal custom or a judicial decision in a particular case), any information conveyed by the child to the examiner may be revealed to the court (and to parents).

Direct Observation

It generally is agreed that interviewing the children with each parent and observing the parent and children engaging in some type of structured or unstructured activity serves to decrease initial anxiety the children may have about the evaluation process and provides helpful information regarding parent-child interactions and the relationship more generally. Examiners should be careful, however, to ensure that each parent is provided similar opportunities with the children, and they must remain aware that such interactions can be affected by a number of extrarelationship factors. Thus, observation of the parent and children on more than one occasion may prove helpful.

Authorities differ with respect to their recommendations regarding observations of and visits with the parent and children in the home setting. Possible benefits of a home visit include that it allows for more naturalistic observation of the family and provides an opportunity to consider the parent's ability to establish a positive and safe home environment. Additionally, younger children may be more comfortable talking about themselves and their family, and may be more likely to do so, in an environment more familiar than the examiner's office and with stimuli readily available to foster discussion and description (Gould, 1998; Stahl, 1994). Downsides to home visits include their potential costs, as such visits will require a considerable number of hours on the examiner's part when travel and observation are considered. Schutz et al. (1989) provide direction to examiners considering home visits in the context of child custody evaluations.

Use of Psychological Testing in Child Custody Evaluation

Although surveys indicate that use of psychological testing in child custody evaluations is common (at least among psychologists; see below for a summary of this research, as well as Otto et al., 2000b), the utility of testing in this context has been questioned by a number of commentators. Many of the psychological tests used by child custody evaluators have been criticized on the grounds that they do not assess constructs or issues most relevant to the child custody question, such as parenting ability, the nature and quality of the parent-child relationship, and the willingness of each parent to facilitate a close relationship with the other parent (Bricklin, 1994, 1995, 1999; Brodzinsky, 1993). Indeed, use of psychological measures that assess general constructs such as intelligence, psychopathology, or academic achievement requires the evaluator, at a minimum, to make an inference from the global construct assessed to a more specific behavior or capacity that is relevant to child custody questions (e.g., ability to meet the child's emotional and behavioral needs). Grisso (1984, cited in Melton et al., 1997) offered a cogent summary of the problem:

> Too often we rely on assessment instruments and methods that were designed to address *clinical* questions, questions of psychiatric diagnosis, when clinical questions bear only secondarily upon real issues in many child custody cases. Psychiatric interviews, Rorschachs, and MMPIs might have a role to play in child custody assessment. But these tools were not designed to assess parents' relationships to children, nor to assess parents' child-rearing attitudes and capacities, and *these* are often the central questions in child custody cases. (p. 484; emphasis in original)

Other evaluation tools and methods purported to assess constructs more specific to custody questions have been criticized on the grounds that they do not comport with basic ethical, scientific, and practice requirements under which psychologists and other mental health professionals must operate (see Heinze & Grisso, 1996; Otto et al., 2000b; and below). In a recent handbook on family law, judges were warned,

"We . . . believe that judges should be wary of a recent trend to make use of supposedly scientific tests claimed to distinguish between potential custodians" (National Interdisciplinary Colloquium on Child Custody [NICCC], 1998, pp. 321–322). Moreover, all three sets of professional custody evaluation guidelines (see above) offer cautions regarding the use of psychological testing in the evaluation process.

A number of assessment techniques are used in the context of a child custody evaluation, all of which can be placed into one of three broad categories: (a) clinical assessment instruments, (b) forensically relevant instruments, and (c) forensic assessment instruments (see Heilbrun, Rogers, & Otto, in press). The appropriateness of using and relying on results of a psychological test in a child custody evaluation will depend on a number of test- and case-specific factors. Based on their review of the APA Ethical Principles and Code of Conduct (1992), the Standards for Educational and Psychological Testing (American Educational Research Association, American Psychological Association, National Council on Measurement in Education, 1999), and Heilbrun's (1992) guidelines for considering use of psychological tests in forensic evaluations, Otto et al. (2000b) offered a template consisting of a number of questions forensic examiners should ask themselves when considering using a psychological test or assessment measure in the context of a custody evaluation (see Table 11.6).

Clinical assessment instruments measure general psychological constructs (e.g., psychopathology, intelligence, academic achievement, personality), were developed for therapeutic applications, and most typically are used in nonforensic settings. If the examiner believes that these tests validly assess general constructs that are relevant to decisions revolving around child custody, then their use in these evaluations is appropriate. For example, in those jurisdictions where emotional stability of the parties is one factor to be considered in making decisions about the custody and placement of children, use of the Minnesota Multiphasic Personality Inventory 2 (MMPI-2;

TABLE 11.6   Considering Use of Tests in Child Custody Evaluations

Is the test commercially published?
Is a comprehensive test manual available?
Are adequate levels of reliability demonstrated?
Have adequate levels of validity been demonstrated?
Is the test valid for the purpose for which it will be used?
Has the instrument been peer-reviewed?
Do I possess the qualifications necessary to use this instrument?
Does the test require an unacceptable level of inference from the construct
   it assesses to the psycholegal question(s) of relevance?

Source: Adapted from Otto et al. (2000b).

Butcher, Dahlstrom, Graham, Tellegen, & Kaemmer, 1994) to assess psychopathology and emotional stability *as it may be related to parenting* is appropriate. Similarly, if an examiner uses the Parenting Stress Index (PSI; Abidin, 1995) to assess how interactions with the child affect the parent, this too would appear to be appropriate use of a validated clinical assessment instrument for purposes of a custody evaluation.

Forensically relevant instruments are assessment techniques that evaluate constructs or issues that most typically arise in the course of forensic evaluations, but are not limited to forensic assessments. Tests of defensiveness, malingering, and psychopathy [e.g., Paulhus Deception Scales (Paulhus, 1999), Crown-Marlowe Scales (Crown & Marlowe, 1960), Structured Interview of Reported Symptoms (Rogers, Bagby, & Dickens, 1992), Test of Memory Malingering (Tombaugh, 1996), Psychopathy Checklist–Revised (Hare, 1991)] are examples of such instruments. Perhaps with the exception of measures of general defensiveness (for an example, see Paulhus, 1999, for a description of the Paulhus Deception Scales), forensically relevant instruments are unlikely to prove helpful in the large majority of child custody evaluations.

Forensic assessment instruments (FAIs) are developed specifically for application in forensic settings. Their purpose is to assess constructs relevant to particular legal issues. Rogers and Webster (1989) observed that in many forensic evaluation contexts, the best validated tests and assessment instruments are general clinical tests, which are least relevant to the psycholegal questions the courts look to mental health professionals for assistance in answering (i.e., the constructs assessed by the best-validated, traditional clinical measures are not directly related to the legal issue at hand). This observation applies in the child custody evaluation context, in which the general clinical assessment instruments that are used typically have better validity data than existing child custody evaluation measures. The constructs they assess (e.g., psychopathology, intelligence, academic achievement, normal personality) are not directly legally relevant, although they may provide useful information nonetheless.

At the current time, there are a number of child custody evaluation instruments that are proffered by their authors as assessing constructs directly relevant to child custody decision making: the Bricklin Perceptual Scales (BPS; Bricklin, 1990a; Bricklin & Elliott, 1997), the Perception of Relationships Test (PORT; Bricklin, 1989), the Parent Perception of Child Profile (Bricklin & Elliott, 1991), the Parent Awareness Skills Survey (PASS; Bricklin, 1990b), the Custody Quotient (Gordon & Peek, 1989), and the Ackerman-Schoendorf Parent Evaluation of Custody Test (ASPECT; Ackerman & Schoendorf, 1992). Other instruments, such as

the Uniform Child Custody Evaluation System (UCCES; Munsinger & Karlson, 1994), which is intended for use in data collection in custody evaluations, are better described as structured clinical approaches to child custody assessment and, thus, are not discussed here. Integrating these tests into the assessment process may be appealing to mental health professionals and the judiciary because, unlike general clinical assessment instruments, they ostensibly address the specific questions involved in forming an opinion in a custody case, such as "Does the parent have adequate parenting skills?" or "With which parent is the child most bonded?" Such questions are not easily answered by making inferences from results of standard measures of psychopathology, intelligence, and personality. However, essentially all of the FAIs developed for use in child custody evaluation have been subjected to significant criticism. In their review of the above instruments, Otto et al. (2000b) recommended that none of these assessment techniques be employed by child custody evaluators, given their significant psychometric and conceptual limitations. (The interested reader is directed to reviews of these FAIs by Arditti, 1995; Bischoff, 1992, 1995; Carlson, 1995; Cole, 1995; Conger, 1995; Fabry & Bischoff, 1992; Hagin, 1992; Heinze & Grisso, 1996; Hiltonsmith, 1995; Kelley, 1995; Melton, 1995; Melton et al., 1997; Shaffer, 1992; Wellman, 1994.)

Although a number of researchers (see below) have investigated child custody evaluators' general assessment practices and their use of tests more specifically, it is unclear how accurately these results depict current practice. All of the surveys to date have been based on the self-report of practitioners, have been conducted using small samples, and have oversampled psychologists. Thus, the studies described below may overestimate the use and significance of psychological tests in custody evaluations.

In the first published study of custody evaluation practices, Keilin and Bloom (1986) surveyed a national sample of psychologists, psychiatrists, and master's-level practitioners. Of the 82 surveys that provided usable data, 78% were completed by doctoral-level psychologists, 18% were completed by psychiatrists, and 4% were completed by master's-level practitioners. No single measure was used by a majority of the respondents when assessing children. Intelligence tests were the instruments most frequently employed by the examiners, with 45% of respondents using some measure of intelligence in the majority (85%) of their cases. The next most frequently used measure was the Thematic Apperception Test (TAT; Murray & Bellak, 1973) or the Children's Apperception Test (CAT; Bellak & Bellak, 1992); 39% of the respondents reported using these measures in most (75%) of their evaluations. The next three most commonly used assessment techniques with children were miscellaneous projective drawings, the Rorschach Inkblot Technique (Rorschach, 1942), and the Bender Visual Motor Gestalt Test (Bender, 1946).

Respondents identified the MMPI (Hathaway & McKinley, 1989) as the most commonly used assessment technique with adults; 70% of the evaluators reported using this instrument in child custody evaluations, and those who used it employed it in almost all (88%) of their cases. The next most commonly used instruments were the Rorschach Inkblot Technique (42%) and the TAT (38%), and evaluators who employed these instruments reported using them in a majority of their cases. Measures of adult intelligence also occasionally were employed, with the Wechsler Adult Intelligence Scale (WAIS; Wechsler & Stone, 1955) being used by 29% of the respondents. Those who used the WAIS reported employing it in a majority (67%) of the cases.

Ackerman and Ackerman (1997) replicated the Keilin and Bloom (1986) survey to obtain a more current picture of the child custody evaluation process. In the 10-year interim between these two surveys, a number of new or revised standard psychological measures were developed (e.g., MMPI-2, WAIS-III; Wechsler, 1997), as were several of the instruments specifically designed for application in cases of child custody noted earlier. Of the 800 questionnaires mailed to psychologists identified by various psychological and legal associations as conducting child custody evaluations, 201 usable protocols were returned by doctoral-level psychologists.

Intelligence tests and projective measures were the instruments most frequently used with children, consistent with the findings of Keilin and Bloom (1986). Fifty-eight percent of the respondents reported using intelligence tests in their evaluations, and those using them reported employing them in about half (45%) of their evaluations. Thirty-seven percent reported using either the CAT or the TAT (in 53% of their evaluations). Also consistent with the earlier findings of Keilin and Bloom were the respondents' reports of how they assessed adults. The MMPI/MMPI-2 remained the most frequently used assessment instrument: 92% of the psychologists reported using a version of this test in the large majority (91%) of their evaluations. The Rorschach Inkblot Technique remained the second most frequently used test with adults; 48% of the respondents indicated they used the test in the context of custody evaluations, and those who used it did so in over half (64%) of their cases. The next most frequently used tests were the revised WAIS (Wechsler, 1981) and the Millon Clinical Multiaxial Inventory (MCMI-II/MCMI-III; Millon, 1987, 1994), with 43% and 34% of the examiners reporting using these tests in their custody evaluations, respectively.

Over one-third of the respondents (35%) reported using the BPS (Bricklin, 1990a), one of the better-known forensic

assessment instruments designed for use in child custody evaluations. On average, those examiners using the BPS relied on it in a majority (66%) of their evaluations. Respondents (16%) also reported use of the PORT (Bricklin, 1989), with those using it reporting that it was employed in a majority (64%) of cases.

Fewer of the respondents reported using specific custody measures designed for use with families or adults. Only 11% of the psychologists reported using the ASPECT (Ackerman & Schoendorf, 1992), but those who used it did so in essentially all (89%) cases. The only other custody-specific measures endorsed were the PASS (Bricklin, 1990b), used by 8% of the respondents (who employed it in 94% of their cases) and the Custody Quotient (Gordon & Peek, 1989), used by 4% of the respondents (in 57% of their cases).

Recently, however, Hagen and Castagna (2001) performed a reanalysis of the survey results presented by Ackerman and Ackerman (1997) and came up with quite different results. Instead of focusing on the percent of respondents who "had ever used in custody evaluations for children and adults and the percentage of time that each of these tests had been used" (Ackerman & Ackerman, 1997, p. 138), Hagen and Castagna computed the *percentage of evaluations* in which a particular test was actually used. Other than the MMPI, which was used in 84% of the 43,195 evaluations examined, no test was used in even one-third of the evaluations. Only the Rorschach, the MCMI-II/III, and the WAIS-R were used in more than 20% of them. In light of this alternative view of the Ackerman data, they concluded,

> It would be highly misleading to represent to the public . . . that there exists at the present time anything approaching a usual and customary practice much less an actual standard of practice for the use of psychological tests in custody evaluations beyond the nearly routine use of the MMPI in the assessment of adults. (Hagen & Castagna, 2001, p. 271)

LaFortune and Carpenter (1998) surveyed mental health professionals about the tests and strategies they employed in their custody evaluations. They received completed surveys from a geographically diverse sample of 165 mental health professionals, the majority of whom were psychologists (89%). Respondents reported the frequency of use of various assessment methods on a 1 (never) to 5 (always) scale. Regarding psychological tests used to assess adults, "parenting scales," such as the ASPECT and the Bricklin measures (the specific Bricklin measures were not identified by the investigators), were second in frequency of use (mean response level of 3.28) only to the MMPI (mean response level of 4.19). Unfortunately, the authors did not report frequency of use for individual custody tests. Nevertheless, it appears that these newer, more specific instruments enjoyed a fairly significant rate of use among these respondents. Data regarding instruments used to assess children apparently were not collected, so it is unclear whether a similarly high rate of use would have been found.

Finally, Bow, and Quinnell (2001; see also, Quinnell & Bow, 2001) replicated the Ackerman and Ackerman (1997) survey regarding the current practice of child custody evaluations. Of the 563 surveys mailed, 198 usable questionnaires were returned. These encompassed mental health professionals from throughout the United States, 96% of whom were doctoral-level psychologists. Reporting of this study is bifurcated, with one article reporting the general procedures used by child custody evaluators (see Bow & Quinnell, 2001) and a second article discussing the current use of psychological testing specifically in this context (Quinnell & Bow, 2001). The use of psychological testing of parents ranked fourth out of 10 custody procedures in importance—behind clinical interviews with parents and children and parent-child observations. Psychological testing of the child ranked sixth. Nevertheless, findings showed that approximately 90% of adults and 60% of children continue to be tested.

By far, the MMPI/MMPI-2 was the most frequently used test (i.e., 94% of respondents reported using it), which reaffirms prior findings (Ackerman & Ackerman, 1997; Hagen & Castagna, 2001; Keilin & Bloom, 1986; LaFortune & Carpenter, 1998). Respondents in this study also reported wide use of the MCMI. Indeed, it emerged as the second most commonly used test (i.e., 52% indicated incorporating its use) out of all categories for both adults and children. Use of projective tests and intelligence tests with adults was essentially similar to earlier surveys. For assessment of children, intelligence tests (48%) and projective measures (ranging from 23% to 45%) were the most frequently used instruments, and the adolescent version of the MMPI followed closely behind (43%). No measure, however, was used in more than half of the child assessments, and generally, children appear to be tested somewhat less frequently by these respondents than by those participating in earlier surveys.

Of the specialized measures examined, parenting inventories were used by more examiners in this survey than by those in prior studies. In fact, the Parent-Child Relationship Inventory (Gerard, 1994) and the Parenting Stress Index (Abidin, 1995) were the fourth (44%) and fifth (41%) most commonly used tests of adults, respectively, out of all categories. This is especially noteworthy considering that in the Ackerman and Ackerman (1997) study, each of these tests were used by only 10% of evaluators overall. In contrast, the use of custody batteries and forensic assessment instruments designed specifically for use in custody evaluations was similar to earlier survey results (e.g., BPS: 28% versus 35%;

PORT: 23% versus 16%; PASS: 21% versus 8%; and ASPECT: 16% versus 11%). Overall however, study participants reported relatively low usage of these instruments.

Third-Party Information

As is the case with any forensic evaluation, contact with knowledgeable third parties and review of various documents can provide valuable information (Committee on Specialty Guidelines for Forensic Psychologists, 1991; Gould, 1998; Melton et al., 1997; Schutz et al., 1989; Weithorn, 1987). For example, baby-sitters may offer insights into the parents' abilities and interactions with the children, teachers may provide information about the children's adjustment and how involved the parents are in their children's education, and physicians may inform the examiner about the parents' ability to protect their children and meet their needs. Custody examiners must use and rely on such information cautiously, however.

Some information that the examiner seeks will be confidential and/or privileged (e.g., medical, mental health, or school records), and access to such information will require formal release by the parties. Other information, although not confidential or privileged, may be sensitive, and the holder of it may not provide such information without the agreement of the party (e.g., employment or day care records). Some information may be inadmissible (e.g., illegally obtained information, such as stolen documents or audio- or videotapes obtained without the party's consent). Whenever possible, before considering or reviewing information that the examiner believes may be inadmissible, he or she should contact the attorneys involved and request direction from them or the court.

In all cases, because the rules of evidence and practice standards indicate that the bases for an examiner's opinion must be revealed, potential third-party informants must first be instructed about how and for what purposes the information will be used, and that nothing they reveal will remain confidential or privileged. Of course, third parties cannot be forced to reveal information to the examiner (e.g., day care personnel cannot be forced to speak with the examiner), although the attorneys representing the parties may seek revelation of information that the parties seek via subpoena.

Report Writing and Testifying

Although custom varies across jurisdictions, it is good practice to write a report that describes the evaluation procedure, information gained, and opinions formed. In addition to forcing the examiner to integrate his or her ideas, the report provides for the efficient communication of information to the parties, their attorneys, and the court (Martindale & Otto, 2000). The report should summarize, using language and concepts understood by laypersons, the evaluator's conceptualization of the parents, their children, and their adjustment, needs, abilities, and limitations. The report and any associated testimony should highlight the most important issues relevant to the custody decision in the case at hand, and the reasoning underlying the examiner's conclusions and recommendations should be made clear. The examiner has failed if, after reviewing the report, the reader cannot describe (a) the examiner's conceptualization of the children, their parents, and the unique family situation, and (b) how the examiner reached these opinions (regardless of whether the reader agrees with the opinions, conclusions, or recommendations). The foundation of these opinions can be considered during the deposition or hearing process (Martindale & Otto, 2000).

Summary

Central to conducting an evaluation that assists the legal decision maker in cases of contested custody is knowledge of (a) the law on which custody decisions are based, (b) practice guidelines, (c) sources of information that may provide important information about the children and their parents, and (d) techniques designed to provide some insight into the parties and their adjustment. Also critically important, however, is knowledge of research related to developmental psychology, parent-child interactions, and custody outcome. Some of the most relevant research is discussed below.

RESEARCH RELEVANT TO CHILD CUSTODY EVALUATION AND DECISION MAKING

Parenting and Child Development

Ideally, parents provide an environment that allows their children to develop and reach their maximum potential intellectually, emotionally, and in other important ways. As a result, psychologists and other mental health professionals who conduct custody evaluations should be knowledgeable about parenting behaviors and their impact on children's development.

The Impact of Parents on Their Children's Development

A central premise of the involvement of mental health professionals in custody disputes is that parents may have psychological characteristics or engage in behaviors or activities that lead to less than optimal outcomes in terms of the development and socialization of their children. This is based on the almost self-evident belief that parental behavior exerts a strong influence on the psychosocial development of children and therefore should be weighted heavily regarding the determination of the best interests of the child. Recently, however, this basic assumption of parental influence has been challenged in the developmental psychology literature by an alternative position claiming that children's socialization is *not* influenced significantly by the behavior of their parents (Harris, 1995, 1998; Rowe, 1994). In reviewing the literature, Harris (1998) argued, "Do parents have any important long-term effects on the development of their child's personality? This article examines the evidence and concludes that the answer is no" (p. 458). Rather than parental behavior, genetic influences and children's peer groups are construed to play more determinative roles in the psychosocial development of children. If supported, such an argument obviously would have far-reaching impact in terms of the weight that should be given to any "psychological" characteristics of the parents when making custody determinations.

Leading developmental psychologists have criticized severely the basic premise that parents are inconsequential in the development of their children and have provided various counterarguments and research findings to contradict this claim. Although an exhaustive review of this issue would go well beyond the scope of this chapter (for an overview, see Collins, Maccoby, Steinberg, Hetherington, & Bornstein, 2000), the key point from this debate as it relates to child custody issues appears to be that the relationship between parenting and children's development and socialization is complex and multifaceted. Simple linear relationships and main effects models, although characteristic of early theorizing about parent-child influence, do not account for the multiplicity of interacting factors that influence children's development and socialization. The implication of this conclusion for those involved in child custody decision making is that overarching statements regarding the effects of parental behavior on child development should be made with considerable reservation and with acknowledgment of the potential mediating and moderating role of a host of other factors unrelated to the parents' behavior.

As noted previously, the legal system provides relatively limited direction to mental health professionals regarding what *specific* factors are to be considered relevant in determining the best interests of the child. Consequently, evaluators may have considerable latitude in terms of what parental characteristics are incorporated into their evaluation and the weight that is given to each factor in terms of their relevance to children's psychosocial development. The following section reviews the extant empirical research regarding the relationship between parental characteristics and children's psychosocial development, focusing on those variables that have been shown (or have been presumed) to serve as significant risk factors for maladjustment. Clinical and developmental researchers have examined a wide range of parental factors, including (a) general features of psychopathology and personality (e.g., depression, substance abuse, antisocial personality disorder); (b) broad parenting styles (e.g., authoritarian, permissive, authoritative); and (c) more circumscribed parenting behavior (e.g., degree of monitoring, disciplinary practices). Empirical research examining the effects of these variables on children's development is summarized below, along with citations for more thorough reviews of this literature.

Mental Disorder

It seems almost a truism that various forms of parental mental disorder are important factors for examiners to consider in custody evaluations. It has been noted that "many mental health experts would place concerns about parental mental and emotional health or status at the top of any list of essential criteria in determining the appropriate custodian for a postdivorce child" (NICCC, 1998, p. 31), and this contention generally has been supported in surveys of custody evaluators. Nevertheless, *the existence of mental disorder should not be dispositive in terms of custody unless it can be shown "to be relevant to that parent's care of the child and to have a negative influence on the child's condition or development"* (p. 32; emphasis added; see also Jenuwine & Cohler, 1999). This is of particular importance as mental health professionals have been criticized in the past as focusing on psychopathology and diagnosis in the context of custody evaluations to the exclusion of more central issues related to parenting and parent-child interactions (APA, 1994; Brodzinsky, 1993; Grisso, 1984, cited in Melton et al., 1997). As such, the research detailed below should be considered from the context of how mental disorder may (or may not) impact parenting practices that, in turn, are associated with negative developmental outcomes for children. Furthermore, it is important to note that the relationship between parental mental disorder and children's functioning may not be a causal one (Jenuwine & Cohler, 1999).

The vast majority of research in this area is correlational or quasi-experimental, and inferences that parental mental disorder *causes* impaired parenting, which in turn *causes* child maladjustment, are largely unsubstantiated. All of the disorders described below have some hereditary component, and children's impairment might be attributable more to direct genetic effects (or, more likely, interactions between hereditary factors and various environmental variables) rather than specifically to inadequate parenting caused by mental disorder (e.g., Collins et al., 2000; Rowe, 1994). Moreover, most of this research has failed to consider the effects of socioeconomic factors, which may account for significant variance in the relationship between parental mental disorder and child adjustment (Oyserman, Mowbray, Meares, & Firminger, 2000). Also, there is evidence to suggest that the behavior of children (particularly externalizing behavior problems) may exert a strong influence on parenting practices (e.g., Dishion & Patterson, 1997). All of these caveats should be considered when attempting to draw conclusions about the relationship between any given mentally disordered parent and the behavior of his or her child. Given these limitations, we review below empirical research related specifically to what is known about parental depression, schizophrenia, substance abuse, and antisocial conduct as they relate to children's psychosocial development and adjustment.

The impact of parental depression on child development is one of the most widely researched areas in developmental psychopathology, although it is noteworthy that most of this research has focused on depressed mothers rather than fathers. Maternal depression has been associated with various negative outcomes for children, including internalizing and externalizing behavior problems and social and achievement difficulties (see, generally, Cummings & Davies, 1999; Downey & Coyne, 1990; Field, 1995; Hammen, 1997; Lovejoy, Graczyk, O'Hare, & Neuman, 2000; Oyserman et al., 2000). For example, findings from one comprehensive review indicated that children of parents with major affective disorders are two to five times more likely to develop some type of psychopathology than children of nondisordered parents (Beardslee, Bemporad, Keller, & Klerman, 1983).

The empirical research examining the association between parental depression and child behavior and emotional problems has used diverse methodologies over various time frames and age ranges. Although depression appears to be associated with dysfunction during all stages of childhood, the effects of maternal depression may be pronounced particularly during infancy and may have a negative impact well beyond the first year (Field, 1995; Lovejoy et al., 2000; Oyserman et al., 2000). For example, maternal depression is associated with the development of insecure parent-child attachment (see below), which predicts various adjustment difficulties during later childhood (Cummings & Davies, 1999).

The specific mechanisms by which parental depression leads to child dysfunction are not completely clear, although several mediating factors have been investigated. Depressed parents tend to provide fewer supportive statements, be more critical and intrusive, and display more depressive affect (e.g., sadness) when interacting with their children. They also report communication difficulties, disaffection, and increased levels of hostility and resentment, which generally have been corroborated by observational studies (see Lovejoy et al., 2000, for a comprehensive review of observational studies). Depression also has been associated with various deficits in child management practices (see below) and subsequent deviance in adolescence (see, generally, Cummings & Davies, 1999; Lovejoy et al., 2000; Oyserman et al., 2000).

Although not as widely researched as parental depression, early reports of the effects of having a parent with schizophrenia suggested that these children were particularly at risk for developing various adjustment problems and forms of psychopathology (see, generally, Jenuwine & Cohler, 1999; Mednick, Parnas, & Schulsinger, 1987; Nuechterlein, 1986; Weintraub, 1987). For example, parents with schizophrenia tend to have children who are disproportionately likely to evince later schizophrenia, personality disorders, and antisocial behavior, as well as social functioning deficits, various information-processing anomalies and cognitive deficits, neurological soft signs, and autonomic abnormalities. However, the existing studies have reported widely varying rates and types of subsequent dysfunction among children of parents with schizophrenia, which make conclusions regarding the specific effects of this disorder on children's development difficult to determine (Jenuwine & Cohler, 1999; Oyserman et al., 2000). Moreover, many children with parents who suffer from schizophrenia do not appear to experience any significant levels of maladjustment. Although the literature is less developed than the parental depression research, there is some evidence in the parental schizophrenia literature to suggest that diagnostic status per se may be less relevant in predicting adjustment problems experienced by offspring than are other factors such as the chronicity of the disorder and the specific deficits in parenting ability evidenced by the parents (see Goodman & Brumley, 1990; Oyserman et al., 2000; Rogosch, Mowbray, & Bogat, 1992).

Another truism in relation to the effects of parents' behavior on children is that exposure to parental substance abuse and dependence will be detrimental to the development and socialization of children (for reviews, see Chassin, Barrera, & Montgomery, 1997; Logue & Rivinus, 1991; Lynskey, Fergusson, & Horwood, 1994; Steinhausen, 1995; Swaim, 1991; West & Prinz, 1987). Specific childhood outcome factors that have been associated with excessive parental alcohol and drug use include various forms of externalizing symptomatology (e.g., aggression, delinquency, attention deficits), internalizing behavior problems (e.g., depression, low self-esteem), adolescent drug use, cognitive deficits, and poor school achievement. It should be noted, however, that the majority of this research (particularly longitudinal studies) has been conducted in relation to alcoholism rather than illicit drugs of abuse.

Similar to earlier qualifications noted about the relationship between parental psychopathology and child adjustment, it should be pointed out that the strength of the relationship between parental substance use and childhood dysfunction has varied considerably across studies and that many children of substance-abusing parents do not exhibit significant subsequent psychopathology. Furthermore, there is some evidence that those parents who desist from alcohol dependence (i.e., those "in recovery") do not have children who exhibit internalizing symptomatology, although relatively little research has been conducted in this area.

Parenting practices have been noted as potential mediators of the relationship between parental substance use and childhood dysfunction. Specifically, Chassin et al. (1997) review data supporting the deleterious effect of alcohol on parents' monitoring of children's behavior, which resulted in increases in association with drug-using peers. Indeed, higher rates of child abuse and neglect are consistently reported among substance-abusing parents (e.g., Black & Mayer, 1980; Mayes, 1995). Other relevant parenting factors that have received empirical support include increased exposure to stressful life events and breakdown of family routines due to parental substance use, and impairments in parent-child attachment status among younger children.

A final area relevant to custody evaluations is research examining the relationship between parental antisocial conduct and childhood dysfunction. One of the most consistent findings in the developmental literature is that parents who engage in significant antisocial behavior tend to have children who evidence various adjustment problems, particularly related to externalizing behaviors such as aggression and delinquency (see, generally, Dishion & Patterson, 1997; Farrington, 1995, 2000; Frick, 1993; Frick & Jackson, 1993; Loeber, 1990; Loeber & Stouthamer-Loeber, 1986; Robins, West, & Herjanic, 1975). Although most of this research has addressed paternal antisocial personality and behavior, maternal criminality and antisocial personality disorder (as well as sibling delinquency) also have been shown to be associated with subsequent impairment among offspring.

Specifically in terms of custody evaluations, it should be noted that parental antisocial conduct not only exerts a significant impact on children's functioning in childhood and adolescence, it also has been associated with long-term consequences reaching well into adulthood. For example, when predicting antisocial behavior at age 32, Farrington (2000) reported that having a criminally convicted parent when the individual was between ages 8 and 10 was the single strongest predictor among a host of risk factors (odds ratio = 3.7) examined in the Cambridge study of delinquent development.

The specific mechanisms that account for the relationship between parental antisocial personality disorder/criminality and subsequent dysfunction have not been clearly explicated, although research has supported the role of both genetic and family socialization factors and has, to some extent, paralleled the research examining the effects of parental depression on parenting and childhood psychopathology. Those specific parenting practices that have received empirical support as predictors of later impairment are reviewed below.

Parenting Practices and Child Development

Aside from parental mental disorder, various other "psychological" characteristics related to parenting more broadly have been investigated in relation to children's psychosocial development. In fact, the bulk of developmental research over the past half-century has focused less on diagnosable psychopathology and more on specific parenting practices. Various practices have been examined in terms of their effects on the development and socialization of children and adolescents, ranging from very concrete microanalyses of observable parental behaviors to more global assessments of latent parenting constructs. Although a wide range of variables has been investigated, much of the research and theorizing about parental influence in the past several years has come to focus on a core set of "family management" factors that appear to be associated strongly with adverse outcomes over the course of development from infancy to adolescence. Much of this research has been conducted in reference to the development of attachment theory (described below), although behavioral models also have been prominent. Regardless of the specific theoretical orientation of researchers, the data derived from these studies have provided empirical support for several parenting factors that appear influential in children's development. Key factors that have emerged from this literature are highlighted below. For more comprehensive reviews of these variables, see Campbell (1997), Dishion and Patterson (1997), Edens (1999), Greenberg, Speltz, and DeKlyen (1993), Kelly and Lamb (2000), Loeber and Stouthamer-Loeber (1986), Reitman and Gross (1995), and Shaw and Winslow (1997).

The quality of parent-child attachment during the first few years of life has received considerable attention in terms of its relationship to children's later adjustment. Attachment theory was initially proposed by Bowlby (1969) as a general theory of personality development that was based heavily in ethnology and evolutionary theory. Attachment is seen as an organized behavioral system designed to maintain "felt security" for the infant by preserving proximity to the caregiver and by providing a "secure base" from which to explore the environment. Much of the attachment research has focused on how early relationship experiences influence infants' development of emotional regulation (a key sociodevelopmental milestone), as well as how these early experiences form the basic "working models" of subsequent relationships in later childhood and adolescence.

Typically, investigators have assessed specific patterns of attachment that are observed in infant-caregiver relationships. The majority of this research has been an outgrowth of the Strange Situation procedure (Ainsworth, Blehar, Waters, & Wall, 1978), in which the parent briefly leaves a 12- to 18-month-old infant in the company of a stranger. Building on Bowlby's initial observations of typical reactions to separation and reunion, the response of the infant to the caregiver upon reunion has been the basis for identifying four basic attachment styles: securely attached, insecure-resistant or ambivalent, insecure-avoidant, and insecure-disorganized. Most children are identified as secure, in that they welcome caregivers upon reunion and seek their proximity if distressed by the separation. Insecurely attached children, however, display various forms of dysfunctional reactions in response to the reunion (see Ainsworth et al., 1978, or Greenberg et al., 1993, for a more thorough description).

Although main effect models have been inconsistent, a wealth of data exists showing that insecure attachment before the age of 2 years, in combination with other risk factors, significantly predicts increased problems with aggression, depression, and peer relationships in the preschool, elementary school, and preadolescent age ranges (see Greenberg & Speltz, 1988; Greenberg et al., 1993). In fact, many of the behaviors and outcomes distinguishing secure and insecure preschoolers are specific symptoms of childhood behavior disorders such as oppositional defiant disorder (Greenberg et al., 1993). Regarding specific patterns of behavior associated with each attachment status, Renkin, Egeland, Marvinney, Mangelsdorf, and Sroufe (1989) found that teachers rated boys who were identified as avoidant in infancy as more aggressive, whereas ambivalent-resistant attachment was associated with passive-withdrawal. More recent research, summarized by Lyons-Ruth (1996), suggests that disorganized attachment status in infancy may be the most predictive of subsequent externalizing behavior problems in the preschool and grade school years. For example, Lyons-Ruth, Alpern, and Repacholi (1993) found that a large percentage of children exhibiting serious hostile behavior problems had disorganized attachment histories. Similarly, Solomon, George, and DeJong (1995) reported that children with disorganized attachment histories were more aggressive (mother- and teacher-report) than nondisorganized children.

Specific parental factors (as well as child variables) have been shown to predict insecure attachment. Aside from obvious risk factors such as abuse and neglect, parents' emotional expressiveness and their sensitivity and responsiveness to infants' emotional cues are associated with attachment status (see Campbell, 1997; Crockenberg & Leerkes, 2000; Cummings & Davies, 1999). Although much of this research has been conducted with mothers, similar relationships appear to exist regarding father-child attachment.

Collectively, the attachment data clearly indicate that the quality of the parent-child relationship plays a central role in children's socioemotional development, and the theory itself provides an explanatory mechanism for understanding how parental relationships affect children. Moreover, the importance of this variable is not limited to the infancy and toddler years, in that relationship quality continues to be an important predictor of maladjustment in later childhood and adolescence. It is worth noting, however, that other paradigms (e.g., learning theory) can be used to explain the results of the attachment data and that much of the research with children beyond the toddler years is not driven from an attachment perspective. In fact, some have argued for a "macroparadigm" in developmental psychology that accommodates results from multiple theories (Reitman & Gross, 1995).

Consistent with this macroparadigm conceptualization, developmental researchers have identified two basic dimensions of parenting that seem to play a prominent role in the socioemotional development of children. The first of these dimensions has been labeled *nurturance,* reflecting the degree of affective warmth or coldness in the relationship. The second broad dimension, sometimes referred to as *control* or restrictiveness, relates to the type and degree of supervision, monitoring, and limit setting used by the parent. These two factors often have been used to classify basic parenting styles (Baumrind, 1967; Campbell, 1997; Reitman & Gross, 1995), such as *authoritative* (high nurturance, high control), *authoritarian* (low nurturance, high control), and *permissive* (high or low nurturance, low control).

Both authoritarian and permissive parenting styles have been linked with undesirable outcomes among children and adolescents, through the use of various research methodologies (e.g., laboratory tasks, home observation, self-report questionnaires). For example, toddlers who have parents whose behavior is consistent with an authoritarian approach tend to show more negative affect and to be more defiant and noncompliant in parent-child interactions. Deficits in

self-regulation also have been noted. Children and adolescents with authoritarian parents are at greater risk for aggression and other forms of externalizing behavior problems and for academic difficulties and tend to perform more poorly on measures of moral development, self-esteem, and self-competence. Parenting practices associated with permissiveness also have been shown to be linked with aggression and poor behavioral controls. More specifically, a meta-analysis conducted by Loeber and Stouthamer-Loeber (1986) found that boys' conduct problems were significantly related to a lack of parental involvement in 22 of the 29 studies reviewed. Level of parental supervision also was strongly correlated with subsequent delinquency and antisocial behavior.

Not surprisingly, parents who engage in what generally can be construed as authoritative approaches to parenting tend to have psychologically healthy children who are more prone to be self-reliant, socially competent, and capable of self-regulation. Moreover, these parenting strategies may serve as a buffer against other risk factors in a child's environment. As Dishion and Patterson (1997) have noted in their summary of the research:

> In every instance, the finding has been that the impact of context on adjustment is mediated through parenting practices. The parents can be subjected to severe stress, but if they manage to keep their parenting practices relatively intact, the negative context will not have a significant impact on child adjustment. Effective discipline, monitoring, and family problem-solving practices are the strongest protective factors that we have seen in the literature. (p. 211)

Divorce

The research literature of the 1970s and 1980s took a narrow view of divorce, focusing on family structure and on adverse outcomes (Hetherington & Stanley-Hagan, 1999) and conceptualizing divorce in a simple cause-effect model (Kaplan & Pruett, 2000). Divorce was not yet recognized for its longitudinal impact. Using anecdotal, cross-sectional, uncontrolled studies, early researchers reported that children from divorced families suffered from a wide range of emotional, behavioral, and academic problems when compared to children from nondivorced families (Kaplan & Pruett, 2000). Mean differences, often using clinical samples, were interpreted inappropriately and sweeping generalizations were made about the effects of divorce. The accumulation of such negative findings led to the inaccurate conclusion that being divorced per se caused ill effects in children (Kelly, 1998). Essentially, divorce was viewed as a single traumatic experience. In retrospect, much of this research has been criticized for various methodological flaws: Most investigators used cross-sectional methodologies and nonrepresentative, poorly defined samples; data often were derived from single sources or measures of questionable validity; researchers failed to distinguish negative effects resulting from marital discord from negative effects resulting from divorce per se; and significant mediating or moderating factors were not considered (Hetherington & Stanley-Hagan, 1999).

The current model of divorce research does not assume that divorce inevitably leads to poor outcome. Instead, developmental, family systems, and ecological models have been adopted that regard divorce as a family transition or disruption that, depending on a variety of individual, family, and extrafamilial factors, places each individual child at risk for variable amounts of time (Hetherington & Stanley-Hagan, 1999). Emphasis is placed on the diversity of children's adjustment to divorce and on the interactions among the influences that undermine or support the child's adjustment (Wolchik, Wilcox, Tein, & Sandler, 2000). Also, replacing the cross-sectional tradition of early research on divorce, leading researchers have adopted a life course, risk, and resiliency perspective (Hetherington, 1999a). From this perspective, it is assumed that "although divorce may be associated with stressful changes and challenges in family members' lives, it also may present a chance for escape from conflict, for more harmonious, fulfilling relationships, and the opportunity for greater personal growth, individuation, and well-being" (Hetherington & Stanley-Hagan, 1999, p. 130). Such a complex approach is made possible by the use of more sophisticated statistical methods (e.g., cluster analysis, structural equation modeling) and research methodologies (e.g., quasi-experimental designs, longitudinal studies, multiple outcome measures, nationally representative samples, studying the adjustment of multiple children in a family).

Unlike earlier reports, more recent research examining the impact of divorce on children indicates that many of the problems suffered by children of divorce cannot be accounted for by the divorce itself. Instead, events and experiences in the years preceding the divorce (e.g., general family conflict and marital discord) are of central importance (Cherlin et al., 1991; Kelly, 2000). For example, families on the verge of breakup have been found to be characterized by less intimate interparental and parent-child relationships, less parental commitment to children's education, and fewer economic and human resources, resulting in more academic, psychological, and behavioral problems for children even before the marital disruption (Sun, 2001). Moreover, children's maladjustment subsequent to divorce can be predicted largely by these pre-disruption factors and by the corresponding changes in family circumstances during the period surrounding the divorce (Sun, 2001). In general, Cherlin et al. concluded that the differences in outcome between children from divorced and intact families derives from three sources: (a) growing up in a poorly functioning family, (b) severe and extended marital conflict, and (c) parents' emotional upset, diminished parenting capacities, and ongoing conflict that continues after separation. Thus, the presence of prolonged marital conflict appears to play a greater role than divorce itself on children's adjustment.

Teasing apart the differential impact of marital conflict and/or divorce proves difficult. Accordingly, there has been a large increase in the number of studies examining complex variables within the marriage that profoundly impact child adjustment, including marital conflict, violence, and related parenting behaviors. The results essentially have confirmed that the deleterious effects of the divorce process and/or the postdivorce family structure on children's adjustment have been overstated and overgeneralized (Hetherington & Stanley-Hagan, 1999; Kaplan & Pruett, 2000; Kelly, 2000).

Finally, studies examining the possible association between genetics to divorce-proneness and to children's adjustment to divorce have begun to accumulate (Jockin, McGue, & Lykken, 1996; O'Connor, Plomin, Caspi, & DeFries, 2000). In a prospective longitudinal comparison of children from adoptive and biological families who divorced, findings for psychopathology (e.g., behavioral problems, substance abuse) appear to be consistent with an environmentally mediated explanation for the association between parent divorce and children's adjustment. Findings for academic achievement and social adjustment, however, were consistent with a genetically mediated explanation (O'Connor et al., 2000). Although the results are intriguing, conclusions derived from a single study should be viewed cautiously.

Effects of Divorce on Children's Adjustment

It is a generally accepted fact that children of divorce, compared with children in never-divorced families, have significantly more adjustment and achievement problems (Kelly, 2000). This is not surprising considering that

> most children of divorce experience dramatic declines in their economic circumstances, abandonment (or fear of abandonment) by one or both of their parents, the diminished capacity of both parents to attend meaningfully to their children's needs (because they are preoccupied with their own psychological, social, and economic distress as well as stresses related to the legal divorce), and diminished contact with many familiar or potential sources of psychosocial support (friends, neighbors, teachers, schoolmates, etc.), as well as familiar living settings. (Lamb, Sternberg, & Thompson, 1997, p. 395)

In the short term, the experience of parental separation and divorce represents a significant crisis for the majority of children and adolescents, who are likely to respond with a multitude of conflicting emotions. For example, anger, sadness, and deep feelings of loss may be apparent, but in situations of extreme parental conflict, considerable relief also may be experienced. Depression, low self-esteem, and anxiety are common under these circumstances, and acting-out may occur.

Certain differences between children of divorce and children of never-divorced families consistently are reported (Amato & Keith, 1991); and a recent, updated meta-analysis suggests that this gap is widening, after a decrease during the 1980s (Amato, 2001). However, recent studies with more sophisticated methodologies report smaller differences between children of divorce and children of never-divorced families than previously believed (Kelly, 2000). Contrary to early research, most children from divorced homes actually fall within the normal range of adjustment on standardized measures (Amato, 1994). There is, of course, considerable disagreement about the size and significance—both statistically and practically—of differences in problems experienced (Hetherington & Stanley-Hagan, 1999). Furthermore, although a variety of problems (e.g., teenage pregnancy, substance abuse, delinquency) in some areas of adjustment are nearly twice as common among children of divorce than among children of nondivorced families, it is important to note that these problems tend to cluster together in the same individuals, potentially exaggerating the true range of impairment and pathology. The vast majority of children whose parents divorce do not exhibit severe or enduring problems and develop into relatively competent and well-adjusted adults (Amato, 1999).

Despite the preceding caveat, disturbances in the social, academic, and physical domains frequently are cited in the literature, in addition to the psychological effects of divorce noted earlier. Poor academic performance and achievement test scores are commonly reported, but differences are modest and are reduced further when researchers take into account the effects of changes in socioeconomic status and parental supervision (McLanahan & Sandefur, 1994). The school dropout rate of divorced children is two to three times that of nondivorced children, and they are less likely to earn a college degree (McLanahan, 1999). In addition, divorced children are twice as likely to give birth to a child as a teenager (McLanahan & Sandefur, 1994), to use alcohol, cigarettes, and marijuana (Kelly, 2000), and to engage in other antisocial or delinquent behavior. Furthermore, children of divorced parents tend to have more illnesses, medical problems, and physician visits, and are three times more likely to receive psychological treatment than never-divorced children (Zill, Morrison, & Coiro, 1993). Finally, children of divorce commonly experience difficulty with peer relationships.

In keeping with the risk and resiliency perspective of divorce research cited above, many researchers have investigated the characteristics of children that cause some to be more vulnerable or resilient than others. The most commonly investigated characteristics are age, sex, and personality. First, it has long been proposed that young children may be more affected by divorce because they are less prepared cognitively, emotionally, and socially to deal with the challenges and changes of divorce. However, most researchers have reported equally negative effects for older children and adolescents (Amato & Keith, 1991). Contrary to popular belief, the majority of children—and especially older ones who have the ability to form cognitively appropriate conclusions—do *not* assume responsibility or blame for causing their parents' marital separation (Kaplan & Pruett, 2000). Furthermore, as Emery (1998) has noted, the results of many studies examining the relationship between children's age and adjustment are inconclusive, as age is often confounded by other factors (e.g., time since parental separation and divorce, age at the time of assessment).

The association between sex and adjustment to divorce is more complex than originally believed. Although earlier researchers often reported more problems pertaining to divorce for boys and to parental remarriage for girls, findings of more recent research do not indicate such sex differences (Hetherington & Stanley-Hagan, 1999). When sex differences are found, they tend to be more likely to occur with younger children than with adolescents (Amato & Keith, 1991). In addition, boys from predivorcing families demonstrate difficulties in the domains of aggression and impulsivity, whereas girls are more likely to demonstrate difficulties with interpersonal relationships (Block, Block, & Gjerde, 1989). Behavior problems appear to increase in children from divorced families during adolescence, with the increased adjustment difficulties being more significant for girls than for boys (Hetherington, 1993; Hetherington et al., 1992). Furthermore, fathers tend to be more involved with their sons subsequent to divorce, which is encouraging considering that such involvement has been found to be more important for the development of boys than of girls (Amato & Keith, 1991). Overall, divorce appears to be more detrimental to females than males, but the differences seem modest. Instead, Hetherington (1999b) notes the complexity of the gender-age-adjustment issue, in that adjustment and achievement in boys and girls after divorce have been found to vary by age, time since divorce, type of parenting, and type and extent of conflict (Kelly, 2000). Finally, intelligent, effective, and pleasant children are more likely to evoke positive responses and support from others and to be able to adapt to new challenges and stressful life experiences (Hetherington, 1989), whereas the psychosocial stress of divorce merely serves to exacerbate the difficulties of already troubled and poorly adjusted children (Block et al., 1989; Hetherington, 1989).

Adjustment problems tend to diminish in intensity over time, but, on average, children of divorced parents remain less socially, emotionally, and academically well-adjusted than children from nondivorced families (Amato & Keith, 1991). Specifically, meta-analyses have revealed that young adults whose parents divorced (when compared to those whose parents did not divorce) reported lower psychological well-being and socioeconomic attainment, more pregnancies outside of marriage and earlier marriages, poorer-quality marital relationships, and increased propensity to divorce (Amato & Keith, 1991). Even when issues apparently have been resolved earlier, problems can emerge or reemerge later in life in the face of new challenges and developmental tasks. Again, however, such effects are modest, and the general view of this research is still that of resiliency rather than dysfunction (Kelly, 2000). For example, in the National Child Development Study, a long-term follow-up of divorced children into adulthood, 94% of men and 82% of women fell below clinical cutoffs for adult emotional disorders (Chase-Lansdale, Cherlin, & Kiernan, 1995). Unfortunately, however, the most enduring effects of divorce during childhood lie in the realm of educational attainment, which in turn affects the occupational achievement and socioeconomic security of those who dropped out of school and entered early marriages and parenthood (Kelly, 2000).

In the most extensive study to date, both in terms of duration (25 years) and method (e.g., based on hundreds of hours of face-to-face interviews), Wallerstein and Lewis (1998) reported anecdotal data on the psychological, economic, and social consequences of marital breakdown on children. Over two decades postdivorce, the young adults in the sample continued to relate sad stories of their "lost childhoods." The developmental tasks of young adulthood—choosing a profession or career, searching for and selecting a life partner, establishing intimacy, and beginning a family—posed special challenges for these adult children of divorce. Specifically, burdened with financing their own education beyond high school, these children of middle- to upper-class parents were forced to select career lines that, in many cases, fell far below those of their parents. As a consequence, 40% fell below their parents' socioeconomic level. Furthermore, they commonly expressed deep concerns about marriage and having children, worrying about committing the same mistakes as their parents. Consistent with other researchers on the topic, Wallerstein and Lewis recognized the resiliency of children, but emphasized that divorce "does superimpose a series of special and difficult tasks on top of the normative tasks of growing up" (p. 375).

Parental/Marital Conflict and Children's Adjustment

As mentioned, marital conflict is a more powerful predictor of children's adjustment than is divorce itself. Marital conflict takes its toll via a number of mechanisms, both direct (e.g., simple extended activation of the body's physiological stress response, modeling effects; Kelly, 1998) and indirect (e.g., less effective parenting). Furthermore, among the most important predictors of the adjustment of the child are a number of central variables: (a) frequency and intensity of parent conflict; (b) style of conflict (e.g., presence and type of interspousal violence and other acts of marital aggression); (c) manner in which conflict is resolved; and (d) presence of buffers to ameliorate the effects of high conflict (e.g., good relationship with at least one parent or caregiver, parental warmth, support of siblings, good self-esteem and peer support; Kelly, 2000). More extreme expressions of parental anger result in a broader range of adjustment problems and significantly higher levels of psychopathology. The most harmful conflicts are those directly concerning the child, those to which the child is directly exposed, those that lead to physical violence, and those in which the child feels caught in the middle (Davies & Cummings, 1994). Furthermore, high marital conflict is associated with less warm parent-child relationships (Kelly, 1998). Parents in high-conflict marriages engage in more erratic disciplinary practices and are more likely to use anxiety- or guilt-inducing techniques to discipline (Kelly, 1998).

Although immediately after divorce children exhibit more problems in adjustment than those in high-conflict nondivorced families, as the children adapt to their new familial structure, the pattern of differences reverses (Hetherington & Stanley-Hagan, 1999). In fact, when divorce is associated with a move to a less stressful situation, children in divorced families show adjustment similar to those in intact families with nondistressed marital relations (Amato, Loomis, & Booth, 1995; Hetherington, 1999b). However, when divorce is associated with continued high levels of conflict, adjustment of divorced children is worse than that of nondivorced children, perhaps because of the lack of a second residential parent, fewer resources, and higher rates of stressful life events (Hetherington & Stanley-Hagan, 1999). The implications of these findings is made clear by Hetherington and Stanley-Hagan (1999): "Essentially, if conflict is going to continue, it is better for children to remain in an acrimonious two-parent household than to suffer divorce; but if there will be a shift to a more harmonious household a divorce is advantageous" (p. 134). This relationship is not fully clear-cut, however. As expected, when marital conflict prior to divorce was high, divorce resulted in positive outcomes as young adults. Conversely, when marital conflict was low and parents divorced (divorce was unexpected), young adults suffered *more* adjustment problems (Amato et al., 1995).

To summarize, children of divorce in general do appear to suffer from a number of problems in behavioral, emotional, and social domains, particularly in the short term after the divorce, in comparison to children of families never impacted by such a major family transition. However, the differences are smaller than originally believed, and most children of divorce fall in the normal range of adjustment, developing into competent, stable adults. Furthermore, review of the recent literature yields less than consistent findings, as researchers have employed very different methodologies, including groups sampled, instruments used, definition of terms, length of follow-up, and the age of children at the time of divorce (Kaplan & Pruett, 2000).

A substantial body of research on the effects of divorce on children has accrued since the 1970s, but there are still many issues left virtually unexplored and others remain open for clarification. Hetherington & Stanley-Hagan (1999), in their extensive literature review, identified a number of suggestions for new directions of research. First, although not entirely new, the need for further longitudinal studies cannot be overstated. There has been an increasing call for research to examine the diverse developmental trajectories and patterns of children's outcomes subsequent to divorce rather than focusing solely on averages. Cross-sectional studies that have so plagued the early research on the topic cannot address adequately the dynamic interaction of risk and protective factors that influence the adjustment of children over time. Second, the use of rigorous methodologies must continue and new strategies for studying this complex topic be proposed and tested. Interdisciplinary efforts, combining the sampling skills of sociologists and the assessment and observational skills of psychologists, are necessary. Third, although research on divorce in White, middle- to upper-class families proliferates, there is an unfortunate dearth of information on other cultural, ethnic, and racial factors that affect adjustment. This must be rectified to be able to draw even remotely adequate, generalizable conclusions. Fourth, more studies should take a family systems approach, considering children's relationships with custodial fathers, noncustodial parents, grandparents, siblings, and other relatively neglected family subsystems. Furthermore, effects of *multiple* transitions and reorganizations of the family (e.g., transitioning into stepfamilies, parental relocation) on children's adjustment must be investigated, given that this is a common reality for many families. Fifth, because the family is but one system in which a child is nested, albeit a critical one, more ecological approaches studying the effects of extrafamilial structures or factors (e.g., neighborhood, school, peers, place of worship) must be undertaken. Finally, long-term systematic examinations of interventions with divorced families must follow.

Parenting after Divorce

When parents divorce, children of all ages express anxiety about caretaking and custody arrangements (Kelly, 1998). In all families, regardless of the number of structural reorganizations or the time since each transition, children's adjustment is associated with the quality of the parenting environment (Hetherington et al., 1992): the degree to which parents are warm and supportive, communicative, responsive to their needs, exert firm, consistent control and positive discipline, and monitor their activities (Hetherington & Stanley-Hagan, 1999). Especially important in single-parent homes in which, by definition, no other residential parent is available, is the ability of the custodial parent to provide these family management practices. It is also important for both parents to be able to minimize the conflict to which their children are exposed. This includes not fostering hostility against the other parent and not allowing the child to get caught in the middle of parental conflict (Hetherington & Stanley-Hagan, 1999).

Considering the stress involved with divorce, psychological and health problems often ensue, compromising the ability of parents to be responsive and sensitive to their children's needs and to be consistently controlling of their behavior (Hetherington, 1993). Children's personal circumstances and developmental needs are often given inadequate attention, particularly among couples characterized by high rates of litigation and relitigation, high degrees of anger and distrust, intermittent verbal and/or physical aggression, difficulty focusing on their children's needs as distinct from their own, and chronic difficulty coparenting and communicating about their children after divorce (Lamb et al., 1997). Furthermore, there is wide variability in the amount of time most individuals, both parents and children, take to achieve stability. The fact remains, however, that the overall psychological and economic well-being of custodial parents is one of the most powerful predictors of children's adjustment following divorce (Lamb et al., 1997).

In accordance with findings in the broader developmental literature, a recent study found both additive and interactive effects between parenting variables and child variables (i.e., temperament) in predicting adjustment problems in children after divorce (Lengua, Wolchik, Sandler, & West, 2000). Utilizing a sample of 231 mothers and children who had experienced divorce within the preceding 2 years, main effects were detected for both parenting (with a focus on parental rejection and inconsistent discipline) and temperament (represented by positive/negative emotionality and impulsivity), in terms of the prediction of child adjustment problems (e.g., depression, conduct problems). Moreover, significant interactions resulted: Parental rejection was more strongly related to depression and conduct problems for children low in positive emotionality. That is, positive emotionality appears to act as a protective factor for children, buffering the impact of maternal rejection. Furthermore, inconsistent discipline was more strongly related to adjustment problems (both depression and conduct problems) for children high in impulsivity, suggesting that children with impulse control difficulties may be at risk for developing problems of various kinds.

Economics and Remarriage

Particularly in mother-headed single-parent households, divorce commonly brings a significant decline in economic resources. Whereas fathers suffer a 10% decline in income following divorce, mothers, who continue to be granted primary physical custody of children despite changing conceptions of gender and parent roles, experience a 25% to 45% drop in family income, further adding to general levels of stress (Furstenberg, 1990). The establishment and maintenance of two separate residences made necessary by separation and divorce impose economic burdens on the family as a whole (Lamb et al., 1997). Given how widespread economic disadvantage is among single-parent mother-headed families, it is unfortunate that economic disadvantage is commonly found to be the most significant risk factor for children's adjustment (e.g., McLanahan, 1999; McLanahan & Sandefur, 1994).

Although one way that custodial mothers can improve their financial situation is by remarrying (Furstenberg, 1990), the benefits of increased income do not appear to counterbalance the additional stresses experienced by children in stepfamilies (Hetherington, 1993). Aside from the stress of adjusting to new family members, remarriage often entails relocation, which means further limiting availability of friends and relatives to provide social and emotional support during stressful times (Lamb et al., 1997). This is extremely problematic because children benefit from regularity, consistency, and continuity, which pertain not only to

parental involvement, but to peers, extrafamilial caregivers, and schools.

Access to the Noncustodial Parent

Meaningful economic and psychological involvement of the noncustodial parent is important in terms of children's postdivorce adjustment. To maintain high-quality relationships with their children, parents need to have sufficiently extensive and regular interaction with them, but research indicates that the amount of time involved is usually of less import than the quality of the interaction (Lamb et al., 1997). From a developmental perspective, it is recommended that time distribution arrangements ensure the involvement of both parents in important aspects of their children's everyday lives, including bedtime/waking rituals, transitions to/from school, and extracurricular activities (Kelly & Lamb, 2000). Together with developmental needs, parents must consider the temperament and dynamic individual circumstances of the individual child, and plans must be continuously adjusted accordingly (Lamb et al., 1997).

Although contact with both parents is valuable, when conflict between the two parents is intense, frequent contact with each actually can be harmful (Lamb et al., 1997). Furthermore, when a parent's adjustment is affected by mental illness or incapacity, serious substance abuse, or domestic violence, the potential costs of continued contact with children may outweigh the benefits (Lamb et al., 1997). Conversely, families headed by parents whose relationship is characterized by cooperation and flexibility in decisions about custody tend to enjoy greater advantages overall, which is not surprising. Specifically, more cooperative families, reflected by parents mediating rather than litigating custody, tended to have nonresidential parents who maintained more contact with their children, were more involved in multiple domains of their children's lives, had a greater influence in coparenting 12 years after the custody dispute, and made more changes in their children's living arrangements over the years (Emery, Laumann-Billings, Waldron, Sbarra, & Dillon, 2001). Moreover, increased contact between parents did not lead to heightened coparenting conflict.

Research has resulted in conflicting findings regarding the importance of children's contact with their father. For example, large-scale national studies have generally found no relationship between frequency of father contact and children's postdivorce adjustment (Kelly, 2000). However, in a meta-analysis of 57 studies, Amato and Gilbreth (1999) found that more recent studies of father-child contact provide stronger evidence of father impact on child adjustment than do earlier studies. Again, the quality of the relationship (e.g., feelings of closeness with the child and active parenting of the father) is more important than frequency of visits. The degree to which father involvement impacts child adjustment, however, ultimately is linked to such factors as degree of conflict, type of paternal and maternal acceptance, and regular payment of child support (Lamb, 1999; McLanahan & Sandefur, 1994; Pruett & Pruett, 1998). Furthermore, one group of researchers reported that even when economic factors were accounted for, children in father-custody families evidenced fewer problems than those in mother-headed families (Clark-Stewart & Hayward, 1996). Nevertheless, while "fathers are important . . . children can develop well in mother-headed families with absent fathers" (Hetherington & Stanely-Hagan, 1999, p. 136).

Type of Custody Arrangements

At a theoretical level, substantial debate remains about which custody arrangement is in the best interests of children. Besides the benefits and detriments to each parent (and how they indirectly affect a child), effects on the child with regard to single-parent versus joint-custody arrangements are mixed. On the one hand, advocates of joint-custody argue that children are expected to experience both higher quality residential parenting and relationships with nonresidential parents, more cooperative coparenting, and ultimately, better adjustment (Emery et al., 2001; Gunnoe & Braver, 2001). Conversely, critics are concerned that joint custody exacerbates family conflict by requiring sustained contact to collaborate in the child's interests and that children will be adversely affected when they are unable to keep their relationships with both parents equal (Gunnoe & Braver, 2001). Moreover, results of research on the adjustment of children from single-parent versus joint custody families also have been mixed. For example, Johnston (1995) asserts that more recent and larger studies find few differences in adjustment between children in sole versus joint physical custody, other than higher parental income and education and regular child support payments among joint custody parents. Conversely, Kelly (2000) notes that joint legal custody has been linked to children's well-being. Yet others have speculated a more complex relationship between type of custody arrangement and adjustment. For example, Gunnoe and Braver (2001) identified 20 variables that predisposed families to be awarded either sole or joint custody, including demographic factors (e.g., education of mother, hours per week worked by father), parental adjustment (e.g., fathers' anger), spousal relations (e.g., mothers' visitation opposition), aspects of both fathers' parenting (e.g., involvement in child rearing, visitation during separation) and mothers' parenting (e.g.,

rejection/acceptance of child), and child adjustment (e.g., male children's antisocial behavior, impulsivity). After controlling for these factors, which were hypothesized to have confounded apparent effects obtained in previous research, results indicated that families with joint custody had more frequent father-child visitation, lower maternal satisfaction with custody arrangement, and more rapid maternal re-partnering. All in all, however, children tended to exhibit fewer adjustment problems. Moreover, Maccoby and Mnookin (1992) reported that when conflict was low after divorce, adolescents in joint physical custody were better adjusted, but not in high-conflict postdivorce families. Finally, in families with extreme and continuing high conflict after divorce, children (particularly girls) with more frequent transitions and shared access were found to have more emotional and behavioral problems than children in sole custody situations (Johnston, 1995). Thus, it appears that interparental conflict continues to be a pivotal factor in children's adjustment well after the marriage has been dissolved. The type of custody arrangement and its likely effects cannot be considered in isolation.

SUMMARY

Child custody evaluations are one of the most difficult areas of forensic practice, given the complexity of the issues at hand (e.g., vague legal doctrines, contentious family dynamics, multiple persons and domains requiring assessment) and the intrinsically tenuous nature of any empirically supported conclusions that examiners reasonably can be expected to draw in most cases. Despite these difficulties, it seems clear from the preceding review that significant improvements in the child custody arena have been made in recent years. These improvements can be seen in the ever-expanding database of empirical research concerning the relationship between parenting behavior and child adjustment, the effects of divorce, and the impact of various custody arrangements on children. Improvements also can be seen in terms of the development of professional guidelines promulgated by various organizations that provide at least some instruction about standards of practice for examiners.

Despite these advances, considerable room for improvement remains in most areas of research and practice, and significant problem areas should be noted (see also Nicholson & Norwood, 2000). First, the existing assessment approaches employed by many examiners remain of questionable value for assessing the psycholegal constructs relevant to child custody issues. Moreover, the recent advent of "custody-specific" tests in particular could be argued to be a step backward in the process of developing appropriate instrumentation. Second, the scientific foundation on which examiners should draw their conclusions and/or recommendations, although considerably improved, remains in its infancy. Furthermore, research in this area always will be constrained by the inability to use true experimental designs to address the most prominent questions related to custody decision making. Additionally, little is known about how child custody evaluators, attorneys, and judges consider information in cases, and on what types of information they base their decisions.

A final and more general area of concern is that many of the fundamental issues needing to be resolved in custody cases (e.g., what is in a child's best interest) ultimately are value judgments that may not be directly amenable to scientific inquiry, although value judgments made by legal decision makers certainly can be informed by scientific data (as noted previously). Some of the more damning critiques of this area of practice assert that it is little more than subjective value judgment dressed up as expert opinion or social science data. In fact, there remains a debate within the field about the fundamental appropriateness of the involvement of mental health professionals in child custody evaluations (Emery, 1999; Koocher, 1999; Melton, 1999; O'Donohue & Bradley, 1999; Weisz, 1999). Despite this debate, it is clear that mental health professionals will continue to be involved in these evaluations for the foreseeable future. As such, attention to improving the quality of practice in this area should remain a priority.

REFERENCES

Abidin, R. R. (1995). *Parenting Stress Index. (PSI).* Odessa, FL: Psychological Assessment Resources.

Ackerman, M. J., & Ackerman, M. C. (1997). Custody evaluation practices: A survey of experienced professionals (revisited). *Professional Psychology: Research and Practice, 28,* 137–145.

Ackerman, M., & Schoendorf, K. (1992). *ASPECT: Ackerman-Schoendorf Scales for Parent Evaluation of Custody manual.* Los Angeles: Western Psychological Services.

Ainsworth, M. D. S., Blehar, M. C., Waters, E., & Wall, S. (1978). *Patterns of attachment: A psychological study of the strange situation.* Hillsdale, NJ: Erlbaum.

Amato, P. R. (1994). Life-span adjustment of children to their parents' divorce. *Future of Children, 4,* 143–164.

Amato, P. R. (1999). Children of divorced parents as young adults. In E. M. Hetherington (Ed.), *Coping with divorce, single-parenting, and remarriage: A risk and resiliency perspective* (pp. 147–163). Hillsdale, NJ: Erlbaum.

Amato, P. R. (2001). Children of divorce in the 1990s: An update of the Amato and Keith (1991) meta-analysis. *Journal of Family Psychology, 15,* 355–370.

Amato, P. R., & Gilbreth, J. G. (1999). Nonresident fathers and children's well-being: A meta-analysis. *Journal of Marriage and Family, 61,* 557–573.

Amato, P. R., & Keith, B. (1991). Parental divorce and the well-being of children: A meta-analysis. *Psychological Bulletin, 110,* 26–46.

Amato, P. R., Loomis, L. S., & Booth, A. (1995). Parental divorce, parental marital conflict, and offspring well-being during early adulthood. *Social Forces, 73,* 895–916.

American Academy of Child and Adolescent Psychiatry. (1997). Practice parameters for child custody evaluation. *Journal of the American Academy of Child and Adolescent Psychiatry, 36,* 57S–68S.

American Educational Research Association, American Psychological Association, & National Council on Measurement in Education. (1999). *Standards for educational and psychological testing* (3rd ed.). Washington, DC: American Educational Research Association.

American Psychological Association. (1992). Ethical principles of psychologists and code of conduct. *American Psychologist, 47,* 1597–1611.

American Psychological Association. (1994). Guidelines for child custody evaluations in divorce proceedings. *American Psychologist, 49,* 677–682.

American Psychological Association. (1995). *Lesbian and gay parenting: A resource for psychologists.* Washington, DC: American Psychological Association.

Arditti, J. A. (1995). Ackerman-Schoendorf Scales for Parent Evaluation of Custody. In J. C. Conoley & J. C. Impara (Eds.), *The twelfth mental measurements yearbook* (pp. 20–22). Lincoln, NE: Buros Institute of Mental Measurements.

Association of Family and Conciliation Courts. (n.d.). *Model standards of practice for child custody evaluation.* Milwaukee, WI: Author.

Baumrind, D. (1967). Child care practices anteceding three patterns of preschool behavior. *Genetic Psychology Monographs, 75,* 43–88.

Beardslee, W., Bemporad, J., Keller, M. B., & Klerman, G. L. (1983). Children of parents with major affective disorder: A review. *American Journal of Psychiatry, 140,* 825–832.

Bellak, L., & Bellak, S. S. (1992). *Children's Apperception Test 1991 Revision.* Larchmont, NY: CPS Inc.

Bender, L. (1946). *Bender Visual-Motor Gestalt Test.* San Antonio, TX: Psychological Corporation.

Bischoff, L. G. (1992). The Custody Quotient. In J. J. Kramer & J. L. Conoley (Eds.), *The eleventh mental measurements yearbook* (pp. 254–255). Lincoln, NE: Buros Institute of Mental Measurements.

Bischoff, L. G. (1995). Parent Awareness Skills Survey. In J. L. Conoley & J. C. Impara (Eds.), *The twelfth mental measurements yearbook* (p. 735). Lincoln, NE: Buros Institute of Mental Measurements.

Black, R., & Mayer, J. (1980). Parents with special problems: Alcohol and opiate addictions. *Child Abuse and Neglect, 4,* 45–54.

Block, J., Block, J. H., & Gjerde, P. F. (1989). Parental functioning and the home environment in families of divorce: Prospective and concurrent analyses. *Annual Progress in Child Psychiatry and Child Development,* 192–207.

Bow, J. N., & Quinnell, F. A. (2001). Psychologists' current practices and procedures in child custody evaluations: Five years after American Psychological Association Guidelines. *Professional Psychology: Research and Practice, 32,* 261–268.

Bowlby, J. (1969). *Attachment and loss. Volume I: Attachment.* New York: Basic Books.

Bricklin, B. (1989). *Perception of Relationships Test manual.* Furlong, PA: Village.

Bricklin, B. (1990a). *Bricklin Perceptual Scales manual.* Furlong, PA: Village.

Bricklin, B. (1990b). *Parent Awareness Skills Survey manual.* Furlong, PA: Village.

Bricklin, B. (1995). *The custody evaluation handbook: Research-based solutions and applications.* New York: Brunner/Mazel.

Bricklin, B. (1999). The contributions of psychological tests to child custody evaluations. In R. M. Galatzer-Levy & L. Kraus (Eds.), *The scientific basis of child custody decisions* (pp. 120–156). New York: Wiley.

Bricklin, B., & Elliott, G. (1991). *Parent Perception of Child Profile manual.* Furlong, PA: Village.

Bricklin, B., & Elliott, G. (1997). *Critical child custody evaluation issues: Questions and answers. Test manuals supplement for BPS, PORT, PASS, PPCP.* Furlong, PA: Village.

Brodzinsky, D. M. (1993). On the use and misuse of psychological testing in child custody evaluations. *Professional Psychology: Research and Practice, 24,* 213–219.

Butcher, J. N., Dahlstrom, W. G., Graham, J. R., Tellegen, A., & Kaemmer, B. (1994). *Minnesota Multiphasic Personality Inventory—2 (MMPI-2).* Minneapolis, MN: NCS Assessments.

Campbell, S. B. (1997). Behavior problems in preschool children: Developmental and family issues. In T. H. Ollendick & R. J. Prinz (Eds.), *Advances in clinical child psychology* (Vol. 19, pp. 1–26). New York: Plenum Press.

Carlson, J. N. (1995). Perception of Relationships Test. In J. C. Conoley & J. C. Impara (Eds.), *The twelfth mental measurements yearbook* (pp. 746–747). Lincoln, NE: Buros Institute of Mental Measurements.

Chase-Lansdale, P. L., Cherlin, A. J., & Kiernan, K. K. (1995). The long-term effects of parental divorce on the mental health of young adults: A developmental perspective. *Child Development, 66,* 1614–1634.

Chassin, L., Barrera, M., & Montgomery, H. (1997). Parental alcoholism as a risk factor. In S. A. Wolchik & I. N. Sandler (Eds.), *Handbook of children's coping: Linking theory and intervention* (pp. 101–129). New York: Plenum Press.

Cherlin, A. J., Furstenburg, F. F., Chase-Lansdale, P. L., Kiernan, K. E., Robins, P. K., Morrison, D. R., et al. (1991). Longitudinal studies of effects of divorce in children in Great Britain and the United States. *Science, 252,* 1386–1389.

Clark, S. C. (1995, March). Advance report of final divorce statistics, 1989 and 1990. In *Monthly vital statistics report* (Vol. 43, No. 9). Hyattsville, MD: National Center for Health Statistics.

Clarke-Stewart, K. A., & Hayward, C. (1996). Advantages of father custody and contact for the psychological well-being of school-age children. *Journal of Applied Developmental Psychology, 17,* 239–270.

Cohen, R. J., & Swerdlik, M. E. (1999). *Psychological testing and assessment: An introduction to tests and measurement* (4th ed.). Mountain View, CA: Mayfield.

Cole, D. E. (1995). Parent Awareness Skills Survey. In J. L. Conoley & J. C. Impara (Eds.), *The twelfth mental measurements yearbook* (p. 735). Lincoln, NE: Buros Institute of Mental Measurements.

Collins, W. A., Maccoby, E. E., Steinberg, L., Hetherington, E. M., & Bornstein, M. H. (2000). Contemporary research on parenting: The case for nature and nurture. *American Psychologist, 55,* 218–232.

Conger, J. (1995). Perception of Relationships Test. In J. C. Conoley & J. C. Impara (Eds.), *The twelfth mental measurements yearbook* (pp. 747–748). Lincoln, NE: Buros Institute of Mental Measurements.

Crockenberg, S., & Leerkes, E. (2000). Infant social and emotional development in family context. In C. H. Zeanah (Ed.), *Handbook of infant mental health* (2nd ed., pp. 60–90). New York: Guilford Press.

Crown, D. P., & Marlowe, D. (1960). A new scale of social desirability independent of psychopathology. *Journal of Consulting Psychology, 24,* 349–354.

Cummings, E. M., & Davies, P. T. (1999). Depressed parents and family functioning: Interpersonal effects and children's functioning and development. In T. Joiner & J. C. Coyne (Eds.), *The interactional nature of depression: Advances in interpersonal approaches* (pp. 299–327). Washington, DC: American Psychological Association.

Daubert v. Merrell Dow Pharmaceuticals, Inc., 509 U.S. 579, 113 S. Ct. 2786 (1993).

Davies, P. T., & Cummings, E. M. (1994). Marital conflict and child adjustment: An emotional security hypothesis. *Psychological Bulletin, 116,* 387–411.

Dishion, T. J., & Patterson, G. R. (1997). The timing and severity of antisocial behavior: Three hypotheses within an ecological framework. In D. M. Stoff, J. Breiling, & J. D. Maser (Eds.), *Handbook of antisocial behavior* (pp. 205–217). New York: Wiley.

Downey, G., & Coyne, J. C. (1990). Children of depressed parents: An integrative review. *Psychological Bulletin, 108,* 50–76.

Edens, J. F. (1999). Aggressive children's self-systems and the quality of their relationships with significant others. *Aggression and Violent Behavior, 4,* 151–177.

Emery, R. E. (1998). *Marriage, divorce, and children's adjustment.* Newbury Park, CA: Sage.

Emery, R. E. (1999). Changing the rules for determining child custody in divorce cases. *Clinical Psychology: Science and Practice, 6,* 323–327.

Emery, R. E., Laumann-Billings, L., Waldron, M. C., Sbarra, D. A., & Dillon, P. (2001). Child custody mediation and litigation: Custody, contact, and coparenting 12 years after initial dispute resolution. *Journal of Consulting and Clinical Psychology, 69,* 323–332.

Fabry, J. J., & Bischoff, R. A. (1992). The Custody Quotient. In D. Keyser & R. Sweetwater (Eds.), *Test critiques* (Vol. 9, pp. 145–148). Austin, TX: ProEd.

Falk, P. (1989). Lesbian mothers: Psychosocial assumptions in family law. *American Psychologist, 44,* 941–947.

Farrington, D. P. (1995). The development of offending and antisocial behavior from childhood: Key findings from the Cambridge study in delinquent development. *Journal of Child Psychology and Psychiatry, 36,* 929–964.

Farrington, D. P. (2000). Psychosocial predictors of adult antisocial personality and adult convictions. *Behavioral Sciences and the Law, 18,* 605–622.

Felner, R. D., Rowlison, R. T., Farber, S. S., Primavera, J., & Bishop, T. A. (1987). Child custody resolution: A study of social science involvement and impact. *Professional Psychology: Research and Practice, 5,* 468–474.

Field, T. (1995). Psychologically depressed parents. In M. H. Bornstein (Ed.), *Handbook of parenting: Applied and practical parenting* (Vol. 4, pp. 85–99). Mahwah, NJ: Erlbaum.

Florida Statutes 61.12(2)9(b)2 (2000).

Frick, P. J. (1993). Childhood conduct problems in a family context. *School Psychology Review, 22,* 376–385.

Frick, P. J., & Jackson, Y. K. (1993). Family functioning and childhood antisocial behavior: Yet another reinterpretation. *Journal of Clinical Child Psychology, 22,* 410–419.

Frye v. United States, 293 F. 1013 (D.C. Cir. 1923).

Furstenberg, F. F. (1990). Divorce and the American family. *Annual Review of Sociology, 16,* 379–403.

Gerard, A. B. (1994). *Parent-Child Relationship Inventory (PCRI): Manual.* Los Angeles, CA: Western Psychological Services.

Goodman, S. H., & Brumley, H. E. (1990). Schizophrenic and depressed mothers: Relational deficits in parenting. *Developmental Psychology, 26,* 31–39.

Gordon, R., & Peek, L. A. (1989). *The Custody Quotient: Research manual.* Dallas, TX: Wilmington Institute.

Gould, J. W. (1998). *Conducting scientifically crafted child custody evaluations.* Thousand Oaks, CA: Sage.

Greenberg, M. T., & Speltz, M. L. (1988). Attachment and the ontogeny of conduct problems. In J. Belsky & T. Nezworski (Eds.), *Clinical implications of attachment* (pp. 177–218). Hillsdale, NJ: Erlbaum.

Greenberg, M. T., Speltz, M. L., & DeKlyen, M. (1993). The role of attachment in the early development of disruptive behavior problems. *Development and Psychopathology, 5,* 191–213.

Grisso, T. (1984, June). *Forensic assessment in juvenile and family cases: The state of the art.* Keynote address at the Summer Institute on Mental Health Law, University of Nebraska, Lincoln.

Grisso, T. (1986). *Evaluating competencies: Forensic assessments and instruments.* New York: Plenum Press.

Gunnoe, M. L., & Braver, S. L. (2001). The effects of joint legal custody on mothers, fathers, and children controlling for factors that predispose a sole maternal versus joint legal award. *Law and Human Behavior, 25,* 25–43.

Hagen, M. A., & Castagna, N. (2001). The real numbers: Psychological testing in custody valuations. *Professional Psychology: Research and Practice, 32,* 269–271.

Hagin, R. A. (1992). Bricklin Perceptual Scales. In J. L. Conoley & J. C. Impara (Eds.), *The twelfth mental measurements yearbook* (pp. 117–118). Lincoln, NE: Buros Institute of Mental Measurements.

Hammen, C. (1997). Children of depressed parents: The stress context. In S. A. Wolchik & I. N. Sandler (Eds.), *Handbook of children's coping: Linking theory and intervention* (pp. 131–157). New York: Plenum Press.

Hare, R. D. (1991). *The Hare Psychopathy Checklist—Revised Manual.* Toronto: Multi-Health Systems, Inc.

Harris, J. R. (1995). Where is the child's environment? A group socialization theory of development. *Psychological Review, 102,* 458–489.

Harris, J. R. (1998). *The nurture assumption: Why children turn out the way they do.* New York: Free Press.

Hathaway, S. R., & McKinley, J. C. (1989). *Minnesota Multiphasic Personality Inventory (MMPI).* Minneapolis, MN: NCS Assessments.

Heilbrun, K. (1992). The role of psychological testing in forensic assessment. *Law and Human Behavior, 16,* 257–272.

Heilbrun, K., Rogers, R., & Otto, R. K. (in press). Forensic assessment: Current status and future directions. In J. Ogloff (Ed.), *Psychology and law: The state of the discipline.* New York: Kluwer/Plenum Press.

Heinze, M. C., & Grisso, T. (1996). Review of instruments assessing parenting competencies used in child custody evaluations. *Behavioral Sciences and the Law, 14,* 293–313.

Hetherington, E. M. (1989). Coping with family transitions: Winners, losers, and survivors. *Child Development, 60,* 1–14.

Hetherington, E. M. (1993). An overview of the Virginia longitudinal study of divorce and remarriage with a focus on early adolescence. *Journal of Family Psychology, 7,* 1–18.

Hetherington, E. M. (Ed.). (1999a). *Coping with divorce, single parenting, and remarriage: A risk and resiliency perspective.* Hillsdale, NJ: Erlbaum.

Hetherington, E. M. (1999b). Should we stay together for the sake of the children? In E. M. Hetherington (Ed.), *Coping with divorce, single parenting, and remarriage: A risk and resiliency perspective* (pp. 93–116). Hillsdale, NJ: Erlbaum.

Hetherington, E. M., Clingempeel, W. G., Anderson, E. R., Deal, J. E., Stanley-Hagan, M., Hollier, E. A., et al. (1992). Coping with marital transitions: A family systems perspective. *Monographs of the Society for Research in Child Development, 57*(2/3, Serial No. 227).

Hetherington, E. M., & Stanley-Hagan, M. (1999). The adjustment of children with divorced parents: A risk and resiliency perspective. *Journal of Child Psychology and Psychiatry, 40,* 129–140.

Hiltonsmith, R. W. (1995). Parent Perception of Child Profile. In J. C. Conoley & J. C. Impara (Eds.), *The twelfth mental measurements yearbook* (pp. 736–738). Lincoln, NE: Buros Institute of Mental Measurements.

Hughes, R. (1996). *Demographics of divorce* [Online]. INTERNET IN-SERVICE ON CHILDREN AND DIVORCE. Available from www.hec.pohio-state.edu/famlife/divorce/index.htm.

Jameson, B., Ehrenberg, M., & Hunter, M. (1997). Psychologists' ratings of the best interests of the child custody and access criteria: A family systems assessment model. *Professional Psychology: Research and Practice, 28,* 253–262.

Jenuwine, M. J., & Cohler, B. J. (1999). Major parental psychopathology and child custody. In R. M. Galatzer-Levy & L. Kraus (Eds.), *The scientific basis of child custody decisions* (pp. 285–318). New York: Wiley.

Jockin, V., McGue, M., & Lykken, D. T. (1996). Personality and divorce: A genetic analysis. *Journal of Personality and Social Psychology, 71,* 288–299.

Johnston, J. R. (1995). Research update: Children's adjustment in sole custody compared to joint custody families and principles of custody decision making. *Family and Conciliation Courts Review, 33,* 415–425.

Kaplan, M. D., & Pruett, K. D. (2000). Divorce and custody: Developmental implications. In C. H. Zeanah, Jr. (Ed.), *Handbook of infant mental health* (2nd ed., pp. 533–547). New York: Guilford Press.

Keilin, W. G., & Bloom, L. J. (1986). Child custody evaluation practices: A survey of experienced professionals. *Professional Psychology: Research and Practice, 17,* 338–346.

Kelley, M. L. (1995). Parent Perception of Child Profile. In J. C. Conoley & J. C. Impara (Eds.), *The twelfth mental measurements yearbook* (pp. 738–739). Lincoln, NE: Buros Institute of Mental Measurements.

Kelly, J. B. (1998). Marital conflict, divorce, and children's adjustment. *Child and Adolescent Psychiatric Clinics of North America, 7,* 259–271.

Kelly, J. B. (2000). Children's adjustment in conflicted marriage and divorce: A decade review of research. *Journal of the American Academy of Child and Adolescent Psychiatry, 39,* 963–973.

Kelly, J. B., & Lamb, M. E. (2000). Using child development research to make appropriate custody and access decisions for young children. *Family and Conciliation Courts Review, 38,* 297–311.

Koocher, G. P. (1999). Afterthoughts on child custody evaluations. *Clinical Psychology: Science and Practice, 6,* 332–334.

Kuehnle, K., & Weiner, I. (2000). *A survey of judges' opinions regarding child custody evaluations.* Unpublished manuscript.

LaFortune, K. A., & Carpenter, B. N. (1998). Custody evaluations: A survey of mental health professionals. *Behavioral Sciences and the Law, 16,* 207–224.

Lamb, M. E. (1999). Non-custodial fathers and their impact on the children of divorce. In R. A. Thompson & P. R. Amato (Eds.), *The post-divorce family: Research and policy issues* (pp. 105–125). Thousand Oaks, CA: Sage.

Lamb, M. E., Sternberg, K. J., & Thompson, R. A. (1997). The effects of divorce and custody arrangements on children's behavior, development, and adjustment. *Family and Conciliation Courts Review, 35,* 393–404.

Lengua, L. J., Wolchik, S. A., Sandler, I. N., & West, S. G. (2000). The additive and interactive effects of parenting and temperament in predicting adjustment problems of children of divorce. *Journal of Clinical Child Psychology, 29,* 232–244.

Loeber, R. (1990). Development and risk factors of juvenile antisocial behavior and delinquency. *Clinical Psychology Review, 10,* 1–42.

Loeber, R., & Stouthamer-Loeber, M. (1986). Family factors as correlates and predictors of juvenile conduct problems and delinquency. In M. Tonry & N. Morris (Eds.), *Crime and justice* (Vol. 17, pp. 29–149). Chicago: University of Chicago Press.

Logue, M. E., & Rivinus, T. M. (1991). Young children of substance-abusing parents: A developmental view of risk and resiliency. In T. M. Rivinus (Ed.), *Children of chemically dependent parents: Multiperspectives from the cutting edge* (pp. 55–73). Philadelphia: Brunner/Mazel.

Lovejoy, M. C., Graczyk, P. A., O'Hare, E., & Neuman, G. (2000). Maternal depression and parenting behavior: A meta-analytic review. *Clinical Psychology Review, 20,* 561–592.

Lynskey, M. T., Fergusson, D. M., & Horwood, J. L. (1994). The effect of parental alcohol problems on rates of adolescent psychiatric disorders. *Addiction, 89,* 1277–1286.

Lyons-Ruth, K. (1996). Attachment relationships among children with aggressive behavior problems: The role of disorganized early attachment patterns. *Journal of Consulting and Clinical Psychology, 64,* 64–73.

Lyons-Ruth, K., Alpern, L., & Repacholi, B. (1993). Disorganized infant attachment classification and maternal psychosocial problems as predictors of hostile-aggressive behavior in the preschool classroom. *Child Development, 64,* 572–585.

Maccoby, E., & Mnookin, R. (1988). Custody of children following divorce. In E. M. Hetherington & J. D. Aresteh (Eds.), *Impact of divorce, single parenting, and stepparenting on children* (pp. 110–149). Hillsdale, NJ: Erlbaum.

Maccoby, E. E., & Mnookin, R. H. (1992). *Dividing the child: Social and legal dimensions of child custody.* Cambridge, MA: Harvard University Press.

Martindale, D., & Otto, R. K. (2000). Communicating with the custody evaluator. *Family Advocate, 23*(1), 30–33.

Mayes, L. C. (1995). Substance abuse and parenting. In M. Bornstein (Ed.), *Handbook of parenting* (Vol. 3, pp. 101–125). Hillsdale, NJ: Lawrence Erlbaum.

McIntosh, J. A., & Prinz, R. J. (1993). The incidence of alleged sexual abuse in 603 family court cases. *Law and Human Behavior, 17,* 95–101.

McLanahan, S. S. (1999). Father absence and children's welfare. In E. M. Hetherington (Ed.), *Coping with divorce, single-parenting, and remarriage: A risk and resiliency perspective* (pp. 117–145). Hillsdale, NJ: Erlbaum.

McLanahan, S. S., & Sandefur, G. (1994). *Growing up with a single parent: What hurts, what helps.* Cambridge, MA: Harvard University Press.

Mednick, S., Parnas, J., & Schulsinger, F. (1987). The Copenhagen high-risk project, 1962–1986. *Schizophrenia Bulletin, 13,* 485–496.

Melton, G. B. (1995). Ackerman-Schoendorf Scales for Parent Evaluation of Custody. In J. C. Conoley & J. C. Impara (Eds.), *The twelfth mental measurements yearbook* (pp. 22–23). Lincoln, NE: Buros Institute of Mental Measurements.

Melton, G. B. (1999). Due care, not prohibition of expert opinions. *Clinical Psychology: Science and Practice, 6,* 335–338.

Melton, G. B., Petrila, J., Poythress, N. G., & Slobogin, C. (1997). *Psychological evaluations for the courts: A handbook for attorneys and mental health professionals* (2nd ed.). New York: Guilford Press.

Melton, G. B., Weithorn, L. A., & Slobogin, C. (1985). *Community mental health centers and the courts: An evaluation of community-based forensic services.* Lincoln: University of Nebraska Press.

Michigan Child Custody Act of 1970, MCL § 722.23 (1993 amended).

Millon, T. (1987). *Millon Clinical Multiaxial Inventory—II (MCMI-II).* Minneapolis, MN: NCS Assessments.

Millon, T. (1994). *Millon Clinical Multiaxial Inventory—III (MCMI-III).* Minneapolis, MN: NCS Assessments.

Munsinger, H. L., & Karlson, K. W. (1994). *Uniform Child Custody Evaluation System.* Odessa, FL: Psychological Assessment Resources.

Murray, H. A., & Bellak, L. (1973). *Thematic Apperception Test (TAT).* San Antonio, TX: Psychological Corporation.

National Interdisciplinary Colloquium on Child Custody. (1998). *Legal and mental health perspectives on child custody law: A deskbook for judges.* Danvers, MA: West Group.

Nicholson, R. A., & Norwood, S. (2000). The quality of forensic psychological assessments, reports, and testimony: Acknowledging the gap between promise and practice. *Law and Human Behavior, 24,* 9–44.

Nuechterlein, K. H. (1986). Childhood precursors of adult schizophrenia. *Journal of Child Psychology and Psychiatry and Allied Disciplines, 27,* 133–144.

O'Connor, T. G., Plomin, R., Caspi, A., & DeFries, J. C. (2000). Are associations between parental divorce and children's adjustment genetically mediated? An adoption study. *Developmental Psychology, 36,* 429–437.

Oddenino, M. (1994). Helping your client navigate past the shoals of a child custody evaluation. *American Journal of Family Law, 8,* 81–95.

O'Donohue, W., & Bradley, A. R. (1999). Conceptual and empirical issues in child custody evaluations. *Clinical Psychology: Science and Practice, 6,* 310–322.

Otto, R. K. (1989). Bias and expert testimony of mental health professionals in adversarial proceedings: A preliminary investigation. *Behavioral Sciences and the Law, 7,* 267–273.

Otto, R. K. (2000). *Child custody evaluation: Law, ethics, and practice.* Tampa, FL: Louis de la Parte Florida Mental Health Institute.

Otto, R. K., Edens, J. F., & Barcus, E. (2000a, August). The family bar's perception of mental health professionals in the context of child custody. In M. Ackerman (Chair), *What judges expect from psychologists in child custody evaluations.* Symposium conducted at the annual meeting of the American Psychological Association, Washington, DC.

Otto, R. K., Edens, J. F., & Barcus, E. (2000b). The use of psychological testing in child custody evaluations. *Family and Conciliation Courts Review, 38,* 312–340.

Oyserman, D., Mowbray, C. T., Meares, P. A., & Firminger, K. B. (2000). Parenting among mothers with a serious mental illness. *American Journal of Orthopsychiatry, 70,* 296–315.

Patterson, C. (1995). Lesbian and gay parenthood. In M. Bornstein (Ed.), *Handbook of parenting* (Vol. 3, pp. 255–276). Mahwah, NJ: Erlbaum.

Paulhus, D. L. (1999). *Manual for the Paulhus Deception Scales.* North Tonawanda, NY: Multi-Health Systems.

Paulhus, D. L. (1999). *Paulhus Deception Scales (PDS): The Balanced Inventory of Desirable Responding—7.* North Tonawanda, NY: MHS/Multi-Health Systems.

Pruett, M. K., & Pruett, K. D. (1998). Fathers, divorce, and their children. *Child and Adolescent Psychiatric Clinics of North America, 7,* 389–407.

Quinnell, F. A., & Bow, J. N. (2001). Psychological tests used in child custody evaluations. *Behavioral Sciences and the Law, 19,* 491–501.

Reidy, T., Silver, R., & Carlson, A. (1989). Child custody decisions: A survey of judges. *Family Law Quarterly, 23,* 75–87.

Reitman, D., & Gross, A. M. (1995). Familial determinants. In M. Hersen & R. T. Ammerman (Eds.), *Advanced abnormal child psychology* (pp. 87–104). Hillsdale, NJ: Erlbaum.

Renken, B., Egeland, B., Marvinney, D., Mangelsdorf, S., & Sroufe, L. A. (1989). Early childhood antecedents of aggression and passive-withdrawal in early elementary school. *Journal of Personality, 57,* 257–281.

Robins, L., West, P., & Herjanic, B. (1975). Arrests and delinquency in two generations: A study of Black urban families and their children. *Journal of Child Psychology and Psychiatry, 16,* 125–140.

Rogers, R., Bagby, R. M., & Dickens, S. E. (1992). *Structured Interview of Reported Symptoms.* Odessa, FL: Psychological Assessment Resources.

Rogers, R., & Webster, C. (1989). Assessing treatability in mentally disordered offenders. *Law and Human Behavior, 13,* 19–29.

Rogosch, F. A., Mowbray, C. T., & Bogat, G. A. (1992). Determinants of parenting attitudes in mothers with severe psychopathology. *Development and Psychopathology, 4,* 469–487.

Rohman, L., Sales, B., & Lou, M. (1987). The best interests of the child in custody disputes. In L. Weithorn (Ed.), *Psychology and child custody determinations* (pp. 59–105). Lincoln: University of Nebraska Press.

Rorschach, H. (1942). *Rorschach Inkblot Test.* Los Angeles, CA: Western Psychological Services.

Rowe, D. (1994). *The limits of family influence: Genes, experience, and behavior.* New York: Guilford Press.

Schutz, B., Dixon, E., Lindenberger, J., & Ruther, N. (1989). *Solomon's sword: A practical guide to conducting child custody evaluations.* San Francisco: Jossey-Bass.

Settle, S. A., & Lowery, C. R. (1982). Child custody decisions: Content analysis of a judicial survey. *Journal of Divorce, 6,* 125–138.

Shaffer, M. B. (1992). Bricklin Perceptual Scales. In J. L. Conoley & J. C. Impara (Eds.), *The twelfth mental measurements yearbook* (pp. 118–119). Lincoln, NE: Buros Institute of Mental Measurements.

Shaw, D. S., & Winslow, E. B. (1997). Precursors and correlates of antisocial behavior from infancy to preschool. In D. M. Stoff, J. Breiling, & J. D. Maser (Eds.), *Handbook of antisocial behavior* (pp. 148–158). New York: Wiley.

Solomon, J., George, C., & DeJong, A. (1995). Children classified as controlling at age six: Evidence of disorganized representational strategies and aggression at home and at school. *Development and Psychopathology, 7,* 447–463.

Stahl, P. (1994). *Conducting child custody evaluations: A comprehensive guide.* Thousand Oaks, CA: Sage.

Steinhausen, H. C. (1995). Children of alcoholic parents: A review. *European Child and Adolescent Psychiatry, 4,* 419–432.

Sun, Y. (2001). Family environment and adolescents' well-being before and after parents' marital disruption: A longitudinal analysis. *Journal of Marriage and Family, 63,* 697–713.

Swaim, R. C. (1991). Childhood risk factors and adolescent drug and alcohol abuse. *Educational Psychology Review, 3,* 363–398.

Tombaugh, T. N. (1996). *Test of Memory Malingering.* Tonawanda, NY: Multi-Health Systems.

U.S. Bureau of the Census. (1989). *Statistical abstract of the United States.* Washington, DC: Author.

Wallerstein, J. S., & Lewis, J. (1998). The long-term impact of divorce on children. *Family and Conciliation Courts Review, 36,* 363–383.

Wechsler, D. (1981). *Wechsler Adult Intelligence Scale—Revised (WAIS-R).* San Antonio, TX: Psychological Corporation.

Wechsler, D. (1997). *Wechsler Adult Intelligence Scale–Third Edition.* San Antonio, TX: The Psychological Corporation.

Wechsler, D., & Stone, C. P. (1955). *Wechsler Adult Intelligence Scale (WAIS).* San Antonio, TX: Psychological Corporation.

Weintraub, S. (1987). Risk factors in schizophrenia: The Stony Brook High Risk Project. *Schizophrenia Bulletin, 13,* 439–450.

Weisz, V. G. (1999). Commentary on conceptual and empirical issues in child custody evaluations. *Clinical Psychology: Science and Practice, 6,* 328–331.

Weithorn, L. (1987). Psychological evaluations in divorce and custody: Problems, principles, and procedures. In L. Weithorn (Ed.), *Psychology and child custody determinations* (pp. 158–181). Lincoln: University of Nebraska Press.

Weitzman, L. J. (1985). *The divorce revolution: The unexpected social and economic consequences for women and children in America.* New York: Macmillan.

Wellman, M. M. (1994). Ackerman-Schoendorf Scales for Parent Evaluation of Custody. In D. Keyser & R. Sweetwater (Eds.), *Test critiques* (Vol. 10, pp. 13–19). Austin, TX: ProEd.

West, M. O., & Prinz, R. J. (1987). Parental alcoholism and childhood psychopathology. *Psychological Bulletin, 102,* 204–218.

Wolchik, S. A., Wilcox, K. L., Tein, J., & Sandler, I. N. (2000). Maternal acceptance and consistency of discipline as buffers of divorce stressors on children's psychological adjustment problems. *Journal of Abnormal Child Psychology, 28,* 87–102.

Wyer, M., Gaylord, S., & Grove, E. (1987). The legal context of child custody evaluations. In L. Weithorn (Ed.), *Psychology and child custody determinations* (pp. 4–22). Lincoln: University of Nebraska Press.

Zill, N., Morrison, D., & Coiro, M. (1993). Long-term effects of parental divorce on parent-child relationships, adjustment, and achievement in young adulthood. *Journal of Family Psychology, 7,* 91–103.

Zusman, J., & Simon, J. (1983). Differences in repeated psychiatric examinations of litigants to a lawsuit. *American Journal of Psychiatry, 140,* 1300–1304.

CHAPTER 12

Assessment of Childhood Trauma

STEVEN N. SPARTA

Over the past two decades, there has been increased attention paid around the world to the causes and effects of traumatic stress on children. Along with this has been an increasing recognition that children may experience a variety of psychological reactions, including posttraumatic stress disorder (Pynoos, Steinberg, & Goenjian, 1996; Shannon, Lonigan, Finch, & Taylor, 1994). These developments, and the nature and consequences of psychological trauma, are of particular interest to both psychologists and attorneys addressing issues related to a variety psycholegal applications involving children.

DEFINITIONS OF TRAUMA

Trauma is discussed in the literature in various ways. Psychological trauma has sometimes been described as an overwhelming experience that can result in a continuum of posttrauma adaptations and/or specific symptoms. At other times, psychologists and lawyers have interchangeably defined trauma as a qualitative degree of suffering within the child (an effect) or as a psychological consequence related to a forensically relevant event (a cause). The forensic psychologist asked to evaluate children in such matters should be careful to avoid assumptions about the nature, extent, and causality of psychological functioning based solely on the existence of a legally contested event and its presumed magnitude of psychological disruption. Whether a child has suffered the effects of trauma that is proximally related to a legally related event can be determined only after a careful analysis of multimodal data gathered within an objective forensic evaluation context.

Melton, Petrila, Poythress, and Slobogin (1997) note that a variety of terms have been used to describe the mental effects associated with emotional distress legal cases, but the trauma-based diagnosis most likely to be involved in mental injury cases is posttraumatic stress disorder (PTSD). Impairment and diagnosis are both relevant to clinical treatment and prognosis. In assessing childhood trauma, concepts of

I wish to thank Marc R. Stein, Esquire, and Robert Kinscherff, PhD, JD, for their very helpful review of the chapter.

damage or disability should include evaluations of whether the child's psychological problems were proximately caused by a legally relevant event. Evaluation of childhood trauma need not be limited to traditional psychiatric diagnostic classifications systems, such as the *Diagnostic and Statistical Manual of Mental Disorders,* fourth edition (*DSM-IV;* American Psychiatric Association [APA], 1994).

The *DSM-IV* states that the essential feature of PTSD is the development of characteristic symptoms following exposure to a situation experienced as stressful. The stressful event can involve direct personal experience that involves actual or threatened death or serious injury or other threat to one's "physical integrity," as well as "witnessing an event that involves death, injury, or a threat to the physical integrity of another person; or learning about unexpected or violent death, serious harm or threat of death or injury experienced by a family member or other close associate" (APA, 1994, p. 424).

Historical accounts of trauma appear early in literature and are varied. For example, as cited in Pynoos et al. (1996), accounts of an adolescent's reactions to the eruption of Mount Vesuvius are reported as early as A.D. 100–113 in the letters of Pliny the Younger (1931). Andreasen (1985) notes that the term post-traumatic stress disorder first appeared in *DSM-III,* but that the concept is considerably older, often found in histories of early warfare. Andreasen describes a stress syndrome in soldiers during the U.S. Civil War that was originally believed to be due to functional cardiac disturbance. The condition of "shell-shock" during World War I was once believed to be due to organic brain syndrome secondary to carbon monoxide gas. World War II gave rise to a great number of "combat neuroses" or "traumatic war neuroses," which led to an increased interest in PTSD, eventually resulting in a category of "gross stress reaction" in the *International Classification of Diseases* (*ICD;* World Health Organization, 1977).

The Web site of the National Institute of Mental Health Public Inquires notes that PTSD is a debilitating condition that follows a terrifying event and can occur at any age, including childhood. About 4% of the population will experience symptoms in a given year. Symptoms typically begin within three months following a traumatic event, although occasionally symptoms do not begin until years later. Once PTSD develops, the duration of the illness varies. The *DSM-IV* reports prevalence ranges from 1% to 14% because of the variability of the methods of ascertainment and sampling of populations. The public information Web site for the American Psychiatric Association (1999) reports that 10% of the population has been affected at some point by clinically diagnosable PTSD. The *DSM-IV* notes that duration of symptoms varies, with complete recovery occurring within three months in approximately half of cases. Andreasen

(1985) notes that chronic PTSD is less common than acute, with symptoms of six months or longer. The foregoing statistics are not specific to children. Therefore, evaluators should appreciate that a given referral involving child trauma may represent a problem with significantly different base rates.

In his manual for the Trauma Symptom Checklist for Children, Briere (1996) notes that researchers have documented a wide variety of psychological effects associated with trauma. As cited by Briere, some of the effects include the murder of a parent (Malmquist, 1986), war (Baker, 1990; Sack, Aangel, Kinzie, & Rath, 1986; Ziv, Kruglanski, & Shulman, 1974), natural disasters such as earthquakes or hurricanes (Green et al., 1991), physical and sexual abuse (Browne & Finkelhor, 1986; Kiser, Heston, Millsap, & Pruitt, 1991; Kolko, Moser, & Weldy, 1988; Lanktree, Briere, & Zaidi, 1991), witnessing spousal abuse (Jaffe, Wolfe, & Wilson, 1990; Kashani, Daniel, Dandoy, & Holcomb, 1992), physical and sexual assaults by peers or caretakers (Boney-McCoy & Finkelhor, 1995; Freeman, Mokros, & Poznanski, 1993; Singer, Anglin, Song, & Lunghofer, 1995) as well as parental divorce or hospitalization of a family member (Evans, Briere, Boggiano, & Barrett, 1994). Studies suggest that half of all sexually abused children meet partial or full criteria for PTSD (McLeer, Deblinger, Atkins, Foa, & Ralphe, 1988; McLeer, Deblinger, Henry, & Orvashel, 1992). In addition to direct threats to children, posttraumatic stress can be experienced indirectly when children perceive threat to their major sources of psychological security. Motor vehicle accidents are considered the major cause of posttraumatic stress in the general population (Norris, 1992). Burns can result in protracted and disfiguring injuries; in pediatric cases, fire and burn injuries are second only to motor vehicle accidents in children ages 1 and 4 years.

Children may be traumatized not only by directly experiencing traumatic experience, but by observing the event (Lyons, 1988). In the growing literature concerning domestic violence, children are described as being subject to serious psychological detriment from the observation or knowledge of violence in the household (Jaffe, 1995). Parent reports of the child's history or their ratings of the child's functioning can be distorted by downplaying the incidence of interpersonal violence in the family or their noting the effects on the child.

Classes of Psychological Trauma

The range of forensically relevant referrals can be grouped into categories of noninterpersonal and interpersonal forms of trauma. Noninterpersonal forms of trauma can include burns, witnessing fires, motor vehicle accidents, floods, earthquakes, and hurricanes, and other forms of natural disaster.

Interpersonal forms of trauma can include sexual/physical abuse, witness to domestic violence or spousal murder, chronic exposure to expressed hostility in divorce conflicts, kidnapping, or shootings in school settings. One case the writer reviewed involved the scalding death of a baby in the presence of multiple siblings. In this case, there were direct and secondary traumatic effects of interpersonal origin. Not only did the children witness the death of a sibling by a parent, but they were also being considered for trial testimony in the prosecution of a parent in a death penalty case. Although each case should be analyzed without preconceptions as to whether a child is necessarily affected or to what degree, DeBellis (1997) noted that when trauma is of interpersonal origin, the resulting disorders may lead to more lasting and/or severe symptoms.

Terr (1991) suggested that two classes of trauma may lead to PTSD in children. The first involves single, sudden and unexpected experiences, such as being the victim of a violent crime; the second involves repeated occurrences, often expected by the victim, such as ongoing physical or sexual abuse. Repeated exposure to traumatic stressors may result in significant psychological disruption for a variety of reasons, including the child's inability to profit from moderating variables of resilience, social support, and positive coping mechanisms. The assessment should be broad enough to examine variables beyond simply the magnitude of the stressor, as mediating variables can significantly affect the child's reaction to a traumatic event.

DSM Diagnoses Related to Childhood Trauma

Relevant DSM diagnoses include, but are not limited to, PTSD, acute stress disorder, and adjustment disorder with anxious or depressed features. Careful differential diagnosis is needed, particularly concerning mood disorders and/or attention-deficit/hyperactivity disorder (ADHD), whose clinical presentations can appear similar and may be comorbid with PTSD. Meyer (1993) has noted that it may be more appropriate at times to use the diagnosis of adjustment disorder, qualified by possible features of anxious or depressed mood, disturbance of conduct, academic inhibition, mixed emotional features or mixed disturbance of emotions and conduct. This can occur when a stressor is more likely within the normal range of experience, with little in the way of a vivid reexperiencing of the event.

Differential Symptomatology of Posttraumatic and Anxiety States

PTSD is classified as one of the anxiety disorders. Although some features of some anxiety disorders can occur in posttraumatic states, there are a number of distinguishing characteristics. Knowledge of these differences can be important when formulating opinions as to whether the symptoms documented in the forensic evaluation are proximately caused by a legally related event or are related to a preexisting or coexisting disorder. For example, panic attacks can be associated features of other anxiety and psychotic disorders. Panic attacks in PTSD are cued by stimuli recalling the stressor, whereas panic attacks that occur in the context of other anxiety disorders are situationally bound, predisposed, or more generalized. Panic attacks in PTSD can generalize to other situations but should originate in stimuli reminiscent of the trauma before generalization. In social phobia, the panic attack is cued by social situations; in specific phobia, by a particular object or situation; and in obsessive-compulsive disorder, by exposure to the object of an obsession (DSM-IV, APA, 1994). Anxiety as a trait has a familial association. Generalized Anxiety Disorder, which includes Overanxious Disorder of Childhood, consists of a variety of anxiety symptoms exclusive of the distinguishing posttraumatic characteristics.

Acute stress disorder is a closely related diagnosis, but is appropriate only for symptoms that occur within one month of an extreme stressor. For symptoms that persist longer than one month, PTSD should be considered. For those children who experience an extreme stressor but do not meet the PTSD criteria of dissociative symptoms, persistent reexperience of the traumatic event, marked avoidance of stimuli associated with the traumatic event, anxiety, or arousal, a diagnosis of adjustment disorder should be considered. When attempting to describe the results of one's forensic evaluation using DSM classifications, it is important to keep in mind that each descriptive term may represent connotations to judges or attorneys not consistent with their meanings and implications understood by mental health professionals. For example, the term acute stress disorder may be understood to be synonymous with PTSD in terms of the severity of symptoms or how long symptoms persist. Therefore, diagnoses described in reports or during testimony should be carefully characterized and distinguished from one another.

Dissociative amnesia is characterized by a difficulty in recalling important personal information, whereas depersonalization can include persistent or recurrent feelings of being detached from one's mental processes or body (DSM-IV, APA, 1994). Dissociative amnesia can occur in PTSD and is not diagnosed when it does. Forensic evaluation of children who have experienced chronic sexual or physical abuse should consider the possibility of dissociative reactions as part of a PTSD. Evaluation of these children requires additional evaluation competencies to ensure defensible interviewing techniques and the reliability of one's opinions.

The range of symptomatology with children is not defined by stage of development or the severity of the disorder. Evaluators should be alert to the widest possible spectrum of manifestations that can differ from those found in the diagnostic criteria for PTSD. The evaluator should be knowledgeable about traumatic reactions in children and carefully assess the possible presence of such problems. Doing so not only increases the evaluator's confidence in the conclusions, but also anticipates possible cross-examination challenges to forensic opinions.

Communicating Trauma in Forensically Relevant Terms

Evaluators should not rely solely on *DSM* diagnostic formulations to define forensically relevant issues. This diagnostic classification system was not developed to address legally relevant questions such as proximate cause in civil cases, the best interests of children in custody disputes, or whether children require the protection of the Juvenile Court in child abuse cases. Although trauma assessment can be undertaken in any of the psycholegal contexts described above, if the forensic psychologist uses only the *DSM* classification system, important areas of legally relevant information related to the child's response to traumatic events may be overlooked. Some children experience problems not detectable on standardized tests. Some have few symptoms; those who do not reach thresholds of clinical concern may yet be at risk for "sleeper" effects, experiencing significant problems later in the developmental sequence. The American Academy of Child and Adolescent Psychiatry (1998) noted that PTSD in children may be underdiagnosed, possibly because the diagnostic criteria are not developmentally sensitive or because available methods for assessment make it difficult to detect these effects.

Phase-Related Trauma Symptomatology

Forensic evaluators of trauma should recognize that the acute, chronic, and delayed-onset phases of the disorder may produce different symptoms of different intensity or frequency in children at different developmental stages. Children in the acute phase may have nightmares, distressing dreams, hypervigilance, difficulty falling asleep, generalized anxiety, and an exaggerated startle response. A different symptom pattern among children whose PTSD had moved into a chronic form was noted by Famularo, Kinscherff, and Fenton (1990) for children suffering long-standing difficulties with detachment, restricted range of affect, sadness, dissociative episodes, estrangement from others, and a future expectation that life will be difficult.

Determinants of Traumatic Effects

How a child reacts to a stressful event is a function of a complex biopsychosocial process, including, but not limited to, the level of stress; the nature of the traumatic event; the individual's coping ability, predisposition for autonomic arousal, and personality; the constructive support available from caretakers following the trauma; and comorbid or premorbid developmental/psychological conditions. The impact of any potentially traumatic experience depends not only on the characteristics of the event, but also on the child's temperament, neurodevelopmental reactivity, attachment status, and a variety of risk-protective factors (e.g., family functioning and emotional resources; Saywitz, Mannarino, Berliner, & Cohen, 2000). Briere (1997) summarized the determiners of posttraumatic responses. He includes such factors as the characteristics of the stress, variables specific to the victim, subjective response to the stress, and the response of others to the victim. These factors can account for significant variability among children who experience what appears to be equivalent stresses. These findings underscore why it is essential for forensic evaluators to view each child's situation as unique. The developmental vulnerability of the child may increase the significance of the response by caretakers or others toward that child, thus highlighting the need for a child forensic evaluation to carefully consider this factor.

Understanding Trauma as Developmental Psychopathology

It is essential that forensic evaluators of childhood trauma understand developmental psychopathology. This provides an integrative framework for understanding the normal trajectory of changes in children in general, and how disruptions in childhood development can occur at later stages in the child's life. Examined in this framework, the disruptive effects of traumatic experience can be understood to have consequences on the child's future ability to process information, regulate affect, and adapt socially (Berliner, 1997). The potential for future developmental disruption to a child's functioning is one distinguishing feature in assessing trauma in children as compared to adults. It is clear, however, that childhood trauma may have profound effects on all of adult functioning, to the extent that childhood trauma may be considered a mitigating factor in death penalty cases (Goldstein & Goldstein, in press). At times, a traumatic event can exacerbate a preexisting psychological condition, such as a child's anxiety and loss following a conflictual divorce in his or her family.

It is always important for the forensic evaluator to recognize that the presence of legitimate psychological symptoms does not necessarily mean that they represent legally relevant evidence of impairment. For example, and as described later, whether psychological impairments are proximately related to legally contested events is an essential consideration for psychological evaluation of damages in a personal injury civil litigation.

Biological Reactions to Trauma

Traumatic events can produce a complex interaction between behavioral and biological stress responses systems. DeBellis and Putnam (1994) noted that multiple, densely interconnected, neurobiological systems were likely to be impacted by acute and chronic stressors associated with the traumatic event. The dysregulation of stress response systems within the child may impact emerging neurodevelopment and thus be potentially more detrimental to a child than to an adult. These major systems can have significant implications for the strength of mood dysregulation, including anxiety and depression. Evaluation should include an assessment of behavioral manifestations of motor restlessness due to hyperaroused stress systems and/or learning and memory deficits that may be secondary to anxiety. In addition, DeBellis and Putnam suggest that it is important to note the biological role in understanding traumatic effects because of the potential use of pharmacological treatments for specific target symptoms. Such treatment may represent an important element that determines the prognosis for the child's recovery. The presence or absence of appropriate treatments after a traumatic event may affect the ultimate settlement in assessing damages. Although the forensic evaluator may not be able to accurately project the response by the child to such recommended interventions, identifying the foregoing issues in an evaluation report can significantly benefit considerations for treatment or legal settlement.

Comorbidity and Preexisting Dysfunction

Traumatic effects with children can assume a variety of divergent symptomatic expressions, requiring a broad-spectrum assessment of major areas of developmental functioning. Broad assessment also can identify conditions that coexist and are *not* proximately related to a legally contested event. Children may be assessed years after a traumatic event following the appearance of a number of psychologically significant symptoms independent of the initial trauma. Forensic evaluators familiar with trauma can conduct careful interviews of children that increasingly focus evaluation questions to clarify the nature of a child's psychological functioning.

Pynoos et al. (1996) note that grief, depression, posttraumatic stress, and separation anxiety are interrelated but can occur independently of one another. It is essential to have as complete a history as possible of the child's functioning over the entire developmental life span up to the time of the traumatic event. Frequently, evaluators focus on present functioning without sufficient inquiry concerning prior functioning. Questions about prior functioning should include inquiries about trauma that may have occurred *before* the legally contested event. Many children are victims of domestic violence, physical and/or sexual abuse, medical emergencies, or fires or are witnesses to extreme violence. These children may have been experiencing symptoms before the legally contested event. The evaluator must, therefore, determine whether the prior trauma has contributed to increased impairment or the child's functioning has been changed by the event. For example, some children who have been removed from their parents due to child protection concerns are subsequently maltreated while in substitute care. Other children evaluated for psychological damages stemming from a fire may have been victims of chronic sexual abuse prior to the legally contested event. Consequently, the evaluator may observe significant symptomatology not caused by a specific traumatic event that was the precipitant for the evaluation referral.

Factors Mediating Traumatic Response

As noted above, prior traumatization can be a factor affecting the duration or severity of the trauma response. The suddenness or severity of the stressor is an important component in predicting the impact on the child, but could increase or decrease potential effects depending on other variables. It is helpful for evaluators to consider that current symptoms may not remain present in the near future. Conversely, positive functioning at the time of the evaluation should not be taken to indicate that the child could not have suffered significant symptoms at an earlier time. Situational factors such as protracted litigation can have a contributing effect at the time of evaluation (Weissman, 1990). Personality traits can create vulnerabilities that limit adaptation and foster chronic impairment. The presence or absence of social support can have a dramatic effect on children's adaptation to traumatic stress.

Shalev (1996) and Shalev, Bonne, and Eth (1996) noted various factors that may predict the likelihood of PTSD, including pretrauma vulnerability, the magnitude of the stressor, immediate responses to the event, and posttrauma responses. Additional factors that can affect the duration or severity of posttraumatic responses include genetic predisposition, prior traumatization, preexisting personality, and the child's stage of development at the time the trauma is experienced (van der Kolk, 1987). These factors provide useful criteria to consider in any forensic trauma assessment.

COMPETENCY, RECALL, AND CREDIBILITY OF CHILDREN'S STATEMENTS

Children's statements during evaluation must be considered in terms of developmental competency to accurately report the experience, accurately recall the chain of events, and in terms of deception. The child's reports should ordinarily be assessed against corroborating data, which usually are more persuasive than clinical observation alone. Kuehnle (1996) noted that in the context of assessing the veracity of statements from children suspected of having been sexually abused, information based on consistent observations by multiple experienced professionals has consensual validity. Reports of teachers, day care staff at preschools, and pediatricians, in addition to mental health professional consultation, can help establish consistency of statements and behavior across settings and time periods. Such methods can assist in the determination of the child's accuracy of recall and developmental competency or indications of deception. Forensic evaluators should never solely rely on subjective appraisals of a child's credibility to answer psycholegal questions.

Weissman (1991) reported that competency in reporting events involves the capacity to perceive facts accurately, to recall, to distinguish truth from falsehood, and to be able to communicate based on personal knowledge of the facts. Expert developmental knowledge of cognitive capacities is required to assess the child's reports and to frame questions in developmentally appropriate language. Preschool children are particularly susceptible to suggestibility as well as to developmentally different ways of expressing or experiencing time and sequence. Because of these developmental limitations, it is sometimes difficult to determine whether an absence of reported symptoms is due to an absence of difficulty, developmental limitations in expression, or *DSM-IV* Cluster B symptoms associated with avoidance of thoughts or feelings caused by the trauma.

When assessing young children's reports about traumatic events, one must recognize the potential complications of recall/memory in adults and children. Accurate recall by children represents a complicated process affected by diverse variables, including ongoing reports by family members and a shifting developmental interpretation for the original experience. As the child learns from others about the traumatic event and their reaction to it, the child can internalize a belief at variance with the actual event. Studies of memory show that events are not simply encoded and later replayed,

analogous to a tape recorder. Accurate recall is malleable, subject to various factors, including suggestibility, the length of time delay until questioned, emotions that existed at the time of the event, and potential selective reinforcement for certain beliefs. In addition, children have a natural tendency to reach closure, which may lead them to construct a "story" explaining what happened. Such perceptions and beliefs reported by children during evaluation may or may not be factually accurate in whole or in part, but they are psychologically important to understanding children's adaptation. Although these points need to be carefully considered, children should not be presumed incapable of accurate reporting of prior events, including child abuse.

EVALUATION OF TRAUMA

Psychological-Legal Contexts for Evaluating Trauma

The nature of the legal proceeding determines the applicable psycholegal constructs to be considered in each case. Psychological assessment involving childhood trauma can occur in a variety of legal proceedings, each with different purposes, court rules, rules of evidence, and culture among attorneys and judges.

The forensic evaluation is different in scope, purpose, and method from a traditional clinical assessment. The selection of assessment instruments and interview formats should be consistent with the psycholegal requirements of the assessment. If traditional clinical instruments are selected, the evaluator should use them with a complete understanding of their limited applicability to the ultimate legal questions.

The purpose of the forensic assessment of trauma is to inform the court with the use of objectively gathered, valid, and relevant information. To assist the court in making informed judgments, evaluators should be open to various alternative hypotheses. Psychological tests can complement interview data by providing standardized administration of various questions or tasks with normative data. Prior to the completion of the report, the evaluator should challenge his or her own conclusions by formulating counterhypotheses to explain the same findings. Melton et al. (1997) suggest that the interpretive results of tests are best considered as hypotheses subject to corroboration from other sources.

Grisso (1986) has noted the problem of employing general psychological constructs as a conceptual basis for assessments related to psycholegal issues. He discussed the need to use, whenever possible, specific forensic formulations and instruments. As with all psychological assessment instruments, forensic assessment instruments operationally define dimensions of behavior, attitude, or ability. Grisso notes that forensic assessment instruments resemble criterion-referenced tests, which can specifically define the legally relevant domain to be measured and formulate specific ways to define mastery of the domain skills or abilities.

To address the causal question of whether measured deficits are proximally related to a traumatic event, the evaluation should address the domain of psychological constructs described in the theories and empirical findings related to the trauma literature. It is important for evaluators to perform this analysis consistent with the general developmental requirements for assessing children and the specialized trauma literature regarding children. The sample evaluation protocol described later in this chapter includes general psychological assessment techniques useful for generating hypotheses and identifying potential areas of subsequent assessment, in addition to specific PTSD instruments.

Because the concept of trauma is *not* limited to one particular type of legal proceeding, there is no single domain or test for application in all legal proceedings. Discussions of trauma in a forensic context should inform the court, in reasonably supported probabilities, about deficits and the potential for stability, change, and rehabilitation. Assessment strategies should be informed by empirical research about trauma effects in children, including those studies that establish links between past traumatic events and current behavioral and psychological functioning. Relationships among trauma variables should be demonstrated. For example, the intensity of the traumatic event combined with the duration of exposure can lead to increased risk for disability (van der Kolk, 1987). Other relationships may mitigate the potential for enduring impacts, such as mediating factors of effective social support, coping strategies, and personality traits involving resiliency.

Grisso (1986) describes how assessment results can identify certain psychological characteristics of the examinee, and that existing research can guide the evaluator's inferences to reject or accept various causal explanations and predictions. At a minimum, the forensic assessment can provide the court with an explanation of functional deficits and strengths with a consideration of the relationship between the results and psychological theories or studies about specific areas of functioning.

Psychological Trauma in Personal Injury Litigation

Trauma often arises in the context of personal injury litigation. When this occurs, it should be viewed as one part of a broader set of psychological and legal issues related to tort law and personal injury. (See the chapter by Greenberg in this volume for information regarding psychological evaluation in tort litigation). Other forensic applications potentially involving trauma include, but are not limited to, child abuse cases and child custody conflicts, including allegations of domestic violence and/or child abuse; special education eligibility determinations; and delinquency cases where PTSD may be relevant to the offense or to the potential for rehabilitation.

Personal injury evaluations of children can occur in civil cases involving the adjudication of alleged wrongs. Tort law is designed to provide monetary compensation for certain types of injuries. In civil proceedings, psychologists are usually involved in assessing alleged damages, not in the liability portion of the proceeding, which determines whether the defendant has responsibility for the plaintiff's allegations. Damages in tort proceedings are set by juries, subject to judicial review.

According to Melton et al. (1997), definitional criteria can vary for different types of torts, but usually, the following elements define whether an actionable event has been committed: (a) The defendant owes a "duty" to the plaintiff, (b) which is violated or "breached" by the defendant, (c) "proximately" causing the injury, and (d) the injury is recognized as compensable.

Psychologists evaluating children for psychological trauma typically do not become involved in the question of whether a duty to the plaintiff existed and/or was breached. However, the concept of proximate cause is an important legal issue and must be understood by the forensic psychologist. Whether conduct was intentional or negligent, it will not lead to liability unless it proximately causes the injury. Explanations of "proximate" include whether one can reasonably foresee that one event causes another or that an unbroken sequence of events causes the injury. Weissman (1985) reported that proximate cause can represent the extent to which the cause of action constitutes a substantial factor in causing impairment or disorder. He described the importance of separating proximate from nonproximate factors in the causal nexus of impairment. When conducting forensic evaluations, psychologists are trained to respect the multiplicity of biological, social, psychological, environmental, and other factors that can influence behavior and functioning. To determine proximally caused impairments, the evaluator must assess the child in a comprehensive and rigorous manner.

Isolating present functioning of a child to one or more legally relevant factors can be extremely complicated and, in some cases, may be impossible to do with confidence. Particularly because children's developmental capabilities evolve at different rates over time, it is often difficult to determine or quantify whether the child's delayed functioning in some areas at the time of evaluation was proximately caused by the legally contested event or by some other factor. Also, comorbid disorders predating or subsequent to the traumatic event may account for some or all of the observed deficits. At the time of evaluation, children may be susceptible to situational events occurring in their home, the need to be evaluated, or possibly being interviewed by other strangers. Even when using standardized methods of assessment with normative data, the evaluator must formulate by a preponderance of the evidence a logically persuasive opinion based on a careful analysis of historical and multimodal assessment data.

Psychological Trauma in Other Legal Proceedings

In contrast to the personal injury evaluation associated with tort litigation, allegations of traumatic effects of child abuse at the hands of a parent or from witnessing domestic violence can occur during a contested divorce child custody dispute. The Uniform Marriage and Divorce Act (1973) served as a model code for various state statutes defining elements of "the best interests of the child," the primary judicial concern in such cases. Statutory definitions of a child's best interests are usually broad enough to include psychological trauma as one of many potentially relevant evaluation factors. The psycholegal standards are different for custody evaluations, personal injury assessments, special educational evaluations, and psychological evaluations for child protection in a Juvenile Court, but all assessments require knowledge of trauma effects with children.

Estimating Future Damages

Forensic evaluators frequently are asked to estimate future damages of an impaired individual. Each case should be viewed as reflecting a unique constellation of factors, not amenable to easy generalizations about future functioning based on epidemiological statistics. Andreasen (1985) notes that most cases are acute, in that symptoms develop quite rapidly after the traumatic event, usually within hours or days. In many of these cases, the symptoms resolve spontaneously without psychiatric treatment. Mediating factors, described later in this chapter, can have significant influence on future functioning. Recognizing that precise estimates of future psychological impairment may not be possible, evaluation opinion can include whether the child's problems are improving or worsening and what types of interventions are likely to improve functioning.

Ultimate Opinion Issues in Trauma Assessment

Melton et al. (1997) caution psychological evaluators that although courts frequently seek opinions about ultimate legal issues, evaluators should be careful not to exceed the limits of what can reasonably be supported on the basis of their specialized knowledge. Even if a court permits such an opinion, the professional should be careful not to exceed the limits of the data from the evaluation. Simon and Wettstein (1997) noted that questions could be asked about whether the traumatic stressor alleged to have caused PTSD is of sufficient severity to produce the disorder. However, in a forensic context, answers to such direct questions could be contaminated by a variety of factors discussed in this chapter. Unless the evaluator can provide a reasonably supported and relevant opinion, it would be ethically incumbent on the evaluator to defer the ultimate judgment to the trier of fact. Instead, the evaluator could provide the trier of fact with specific results and analyses based on the evaluation that do not answer the ultimate questions before the court.

Forensic Expert Qualification in Child Trauma Assessment

Who is an expert in childhood trauma assessment? Federal Rule of Evidence 702 defines testimony by experts. Each state may have different statutes, but they generally parallel Rule 702: "If scientific, technical, or other specialized knowledge will assist the trier of fact to understand the evidence or determine a fact at issue, a witness qualified as an expert by knowledge, skill, experience, training or education, may testify thereto in the form of an opinion or otherwise." (For a more comprehensive discussion of this issue, see the chapter by Packer & Borum in this volume.)

In performing evaluations of children and adolescents in legal proceedings, specialized knowledge and training requires specialized competence to assess general developmental functioning to differentiate normal childhood experience from extraordinary, such as that experienced by traumatized children. Special knowledge in childhood psychopathology is required to differentiate traumatic effects from possible comorbid or premorbid conditions. The evaluator must know how to properly interview, test, or otherwise evaluate children and have specialized forensic knowledge for the type of assessment being performed. The expert must be familiar with the requirements of the relevant law specific to the appropriate jurisdiction and the type of legal referral question when performing assessments involving trauma. As suggested by the foregoing forensic examples involving childhood trauma, the evaluator may potentially be called on to examine a divergent range of highly specific childhood problems, each type requiring unique training and knowledge.

Trauma Assessment or Treatment of Trauma?

Greenberg and Shuman (1997) discussed the significant differences in roles between an evaluator and a psychotherapist. The evaluator strives for objectivity and to provide relevant, balanced information for the court, not to rehabilitate or cure the client's problems. The treatment alliance includes a quasi-advocacy role for the stated preferences of the patient, whereas forensic psychologists can be said to advocate for the data instead of the person. This principle can be easily violated in assessing childhood trauma victims, who have suffered in their past and thereby elicit, within the evaluator, protective and empathetic identifications. Parents who accompany children for their appointments may ask for advice or information, more easily creating in the evaluator blurred boundaries of roles. In these situations, the writer does not believe it is ethical to withhold potentially helpful information, but imparting information may be more suitably accomplished by directing the parents to appropriate resources.

Situational Factors Affecting Trauma Evaluation

Those working with children often note the potentially significant effects that interviews or other procedures can exert on the child. Weissman (1990) noted that protracted litigation itself may have effects on litigants, referring to this effect as "jurisogenic" conditions. Applying this concept, the writer frequently has noted that parents involved in litigation may experience altered emotional reactions that can affect their children and the child's response to the evaluation itself. Thus, evaluations should consider the potential influence of situational variables such as parental stress and the child's understanding of his or her own role as related to the goals of litigation.

Developmental Factors and Personality

The failure to adequately factor into an assessment developmental knowledge of a child's level of language and cognition can result in excluding important information. Communicating in terms understandable to children and eliciting responses that can be reliably interpreted are essential elements of any child assessment. It is essential to elicit relevant symptoms and to make reliable estimates of the intensity of evaluated deficits, particularly as an element of compensable injury. In child custody assessments, formulating opinions about child protection risk can be compromised by evaluation interviewing that exceeds the child's developmental capability to comprehend what is asked or due to the child's inability to adequately express significant information. Evaluations of trauma-related issues in special education cases may be compromised by comorbid factors of developmental delays in language or communication.

Children may lack the language and cognitive competence to adequately express the nature of their experience. Special attention should be given to reports by children so that attorneys and evaluators do not prematurely accept erroneous information or reject important data that the child is unable to express. For example, in determining the magnitude of psychological distress, attorneys and evaluators frequently ask children to estimate the degree of their distress (e.g., anxiety or depression) on a 10-point scale. Such a technique may permit a useful starting point for relative comparisons, but there may be significant psychological scaling differences between number points within or among categories or time periods. What a child means in assigning a low number in one category and what verbal labels such as "a little" mean vary tremendously and can have important legal consequences. To clarify these issues, consensual validation in the interview is useful and can be achieved by examining the same issue from a variety of vantage points. For example, the use of a 10-point scale can be complemented by having the child determine "greater than" and "less than" responses in reference to important life events as well as the traumatic incident. Temporal estimates can be assessed by reporting functioning in reference to *known* events, such as the birth of a sibling or a major holiday. Similarly, asking the child to respond via visual representational aids, such as coloring in the correct number of equal-size blocks on a bar graph, allows the evaluator to examine the child's responses according to nonverbal quantification.

To differentiate affect regulation and psychological defenses related to traumatic injury from other factors, it is important for the evaluator to assess general personality/temperament functioning. For example, teacher and parent characterizations of the child as shy and withdrawn in a variety of situations predating the traumatic incident would temper interpretations that *all* of a child's withdrawal or avoidance could be ascribed to the traumatic event. Collateral sources of information and the child interview should attempt to reconstruct the child's functioning in general and his or her adaptation to stressful life events prior to the traumatic incident. The evaluator could inquire about the child's reactions to hospitalizations/medical treatments, the first day of school, marital conflicts/separations, and other noteworthy events.

DeBellis (1997) suggested that the potential impact of trauma may be associated with a delay or deficiency in developmental achievements. For example, DeBellis notes the following: The anxious toddler, age 2 or 3, may show regression in motor and verbal skills, bed-wetting, and deficiencies in ability to self-regulate emotions; the 3- to 6-year-old may exhibit psychomotor retardation or restlessness or possible guilt; between 7 and 11 years, androgens are associated with increased aggressive behaviors and inability to regulate emotions; and during adolescence, trauma may impact identity formation, separation-individuation, future goals, and intimate relationships. Pynoos et al. (1996) suggest that children be examined in the context of traumatic stress interacting with the acquisition of developmental competencies. That is, the manner in which a child shows the effects of trauma is partly dependent on what is developmentally characteristic for the child's age, recognizing that the child is continuing to evolve developmental capabilities. Considering the impact of trauma on development gives rise to issues of future difficulties that have not yet emerged and that may have significant implications for estimating damages.

Traumatic Reminders and Secondary Adversities

Assessment should consider that reminders of the trauma may trigger chronic or phasic recurrence of fears or other symptoms. Berkovitz, Wang, Pynoos, James, and Wong (1994) studied children who experienced the 1994 Northridge, California earthquake. They found that reactivity to reminders and an inability to feel calm were predictive of chronic PTSD. Assessment interviews should focus on children's reactions to family discussions, television news reports, and school subjects. Traumatic reminders need not be direct. For example, in one case involving a wildfire that destroyed an entire community, a child had to evacuate his home and described emotional reactions of fear and anticipatory dread while on his school bus going home. These reports were not provided in response to direct questions about PTSD symptoms but, rather, in the course of describing his daily experiences. After a careful interview about this experience, he revealed that he would look to the sky and see cloud formations, reminding him of how he saw smoke gradually accumulating in the sky. When he saw treetops from his school bus window, he thought of how the trees could easily catch fire. Evaluators should be careful to distinguish the above reactions from simple questions by the evaluator that cause recollections of past traumatic events. During litigation, it is not uncommon for parents, other family members, or attorneys to create recollections based on their questions. Answers to direct questions about past experience is not an intrusive recollection.

Pynoos et al. (1996) note that secondary adversities can accompany traumatic suffering of children, including medical and surgical procedures. One such example was a child burn victim who required an ongoing series of surgeries to treat skin contractures. As the child recovered from the disruption of school and family, along with the pain associated with surgery, he had to endure additional treatments. The continued surgeries, daily pain, and physical disfigurement constituted chronic secondary reminders of the traumatic event.

Melton et al. (1997) have noted that symptoms contained in *DSM* or in suggested checklists, such as one described by Wilkinson (1983), need not be present for compensation if the requisite causation element is met. Although PTSD receives the predominant attention in terms of traumatic events, grief and sorrow (Smith, 1982) and changes in self-perception or "body image" in the aftermath of physical injury have also been found to be compensable (Roberts & Wilkinson, 1983). Children's grief or sorrow can be considerable when there is loss associated with major psychological attachment figures on whom the child has depended for security and stability.

In traumatic situations, the magnitude of the threat can be used to estimate the degree of psychological distress. Some studies have examined the subjective perception of threat with children (Schwartz & Kowalski, 1991), and evaluators should always inquire into the meaning of the experience to the child being psychologically assessed. Pynoos et al. (1996) note that a contributing factor to the child's experience of external threat is the unavailability or ineffectiveness of contemplated or actual protective actions. Sparta (1982) noted children's reactions of learned helplessness following traumatically induced neurological impairment. Children with hemiplegia/quadriplegia following sudden traumatic impairment can suffer pervasive disruption to major life activities, in functions not physiologically impaired, because of generalized cognitive attributions or beliefs about their abilities. Assessment of childhood trauma should always include inquiry about the child's subjective experience, the role or expectation, and interpretations of traumatic experience.

Childhood Trauma Case Examples

In child trauma cases, the exposure to trauma can be more intense due to developmental context because children have a greater dependency on caretakers. Social supports are necessary to maintain even normal functioning in addition to representing a potential mediating factor and facilitating healthy adaptation. Secondary gain can be unconscious, shaped by the child's desire to respond to the needs of parents or other attachment figures.

The forensic evaluator should avoid rigid categorizations or preconceptions when determining how events can result in potential trauma in children. Consider the following example: An 8-year-old child and his younger brother in a rural setting wander to a grain elevator. While playing, one of the brothers falls into a large grain tower and begins to sink deeper and deeper. As the child becomes more desperate to free himself, his anxious brother is holding one of his arms, attempting to pull him free. The child's brother eventually disappears beneath the grain. After running for help, the surviving brother learns that it is too late to save the victim from asphyxiation. There is tremendous loss, which is vicariously reexperienced in the secondary reminders promoted by his mother's grief.

The interview revealed pervasive references to survivor guilt and a burden of responsibility and guilt for his failure to save his brother. Intrusive recollections were actively avoided by the child and not known to the child's mother. Initially, the child denied any intrusive recollections. Later in the evaluation, feelings of loss and fear were suggested in drawings. The content of the drawings provided an opportunity for follow-up questions, yielding elaborate explanations for specific emotional distress associated with the traumatic event, triggered by specific situations. The child's potential for developing autonomy and independence was compromised by his perception of his mother's separation anxiety if he was not in close proximity. No psychological treatment had been provided. The child experienced multiple disruptions in a variety of areas, including learning due to intrusive thoughts, increased anxiety when away from his mother or home, increasing withdrawal of effort in response to challenges previously mastered, and sad mood and/or anhedonic experience during much of his daily routine.

Consider another example: Two children are driving with their father in his truck. When it swerves to avoid debris on the highway, the truck overturns, falling into an adjacent canal filled with water. The father is unconscious and trapped, as are the two children, who remain conscious. As the water continues to fill the cab, the oldest child recognizes that she and her family are being increasingly submerged but is unable to free herself. Eventually, a passerby runs to help all the victims, discovers all submerged below water, and reaches below the surface, successfully pulling one of the children to safety. The second child, who was very young, also survived, but the father died. In this case, the mother provided tremendous support, continuity, and reassurance to the surviving children. There were many extended family members who also provided the children with a continuing sense of stability, maintaining preexisting school relationships and routines. Personality traits of the child being evaluated found her to be resilient, with excellent coping skills. The acute effects of the traumatic experience were greatly mediated by other factors. Although the traumatic events are serious in *both* examples,

the psychological outcomes could be significantly different because of a number of mediating factors.

Interviewing and Testing Issues When Evaluating Trauma Effects

Considerations When Interviewing

Sattler (1998) has proposed the following techniques as useful for interviewing children: Use appropriate intonation and do not lead; ask for examples; be open to what children tell you; rephrase children's answers for confirmation; give praise frequently for talking about their experience, but avoid *selective* reinforcement for only certain topics or responses; consider the child's age in setting the tempo and length of the interview; and use simple questions and, where appropriate, concrete referents. A concrete referent can be line drawings depicting emotional expressions on faces to create affect labels or concrete representations of the strength of the child's psychological experience.

Sattler (1998) has also suggested avoiding yes-no questions unless a specific fact is being verified. Questions should avoid compound elements within the same question, in which the child is confronted with two persons or situations at once. The child may be confused and interpret the question in a manner completely different from that intended, or respond to selective elements in a manner that is not clearly understood by the interviewer.

When conducting interviews, the evaluator should be careful not to offer suggestions, distort the meaning of child communications, or follow misleading avenues of questioning due to the examiner's prior expectancies. Possible contamination in a trauma assessment could result from an evaluator's starting the evaluation by asking the child questions with specific content reflecting the *DSM* criteria. Instead, the examiner might begin asking open-ended questions that elicit the child's descriptions. This is especially important when working with preschool children, who may be deferential to older/authority figures. Additionally, because recall may be a function of a malleable and reconstructive process subject to various contaminating influences, the interviewer may wish to inquire about how many prior occasions the child was interviewed and under what conditions.

An interesting analogy may be drawn to techniques used by a recognized sketch artist who consults with the FBI and other law enforcement agencies (Boylan, 2000). The artist recognized the potential contamination caused by conventional police techniques of showing children photos and asking them multiple questions about a criminal suspect before the children have had an opportunity to *spontaneously* report their own experiences in their own words and at their own pace. Interviewing children should begin by establishing rapport. When the child is relaxed and talking, the interviewer carefully introduces selected elements. Only after a thorough reconstruction of the child's account does the interviewer ask specific confirmatory questions. Similarly, when conducting trauma interviews, the mental health professional must be alert to such effects. Ceci and Bruck (1995) have described various potential examiner effects on children interviewed in the context of child sexual abuse investigation. Such cautions are relevant to trauma assessments.

Other commentators have addressed similar issues in the forensic context (e.g., Faust, Ziskin, & Hiers, 1991), recognizing that examinee responses may be affected by the characteristics or behavior of the examiner.

Ware (1998) noted that direct observation is an effective complement to parent and/or self-report. When observing the child in various settings, the evaluator should consider the timing of the observation in relation to when the trauma occurred. There are a number of structured and semistructured tools for assessment, ranging from generalized behavior to specific quantification within particular populations. The examiner's choice of instrument should be guided by the findings that emerge as the evaluation proceeds.

Considerations When Conducting Psychological Testing

When using psychological tests, it is important to recognize that most were developed for traditional psychotherapeutic needs rather than for forensic evaluation of specific traumatic effects. Therefore, caution must be exercised in interpreting the results from such instruments. Briere (1997) noted that results obtained on traditional tests can be misinterpreted by confusing intrusive recollections caused by PTSD with hallucinations or obsessions, dissociative avoidance related to trauma with fragmented thinking, or hypervigilance with paranoid processes. Checklists or structured interviews that specifically parallel posttraumatic symptomatology can provide an opportunity to more precisely differentiate the causes of various symptoms.

Trauma effects can vary in frequency of symptoms and their respective intensity and duration. Therefore, the evaluator should be open to consider the broadest range of possible effects. Because the type of psychological testing instrument used can produce different information about the same child, the evaluator should consider a range of different types of assessment techniques or instruments. Rating scales vary in their format and type of information revealed. Some scales ask whether a symptom is present, the degree to which it is experienced by the child, and the frequency and/or intensity

with which it is experienced. Nader (1997) noted that sometimes just asking about symptoms can produce them temporarily in a traumatized child, and that specific symptoms may occur with a relatively healthy child.

Kuehnle (1996) noted that dissociation has been reported as a common consequence of trauma and specifically sexual abuse. (See Chapter 22 for more information regarding this topic.) Dissociation is a complex psychophysiological process, representing, on the severe end of the continuum, a significant disruption in the child's everyday life. This process needs to be differentiated from common developmental experience related to daydreaming, forgetfulness, or changes in attention (Hornstein & Putnam, 1992). Among the instruments that assess dissociation are the Child Dissociative Checklist (Putnam, 1990) and the PTSD Reaction Index (Pynoos et al., 1987).

Concordance in reporting between child and parent can provide corroboration regarding the validity of some test findings. However, some parents may not wish to recognize their child's suffering (Sternberg et al., 1993). This may depress estimates on rating scales for frequency or intensity of symptoms. Nader (1997) has noted some indications that long-term and ongoing trauma may produce greater reexperiencing and avoidance, creating more challenges for accurate assessment.

Third-Party Interviews

Information from parents, teachers, and other care providers can provide important information about the child's reactions to a traumatic event. Prior to weighing the relative importance of such information, the forensic evaluator should assess whether the third-party respondent is minimizing or otherwise distorting the impact of events. For example, one study noted that after a tornado, parents attempted to control their own anxiety by minimization or denial of the event's impact (Bloch, Silber, & Perry, 1956). In personal injury evaluations, where monetary gain or loss is possible depending on the outcome of the evaluation, respondents can perceive or report exaggerated disability.

As part of a comprehensive evaluation, parental history is sought regarding the child's family, educational, social, and health history. Educational, medical, and other professionals who have observed the child should ordinarily be included as collateral sources of information. Parents are also potential sources of important information as to the child's functioning both before and after the traumatic event.

Interview questions may begin assessing general categories of developmental functioning, including, but not limited to, questions related to the child's behavior in learning situations, social relationships, mood, academic functioning, family relationships, mastery of activities of daily living, motivation in completing tasks, and health status.

More specific questions may include symptoms described in *DSM-IV* (APA, 1994), such as sleep disturbance, diminished interest or participation in activities, deliberate attempts to avoid certain situations or thoughts, or statements suggesting a foreshortened future (e.g., not expecting a normal life span or a career). The evaluator should be alert to probe when reports suggest altered behavioral or emotional reactions representing different functioning compared to pretrauma functioning. As the interview continues, the evaluator should inquire about possible symptoms, traumatic reminders, and secondary effects. Later sections of this chapter provide references for various instruments that survey childhood reactions to trauma. (For further information on third-party interviews, see the chapter by Heilbrun and Warren in this volume.)

Interview Preparation, Phase-Related Trauma Responses, Follow-Up Clarifications

The forensic evaluator must be familiar with all known aspects of the traumatic event(s), including the sequence of events, the reported reactions of the child and/or family, and all external source of information, such as police reports, witness statements, news accounts, and other collateral sources. Forensic evaluations are typically undertaken significantly after the traumatic event has occurred, resulting in an assessment conducted considerably later in the child's reaction to the trauma. Children can make a successful adaptation to an acute traumatic response within six months. Andreasen (1985) noted that most cases of PTSD are acute, involving symptoms within hours or days of the event, and that in many of these cases, symptoms resolve without treatment. However, children may continue to experience intense psychic numbing and avoidance, which can mask psychological difficulty, and there can be a risk to underestimate the complexity of children's traumatic experiences (Pynoos et al., 1996). The *DSM-IV* (APA, 1994) notes that complete recovery occurs within three months in approximately half of the cases, whereas many other cases reflect persisting symptoms of experience of the trauma, avoidance, and hyperarousal longer than 12 months.

Following the completion of assessment instruments in the standardized fashion, a follow-up interview with the child is essential. As Nader (1997) noted, children and adolescents more accurately convey their true psychological experience when they can comfortably ask questions of a skilled interviewer, one who can probe when necessary while avoiding leading questions. Because of age-related variables in comprehension and expression, possible limitation in item construction, and possible avoidance features of posttraumatic response, follow-up validation is important. For example, a 9-year-old child who survived a sniper shooting that killed her sibling and wounded her mother reported on the Children's Depression Inventory (Kovacs, 1992), "I'm tired all the time." This raised questions about possible lethargy, anhedonia, and withdrawal from activities of daily living. Subsequent interviews revealed that her answer was actually quite benign, as the child explained that in the morning she "likes to sleep in all the time." Particularly with younger children, adults can frequently infer meanings that are not accurate reflections of the child's experience. In the same protocol, the child denied mood disturbance, but a follow-up interview revealed dysphoric mood, intrusive recollections of the event, and an acute grief reaction that immediately followed the trauma and her mother's bouts of depression associated with the trauma.

A follow-up interview is also important because secondary trauma can cause effects that would not be predicted from a logical understanding of the traumatic event itself. For example, a child of 2 years of age at the time of a sniper shooting would not likely be able to fully comprehend the seriousness of the presence of emergency response vehicles, smoke accumulating in the residence complex, or fearful expectations about future threats. However, the child's dependence on the quality of attachment with her primary caregiver could lead to significant disruption because of the adverse impact on the child's mother. The child's vicarious identification with the mother's fears and depression or the mother's withdrawal behavior can secondarily produce significant impact on the child's functioning.

Arrangements with Legal Representatives and Informed Consent from Guardians

Evaluators should explain to the minor's legal guardian, in terms that are understandable and noncoercive, what their role will be. A separate explanation should also be provided to the minor in developmentally appropriate terms. The agreement should make clear to the legal guardian that you are assessing the child for purposes of formulating general psychological opinions and, to the extent possible, *specific* psychological opinions related to the child's psychological functioning relative to the legal case. Because all states have some form of legally mandated child-abuse reporting laws, the evaluator should inform the appropriate parties about these responsibilities. The possibility of child abuse is a potentially significant factor in differentiating whether symptoms preexisted traumatic events.

A letter of engagement from the attorney or court that retained the expert should memorialize his or her role prior to assessment. This letter should include fees and how they are to be paid and clearly state that a contingency agreement does not exist. Any payment contingency creates an actual or perceived contamination influence on the objectivity of the evaluator's opinions and is specifically prohibited in the "Specialty Guidelines for Forensic Psychologists" (Committee on Ethical Guidelines for Forensic Psychologists, 1991). Evaluators should explain who retained them, that they may be communicating directly to the retaining party any information they may gather or opinion they may form, and that interpretation and opinion may be used in the case.

Evaluators may be asked to audiorecord the session, particularly during personal-injury-related cases. Some evaluators decline participation of an evaluation under such conditions because it is believed to violate standardized assessment protocol. Regarding audiotaping the session, frequently, one machine records for the requesting party, and another machine simultaneously records for the examiner/retaining party. In general, this writer does not consent to requests to videorecord, as he considers it too intrusive to the evaluation process when compared to an audiorecording that can preserve an accurate record of the examination.

The expert may be asked to allow legal counsel to be present during the examination. This writer will not agree to conducting an evaluation under this condition, as it violates the standardized nature of the assessment process, with potential effects on subject and/or examiner. Some states have legal cases supporting the exclusion of legal counsel during psychological evaluation.

Ragge v. MCA (1995) resulted in a court ruling that the plaintiff's attorney was not entitled to disclosure of the specific psychological tests that would be used in the evaluation and declined to allow a third-party observer to be present during the psychological examination. In evaluations of trauma with children, it is common to request from parents behavior rating forms, such as the Achenbach Child Behavior Checklist (Achenbach, 1992). Prior release of such forms to parents and legal representative(s), outside of the evaluator's office, results in a situation whereby the evaluator does not know the conditions under which the forms were discussed and potentially influenced by others.

If the expert was retained by a defense attorney involving a personal injury matter, the family's lawyer frequently will prohibit the parent from being drawn into the evaluation process in any way. If this cannot be resolved by the evaluator, it should be referred to the attorneys for resolution. If the parent does not provide information, evaluators should note in the report possible limitations of the findings.

Sample Evaluation Protocol

Identifying Information and Reason for Referral

The evaluator should describe who was seen and whether they were seen individually and/or conjointly. Report how many sessions occurred and the total amount of time spent with each person. Report who retained the expert and for what purpose. Describe the nature and date of the legal event and/or alleged psychological injury. Describe the fact pattern that gave rise to the cause of action, describing the events and reactions of the child and the child's family. Report whether the evaluation was recorded and, if so, by whom.

Personal, Family, Educational, and Medical History

The evaluator should describe the child's educational experience, including reports of teacher concerns and student successes, special education assessments, and any type of educational remediation. Describe the child's family history, including household composition, divorce and custody arrangements, and conflicts associated with child custody. Characterize family relationships, including any problems that required police responses, social service interventions, or relocations, and special health problems of family members. Report the developmental history of the child, including any specific delays, birth complications, including causes of anoxia/hypoxia, and any history of accidents/injuries. For older children and adolescents, review any past alcohol or drug use. Report health status and the reasons for past medication. Inquire about possible mental health treatment or school counseling, and report the results of the review of records of these interventions and interviewees of providers or parents.

Review of Records and Other Data Sources

List *all* sources of information reviewed in formulating opinions, including testing previously administered. List all evaluation procedures, including all psychometric instruments, clinical interviews, mental status examinations, developmental history, and observations of the child during conjoint meetings.

Interviewing Protocol

Create the proper interview environment. Build rapport by showing interest, being attentive, offering encouragement and compliments when appropriate, encouraging spontaneous discussion, and inviting discussions presumed to be nonthreatening and enjoyable to the child. Inquire about general interests and past experiences. During the interview, invite projective responses for which there are no clear answers, such as: "What do want to be when you grow up?"; "Tell me about your favorite books, movies, or TV programs"; "Tell me about your happiest memory"; "What was so special about it?"; "If you had three wishes, what would you wish for? Why?" The forensic evaluator should be alert to responses in the context of the psycholegal questions related to trauma. For example, what the child wants to be when he or she becomes an adult may reveal whether the child has a foreshortened sense of the future or has specific fears, or may suggest whether the child has positive expectations for the future.

When the evaluator is ready to transition to more formal questioning, the content of the forensic interview can include the following.

General Psychological Functioning. This includes major developmental/psychological areas of functioning. Inquire about family and other interpersonal relationships and academic and behavioral functioning in school. Examine activities of daily living, but with the perspective of what is known from the trauma literature. Examples to consider when reviewing the child's general experience include disturbed sleep and the time course for its existence, possible acting or feeling as if the traumatic event were recurring, and intrusive recollections of the traumatic event. When questioning the child about everyday experience or past history, the evaluator should be alert to probe areas suggesting altered emotional responses during the interview. Having the benefit of prior records review or interview data from third parties, the evaluator can identify potential areas of differential functioning compared to pretrauma functioning. It is not uncommon to begin questioning about general experience and then refocus inquiry in specific areas of trauma-related symptoms.

Specific Interview about the Legal Cause of Action. This includes questions about precipitating events and the child's narrative of what occurred. The child should be questioned about his or her reactions to reported events as well as reactions to potential intervening factors or events that may have exaggerated or moderated the child's reaction. The evaluator should ask the child to describe his or her functioning over time, up to the time of evaluation. Question subjective symptoms, including their onset, frequency, and intensity, and whether the child reports feeling different in any way since the legally relevant event. Interview the parents for their observations and impressions about these areas.

Medical/Health History. This should include inquiries about all medications that are being taken and for what purpose, emergency room consultations, and consultations with physicians or other health care professionals. The child's reports should be compared to those of the parent and the medical record. Inconsistencies should be investigated for possible distortions by the child and/or parent or possible signs of avoidance or inability to recall important aspects of the trauma.

Family History. Ask the child and the family about the trauma's impact on various family members. Inquire about possible preexisting/coexisting sources of trauma, including questions designed to rule out all forms of prior child abuse, exposure to domestic violence, alcohol/drug abuse in the child's environment, divorce conflicts, and frequent dislocations of home and school environments. In some cases, collateral sources of information may have to be interviewed about these factors.

Interviews Specific to Traumatic Events

The Diagnostic Interview Schedule for Children, Version IV, PTSD Subscale. The highly structured Diagnostic Interview Schedule for Children (Shaffer, Fisher, Lucas, Dulcan, & Schwab-Stone, 2000) has been in development since 1979, and the current version is based on the *DSM-IV*. The schedule also includes a PTSD subscale. Separate questionnaires are used for children ages 6 to 12 and for adolescents ages 13 to 17. The interview is available in English and Spanish and can be used by nonprofessionals. This interview schedule will guide the evaluator asking questions sufficient to address the nature of the traumatic experience and *DSM-IV* symptomatology including reexperiencing symptoms, numbing/avoidance, and hyperarousal.

Mental Status Exam. The evaluator may perform a clinical assessment of the child according to the traditional criteria of a mental status exam, enabling the evaluator to make comparisons of the child with other children previously evaluated. Mental status examination criteria may focus on areas of functioning found in the literature on childhood trauma. Assessment of orientation and alertness could include questions regarding physiological reactivity to internal cues that resemble or symbolize an aspect of the traumatic event.

When assessing the child's range of emotional expression and predominant mood, the evaluator should note altered states of emotional functioning, intense psychological distress, the presence of a foreshortened future, and diminished interests. In assessing the child's thinking process, the evaluator may include questions about possible anticipatory fears for future events and anxious beliefs related to the traumatic event. The child's responses should be analyzed for possible perceptual distortions associated with sensory cues and other events. An assessment of the child's thought content may include questions about intrusive thoughts and persistent reexperience of the traumatic event.

Evaluation of cognition may include questions about alterations of attention and concentration. The evaluator should inquire about possible hypervigilance. Questions about the child's insight and judgment may include the child's understanding of the relationship between the traumatic event and present functioning. Motor functioning, including exaggerated startle response, hyperactivity, and psychomotor retardation should be assessed and differentiated from possible preexisting disorders, such as ADHD.

Psychological Testing

The evaluator may administer a broad battery of testing sufficient to assess the general emotional, cognitive, and educational functioning of the child, combined with specific interview instruments or techniques related to childhood trauma. Standardized testing for cognitive/neuropsychological functioning may include a full intelligence test battery. Assessment of personality traits, emotional states, withdrawal tendencies, reports of somatic symptoms, disturbances of mood, and interpersonal conflicts can be evaluated with a variety of standardized measures, some of which are described later in this chapter. Standardized testing instruments using developmental norms assist the evaluator in making comparisons among different test scores with the same child. This can potentially reveal inconsistencies in reporting, useful for determining possible exaggeration or minimization of symptoms. Standardized measures of aptitude and achievement could potentially reveal significant decrements in functioning compared to pretrauma functioning. The evaluator should note differential responsiveness to direct versus indirect questioning of trauma so that the interview process can be adjusted to comport with the child's ability to proceed.

Traditional Clinical and Specific Trauma Assessment Techniques and Instruments

The forensic evaluator may consider using the traditional clinical instruments described below, recognizing that those developed for traditional clinical purposes may suffer considerably in accurately generalizing results to addressing psycholegal issues. Because there are severe limitations in methodology in assessing emotional states in young children, the following traditional clinical procedures may be

considered for purposes of generating hypotheses subject to corroboration. Additionally, as children may experience a wide range of reactions that are not directly PTSD-related, it is important to use instruments that can assess a broad spectrum of symptoms (Ruggiero, Morris, & Scotti, 2001). Information generated from such instruments may lead the examiner to inquire in areas that may not have been apparent. Evaluators should guard against formulating unsupported opinions, which can be helped by examining results in the context of standardized protocols reflecting the current research about traumatic effects in children.

Traditional Clinical Assessment Techniques and Instruments

The Children's Depression Inventory.   For use with children between 7 and 17 years of age, the Children's Depression Inventory (Kovacs, 1992) quantifies a range of depressive symptoms, including disturbed mood, hedonic capacity, vegetative functions, self-evaluation, and interpersonal behaviors. Items from this instrument can help identify possible intrusive ideation and attentional inconsistencies, isolating or withdrawing behaviors as possible defenses against unresolved psychic trauma. Body image distortions, which can be particularly important in cases involving actual or feared disfigurement, such as from fire/burns, physical trauma secondary to motor vehicle accident, dog bite attacks, and physical assaults, can be revealed on items pertaining to self-image and self-esteem.

The Draw-a-Person and Kinetic Family Drawing Techniques.   Although among the weakest in terms of empirical validation, these instruments, when used in a limited fashion, can facilitate communication and hypotheses about the child's psychological experience (Pihl & Nimrod, 1976). The examiner should recognize that such techniques do *not* meet definitions of formal tests with manuals describing standardized procedures, reliability/validity studies, and descriptions of their development in reference to the population being studied. However, when used in a child assessment as a basis for generating hypotheses or facilitating the child's expression of past experiences or psychological states, the use of drawings can be an intrinsically rewarding opportunity for the child to overcome avoidant defenses. Systematic scoring techniques have been developed for childhood cancer victims as one example of preserving the intrinsic interest by children for drawing while maintaining methodological standardization for administration and interpretation (Spinetta, McLaren, Fox, & Sparta, 1981).

Sentence Completion Techniques. These techniques do not qualify as tests, but can facilitate expression, generating associations within the child about trauma-related experience. Follow-up interview concerning the child's responses can yield important information not previously disclosed during any other portion of the evaluation, or can provide additional information about subjects reported at another time.

Thematic Apperception Test/Children's Apperception Test and Roberts Apperception Test. The child's story constructions can help reveal the child's perceptions of the environment, defense mechanisms for resolving conflicts, predominant moods, and relationships with others. Using the Thematic/Children's Apperception Test (Bellak, 1993) or Roberts Apperception Test (McArthur & Roberts, 1990), children who have experienced traumatic effects may elaborate on threats of harm, hypervigilance, or avoidance toward particular elements of the traumatic event. In the context of such discussions, where the secondary gain for exaggerating symptoms is less obvious, such data can provide a corroborating source of evaluation findings.

Behavior Rating Scales. These scales can be completed by teachers and parents, providing important data complementing self-reports by the child or collateral information contributed by sources independent of litigation. The Child Behavior Checklist (Achenbach, 1992) includes scales of attentional difficulties, depression/anxiety, and specific items within each scale potentially relevant to the assessment of trauma effects. Information can be immediately scanned for significant items on the day of the child's examination. Consistency among items endorsed by parents and problem areas elicited from the child during the forensic interview provides convergent validity or suggestions for over/underreporting. Assessment of a broad spectrum of developmental functioning is helpful for examining the potential presence of comorbid or preexisting problems. Teachers can provide valuable information in helping to establish diagnoses regarding the spectrum of childhood psychopathology. Parents can report changes in behaviors in the home and with peers (Reich & Earls, 1987). Ratings of children should consider source variance (consisting of rater biases), setting variances (consisting of differences in the child's functioning by environment), and temporal variance (referring to changes in behavior over time; Martin, Hooper, & Snow, 1986).

The Children's Attributions and Perceptions Scale. This brief 18-item scale was designed to measure children's attributions and perceptions of self in a sexual abuse context (Mannarino, Cohen, & Berman, 1994). This scale includes questions assessing feeling different from peers, reduced interpersonal trust, and personal attributions for negative events. In the context of trauma assessment, information from this scale may yield information about guilt and helplessness following sudden traumatic experience or sexual abuse. Two of the subscales were reported to correspond to the stigmatization and betrayal factors described by Finkelhor (1987).

Specific Trauma Assessment Techniques and Instruments

The instruments described below more closely follow the theory and empirical research regarding the trauma literature related to children. Many of the instruments are focused on PTSD or other trauma-related conditions and should be considered as part of a comprehensive assessment of trauma. Nader (1997) provides excellent critiques on reliability, validity, training, and issues related to the use of these scales.

The Trauma Symptom Checklist for Children. Briere's (1996) instrument is one of the most psychometrically developed in terms of item relevance and empirical investigation. It is a self-report measure of posttraumatic stress and related psychological symptomatology, for use with children between 8 and 16 years of age. Because the child provides direct responses to the items, it is an excellent complement to rating data completed by parents or teachers. The range of posttraumatic symptomatology is broad, including items concerning sexual victimization. Two validity scales are included along with six clinical scales. After the standardized completion of the instrument, the evaluator can interview the child about items that contain significant answers. This posttest interviewing can provide important clarification regarding the underlying psychological experience of the child, often including essential clarifications related to proximate cause, secondary traumatic effects and comorbid or premorbid factors. Promising preliminary psychometric support has been established for a version of the instrument for children younger than 8 years (Briere et al., 2000).

The Clinician-Administered PTSD Scale for Children. Developed by Nader, Kriegler, Blake, and Pynoos (1994), this instrument has more direct relevance to forensic assessment as compared to more traditional assessment tools. Frequency and intensity of PTSD symptoms are evaluated, as well as their impacts on social functioning. Symptoms include those reported in *DSM-IV* and from the literature concerning childhood trauma. This is a relatively new instrument without extensive validity or reliability data.

The Child Dissociative Checklist. This instrument (Putnam, 1990; Putnam & Peterson, 1994) is completed by someone familiar with the child's functioning during the previous 12-month period. It is short and can be completed in a brief amount of time. The items were derived from professional experience with dissociative disorders, including amnesia, rapid shifts in demeanor, access to information, ability and age-appropriateness of behavior, spontaneous trance states, alteration in identity, aggressive or sexual behavior, and hallucinations. Because of the brevity of the instrument, it is possible to easily perform repeated assessments during different times and circumstances in the child's life, although this often is not possible in forensic assessment.

The Child Posttraumatic Stress Reaction Index. This 20-item scale developed by Frederick, Pynoos, and Nader (1992) considers the main symptoms of *DSM-IV,* including questions related to reexperiencing trauma, numbing/avoidance, and physiological arousal. Items are scored on a 5-point Likert scale ranging from "none" to "most of the time." Realmuto et al. (1992) note some inconsistency between the items on the scale and symptoms listed in the *DSM-III-R* and *DSM-IV,* including some items asked more than once and some symptoms not addressed by the scale. In using this scale and others related to forensic assessment of trauma, it is particularly important to conduct posttesting interviews about symptom duration, frequency, and intensity (Nader, 1997).

The Children's Impact of Traumatic Events Scale. First developed by Wolfe, Wolfe, Gentile, and Larose (1986), the scale was revised based on factor analysis of the original 54-item instrument (Wolfe & Gentile, 1991). Dimensions include PTSD (intrusive thoughts, avoidance, hyperarousal, and sexual anxiety); social reactions (negative reactions from others and social support); abuse attributions (self-blame/guilt, empowerment, vulnerability, and dangerous world); and eroticism (particularly relevant to trauma caused by sexual abuse). The scale can be used for noninterpersonal types of traumatic experiences as well as interpersonal trauma resulting from sexual abuse. The sexual anxiety scale was patterned after the traumagenic factors described by Finkelhor and Browne (1985), consisting of helplessness, stigmatization, betrayal, and traumatic sexualization.

Child Rating Scales of Exposure to Interpersonal Abuse. Nader (1997) reports that the Child Rating Scales of Exposure to Interpersonal Abuse (Praver, 1994) assesses both the frequency and severity of children's exposure to interpersonal abuse. This instrument can be used for children 6 to 11 years of age. A version of this instrument, the Angie/Andy Child Rating Scale (Praver, Pelcovitz, & DiGiuseppe, 1994), uses an illustrated format based on cartoon characters. The child is asked whether a character has been exposed to sexual abuse, physical abuse, witnessing family violence, and community violence. An earlier scale by Richters and Martinez (1990), called Things I Have Seen and Heard, is described as a structured interview for assessing young children's violence exposure and also uses a cartoon character. These scales may be useful in trauma assessment for young and/or developmentally delayed children who have experienced interpersonal forms of trauma.

When Bad Things Happen Scale. Similar to the Trauma Symptom Checklist for Children, this scale (Fletcher, 1991) is completed by the child. The scale can be used for children age 8 and older and assesses PTSD symptoms and other trauma-related items. An additional scale, Dimensions of Stressful Events, measures trauma-exposure variables and results. Examples of what is assessed include number of traumas and whether there is a sense of stigmatization. This scale and many others focused on trauma assessment are continually being revised and undergoing psychometric validation.

The Child's Reaction to Traumatic Events Scale. Jones's (1994) 15-item self-report measure assesses the child's reactions to stressful events. Item content focuses on *DSM* criteria of PTSD and from reported reactions to people following traumatic experiences using a 4-point rating scale from "not at all" to "often." Particular attention is given to items related to intrusions and avoidance.

March (1999) provided an excellent review of assessment instruments related to childhood trauma. Additional instruments related to PTSD criteria include the Kiddie Post-Traumatic Symptomatology Scale (March & Amaya-Jackson, 1999, as cited in March, 1999) and the Children's PTSD Inventory (Saigh, 1997).

As Ruggiero et al. (2001) note, trauma researchers typically distinguish among various distinct events. For example, sexual abuse represents a distinct form of interpersonal violence. Consistent with Grisso's (1986) recommendations, assessment instruments used for forensic purposes should match the psycholegal dimensions of behavior, attitude, and ability. The Trauma Symptom Checklist for Children (Briere, 1996) contains items related to sexual abuse in a separate subscale. The Child Sexual Behavior Inventory (Freidrich, 1997) assesses a wide variety of sexual behaviors by children and provides normative behavior for abused and nonabused child populations. It provides a greater amount of psychometric information regarding its development and validation relative to many PTSD surveys. The Child Rating Scales of Exposure to Interpersonal Violence (Praver, 1994) are emerging measures concerned with children's exposure to interpersonal violence, including frequency and severity. Enns et al. (1988) reported a number of trauma-related assessment techniques in connection with adults who may have experienced sexual abuse as children. Kuehnle (1996) provides an excellent review of assessment techniques of child sexual abuse (see also the chapter by Kuehnle in this volume). Strategies for assessment should include measures reflecting the unique nature of each type of trauma, not simply generalized PTSD responses.

SUMMARY

Concerns about violence underscore the need for accurate assessment of how traumatic events affect children. The increased attention in the trauma literature improves the ability of experts to provide effective treatment and answer forensic questions.

Legally contested issues involving children may include a variety of traumatic events. Forensic referrals differ in purpose, including, but not limited to, those associated with personal injury litigation, child abuse cases, child custody conflicts (including allegations of child abuse or domestic violence), special education eligibility, and delinquency cases in which PTSD may be relevant to the offense or to the potential for rehabilitation. Each type of referral demands knowledge of the specifically relevant law of the applicable jurisdiction. Forensic evaluation of trauma with children involves developmentally appropriate and empirically supported methods, and must focus on the relevant psycholegal questions. Evaluations that are objectively performed use multimodal traditional clinical and forensic methods, and integrate specialized knowledge about trauma and its effects can provide the trier of fact with valuable information necessary to a verdict.

As Melton et al. (1997) note, the ultimate practical usefulness of a forensic report, or testimony based on that report, is a persuasive message to the referral source about the findings and opinions resulting from the evaluation. To facilitate the understanding of legal consumers, several areas are worthy of further investigation. Forensic evaluations of young children are particularly challenging because of the limitations in methodology in assessing the potentially broad range of emotional states associated with childhood trauma. Traditional assessment methods may be used to generate hypotheses subject to other validation, but such instruments can have serious limitations.

One reason forensic assessment instruments are usually superior to traditional forms of techniques in forensic proceedings is that they more directly sample and measure the specific legal application appropriate to the referral. When the inferential components between assessment procedure and forensic conclusion are reduced, the forensic evaluator has a better chance of more accurately addressing the domain of psycholegal issues and to clearly communicate with the legal consumers of trauma evaluations. Future specialized assessment methods, more sensitive and specific to trauma issues, will address Briere's (1997) cautions about the risks of misinterpretation based on the use of *only* traditional clinical assessment methods.

For example, in a personal injury case involving a child burn victim, assessment could go beyond questions that mirror the PTSD diagnostic criteria. Questions regarding the nature and extent of pain, whether there is anticipatory fear for repeated medical procedures or surgery, and psychological identity issues resulting from disfigurement may yield important data not elicited by other PTSD or dissociation instruments. The potential identification of these issues may increase the likelihood for determining secondary adversities not typically associated with the traumatic event. Each type of childhood trauma represents a relatively unique and important area deserving specialized investigation. It may be particularly difficult for the forensic evaluator to appropriately transpose broad categories of PTSD symptomatology into relevant psychological experience among the many different types of childhood trauma.

Given the developmental factors that make accurate understanding of a child's psychological experience sometimes difficult, more specialized assessment methods may make it easier for children to communicate their experience. The PTSD symptom of avoidance against revealing traumatic experience emphasizes the need for developmentally sensitive and specialized assessment. The literature has described problems that arise when questioning children. These difficulties may be due to the child's perception of the interviewer, the wording of questions, and the absence of concrete referents in eliciting or cross-validating answers. The development of solidly conceptualized and rigorously validated instruments specific to each type of trauma experience would greatly enhance forensic assessment conclusions.

REFERENCES

Achenbach, T. M. (1992). *Manual for the Child Behavior Checklist/2–3 and 1992 profile.* Burlington: University of Vermont, Department of Psychiatry.

American Academy of Child and Adolescent Psychiatry. (1998). Practice parameters for the assessment and treatment of children and adolescents with posttraumatic stress disorder. *Journal of the American Academy of Child and Adolescent Psychiatry, 37,* 4S–26S.

American Psychiatric Association. (1994). *Diagnostic and statistical manual of mental disorders* (4th ed.). Washington, DC: Author.

American Psychiatric Association. (1999). *Public information online, post-traumatic stress disorder.* (Available from 1400 K Street, N.W. Washington, DC; www.psych.org)

Andreasen, N. C. (1985). Posttraumatic stress disorder. In H. Kaplan & B. Sadock (Eds.), *Comprehensive textbook of psychiatry/IV.* Baltimore: Williams & Wilkins.

Baker, A. (1990). The psychological impact of the Intifada on Palestinian children in the occupied West Bank and Gaza: An exploratory study. *American Journal of Orthopsychiatry, 60,* 496–505.

Bellak, L. (1993). *The T.A.T., & C.A.T., & S.A.T. in clinical use* (5th ed.). Needham Heights, MA: Allyn & Bacon.

Bellak, L., & Bellak, S. (1949). *Children's Apperception Test.* Larchmont, NY: C.P.S.

Berkovitz, I. H., Wang, A., Pynoos, R., James, Q., & Wong, M. (1994, October). *Los Angeles earthquake, 1994: School district reduction of trauma effects.* Symposium presented at the annual meeting of the American Academy of Child and Adolescent Psychiatry, New York.

Berliner, L. (1997). Intervention with children who experience trauma. In D. Cicchetti & S. Toth (Eds.), *Developmental perspectives on trauma: Theory, research and intervention.* Rochester, NY: University of Rochester Press.

Bloch, D., Silber, E., & Perry, S. (1956). Some factors in the emotional reaction of children to disaster. *American Journal of Psychiatry, 113,* 416–422.

Boney-McCoy, S., & Finklehor, D. (1995). Psychosocial sequelae of violent victimization in a national youth sample. *Journal of Consulting and Clinical Psychology, 63,* 726–736.

Boylan, J. (2000). *Portraits of guilt: The woman who profiles the faces of America's deadliest criminals.* New York: Pocket Books.

Briere, J. (1996). *Trauma symptom checklist for children: Professional manual.* Odessa, FL: Psychological Assessment Resources.

Briere, J. (1997). *Psychological assessment of adult posttraumatic states.* Washington, DC: American Psychological Association.

Briere, J., Johnson, K., Damon, L., Bissada, A., Crouch, J., Gil, E., et al. (2000, January). *The Trauma Symptom Checklist for Young Children: Reliability and predictive data from a multi-site study.* Paper presented at the San Diego Conference on Responding to Maltreatment, San Diego, CA.

Browne, A., & Finklehor, D. (1986). Impact of child sexual abuse: A review of the research. *Psychological Bulletin, 99,* 66–77.

Ceci, S. J., & Bruck, M. (1995). *Jeopardy in the courtroom: A scientific analysis of children's testimony.* Washington, DC: American Psychological Association.

Committee on Ethical Guidelines for Forensic Psychologists. (1991). Specialty guidelines for forensic psychologists. *Law and Human Behavior, 15,* 655–665.

Crandall, V., Crandall, V., & Katkovsky, W. (1965). A children's social desirability questionnaire. *Journal of Consulting Psychology, 29,* 27–36.

DeBellis, M. D. (1997). Posttraumatic stress disorder and acute stress disorder. In R. T. Ammerman & M. Hersen (Eds.), *Handbook of prevention and treatment with children and adolescents: Intervention in the real world context.* New York: Guilford Press.

DeBellis, M. D., & Putnam, F. W. (1994). The psychobiology of childhood maltreatment. *Child and Adolescent Clinics of North America, 3,* 663–677.

Enns, C. Z., Courtois, C. A., Lese, K. P., Campbell, J., Gottlieb, M. C., Gilbert, M. S., et al. (1988). Working with adults who may have experienced childhood abuse. *Professional Psychology: Research and Practice, 29*(3), 245–256.

Evans, J., Briere, J., Boggiano, A., & Barrett, M. (1994, January). *Reliability and validity of the Trauma Symptom Checklist for children in a normal sample.* Paper presented at the San Diego Conference on Responding to Maltreatment, San Diego, CA.

Famularo, R. A., Kinscherff, R. T., & Fenton, T. (1990). Symptom differences in acute and chronic presentation of childhood posttraumatic stress disorder. *Child Abuse and Neglect, 14,* 439–444.

Faust, D., Ziskin, J., & Hiers, J. B. (1991). *Brain damage claims: Coping with neurological evidence.* Los Angeles: Law and Psychology Press.

Federal Rule of Evidence, Section 702, 28 U.S.C. 539–605 (1976).

Finkelhor, D. (1987). The trauma of sexual abuse: Two models. *Journal of Interpersonal Violence, 2,* 348–366.

Finkelhor, D., & Browne, A. (1985). The traumatic impact of child sexual abuse: A conceptualization. *American Journal of Orthopsychiatry, 55,* 530–541.

Fletcher, K. (1991). *When Bad Things Happen Scale.* (Available from the author, University of Massachusetts Medical Center, Dept. of Psychiatry, 55 Lake Ave. North, Worcester, MA 01655)

Frederick, C., Pynoos, R., & Nader, K. (1992). *Childhood PTSD Reaction Index.* (Available from Frederick and Pynoos, 760 Westwood Plaza, Los Angeles, CA 90024)

Freeman, L. Mokros, H., & Poznanski, E. (1993). Violent events reported by normal school-aged children: Characteristics and depression correlates. *Journal of the American Academy of Child and Adolescent Psychiatry, 32,* 419–423.

Freidrich, W. N. (1997). *The Child Sexual-Behavior Inventory manual* [Mayo Clinic Foundation]. Odessa, FL: Psychological Assessment Resources.

Freidrich, W. N., Grambsch, P., Damon, L., Hewitt, S., Koverola, C., Lang, R., et al. (1992). Child Sexual Behavior Inventory: Normative and clinical comparisons. *Psychological Assessment, 4,* 303–311.

Goldstein, A. M., & Goldstein, N. E. (in press). Relevance of childhood trauma and childhood developmental factors to juvenile and adult death penalty cases. In S. N. Sparta & G. P. Koocher (Eds.), *Forensic assessment of children and adolescents: Issues and applications.* New York: Oxford University Press.

Green, B. L., Korol, M., Grace, M. C., Vary, M. G., Leonard, A. C., Glesser, G. C., et al. (1991). Children and disaster: Age, gender, and parental effects on PTSD symptoms. *Journal of the American Academy of Child and Adolescent Psychiatry, 30,* 945–951.

Greenberg, S. A., & Shuman, D. W. (1997). Irreconcilable conflict between therapeutic and forensic roles. *Professional Psychology: Research and Practice, 28,* 50–57.

Grisso, T. (1986). *Evaluating competencies: Forensic assessments and instruments.* New York: Plenum Press.

Hornstein, N. L., & Putnam, F. W. (1992). Clinical phenomenology of child and adolescent dissociative disorders. *Journal of the American Academy of Child and Adolescent Psychiatry, 31,* 1077–1085.

Jaffe, P. G. (1995). Children of domestic violence: Special challenges in child custody and visitation dispute resolution. In J. Carter, B. Hart, & C. Hostler (Eds.), *Domestic violence and children: Resolving custody and visitation disputes, a national judicial curriculum* (pp. 19–30). San Francisco: Family Violence Prevention Fund.

Jaffe, P. G., Wolfe, D. A., & Wilson, S. K. (1990). *Children of battered women.* Newbury Park, CA: Sage.

Jones, R. T. (1994). *Child's Reaction to Traumatic Events Scale (CRTES): A self report traumatic stress measure.* (Available from the author, Dept. of Psychology, Virginia Polytechnic Institute and State University, 4102 Derring Hall, Blacksburg, VA 24060)

Kashani, J. H., Daniel, A. E., Dandoy, A. C., & Holcomb, W. R. (1992). Family violence: Impact on the child. *Journal of the American Academy of Child and Adolescent Psychiatry, 31,* 181–189.

Kiser, L. J., Heston, J., Millsap, P. A., & Pruitt, D. (1991). Physical and sexual abuse in childhood: Relationship with posttraumatic stress disorder. *Journal of the American Academy of Child and Adolescent Psychiatry, 30,* 776–783.

Kolko, D. J., Moser, J. T., & Weldy, S. R. (1988). Behavioral/emotional indications of sexual abuse in child psychiatric inpatients: A controlled comparison with physical abuse. *Child Abuse and Neglect, 12,* 529–542.

Kovacs, M. (1992). *Children's Depression Inventory.* New York: Multi-Health Systems.

Kuehnle, K. (1996). *Assessing allegations of child sexual abuse.* Sarasota, FL: Professional Resource Press.

Lanktree, C. B., Briere, J., & Zaidi, L. Y. (1991). Incidence and impacts of sexual abuse in a child outpatient sample: The role of direct inquiry. *Child Abuse and Neglect, 15,* 447–453.

Lyons, J. (1988). Posttraumatic stress disorder in children and adolescents: A review of the literature. *Journal of Developmental and Behavioral Pediatrics, 8,* 349–356.

Malmquist, C. P. (1986). Children who witness parental murder: Post-traumatic aspects. *Journal of the American Academy of Child and Adolescent Psychiatry, 25,* 320–325.

Mannarino, A. P., Cohen, J. A., & Berman, S. R. (1994). The Children's Attributions and Perceptions Scale: A new measure of sexual-abuse related factors. *Journal of Clinical Child Psychology, 23,* 204–211.

March, J. S. (1999). Assessment of pediatric posttraumatic stress disorder. In P. A. Saigh & J. D. Bremner (Eds.), *Posttraumatic stress disorder: A comprehensive text* (pp. 199–218). Needham Heights, MA: Allyn & Bacon.

Martin, R. P., Hooper, S., & Snow, J. (1986). Behavior rating scale approaches to personality assessment in children and adolescents. In H. Knoff (Ed.), *The assessment of child and adolescent personality* (pp. 309–351). New York: Guilford Press.

McArthur, D. S., & Roberts, G. E. (1990). *Roberts Apperception Test for Children.* Los Angeles: Western Psychological Services.

McLeer, S. V., Deblinger, E., Atkins, M. S., Foa, E., & Ralphe, D. (1988). Posttraumatic stress disorder in sexually abused children. *Journal of the American Academy of Child and Adolescent Psychiatry, 27,* 650–654.

McLeer, S. V., Deblinger, E., Henry, D., & Orvashel, H. (1992). Sexually abused children at high risk for PTSD. *Journal of the American Academy of Child and Adolescent Psychiatry, 31,* 875–879.

Melton, G. B., Petrila, J., Poythress, N. G., & Slobogin, C. (1997). *Psychological evaluations for the courts: A handbook for mental health professionals and lawyers* (2nd ed.). New York: Guilford Press.

Meyer, R. G. (1993). *The clinician's handbook: Integrated diagnostics, assessment and intervention in adult and adolescent psychopathology.* Boston: Allyn & Bacon.

Nader, K. O. (1997). Assessing traumatic experiences in children. In J. P. Wilson & T. M. Keane (Eds.), *Assessing psychological trauma and PTSD.* New York: Guilford Press.

Nader, K. O., Kriegler, J. A., Blake, D. D., & Pynoos, R. S. (1994). *Clinician administered PTSD Scale: Child and adolescent version (CAPS-C).* White River Junction, VT: National Center for PTSD.

National Institute of Mental Health Public Inquires. (2000). *Anxiety disorders, post-traumatic stress disorder.* (Available from 6001 Executive Blvd. Rm 8184 MSC 9663, Bethesda, MD, www.nimh.nih.gov)

Norris, F. (1992). Epidemiology of trauma: Frequency and impact of different potentially traumatic events on different demographic groups. *Journal of Consulting and Clinical Psychology, 60,* 409–418.

Pihl, R., & Nimrod, G. (1976). The reliability and validity of the draw-a-person test in IQ and personality assessment. *Journal of Clinical Psychology, 32*(2), 470–472.

Pliny the Younger. (1931). Letters. (W. Melmoth, Trans., revised by W. M. L. Hutchinson). London: Heinemann. (Original works written A.D. 100–113)

Praver, F. (1994). *Child Rating Scales: Exposure in interpersonal abuse.* Unpublished copyrighted material. (Available from the author, 5 Marseilles Drive, Locust Valley, New York 11560)

Praver, F., Pelcovitz, D., & DiGuseppe, R. (1994). *The Angie/Andy Child Rating Scales.* (Available from F. Praver, 5 Marseilles Drive, Locust Valley, New York 11560)

Putnam, F. W. (1990). *Child Dissociative Checklist* (Version 3.0–2/90). Bethesda, MD: National Institute of Mental Health, Laboratory of Developmental Psychology.

Putnam, F. W., Helmers, K., & Trickett, P. K. (1993). Development, reliability and validity of a child dissociation scale. *Child Abuse and Neglect, 17,* 731–741.

Putnam, F. W., & Peterson, G. (1994). Further validation of the Child Dissociative Checklist. *Dissociation, 7,* 204–211.

Pynoos, R. S., Frederick, C., Nader, K., Arroyo, W., Steinberg, A. M., Eth, S., et al. (1987). Life threat and posttraumatic stress in school age children, *Archives of General Psychiatry, 44,* 1057–1063.

Pynoos, R. S., Steinberg, A. M., & Goenjian, A. (1996). Traumatic stress in childhood and adolescence: Recent developments and current controversies. In B. A. van der Kolk, A. C. McFarlane, & L. Weisaeth (Eds.), *Traumatic stress: The effects of overwhelming experience on mind, body and society* (pp. 331–358). New York: Guilford Press.

Ragge v. MCA/Universal Studios 165 F.R.D. 605 (C.D. Cal. 1995).

Realmuto, G. M., Masten, A., Carole, L. F., Hubbard, J., Groteluschen, A., & Chun, B. (1992). Adolescent survivors of massive childhood trauma in Cambodia: Life events and current symptoms. *Journal of Traumatic Stress, 5*(4), 589–599.

Reich, W., & Earls, F. (1987). Rules for making psychiatric diagnoses in children on the basis of multiple sources of information: Preliminary strategies. *Journal of Abnormal Psychology, 15,* 601–616.

Richters, J. E., & Martinez, P. (1990). *Things I have seen and heard.* Rockville, MD: National Institute of Mental Health, Child and Adolescent Disorders Research Branch.

Roberts, A., & Wilkinson, A. (1983). Developing a positive posture at trial. *Trial, 19,* 56.

Ruggiero, K. J., Morris, T. L., & Scotti, J. R. (2001, Summer). Treatment for children with posttraumatic stress disorder: Current status and future directions. *Clinical Psychology: Science and Practice, 8*(2), 210–227.

Sack, W. H., Aangel, R. H., Kinzie, J. D., & Rath, B. (1986). The psychiatric effects of massive trauma on Cambodian children. II: The family, the home and the school. *Journal of the American Academy of Child and Adolescent Psychiatry, 25,* 377–383.

Saigh, P. A. (1997). *The Children's Posttraumatic Stress Disorder Inventory.* New York: City University of New York Graduate School.

Sattler J. M. (1998). *Clinical and forensic interviewing of children and families.* San Diego, CA: Jerome M. Sattler.

Saywitz, K. J., Mannarino, A. P., Berliner, L., & Cohen, J. A. (2000). Treatment for sexually abused children and adolescents. *American Psychologist, 55,* 1040–1049.

Schwartz, E. D., & Kowalski, J. M. (1991). Malignant memories: PTSD in children and adults after a school shooting. *Journal of the American Academy of Child and Adolescent Psychiatry, 30,* 936–944.

Shaffer, D., Fisher, P., Lucas, C. P., Dulcan, M. K., & Schwab-Stone, M. E. (2000). NIMH Diagnostic Interview Schedule for Children, version IV (NIMH DISC-IV): Description, differences from previous versions, and reliability of some common diagnoses. *Journal of the American Academy of Child and Adolescent Psychiatry, 39,* 28–38.

Shalev, A. Y. (1996). Stress versus traumatic stress: From acute homeostatic reactions to chronic psychopathology. In *Traumatic stress: The effects of overwhelming experience on mind, body and society.* New York: Guilford Press.

Shalev, A. Y., Bonne, O., & Eth, S. (1996). Treatment of posttraumatic stress disorder: A review. *Psychosomatic Medicine, 58,* 165–182.

Shannon, M. P., Lonigan, C. J., Finch, A. J., & Taylor, C. M. (1994). Children exposed to disaster. I: Epidemiology of posttraumatic symptoms and symptom profiles. *Journal of the American Academy of Child and Adolescent Psychiatry, 33,* 80–93.

Simon, R. I., & Wettstein, R. M. (1997). Toward the development of guidelines for the conduct of forensic psychiatric examinations. *Journal of the American Academy of Psychiatry and Law, 95,* 17–30.

Singer, M. I., Anglin, T. M., Song, L. Y., & Lunghofer, L. (1995). Adolescents' exposure to violence and associated symptoms of psychological trauma. *Journal of the American Medical Association, 273,* 477–482.

Smith, J. (1982). The expert witness: Maximizing damages for psychic injuries. *Trial, 18,* 51.

Sparta, S. N. (1982). Learned helplessness after traumatically induced neurological impairment. In J. M. Tuma (Ed.), *Handbook of pediatric psychology.* New York: Wiley.

Spinetta, J. J., McLaren, H. H., Fox, R. W., & Sparta, S. N. (1981). The Kinetic Family Drawing in childhood cancer: A revised application of an age-independent measure. In J. J. Spinetta & P. Deasy-Spinetta (Eds.), *Living with childhood cancer.* St. Louis, MO: Mosby.

Sternberg, K. J., Lamb, M.E., Greenbaum, C., Cicchetti, D., Dawud, S., Cortes, R. M., et al. (1993). Effects of domestic violence on children's behavior problems and depression. *Developmental Psychology, 29,* 44–52.

Terr, L. C. (1991). Childhood trauma: An outline and review. *American Journal of Psychiatry, 148,* 10–20.

Uniform Marriage and Divorce Act, 9A U.L.A. 561 § 402 (1973).

van der Kolk, B. A. (1987). *Psychological trauma.* Washington DC: American Psychiatric Press.

Ware, J. (1998). Child behavior observations. In G. P. Koocher, J. C. Norcross, & S. S. Hill (Eds.), *Psychologists' desk reference.* New York: Oxford University Press.

Weissman, H. N. (1985). Psychological standards and the role of psychological assessment in personal injury litigation. *Behavioral Sciences and the Law, 3,* 135–147.

Weissman, H. N. (1990). Distortions and deceptions in self presentation: Effects of protracted litigation on personal injury cases. *Behavioral Sciences and the Law, 8,* 67–74.

Weissman, H. N. (1991). Forensic psychological examination of the child witness in cases of alleged sexual abuse. *American Journal of Orthopsychiatry, 61,* 48–58.

Wilkinson, C. B. (1983). Aftermath of a disaster: The collapse of the Hyatt Regency skywalks. *American Journal of Psychiatry, 140,* 1134.

Wolfe, V. V., & Gentile, C. (1991). *Children's Impact of Traumatic Events Scale–Revised.* (Available from Wolfe, Dept. of Psychology, London Health Sciences Center, 800 Commissioners Road East, London, Ontario, Canada N6A4G5)

Wolfe, V. V., Wolfe, D. A., Gentile, C., & Larose, L. (1986). *Children's Impact of Traumatic Events Scale.* (Available from Wolfe, Dept. of Psychology, London Health Sciences Center, 800 Commissioners Road East, London, Ontario, Canada N6A4G5)

World Health Organization. (1977). International Classification of Diseases, rev 9. World Health Organization, Geneva.

Ziv, A., Kruglanski, A. W., & Shulman, S. (1974). Children's psychological reaction to wartime stress. *Journal of Personality and Social Psychology, 30,* 24–30.

CHAPTER 13

Personal Injury Examinations in Torts for Emotional Distress

STUART A. GREENBERG

Public policy usually allows persons who have been harmed to collect compensation from perpetrators of that harm, even when a crime is not involved. According to a variety of legal rules, most jurisdictions allow an injured party (the plaintiff) to sue a responsible party (the defendant) for the harm (the damage) to the psychological well-being that the defendant allegedly caused to the plaintiff. If the defendant is held liable, the plaintiff may receive a monetary award (the damages) as compensation for that harm. In other words, the victim of the wrong (the plaintiff) makes a claim (the complaint) against the perpetrator of the wrong (the defendant) for each wrong allegedly committed by the defendant. This claim is for compensation for the harm that the victim suffered and the perpetrator inflicted. The viability of this claim usually requires a showing that the defendant has breached a legal duty that was owed by the defendant to the plaintiff. Such is the basic nature of personal injury claims for psychological damages. These claims are pursued in civil court as disputes

between private parties and in an attempt by the plaintiff to gain compensation for the loss that was caused by the actions of the defendant (Greenberg & Shuman, 1999).

THE LAW OF TORTS

The legal framework of personal injury cases is the law of torts. The legal claim or complaint, in the form of a lawsuit, is properly known as a tort. A tort can be for almost any type of injury to the person, including psychological as well as physical damage. When psychological damage is claimed, the claim or complaint may be referred to as a tort for emotional distress, emotional damage, emotional harm, or pain and suffering, depending on the custom or rule of the jurisdiction in which the claim is filed. A tort is basically a civil, as opposed to a criminal, wrong that one person commits against another. For the tort claim to be legally viable, there must always be a violation of some duty owing from a defendant to a plaintiff, a breach of that duty, and damage to the plaintiff as a proximate result (Greenberg & Shuman, 1999).

Selected parts of this chapter are adapted from Greenberg and Brodsky (2001).

More formally, *Black's Law Dictionary* (Garner, 1999) defines tort as "A civil wrong for which a remedy may be obtained, usually in the form of damages; a breach of a duty that the law imposes on everyone" (p. 1496). Garner then defines personal tort as "A tort involving or consisting in an injury to one's person, reputation, or feelings, as distinguished from an injury or damage to real or personal property" (p. 1497). Keeping in mind the English law heritage of U.S. common law, it is instructive to note that English law (Martin, 1990) similarly defines a tort as:

> [Old French: harm, wrong; from Latin *tortus,* twisted or crooked] *n.* A wrongful act or omission for which damages can be obtained in a civil court by the person wronged, other than a wrong that is only a breach of contract. . . . Most torts are actionable only if they have caused damage. . . . The person principally liable is the one who committed the tort (the tortfeasor). . . . The main remedy for a tort is an action for damages. . . . Many torts are also crimes. Assault is both a crime and a tort. Reckless driving is a crime and may give rise to an action in tort if it causes injury to another person. (p. 415)

In fact, the only substantial difference between the U.S. law definition and English law definition of a tort is that the English law definition goes on to state that "The crime is prosecuted by agents of the state in the name of the *Crown*" (emphasis added). Under both legal systems, it is left to the injured person, the plaintiff, to seek compensation from the wrongdoer, the tortfeasor or defendant, by means of an action in tort that is filed in a civil court complaint.

Professional Roles

To better understand the roles that psychologists may play in tort litigation and the tasks that may be asked of them, it is helpful to conceptualize tort cases into *liability* and *damage* determinations. In the realm of liability is the determination of whether the defendant is legally responsible, (i.e., whether substantive tort law grants the plaintiff a right to recover under the facts of the case). This includes the adjudication of questions such as: Have the actions of a therapist-defendant breached a legal duty that the therapist owed to the patient and, if so, has the patient-plaintiff sustained his or her burden of persuasion on the elements of this claim? Such a legal duty is usually expressed in terms of whether the therapist's actions fell below a standard of care for treatment that would have been reasonable to provide to this patient. In the realm of damages is the determination of compensation (i.e., the amount of money that is appropriate to compensate the plaintiff for the injury suffered at the hands of the defendant). This includes the adjudication of questions such as: Does the law permit recovery for emotional distress caused by words

alone (e.g., the therapist's use of extensive profanity, sexual innuendo, and religious symbolism allegedly as part of treatment) and, if so, what loss has the plaintiff suffered due to the distress caused by these words?

The court ultimately decides questions regarding what is reasonable and just, what is the standard of care, what is the cause of the damage, and how much compensation is to be awarded, and psychologists may play an important role in the court's determinations. Numerous substantive legal rights to recover turn on issues to which psychological expert testimony may be relevant. In psychological malpractice cases, for example, the standard of care is ordinarily proved by expert psychological testimony; in sexual harassment cases, psychological expert testimony may be introduced on the issues of hostile work environment and the reasonable person standard (see the chapter by Vasquez, Baker, & Shullman in this volume). When a plaintiff claims damages for emotional distress, expert psychological testimony may be relevant to assess the cause and extent of that injury (to help the jury determine compensatory damages) and the amount of therapy that might be needed to ameliorate the injury (to help the jury determine special damages), including providing an estimate as to how long therapy is likely to take to accomplish this goal.

The forensic psychologist, when retained in the role of the forensic examiner of a tort claim, has five basic tasks as the plaintiff's or the defense's damages expert in most personal injury matters. These tasks are to assess (a) the baseline state of psychological functioning of the plaintiff before the harm occurred; (b) the nature and extent of any distress that was caused to the plaintiff by the actions of the defendant; (c) the nature and extent of any significant impairments or injuries to the plaintiff's functioning; (d) the likely psychological cause of each impairment or injury; and (e) the nature of any psychological intervention that might be helpful in assisting the plaintiff to return to the preincident baseline level of functioning. These five forensic examination tasks, undertaken as a damages expert, may be in addition to the tasks of forming an opinion regarding such liability issues as the standard of care in the matter, whether most "reasonably constituted" persons would have been injured by what the plaintiff experienced, and whether the plaintiff has reasonably attempted to mitigate the harm suffered.

As with most other types of forensic examinations for criminal, parenting, and competency examinations, the forensic examiner's role in personal injury claims is very different from that of the role of the therapist who works in a treatment context (Greenberg & Shuman, 1997). The forensic examination is initiated by attorneys, not patients. The forensic examiner's client is the retaining attorney, not the party being examined. The purpose of the examination is litigation, not therapy. The anticipated outcome is public testimony, not privacy. The attorney-client privilege usually applies to the examiner-litigant relationship; the therapist-patient privilege does not. Rather than striving to help the party, the examiner attempts to help the court. And, although principles of benevolence apply to therapist-patient relationships, the product of the forensic examination and testimony may not be beneficial either to the examined or to the retaining client-attorney. In all such ways, the forensic examiner's role is different from that of the therapist. The examiner must be independent and objective in his or her task of assisting the trier of fact to come to the most accurate and just conclusion about the party that the examiner has examined (Greenberg, 2001b). Providing the candor and objectivity that are required to be of such assistance to the court would ordinarily mean risking the very private and supportive relationship that forms the basis of a therapeutic alliance between therapist and patient. For that reason, even if the therapist has information that may help the patient's legal case, prudence dictates that the therapist not risk the therapeutic relationship, but instead, let the court acquire the helpful information from other sources (Shuman, Greenberg, Heilbrun, & Foote, 1998).

Much has been written about the professional and ethical role of the expert, and this is well stated in the "Specialty Guidelines for Forensic Psychologists" (Committee on Ethical Guidelines for Forensic Psychologists, 1991). In essence, the Guidelines encourage, advise, and admonish that the essential role of the forensic psychologist is as expert to the court, whose task it is to assist the trier of fact to understand the psychological aspects of the evidence and legal issues before the court. In so doing, the forensic psychologist is to present findings and opinions in a fair and objective manner, to not engage in nor participate in a partisan distortion or misrepresentation of evidence, and generally to provide services in an objective manner and in a way consistent with the highest standards of the profession. These obligations extend to all parties in the proceedings, even those whom the forensic psychologist has not been retained by nor even ever met.

One might ask, Why is this so? After all, we have an adversarial system of justice in which each side presents its best arguments in an attempt to persuade the trier of fact of the rightness and justness of its cause. Although this is the defined role of the attorney in this struggle, the reason that this is *not* the role of the forensic psychologist is actually quite simple. The forensic expert cannot assist a third party, in most cases, a jury, to most accurately understand evidence from and about a party that has been examined if the expert's testimony about that party is slanted or distorted for or against that individual. That, by definition, would be misleading to the trier of fact, whom the expert is supposed to be assisting. Only by fairly and accurately providing facts and opinions to the trier of fact can the expert assist that trier of fact come to

a just conclusion. Anything else would result in less accuracy and less justice (Shuman & Greenberg, 1998).

The Rules of Civil Procedure

The forensic psychologist ultimately has a role in this legal process because the state has an interest in the resolution of civil disputes. Such cases proceed through the federal and state legal systems according to what is referred to as the Rules of Civil Procedure of each jurisdiction. These rules usually allow each side to the dispute to discover from the other side any information that might reasonably lead to admissible evidence in the trial resolving the disputed matter.

As part of this discovery process, examining experts first serve as agents of discovery for the side that retains them. They then serve as the objects of the discovery by the other side of the dispute. As an agent of discovery, the forensic examiner assesses the plaintiff's damage for the retaining counsel. Then, as an object of the discovery process, the forensic examiner becomes a source of information to the opposite side through submission of the expert's forensic report and witnesses' statement and through the use of a subpoena of the expert's records and deposition testimony. Thus, the expert first informs retaining counsel and then informs opposing counsel what facts have been learned from and about the plaintiff, what opinions have been formed regarding the plaintiff's allegation, and what are the bases for those facts and opinions. Most states support such extensive mutual pretrial discovery in the interest of both sides knowing the facts, theories, and opinions that the other side will eventually offer at trial. Although there are exceptions, few state legal systems encourage trial by ambush, or blindsiding the opposition, or "Perry Mason"-style intrial discovery in civil matters.

A civil action for damages is begun with the filing of a complaint by the plaintiff. This is conceptually similar to a criminal action that is begun by the filing of an indictment by a prosecutor. Although there may have been prior efforts to negotiate a settlement of a dispute, filing the complaint formally places the case before the court. In the complaint, the plaintiff typically states why the court has jurisdiction to hear the plaintiff's claims, why the plaintiff is entitled to relief, and what relief the plaintiff seeks. Each claim for relief that the plaintiff pleads is referred to as a cause of action and is conceptually similar to each count of an indictment that is offered by the prosecution in a criminal matter.

The participants in this civil legal process typically include the trier of law, the trier of fact, the parties, the counsel for each party, the court personnel, the witnesses, and members of the public. The trier of law is the judge, whose task it is to make rulings of law. The trier of fact has the task of making decisions of fact (i.e., deciding the facts of the case).

The trier of fact is usually the jury, but in some jurisdictions, one or both parties may have the right to waive the presence of a jury. When this occurs, the judge serves as both the trier of law and the trier of fact in what is referred to as a bench trial. The parties are the plaintiffs and the defendants, and each has an attorney or counsel who argues that party's case. There are typically court personnel who assist the judge, and these may include a clerk of the court, bailiff, court reporter, law clerk, and legal intern. The witnesses offer testimony for the trier of fact to consider. Witnesses may be fact witnesses or expert witnesses. Members of the public, such as trial observers and the press, are also considered an integral part of the process. This is because, on a societal basis, it is the openness of the judicial process to public and press scrutiny that help ensure a fair and equitable process.

The Civil Trial Process

Although there are many variations, the steps through the civil process in personal injury matters in most jurisdictions approximate the pattern outlined in Table 13.1.

TABLE 13.1   Typical Steps through the Civil Complaint and Trial Process

1. Prefiling settlement negotiation (settlement negotiations may continue throughout).
2. Plaintiff files complaint specifying causes of action and serves defendant.
3. Defendant may file motions to dismiss, motions for counterclaims, and notice of any affirmative defenses.
4. Defendant files answer.
5. Defendant answers elements of complaint not dismissed.
6. Discovery (discovery may continue throughout):
   Requests for production of documents.
   Interrogatories.
   Depositions and subpoenas for documents.
   Physical and mental examinations under Civil Rule 35.
7. Motion(s) for summary judgment (motions may continue throughout).
8. Pretrial conference:
   Motions *in limine* and motions to seal file.
   Witness lists, witness statements, and exhibits lists.
   Discovery cutoff.
9. Trial:
   Plaintiff's case in chief:
      Plaintiff rests.
      Motion for directed verdict by defendant.
   Defendant's case in chief:
      Defense rests.
      Motion for directed verdict by plaintiff.
10. Verdict by trier of fact.
11. Motion for judgment notwithstanding the verdict by nonprevailing party.
12. Entry of judgment by trier of law.
13. Motions for reconsideration.
14. Appellate process.
15. Renewed settlement negotiations.

Source: Adapted from Greenberg (2001b).

If initial settlement efforts are unsuccessful, the plaintiff may file a complaint setting forth a claim for relief, in this case, damages. The matter is now filed and said to be before the court. The complaint usually contains relatively short statements, considering the reams that may follow, of the grounds on which the court's jurisdiction depends, the events giving rise to the dispute, the legal causes of action, the claim showing why the plaintiff is entitled to damages, and a demand for a judgment for damages or other relief. The complaint and a summons are then served on the defendant.

The defendant may then file a motion to dismiss the complaint for intrinsic flaws that are apparent from the face of the complaint. This might occur because of the plaintiff's failure to state a claim on which relief can be granted, because of the plaintiff having filed in the wrong jurisdiction, or because of an untimely filing of the complaint. A successful motion to dismiss can result in a case being dismissed with prejudice or without prejudice. Dismissal with prejudice means that the matter is permanently resolved. Dismissal without prejudice means that the court has dismissed the complaint in its current form but has left open the possibility that the flaws that caused the dismissal may be cured, such as by refiling in a proper venue or jurisdiction. In a dismissal without prejudice, a new suit may be refiled for the same cause of action and the matter remains unsettled.

The defendant may counterclaim that the defendant has causes of action against the plaintiff and may file these before the court. The proceedings for these claims usually take place within the same trial process that was initiated by the plaintiff, but the defendant has the burden to prove these claims against the plaintiff much in the same way, and usually to the same standards, as does the plaintiff to prove the initial claims that the plaintiff filed against the defendant.

The defendant may also claim what are known as *affirmative defenses* to the plaintiff's claim. These are defenses that, if proven true, reduce or eliminate the defendant's liability, even if the plaintiff is able to prove the plaintiff's claims against the defendant. An affirmative defense is a defense that negates all or part of the plaintiff's right to recover, even if the plaintiff proves all of the elements of the plaintiff's case.

Although both plaintiff and defendant seek to introduce evidence on all of the issues, the plaintiff ordinarily bears the burden of proof on all elements of the plaintiff's claims, and the defendant ordinarily bears the burden of proof on all affirmative defenses. The legal process thus allows the plaintiff the opportunity to prove each of the necessary elements of the claims that are identified in the plaintiff's complaint and allows the defendant to cast doubt on the plaintiff's claims and to offer other defenses. If the defendant does offer affirmative defenses, it becomes the plaintiff's task to similarly cast doubt on the defendant's assertions as the defendant has done to the plaintiff's assertions. Thus, for example, in a case in which the plaintiff claims damages for loss of consortium based on the defendant's causing the death of the plaintiff's spouse, the plaintiff bears the burden of proof to show, among other things, that the defendant's negligent driving caused the death of his spouse. Such may be the case if the defendant can prove that the deceased contributed to the accident or had a last clear chance to avoid any harm despite the defendant's negligent driving. This might occur in a situation where a hurrying pedestrian had the opportunity to stop before running into the street but instead decided to try to beat the oncoming vehicle.

If a motion to dismiss based on the pleadings is not successful, based on evidence revealed during discovery all parties may file motions for *summary judgment* to resolve the plaintiff's claims or defendant's defenses, in whole or in part. The standard for granting a motion for summary judgment is that there is no genuine issue as to any material fact and that the moving party is entitled to judgment as a matter of law. Thus, summary judgment is designed for questions in which there is nothing factually for the jury to resolve, but instead, the question is one of law for the court. Summary judgment is granted to a party who successfully demonstrates that there are no genuine factual disputes on any legally salient issues when the issues are viewed in the light most favorable to the nonmoving party. If successful, this implies that the judge decided that there is no need to waste the court's resources by putting such a case before a jury.

Forensic experts may play a critical role in summary judgment proceedings by testifying, essentially, that facts are disputed. For example, a malpractice defendant's claim for dismissal that he could not have reasonably foreseen a particular harm to a patient may be rebutted by plaintiff's expert, who may assert that such harm should have been foreseeable by the reasonably competent practitioner. By this assertion, the plaintiff has put the issue in dispute. The court will view the dispute in the light most favorable to the plaintiff because the plaintiff is the nonmoving party in the summary judgment motion. The claim, then, most probably will not be dismissed in favor of the defendant's motion for summary judgment but instead will proceed to trial.

Even when all the issues in a case are not resolvable by summary judgment, motions often are successful at removing some of the claims or defenses. Reducing the issues in this way facilitates the potential for negotiated settlement, simplifies and shortens trials, or leads to the abandonment of causes because a party decides the remaining claims do not warrant the expense and risk of trial.

Anytime after the complaint is filed, up to the time that the court has established a discovery cutoff, the parties may engage in *discovery*. It is during this period that the forensic examiner must complete his or her examination and disclose its results and any opinions that may be offered at trial. In most jurisdictions, retaining counsel must make any potential expert witness available for discovery of these facts and opinions by opposing counsel before discovery cutoff or risk having that expert's testimony excluded at trial.

The *standard of persuasion* describes the degree of certainty with which the party who bears the burden of proof on an issue is required to sustain that burden. In other words, the standard of persuasion defines what level of surety or confidence the trier of fact must have to be convinced of the facts and opinions asserted by each side. In civil matters, as well as criminal matters, reasonable doubt is said to exist when the party with the burden fails to persuade the trier of fact to the degree of certainty required for the type of matter or issue that is before the court.

In personal injury matters, the relevant degree of certainty or standard of persuasion to establish claims and defenses to the fact finder is referred to as a *preponderance of the evidence*. It is usually referred to as the "more likely than not standard" or, stated more formally, as more overall evidence for a proposition than not. A preponderance of evidence is said to be evidence that is more convincing than the evidence offered in opposition to it. It is the evidence that is more credible, convincing, reasonable, and probable. The word "preponderance" is intended to mean something close to the sense of outweighing overall. To be a preponderance, the weight of evidence for one side must outweigh the evidence for the other. This is not simply the number of witnesses, documents, or simple arguments and facts in favor, but rather, the overall composite balance of which side's argument, opinion, and information is likely to be correct or is more persuasive. This standard is basically considered to be a majority of the evidence or, said another way, more evidence than would be merely reasonable to some persons but less than would be clear and convincing to most persons.

The concept of preponderance of evidence plays a central role in expert witness testimony. For an expert's opinion to be admissible, the expert must also testify that the opinion is supported by a preponderance of the evidence that the expert has considered and relied on. These sources of support or foundation include the expert's training, experience, special expertise, literature research, and facts of the immediate case. Attorneys may ask questions similar to the following of their expert witnesses: "Doctor, based on your examination and your expertise, will you tell this jury your opinion, on a more likely than not basis, as to whether this plaintiff is experiencing significant psychological impairments in her functioning?" and "Doctor, is this damage manifested by her inability to sleep, keep basic hygiene, care for her children, drive, perform effectively at work, and be intimate with her husband?" The expert need not be 95% or 99% certain that this opinion is correct, but need only be reasonably certain that the opinion is more probably true than any competing or alternative conclusion.

In the absence of an admission of liability, the trier of fact is asked to determine if the plaintiff has adequately proven each of the necessary elements of the claim. If this is the verdict, then the defendant is held to be liable. Civil defendants are not thought of as having been found guilty or not guilty, but rather as liable or not liable. The legal term "liability" means, in this context, that the defendant has been found by the jury to have legal responsibility for the tort and has an obligation to pay compensation for the damage that was caused to the plaintiff by the defendant's breach of duty.

However, judges in their role as the triers of law have the final say. Judges can preempt the jury's deliberation by preventing the case from even being submitted to the jury. In what is called a *directed verdict,* the judge can determine that the party with the burden of proof has failed to present a sufficient prima facie case to proceed to jury consideration. This means that the party has not met the necessary burden of proof on at least one of the necessary legal elements. Judges can even override the jury's finding after a verdict has been reached. The acronym JNOV refers to the Latin judgment *non obstante veredicto,* which means judgment notwithstanding the verdict by the jury. On successful motion by the nonprevailing party, JNOV sets aside the jury verdict and renders in favor of one party notwithstanding the finding of a jury verdict in favor of the other party. Either plaintiff or defendant may win a judgment JNOV in qualifying cases in which it is the opinion of the judge that evidence overwhelmingly favors a different conclusion than that reached by the jury.

Judges alone control the legal process, interpret the law, and apply rules of procedure and evidence, all of which may have an important effect on the outcome of the case. Consider the popular book *A Civil Action* (Harr, 1996). The judge's ruling to bifurcate the liability and damages aspects of the legal process was portrayed to have had a huge effect on the outcome of the matter. The rules of procedure, as a part of due process, are intended to keep the judicial process orderly, to ensure fairness to each side, and to guarantee each participant's rights under the law. At the broadest level, the conduct of judicial proceedings is defined by the constitutional requirement that no person be deprived of life, liberty, or property without due process of law. Due process requires that parties be given notice and the opportunity to be heard before governmental action that deprives them of life, liberty, or property. State and federal rules of evidence and rules of procedure are designed to implement these constitutional guarantees. If the attorneys use the rules effectively and appropriately, the evidence and arguments that will be presented at trial are known well in advance of the trial. This generally permits a better opportunity to settle cases fairly or to try cases that do not settle without surprises.

Trial tactics, however, also play a significant role in personal injury cases. Within the rubric of an adversary system, it is understood and expected that lawyers will make tactical uses of these rules for the benefit of their clients. Thus, the operation of these procedural rules, designed to achieve lofty conditional goals, is shaped by their adversarial implementation. Most procedural rules create rights that a party may waive. For example, if a party does not object to an opponent's expert's qualification, the court will not prevent the witness from testifying as an expert. Although the judge in the U.S. judicial system is expected to ensure that justice is done, in the main, the judge is expected to intercede in the presentation of evidence only when the fundamental fairness of the proceeding is threatened, but not to interfere with tactical decisions of the lawyers as to how they choose to try their cases. In this sense, the judge typically does not act as would the referee in a sporting event, who, on the occasion of a foul, blows a whistle or throws down a flag. Rather, the judicial "referee" usually waits until one of the "players" objects (i.e., cries foul), and then resolves the dispute. Thus, it is rare in a tort case for the judge to raise an objection on his or her own. As an example of this, consider that it is unlikely that judges will, on their own motion, raise a privilege objection when a psychologist or psychiatrist is asked about his or her treatment of the plaintiff.

Similarly, many times, opposing counsel make no objection to technically improper procedure, simply because that wrong process or procedure has no effect or is working to their benefit. Strategy, not rule, ultimately guides the objector's decision. In the same sense, other rules get broken without objection. It is not that expert opinions can be offered *only* by experts, that opinions *must* have proper foundation, that previously undisclosed opinions *cannot* be offered at trial, that the scope of cross-examination *must not* exceed that of direct examination, or that one *must not* testify as to uncorroborated hearsay. Instead, an objection to each of these, if offered, is likely to be sustained. The primary concern to the attorney is the effect on the jury of the way each witness and each counsel presents themselves for personal and professional scrutiny by the jury, rather than the technical propriety or impropriety of any question or answer. What is left is not hard and fast rules, but art and style, silence and assertion, which play themselves out behind the scenes repeatedly throughout the trial process.

Discovery

Usually well before trial, the attorneys engage in an attempt to discover evidence that may be helpful to them or prejudicial to the opposing counsel at the upcoming trial. As part of this pretrial discovery process, each side is allowed to investigate its case very broadly, essentially given the opportunity to discover anything that might reasonably lead to admissible evidence. In this process, examining experts serve as agents of discovery for the side that retains them, usually by conducting a forensic examination of the plaintiff. Consistent with the rules of discovery, this examination can also be rather broad in its scope, as long as the questions asked by the examiner are reasonably calculated to lead to information that may be admissible at trial.

Conceptually, this examination is allowed because the plaintiff has put his or her emotional well-being at issue before the court by claiming psychological damages. This claim for damages for emotional distress results in the defendant's right to discover (i.e., to independently assess that claim). In the interest of fairness, the court usually grants the defendant discovery of the plaintiff's claim in the form of the right to force the plaintiff to undergo a physical or mental examination performed by an expert of the defendant's choosing. Plaintiffs can also elect to be examined by an expert of their choice and this elective examination can take place either before or after the examination conducted by the expert retained by the defense.

Also in the interest of fairness, the plaintiff has a right to discover the results of the forensic examination conducted by the expert selected by defense. In exchange for learning about the results of this examination from the defendant, the plaintiff must provide to the defendant all similar information that the plaintiff has accumulated, usually including the plaintiff's own elective forensic examination as well as the plaintiff's treatment records, if any, that bear on the liability or damage being claimed.

Federal Rules of Civil Procedure: Rule 35 (Fed. R. Civ. Proc. 35)

Examinations of the plaintiff by the defense expert are typical but not automatic. They may occur under the authority of Federal Rule of Civil Procedure 35 or, more simply, Civil Rule 35 or CR35, or its state equivalent. These examinations may be ordered by a court against the wishes of the plaintiff when the plaintiff's mental or physical condition is in controversy. When the plaintiff resists being examined, the court may ask the defense to show good cause as to why such an examination would be helpful to the court's deliberations. If the defense motion for the CR35 examination is granted, this usually results in what is referred to as the litigation exception to privilege, which basically waives most of plaintiff's claims to privacy and to therapist-patient privilege that the plaintiff might otherwise have.

A good cause affidavit or declaration that is submitted by the proposed CR35 examiner begins with the court, cause, and caption information, an oath that the statement is true, and an affirmation that the declarant is competent to make the declaration. The substance of the statement describes the examiner's qualifications, the basic relevant facts of the current matter, and the process of the examination. This includes plans for testing, interviews, and collateral contacts and the general nature of the inquiry. Although the expert usually does not need to identify the individual instruments to be used, there would be indication of the plan to perform cognitive testing, personality testing, and assessment of areas of well-being as well as injuries focusing on trauma, anxiety, depression, and other impairments.

The expert's declaration in support of the motion for a CR35 examination then states the number of testing and interview sessions, the approximate number of hours needed, any concerns about having an observer present for the testing or interviews, and that the assessment is better performed over several sessions; this is to sample the plaintiff's status at more than one moment in time and to keep fatigue from distorting the examination results. The description of the content of the interviews includes the intent to explore the plaintiff's condition before and after the alleged event, the nature of the alleged event, the likely psychological causes of any impairments that the plaintiff is experiencing, and the plaintiff's likely future needs to recover from any residual impairments. Similarly, persons to be interviewed as collaterals are described in terms of their relationship to the case or to the plaintiff, the nature of the information likely to be acquired from them, and the general way in which it is likely to be helpful. The expert then needs to state how this process is warranted in terms of the information that may result, how that information is relevant to the matter, and how the overall product of the examination may be helpful to the court when provided as testimony.

Whether retained by the defense attorney to formally provide a forensic examination under CR35, or retained voluntarily by plaintiff's counsel to examine the plaintiff, the procedural model that experts should follow is CR35. If not in federal court, examiners should be familiar with the state version of this rule for the jurisdiction in which the matter is being tried. Whereas ethics codes and specialty practice guidelines are the conceptual guiding principles for the psychological aspects of this process, the Rules of Civil Procedure, especially Rule 35, and the Rules of Evidence, especially Rules 702 through 705, are the guiding principles for the legal aspect of the process. These combine to provide the governing principles for civil forensic examinations and testimony. Forensic practice can be thought of as the

TABLE 13.2 Federal Rules of Civil Procedure: Rule 35 (Fed. R. Civ. Proc. 35): Physical and Mental Examination of Persons

(a) Order for Examination.

When the mental or physical condition (including the blood group) of a party, or of a person in the custody or under the legal control of a party, is in controversy, the court in which the action is pending may order the party to submit to a physical or mental examination by a suitably licensed or certified examiner or to produce for examination the person in his custody or legal control. The order may be made only on motion for good cause shown and upon notice to the person to be examined and to all parties and shall specify the time, place, manner, conditions, and scope of the examination and the person or persons by whom it is to be made.

(b) Report of Examiner.

(1) If requested by the party against whom an order is made under Rule 35(a) or the person examined, the party causing the examination to be made shall deliver to the requesting party a copy of the detailed written report of the examiner setting out the examiner's findings, including results of all tests made, diagnoses and conclusions, together with like reports of all earlier examinations of the same condition. After delivery the party causing the examination shall be entitled upon request to receive from the party against whom the order is made a like report of any examination, previously or thereafter made, of the same condition, unless, in the case of a report of examination of a person not a party, the party shows that the party is unable to obtain it. The court on motion may make an order against a party requiring delivery of a report on such terms as are just, and if an examiner fails or refuses to make a report the court may exclude the examiner's testimony if offered at trial.

(2) By requesting and obtaining a report of the examination so ordered or by taking the deposition of the examiner, the party examined waives any privilege the party may have in that action or any other involving the same controversy, regarding the testimony of every other person who has examined or may thereafter examine the party in respect of the same mental or physical condition.

(3) This subdivision applies to examinations made by agreement of the parties, unless the agreement expressly provides otherwise. This subdivision does not preclude discovery of a report of an examiner or the taking of a deposition of the examiner in accordance with the provisions of any other rule.

---

convergence point of these principles. CR35, though relatively short, is complex; it is presented in Table 13.2.

Part (a) of the rule addresses the provisions for the examination. It refers to the plaintiff's claim of emotional pain and suffering (i.e., psychological impairment) as a basis for receiving damages and to the defendant's dispute of at least part of that claim. The examination is to be conducted by a "suitably licensed or certified examiner," which may include any person with recognized expertise in the area of the plaintiff's claim. Although the defense may have to convince the court of "good cause" for the examination, CR35 exams often are arranged by agreement of counsel when the attorneys

recognize that there are insufficient grounds to resist the request. If disputed, the determination of "good cause" is within the judge's discretion. At the request of the plaintiff, the defense may have to state in advance the identity of the examiner, the amount of time that the examination will require, the location for the exam, the procedures to be used, and the general areas of inquiry.

Part (b) subpart (1) of the rule provides for the examiner's report. This section spells out the requirement that the defense must provide a copy of the detailed written report of the examination to the plaintiff before discovery cutoff. The report needs to be complete on all issues that bear directly on the legal question and, in particular, all areas that are likely to be the subject of future testimony. At a minimum, the report should contain all procedures used, all opinions evident at the time, and the foundation or basis for each opinion. Upon receipt of the defense expert's examination report, the plaintiff must provide to the defense any reports in plaintiff's control regarding the same condition or claim. This provision may be the basis for the plaintiff having to turn over his or her therapy notes to the defense as an ongoing report of the same condition. As stated in the rule, "If an examiner fails or refuses to make a report, the court may exclude the examiner's testimony if offered at trial." Thus, failure to write a requested report may result in the exclusion of the expert's testimony. However, a report is to be written only if requested by the attorney who has retained the expert and not automatically. This is because the attorney who retained the expert may want that testimony to be excluded. If the expert's findings or opinions are not sufficiently favorable to the defense, then not having that expert testify may be exactly what the side retaining that expert desires.

Part (b) subpart (2) explains the provisions for the reciprocal waiving of privilege. It provides that, in consideration for the defense having to reveal its report to the plaintiff, the plaintiff waives any privilege and reciprocates by providing all information available about the plaintiff regarding the condition in question. Because the plaintiff has waived privilege in requesting the defense's report of the plaintiff, then the plaintiff must waive privilege in making available all reports of similar conditions that are under the plaintiff's control. In effect, the rule provides that a release to one person regarding the plaintiff's condition is a release to all regarding the same condition.

Part (b) subpart (3) establishes that agreements between counsel are as binding as court orders and clarifies that neither party is relieved of any obligation to allow discovery and deposition, even if the examination is conducted by agreement and the report is provided as described.

THE NATURE OF THE FORENSIC EXAMINATION PROCESS

Because the nature of the forensic examination flows directly from the law that is relevant to the matter, the forensic examiner should be familiar with the underlying legal standards as well as the scientific foundations of psychology that are applicable to the issue being assessed. The forensic examiner's overarching consideration is that his or her primary and essential role is that of expert to the court. If others are to rely on the examiner's statements of facts and opinions, these need to be thorough, objective, and impartial. The forensic examiner is an advocate only for that which most accurately represents the state of psychological knowledge and the results of the forensic examination in question. It is not the examiner's role to be a partisan for the cause of the retaining attorney. Because forensic practice is among the most public of all mental health professional practices, the statements and actions of the forensic professional may have a profound impact on the parties to the suit, the attorneys, the profession, and the forensic examiner himself or herself. The examination process of comparable legal questions should be essentially the same whether the examiner is retained by plaintiff's counsel or defense counsel. Record keeping should reflect thoroughness and impartiality, avoiding passive or active distortion by selection or recording of quotes out of context. All contact with any party or witness is "on the record."

Whereas clinical assessments attempt to assess the strengths and weaknesses of a patient when compared either to a population average or to an aspired ideal, forensic examinations are basically a pre/post comparison of how the plaintiff was functioning before an alleged event with how plaintiff has been functioning since the alleged event. Having said this, it should immediately be acknowledged that the field has not generated a detailed, "gold standard" model for how to perform the examinations. The elements culled and combined from a variety of sources suggest the following procedures, though these suggestions should not be considered mandates and decisions must be made by each expert on a case-by-case basis.

The elements of the assessment to be considered are the examiner's informed consent from the client-attorney, collateral information, informed consent from the party being examined, testing and other assessment instruments to be administered, substantive interviews of the party, interviews of collaterals, the examiner's report, and the examiner's deposition, and courtroom testimony (see Table 13.3).

TABLE 13.3   Sequence of the Typical Examination Process

Although time and court demands often change this, a general model for the forensic examination process is the following:

Attorney's referral contact to the examiner's office.
- Attorney's basic description of case.
  - Referral counsel's theory of the case and the facts that support it.
  - Opposing counsel's theory of the case and the facts that support it.

Practice, expertise, availability, and fee information that the examiner provides to the referring attorney.
- Attorney-client provides informed consent and documents in letter or contract form.

Retainer paid by client-attorney.

Records of both sides reviewed.

Interview #1: Brief introductory interview of plaintiff.
- Not a case-substantive interview.
- Informed consent from plaintiff as to examiner's role and as to examination process.
- Inform plaintiff of information and documents received thus far by examiner.
- Ask plaintiff if wishes to provide names of additional collaterals and additional documents.

Plaintiff completes in-office testing and take-home history questionnaires.

Read plaintiff's questionnaires, test results, and remaining records.

Interview #2: First case-substantive interview of plaintiff.

Conduct collateral interviews.

Interviews #3+.

Review of data and results.
- Organize as to the five conceptual parts of the examination.
  - Preallegation history.
    - Strengths and competencies.
    - Preexisting vulnerabilities.
    - Preexisting impairments in functioning.
  - The trauma and distress.
    - What the plaintiff was exposed to.
  - Sequelae.
    - Substantial impairments in functioning that the plaintiff suffered.
    - Ways in which the plaintiff was resilient.
  - Proximate cause.
    - Impairments that would not have occurred but for the alleged events.
    - Impairments that would have occurred otherwise.
  - Prognosis.
    - Degree of future impairments (partial or complete, temporary or permanent).
    - Interventions or accommodations indicated.

Conclusions.
- Opinions and recommendations.
- Consult with colleagues as needed.
  - Use colleagues as a check against hindsight bias.

Consultation with the retaining client-attorney.

Written report (if requested).

Deposition.

Testimony.

Source: Adapted from Greenberg (2001b).

Informed Consent from the Retaining Client-Attorney

Because the attorney is the client who retains the forensic examiner on behalf of that attorney's client, the plaintiff or the defendant, the examiner first acquires informed consent from the client-attorney regarding the cost and nature of any professional responsibilities and services the examiner is expected to perform. These may include consultation, document review, CR35 examination, report writing, and testimony. It is advisable to have the attorney write a letter that identifies and commemorates the salient aspects of the retainer agreement, especially an acknowledgment that the attorney is the client of the forensic examiner and is responsible for the expert's fees regardless of the outcome of the matter. The expert should request a retainer that will cover at least what the typical matter of this sort would cost to evaluate. If asked by counsel or the party, remember that health insurance is basically a contract between an insurance company that agrees to provide reimbursement for services that are covered under that contract and an insured who agrees to pay for the cost of that coverage. Because health insurance rarely is intended to reimburse for legal purposes as opposed to health purposes, it is usually not appropriate to use health insurance as a means to pay for a forensic examination (see Greenberg, 2000, for further discussion of this issue).

The attorney may specify that the examiner is being retained as a trial consultant, as long as it is clear that this is done to avoid premature discovery of the expert and that, once identified as a witness, everything that the expert has accumulated will become available to both sides. No information that was considered and relied on by the examiner in the forming of his or her opinion should be withheld from judicial scrutiny.

Acquiring Collateral Documents

The client-attorney should be asked in the initial contact to provide to the expert all documents and records that are relevant to the expert's responsibilities, especially those that may help the expert understand opposing counsel's theories of the case, and any evidence that might support those theories. Potential duplications and complications may be less likely to occur if the retaining attorney is responsible for acquiring and providing to the expert all of the documents that the expert requests, rather than having the expert request documents directly.

Informed Consent from the Plaintiff

Having learned from the documents the essential positions of each side in the matter, the examiner should conduct a brief informed consent initial meeting with each party being examined. This meeting is not a substantive interview about the facts and allegations of the case. It is an opportunity for the party to learn about the process and about what to expect. The meeting also should help the party become more comfortable with the idea of being examined. According to Fink and Butcher (1972), doing so may encourage some parties to be less defensive or less resentful of psychological testing. The party should be informed which attorney is the examiner's client, that the exam is being conducted by court order or by agreement, that it is a forensic examination for which there is not intended to be any therapeutic benefit, and that therapist-patient privilege does not apply. The party, and any collateral, should expect "publicness" in the form of professional consultations, reports, and testimony. As part of the process, the party should expect to be administered standardized psychological testing, history taking, interviews about status before and after the claimed event, and any ways in which he or she may have been damaged.

Tests and Other Instruments

Assessment of the party should follow the informed consent interview, but may precede it if the informed consent has been accomplished with the party's attorney or by providing the party written forms that describe the same consent information.

Unfortunately, there is no universally agreed on set of assessment tools that has been developed for personal injury examinations, nor any tests that directly answer the legally relevant questions regarding preexisting conditions, proximately caused damage, or the severity of the distress caused by the defendant's behavior. In general, civil forensic examiners tend to use the same core battery of test instruments that typically are used in clinical assessment. In 1992, Lees-Haley found from a relatively small sample ($n = 69$) of forensic examiners that these tests tended to include the Minnesota Multiphasic Personality Inventory (MMPI) and MMPI-2, the Wechsler Adult Intelligence Scale–Revised (WAIS-R), the Rorschach Inkblot, and the Bender-Gestalt Test. In a more recent survey with a slightly larger sample ($n = 80$), Boccaccini and Brodsky (1999) found that most commonly used instruments in forensic assessments were the MMPI-1 or -2, the WAIS-R or -III, the Millon Clinical Multiaxial Inventory II or III, the Rorschach, the Beck Depression Inventory, the Trauma Stress Inventory, and the Symptom Checklist 90–Revised. Interestingly, each of these studies found that among these two groups of clinicians, no two forensic examiners of emotional injury claims used an identical battery of tests and instruments.

Regardless of which specific instruments are used, the results should be used to generate hypotheses that then need to be corroborated or disconfirmed when tested against the other information available in the matter. Whichever instruments the examiner prefers and is skilled with administering and interpreting, the same core battery of assessment instruments and procedures should be used in most examinations. These instruments are then supplemented with specialized tests as necessary to further assess cognitive or intellectual impairment, trauma, anxiety, depression, substance misuse, and so on. (See Heilbrun, 1992 for further discussions of the role of psychological testing in forensic assessment.)

When interpreting testing results, especially the results of personality testing, the examiner needs to exercise caution to understand the results in the context of the forensic process and should not assume that the standard clinical interpretation applies. For example, plaintiffs often believe that they have been mistreated unfairly by authority figures and are particularly untrusting, guarded, and suspicious of the arcane motives of an expert hired by the defense. Such influences, taken together, can result in a significant elevation on MMPI-2 Scale 6 (Pa) without necessarily indicating that the person warrants the standard clinical interpretation of such a score. Prefacing any interpretation with an explanatory statement, as is recommended by the "Ethical Principles of Psychologists and Code of Conduct" (APA, 1992) and the "Specialty Guidelines for Forensic Psychologists" (Committee on Ethical Guidelines for Forensic Psychologists, 1991), may help readers of the report to understand the limitations of the testing process in this context. Such an explanatory statement might approximate the following:

Note to the Reader about the Interpretation of Psychological Tests:

The interpretations of the psychological tests presented in this report are hypotheses and should not be used in isolation from other information in this matter. The interpretive statements are primarily computer-generated, actuarial, and expert predictions based on the test patterns. The interpretations reflect characteristics of persons who have provided test response patterns that are similar to those of the current individual. Test results are probabilistic in nature and should be interpreted cautiously, in that it is impossible to tell, from test results alone, if these patterns and deficits preexisted the events in question, or are the sequelae of the events. Therefore, the reader should examine the test interpretations for general trends and put limited weight on any one specific statement. In the integration and presentation of the test data, where results were unclear or in conflict, I selected the most likely hypotheses for presentation here.

This conservative approach should then be echoed in the language that is used in the actual interpretation. Instead of writing that "Mr. Jones's MMPI-2 results indicate that he is experiencing significant depression," the examiner can hypothesize that "Persons who score similarly to Mr. Jones may be significantly depressed." Although in some ways the two statements suggest the same outcome, the latter style reminds the reader that the interpretation is based only on the assumption that, because Mr. Jones scores in the range of the members of a group with depression as a known characteristic, he is more likely to resemble them than persons without scores such as his. This is different from implying that the test result demonstrates that he is depressed.

This approach also helps inoculate the examiner, when in the role of expert witness, against three common cross-examination strategies that are suggested to the attorney by the "Specialty Guidelines" and the "Ethical Principles." First, as suggested by these guidelines, the examiner has affirmatively stated that there are limitations to the methods and procedures that were employed. Second, inadvertent or apparent overstatement of the implied meaning of the test results is reduced. Third, apparently conflicting test data are properly conceptualized as being competing hypotheses generated by different aspects of the test protocols and not as contradictory results.

In deciding the content and substance of what to state in the report regarding the test interpretation, experts should be mindful of the "Specialty Guidelines" admonition to present in forensic reports only that which bears directly on legally relevant issues. Simply because an interpretative statement is accurate is not, by itself, sufficient reason for the statement to be included. For example, suppose that an MMPI-2 text cited research that a disproportionate number of females with a particular code were significantly more likely than the average woman to have had an abortion. The knowledge of that citation for this person's code type would not be adequate reason to include that likelihood in the forensic examiner's report in a matter in which having or not having had an abortion did not bear directly on the plaintiff's claim or damage.

Interpretative statements need to be not only relevant, they need to be understood in the forensic context. Elevated defensiveness or elevated self-criticalness in test results can merit very legal-case-specific interpretations rather than the more usual interpretative statements that would be offered if the MMPI-2 were taken in the anticipation of therapy or as part of "self-exploration" without the very significant consequences attendant to the legal struggle. Similarly, experts must exercise special caution in making clinical interpretations of elevated test scale scores that are substantially adjusted for defensiveness. Consider an example similar to the

Scale 6 example cited previously. In a stylistically defensive person who has been intrusively assaulted and who is now a personal injury plaintiff, Scale 8 (Sc) in particular can become highly elevated in large part due to a combination of K Scale correction and intrusive recollections of the event. This plaintiff may have few of the typical "Hi-8" qualities that otherwise would be attributed to such a score. In general, before being accepted by the examiner, hypotheses generated as a result of personality testing must be corroborated by real-world evidence.

Case-Substantive Interviews of Plaintiffs

Interviews with the parties should be conducted in a respectful and straightforward manner and never with the intent of tricking, confusing, or angering any individual. Interviewees have the right to refuse any part of the examination they consider to be unduly intrusive, emotionally stressful, or demanding. If the interview becomes too difficult for them, they can always leave and have their attorney ask the court for relief from any allegedly inappropriate procedures. There is simply no valid reason not to treat all parties in the same cordial and respectful manner, regardless of the side retaining the expert. This is not therapy, but neither should it resemble an interrogation or inquisition.

The interview should begin with the examiner informing the plaintiff of the general nature of the information needed by the expert. One method is to explain to the plaintiff that the examination will cover five areas and provide the reasons that each should be covered. These include (a) establishing a baseline of what plaintiff's life was like before the incident in question; (b) the nature of the incident itself; (c) how the person has been functioning since the incident; (d) why the person thinks the incident is the cause of the claimed difficulties and not something else; and (e) how the person is likely to function in the future. Elaborating on these five areas calls for descriptive accuracy and is also an opportunity for the examiner to set a tone of openness and even-handedness in the way the issues will be explored.

Establishing a Baseline

Because personal injury assessments are basically pre- and postincident examinations, exploring what the person's life was like before the incident is necessary to establish a baseline for the purpose of comparing "then and now." The plaintiff can be told that this is important because the examiner will be asked to testify about what problems and strengths the plaintiff already had at the time of the incident, whether any psychological damage was caused by the actions of the defendant, whether any preexisting problems were exacerbated, whether any of the strengths were impaired, and whether any areas of functioning proved to be resilient to the distress. The examiner may also be asked if the plaintiff was especially vulnerable to certain kinds of stressors; if so, this might establish the plaintiff as being what is referred to as an "eggshell" plaintiff. Such might be the case of a person who was sexually abused as a child, but who was nevertheless functioning without significant impairment 30 years later at the time of being sexual harassed on the job. Although this person's baseline level of function at the time of being harassed was normal, if this person's damage in response to the harassment was more profound than would be typical of most persons, the law considers the person to have been as vulnerable as an eggshell. Such plaintiffs usually are held to be entitled to compensation for all the damage suffered and not only that which would have been experienced by the average person suffering the same experience.

The Nature of the Stressor Incident

Second, the plaintiff should be told that the examiner is likely to be asked about the severity of the stressor to which the plaintiff was subjected. This is not for the purpose of testifying about whether the plaintiff is telling the truth about what is alleged to have happened. Plaintiffs frequently worry about exactly that, and they should be disabused of the notion that forensic examiners are "truth-tellers" or that the expert would testify that an incident did or did not occur in the way claimed by the plaintiff. The plaintiff should understand that the expert likely will be asked at least two questions about the claimed incident(s). One is that, if the incidents occurred as described, would the nature and degree of the stress experienced be severe enough to significantly impair the functioning of the average person. The other is whether the claimed impairment is clinically consistent with the nature and the severity of the stressor that is alleged. Basically, the plaintiff is informed that the forensic examiner wants to know what the experiencing of the events was like for the plaintiff and, if the plaintiff reacted differently to the stressor than other people might have, why the plaintiff thinks that would have been the case.

Sequelae

This third area focuses on how the plaintiff has been functioning since the incident. This includes not just how the plaintiff is functioning today, but how the person has been doing since this first happened. Consideration also needs to be given to ways in which the plaintiff proved to be resilient to the stressor. A chronology is especially helpful so that the forensic examiner may determine if the plaintiff is improving, getting worse, or remaining about the same. Occasionally, there is a silver lining to the cloud; that is, if one plaintiff and another person have rallied together in support of this claim, if plaintiff has gained insight or personal effectiveness as a result of treatment, if plaintiff has since found a better job, or if plaintiff and spouse are more intimate or open about feelings with each other, these are factors to be considered in the ways in which the plaintiff was damaged. A majority of plaintiffs probably somewhat exaggerate their psychological damage; the expert should keep in mind that exaggeration does not necessarily indicate that the entire damage is malingered. Even if damage is malingered, does this necessarily mean that the stressor events did not occur as claimed? There is no psychological test or interview procedure that can indicate with certainty whether or not a specific event occurred as claimed.

Cause in Fact

While policy decides what is to be considered the legally proximate cause of a harm, the forensic examiner can help the trier of fact decide if alleged impairments would have been unlikely to occur but for the actions the defendant is alleged to have committed. Again, because no psychological test indicates the specific cause of the plaintiff's problems, this needs to be the subject of detailed interviewing. Especially if the examiner is skeptical of the plaintiff's claimed damage and its cause, the plaintiff's statements in this regard should be fully and fairly represented in the examiner's notes and report, and then the expert should explain the basis for doubting the claims.

Prognosis

Legally, this refers to future damages, the consideration of ways that the plaintiff is likely to remain damaged and to need future treatment. One element should be simply asking the plaintiff about what the plaintiff expects in terms of recovery and future needs for treatment, job retraining or accommodation, or schooling. Psychological testing, as well as plaintiff's previous real-life experiences, can help estimate how plaintiff is likely to respond to treatment and to whether plaintiff is prone to become helpless or to be a survivor. Counsel will probably appreciate, where possible, an estimate of plaintiff's future treatment needs and the likely cost at the going rate in plaintiff's community.

Documentation of the interviews is critical. The "Specialty Guidelines" spells out clearly that it is the forensic expert's responsibility to document evidence in a clear and complete manner, anticipating judicial scrutiny, and more so than one would for the purposes of treatment. The forensic examiner is acting as an agent of discovery. This is not testimony. The operative rule for the forensic examiner is to ask about anything relevant to the psycholegal aspects of the case that might reasonably lead to admissible evidence and to record the same.

Sometimes, plaintiffs reveal information that is unfairly prejudicial to their case. If it is likely to be relevant to the issues before the court, the forensic examiner needs to document it. Applying a decision rule of keeping the plaintiff from harm, or of serving the purposes of the attorney who retains the forensic examiner, only serves to distort the process. Selective note taking, which depends on who the information favors, is not neutral, impartial, or objective. Unfairly prejudicial information is still usually discoverable. It is up to the trier of law, not the examiner, to decide if it is admissible.

The professional discretion that the forensic examiner is expected to exercise is in deciding what information gained is directly relevant to the forensic opinions to be offered. Those professional decisions are reflected in what the examiner puts in the report, not what gets put in the notes of the examination. Except for issues of legal privilege, relevance, and repetition, notes should be uncensored "raw data" for both sides to discover and use as the court allows. The forensic examiner should be documenting anything learned that is potentially relevant, meaning that, if admissible by a trier of law, it may assist the trier of fact. This is because the law's limits to discovery are couched in terms of relevance, and not in terms of admissibility. Unfair prejudice is a consideration to admissibility. Federal Rule of Civil Procedure 26 (Fed.R.Civ.P.26) and its state equivalents define the scope of discovery as "any matter, not privileged, which is relevant to the subject matter involved in the pending action . . . [and] need not be admissible at the trial if the information sought appears reasonably calculated to lead to the discovery of admissible evidence." The limits of discovery are usually objections that discovery is privileged, unduly burdensome, overbroad, or repetitive, not objections in terms of unfair prejudice and certainly not to be exercised unilaterally by the forensic examiner. Experts should not preempt the court's discovery process by acting as censors on the basis of the examiner's understanding of what might constitute potential unfair prejudice.

History taking should be structured so that important areas do not get overlooked. The regular use of a forensic history questionnaire (Greenberg, 2001a) allows for uniformity and thoroughness of questioning on examination after examination, providing the forensic examiner an opportunity to learn how different persons respond to exactly the same question. The basic areas to question in forensic history taking are identified in Table 13.4.

TABLE 13.4   Forensic History Interview Outline

Family of Origin

Name of each sibling, parent, grandparent, aunt, and uncle.
Year of birth and current age.
Nature of relationship (e.g., paternal aunt, foster brother).

Nonromantic Relationship History

Nature of their relationship to you (e.g., coach, boss, neighbor).
Other person's name.
Your age and other person's at the start of relationship.

Romantic Relationship History

Nature of their relationship to you (e.g., dated, partner, cohabitated).
Other person's name.
Your age and other person's at the start of relationship.

Children

Name of each daughter and son.
Nature of relationship (e.g., daughter, stepson).
Date of birth and current age (or age when deceased).
Names of biological mother and father.

Residential History

Location: city and state.
Dates lived there.
Type of residence (e.g., house, apartment, school, foster home).
Name of each person who lived (not just visited) in the residence with you.

Educational History

Name of school.
Type, city, state of school.
Years and grades attended.
Major area or program.
Certification or degree earned.
Last grade attended (e.g., eighth, H.S. sophomore, college senior).

Spiritual, Philosophical, Ethical, or Religious Training

Nature of participation.
Years attended or involved.

Recreational and Leisure Activities

Name or type of activity.
Description of participation.
Years participated.

Hobbies and Leisure Activities

Name or type of activity.
Description of participation.
Years participated.

Employment History

How earned money while growing up.
Adult jobs, positions, and responsibilities.
Employer.
Dates of employment.
Age when job started.
Hours worked per week.
Reason for leaving position.

Charitable Contributions

Work for charity and nonprofit organizations.
Donations.

Military Service

Service.
Branch, rate, and rank.
Locations where stationed.
Dates at location.
Age at the time.
Combat experience.

Current and Past Legal History

Juvenile, divorce, paternity, family law, or matrimonial law matters.
Agency, union grievance, or administrative law matters.
Civil law or business law matter.
Criminal misdemeanors or other criminal activity, allegations, or charges.
Posted a bond, paid damages, or paid compensation.
Placed on probation or parole or under someone's legal supervision.
Placed in a detention center, halfway house, or correctional institution.

Alcohol Use History

What (e.g., beer, wine, wine coolers, hard liquors, cocktails, mixed drinks, sherries, cognacs, cordials).
Where (e.g., home, job, bars, parties, sporting events, restaurants).
When (e.g., days, before dinner, with dinner, evenings, weekends, holidays).
How often (e.g., number of times each day, week, month).
How much you drank each time (e.g., number of 10-oz. drinks).

Drug and Substance Use History

What (e.g., cocaine, acid, marijuana, hash, Percocet, Valium).
Where (e.g., home, job, restaurants, parties).
When (e.g., days, evenings, weekends, holidays).
How often (e.g., number of times each day, week, or month).
How much you used each time (e.g., number of grams, joints, pills).

Physical Health History

Type of disorder, illness, or injury.
Date of each injury or condition.
Name of doctor or hospital.
Medications prescribed.
Degree of recovery.

Mental Health History

Type of counseling (e.g., individual, group, psychoanalytic, pastoral).
Name of counselor or therapist.
Total number of sessions.
Starting and ending dates.
Medications prescribed.

Psychological Educational Experience

Psychologically oriented meetings, information schools, classes.
Name or type of class, group, or seminar.
Total number of hours attended.
Starting and ending dates.

Other Pleasant and Unpleasant Experiences and Memories

Source: Adapted from Greenberg (2001b).

Site Observation

Experts should consider visiting the site of any relevant alleged event and interviewing relevant parties at such sites. In some cases, seeing the location of an alleged incident can help the forensic examiner understand and appreciate both the claims and the defenses being offered.

Collateral Interviews

Persons who have significant contact with the parties being examined (employers, coworkers, employees, neighbors, family members, teachers, coaches, pastors, health care providers) should be considered for collateral interviews. If permissions for privileged contacts are declined by the plaintiff, the forensic examiner will have to decide if an adequate examination can be conducted without such information. If not, the retaining attorney should be apprised of the need for such interviews, along with the professional literature supporting their use. The forensic examiner should never convey to the plaintiff that he or she must agree to collateral interviews. Plaintiffs can always have their attorneys ask the court to limit such discovery, just as defendants can always have their attorneys ask the court to order discovery and to waive privilege. The forensic examiner should indicate what is required and then let the legal process run its course.

On a related matter, all parties should understand that the relationship between the plaintiff and the forensic examiner is not privileged unless it happens to be protected by the attorney-client privilege. The forensic expert is not providing therapy, and the plaintiff should have no reasonable anticipation of confidentiality because the forensic examiner was retained in anticipation of public testimony. Therefore, technically, it is not the forensic examiner who, for example, needs a release to talk to a plaintiff's therapist; rather, it is the plaintiff's therapist who needs plaintiff's release to talk to the forensic examiner. This notwithstanding, it is still advisable when possible to request plaintiff's consent to discuss plaintiff with anyone to avoid surprises and misunderstandings. This may not be possible when the forensic examiner is retained by the defense and it is the defense counsel who wishes the forensic examiner to talk to defense witnesses and collaterals about their observations of the plaintiff. In that case, the plaintiff should be informed, as part of the initial informed consent interview, that there may be persons the defense will request the forensic examiner interview; if the plaintiff objects to that, then plaintiff should inform plaintiff's attorney of the objection.

The plaintiff should be encouraged to provide names of collaterals for the forensic examiner to interview, regardless of who has retained the forensic examiner. Even if the suggestion is declined, this puts the forensic examiner in the position at trial of having made the request rather than having to defend why the forensic expert received collateral information from only one side. Similarly, the forensic examiner should ask the plaintiff, through his or her attorney, for any documents that might help corroborate the plaintiff's case. Plaintiffs may forget to provide to their attorneys such things as diaries, family calendars, and day planners.

Two valuable sources of information about daily activities are checkbook registers and credit card statements. These may indicate if a person's lifestyle has changed before or after an incident. The person who was regularly going to movies or shows, dining out, purchasing music or art supplies, skiing, travelling, gardening, or doing home improvements may or may not continue such activities after an alleged harm. Financial records can be a ready source for corroboration of such claims. If not otherwise available, such records should be requested of the retaining attorney, who can use subpoena powers to acquire them, rather than the forensic examiner doing anything more than suggesting to the plaintiff that he or she might want to provide them directly, after consulting with counsel.

Experts should remember that consent should be received from a collateral before an interview is begun. At a minimum, the collateral should be informed of the role of the forensic examiner, that the expert is not providing therapy to anyone in the matter, and that what is discussed may not be confidential. In fact, what the collateral tells the forensic examiner may be discussed with others as part of corroborating the information. Finally, the collateral should be asked to focus on what is known through firsthand knowledge rather than anything that has been learned through hearsay. Collaterals should be told to not reveal anything to the forensic examiner that they do not want repeated and that they may request that the examiner read back the notes of the conversation so that they may be satisfied as to the accuracy of the record.

Results

It is important to complete the examination before issuing any opinions. Although this may seem obvious, attorneys often ask experts for verbal progress reports as a tactic for gently influencing the forensic examiner's opinion as the assessment proceeds. Bias may unknowingly creep into the forensic examiner's opinion if care is not taken to proceed fairly and systematically, forcing oneself to look at the forensic hypotheses from all reasonable perspectives and to be constantly alert to hindsight and confirmatory bias.

In considering the results of the examination, experts must think in forensic and not diagnostic terms. The law defines the elements of the exam. If the defendant is held liable, the plaintiff will get compensated based on the amount of impairment in the plaintiff's functioning, not on the diagnosis that the plaintiff carries. The forensic examiner should compare the plaintiff's state in the three to six months before the insult or trauma with the plaintiff's subsequent state. Part of the process is to determine what aspects of plaintiff's functioning before and after the event were average, were strengths, or were impaired.

In attempting to avoid hindsight bias, the forensic examiner should not let the tail wag the dog; that is, the expert should not let the knowledge that something traumatic may have happened to the plaintiff cloud the assessment of whether the plaintiff was impaired by it. Some people are remarkably resilient; others are remarkably fragile. Next, in assessing damages, the forensic examiner should form an opinion as to how vulnerable the plaintiff was at the time of the trauma, even if not then impaired. As to the stressor itself, was it of a nature and degree that would have been likely to damage most persons subjected to it?

Experts should consider future damages. What are the indications that the plaintiff is likely to need future treatment? Also, consider likely affirmative defenses. Did the plaintiff contribute to his or her own harm? Could the plaintiff have avoided the harm altogether by some reasonable action? Has the plaintiff acted reasonably in reducing his or her own damage by attending treatment and by not acting in self-defeating ways? Finally, were there any silver linings to this cloud? Did anything substantial in plaintiff's life actually improve as a result of what happened?

Forensic Report

Results initially should be communicated verbally to the retaining attorney. This is because many jurisdictions allow the retaining attorney to prevent the attorney's own expert from being used against the retaining attorney's case should the results of the examination fail to be adequately helpful to the case. There is no reason to bill a client to prepare a written report when it will not be used. At the same time, this is not an opportunity for the attorney to influence the forensic examiner's opinion. This discussion is to be a report of the findings, not a debate.

Assuming that the decision by the retaining attorney is to proceed, a report should be written in a standard format. One

way to begin the report is to describe the nature of a forensic report. The following language may be useful:

> As requested, this is the report of my forensic psychological examination of Ms. Smith, one of the plaintiffs in this matter. This examination was conducted and this report was prepared in anticipation of the current litigation, and should not be relied on for any other purpose. Prior to commencing the first interview, I explained to the plaintiff my role, by which attorney I was retained, the nature of the forensic examination process, that the examination was not therapy, and that forensic examinations are not covered by therapist-patient privilege, but may be covered under other legal privilege. When considering the interviews, psychometric testing, and collateral records and interviews in this matter, and when formulating my opinions, I view my role as expert to the court, attempting to assist the trier of fact. The plaintiff indicated that she understood each of the above, agreed to proceed, and signed the appropriate consent forms. Please notify me promptly of any significant incorrect facts (e.g., ages, names, dates, events) that need to be corrected in this report. Thank you for your cooperation during this examination.

When choosing the language of the report itself, unnecessarily pejorative descriptive language or test interpretations should be avoided. Although some psychologically driven recommendations contain financial implications (e.g., a party's need to have a certain amount of therapy), examiners usually avoid discussions of financial matters. Referrals to specific providers usually should be deferred until the time when the examiner will have no further involvement in the matter. Although there is no one universally accepted format, the report model outlined in Table 13.5 may be of assistance.

In writing reports and testifying orally, experts should always keep in mind that their obligation is to be fair to all sides. In so doing, experts should present fairly and completely all relevant information that might assist an opposing counsel to persuade the court to act contrary to the examiner's own recommendations. This is not to preclude the examiner from arguing persuasively for his or her opinions, but it does preclude the omission or distortion of data that may be contrary to the examiner's opinions. The examiner cannot be helpful to the court if the information being provided by the examiner is distorted by partisanship, bias, or the examiner's personal issues.

TESTIMONY

Being Discovered

The basic methods for discovery by opposing counsel are, first, to subpoena the examiner's records and, then, to depose the expert. In some jurisdictions, opposing counsel receives

TABLE 13.5   Personal Injury Report Model Outline

Referral Information

Source of referral.
Professional role.
Reason/purpose of referral.
Understanding of the legal complaint.
Psycholegal issues to be examined.
Intended use of report.
Any confidentiality/privilege/access issues.
Statement as to the nature of a forensic report.

Informed Consent

Attorney informed consent.
Party informed consent.

Process of Exam and Nature of Information Sources

Assessment instruments and dates.
Questionnaires completed and dates.
Party interviews and dates.
Collateral sources.
  Documents reviewed.
  Persons interviewed and dates.
  Other professional consults.
Comment on any nonstandard processes.

Party's Current Presentation

Mental status exam or description.

History as May Be Directly Relevant

Family of origin.
Relationship history.
  Family members, partners, and children.
  Other significant persons.
Residential history.
Educational history.
  Religious, spiritual, or philosophical training.
Recreation
  Leisure activities, hobbies.
  Charitable contributions of time and resources.
Employment history.
  Employment/unemployment history.
  Military service.
  Military and employment personnel records.

Current and past legal history.
  Juvenile, divorce, paternity, or family law matters.
  Agency, union grievance, governmental, or administrative
    law matters.
  Civil law or business law matters.
  Criminal misdemeanors.
  Other criminal activity allegations or charges.
Alcohol use history.
Drug and other substance use history.
Physical health history.
  Health and fitness.
  Current treatments and medications.
  Injuries, illnesses.
  Hospitalizations, surgeries, and major treatments.
Mental health history.
  Therapy and counseling treatment.
  Psychoeducational experiences, seminars, workshops.

History Specifically as Regards the Psycholegal Issues

Party's description of events.
Information from other sources.
  Regarding the events in question.
    Collateral documents.
    Collateral party interviews.

Assessment Results

Information regarding meaning of test interpretations.
Testing results and interpretations.
  Comment on any prior testing.

Opinion

Summary of information acquired.
Any extra examination information on which examiner relied
  (e.g., research, literature).
Opinion as to each psycholegal issue.
Caveats as to opinions.
  Limitations.
  Additional information needed.
  Offer to make corrections of any factual errors.
Recommendations, if any.

Sworn Statement and notarized or attested signature.

Source: Adapted from Greenberg (2001b).

additional discovery in the form of a detailed expert witness statement that must be provided before a court-imposed deadline. The process of being discovered usually begins with the receipt of a subpoena for a records deposition. The following is an example of such a subpoena, technically called a *Subpoena Duces Tecum*. As indicated at the end of this document, if the records are provided in advance, the expert usually need not personally appear.

Subpoena Duces Tecum for Records Deposition

YOU ARE, HEREBY, COMMANDED to appear at the office of _____ at _____ on _____, commencing at the hour of

1:00 P.M. on said day, and to remain in attendance upon the undersigned or any other Notary Public until discharged, AND YOU ARE FURTHER COMMANDED TO BRING WITH YOU AT SAID TIME AND PLACE the following instruments, papers, and documents, to wit:

Your entire file and records pertaining to the forensic examination performed of ____, including but not limited to all transcriptions and notes made of interviews with any person done in connection with this examination; all testing and other assessment instruments completed by either of the parties and/or any child of the parties, and all raw test data and scoring reports, all reports, evaluations, letters, declarations, and other written communications of any kind whatsoever received by you in connection with this examination, from any person or entity; all of your billing records pertaining to this examination; and all of your written communications with any person or entity made in connection with this examination.

NOTE: YOU NEED NOT APPEAR AS INDICATED IF PHOTOCOPIES OF ALL SUBPOENAED MATERIALS ARE TIMELY DELIVERED PURSUANT TO THE ABOVE DESCRIPTION OF INSTRUMENTS, PAPERS, AND DOCUMENTS. HEREIN FAIL NOT AT YOUR PERIL.

The Expert's Deposition

Deposition discovery of experts, which also includes the right to discover forensic examination notes, other documents, methods, and results, as well as the credentials of the examiner, typically is conducted by opposing counsel. Opposing counsel wants to know what the expert has learned from and about the plaintiff, what the opinions of the expert are, the bases for those opinions, and the expert's ability to present those in front of the jury. The expert is subpoenaed and questioned under oath to test the expert's limits of expertise, knowledge, and personal mettle. Opposing counsel is interested in the information but is also focused on the expert's fortitude in dealing with verbal adversity as a preview of what trial testimony may be like. In some cases, the expert may be subjected to a more severe and impolite questioning during the deposition than at trial because the attorney is operating without the countervailing concern of potentially alienating the jury by rudeness.

One federal rule directly addresses the discovery of information from experts. It is indicative of what is expected of the expert and how the expert is to be paid. It is found in Table 13.6.

TABLE 13.6   Procedural Rules Pertaining to the Discovery of Expert Testimony: Federal Rules of Evidence: Rule 26(b)(4)

Trial Preparation Experts. Discovery of facts known and opinions held by experts, otherwise discoverable under the provisions of subdivision (b)(1) of this rule and acquired or developed in anticipation of litigation or for trial, may be obtained only as follows:

A party may through interrogatories require any other party to identify each person whom the other party expects to call as an expert witness at trial, to state the subject matter on which the expert is expected to testify, and to state the substance of the facts and opinions to which the expert is expected to testify and a summary of the grounds for each opinion. Unless manifest injustice would result, (i) the court shall require that the party seeking discovery pay the expert reasonable fee for time spent in responding to discovery under . . . of this rule; and (ii) with respect to discovery obtained under . . . of this rule. The court . . . shall require the party seeking discovery to pay the other party a fair portion of the fees and expenses reasonably incurred by the latter party in obtaining facts and opinions from the expert.

Trial Testimony

Under both *Frye v. United States* (1923) and *Daubert v. Merrell-Dow Pharmaceuticals, Inc.* (1993), expert testimony needs to be reliable to be admissible. *Frye* requires the court to ascertain whether the expert's methods and procedures have gained general acceptance in the relevant professional community to assess their reliability. *Daubert* requires federal courts to determine "whether the reasoning or methodology underlying the testimony is scientifically valid and whether that reasoning properly can be applied to the facts in issue" (p. 2796). The expert witness staying within the guidelines of the "Ethical Principles" and the "Specialty Guidelines" goes a long way toward meeting the admissibility requirements articulated in both *Frye* and *Daubert.* Although compliance with an ethical code or guideline provides no necessary assurance that the reasoning and methodology underlying the testimony is scientifically valid, failure to comply with them is powerful evidence that such reasoning and methodology may well be invalid (Shuman & Greenberg, 1998).

There is also no substitute for being well prepared. Attorneys may blanch at the cost for the time needed to do adequate preparation for trial, but the expert who is the master of the case facts is usually the master of the give and take of questioning. This also applies to preparation for the legal process in general. Being familiar with texts such as *Psychiatric and Psychological Evidence* (Shuman, 2000), as the name implies, will help expert witnesses understand the legal process and anticipate what is likely to be admissible testimony in this legal area.

Seasoned attorneys usually do an adequate job of inquiring about the expert's qualifications by following the basic format of the expert's vita; however, a better presentation may result if the expert prepares qualifying questions in advance, tailored to the expert's expertise and to the specific issues of the case. This will vary for each expert and each case, but a rough outline might include questioning regarding the expert's identification, professional address, licensure, and nature of practice. The second set of questions would inquire regarding educational background, postdoctoral training, specialized training, and advanced certifications. Next might come professional organization membership, volunteer and elected positions, and university or hospital affiliations. Continuing education, especially in areas related to the current matter, is extremely important so that the jury can hear that the expert keeps current on issues that are related to this case. Research, training of students and of other professionals, other strategies for keeping current in professional practice, and a description of the experience the expert has had with similar cases can all dovetail into the current case issues. Qualifying should end with a description of what tasks were requested by the retaining attorney in the present matter and what procedures the expert undertook to complete those tasks.

If the matter is before a jury, a discussion during qualifying of the expert's role when testifying in court should be considered. By telling the jury that the expert's role is to impartially assist the trier of fact and that there are limitations to what an expert can reasonably conclude, the expert is likely to surprise at least some of the jurors. However, it is also likely to set very high expectations of the expert by the jury–expectations that must be met. After such pronouncements, for the expert to have any credibility, testimony must be measured, fair, and impartial. On the other hand, the reward for actually providing such trustworthy testimony is likely to be the opportunity to persuade the jury of the merits of the expert's examination and testimony. Trials are mostly decided on issues of credibility. Facts and opinions do not count for anything if they are not believed by the trier of fact.

Sample Testimony

In 1993, there was an appeal heard in the U.S. Court of Appeals in the matter of *Darreyl Wayne Gough v. Natural Gas Pipeline Co. of America (NGP)*. This interesting, if tragic, case illustrates a number of the aspects typical of personal injury matters in which psychological damages are sought. Below is a completely fabricated transcript of what might have been some of the direct and cross-examination testimony at trial of a forensic expert called by the plaintiff in this matter. The actual case "facts" have been altered or fabricated for the purposes of this example.

While reading this testimony, consider a number of things. The witness, despite being retained by the plaintiff's counsel, mostly testifies as a neutral expert who is helping the court. While being fair, he tries to persuade the jury of the accuracy of his opinions by presenting them persuasively in an expert, trustworthy, and dynamic manner. At the same time, he is even-handed. On direct examination, he presents data from both sides of the case, arguing forcefully for his conclusions but granting the devil his due when appropriate. Be mindful that "the devil" is not the opposite attorney or opposing expert. "The devil" in this context is the data that support opinions that are contrary to those that the expert has reached. After testimony as to his qualifications, the expert presents the opinions that he has reached and the data that support those opinions. He then discusses the limitations of his opinions and the data and opinions that rival his own opinions. He explains why the contrary facts and opinions are outweighed by other data and considerations, and then emphasizes to the jury why the opinions he has offered are more consistent with the data than are any others.

It is important that this open debate with himself occur on direct examination. This provides the opportunity for him to fully testify as to both sides of the conceptual arguments without having to do so in the face of what might be selective or hostile questioning by opposing counsel. Additionally, this "supports and rivals" testimony process on direct examination helps inoculate the jury against opposing arguments on cross-examination and later in the trial. It also may steal the thunder of opposing counsel on cross-examination. Most important, it lets the jury know that the expert can be trusted to tell them both sides of the story and to do so fairly, objectively, and voluntarily. The alternative is to testify on direct examination only to that which favors one's opinions and then wait to see what questions are asked on cross-examination. This latter approach runs the risk of giving the jury the impression that the witness is hiding the ball and is willing to acknowledge the presence of contrary facts and arguments only when he is forced to do so by opposing counsel. Such witnesses risk not being viewed as particularly trustworthy.

In reading the fabricated transcript, also be aware that much was left out. The totality of the testimony is very abbreviated and, also in the interest of brevity, the Q and A is presented in "big," sometimes compound, questions and answers rather than in the more incremental, stepwise process that is more typical in most courts.

Also note that some of the questions and answers are clearly objectionable as written. However, only some objections are offered and others are waived. For example, the questions regarding whether most people would respond to the distress as did Captain Gough beg for a challenge of lacking adequate foundation. Further, some of the expert's answers are expansive and therefore unresponsive. For example, questions such as "Doctor, do you have an opinion regarding X?" technically call for a yes or no response and not for an extended colloquy. However, objections to such responses may not be offered for several reasons. Objecting too frequently can make the attorney who does so look pedantic in the eyes of the jury. Both counsel know that the expansive and nonresponsive parts of the witness's answer can simply be requested in counsel's next question anyway. And the making of the objection may have the unwanted effect of drawing the jury's attention to the witness's unhelpful answer. Lodging technically correct but trivial objections to opposing counsel's questions may also leave counsel open to ridicule by opposing counsel. Taking care not to offend the judge, counsel may say in a painfully frustrated and sarcastic tone, "Doctor, I apologize. Defense counsel has requested that we take this one step at a time. Now that the jury has heard that you have an opinion, would you take it the next step and tell us what that opinion is?"

To understand the context of the imaginary expert's testimony, assume that when a fishing vessel piloted by her captain, Darreyl Wayne Gough, backed over a natural gas pipeline that was supposed to have been buried six feet into the seabed, his vessel struck the exposed pipeline, ruptured it, and a fireball swept the ship, killing 11 of its 14 crew. As Captain Gough attempted to escape the flames, the ship exploded. Despite being almost unconscious, he attempted, but failed, to keep an injured crew member from drowning. He was hospitalized for both medical and psychiatric reasons. He sued the pipeline owner, NGP, under general maritime law for a variety of physical and mental damages, as well as other losses.

Fabricated Transcript

Keep in mind that the following is not provided as an example of a uniformly ideal way to testify. Rather, it attempts to provide for the reader a typical example of what expert witnesses might expect on direct and cross-examination and it tries to exemplify how the expert's answers on direct examination try to anticipate counsel's questions on cross-examination. Also assume that there has been extensive pretrial discovery, including detailed reports from and depositions of the plaintiff's expert. As you will see, the plaintiff's attorney chooses to raise "unhelpful" issues on direct examination rather than wait for defense counsel to do so on cross-examination. The testimony of the plaintiff's forensic expert begins after the point at which the witness has described his impeccable credentials.

Abbreviated Direct Examination by Plaintiff's Counsel

Q: Doctor, would you please tell us what you did to complete this forensic examination?

A: In February and March of last year, I reviewed an extensive set of documents, perhaps 5,000 pages. This included accident reconstruction, employment, medical, and psychological records, as well as many of the other legal documents and transcripts in this matter. During that period, and later, I also reviewed the clinical and forensic literature as it relates to these kinds of matters. In April, I administered to Captain Gough a battery of seven psychological questionnaires and tests, and then spent about nine hours interviewing Captain Gough directly. These interviews of Captain Gough were spaced over three days. I also conducted interviews of

seven collateral individuals, which included the two survivors of this accident and Captain Gough's wife. I started interviewing the collaterals after his first interview and completed them before his last interview.

Q: Doctor, would you please describe for the court what your examination revealed about the psychological status of Captain Gough in the period before the pipeline explosion?

A: In most ways, Captain Gough was functioning normally before this incident. He had been through several shipboard tragedies before, with no lasting ill effect. There were no reports that his job performance was psychologically impaired in any way. He was working hard, sleeping well, doing his job, and his relationship with his crew members was positive. He was described as an effective leader and as a man that the crew respected, despite the fishing having been particularly poor on this trip. But his family life was not as positive. He reported that his wife had been complaining bitterly about his long absences, low and sporadic income, and seasonal employment. He was concerned that she might be considering leaving him and he had resolved to try to work things out with her on his next furlough. He also was sad that his son had decided not to accompany him on this trip but, in hindsight, was relieved that he had not done so because of the accident. Overall, I evaluated him or reviewed records regarding his physical health, mental health, employment history, occupational functioning, social functioning, and so on, and in most ways, found that his prior functioning was unimpaired in major life areas.

Q: From the records that you reviewed, from the collateral individuals that you interviewed, and from the many hours you spent testing and interviewing Captain Gough himself, what did you learn about what happened to Captain Gough and his crew on October 3, 1989?

A: On that day, his boat was trawling about one-half mile from shore. Captain Gough had recently returned to the pilot house from one of the smaller work boats and resumed command. He began backing the ship away from the shore when the boat suddenly stopped and there was an immense explosion. The ship had struck and ruptured a gas pipeline and, within seconds, a fireball swept almost the entire ship. Captain Gough escaped the pilot house, was blown overboard, and swam away from the heat and flames. Soon afterwards, spotter helicopters dropped rafts and tried to assist the survivors. Although in shock from the explosion,

Captain Gough tried to assist one injured seaman who, because of all of the fuel and oil in the water, slipped away from him and drowned. In all, 11 crew members died; his brother and another crewman were severely burned. All three survivors were pulled from the water and airlifted to a local medical hospital by helicopter.

Q: Doctor, in your opinion, is that the kind of event that would severely affect most people?

A: Although there is no research that directly answers that question, it is my opinion that such an intense and frightening set of events would traumatize most people.

Q: Why is that, Doctor?

A: Captain Gough was located in the pilot house when his ship collided with the pipeline. Within seconds, flames spread toward him. He could feel the heat, and immediately after he left the pilot house, fire engulfed it. Attempting to avoid the flames, Captain Gough started to jump overboard into the Gulf of Mexico when the ship exploded. The explosion threw him 75 feet into the air, rendering him almost unconscious. Even in the water, the heat was reported to have been unbearable. The medical records indicated that Captain Gough inhaled fumes from the fire and ingested salt water as another victim of the disaster pulled him underwater. Besides being submerged in the ocean, Captain Gough suffered multiple contusions. Finally, some testimony suggests that Captain Gough suffered from minor burns, although no medical record confirmed these opinions. It is my opinion that, based on exposure to this combination of experiences, most people would be significantly psychologically harmed.

Q: Doctor, how in fact was Captain Gough harmed by what he was subjected to?

A: Captain Gough was in the medical ward of a local hospital for two days, but he soon began experiencing nightmares, flashbacks, and depression and needed to be moved to a psychiatric inpatient facility. Psychiatrists and psychologists diagnosed posttraumatic stress disorder, and Captain Gough, after discharge from the psychiatric hospital, began individual psychotherapy.

Q: Doctor, does being psychiatrically diagnosed PTSD by itself demonstrate that Captain Gough has been harmed?

A: No, it does not. Diagnosis, by itself, primarily describes a predefined and standard constellation of symptoms that occur together with greater-than-chance frequency. As the standard diagnostic manual itself says, the clinical diagnosis of a mental disorder is not suffi-

cient to establish the existence or extent of a disability for legal purposes. In determining whether an individual meets a specified legal standard, additional information is usually required beyond that contained in a diagnosis.

Q: Well, then, Doctor, in what ways has Captain Gough been psychologically harmed?

A: Captain Gough is experiencing insomnia, depression, anxiety, and a variety of trauma-related symptoms that he would probably not be suffering but for this experience. He is phobic of boats, deep water, and fires, making it impossible for him to return to work as a mariner. He has intrusive recollections of various aspects of what he experienced, and these prevent him from concentrating, solving problems, or even just relaxing. While his relationship with his wife was already strained, he now is not able to engage in any emotional or sexual intimacy with her. In fact, they barely talk to each other. Any visual entertainment that involves boats, fishing, water, fires, or natural gas—even otherwise innocuous scenes of kitchen stoves or fireplaces—causes him intense anxiety and physical trembling. He is constantly vigilant, scanning the environment for any threat. He startles when anyone lights a cigarette or gas stove. He has difficulty falling asleep, sleeps restlessly with frequent awakenings, and wakes up early still feeling fatigued and exhausted. He feels what is called "survivor's guilt" and at times wishes he had perished with his friends and crewmembers. He is sad and irritable with most people, and his friends told me in the collateral interviews that he won't let them try to help or comfort him. He generally avoids friends and avoids most social engagements. When I interviewed his therapist, she told me that although he was attending regularly, he was making little progress in therapy.

Q: Doctor, his therapist has testified that she thinks he will need three to four more years of weekly, sometimes twice-weekly, treatment to improve back to the state that he was in before the accident. Is that your opinion also?

A: No, I'm afraid it is not. In the nine months in which he has been in twice-weekly therapy, he has made little progress, and I believe that this suggests that Captain Gough is not a good candidate for psychotherapy. While a basically healthy individual before, he did not have the characteristics of someone who was well suited to benefit from therapy. He was a man of few words, not psychologically minded, and disparaging of people who needed therapists. He called them "head shrinkers," because he thought that being a patient of such people meant to be weak and shameful. This was pretty much what he had told his wife before the last trip, when she requested that they seek marital counseling. My opinion of his ability to improve from therapy is also consistent with his performance on psychological testing, which reflects significant negative treatment indicators. This is also consistent with his therapist's notes regarding his lack of therapy progress. He is an individual who believes that, if left to his own resources, he can solve or at least overcome any psychological problem. I would have to say that, given these predisposing attitudes and his current lack of progress in treatment, he is not likely to benefit substantially more from psychotherapy than he already has.

Q: Does this mean that he is voluntarily or intentionally failing to ameliorate his own problems?

A: No. Only that he has probably already achieved maximum benefit from this type of treatment for now. He is unlikely to benefit significantly from additional psychotherapy at this time. Also keep in mind that he is receiving medication management and follow-up from his family doctor, and those records indicate that he is benefiting in the form of reduced depression, anxiety, and insomnia.

Q: Doctor, do you think that the problems that you testified to regarding Captain Gough are significantly overstated, as is being suggested by the expert that the defense has retained?

A: No, I do not. However, I can see why the defense expert might be saying that. Plaintiffs do often exaggerate and may especially do so in an attempt to persuade or express their outrage to experts retained by the defense. Most plaintiffs are at least suspicious of the expert retained by what they consider to be their adversary, if not enemy. In addition, when you are as vulnerable as is Captain Gough, molehills seem like mountains. When you are that frightened of not getting better, you may exaggerate to get help. When you don't trust someone hired by your adversary, you may exaggerate, assuming that the person will discount what you say. When you are intensely angry at something that has happened to you, you may overstate your case. He may indeed have presented himself differently to the defense expert than he did to me, and, in fact, differences between his two psychological testings support that perception. I am not suggesting that the defense expert is incorrect, only that I considered these factors before I offered my opinions regarding Captain Gough's degree of damage.

More important, what exaggeration Captain Gough may have engaged in pales against the severe psychological problems that he undoubtedly has.

Q: What, then, is your prognosis for Captain Gough?

A: It is my opinion that some of his distress will dissipate reasonably soon after the legal process stops requiring him to relive and thereby reexperience the trauma. After that, his anxiety symptoms will probably slowly dissipate over time, but he is unlikely to be able to ever completely recover or completely forget what he experienced. It is possible that after the anxiety dissipates, he may be better able to use therapy than he is currently, in that he is currently almost immobilized by worry and apprehension. Another trial of medication management may also be considered. More exact predictions are impossible for me to offer.

Q: Thank you, Doctor. That's all for now. Your witness.

Abbreviated Cross-Examination by Defense Counsel

Q: Good afternoon, Doctor.

A: Good afternoon, Counsel.

Q: Doctor, would it be correct to say that the treatment of trauma-induced anxiety disorders is relatively well researched and established in the psychological literature?

A: Yes it would. There are reasonably effective methods for treating many victims of trauma.

Q: So then, you are not testifying that the failure of Captain Gough to get better is due to there being no established method of treating such problems?

A: No, I am not. That was not my testimony.

Q: Thank you for clarifying that. We wouldn't want the jury to think that Captain Gough's failure to get better was due to incompetence on the part of his therapist. You didn't see any signs of incompetence on her part as you reviewed his therapy notes, did you, Doctor?

A: No, I did not.

Q: You testified that you thought that most people would be significantly injured by what Captain Gough experienced?

A: Yes, I did.

Q: Doctor, based on your experience, would most people have been injured as much as Captain Gough says he was injured?

A: No, I don't think so. Captain Gough appears to be more harmed by this experience than would most people.

Q: Doctor, as far as you know, have either of the other two survivors of this accident claimed to have developed symptoms as severe as those that Captain Gough has claimed?

A: No, they have not. Both of the survivors were included in the collaterals whom I interviewed. They reported fewer and less severe psychological injuries than did Captain Gough, and they also reported that they have mostly recovered.

Q: Doctor, isn't it possible that this plaintiff is exaggerating—just making things look worse—so he can collect money? After all, we agree that his coworkers are doing fine?

A: I did not testify that his coworkers were "doing fine." I said that they were experiencing fewer problems and mostly recovered. In fact, they are still experiencing some residual problems from the trauma they experienced. As to this plaintiff "just" making things look worse, I testified earlier that a plaintiff's exaggerating is not unusual. However, given the results of my examination of him and the extensive documentation of problems that Captain Gough has suffered, it is very unlikely that he is "just" making things look worse, as you put it, but rather that, even if there is some exaggeration, he has nevertheless suffered severely from this tragedy.

Q: Doctor, when you testified that you thought that most people would be injured by what Captain Gough experienced, were you comparing him to the average person in general, or were you comparing him to other persons with life experiences similar to his?

A: Other people in general.

Q: Doctor, if Captain Gough claims more damage from this incident than the other two survivors who experienced basically the same thing, would it be reasonable to consider that this was because he was somehow more vulnerable to it by virtue of his personality makeup or his previous experiences?

A: Yes, that would have been a reasonable hypothesis to test.

Q: Doctor, would you please tell the jury if the computerized test interpretations of his personality that you discussed in your deposition state in various places that he may be, and I quote: "overreporting his problems," that he may have "a tendency to magnify illness," and have

"an inclination to whine and complain," and that "treatment is unlikely to improve his condition," and also that "he is not motivated to work to do so"? Did the computerized interpretations of his personality tests say those things, Doctor?

A: Yes, they did, but . . .

Q: Doctor, excuse me. You answered my question. If the counsel that is paying you to testify would like to ask you further questions about this, he is entitled to do so later. Thank you for your answer.

Plaintiff's Counsel: Your honor, I object. Counsel interrupted the witness's answer. First of all, the doctor has already testified that he is being compensated for his time and that what opinions he offers to this court are not under the control of either counsel and, second, if the expert feels that he needs to clarify an answer in order to not mislead the jury, he should be allowed to do so.

Defense Counsel: Your honor, that is exactly what I said. "The counsel that is paying you to testify" and, as to the second part, I asked the witness a simple yes-no question, which he answered. Plaintiff's counsel is now trying to testify for his witness.

The Court: Plaintiff's objections are overruled, counsel. The witness will have ample opportunity to elaborate on any of his answers on redirect examination should plaintiff's counsel decide to question him about those at that time. The jury is instructed to disregard the comments of both counsel. Defense counsel, please proceed.

Defense Counsel: Thank you, your honor. Doctor, my last question: You answered earlier that you thought it likely that most persons would have been significantly psychologically injured by being subjected to that which Captain Gough was subjected. Suppose the same question of likelihood had been posed to you, but with regard instead to a group of seasoned sea captains with over 20 years of experience, who had themselves previously weathered a number of equivalently severe sea-going incidents, who sustained the same kinds of limited physical injuries as did Captain Gough in the current incident, and who had emerged from the previous incidents unscathed and with no significant or long-lasting psychological disorders. Would you say that that group—the group more like Captain Gough himself—would be less likely to have been significantly psychologically injured than the average person who has never been a sea captain?

A: Yes, I would say that the experienced sea captain group, with no prior history of trauma response to stress, would be less likely to become significantly impaired than the average person would.

Q: Doctor, would it be accurate to say that Captain Gough has a lot more of those factors in common with the group of sea captains whom I just described than he does with the average person?

A: Yes, that would be accurate.

Q: Thank you very much. No further questions. Counsel, redirect?

Testimony Postmortem

What should be evident in this transcript? While the plaintiff's counsel and plaintiff's expert do an admirable job of attempting on direct examination to inoculate the jury to some of the facts that are unhelpful to the plaintiff's case, the defense counsel's pointed questions of the expert regarding the personality testing results are presented to demonstrate how potentially damaging to testimony it can be to fail to "steal the thunder" and inoculate the jury to the opposing argument, especially when something is so obvious. In this instance, the expert has spoken on direct examination of the testing's "negative treatment indicators," but did not testify as to some of the more dramatically damaging "whine" and "complain" language of exaggeration and of the plaintiff not being motivated to do the work of therapy. Certainly, one must not always do so, but careful consideration of the pro's and con's, and not succumbing to overconfidence, is prudent.

This expert's response of "Yes they did, but . . ." to the attorney's question about the computerized interpretative language can be seen in two lights. In the light most unfavorable to the expert, the witness has heard how awful that language sounds and has seen in the faces of the jury their reaction to the implication that he left that information out of his answers on purpose. In that negative light, the defense has made an arguably valid point, and the expert was not content to let it sit that way with the jury until redirect. Because he did not want to look bad in their eyes and perhaps have his testimony be doubted by them, he tried to explain his answer. In the light most favorable to the expert, the defense counsel has quoted the computerized testing interpretations unfairly out of context and without the appropriate caveats. The expert did not want to let the misleading testimony stand uncorrected. The judge has settled the issue in favor of the defense, leaving the lesson learned for the expert: Next time, bring it up on direct first, so this doesn't happen.

Finally, what is also left out is what cannot be seen or heard in a transcript. The witness has kept himself organized; spoken loudly and clearly; has, without being rude to the attorneys, spoken mostly to the jury, who is supposed to be the recipient of what he says; has not let himself be drawn into the game playing and theatrics of the attorneys; and has, by tone and inflection, treated opposing counsel with respect.

CONCLUDING THOUGHTS

As was so astutely recognized by Grisso (1986) in his landmark text, forensic examination is essentially the evaluation of competency. Be it competency to parent, to execute a will, to stand trial, to refuse medication, to live independently in the community, or to be executed, forensic examination is, at its most basic level, a functional analysis of a party's abilities and impairments. At this most basic level, conducting an examination for personal injury is no different. It is the assessment of whether and how a person's functioning has become damaged or impaired.

What sets personal injury assessments apart from other types of forensic examinations is the pre/post nature of the examination. The defendant is potentially responsible to compensate the plaintiff for all of the damage and impairment that the defendant caused the plaintiff. That harm is the plaintiff's "pain and suffering." The defendant is not responsible for any pain, suffering, damage, or impairment that the plaintiff experienced prior to the defendant's wrongful action. In that light, each personal injury examination is really two assessments: one of plaintiff's functioning before and one of plaintiff's functioning since the allegedly wrongful actions of the defendant. The differences found in the plaintiff's functioning between these two points in time reveal the nature and degree to which the plaintiff has or has not been damaged. This becomes one of the primary bases on which juries decide whether to award damages to injured parties and, if so, how much.

Contributing as a forensic examiner to this legal process can be both intellectually rewarding and emotionally draining. Preparation and prudence are indicated. Because of the potentially huge and immediate impact that forensic examiners may have on the well-being of others, the "Specialty Guidelines" reminds us that forensic psychologists have an obligation to provide services in a manner consistent with the highest standards of the profession. For those willing to attempt to do so, this can be a fascinating and challenging professional task.

REFERENCES

American Psychological Association. (1992). Ethical principles of psychologists and code of conduct. *American Psychologist, 47,* 1597–1611.

Boccaccini, M. T., & Brodsky, S. L. (1999). Diagnostic test usage by forensic psychologists in emotional injury cases. *Professional Psychology: Research and Practice, 30*(3), 253–259.

Committee on Ethical Guidelines for Forensic Psychologists. (1991). Specialty guidelines for forensic psychologists. *Law and Human Behavior, 15,* 655–665.

Darreyl Wayne Gough, Plaintiff-appellee, Cross-appellant, v. Natural Gas Pipeline Co. of America, ("NGP"), Defendant-appellant, Cross-appellee. (U.S.C.A., 5th Cir. 1993). LEXIS No. 92-4220.

Daubert v. Merrell-Dow Pharmaceutical, Inc., 509 U.S. 579, 113 S. Ct. 2786 (1993).

Fink, A. M., & Butcher, J. N. (1972). Reducing objections to personality inventories with special instructions. *Educational and Psychological Measurement, 32*(3), 631–639.

Frye v. United States. 293 F. 1013 (D.C. Cir. 1923).

Garner, B. A. (Ed. in Chief). (1999). *Henry Campbell's Black's law dictionary* (7th ed.). New York: West Group.

Greenberg, S. A. (2000). Health insurance reimbursement for forensic services: A minefield to be avoided. *Bulletin of the American Psychology-Law Society, 20*(2).

Greenberg, S. A. (2001a). *Forensic History Questionnaire.* Unpublished manuscript. (Available from Stuart Greenberg, 2815 Eastlake Ave E, Ste. 220, Seattle, WA 98102)

Greenberg, S. A. (2001b). *Personal injury examinations: Ethics, case law, and practice.* Unpublished manuscript, Continuing Education Workshop of The American Academy of Forensic Psychology, San Jose, CA, & Vancouver, British Columbia, Canada.

Greenberg, S. A., & Brodsky, S. (2001). *The practice of civil forensic psychology.* Washington, DC: American Psychological Association.

Greenberg, S. A., & Shuman, D. W. (1997). Irreconcilable conflict between therapeutic and forensic roles. *Professional Psychology: Research and Practice, 28,* 50–57.

Greenberg, S. A., & Shuman, D. W. (1999, Summer). *Personal injury examination: The application of psychology to the law of torts.* Unpublished manuscript. Portland, OR: The American Board of Professional Psychology, Continuing Education Workshop.

Grisso, T. (1986). *Evaluating competencies: Forensic assessments and instruments.* New York: Plenum Press.

Harr, J. (1996). *A civil action.* New York: Vintage Books.

Heilbrun, K. (1992). The role of psychological testing in forensic assessment. *Law and Human Behavior, 16,* 257–272.

Lees-Haley, P. R. (1992). Psychodiagnostic test usage by forensic psychologists. *American Journal of Forensic Psychology, 10*(1), 25–30.

Martin, E. A. (Ed.). (1990). *Oxford reference: A concise dictionary of law* (2nd ed.). Oxford, England: Oxford University Press.

Shuman, D. W. (2000, with yearly supplements). *Psychiatric and psychological evidence* (2nd ed.). New York: West Group.

Shuman, D. W., & Greenberg, S. A. (1998). The role of ethical norms in the admissibility of expert testimony. *The Judges' Journal: A Quarterly of the Judicial Division, 37*(1), 5–43.

Shuman, D. W., Greenberg, S. A., Heilbrun, K., & Foote, W. E. (1998). An immodest proposal: Should treating mental health professionals be barred from testifying about their patients? *Behavioral Sciences and the Law, 16,* 509–523.

CHAPTER 14

Assessing Employment Discrimination and Harassment

MELBA J. T. VASQUEZ, NANCY LYNN BAKER, AND SANDRA L. SHULLMAN

The psychologist who performs forensic assessment in employment discrimination litigation faces several significant tasks and must be knowledgeable in a variety of areas. This chapter provides an overview of those tasks and knowledge domains. Specifically, the authors (a) review the legal basis of discrimination and harassment litigation; (b) identify social science research concerning discrimination and harassment; (c) discuss various roles for psychologists providing evidence relevant to discrimination and harassment; and, (d) suggest a framework for performing an assessment of the psychological effects of discrimination and harassment on an individual. Conclusions and future directions also are addressed.

Employment discrimination and harassment occur in the workplace for a variety of reasons. The Civil Rights Act of 1964 identified race, sex, religion, and national origin as discrimination criteria. Additional laws, notably the Age Discrimination in Employment Act and the Americans with Disabilities Act (ADA), have added protection against discrimination based on

age and disability status. Although this chapter specifically addresses only those issues covered under the Civil Rights Act, many of the psychological concerns for any type of *employment* discrimination are parallel. Additionally, as the EEOC notes, age discrimination and harassment claims parallel Civil Rights claims because "the substantive prohibitions of the Age Discrimination in Employment Act (ADEA) were copied verbatim from Title VII" (*EEOC Compliance Manual,* Section 615.11, 6/87). Claims under the ADA are addressed separately in this volume (see the chapter by Foote).

THE LEGAL BASIS OF DISCRIMINATION COMPLAINTS

For the most part, sorting out complex legal issues is not the task of the psychologist. However, it is essential to have some understanding of what claims are being made to ensure that the assessment provides information relevant to those claims. When performing an assessment concerning employment discrimination or harassment for any legal action, it is important to review the relevant legal standards and procedures.

Discrimination and harassment in employment, especially when resulting in significant psychological consequences, can give rise to legal claims or actions under workers compensation, unemployment, and civil rights statutes. Additionally, severe or pervasive harassment may give rise to various common law tort claims for injuries, including negligent or intentional infliction of emotional distress, assault and battery, false imprisonment, and invasion of privacy (Lindermann & Kadue, 1999). This chapter focuses on federal litigation of civil rights statutes (workers compensation issues are covered elsewhere in this volume; see the chapter by Greenberg). Although state laws and standards frequently follow federal laws and standards, state law claims are not addressed specifically, given the variability of state statutes.

Workers compensation claims for the psychological consequences of harassment are not covered here. The legal issues are very different from those that apply to civil rights claims. Additionally, there is a wide variability among state jurisdictions concerning whether harassing conduct, especially if it does not include physical assault and results in a purely psychological injury, is compensable.

The rules concerning issues of compensability, standards of proof, and procedure are, or at least can be, significantly different. This depends on whether the legal claim is for compensation under workers compensation statutes or for damages as a consequence of an alleged violation of the individual's civil rights. Civil rights claims can be based on violations of federal law, state fair employment practices law, and, in some cases, local antidiscrimination ordinances. There are also at least potential differences between the rules and procedures for civil rights claims based in federal law and those based in state law or local ordinance. For example, the Federal Rules of Evidence and the U.S. Supreme Court decision in *Daubert v. Merrell Dow Pharmaceuticals* (1993) establish the requirements for expert testimony in federal court. In some states, the prior federal standard, as established by the Supreme Court in *Frye v. United States* (1923), was codified into state law and remains the standard, at least for now. Although the standards of proof are essentially the same for common law torts and civil rights claims filed within the same jurisdiction, the legal issues are slightly different. In most cases, especially at the state level, both violations of civil rights under fair employment statutes and violations of common law rights, if claimed, will be part of the same legal action.

Discrimination Law: Title VII of the Civil Rights Act of 1964

Title VII of the Civil Rights Act of 1964 prohibits discrimination on the basis of race, sex, color, religion, or national origin. Title VII provides the basis for federal claims of employment discrimination based on those factors. It is interesting to note that sex discrimination was not included in the original bill introduced into Congress. It was added to the Civil Rights Act as an amendment by legislators seeking to defeat the bill, but the bill passed with the amendment, establishing legal prohibition for sex-based discrimination as part of Federal Civil Rights Law.

At the time the Civil Rights Act of 1964 was passed, there was a wide range of overtly discriminatory practices in employment. The "Help Wanted" ads of that time were divided into "men's work" and "women's work" and, in some places, further divided into categories based on race. Only a relatively small number of job openings were listed as available to any candidate. Many jobs were exclusively gendered, like that of policeman, fireman, and airline pilot. Other jobs were subject to a variety of discriminatory practices and policies. For example, in a number of factories, unionized and nonunionized, there were essentially equivalent job classifications, differing only by the sex or race of the job holders, yet providing significant differences in the rate of pay. Legal restrictions, in the form of protective legislation, restricted women's work hours or put limits on the weight women could lift. In effect, such laws functionally kept women out of other jobs (Freeman, 1984).

During the 1960s and early 1970s, legal and legislative processes successfully challenged a system that had functionally segregated all women, immigrants, and non-White men into the lowest-paying jobs and limited the openings for and advancement in the professions by such groups (Bergmann, 1986). Protective legislation for women, which ostensibly protected women by restricting work hours and weight lift limits, was voided. By the early to middle 1970s, formal barriers to full participation in the labor force by members of groups protected by the Civil Rights Act of 1964 had generally been held to be unlawful. Affirmative Action was instituted to increase employment in those jobs that had previously been closed by discriminatory restrictions.

Forms of Legal Discrimination Claims

Legal claims concerning discrimination can allege either *discriminatory effects* or *discriminatory treatment*. Complaints concerning discriminatory effects, called disparate impact, require showing that an entire *group* was adversely affected by a policy or practice. Discriminatory or disparate treatment claims address the adverse treatment of a particular *individual* and require showing harm to only one individual.

In addition to prohibiting employers from engaging in such unlawful conduct, the Civil Rights Act of 1964, as amended by the Civil Rights Act of 1991, provides for injunctive relief (i.e., correction of the problem) and, in some cases, for monetary damages for those harmed by discriminatory practices. These monetary damages are compensation for loss of wages and benefits and for emotional pain and suffering. When the conduct is found to be particularly offensive, punitive damages can be awarded. Under Title VII, as amended by the Civil Rights Act of 1991, punitive damages are awarded only when the employer acted with "malice or reckless indifference to the federally protected rights of an aggrieved individual" (Lindermann & Kadue, 1999, p. 317). Additionally, monetary damages are generally allowed only where the discriminatory result was found to be intentional (for further discussion of damages, see EEOC Policy Guidance on Compensatory and Punitive Damages under the Civil Rights Act of 1991). This can create a significant legal hurdle for those bringing discrimination complaints.

Harassment as a Form of Discrimination

Complaints concerning harassment constitute a somewhat special category. The EEOC (Commission Decision No. YSF 9-108, CCH EEOC Decisions, 1973, ¶6030) and Federal Courts (*Anderson v. Methodist Evangelical Hospital, Ind.,* Civil No. 6580, 3 EPD, ¶8282, W.D. KY., June 1971, aff'd, 464 F.2d 723, 4 EPD ¶7901, 6th Cir. 1972) first defined harassment as discriminatory, alleging that racial harassment is discrimination. The courts ruled that employers have "a duty to provide employees with a workplace free from hostility, intimidation, or insult based on race, sex, color, religion, or national origin" (*EEOC Compliance Manual,* Harassment, 1994). Where that was not the case, the resulting harassment was considered based in *animus* or hostility, making the specific demonstration of discriminatory intent generally unnecessary. This has been considerably beneficial for legal claims of harassment.

To prevail in a case alleging harassment, it has been necessary to show that the harassment altered the conditions of employment (*EEOC Compliance Manual,* Harassment, 1994). This can be based on demonstrating that the harassment was the cause or basis of some adverse employment action. It can also be based in showing that the conduct was sufficiently severe to alter the conditions of employment in ways that are essentially psychological. The legal standards for what is required to establish that the work environment has been psychologically altered have developed over time and vary, to some extent, by jurisdiction. There is generally an expectation, at least in federal jurisdictions, that conduct be sufficiently severe enough that a "reasonable person similarly situated" would experience this conduct as altering the work environment.

In the evaluation of the harassment, factors to consider include (a) the degree to which the conduct was threatening or offensive, (b) how frequently it occurred, and (c) the status of the person or persons engaging in the conduct. Obviously, the determination of whether harassing conduct would be expected to alter the work environment for a reasonable person, as well as the question of whether it altered the work environment for a given plaintiff, are issues for which psychological experts can provide the court with important information.

Sexual Harassment: A Special Case of Harassment

The legal understanding of sexual harassment has had a somewhat unique development. In the mid-1970s, feminist legal scholars began to argue that unwanted sexual attention, even if ostensibly or superficially expressed in a positive manner, could constitute discrimination (MacKinnon, 1979). The argument put forward was that women were subjected to this sexual attention because they were women. That is, sexual attention is not, generally, gender-neutral in its origin. People receive sexual attention because of physical factors specifically linked to their sex. A boss using the power of the employer role does not randomly or equally direct requests for sexual favors to men and women alike. In our society, the argument continues, most people are heterosexual and men are socialized to view the sexual objectification of women as part of their basic rights. The male boss thus directs sexual attention and requests for sexual favors at the female subordinate because of her sex-linked physical attributes and because of his gender socialization. Further, it was argued that this conduct had a negative effect on women's employment. Thus, such unwanted sexual attention was alleged to be discrimination on the basis of sex.

The first cases brought under this theory dealt with the experiences of women who quit their jobs because of being pressured for sexual favors (*Garber v. Saxon Business Products, Inc.,* 1977; *Williams v. Saxbe,* 1978). In one case, the plaintiff reported tiring of being regularly chased around the desk by her boss in his efforts to grab her and engage in sexual behavior. In each case, the women were the direct subordinates of male harassers, required to report, when summoned, to their harassing boss as part of their job duties. In both cases, the supervisors used these encounters, which were created by their supervisory authority, as an opportunity to seek sexual favors. In both cases, the women articulated their desires for the attention to cease, but it did not.

Initially, the lower courts were not supportive of the argument that this type of conduct represented employment discrimination based on sex (*Williams v. Saxbe,* 1978). The courts held that the conduct was the private and personal action of the pursuer (in these cases, male supervisors), directed at the pursued (female subordinates). Within several years, as some of these cases made their way through the Courts of Appeals, the role of the employment relationship in the harassment was acknowledged and sexual harassment was held to be an unlawful form of sex discrimination. The legal argument is that sexual harassment is unlawful not because it is sexual but because the recipient of the harassment is being targeted because of her (or his) sex.

In 1981, the Equal Employment Opportunity Commission (EEOC), established by Congress and charged with implementation of the Civil Rights Act of 1964, provided a definition of sexual harassment. The EEOC guidance on sexual harassment states:

> Harassment on the basis of sex is a violation of Sec. 703 of Title VII [of the U.S. Civil Rights Act of 1964]. Unwelcome advances, requests for sexual favors, and other verbal or physical conduct of a sexual nature constitute sexual harassment when:
>
> 1. Submission to such conduct is made either explicitly or implicitly a term or condition of the individual's employment.
> 2. Submission to or rejection of such conduct by an individual is used as the basis for employment decisions affecting such individual.
> 3. Or such conduct has the purpose or effect of unreasonably interfering with an individual's work performance or creating an intimidating, hostile, or offensive work environment.
>
> (EEOC Guidelines on discrimination because of sex, 45 Fed. Reg. 74676, 1980)

This definition clarified and formalized the rationale, which had been developed in the early appellate decisions defining sexual harassment as a form of sexual discrimination. The definition is still in use, but understanding of it has been modified over the years by court decisions.

Sexual Harassment and the Evolution of Hostile Environment Claims

The U.S. Supreme Court first upheld the EEOC Guidelines on Sexual Harassment in 1986 (*Meritor Savings Bank v. Vinson,*

1986). In the *Vinson* case, the plaintiff, a bank teller, complained that she felt pressured to engage in unwanted sexual relations with her supervisor. The unwanted sexual relationship extended for several years and included lunchtime trysts at a nearby hotel. The plaintiff claimed that she was coerced into the relationship because of the supervisor's power over her employment, even though there was no evidence of explicit threats by the supervisor. There was evidence that she did not initiate the sexual relationship and was seriously distressed by it. The Court affirmed that demand for sexual conduct could create a hostile environment even when there was no explicit threat of adverse employment action. If the sexual conduct created a hostile or offensive work environment, the conditions of employment were altered.

Unlike other forms of harassment, in which the inherently hostile nature of the conduct is assumed, sexual harassment requires showing that the conduct in question was unwelcome. In the *Vinson* case, the Supreme Court noted that the issue of "welcomeness" is not synonymous with the issue of being "voluntary." Thus, this was interpreted to mean that, in a work environment where going out with the supervisor is known to be the best or only way to get a promotion, an employee who willingly accepts the supervisor's invitation for a date may have a sexual harassment claim.

The standards for what constitutes showing unwelcomeness, like the definitions of harassment and sexual harassment, continue to evolve through case law and vary across different jurisdictions. In general, such factors as verbal and nonverbal indications of disapproval, discomfort, disinterest, or disdain are part of the evidence. Some courts allow evidence about the complaining party's behavior, including style of dress, as evidence of the welcomeness of the behavior. EEOC Guidance (EEOC Policy Guidance: Sexual Harassment, N-915-050, 3/19/1990) notes that such evidence must be of a parallel nature. For example, while "using sexual terms or telling off-color jokes may suggest the sexual comments by others in that situation were not unwelcome, more extreme and abusive or persistent comments or a physical assault would not be excused," nor would an adverse employment action (EEOC, 1990).

Harassment and Employer Liability

Another central issue in the *Vinson* case was the question of employer liability for the actions of supervisors. Specifically, the issue has focused on the conditions under which an employer can be held liable for the harassing conduct of its individual supervisors (*Meritor Savings Bank v. Vinson,* 1986). At one extreme, the argument held that an employer is always liable for the actions of supervisors because the supervisor is acting as the agent of the employer. At the other extreme, the argument held that, unless the act of sexually harassing employees was part of the supervisor's job, the employer should be liable only if the employer was negligent. Negligence in this context has come to be defined as "the employer knew or should have known and failed to exercise reasonable care to prevent or promptly correct the harm" (*Burlington Industries, Inc. v. Ellerth,* No. 97-569, 1998). Although this case was a sexual harassment claim, the Court's analysis applied to all Title VII harassment.

In the first 12 years following the *Vinson* decision, the lower courts centered the issue of employer liability on the questions of *quid pro quo* versus *hostile environment* harassment. This meant that, if submitting to the harassment was a condition of employment, there was liability for the supervisor's conduct; if not, the negligence standard would apply. This led to a variety of arguments that sought to stretch or shrink the definition of what constituted a quid pro quo claim. In 1998, the U.S. Supreme Court issued two decisions, further clarifying the issue of employer liability for supervisor harassment (*Burlington Industries v. Ellerth,* 1998; *Faragher v. City of Boca Raton,* 1998). In these cases, the Court distinguished between situations in which there was a tangible adverse job action versus those where there was not. The Court stated:

> An employer is subject to vicarious liability to a victimized employee for an actionable hostile environment created by a supervisor with immediate (or successively higher) authority over the employee. When no tangible employment action is taken, a defendant employer may raise an affirmative defense to liability or damages, subject to proof by a preponderance of evidence. . . . The defense comprises two necessary elements: (a) that the employer exercised reasonable care to prevent and correct promptly any sexually harassing behavior, and (b) that the plaintiff employee unreasonably failed to take advantage of any preventive or corrective opportunities provided by the employer or to avoid harm otherwise. . . . No affirmative defense is available, however, when the supervisor's harassment culminates in a tangible employment action such as discharge, demotion, or undesirable reassignment. (*Burlington Industries v. Ellerth,* 1998)

Following these two decisions, the standard for employer liability can be summarized with relative clarity. The employer is deemed liable for coworker harassment that it knew of or should have known of. This is considered the negligence standard. The employer is liable for the actions of supervisors whether the employer knew about them or not. However, where there was no tangible adverse action, the employer's liability is subject to the affirmative defense outlined above. That same affirmative defense is often applied in the negligence or coworker harassment cases, especially in the determination of damages. At this time, however, the U.S. Supreme Court has not affirmed that extension of the employer's affirmative defense in coworker harassment cases.

What Is a Hostile Environment?

Another critical issue developed in the context of sexual harassment litigation is the question of what constitutes a hostile environment. This issue has considerable overlap with legal issues in other forms of harassment. In essence, the issue considers the conditions under which an environment becomes so affected by harassment that the conditions of work have been altered. In the years following the *Vinson* case, various federal appellate courts developed various standards on this question. The Sixth Circuit developed the standard that the conduct must be so severe that it both interfered with a person's work performance and seriously affected the individual's psychological well-being. This was the standard used by the Sixth Circuit in rejecting the claim of the plaintiff *in Harris v. Forklift Systems, Inc.* (1993). In this case, Harris, the only female in her job classification, complained about her boss, a man described by the court as crude and offensive. His conduct was upsetting and humiliating to Harris, resulting in her decision to quit. However, the Sixth Circuit rejected her claim on the grounds that there was no evidence that Harris had suffered a significant injury even though they agreed that her boss's conduct was both pervasive and offensive.

The U.S. Supreme Court rejected the Sixth Circuit standard of psychological injury (*Harris v. Forklift Systems, Inc.,* 1993), noting, "even though discriminatory incidents may not seriously affect an employee's psychological well being, a discriminatorily abusive work environment may, among other things, affect an employee's job performance or advancement" (EEOC, 1994 N: 4072). The Court went on to state that, even when there is no tangible effect, there is a violation of Title VII when the "discriminatory conduct was so severe or pervasive that it created a work environment abusive to employees because of their race, gender, religion, or national origin" (EEOC, 1994 N: 4073).

There was hope among some that the Supreme Court would have used the *Harris* ruling to specify exactly what actions can cause an abusive environment, or what effects are characteristic of abusive environments (Zigarelli, 1995). In the *Harris* case, however, the Court held that both the welcomeness and the severity or pervasiveness of conduct in question must be evaluated in their context. The Court directed that the determinations must be made on "the record as a whole and at the totality of the circumstances," including the nature of the conduct and the context in which it occurred. The two criteria developed in the *Harris* decision for a hostile environment are (a) that the conduct must be sufficiently severe to be objectively offensive to a reasonable person similarly situated; and (b) that the complaining party must have been subjectively offended (EEOC, 1994). This decision by the Court is consistent with the position taken by many psychologists working in the area of sexual harassment. That is, context is critical in determining whether a hostile environment has been created (Fitzgerald, Swann, & Magley, 1997).

The task of assisting the trier of fact in determining whether a hostile environment was created is a task for which psychological evidence and psychological expertise can play a significant role. For example, psychologists have determined that men and women can differ in what they interpret as sexual harassment, with women interpreting and experiencing a wider range of behaviors as harassing (Pryor, Giedd, & Williams, 1995). In general, men and women are more likely to differ in their perceptions of more ambiguous or less severe behaviors, such as verbal harassment (e.g., coarse language and sexual remarks), sexual looks, flirting, and nonsexual touching. Women are more likely than men to view these behaviors as harassment, yet the majority of both men and women do not define those behaviors as harassment. On the other hand, the majority of both men and women tend to agree that more severe behaviors, such as sexual bribery and explicit propositions, are harassment (Frazier, Cochran, & Olson, 1995). Other psychological research has identified the common responses of women when they experience harassment (Fitzgerald, 1992). Fitzgerald's framework identifies internally focused or externally focused responses. Internally focused responses include the common response of "endurance," which is simply to ignore the harassment and do nothing, and "denial," which is to pretend that the situation is not happening or has no effect, especially in response to less severe situations. Other internally focused responses include detachment, illusory control (including self-blame), reattribution (reinterpreting the situation in such a way that it is not defined as harassment, or identified extenuating circumstances, such as the harasser was lonely, intentions were benign) as coping strategies. Externally focused responses include avoidance, appeasement (attempt to "put off" the harasser without direct confrontation, using humor, excuses, delaying), seeking of social support, a variety of assertive responses, and seeking institutional/organizational relief. In their research, the most common response reported by women was to have done nothing, and the response of seeking institutional relief was an extremely infrequent response (Fitzgerald, Swan, et al., 1995).

Traditionally Male Jobs: A Case of Gender Hostility

Another area in which psychologists and psychological research has played a role in increasing understanding has been the harassment encountered by women in traditionally male occupations. Psychologists have consistently found that women in such jobs experience high levels of harassment. Such harassment includes a variety of expressions of gender-based animus and explicit sexually verbal and physical behavior (Baker, 1995; Gold, 1987). The elevated levels of harassment include everything from more extreme acts such as exposure to male nudity, sexual assault, and attempts to cause physical harm, to more mundane acts, such as sexually explicit cartoons and pictures, offensive graffiti, and graphic sexual language. Interestingly, the only category of harassment that appears to be unique to women in traditionally male jobs is that of attempts by male coworkers to cause physical harm (Baker, 1995).

Beyond the information about the prevalence of the harassment faced by the women introduced into formerly all-male work domains, social psychological research on stereotyping and prejudice provides important information about the particularly difficult situation that women face in traditionally male occupations (Fiske, 1998). The high levels and frequently extreme nature of the harassment faced by women in traditionally male jobs can be both predicted and explained by the psychological research on group threat (Smith, 1993). The addition of women can threaten the previously male/macho identity of the work group, creating significant hostility. In addition to the hostility that women in such jobs encounter, their participation in male-dominated occupations may also create the stereotype-based expectation that such women are so "tough" that they will not be affected by the harassment (Burgess & Borgida, 1997, cited in Deaux, 1998).

Same-Sex Harassment: Gender and Sexual Orientation Hostility

Federal civil rights law and most state fair employment statutes do *not* include sexual orientation as a protected category. In most jurisdictions, there is no explicit legal protection from discrimination or harassment based on the target's sexual orientation. Nonetheless, courts have, in many cases, found same-sex sexual harassment to be a violation of Title VII of the Civil Rights Act of 1964. This issue resulted in a variety of decisions and theories among the various jurisdictions of the U.S. Federal Courts of Appeals. Some courts held that such claims required that the harasser be a homosexual (*McWilliams v. Fairfax County Bd. of Supervisors*, 1996). Others held that the issue focuses on whether members of one sex were faced with different conditions of employment than members of the other sex (*Quick v. Donaldson Co.,* 1996). The Seventh Circuit Court held that anyone experiencing offensive conduct of a sexual nature could state a claim for sexual harassment, regardless of the gender or sexual orientation of the harasser or the target of the harassment (*Doe v. City of Belleville,* 119 F.3d 563, 74 FEP Cases 625, 7th Cir. 1997). The Fifth Circuit Court took a position at the opposite extreme, stating that no claim for sexual harassment could exist for male-on-male harassment (*Garcia v. Elf Atochem N. Am.,* 1994; *Oncale v. Sundowner Offshore Oil,* 1996).

In 1998, the U.S. Supreme Court reversed the Fifth Circuit's ruling in *Oncale,* noting that nothing in Title VII of the Civil Rights Act of 1964 bars a claim because the plaintiff and the harasser are of the same sex (*Oncale v. Sundowner Offshore Oil,*118 S. Ct. 998, 76 FEP Cases 221, 1998). However, the Supreme Court also limited the more sweeping definition of the Seventh Circuit in the *Doe* case, noting that the harassment must be discriminatory based on the plaintiff's gender. This decision has given rise to the "equal opportunity harasser" line of defense in harassment cases, where it is argued that both men and women are faced with the same objectionable conduct. Social psychology research on the gendered nature of experience may be of particular import to triers of fact in such cases. For example, previously cited research by Pryor and his colleagues (Pryor et al., 1995) suggests that the same behavior is not interpreted, labeled, or experienced in the same way by men and women. Other research (Waldo, Berdahl, & Fitzgerald, 1998) finds that men and women differ in their psychological reaction to harassment experiences.

Retaliation: Another Hostile Environment

In addition to claims for injury as a result of discrimination or harassment, there can be claims for retaliation. These claims cover situations in which individuals have experienced discrimination or harassment as a consequence of their opposition to or reporting of what they reasonably believe to be employment discrimination, including discriminatory harassment. It is unlawful under Title VII of the Civil Rights Act to discriminate against individuals for making a claim or for participating in any manner in the investigation of a Title VII claim (*EEOC Compliance Manual,* Retaliation, 1988). This is important because many individuals who make claims for harassment or discrimination in the workplace also report significant experiences of retaliation. Claims of retaliation do not require that the original complaint be legally upheld; complaints of retaliation require only that the original

complaint was based on a reasonable belief that it was a legitimate complaint.

Harassment and Evolving Legal Standards

As the previous sections on the legal issues in harassment and discrimination has made clear, the legal standards for claims concerning discrimination and harassment in the workplace are constantly changing and evolving. New legislation, new regulations, and new court decisions alter the legal issues. Psychologists providing forensic assessments in such cases are not required to have a lawyer's knowledge of the legal issues. However, it is important to stay reasonably current in one's understanding of the developments in the law. This will assist in determining what specific psycholegal questions are being asked and what psychological research and assessment techniques will best assist in providing the answers to such questions.

PSYCHOLOGICAL LITERATURE ON DISCRIMINATION AND HARASSMENT

There is a substantial body of psychological research that is relevant to the issues of discrimination and harassment in employment. This includes the general research on stereotyping and prejudice (Fiske, 1993, 1998; Macrae, Stangor, & Hewstone, 1996), group dynamics (Brewer & Brown, 1998; Mackie & Hamilton, 1993), social stigma (Crocker, Major, & Steele, 1998), gender (Deaux, 1998), and information processing and decision making (Sedikides, Insko, & Schopler, 1997). A general review of these issues can be found in the *Handbook of Social Psychology* (D. Gilbert, Fiske, & Lindsey, 1998). There is also a significant body of literature on the effects of stress, which is informative in understanding the effects of the particular stressors of discrimination and harassment. Further, there is a substantial body of research specifically addressing the issues of discrimination and harassment and their effects on people.

Social science research examines the behaviors and contextual factors that affect whether experiences are perceived as discriminatory or harassing. For example, one of the most important situational characteristics in harassment is the power and status of the harasser relative to the harassment recipient (Fiske, 1993). Root (2001) suggests that White supervisors may rely on the power of "White privilege" in addition to their authority role to provide them the status to lie or to be perceived as more credible than subordinate employees. Similarly, others have argued that the power of the male gender role itself is a factor in power relations between men and women in the workplace (L. Gilbert, 1992).

Familiarity with the research on stereotyping is particularly useful in understanding the dynamics of discrimination in the workplace. The process of stereotyping, a relatively ubiquitous psychological information-processing phenomenon, influences how people are seen, how their behavior is evaluated, and what is remembered about them. Those in groups that have power are more likely to engage in stereotyping about members of other groups with less power. Further, those in groups without power are more likely to become the focus of stereotyping (Fiske, 1993). Stereotype-consistent information is more easily recognized and remembered, and members of devalued groups are perceived as more homogeneous, more stereotype-consistent, than they actually are. Although stereotype-incongruent information may be more noticed in some circumstances because it is unusual, it is less likely to be recalled. A full review of this literature can be found elsewhere (Fiske, 1998).

Stress is well known as a source of a variety of negative physical and emotional consequences (Everly, 1989; Kiecolt-Glaser & Glaser, 2001). There is some specific research on the negative physiological effects of stressors such as racism (Fang & Myers, 2001) and on the specific effects of sexual harassment (Dansky & Kilpatrick, 1997). However, the expert providing testimony concerning discrimination and harassment in employment would be well advised to be familiar with the basic research on the effects of both cumulative and traumatic stress.

Sex Discrimination and Sexual Harassment Research

A meta-analysis of 30 years (1964 to 1994) of empirical studies that examined sex discrimination in employment generally found that job sex-type and job-relevant information affected discrimination (Davison & Burke, 2000). Both female and male applicants received lower ratings when being considered for an "opposite-sex" job. The difference in ratings decreased as more job-relevant information was provided.

Sexual harassment, given its controversial nature as a legal and social issue, has received considerable research attention. (The focus on sexual harassment may also have some relationship to racism, in that sex discrimination and harassment can occur to people of all ethnicities, but racial discrimination is most often only an issue for non-White and nonethnic persons. An evaluation of the relative role of these two factors is beyond the scope of this chapter.) Early research focused on establishing that sexual harassment, as a social phenomenon, was sufficiently pervasive and severe to warrant attention. Some research has also focused on the

characteristics of harassers (Pryor et al., 1995). Pryor et al. (1995) developed a model of sexual harassment that suggested that sexually harassing behavior may be predicted from an analysis of social situational and person factors. Sexual harassment is more likely to occur in situations where it is perceived as socially permissible, including positive reactions of work group leaders. Pryor (1987) developed the Likelihood to Sexually Harass Scale in an attempt to identify person factors associated with those who harass. Some of those factors are characteristics including sexual aggressiveness, hostility, antifemininity, status, toughness, and hypermasculinity; and a cognitive tendency to link ideas about social dominance and ideas about sexuality. The development of assessment scales and models such as those developed by Pryor (1987) and Pryor et al. (1995) are likely to be particularly useful in identifying the causes of certain types of sexual harassment incidents, including stalking, sexual assault, and coerced sexual behavior. These behaviors can be called predatory forms of harassment and are relatively rare forms of sexual harassment (Fitzgerald et al., 1988; Hay & Elig, 1999).

More recent research has focused on identifying the antecedents and consequences of sexual harassment, those factors that contribute to its occurrence, and the resulting harmful outcomes of its occurrence (Fitzgerald, Drasgow, Hulin, Gelfand, & Magley, 1997). Various studies have indicated that certain social norms in specific organizational settings may "permit" sexual harassment (Pryor et al., 1995). Fitzgerald and her colleagues (Fitzgerald, Drasgow, et al., 1997; Glomb et al., 1997) present a theoretical model for understanding sexual harassment and provide empirical support for it. Their data support the theory that the organizational climate (Naylor, Pritchard, & Ilgen, 1980) and the job-gender context are the main factors determining the prevalence level of sexual harassment in an organization.

Fitzgerald et al. (1997) also posit that harassment has a negative outcome on job factors, including (a) organizational participation and job satisfaction; (b) stress-related psychological outcomes, including anxiety and depression; and (c) stress-related health problems, including headaches, gastrointestinal disorders, and sleep disturbance (Fitzgerald et al., 1997a; Glomb et al., 1997).

Consistent with previous research (U.S. Merit Systems Protection Board, 1981, 1987; Goldenhar, Swanson, Hurrell, Ruder, & Deddens, 1998; Hesson-McInnis & Fitzgerald, 1997), all of these predictions were supported by the empirical data. Whereas data have supported the importance of organizational intervention, research findings have suggested that assertive responses may increase rather than decrease negative consequences for harassment victims (Stockdale, 1998).

In evaluating research on workplace experiences, it may be important to consider whether the research is based on actual experiences or on hypothetical scenarios. When dealing with hypothetical situations or analog research, participants are indicating what they believe they would or should do and what they think others would or should do. This more closely represents a measure of attitudes than a description of actual behavioral responses. When the responses of analog research concerning the reporting of sexual harassment experiences were directly compared to the actual behaviors of harassment targets, there were significant differences (Perry, Kulik, & Schmidtke, 1997).

Another issue of significance in the psychological literature is how men and women experience harassment. Early research demonstrated that men as well as women report sexual harassment experiences (U.S. Merit System Protection Board, 1981). However, relatively little research has specifically compared the experiences of men and women who report that they have been sexually harassed. One study directly comparing these experiences, using reports of women and men in the military, found both similarities and differences (Magley, Waldo, Drasgow, & Fitzgerald, 1999). Both male and female harassment victims appear to experience negative psychological, health, and job outcomes. Job outcomes can include poor performance and poor attendance, as well as loss of interest in the job. However, women were more likely to experience sexual harassment, more likely to experience high levels of harassment, and were almost always harassed by men rather than experiencing same-sex harassment (Magley et al., 1999).

Racial Discrimination and Harassment Research

Significant documentation abounds regarding discrimination on the basis of race and ethnicity (Eberhardt & Fiske, 1998). Studies have identified key factors related to the probability of occurrence of race discrimination. For example, Brief, Dietz, Cohen, Pugh, and Vaslow (2000) found that research participants were more likely to engage in discrimination against minorities in hiring situations when a legitimate authority figure provided a business-related justification for the discrimination.

Dovidio and Gaertner (2000) conceptualized a new form of racism that predicts discriminatory conduct when the decision is more ambiguous. Dovidio (2001) demonstrated that a new form of "modern" White racism—essentially unconscious—reflects a surface belief in racial equality that masks latent, unconscious prejudicial feelings that can affect the ability of Blacks to get jobs and to do well in them. Dovidio found that nearly half of all Whites demonstrate this propensity and find

ways to rationalize their biases on the basis of factors that seem, on the surface, to be unrelated to race. Although this motivation is hidden to Whites, Blacks identify it clearly. Dovidio's results demonstrated that Blacks pick up Whites' negative facial cues in situations in which Whites show no overt bias and that Whites remain "clueless" to their own subtle behaviors (DeAngelis, 2001; Dovidio, 2001).

Mueller, Parcel, and Tanaka (1989) found that homosocial reproduction (the notion that managers promote persons similar to themselves) operates mainly for Whites. Promotion decisions for Blacks are based on more observable, identifiable criteria. Racial discrimination may be a factor generating differences in the desires and expectations of racial and ethnic minority workers.

Kirby and Jackson (1999) studied 100 Black workers (blue-collar and white-collar) to determine the relationship between perceptions of racial discrimination and traditional organizational attitudes such as job satisfaction, mediated by having either a supervisor of the same or of a different race. Overall, their findings indicate that Black workers who worked for Black supervisors in work groups that were entirely or predominantly Black had a more positive experience than those workers with White supervisors. Apparently, the race of the participant's supervisor did not affect job satisfaction, but it was shown to influence perceptions of job opportunity and discrimination (Kirby & Jackson, 1999). The results also suggested that it was especially problematic for Blacks in entirely Black work groups to have White supervisors. Job satisfaction was found to be dependent on the racial composition of the participant's immediate work group (Kirby & Jackson, 1999).

Research on the Effects of Racial Discrimination

The effects of racism have been documented in various ways. Allport (1954) listed traits that develop in response to being a target of prejudice and discrimination. Steele (1997) has more recently introduced the notion of stereotype threat: the fear of proving that a negative stereotype is true. In a series of experiences, Steele and his associates demonstrated that such fears can lead to lower performance and a desire to disidentify with important social domains, such as schooling and other achievement-oriented activities (Steele, 1997; Steele & Aronson, 1995). For example, in one study, when women were told that a difficult math test produced gender differences that replicated women's underperformance, the women performed worse than men. However, they performed equally to men when the test was described as insensitive to gender differences, even though the same difficult "ability" test was used in both conditions (Steele, 1997). This experiment has been replicated in a variety of situations with Blacks and other groups, including White males, who underperformed when told that they were taking a test on which Asians do better than Whites (Steele, 2001). In addition to diminishing people's performance, stereotyped threat can heighten blood pressure (Steele, 2001). Although the effects of stereotype threat can occur for any group, including White males, it affects women and minorities more strongly because negative stereotypes about them are more relevant to the important domains of schooling and achievement, especially for those invested in performing well (DeAngelis, 2001; Steele, 2001).

Recent research on the effects of racism and racial harassment has also included a focus on developing scales for measuring and quantifying the effects of racial discrimination. A variety of scales have been developed to assess the effects on Black Americans of experiencing racism, including the Racism Reaction Scale, Perceived Racism Scale, Index of Race-Related Stress, Racism and Life Experience Scale–Brief Version, Schedule of Racist Events, and the Perceptions of Racism Scale (Utsey, 1998). Although these scales have not been extensively validated, their development may be of value in assessing the effects of racism, especially where large numbers of individuals have experienced such.

Double Jeopardy Research: Race and Gender in Discrimination and Harassment

In a study of the relationship between perceived race-based discrimination and sociodemographic factors and job participation and stress, Mays, Coleman, and Jackson (1999) found that these factors differentially affected the employment patterns and stress levels of Black women. There is more limited research on the labor force participation of Latinas, and mostly from secondary sources (Yaffe, 1995). Approximately 75% of Latinas report experiencing race or gender discrimination (Yaffe, 1995). Others have noted that the double jeopardy for women of color creates some variability in whether a particular experience of discrimination or harassment is considered to be based on race or gender. This may be of special importance in the evaluation of discrimination complaints put forth by those in double jeopardy situations because the plaintiff may not fully report incidents of harassment or discrimination if the questioner asks specifically about only one type of harassment.

Remediation of Discrimination

Expert witnesses are sometimes asked to recommend remediation and/or interventions in organizations deemed to have problems with racism, discrimination, and prejudice.

For example, a racial discrimination settlement involving Texaco, Inc. called for a court-appointed blue ribbon panel to provide oversight of its reform efforts. Van Duch (2001) reports that similar approaches have been taken in more recent settlements involving Mitsubishi (sexual discrimination) and Coca Cola (racial discrimination).

Although it is beyond the scope of this chapter to offer other than a brief overview of key issues, it may be helpful to identify social science research that has offered attempts to provide an interface between basic research and programmatic intervention in reducing prejudice and promoting respectful interactions. Allport's (1954) contact theory and the social identity theory developed by Tajfel (Tajfel, Flament, Bilig, & Bundy, 1971) have informed many of the desegregation and integration efforts in schools and workplaces. For example, there is encouraging evidence that mixed-race groups of problem solvers work together effectively under certain conditions, according to laboratory analog studies (Cook, 1985). Actual translation into real programs, however, has proven difficult (Aboud & Levy, 1999).

Another body of research has explored social cognitive factors, including the reality that categorization is inevitable and adaptive (Fiske, 1998). Most people have access to a variety of social schema and skills, which can be differentially strengthened through training or social influence. Categorization could apply to both those who hold negative stereotypes as well as those affected by such stereotypes (Fiske, 1998). Graves (1999) reviewed several decades of research and programming and described two new effective media interventions. One of these interventions is based on the notion that vicarious contact through the media can have a more beneficial impact when it arouses anger directed at unjustified discrimination. The other intervention is based on the notion that beneficial impact can occur when media produce an emotional identification with outgroup members. The underlying principle is to engage emotions through empathy (Graves, 1999).

A Note on Moving Targets

The forensic psychologist is bolstered by familiarity with the research identifying evidence of, effects of, and interventions with discrimination and harassment. Definitions of race, sex, gender, religion, ethnic origin, age, disability, and sexual orientation as well as the people who are defined by such criteria play a very different role in the United States today relative to five decades ago, when the Civil Rights Act of 1964 was first enacted. More minority group members hold higher-status and better-paying jobs, are more often college-educated, and may live in integrated neighborhoods. Prejudice and discrimination by dominant groups currently range from more virulent to more subtle forms, both in general and in the workplace. Psychologists have a role to play in assessing the presence and effects of those experiences.

COMBINING LEGAL ISSUES AND SOCIAL SCIENCE: PSYCHOLOGISTS' ROLES IN COURT

Psychologist's assessments of individuals making claims concerning discrimination and harassment in employment require the application of social science research in the context of the legal issues. This can take place either in the course of providing psychological treatment to individuals claiming discrimination or harassment or as an expert evaluator retained for the purpose of providing expert testimony to an adjudicative body (e.g., a jury or administrative law judge). Forensic psychologists recognize that these two types of intervention are significantly different and represent separate roles (Greenberg & Shuman,1997; Committee on Ethical Guidelines for Forensic Psychologists, 1991). The "Specialty Guidelines for Forensic Psychologists" specifically prohibit performing multiple roles in the same case. Additionally, the "Ethical Principles of Psychologists and Code of Conduct," Standard 7.03 (APA, 1992) raises significant caution for any psychologist considering undertaking dual roles. Lawyers do not always recognize the difference between these roles and may encourage psychologists to provide *both* forensic expert testimony and psychological treatment in the same case. Although a full discussion of this issue is beyond the scope of this chapter, psychologists not convinced of the inappropriateness of providing expert assessment testimony concerning those for whom they provide treatment are encouraged to further review the literature on this topic.

Psychologists testifying in litigation on employment harassment or discrimination in their role as experts may present testimony based on the psychological research about workplaces and psychological processes (i.e., stereotyping, prejudice, workplace culture) or the psychological assessment of a particular individual. Although these functions can, to some extent, be separated, they are both forms of expert testimony. Thus, psychologists testifying about both of these issues are filling only one role: the role of expert. Even when a psychologist is asked to address only the psycholegal question of the extent to which an individual has been psychologically harmed by a particular set of workplace experiences, knowledge about work environments and about the dynamics of discrimination and harassment is an essential part of the required knowledge base.

THE ASSESSMENT PROCESS IN EMPLOYMENT DISCRIMINATION AND HARASSMENT

In addition to knowledge about those legal and psychological issues previously discussed, individuals performing forensic psychological evaluations in employment discrimination and harassment cases need to have a sound foundation in the process of psychological assessment. This includes a basic understanding of the construction and proper use of psychological tests and assessment tools. The evaluator should also be aware of the psycholegal issues and defenses typically raised in a discrimination or harassment case and the specific assessment tasks or questions raised by them.

PSYCHOLOGICAL ISSUES RAISED BY THE HARASSMENT CLAIM

When a claim for harassment or discrimination is made, it raises the following questions: (a) whether the alleged events occurred; (b) why the alleged events occurred; and (c) the nature and extent of the effects of the events on the plaintiff. The plaintiff must include in the complaint some variation on the view that the events did occur, that the events occurred because of the employer's action or inappropriate (i.e., negligent) inaction, and that the events had a serious effect on the plaintiff.

The defense's response to a complaint is generally some variation of the position that these events did not occur; that if, indeed, they did occur, they were either caused by the plaintiff, outside of the employer's knowledge and control, or were the result of some misinterpreted innocent conduct; and that the events resulted in no significant effect on the plaintiff. In such a complaint situation, the plaintiff must prevail on all three issues to prove a claim, whereas the defense need only prevail on one to disprove a claim.

Did It Occur?

The first question, addressing whether the events occurred, is primarily an issue for the trier of fact. The Federal Rules of Evidence do not permit expert opinion testimony on the issue of whether a particular party to the complaint is telling the truth. However, especially in sexual harassment cases, the claim is sometimes made that the plaintiff is sufficiently psychologically disturbed (often proposed as a result of a personality disorder) to render the plaintiff unable to accurately report reality. This argument raises an issue different from the issue of the relative contribution of the alleged conduct versus prior events to any psychological problems experienced by the plaintiff. The issue of plaintiff psychological disturbance precluding an accurate assessment of reality has *not* been supported in the empirical psychological research literature (Fitzgerald, Buchanan, Collinsworth, Magley, & Ramos, 1999). Nonetheless, an evaluation of the possibility of a personality disorder is generally advisable in a forensic psychological examination in sexual harassment cases.

Why Did It Occur?

The second question, involving whether the plaintiff in some way caused, welcomed, or misinterpreted the behavior subject to complaint, has multiple manifestations. In some cases, the argument is made that the plaintiff *caused* the harassment or punitive conduct of management by being a poor employee. This is a particularly complex issue to evaluate because many of the behaviors typically cited to demonstrate that an individual is a bad employee (e.g., absenteeism, irritability or difficulty getting along with others in the workplace, and poor work performance) are among the predictable and common results of experiencing harassment.

An adequate analysis must include consideration of the time line involved (i.e., the relationship in time between the behavior alleged as harassment and the plaintiff's problem conduct); not necessarily the time of the harassment complaint and the plaintiff's problem conduct. Furthermore, some individuals with poor work performance records tolerate harassment as part of what they perceive to be a quid pro quo bargain, often experienced as "I will put up with your policy-violating behavior if you will put up with mine." Such individuals complain of long-standing harassing conduct if they are suddenly disciplined for their problem (e.g., tardiness). Ultimately, it is important to remember that the Title VII promise of a nondiscriminatory workplace is not limited to model employees. Thus, when the conduct subject to complaint is sufficiently egregious, the work performance of the plaintiff is generally irrelevant.

Welcomed or Unwelcomed, Not Voluntary or Coerced?

The issue of unwelcomeness is a central requirement for proof of a sexual harassment compliant. As noted before, this is not synonymous with voluntary conduct, although coerced conduct is, by definition, unwelcome. The analysis must include any evidence indicating that the plaintiff welcomed the conduct and any evidence that the plaintiff did not welcome the conduct.

Misinterpretation

The issue of misinterpretation relates to the legal requirement that the conduct subject to complaint is sufficiently severe to offend and alter the working conditions of a reasonable person similarly situated. This is *not* a requirement that the hypothetical reasonable person would be as offended or as severely affected as the plaintiff. What is required is that the level of offense could be expected to alter the working conditions of that hypothetical reasonable person.

Although none of these questions are necessarily the province of the forensic psychologist, a psychologist well-versed in the relevant social psychological literature may offer opinions useful to the trier of fact. These opinions may be developed either as part of the assessment of a particular plaintiff or as part of a more general psychological assessment of the workplace and the situation. It is important, however, that such opinions be based on an understanding of the relevant research literature, not simply the clinical experience of the psychological expert.

Was There Any Harm?

Whether the alleged conduct, if it occurred, significantly affected the plaintiff is obviously central to the task of the forensic psychological evaluator. To answer this question, the evaluator must determine whether there is evidence that (a) the plaintiff is currently showing harmful effects from the behavior subject to the complaint, or (b) the plaintiff has previously shown effects from the behavior subject to the complaint that are no longer evident. If there is evidence of harmful or negative effects, the evaluator must further consider the issue of whether this negative effect was *caused* by the behavior subject to the complaint. As most people have multiple sources of stress in their life, the issue here is often more accurately stated as an assessment of the extent to which any harm was caused by the behavior subject to the complaint. In essence, the evaluator asks, "To what extent was any harm caused by the behavior in question?"

In evaluating the extent to which any harm or psychological injury was caused by something other than the behavior that is the subject of complaint, it is important to distinguish between increased vulnerability and actual dysfunction. Legally, an event is the proximate cause of an outcome if that outcome would not have occurred but for this event, even if the event caused the outcome only because of numerous other factors that created conditions of vulnerability, opportunity, or resilience. The evaluator needs to ask, "Did other stressors or psychological problems leave the plaintiff functioning effectively but more vulnerable to the effects of harassment and discrimination?" Or, by contrast, the evaluator needs to ask, "Was the plaintiff already demonstrating all of the various areas of dysfunction (e.g., having relationship problems, health problems, emotional problems, or job-related performance problems), which may or may not have been exacerbated by the behavior subject to complaint?"

Obviously, although psychological tests may be of value in determining whether the plaintiff is currently demonstrating signs of psychological distress, the full evaluation requires additional sources of information. This includes the information provided by a detailed personal history, a thorough clinical interview, a review of collateral documents, and the input of others, either through written statements, transcripts of depositions, or interviews. The importance of addressing collateral documents and input of others in the process provides substantial rationale for the perspective that a treating therapist is not an appropriate source of information concerning the psycholegal question of extent of harm caused by the behavior subject to the complaint.

Chronic or Traumatic Stress?

In forensic assessments of discrimination and harassment, it is useful to distinguish between harmful effects of *chronic* stress and those of *traumatic* stress. The existence of significant negative psychological and physical effects from both are well established (Everly, 1989; Kiecolt-Glaser & Glaser, 2001). Thus, the distinction between the two forms of stress is not central to the determination of whether the conditions of work were effected (i.e., the existence of a hostile environment). This distinction may, however, be of significance in evaluating expected recovery.

Prior to 1994, it was often quite difficult to demonstrate that discrimination or harassment had resulted in traumatic stress disorder. In 1994, with the publication of the fourth edition of the *Diagnostic and Statistical Manual of Mental Disorders* (American Psychiatric Association, 1994), both the criterion for posttraumatic stress disorder and the accompanying accepted definition of what constitutes a psychologically traumatic event changed to more accurately reflect the experience of mental health experts working with trauma. Criterion A, the definition of the psychological traumatic event, now reads:

A. The person must have been exposed to a traumatic event in which both of the following were present:

1. The person experienced, witnessed, or was confronted with an event or events that involved actual or threatened death or serious injury, or a threat to the physical integrity of self or others.

2. The person's response involved intense fear, helplessness, or horror. (pp. 427–428)

This definition acknowledges the possibility of traumatic psychological injury from events in which the physical harm was only threatened. Harassment cases can and do include actual physical assaults, but many harassment cases and most, if not all, discrimination cases deal with events in which no physical assault took place. In many of these cases, the psychological injury is the result of the chronic stress of being demeaned, devalued, and disadvantaged. However, when the behavior subject to complaint results in an experience of significant threat, the possibility of a traumatic psychological injury exists and should be evaluated.

It has been suggested (Baker, 1995) that the traumatic effects of harassment come from the implicit message that the targeted individual or group is not welcome in the workplace and may be forced out, or, in the case of sexual harassment, possibly that the target may be sexually or physically assaulted. The point at which discriminatory or harassing conduct becomes threatening may be thought of as an interaction between the actual conduct in its full context and the prior experience of the individual with violence or threatened violence (Fitzgerald, Swan, et al., 1997).

Feigning and Malingering

In performing a forensic evaluation for employment discrimination and harassment issues, it is essential to include an assessment of feigning and malingering. Given the potential benefits to the plaintiff of prevailing in a discrimination or harassment complaint, there is more incentive to invent or exaggerate psychological problems than there is for a person seeking only clinical treatment. Unlike a clinical relationship, which exists for the purpose of helping the client or patient, the forensic evaluation exists for the purpose of determining information of use to the trier of fact, regardless of which party in the case has requested the evaluation. At the same time, it is important to remember that, even if a person is exaggerating injuries, it does not mean that injuries do not, in fact, exist (Rogers, 1997). Thus, the psychologist, in identifying evidence of feigning or malingering, should neither understate nor overstate the meaning and significance of that evidence (see the chapter by Rogers & Bender for a discussion on evaluating malingering and exaggeration).

Effects of Discrimination/Harassment versus Effects of Lawsuit

Another assessment issue for the evaluator to consider is the distinction between the psychological effects of the conduct subject to the harassment or discrimination complaint versus the psychological effects of participation in a lawsuit. The distinction is an important one because the psychological effects of harassment or discriminatory behavior are compensable, whereas the psychological effects of participation in a lawsuit are not. The distinction is further complicated by the fact that frequent defense positions (e.g., the behavior did not occur, the behavior was of no consequence, the behavior was caused by the plaintiff) become a continuation experience of the behavior subject to the complaint itself. A useful heuristic in attempting to make this distinction is to ask the evaluator to consider the degree to which the plaintiff's stress would be different if the defense had agreed on all points except the issue of the size of the damages. Such a framework separates the emotional effects of extension of the behavior subject to complaint from the emotional effects of dealing with the legal system. This is an issue that may be a topic of both further judicial clarity and psychological research.

Conducting the Assessment

The specifics of any given psychological assessment will be somewhat unique to the particular case, and therefore, must be determined on a case-by-case basis. However, there are some general guidelines about the content and conduct of the assessment that should be considered. These are, for the most part, similar to the issues present in any forensic psychological evaluation.

Prior to beginning the assessment, the psychologist should clarify the nature of the assignment with the referring attorney. This includes establishing what psycholegal questions or issues the attorney expects the psychologist to explore. It is, of course, not possible to know what one's opinions will be until after the evaluation is complete, but the scope and nature of the task (e.g., assessing degree of injury, exploring reasons for the manner in which the plaintiff dealt with the various alleged instances of harassment, or attempting to estimate future treatment needs) should be clarified as much and as soon as possible. It is advisable to clarify in writing details of the retention agreement, including fees and schedule issues. In practice, forensic psychologists do not perform expert evaluations where payment is contingent on the outcome of the case, for obvious ethical reasons.

Prior to the actual clinical evaluation, the forensic psychologist generally reviews a variety of documents relevant to the case. These documents include depositions by the plaintiff and other relevant witnesses to the alleged conduct. The evaluator also reviews available medical records, including therapy records. Other material of value includes the employment records of the plaintiff. Although most evaluators prefer to review these documents prior to seeing the plaintiff, this will not always be possible.

The actual face-to-face assessment process must begin with obtaining the informed consent of the person being evaluated. That includes providing the individual with sufficient information to understand the process and what will happen to the results of the evaluation. It is not the task of the forensic evaluator to force an assessment on an unwilling participant. The forensic evaluator should document the informed consent in writing before conducting the examination or testing of the plaintiff.

The selection of psychological tests and structured interviews should be based on their relevance to the psycholegal issues in question. Selection should include full consideration of the appropriateness of the test for the given plaintiff, based on language, culture, and standardization sample issues. Selection also should be based on adequate evidence that the plaintiff has the necessary language skills to comprehend the test fully. The administration should be in compliance with the administration procedures outlined in the test manual. Any nonstandard use or administration should be identified and its limitations fully disclosed. Although the actual tests used in evaluations may vary, based on a variety of factors, the question of whether the plaintiff or the defense in a legal action has retained the expert is *not* a legitimate basis for determining the appropriate assessment tools. Empirical or actuarially constructed tests, such as the Minnesota Multiphasic Personality Inventory 2 (MMPI-2) and the Personality Assessment Inventory (PAI), useful only as sources of hypotheses, should be administered in the early stages of the assessment and used to inform other aspects of the evaluation, especially the interview.

Although some plaintiff attorneys oppose psychological testing on the grounds that it is overly intrusive into client privacy, properly selected psychological tests, administered and interpreted by knowledgeable forensic psychologists, can be of significant value in the evaluation process. As noted previously, the actual tests used necessarily vary from case to case due to a variety of factors, including the nature of the psychological problems the plaintiff reports and the cultural and language background of the plaintiff. A full test battery in an employment discrimination or harassment case generally includes a general personality measure, such as the MMPI-2 or the PAI; a tool to assess the current status or complaints of the plaintiff, such as the Symptom Checklist 90–Revised; and a measure to assess feigning or malingering. Additional assessment instruments might be chosen to assess the presence of personality disorders and specific psychological disorders, such as posttraumatic stress disorder, anxiety disorders, and depression, if the plaintiff's clinical presentation or reported situation suggests that such tests are relevant. In some situations, especially where significant cognitive effects, resulting from psychological reaction to the discrimination or harassment, are alleged, a cognitive or neuropsychological test may be appropriate.

In selecting psychological tests, the forensic evaluator should seek tests that are appropriate for legal decision making, thereby avoiding tests that are unreliable. Similarly, an evaluator should use only tests for which the evaluator has adequate training in administration and interpretation. Because psychological tests are best used as a source of potential hypotheses, they are best administered early in the assessment. Tests can then be scored and used to provide direction for the assessment process. This practice necessitates either seeing the plaintiff on multiple days and/or having the ability to score the tests quickly. Actuarially constructed tests like the MMPI should be given in this way, as they provide only possible hypotheses and cannot be purported as proof of anything.

In addition to psychological tests, the forensic evaluator needs to obtain a full history, both of the plaintiff's life and of the specific employment situation. Various structured information forms and interviews may be of use in this process. When multiple plaintiffs are involved in a single legal action, it is advisable to use the same protocol, including a structured interview, with all plaintiffs.

To the fullest extent possible, all issues being evaluated should be assessed through multiple methods. This process conforms to the best standards of obtaining information and developing conclusions. Although the potential for error of each method of assessment may be high, the probability of error decreases greatly when the same information is obtained and corroborated through multiple independent means. Thus, for example, it may be useful to obtain information about the incidents of alleged harassment through paper-and-pencil measures or structured interviews, unstructured or semistructured interviews, and collateral documentation and interviews. Similarly, psychological dysfunction should be assessed using psychological tests, clinical observations, plaintiff self-report, and collateral documentation. Collateral documentation might include medical records, school records, personnel records, life history information, depositions, collateral interviews, and similar sources of information.

FUTURE DIRECTIONS AND CONCLUSIONS

Psychological experts have substantial expertise about employment discrimination and harassment. This information is important and helpful to the litigation process and the court system. Expertise is best provided by forensic psychologists trained in assessment and well-versed in the relevant legal issues and psychological research. As both legal standards and the psychological research are constantly evolving, no article, chapter, or book, including this one, can substitute for maintaining familiarity with the field. Psychological experts interested in providing such evaluations are well advised to continue updating their knowledge of the legal standards and the psychological literature addressing these issues.

Daubert and Junk Science

Undoubtedly, psychologists in this area, like psychologists working in other areas of assessment, will find their work subject to the scrutiny of the standards created by *Daubert* and its progeny (*General Electric v. Joiner,* 118 S.Ct. 512, 1997 and *Kumho Tire v. Carmichael,* 526 U.S. 137, 1999). Lawyers are likely to seek experts to support the view that *any* psychological research or testimony they do not like is "junk science" or no science at all. Psychologists are advised to be prepared for such challenges. One useful tool in that preparation is to evaluate any proposed testimony in light of the National Conference of Commissioners on Uniform State Laws Uniform Rule 702 (O'Connor, 2001). This is particularly important for those testifying in state courts.

Recent Court Decisions and Complaint Policies

Recent Supreme Court decisions on sexual harassment, particularly in the *Faragher* and *Ellerth* cases, have increased concerns about the nature of an acceptable policy and complaint mechanism. As noted previously, in those decisions, issued on the same day, the Supreme Court ruled that, when there was no direct adverse job action involved, an affirmative defense against claims of supervisor harassment can be made. This affirmative defense requires that (a) the employer exercised reasonable care to prevent and correct promptly any harassment and (b) the plaintiff unreasonably failed to take advantage of the opportunities to prevent, avoid, or correct the harm. There is psychological research relevant to the issues of effective policies, investigation processes, and what constitutes a reasonable or unreasonable failure to use an available complaint mechanism. However, further research and better articulation of existing research, written in a way that makes it more accessible to lawyers and the court, would be of value.

One important area of research concerns the psychological and employment effects/consequences of making complaints, both generally and, in particular, in work settings. Some research has suggested that those who complain have worse job outcomes than individuals not making complaints (Fitzgerald, Swan, & Fisher, 1995). There is significant need for clearer identification of the conditions under which complaint about harassment or discrimination makes the situation worse for an employee and when it prevents or reduces harm. Such research has important legal and policy implications.

This line of research likely will include more exploration of what factors increase or inhibit retaliation by harassers and others against those individuals making complaints of discrimination or harassment.

Similarly, additional research on which factors in a complaint policy (and the application of the policy) facilitate and inhibit the willingness of targeted individuals to come forward will be of significant value. Significant questions remain unaddressed in this area: What types of wording increase use of complaint policy and procedure? What role do promises of confidentiality or the lack of confidentiality have on willingness to come forward? What role do organizational factors play in shaping the type of policy needed? For example, does formal wording and a formal procedure in a small company have similar value or effect as it does in a large company? Psychological research can play an important role in providing employers, policymakers, and the courts information on these questions.

Oncale and Equal Opportunity Harassers

The *Oncale* decision has established that Title VII requires an individual to be disadvantaged due to membership in an identified class. This decision places the focus on the discriminatory nature of the conduct, not just the egregious nature of the conduct. Although important, it may unfortunately give rise to certain arguments that require additional psychological commentary. The argument that "equal opportunity harassers," those who use abusive language and/or grope or proposition both men and women, are not violating Title VII creates urgency for additional research and better translation of the existing research. Both old and new research that deals with the gendered difference in the experience of the same conduct will be relevant in addressing this area of legal analysis.

CONCLUSION

Psychological research, especially on sexual harassment, has been important in the evolution of both legal standards and litigation strategies. As legal standards continue to evolve, it will be important for psychological research to continue to inform that process. In general, the field will benefit from a closer relationship between those performing the psychological research and those developing the legal theory and litigation strategies. Such interactions between the disciplines may improve the relevance and use of psychological research for legal proceedings and increase the degree to which legal decisions accurately reflect people's lived psychological experiences.

REFERENCES

Aboud, F. E., & Levy, S. R. (1999). Introduction: Are we ready to translate research into programs? *Journal of Social Issues, 55,* 621–626.

Allport, G. W. (1954). *The nature of prejudice.* Reading, MA: Addison-Wesley.

American Psychiatric Association. (1994). *Diagnostic and statistical manual of mental disorders* (4th ed.). Washington, DC: Author.

Anderson v. Methodist Evangelical Hospital, Ind., Civil No. 6580, 3 EPD, § 8282, W.D. KY., June 1971, aff'd, 464 F.2d 723, 4 EPD § 7901 (6th Cir. 1972).

Baker, N. L. (1995). The sex role construction of occupational roles: That's why they call it a man's world. *Feminist forensic psychology.* Paper presented at symposium conducted at the American Psychological Association Annual Convention, New York.

Bergmann, B. C. (1986). *The economic emergence of women.* New York: Basic Books.

Brewer, M. B., & Brown, R. J. (1998). Intergroup relations. In D. T. Gilbert, S. T. Fiske, & G. Lindsey (Eds.), *The handbook of social psychology* (4th ed., pp. 554–594). New York: Oxford University Press.

Brief, A. P., Dietz, J., Cohen, R. R., Pugh, S. D., & Vaslow, J. B. (2000). Just doing business: Modern racism and obedience to authority as explanations for employment discrimination. *Organizational Behavior and Human Decision Processes, 81,* 72–97.

Burgess, D., & Borgida, E. (1997). Sexual harassment: An experimental test of sex-role spillover theory. *Personality and Social Psychology Bulletin, 23,* 63–75.

Burlington Industries, Inc. v. Ellerth, Pub. L. No. 97–569 (1998).

Civil Rights Act of 1964, 42 U.S.C. § 1983.

Committee on Ethical Guidelines for Forensic Psychologist. (1991). Specialty guidelines for forensic psychologists. *Law and Human Behavior 15,* 655–665.

Cook, S. W. (1985). Experimenting on social issues: The case of school desegregation. *American Psychologist, 40,* 452–460.

Crocker, J., Major, B., & Steele, C. (1998). Social Stigma. In D. T. Gilbert, S. T. Fiske, & G. Lindsey (Eds.), *The handbook of social psychology* (4th ed., pp. 504–553). New York: Oxford University Press.

Dansky, B. S., & Kilpatrick, D. G. (1997). Effects of sexual harassment. In W. O'Donohue (Ed.), *Sexual harassment: Theory, research, and treatment* (pp. 152–174). Boston: Allyn & Bacon.

Daubert v. Merrell Dow Pharmaceutical, Inc. 509 U.S. 579, 113 S. Ct. 2786 (1993).

Davison, H. K., & Burke, M. J. (2000). Sex discrimination in simulated employment contexts: A meta-analytic investigation. *Journal of Vocational Behavior, 56,* 225–248.

DeAngelis, T. (2001). Thwarting modern prejudice. *Monitor on Psychology, 32,* 26–30.

Deaux, K. (1998). Gender. In D. T. Gilbert, S. T. Fiske, & G. Lindsey (Eds.), *The handbook of social psychology* (4th ed., pp. 788–827). New York: Oxford University Press.

Doe v. City of Belleville, 119 F.3d 563, 74 FEP 625 (7th Cir. 1997).

Dovidio, J. F. (2001, January). *Why can't we get along? Interpersonal biases and interracial distrust.* Paper presented at the National Multicultural Conference and Summit II, Santa Barbara, CA.

Dovidio, J. F., & Gaertner, S. L. (2000). Aversive racism and selection decisions: 1989 and 1999. *Psychological Science, 11,* 315–319.

Eberhardt, J. L., & Fiske, S. T. (Eds.). (1998). *Racism: The problem and the response.* Thousand Oaks, CA: Sage.

Equal Employment Opportunity Commission. *EEOC Compliance manual.* Washington, DC: Bureau of National Affairs.

Equal Employment Opportunity Commission. (1980). Guidelines on discrimination because of sex (Sect. 1604.11). *Federal Register, 45,* 74676–74677.

Equal Employment Opportunity Commission Decision No. YSF 9–108, CCH EEOC Decisions, § 6030 (1973).

Equal Employment Opportunity Commission Compliance Manual. (1988, April). Retaliation, Section 614. Washington, DC: Bureau of National Affairs.

Equal Employment Opportunity Commission Compliance Manual. (1994, June). N: 4072–4073 Harassment, Section 615. Washington, DC: Bureau of National Affairs.

Equal Employment Opportunity Commission Policy Guidance: Sexual Harassment. (1990). N-915–050 (March 19, 1990).

Everly, G. (1989). *A clinical guide to the treatment of the human stress response.* New York: Plenum Press.

Fang, C. Y., & Myers, H. F. (2001). The effects of racial stressors and hostility on cardiovascular reactivity in African American and Caucasian men. *Health Psychology, 20*(1), 64–70.

Faragher v. City of Boca Raton, 118 S. Ct. 2275 (1998).

Fiske, S. T. (1993). Controlling other people: The impact of power on stereotyping. *American Psychologist, 48,* 621–628.

Fiske, S. T. (1998). Stereotyping, prejudice, and discrimination. In D. T. Gilbert, S. T. Fiske, & G. Lindsey (Eds.), *The handbook of social psychology* (4th ed., pp. 357–411). New York: Oxford University Press.

Fitzgerald, L. F. (1992). *Breaking silence: The harassment of women in academia and the workplace.* Washington, DC: Federation of Cognitive, Psychological, and Behavioral Sciences.

Fitzgerald, L. F., Buchanan, N. T., Collinsworth, L. L., Magley, V. J., & Ramos, A. (1999). Junk logic: The abuse defense in sexual harassment litigation. *Psychology, Public Policy, and Law, 5,* 730–759.

Fitzgerald, L. F., Drasgow, F., Hulin, C. L., Gelfand, M. J., & Magley, V. J. (1997a). Antecedents and consequences of sexual harassment in organizations: A test of an integrated model. *Journal of Applied Psychology, 82,* 578–589.

Fitzgerald, L. F., Shullman, S. L., Bailey, N., Richards, M., Swecker, J., Gold, Y., et al. (1988). The incidence and dimensions of sexual harassment in academia and the workplace. *Journal of Vocational Behavior, 32,* 152–175.

Fitzgerald, L. F., Swan, S., & Fisher, K. (1995). Why didn't she just report him? The psychological and legal implications of women's responses to sexual harassment. *Journal of Social Issues, 51,* 117–138.

Fitzgerald, L. F., Swan, S., & Magley, V. J. (1997b). But was it really sexual harassment? Legal, behavioral, and psychological definitions of the workplace victimization of women. In W. O'Donohue (Ed.), *Sexual harassment: Theory, research, and treatment* (pp. 5–28). Boston: Allyn & Bacon.

Frazier, P. A., Cochran, C. C., & Olson, A. M. (1995). Social science research on lay definitions of sexual harassment. *Journal of Social Issues, 51,* 21–37.

Freeman, J. (1984). Women, law, and public policy. In J. Freeman (Ed.), *Women: A feminist perspective* (3rd ed.). Palo Alto, CA: Mayfield.

Frye v. United States, 293 F. 1013 (D.C. Cir. 1923).

Garber v. Saxon Business Products, 552 F.2d 1032, 14 EPD § 7598 (4th Cir. 1977).

Garcia v. Elf Atochem N. Am., 28 F.3d 446, 66 FEP § 1700 (5th Cir. 1994).

General Electric Company et al. v. Joiner *et ux,* 522 U.S. 136 (1997).

Gilbert, D. T., Fiske, S. T., & Lindsey, G. (Eds.). (1998). *The handbook of social psychology* (4th ed.). New York: Oxford University Press.

Gilbert, L. A. (1992). Gender and counseling psychology: Current knowledge and directions for research and social action. In S. D. Brown & R. W. Lent (Eds.), *Handbook of counseling psychology* (2nd ed., pp. 383–419). New York: Wiley.

Glomb, T. M., Richman, W. L., Hulin, C. L., Drasgow, F., Schneider, K. T., & Fitzgerald, L. F. (1997). Ambient sexual harassment: An integrated model of antecedents and consequences. *Organizational Behavior and Human Decision Processes, 71,* 309–328.

Gold, Y. (1987). *Sexual harassment in the workplace: Pink, white, and blue collar women.* Paper presented at the annual meeting of the American Psychological Association, New York.

Goldenhar, L. M., Swanson, N. G., Hurrell, J. J., Jr., Ruder, A., & Deddens, J. (1998). Stressors and adverse outcomes for female construction workers. *Journal of Occupational Health Psychology, 3,* 19–32.

Graves, S. B. (1999). Television and prejudice reduction: When does television as a vicarious experience make a difference? *Journal of Social Issues, 55,* 707–728.

Greenberg, S., & Shuman, D. (1997). Irreconcilable conflict between therapeutic and forensic roles. *Professional Psychology: Research and Practice, 28,* 50–57.

Harris v. Forklift Systems, 510 U.S. 17,114 S.Ct. 367, 63 FEP. (1993).

Hay, M. S., & Elig, T. W. (1999). The Department of Defense sexual harassment survey: Overview and methodology. *Military Psychology, 11,* 233–242.

Hesson-McInnis, M. S., & Fitzgerald, L. F. (1997). Sexual harassment: A preliminary test of an integrative model. *Journal of Applied Social Psychology, 27,* 877–901.

Kiecolt-Glaser, J. K., & Glaser, G. (2001). Stress and immunity: Age enhances the risks. *Current Directions in Psychological Science, 10,* 18–21.

Kirby, D., & Jackson, J. (1999). Mitigating perceptions of racism: The importance of work group composition and supervisor's race. In A. J. Murrell & F. J. Crosby (Eds.), *Mentoring dilemmas: Developmental relationships within multicultural organizations* (pp. 143–155). Mahwah, NJ: Erlbaum.

Kumho Tire v. Carmichael, 526 U.S. 137, 1999.

Lindermann, B. T., & Kadue, D. D. (1999). *Sexual Harassment in Employment Law 1999 cumulative supplement.* Washington, DC: Bureau of National Affairs.

Mackie, D., & Hamilton, D. L. (Eds.). (1993). *Affect, cognition, and stereotyping: Interactive processes in group perception.* San Diego, CA: Academic Press.

MacKinnon, C. (1979). *Sexual harassment of working women: A case of sex discrimination.* New Haven, CT: Yale University Press.

Macrae, C. N., Stangor, C., & Hewstone, M. (Eds.). (1996). *Stereotypes and stereotyping.* New York: Guilford Press.

Magley, V. J., Waldo, C. R., Drasgow, F., & Fitzgerald, L. F. (1999). The impact of sexual harassment on military personnel: Is it the same for men and women? *Military Psychology, 11,* 283–302.

Mays, V. M., Coleman, L. M., & Jackson, J. S. (1999). Perceived race-based discrimination, employment status, and job stress in a national sample of Black women: Implications for health outcomes. *Journal of Occupational Health Psychology, 1,* 319–329.

McWilliams v. Fairfax County Bd. of Supervisors, 72 F.3d 1191, 69 FEP 1082 (4th Cir. 1996).

Meritor Savings Bank v. Vinson, 106 S. Ct. 2399, 40 EPD § 36, 159 (1986).

Mueller, C. W., Parcel, T. L., & Tanaka, K. (1989). Particularism in authority outcomes of Black and White supervisors. *Social Science Research, 18,* 1–20.

Naylor, J. C., Pritchard, R. D., & Ilgen, D. R. (1980). *A theory of behavior in organizations.* New York: Academic Press.

O'Connor, M., & Krauss, D. (2001). Legal update: New developments in Rule 702. *American Psychology-Law Society News, 21,* 1–4.

Oncale v. Sundowner Offshore Oil, 83 F.3d 118, 70 FEP 1303 (5th Cir. 1996).

Oncale v. Sundowner Offshore Oil, 118 S. Ct. 998, 76 FEP 221 (1998).

Perry, E. L., Kulik, C. T., & Schmidtke, J. M. (1997). Blowing the whistle: Determinants of responses to sexual harassment. *Basic and Applied Social Psychology, 19,* 457–482.

Pryor, J. B. (1987). Sexual harassment proclivities in men. *Sex Roles, 17,* 269–290.

Pryor, J. B., Giedd, J. L., & Williams, K. B. (1995). A social psychological model for predicting sexual harassment. *Journal of Social Issues, 51,* 69–84.

Quick v. Donaldson Co., 90 F.3d 1372, 71 FEP 551 (8th Cir. 1996).

Rogers, R. (Ed.). (1997). *Clinical assessment of malingering and deception* (2nd ed.). New York: Guilford Press.

Root, M. P. P. (2001). *Hate crimes and the trauma of discrimination.* Paper presented at the National Multicultural Conference and Summit II, Santa Barbara, CA.

Sedikides, C., Insko, C., & Schopler, J. (Eds.). (1997). *Inter-group cognition and behavior.* Mahwah, NJ: Erlbaum.

Smith, E. R. (1993). Social identity and social emotions: Towards new conceptualizations of prejudice. In D. Mackie & D. L. Hamilton (Eds.), *Affect, cognition, and stereotyping: Interactive processes in group perception.* San Diego, CA: Academic Press.

Steele, C. M. (1997). A threat in the air: How stereotypes shape intellectual identity and performance. *American Psychologist, 52,* 613–629.

Steele, C. M. (2001, January). *Institutional climate and stereotype threat: Enhancing educational performance and identification in the face of negative group stereotype.* Paper presented at the National Multicultural Conference and Summit II, Santa Barbara, CA.

Steele, C. M., & Aronson, J. (1995). Stereotype threat and the intellectual performance of African Americans. *Journal of Personality and Social Psychology, 69,* 797–811.

Stockdale, M. S. (1998). The direct and moderating influences of sexual-harassment pervasiveness, coping strategies, and gender on work-related outcomes. *Psychology of Women Quarterly, 22,* 521–535.

Tajfel, H., Flament, C., Bilig, M., & Bundy, R. (1971). Social categorization and intergroup behavior. *European Journal of Social Psychology, 1,* 149–178.

Title VII of the Civil Rights Act of 1964, 42 U.S.C. 2000e *et seq.* (1982).

U.S. Merit System Protection Board. (1981). *Sexual harassment of federal workers: Is it a problem?* Washington, DC: U.S. Government Printing Office.

Utsey, S. O. (1998). Assessing the stressful effects of racism: A review of instrumentation. *Journal of Black Psychology, 24,* 269–288.

Van Duch, D. (2001, June 11). Coke employment bias settlement follows Texaco's task force approach. *National Law Journal.*

Waldo, C. R., Berdahl, J. L., & Fitzgerald, L. F. (1998). Are men sexually harassed? If so, by whom? *Law and Human Behavior, 22,* 59–79.

Williams v. Bell, 587 F.2d 1240, 17 EPD § 8605 (D.C. Cir. 1978).

Williams v. Saxbe, 413 F. Supp. 654, 11 EPD § 10,840, D.D.C. 1976, rev'd and remained on other grounds sub nom.

Yaffe, J. (1995). Latina managers in public employment: Perceptions of organizational discrimination. *Hispanic Journal of Behavioral Sciences, 17,* 334–346.

Zigarelli, M. A. (1995). Clarifying the boundaries of sexual harassment and employer liability: Judicial application of *Harris v. Forklisft Systems. Employee Responsibilities and Rights Journal, 10,* 49–63.

CHAPTER 15

Forensic Evaluation in Americans with Disabilities Act Cases

WILLIAM E. FOOTE

In July 1990, President George Bush signed the Americans with Disabilities Act (ADA), which became effective two years later. In writing the most sweeping civil rights legislation since the Civil Rights Act of 1964, the framers of this legislation intended to assist people with disabilities to obtain jobs and achieve the goal of full functioning in the workplace. The ADA contains provisions that outlaw discrimination against people with disabilities in hiring, training, compensation, and benefits (Bell, 1997). The statute makes it illegal to use employment classifications based on disability or to participate in contracts that have an effect of discriminating against people with disabilities. The statute also indicates that it is unlawful for an employer to use tests or other qualification standards that are not job-related and that have the impact of screening out individuals with disabilities. The ADA protects individuals against retaliation for filing a charge or otherwise being involved in an Equal Employment Opportunity Commission (EEOC)-related action. In addition, the law mandates that employers provide "reasonable accommodation" for disabled workers who could qualify for jobs if such assistance is provided (Parry, 1996).

Although the ADA has yet to fulfill its full promise (Blanck, 1995, 1996; Stefan, 2001; Wylonis, 1999), this remarkable and sweeping legislation has had an impact on many aspects of American life, including public accommodations, telecommunications, and transportation. This chapter focuses on how forensic mental health professionals can inform decisions made by people with disabilities, employers, and courts as they engage both the opportunities and the conflicts provided by the ADA.

The author wishes to express his appreciation to Susan Stefan for her comments on an earlier draft of the chapter; Marcia Lubar for her review of the final draft; Alan Goldstein for his encouragement and editing; Kerri Repa for her work with references; Krisan Smith for her work on the many drafts of the paper and her excellent work on the references; and Cheryl Foote for her support and careful editing.

Correspondence may be addressed to William E. Foote, Ph.D., 212 Gold, SW, Suite 202, Albuquerque, New Mexico 87102, 505-243-2777.

The chapter introduces the reader to some general information about disability in the workplace and how the ADA fits into existing disability systems. The second section deals with mental disabilities under the ADA. The third section deals with how psychologists may work with employers to accommodate workers with disabilities. The fourth section examines litigation-related psychological evaluations and how psychologists may assist the court in determining damages in cases of discrimination and failure to provide reasonable accommodation. The final section provides some concluding remarks. Because of space limitations, this chapter does not focus on the legal structure of the ADA nor how the ADA applies to the hiring process. For information on these topics, the interested reader is directed to Parry (1997), Stefan (2001), and Carling (1993) for information concerning the law and to Parry (1997) and Hall and Cash (1992) for material related to hiring issues.

THE EMPLOYMENT OF PEOPLE WITH DISABILITIES

According to recent statistics (Kraus, Stoddard, & Gilmartin, 1996), about 48.9 million Americans have some type of disability. This number constitutes an estimated 19.4% of the noninstitutionalized civilian population and nearly one in five people. About half of these people, or 24.1 million, are considered to be severely disabled.

The extent to which people with disabilities participate in the labor market depends on a number of factors, including sex and age. In the general population, some 91.4% of men and 74.9% of women participate in the labor force (Kraus et al., 1996). However, people with disabilities participate at a lower rate, with disabled men participating at a rate of 58.8% and disabled women participating at a rate of 45.6%. The same source notes that full-time participation in the labor force also varies as a function of age, with both disabled men and women achieving the highest rate of participation in their late 20s and early 30s. However, disabled men keep approximately the same level of labor force participation through their mid-50s, whereas women experience a sharp age-related decline.

The income of people with disabilities is generally lower than is the income of those without such limitations. In general, if a nondisabled worker earns $1.00, a person with a nonsevere disability would earn $.90, and a person with a severe disability would earn $.70 (Kraus et al., 1996). The differences in income are less marked for younger workers, among whom both disabled and nondisabled persons earn approximately the same. For workers between the ages of 35 and 64, the differences are greater. In this age group, if the nondisabled worker earned $1.00, the person with a nonsevere disability would earn $.82, and the person with a severe disability would earn $.63.

In addition, people with disabilities constitute a substantial cost to the U.S. government for support and medical care. O'Keeffe (1993) notes that in 1991, the government spent $92 billion to assist persons with disabilities to meet their basic living needs.

Baldwin (1999) reviewed employment patterns in the six years before the ADA was passed in 1990. In general, people with physical disabilities are more diverse and may have years of work experience prior to onset of disability. On the other hand, people with psychological disabilities may have experienced those problems since school years. Baldwin's study was designed to look at a range of people with disabilities and to determine the impact of those disabilities on work and income opportunities. The researcher attempted to factor the impact of impairments by clustering them into five groups: cardiovascular, mental, musculoskeletal, respiratory, sensory, and "other," which included people with AIDS, cancer patients, people with cerebral palsy and paralysis, and individuals with diabetes and epilepsy. The data reviewed by Baldwin from the year 1990 indicated that the largest category (about 44%) of people with disabilities suffered from some form of musculoskeletal disorder. Of the sample, men and women with mental disorders constituted about 10% and 6%, respectively.

Employment rates of workers with mental disabilities fell significantly below that of all other groups. The employment rates of nondisabled male and female workers were 89% and 74%, respectively. For most other disabilities, the rates for men had an average in the low 70% range. However, men with mental disabilities had a rate of 53%. For women, as noted above, the overall employment rate is lower, and the variation in employment rates was greater, between 41% and 62%. For disabled women, the employment rate was at the low end of this continuum, at a rate of 41%.

Similar rates of employment for people with mental disorders were found by Milazzo-Sayre, Henderson, and Manderscheid (1997). They noted that the Ecological Catchment Area study revealed that 22% of the U.S. adult population have a diagnosable mental disorder, and some 6% have a substance abuse disorder. About one-third of those with substance abuse disorders have a comorbid Axis I or Axis II disorder. Of the overall population, 2.3% have a severe mental disorder.

Yelin and Cisternas (1997) demonstrated that diagnosis per se did not dictate whether a disabled worker could function in the workplace. This research found that a number of variables determine the employability of people with mental illnesses. Primary among these are the presence of a prior work history. In addition, the provision of a nonpsychotic diagnosis, the presence of an affective disorder diagnosis, and a positive reaction to work stressors predict better work performance.

These data echo a much older study (Anthony & Jansen, 1984) that reported a number of findings relevant to how people with mental illness function in the workplace. They determined that neither diagnosis nor specific symptoms effectively predict work performance. Surprisingly, intelligence, aptitude, and personality tests are poor predictors, but paper-and-pencil measures of ego strength and self-concept are good predictors of work functioning. The best predictors of future work performance were the workers' past vocational history and how well they functioned in a worklike setting (e.g., a sheltered employment or workshop).

IMPACT OF DISCRIMINATION

In the study discussed above, Baldwin (1999) noted, "Overall, the results are consistent with the hypothesis that declining employment rates for men with impairments between 1984 and 1990 are at least partly explained by increasing employer discrimination against men with disabilities" (p. 19). The presence of attitudes that support discrimination is frequently reported by people with disabilities.

Stefan (2001) conducted a brief survey with a broad array of mentally disabled people. Three-quarters of the sample (74%) reported that they had experienced some form of discrimination based on disability. The most painful type of discrimination came in the form of how people with disabilities are treated by others on a daily basis. Some 65% of respondents reported that family, neighbors, friends, churchgoers, or fellow students had discriminated against them. Employment was the next highest area of discrimination, with 55% reporting some form of work-related discriminatory activity. Negative experiences of differential treatment by others was also reported in institutional settings (34%), educational institutions (30%), medical care (29%), insurance (29%), the court system (24%), housing (23%), and commercial establishments (stores and restaurants; 9%).

In a larger study of stigma, Wahl (1999) surveyed 1,301 consumers of mental health services to determine whether they had been victims of stigma and stereotyping. About 80% of the sample reported overhearing someone utter a hurtful or offensive comment; more than half reported experiences of being shunned or avoided by others; Seven of ten reported that they had been treated as less competent because of their disability status. Over half of the respondents experienced job discrimination; of these, however, only about 15% said

that they had been frequently turned down for a job for which they were qualified. An even smaller proportion (34%) indicated that they had been denied educational opportunities because of discrimination. However, 82% indicated that they had attempted to conceal their disability from others on written job applications for fear that the potential employer would discriminate against them.

Thus, the decision to disclose the presence of a mental disorder is often a complicated one. Stefan (1998) noted that people with mental disabilities often are able to conceal their disability in the workplace. However, their mental disorder becomes disabling when they encounter a supervisor or employer who is overbearing, threatening, or overly critical. Hostile work environments test the worker, and those with limited stamina and resilience begin to show impairment in work-related tasks. Stefan notes that courts often assume that the ability to function in a stressful work environment should be a fundamental qualification for most workers.

SUMMARY

The research on worker participation in the workforce indicates that people with mental disorders generally participate at a lower rate than those who do not suffer from those conditions. The impact of sex is additive to that of mental disorder, as shown by the uniformly lower workplace participation of both nondisabled and disabled women.

Generally, people with psychotic disorders who have little work history and few worklike experiences have the greatest difficulty integrating into the workplace. Those who have more work history, have an affective disorder diagnosis, and who enter the workplace with some degree of self-confidence are better able to obtain and maintain employment. However, many people with mental disorders do not disclose their disability to employers or coworkers for fear of discrimination and stigmatization (Ravid, 1992; Ravid & Menon, 1993). This fear appears to be well founded based on the experience of many (Stefan, 2001). This is, however, a feature of the American workplace that the ADA was designed to address.

PSYCHIATRIC/PSYCHOLOGICAL DISABILITIES AND THE ADA

Mental Disabilities under the ADA

The ADA includes a three-prong definition of disability: "(1) A physical or mental impairment that substantially limits

one or more of the major life activities of such individuals;
(2) a record of such an impairment; (3) being regarded as having such an impairment" (29 C.F.R. Chapter XIV, Part 1630.2 (g(1))-(3)). The Act defines a *qualified individual with a disability* as a person with a disability who has the proper skills, experience, education, and other job-related requirements required by the job that the person either currently holds or wishes to obtain. Critically, a qualified individual with a disability, with or without reasonable accommodation, can perform the essential functions of that job.

In the ADA, a *mental impairment* includes "any mental or psychological disorder, such as . . . emotional or mental illness." Examples of emotional or mental illness include major depression, bipolar disorder, anxiety disorders (which include panic disorder, obsessive-compulsive disorder, and posttraumatic stress disorder), schizophrenia, and personality disorders. Note that the EEOC regulations include personality disorders, which were not listed in the ADA statute. EEOC publications (United States Equal Employment Opportunities Commission, 1997) suggest that the current edition of the American Psychiatric Association's (2000) *Diagnostic and Statistical Manual of Mental Disorders* (now the text revision of the fourth edition, *DSM-IV-TR*) is an appropriate source of information to identify such disorders. The term disability *excludes*

(1) transvestism, transexualism, pedophilia, exhibitionism, voyeurism, gender identity disorders not resulting from physical impairments, or other sexual behavior disorders; (2) compulsive gambling, kleptomania, or pyromania; or (3) psychoactive substance abuse disorders resulting from current illegal use of drugs. (e) Homosexuality and bisexuality are not impairments and so are not disabilities as defined in this part. (29 C.F.R. Chapter XIV, Part 1630.3 (a)(1).)

An *impairment* constitutes a disability under the ADA when it adversely affects one or more major life activities. The worker need not demonstrate that the impairment interferes with work. In fact, the inquiry begins with non-work-related life activities, including caring for oneself, sleeping, reading, and concentrating. It is only after it is determined that no other major life activity is impaired that the worker should consider impairments in working as a basis for disability.

When one evaluates psychiatric disorders in light of the ADA, the determination of whether a particular person has an impairment that substantially limits a major life activity should be based on how the condition affects that particular individual's life. Decisions should not be made on the basis of stereotypes about people with mental illness or assumptions about the particular disorder of that individual. For example, stereotypes such as "no schizophrenic could do this job" reflect this kind of inappropriate generalization (United States Equal Employment Opportunities Commission, 1997).

An evaluation of a psychological disability case begins by examining evidence of how the worker functions at home, at work, and in a variety of other settings. It is critical to connect the individual's functional limitations to impairments, although it is not necessary to use the testimony of experts to make this connection. The worker, family members, friends, or coworkers may provide sufficient evidence for such determinations. The threshold for determining if a condition is sufficiently *severe* to constitute a disability can be met by reference to whether the condition prevents a person from engaging in a major life activity or otherwise restricts the person in the performance of a major life activity. If the impairment results in only *mild* limitations, it may not meet this threshold. The duration of the impairment is also of importance because impairments of several weeks or months do not constitute a disability. Many mental disorders that are chronic and episodic would be considered substantially limiting while they are active or if they are likely to recur.

The ability to interact with others may be a focus for the determination of substantial disability. In this case, the claimant is compared to the average person in the general population. If the person is significantly restricted compared to that average person, the condition is considered to constitute a substantial limitation. The threshold for impairments of abilities to interact with others would *not* be met in the case of one who was simply unfriendly or unpleasant in interactions with supervisors or coworkers. However, if the person demonstrated social withdrawal, high levels of hostility, or impairments in necessary communications, the threshold may be met.

Issues of Conduct

People with disabilities are no different from nondisabled workers in that they may be subject to discipline from employers because of employee misconduct. However, when mental disabilities affect conduct in the workplace, the employer may be required to accommodate that conduct. In general, the employer may discipline an employee with a disability if that employee has engaged in misconduct that would provoke the same discipline for a nondisabled employee (Rothstein, 1997). However, if the conduct standard does not relate to job functions and is not consistent with business necessity, then the imposition of that conduct standard could constitute a violation of the ADA. In such circumstances, the employer must provide reasonable accommodations that would enable a person who is otherwise qualified to meet those conduct requirements in the future, if those accommodations do not pose undue hardship to the employer. This requirement does not compel an employer to excuse past conduct, as reasonable accommodations determinations are prospective.

Direct Threat

The ADA recognizes that the workplace should be a safe place for employees, customers, vendors, supervisors, and the general public. Generally, these safety concerns take precedence over principles of fairness to an individual worker. The ADA requires that the employer demonstrate that a worker constitutes a *direct threat*. The application of safety rules and the *direct threat* standards must be uniformly applied by the employer, who may not inappropriately use safety rules as a means of excluding persons with disabilities (United States Equal Employment Opportunity Commission, 2000).

Direct threat is defined as "a significant risk of substantial harm to the health and safety of the individual or others that cannot be eliminated or reduced by reasonable accommodation" (United States Equal Employment Opportunity Commission, 1992, 29 C.F.R. §1630.2(r)). To meet this definition, the risk must be high, more than a slightly increased risk. The decision must be based on an individualized assessment of the worker's current ability to perform the functions of the job safely (see *School Bd. of Nassau Cty., Fla. v. Arline*, 1987). A physician's (or other appropriate professional's) evaluation based on the most current knowledge should determine if the worker is capable of safely performing job functions.

This assessment should include reference to the following factors: the duration of the risk; the nature and severity of the potential harm; the likelihood that potential harm will occur; and the imminence of potential harm. An employer must specify the behavior that constitutes the threat. The mere presence of a psychiatric diagnosis or a history of psychiatric treatment does not prove that the worker poses a direct threat. Also, the impact of the employer's reasonable accommodation must be taken into account. If the employer can eliminate the direct threat by accommodations, the worker may be considered a qualified individual with a disability. If, on the other hand, no amount of reasonable accommodation can reduce the threat, the worker is no longer qualified for the job and is not considered a qualified individual with a disability. For example, Parry (1997) notes that a New York Federal Court case (*Altman v. New York City Health and Hosp. Corp.*, 1995) found that a physician who was discovered drinking on the job could not demand reinstatement because no reasonable accommodation could be fashioned to allow him to safely treat patients.

Violence and Threats of Violence

A worker who has threatened violence or committed violent acts may face sanctions, including discharge, from the employer. If the worker files suit against the employer for those job actions, the employer may use a defense based on direct threat. However, as Rothstein (1997) observes, the employer is in a difficult position. If the employer inappropriately discharges or disciplines a worker for threatening behavior, the probability of an ADA lawsuit increases. If the employer fails to act in the face of a worker who poses a direct threat, the employer faces liability to those harmed by the worker.

Some courts have ruled that a worker who engaged in threatening behavior was not considered a qualified individual with a disability (e.g., *Mazzarella v. United States Postal Service*, 1994). In this case, the ability to do the job without posing a threat to others or without being involved in violent behavior was viewed as an essential job function. A history of violence or threats of violence may be used as a basis for not hiring an otherwise qualified job applicant if it can be shown that the worker continues to pose a direct threat.

Suicidal Workers: Danger to Self Issues

Although the ADA relates the direct threat language only to the health and safety of others, EEOC regulations (29 C.F.R. §1630.2 (r)) include danger to self as an element. Parry (1997) notes that courts have handled this issue in different ways. Some have ruled that a history of suicide attempts does not necessarily translate into a direct threat in the workplace. As above, the employer must initiate an individualized determination based on current and thorough professional assessment of the worker. As always, the central issue is whether the worker can perform job functions. Some cases (e.g., *EEOC v. Amego*, 1997) suggest that dangerousness to self could bar employment for a disabled person if that self-destructive behavior could result in harm to others. In the *Amego* case, a medical professional whose duties included dispensing medications to patients came to work in a partially sedated state after a suicide gesture by drug overdose (Foote, 1997). In other cases (e.g., *Kohnke v. Delta Airlines, Inc.*, 1996), the court noted that the EEOC's interpretation of the ADA was untenable and that expanding the language to include danger to self was inappropriate.

Substance Abuse Disorders and the ADA

For the ADA, all substance abuse disorders are not created equal but are treated very differently, depending on whether the abused substance is illegal or legal. In general, a worker currently using illegal drugs is not protected by the ADA (LaPorte, 1996). Likewise, one who abuses prescribed drugs in such a way as to violate the law is considered to use illegal drugs (Parry, 1993). The ADA attempts to be neutral on the issue of drug testing, although the Act allows an employer to conduct drug tests with employees or applicants in contexts in which other sorts of medical evaluations are prohibited (Jones, 1993). Thus, a worker who is not hired or is discharged for testing positive for illegal drugs is not usually protected by the Act.

It is the rehabilitated illegal drug user who is protected by the law. Consequently, a history of illegal drug use cannot be used as a basis for nonhire or discharge. However, if a worker who has been drug-free for some time experiences a relapse of illegal drug use, he or she may be fired without protection from the ADA. Unfortunately, as Jones (1993) notes, such extreme consequences of a relapse could encourage a worker to conceal a relapse from an employer.

A worker with an alcohol problem must experience a substantial limitation in a major life activity to be covered by the ADA (Aristeiguieta, 1998). A casual drinker would probably not be considered disabled, whereas one who is alcohol-dependent would be (Allison & Stahlhut, 1995). The implications of relapses for workers with alcohol problems are more serious when the alcohol use results in conduct that would trigger discipline for other workers. A worker considered disabled because of alcohol-related disorders is not shielded from discipline or discharge resulting from absenteeism during a binge or reporting to work drunk. The principle of direct threat applies to substance abuse disorders. As noted above, the worker with an alcohol dependence diagnosis engaging in conduct that places anyone in danger could be disciplined in the same way as other workers.

In general, the courts have been unfriendly to anyone claiming discrimination on the basis of illegal drug use (Parry, 1997). In a number of jurisdictions, courts have ruled that many forms of current illegal drug use can serve as one basis for discharge or for not hiring an applicant. Courts have expanded the meaning of "current" in relation to illegal drug use. Courts in the Ninth and Fourth Circuits have interpreted past—but recent—drug use as reflecting an "ongoing problem rather than a problem in the past" (e.g., *Trans Mart, Inc., v. Brewer,* 1993).

DEALING WITH MENTAL DISABILITIES UNDER THE ADA

The ADA provisions for psychological and psychiatric disabilities are designed to treat these disabling conditions as similar to more familiar disabilities, such as orthopedic or cardiac impairments. As the research cited above demonstrates, however, when the disability is based on a mental disorder, stigma and adverse stereotypes abound. Stefan (2001) notes that illnesses that express themselves in abnormalities of behavior are often subject to value judgments, equating these problems with moral failings. These value judgments are evident in the government's discomfort with mental disorders, which becomes obvious when one reads the statute and the enabling regulations (see Stefan, 1998, for discussion of the legislative history of the Act).

Because mental disorders often are not easily observable, employers may be unaware that workers have such disorders (Calfee, 1998). The complicated natural history of chronic psychiatric disorders implies that the accommodations necessary to deal with mental disorders may change with time. Mental disorders frighten laypeople because of common misconceptions about such illnesses (Wahl, 1999).

Because the ADA requires the employer to undertake an individualized approach to each case, it is difficult for employers (or even observers) to develop clear-cut rules for decision making in future cases (Stefan, 2001). Each new case that involves developing reasonable accommodations for those with mental disabilities may cause the employer to feel like one lurching into unknown and frightening territory.

A limited body of research exists on specific mental disorders as they are viewed through the lens of the ADA. The following section examines this literature.

Depression

For some mental disorders, accommodation may be complicated by the inherent characteristics of the disorder. The workplace is one setting in which the complications presented by depressive disorders become clearly evident. Croghan, Kniesner, and Powers (1999) observe that the impact of depression on functioning in the workplace is greater than low-back pain, heart disease, high blood pressure, and diabetes mellitus combined. Because of antidepressant medications that currently have widespread use, many people with depression are able to seek and obtain jobs. However, these people may still suffer relapses of depression while they are on the job. Thus, many concerns about depression relate to accommodations for already employed workers instead of those who are dealing with disability issues at the time of hiring.

For example, a supervisor may become aware of the worker's depression-related symptoms: poor concentration, impaired cognitive ability, irritability, or loss of interest in work. These observations may trigger an obligation on the part of the employer to accommodate the disorder. As noted above, the diagnosis alone does not determine eligibility. And, as noted by Foote (2000), worker and employer may find themselves in the quandary of finding too little distance between being disabled enough to meet entry definition for qualified individual with a disability and a person too disabled to be qualified even with reasonable accommodation. Depressed people face another barrier to seeking accommodation because the disorder itself may deprive the worker of sufficient energy to proactively seek ADA accommodations. Depressed workers who are concerned about the stigma associated with their disability may believe that the ADA does not provide sufficient incentives to outweigh the disadvantages of making their disability known to supervisors and coworkers.

Croghan et al. (1999) argue that the employer must play an active role in addressing a worker's depression. In general, treatment for depression does not cost much and results in improved productivity, reduced hospitalization, reduced absences, and lower turnover. If either the employer or employee triggers the accommodation process, the employer may require treatment as the first accommodation. In one case (*Roberts v. County of Fairfax, Va.,* 1996), an employer placed a worker on medical leave of absence and instructed the worker to obtain treatment, which was available through the employer's Employee Assistance Program and county emergency services. The employee's doctor believed that, with treatment, the employee could function on the job. However, a year went by and the worker failed to get treatment. The court ruled that the employee was not a qualified individual with a disability because he refused to accept his employer's efforts to accommodate his condition.

Courts agree that it is reasonable for an employer to require treatment as a condition of employment. There is also precedent that indicates that the employer's duty to accommodate ends when the employee is noncompliant with treatment (*Keoughan v. Delta Airlines, Inc.,* 1997). In this case, an employee with bipolar disorder who had problems with performance, dependability, and attendance was deemed not otherwise qualified because she had failed to comply with her medication regimen. In this case, the medications would have controlled the condition. Courts and employers have considered that people who will not take medication when the medication will effectively remediate their disorder experience a "voluntary disability" (Croghan et al., 1999).

One frequent feature of depressive disorders is a pattern of recurrent exacerbations separated by periods of substantial remission. Often, these periods of remission are accomplished by compliance with the medication regimen and its associated side effects. A trio of recent Supreme Court cases have changed how courts may view the use of such mitigating measures. In *Sutton v. United Airlines* (1999), *Albertson's v. Kirkingberg* (1999), and *Murphy v. United Parcel* (1999), the Court determined that the definition of an impairment that substantially limits a major life activity must consider any mitigating measures that the individual uses to eliminate or reduce the effects of the impairment. These mitigating measures may include any means that an individual uses to eliminate or reduce the effects of an impairment, including medications for conditions like epilepsy or major depression, insulin used to control diabetes, and assistive devices such as prosthetic devices, walkers, canes, crutches, and hearing aids.

Some (e.g., United States Equal Employment Opportunity Commission, 2000) consider the *Sutton* decision as a lever to force the employer or court to make an individualized determination of disability when examining a specific case. A person may still have a substantial limitation in performing a major life activity in spite of a mitigating measure. Also, some mitigating measures may produce side effects that in themselves may limit a major activity. In addition, a person who uses a mitigating measure may also meet one of the other criteria of the definition of disability in the Act.

Others (Honberg, 1999) are concerned that in the case of mental disabilities, the Court is unduly restricting the range of disabilities covered by the ADA. By eliminating those individuals whose disabilities are substantially mitigated by corrective measures such as medication, the Court ignores the fact that medications do not cure mental illnesses, but only control them.

As Croghan et al. (1999) noted, even a person with a diagnosis of depression who is controlling the expression of the illness through psychotherapy may run afoul of the ADA's emphasis on the employer's ability to maintain requirements related to attendance and performance. The depressed worker who has to miss work to attend psychotherapy sessions may face adverse job actions or discharge, without protection from the ADA. Also, when accommodations involve modification of hours, job responsibilities, or levels of structure, the costs of such accommodations may become an "undue burden" to the employer and may seem unfair to other workers.

Learning Disabilities

Learning disabilities may interfere with the functioning of an adult in the same way that they do in a school-age child (Resnick, 2000). Reading is the most frequent problem area, and impairments of written expression occur with nearly equal frequency (Anderson, Kazmierski, & Cronin, 1995). As these areas form the basis for basic literacy, adults with learning disabilities often have difficulty functioning in work contexts. Anderson et al. note that even with specific education experiences directed toward remediating the learning disability, many people still find themselves unprepared for employment. Because these impairments are not visible to employers and because the impact of learning problems is not as clear-cut as that of better-known disabilities, employers may be less willing to provide reasonable accommodation.

Gerber (1992) notes that learning disabled people must frequently compete head to head with people who are not disabled. Often, they come out of educational institutions in which people understood their problems and offered accommodations. However, the business world is one in which economic incentives often hold sway. To function in the workplace, learning disabled people must become competitive in the interview and job acquisition process. Rapid workplace changes involving downsizing and corporate takeovers may give learning disabled people some pause about disclosing their disability. Gerber recommends that learning disabled workers would be wise to carefully work out a plan for disclosure of disability to determine if disclosure is in their best interests. This same author notes that learning disabilities often are misunderstood by employers, supervisors, and coworkers. Not only do others fail to understand how learning problems are manifested, they may also confuse this form of disability with other stigmatizing impairments such as mental illness and mental retardation.

Courts appear to have difficulty dealing with learning disabilities. In some cases, judges place the threshold for considering a learning problem a "significant impairment" so high that hardly anyone in the workplace could meet the criterion. For example, in *Davidson v. Midelfort Clinic, Ltd.* (1998), a psychotherapist employed by a mental health clinic had a long-standing problem with concentration and other difficulties related to learning. She had problems completing her paper work and asked her employer to provide the accommodation of a transcription device. Her employer refused the accommodation and, when Davidson could not make up the backlog of her dictation, she was discharged. The trial court and the Seventh Circuit agreed with the employer, holding that her learning problem did not constitute a disability because it did not substantially limit her ability to work, speak, or learn.

Summary

Depression and learning disabilities illustrate how mental disabilities interfere with functioning in the workplace. Depression is a condition manifested by chronicity and fluctuation in levels of functioning. Depressed workers seeking accommodation through the ADA may be denied because medications and other treatment mitigate their condition for much of the time. Because such mitigation must be taken into account when determining the presence of a disability in the ADA, people with depression may not be considered disabled and thus are not eligible for ADA coverage.

In contrast, people with learning disabilities often have difficulty mitigating their condition but may be able to conceal their problems from employers until faced with a task that requires concentration or extensive verbal or written work. Because they have been able to "cover" through much of their lives or have been able to complete educational tasks because of accommodations, they often are not perceived to be suffering from any disability.

PSYCHOLOGICAL CONSULTATIONS WITH EMPLOYERS AND WORKERS

Because Title I of the ADA requires employers to provide reasonable accommodation to qualified workers with disabilities, an employer may request the assistance of a psychologist to determine the best course of action for that accommodation plan (Crist & Stoffel, 1992; Foote, 2000; Mancuso, 1990). Some of the material in this section was previously published in an article in *Professional Psychology* (Foote, 2000). Please refer to that paper for a more detailed elaboration of issues in this area. The ADA requires that the employer work with each employee as an individual and attempt to develop a plan that takes into account the worker's specific disability, the worker's strengths, and the context of the worker's job (Moss, Ullman, Johnsen, Starrett, & Burris, 1999; Parry, 1997). In some cases, accommodations for mental disabilities may be relatively straightforward: time off for psychotherapy sessions or special breaks so that the worker may take psychotropic medication (Mancuso, 1990). In other cases, the accommodations may be less obvious and may require expert assistance to both the employer and employee to fashion accommodations that fit the worker and the organization (Carling, 1993; Croghan et al., 1999; Mancuso, 1990).

Conceptualizing ADA Disability

The definitions of disability and of a qualified individual with a disability in the ADA present the psychologist with a dilemma. On the one hand, the worker has to experience substantial limitations in one or more major life activities to be considered disabled under the statute (Bell, 1997). As noted above, courts frequently have assumed that those limitations

Essential Job Functions	Skills of Worker
Color vision.	Color vision.
Gross motor dexterity.	Gross motor dexterity.
Fine motor dexterity.	Fine motor dexterity.
High school mathematics skills.	High school mathematics skills.
Planning.	
Sequencing.	Skills to be compensated by reasonable accommodation.
Social skills.	

Figure 15.1   Reasonable accommodation of work-related deficits.

must be relatively pervasive and severe for the worker to be considered disabled. At the same time, the worker has to meet the educational and experiential requirements for the position and must be able to perform the essential functions of the job with or without reasonable accommodation.

As Foote (2000) suggested, one may conceptualize the problem this way. If a job may be described in terms of skills (essential job functions) necessary for working in that position, those may be listed as shown in Figure 15.1. An incumbent in the position may have a broader array of skills than those listed and may be deserving of a promotion to a position with greater responsibilities. Those skills may be compared to those of a worker who has suffered a traumatic frontal lobe brain injury. In this case, the injury resulted in impaired planning and sequencing abilities and reduced abilities to engage in social interaction (Prigitano, 1991). Those skills require reasonable accommodation.

An assessment of the worker with frontal lobe impairment begins with an inquiry to determine if the individual is otherwise qualified for the position. That is, can the employee perform the essential functions of the position with or without reasonable accommodation? The first step is to review the experiential and educational requirements of the position (Blanck, Andersen, Wallach, & Tenney, 1994). If the worker meets these standards, then the examination of the other job skills would be as described above. If reasonable accommodation can alter the work situation such that the worker can fulfill the job requirements, the worker is a qualified individual with a disability.

This accommodation can be accomplished in several ways. One is to change the job qualifications to better match the worker's skills (Carling, 1993). For example, whereas most electronics technicians work independently, the worker with a brain injury, as described above, may work under supervision (Hantula & Reilly, 1996). In this case, a supervisor would do planning and sequencing and provide the worker with a written "punch list" of tasks to be performed. Using a written list would eliminate one social component, another area of weakness for this worker. Additional accommodations would include added time for using lists or dispensation from worker meetings.

ADA-Related Employer Consultation: Return to Work

Some workers with mental disabilities experience fluctuations in their illnesses that cause them to take extended sick leave or leave without pay. For example, a worker with schizophrenia may experience an acute psychotic episode. This exacerbation may be an element of a pattern of exacerbations and remissions that have been a previous part of the worker's performance on this job. In contrast, especially in the case of mood disorders, it may be the first time the illness has become manifest. For some workers who have concealed their disability, symptoms may become evident only under situations of unusual stress (Stefan, 1998). Stress may arise from the actions of the supervisor or may occur if the worker is promoted and not used to the stresses associated with increased responsibilities. However, once the worker is stabilized on medication and is in supportive treatment, the employer then would consider the issue of whether the worker can return to work.

In general, for return-to-work evaluations, the referral from the employer should contain specific questions to be answered. (In this and subsequent sections, "employer" is used to denote the actual employer in smaller organizations or the human relations person or supervisor in larger concerns.) The essential question is whether the worker has regained a level of functioning so that he or she would qualify as a qualified individual with a disability (Pollet, 1995). That is, is the worker able, with or without reasonable accommodation, to perform the essential job functions of that position? If the worker is a qualified individual with a disability, the consultation may focus on adapting to particular characteristics of the job, such as shift work, interpersonal demands, environmental conditions, and workplace dangers, noise, or distractions.

Initial Considerations

The consultant's job is to first review the employee's work history with the company. To gather this history, the psychologist may rely on personnel documents. Work records also provide clues about how the disability developed. In some cases, medical records and evaluation reports provide this documentation. These records may have been provided by the worker if he or she disclosed the disability and requested reasonable accommodation.

The consultant's second duty is to determine what tasks constitute the job. This determination may require the consultant to visit the workplace. In that setting, the consultant may talk with the worker's supervisor concerning demands not listed in official job descriptions or other documentation. The consultant may want to observe what the worker actually does to accomplish the job. In addition, the consultant may wish to assess the noise, distraction, and activity level of the workplace. The consultant's third responsibility is to consider the parameters for the job. These include the hours that the worker puts in, the nature and duration of shifts, and whether the worker is required to function in the context of rolling or graveyard shifts. The consultant's fourth job is to assess the social environment of the position. This involves examination of the chain of command, composition of the pool of coworkers, and the demands of the position for the worker to cooperate and work closely with others. The fifth responsibility of the consultant is to determine the cognitive skills the position requires. Again, this determination begins with the job requirements as detailed through the listed job description. These may include requisite education and training. In addition, the consultant may want to perform an actual job analysis (Colledge, Johns, & Thomas, 1999). To do this, even experienced psychologists may require additional training (Colledge et al., 1999; Pape & Tarvydas, 1994).

Psychological Evaluation

Once the appropriate background information has been gathered, it is usually necessary to conduct a formal psychological evaluation. Before the initiation of the assessment, the psychologist is required by ethical standards and standards of practice (American Psychological Association, 1992; Committee on Ethical Guidelines for Forensic Psychologists, 1991) to obtain informed consent from the client. In this case, the informed consent includes a discussion of who is requesting the evaluation, the purpose of the evaluation, who will have access to the evaluation report, and any limitations on confidentiality. If the psychologist is concerned that the worker may have some disability that interferes with understanding the informed consent procedure, it may be appropriate to contact the employer for further guidance.

The accommodation evaluation typically includes psychological testing. Cognitive testing is usually necessary to determine the skills that the worker possesses. For example, the consultant may want to include measures of reading, visual-motor functioning, and specific vocationally related tests. Mainly, the evaluation procedures should address those specific deficits raised by the client or the employer.

In the course of selecting and administering tests, the psychologist should be sensitive to several issues in relation to the specific worker who is being evaluated. First, cultural issues may be an important consideration (Smart & Smart, 1993). If the worker's first language is not English or if the worker is from a cultural group with characteristics that may affect the evaluation procedures, the psychologist must take those into account. If the worker has a disability that may affect the testing process, the psychologist should, to the extent possible, modify the testing situation or the tests administered to accommodate the disability (Council on Licensure, Enforcement and Regulation, 1996; Fischer, 1994; Tenopyr, Angoff, Butcher, Geisinger, & Reilly, 1993; Zuriff, 1997). Modification of standardized testing procedures should be reflected in any written report of the evaluation. Of course, one of the main purposes of conducting the testing is to determine what disabilities the worker has. To substantially accommodate a worker's anticipated disabilities may yield little information concerning what the worker can and cannot do.

In the interview with the worker, the psychologist should obtain a full vocational history, including a review of the duties and pay levels of previous positions. When examining these jobs, it is important to determine if the person has experienced similar difficulties in prior jobs to discern whether he or she had an unrecognized disability (or a disability that the worker chose to keep confidential). This discussion should include an exploration of other behavioral patterns that may have negatively affected job tenure but are unrelated to the worker's disability. For example, a worker may have a short temper or low frustration tolerance and report a history of workplace discipline or frequent discharge from employment. As part of the vocational history, it is often helpful to determine if the worker has other recurrent behavioral or symptom patterns in the workplace. These might include exacerbations following a change of supervisor or coworkers, problems in adapting to changes in duties, or failure on promotion or job change.

In the course of the evaluation, it is essential to determine if the worker is a qualified individual with a disability. In some cases, the worker may experience personality traits or predispositions that do not qualify as disabling conditions under the ADA (Mickey & Pardo, 1993).

The next task is to determine if reasonable accommodation is required (Blanck et al., 1994). Would reasonable accommodations allow the worker to perform "essential job functions"? If that question is answered in the affirmative, then the next question is whether the accommodation is feasible (Pollet, 1995). This determination cannot be made in isolation, however, because the employer must provide sufficient information to determine feasibility (Croghan et al., 1999). Recall that the employer is not required to implement accommodations that constitute an "undue burden" (Rothstein, 1997). The psychologist must ask a series of questions concerning the accommodations suggested. First, is there such a job consistent with the worker's experience, training, and skills in the organization? In general, employers are not required to create a job for a qualified disabled employee. Will implementing the accommodation tax the resources of the organization? Is the accommodation in scale with the size of the company? Is adequate staff available for supervision or other aspects of the accommodation (Hantula & Reilly, 1996)? Can the accommodation be made without disrupting the work of the organization? Finally, what will the accommodation cost?

After making these determinations, the evaluator may meet with the employer or the worker's supervisor. In that discussion, evaluator and employer may help choose an alternate position for the worker to develop an alternative work context for the same job. In discussions with the employer, the psychologist may also want to develop a written return-to-work plan or contract (Blanck et al., 1994). This plan should explicitly consider the responsibilities of the employer and the worker. On the employer's side, it enumerates the accommodations that the employer will provide the returning worker. These may include a physical aid (Berven & Blanck, 1999) or assistive technology that can allow the worker to perform the task. For example, a worker with a learning disability may require a laptop computer to keep notes in business meetings. The employer should also list people who are part of the plan in the written report. For example, if the supervisor is to devote additional time to assisting or planning for the worker (Hayes, Citera, Brady, & Jenkins, 1995), the written document should outline those assignments. In addition, the plan should include a section directed toward the worker. The worker will be expected to use accommodations to compensate for the disability. The employee may be required to attend psychotherapy sessions, to take medicine (although this may be controversial; Rothstein, 1997), or to advise a particular supervisor when emotional problems are developing to a level sufficient to impair functioning. The plan may include a "ramping up" period in which the worker would begin on a part-time basis for several weeks or months, then gradually increase the time on the job until full-time functioning is resumed. In this regard, the plan should be coordinated with the worker's therapist so that it coordinates with the therapeutic regimen already in place.

Given the confidentiality provisions of the ADA (Ravid & Menon, 1993), disclosure of the worker's disability status and proposed accommodations should be limited to those with a need to know to implement the plan. The accommodation plan itself should be kept in a confidential file (along with the psychologist's report) maintained by the employer. It may be necessary to discuss the implementation plan with the disabled worker's coworkers as a means of smoothing the return-to-work transition. To the extent possible, those changes should be discussed as a supervisory decision and no reference should be made to the worker's disabled status. If it is not possible to make these arrangements without disclosing the worker's disability status, written authorization should be obtained from the worker.

The psychologist may want to maintain continuing consultation with the employer to determine if the suggested accommodations are effective and to provide guidance on the implementation of modifications as the person returns to the workplace. This will allow for some fine-tuning of the program to reflect the realities of how worker and employer deal with the return to work.

As Blanck et al. (1994) note, one advantage to these kinds of workplace consultations is increased employer sensitivity to people with disabilities in general and, specifically, those with mental disabilities. The negotiation process in which worker and employer (along with a consulting psychologist) develop and implement an accommodation plan can serve as a template for other uses of alternative dispute resolution procedures in the workplace (Parry, 1997).

Case Example: Return-to-Work Evaluation

Janet Baker's childhood was spent in the disarray caused by a psychotic mother and a father who was disengaged from both his children and his emotionally inaccessible wife. Janet was the second in a sibline of four girls, and was mothered by her older sister. After age 6, she in turn mothered her younger sisters. By the time she was 10, she did most of the ironing, about half the cooking, and made a stab at cleaning a house that her mother insisted on cluttering with her "valuables." Her mother spent most of her time in her bedroom in conversation with voices that no one else could hear.

Because of her mother's bizarre behavior and deficiencies as a housekeeper, Janet never brought friends home. Although she was talented in music, the only training she got was in junior high and high school band, in which she excelled. She also excelled in most academic subjects, and by the time she was in high school, her keen intellect was recognized by her teachers, who recommended her for National Honor Society and ensured that she was in accelerated and college prep courses. Janet graduated from high school in 1990 as second in her class and was immediately accepted into a large Midwestern university. She was interested in optical physics and was able to do work-study to supplement the meager amount she obtained from her parents for tuition. In her junior year, she started taking advanced optics courses and spent her senior year on co-op at a nearby telephone equipment design firm.

In her senior year, she began experiencing instances in which she became alienated from friends who she felt had treated her badly. When these instances were explored in the clinical interview, it became apparent that Janet had taken something that the person said as impugning her integrity or intellect. Most of these relationships were never recovered, and by the end of her senior year, she had few friends and spent most of her time at work, putting in 60- to 80-hour weeks in her job. Her work was rated as outstanding by her co-op supervisors, and at the end of 1994, she graduated with an A average from one of the country's most difficult physics programs.

She was recruited by a large communications firm even before she graduated, and they paid for her move to a large Western city to work in their plant. She was placed in a section in which she engaged in advanced design and manufacture of state-of-the-art optical interfaces. She quickly got "up to speed" and was functioning in the job at an advanced level.

However, this particular company relies on close collaboration among design personnel, who work together as a team. Team leaders meet with the group several times a week and ideas are shared, criticisms are offered about how things are done, and problems are ironed out. These meetings became occasions of great stress for Janet. She dreaded the sessions where she was called on to "think on her feet" and to put herself and her ideas before the group for review and critique. She also took everything that was said about her work very personally and came to view several of the people on the team as harsh and unfair critics. She began to avoid these meetings whenever she could, which drew the attention of her team leader and resulted in a memo regarding meeting attendance in the summer of 1995. Nevertheless, her work was brilliant; her team came to view her behavior as a little eccentric, but she was considered valuable to the team and the company. She worked very hard, putting in 60 hours of work a week at the plant and taking work home to do on her laptop. She reported actual work weeks of about 80 hours.

Although her work was intense, her personal life deteriorated. She had an apartment and had tried to make friends through a local church. These friendships rapidly dwindled in number as her work took priority. Somehow, all the boxes she had brought from her college never did get unpacked; they were kept in the corners of all the rooms in her small apartment. She rarely cooked a whole meal for herself, but often ate fast food or ate her meals at the plant cafeteria.

By the end of 1997, she had no friends. Her life consisted solely of work, and there were times when her team leader arrived at the beginning of the shift and found her asleep at her desk, wearing the same clothes she had worn the day before. At about the same time, her supervisor noticed Janet's hair. She had been pulling her hair as part of a pattern in which she would twist a hair around her finger, then yank it out. This left her hair very thin, with clumps missing from some areas. Janet seemed oblivious to how her hair looked and to the dismay that her appearance provoked in others.

In mid-1998, Janet was sent on a temporary assignment to the company's Minnesota plant. As a key person in designing and implementing the manufacturing process in the Western U.S. plant, she was to train the Minnesota engineers in new procedures and to learn from them innovations that they had made in creating new electronic wonders. The move to Minnesota was a disaster. She had difficulty getting an apartment, even though the company staff had procured one for her. The company also had a contract from a furniture rental company to provide full furnishings for her flat, but she was able to get only a bed, a desk, and a kitchen table and chairs. Boxes from her Western U.S. apartment, some the same that had never been unpacked from college, filled the rest of the space.

In the Minnesota plant, she was never quite able to connect with her professional counterparts. She saw them as hypercritical; she began to worry that they were talking behind her back, and she often felt that cafeteria conversations of coworkers sitting some distance away were about her. Her sleep deteriorated; she found herself working similar long hours, but she was not able to get restful sleep because she kept hearing people shouting in the next apartment. It was several months later that she learned that the next apartment was vacant. She had trouble washing her clothes, and often went to work in clothing that was dirty, unironed, and stained. Her dental hygiene deteriorated, and she started getting periodontal infections.

Her work performance began to deteriorate, and she started acting so peculiarly that her supervisor referred her to the occupational health nurse. On brief examination, the nurse referred her to a local psychiatrist, who immediately hospitalized her in a psychiatric hospital. She was there for three weeks while she was stabilized on antipsychotic medication, and her agitation, auditory hallucinations, and ideas of reference came under some control. She stayed at home for several more weeks of outpatient therapy and returned to work in September 1998.

Her supervisor noted that she was much less "weird" than she was before, and was pleased that she seemed able to focus on her work better. She was at least able to tolerate meetings again, but her self-care remained problematic. Her grooming was poor and clothing was still unkempt, and her hair never did look right. Her work was within expectations until late fall of 1998, when she did not come into work on her scheduled shift. The company occupational nurse later learned that she had been found in a local airport, confused, disoriented, and asking for her family. The police connected her with her physician, who put her back in the hospital for a three-week stay.

She again stabilized, and her physician learned that she had stopped taking her medications six weeks before "because they stifled my creativity." She returned to work within days out of the hospital, and was to return to the Western U.S. city in February. This move was accomplished, although she moved into a short-term apartment of the sort used by college students traveling through town. Her boxes followed; few of these were opened and almost filled the small space. Her car broke down and stayed at a local garage; for a reason still unknown, in spite of her having sufficient income to cover repairs, arrangements could not be made to fix it. She started taking the bus to get to work, no mean task in an automobile-oriented town like hers.

She never seemed to get reintegrated into her old team on return to the Western U.S. city. She felt that she was treated indifferently or with hostility by her supervisors. She felt that they did not instruct her properly on changes that had been made since she left, and she felt that she was "out of the loop." Her supervisors saw her as much less efficient, remote, and never quite up to even relaxed company standards for dress or grooming. One morning in the fall of 1999, her supervisor found her asleep at her desk wearing clothing she had worn for three days. He learned that she had not been home that whole time, and that the work that she had done was largely incomprehensible. He referred her to the occupational health nurse, and she was sent for a fitness-for-duty evaluation.

Upon evaluation, I observed a woman who was wearing stained, dirty, and unironed jeans and sweatshirt. Her lips were cracked and bleeding, and her scalp showed the effects of her hair pulling. She seemed distracted throughout the interview, and her answers were often tangential and guarded. She admitted to hearing auditory hallucinations and experiencing olfactory hallucinations and ideas of reference. She had stopped taking her medication in late October. Her personality assessment revealed a 6-8-2 pattern on the Minnesota Multiphasic Personality Inventory 2 (MMPI-2), a Rorschach X+% of 53, and a positive Schizi index. Her intellectual assessment showed an IQ diminished by serious impairments of attention and concentration and by intrusions of irrelevant material into verbal responses.

After reviewing the data, in a discussion with the occupational health nurse, my verbal recommendation was that she should be placed on medical leave of absence and returned to her physician for resumption of medication. She spent much of the holidays at home with her sister and was to return for evaluation at the end of January.

On return for reevaluation, her self-care had improved to the point that her clothing, though unironed, was at least clean. Her lips looked cared for, and much of her hair had grown back. She was able to respond to questions in a coherent manner and was distinctly less guarded. She expressed an interest in returning to work as soon as possible.

I secured permission to talk with her sister. She confirmed Janet's history and discussed her behavior at her visit home. She indicated that he could tell when Janet had been taking her medication just by looking at her hair. Retesting revealed reductions in elevations of the MMPI scales, although the code type remained generally the same. Repeat Rorschach testing showed few changes, save improvements in scales related to psychotic thinking processes.

A review of the data from the interviews and testing yielded a number of conclusions. Janet suffers from chronic paranoid schizophrenia. This illness is primarily expressed in interpersonal alienation caused by disordered thinking processes, and a suspicious perspective relative to others. Her illness is characterized by exacerbations and remissions. The exacerbations appear when she is exposed to stress from external changes, such as the move to Minnesota, or by deteriorations in her own functioning that generate work-related problems. She responds to antipsychotic medications, but has a pattern of noncompliance that contributed significantly to her three previous decompensations. Between decompensations, she still has significant negative symptoms of the psychosis, which cause her to have some degree of inherent stress because of her problems in maintaining her residence, vehicle, and personal hygiene. Her personal hygiene appears to be a good barometer of the severity of negative symptoms.

I participated in a conference call with her immediate supervisor, the occupational health nurse, the plant human relations director, and the firm's lawyer. In that call, we discussed a number of different aspects of returning Janet to work. In discussions with her supervisor, it was evident that Janet was still considered a valuable asset to the development division. Her insights into leading-edge design were exceptional, and some of her innovations had allowed the state of the art in her area of expertise to advance significantly. The supervisor wanted her to return to her old job, if she was capable of doing it without totally disrupting the work of the others in the workplace. Discussions with the human relations director and the occupational health nurse indicated that they were willing to provide sufficient support to allow Janet to return to the workplace. Specifically, the occupational health nurse was willing to assume a monitoring function with her.

On the basis of this discussion, we developed a return-to-work contract for Janet. This contract included the following components. First, she was to take her antipsychotic medication as prescribed by her physician. To ensure compliance and safety with the medication, she would go to her doctor for blood levels of the medication on a regular basis. Second, she would meet with the occupational health nurse on a regular basis. This would allow for the nurse to assess her hygiene and other metrics of her condition to ensure that she was functioning in spite of some negative schizophrenic symptoms. Third, her supervisor would be alert to specific behaviors that would indicate deterioration of her condition. These included increased social isolation, unusual speech, and changes in her personal hygiene or work habits. Long work hours, though occasionally necessary, were to be monitored to ensure that she did not become exhausted and vulnerable to breakdown.

The program has been in place for over a year at the time of this writing. Her physician has made changes in her medication regimen on several occasions in an attempt to fine-tune the control of her illness. She has had no further decompensations, although she took two weeks of sick leave to recover emotionally from the loss of her grandmother in the fall of last year. Overall, her work performance has been within the high-level parameters expected by her employer.

LITIGATION-RELATED EVALUATIONS AND CONSULTATIONS

The second general role of a psychologist is as an expert working for the plaintiff, defendant, court, or administrative law judge in the context of litigation of ADA cases. Plaintiffs may file cases under the ADA for discrimination under several theories (Goodman-Delahunty, 2000). These include the employer's failure to make reasonable accommodation, disparate treatment and disparate impact, reprisal for protected conduct, and disability harassment and hostile work environment. This section deals with the psychological evaluation of plaintiffs who file claims based on each of these issues in order.

Failure to Provide Reasonable Accommodation

An employer's failure to make reasonable accommodation as requested by a worker is a basis for a discrimination claim under the ADA (Parry, 1997). In addition, the employer may not refuse to hire a potential employee because it is evident that the worker will require reasonable accommodation.

The forensic evaluation of plaintiffs who have filed claims based on failure to accommodate are similar in many ways to the evaluations noted above for return-to-work assessments. The similarity centers around the comparison of the worker's skills with the job requirements in such a way as to illuminate the compatibility of the worker's existing or potential capacity (with reasonable accommodation) to perform the essential job functions of the position. This determination is central because the employer has four basic defenses against a reasonable accommodation case: (a) The employee is not a qualified individual with a disability; (b) the proposed accommodations are not feasible or will impose an undue hardship on the employer; (c) the employer, in fact, provided an accommodation that was reasonable, but the plaintiff did not accept it; and (d) for the particular work situation in which the worker and employer encounter each other, no effective accommodation exists (Goodman-Delahunty, 2000).

Psychological evaluations in these cases should, of course, be conducted with appropriate informed consents and other ethical and legal elements of any proper forensic evaluation (American Psychological Association, 1992; Committee on Ethical Guidelines for Forensic Psychologists, 1991). However, in addition to the elements noted above in the section on return-to-work evaluations, the following elements should be added.

Record Review

The evaluation for psychological damages of a plaintiff with a reasonable accommodation claim should begin with a review of available documentation (Goodman-Delahunty & Foote, 1995). This documentation should, as above, include job descriptions, job advertisements, and the employee's personnel file. In addition, the psychologist should review the worker's vocational records, medical and psychiatric treatment records, school records, military records, records from prior litigation, criminal records, and any other documents related to the case.

In reviewing the vocational records, the psychologist should be alert for the total number of positions held by the worker over his or her life. Reasons for changing jobs should be a focus of that search, along with the pattern of employment. Examining those records allows the psychologist to determine if the worker has a pattern of job success with repeated promotions or job changes to higher-paying positions, as opposed to a pattern of impairment reflected by repeated firing, downsizing, moves to new locations, or lateral transfers.

Medical and psychiatric treatment records provide not only the basis for determining whether the worker has a disability that substantially impairs major life functions, but also provide a record of exacerbations and remissions of chronic conditions such as schizophrenia or bipolar disorder. In addition, these records may identify the situations or stressors that trigger episodic breakdowns and mark the severity, duration, and residuals of those breakdowns. The impact of treatment may be evident in these records, including the viability of medication, compliance with the treatment regimen, and the efficacy of individual or group treatment.

School records provide evidence of basic academic skills not only though grades earned but also through the periodic large-group achievement testing. For people with learning disabilities, the evidence of their disability should be early and pervasive (Resnick, 2000). For younger workers who have been schooled since the enactment of the Individuals with Disabilities Education Act (IDEA) (Roberts & Mather, 1995), school records may include psychological evaluations conducted during the worker's childhood. Again, the impact of remediation may be evident in these records.

Military records are often an excellent source of information concerning the worker's ability to adapt to novel situations. Of course, many workers with physical disabilities may not have served, but those with mental disorders may have experienced their first serious episode during military service and may have a Veterans Administration file documenting the condition and disabling aspects thereof. In addition, for those workers for whom conduct problems are a major issue, the demands of military service may highlight those difficulties. A history of courts-martial or captain's mast, Article 15, or other forms of nonjudicial punishment may reflect impulse control and anger management problems.

Records of prior litigation may be important. In some cases, the disability issue may arise after a worker's compensation action or may occur in the context of a Social Security claim (Pincus et al., 1991; Pryor, 1997). The filing of a claim for disability under one system does not preclude the filing of a claim under another (*Cleveland v. Policy Management Systems Corp.,* 1999), as these systems differ in scope and goals. For the psychologist evaluating a plaintiff in an ADA-related lawsuit, these records may provide expert evaluations conducted in those contexts. In some cases, it may be possible to obtain testing from the earlier evaluations that provide excellent baseline data to determine the later impact of allegedly discriminatory activities on the part of the employer.

Other records of interest include information gathered from sources reflecting a plaintiff's criminal history, including prison, probation, or parole records. In workers with these histories, records may provide information concerning the issue of direct threat (see previous text).

In some cases, financial records can assist the examiner to determine changes in spending habits from before to after the alleged discriminatory activity. Credit card receipts and check registers can provide an empirical basis for reviewing the impact of discriminatory actions (Greenburg, 2000).

In addition, it is always critical to review legally related documents. At minimum, these include a copy of the claim, which lays out the plaintiff's case and its basis. Interrogatories and depositions of the plaintiff, supervisor, coworkers, and other experts are often invaluable sources of cross-validation and corroboration of information gathered through interview and other sources.

Interviews

Interviews with the plaintiff should follow the procedures noted for return-to-work evaluations. It is often helpful to have several interviews with the plaintiff to observe behavior on several occasions and under different circumstances. However, in the interviews associated with litigation, it is also critical to focus on issues of damages (Goodman-Delahunty & Foote, 1995). That is, if the worker has filed a lawsuit, a critical element of the case is the injury that the worker claims was suffered as a result of the employer's adverse actions. Thus, in addition to the personal, medical, social, vocational, and military history gathered above, it may be appropriate to conduct a mental status examination and other inquiries into the worker's current psychological status.

Structured interview methods are often useful. For example, the examining psychologist may use the Structured Clinical Interview for the *DSM-IV* (First, Spitzer, Gibbon, & Williams, 1997) or the Structured Interview for *DSM-IV* Personality (Pfohl, Blum, & Zimmerman, 1997). These provide not only a systematic method for information gathering, but may have better reliability and validity than standard unstructured interviews and even traditional psychometric testing (Rogers, 1995).

A review of the client's life before and after the alleged discrimination is a critical part of the interview. In all damages evaluations, it is critical to establish the *baseline* (e.g., the plaintiff's condition before the alleged discriminatory activity). This is sometimes difficult because people in litigation are likely to view their life before events that are the focus of litigation as being more problem-free and happier than following the events leading to the litigation (Lees-Haley et al., 1997). A careful consideration of life activities, including hobbies, religious life, family life, and social contacts, can help elucidate the worker's state before the alleged discrimination began. Likewise, a review of all those features can help establish the losses experienced by the worker. For example, an employee who experienced humiliation as a result of the employer's actions may significantly change life activities, avoiding social contacts made through work and other social situations.

Psychological Testing

The use of psychometric testing is often an essential element of the psychologist's assessment armamentarium. As noted above, cognitive testing, such as the Wechsler Adult Intelligence Scale III (Wechsler, 1997), is a critical part of the ADA reasonable accommodation evaluation; an assessment of the ability of the worker to engage in worklike activities is important to determine what work the plaintiff can do. Similarly, some vocationally related tests might be appropriate to determine specific job-related skills (Pape & Tarvydas, 1994). Personality measures including the MMPI-2 (Greene, 2000; Pope, Butcher, & Seelen, 1997) and the Personality Assessment Inventory (PAI; Morey, 1991) can provide a means of assessing symptoms and character patterns. Projective testing such as the Rorschach (Exner, 1986) may also provide supportive data indicating a mental disorder.

Any forensic battery of psychological tests should contain some measures of malingering (Rogers, 1997). These may include measures of effort, such as the Test of Memory Malingering (Tombaugh, 1997) and the Validity Indicator Profile (Frederick, 1997). In some cases in which the feigning of psychosis or depression is of concern, the Structured Interview of Reported Symptoms (Rogers, 1992) may be helpful. Of course, measures such as the MMPI-2 and PAI also contain measures of exaggeration and minimization and can provide information concerning the plaintiff's tendency to overreport or underreport emotional distress. (For a discussion of the evaluation of malingering and defensiveness, see the chapter by Rogers & Bender in this volume.)

Of course, the examiner should be careful to administer only tests that are valid and appropriate for those who are being tested, taking into account cultural and disability issues as part of the test administration and interpretation process (American Educational Research Association, American Psychological Association, & National Council on Measurement in Education, 1999). As noted above, to fail to take the plaintiff's disability into account in the assessment process is itself a violation of the ADA.

Collateral Interviews

A developing standard in forensic evaluations is the conduct of interviews with people who know the examinee in some significant way. These "collateral sources" or third-party interviews (Heilbrun, Rosenfeld, Warren, & Collins, 1994) are invaluable sources of information concerning the activities of the plaintiff before and after the alleged discrimination. The plaintiff's spouse or other appropriate family members, neighbors, and fellow members of religious organizations and clergy are useful sources of information concerning the worker. In these cases, coworkers and supervisors are also sources of data concerning the worker's life. Care should be taken to obtain the plaintiff's written informed consent to contact these people, and the informant should provide verbal informed consent before the interview takes place. In addition, it may be helpful to get a list of collateral sources from the employer. This provides for balance and may allow for a perspective on the worker otherwise unavailable through the worker alone.

Reports, Depositions, and Court Testimony

In many cases, the retaining party (either the defendant's counsel or plaintiff's counsel) may request a written report of the evaluation findings. As required by ethical and forensic standards (APA, 1992; Committee on Ethical Guidelines for Forensic Practice, 1991), the report should accurately reflect the procedures conducted and the results of the evaluation. To the extent possible, the legal issues in the case, such as causation of damages and future damages (Goodman-Delahunty & Foote, 1995), should be addressed.

Either the hiring party or the opposing party in a case may subpoena the expert for a deposition. In many cases, this is a *subpoena duces tecum,* which demands not only that the psychologist submit for an oral deposition, but that the psychologist bring along all test and interview data that serve as the foundation for professional opinions in the case. Preparation for depositions is critical and should be commensurate with the complexity and detail of the case.

For the small proportion of ADA cases that do not settle, it may be necessary for the examining psychologist to testify in court as an expert witness. Again, before the psychologist testifies in court, it is appropriate to prepare extensively so that testimony is accurate and resistant to cross-examination. As always, fairness, truthfulness, and clarity are goals to guide courtroom testimony.

Disparate Treatment and Disparate Impact Evaluations

Disparate treatment is a legal theory in which the disabled person must establish that he or she is disabled according to the criteria of the ADA; has suffered adverse treatment from the employer in the form of being fired, not hired, or not promoted; and that "a similarly situated nondisabled employee was treated more favorably" (Goodman-Delahunty, 2000, p. 202). In the alternative, if the employer states or does something indicating that bias against disabled employees, a similar presumption arises. In either case, the employer has the opportunity to present evidence that the actions were based on a legitimate, nondiscriminatory reason. The employee has the burden to prove that the basis for the adverse treatment was the worker's disability. In effect, the employee has to prove that the supposed legitimate basis offered by the employer is, in fact, a *pretext* for discrimination (Parry, 1997).

Disparate impact differs from disparate treatment in that the adverse job action that the worker suffered is not a result of the employer's deliberate discrimination but a result of a policy or plan that, on its face, was designed to be neutral toward people with disabilities. If the policy has a more adverse impact on people with disabilities, causing them not to be hired or not promoted in comparison with nondisabled workers, then the policy can be said to have disparate impact (Goodman-Delahunty, 2000).

Evaluations of plaintiffs in disparate treatment and impact cases generally focus on the impact of nonhire, nonpromotion, or termination. Emotional damages in such cases may be significant if the worker has a strong emotional stake in the position or promotion (Goodman-Delahunty & Foote, 1995). The loss of a job has strong emotional consequences (French, Caplan, & VanHarrison, 1982; Kasl & Cobb, 1980; Merriam, 1987; Schlossberg & Leibowitz, 1980). Discharged workers may experience increased depression, sleep disturbance, family problems, and increased vulnerability to serious illness. Workers who lose their jobs experience a loss of self-esteem and a general reduction in well-being (Prussia, Kinicki, & Bracker, 1993). Loss of contact with fellow workers and loss of contacts for obtaining future employment can have serious emotional consequences as well. In many cases, the worker who has lost an expected promotional opportunity or a job feels as if he or she has lost an important piece of property. In some cases, social status is diminished and income suffers significantly (Goodman-Delahunty & Foote, 1995). The desire to actively search for a new position may be diminished by the emotional reaction to the job loss (Prussia et al., 1993).

In these cases, consultation with the worker's family is especially important. If the worker has been fired, he or she frequently is spending more time at home and has lost a primary role identification. These changes sometimes alter family dynamics, having an adverse impact on both spouse and children.

Reprisal for Protected Conduct

If a worker is the recipient of adverse treatment or discharge following participation in an EEOC case, that employee may file a claim for reprisal. In general, such cases are easier to prove than disparate impact and intent cases (Goodman-Delahunty, 2000). These claims may be based on coercion, harassing, or intimidating the employee (Parry, 1997).

In general, the evaluation of these cases is similar to the evaluation of disparate impact cases, noted above. Discharge or other adverse job action may affect a worker in a variety of ways that a psychological evaluation may reveal. In these cases, accounts of coworkers are especially important to determine whether others observed the alleged adverse job actions.

One problem that arises especially in reprisal cases is the finding of paranoid or hypervigilant elements in the worker's presentation or test data. This is of special importance in such cases because the perception that the employer's actions were connected to the protected activity of the worker is sometimes a subjective one (McDonald & Lees-Haley, 1996). When a worker's evaluation produces evidence of paranoid thinking, the clinical issue becomes one of causation. One alternative to consider is whether the worker became paranoid because the employer repeatedly treated the employee inappropriately or overreacted to the worker's appropriate behavior. Such repeated experience would cause a worker to become hypervigilant and distrustful, thus raising scales designed to measure such traits on instruments like the MMPI-2 and PAI.

The other alternative to consider is that the employee has come to look at the world as a hostile place in which he or she has become the focus of undeserved bad treatment. This could arise from a personality disorder (paranoid or narcissistic) or a frank delusional system (paranoid delusional disorder or paranoid schizophrenia). The psychologist evaluating the worker can assess this causation issue through an overall review of the test data to determine the pervasiveness and severity of the cognitive distortions. If the cause of the paranoid thinking arises from an Axis I or Axis II disorder, in most cases (notwithstanding paranoid delusional disorder, which may be narrow in scope), those distortions should be pervasive. Also, the paranoid pattern should be reflected in nonwork situations. The paranoid individual should have a history of difficulty establishing and maintaining relationships, frequently demonstrating jealousy, distrust, and retributive actions.

More difficult to discriminate is a paranoid pattern that emerges following clearly inappropriate employer actions, such as public humiliation or blatant discrimination. Even if the difficulty is apparently resolved through arbitration or court action, the employee may still be sensitized to the employer's behavior. This sensitivity may cause the worker to perceive subsequent neutral job actions or actions that are rationally based as evidence of reprisal. In such circumstances, the causation issue is more difficult to assess because the worker is not suffering from a frank mental disorder. Rather, the worker has experienced a situationally bound change in perceptual predisposition. Generally, the only way to differentiate between this mild paranoid pattern and a reaction to real-world events is to interview coworkers who may have observed the allegedly retaliatory conduct.

Disability Harassment and Hostile Work Environment

In situations in which the worker with a disability experiences harassment because of his or her disability, a claim for "hostile work environment" may be filed (Goodman-Delahunty, 2000). To file such a claim, the worker must

> demonstrate that (a) he or she meets the definition of a disabled employee under the ADA, (b) he or she was subjected to physical or verbal conduct because of the disability, (c) the conduct was offensive to a reasonable person in the position of the plaintiff, (d) the conduct created a hostile work environment, (e) the employer knew or should have known of the harassment, and (f) the employer failed to take prompt remedial action. (Goodman-Delahunty, 2000, p. 203)

In recent U.S. Supreme Court decisions (*Burlington Industries, Inc. v. Ellerth,* 1998: *Faragher v. City of Boca Raton,* 1998), the Court placed the responsibility for the behavior of supervisors and managers squarely on the employer's shoulders. The Court attempted to balance the duty of the employer to provide a harassment-free environment through appropriate procedures and notification mechanisms with the responsibility of the aggrieved worker to use available means of registering complaints. As applied to ADA hostile work environment claims, these cases clearly extended the legal principle of *respondent superior* (the employer is responsible for the actions of subordinates) to cases involving harassment.

Holzbauer and Berven (1996) explored the harassment of people with disabilities. In their research, they determined that people with disabilities who experienced harassment reported a number of adverse emotional reactions, including self-doubt following the experience of an attack on their personal functioning. Denial and self-blame discourages people from taking action by preventing their recognition of being harassed. Humiliation and devaluation are frequent reactions to harassment experiences, as are anger and depression.

The psychological evaluation of people who claim that they experienced a hostile work environment follows the same general outline noted above. However, several components are included for harassment claims. A reasonable expectation is that a harassed worker experiences more anxiety-related symptoms than do other workers. If the harassment is of a relatively low level, such as the use of derogatory terms or the posting of cartoons that make fun of people with disabilities, the worker may experience a steady low to moderate level of tension related to the work environment. Similar patterns are seen in workers who are sexually harassed in the workplace (Fontana & Rosencheck, 1998; Richman, Flaherty, & Rospenda, 1996; Rosell, Miller, & Barber, 1995). For many harassed workers, their desire to work diminishes, they become more hesitant to go to work, have more sick days, and are more likely to leave employment. In general, a hostile work environment is experienced by workers as a "war of attrition" in which their will to continue functioning in the workplace is tested by frequent humiliations and slights.

For situations that involve public humiliation, such as singling out a disabled person on the basis of the disability or a practical joke involving the disabled person's impairments, anxiety symptoms similar to posttraumatic stress disorder (PTSD) may develop. In sexual harassment settings, similar events have been shown to produce PTSD-like symptom patterns (Fitzgerald, Drasgow, Hulin, Gelfand, & Magley, 1997; Schneider, Fitzgerald, & Swan, 1997). The reexperiencing of the traumatic events through waking recollections and nightmares, social isolation and withdrawal from favored activities, and symptoms of hyperarousal may characterize the emotional reactions of those who experience such humiliating events.

CONCLUSION

The ADA was designed to address a societal ill: discrimination against people with disabilities. Although the impact of the ADA on public accommodations and transportation is seen every time one enters a public building or boards a bus, the impact of the statute on the lives of people with disabilities generally and on people with mental disabilities in particular is harder to discern (Stefan, 2001). Psychologists can be agents in the implementation of the ADA. Our role as consultants to workers and employers can enable us to bring our knowledge of behavior, mental illness, and rehabilitation into a context in which that knowledge can improve the lives of workers as well as the bottom line of employers. Our role as expert witnesses in ADA litigation can enable us to provide information gained through clinical procedures and forensic assessment to the judges, administrative panels, and juries who must decide whether the worker has been treated fairly, and if not, what the legal remedy for that adverse treatment should be.

As in other areas of psychology and the law, the clinical and legal aspects of our work are a constantly changing vista. Nowhere is that more true than in disability law, where U.S. Supreme Court decisions can at times hew great swaths through the accepted legal landscape. Knowing that territory is a critical part of forensic work in ADA cases. Equally critical, however, is the knowledge of how disability alters the lives of people for good and for ill. Psychologists cannot "level the playing field," but we can do our work with sensitivity to both the strengths and impairments of people with disabilities. Exercising this sensitivity (whether we are hired by the worker, the employer, or the court), we can be agents of fairness for the worker and the employer.

REFERENCES

Albertson's v. Kirkingberg, U.S. 98–591 (1999).

Allison, L. K., & Stahlhut, E. H. J. (1995, March). DOT, ADA, and FMLA: Overlap, similarities, and differences with respect to the new alcohol and drug testing rules. *Labor Law Journal,* 153–161.

Altman v. New York City Health and Hosp. Corp., 503 F. Supp. 903 (S.D.N.Y., 1995).

Americans with Disabilities Act of 1990, 42 U.S.C. §§12101–12213 *et seq.*

American Educational Research Association, American Psychological Association, & National Council on Measurement in Education. (1999). *Standards for educational and psychological testing.* Washington, DC: American Educational Research Association.

American Psychiatric Association. (2000). *Diagnostic and statistical manual of mental disorders* (4th ed.). Washington, DC: Author.

American Psychological Association. (1992). Ethical principles of psychologists and code of conduct. *American Psychologist, 47,* 1597–1611.

Anderson, P. L., Kazmierski, S., & Cronin, M. E. (1995). Learning disabilities, employment discrimination, and the ADA. *Journal of Learning Disabilities, 28*(4), 196–204.

Anthony, W. A., & Jansen, M. A. (1984). Predicting the vocational capacity of the chronically mentally ill. *American Psychologist, 39*(5), 537–544.

Aristeiguieta, C. A. (1998). Substance abuse, mental illness, and medical students: The role of the Americans with Disabilities Act. *Journal of the American Medical Association, 279*(1), 80.

Baldwin, M. L. (1999). The effects of impairment on employment and wages: Estimates from the 1984 and 1990 SIPP. *Behavioral Sciences and the Law, 17*(1), 7–28.

Bell, C. (1997). The Americans with Disabilities Act, mental disability and work. In R. J. Bonnie & J. Monahan (Eds.), *Mental disorder, mental disability and the law* (pp. 203–219). Chicago: University of Chicago Press.

Berven, H. M., & Blanck, P. D. (1999). Assistive technology patenting trends and the Americans with Disabilities Act. *Behavioral Sciences and the Law, 17*(1), 47–72.

Blanck, P. D. (1995). Assessing five years of employment integration and economic opportunity under the Americans with Disabilities Act. *Mental and Physical Disability Law Reporter, 19*(3), 384–392.

Blanck, P. D. (1996). Empirical study of the Americans with Disabilities Act: Employment issues from 1990 to 1994. *Behavioral Sciences and the Law, 14*(1), 5–27.

Blanck, P. D., Andersen, J. H., Wallach, E. J., & Tenney, J. P. (1994). Implementing reasonable accommodations using ADR under the ADA: The case of a white-collar employee with bipolar mental illness. *Mental and Physical Disability Law Reporter, 18*(4), 458–464.

Burlington Industries. v. Ellerth, 524, 18 S. Ct. 2257, 141 L. Ed.2d 662 U.S. 742 (1997).

Calfee, B. E. (1998). Health care workers with mental illness: What does the Americans with Disabilities Act offer? *American Association of Occupational Health Nurses Journal, 46*(4), 221–222.

Carling, P. J. (1993). Reasonable accommodations in the workplace for individuals with psychiatric disabilities. *Consulting Psychology Journal, 45*(2), 46–67.

Civil Rights Act of 1964, 42 U.S.C. § 2000e *et seq.* (as amended).

Cleveland v. Policy Management Systems Corp., 120 F.3d 513 (5th Cir. 1997).

Colledge, A. L., Johns, R. E., Jr., & Thomas, M. H. (1999). Functional ability assessment: Guidelines for the workplace. *Journal of Occupational and Environmental Medicine, 41*(3), 172–180.

Committee on Ethical Guidelines for Forensic Psychologists. (1991). Specialty guidelines for forensic psychologists. *Law and Human Behavior, 15*(6), 655–665.

Council on Licensure, Enforcement and Regulation. (1996). *The Americans with Disabilities Act: Information and recommendations for credentialing examination.* Lexington, KY: Council on Licensure, Enforcement and Regulation.

Crist, P. A. H., & Stoffel, V. C. (1992). The Americans with Disabilities Act of 1990 and employees with mental impairments: Personal efficacy and the environment. *American Journal of Occupational Therapy, 46*(5), 434–443.

Croghan, T. W., Kniesner, T. J., & Powers, R. H. (1999). Does the Americans with Disabilities Act accommodate depressed workers? *Health Affairs, 18*(5), 249–253.

Davidson v. Midelfort Clinic, Ltd., 133 F.3d. 499 (7th Cir. Jan. 7, 1998).

EEOC v. Amego, 110 F.3d. 135 (1st Cir. 1997).

Exner, J. (1986). *The Rorschach: A comprehensive system.* New York: Wiley.

Faragher v. City of Boca Raton, 118 U.S. 2275 (1998).

First, M. B., Spitzer, R. L., Gibbon, M., & Williams, J. B. (1997). *Structured Clinical Interview for the DSM-IV Axis I disorders (SCID-I): Clinician version.* Washington, DC: American Psychiatric Press.

Fischer, R. J. (1994). The Americans with Disabilities Act: Implications for measurement. *Educational Measurement: Issues and Practice, 13*(3), 17–26.

Fitzgerald, L. F., Drasgow, F., Hulin, C. L., Gelfand, M. J., & Magley, V. J. (1997). Antecedents and consequences of sexual harassment in organizations: A test of an integrated model. *Journal of Applied Psychology, 82*(4), 578–589.

Fontana, A., & Rosencheck, R. (1998). Duty-related and sexual stress in the etiology of PTSD among women veterans who seek treatment. *Psychiatric Services, 49*(5), 658–662.

Foote, W. E. (1997, August). History of pill overdose means adios amego. *Forensic Psychiatry Echo,* 5–7.

Foote, W. E. (2000). A model for psychological consultation in cases involving the Americans with Disabilities Act. *Professional Psychology: Research and Practice, 31*(2), 190–196.

Frederick, R. (1997). *The Validity Indicator Profile manual.* Minneapolis MN: National Computer Systems.

French, J. R. P., Caplan, R. D., & VanHarrison, R. (1982). *Mechanisms of job stress and strain.* New York: Wiley.

Gerber, P. J. (1992). At first glance: Employment for people with learning disabilities at the beginning of the Americans-with-Disabilities-Act era. *Learning Disability Quarterly, 15,* 330–332.

Goodman-Delahunty, J. (2000). Psychological impairment under the Americans with Disabilities Act: Legal guidelines. *Professional Psychology: Research and Practice, 31*(2), 197–205.

Goodman-Delahunty, J., & Foote, W. E. (1995). Compensation for pain, suffering, and other psychological injuries: The impact of *Daubert* on employment discrimination claims. *Behavioral Sciences and the Law, 13,* 183–206.

Greenberg, S. (2000). *Psychological evaluation in personal injury cases.* American Board of Forensic Psychology Intensive Workshop, Tampa, FL.

Greene, R. L. (2000). *The MMPI-2: An interpretive manual.* Boston: Allyn & Bacon.

Hall, E. A., & Cash, M. H. (1992). ADA concerns: The hiring process. *Texas Bar Journal, 55*(2), 814–817.

Hantula, D. A., & Reilly, N. A. (1996). Reasonable accommodation for employees with mental disabilities: A mandate for supervision? *Behavioral Sciences and the Law, 14,* 107–120.

Hayes, T. L., Citera, M., Brady, L. M., & Jenkins, N. M. (1995). Staffing for persons with disabilities: What is "fair" and "job related"? *Public Personnel Management, 24*(4), 413–427.

Heilbrun, K., Rosenfeld, B., Warren, J. I., & Collins, S. (1994). The use of third-party information in forensic assessments: A two state comparison. *Bulletin of the American Academy of Psychiatry and Law, 22*(3), 399–406.

Holzbauer, J. J., & Berven, N. L. (1996). Disability harassment: A new term for a long-standing problem. *Journal of Counseling and Development, 74*(5), 478–483.

Honberg, R. (1999). Supreme Court decisions could limit ADA protections. *National Alliance for the Mentally Ill Legal Letter, 1*(1).

Jones, N. L. (1993). The alcohol and drug provisions for the ADA: Implications for employers and employees. *Consulting Psychology Journal, 45*(2), 37–45.

Kasl, S. V., & Cobb, S. (1980). The experience of losing a job: Some effects on cardiovascular functioning. *Psychotherapy and Psychosomatics, 3*(4), 88–109.

Keoughan v. Delta Airlines, No. 96–4072, 1997 U.S. App. LEXIS 12232 (10th Cir. 1997).

Kohnke v. Delta Airlines., 1520 F. Supp. 956 (N.D. Cal. 1996).

Kraus, L. E., Stoddard, S., & Gilmartin, D. (1996). *Chartbook on disability in the United States, 1996.* Washington, DC: U.S. National Institute on Disability and Rehabilitation Research.

LaPorte, D. L. (1996). The conflict and interaction of the Americans with Disabilities Act with the Omnibus Transportation Employee Testing Act: Two modest proposals to achieve greater synchrony. *DePaul Law Review, 45,* 537–602.

Lees-Haley, P. R., Williams, C. W., Zasler, N. D., Margulies, S., English, L. T., & Stevens, K. B. (1997). Response bias in plaintiffs' histories. *Brain Injury, 11*(11), 791–799.

Mancuso, L. (1990). Reasonable accommodation for workers with psychiatric disabilities. *Psychosocial Rehabilitation Journal, 14*(2), 3–19.

Mazzarella v. United States Postal Serv., 849 F. Supp. 89 (D. Mass. 1994).

McDonald, J. J., Jr., & Lees-Haley, P. R. (1996). Personality disorders in the workplace: How psychological problems often are confused with employment law violations. *Employee Relations Law Journal, 22*(2), 57–81.

Merriam, S. B. (1987, September). The experience of job loss as perceived by young and middle-aged adults and those near retirement. *Journal of Employment Counseling,* 107–114.

Mickey, P. F., & Pardo, M. (1993). Dealing with mental disabilities under the ADA. *Labor Lawyer, 9,* 531.

Milazzo-Sayre, L. J., Henderson, M. J., & Manderscheid, R. W. (1997). Serious and severe mental illness and work: What do we know? In Richard J. Bonnie, John E. Monahan, et al. (Eds.), *Mental disorder, work disability, and the law* (pp. 13–24). Chicago: University of Chicago Press.

Morey, L. C. (1991). *Personality Assessment Inventory professional manual*. Odessa, FL: Psychological Assessment Resources.

Moss, K., Ullman, M., Johnsen, M. C., Starrett, B. E., & Burris, S. (1999). Different paths to justice: The ADA, employment and administrative enforcement by the EEOC and FEPAs. *Behavioral Sciences and the Law, 17*(1), 29–46.

Murphy v. United Parcel Services., 527 U.S. 471, 119 S. Ct. 2139 (1999).

O'Keeffe, J. (1993). Disability, discrimination and the Americans with Disabilities Act. *Consulting Psychology Journal, 45*(2), 3–9.

Pape, D. A., & Tarvydas, V. M. (1994). Responsible and responsive rehabilitation consultation on the ADA: The importance of training for psychologists. In S. M. Bruyere & J. O'Keeffe (Eds.), *Implications of the Americans with Disabilities Act for psychology* (pp. 169–185). Washington, DC: American Psychological Association.

Parry, J. W. (1993). Mental disabilities under the ADA: A difficult path to follow. *Mental and Physical Disability Law Reporter, 17*(1), 111–112.

Parry, J. W. (1996). *Regulation, litigation and dispute resolution under the Americans with Disabilities Act: A practitioner's guide to implementation*. Washington, DC: American Bar Association, Commission on Mental and Physical Disability Law.

Parry, J. W. (1997). *Mental disabilities and the Americans with Disabilities Act* (2nd ed.). Washington, DC: American Bar Association, Commission on Mental and Physical Disability Law.

Pfohl, B., Blum, N., & Zimmerman, M. (1997). *Structured interview for DSM-IV personality*. Washington, DC: American Psychiatric Press.

Pincus, H. A., Kennedy, C., Simmens, S. J., Goldman, H. H., Sirovatka, P., & Sharfstein, S. S. (1991). Determining disability due to mental impairment: APA's evaluation of Social Security Administration guidelines. *American Journal of Psychiatry, 148*(8), 1037–1043.

Pollet, S. L. (1995). Mental illness in the workplace: The tension between productivity and reasonable accommodation. *Journal of Psychiatry and Law, 23*, 155–184.

Pope, K. S., Butcher, J. N., & Seelen, J. (1997). *The MMPI, MMPI-2 and MMPI-A in court*. Washington, DC: American Psychological Association.

Prigitano, G. P. (1991). The relationship of frontal lobe damage to diminished awareness: Studies in rehabilitation. In H. S. Levin, H. M. Eisenberg, & A. L. Benton (Eds.), *Frontal lobe function and dysfunction* (pp. 381–400). New York: Oxford University Press.

Prussia, G. E., Kinicki, A. J., & Bracker, J. S. (1993). Psychological and behavioral consequences of job loss: A covariance structure analysis using Weiner's (1985) attribution model. *Journal of Applied Psychology, 78*(3), 382–394.

Pryor, E. S. (1997). Mental disabilities and the disability fabric. In R. J. Bonnie & J. Monahan (Eds.), *Mental disorder, mental disability and the law* (pp. 153–198). Chicago: University of Chicago Press.

Ravid, R. (1992). Disclosure of mental illness to employers: Legal recourses and ramifications. *Journal of Psychiatry and Law, 20*(1), 85–102.

Ravid, R., & Menon, S. (1993). Guidelines for disclosure of patient information under the Americans with Disabilities Act. *Hospital and Community Psychiatry, 44*(3), 280–281.

Resnick, R. J. (2000). *The hidden disorder: A clinician's guide to attention deficit hyperactivity disorder in adults*. Washington, DC: American Psychological Association.

Richman, J. A., Flaherty, J. A., & Rospenda, K. M. (1996). Perceived workplace harassment experiences and problem drinking among physicians: Broadening the stress/alienation paradigm. *Addiction, 91*(3), 391–403.

Roberts, R., & Mather, N. (1995). Legal protections for individuals with learning disabilities: The IDEA, Section 504, and the ADA. *Learning Disabilities Research and Practice, 10*(3), 160–168.

Roberts v. County of Fairfax, 937 F. Supp. 541 (E.D. Va. 1996).

Rogers, R. (1992). *Structured interview of reported symptoms (SIRS)*. Odessa, FL: Psychological Assessment Resources.

Rogers, R. (1995). *Diagnostic and structured interviewing: A handbook for psychologists*. Odessa, FL: Psychological Assessment Resources.

Rogers, R. (1997). *Clinical assessment of malingering and deception* (2nd ed.). New York: Guilford Press.

Rosell, E., Miller, K., & Barber, K. (1995). Firefighting women and sexual harassment. *Public Personnel Management, 24*(3), 339–350.

Rothstein, L. F. (1997). The employer's duty to accommodate performance and conduct deficiencies of individuals with mental impairments under disability discrimination laws. *Syracuse Law Review, 47*, 931–986.

Schlossberg, N. K., & Leibowitz, Z. (1980). Organizational support systems as buffers to job loss. *Journal of Vocational Behavior, 17*, 204–217.

Schneider, K. T., Fitzgerald, L. F., & Swan, S. (1997). Job-related psychological effects of sexual harassment in the workplace: Empirical evidence from two organizations. *Journal of Applied Psychology, 82*(3), 401–415.

School Bd. of Nassau Cty., Fla. v. Arline, 480 U.S. 273 (1987).

Smart, J. F., & Smart, D. W. (1993). Vocational evaluation of hispanics with disabilities: Issues and implications. *Vocational Evaluation and Work Adjustment Bulletin, 26*(3), 111–122.

Stefan, S. (1998). "You'd have to be crazy to work here": Worker stress, the abusive workplace and Title I of the ADA. *Loyola Law Review, 31*(3), 795–846.

Stefan, S. (2001). *Unequal rights: Discrimination against people with mental disabilities and the Americans with Disabilities Act.* Washington, DC: American Psychological Association.

Sutton v. United Airlines., 527 U.S. 471, 119 S. Ct. 2139 (1999).

Tenopyr, M. L., Angoff, W. H., Butcher, J. N., Geisinger, K. F., & Reilly, R. R. (1993). Psychometric and assessment issues raised by the Americans with Disabilities Act. *Score, 15*(4), 1–15.

Tombough, T. M. (1997). The Test of Memory Malingering (TOMM): Normative data from cognitively intact and cognitively impaired individuals. *Psychological Assessment, 9,* 260–268.

Trans Mart. v. Brewer, 630 So.2d 469 (Ala. Civ. App. 1993).

United States Equal Employment Opportunity Commission, 29 C.F.R., 1630 *et seq.* (1992).

United States Equal Employment Opportunity Commission. (1997). *EEOC enforcement guidance on the Americans with Disabilities Act and psychiatric disabilities.* (EEOC Notice Number 915.002 ed.). Washington, DC: U.S. Government Printing Office.

United States Equal Employment Opportunity Commission. (2000). *Questions and answers on amending the interpretive guidance on Title I of the Americans with Disabilities Act* [OnLine]. Available from www.eeoc.gov/regs/1630-mitigating-qanda.html

Wahl, O. F. (1999). Mental health consumers' experience of stigma. *Schizophrenia Bulletin, 25*(3), 467–478.

Wechsler, D. (1997). *Wechsler Adult Intelligence Scale–Third edition administration and scoring manual.* San Antonio, TX: Psychological Corporation.

Wylonis, L. (1999). Psychiatric disability, employment and the Americans with Disabilities Act. *Psychiatric Clinics of North America, 22*(1), 147–158.

Yelin, E. H., & Cisternas, M. G. (1997). Employment patterns among persons with and without mental conditions. In Richard J. Bonnie, John E. Monahan, et al. (Eds.), *Mental disorder, work disability, and the law* (pp. 25–54). Chicago: University of Chicago Press.

Zuriff, G. E. (1997). Accommodations for test anxiety under ADA? *Journal of American Academy of Psychiatry Law, 25*(2), 197–206.

CHAPTER 16

Substituted Judgment: Roles for the Forensic Psychologist

ERIC Y. DROGIN AND CURTIS L. BARRETT

"Substituted judgment" is a term that addresses several domains of forensic psychology practice. These domains all involve the replacement of an individual's judgment with that of another person or agency. This replacement may or may not be mandated by court order, but in all cases, it must be sanctioned by law. The roles of guardians, conservators, curators, surrogates, and executors may be determined by a variety of wills, testaments, and other advance directives.

SUBSTITUTIONS FOR PRIOR JUDGMENT

Wills and other "advance directives" (such as "living" wills, durable powers of attorney, and health care surrogacies) are means by which individuals attempt to ensure that their wishes will be followed in the future. When the time comes to implement the instrument in question, it may also become necessary to determine whether, at the time of execution, the person's capacity was so lacking that the judgment of others must now be substituted.

Legal and Historical Background

As early as the late twelfth century, English law began to recognize the rights of persons to bequeath personal property. It was not until the *Statute of Wills* in 1540 that ownership of various classes of real property could be transmitted on a similar basis (Robitscher, 1966). When feudalism was outlawed in 1660, all barriers to disposition by will were eradicated (Kempin, 1973).

Variously dated in the forensic literature as 1572 (Smith & Meyer, 1987) and even 1839 (Robitscher, 1966), it was actually in 1542 (Garner, 1999) that an amendment to the *Statute of Wills* barred "any person *de non sane* memory" (Spaulding, 1985, p. 114) from making a will. This exception persists to the present, defined (without elaboration) in most American jurisdictions as the requirement that persons wishing to bequeath property be "of sound mind" (Melton, Petrila, Poythress, & Slobogin, 1997, p. 359). As a general rule, "if a person is unable to communicate orally, in written fashion or by behavior his [or her] wishes, then that person will not be considered competent to make a will" (Perr, 1981, p. 15).

In the landmark case of *Cruzan v. Missouri Department of Health* (1990), the U.S. Supreme Court extended the testamentary concept into the health care arena. It upheld the constitutionality of a requirement that a judge could not order termination of life support without clear and convincing evidence that the patient would have wished this to occur. *Cruzan* left states with the ability to set their own standards in this regard, such that "the outcome for a person who has become permanently unconscious may very well depend on geography" (Gilfix & Gilfix, 1992, p. 44). In most states, the recognition and components of a valid living will are now specified by statute (Hawkins, 1992).

The durable power of attorney "remains in effect during the grantor's incompetency" and "commonly allow[s] an agent to make healthcare decisions for a patient who has become incompetent" (Garner, 1999, p. 1191). The theory underlying this instrument, distinct from that of the living will, is that the individual may eventually regain his or her capacity for independent decision making (Insel, 1995).

In many jurisdictions, the right to make such designations is buttressed with statutory guidelines for "health care surrogacy," dictating the form of these documents and boundaries for those who may implement them in the future (High, 1994). The uniformity and predictability of surrogate laws have been praised as a necessary supplement to living wills and durable powers of attorney (Hamann, 1993), as well as an alternative to the perceived lack of procedural safeguards associated with guardianship proceedings (Herr & Hopkins, 1994).

Forensic Assessment of Prior Judgment

Forensic psychological assessment of prior judgment is sought at two distinct stages: during the development and execution of a guiding document and subsequent to the individual's demise or incapacity. The first stage is designed to ensure that, in effect, judgment is never "substituted." The second stage involves a determination of whether valid judgment was ever exercised or expressed at all. In the following, we consider these in more detail.

Development and Execution

Sprehe and Kerr (1996) caution attorneys to implement a range of "safeguards" in cases where "the will is going to be controversial":

- Procure detailed information from the client relating to assets and relatives. If close relatives are being excluded from the will, inquire as to the reasons for the exclusion.
- Procure a psychiatric opinion as to competency as close to the will execution date as possible.
- Permit the witnesses to participate in both the preliminary conference with the client and the conference immediately prior to execution of the will.
- Prepare detailed memoranda of the preliminary conference with the client and the conference and the execution conference, including memoranda by the witnesses.
- Be alert to circumstances that may cause the validity of the will to be questioned. If such circumstances exist, conduct the conference and execution as if such a will contest were a certainty. Preserve all documentation and consider the desirability of recording by video tape.
- Be ever conscious of the fact that attorneys may be called upon to testify years after the will execution. Records should be kept in perpetuity (p. 259).

In terms of the specific forensic approach within which these determinations are made, the psychologist will naturally review, with counsel's guidance and support, the relevant law in the jurisdiction in which the will or advance directive will be made and/or interpreted. These laws are essentially uniform in most states (Redmond, 1987); the document's validity rests on knowing what one has, possessing a rational plan for distribution, and recognizing the expected recipients of the contents of one's estate.

Melton et al. (1997) addressed the assessment of testamentary capacity, offering several suggestions for avenues of forensic inquiry. Concerning the act of making a will, they suggest asking about a testator's "conception of a will, what it is intended to do, and why they are preparing theirs at this time" (p. 360). The issue of the nature and extent of one's property includes questions about "occupation," "salary," "living accommodations," "personal possessions," "intangibles," and "any other possessions." Regarding estate disposition, evaluators are advised to inquire into the "general consequences" of the planned disposal of property. In terms of the natural objects of one's bounty, testators "should be asked to identify family, friends, and those who might have played a major role in their lives" (pp. 360–362).

Numerous factors have been identified as interfering with testamentary capacity, including organic brain dysfunction, psychosis, paranoia, and psychoactive medication (Bolton, 1977). For decades, deficits in "abstract thinking" (Eliasberg, 1953) have been recognized as relevant warning signs for incapacity, although a natural emphasis on more concrete, factually bound information tends to obscure this consideration in less comprehensive assessments.

Often, the potentially disruptive issue is one of "undue influence," defined as "engaging in manipulation or deception to significantly impair the ability of testators to freely decide on the distribution of their property" (Regan & Gordon, 1997), identifiable in part on the basis of the following "clues":

- The person requesting the examination indicates the competency statement is routine because of the testator's age.
- The examination appointment is made by someone other than the testator and his [or her] attorney.
- The testator is brought to the examination office by someone who is reluctant to allow the testator to be interviewed alone.
- Specifics about the will are not given or the testator seems unclear about specific items in the will.
- The testator is reluctant to give information about the potential heir and their relationship (p. 14).

The form of preservation of interview data may be a crucial factor in its ultimate persuasiveness for a judge or jury.

For this reason, as suggested by Sprehe and Kerr (1996), there has been increasing acceptance, and even encouragement, of videotaped wills and advance directives. Buckley (1988) convincingly asserts that this medium offers "special advantages," as "the video recording provides a visual nexus between declarant and document so that intentions are crystallized and mental competency is undeniably demonstrated" (p. 30). Caution, of course, is appropriate in choosing the technology to be used, because some data recording media are likely to be unusable within a relatively short time. The following circumstances are likely to enhance the likelihood that such evidence will be admissible in the event of a subsequent contest:

- The videotape recorder was capable of recording testimony.
- The video machine operator was competent.
- The recording had not been altered.
- The videotape was appropriately preserved.
- The recording was both visually and audibly clear so as not to be unintelligible or misleading.
- The testimony was voluntary.
- The speakers on the videotape can be identified (p. 31).

Forensic evaluators wishing to preserve their examinations on videotape must consider ethical (and, in some jurisdictions, legal) proscriptions against the revelation of raw psychological test data in a way that may serve to invalidate them for future examinees (American Psychological Association, 1996).

Determining the validity of a client's directive intent requires a proper clinical as well as forensic assessment strategy, including appropriate tests and relevant interview techniques. Where the client is an older adult, the American Psychological Association (1998) has adopted "Guidelines for the Evaluation of Dementia and Age-Related Cognitive Decline."

In particular, these Guidelines come to life when interpreted and applied in the context of another American Psychological Association resource, *What Practitioners Should Know about Working with Older Adults* (Abeles, 1997). This reference describes "Basic Principles in the Assessment of Older Adults," including the following:

- Familiarize the older adult with the purpose and procedures of testing. Older adults, especially those with little formal education, are often less familiar with testing than younger adults and may be more cautious in responding.
- Ensure optimal performance. Older adults should be prepared in advance for testing. They should be given prior notice to bring all assistive devices (e.g., hearing aids, eyeglasses).
- Create a well-lighted and quiet environment. Glare should be minimized. Arrange the space to accommodate a wheelchair or other device for those with physical limitations.
- Preferably use tests that have been constructed specifically for older adults. Most commonly used psychological tests have not been developed for use with older people, although some have age-related norms.
- Ensure that the older adult understands the test directions. Speak in clear, simple language but do not shout. Query and repeat if necessary. If needed, use large print materials.
- Determine if the older adult patient is experiencing pain or discomfort and attempt to reduce it when possible. Find out what medication(s) the patient is taking and assess effect on performance.
- Adjust the testing time to suit the optimal functioning of the older adult. Older adults tire more easily than younger adults. Plan for frequent rest and bathroom breaks. If fatigue sets in, resume testing at another time.
- Use encouragement and verbal reinforcement liberally when testing.
- Utilize multiple testing sessions to gauge how the older adult performs at varied times of the day (pp. 20–21).

Experts should note that such resources are increasingly likely to form the basis of focused cross-examination, as attorneys become increasingly familiar with documented guidelines for forensic psychological assessment (Drogin, 2000a).

Regarding the selection of assessment domains and testing instruments, *What Practitioners Should Know about Working with Older Adults* (Abeles, 1997) offers practical guidance concerning the perceived attributes and deficiencies of specific measures:

- *Brief Assessment of Cognitive Ability.* The Mini-Mental State Examination (MMSE; Folstein, Folstein, & McHugh, 1975) is touted as "easy to administer" and "specifically developed for the older age group," although it is appropriately noted that the MMSE should not be used as a "stand-alone" diagnostic test.
- *Assessment of Acute and Reversible Changes.* No single test is recommended, but "a review of the medical record," "consultation with a physician," and "repeat testing in the acute phases" are recommended.
- *Assessment of Dementia.* The lack of any "single accepted battery of tests" is acknowledged, but the Mattis Dementia Rating Scale (Smith, 1994) and the Cognistat

(Neurobehavioral Cognitive Status Examination; Logue, Tupler, D'Amico, & Schmitt, 1993) are cited with approval, as "easily administered, well-validated tests of general cognitive functioning that can be useful in the assessment of dementia."

- *Psychopathology.* Regarding depression, the Hamilton Depression Rating Scale (Williams, 1988), Beck Depression Inventory (Kendall, Hollon, Beck, Hammen, & Ingram, 1987), and Geriatric Depression Scale (GDS; Hyer & Blount, 1984) are recommended. The GDS is described as particularly appropriate, given "age-related norms," administration in "oral and written forms," and the omission of "somatic items that can elevate depression scores." For alcohol screening, the Michigan Alcoholism Screening Test–Geriatric Version (Knight & Mjelde-Mossey, 1995) is seen as having "demonstrated potential."

- Among more comprehensive personality measures, the Minnesota Multiphasic Personality Inventory 2 (MMPI-2) (Ben-Porath & Butcher, 1989) is characterized as well-normed but perhaps overly lengthy and demanding in the area of "reading level"; the Brief Psychiatric Rating Scale (Ownby & Seibel, 1994) is recommended in its stead. Noting that the Rorschach should be used "with caution," preferred projective measures are said to include the Senior Apperception Test (Foote & Kahn, 1979), and the Gerontological Apperception Test (Fitzgerald, Pasewark, & Fleisher, 1974) (pp. 22–25).

This overview of diverse assessment measures comports well with the classic multimethod-multitrait forensic evaluation principle. By this device, "psychologists frequently require that their interpretations of assessment results be grounded in more than one data source and that enough information has been obtained to rule out optional interpretations" (Grisso, 1986, p. 109). In a similar vein, Kennedy (1986) has warned against the employment of "short of optimal" batteries, characterized as "the height of folly in an expert" (p. 502).

Demise or Incapacity

In one popular turn-of-the-century novel, the murderer's identity was revealed when a powerful microscope was trained upon the victim's retina, wherein the image of her killer was retained (Dixon, 1905). Despite such fanciful notions, the succeeding decades failed to produce instruments and methods capable of divining the intent, actions, or experiences of deceased or permanently noncommunicative persons.

Psychologists have been left to their own inferential devices in regard to assessing testamentary capacity. The

methodology employed is often similar to that associated with "psychological autopsies" in cases of alleged suicide (Selkin, 1994; Shneidman, 1994). Such a procedure "consists essentially of interviews with survivors and examination of public and private documents that reveal the personality of the deceased party" (Selkin, 1994, p. 74). Nursing home records, medical charts, personal correspondence, institutional staff and family interviews, financial records, and other resources are reviewed in an attempt to divine the intent and functional capabilities of the testator.

The trier of fact may glean considerable useful information from a retrospective evaluation that has been systematic in its approach (Spar & Garb, 1992). Kosloski, Datwyler, and Montgomery (1994) identified moderate to high retrospective reliability for information obtained from caretaker interviews, and Derouesne, Guigot, and Chatellier (1995) have reported mixed but overall encouraging results in the retrospective examination of progressive dementia. Considerable care must be taken to ensure that the psychologist neither overinterprets nor overextrapolates from retrospectively obtained data (Henry, Moffitt, Caspi, Langley, & Silva, 1994). Without further research, such methods may be viewed as speculative, despite the powerful lure of evolving techniques for practitioners and judges alike (Drogin, 2000b).

SUBSTITUTIONS FOR PRESENT JUDGMENT

The right to refuse treatment and the doctrine of informed consent constitute an affirmation of patient and client autonomy. Only when an individual's current decision-making capacity is impaired will these principles bow to emergent concerns. This may occur when the health and safety of those whom the mental health professional seeks to treat and, occasionally, the health and safety of others are threatened indirectly should treatment not be imposed.

Legal and Historical Background

In a landmark case for the legal doctrine of informed consent, the District of Columbia Circuit Court of Appeals in *Canterbury v. Spence* (1972) held:

> True consent to what happens to one's self is the informed exercise of a choice, and that entails an opportunity to evaluate knowledgeably the options available and the risks attendant upon each. The average patient has little or no understanding of the medical arts, and ordinarily has only his physician to whom he can look for enlightenment with which to reach an intelligent decision. From these almost axiomatic considerations springs the need, and in turn the requirement, of a reasonable

divulgence by physician to patient to make such a decision possible. (p. 780)

The court's ruling acknowledged an exception to this general requirement, "when the patient is unconscious or otherwise incapable of consenting, and harm from a failure to treat is imminent and outweighs any harm threatened by the proposed treatment" (*Canterbury v. Spence,* 1972, p. 788). As reflected in virtually every jurisdiction today, "the translation of ethical principles into concrete requirements for physicians' behavior has been largely a function of the courts (usually state, occasionally federal). . . . State legislatures to a lesser extent have been involved in making law in this area" (Appelbaum, Lidz, & Meisel, 1987, p. 35).

To the extent that consent has been obviated by commitment proceedings, the District of Columbia Circuit Court of Appeals in *Rouse v. Cameron* (1966) confirmed that the purpose of involuntary hospitalization was treatment, not punishment. This ruling required hospitals to show that periodic inquiries were made into needs and conditions of patients, with a view toward providing suitable treatment (which could not be justified by a lack of staff or facilities). An Alabama federal court drew a similar distinction in *Wyatt v. Stickney* (1972), further maintaining that mere custodial care was insufficient for commitment purposes. The *Wyatt* court compelled state facilities to observe mail and telephone privileges, minimum staff qualifications, allotments for clothing, minimum available living spaces, essential nutrition, educational programs, review committees, individual treatment planning, and written orders for medication and restraint.

These progressive decisions concerning treatment and living conditions for involuntary hospitalization were allayed somewhat by the U.S. Supreme Court's holding in *Youngberg v. Romeo* (1982). The Court maintained that although rights to safe conditions and freedom from bodily restraint are supported by the 14th Amendment, state facilities owe no duty of "habilitation." Instead, the requisite standard consisted of that degree of training reasonable in light of a patient's safety and freedom interests, with deference to the judgment exercised by a qualified professional.

Along with this development of a patient's "right to treatment" came a growing delineation of the "right to refuse treatment." In *Kaimowitz v. Michigan Department of Mental Health* (1973), a local court determined that involuntarily detained mental patients may not consent to psychosurgery, because the basic elements of informed consent may not be ascertained reliably under these circumstances.

A string of regional cases in the 1970s and 1980s elaborated on this theme. In *Rennie v. Klein* (1978), a New Jersey federal court ruled that patients must be informed of and participate in the decision-making aspects of their treatment, with entitlement to legal assistance and outside psychiatrists of their choosing, unless the state sets up an independent review board. A Massachusetts federal court held in *Rogers v. Okin* (1979) that failure to adhere to proper procedures for seclusion and forced medication provided grounds for an injunction. In *Rivers v. Katz* (1986), the New York Court of Appeals ruled that neither mental illness nor involuntary commitment constitutes an independently sufficient basis to conclude that patients lack the mental capacity to make informed decisions regarding a decision to refuse medication. The court mandated that there must be a de novo judicial determination in this regard once institutional review processes have been exhausted. Judicial determinations focus on patients' best interests, benefits to be gained from treatment, adverse side effects, and less intrusive alternative treatments.

More recently, the U.S. Supreme Court ruled in *Washington v. Harper* (1990) that inmates' interests are adequately protected when involuntary medication decisions are made by medical personnel. This conclusion applies as long as sufficient institutional safeguards are in place and as long as there is overriding justification and a determination of medical appropriateness. In *Riggins v. Nevada* (1992), the Court further found that forced administration of psychotropic medication to achieve competency to stand trial does not meet the *Harper* standards of overriding justification or medical appropriateness, particularly in light of the substantial probability of trial prejudice. The Court made clear in *Zinermon v. Burch* (1990) that the *failure* to substitute judgment could amount to a violation of civil rights, indicating that there may even be a *duty* to provide judgment. As the Court emphasized, the voluntary civil commitment of an individual not competent to provide informed consent gives rise to a cause of action.

Forensic Assessment of Present Judgment

Beck (1987) identified two common errors in assessing competence relative to a patient's right to refuse treatment:

- *Every psychotic person is incompetent to decide about whether or not to take psychotic medication.* Not so. There are psychotic people who are nevertheless able to meet the standard for competent refusal. . . . Determining whether a psychotic person is incompetent is always an empirical question.
- *A person who is involuntarily committed to a psychiatric hospital is ipso facto incompetent to make treatment decisions.* [Generally], there is no necessary relationship between involuntary hospitalization and competence to decide about medication (p. 369).

Moving beyond these initial conceptual barriers, Erlen (1995) noted "various criteria used for determining decision-making capacity," including the patient's ability to "make a decision," "understand in a general sense," "understand the information in a particular sense," "provide a reason for the selected alternative," "give a plausible reason for the decision," and "weigh the potential risks and benefits" (p. 52).

Swartz (1985) identified a series of standards for judging whether treatment providers had adequately ascertained "a patient's preference." These included "the ward's prognosis if he chose no treatment, the prognosis if he chose one treatment over another, the risk of adverse side effects from the proposed treatment, [and] the ability of the ward to cooperate with post-treatment therapy" (pp. 175–176). In anticipation of such judicial review, it appears that treatment facilities have implemented varying, broader methods of responding to "administrative and legal demands," including "transfer of the patient refusing treatment," "discharg[ing] patients either to their families or to their own living arrangements," and attempts to "avoid the use of the judicial mechanism" where possible, to "facilitate all-important clinical approaches to working with patients refusing treatment" (Ciccone, Tokoli, Clements, & Gift, 1990, p. 212).

Some authors have approached analysis of a patient's decision-making processes from a more theoretically abstract perspective. Gigliotti and Rubin (1991) explored "characteristics of competent choice" from the perspective of "expected utility models," isolating assumptions that the "competent" individual will be able to:

- Use sensible probability weights for possible outcomes, when such weights are available or computable.
- Evaluate, that is, determine the utility of, the possible outcomes of risky prospects.
- Calculate the expected utility of risk prospects correctly, given sensible probability weights and evaluations of outcomes (p. 413).

The forensic clinician whose head is left spinning by such notions will take comfort in the availability of psychological tests purporting to assess the relevant constructs. "The best appears to be the MacArthur Competence Assessment Tool for Treatment Decisions (MacCAT-T), which uses features [of] the Understanding Treatment Disclosures (UTD) instrument, the Perceptions of Disorder (POD) instrument, and the Thinking Rationally about Treatment (TRAT) instrument" (Melton et al., 1997, p. 356).

Studies performed with the MacCAT-T appear to underscore its reliability, validity, and overall practical utility in assessing the capacity to make treatment decisions. Grisso, Appelbaum, and Hill-Fotouhi (1997) have been particularly complimentary of this measure's flexibility, which does not appear to have come at the expense of structure. Examiners should, of course, bear in mind that "while various instruments can provide evidence that is useful in the courtroom, it has been observed that none of these measures alone is a substitute for judicial determinations of legal incompetency to consent to treatment" (Parry, 1998, p. 96).

SUBSTITUTIONS FOR FUTURE JUDGMENT

The related interventions of guardianship and conservatorship represent the state's obligation to infer from a present incapacity that a disability may manifest itself at some later date, involving personal and financial affairs, respectively. A respondent's failure to identify adequate strategies for discharging responsibilities in a range of hypothetical situations may result in a pervasive denial of basic civil functions, including voting, choosing among health care options, self-determined transportation, and determining one's own residence.

Legal and Historical Background

Guardianship may represent the earliest historical manifestation of mental health law (Melton et al., 1997). During the period of the Roman Empire, "the need for surrogates to handle the property and commercial affairs of disabled citizens was first legally recognized" (Appelbaum, 1982, p. 183). By the sixteenth century in England, the system had evolved into one recognizable in many aspects by modern standards, such as supervision of persons with disabilities by court-appointed guardians (Neugebauer, 1989, p. 1582).

The first guardianship petition in the New World was decided under English law in 1637. Benoni Buck, a person with mental retardation, had become the subject of considerable dispute in English courts, over the cost of his maintenance in Jamestown, Virginia. Unfortunately, his revenues eventually "were to be used almost entirely for purposes other than his upkeep; no guardian accounted for his stewardship; [and] surplus estate profits were not preserved for any heirs," although "exploitative guardianships of this form had been abandoned in England at least 80 years earlier and, from this perspective, were socially regressive" (Neugebauer, 1987, p. 481).

In America, through the later twentieth century, "guardians came to have control of their wards' place of residence, choice of life style, and selection of care-givers," with the result that "the consent of the guardian alone was sufficient for the provision of most medical treatment" (Appelbaum, 1982, p. 183).

As noted by Hafemeister and Sales (1982), "all 50 states and the District of Columbia provide for some form of guardianship and/or conservatorship" (p. 255). An increasing tendency has been noted in these statutes toward the availability of "limited" or "partial" guardianship, which "allow competency, and, therefore, decision-making autonomy, to be determined issue-by-issue, thereby respecting individual strengths as well as disabilities" (Rosoff & Gottlieb, 1987, p. 18).

Despite such innovations, "procedural deficiencies" remain in many states (Pleak & Appelbaum, 1985, p. 78). The American Bar Association (1989) has projected that "by the year 2035, there will be nearly 71 million elderly persons, almost one quarter of the United States' population" (p. iii), highlighting the urgency of broad reform of existing guardianship laws.

Forensic Assessment of Future Judgment

Anderer (1990) noted that "the literature provides little practical advice for performing assessments specifically geared toward guardianship cases" (p. 19). To some extent, this may reflect the broad variability of standards across American jurisdictions (Baker, Perr, & Yesavage, 1986), as well as the differing adherence to such standards, even on a county-by-county basis.

In terms of guardianship-specific forensic psychological tests: "Clearly they are needed. Just as clearly they do not exist" (Quinn, 1996, p. 139). This is not to suggest that psychologists lack formal measures of functional ability, in different specific or overlapping task domains, although these may fail to capture the elusive construct of guardianship competency as a whole. Some of these include:

- *The Community Competency Scale* (CCS; Searight & Goldberg, 1991): This measure comprises 180 items of 15 components, calling in each case for "the older person to perform some function related to the subscale in question," such as Handling Emergencies, in which "examinees are provided a telephone and asked to do what they would do if they needed help immediately," and Managing Money, in which they "are given a blank check and asked to fill it out to a payee for a certain amount, then to subtract the amount from a facsimile of a checkbook balance page" (Grisso, 1994, p. 128). The CCS requires approximately 1 to 1.5 hours to administer (Willis, 1996).

- *The Multidimensional Functional Assessment Questionnaire* (MFAQ; Fillenbaum & Smyer, 1981): This test consists of two parts. The first obtains information in five functional areas (social resources, economic resources, mental health, physical health, and activities of daily living); the second gauges a respondent's utilization of a broad range of services (such as transportation, employment, physical therapy, and relocation and placement; Grisso, 1986). The MFAQ has been adapted for use with a Spanish-speaking population (Santisteban & Szapocznik, 1981), and takes approximately one hour to administer (Grisso, 1986).

- *Direct Assessment of Functional Status* (DAFS; Klapow, Evans, Patterson, & Heaton, 1997): Presenting elderly adults with "specific tasks of daily living" (Willis, 1996, p. 113), this measure "requires actual demonstration of abilities associated with day-to-day instrumental functions, such as performing grooming functions, remembering items on a grocery list, and identifying street and roadway signs" (Grisso, 1994, p. 128). The DAFS has fared well in research regarding older adults with schizophrenia as well as those with dementia (Klapow et al., 1997). Briefer than the CCS (Grisso, 1994), it may be administered in less than one hour.

Two often-used, general rating scales are the MMSE (Folstein et al., 1975; Mungas, 1991) and the Cognitive Capacity Screening Examination (Jacobs, Bernhard, Delgado, & Strain, 1977). These measures provide little by way of specific information regarding current functional abilities, but they serve to provide context for more focused inquiries by establishing the general cognitive status of an examinee. Both were normed on inpatient psychiatric and neurological treatment samples (Baker, 1989) and have been applied successfully in outpatient settings (Balster, Bienenfeld, Marvel, Pollock, & Somoza, 1990), with specific (and essentially equal) applicability for assessing cognitive impairment with elderly patients (Yazdanfar, 1990).

Beyond formal testing measures, various researchers and clinicians have developed patterned, often detailed outlines for the assessment of competency domains relevant to guardianship and conservatorship. Anderer (1990) recommends a stepwise method of inquiry comprising three main stages:

1. *Disorder/Disability Inquiry.* Evaluators determine the presence of "any diagnosis given the respondent's mental or physical condition," given that this "may be necessary to determine if the statutory disorder/disability

requirement has been met," as well as "to determine the stability of the deficits resulting from the condition or disability and to make a proper disposition after a finding of incapacity."

2. *Functional Capacity Inquiry.* This investigation is conducted "so that the court can determine which areas of decision-making capacity need to be examined." Two distinct areas of capacity are evaluated: "care for self" and "care for property."

3. *Decision-Making/Communicating Capacity Inquiry.* This level of analysis attaches to a respondent's ability to "receive and evaluate information" or to "make or communicate decisions," and "separates the relevant decisionmaking universe into three domains." These include "personal decisionmaking," "property decisionmaking," and "decisionmaking on other legal actions" (pp. 25–36).

Saunders and Simon (1987) developed the Individual Functional Assessment "to assist extended care facilities in determining a resident's need for guardianship or other protective services" (p. 60). Designed to meet "the stringent requirements of New Hampshire's guardianship law," this measure addresses "alternatives to guardianship" as well as the "scope of guardianship" (pp. 60–61), examining relevant factors in considerable detail.

Representative of the highly detailed, specific statutory schemes instituted in some jurisdictions, Kentucky's guardianship law requires court-appointed examiners to provide:

1. A description of the nature and extent of the respondent's disabilities, if any.

2. Current evaluations of the respondent's social, intellectual, physical, and educational condition, adaptive behavior, and social skills. Such evaluations may be based on prior evaluations not more than three months old, except that evaluations of the respondent's intellectual condition may be based on individual intelligence test scores not more than one year old.

3. An opinion as to whether guardianship or conservatorship is needed, the type of guardianship or conservatorship needed, if any, and the reasons therefor.

4. An opinion as to the length of time guardianship or conservatorship will be needed by the respondent, if at all, and the reasons therefor.

5. If limited guardianship or conservatorship is recommended, a further recommendation as to the scope of the guardianship or conservatorship, specifying particularly the rights to be limited and the corresponding powers and duties of the limited guardian or limited conservator.

6. A description of the social, educational, medical, and rehabilitative services currently being utilized by the respondent, if any.

7. A determination whether alternatives to guardianship or conservatorship are available.

8. A recommendation as to the most appropriate treatment or rehabilitation plan and living arrangement for the respondent and the reasons therefor.

9. A listing of all medications the respondent is receiving, the dosage, and a description of the impact of the medication upon the respondent's mental and physical condition and behavior.

10. An opinion whether attending a hearing on a petition would subject the respondent to serious risk of harm.

11. The names and addresses of all individuals who examined or interviewed the respondent or otherwise participated in the evaluation.

12. Any dissenting opinions or other comments by the evaluators (Guardians; Conservators; Curators of Convicts, 1998).

To respond to this array of considerations, Barrett and Drogin (1991) developed a "Disability Court Psychologist's Outline" to assist examiners in addressing the indicated domains in detail (see Table 16.1).

Psychologists must remain aware of the many alternatives to guardianship, should some incapacity be present that fails to meet the relevant statutory standard, or if, for some other reason, a less restrictive alternative should be recommended (Appelbaum, 1982). The American Bar Association (1998) has developed a comparative description of the range of different options that may be available in such situations, depending on the laws of a particular jurisdiction. Some of these alternatives potentially involve substitutions of prior judgment (e.g., living wills and powers of attorney). To this list can be added curatorship, often construed as a form of "temporary" guardianship or conservatorship (Garner, 1999, p. 387), requiring the informed consent of the individual for its initiation. Reversal of the curatorship must be requested by the individual, but, as well, the Court must find the person capable of performing the required functions again.

CONCLUSION

Those in the field of forensic psychology have traditionally regarded criminal law issues such as criminal nonresponsibility and competency to stand trial as the most interesting

TABLE 16.1   Selected Issues Addressed in the *Disability Court Psychologist's Outline*

1. Identifying Information
    Respondent's name.
    Respondent's age and date of birth.
    Respondent's social security number.
    Respondent's race.
    Date of evaluation.
    Site of evaluation.
    Date of admission.
    Physician name and contact information.
    Diagnoses.
    Medication.
    Assistance needs.
    Notable characteristics.
    Examination setting.
    Respondent's initial presentation.
2. Orientation
    Reason for examination.
    Definitions of guardianship and disability.
    Identity of petitioner.
    Reason for petition.
    Identity of attorney.
    Respondent's name, age, and date of birth.
    Current date.
    Current location.
    Respondent's marital status.
    Identity of respondent's spouse.
    Respondent's home address and telephone number.
3. Education
    Extent of education.
    Alphabet recitation.
    Counting from 1 to 20.
    Basic calculations: addition.
    Basic calculations: subtraction.
    Basic calculations: multiplication.
    Basic calculations: division.
4. Finances
    Social security number.
    Location and contents of bank account.
    Home ownership and value.
    Additional property.
    Monthly and annual income.
    Source and nature of income.
    Calculation of change: basic transactions.
5. Self-Care
    Clothing for 95-degree, 70-degree, 5-degree weather.
    Suicidal and/or interpersonally aggressive ideation.
    Responding to fire in the home.
    Responding to burglary.
    Responding to natural disasters.
    Responding to being lost in public.

    Responding to the need to make telephone contact.
    Use of microwave oven and other appliances.
6. Social Contact and Leisure Pursuits
    Friends and acquaintances: names and occupations.
    Frequency of social contact.
    Television: favorite programs.
    Movies: favorite films.
    Use of spare time in general.
    Community involvement.
7. Testamentary Capacity
    Definition of a will.
    Existence of a will.
    Date of drafting of a will.
    Property to be devised or bequeathed.
    Beneficiaries.
8. Medical Care
    Name of physician.
    How physician would be contacted.
    Illness/medical conditions.
    Current physician's orders.
    Medications: name/dosage/frequency/purpose.
    Medications: prescriber/payment.
    Medical insurance.
9. Driving an Automobile
    Driver's license.
    Last time driving an automobile.
    Traffic signals.
    Road markings.
    Signs.
    Speed limits.
    Intentions regarding driving.
    Reasons for any limitations.
10. Voting
    Last time voted.
    Frequency of presidential elections.
    Year next presidential election to occur.
    Registration: status and mechanics.
    Purpose and importance of voting.
    Identity of president and governor.
    Capitals of country and state.
11. Behavioral Response
    Counting fingers.
    Touching nose.
    Raising left and right hands.
    Looking up and to the right.
12. Review
    Purpose of visit.
    Issues discussed.
    Ability to conduct personal and financial affairs.

Source: Barrett & Drogin (1991).

and challenging of forensic areas. Candidly speaking, we too held this view at one time. With experience, however, we have come to believe that the arena of substituted judgment pushes the theories, measures, and instruments of forensic psychology to their very limits. Although criminal issues are important in liberty interests, substituted judg-ment issues speak directly to the capacity to experience, in whatever way is possible, the full potential of one's quality of life. There can be no doubt that the forensic psychologist's role, in contributing to the ability of a trier of fact to reach a sound decision, can be crucial. What more rewarding role for a forensic psychologist is available?

REFERENCES

Abeles, N. (1997). *What practitioners should know about working with older adults.* Washington, DC: American Psychological Association.

American Bar Association. (1989). *Guardianship: An agenda for reform.* Washington, DC: Author.

American Bar Association. (1998). *Facts about law and the elderly.* Washington, DC: Author.

American Psychological Association. (1996). Statement on the disclosure of test data. *American Psychologist, 51,* 644–648.

American Psychological Association. (1998). Guidelines for the evaluation of dementia and age-related cognitive decline. *American Psychologist, 53,* 1298–1303.

Anderer, S. J. (1990). *Determining competency in guardianship proceedings.* Washington, DC: American Bar Association.

Appelbaum, P. S. (1982). Limitations on guardianship of the mentally disabled. *Hospital and Community Psychiatry, 33,* 183–184.

Appelbaum, P. S., Lidz, C. W., & Meisel, A. (1987). *Informed consent: Legal theory and clinical practice.* New York: Oxford University Press.

Baker, F. M. (1989). Screening tests for cognitive impairment. *Hospital and Community Psychiatry, 40,* 339–340.

Baker, F. M., Perr, I. N., & Yesavage, J. A. (1986). *An overview of legal issues in geriatric psychiatry.* Washington, DC: American Psychiatric Press.

Balster, G. A., Bienenfeld, D., Marvel, N. T., Pollock, G., & Somoza, E. (1990). Cognitive impairment among geropsychiatric outpatients. *Hospital and Community Psychiatry, 41*(5), 556–558.

Barrett, C. L., & Drogin, E. Y. (1991). *Jefferson County Disability Court psychologist's outline.* Unpublished manuscript, University of Louisville, KY.

Beck, J. C. (1987). Right to refuse antispsychotic medication: Psychiatric assessment and legal decision-making. *Mental and Physical Disability Law Reporter, 11,* 368–371.

Ben-Porath, Y. S., & Butcher, J. S. (1989). The comparability of the MMPI and MMPI-2 scales and profiles. *Psychological Assessment, 1,* 345–347.

Bolton, J. (1977). Testamentary capacity. *Law and Psychology Review, 3,* 107–114.

Buckley, W. R. (1988). The case for the videotaped living will. *Probate and Property, 2,* 30–31.

Canterbury v. Spence, 464 F.2d 772 (D.C. Cir. 1972).

Ciccone, J. R., Tokoli, J. F., Clements, C. D., & Gift, T. E. (1990). Right to refuse treatment: Impact of *Rivers v. Katz. Bulletin of the American Academy of Psychiatry and the Law, 18,* 203–215.

Cruzan v. Missouri Department of Health, 497 U.S. 261 (1990).

Derouesne, C., Guigot, J., & Chatellier, G. (1995). An index for retrospective evaluation of the rate of cognitive decline in Alzheimer's disease. *International Journal of Geriatric Psychiatry, 10,* 805–807.

Dixon, T. (1905). *The clansman.* New York: Doubleday.

Drogin, E. Y. (2000a). Evidence and expert mental health witnesses: A "jurisprudent therapy" perspective. In E. Pierson (Ed.), *New developments in personal injury litigation* (pp. 295–333). New York: Wiley.

Drogin, E. Y. (2000b). In search of psychology. *Advocate, 22,* 17–19.

Eliasberg, W. G. (1953). To examine testamentary and testimonial capacity. *Journal of Criminal Law and Criminology, 44,* 320–329.

Erlen, J. A. (1995). When the patient lacks decision-making capacity. *Orthopaedic Nursing, 14,* 51–54.

Fillenbaum, G., & Smyer, M. (1981). The development, validity, and reliability of the OARS Multidimensional Functional Assessment Questionnaire. *Journal of Gerontology, 36,* 428–434.

Fitzgerald, B. J., Pasewark, R. A., & Fleisher, S. (1974). Responses of an aged population on the Gerontological and Thematic Apperception Tests. *Journal of Personality Assessment, 38,* 234–235.

Folstein, M. F., Folstein, S. E., & McHugh, P. R. (1975). "Mini-Mental State": A practical method for grading the cognitive state of patients for the clinician. *Journal of Psychiatric Research, 12,* 189–198.

Foote, J., & Kahn, M. W. (1979). Discriminative effectiveness of the Senior Apperception Test with impaired and nonimpaired elderly persons. *Journal of Personality Assessment, 43,* 360–364.

Garner, B. A. (Ed.). (1999). *Black's law dictionary.* St. Paul, MN: West Group.

Gigliotti, G. A., & Rubin, J. (1991). The right to refuse treatment: An application of the economic principles of decision-making under uncertainty. *International Journal of Law and Psychiatry, 14,* 405–416.

Gilfix, M. G., & Gilfix, M. (1992). Protecting patients' rights: Living wills. *Trial, 28,* 42–47.

Grisso, T. (1986). Psychological assessment in legal contexts. In W. Curran, A. McGarry, & S. Shah (Eds.), *Forensic psychiatry and psychology* (pp. 103–128). Philadelphia: Davis.

Grisso, T. (1994). Clinical assessments for legal competence of older adults. In M. Storandt & G. R. VandenBos (Eds.), *Neuropsychological assessment of dementia and depression in older adults: A clinician's guide* (pp. 119–139). Washington, DC: American Psychological Association.

Grisso, T., Appelbaum, P. S., & Hill-Fotouhi, C. (1997). The MacCAT-T; A clinical tool to assess patients' capacities to make treatment decisions. *Psychiatric Services, 48*(11), 1415–1419.

Guardians; Conservators; Curators of Convicts, Ky. Rev. Stat. §387.540 (1998).

Hafemeister, T., & Sales, B. D. (1982). Responsibilities of psychologists under guardianship and conservatorship laws. *Professional Psychology, 13,* 354–371.

Hamann, C. M. (1993). Family surrogate laws: A necessary supplement to living wills and durable powers of attorney. *Villanova Law Review, 38,* 103–177.

Hawkins, L. A. (1992). Living-will statutes: A minor oversight. *Virginia Law Review, 78,* 1581–1615.

Henry, B., Moffitt, T. E., Caspi, A., Langley, J., & Silva, P. A. (1994). On the "remembrance of things past": A longitudinal evaluation of the retrospective method. *Psychological Assessment, 6,* 92–101.

Herr, S. S., & Hopkins, B. L. (1994). Health care decision making for persons with disabilities: An alternative to guardianship. *Journal of the American Medical Association, 271,* 1017–1022.

High, D. M. (1994). Surrogate decision making. *Clinics in Geriatric Medicine, 10,* 445–462.

Hyer, L., & Blount, J. (1984). Concurrent and discriminant validities of the Geriatric Depression Scale with older psychiatric patients. *Psychological Reports, 54,* 611–616.

Insel, M. S. (1995). Durable power can alleviate effects of client's incapacity. *Estate Planning, 22,* 37–43.

Jacobs, J. W., Bernhard, M. R., Delgado, A., & Strain, J. J. (1977). Screening for organic mental syndromes in the medically ill. *Annals of Internal Medicine, 86,* 40–46.

Kaimowitz v. Michigan Dept. of Mental Health, 42 U.S.L.W. 2063 (Civil Action No. 73–19434-AW, Cir. Ct. Wayne Cty. Mich. July 10, 1973).

Kempin, F. G. (1973). *Historical introduction to Anglo-American law.* St. Paul, MN: West.

Kendall, P. C., Hollon, S. D., Beck, A. T., Hammen, C. L., & Ingram, R. E. (1987). Issues and recommendations regarding use of the Beck Depression Inventory. *Cognitive Therapy and Research, 11,* 289–299.

Kennedy, W. A. (1986). The psychologist as expert witness. In W. Curran, A. McGarry, & S. Shah (Eds.), *Forensic psychiatry and psychology* (pp. 487–511). Philadelphia: Davis.

Klapow, J. C., Evans, J., Patterson, T. L., & Heaton, R. K. (1997). Direct assessment of functional status in older patients with schizophrenia. *American Journal of Psychiatry, 154,* 1022–1024.

Knight, B. G., & Mjelde-Mossey, L. A. (1995). A comparison of the Michigan Alcoholism Screening Test and the Michigan Alcoholism Screening Test–Geriatric version in screening for higher alcohol use among dementia caregivers. *Journal of Mental Health and Aging, 1,* 147–155.

Kosloski, K., Datwyler, M. M., & Montgomery, R. J. (1994). Evaluating retrospective measures in gerontological research. *Research on Aging, 16,* 389–400.

Logue, P. E., Tupler, L. A., D'Amico, C. J., & Schmitt, F. A. (1993). The Neurobehavioral Cognitive Status Examination: Psychometric properties in use with psychiatric inpatients. *Journal of Clinical Psychology, 49,* 80–89.

Melton, G. B., Petrila, J., Poythress, N. G., & Slobogin, C. (1997). *Psychological evaluations for the courts* (2nd ed.). New York: Guilford Press.

Mungas, D. (1991). In-office mental status testing: A practical guide. *Geriatrics, 46,* 54–66.

Neugebauer, R. (1987). Exploitation of the insane in the New World. *Archives of General Psychiatry, 44,* 481–483.

Neugebauer, R. (1989). Diagnosis, guardianship, and residential care of the mentally ill in medieval and early modern England. *American Journal of Psychiatry, 146,* 1580–1584.

Ownby, R. L., & Seibel, H. P. (1994). A factor analysis of the Brief Psychiatric Rating Scale in an older psychiatric population. *Multivariate Experimental Clinical Research, 10,* 145–156.

Parry, J. (1998). *National benchbook on psychiatric and psychological evidence and testimony.* Washington, DC: American Bar Association.

Perr, I. N. (1981). Wills, testamentary capacity and undue influence. *Bulletin of the American Academy of Psychiatry and the Law, 9,* 15–22.

Pleak, R. R., & Appelbaum, P. S. (1985). The clinician's role in protecting patients' rights in guardianship proceedings. *Hospital and Community Psychiatry, 36,* 77–79.

Quinn, M. J. (1996). Commentary: Everyday competencies and guardianship: Refinements and realities. In M. Smyer, K. W. Schaie, & M. B. Kapp (Eds.), *Older adults' decision-making and the law* (pp. 128–141). New York: Springer.

Redmond, F. C. (1987). Testamentary capacity. *Bulletin of the American Academy of Psychiatry and the Law, 15,* 247–256.

Regan, W. M., & Gordon, S. M. (1997). Assessing testamentary capacity in elderly people. *Southern Medical Journal, 90,* 13–15.

Rennie v. Klein, 462 F. Supp. 1131 (D.N.J. 1978).

Riggins v. Nevada, 504 U.S. 127 (1992).

Rivers v. Katz, 495 N.E.2d 337 (N.Y. 1986).

Robitscher, J. B. (1966). *Pursuit of agreement: Psychiatry and law.* Philadelphia: Lippincott.

Rogers v. Okin, 478 F. Supp. 1342 (D. Mass. 1979).

Rosoff, A. J., & Gottlieb, G. L. (1987). Preserving personal autonomy for the elderly. *Journal of Legal Medicine, 8,* 1–47.

Rouse v. Cameron 373 F.2d 451 (D.C. Cir. 1966).

Santisteban, D., & Szapocznik, J. (1981). Adaptation of the Multidimensional Functional Assessment Questionnaire for use with Hispanic elders. *Hispanic Journal of Behavioral Sciences, 3,* 301–308.

Saunders, A. G., & Simon, M. (1987). Individual functional assessment: An instruction manual. *Mental and Physical Disability Law Reporter, 11,* 60–70.

Searight, H. R., & Goldberg, M. A. (1991). The Community Competence Scale as a measure of functional daily living skills. *Journal of Mental Health Administration, 18,* 128–134.

Selkin, J. (1994). Psychological autopsy: Scientific psychohistory or clinical intuition? *American Psychologist, 49,* 74–75.

Shneidman, E. S. (1994). The psychological autopsy. *American Psychologist, 4,* 75–76.

Smith, G. E. (1994). Psychometric properties of the Mattis Dementia Rating Scale. *Assessment, 1,* 123–131.

Smith, S. R., & Meyer, R. G. (1987). *Law, behavior, and mental health: Policy and practice.* New York: New York University Press.

Spar, J. E., & Garb, A. S. (1992). Assessing competency to make a will. *American Journal of Psychiatry, 149,* 169–174.

Spaulding, W. J. (1985). Testamentary competency: Reconciling doctrine with the role of the expert witness. *Law and Human Behavior, 9,* 113–139.

Sprehe, D. J., & Kerr, A. L. (1996). Use of legal terms in will contests: Implications for psychiatrists. *Bulletin of the American Academy of Psychiatry and the Law, 24,* 255–265.

Swartz, M. (1985). The patient who refuses medical treatment: A dilemma for hospitals and physicians. *American Journal of Law and Medicine, 11,* 147–194.

Washington v. Harper, 494 U.S. 210 (1990).

Williams, J. B. (1988). A structured interview guide for the Hamilton Depression Rating Scale. *Archives of General Psychiatry, 45,* 742–747.

Willis, S. L. (1996). Assessing everyday competence in the cognitively challenged elderly. In M. Smyer, K. W. Schaie, & M. B. Kapp (Eds.), *Older adults' decision-making and the law* (pp. 87–127). New York: Springer.

Wyatt v. Stickney, 344 F. Supp. 387 (M.D. Ala. 1972).

Yazdanfar, D. J. (1990). Assessing the mental status of the cognitively impaired elderly. *Journal of Gerontological Nursing, 16,* 32–36.

Youngberg v. Romeo, 457 U.S. 307 (1982).

Zinermon v. Burch, 494 U.S. 113 (1990).

PART FIVE

CRIMINAL FORENSIC PSYCHOLOGY

CHAPTER 17

Forensic Evaluation in Delinquency Cases

THOMAS GRISSO

Psychologists have been providing specialized evaluations for the courts in delinquency cases for about 100 years. In contrast, forensic psychologists have routinely performed adult competence to stand trial and criminal responsibility assessments for the courts for only the past 30 years. Yet the specialized knowledge base that serves forensic examiners in delinquency cases lags behind other areas of forensic psychology, most of which have seen more significant advances in research and systematic guidance for the practitioner.

This anomaly provides a subtext that guides the present chapter, which focuses on the needs and current opportunities for improving the quality of forensic evaluations in delinquency cases. The chapter begins with a brief history of juvenile courts and evaluations in delinquency cases, showing how the subfield evolved to create some of our more complex forensic questions. The next three sections describe the current status of specific types of evaluations, including limitations and need for research and development. They address evaluation of mental health and dispositional needs of

delinquent youths, assessing risk of violence and recidivism, and specific psycholegal questions arising in delinquency cases, including waiver to criminal court, competence to stand trial, and capacities to waive *Miranda* rights. The final section reviews selected conceptual issues in this area that are in need of research and applied solutions during the next few decades.

ONE HUNDRED YEARS OF PSYCHOLOGICAL EVALUATIONS IN DELINQUENCY CASES

The scope of forensic evaluations in delinquency cases has changed dramatically during the history of juvenile justice in the United States. To understand this, we must briefly visit the origins of the juvenile court and its early clinics. Then we examine two reforms in juvenile justice during the past century that raised new legal questions in juvenile courts, as well as the need for forensic evaluations to address them. Finally, we consider this field's search for identity as a forensic evaluation specialty.

1899–1965: The Early Juvenile Court

Late in the nineteenth century, there were significant changes in Western thought about the nature of children in their teen years (Cicourel, 1968; Scott, 2000). Evidence of this change in the United States was the development of a public education system, child labor laws, and the rise of the new concept of "adolescence," advanced by G. Stanley Hall, as a distinct developmental stage.

Together with this change in the perception of youths came reform in the way that society responded to their transgressions. Because adolescents were still developing and were not yet adultlike, it was argued that their offenses were signs that they were misguided, not inevitably destined for adult criminal careers. This placed an obligation on society not to punish them, but to redirect their development in positive ways (Platt, 1977). Rehabilitation was seen as more appropriate than punishment and retribution as a response to youths' illegal behaviors. This notion of child welfare and rehabilitation became the foundation for a new system of law to be applied to youths before a certain age (often, 16 or 17). This new legal system would not find youths guilty of crimes, but rather "delinquent" or "wayward" and not subject to the penalties that would have been associated with their offenses if they were adults.

The new juvenile justice system had courts and judges, but instead of deciding guilt and punishment, they were instructed to deal with juvenile cases according to the doctrine of *parens patriae,* as "a wise, merciful father handles his own child whose errors are not discovered by the authorities" (Mack, 1909). As expressed by Jane Addams (1935), one of the moving forces behind the development of Chicago's juvenile court, the first in the United States, in 1899:

> The child was brought before the judge with no one to prosecute him and with no one to defend him—the judge and all concerned were merely trying to find out what could be done on his behalf. The element of conflict was absolutely eliminated and with it, all notion of punishment. (p. 137)

Many of the juvenile court's evolving features were consistent with this philosophy. The court often functioned as a social service agency that had the authority and structure of a legal institution. The judge was given wide discretion in deciding what was best for the child. Burdens of proof were unnecessary, as were most matters of due process, because the state was intervening in the child's life not to confine for purposes of punishment but to address the child's needs.

The judge's primary staff included child welfare specialists (often, social workers); defense attorneys were unnecessary in a system that was intended to be benevolent, not adversarial. Training schools, reformatories, and child community services developed with the intention of providing the services that would carry out the juvenile court's rehabilitation philosophy.

Judges needed guidance from clinicians in reaching their decisions about the services that wayward children required, and in larger communities, they were assisted by psychologists and psychiatrists at court-related evaluation clinics. One of the earliest models for clinical evaluation services for juvenile courts was an institute developed in 1909 by Healy, a neurologist, and Fernald, a psychologist, to serve the Cook County (Chicago) juvenile court (Schetky & Benedek, 1992). Their assessments are said to have been comprehensive, multidisciplinary studies of youths' life situations, including developmental histories, diagnostic information, and rehabilitation recommendations.

The new juvenile court did not "sentence" youths; their cases were merely "settled" or "disposed." Thus, the evaluations that assisted the judge in determining the future placement of youths were termed "dispositional evaluations." They were virtually the only "forensic" evaluation in the early juvenile courts, and they remain today the most frequent type of clinical evaluation provided by psychologists in delinquency cases.

The actual functioning of social institutions often is not consistent with its formal philosophy, and the juvenile court of the first half of the twentieth century was no exception. As Tanenhaus (2000) has described, early juvenile courts (and their communities) were often in conflict about the new conceptualization of adolescence and delinquency, especially in cases involving serious offenses. Mechanisms soon arose for assuring that at least some adolescents would be tried not as juveniles but in criminal courts under criminal law as though they were adults. Moreover, even the dispositions of youths who were retained in the juvenile justice system often amounted to no more than punishment, in that the reformatories and training schools that evolved often provided little that could be construed as an effort at treatment or rehabilitation. Confidentiality associated with juvenile court proceedings, intended for the protection of youths, also acted as a curtain that shielded from public view the abuses that sometimes occurred as a result of the broad discretion that was allowed in the courts in their decisions about youths' confinement. In the latter half of the twentieth century, these conditions fueled two important reforms in juvenile justice that changed the forensic evaluation needs of juvenile courts.

1965–1995: From Judicial Discretion and Rehabilitation to Rights and Punishment

The Rights Reform

The first of these reforms was ushered in by two U.S. Supreme Court cases: *Kent v. U.S.* (1966), and *In re Gault* (1967). *Kent* required the application of certain due process rights in cases in which the juvenile court contemplated waiving its legal jurisdiction over a youth, allowing the youth to be remanded to the adult criminal courts for trial. *Gault* recognized several constitutional rights of youths throughout the adjudication process in all delinquency cases. Whereas those rights had not been considered necessary in a system that was intended to operate solely for the welfare of the child, the U.S. Supreme Court now required them, explaining that the juvenile court had failed to live up to its promise, typically providing custodial care without rehabilitative efforts.

The juvenile court was still obligated to provide rehabilitation, the Court said, but to take custody of the youth (that is, to find the youth "delinquent" to then provide a rehabilitative disposition) would require procedures and rights that more closely resembled the protections for adults in criminal court. Among these were adequate notice of charges, representation by legal defense counsel, the privilege against self-incrimination, and the right to confront and cross-examine opposing witnesses.

Juvenile justice systems throughout the country gradually adjusted to these requirements. Typically, they developed a system of adjudication for delinquency that provided legal protections for the defense, while retaining significant judicial discretion for the dispositional stage of the process after the youth was found delinquent.

The Punishment Reform

The second reform occurred in the late 1980s and early 1990s in response to a sudden increase in the rate of adolescents' violent offenses, especially homicide (Zimring, 1998). Within a few years, almost all states changed their statutes in ways that de-emphasized a rehabilitative response to offenses by juveniles and increased the likelihood and severity of punishment (Grisso, 1996).

This took several forms, especially the lowering of ages and expansion of offenses for which youths could be automatically sent to criminal court for trial and sentencing as adults. Moreover, legislatures in many states explicitly changed the legal purposes of juvenile justice, making public safety its first priority rather than rehabilitation. In many states, youths who were adjudicated delinquent now faced much harsher consequences, including the possibility of sentences that would begin in juvenile facilities and continue in adult correctional facilities after they had reached their majority.

2000: The New Field of Juvenile Forensic Evaluation

These juvenile justice reforms of the late twentieth century confronted courts with the need for certain types of forensic evaluations that had never existed for most of the juvenile court's history. Until the recent reforms, clinicians' evaluations for juvenile courts were basically clinical evaluations, or "child studies," designed to assist courts in understanding youths' delinquent behaviors for purposes of dispositional (rehabilitation) recommendations. They were "forensic" in that they were performed for courts, but they did not require much by way of specialized interpretation to address legal questions. They used the clinician's knowledge in developmental and child clinical psychology, as well as theories of delinquency and a rather modest literature on the treatment of delinquent youths.

The later reforms, however, raised a number of new questions that juvenile court judges and attorneys had to address to apply new laws in delinquency cases. No longer was it sufficient simply to identify a youth's needs. Now one needed to know whether youths had capacities that were related to the fair application of their rights under a primarily adversarial and punitive system of justice:

- Could youths understand their *Miranda* rights (and therefore validly waive their constitutional right to self-incrimination)?

- Was there sufficient evidence of a youth's potential danger to the community to meet legal requirements for deprivation of liberties associated with secure pretrial or posttrial detainment?

- What psychological evidence could be offered to determine whether a youth met the new legal criteria for deciding whether he or she was "unamenable to treatment" and therefore could be sent to adult criminal court for trial?

- When was a youth competent to participate in the trial process ("competent to stand trial") in a way that met a standard of fairness that the new juvenile laws required?

Courts' and attorneys' requests for forensic evaluations to address these questions gradually began to increase and became quite frequent in many courts in the 1980s and 1990s. As a consequence, many forensic examiners in juvenile courts were suddenly required to perform assessments for questions that were fundamentally outside their experience. Unlike requests for dispositional evaluations, these requests asked whether youths had various behaviors and capacities that were related to specific legal concepts. They required evaluations that were forensic not merely because they were performed for courts, but also because they addressed specific legal standards regarding the protection of youths' rights.

Psychologists who provided evaluations for juvenile courts had little to guide them in meeting these requests. Many of the legal standards themselves were ill-defined in the new legislative reforms, creating ambiguity regarding what was to be evaluated and concluded. For most of the new questions, the field had developed neither systematic approaches to assessment nor special assessment methods for use in delinquency cases.

Thus, in the past few years, we have witnessed a significant transformation of the field of forensic evaluation in delinquency cases. It continues its tradition of dispositional evaluations and its close ties to child clinical and developmental psychology, as well as specialized knowledge of delinquent youths. But currently, it is searching for its foundations, methods, and identity associated with the new psycholegal evaluations that arose near the end of the twentieth century and that will dominate its future.

In Search of a Specialty

What is the status of this area of juvenile forensic evaluations in delinquency cases as a specialty in forensic psychology? Given its 100-year history, is it a mature specialty? Or is it only evolving, in that it is beginning anew in response to demands created by recent changes in juvenile law? Let us briefly review its status on some of the criteria one uses to judge the maturity of a professional specialty in psychology: (a) a specialized knowledge base, (b) an organized body of specialists, (c) a training base, and (d) a set of standards to guide the specialty's applications.

Knowledge Base

Despite its 100 years of practice, the field of psychological evaluations for juvenile courts in delinquency cases has proceeded primarily on the knowledge base offered by general developmental and child clinical psychology. As described later, a specialized literature on the causes of delinquency and the classification of delinquent youths did arise in the 1950s through the 1970s. But not until the 1980s did there appear textbooks on the practice of clinicians in juvenile courts (Rosner & Schwartz, 1989; Schetky & Benedek, 1980, 1985,

1992), and these were not by psychologists. Moreover, neither these texts nor psychology's general forensic texts (e.g., Melton, Petrila, Poythress, & Slobogin, 1986, 1997) provided detailed, systematic guidance for evaluations in delinquency cases. Thus, during most of the history of the juvenile court there has been little evidence that forensic evaluation of delinquent youths involved a body of knowledge that differed from general child clinical psychology.

Concerning evaluations for the psycholegal questions recently raised by changes in juvenile law pertaining to delinquency cases, the first text to describe a systematic, conceptual approach to such evaluations did not appear until 1998 (Grisso, 1998a). Moreover, that text was based far less on a sound empirical foundation and far more on clinical experience than is desirable for a professional specialty.

For example, serious research on the estimation of youths' risk for future violence has appeared only in the past decade (e.g., Loeber & Farrington, 1998), and translations of these results into guidance for forensic examiners (e.g., Borum, 2000; Grisso, 1998a, 2000), though promising, have been without evidence for their validity in forensic practice. Similarly, at this writing, current literature provides no substantial studies of youths' capacities related to competence to stand trial. Our only current guidance for evaluating competence for juvenile courts is in the form of recommendations based on inferences from developmental and child clinical theory, together with structure borrowed from our experience in evaluating competence to stand trial in adult criminal cases (e.g., Grisso, 1997; Grisso & Schwartz, 2000).

It is almost certain that these circumstances will change. The late 1990s witnessed a dramatic increase in attention to juvenile forensic assessment issues at psychological conferences, which is often a bellwether for future research and professional developments. Those developments will be important for growing the type of knowledge base that is needed to support a specialty in forensic evaluations for delinquency cases.

Organizational Identity

Forensic psychology became officially organized in the 1970s (e.g., the American Psychology-Law Society, and the American Board of Forensic Psychology; see Grisso, 1991), as did some subspecialty organizations (e.g., the American Association of Correctional Psychologists). In contrast, forensic psychologists working in juvenile courts have no national organization representing their special practice in delinquency cases. They have no national newsletters and no journal devoted specifically to psychological evaluations in the juvenile justice system.

However, the components for national organizational identity do exist. Court clinics to serve juvenile courts in delinquency cases can be found in the majority of moderate to large communities, and in other communities, the juvenile courts have contractual arrangements with psychologists in private practice who provide necessary evaluations (Grisso, 1998a). But these local systems have developed in relative isolation, few of them having any systematic and continuing communication with other juvenile court clinics or practitioners outside their own state. We have yet to perform any surveys that would describe juvenile court clinical services in ways that would identify the body of psychologists in practice, the number of clinics, their structural and operational models, and their functions. If a specialty requires an organizational identity, the field of forensic juvenile evaluation does not yet meet that requirement.

Training

Specialized training programs in forensic psychology arose during the past two decades and have increased in number (Vant Zelfde & Otto, 1997), but few of them currently provide specialized preparation for juvenile forensic evaluations. The majority of psychology graduate schools provide the basic child clinical preparation that continues to be the foundation for juvenile court evaluations. However, specialized experience in providing evaluations for delinquency cases is rarely found in psychology predoctoral internship programs or even in forensic psychology postdoctoral programs.

Professional Standards

Standards for the professional and ethical practice of forensic psychology did not appear until 1991 (Committee on Ethical Guidelines for Forensic Psychologists, 1991). Subsequently, the American Psychological Association (1994) developed guidelines for the ethical practice of psychological evaluations in other types of child forensic cases (e.g., child custody). Currently, there are no specialized standards for the professional and ethical practice of psychological evaluations in delinquency cases. Thus, there have been no clear definitions of the necessary qualifications for psychologists who practice in this field.

Summary

This review of the lack of evidence for a specialty in juvenile forensic evaluations for delinquency cases presents an irony. As the remaining sections of this chapter show, psychologists cannot competently perform evaluations in most delinquency cases without certain types of knowledge and experience that go well beyond those of the general child clinical psychologist. Moreover, although no one has documented it, there are a large number of psychologists nationally who have that knowledge and experience and who therefore can be construed as "specialists." Yet it is difficult to identify the specialty because of (a) the historical lack of attention to developing its specialized research base and documenting its knowledge domain, (b) its lack of professional organization, and (c) the absence of professional standards and training programs related to the practice of juvenile forensic evaluation.

The next decade is very likely to bring a change in these conditions, resulting in the evolution of a specialty that has been with us for a century but that has only recently discovered itself. The remainder of this chapter provides an overview of the concepts, research questions, and issues in evaluation practice that will provide the context for the evolution of this old field of practice into a young forensic specialty.

CLINICAL AND DISPOSITIONAL ASSESSMENTS IN DELINQUENCY CASES

As noted earlier, psychologists' most frequent evaluations in delinquency cases have involved describing youths' psychological needs and rehabilitation potentials. There are two broad contexts in which these evaluations occur in delinquency cases. One is at the pretrial stage to assess the potential need for emergency mental health intervention; this may be in the form of routine psychological screening or clinical evaluation. The second is an assessment to assist the court at the posttrial stage of the delinquency proceeding in arriving at a dispositional decision about appropriate intervention. After describing some fundamentals, this section describes methods available for performing these evaluations.

Some Fundamentals

Grisso (1998a) has outlined four basic questions that dispositional evaluations should answer in delinquency cases:

1. What are the youth's important characteristics (e.g., personality, family factors, mental or intellectual problems, delinquency history)?
2. What needs to change (e.g., what factors that have contributed to delinquency will need to be modified to reduce the likelihood of recidivism)?
3. What modes of intervention could be applied toward the rehabilitation objective?
4. What is the likelihood of change, given the relevant interventions?

Certain factors are fundamental to the practice of evaluating the psychological needs and rehabilitation potentials of delinquent youths to address these questions. Some of them are shared with general child clinical psychology; others are more specific to delinquency cases. Similarly, some of them are shared with other areas of forensic psychology, and others are not.

Development

It is axiomatic that evaluations of youths' psychological and rehabilitation needs must always be performed with a developmental perspective. Unlike adults, most youths change intellectually and behaviorally throughout the teen years. The normative nature of those changes, and their implications for future offending, always need to be considered in delinquency cases. For example, the normative process of development in adolescence is responsible for the well-documented facts that the majority of adolescent males engage in behaviors that would be misdemeanors or felonies if they were arrested (Elliott, Ageton, Huizinga, Knowles, & Canter, 1983), and the great majority of youths who commit serious violent offenses do not continue their offending into adulthood (Howell, Krisberg, Hawkins, & Wilson, 1995).

Family

Youths typically are dependent on their families. An assessment of a youth's psychological needs and rehabilitation potential that does not include information about the family will be inadequate for most dispositional evaluation questions in delinquency cases. More than in most other areas of forensic evaluation, assessments in delinquency cases are, in part, evaluations of youths in various social contexts, including family, school, and peer interactions.

Mental Disorder

As described later, current evidence indicates that the prevalence of mental disorders among youths in the juvenile justice system is at least twice that among youths in the general U.S. population (Kazdin, 2000). The diagnosis of mental disorders among adolescents is considerably more complex and ambiguous than among adults. There are difficulties with our present diagnostic classification system for adolescents. But beyond this, the developmental process that adolescents are undergoing nearly guarantees greater instability, less reliability, and greater apparent comorbidity in mental disorders during adolescence than during adulthood.

Race and Gender

Our theories of delinquency and our methods for assessing psychological and clinical needs of juveniles have been developed primarily with a focus on the White male delinquent youth. These guides cannot automatically be applied to girls in the juvenile justice system. Moreover, whereas minority youths comprise about one-third of the U.S. population of teenagers, they make up about two-thirds of youths in our juvenile detention and correctional facilities (Community Research Associates, Inc., 1997). As will be discussed later, our assessment knowledge base often does not allow us to apply it with confidence to minority youths. The challenges posed by the discontinuity between our knowledge base and the populations of youths actually served in the juvenile justice system have too often been ignored.

Systemic Knowledge

Psychologists who perform evaluations for dispositional questions in delinquency cases must know as much about the rehabilitation resources of the juvenile justice and correctional system as they do about the needs of youths. Ultimately, the objective of a dispositional evaluation is to match the needs of youths with the services that the system can provide.

General Methods for Assessing Personality and Mental Disorder

Every dispositional evaluation includes an assessment of the youth's intellectual and social development, personality, and possible mental disorder. In this respect, dispositional evaluations for delinquency cases are most like general child clinical evaluations and may borrow on our general knowledge of child psychopathology and its assessment. Hoge and Andrews (1996) have provided a helpful review of methods pertaining to this area of assessment with delinquent youths.

Examiners have the benefit of a number of relatively new assessment tools for describing youths' personality, developmental problems, and symptoms of mental disorder. Among them are the Minnesota Multiphasic Personality Inventory–Adolescent (MMPI-A; Butcher et al., 1992) and the Millon Adolescent Clinical Inventory (MACI; Millon, 1993). They have their limitations for use in delinquency cases, however. Neither has yet been used extensively in research in juvenile justice settings, and research has not yet provided a confident view of the application of the instruments to ethnic minority youths. The Child Behavior Checklist (Achenbach, 1991) provides a better research foundation for application to delinquent youths of various ethnic backgrounds, as well as offering parent-response, teacher-response, and youth self-report versions. In addition, the less well known Basic Personality Inventory (Jackson, 1995) is shorter than the MMPI-A or MACI and offers norms for delinquent samples.

Until recently, research on the prevalence of mental disorders among youths in the juvenile justice system has been piecemeal, offering widely varying estimates (Otto, Greenstein, Johnson, & Friedman, 1992). Based on several comprehensive studies in the past few years (e.g., Teplin, Abrams, & McClelland, 1998; Timmons-Mitchell et al., 1997), the prevalence of mental disorders among youths in juvenile justice facilities appears to be about 40% (excluding conduct disorders), roughly twice that of youths in the general population.

Conduct disorder, of course, is the most frequent diagnosis among delinquent youths. Its usefulness as a diagnostic classification is limited by the fact that the "disorder" is little more than an identification of the fact that a youth has been habitually delinquent. The distinction in the *Diagnostic and Statistical Manual of Mental Disorders* (*DSM-IV;* American Psychiatric Association, 1994) between the onset of conduct disorder prior to adolescence and during adolescence, however, has some value, in that a body of literature indicates that early onset increases the likelihood that a youth will continue to engage in illegal behaviors beyond adolescence (e.g., Moffitt, 1993; Loeber & Farrington, 1998). Frick (1998b) has provided a useful set of guidelines for the diagnosis of conduct disorder and its use in dispositional planning.

The literature (e.g., Teplin et al., 1998) makes it clear that special attention should be given in dispositional evaluations of delinquent youths to mood disorders (especially depression), anxiety disorders, and posttraumatic stress disorder. In addition, attention-deficit/hyperactivity disorder (Barkley, 1990) and substance abuse disorders play a significant role in describing and explaining the delinquent histories of some youths.

Unfortunately, the diagnosis of mental disorders among juvenile justice youths in clinical evaluations is hampered by controversy regarding theories and taxonomy in child psychopathology (Mash & Barkley, 1996) and issues of comorbidity. Moreover, structured tools for arriving at *DSM-IV* diagnoses, like the Diagnostic Interview Schedule for Children (Schaffer, Schwab, & Fisher, 1993), are very time-consuming and thus not amenable to many clinical referral situations in delinquency cases.

Personality and Problem Scales Specifically for Delinquency Cases

A number of typologies for categorizing delinquent youths were developed in the 1960s and 1970s, and they persist today along with assessment methods for classifying youths according to these typologies. For example, classification of youths according to interpersonal maturity level can be based in part on scores on the Jesness Inventory (Jesness & Wedge, 1985), developed specifically for use with delinquent youths. Quay (1964, 1966) has long had a useful typology for classifying delinquent youths, objectified in his Revised Behavior Problem Checklist (Quay & Peterson, 1987). More recently, the Youth Level of Service/Case Management Inventory (Hoge & Andrews, 1994) was developed to identify specific problem areas around which to formulate rehabilitation plans for youths in the juvenile justice system.

Most of these instruments have been intended for use with youths after they have been identified as in need of intervention. That is, typically, they would not be used to screen every youth entering a juvenile justice facility at the pretrial or posttrial stage. Several other instruments have been developed for routine screening of youths as they enter the juvenile justice system. Typically, they are used to identify youths who may be in need of immediate referral for further evaluation. Among these are the Child and Adolescent Functional Assessment Scale (Hodges, 1995), the Problem Oriented Screening Instrument for Teenagers (McLellan & Dembo, 1993), and the Massachusetts Youth Screening Instrument–Second Version (Grisso & Barnum, 2000; Grisso, Barnum, Fletcher, Cauffman, & Peuschold, 2001).

These screening instruments have the advantage of being amenable to routine administration to all youths entering the juvenile justice system. Thus, they are useful as "triage" instruments and as methods for suggesting problem areas that need to be explored in further assessment directed toward intervention planning. The more an instrument is amenable to routine use, however, the greater has been the requirement to keep the instrument brief, to rely on the youth's own self-report, and to allow that the instrument may be influenced by immediate and potentially transient psychological states rather than primarily characterological traits. These features may decrease the reliability and validity of the instruments for some purposes (e.g., diagnosis), while allowing them to be satisfactory as triage instruments that signal potential needs. Typically, they should not be used in place of clinical expertise or more complete measures when performing comprehensive dispositional evaluations.

Assessment of Social Contexts

As noted earlier, dispositional evaluations in delinquency cases require an evaluation of potential resources and interventions that may be relevant in developing a rehabilitation plan. A few methods are available for assessing the qualities of youths' families and their potential as a focus for rehabilitation efforts. Examples include the Family Environment Scale (Moos & Moos, 1986) and the Family Adaptability and Cohesion Evaluation Scales II (Olson et al., 1982). At present, they can be of value descriptively, but there is little research to guide the clinician in using the data for rehabilitation planning.

Especially noteworthy is the absence of methods to describe and classify rehabilitation programs in ways that are clinically useful. Recent research has demonstrated the value of some types of rehabilitation programs for delinquent youths in general (e.g., Tate, Reppucci, & Mulvey, 1995). However, research has provided little guidance for valid matching of types of youths with types of rehabilitation programs. As essential as this information may seem, it is simplistic to imagine that a call for such research will provide it. Before even beginning to test the value of specific programs with certain youths, researchers need a reliable way to classify youths and to classify rehabilitation programs according to some theory of rehabilitation, neither of which currently exists. Moreover, the application of such research would have to presume that local versions of the rehabilitation programs practiced the intervention methods in question reliably and consistently. Thus, it is unlikely that researchers will be able to provide empirically validated guidelines for matching types of youths with types of programs in the near future.

Dispositions and Public Safety

The juvenile justice system has always had two primary objectives: to provide for youths' positive development, and to protect the community. In recent years, juvenile justice systems increasingly have acknowledged that youths' rehabilitation in a juvenile correctional system exists *primarily* to reduce the likelihood of future harm to others, not simply to meet youths' psychological needs. Public safety is not only a long-range objective, but also a more immediate concern during the process of rehabilitation. Therefore, virtually every evaluation for the needs and rehabilitation potential of a youth in the juvenile justice system requires an assessment of the short-range and long-range risk of future harm to others. Assessment for likelihood of future harm is described in the next section as a separate type of evaluation. However, these assessments have always been a part of disposition evaluations as well.

ASSESSMENTS FOR VIOLENCE RISK

Substantial advances have been made in recent years in the assessment of the risk of future violence among adults (see the chapter by Monahan in this volume). The assessment of risk of violence in youths has borrowed from that research certain general principles, which are described below. Research on methods for risk assessment with youths lags behind the adult research in identification of specific risk factors and the development of assessment instruments. As noted below, however, the field shows promise for meeting those needs in the near future.

Clinicians are asked to evaluate youths' risk of future violent behavior at a number of points in the adjudicative process in delinquency cases:

- Determining the need for secure pretrial detention.
- Addressing the "public safety" standard in juvenile court hearings on waiver of a juvenile to criminal court for trial.
- For youths adjudicated delinquent, to assist the court in determining degree of security needed during rehabilitation.
- After a period of commitment to a secure rehabilitation program, assessing whether rehabilitative efforts have resulted in reduced risk of future harm (allowing transitional placement in a less secure program).
- Assessing the need for extended juvenile court custody in states that allow such extension beyond the usual age jurisdiction for juvenile court.

The scope and method of risk assessments will differ somewhat for these various purposes, but most of the points raised below are applicable across these various types of risk assessments.

Some Fundamentals

From research on adult violence risk assessment, we have learned a number of lessons that can be applied to risk assessment with adolescents. These fundamentals are now widely recognized among forensic psychologists who perform violence risk assessments (e.g., Borum, Swartz, & Swenson, 1996; Grisso, 1998a; Monahan, 1981; Otto, 1992).

Use Risk Factors

Clinicians should bring to the task a set of factors or variables that, based on research evidence, have known relations to future violence. Research has identified such factors for use with adolescents (e.g., see Loeber & Farrington, 1998). None of these risk factors is highly correlated with future violence, but their modest empirical relations to violence provide a reasonable, logical foundation for any risk assessment. Those factors are reviewed later in this section.

Make Risk Estimates, Not Predictions

When clinicians treat risk assessment as a dichotomous question (that is, whether the individual "will or won't" engage in a violent behavior in the future), their predictions that a person will engage in a violent behavior are more often wrong than right (Monahan, 1981). Violence in most populations is a low-base-rate behavior, raising the rate of false-positive predictions. Clinicians, therefore, are urged to see their task as estimating the relative likelihood of future violence (e.g., a statistical probability estimate, or a designation of "less likely, as likely, or more likely" than others in a specific population).

Use Actuarial Methods and Base Rates

Clinicians are encouraged to use any valid methods that research provides for combining risk factors to arrive at probability estimates of future violence. Unfortunately, no such methods currently exist for use with adolescents in delinquency cases. This is an area that is in need of research, and, as noted later, current efforts in that direction are underway. When validated actuarial tools for this task are available, they will be the preferred method for performing adolescent violence risk assessments.

Recognize Social Context

Acts of violence are only partly a function of personal characteristics. They are also a function of situations and social contexts that increase or decrease the likelihood of an aggressive reaction. A youth with aggressive tendencies may be more likely to be violent in one context than in another (e.g., when not under supervision versus when in custody in a structured delinquency program). Clinicians should recognize, assess, and consider those social situations in which the youth is likely to be functioning in the future. Moreover, risk estimates should be conditional, based on reference to a specific context.

Recognize Difficulties in Long-Range Estimates

Sometimes, clinicians are asked to make estimates of the likelihood that a youth will engage in violent behavior several years in the future, or when the youth becomes an adult. The process of ongoing development in adolescence suggests that a youth's present behavior, though important to consider, is less likely than an adult's to be a good indicator of future behavior when the future in question is more extended. Moreover, it is well documented that most youths who engage in violent behavior as adolescents do not continue to engage in violent behavior as adults (e.g., Elliott et al., 1983; Gottfredson & Hirschi, 1990).

Risk Factors

The following factors have been identified as empirically related to future violence in youths, although none of them is highly predictive. Borum (2000) and Grisso (1998a) have provided commentary on their application in assessment cases, and the following comments on each factor are consistent with those recommendations.

- *Past Violent Behavior.* Clinicians should examine the nature and history of youths' past violence. Typically, the mere fact that the youth is charged with a violent offense is less critical for estimates of future violence than whether the youth's first harmfully aggressive behaviors began to emerge in preadolescence or in adolescence. Earlier onset is more suggestive of continued aggression beyond adolescence (e.g., Elliott, 1994; Moffitt, 1993).
- *School Problems.* Truancy, dropout, and other signs of poor attachment to school are related to increased risk of future violence (Lipsey & Derzon, 1998). This factor is more critical when incidents of school problems began earlier in a youth's school history.
- *Substance Abuse.* Alcohol and drug use increases the risk of violence both directly (as a condition during which violence may occur) and indirectly (as an activity that frequently brings youths into social situations that encourage aggressive behaviors).
- *Personality Traits.* Personality characteristics such as anger, impulsiveness, and lack of empathy have been related to youth violence. Research currently underway examines the construct of psychopathy as a personality type in adolescence (e.g., Frick, Bodin, & Barry, 2000) and as a factor in risk assessment (as discussed later in this chapter).
- *Mental Disorder.* Although not highly predictive, mood disorders, posttraumatic stress disorder, and attention-deficit/hyperactivity disorder contribute to the risk of harmful aggression.
- *Family Conflict.* The modeling of aggression by parents, as well as youths' experience as victims of family abuse and neglect (Widom, 1989; Widom & Maxfield, 1996), have been shown to be related to an increase in risk of harm to others.

- *Peers.* Social interaction with peer groups that have patterns of aggression increases the risk of violent behavior, as well as proximity to neighborhoods in which the base rate of violence is high.

- *Opportunity.* Risk assessments should attend to external factors that may increase the likelihood that violent acts may occur among youths who are high in other risk factors (e.g., the availability of weapons, the accessibility of a specific person with whom a youth may be in conflict).

Methods and Instruments

There is a significant need for systematic methods that would allow clinicians to collect reliable information on these factors for a given youth and to refer to research-based rates of violence for youths who were known to have this same combination of factors. Such instruments have been developed for use with adults (e.g., Quinsey, Harris, Rice, & Cormier, 1998), but they have not yet been developed for adolescents. Actuarial methods of that type are in progress, including the Early Assessment Risk List for Boys (Augimeri, Webster, Koegl, & Levene, 1998) and the Structured Assessment of Violence Risk in Youth (Bartel, Borum, & Forth, 1999). Before these instruments can be used clinically, however, it is necessary to complete substantial research to validate and cross-validate their use in delinquent samples, with adequate attention to their use with both boys and girls and with ethnic minority youths.

Risk of Sex Reoffending

The development of assessment methods in this area has focused primarily on identifying types of juvenile sex offenders, discovering their special characteristics to improve treatment efforts, assessing treatment progress, and evaluating risk of future sex reoffending when discharge from treatment programs is being considered. Assessment in this area can employ some of the general risk assessment factors discussed earlier, but it also requires additional factors as well as special attention to specific diagnostic features of youthful sex offenders (American Academy of Child and Adolescent Psychiatry, 1999).

Considerable progress has been made in recent years in providing examiners with structured methods for classification of juvenile sex offenders and identifying important factors for guiding their treatment (e.g., American Academy of Child and Adolescent Psychiatry, 1999; Barbaree, Marshall, & Hudson, 1993; Perry & Orchard, 1992). Several methods also have been made available for risk assessment and treatment

planning for youthful sex offenders. Although these methods have not yet demonstrated adequate validity, some methods now in development have reported more promising results (e.g., Knight & Cerce, 1999; Knight, Prentky, & Cerce, 1994; Prentky, Harris, Frizzell, & Righthand, 2000).

ASSESSMENTS FOR PSYCHOLEGAL CONCEPTS IN DELINQUENCY CASES

In contrast to dispositional and violence risk evaluations, some assessments in delinquency cases call for examiners to provide information that assists the courts in addressing youths' capacities in relation to specific legal criteria. One of these evaluations addresses criteria for waiver of juvenile court jurisdiction, allowing youths to be tried in criminal court. Clinicians have provided waiver evaluations for juvenile courts for many decades. Other types of evaluations addressing specific legal criteria have a shorter history because, as noted earlier, they have arisen as a consequence of relatively recent changes in juvenile law. Among these are assessments of youths' capacities as trial defendants (i.e., their competence to stand trial) and evaluations for youths' capacities to waive *Miranda* rights.

Some Fundamentals

The field of forensic psychological assessment has developed a consensus about some fundamental principles when performing evaluations to address legal standards related to capacities and characteristics of individuals before the courts. Elaboration on these principles can be found in Grisso (1986, 1988, 1998a), Melton et al. (1997), and a number of texts that describe basic standards for forensic evaluations (e.g., Heilbrun, 2001; Schwartz & Rosado, 2000).

Clinicians who assist courts in addressing a person's capacities in relation to a legal standard should at least engage in the following procedures:

- Know the legal standard and how it has been used in law, and translate it into psychological or psychiatric constructs that bear a conceptual relation to the legal standard as it has been applied by courts.

- Perform evaluations using methods that collect information relevant to the psychological constructs derived from the preceding translation.

- Interpret and communicate the evaluation's results in a way that assists the court in understanding their relevance for the legal standard that guides the court's decision.

Waiver to Criminal Court

The Legal Standard

All states provide legal mechanisms whereby a youth who is charged with an offense may be waived (in some states, "transferred" or "certified") to stand trial in criminal court as an adult (Snyder & Sickmund, 1999). In recent years, many states have put in place laws that require that cases involving youths of certain ages and charged with specific offenses must "automatically" be filed in criminal court. Almost all states, however, have retained laws and procedures that allow juvenile court judges the discretion to waive jurisdiction for other juveniles, following a "waiver hearing" to determine whether the evidence meets the legal criteria. These criteria vary somewhat from state to state, but typically, they include a finding that the youth presents a significant risk of harm to others (a "public safety" standard) and that the youth is very unlikely to be rehabilitated if retained in the juvenile justice system (an "unamenable to rehabilitation" standard). Clinicians sometimes are asked to evaluate youths prior to waiver hearings to provide information about risk of harm and likelihood of rehabilitation.

The historical vagueness of legal standards for waiver has made it difficult for clinicians to translate the legal standards into psychological constructs for assessment purposes. Criteria offered by the U.S. Supreme Court in *Kent v. U.S.* (1966) often have been used but are inadequate for this purpose. Several of *Kent's* eight criteria are not psychological at all (e.g., "seriousness of the offense"), others are psychological but nonspecific (e.g., "sophistication and maturity of the child"), and still others are so vague as to offer virtually no guidance (e.g., "previous history of the child").

Most states' "public safety" or "danger to others" criteria are similarly vague. This at least allows clinicians to employ factors that have known empirical relations to future violence among youths, as previously discussed, but usually, the standards do not describe the context in which estimates of risk for violence are to be made. For example, does the court wish to know whether the youth, if retained in the juvenile justice system, would be a significant risk *while being treated,* or is the question the risk of violence *in adulthood after the youth has been treated?* Standards usually are silent on such matters, although attorneys and judges sometimes can offer guidance regarding local interpretations.

Likewise, states' definitions of "unamenable to rehabilitation" often are nonspecific. Most, however, do not consider merely whether the youth's condition is modifiable *in general:* They ask whether it is reasonable to expect *the state's rehabilitation programs* for delinquent youths to be able to bring about necessary change with *this particular youth.* In other words, the question of amenability to rehabilitation requires addressing the match of the youth to rehabilitation options, and the likelihood of reduced recidivism under the "best fit" of these possible matches. Moreover, courts typically require an estimation of the time that may be needed to achieve the desired low level of recidivism risk, because the juvenile justice system in most states must release a youth at an age specified by law as the extent of the juvenile court's age jurisdiction.

Assessment Concepts and Methods

The two criteria that guide waiver decisions allow evaluations to be based substantially on methods that were discussed earlier in this chapter for dispositional evaluations (pertaining to rehabilitation potentials and recommendations) and in another section for evaluating risk of future harm to others. Evaluations for waiver cases, however, have many features that require more than simply combining a "risk assessment" with a "rehabilitation assessment" in one package. For example, they require more specific attention than do either of these two evaluations alone to such matters as the youth's potential responsiveness to intervention, the real or questionable significance of past unsuccessful interventions with the youth, and the estimated time that will be required for rehabilitation.

Systematic guidance for dealing with these special issues, and for integrating information from risk and rehabilitation data to satisfy the requirements of waiver questions, has only recently begun to appear (Grisso, 1998a, 2000). Thus, there is no consensus regarding the manner in which waiver evaluations should be performed. The field is producing information that someday may offer more confident guidance for waiver evaluations. For example, recent reviews of evaluation research have provided helpful information on the relative effectiveness of various types of rehabilitation interventions for delinquent youths (e.g., Kendall & Braswell, 1993; Lipsey & Wilson, 1998; Mulvey, Arthur, & Reppucci, 1993; Schoenwald, Scherer, & Brondino, 1997). But considerably more research is needed before clinicians can speak with confidence about the potential results of these interventions with youths having specific clinical and offense characteristics.

Adjudicative Competence (Competence to Stand Trial)

As noted earlier, the issue of competence to stand trial has virtually no tradition or history in the juvenile justice system. It was first raised with any frequency little more than a decade ago, in response to changes in juvenile law that increased the penalties associated with delinquency adjudication, and therefore increased the need for attention to due process requirements more like those provided to adults in criminal court. Clinicians who perform evaluations in delinquency cases increasingly are being asked to evaluate youths' capacities as trial defendants in juvenile court proceedings, and this demand is expected to continue. (See the chapter by Stafford for a discussion of trial competence of adults.)

The Legal Standard

During the past 15 years, over half of the states came to recognize the right of juveniles to be competent to stand trial in delinquency cases in juvenile court. In many states, this has been established by new statutes (Bonnie & Grisso, 2000); in others, it has been recognized as a consequence of litigation (e.g., *In the Interest of S.H.*, 1996). Often, these new laws have not specifically stated the standard for competence to be applied in juvenile court. But in all cases in which the issue has been raised, courts have applied to juvenile cases the modern standard for competence to stand trial as formulated in *Dusky v. U.S.* (1960) for criminal cases referring to comprehension of the trial and the ability to assist counsel.

Three other matters of definition for competence in juvenile court are far less certain (Bonnie & Grisso, 2000). First, most states' laws are unclear as to whether the *degree* of ability that is required within this definition is the same for participating in juvenile proceedings as for participating in criminal proceedings. Second, whereas incompetence to stand trial typically is related to mental disorder or mental retardation in criminal cases, some youths may lack the abilities identified in the *Dusky* standard not because of disorder or disability, but due to immaturity. Only a few states explicitly recognize the possibility of incompetence due to immature abilities; most are silent on this matter. Third, the disposition of juveniles found incompetent is still a matter of uncertainty in many states. In adult cases, persons found incompetent are provided appropriate treatment for the mental disorder or developmental disability that is responsible for their functional deficits associated with incompetence. Although many states presume that this applies to juveniles as well, it does not provide a remedy for youths whose deficits are simply a result of their immaturity.

Assessment Concepts

Only recently have clinicians been provided guidance for conceptualizing and performing evaluations of juveniles'

competence to stand trial (Barnum, 2000; Grisso, 1997, 1998a, 2000; Grisso, Miller, & Sales, 1987; Schwartz & Rosado, 2000). These efforts borrow on established concepts in adult competence evaluations, but they leave unanswered a host of questions raised by the developmental status of adolescents and its potential relation to youths' functional abilities as trial defendants.

Concerning the *functional* component of competence to stand trial, several decades of legal and clinical forensic analysis have established a consensus regarding the functional abilities to which the *Dusky* standard refers. These are outlined elsewhere in this volume. These functional abilities should apply to juvenile proceedings as well as adult criminal proceedings with only a few minor exceptions (e.g., knowledge of the jury process is irrelevant in most states in that they do not provide for jury trials in juvenile court proceedings). Some of the more important functional abilities include (a) understanding of the charges and possible consequences of the trial; (b) understanding and appreciation of the role of participants in the trial; and (c) the ability to make decisions about the exercise or waiver of important rights, such as may occur when one waives the right to a trial by pleading guilty or waives the right to be represented by legal counsel.

Concerning the *causal* component of competence to stand trial, it is presumed that deficits in these abilities due to mental disorder or mental retardation are as applicable in juvenile cases as in criminal cases. However, as noted earlier, in many states, it is not clear whether youths may be found incompetent when their deficits in relevant functional abilities are due merely to immaturity.

A number of recent reviews have used developmental psychological theory and research to identify children's and adolescents' cognitive and emotional capacities potentially associated with their adjudicative competence (Abramovitch, Peterson-Badali, & Rohan, 1995; Grisso, 1997, 1998a, 2000; Scott, Reppucci, & Woolard, 1995; Steinberg & Cauffman, 1996). Typically, they suggest that children younger than the teen years are not expected to match the knowledge and capacities of adults for grasping the trial process. Reviews suggest that "average" adolescents may have adultlike abilities for basic understanding of trials, but that adolescents with mental disorders and developmental delays (especially common in delinquent populations) may have poorer capacities for understanding their legal circumstances than do adults with similar disabilities.

Moreover, even "average" adolescents may not yet have achieved their own potential (i.e., the capacities they will have when they reach adulthood) for making critical decisions about the exercise of rights in the trial process. Decision making is significantly influenced by a number of factors for which there is evidence of normative differences between adolescents and adults: for example, in risk-benefit analyses (Benthin, Slovic, & Severson, 1993; Furby & Beyth-Marom, 1992; Mann, Harmoni, & Power, 1989; Peterson-Badali, Abramovitch, & Duda, 1997), in time perspective and future orientation (Greene, 1986; Nurmi, 1991), and in risk-taking tendencies (Arnett, 1992).

These opinions about youths' capacities as trial defendants, however, have been based primarily on theoretical analyses rather than on empirical research specific to their legally relevant functional abilities. Thus, greater certainty about the nature and scope of youths' trial-related deficits as a result of immaturity awaits additional empirical information from future research on the question.

Concerning the *interactive* component of competence to stand trial, one might suppose that the demands on youths for participation in their trials would be less than for adults, in that they have the benefit of parents who may assist them in understanding the proceedings and making important decisions. Some observations, however, suggest that too often, parents are not able to provide such assistance (Tobey, Grisso, & Schwartz, 2000). Attorneys can sometimes improve their young clients' understanding or decision making, but commentators typically have expressed misgivings about their ability to do so routinely (e.g., American Bar Association Juvenile Justice Center, 1995; Buss, 1996).

Assessment Methods

Guidelines for evaluating youths' competence to stand trial (e.g., Barnum, 2000; Grisso, 1998a) generally have recommended procedures and methods that are patterned after those employed with adults (see the chapter by Stafford; Grisso, 1988; Melton et al., 1997). They recommend a clinical and developmental assessment, intelligence testing when necessary, the collection of relevant historical information (e.g., academic records), and a direct assessment of the youth's current functional abilities associated with the competence standard. A number of structured tests and interview procedures have been developed for assessing the relevant functional abilities in adult criminal cases (for a review, see Grisso, 1986; more recently, the MacArthur Competence Assessment Tool for Criminal Adjudication: Poythress et al., 1999). Although some of the instruments may have potential for application in delinquency cases, and a few research reports have used structured competence assessment tools in small samples of youths (Cooper, 1997; Savistsky & Karras, 1984), to date, there is no body

of research providing adequate normative data for adolescents on these instruments.

Youths' Capacities to Waive *Miranda* Rights

The issue of youths' capacities to waive *Miranda* rights became an issue during the decade following *In re Gault* (1967), in which the U.S. Supreme Court ruled that youths in delinquency cases had many of the same rights as adults facing criminal charges. Among these were the constitutional rights to avoid self-incrimination and to have counsel present at the time of any police interrogation. The 1970s saw an increase in appellate cases that addressed whether juveniles in delinquency investigations were capable of waiving these rights when they were informed of them by police, and therefore whether their confessions were obtained in a manner that would allow them to be admitted as evidence against them (Feld, 2000). Eventually, clinicians began receiving requests for evaluations of youths' cognitive and emotional capacities to have understood and waived their rights prior to the confessions they gave to police officers. Requests increased in the 1990s, as new juvenile laws lowered the ages at which youths could be waived to criminal court (where their confessions would have considerably greater consequences).

The Legal Standard

Any confessions used against criminal or delinquency defendants must be preceded by warnings to them regarding their constitutional rights to legal counsel and to avoid self-incrimination, as required by *Miranda v. Arizona* (1966). For their confessions to be admissible as evidence, their waiver of the rights must be made "voluntarily, knowingly and intelligently" (*Fare v. Michael C.*, 1979). Whether this standard is met in a particular case is dependent on the court's weighing of the "totality of circumstances" (*People v. Lara*, 1967; *Fare v. Michael C.*, 1979).

The U.S. Supreme Court's decision in *Colorado v. Connelly* (1986) indicated that confessions typically will be seen as *voluntary* as long as they are not the product of obvious police coercion. Courts have not settled the application of this standard to youths, although U.S. Supreme Court commentary in *In re Gault* (1966) and *Fare v. Michael C.* (1979) appears to acknowledge that greater protection from coercion may be necessary for youths than for adults because of their psychological immaturity. Some states require that parents be present to advise youths regarding their decision to waive the rights (Grisso, 1981), but parents themselves may not waive their child's constitutional rights in police investigations that may lead to delinquency charges.

Assessment Concepts

Concerning the *functional* component of the question of valid waiver of rights, the *Miranda* warnings themselves define the specific information that youths must be able to understand, but they do not define all of the information that is relevant. For example, a youth may understand that he or she can have an attorney present at the interrogation (as stated in the third *Miranda* warning). But the youth is unprepared to use this information if he or she does not understand that an attorney is an advocate who works on his or her behalf (which is not explained in the *Miranda* warnings). Grisso (1981, 1998a) has outlined the additional types of knowledge that youths should have, beyond "understanding" of the *Miranda* warnings themselves, to ensure that they "appreciate" the significance of the warnings.

Concerning the *causal* component, possible explanations for youths' deficits in understanding and appreciation of the *Miranda* warnings might include any of the clinical and psychological reasons that one might imagine for impairment or immaturity in intellectual functioning, attention, memory, and other cognitive functions. They might also include simple lack of knowledge or, at the time of the evaluation, the possibility of feigning an inability to understand the *Miranda* warnings.

In a substantial research project, Grisso (1980, 1981) examined the capacities of youths to understand and appreciate *Miranda* warnings, using objective assessment methods with large samples of youths (in pretrial detention) and adults (in the criminal justice system). Age and intelligence were the most significant correlates of performance on the measures of understanding and appreciation of *Miranda* rights. Youths below age 14 generally had significantly poorer performance than did adults, and midadolescents with low intelligence performed significantly more poorly than most adults, even those with similarly low intelligence. Contrary to common judicial presumptions, youths with more prior experience with the justice system did *not* perform better than youths with less prior involvement with attorneys and courts.

Concerning the *interactive* component, opinions about a youth's capacities to have waived *Miranda* rights at the time of interrogation typically require not only consideration of the youth's capacities, but also the circumstances of the interrogation itself. For example, a youth with marginal capacities for understanding the warnings at the time of an evaluation may have been far less able to comprehend them

at the time of police questioning, depending on how the *Miranda* warnings were given (e.g., in a cursory fashion, or if a youth with serious reading deficits was expected to read them). Examples of other interrogation circumstances (Grisso, 1998a) that might be relevant because they could influence the youth's capacities to attend to, understand, and appreciate the significance of the *Miranda* warnings include, for example:

- The length of time the youth was held in isolation prior to questioning.
- Physical conditions of the holding cell.
- Whether the youth was provided food and other necessities.
- Whether parents were present and were capable of offering advice.

Assessment Methods

Current guidelines (Grisso, 1998a; Schwartz & Rosado, 2000) suggest that evaluations for juveniles' capacities relevant for questions of valid waiver of *Miranda* rights should involve extensive investigation of the circumstances of the police questioning, including information from police records, from the youth, and from the youth's parents (even if they were not present, because they often can provide information about the youth's psychological condition during the days preceding the arrest). Clinical and developmental assessment is needed to describe the youth's psychological and mental health status in relation to the causal component of the evaluation. Psychological testing, especially intelligence testing, will usually be used to assist in this description.

The functional component requires a direct assessment of the youth's ability to understand the *Miranda* warnings and their significance. This will not necessarily describe what the youth knew or was able to understand at the time of police questioning, but knowing the youth's current ability to understand the warnings is a prerequisite to making such inferences. This part of the assessment can be done by interview. However, specialized tools for this purpose (Grisso, 1998b) allow for objective scoring and comparison of the youth's scores to those of a large sample of youths and adults.

Of concern in this area of assessment is its current reliance on one substantial research project (Grisso, 1981, 1998a) for its methods and normative data. Further research is needed to replicate its findings, provide greater evidence for validity of the measures that it produced, and develop more sophisticated methods for integrating assessment data to address the complex retrospective question of youths' capacities to have provided valid waiver of *Miranda* rights.

FUTURE ADVANCES IN FORENSIC ASSESSMENTS IN DELINQUENCY CASES

As the twentieth century drew to a close, there was evidence that this field would be seeing significant research in several areas that could have an impact on the quality of forensic assessments in delinquency cases. Four of those areas are briefly reviewed here, representing one topic from each of the preceding sections of this chapter: (a) mental health needs of delinquent youth; (b) adolescent psychopathy, related to risk assessment; (c) adolescents' adjudicative competence; and (d) systems issues in evaluation services to juvenile courts.

Identifying Mental Health Needs of Youths in the Juvenile Justice System

The 1990s was a "get tough" era in juvenile justice law and policy. As noted earlier, many states changed their laws to identify public safety, accountability, and punishment, not the best interests of youth, as the primary objectives of their juvenile justice systems. Dramatic and extreme swings in social policy, however, often produce a reaction. As the 1990s closed, there was significant evidence for a counteraction among juvenile advocates who sought to moderate the juvenile justice system's new, punitive objectives. This took the form of increased concern about the mental health needs of youths in the juvenile justice system.

This concern was fueled by preliminary evidence from research studies (e.g., Otto et al., 1992; Teplin et al., 1998) that the prevalence of mental disorders among youths entering the juvenile justice system was very high (compared to the general population) and that it was rising. The cause of this increase has been unclear, but it may have been influenced by (a) increased trauma in high-crime neighborhoods during the wave of juvenile violence in the early 1990s; (b) new juvenile laws that inhibited discretionary diversion of mentally disordered youths from the courts to mental health services; and/or, (c) in many communities, a deterioration of inpatient and community mental health services for youths during the 1990s.

As the century came to a close, federal agencies (e.g., Office of Juvenile Justice and Delinquency Prevention) and private foundations (e.g., the John D. and Catherine T. MacArthur Foundation) began to fund a number of new initiatives that were intended to address this issue. Chief among their objectives were:

- Better estimates of the degree and types of mental health and substance abuse needs of youths in pretrial detention and posttrial custody.

- The development of more valid and reliable methods for screening and thus identifying youths with these special needs.
- Improving mechanisms for responding to those needs with effective intervention.

Clinicians may expect a significant increase in information in these areas over the next decade, as well as the appearance of new screening and assessment methods for use specifically in delinquent populations for identifying their mental health and substance abuse needs.

Child and Adolescent Psychopathy

The 1990s produced a small explosion of research reports on theories, measurements, and empirical evidence for psychopathy in children and adolescents. Considerably more research on this topic will appear in the next decade. Clinicians who perform evaluations in delinquency cases must be prepared to review and respond to it because it will have significant implications for assessments of risk of violence as well as questions of amenability to rehabilitation.

Psychopathy as a personality type was proposed by Cleckley (1976) and then operationalized and studied extensively in the 1980s and 1990s by Hare and a number of his colleagues (Hart & Hare, 1997 for a review; also see the chapter by Hemphill & Hart). Psychopathy is a particularly important personality construct in forensic psychology. Adults who possess its two main sets of characteristics—a cluster of "antisocial" markers together with a second cluster of "callous/unemotional" traits that distinguish the psychopathic individual from other antisocial types—make up only a minority of adult criminals. However, psychopathic individuals tend to be the more frequently violent and more persistent offenders in society and are also the least amenable to interventions intended to reduce recidivism. As measured by the Psychopathy Checklist–Revised (Hare, 1991), psychopathy has been shown to be one of the most important and reliable factors in identifying adults at high risk of violent behavior.

It is no surprise, therefore, that the concept eventually began to be studied in children and adolescents by researchers seeking possibilities for early identification of individuals at high risk for developing psychopathy. The search was fueled by parallel findings in criminology and clinical developmental psychology in the 1980s. For example, evidence was mounting that a relatively small percentage of youths who have delinquent histories in adolescence continue their offending in adulthood, and that those who persisted began their offending prior to adolescence (e.g., Elliott, 1994; Elliott,

Huizinga, & Morse, 1986; Moffitt, 1993). Might these youths become tomorrow's psychopathic adults? And can they be identified sufficiently early to alter the course of their personality development?

Research on this question in the 1990s was stimulated by the development of several research measures for identifying psychopathic-like characteristics among children and adolescents: the Psychopathy Checklist: Youth Version (Forth, Kosson, & Hare, 1997), the Psychopathy Screening Devise (Frick et al., 2000; Frick, O'Brien, Wootton, & McBurnett, 1994), and the Childhood Psychopathy Scale (Lynam, 1997, 1998). Theories were developed regarding the potential relation of psychopathy to childhood disorders such as ADHD and conduct disorder (e.g., Frick, 1998a, 1998b; Lynam, 1996), and research evidence testing these theories began to accumulate.

This area of research shows promise but must develop much further before it provides a resource for forensic examiners in delinquency cases. Currently, researchers are working to resolve a number of methodological problems, such as difficulties in examining the relation between psychopathic characteristics and diagnostic conditions (e.g., conduct disorder) when measures of the two constructs have similar item content (Burns, 2000; Frick, Bodin, & Barry, 2000). Other issues pertain to potential problems in the application of an "adult" personality construct to youths who are still undergoing developmental change (Seagrave & Grisso, in press). For example, some behavioral characteristics that define psychopathy—such as risk taking, impulsiveness, and self-centeredness—bear a similarity to many "normal" though developmentally transient behavior tendencies among adolescents. Before knowing the meaning of adolescents' scores on psychopathy scales, we need evidence from longitudinal studies that those scores are indeed related to enduring psychopathic traits in adulthood. If the evidence is positive, clinicians may find a number of uses for measures of psychopathy in delinquency cases (e.g., violence risk assessment, or identification of youths who may be less amenable to rehabilitation in the juvenile justice system).

Adjudicative Competence

Late in the 1990s, researchers at several centers in the United States were at work on substantial projects to increase our knowledge of youths' capacities associated with competence to stand trial. The most ambitious of these projects began with a volume of conceptual papers, commissioned by the John D. and Catherine T. MacArthur Foundation, that provided the groundwork for future work in this area (Grisso & Schwartz, 2000). That initiative is continuing with a study currently being performed by the MacArthur Research Network on Adolescent Development and Juvenile Justice. The study compares 1,000 youths and 500 adults on measures of abilities related to adjudicative competence, especially their decision-making capacities in legal contexts. The project will provide information for both policy and practice, including specialized measures and norms that will be useful in clinical forensic evaluations of youths' competence to stand trial.

Systemic Issues Influencing Forensic Evaluations in Delinquency Cases

As noted earlier, there has been an absence of organizational support for clinicians who perform forensic evaluations in delinquency cases and a lack of information on models for the delivery of those services. This contrasts with the fact that in the past decade, clinical and forensic services for youths in the juvenile justice system have suddenly become the focus of public attention, new governmental initiatives, and professional interest within forensic psychology.

The quality of forensic evaluations depends on many factors, including a theoretical and research foundation, the development of appropriate assessment methods, and adequate professional training. But ultimately, the quality of forensic evaluations cannot rise higher than the organizational systems in which they are performed. Currently, we have almost no meaningful knowledge of the organizational structure of juvenile courts' forensic evaluation services. We know that many juvenile courts have court clinics, but we do not know specifically where they are, how they are organized and financed, how they are staffed, what they do, and how well they function. We have no models for forensic evaluation services in juvenile courts, no established standards for their delivery in delinquency cases, and no criteria for professional competence to perform these evaluations. In short, we have virtually no systematic knowledge about the actual delivery of forensic evaluations in delinquency cases in the United States.

Research is advancing at a rapid pace toward improving the conceptual and methodological foundation for practice in this area. But it will be of little value if we do not pay adequate attention to the study of the organizational systems in which our juvenile forensic evaluations are performed. In contrast to the other three areas of research reviewed above, there is, as yet, no research on the horizon to fill this need. Thus, to improve forensic evaluations in delinquency cases, the most urgent call for research might be made not to clinicians and the developers of assessment methods, but to researchers who identify current methods for the delivery of mental health services, evaluate their effectiveness, and study the evolution of accepted standards of practice.

REFERENCES

Abramovitch, R., Peterson-Badali, M., & Rohan, M. (1995). Young people's understanding and assertion of their rights to silence and legal counsel. *Canadian Journal of Criminology, 37,* 1–18.

Achenbach, T. (1991). *Manual for the Child Behavior Checklist/4–18 and 1991 profile.* Burlington: University of Vermont, Department of Psychiatry.

Addams, J. (1935). *My friend Julia Lathrop.* New York: Macmillan.

American Academy of Child and Adolescent Psychiatry. (1999). Practice parameters for the assessment and treatment of children and adolescents who are sexually abusive of others. *Journal of the American Academy of Child and Adolescent Psychiatry, 38,* 55–76.

American Bar Association Juvenile Justice Center. (1995). *A call for justice: An assessment of access to counsel and quality of representation in delinquency proceedings.* Washington, DC: Office of Juvenile Justice and Delinquency Prevention.

American Psychiatric Association. (1994). *Diagnostic and statistical manual of mental disorders* (4th edition). Washington, DC: American Psychiatric Association.

American Psychological Association. (1994). Guidelines for child custody evaluations in divorce proceedings. *American Psychologist, 49,* 677–680.

Arnett, J. (1992). Reckless behavior in adolescence: A developmental perspective. *Developmental Review, 12,* 339–373.

Augemeri, L., Webster, C., Koegl, C., & Levene, K. (1998). *Assessment Risk List for Boys: EARL-20B, Version 1: Consultation edition.* Toronto, Ontario, Canada: Earlscourt Child and Family Centre.

Barbaree, H., Marshall, W., & Hudson, S. (Eds.). (1993). *The juvenile sex offender.* New York: Guilford Press.

Barkley, R. (1990). *Attention-deficit hyperactivity disorder: A handbook for diagnosis and treatment.* New York: Guilford Press.

Barnum, R. (2000). Clinical and forensic evaluation of competence to stand trial in juvenile defendants. In T. Grisso & R. Schwartz (Eds.), *Youth on trial: A developmental perspective on juvenile justice* (pp. 193–224). Chicago: University of Chicago Press.

Bartel, P., Borum, R., & Forth, A. (1999). *Structured Assessment for Violence Risk in Youth (SAVRY): Consultation edition.* Author.

Benthin, A., Slovic, P., & Severson, H. (1993). A psychometric study of adolescent risk perception. *Journal of Adolescence, 16,* 153–168.

Bonnie, R., & Grisso, T. (2000). Adjudicative competence and youthful offenders. In T. Grisso & R. Schwartz (Eds.), *Youth on trial: A developmental perspective on juvenile justice* (pp. 73–104). Chicago: University of Chicago Press.

Borum, R. (2000). Assessing violence risk among youth. *Journal of Clinical Psychology, 56,* 1263–1288.

Borum, R., Swartz, M., & Swanson, J. (1996). Assessing and managing violence risk in clinical practice. *Journal of Practice in Psychiatry and Behavioral Health, 4,* 205–215.

Burns, G. (2000). Problem of item overlap between the psychopathy screening device and attention deficit hyperactivity disorder, oppositional defiant disorder, and conduct disorder rating scales. *Psychological Assessment, 12,* 447–450.

Buss, E. (1996). You're my what? The problem of children's misperceptions of their lawyers' roles. *Fordham Law Review, 64,* 1699–1762.

Butcher, J., Williams, C., Graham, J., Archer, R., Tellegen, R., Ben-Porath, Y., et al. (1992). *MMPI-A: Manual for administration scoring and interpretation.* Minneapolis: University of Minnesota Press.

Cicourel, A. (1968). *The social organization of juvenile justice.* New York: Wiley.

Cleckley, H. (1976). *The mask of sanity* (5th ed.). St. Louis, MO: Mosby.

Colorado v. Connelly, 479 U.S. 157 (1986).

Committee on Ethical Guidelines for Forensic Psychologists. (1991). Specialty guidelines for forensic psychologists. *Law and Human Behavior, 15,* 655–665.

Community Research Associates. (1997). *Disproportionate confinement of minority juveniles in secure facilities: 1996 national report.* Washington, DC: Office of Juvenile Justice and Delinquency Prevention.

Cooper, D. (1997). Juveniles' understanding of trial-related information: Are they competent defendants? *Behavioral Sciences and the Law, 15,* 167–180.

Dusky v. United States, 362 U.S. 402, 80 S. Ct. 788 (1960).

Elliott, D. (1994). Serious violent offenders: Onset, developmental course, and termination: American Society of Criminology presidential address. *Criminology, 32,* 1–21.

Elliott, D., Ageton, S., Huizinga, D., Knowles, D., & Canter, R. (1983). *The prevalence and incidence of delinquent behavior: 1976–1980* (The National Youth Survey Report No. 26). Boulder, CO: Behavioral Research Institute.

Elliott, D., Huizinga, D., & Morse, B. (1986). Self-reported violent offending: A descriptive analysis of juvenile violent offenders and their offending careers. *Journal of Interpersonal Violence, 1,* 472–514.

Fare v. Michael C., 442 U.S. 707 (1979).

Feld, B. (2000). Juveniles' waiver of legal rights: Confessions, *Miranda,* and the right to counsel. In T. Grisso & R. Schwartz (Eds.), *Youth on trial: A developmental perspective on juvenile justice* (pp. 105–138). Chicago: University of Chicago Press.

Forth, A., Kosson, D., & Hare, R. (1997). *The Psychopathy Checklist: Youth version.* Toronto, Ontario, Canada: Multi-Health Systems.

Frick, P. (1998a). Callous-unemotional traits and conduct problems: A two-factor model of psychopathy in children. In R. Hare, D. Cooke, & A. Forth (Eds.), *Psychopathy: Theory, research, and implications for society* (pp. 161–187). Dordrecht, the Netherlands: Kluwer Press.

Frick, P. (1998b). *Conduct disorders and severe antisocial behavior.* New York: Plenum Press.

Frick, P., Bodin, S., & Barry, C. (2000). Psychopathic traits and conduct problems in community and clinic-referred samples of children: Further development of the Psychopathy Screening Device. *Psychological Assessment, 12,* 382–393.

Frick, P., O'Brien, H., Wootton, J., & McBurnett, K. (1994). Psychopathy and conduct problems in children. *Journal of Abnormal Psychology, 103,* 700–707.

Furby, M., & Beyth-Marom, R. (1992). Risk-taking in adolescence: A decision-making perspective. *Developmental Review, 12,* 1–44.

Gottfredson, M., & Hirschi, T. (1990). *A general theory of crime.* Stanford, CA: Stanford University Press.

Greene, A. (1986). Future-time perspective in adolescence: The present of things future revisited. *Journal of Youth and Adolescence, 15,* 99–113.

Grisso, T. (1980). Juveniles' capacities to waive Miranda rights: An empirical analysis. *California Law Review, 68,* 1134–1166.

Grisso, T. (1981). *Juveniles' waiver of rights: Legal and psychological competence.* New York: Plenum Press.

Grisso, T. (1986). *Evaluating competencies: Forensic assessments and instruments.* New York: Plenum Press.

Grisso, T. (1988). *Competency to stand trial evaluations: A manual for practice.* Sarasota, FL: Professional Resource Press.

Grisso, T. (1991). A developmental history of the American Psychology-Law Society. *Law and Human Behavior, 15,* 213–231.

Grisso, T. (1996). Society's retributive response to juvenile violence: A developmental perspective. *Law and Human Behavior, 20,* 229–247.

Grisso, T. (1997). The competence of adolescents as trial defendants. *Psychology, Public Policy, and Law, 3,* 3–32.

Grisso, T. (1998a). *Forensic evaluation of juveniles.* Sarasota, FL: Professional Resource Press.

Grisso, T. (1998b). *Instruments for assessing understanding and appreciation of Miranda rights.* Sarasota, FL: Professional Resource Press.

Grisso, T. (2000). Forensic clinical evaluations related to waiver of jurisdiction. In J. Fagan & F. Zimring (Eds.), *The changing borders of juvenile justice: Transfer of adolescents to the criminal court* (pp. 321–352). Chicago: University of Chicago Press.

Grisso, T., & Barnum, R. (2000). *Massachusetts Youth Screening Instrument–Second version: Users manual and technical report.* Worcester, MA: University of Massachusetts Medical School, Law and Psychiatry Program.

Grisso, T., Barnum, R., Fletcher, K., Cauffman, E., & Peuschold, D. (2001). Massachusetts Youth Screening Instrument for mental health needs of juvenile justice youths. *Journal of the American Academy of Child and Adolescent Psychiatry, 40,* 541–548.

Grisso, T., Miller, M., & Sales, B. (1987). Competency to stand trial in juvenile court. *International Journal of Law and Psychiatry, 10,* 1–20.

Grisso, T., & Schwartz, R. (Eds.). (2000). *Youth on trial: A developmental perspective on juvenile justice.* Chicago: University of Chicago Press.

Hare, R. (1991). *The Hare Psychopathy Checklist–Revised manual.* Tonawanda, NY: Multi-Health Systems.

Hart, S., & Hare, R. (1997). Psychopathy: Assessment and association with criminal conduct. In D. Stoff, J. Breiling, & J. Maser (Eds.), *Handbook of antisocial behavior* (pp. 22–35). New York: Wiley.

Heilbrun, K. (2001). *Principles of forensic mental health assessment.* New York: Kluwer Academic/Plenum Publishers.

Hodges, K. (1995). *Child and Adolescent Functional Assessment Scale (CAFAS).* Ann Arbor, MI: Author.

Hoge, R., & Andrews, D. (1994). *The Youth Level of Service/Case Management Inventory and manual.* Ottawa, Ontario, Canada: Carleton University, Department of Psychology.

Hoge, R., & Andrews, D. (1996). *Assessing the youthful offender.* New York: Plenum Press.

Howell, J., Krisberg, B., Hawkins, J., & Wilson, J. (Eds.). (1995). *A sourcebook: Serious, violent, and chronic juvenile offenders.* Thousand Oaks, CA: Sage.

In re Gault, 387 U.S. 1 (1967).

In the Interest of S.H., 469 S.E.2d 810 (Ga. Ct. App., 1996).

Jackson, D. (1995). *The Basic Personality Inventory manual.* Port Huron, MI: Sigma Assessment Systems.

Jesness, C., & Wedge, R. (1985). *Jesness Inventory classification system: Supplementary manual.* Palo Alto, CA: Consulting Psychologists Press.

Kazdin, A. (2000). Adolescent development, mental disorders, and decision making of delinquent youths. In T. Grisso & R. Schwartz (Eds.), *Youth on trial: A developmental perspective on juvenile justice* (pp. 33–65). Chicago: University of Chicago Press.

Kendall, P., & Braswell, L. (1993). *Cognitive-behavioral therapy for impulsive children* (2nd ed.). New York: Guilford Press.

Kent v. United States, 383 U.S. 541 (1966).

Knight, R., & Cerce, D. (1999). Validation and revision of the multidimensional assessment of sex and aggression. *Psychologica Belgica, 39,* 135–161.

Knight, R., Prentky, R., & Cerce, D. (1994). The development, reliability, and validity of an inventory for the multidimensional assessment of sex and aggression. *Criminal Justice and Behavior, 21,* 72–94.

Lipsey, M., & Derzon, J. (1998). Predictors of violent or serious delinquency in adolescence and early adulthood: A synthesis of longitudinal research. In R. Loeber & D. Farrington (Eds.), *Serious and violent juvenile offenders: Risk factors and successful interventions* (pp. 86–105). Thousand Oaks, CA: Sage.

Lipsey, M., & Wilson, D. (1998). Effective intervention for serious juvenile offenders: A synthesis of research. In R. Loeber & D. Farrington (Eds.), *Serious and violent juvenile offenders: Risk factors and successful interventions* (pp. 313–345). Thousand Oaks, CA: Sage.

Loeber, R., & Farrington, D. (Eds.). (1998). *Serious and violent juvenile offenders: Risk factors and successful interventions.* Thousand Oaks, CA: Sage.

Lynam, D. (1996). Early identification of chronic offenders: Who is the fledgling psychopath? *Psychological Bulletin, 120,* 209–234.

Lynam, D. (1997). Pursuing the psychopath: Capturing the fledgling psychopath in a nomothetic net. *Journal of Abnormal Psychology, 106,* 425–438.

Lynam, D. (1998). Early identification of the fledgling psychopath: Locating the psychopathic child in the current nomenclature. *Journal of Abnormal Psychology, 107,* 566–575.

Mack, J. (1909). The juvenile court. *Harvard Law Review, 23,* 104–122. Academic Press.

Mann, L., Harmoni, R., & Power, C. (1989). Adolescent decision-making: The development of competence. *Journal of Adolescence, 12,* 265–278.

Mash, E., & Barkley, R. (1996). *Child psychopathology.* New York: Guilford Press.

McLellan, T., & Dembo, R. (1993). *Screening and assessment of alcohol and other drug abusing adolescents.* Rockville, MD: U.S. Department of Health and Human Services, Substance Abuse and Mental health Services Administration.

Melton, G., Petrila, J., Poythress, N., & Slobogin, C. (1986). *Psychological evaluations for the courts.* New York: Guilford Press.

Melton, G., Petrila, J., Poythress, N., & Slobogin, C. (1997). *Psychological evaluations for the courts* (2nd ed.). New York: Guilford Press.

Millon, T. (1993). *Millon Adolescent Clinical Inventory.* Minnesota, MN: National Computer Systems.

Miranda v. Arizona, 384 U.S. 436 (1966).

Moffitt, T. (1993). Adolescence-limited and life-course-persistent antisocial behavior: A developmental taxonomy. *Psychological Review, 100,* 674–701.

Monahan, J. (1981). *The clinical prediction of violent behavior.* Rockville, MD: National Institute of Mental Health.

Moos, R., & Moos, B. (1986). *The Family Environment Scale manual* (2nd ed.). Palo Alto, CA: Consulting Psychologists Press.

Mulvey, E., Arthur, M., & Reppucci, N. (1993). The prevention and treatment of juvenile delinquency: A review of the research. *Clinical Psychology Review, 13,* 133–167.

Nurmi, J. (1991). How do adolescents see their future? A review of the development of future orientation and planning. *Developmental Review, 11,* 1–59.

Olson, D., McCubbin, H., Barnes, H., Larsen, A., Muxen, M., & Wilson, M. (1982). *Family inventories: Inventories used in a national survey of families across the family life cycle.* St. Paul: University of Minnesota.

Otto, R. (1992). Prediction of dangerous behavior: A review and analysis of second-generation research. *Forensic Reports, 5,* 103–113.

Otto, R., Greenstein, J., Johnson, M., & Friedman, R. (1992). Prevalence of mental disorders among youth in the juvenile justice system. In J. Cocozza (Ed.), *Responding to the mental health needs of youth in the juvenile justice system* (pp. 7–48). Seattle, WA: National Coalition for the Mentally Ill in the Criminal Justice System.

People v. Lara, 432 P.2d 202 (1967).

Perry, G., & Orchard, J. (1992). *Assessment and treatment of adolescent sex offenders.* Sarasota, FL: Professional Resource Press.

Peterson-Badali, M., Abramovitch, R., & Duda, J. (1997). Young children's legal knowledge and reasoning ability. *Canadian Journal of Criminology, 39,* 145–170.

Platt, A. (1977). *The child savers: The invention of delinquency* (2nd ed.). Chicago: University of Chicago Press.

Poythress, N., Nicholson, R., Otto, R., Edens, J., Bonnie, R., Monahan, J., et al. (1999). *MacCAT-CA: The MacArthur Competence Assessment Tool–Criminal Adjudication: Professional manual.* Odessa, FL: Psychological Assessment Resources.

Prentky, R., Harris, B., Frizzell, K., & Righthand, S. (2000). An actuarial procedure for assessing risk with juvenile sex offenders. *Sexual Abuse: A Journal of Research and Treatment, 12,* 71–93.

Quay, H. (1964). Personality dimensions in delinquent males as inferred from the factor analysis of behavior ratings. *Journal of Research in Crime and Delinquency, 1,* 33–37.

Quay, H. (1966). Personality patterns in preadolescent delinquent boys. *Educational and Psychological Measurement, 16,* 99–110.

Quay, H., & Peterson, D. (1987). *Manual for the Revised Behavior Problem Checklist.* Miami, FL: University of Miami.

Quinsey, V., Harris, G., Rice, M., & Cormier, C. (1998). *Violent offenders: Appraising and managing risk.* Washington, DC: American Psychological Association.

Rosner, R., & Schwartz, H. (Eds.). (1989). *Juvenile psychiatry and the law.* New York: Plenum Press.

Savitsky, J., & Karras, D. (1984). Competency to stand trial among adolescents. *Adolescence, 19,* 349–358.

Schaffer, D. D., Schwab, M., & Fisher, W. (1993). The Diagnostic Interview Schedule for Children (DISC): Preparation, field testing, interrater reliability and acceptability. *Journal of the American Academy of Child and Adolescent Psychiatry, 32,* 643–650.

Schetky, D., & Benedek, E. (Eds.). (1980). *Child psychiatry and the law.* New York: Brunner/Mazel.

Schetky, D., & Benedek, E. (Eds.). (1985). *Emerging issues in child psychiatry and the law.* New York: Brunner/Mazel.

Schetky, D., & Benedek, E. (Eds.). (1992). *Clinical handbook of child psychiatry and the law.* Baltimore: Williams & Wilkins.

Schoenwald, S., Scherer, D., & Brondino, M. (1997). Effective community-based treatments for serious juvenile offenders. In S. Henggeler & A. Santos (Eds.), *Innovative approaches for difficult to treat populations* (pp. 65–82). Washington, DC: American Psychiatric Association.

Schwartz, R., & Rosado, M. (Eds.). (2000). *Evaluating youth competence in the justice system.* Washington, DC: American Bar Association Juvenile Justice Center, Juvenile Law Center, and Youth Law Center.

Scott, E. (2000). Criminal responsibility in adolescence: Lessons from developmental psychology. In T. Grisso & R. Schwartz (Eds.), *Youth on trial: A developmental perspective on juvenile justice* (pp. 291–324). Chicago: University of Chicago Press.

Scott, E., Reppucci, N., & Woolard, J. (1995). Evaluating adolescent decision making in legal contexts. *Law and Human Behavior, 19,* 221–244.

Seagrave, D., & Grisso, T. (in press). Adolescent development and the measurement of juvenile psychopathy. *Law and Human Behavior.*

Snyder, H., & Sickmund, M. (1999). *Juvenile offenders and victims: 1999 national report.* Washington, DC: Office of Juvenile Justice and Delinquency Prevention.

Steinberg, L., & Cauffman, E. (1996). Maturity of judgment in adolescence: Psychosocial factors in adolescent decision making. *Law and Human Behavior, 20,* 249–272.

Tanenhaus, D. (2000). The evolution of transfer out of the juvenile court. In J. Fagan & F. Zimring (Eds.), *The changing borders of juvenile justice: Transfer of adolescents to the criminal court* (pp. 13–44). Chicago: University of Chicago Press.

Tate, D., Reppucci, N., & Mulvey, E. (1995). Violent juvenile delinquents: Treatment effectiveness and implications for future action. *American Psychologist, 50,* 777–781.

Teplin, L., Abrams, K., & McClelland, G. (1998, March). *Psychiatric and substance abuse disorders among juveniles in detention: An empirical assessment.* Paper presented at the convention of American Psychology-Law Society, Redondo Beach, CA.

Timmons-Mitchell, J., Brown, C., Schultz, S., Webster, S., Underwood, L., & Semple, W. (1997). Comparing the mental health needs of female and male incarcerated juvenile delinquents. *Behavioral Sciences and the Law, 15,* 195–202.

Tobey, A., Grisso, T., & Schwartz, R. (2000). Youths' trial participation as seen by youths and their attorneys: An exploration of competence-based issues. In T. Grisso & R. Schwartz (Eds.), *Youth on trial: A developmental perspective on juvenile justice* (pp. 225–242). Chicago: University of Chicago Press.

Vant Zelfde, G., & Otto, R. (1997). *Directory of practicum, internship, and fellowship training opportunities in clinical-forensic psychology.* Tampa, FL: University of South Florida.

Widom, C. (1989). Does violence beget violence? A critical examination of the literature. *Psychological Bulletin, 106,* 3–28.

Widom, C., & Maxfield, M. (1996). A prospective examination of risk for violence among abused and neglected children. In C. Ferris & T. Grisso (Eds.), *Understanding aggressive behavior in children* (Vol. 794, pp. 224–237). New York: Annals of the New York Academy of Sciences.

Zimring, F. (1998). *American youth violence.* New York: Oxford University Press.

CHAPTER 18

Competence to Confess

LOIS B. OBERLANDER, NAOMI E. GOLDSTEIN, AND ALAN M. GOLDSTEIN

A confession serves as a strong source of evidence against a defendant in a criminal trial. Once offered into evidence, it is extremely difficult for defense counsel to overcome the impact a defendant's inculpatory statements might have on a judge or jury. If left unchallenged, the defendant's confession is highly influential on the trial outcome. In many cases, a confession serves as the single most influential factor in leading the trier of fact to reject the attorney's defense strategy and render a verdict of guilty. Sometimes, impairments in the defendant's functioning compromise the defendant's abilities relevant to the confession process. In this chapter, we consider two major psycholegal issues related to confessions given by those arrested for crimes.

First, we focus on the origins of the *Miranda* rights and subsequent case law. Legal issues related to assessing the ability of individuals, especially those of special populations, to waive their rights are reviewed. We describe methodological approaches to the assessment of comprehension of *Miranda* rights. We review empirical research on the ability of suspects to make knowing, intelligent, and voluntary waivers of their constitutional rights, along with appropriate methodology for forensic psychologists to use in evaluating such cases. Methodology is considered in light of relevant

ethical issues and limits of testimony. In the second section, we address issues related to *false* confessions. That is, we consider inculpatory statements made by defendants that may not be trustworthy. We review relevant case law on the admissibility of such testimony, and we discuss the strengths and limitations inherent in presenting expert opinions on this topic in a court of law. We describe empirical research on false confessions and assessment methodology for evaluating the trustworthiness of confessions.

EVALUATING THE VALIDITY OF *MIRANDA* RIGHTS WAIVERS

Constitutional Law and the *Miranda* Warning

A defendant's confession often serves as the most persuasive evidence in criminal trials, and it is particularly influential when it serves as the sole or primary source of evidence offered by the prosecution. When a suspect is placed under arrest or is given the impression that he or she is not free to leave, police officers are expected to read the *Miranda* warning. The constitutional basis for the *Miranda* warning and the conditions for a valid waiver of the *Miranda* rights were

336 Competence to Confess

stated by the U.S. Supreme Court in *Miranda v. Arizona* (1966) and affirmed in *Dickerson v. U.S.* (2000).

The Evolution of the Miranda Warning

The concept that the courts should play a primary role in ensuring the constitutional rights of defendants in criminal cases evolved gradually. At first, the U.S. Supreme Court ruled that physical brutality could not be used as a means to extract a confession from a suspect. In *Brown v. Mississippi* (1936), the Court reviewed a trial transcript in which police officers testified, "they had seized him [the African American suspect], and with participation of the deputy they hanged him by a rope to the limb of a tree, and having let him down, they hung him again, and when he was let down the second time, and he still protested his innocence, he was tied to a tree and whipped, and still declined to accede to the demands that he confess.... [The next day he was] again severely whipped . . . and the defendant then agreed to confess." The Court ruled that convictions based solely on confessions demonstrated to be extorted by police officers through "brutality and violence" represented a violation of the due process clause of the 14th Amendment. In a decision that clearly indicated that confessions could no longer be physically coerced, the Court opined, "the rack and torture chamber may not be substituted for the witness stand."

In *Spano v. New York* (1959), the U.S. Supreme Court extended the concept of coercion to include not only physical brutality, but psychological pressure as well. The Court acknowledged the conflict that exists between society's need for prompt and effective law enforcement versus protecting the rights of all individuals from violation by "unconstitutional methods of law enforcement." The Court indicated that not only do police officers enforce the law, they "must obey the law" as well. It argued that coercive methods may not only encourage "untrustworthy" confessions, but "in the end life and liberty can be as much endangered from illegal methods used to convict those thought to be criminals as from the actual criminals themselves." Among the factors the Court cited in overturning the petitioner's conviction were that his "will was overborne by official pressure, fatigue and sympathy falsely aroused."

In 1964, the Court considered *Esobedo v. Illinois,* in which the defendant had requested to consult his attorney during the course of police interrogation. Despite several such requests, the suspect and his retained lawyer were not provided the opportunity to meet until the confession was obtained. The Court opined that the "petitioner had become the accused, and the purpose of the interrogation was to 'get him' to confess his guilt despite his constitutional right not to do so," in violation

of the 6th Amendment. Acknowledging that many confessions occur between the time of arrest and indictment, this time period "points up its critical nature as a stage when legal aid and advice are surely needed." In a strongly worded opinion, the Court stated, "The right to counsel would indeed be hollow if it began at a period when few confessions were obtained." Going further, it argued, "No system of criminal justice can, or should, survive if it comes to depend for its continued effectiveness on the citizens' abdication through unawareness of their constitutional rights." These and other earlier opinions set the stage for the *Miranda* case that was to follow.

Miranda v. Arizona (1966) resolved four separate criminal appeals, all questioning the role of the 5th Amendment to the Constitution (the right against compelled self-incrimination) in the context of interrogation of a criminal suspect in police custody. Because *Miranda* was the lead case of the four, the case took on the defendant's name. Ernesto Miranda, an indigent defendant, had been convicted by an Arizona jury of kidnapping and rape on the basis of a signed confession given to Phoenix police officers. He was interrogated for two hours, without a lawyer present. The other three defendants experienced similar interrogations in the states of New York, California, and Missouri. The conviction of the California murder defendant already had been overturned by the California Supreme Court because there was no evidence that the defendant had been advised of his right to counsel and his right to remain silent.

In *Miranda v. Arizona* (1966), the U.S. Supreme Court affirmed the California Supreme Court's ruling, and it reversed the convictions of Ernesto Miranda and the other defendants. In his opinion, Chief Justice Warren wrote that the case raised questions "which go to the roots of our concepts of American criminal jurisprudence: the restraints society must observe consistent with the federal Constitution in prosecuting individuals for crimes." The Court ruled that any statement by a criminal suspect stemming from a custodial police interrogation would be presumed involuntary and inadmissible unless police detectives provided the suspect with four warnings to remind the defendant of his or her constitutional rights: (a) the right to remain silent; (b) statements made by the suspect may be used as evidence in court against the suspect; (c) the right to an attorney during and after the interrogation; and (d) the right to a court-appointed attorney, if the suspect cannot afford one. The Court also ruled that a defendant may waive his or her rights, provided the waiver is made knowingly, intelligently, and voluntarily.

Concern about Coerced Confessions

In its *Miranda* decision, the Court noted that the advent of modern custodial police interrogations raised increased concern about coerced confessions (no claims of police coercion were made in the four cases before the Warren Court). Custodial police interrogations, by their very nature, isolate and pressure the suspect. Thus, custodial interrogations, even without physical or other coercive strategies, were construed by the Court as exacting a heavy toll on individual liberty. In its decision, the Court quoted from *Criminal Interrogation and Confessions* (Inbau & Reid, 1967), a police training manual for eliciting confessions. The manual offers physical and verbal interrogation suggestions for obtaining confessions. With respect to the physical section, interrogators are advised to dress in civilian clothing, use a small soundproof room removed from familiar sights and sounds, leave the room bare of telephones and décor, furnish the room sparsely with armless straight-backed chairs and a desk, and include a one-way mirror in the room's design. Officers are advised to periodically invade the suspect's personal space, adding loss of personal control to the social isolation and sensory deprivation of the room. Other suggested strategies include nonexcessive use of restraint and nonexcessive deprivation of food and sleep. The Court concluded that the coercion inherent in custodial interrogations blurred the line between voluntary and involuntary statements because it heightened the risk of the individual's being denied the privilege against self-incrimination (from the Rehnquist opinion in *Dickerson v. U.S.,* 2000).

Recent Developments in Constitutional Law

Attempts to Overturn **Miranda**

The U.S. Congress attempted to overrule *Miranda* in 1968. Congress passed a law, 18 U.S.C. 3501, allowing for a case-by-case "totality of circumstances" test of whether a confession was voluntary. The law essentially returned interrogation procedures to the pre-*Miranda* era. That is, under 18 U.S.C. 3501, the *Miranda* warning was not required. In the pre-*Miranda* era, courts often considered elements of what eventually became the *Miranda* warning, but courts had the latitude to consider other factors and their rulings were not bound by the contents of the *Miranda* warning. Confessions were not presumed involuntary if the *Miranda* warning was not delivered prior to interrogation. Because of the relationship between the legislative powers of Congress and the judicial powers of the Supreme Court, the new law, 18 U.S.C. 3501, could be upheld only if successful legal challenges were made to *Miranda*.

In 1975, *U.S. v. Crocker* held that 18 U.S.C. 3501 governed the admissibility of confessions in federal court. Despite the ruling, 3501 generally was ignored in federal cases until many years later, when it was used as a basis for the

Dickerson v. U.S. challenge to *Miranda*. On June 26, 2000, the U.S. Supreme Court upheld *Miranda* in *Dickerson* on a 7-to-2 vote, stating that *Miranda* had "become embedded in routine police practice" without causing any measurable difficulty for prosecutors or law enforcement officers. The ruling also affirmed that Congress could not pass laws that contravened Supreme Court decisions.

Dickerson v. U.S.

Dickerson v. U.S. (2000) overturned a February 8, 1999, ruling by the U.S. Court of Appeals for the Fourth Circuit. The court had attempted to narrow the relevance of the *Miranda* warning for federal law enforcement officials. It ruled that confessions obtained voluntarily by federal law enforcement officials may not be suppressed simply because a defendant was not given the *Miranda* warning. In her opinion, Judge Karen Williams said that *Miranda* was a rule of law, not a constitutional requirement. The Fourth Circuit found that 18 U.S.C. 3501 was passed by Congress to reinstate a rule that had been in effect for 180 years before *Miranda,* specifically, that statements by suspects could be used against them, provided they were voluntary. Voluntariness was to be judged on a case-by-case basis. Had the U.S. Supreme Court not overturned the Fourth Circuit, 18 U.S.C. 3501 would have applied to federal cases in Maryland, North Carolina, South Carolina, Virginia, and West Virginia. Even if all federal jurisdictions overturned *Miranda,* the states would have remained bound by *Miranda* because the law at issue applied only to federal officials.

In *Dickerson v. U.S.,* Chief Justice Rehnquist (who, for over 25 years, made statements about *Miranda*'s lack of a clear constitutional foundation) wrote, "Whether or not we would agree with *Miranda*'s reasoning and its resulting rule, were we addressing the issue in the first instance, the principles of *stare decisis* weigh heavily against overruling it now." The court held that *stare decisis* (to let stand that which was decided), a doctrine that typically is of limited application to constitutional law, required the Court to defer to the *Miranda* precedent. The Court argued that *Miranda* was more straightforward than pre-*Miranda* procedures. Chief Justice Rehnquist wrote, "*Miranda,* being a constitutional decision of this court, may not be in effect overruled by an act of Congress, and we decline to overrule *Miranda* ourselves."

The impact that the *Miranda* decision has had on law enforcement has been debated since the decision was issued in 1966. Many warned that the consequences of reminding suspects about their constitutional rights would significantly reduce the rate of confessions and, ultimately, the rate of convictions. Leo (2001a, 2001b) reviews a series of impact studies assessing the overall effects of the requirement that *Miranda* rights be provided on the criminal justice system. He concludes that it has had a very limited impact, either positive or negative.

Totality of Circumstances Approach

A totality of the circumstances approach examines all of the circumstances surrounding an alleged *Miranda* violation; it prohibits either validating or invalidating a waiver based solely on a single factor (e.g., age or intelligence of the defendant). Early cases suggested that the suspect's background, experience, and conduct (*Johnson v. Zerbst,* 1938) were factors worthy of consideration. *Coyote v. U.S.* (1967) provided a list of characteristics to be considered in determining the capacities of suspects to waive *Miranda* rights (i.e., age, intelligence, education, amount of prior contact with police officers, conduct, physical conditions, and background). Courts usually do consider factors such as level of education, IQ, language ability, literacy, age, mental illness, and experience with the police and the court system (Frumkin, 2000, Grisso, 1998b; Oberlander, 1998; Oberlander & Goldstein, 2001).

Courts also consider factors such as who was present at the interrogation, the physical arrangements of the interrogation, police strategies for interrogation, number of times the *Miranda* warning was given, method of delivery (e.g., silently, aloud, from a wall poster, from a piece of paper or small card, read by a law enforcement officer, read by the defendant, read together), time elapsed between the warning and the interrogation, and the methods law enforcement officers used to assess the suspect's comprehension of the warning (e.g., no methods, signing an acknowledgment that the warning was given, inquiring whether the suspect waives each element of the warning, waiving each element in writing, paraphrasing each element of the warning; Grisso, 1986; Oberlander, 1998; Oberlander & Goldstein, 2001).

Other Relevant U.S. Supreme Court Cases

Since *Miranda* (1966), other U.S. Supreme Court cases have tended to narrow the scope of an involuntary waiver of *Miranda* rights. For example, in *Colorado v. Connolly* (1986), the Court held that a waiver was voluntary as long as it was not the product of coercive police activity. *Connolly* involved a defendant who followed the "voice of God" in confessing to a murder. A psychiatrist testified that the defendant had a psychosis that interfered with his ability to make a rational and free choice to confess. The lower court found the waiver invalid, but the Supreme Court reversed the ruling,

stating that a waiver need not be the product of free will to be voluntary. The Court ruled that significant mental impairment does not automatically render a waiver and confession invalid; an invalid confession must be the direct result of police conduct. In most subsequent state cases, coercion was interpreted to mean only physical coercion (Oberlander, 1998; Oberlander & Goldstein, 2001). However, some cases recognized psychological coercion (e.g., *Blackburn v. Alabama,* 1960).

When Is *Miranda* Relevant?

Law enforcement officers question suspects in a variety of ways. They might ask casual questions in community settings; they might ask semiformal questions in a suspect's home or on the way to the police station; they might record a formal videotaped statement at police headquarters (frequently *after* a verbal statement has been given by the defendant under conditions in which a formal record is not made). Any of these encounters might lead to a confession, but not all of them require a *Miranda* warning. The warning is required when a suspect is questioned while in police custody (Grisso, 1998b) and when the police detectives intend to use the confession as evidence (Oberlander, 1998; Oberlander & Goldstein, 2001). Custody typically involves formal arrest, but states define it subjectively, usually using the *reasonable person* standard.

The Reasonable Person Standard

The benchmark of the reasonable person standard is whether a reasonable person would know or might believe that he or she was in custody. Factors contributing to a "custodial situation" include time elapsed between arrest and confession, whether the confession was made between arrest and arraignment, and whether the defendant knew he or she was a suspect. Additional factors include whether the defendant knew the nature of the charge and whether the defendant realized a statement was not required (Grisso, 1981, 1998b). Other factors include whether the suspect was questioned in familiar or neutral surroundings or at a police station, the duration of the interrogation, the degree of physical restraint placed on the suspect, the number of law enforcement officers present, and whether the interview was aggressive or formal (Grisso, 1998b).

Grisso (1998b) described other extensions from case law (e.g., *West v. U.S.,* 1968), including time spent in a holding cell prior to interrogation, the physical condition of the holding cell, the presence of other incarcerated persons, whether the suspect was provided food and other necessities, and behaviors of law enforcement officers that might be interpreted as an attempt to instill fear. In New York (*People v. Rodney P.,* 1967) and Texas (*Orozco v. Texas,* 1969), a person is in custody if police officers offer the impression that the individual they are questioning is not free to leave. Such an impression can be given when police detectives watch the suspect dress before accompanying him or her to the police station (implying that he or she might escape if not observed) or if police officers do not permit the suspect to drive there in his or her own vehicle.

If a suspect confesses prior to being taken into police custody, the validity of the confession depends on a number of factors: whether the confession was spontaneous (i.e., not elicited by police detectives' questions), whether questions were directed toward obtaining a confession, whether the suspect subsequently was taken into custody, and whether procedural requirements subsequently were followed (e.g., providing the warning, obtaining a waiver, asking the suspect to repeat the confession; Grisso, 1998b). If a suspect offers a spontaneous confession or volunteers to remain in police custody, or if the police detectives do not expect the prosecutor to use the confession as evidence, then *Miranda* does not pertain (Oberlander, 1998; Oberlander & Goldstein, 2001).

Jurisdictional Versions of the Miranda Warning

Although *Miranda* established and *Dickerson* affirmed the required content of the warning, the actual wording of the *Miranda* warning varies within and across jurisdictions. The complexity of the language differs, with most jurisdictions using simpler language than that used in the 1960s and 1970s. For example, most jurisdictions use the word "questioning" in place of "interrogation," "talk" instead of "consult," and "lawyer" rather than "attorney." Most jurisdictions also use non-English versions when necessary.

The original *Miranda* ruling set forth the four prongs of the warning (see above). Most jurisdictions have added a fifth prong, specifically stating that the defendant has the right to stop the police interrogation at any time to ask for an attorney (Oberlander, 1998; Oberlander & Goldstein, 2001). A warning that typifies more modern versions (from the Chelmsford, Massachusetts, Police Department) appears below. Words appearing in italics are often absent in simplified versions:

- You have the right to remain silent.
- Anything you say can be used against you in court.
- You have the right to talk to a lawyer *for advice* before we ask you any questions and to have him with you during questioning.

- If you cannot afford a lawyer, one will be appointed for you before questioning *if you wish.*
- If you decide to answer questions now without a lawyer present, you will still have the right to stop answering at any time until you talk to a lawyer.

Some versions contain remnants of earlier language in warnings, such as "court of law" rather than "court." No research has been conducted to determine if the simplified language or the inclusion of the fifth component facilitates comprehension (however, see Oberlander, Goldstein, & Grisso, 2002), nor have there been any legal challenges to the constitutionality of either including or excluding the fifth component (or any other supplementary information).

Case Law Developments for Juveniles

Developments in *Miranda* procedures have focused on special populations, as reflected in *People v. Higgins* (1993). In this case, the court mandated that police detectives do "something more" than a rote reading and explanation of rights in special circumstances. Special populations include children and adolescents, individuals with mental illness, those with mental deficiencies, and individuals with organic impairment. Most empirical research on special populations has focused on juveniles and individuals with cognitive limitations.

Extending Miranda Protections to Juveniles

Miranda originally applied only to adults. Its protections were extended to adolescents in *Kent v. U.S.* (1966) and *In re Gault* (1967). The U.S. Supreme Court did not directly apply the requirements of *Miranda v. Arizona* (1966) to juvenile proceedings, but it assumed its applicability in *Fare v. Michael C.* (1979). Prior to the 1960s, the only case to consider the due process right of juveniles was *Haley v. Ohio* (1948), wherein the Court concluded that a coerced juvenile confession could not be used. The *Kent* and *Gault* cases affirmed that 5th Amendment (protection against self-incrimination) and 14th Amendment (due process) protections applied to juveniles at all stages of delinquency proceedings. Thereafter, cases soon emerged questioning the capacities of juveniles to comprehend their *Miranda* rights and to waive their rights voluntarily, knowingly, and intelligently.

In *People v. Lara* (1967), the Court distinguished between "knowing" and "intelligent," explaining that an adolescent defendant might not "fully comprehend the meaning of the effect of the waiver." In *Fare v. Michael C.* (1979), a 16-year-old defendant offered a confession without a waiver and asked to speak with his probation officer instead of his attorney. In this case, the U.S. Supreme Court extended the "totality of circumstances" standard to adolescent cases. *People v. Lara* (1967), *West v. U.S.* (1968), and *Fare v. Michael C.* (1979) ruled that adolescent status did not automatically invalidate a waiver of *Miranda* rights, but the Court recognized that adolescents, as a class, were at greater risk than adults for deficits in intelligence and functioning relevant to the standard for a valid waiver (see Grisso, 1998b; a comprehensive review of legal cases related to juveniles' waiver of *Miranda* rights is found in Feld, 2000).

The Interested Adult

In *Gellegos v. Colorado* (1962), the U.S. Supreme Court found that adult advice might help ensure the voluntariness of youthful suspects' confessions. In *Gellagos,* the Court found that the advice of a lawyer, adult relative, or friend might obviate effects of adolescent immaturity, putting the adolescent "on a less unequal footing" with interrogators. Following the lead of *Gellagos,* many state legislatures and courts (e.g., *Commonwealth v. Roane,* 1974) added a procedural requirement that provided juveniles with a higher level of protection during interrogation than adult suspects were afforded. Law enforcement officers were required to provide the youth with the opportunity for contact with an adult (a parent, guardian, or other adult) prior to a waiver of *Miranda* rights. The adult became known as the *interested adult,* whose job it was to provide the youth with consultation about the desirability of a waiver prior to interrogation. The requirement was intended to reduce the risk of invalid waivers and confessions among juveniles (Grisso, 1981, 1998b).

The interested adult need not be the youth's parent, but must be an interested party. For example, *Commonwealth v. MacNeill* (1987) held that a grandfather was sufficiently interested; *Commonwealth v. Guyton* (1989) held that a minor, such as an older sibling, could not satisfy the interested adult requirement; *Commonwealth v. a Juvenile* (1989) held that an employee of the Department of Youth Services could not serve as an interested adult. Some states have taken exception to the interested adult requirement, expressing concern that it unnecessarily restricts the prosecution of sophisticated or repeat juvenile offenders (Grisso, 1981).

Although most states require the opportunity for consultation with an interested adult, the adult is not empowered to make decisions for the adolescent (Grisso, 1998b). Based on *Kent* and *Gault,* adolescents have legal autonomy, independent of parents or guardians, for waiving *Miranda* and making other legal decisions in delinquency proceedings. Attorneys also should not waive *Miranda* rights for adolescent clients (Grisso, 1998b). However, regardless of adolescents' autonomous legal role in waiving *Miranda* rights, courts

have been reluctant to invalidate waivers based on the type or quality of adult advice. For example, in *Commonwealth v. Philips* (1993), the court rejected the notion that a parent who fails to tell the child not to talk, who advises the child to tell the truth, or who fails to seek immediate legal assistance is a "disinterested adult."

Research showed that although the absence of opportunity for consultation with an interested adult sometimes invalidates a youth's waiver and confession, the presence of an interested adult does not guarantee the waiver's validity (Grisso, 1998b). The interested adult might be anxious, fearful, confused, or mentally incapacitated at the time of the consultation and, thus, be unable to provide guidance for a knowing, intelligent, and voluntary waiver. The interested adult procedure does not necessarily result in more adolescent refusals to waive *Miranda.* Parents often assume an authoritative or disciplinary role in the presence of law enforcement officers, not a role of legal advocacy. They encourage their children to tell the truth and accept responsibility for what might have happened, but not for reasons of legal strategy. In doing so, they effectively offer advice, directly or indirectly, to the child or adolescent to waive *Miranda* rights. Grisso (1981) and Grisso and Ring (1979) found that parents often believe they should pressure their arrested children to cooperate with law enforcement officers. In many parent-adolescent consultations, parents offered no advice about waiver of *Miranda* rights (70% failed to do so in Grisso and Ring's study, 1979). In fact, there was silence between parents and adolescents during most consultations (66% did not exchange words in that same study). When advice was given, it favored waiving rights by a ratio of 3 to 1.

Most states have an age threshold for requiring the presence of an interested adult (usually set between 14 and 16 years). Because of their relative maturity, older adolescents typically are viewed as having little or no need for consultation. Courts have not interpreted age cutoffs as implacable, however. In *Commonwealth v. King* (1984), the court held that a waiver by a young adolescent was valid, despite a lack of parental consultation, because the adolescent was "capable and mature" and "two weeks earlier had exercised his right to remain silent." In most jurisdictions, the interested adult requirement applies only to the rendering of *Miranda* rights. Police detectives are not required to provide the adult with an opportunity to be present during the interrogation or confession.

Case Law Developments for the Mentally Retarded

Courts historically have recognized that confessions of mentally retarded individuals might be invalid. In *Ford v. State* (1897), the Supreme Court of Mississippi ruled invalid the confession of an individual who was "not bright." Ford's employer testified, "He is going to give you the answer you desire. If you want a 'yes,' he will give it to you; and if you want a 'no,' he will give you that" (see Fulero & Everington, 1995, for a complete description of the case). Based on the "knowing" component, *U.S. ex rel. Simon v. Maroney* (1964) held that a mentally retarded client was presumed incompetent, even though police officers stated the warnings clearly and properly.

Mental retardation is not synonymous with invalidity of a waiver. In *People v. Williams* (1984), although the defendant was mentally retarded and organically impaired, the court ruled that a waiver was valid because the detective paraphrased and explained the warning. In this New York case, the court stated that it is the responsibility of neither the police detectives nor the prosecutor to provide a legal education for those under arrest. The defendant does not need to understand the advantages of remaining silent, how statements can be used in court, or the advantages of having an attorney. Simply stated, defendants must possess only a minimal or concrete understanding of the *Miranda* warning.

Methods for Delivering the *Miranda* Warning and Obtaining Confessions

Grisso (1998b) described a wide variety of methods for delivering the warning, including reciting it carefully and slowly, delivering it in a rapid and rote fashion, reciting the warning and then placing a written form in front of the suspect, giving only a written version without a verbal rendering, asking the suspect to read it aloud, giving an explanation of the warning, and having the suspect explain what it means. The degree of documentation in investigation records of *Miranda* delivery methods, methods of discerning comprehension, and the suspect's statements relevant to comprehension varies across and within jurisdictions (Oberlander, 1998; Oberlander & Goldstein, 2001). The court weighs the necessity of careful procedures on a case-by-case basis. In *State v. Prater* (1970), the court ruled that the suspect understood his rights because of his extensive arrest history and repeated exposure to police arrest procedures. The suspect's familiarity with police proceedings meant that the hasty and incomplete reading of the rights by officers did not invalidate the wavier.

Courts have addressed the degree to which law enforcement officers can use ploys to encourage confessions. *Commonwealth v. Meehan* (1979) and *Commonwealth v. Mandile* (1986) addressed whether a confession given subsequent to police inducement was valid. Both rulings held that promises and other inducements are included in the totality of circumstances. In both cases, the court allowed officers to suggest it would be better for the suspect to tell the truth because it would indicate a degree of cooperation. The court

prohibited, however, expressed or implied assurances that a statement would aid the defense or result in a reduced sentence. Rulings on police detectives' questioning tactics are not consistent, however. In *State v. Jackson* (1983), the North Carolina Supreme Court ruled that the confession was valid even though the police had misled Jackson by citing nonexistent evidence. Jackson was led to believe that the victim's blood was on his pants, his shoes matched footprints at the crime scene, his fingerprints were found on the murder weapon, and an eyewitness saw him. The court ruled that Jackson's confession was valid because he was not physically restrained, offered leniency, or threatened. In contrast, in *People v. Higgins* (1993), the court ruled that a suspect's waiver was not knowing, intelligent, or voluntary because the police detectives had misrepresented information when they deceived him, stating, for example, that his fingerprints were found at the crime scene.

Because of concern about the likelihood that particularly suggestible, but innocent, suspects might give false confessions, courts have placed limitations on police methods for obtaining confessions. *Colombe v. Connecticut* (1961) ruled that there is no absolute standard, but a coerced confession should be based on police misconduct (e.g., the use of physical force or assault, prolonged isolation of the suspect, deprivation of food or sleep, threats of harm or punishment, or promises of immunity or leniency; see also, Kassin, 1997). Case law limitations on police conduct are not as restrictive as proponents of defendants' rights would like, however. Police manuals for eliciting confessions describe the use of a broad spectrum of techniques, some of which are similar to those described in *Colombe* (Aubry & Caputo, 1980; Inbau, Reid, & Buckley, 1986; MacDonald & Michaud, 1987; O'Hara & O'Hara, 1981).

Research Relevant to *Miranda* Comprehension

Research on *Miranda* comprehension has focused on individual factors cited in case law as relevant to a lack of comprehension. These include age, socioeconomic status, experience with the legal system, intelligence, education, and literacy. There is no single individual factor or circumstance that, per se, obviates comprehension in the eyes of the court. Courts decide comprehension on a case-by-case basis. Because of this iterative approach, it is impossible to weigh any one variable or cutoff score as particularly influential on judicial decisions of *Miranda* comprehension (Grisso, 1981).

Research on *Miranda* comprehension has focused on the "knowing" and "intelligent" requirements for a valid waiver of these rights. "Knowing" is reflected in an understanding of the words and phrases of the warning or an ability to read the warning (if administered by police detectives in written form). It also includes the ability of the suspect to understand the language, especially if English is not his or her first language. "Intelligent" is interpreted as the defendant's ability to appreciate and apply the rights to the custodial situation and, in some jurisdictions, to comprehend the inalienable quality of rights (Frumkin, 2000; Oberlander, 1998). Because of difficulty objectively defining or establishing the use of physical or psychological coercion during an interrogation, little research has been conducted on the issue of "voluntariness" of confessions. In part, the difficulty lies in the lack of corroborative evidence of coercion. It is highly unlikely that an audio- or videotape exists of interrogators physically threatening or assaulting the suspect; rather, suspects may claim they were coerced, and police officers vehemently deny employing any form of coercion. Forensic psychologists are not in position to offer opinions about the accuracy of these assertions, but in many cases it is possible to examine abilities related to the "trustworthiness" of confessions. There is a relationship between the legal construct of the voluntariness of a confession and the construct of the "trustworthiness" or credibility of a confession (see below for further information).

Children and Adolescents

The courts have avoided specific age cutoffs for *Miranda* comprehension. However, case law suggests that courts are more likely to find that adolescents under age 13 lack comprehension (Grisso, 1981, 1986; for additional information on this topic, see the chapter by Grisso in this volume). Adolescent cases of *Miranda* comprehension have involved youths from ages 7 to 19. In his research, Grisso (1981) found that understanding of *Miranda* was generally inadequate among juveniles age 12 or below and more variable in the 13- to 15-year-old age range. Despite their better understanding, Grisso still found a high degree of variability in adolescents age 16 or older. Because of high variability within age groups, Grisso found that age was limited in its ability to guide *Miranda* comprehension decisions. Although preteens had poorer comprehension, there was a plateau at age 14. Above 13 years, age alone ceased to account for individual differences in understanding. Above 13, age was a better predictor of understanding when it was combined with level of intelligence.

Adult Comprehension of Miranda Rights

Grisso (1981) questioned whether the plateau in comprehension scores between ages 14 and 16 carried through to adulthood. Using the same *Miranda* instruments, he evaluated

adult offenders sent to a halfway house during or after probation. He also studied a smaller sample of nonoffender adults matched for age and IQ. Data were obtained on the number of prior arrests for felonies, misdemeanors, and total arrests for the offender group. When compared to juveniles (Grisso, 1981), adults more frequently obtained perfect scores on the *Miranda* instruments. That is, "most of the differences between juveniles and adults occurred on Warning II (use of incriminating information in court) and Warning III (right to counsel before and during interrogation)" (p. 100). Few differences existed between the offender and nonoffender groups. When age was statistically controlled, nonoffenders performed significantly better than offenders on a comprehension measure of *Miranda* vocabulary (CMV; the measures are described below), suggesting that experience with the criminal justice system did *not* translate into a greater understanding of the vocabulary contained in the warnings. Grisso found that when other factors were statistically controlled, "differences among adults in understanding of *Miranda* warnings are related primarily to differences among them in general intellectual functioning" (p. 101). He found that "those offenders with a large number of felony arrests (a great deal of police or court experiences) do acquire a greater understanding of the *Miranda* warnings than do nonoffenders or less experienced offenders" (p. 102). In comparing juveniles to adults, Grisso concluded that comprehension (CMR) scores were higher at all adult ages and at every IQ level. The scores of 16-year-olds were not significantly different from those of 17- to 22-year-olds. However, they were significantly lower than those individuals 23 years of age and older.

IQ, Academic Achievement, and Reading Ability as Moderators of Comprehension

Despite court rulings that no particular IQ score can serve as the sole indicator of invalid comprehension of *Miranda*, Grisso (1981) found a relationship between judicial decisions and IQ scores of juveniles. Almost all cases involving a lack of comprehension of *Miranda* involved juveniles with IQ scores below 75. Grisso's results also suggested that the courts might overestimate the capacities of youth in the 75 to 80 IQ range. Even among adolescents with IQs between 80 and 100, the probability of adequate understanding in 14- to 16-year-old youths was between 40% and 50%.

Reading skills and reading comprehension are especially relevant to *Miranda* comprehension when the warning is administered by asking the suspect to read it. For many persons with mental deficiencies, the vocabulary and syntax of the *Miranda* warning are above their reading and comprehension levels (Fulero & Everington, 1995). In 1977, the Fry readability analysis placed the typical *Miranda* warning at the seventh-grade level of reading ability (Fulero & Everington, 1995). Though more simplified versions of the warning might be at a lower grade level, it is unlikely (in part because of interjurisdictional differences) that most warnings are at a third-grade level, the average reading level of a defendant with diagnosable mental retardation.

Cases involving grade level and reading ability are relevant in two ways. Placement in a special education classroom for mentally retarded children has served as evidence of low intelligence (*State v. Toney*, 1976). In contrast, a few cases cited reading comprehension scores at a fifth-grade level or higher as evidence of adequate understanding (*Commonwealth v. Youngblood*, 1973; *United States ex rel. Simon v. Maroney*, 1964).

Familiarity with the Criminal Justice System as a Moderator of Comprehension

The courts have considered a youth's prior experience with the juvenile justice system as a factor when deciding *Miranda* comprehension. In some cases, extensive prior experience has negated the importance of carefully reviewing the warning (*In re Morgan*, 1975; *State v. Prater*, 1970). Despite these court decisions, Grisso (1981) found no simple relationship between indices of prior experience and understanding of *Miranda*. He hypothesized that the emotionally arousing conditions of being arrested might interfere with incidental learning of the warning's content. He further hypothesized that although repetition might lead to familiarity, familiarity does not guarantee understanding.

Race and Socioeconomic Status as Moderators of Comprehension

Grisso (1981) reported a relationship between race and poor comprehension at low IQ levels (below approximately 80 to 90), with Blacks obtaining lower understanding scores than Caucasians. Racial differences were insignificant at higher IQ levels. Grisso also found that impoverished Caucasians with felony experience showed better understanding of *Miranda* than impoverished Blacks with felony experience. Overall scores of understanding were poorer for lower-socioeconomic Caucasians than for lower-socioeconomic Blacks, even within the same IQ range. The courts have not considered socioeconomic status or race as relevant factors when making judicial determinations about *Miranda* comprehension.

Forensic Evaluation of *Miranda* Rights Waivers

Based on the recommendations of Grisso (1981, 1998b) and Frumkin (2000), the evaluator of an examinee's *Miranda* waiver's validity should conduct a clinical interview for historical factors relevant to the case and a specific interview focusing on the circumstances of the arrest and confession. Assessment data, if relevant to hypothesized impairments, should include the client's level of intellectual functioning and academic achievement. Personality assessment measures and symptom or diagnostic checklists often are used when mental illness or personality variables may have influenced suggestibility or deference to authority. Specific measures of *Miranda* comprehension are often used, but some evaluators prefer to gather *Miranda* comprehension data through semistructured interview methods that use specific measures only as a guideline (see Frumkin, 2000; Grisso, 1998b; and Oberlander & Goldstein, 2001, for an analysis of the tension between external and internal validity in *Miranda* comprehension evaluations). Records relevant to the evaluation should be reviewed, and specific attention should be paid to records documenting previous *Miranda* comprehension.

Methodology

The first step in the evaluation process is gathering relevant records. Records should include a copy of the signed *Miranda* waiver form and any related documentation or descriptive information of how, when, and how many times the *Miranda* warning was delivered. The *actual* waiver form signed by the defendant must be reviewed to determine the wording and sentence length used in the relevant jurisdiction. The evaluator also should obtain any existing transcripts or audio/video recordings of the interrogation (Frumkin, 2000; Grisso, 1998b). Complete records relevant to the *Miranda* warning process are rare, especially those documenting the first administration of the warning. However, law enforcement officers' depositions sometimes clarify how many times the warning was given and under what circumstances (Frumkin, 2000). Arrest records, records documenting the procedures for delivering *Miranda*, and confession transcripts also aid in evaluations of *Miranda* comprehension. Other relevant records include prior psychological assessment data (such as past IQ scores and educational achievement scores), school records relevant to grade level and academic performance, records of prior criminal justice involvement, court clinic and probation reports relevant to intellect or prior arrest history, and relevant medical and mental health records.

In gathering information about the *Miranda* warning used in the suspect's jurisdiction, the evaluator should be aware of the periodic use of non-English versions of the warning. If *Miranda* was delivered in a non-English form, the evaluator should be fluent in that language, should refer the retaining attorney to the services of an evaluator who is fluent in that language (and qualified to conduct the evaluation), or should retain the services of a certified court interpreter. The evaluator should determine if the language used in the *Miranda* warning is consistent with the language or dialect used by the defendant. For example, a Mexican American defendant who speaks Spanish might not understand some of the words used in a Spanish-language warning written for individuals originating from Puerto Rico. In cases of non-English-speaking or bilingual clients, the evaluator also should clarify in which language the confession was given, the language in which it was recorded and signed, and whether the law enforcement officer interviewing the defendant was fluent and used the relevant language or dialect.

Interviewing the Defendant

Informed consent, the first step prior to interviewing the defendant, requires a specific description of the purpose of the evaluation and the lack of confidentiality that will apply if the defendant consents to participate. As in all forensic assessments, the informed consent procedure (what the examiner told the defendant, as well as the defendant's attempts to paraphrase this information) should be carefully documented. However, in cases involving the assessment of *Miranda* rights waivers, this procedure takes on additional significance. The forensic psychologist tells the defendant that anything he or she says during the assessment potentially will appear in the report and/or be discussed during testimony. Similarly, the defendant is warned that all notes on this issue might be discoverable and, consequently, opposing counsel would see them. The defendant is told that anything he or she says on this issue will not be confidential. Questions sometimes are raised during expert testimony about the similarity between comprehension of a waiver of *Miranda* rights and comprehension of the limits of confidentiality in forensic evaluations. The evaluator should be prepared to address the similarities and differences in the content of the information, the requirements of the defendant, the methods in which the information was delivered, and the role of defense counsel. A key difference, for example, is the defendant's access to consultation with defense counsel prior to agreeing to a forensic evaluation, compared to the frequent lack of legal representation or access to defense counsel prior to waiving *Miranda* rights.

After consent is obtained, evaluators usually begin with a clinical interview. The interview should focus on gathering data regarding the defendant's understanding of the warning at the time of interrogation and arrest, not at the time of the evaluation interview. Incarcerated defendants often spend a considerable amount of time discussing their case with other inmates (as well as with "jailhouse lawyers"). They may have acquired information from their own attorneys regarding the nature and content of the *Miranda* warnings. The forensic psychologist must distinguish between pre- and postincarceration knowledge, and identify the defendant's learning while incarcerated and awaiting trial.

The purpose of interviewing the defendant is to (a) obtain relevant background information; (b) locate sources of corroborative data (e.g., schools attended by the defendant, prior places of employment, records of prior hospitalizations); (c) assess the defendant's psychological functioning; (d) obtain the defendant's account of what transpired before and during the interrogation; and (e) specifically assess his or her comprehension of *Miranda* rights (Frumkin, 2000; Grisso, 1998b; Oberlander, 1998; Oberlander & Goldstein, 2001). Relevant background information includes educational, medical, mental health, and prior arrest data (Grisso, 1981; 1998a, 1998b). A history of substance use and abuse might be relevant if the defendant was intoxicated at the time of interrogation (Frumkin, 2000).

Psychological Assessment

Psychological assessment measures usually are chosen on the basis of reasonable hypotheses concerning specific impairments. Because they may serve as indicators of comprehension, most evaluations include assessments of intellectual functioning and educational achievement. In addition, case-specific information generates further hypotheses to guide the selection of additional psychological assessment instruments. Neuropsychological or neurological evaluations sometimes are appropriate to determine whether organic conditions interfered with the defendant's functioning during the interrogation and confession process. Consultation should be sought when indicated with known experts or by consulting such sources as the American Board of Professional Psychology directory of Board Certified Psychologists (www.abpp.com). The amount of psychological assessment often depends on the amount of background documentation available, and, the recency of past assessments. Also, additional hypotheses may arise during the clinical interview process that alter the focus of the assessment phase.

Assessment of Malingering

Defendants sometimes malinger symptoms of mental retardation or mental illness in an attempt to convince the examiner and court that, at the time the *Miranda* warning was given, impairments interfered with the ability to give a knowing and intelligent waiver. Sometimes a review of the defendant's presentation in comparison to prior records yields data relevant to the issue of possible malingering. When the data are less clear, evaluators frequently use specific assessment measures to address the issue of malingering. For example, if a defendant malingers mental retardation, it is helpful to administer a cognitive-based forensic malingering instrument, such as the Validity Indicator Profile (Frederick, 1997). Scores on standardized intelligence tests obtained during the evaluation may be compared to school achievement or reading test scores administered prior to the crime to assess consistency.

To assess the possibility that the defendant might be malingering symptoms of mental illness, it is useful to observe the pattern of symptoms or reported symptoms in terms of their diagnostic integrity, to inquire about "foible" or nonsensical symptoms (as an initial clinical screening), and to see whether the defendant is willing to endorse symptoms that have no relationship to the mental illness(es) of concern. The defendant's reported pattern of symptoms should be compared to records and other historical data concerning mental health history. It often is helpful to refer to validity indices on symptom checklists or personality inventories and to examine the pattern of clinical scores to determine whether they support the defendant's presentation. Specific forensic measures, such as the Structured Interview of Reported Symptoms, are widely used to assess malingering of symptoms of schizophrenia (Rogers, 1992; see the chapter by Rogers & Bender in this volume for a discussion of methods used to assess malingering and defensiveness for a range of forensic issues).

If a determination has been made that the defendant is malingering, the examiner should not terminate the evaluation. Resnick (1997) and Rogers, Sewell, and Goldstein (1994) emphasize that malingering falls on a continuum. That is, while some individuals may totally fabricate symptoms of mental retardation or mental illness, others may attempt to falsely attribute a claim of a lack of understanding of *Miranda* rights to symptoms that may be present, but at a level insufficient to account for the claimed deficits. Malingering and exaggeration in a forensic context is seen by forensic psychologists as an attempt to cope or make the best out of a threatening, negative situation and not necessarily as an aspect of an antisocial personality (Rogers, Sewell, & Goldstein, 1994; Rogers, Salekin, Sewell, Goldstein, & Leonard, 1998). Braginsky and Braginaski (1970) and Resnick (1993) report that the mentally retarded are capable of appearing more severely impaired if it would enhance their chances of obtaining desirable goals. As such, evidence

of malingering does not, by itself, preclude the possibility of the coexistence of symptoms of mental defects or deficits (Otto, 2001).

Measures and Procedures Specific to *Miranda* Comprehension

Grisso's original research (1981) focused on the ability of juveniles to make knowing, intelligent waivers of their *Miranda* rights. To conduct an objective study, Grisso designed four instruments to evaluate juveniles' comprehension of the *Miranda* warning, instruments that also were used to assess adults' comprehension of the warnings. Use of these instruments is considered by many to be an integral part of any competence evaluation of juveniles or adults to waive their *Miranda* rights. Grisso (1998a) provides guidelines for administration and scoring and discusses issues of internal and external validity. He describes the intended uses of the instruments, with recommendations for data interpretation.

- *Comprehension of* Miranda *Rights* (CMR) requires the defendant to paraphrase each element of the *Miranda* warning, assessing general comprehension.
- *Comprehension of* Miranda *Rights–Recognition* (CMR-R; also referred to in Grisso, 1981, publication as *Comprehension of* Miranda–*True-False*), asks the defendant to identify statements that are the same as or different from the elements of the warning. This instrument provides information on whether defendants can recognize the meaning of their rights.
- *Comprehension of* Miranda–*Vocabulary* (CMV) asks for definitions of six words used in the warning to assess, in part, where confusion about rights may have originated.
- *Function of Rights in Interrogation* (FRI) uses hypothetical police interrogation vignettes, accompanied by pictures, to determine whether the defendant understands the function of rights in the context of arrest and interrogation.

Grisso conducted his research on specific population samples in St. Louis County, Missouri. The version of the *Miranda* warning used in his instruments is based on the wording used in that jurisdiction. The actual waiver used with each defendant will vary in terms of vocabulary, sentence length, and reading level. Grisso describes several recommended methods to accommodate the administration of the measures to integrate the actual *Miranda* wording used in the defendant's jurisdiction. The Grisso instruments serve as a useful tool to compare a defendant's comprehension of the actual rights he or she waived to the norms developed by Grisso.

A revised version of the first three instruments is in development, along with a fifth instrument, Perceptions of Coercion in Holding and Interrogation Procedures (P-CHIP). The P-CHIP asks the defendant to specify the likelihood that he or she might offer a true or false confession under various circumstances (Oberlander, Goldstein, & Grisso, 2002). The researchers are currently updating norms for all five instruments. Norms will be based on a larger and more diverse population sample than the Grisso, 1981, data.

If records indicate that the defendant was asked to read the *Miranda* warning silently or aloud, and sometimes even when the defendant was not asked to do so, the evaluator might also wish to ask the defendant to read the warning. The evaluator records how long it takes the defendant to read the warning, whether the defendant reads poorly or is illiterate, and whether poor reading skills might have altered the meaning of the warning by omitting or changing words (Frumkin, 2000; Grisso, 1998b; Oberlander, 1998; Oberlander & Goldstein, 2001). Independent measures of reading level should be used to corroborate the performance of the defendant.

For juvenile defendants who waive *Miranda* in consultation with an interested adult, the evaluation usually includes an interview of the adult. This interview focuses on the adult's account of the consultation and the *Miranda* warning process (if the adult was present during the warning). Usually, the interested adult is given an independent *Miranda* warning; however, the adult might not have been present when the juvenile was given the warning. If an appropriate referral is made, a more complete assessment of the adult might be indicated if there is concern regarding mental retardation, mental illness, or other problems that may have impaired the adult's ability to provide consultation to the juvenile (Grisso, 1981, 1998b; Oberlander, 1998; Oberlander & Goldstein, 2001).

Establishing a Causal Link between Impairments and *Miranda* Comprehension

Data interpretation is the phase in which the evaluator considers whether the full range of evaluation data support a connection between impairments in the defendant's functioning and deficits in *Miranda* comprehension. First, let us examine cases where deficits seem causally linked to a legally relevant factor. If the interview and assessment data relevant to *Miranda* comprehension are consistent with what might be expected from school and other relevant records, and if malingering or exaggeration is ruled out, it is helpful to the court to offer a descriptive explanation of the poor performance. Interview data, data from records or collateral contacts, and psychological assessment data usually help establish *reasons* for the defendant's impairments in *Miranda* comprehension. The deficits in *Miranda* comprehension should be described

with clarity and specificity. A defendant might have comprehended some of the rights in the warning, but not others. The nature and extent of poor comprehension or partial comprehension should be described based on data.

It is usually helpful to specify why malingering or exaggeration were ruled out, and why a clinical (and legally relevant) explanation seems more compelling as a causal link. Providing data-based information in a scientifically sound but descriptive format enhances the likelihood that the fact finder will find the report data useful, necessary, and relevant to a legal determination about the validity of the waiver. In some cases, the evaluator will write a report that is not favorable to a potential legal determination of the validity of the *Miranda* waiver. The evaluator should be equally careful in providing descriptive data in support of the conclusions, explaining why legally relevant causal links do not appear to be clinically compelling.

Expert Testimony, Standards of Practice, and Ethical Issues

Testimony should describe how informed consent was obtained and any difficulties in obtaining it. The sources of data relied on, the methods used, and an explanation of the link between data and conclusions should be included in the testimony. An unbiased summary of relevant records should be presented along with descriptions of interviews conducted with third parties. Results specific to *Miranda* comprehension should be presented as they relate to the ability of the defendant to comprehend each right contained in the warning. Results of psychological assessment data (if relevant) and information from records and collateral contacts should be described in enough detail to illustrate the link (if any) between these data and poor or partial *Miranda* comprehension. The data should be described in a manner that is readily understandable to the trier of fact and all parties to the proceedings. The court makes the legal determination of whether rights were waived knowingly, intelligently, and voluntarily. The degree to which the evaluator's opinion approaches the ultimate issue is a question of professional judgment and sometimes is influenced by judicial expectations favoring or overruling such testimony. (Some would argue that ultimate issue testimony is a question of ethics; see the chapter by Weismann & DeBow in this volume.)

An Illustrative Case

Aaron Wilson, a 19-year-old African American man, was arrested approximately one month before the referral. (All identifying information has been altered.) He was accused of robbery in the first degree and criminal possession of a weapon. According to his attorney, Aaron was in special education classes throughout his school career. It was reported that he was unable to read and write, and he had a long-standing diagnosis of fetal alcohol syndrome. Because of his background and his difficulty in communicating with his attorney, it was requested that I (A. M. Goldstein) evaluate his ability to make a knowing and intelligent waiver of his *Miranda* rights.

Aaron was seen for two sessions at the Bronx County Jail over a period of approximately eight hours. In addition to interviews focusing on his background and history, the circumstances under which the statement was obtained, and his understanding of his constitutional rights as expressed in the *Miranda* waiver used in his jurisdiction, a battery of tests was administered to him: the Wechsler Adult Intelligence Scale III (WAIS-III), Wide Range Achievement Test 3 (WRAT-3), Symbol Digit Modalities Test, Bender-Gestalt, and the four instruments developed by Grisso (1981) described in this chapter. Copies of the following documents were reviewed: the indictment, the defendant's record of prior arrests and convictions, the defendant's statement, school records, records from the Office of Family and Children's Services, home assistance reports, mental health crisis team intervention records, and two prior trial competency evaluations. His father was interviewed as well.

Records consistently indicated a long-standing history of "learning disability and intellectual impairment." In the first grade, Aaron was diagnosed with Mild Mental Retardation and placed in a special education class. He repeated both the second and fifth grades. Teacher notes frequently referred to his inability to follow simple instructions, his problems focusing attention, his distractibility, and his difficulty recalling what he had been told. Psychological testing at age 14 with the Stanford Binet found an IQ of 57, and his Vineland Adaptive Behavioral Scale scores ranged from 46 to 54. Educational evaluations resulted in scores significantly below grade level. Psychological assessment records reflected his "lack of critical thinking skills" at age 17 and a need for continued special educational services to improve his receptive language abilities. Fetal alcohol syndrome was included in the diagnoses.

Records from the Office of Family and Children's Services reflected that both parents were substance abusers and that his mother "ingested alcohol throughout her pregnancy." When seen by the mental health crisis team two weeks prior to his arrest, it was reported that "Aaron was noncommunicative and did not appear to understand the questions posed to him. To those questions which he was able to give answers, Aaron responded with simple yes or no." He was described as highly anxious, agitated, and confused. Two psychiatrists who had evaluated his fitness for trial reported that he appeared to be "borderline retarded."

His father revealed that both he and his common-law wife were heroin users throughout her pregnancy with their son. In addition, he recalled that Aaron's mother had constantly abused alcohol before, during, and immediately after her pregnancy. He confirmed that his son had been diagnosed with the symptoms of fetal alcohol syndrome and "brain problems" and that he had been placed in special education classes throughout his school career. In addition, his father explained that his son had been placed on Ritalin approximately eight years before "to make him calm down." He recalled that although the prescription had run out two weeks before his son's arrest, it had not been renewed because of difficulty with the family's health insurance. According to the father, his son had become hyperactive, anxious, and unable to concentrate.

Aaron was unable to provide informed consent to participate in this assessment. Although several attempts were made to explain the purpose of this assessment and the limits of confidentiality (using simple language), he could not meaningfully paraphrase the information. The assessment continued with authorization from his attorney. Aaron was frequently distracted by outside noise and movements and appeared highly agitated and anxious. During the interview, he had difficulty providing a meaningful, logical, sequential history. He believed he had attended "private schools" for his earliest grades, but was unable to recall the names of these schools. He explained that he left school in the eighth grade because "I was roaming the streets too much." He reported that he never worked because "I can't fill out an application. I never picked up a book to read."

When asked what rights the police had read to him, Aaron stated, "They didn't give me none." When asked what rights he *should* have been provided, he stated, "the lineup." He was again questioned about which rights he was aware of, and he responded, "I'm trying to think. It means to stay out of trouble?" When asked what the police officers on television say to someone they are arresting, he stated, "You're going to jail." He could not spontaneously offer any of the *Miranda* rights.

Aaron was read the waiver on which he had printed his name. He explained that the right to remain silent means "The police don't want you to ask them no questions and they want you to be quiet and say nothing and to just sit down until they're ready for you." Regarding the use of his statements in court, he believed it meant "Anything that you say, your lawyer writes down and he'll tell the judge." Regarding the right to an attorney during interrogation, he first indicated, "I don't know what that means." He added, "It means you talk to your lawyer and tell him what happened or you tell the police what happened. Then my lawyer goes to court and he tells the judge what I said or when he calls him on the phone." Several times during both evaluation sessions, he expressed his belief that "The police will help you by putting you back on the right track." With regard to being assigned an attorney if he could not afford one, he explained, "If I can't pay for one, somebody will be your lawyer to help you with your case and help you out." Later, when asked if he could have had a lawyer present *during* interrogation, he stated, "No, I don't have that kind of money. I get one in court."

On the WAIS-III, Aaron obtained Verbal and Performance IQs of 63 and 59, respectively. His Full Scale IQ was 58. Similar scores were obtained on the indices that comprise this instrument (Verbal Comprehension was 68; Perceptual Organization was 64; Working Memory was 57; and Processing Speed was 68). His scores on the Vocabulary, Comprehension, Digit Span, and Information subtests fell between the first and second percentiles. He experienced difficulty defining relatively simple words, such as "penny" ("It's brown"). His scores on the WRAT-3 were consistent with those obtained on the WAIS-III. Reading, Spelling, and Arithmetic-grade equivalent scores fell within the first grade level and below the first percentile. On the Bender-Gestalt, he made nine errors using the Hutt and Briskin scoring system (five errors or more generally is accepted as suggesting the possibility of organic impairment). On the Symbol Digit Modalities Test, he completed 22 items (the completion of 38 items or fewer for a person his age would strongly suggest the presence of neurological impairment). These scores were highly consistent with his school records. Because the past diagnosis of fetal alcohol syndrome and its effects on his functioning were well documented, no further neuropsychological testing was administered.

On the Grisso (1981) instruments, Aaron's performance was consistent with scores obtained by those with similar levels of intellectual functioning. On the CMR instrument, requiring him to paraphrase the St. Louis County version of the *Miranda* rights, he obtained a score of 1 out of a possible 8. On the CMR-V, the measure requiring him to define six words contained in that version of the waiver (four words are identical to the waiver he signed), his score was 2 out of a possible 12. On the CMR-R, which evaluated his ability to recognize the similarity between each right and three related sentences, his score was 8 out of a possible 12. On the FRI, the instrument in which he was shown a series of pictures and asked questions designed to elicit his understanding of legal situations, his score fell significantly below the mean.

Aaron's understanding of each right was highly consistent across all four measures. In addition, when questioned with the actual version of the waiver he had been given, his comprehension (or lack thereof) of each right was highly consistent with his performance on the Grisso instruments. This assessment revealed that he did not understand the right to remain silent, nor did he comprehend that anything he told the police detectives (or his lawyer) might be used as evidence against him in court. He did not comprehend the confidential nature that existed between him and his attorney. Although he initially understood that if he could not afford a lawyer, one would be assigned by the court, he later stated, "I don't have that kind of money [to get an attorney during interrogation]." Thus, he believed that a lawyer would be appointed *only* after his case was placed on the court docket.

Based on the multiple sources of data, it is clear that Aaron was mildly mentally retarded. Impairments were found in his vocabulary, his ability to express himself, and in his overall judgment and reasoning. He had difficulty concentrating and paying attention, and his thinking was overly concrete and simplistic. His responses to questions were poor regarding his comprehension of the specific *Miranda* warning that he was read. His scores on tests objectively evaluating his understanding of these rights were low. There was a link between his poor comprehension of the *Miranda* warning and his cognitive limitations. Based on the correspondence between past records of his functioning and his current functioning, malingering was ruled out as a possible explanation for his deficits in *Miranda* comprehension. The assessment raised questions about the impact of his poor understanding of these rights on his ability to have made a knowing and intelligent waiver of his constitutional rights at the time of arrest.

EVALUATING THE VALIDITY OF CONFESSIONS

A psycholegal issue infrequently addressed in forensic practice is the trustworthiness or validity of a defendant's confession. Among the reasons that minimal attention has been paid to this topic are: (a) the issue of admissibility of such testimony; (b) the lack of a "profile" or "syndrome" of those likely to proffer false inculpatory statements; and (c) court decisions that have narrowed the application of the constitutional rights delineated in *Miranda v. Arizona* (1966). This section considers the significance of confessions in a criminal trial, the reported frequency of false confessions, why defendants may confess to a crime they did not commit, and models for the assessment of those issues related to untruthful confessions.

Crane v. Kentucky

The U.S. Supreme Court ruled in *Crane v. Kentucky* (1986) that jurors are entitled to hear any evidence regarding the possible lack of truthfulness of a confession. The Court stated that such evidence might assist the trier of fact in deciding how much weight to give the confession in its deliberations. It ruled "Evidence about the manner in which a confession was secured, in addition to its bearing on voluntariness, often bears on its credibility, a matter that is exclusively for the jury to assess."

In *Crane v. Kentucky*, a 16-year-old defendant had been convicted of murder committed during the course of a robbery. The defendant had given an inculpatory statement to the police detectives. Prior to trial, his attorney moved to suppress the confession. However, following a pretrial hearing in which the validity of the *Miranda* waiver was considered, the judge ruled that the confession was voluntarily obtained and the motion was denied. During trial, the court ruled as inadmissible testimony that might indicate that the methods used during interrogation and the length of the interrogation process encouraged a false confession. Among the claims made by the defendant were that he was badgered into making a false confession and that his requests to telephone his mother were denied. It was also claimed that he was surrounded by as many as six police officers at a time and that interrogation continued in a windowless room for a protracted period of time. The trial court ruled that this issue was related solely to the question of voluntariness, previously decided by the court, and was, therefore, inadmissible. The Kentucky Supreme Court upheld this decision.

In considering this case, the U.S. Supreme Court ruled,

> The physical and psychological environment that yielded a confession is not only relevant to the legal question of voluntariness, but can also be of substantial relevance to the ultimate factual issue of the defendant's guilt or innocence, especially in a case . . . where there apparently was no physical evidence to link the petitioner to the crime.

Consequently, the court drew a clear distinction between the determination of the voluntariness of a confession and whether that confession is a truthful one. The defendant is, therefore, entitled to offer evidence that goes to the trustworthiness of a confession.

The Significance of Confessions

When introduced at trial, a confession tends to be evaluated by a jury as providing the clearest sign of a defendant's guilt. Confessions have been described as valuable legal and psychological commodities (Driver, 1968) that, once offered, make it difficult for a defendant to purge himself or herself of guilt. Kassin (1997, p. 221) described a confession as "a prosecutor's most potent weapon." He cited McCormick (1972, p. 316) who

contended that when a confession is introduced into evidence, "[it] makes the other aspects of a trial superfluous." In their research, Kassin and Neumen (1997, p. 481) found support for the belief that "confessions are devastating to a defendant." Similarly, Kassin and Sukel (1997, p. 42) found that "confession evidence is inherently prejudicial." According to Wrightsman and Kassin (1993), confessions are given in approximately 50% of criminal cases. They report that approximately 20% of these confessions are eventually challenged in court. Similarly, Gudjonsson (1992) indicated that retractions of confessions are relatively common occurrences.

Reported Frequency of False Confessions

For several reasons, it is difficult to reliably measure the rate of false confessions. Defendants may claim to have given an untrue confession to avoid responsibility for their criminal acts. The "proof" of a false confession is typically established by physical evidence of innocence (e.g., DNA testing) in the presence of a confession or by the subsequent arrest of another person who admits committing the same crime (with accompanying physical evidence to support the new confession). The lack of a "clearinghouse" for gathering such information makes accurate data impossible.

Borchard (1932) identified "several cases" involving false confessions among 64 defendants found innocent by irrefutable evidence. Kalven and Zeisel (1966) reported that of all cases that proceed to trial, confessions are recanted in 20% of cases. Of 70 British cases involving wrongful imprisonment, Brandon and Davies (1973) reported that the most common factor related to their release was false confessions. Bedau and Radelet (1987) reviewed 350 death penalty convictions in which miscarriages of justice were involved; they reported that 49 cases involved false confessions. Of 205 cases involving wrongful imprisonment, 8% involved false confessions, according to Rattner (1988). Estimates of false confessions range from fewer than 35 per year (Cassell, 1996a, 1996b) to as high as 600 per year in the United States (Huff, Rattner, & Sagarin, 1986). Kassin and McNall (1991) estimated the rate of false confessions falls between fewer than 30 to 60 per year. Gudjonsson and Sigurdsson (1994) reported that 12% of offenders they surveyed in Iceland *claimed* to have provided false confessions. Ofshe (1989), Gudjonsson (1992), Leo (1992), Wrightsman and Kassin (1993), Ofshe and Watters (1994), and Scheck, Neufeld, and Dwyer (2000) provide case examples of false confessions by innocent individuals, some of which resulted in executions for crimes they did not commit. A detailed case history involving an allegedly false confession in a military court marshall is described by Talmadge (2001).

Why Defendants May Provide a False Confession

Münsterberg (1908), frequently credited with founding the field of forensic psychology (see the chapter by Goldstein in this volume), wrote that it is a misconception to believe that false confessions do not occur. He acknowledged the common sense belief that, "It would be inconceivable that any man who was innocent . . . should claim the infamy of guilt" (p. 142). He proposed a wide range of hypotheses for reasons someone might confess to a crime for which they are innocent. Münsterberg cited as reasons for false confessions such factors as "a weak mind," threats, promises, social motives, fatigue, "passive yielding," fear, dissociation, depression, and suggestibility. Much of the research conducted since Münsterberg's original thesis tends to confirm these hypotheses, as well as other factors, as contributing to false confessions.

Factors associated with false confessions may be divided into three major categories: *situational,* related to the demands of the interrogation process itself and the difficulty defendants may have in coping with the pressures of interrogation; *intellectual,* related to the defendant's cognitive abilities, including judgment, suggestibility, and naïveté; and *personality,* related to such traits and characteristics as acquiescence to authority.

Situational Factors Contributing to False Confessions

Inbau et al. (1986) suggested a nine-step strategy for confronting a suspect: (a) Confront the suspect with his or her guilty actions; (b) develop psychological "themes" that help the suspect justify or excuse the crime; (c) interrupt all statements of denial by the suspect; (d) overcome the suspect's factual, moral, or emotional objections to the charges (e.g., reframe the crime so that the suspect will find it more acceptable to admit guilt); (e) ensure that passive suspects pay attention; (f) express sympathy and understanding when urging the suspect to tell the truth; (g) offer face-saving alternative explanations for the suspect's actions; (h) encourage the suspect to give a detailed account of the crime; and (i) convert the suspect's account to a full written confession (which has been interpreted as convincing a reluctant suspect to sign a written confession).

Kassin (1997) summarized the specific ploys of interrogation described by Inbau and colleagues (1986) in more psychologically oriented terms and methodology. These ploys include maximization, minimization, communicating implied threats or promises, and using negative and positive incentives. *Maximization* includes overstating the seriousness of the offense or charge, confronting the suspect with exaggerated or false evidence, and blaming the suspect for all troubles

in life. *Minimization* includes understating the magnitude of the offense or charge, offering a face-saving story reconstruction, and offering statements of tolerance for the suspect's actions. *Communicating implied threats or promises* includes implying leniency or immunity and using scare tactics to intimidate a suspect. *Negative incentives* include telling the suspect that the longer he or she denies committing the crime, the longer the interrogation will continue; yelling at the suspect whenever a denial is expressed; and blaming the suspect for destroying family or religion by lying about a crime. *Positive incentives* include offers of sympathy or friendship, offering praise for the suspect's incriminating statements, and offering tangible rewards (e.g., food, soda, cigarettes) for discussing the crime.

Such strategies are designed to play on the weaknesses of defendants and to break down their resistance. In some cases, the strategies might lead to false confessions. In fact, in *Miranda v. Arizona* (1966), the Court opined that these and similar methods advocated by Inbau and Reid (1967) might result in involuntary confessions that might raise questions regarding their "inherent trustworthiness." Inbau et al. (1986) contend that this is a valid approach to interrogation because it is possible to distinguish between true and false denials using verbal and nonverbal cues. Despite this assertion, empirical evidence suggests that people are poor judges of truth and deception (Ekman & O'Sullivan, 1991; Kassin, 1997). Kassin and Fong (1999) found that those who underwent training to distinguish between true and false confessions were *less* able to do so than those without such training (despite expressing a greater degree of confidence in their ability to do so).

Many interrogation techniques are designed to frighten suspects, and their effects are not limited solely to those who are guilty of a crime. The nature of the interrogation process is such that police pressure, persuasiveness, overzealous questioning, browbeating, ignoring contradictory evidence, and fear of confinement may serve to encourage false confessions (Gudjonsson, 1992). The source of a false confession may be related to the defendant's "perceived inability to cope with the police interrogation" (p. 78). Gudjonsson wrote, "Confessing behavior [is linked] primarily with the suspect's ability to cope with pressure, rather than their tendency to give in to leading questions per se" (p. 157). Similarly, Wrightsman and Kassin (1993) emphasized the inability of suspects to cope with interrogation as a factor contributing to false confessions. Grisso (1981, 1986) believes that those who have a poor capacity to resist police pressure during interrogation may comply with demands for a confession to avoid jail. Despite the significance of the demands of the interrogation process, "false confessions can occur, even in the absence of any obvious interrogation pressure" (Gudjonsson, 1992, p. xi).

Because confessions are typically obtained "behind closed doors," Leo (2001a, 2001b) recommends that videotaping of interrogations be mandatory. By memorializing the interrogation, questions regarding suggestions, pressure, and subtle promises and threats might be more validly addressed.

Intellectual Factors Contributing to False Confessions

According to Shaw and Budd (1982), mentally retarded individuals have a stronger need to please others, especially those they identify as authority figures. They are more likely to demonstrate acquiescent behavior by providing socially desirable responses to comply with the demands of others. Parry (1987) discussed mental impairments as factors contributing to involuntary confessions. Gudjonsson (1992) associated low intelligence with increased suggestibility, a factor he cited as contributing to false confessions. Similarly, Wrightsman and Kassin (1993) reported that low intelligence is a factor related to untruthful confessions.

Everington and Fulero (1999) found increased levels of suggestibility in the mentally retarded. They were more likely to respond to suggestive questions and were likely to modify their answers when requested to do so. Research on individuals with mental deficiencies (e.g., mental retardation) indicates that they are more likely to respond to leading questions containing false or misleading information (Perlman, Ericson, Esses, & Isaacs, 1994). They have a strong desire to please others, particularly authority figures (Ellis & Luckasson, 1985). Yes/no questions raise the likelihood of response biases in mentally deficient individuals (Sigelman, Budd, Winer, Shoenrock, & Martin, 1982), and the tendency to acquiesce is so powerful that even absurd questions yield affirmative answers (Sigelman, Budd, Spanhel, & Shoenrock, 1981).

The relationship between intelligence and suggestibility is a critical one in evaluating the validity of a confession. The work of Gudjonsson (1984, 1989, 1991) revealed significant differences in IQ and suggestibility between alleged false confessors and resisters in criminal trials. Alleged false confessors were found to have lower IQ and were more suggestible than were resisters, with a greater magnitude of difference in suggestibility scores than IQ scores. Clare and Gudjonsson (1993) found that individuals with a Full Scale IQ in the range of 57 to 75 were more suggestible than individuals with an average IQ because they were much more susceptible to leading questions. In addition, they confabulated more, and such individuals were more acquiescent. Individuals with low IQ may be more likely to offer confessions, regardless of their truth.

Personality Factors Contributing to False Confessions

A suspect's personality traits and characteristics may contribute to a false confession. However, whether these traits prompt an untrue confession depends greatly on the demands of the interrogation situation itself. Typically, personality factors cannot be considered in isolation from the interrogation process. Gudjonsson (1992) hypothesized that unresolved childhood conflicts (related to such factors as self-image, the need to please, and poor coping skills) might lay the foundation for personality characteristics likely to produce a false confession. He described a number of personality traits that may be associated with false confessions: the need for approval, the need to please, and the need to avoid unpleasant conflicts, including susceptibility to self-criticism. Wrightsman and Kassin (1993) described similar factors, including the need to avoid controversy, suggestibility, and acquiescence when interrogated. Also associated with the likelihood of conforming to the demands of the interrogator are low self-esteem, anxiety proneness, feelings of powerlessness, need to fulfill role expectations, fear of negative evaluations and social disapproval, uncritical obedience to authority, and lack of assertiveness (Gudjonsson, 1992). Leo and Ofshe (1998) wrote that increased anxiety associated with interrogation may serve to increase the likelihood of an invalid confession. Shuy (1998) argued that the need for self-aggrandizement may contribute to a false confession. Ofshe (2000) opines that people confess as a means of coping with a threatening situation, seeing the confession as the best option available.

Other Factors Associated with False Confessions

Bedau and Radelet (1987) reported cases of false confessions designed to impress a girlfriend and to hide the fact that, at the time of the crime, the suspect was sexually intimate with another woman. Gudjonsson (1992) cited mental illness, recent bereavement, and language difficulties as factors that may affect the ability of the suspect to cope with interrogation pressures. Similarly, he cited age, lack of experience with the police, memory impairments, locus of control, and tendencies to confabulate as relevant factors to consider. The need to protect another individual from being accused of the crime may be a reason for providing an untruthful confession (Gudjonsson & Sigurdsson, 1994). Kassin and Fong (1999) cited the desire "to go home" as a possible motivating factor contributing to a false confession. Wrightsman (2001) believes some false confessions may be offered "by a desire for publicity or by generalized guilt or they may reflect some form of psychotic behavior" (pp. 143–144). A summary of police interrogation's methods and strategies that may contribute to false confessions can be found in Leo (2001b).

Types of False Confessions

The mere fact that a defendant recants a confession or challenges its veracity does not necessarily make the confession false (Wrightsman, 2001). However, for those that are untruthful, three types of false confessions have been identified (Kassin & Wrightsman, 1985; Wrightsman & Kassin, 1993). These three models, based on theories of attitude change as well as on anecdotal cases, attempt to explain reasons suspects offer false confessions. Others working in this area, including Gudjonsson (1992) and Shuy (1998), have cited these models in their work. Although these models of false confessions imply three distinct categories, for an individual defendant, they sometimes overlap (Gudjonsson, 1992).

Voluntary False Confessions

Voluntary false confessions are offered willingly, free from external pressure from interrogators. Often, such individuals have seen a crime on television or read about it in the newspaper and voluntarily go to the police station to confess. Frequently, these false confessions are motivated by a desire for publicity or may represent a need to reduce guilt from other real or imagined prior transgressions. A confession may be symptomatic of an underlying psychosis, and, at times, the person confessing may be truly convinced of his or her guilt. Some individuals may offer voluntary false confessions to protect others from being blamed for the crime. As discussed by Gudjonsson (1992), it is unclear how readily police detectives can recognize a voluntary false confession.

Coerced-Compliant False Confessions

Coerced-compliant confessions are given by suspects who are aware of their innocence, but, for a number of reasons, are unable to withstand the pressure of interrogation. As described by Wrightsman (2001), confessions may be given "to escape further interrogation, to gain a promised benefit, or to avoid threatened punishment" (p. 144). The suspect is aware that he or she did not commit the crime to which the confession is given. Their compliance behavior is "a means of coping with the demand characteristics including the perceived pressure of the situation" (Gudjonsson, 1992, p. 228).

Such individuals may have partial or full recognition of the consequences of their confessions. However, frequently, they may believe "that somehow the truth will come out later or that the solicitor will be able to rectify their false confession"

(Gudjonsson, 1992, p. 228). One of the authors (Goldstein) had a case in which a woman found to be both highly suggestible and very naïve may have provided a false confession based on police pressure. After several hours of interrogation, during which time she denied involvement in a conspiracy to commit murder, she "confessed" so that she could return home to care for her young child and avoid incarceration "with tough ladies who will definitely enjoy a new piece of meat." Her concern for the well-being of her child, her fear of being brutalized by other inmates, and the promises made to her by police detectives that they would quickly get things straightened out and allow her to return home, contributed to her suspension of judgment and her decision to confess to a crime that she claimed that she did not commit. Another defendant, who was found to be somewhat mentally slow, confessed to two murders, having been convinced of the futility of his protestations of innocence. He claimed that he had purposely provided inaccurate details regarding the crimes, believing that he would later sue the police for "entrapment" and brutality. In this case, there was no physical evidence tying the defendant to the crime itself. He believed that his attorney would "straighten things out later." (See Johnson & Hunt, 2000, for a description of a case of a 13-year-old involving his ability to waive *Miranda* rights, as well as the likelihood that he gave a false confession.)

Coerced-Internalized False Confessions

With prolonged interrogation and pressure, some innocent suspects gradually begin to adopt the fact pattern presented by interrogating officers. They do so despite a lack of memory regarding details of the offense. They begin to question their judgment and may be quick to adopt suggestions that they have "repressed" details of the crime, allowing them to endorse those details provided to them by interrogators. As described by Gudjonsson and MacKeith (1982), such confessions tend to come from passivity, self-doubt, and "memory distrust."

Implications for Forensic Assessment and Testimony Regarding False Confessions

Forensic psychologists may be asked to evaluate defendants' allegedly false confessions. As discussed in the first section of this chapter, this represents a different referral question, both legally and psychologically, from assessing the validity of a defendant's *Miranda* waiver. Although *Miranda* rights may have been validly waived, questions may remain regarding the trustworthiness of the confession. Referrals cover a broad spectrum of concerns about the defendant's functioning and its relevant to the likelihood that he or she might have given a false confession.

Experts are not in a position to offer an opinion on whether a defendant's confession is, indeed, a false one; clearly, such an ultimate opinion should be left to the trier of fact to determine. However, forensic psychologists can evaluate factors associated with providing false confessions: overall intelligence, judgment, tendencies to suspend critical thinking, decision-making abilities under stress, the capacity to cope with pressure (especially that associated with interrogation), tendencies to acquiesce to the demands of those identified as authority figures, and the need to please others and avoid criticism and conflict. A common topic for this type of assessment is the role psychotic symptoms (including delusions) and underlying feelings of guilt might have played in affecting cognitive skills and judgment. Forensic psychologists might evaluate suggestibility (as a personality construct and as an interactive process), a major factor hypothesized to contribute to false confessions.

Interview of Defendant

All evaluations on issues related to false confessions should include interviews of the defendant. A detailed background history provides a sense of the defendant's overall mental state and reveals sources of corroborating records to establish the defendant's credibility. In addition, instances of marked suggestibility and/or acquiescence to authority figures that predate the confession may serve as real-life validation of traits or characteristics that would contribute to a false confession. For example, in one case, a defendant claimed that she had been coerced by the police into signing a statement admitting to a serious felony that she claimed she had not committed. A review of her background found that on a number of occasions, she had been "talked into" making decisions not in her best interests or contrary to her intended plans: She had gone to a physician for birth control pills, but was talked into a tubal ligation; on another occasion, she closed a successful business for fear of offending a close friend she respected. In reviewing the assessment data, the evaluator must consider the defendant's rendition of the reasons a confession was given and is being challenged as false.

Third-Party Sources

School, employment, and mental health records, along with interviews of others familiar with the defendant, are frequently a valuable source of corroborating information. (A discussion of the use of such sources of data can be found in the chapter by Heilbrun, Warren, & Picarello in this volume.)

A review of the video- or audiotape of the interrogation (if one exists) may serve as an essential source for both framing questions to ask the defendant and determining the source of some details in the confession (however, the defendant may have first given a statement "off-camera" and may merely be repeating what he or she had stated earlier). Instances of the defendant "giving in" to the demands of others, naïveté, suggestibility, and examples of a need to please or to avoid criticism represent relevant data to consider in conducting such examinations. Similarly, descriptions of the defendant as headstrong, stubborn, a leader, and self-assertive are of equal relevance.

Psychological Testing

If cognitive limitations are suggested, a full intellectual assessment is indicated. In addition, neuropsychological testing focusing on executive decision making may be relevant should there be issues related to neuropsychological impairments. The specific tests and forensic assessment instruments must be determined on a case-by-case basis. There is no established battery for conducting such assessments. Personality testing, especially with well-validated instruments (Minnesota Multiphasic Personality Inventory 2, Personality Assessment Inventory), may contribute to an understanding of the defendant's traits, characteristics, self-image, and coping skills. These factors may be relevant in considering those characteristics unique to the defendant that may have contributed to a false confession.

An instrument of potential value is a suggestibility measure such as the Gudjonsson Suggestibility Scale (Gudjonsson, 1984, 1987). Defendants are read a narrative paragraph describing a fictitious crime and are asked to recall as much as they can about the story, both immediately and after approximately 50 minutes. Questions are then asked of the defendant, most of which are "subtly misleading." Even if questions are answered correctly, the defendant is informed that a number of errors have been made and that the questions must be asked again and he or she should try to answer them more accurately. Changes in answers are recorded along with the degree to which defendants give in to the misleading questions. A Total Suggestibility score is obtained. The results of this measure, in the context of a multimodal assessment, sometimes provide useful data regarding the existence of suggestibility as a long-standing characteristic of the defendant.

The relevance of psychological assessment measures depends on their relationship to hypothesized characteristics of the defendant that might be related to a tendency to offer a false confession. Reasonable hypotheses are formed by reviewing records, interviewing relevant collateral contacts, consulting with defense counsel and other individuals with knowledge of the defendant's functioning in legal settings, and observational and interview data. Psychological testing tends to be standard practice in evaluations of abilities related to the trustworthiness of confessions, but sometimes, relevant variables of concern are sufficiently documented in records or sufficiently apparent in observational and interview data. (Even in those cases, assessment data might be used to bolster conclusions or to ensure sufficient reliance on multiple sources of data.) Relevant variables should be described in reports and linked (either clinically or in response to hypothetical questions) to the defendant's functioning at the time the confession took place.

Summary

Although forensic psychologists, like those in other professions, are not in a position to offer the opinion that a specific confession is untruthful, they can evaluate situational, intellectual, and personality characteristics that might have "pushed" a suspect into providing a false confession. It clearly is up to the trier of fact to determine if the expert's findings and testimony are credible and relevant when they determine how much weight to give the defendant's inculpatory statement. *Crane v. Kentucky* (1986) permits testimony bearing on the credibility of the defendant's confession. In conducting these assessments and in the provision of testimony, theoretical and empirical knowledge of why people provide false confessions, knowledge of models of false confessions, and familiarization with appropriate assessment methodology are required as part of the field's standard of care.

CONCLUSION

The validity of *Miranda* rights waivers carries legal significance because a confession typically is viewed as highly persuasive evidence. The validity of the waiver is especially legally relevant when the prosecution expects to offer the confession as a primary or sole source of evidence to convict the defendant. Convictions can result from both illegally obtained confessions as well as confessions that are unreliable. Both *Miranda* comprehension and confessional competence are significant forensic assessment issues. The behavioral sciences offer theories, assessment methods, and methods for analyzing the significance of individual variables in assessing abilities related to *Miranda* comprehension, the validity of

waivers, and the trustworthiness of confessions. Forensic psychologists who conduct assessments of the validity of *Miranda* waivers and factors that may have contributed to false confessions are encouraged to familiarize themselves with jurisdictional concerns. These include factors such as the nature of the *Miranda* warning used in local jurisdictions, common interrogation practices in local jurisdictions, and idiosyncratic rulings in binding case law relevant in specific regions.

In recent years, the U.S. Supreme Court frequently has been closely divided on rulings addressing 5th, 6th, and 14th Amendment rights. Where discretion is permitted, judicial approaches to cases involving competence to waive *Miranda* and the credibility of confessions have been more conservative in the past decade than in previous decades. When there are changes in the composition of the Court, these authors anticipate that significant changes may occur in Court decisions focusing on these issues. When case law changes in significant ways, forensic assessment methodology sometimes must be revised to address legally and clinically relevant standards cited in rulings. Forensic psychologists conducting assessments in these areas must keep abreast of the latest state and U.S. Supreme Court decisions to conduct legally relevant evaluations.

REFERENCES

Aubry, A. S., & Caputo, R. R. (1980). *Criminal interrogation* (3rd ed.). Springfield, IL: Charles C. Thomas.

Bedau, H. A., & Radelet, M. L. (1987). Miscarriages of justice in potentially capital cases. *Stanford Law Review, 40,* 21–179.

Blackburn v. Alabama, 361 U.S. 199 (1960).

Blagrove, M., Cole-Morgan, D., & Lambe, H. (1994). Interrogative suggestibility: The effects of sleep deprivation and relationship with field dependence. *Applied Cognitive Psychology, 8,* 169–179.

Borchard, E. M. (1932). *Convicting the innocent: Sixty-five actual errors of criminal justice.* Golden City: Doubleday.

Braginsky, B., & Braginaski, Y. (1970). Manipulation of "intelligence" by institutionalized mental retardates. *Proceedings of the Annual Convention of the American Psychological Association, 5,* 523–524.

Brandon, R., & Davies, C. (1973). *Wrongful imprisonment.* London: Allen & Unwin.

Brown v. Mississippi, 297 U.S. 278 (1936).

Cassell, C. K. (1996a). All benefits, no costs: The grand illusion of *Miranda*'s defenders. *Northwestern University Law Review, 90,* 1084–1124.

Cassell, C. K. (1996b). *Miranda*'s social costs: An empirical re-assessment. *Northwestern University Law Review, 90,* 387–499.

Clare, I. C. H., & Gudjonsson, G. H. (1993). Interrogative suggestibility, confabulation, and acquiescence in people with mild learning disabilities (mental handicap): Implications for reliability during police interrogations. *British Journal of Clinical Psychology, 32,* 295–301.

Clare, I. C. H., Gudjonsson, G. H., Rutter, S. C., & Cross, P. (1994). The inter-rater-reliability of the Gudjonsson Suggestibility Scale (Form 2). *British Journal of Clinical Psychology, 33,* 357–365.

Colorado v. Connelly, 479 U.S. 157 (1986).

Commonwealth v. Guyton, 405 Mass. 497, 502 (1979).

Commonwealth v. a Juvenile, 389 Mass. 128 (1983).

Commonwealth v. a Juvenile, 402 Mass. 275, 279 (1989).

Commonwealth v. King, 17 Mass. App. Ct. 602 (1984).

Commonwealth v. Lamb, 365 Mass. 265, 270, 311 NE.2d 47 (1974).

Commonwealth v. MacNeill, 399 Mass. 71 (1987).

Commonwealth v. Mandile, 497 Mass. 410 (1986).

Commonwealth v. Meehan, 377 Mass. 522 (1979).

Commonwealth v. Philips, 414 Mass. 804 (1993).

Commonwealth v. Roane, 459 Pa. 389, 394, 329 A.2d 286, 289–290 (1974).

Coyote v. United States, 380 F.2d 305 (1967).

Crane v. Kentucky, 106 S. Ct. Rptr. 2142 (1986).

Culombe v. Connecticut, 367 U.S. 568 (1961).

Dickerson v. United States, 166 F.3d 667 (2000).

Driver E. D. (1968). Confessions and the social psychology of coercion. *Harvard Law Review, 82,* 42–61.

Ekman, P., & O'Sullivan, M. (1991). Who can catch a liar? *American Psychologist, 46,* 913–920.

Ellis, J., & Luckasson, R. (1985). Mentally retarded criminal defendants. *George Washington Law Review, 53,* 414–493.

Escabedo v. Illinois, 378 U.S. 478 (1964).

Everington, C., & Fulero, S. M. (1999). Competence to confess: Measuring understanding and suggestibility of defendants with mental retardation. *Mental Retardation, 37,* 212–220.

Fare v. Michael C., 442 U.S. 707 (1979).

Feld, B. C. (2000). Juveniles' waiver of legal rights: Confessions, *Miranda* and the right to counsel. In T. Grisso & R. G. Schwartz (Eds.), *Youth on trial: A developmental perspective on juvenile justice* (pp. 105–138). Chicago: University of Chicago Press.

Ford v. State, 75 Miss. 101, 21 So. 524 (1897).

Frederick, R. I. (1997). *Validity Indicator Profile manual.* Minneapolis, MN: National Computer Systems.

Frumkin, B. (2000). Competency to waive *Miranda* rights: Clinical and legal issues. *Mental and Physical Disability Law Reporter, 24,* 326–331.

Fry, E. (1977). Fry's readability graph: Clarification, validity, and extension to level 17. *Journal of Reading, 21,* 249.

Fulero, S. M., & Everington, C. (1995). Assessing competency to waive *Miranda* rights in defendants with mental retardation. *Law and Human Behavior, 19,* 533–543.

Gallagos v. Colorado, 370 U.S. 49, 54–55 (1962).

Grisso, T. (1981). *Juveniles' waiver of rights: Legal and psychological competence.* New York: Plenum Press.

Grisso, T. (1986). *Evaluating competencies.* New York: Plenum Press.

Grisso, T. (1998a). *Assessing understanding and appreciation of Miranda rights: Manual and materials.* Sarasota, FL: Professional Resources Press.

Grisso, T. (1998b). *Forensic evaluation of juveniles.* Sarasota, FL: Professional Resources Press.

Grisso, T., & Ring, M. (1979). Parents' attitudes toward juveniles' rights in interrogation. *Criminal Justice and Behavior, 6,* 211.

Gudjonsson, G. H. (1984). A new scale of interrogative suggestibility. *Personality and Individual Differences, 5,* 303–314.

Gudjonsson, G. H. (1987). A parallel form of the Gudjonsson Suggestibility Scale. *British Journal of Clinical Psychology, 26,* 215–221.

Gudjonsson, G. H. (1989). Compliance and an interrogation situation: A new scale. *Personality and Individual Differences, 10,* 535–540.

Gudjonsson, G. H. (1991). The effects of intelligence and memory on group differences in suggestibility and compliance. *Personality and Individual Differences, 5,* 503–505.

Gudjonsson, G. H. (1992). *The psychology of interrogations, confessions, and testimony.* London: Wiley.

Gudjonsson, G. H., & MacKeith, J. A. C. (1982). False confessions, psychological effects of interrogation. In A. Trankell (Ed.), *Reconstructing the past: The role of psychologists in criminal trials* (pp. 253–269). Deventer, Holland: Kluwer Press.

Gudjonsson, G. H., & Sigurdsson, J. F. (1994). How frequently do false confessions occur? An empirical study among prison inmates. *Psychology, Crime and Law, 1,* 21–26.

Haley v. Ohio, 332 U.S. 596 (1948).

Huff, C. R., Rattner, A., & Sagarin, E. (1986). Guilty until proven innocent: Wrongful conviction and public policy. *Crime and Delinquency, 32,* 518–544.

Illinois v. Higgins, 278 N.E.2d 68 (1993).

Inbau, F. E., & Reid, J. E. (1967). *Criminal interrogations and confessions* (2nd ed.). Baltimore: Williams & Wilkins.

Inbau, F. E., Reid, J. E., & Buckley, J. P. (1986). *Criminal interrogation and confessions* (3rd ed.). Baltimore: Williams & Wilkins.

In re Gault, 387 U.S. 1 (1967).

In re Morgan, 35 Ill. App. 3d 10, 341 NE.2d 19 (1975).

Johnson, M. B., & Hunt, R. C. (2000). The psycholegal interface in juvenile *Miranda* assessment. *American Journal of Forensic Psychology, 18,* 17–35.

Johnson v. Zerbst, 304 U.S. 458 (1938).

Kalven, H., & Zeisel, H. (1966). *The American jury.* Boston: Little, Brown.

Kassin, S. M., & Wrightsman, L. S. (1985). Confession evidence. In S. M. Kassin & L. S. Wrightsman (Eds.), *The psychology of evidence and trial procedure* (pp. 67–94). Thousand Oaks, CA: Sage.

Kassin, S. M. (1997). The psychology of confession evidence. *American Psychologist, 52,* 221–233.

Kassin S. M., & Fong, C. T. (1999). "I'm innocent!": Effects of training on judgments of truth and deception in the interrogation room. *Law and Human Behavior, 23,* 499–516.

Kassin, S. M., & McNall, K. (1991). Police interrogations and confessions: Communicating promises and threats by pragmatic implication. *Law and Human Behavior, 15,* 233–251.

Kassin, S. M., & Neumann, K. (1997). On the power of confession evidence: An experimental test of the fundamental difference hypothesis. *Law and Human Behavior, 21,* 469–484.

Kassin, S. M., & Sukel, H. (1997). Coerced confessions and the jury: An experimental test of the "harmless error" rule. *Law and Human Behavior, 21,* 27–46.

Kent v. United States, 383 U.S. 541 (1966).

Leo, R. A. (1992). From coercion to deception: The changing nature of police interrogation in America. *Crime, Law, and Social Change, 18,* 35–39.

Leo, R. A. (2001a). Questioning the relevance of *Miranda* in the twenty-first century. *Michigan Law Review, 99,* 1000–1029.

Leo, R. A. (2001b). False confessions: Causes, consequences, and solutions. In S. D. Wostervelt & J. A. Humphrey (Eds.), *Wrongly convicted: Perspectives on criminal justice.* New Brunswick, NJ: Rutgers University Press.

Leo, R. A., & Ofshe, R. (1998). The consequences of false confessions. *Journal of Criminal Law and Criminology, 88,* 429–496.

MacDonald, J. M., & Michaud, D. L. (1987). *The confession: Interrogation and criminal profiles for police officers.* Denver, CO: Apache.

Malloy v. Hogan, 378 U.S. 1 (1964).

McCormick, C. T. (1972). *Handbook of the law of evidence* (2nd ed.). St. Paul, MN: West.

Miranda v. Arizona, 384 U.S. 436 (1966).

Münsterberg, H. (1908). *On the witness stand: Essays on psychology and crime.* New York: Doubleday.

Oberlander, L. B. (1998). *Miranda* comprehension and confessional competence. *Expert Opinion, 2,* 11–12.

Oberlander, L. B., & Goldstein, N. E. (2001). A review and update on the practice of evaluating *Miranda* comprehension. *Behavioral Sciences and the Law.*

Oberlander, L. B., Goldstein, N. E., & Grisso, T. (2002). *Comprehension of* Miranda *rights.* Manuscript in preparation.

Ofshe, R. (1989). Coerced confessions: The logic of seemingly irrational action. *Cultic Studies Journal, 6,* 1–5.

Ofshe, R. (2000, March 10). The decision to confess: The process of eliciting true and false confessions. Paper presented at biennial meeting of the American Psychology-Law Society, New Orleans, LA.

Ofshe, R., & Watters, E. (1994). *Making monsters: False memories, psychotherapy, and sexual hysteria.* New York: Scribner.

O'Hara, C. E., & O'Hara, G. L. (1981). *Fundamentals of criminal investigation.* Springfield, IL: Charles C. Thomas.

Orozco v. Texas, 89 S. Ct. 1095, 324 U.S. (1969).

Otto, R. K. (2001, February 15). *Assessing malingering and deception.* Seminar presented at American Academy of Forensic Psychology Workshop, San Antonia, TX.

Parry, J. (1987). Involuntary confessions based on mental impairments. *Mental and Physical Disabilities Law Reporter, 11,* 2–4.

People v. Higgins, 278 N.E.2d 68 (1993).

People v. Lara, 432 P.2d 202 (1967).

People v. Rodney P., 286 N.Y.2d 225 (1967).

People v. Williams, 62 N.Y.2d 285 (1984).

Perlman, N. B., Ericson, K. L., Esses, V. M., & Isaacs, B. J. (1994). The developmentally handicapped witness: Competence as a function of question format. *Law and Human Behavior, 18,* 171–187.

Rattner, A. (1988). Convicted but innocent: Wrongful conviction and the criminal justice system. *Law and Human Behavior, 12,* 283–293.

Resnick, P. J. (1993). Defrocking the fraud: The detection of malingering. *Israel Journal of Psychiatry and Related Sciences, 30,* 93–101.

Resnick, P. J. (1997). Malingering of posttraumatic disorders. In R. Rogers (Ed.), *Clinical assessment of malingering and deception.* New York: Guilford Press.

Rock v. Arkansas, 483 U.S. 44 (1987).

Rogers, R. (1992). *Structured Interview of Reported Symptoms.* Odessa, FL: Psychological Assessment Resources.

Rogers, R., Salekin, R. T., Sewell, K. W., Goldstein, A. M., & Leonard, K. (1998). A comparison of forensic and nonforensic malingerers: A protypical analysis of explanatory models. *Law and Human Behavior, 22,* 353–368.

Rogers, R., Sewell, K. W., & Goldstein, A. M. (1994). Explanatory models of malingering: A protypical analysis. *Law and Human Behavior, 18,* 543–552.

Scheck, B., Neufeld, P., & Dwyer, J. (2000). *Actual innocence.* New York: Doubleday.

Shaw, J. A., & Budd, E. D. (1982). Determinants of acquiescence and nay saying of mentally retarded persons. *American Journal of Mental Deficiency, 87,* 108–110.

Shuy, R. W. (1998). *The language of confession, interrogation, and deception.* Thousand Oaks, CA: Sage.

Sigelman, C. K., Budd, E. C., Spanhel, C. L., & Shoenrock, C. J. (1981). When in doubt, say yes: Acquiescence in interviews with mentally retarded persons. *Mental Retardation, 19,* 53–58.

Sigelman, C. K., Budd, E. C., Winer, J. L., Shoenrock, C. J., & Martin, P. W. (1982). Evaluating alternative techniques of questioning mentally retarded persons. *American Journal of Mental Deficiency, 86,* 511–518.

Spano v. New York, 360 U.S. 315 (1959).

State v. Jackson, 304 S.E.2d 134 (1983).

State v. Prater, 77 Wash. 2d 526 529, 463 P.2d 640, 641 (1970).

Talmadge, S. A. (2001). Possible false confession in a military court martial: A case study. *Military Psychology, 13,* 235–241.

United States ex rel. Simon v. Maroney, 228 F. Supp. 800 W.D. Pa. (1964).

United States v. Crocker, 510 F.2d 1129 (1975).

West v. United States, 399 F.2d 467 (1968).

Wrightsman, L. S. (2001). *Forensic psychology.* Stamford, CT: Wadsworth.

Wrightsman, L. S., & Kassin, S. M. (1993). *Confessions in the courtroom.* Newbury Park, CA: Sage.

CHAPTER 19

Assessment of Competence to Stand Trial

KATHLEEN POWERS STAFFORD

Competence to stand trial has been termed "the most significant mental health inquiry pursued in the system of criminal law" (Stone, 1975, p. 200). According to Steadman, Monahan, Hartstone, Davis, and Robbins (1982), 25,000 defendants were evaluated for trial competency in the United States in 1978, and 6,500 were hospitalized as incompetent to stand trial. Hoge, Bonnie, Poythress, and Monahan (1992) estimated that pretrial competence evaluations are sought in 2% to 8% of all felony cases. LaFortune and Nicholson (1995) reported that judges and attorneys estimate that competency is a legitimate issue in approximately 5% of criminal cases, although only two-thirds of these defendants whose competency is questionable are actually referred for formal competency evaluations. With deinstitutionalization of mentally ill persons, concern has been expressed about the "criminalization" of the mentally ill (Teplin, 1994). The proportion of patients in public psychiatric hospitals who have been committed by criminal courts has significantly increased (Linhorst & Dirks-Linhorst, 1997). Cooper and Grisso

(1997) noted the possibility that findings of incompetence or referrals for inpatient competence evaluations have become a mechanism for committing mentally ill persons who would otherwise not be provided inpatient care.

Trial competency is a legal construct rooted in English common law. Wulach (1980) identified four major legal rationales for trying only competent defendants. First, the accuracy of the proceedings demands the assistance of the defendant in acquiring the facts of the case. Second, due process depends on defendants' ability to exercise their rights, including the rights to choose and assist legal counsel, confront their accusers, and testify in their own behalf. Third, the integrity and dignity of the process is undermined by the trial of an incompetent defendant, both in terms of its inherent morality and its outward appearance. Finally, the objectives of punishment are not served by sentencing a defendant who fails to comprehend the punishment and the reasons for imposing it. According to Bonnie (1992), the dignity, reliability, and autonomy of the legal process itself precludes adjudication of incompetent defendants.

This chapter begins with a discussion of the legal framework of competence to stand trial. Conceptual formulations of these legal standards that have been developed to guide psychological assessments of trial competence are then considered. The empirical literature on variables relevant to competence is reviewed. Evaluation issues, including clinical approaches, competence assessment instruments, psychological testing, and report issues, are covered. Trial competence issues posed by special populations are reviewed. Finally, dispositional issues, such as competency assistance, treatment of incompetent defendants, prediction of restorability, and the issue of permanently incompetent defendants, are summarized.

LEGAL FRAMEWORK

Early History

The earliest foundation of the legal construct of competence to stand trial may be the common law prohibition against trials in absentia. Just as a criminal defendant has the basic right to be *physically* present at trial to confront his or her accusers, a defendant must be *mentally* present, or aware enough of the legal situation to meaningfully confront his or her accusers. In tracing the legal roots of trial competency, Melton, Petrila, Poythress, and Slobogin (1997) discussed the practice of seventeenth-century English courts in determining whether defendants who stood mute and did not enter a plea at trial were "mute of malice" or "mute by visitation of God." (p. 120) The former were subjected to placement of increasingly heavy weights on their chests to force a plea. Those considered mute by visitation of God (the deaf, the mute, and later, the lunatic) were not expected to enter a plea. This thinking evolved in the eighteenth century, as reflected by *Frith's Case* (1790), in which the court delayed trial until such time as the defendant, "by collecting together his intellects, and having them entire, he shall be able so to model his defense and to ward off the punishment of the law" (p. 121).

English common law has influenced the development of American criminal law, including the concept of competency. Federal case law linking trial competency to the U.S. Constitution began with the 1899 Court of Appeals case of *Youtsey v. United States*. Youtsey had been tried and convicted of embezzlement after an initial delay of several months, during which he had been physically and mentally unable to appear, due to epilepsy. The court denied his lawyer's motion for an additional continuance, to be based on expert testimony that the epilepsy had resulted in severe memory impairment that prevented the defendant from providing counsel with information about "many of the vital transactions covered by said indictment which ought to be personally within his knowledge" (p. 939). The Sixth Circuit Court of Appeals reversed the conviction and remanded the case for retrial and for a hearing on Youtsey's competency. The Court of Appeals based this finding on evidence that the memory and mind of the defendant were impaired before and during the trial, that epilepsy is progressive, and that it was "doubtful whether the accused was capable of appreciating his situation, and of intelligently advising his counsel as to his defense, if he had any" (p. 947).

Competency Defined

The U.S. Supreme Court, in *Dusky v. United States* (1960), established the minimal constitutional standard for competency to stand trial. The Court ruled that competency to stand trial is based on whether the defendant "has sufficient present ability to consult with his lawyer with a reasonable degree of rational understanding—and whether he has a rational as well as factual understanding of the proceedings against him" (p. 789).

The characteristics of a competent defendant were further articulated in the 1961 case of *Wieter v. Settle:*

> (1) that he has mental capacity to appreciate his presence in relation to time, place and things; (2) that his elementary mental processes be such that he apprehends (i.e., seizes and grasps with what mind he has) that he is in a Court of Justice, charged with a criminal offense; (3) that there is a Judge on the Bench; (4) a Prosecutor present who will try to convict him of a criminal charge; (5) that he has a lawyer (self-employed or Court-appointed) who will undertake to defend him against that charge; (6) that he will be expected to tell his lawyer the circumstances, to the best of his mental ability, (whether colored or not by mental aberration) the facts surrounding him at the time and place where the law violation is alleged to have been committed; (7) that there is, or will be, a jury present to pass upon evidence adduced as to his guilt or innocence of such charge; and (8) he has memory sufficient to relate those things in his own personal manner:—such a person from a consideration of legal standards, should be considered mentally competent to stand trial under criminal procedure, lawfully enacted. (pp. 321–322) The Court laid out functional criteria for determining competence, and it clarified that mental illness does not necessarily mean that a defendant lacks the mental faculties required to stand trial.

Basis for Raising the Issue of Competence

In the 1966 case of *Pate v. Robinson,* the U.S. Supreme Court held that a trial judge must raise the issue of competency if either the court's own evidence, or that presented by the prosecution or defense, raises a "bona fide doubt" about the defendant's competency. In *Drope v. Missouri* (1975), the Court clarified that evidence of the defendant's irrational behavior, demeanor at trial, and any prior medical opinion on competence to stand trial are relevant to determining whether further inquiry is required.

Amnesia and Competence

The tendency of federal courts to articulate functional criteria for determining competence to stand trial continued in the case of *Wilson v. United States* (1968). The court upheld the conviction of a man who sustained head injuries in an accident in the course of a high-speed chase by police and was therefore amnesiac for the offenses. However, the court remanded the case for more extensive posttrial findings on the issue of whether amnesia deprived the defendant of a fair trial and effective assistance of counsel. Six factors were articulated to assist the trial court in determining whether the fairness and accuracy of the proceedings had been compromised and the conviction should be vacated:

1. The extent to which the amnesia affected the defendant's ability to consult with and assist his lawyer.
2. The extent to which the amnesia affected the defendant's ability to testify in his own behalf.
3. The extent to which the evidence in suit could be extrinsically reconstructed in view of the defendant's amnesia. Such evidence would include evidence relating to the crime itself as well as any reasonably possible alibi.
4. The extent to which the Government assisted the defendant and his counsel in that reconstruction.
5. The strength of the prosecution's case. Most important here will be whether the Government's case is such as to negate all reasonable hypotheses of innocence. If there is any substantial possibility that the accused could, but for his amnesia, establish an alibi or other defense, it should be presumed that he would have been able to do so.
6. Any other facts and circumstances which would indicate whether or not the defendant had a fair trial (pp. 463–464).

The court's reasoning in the *Wilson* case not only illustrates the functional, situation-specific analysis demanded by determination of competency; it also emphasizes that the finding of competency is a legal decision designed to ensure the fairness and accuracy of court proceedings.

Competence to Waive Rights

Implicit in the competency of a defendant to participate in proceedings to resolve criminal charges against him or her is the capacity to waive certain rights.

Competence to Plead Guilty

Over 90% of criminal cases in the United States are resolved by pleas of guilty, often the result of plea bargaining. The competency of defendants to plead guilty involves the waiver of the right to a jury trial, of the right to confront one's accusers, and of the privilege against self-incrimination. This issue was considered by the U.S. Court of Appeals case of *Sieling v. Eyman* (1973). The court held that competency to stand trial and competency to plead guilty are not necessarily identical, and that, to the extent that they differ, there is a higher standard for competency to waive constitutional rights and to plead guilty than for competency to stand trial. The court adopted the following standard: "A defendant is not competent to plead guilty if mental illness has substantially impaired his ability to make a reasoned choice among alternatives presented to him and to understand the nature of the consequences of his plea" (p. 215).

However, the majority of the circuits have concluded that the standard of incompetence to plead is the same as the standard of incompetence to stand trial (*Allard v. Hedgemoe,* 1978). The *Allard* court agreed that the waiver of rights and the plea of guilty need to be closely examined, but suggested that the capacity to make such decisions be considered part of the *Dusky* standard.

In an earlier federal court decision (*North Carolina v. Alford,* 1970), the court had ruled in a capital case that defendants may waive their right to trial and plead guilty even if they deny their guilt. The court focused on the logic of Mr. Alford's reasoning in choosing to enter a guilty plea to a murder he stated he did not commit.

Competence to Waive Counsel

The Supreme Court ruled in *Westbrook v. Arizona* (1966) that a competency to stand trial hearing was not sufficient to determine defendants' competence to waive their constitutional right to the assistance of counsel and to conduct their own defense. In the 1975 case of *Faretta v. California,* the Supreme Court noted that waiver of counsel must be knowing and intelligent, but defendants' ability to represent themselves has no bearing on their competence to choose self-representation.

Godinez v. Moran

The 1993 U.S. Supreme Court case of *Godinez v. Moran* considered in detail the issue of waiver of rights in the context of trial competency. The facts of the case are important to consider in view of the significance of this landmark decision. Moran killed two people in a bar and removed the cash register. Several days later, he shot and killed his former wife, shot himself in the abdomen, and attempted to slit his wrists. Two days after the latter incident, Moran summoned police to his hospital bed and confessed to the killings. He was charged with capital murder and found competent to stand trial. Nearly three months later, he appeared in court and stated that he wanted to discharge his attorneys and plead guilty, primarily to prevent the presentation of mitigating evidence at sentencing.

Based on the prior competency evaluations and the court's inquiry of the defendant on the record, the trial court ruled that Moran knew the consequences of entering a guilty plea and could intelligently and knowingly waive his right to counsel. The competency evaluations had noted the presence of depression that affected the defendant's motivation to actively work with counsel in his defense. The court record noted that Moran was taking medication, but did not include an inquiry regarding the type, dosage, or effect on the defendant.

Moran was sentenced to death. When the defendant later sought postconviction relief, the trial court held an evidentiary hearing. Testimony indicated that he had been prescribed phenobarbitol, Inderal, Vistaril, and Dilantin at the time of the court proceedings, and that these medications had a "numbing" effect on him. The trial court rejected the claim that he had been mentally incompetent to represent himself.

The Ninth District Court of Appeals reversed the lower court rulings and concluded that due process required the trial court to determine Moran's competency prior to accepting his decisions to waive counsel and plead guilty. The court also held that the standard for competency to waive counsel or plead guilty is not the same as the standard for competency to stand trial. Rather, competency to make these decisions requires the capacity for reasoned choice among the available alternatives.

The U.S. Supreme Court reviewed the appellate court's decision and held that the competency standard for pleading guilty or waiving the right to counsel is the same as the *Dusky* standard for competency to stand trial. In reaching this decision, the Court reasoned that the defendant has to make a number of complicated decisions during the course of a trial, and that a separate, higher standard is not necessary to determine whether he has the capacity to make the decision to waive counsel. The Court acknowledged:

> In addition to determining that a defendant who seeks to plead guilty or waive counsel is competent, a trial court must satisfy itself that the waiver of his constitutional rights is knowing and voluntary. . . . In this sense there *is* a 'heightened' standard for pleading guilty and for waiving the right to counsel, but it is not a heightened standard of *competence*. (p. 2687)

The concurring opinion suggests that the *Dusky* competence standard should not be viewed too narrowly, as a defendant must be competent throughout the proceedings, from arraignment to pleading, trial, conviction, and sentencing, and whenever the defendant must make a variety of decisions during the course of the proceedings.

Although the Supreme Court did not articulate a separate standard for competence to waive counsel or plead guilty, Justice Thomas in the majority opinion acknowledged that "psychiatrists and scholars may find it useful to classify the various kinds and degrees of competence." Felthous (1994) noted that the Court "did not forbid legislatures, courts, attorneys and mental health witnesses from addressing de facto those abilities that are embodied in decisions about competency to waive counsel and to make one's own defense" (p. 110). Melton et al. (1997) speculated that *Godinez v. Moran* may well increase the level of competency evaluators and judges associate with competency to stand trial, as trial competency includes competency to waive counsel.

The Standard of Proof

In 1996 (*Cooper v. Oklahoma*), the U.S. Supreme Court reviewed the requirement of Oklahoma that a defendant prove incompetence by clear and convincing evidence, rather than the lower standard of preponderance of the evidence. The Court ruled unanimously that to impose the higher standard of clear and convincing evidence violated due process by allowing "the State to put to trial a defendant who is more likely than not incompetent." The Court termed the consequences of an erroneous competency determination in Cooper's case "dire," impinging on his right to a fair trial. In contrast, the consequence to the state of an erroneous finding of incompetence when a defendant is malingering was termed "modest," as it is unlikely that even an accomplished malingerer could "feign incompetence successfully for a period of time while under professional care" (p. 1382). The Court affirmed the importance of competence to stand trial, stating that "the defendant's fundamental right to be tried only while competent outweighs the State's interest in the efficient operation of its criminal justice system" (p. 1383).

Mental Retardation

The U.S. District Court for the Western District of Louisiana, in *United States v. Duhon* (2000), emphasized the ability to make decisions in rejecting the opinion of hospital forensic examiners that a mentally retarded defendant was competent to stand trial. The court ruled that the defendant's factual understanding of the proceedings, after hospital staff taught him to memorize and retain some information, was insufficient. Rather, the defendant lacked the ability to consult with an attorney with a reasonable degree of rational understanding, to otherwise assist in his defense, and to have a rational understanding of the proceedings.

Competency to Refuse the Insanity Defense

Federal appeals courts have considered the issue of a defendant's competency to refuse an insanity plea, separate from the issue of competency to stand trial. The prevailing view was articulated in *Frendak v. United States* (1979). The court held that a trial judge may not impose a defense of insanity over the defendant's objections if a competent defendant intelligently and voluntarily decides to forgo a defense of insanity. An earlier case, *Whalem v. United States* (1965), did provide that a trial judge may impose an insanity defense when the defense would be likely to succeed, but it was overturned by *United States v. Marble* (1991) and is not followed in most jurisdictions. If it appears that competency to waive an insanity defense may be an issue in a given case, it is prudent for the evaluator to address it as part of the trial competency evaluation.

Case Law on Treatment of Incompetent Defendants

A final group of cases addresses the issue of treatment of defendants found incompetent to stand trial.

Length of Commitment

In *Jackson v. Indiana* (1972), the U.S. Supreme Court reviewed the commitment of a deaf mute who had been found incompetent to stand trial on two charges of robbery. He had been ordered to be hospitalized until he became competent, even though the treatment staff did not believe he would ever learn the communication skills necessary to stand trial. The Court ruled that incompetent defendants can be hospitalized only for the "reasonable" period of time necessary to determine whether there is a substantial probability that competency can be attained in the foreseeable future. The Court also held that continued commitment could be justified only on the basis of progress toward the goal of competency restoration. If these conditions could not be met, then the Court considered the alternatives to be releasing the defendant or initiating civil commitment proceedings.

More recently, in *United States v. Duhon* (2000), the U.S. District Court for the Western District of Louisiana ordered the release of a mentally retarded defendant who was not

dangerous to any persons or property and would never achieve trial competency.

Involuntary Medication

The issue of involuntary medication of defendants during trial was addressed by the U.S. Court of Appeals in a case heard twice, *United States v. Charters*. In 1987, the court held that forced administration of psychotropic medication to an incompetent defendant requires a separate judicial decision, using the substituted judgment/best interests standard. In 1988, the court en banc endorsed a reasonable professional judgment standard, with the availability of judicial review. The *Charters* case was not appealed to the U.S. Supreme Court in light of the Court's 1990 decision in *Washington v. Harper*. In this prison case, the Court held that the reasonable professional judgment review of involuntary medication in the treatment of prisoners was constitutional.

The U.S. Supreme Court did consider the issue of involuntary administration of psychotropic medication of pretrial detainees in the case of *Riggins v. Nevada* (1992). Riggins argued that continued administration of medication was an infringement on his freedom, and that drug effects on his mental state during trial would deny him due process by not allowing him to show the jurors his true mental state as part of his insanity defense. The trial court found Riggins competent and denied his motion to suspend administration of psychotropic medication during his murder trial. He was subsequently convicted and sentenced to death. The U.S. Supreme Court reversed Riggins's conviction and extended the *Washington v. Harper* (1990) ruling on the right to refuse medication, absent an "overriding justification and a determination of medical appropriateness" (p. 1815), to pretrial detainees. Once the defendant stated that he wanted his medication discontinued, the state had to "establish the need for Mellaril and the medical appropriateness of the drug" (p. 1815). This could have been established by showing that the medication was essential for the defendant's safety or the safety of others, or that the state could not obtain an adjudication of "guilt or innocence with less intrusive means" (p. 1815).

The case law regarding treatment of incompetent defendants appears to attempt to balance the liberty interests and due process concerns of a defendant who has not been convicted of a crime with the state's interest in a fair and accurate adjudication of criminal cases. Involuntary treatment of incompetent defendants is permissible as long as treatment is likely to restore the defendant to competence and there is no less intrusive means to do so.

Statutory Criteria for Competency to Stand Trial

Although the *Dusky* case established the minimal constitutional standard for competency to stand trial, states are permitted to expand on this standard. Statutory criteria for the determination of trial competency vary across states, and some states, such as Michigan, Florida, and Utah, have elaborated on the *Dusky* standard. For example, the Utah statute (described by Skeem & Golding, 1998) mandates that examiners address the defendant's present capacity to comprehend and appreciate the charges against him or her, disclose to counsel pertinent facts and states of mind, comprehend and appreciate the range and nature of possible penalties that may be imposed, engage in reasoned choice of legal strategies and options, understand the adversary nature of the proceedings, manifest appropriate courtroom behavior, and testify relevantly, if applicable. It also mandates consideration of the impact of mental disorder or mental retardation on the defendant's relationship with counsel, and of the effect of any psychoactive medication currently being administered on the defendant's demeanor and affect and ability to participate in the proceedings.

THE CONCEPTUALIZATION OF COMPETENCY TO STAND TRIAL

The legal doctrine of competency to stand trial has been the subject of conceptual analysis regarding its meaning and application to psychological assessment and legal decision making. For example, Roesch and Golding (1980), in discussing the assessment of competency to stand trial under the *Dusky* standard, phrased the question as "whether or not *this* defendant, facing *these* charges, *in light of the existing evidence,* will be able to assist his attorney in a rational manner" (pp. 18–19). They further noted: "Testimony about mental and physical illnesses is relevant, but only insofar as it speaks to the functional ability of a defendant to *reasonably understand and assist in his/her own defense.* Defendants are not expected to be amateur lawyers, nor paragons of mental health, nor admirers of and true believers in the criminal justice system" (p. 23).

Grisso (1986) reiterated that a defendant's competence depends on the seriousness and complexity of the charges, on what is expected of the defendant in the given case, on the client's relationship with the attorney, on the attorney's skill, and on other interactive factors. This focus on the functional, individual, and situation-specific nature of competency to stand trial is a natural extension of the case law.

More recently, Bonnie (1992) proposed a two-pronged model of competence to stand trial from a theoretical perspective. The first dimension, *foundational competence,* or competence to assist counsel, consists of (a) the capacity to understand the charges, the purpose of the criminal process, and the adversary system, particularly the role of the defense attorney; (b) the capacity to appreciate one's situation as a defendant in a criminal prosecution; and (c) the ability to recognize and relate pertinent information to counsel concerning the facts of the case. This dimension meets the societal need to maintain the dignity of the proceedings and the reliability of the outcome. The second dimension proposed by Bonnie is *decisional competence,* the capacity to make whatever decisions a defendant is required to make to defend himself or herself and/or to resolve the case without a trial. These decisions may include waiver of constitutional rights, such as the right to confront one's accusers at trial, the right to counsel, and the right to a trial by jury. Bonnie noted that the capacity to make decisions may require reassessment at decision points throughout the proceedings, and that assessment of competence at any one point is, in this respect, provisional.

Bonnie (1992) also referred to the literature on competencies in other legal contexts as relevant to assessing decisional competence. For example, Grisso and Appelbaum's (1995) conceptualization of an individual's competency to consent to treatment involves four levels: the ability to (a) communicate a preference, (b) understand relevant information about a particular decision, (c) appreciate the significance of that information to his or her own case, and (d) rationally manipulate or weigh information in reaching a decision. Understanding information does not necessarily enable individuals to apply that information to their situations in a rational manner to make intelligent decisions.

EMPIRICAL LITERATURE

Studies of Attorneys

Because competency to stand trial is a legal concept, it is useful to start with the literature on attorneys' views and practices regarding potentially incompetent defendants. Berman and Osborne (1987) surveyed 20 attorneys who questioned their clients' competence. They found that attorneys reported a broader range of problematic behaviors in terms of competence than did clinicians.

Hoge et al. (1992) conducted structured interviews of attorneys in a public defender office regarding 122 randomly selected felony cases resolved in a six-month period. The attorneys had doubted competence at some point in nearly 15% of these cases, but they referred only about half of those defendants for competency evaluations. Attorneys chose not to refer their clients for evaluations for three basic reasons: (a) Their clients were unlikely to be considered incompetent due to the low threshold for competency findings; (b) there were limited resources for such evaluations; or (c) a finding of incompetence might not be in the best interest of the client. Attorneys were more likely to express doubts about competence when clients were rejecting of their advice or unusually passive in making decisions about their defense.

In a series of three studies, Poythress, Bonnie, Hoge, Monahan, and Oberlander (1994) reviewed 200 felony and misdemeanor cases, 92.5% of which were resolved by plea, and 200 felony and misdemeanor cases resolved by trial, and then interviewed attorneys and clients in 35 recently closed felony cases. Although attorneys doubted the competence of 8% to 15% of their clients in felony cases and 3% to 8% of their clients in misdemeanor cases, only 20% to 45% of these clients were referred for competency evaluations. Attorneys' doubts about competence were based on the degree of the client's helpfulness in developing the facts of the case, particularly when lack of helpfulness was perceived to be due to impaired ability rather than to intentional unwillingness. Attorneys also were more likely to express doubts about clients who faced serious charges, who were unusually passive, or who tended to reject the attorneys' advice. Attorneys reported spending significantly more time on the case in total and directly with the client when they had concerns about the client's competence. They also tended to consult with other attorneys and with clients' relatives or significant others in cases of doubted competence. These studies highlight the interactive, situation-specific nature of competence to stand trial and the importance of involving attorneys in the process of competency assessment.

Clinical Studies

Nicholson and Kugler (1991) conducted a meta-analysis of 30 studies of competent and incompetent criminal defendants. An average of 30% of the defendants evaluated were considered incompetent to stand trial by the forensic examiner. Incompetent defendants performed significantly worse on competency assessment instruments assessing legally relevant, functional abilities. The magnitude of the relationship between incompetence and performance on the Competency Screening Test ($-.37$), the Georgia Court Competency Test ($-.42$), the Competency Assessment Instrument ($-.52$) and the Interdisciplinary Fitness Interview ($-.42$) far exceeded the relationships found for traditional psychological tests, such as intelligence tests ($-.16$), and scales F, 6, and 8 on the Minnesota Multiphasic Personality Inventory (.08). (These instruments are fully reviewed in Competence Assessment Instruments section of this chapter.) The greater

effectiveness of the competency assessment instruments is particularly noteworthy because these were validation studies of these instruments, in which competency status was the criterion and the examiners did not have access to the results of the competency assessment instruments in forming their opinions. In contrast, the results of the traditional psychological tests had often been considered in forming opinions about competency. Even with the lack of independence between the traditional test results and the competency criterion, the traditional tests produced correlations of small magnitude.

Nicholson and Kugler (1991) also found that incompetent defendants were more likely to have a psychotic diagnosis, although only half of the defendants with a psychotic diagnosis were found incompetent. Symptoms of major psychopathology, including delusions, hallucinations, impaired memory, impaired thought or communication, and disturbed behavior, significantly differentiated incompetent from competent defendants. Older defendants, those with a prior history of psychiatric hospitalization, and defendants without a prior legal history were more apt to be found incompetent. The severity of the offense was more strongly related to the decision to refer defendants for competency evaluations than it was to an actual finding of incompetence.

The finding of an approximately 30% rate of incompetence in defendants referred for evaluation over the 25 years of studies reviewed by Nicholson and Kugler (1991) is consistent with the findings of Warren, Rosenfeld, Fitch, and Hawk (1997). These investigators reviewed data from Ohio, Michigan, and Virginia from 1987 to 1988 and discovered rates of incompetence of 29%, 18%, and 13%, respectively. The greater incidence of incompetence findings in Ohio most likely is related to the regional, outpatient system of providing competence evaluations, which leads to a greater percentage of defendants charged with public order offenses, and a greater percentage of defendants diagnosed with schizophrenia, referred for competency evaluations. In all three states, a significantly greater likelihood of incompetence findings occurred in cases of public order offenses; defendants charged with sexual offenses or homicide were less likely to be found incompetent. Defendants diagnosed with schizophrenia, organic disorders, other psychotic disorders, and affective disorders were significantly more likely to be considered incompetent.

In a study of 1436 defendants referred for competency evaluation to a federal medical center, Cochrane, Grisso, and Frederick (2001) found a 19% rate of incompetence opinions. When diagnosis was controlled, there was no significant difference in rates of incompetence opinions between categories of offense. It appears that diagnosis, not category of offense, is related to the incidence of incompetence, and that the prevalence rate for various diagnoses may differ among offense categories. Consistent with the literature, the diagnoses most closely associated with incompetence were psychotic disorders, affective disorders, and mental retardation.

Systems Issues

Warren et al. (1997) reported a decreased likelihood of incompetence findings when evaluations were performed on an inpatient rather than outpatient basis in Virginia. However, they did not indicate whether defendants evaluated on an inpatient basis also received treatment so that their mental states improved over the course of the evaluation period. In contrast, Nicholson and Kugler (1991), in their review, found a slightly greater rate of findings of incompetence in inpatient than outpatient settings: 32.2% versus 25.8%, respectively. Correlations between competency status and defendant characteristics were similar across both settings.

Grisso, Cocozza, Steadman, Fisher, and Greer (1994) surveyed the 50 states and District of Columbia regarding systems of service delivery for pretrial forensic evaluations. A typology of the states' systems was developed that allowed classification of 43 states. Ten states were classified as *traditional* in providing most pretrial evaluations in an inpatient setting, using public mental health funds and multidisciplinary staff, with secondary reliance on outpatient evaluations. Nine states relied on *private practitioners* performing outpatient evaluations on a case-by-case basis, financed by court or criminal justice funds. Eleven states had a *community-based* system of local outpatient mental health facilities or court clinics funded primarily by mental health dollars. In five states, classified as *modified traditional,* most evaluations were conducted at centralized mental health facilities, but on an outpatient basis. The eight states with a *mixed* model had a balance of outpatient evaluations funded by court or mental health funds and inpatient evaluations funded by state mental health funds. No data about these different delivery systems were presented.

EVALUATION ISSUES

Grisso (1988) published a practice manual outlining five objectives for competency evaluations. On a *functional* level, the defendant's strengths and weaknesses in terms of specific legal abilities should be directly assessed. A *causal* analysis focuses on the most plausible explanation for any observed deficits, based on clinical observations and data. The *interactive* objective of a competency evaluation is concerned with assessment of the significance of deficits in light of the demands of the case. The opinion about the ultimate legal issue of competency to stand trial is the *conclusory* objective. For the defendant who is likely to be found incompetent, assessment of the potential for remediation of deficits and recommendations for treatment constitutes the *prescriptive* objective of the evaluation.

There is some controversy about giving a conclusory opinion about the ultimate legal issue. Grisso (1988) does not recommend giving a conclusory opinion, but he acknowledges that there are jurisdictions in which the examiner is permitted or required to give an ultimate opinion about competence.

Although apparent deficits in knowledge and reasoning about one's legal situation trigger concerns about competence, the issue of competence is not only a functional, but a capacity issue as well. Apparent difficulties with competence may be a function of lack of information, failure of an attorney to spend sufficient time in counseling an understandably anxious defendant, or malingering. To conclude that a defendant lacks present *capacity* to proceed with the case requires a thorough assessment of relevant psychological conditions. Therefore, evaluation of competence to stand trial requires two levels of assessment. First, the psychologist assesses the defendant's understanding of his or her legal situation and ability to make decisions about it, through interview, use of competency assessment instruments, review of prosecutor's information, and input from defense counsel about doubts regarding competence. Second, relevant psychological conditions are assessed through self-report, clinical observation, third-party information, and psychological testing of cognitive functioning, psychopathology, and response sets, especially malingering.

Competence Assessment Instruments

Competency to Stand Trial Assessment Instrument and Competency Screening Test

Lipsitt, Lelos, and McGarry (1971; Laboratory of Community Psychiatry, 1974) made the first systematic attempt to structure the assessment of competence to stand trial. The Competency to Stand Trial Assessment Instrument (CAI) is a rating scale for considering 13 functions related to the ability to proceed in a self-protective manner. The functions were derived from appellate cases, the legal literature, and the clinical and courtroom experience of the multidisciplinary team that developed the instrument. The handbook provides illustrative questions and clinical examples to use in rating the degree of incapacity on each of these functions. However, there is no standardized administration or well-defined rules for making ratings. The CAI primarily assesses the competence to assist counsel, or knowledge, aspect of competence. There has been little research on this instrument, although studies indicate high levels of interrater reliability (.87 to .90) and significant correlations between competency status and overall ratings (Nicholson & Kugler, 1991). In practice, the CAI has been used as an interview guide rather than a psychometric instrument (Schreiber, 1978). The major contribution of the CAI has probably been its early impact on educating clinicians about the concept of competence to stand trial and guiding their assessments along legally relevant lines.

The Competency Screening Test (CST) is a sentence completion test with 22 sentence stems that suggest various case scenarios. Responses to each item are scored on a 0 to 2 range based on defined criteria, and a cutoff score of 21 has been established to suggest incompetence. Interscorer reliability has been reported to be excellent, ranging from .88 to .95, and classification accuracy has been reported to be 71% to 84% (Nicholson, Robertson, Johnson, & Jensen, 1988). These investigators found a high false-positive rate of 76%; that is, of the 46 defendants classified as incompetent by the instrument, 35 were actually considered competent by hospital staff. But there was a low, 3.5% false-negative rate, as only 3 of 86 defendants classified as competent by the CST were actually considered incompetent. Therefore, in this sample, with the relatively low base rate of 10% incompetent, the CST appeared to function well as a screening measure, in that few defendants who were actually incompetent were screened out from a full competency assessment.

Nicholson and Kugler (1991) reviewed 11 studies of the CST and report a significant mean weighted correlation (−.37) between the measure and findings of incompetence. However, Bagby, Nicholson, Rogers, and Nussbaum (1992) found there was little stability in factor structure across studies for the CST, making it difficult to determine just what aspects of competency this instrument measures. The Bagby et al. study appears to be the last major research published on the CST (Cooper & Grisso, 1997). However, aspects of its methodology are reflected in the development of the MacArthur instrument, discussed below.

The Interdisciplinary Fitness Interview

Golding, Roesch, and Schreiber (1984) developed the Interdisciplinary Fitness Interview (IFI) to assess symptoms of psychopathology and to assess understanding of legal concepts and functions through a joint interview by a psychologist and a lawyer. Each legal item is rated on a 0 to 2 scale for capacity and for relevance or importance. Symptoms of psychopathology are rated as present or absent and for significance. An overall rating of fit or unfit, and a rating of confidence in that judgment, are made. The potential strength of the instrument lies in its attempt to assess the defendant's functioning in the context of the anticipated demands of his or her particular legal situation. Preliminary data found 95% agreement among the IFI interviewers on opinions regarding competence, and substantial interrater reliability on most of the psychopathology items. Golding (1993) developed the Interdisciplinary Fitness Interview–Revised (IFI-R) in the context of a large-scale study of competency reports (Skeem, Golding, Cohn, & Berge, 1998), but empirical studies of the instrument itself have not yet been published. The IFI-R is a promising interview guide that tailors the assessment to the individual case, ensures lawyer input, and highlights the connection between psychopathology and psycholegal impairment.

Fitness Interview Test

Roesch, Webster, and Eaves (1984) developed the Fitness Interview Test (FIT), a Canadian interview schedule similar to the CAI and the IFI. It contains items focused on legal issues and on assessment of psychopathology. McDonald, Nussbaum, and Bagby (1991) reported a high degree of correspondence between FIT ratings and legal decisions about competence, but the legal decisions were not independent of the FIT ratings. Bagby et al. (1992) found that factor analyses of the FIT legal items failed to yield a stable factor structure across samples, most likely due to the uniformity of item content. The FIT legal items appear to be fairly unidimensional and may not assess multiple aspects of competence. Moreover, the lack of concrete definitions for rating the items may lead to generalization of ratings across items. The Fitness Interview Test–Revised (FIT-R) has subsequently been tested on groups of Canadian defendants referred to an inpatient setting for competency evaluation. Zapf and Roesch (1997) reported that the FIT-R demonstrated perfect sensitivity and negative predictive power as a screening instrument in a study of 57 male defendants. Based on the FIT-R, 82% of the defendants who were clearly fit to stand trial would have been screened out before being remanded for a lengthy inpatient competence evaluation. Whittemore, Ogloff, and Roesch (1997) analyzed responses of a similar sample to the FIT-R and to FIT-R items that address ability to make a guilty plea. They suggested the need for a stage-specific approach to forensic competency assessment, with specialized instruments designed to assess the legal issues of competency at various stages of the proceedings.

Computer-Assisted Determination of Competency to Proceed

The CADCOMP is a computer-administered interview, with over 200 questions pertaining to history, demographics, the day of the crime, behavior since arrest, psycholegal ability, and psychopathology (Barnard et al., 1991, 1992). The initial study found a correlation of .55 between competency judgments based on the CADCOMP and competency judgments based on interview by a forensic examiner, with agreement in 88% of the 50 cases. This is consistent with the level of predictive validity reported for other competency assessment instruments in the literature. The second study analyzed 18 conceptually developed scales from the CADCOMP, using the data obtained from incompetent defendants treated in the same inpatient setting who were either restored to competency or persistently incompetent. The scales most predictive of competency opinions reflect lack of knowledge of the adversarial process, lack of appreciation of appropriate courtroom behavior, prominent psychotic features, and cognitive impairment. The two scales thought to measure relationship with attorney did not significantly correlate with competency status, perhaps because the defendants in this hospitalized sample did not have an active relationship with their attorney. The only scales measuring historical variables that significantly correlated with incompetence were criminal history, in a negative direction, and childhood/educational problems, in a positive direction. The defendants restored to competency endorsed more items reflective of substance abuse and antisocial features, whereas the unrestored defendants were more likely to have a history of educational problems and/or persisting impairment in thinking, perception, and legal ability. This instrument is recommended for research use, although it does provide a standardized database for assessing competence.

Georgia Court Competency Test

The GCCT was developed by Wildman et al. (1978). It is unique in its use of a courtroom drawing as a reference point for 12 questions about the physical positions and functional roles of court participants in a trial. It also consists of five questions about the defendant's charge(s) and defense. The GCCT takes approximately 10 minutes to administer. Initial findings indicated reliability of .79 across two examiners and scorers on two different administrations, and classification accuracy of 68% to 78%. Nicholson et al. (1988) revised the GCCT to create a Mississippi State Hospital version (GCCT-MSH), which has been subjected to further research. They added four questions about the defendant's knowledge of courtroom proceedings, changed the weights of some items,

and clarified scoring, but they did not change the total or cut-off score. Nicholson et al. reported excellent interscorer reliability ($r = .95$). Classification accuracy was 81.8%, with a false-positive rate of 67.7% but a false-negative rate of only 3.8%. Classification and false-positive rates improved when the interval between testing and examiner assessment was less than the average time of two weeks. The study found that the GCCT-MSH compared favorably to the CST in this setting, even though the base rate of incompetence findings was only 10%. Nicholson and Johnson (1991) found that the GCCT or GCCT-MSH was the strongest predictor of competency decisions on an inpatient unit, and that the GCCT did not correlate highly with diagnosis. However, all of the variables combined accounted for a relatively small proportion of the variance in competency findings. A factor analytic study (Bagby et al., 1992) of the CST, the FIT, and the GCCT-MSH found that only the GCCT-MSH yielded stable, independent factors: general knowledge, courtroom layout, and specific legal knowledge. The investigators noted, however, that the GCCT-MSH does not appear to address ability to consult counsel and assist in one's defense in a comprehensive or conceptually reliable way.

The Competence Assessment for Standing Trial for Defendants with Mental Retardation

The CAST-MR was developed by Everington and Luckasson (1992) to assess knowledge of basic legal concepts, skills to assist defense, and understanding of case events in mentally retarded defendants. Knowledge of basic legal concepts is assessed through 25 multiple choice questions, with three response options, measuring knowledge of basic legal terms. Skills to assist defense are measured by multiple choice questions about hypothetical situations the defendant may face in the course of criminal proceedings; there are three courses of action from which the defendant chooses for each situation. The final section of the test consists of 10 open-ended questions about the defendant's case, designed to measure his or her understanding of case events. Responses are rated on a numerical scale, with rating criteria defined in the manual. Initial studies of reliability and validity were conducted on group home residents with mental retardation and four groups of defendants at the pretrial level: "normal" defendants, defendants with mental retardation who were not referred for competence evaluation, defendants with mental retardation evaluated as competent to stand trial, and defendants with mental retardation evaluated as incompetent to stand trial (Everington, 1990). These initial studies produced high levels of internal consistency for the three sections of the test, comparable to those obtained with the CST and the GCCT-MSH.

A second validation study was conducted with mentally retarded defendants ordered for evaluation to the regional outpatient forensic centers in Ohio (Everington & Dunn, 1995). Of the 35 defendants, 15 were considered competent and 20 incompetent by the examiners, who completed their evaluation reports prior to the CAST-MR administration. The 12 of 15 "competent" defendants administered the Wechsler Adult Intelligence Scale–Revised (WAIS-R) as part of the evaluation had an average IQ of 66, whereas the 19 of 20 "incompetent" defendants given the WAIS-R had an average IQ of 57, a significant difference. Social workers trained by the investigator to administer and score the Understanding Case Events Section of the CAST-MR, using tapes of mentally retarded inmates, produced interrater reliability of 87% on average. Total scores and scores on each of the scales were significantly higher for the competent group than for the incompetent group. All CAST-MR scores were significantly correlated with IQ, but the discriminant function yielded a stepwise function for IQ and the Understanding Case Events score, suggesting that this section of the test contributes to assessment of competence, independent of intelligence. Agreement between CAST-MR results and examiners' opinions was 70% to 80%, with one less-experienced examiner producing four of the seven disagreements. This instrument contributes legally relevant data and norms to the assessment of mentally retarded or otherwise cognitively impaired defendants.

The MacArthur Competence Assessment Tool–Criminal Adjudication

Otto et al. (1998) developed this competency assessment instrument from a more extensive research instrument, the MacArthur Structured Assessment of the Competencies of Criminal Defendants (MacSAC-CD). The MacSAC-CD had been designed to investigate Bonnie's (1992) theory of competence, to assess capacity rather than merely current knowledge, and to provide quantitative measures of distinct competence-related abilities, such as reasoning (Hoge et al., 1997). The MacSAC-CD was found to distinguish between competent and incompetent defendants and to reflect changes in competence status. It correlated positively with clinical judgments, and negatively with measures of psychopathology and impaired cognitive functioning. On the MacSAC-CD, significant impairments in competence-related abilities were found in about half of defendants with schizophrenia, but there was substantial overlap in scores obtained by defendants with schizophrenia and those without mental illness. Hallucinations and delusions were associated with impairment in defendants with affective disorders, and conceptual disorganization was associated with competency impairment in defendants with schizophrenia as well as those with affective disorders.

The MacArthur Competence Assessment Tool–Criminal Adjudication (MacCAT-CA) is an abbreviated, clinical version of the research instrument. It also attempts to measure the ability to *understand* information related to law and adjudicatory proceedings, and the ability to *reason* about specific choices that confront a defendant in the course of adjudication. The Understanding and the Reasoning scales each contain eight items that are based on a hypothetical legal scenario. The Appreciation scale taps the ability to *appreciate* the meaning and consequences of the proceedings in the defendant's own case, through six items that refer to the specific legal situation.

The initial validation study of the MacCAT-CA was based on 729 felony defendants between 18 and 65 years of age, in eight states, who spoke English and had a prorated WAIS-R IQ of at least 60. Three groups were tested: untreated defendants in jail, defendants in jail receiving mental health treatment but not referred for competency evaluations, and recent admissions to forensic psychiatric units who had been adjudicated incompetent to stand trial. The study found good internal consistency for the three measures and very good to excellent interrater reliability. The MacCAT-CA correlated negatively with measures of psychopathology, including the Brief Psychiatric Rating Scale and the MMPI-2 Psychoticism scale, and correlated positively with the measure of cognitive functioning, the WAIS-R prorated IQ. Differences between competent and incompetent defendants on the MacCAT-CA were comparable to those obtained on the CST and the GCCT-MSH.

The effect sizes for the Reasoning and Appreciation scales were more robust than those for the Understanding scale. The strength of the Reasoning and Appreciation scales lies in the assessment of different aspects of competence, relevant to decisional competence, and not tapped by the Understanding scale or by most other competency assessment instruments. However, the unique contribution of the Reasoning Scale may be somewhat limited by the hypothetical rather than case-specific nature of the items on which it is based. The authors note that the MacCAT-CA does not include measures of response set, and that the possibility of malingering needs to be assessed through other methods. They advocate for the clinical use of the MacCAT-CA in the context of a comprehensive competency evaluation.

The Evaluation of Competency to Stand Trial–Revised

Rogers, Grandjean, Tillbrook, Vitacco, and Sewell (2001) reported on the early development of a currently unpublished instrument, the Evaluation of Competency to Stand

Trial-Revised (ECST-R). The goal of the instrument is to address systematically both aspects of the *Dusky* standard, rational understanding and ability to consult with counsel, and to assess feigned incompetency in a standardized manner. Preliminary research suggests that the instrument may potentially contribute to competence evaluation by assessing rational abilities as they relate to defense counsel and legal proceedings in the defendant's own case rather than hypothetical cases.

Summary

In general, the interview-based instruments, such as the CAI, the IFI and IFI-R, the FIT and FIT-R, and the CADCOMP, appear to be useful in structuring competency evaluations to include assessment of specific aspects of knowledge-based competence. In addition, the IFI and the IFI-R introduce lawyer input and emphasize the relationship between psychopathology and psycholegal impairment. Other instruments, such as the CST, the GCCT-MSH, the CAST-MR, and the MacCAT-CA, yield scores with norms and psychometric properties important for research and for more standardized assessment. The MacCAT-CA shows some promise in contributing incremental validity to a competency evaluation by measuring the understanding and reasoning underlying decisional capacity, an aspect of competence not comprehensively tapped by instruments that assess primarily knowledge-based competence. Nicholson and Kugler (1991) concluded from their meta-analysis that structured interviews or standardized instruments increase examiner reliability in competency assessment.

Role of Psychological Testing

Although competency assessment instruments focus on functional aspects of competency to stand trial, they do not truly measure capacity or whether there is an underlying condition that actually causes a defendant to appear to function poorly in areas relevant to the adjudication of a criminal case. Psychological testing is particularly helpful in objectively assessing whether displayed deficits are genuine or malingered; the product of mental retardation; associated with cognitive deficits due to traumatic brain injury, brain disease, or dementia; or caused by mood or psychotic disorders. Whereas competency assessment instruments identify possible impairments in competency-related functions, traditional psychological tests may clarify the cause of these potential impairments.

Nestor, Daggett, Haycock, and Price (1999) found significant differences on tests of verbal reasoning, episodic memory, and social judgment between competent and incompetent defendants. Such neuropsychological data can establish a causal link between observed deficits in competence functions and underlying cognitive disorders. For mentally retarded defendants, Everington and Dunn (1995) found a high correlation between WAIS-R IQ and performance on the knowledge-based competency scales of the CAST-MR. Nicholson and Kugler (1991) found small but significant correlations for scales F, 6, and 8 of the MMPI-2 and for IQ with findings of incompetence.

Psychological testing can objectively evaluate the probability of malingering of cognitive deficits motivated by the goal of being found incompetent to avoid prosecution. A number of measures have been developed to assess the malingering of cognitive difficulties, including the Validity Indicator Profile (Frederick, 1997) and the Recognition Memory Test (Warrington, 1984). Particularly promising in assessing the malingering of memory difficulties is the Test of Memory Malingering, which has been reported to have levels of sensitivity of 96% to 98% and specificity of 100% (Rees, Tombaugh, Gansler, and Moczynski, 1998). The MMPI-2 is widely used in forensic cases to assess malingering, particularly of psychosis, and to provide an actuarial measure of symptom patterns associated with particular classes of psychopathology (Pope, Butcher, & Seelen, 2000). (See the chapter by Rogers & Bender in this volume for a discussion of the assessment of malingering.)

Competency assessment instruments have not been designed to measure response set and generally possess face validity, making them vulnerable to malingering. In an attempt to overcome this problem, Gothard, Rogers, and Sewell (1995) developed an Atypical Presentation Scale for the GCCT, consisting of eight questions, varying in level of bizarreness. Pretrial defendants evaluated as competent, incompetent, or suspected malingerers were administered the test. A control group of sentenced inmates and a group of sentenced inmates instructed to feign incompetence, both without histories of psychiatric treatment or findings of incompetence, were also tested. The simulators and suspected malingerers scored significantly below the control, competent, and incompetent groups on the GCCT, and scored significantly above these groups on the Atypical Presentation Scale. These results confirm that individuals with experience in the criminal justice system can modify their responses to a face-valid competency assessment instrument such as the GCCT. However, the specificity and sensitivity of cutoff scores in differentiating malingerers from incompetent defendants on the GCCT was found to be low. Classification accuracy for the Atypical Presentation Scale was 90% overall and 82.6% in distinguishing malingerers from the incompetent group, but this result requires cross-validation.

Gothard, Viglione, Meloy, and Sherman (1995) reported on the administration of the Structured Interview of Reported Symptoms (SIRS; Rogers, Bagby, & Dickens, 1992), a measure of malingering, to these same groups. They found that the SIRS criterion of three or more elevations on the primary scales produced a 97.8% hit rate for detection of malingering. The investigators suggested that a total GCCT score of less than 60, endorsement of items on the Atypical Presentation Scale, and an unexpected pattern of correct and incorrect responses based on item difficulty are promising approaches to assessment of malingering of incompetence. However, they caution that the assessment of malingering requires a comprehensive, multimethod assessment, including the SIRS, the MMPI-2, and measures of malingering of cognitive deficits when appropriate.

Rogers, Grandjean, Tillbrook, Vitacco, and Sewell (2001) recommend the clinical use of the GCCT, without cut scores, as a screening instrument to identify potential competency deficits and potential feigning for further evaluation.

Competency Reports

Skeem, Golding, Cohn, and Berge (1998) noted that the literature tends to base the quality of competency reports on the high rate of concordance between examiners' opinions and court findings, and the generally favorable views of competency reports by judges. However, this approach does not address professional standards, such as the nature and reliability of the reasoning presented, and the way competency is operationalized in reaching the psycholegal opinion.

Skeem et al. (1998) analyzed 100 competency reports completed by examiners on 50 defendants, primarily on an outpatient basis. A coding manual was developed for 11 global psycholegal domains and 31 subdomains, and for 9 categories of symptoms of psychopathology, based on the IFI-R. The reports were coded for documentation of statutory criteria, the demands of the defendant's specific legal situation, substantiation of diagnosis, medication issues, possible malingering, use of psychological testing, and disclosure regarding the purpose and confidentiality of the evaluation. In 53% of the reports, the examiners opined that the defendant was incompetent to stand trial. Most reports addressed the defendant's appreciation of the charges and proceedings, but decisional abilities were addressed relatively infrequently. For example, only 12% of reports addressed the implications of a guilty plea, even though all of the defendants who returned to court engaged in plea bargaining. Although most reports adequately supported clinical findings, they generally did not link psycholegal deficits to symptoms of psychopathology. Examiners agreed in 82% of the cases on the defendant's global competence. However, they agreed only an average of 25% of the time about the particular psycholegal impairments on which the global opinions were based. Competency assessment instruments were rarely used, and the results of psychological testing were linked to opinions about competence in fewer than half of the cases in which testing was employed. Few examiners contacted the defendant's attorney or reviewed treatment records for the evaluation.

Skeem and Golding (1998) formulated recommendations for examiners based on the findings of this research. First, they recommend that examiners address key psycholegal abilities and consider the demands of the case, particularly in terms of the decisions the defendant will be expected to make. All defendants must choose a plea and must decide whether to plead guilty. Their ability to make decisions that involve the waiver of other constitutional rights, such as the right to counsel, the right to a jury trial, and the right to testify, must be considered as well. When other decisions about strategy, such as proceeding with the insanity defense, are an issue, the capacity to make a knowing and intelligent decision about this specific issue must be addressed. Because it is sometimes difficult to predict the decisions a defendant may face, the authors recommend noting which decisions were directly assessed and the level of ability the defendant displayed in considering those specific decisions. For defendants on psychotropic medication, the effect of the medication on the defendant's demeanor and awareness, and changes in mental state from his or her mental state at the time of the offense, should be noted.

Second, Skeem and Golding (1998) recommend providing psycholegal reasoning to support conclusions about the defendant's psychopathology, specific psycholegal abilities and impairments, and the relationship, if any, between psychopathology and deficits in competence. Reports should contain the facts and reasoning underlying the opinion in detail sufficient for the judge to understand the basis for the opinion and make an independent finding.

Third, the authors recommend the use of third-party information, competency assessment instruments, and targeted psychological testing. Third-party information should be obtained from legal and mental health records. Defense counsel provide critical input regarding legal concerns about the defendant's competence, including the likely demands of the case and the defense strategy, the attorney-client relationship, and the attorney's skill and experience in working with mentally disordered defendants. Competency assessment instruments structure the assessment of psycholegal strengths and weaknesses and contribute to interexaminer reliability. Traditional psychological testing should be used to address specific concerns raised by the evaluation. Test results should be discussed in terms of whether they are indicative of underlying psychological conditions that can account for observed impairments in the defendant's psycholegal functioning.

TRIAL COMPETENCY IN SPECIAL POPULATIONS

Three special populations of defendants with potential competence disabilities—those with psychosis, with mental retardation, and with severe hearing and communication impairments—have been discussed in the literature. (For discussion of a fourth special population, juvenile defendants, see the chapter by Grisso in this volume.)

Psychosis

Nicholson and Kugler's (1991) meta-analysis found significant correlations between symptoms of psychosis and findings of incompetence, of a magnitude exceeded only by the correlation between competency assessment instruments and competency status. The correlations between incompetence, on the one hand, and psychosis, delusions, hallucinations, and disturbed behavior, on the other, ranged from .25 to .45. Psychotic symptoms, although not synonymous with incompetence, contribute significantly to consideration of the capacity of the defendant to proceed to trial.

Goldstein and Burd (1990) published a review of the case law on the role of delusions in trial competency and the clinical implications of this body of law for competency evaluation. They reported that delusional defendants may appear to have a rational and factual understanding of the proceedings against them, and they may appear to demonstrate the ability to consult rationally with their attorneys, during a cursory, structured interview. However, a thorough assessment is often required before delusional thinking surfaces, and the impact of such thinking on trial competency needs to be explored fully. Delusions may directly interfere with the defendant's perception of the nature and objectives of the proceedings and with the ability to assist in his or her defense. For example, the New Hampshire Supreme Court in *State v. Champagne* (1985) noted that the defendant could accurately answer simple yes-no questions about the proceedings, but if "the questioning proceeded at any length . . . the defendant's delusions and loosening of association took over, so that his first answer would not be a reliable indicator of his thinking" (p. 1247). The court ruled that, although the defendant understood the roles of various court personnel, the role of the jury in determining guilt or innocence, and the charges against him, he was incompetent to stand trial. His paranoid

delusions impaired his "ability to communicate meaningfully with his lawyer so as to make informed choices regarding trial strategy" (p. 1245) and "so imbued the defendant's thought processes that he could not rationally understand the nature of the proceedings against him" (p. 1246). This case and others reviewed by the authors emphasize the importance of a comprehensive evaluation to assess the impact of delusions on trial competency, competency to waive counsel, and competency to waive the insanity defense.

Goldstein and Burd (1990) further noted that competency assessment of psychotic defendants requires consideration of the likelihood of deterioration in the defendant's mental state prior to the resolution of the case, factors likely to precipitate deterioration, and possible signs of such deterioration. Other cases cited by the authors (e.g., *State v. Hahn,* 1985; *Pride v. Estelle,* 1981) have reinforced the need for inquiry into the defendant's education, literacy, background, prior court experience, and psychiatric treatment history and for psychological testing in competency assessment.

Mental Retardation

The development of the CAST-MR by Everington and Luckasson (1992) illustrates the particular challenge of determining whether mentally retarded defendants are competent to proceed with their criminal cases. Bonnie (1990) reported that mentally retarded defendants constitute 2% to 7% of competence evaluation referrals, but that as many as half of mentally retarded defendants are not referred for competence evaluation. Everington and Dunn (1995) found that 57% of 35 mentally retarded defendants referred for competency evaluations to outpatient forensic centers in Ohio were considered incompetent to stand trial.

Cochrane, Grisso, and Frederick (2001) reviewed literature reporting a 12% to 36% rate of incompetence among mentally retarded defendants referred for competency evaluation. Their own study of 1436 defendants referred for competency evaluation to a federal medical center found that of the 33 mentally retarded defendants evaluated, 30% were considered incompetent to stand trial.

In a Canadian study, Ericson and Perlman (2001) compared developmentally disabled adults (IQ 50–75) with non-disabled adults on knowledge of 34 legal terms. The developmentally disabled adults scored significantly lower on conceptual understanding of all terms except police officer. The concept of guilty was not understood by 45% of the disabled group. Only 8 of the 34 terms were reasonably understood by at least 75% of the developmentally disabled adults. In addition, there were discrepancies of approximately 20% between subjects' report of familiarity with concepts and their actual understanding of the concepts. Disabled subjects frequently reported familiarity with a term when they clearly did not understand what it meant. This result is consistent with other findings in the literature indicating that mentally retarded individuals are likely to acquiesce rather than report they do not know information, particularly to authority figures. The authors recommend the use of open-ended, rather than yes-no questions, in assessing the competency of developmentally disabled defendants, and the use of language appropriate to their level of understanding to facilitate participation in court proceedings.

In assessing the competence of mentally retarded defendants, Appelbaum (1994) recommended techniques such as confrontational questioning to assess the defendant's ability to withstand cross-examination. Observation of defendants in court or in consultation with their attorneys provides relevant information about their strengths and weaknesses in handling these situations. Appelbaum also recommended providing simple explanations of legal concepts to assess the mentally retarded defendant's ability to understand and remember newly presented information over the course of the evaluation.

Speech and Hearing Impairment

The special case of the deaf defendant is epitomized by Theon Jackson, the defendant in *Jackson v. Indiana* (1972), who was indefinitely committed as incompetent to stand trial with virtually no likelihood of becoming competent.

Vernon, Steinberg, and Montoya (1999) presented data on 28 deaf defendants charged with murder and referred for evaluations to assist in trial or treatment planning. Twenty-eight percent had been psychiatrically hospitalized in the past, and an additional 32% had been treated as outpatients. Fifty percent of the defendants were diagnosed with antisocial personality disorder and had prior criminal histories, and 64% had a history of substance abuse. The average IQ of the group was 100.7, but more than half had indications of neurological impairment associated with the underlying etiology of deafness and of violent behavior. Fewer than half were proficient in American Sign Language (ASL).

Of these 28 defendants, 18 were convicted or pled guilty; three were found incompetent to stand trial due to mental illness. Although five were released because of linguistic incompetence or failure to give the *Miranda* warning in a manner comprehensible to the deaf defendant, the evaluators reported that 13 of the defendants were linguistically incompetent to stand trial or sufficiently limited linguistically that a strong case could have been made for their incompetence. Vernon et al. (1999) discussed particular conceptual

difficulties with trial competence for deaf defendants, who may be illiterate, have a poor understanding of sign language, have considerable information gaps, and may never have developed a formal language system.

Practitioners not competent in sign language need to use interpreters, preferably those with legal interpreting certificates, in conducting competency evaluations of deaf defendants. Vernon et al. (1999) reported that there are few formal signs for most legal concepts and vocabulary used in court proceedings. Therefore, a team of interpreters is often necessary in court, so that one interpreter can translate from English to ASL, and a second from ASL to the defendant's own idiosyncratic "language" of gestures, signs, and mime.

Wood (1984) reviewed case law relevant to the efforts of courts to protect the rights of deaf suspects to understand criminal proceedings, with a particular emphasis on sign language interpreting, and including a model statute. The National Center for Law and Deafness (1992) has published a guide to legal rights for deaf and hard-of-hearing people.

INTERVENTIONS FOR COMPETENCE DEFICITS

Although this chapter primarily addresses assessment of competence to stand trial, some brief remarks on the restoration of competence and handling of competence deficits are relevant.

Competency Assistance

The theory of competency assistance, articulated by Keilitz, Monahan, Keilitz, and Dillon (1987), is consistent with the view of competency as a situational and fluid concept, dependent on factors such as the demands of the defendant's own case. They note a number of provisions, short of a finding of incompetence, that are used to enhance defendants' ability to understand the proceedings and to assist in their defense.

Interpreters for defendants who are deaf or hearing impaired or not facile in English are broadly mandated. Continuation of psychotropic medication to maintain competence is allowed by law with some safeguards (e.g., *Riggins v. Nevada,* 1992). Keilitz et al. (1987) reported that some courts permit counsel to proceed with defenses that do not require the assistance of incompetent defendants, such as insufficiency of the indictment, statute of limitations, and double jeopardy. In some states, defense counsel may request "innocence-only trials," in which the court hears evidence and decides whether charges should be dropped.

In a mail survey of judges, Keilitz et al. (1987) found that most judges estimated that fewer than 10% of the criminal defendants in their courts presented with suspected "trial disabilities" (sensory and communication problems, mental illness, mental retardation, learning disabilities, or epilepsy). The judges reported making a number of accommodations to assist such defendants. They might appoint defense lawyers with experience working with trial-disabled defendants or allow a "support person" to sit at the defense table. A *guardian ad litem* might be appointed. Judges were willing to schedule hearings at less hectic times of the day, to take a more tolerant approach to aberrant behavior in the courtroom, and to conduct the proceedings with simpler language and at a slower pace. Judges also reported that they would allow testimony about the defendant's difficulties at trial, if relevant.

The notion of competence assistance is also consistent with the recommendations of the court in *Wilson v. United States* (1968). For amnesiac defendants, the court suggested that providing additional discovery information to the defense might assist in the reconstruction of events at the time of the offense and increase the likelihood that the defendant could proceed with the case.

Research by Poythress et al. (1994) indicates that attorneys who doubt their clients' competence but do not seek competence evaluations use compensatory strategies to facilitate their clients' competent participation in the proceedings. These accommodations include spending more time with the client, involving family members in decision making, modifying their approaches to consulting with clients to minimize impairments, and consulting other attorneys for advice.

As part of the competency evaluation report, the evaluator might consider making specific recommendations to enhance the competency of defendants who appear marginal in their capacity to proceed. When defendants with paranoid psychopathology have difficulty working with a particular attorney, it may be possible to tactfully recommend a change in court-appointed counsel. A referral for supportive counseling for an anxious, otherwise competent defendant awaiting trial may enhance his or her ability to work actively with counsel. It may be prudent to raise the possibility that a defendant with a history of deteriorating under stress or discontinuing treatment may require an updated competence evaluation if he or she appears to deteriorate before the case is resolved.

Similarly, given the comprehensive view of competence to stand trial articulated in *Godinez v. Moran* (1993), it may be critical to include a cautionary statement about the need for reevaluation should a trial-disabled defendant face an unforeseen complication in the proceedings (such as an attempt to waive the right to counsel or a supplementary indictment for a more serious or complex charge). This is consistent with the notion raised by Whittemore et al. (1997) about a "stage-specific" approach to competency assessment.

Predicting Competency Restoration

In some jurisdictions, the prediction of a defendant's restorability to competence is mandated at the time of evaluation; other jurisdictions, including the federal system, allow for a trial of treatment to determine whether the defendant is likely to become competent to stand trial. In *Jackson v. Indiana* (1972), the U.S. Supreme Court ruled that an incompetent defendant cannot be committed longer than "a reasonable period of time necessary to determine whether there is a substantial probability that he will attain the capacity in the foreseeable future" (pp. 737–738).

The literature on competency restoration indicates that most defendants are restored to competency. Cuneo and Brelje (1984) reported a restoration rate of 74% within one year. Restoration rates of 95% after an average of two months were reported by Nicholson and McNulty (1992), and of 90% after a mean stay of over 280 days (Nicholson, Barnard, Robbins, & Hankins, 1994). Carbonell, Heilbrun, and Friedman (1992) reported about 62% of incompetent inpatients had been restored after three months of treatment. None of these investigators were able to develop prediction models that improved on predictions that all incompetent defendants would be restored to competence. Because psychosis correlates highly with findings of incompetence, assessments do not carefully distinguish between psychotic symptoms and psycholegal impairments, and competency treatment programs rely primarily on treatment with psychotropic medication, predicting restorability often becomes a matter of predicting response to antipsychotic medication (Golding, 1992).

Given the low base rate associated with failure to be restored to competence, it is probably most accurate to predict that all psychotic defendants will be restored to competence. Carbonell et al. (1992) recommended a "demonstration model" with a period of varied treatment for all incompetent defendants until competency appears to have been restored or until it seems reasonably clear that competency will *not* be restored in the foreseeable future. However, there are a small number of incompetent defendants with major, irreversible cognitive disorders, such as dementia or moderate mental retardation, for whom it may be reasonable to predict unrestorability without an attempt at treatment designed for competency restoration.

Treatment of Incompetence

Descriptions of treatment programs in the literature describe hospital-based treatment consisting primarily of psychotropic medication and didactic programming focused on knowledge-based competence. A program in Ohio described by Davis (1985) was unique in its focus on individually tailored treatment plans "to address the actual reasons the person was found to be incompetent" (p. 269). Davis noted that "when the patient is restored (or not restored) to competency, the treatment plan serves as the basis for a functional report to the referring court" (p. 269). Defendants were assigned to different didactic and problem-solving groups based on their level of functioning and the areas of deficits in competence they displayed. Some defendants received primarily individual treatment. Patients participated in mock trials to apply information they learned and to allow assessment of their ability to generalize their understanding of these concepts. Brown (1992) described a didactic program in Illinois with seven modules: written information, videotaped vignettes, simulated dialogue between defense attorney and defendant, simulated courtroom proceedings and role play, a videotaped presentation by an experienced public defender on the topic of working with a defense attorney, and short tests.

Siegel and Elwork (1990) conducted an experimental study of a competency treatment program, consisting of a didactic component using a videotape and courtroom model and problem-solving groups. The control group saw videotapes about humor in psychotherapy and participated in groups dealing with general mental health concerns. The treatment and control groups were matched for initial scores on the CAI. They differed significantly on the posttest CAI, as the control group did not improve, whereas the experimental group improved significantly on 10 of 11 elements of the measure. Forty-five days after the posttest, staff had independently assessed as competent 43% of the experimental group but only 15% of the control group. Higher scores on the CAI posttest were significantly correlated with hospital staff assessment of competence.

Other reports in the literature indicate that restoration of competence requires an average of four to six months of hospitalization (Bennett & Kish, 1990; Rodenhauser & Khamis, 1988). Beckham, Annis, and Bein (1986) reported that 14% of defendants restored to competence over a two-year period deteriorated and required rehospitalization prior to resolution of their cases. Decrease in medication at the time of hospital discharge to return to pretrial detention and more serious charges were associated with rehospitalization. The failure of defendants with more serious charges to remain competent after discharge may be due to the greater stress, the greater demands for participation by the defendant in the defense, and the greater incentive to malinger associated with serious charges. Ladds, Convit, Zito, and Vitrai (1993) reported on the outcomes of cases for defendants who had been restored to competence with the assistance of forced medication. They found no adverse effect of forced medication on the

resolution of these defendants' cases, either in terms of negotiating a favorable plea bargain or prevailing at trial on an insanity defense, when compared to defendants who had voluntarily accepted treatment with medication.

Some jurisdictions (e.g., Ohio) permit court-ordered treatment for competency restoration in the community. This option is used for a small number of defendants who do not pose a risk to self or others in the community, consent to treatment, and can be provided, or have, a stable residential placement and community support system.

Permanently Incompetent Defendants

Morris and Meloy (1993) reviewed the legal options for implementing the limitation on competency restoration commitment established by *Jackson v. Indiana* (1972). They summarized data on permanently incompetent criminal defendants confined in California hospitals. These defendants had been confined on average for over four years after being adjudicated as permanently incompetent and eligible for special conservatorship due to dangerousness by reason of a mental disorder. These defendants had already been hospitalized for up to three years prior to conservatorship in failed attempts to restore them to competence. Ninety-three percent of the sample studied were diagnosed with schizophrenia or schizoaffective disorder, and 64% had a history of substance abuse. Mental retardation and organic brain syndrome were virtually nonexistent in this sample, and personality disorders were diagnosed in only 7%. The statute provided that these defendants could be held under conservatorship only if found to represent a substantial danger of physical harm to others beyond a reasonable doubt. However, in only 26% of the cases had the defendant committed more than two violent acts in the hospital before conservatorship was granted and also committed a violent act afterwards. Morris and Meloy concluded that the *Jackson* case has been circumvented in many jurisdictions by statutory provisions that permit civil commitment of permanently incompetent defendants using criteria different from those applied to other civil patients.

CASE EXAMPLE

This vignette illustrates several points that have been made throughout this chapter. First, it demonstrates that competence to stand trial goes beyond foundational competence and encompasses, in addition, rather complex issues of decisional competence, as described by Bonnie (1992) and implicit in *Godinez v. Moran* (1993). Second, it emphasizes the fluid nature of competence, in terms of the specific legal situation and demands placed on the defendant, and changes over time in his or her capacity to meet these situational demands. Third, it raises medication issues discussed in *Riggins v. Nevada* (1992) and by Skeem and Golding (1998). Fourth, it demonstrates the need for forensically relevant assessment techniques, including input from defense counsel, third-party information, competency assessment instruments, and targeted use of traditional psychological testing. Fifth, this case exemplifies the need to specifically address the relationship between symptoms of psychopathology and psycholegal deficits in assessing competence to stand trial. Finally, this case reflects the course of competency restoration of a hospitalized incompetent defendant.

Jason, a single man in his early 20s with a ninth-grade education, is charged with felony assault of a hospital worker. The offense occurred while he was civilly committed and had just been informed that the court had ordered forced medication. Jason first developed symptoms of schizophrenia at age 18. He became religiously preoccupied and secluded himself in his room, where he wrapped himself in sheets, prayed, laughed, and talked to himself, and stated that Jesus talked to him. He also developed delusional thinking about the involvement of family, friends, and neighbors in drug activity, prostitution, the Mafia, and the Masons. He repeatedly refused treatment and became aggressive toward his family, leading to treatment in hospitals, where he refused medication and was combative and threatening with treatment staff. Shortly before the hospitalization leading to the alleged offense, he had traveled to Washington, D.C., and was hospitalized there after he attempted to meet with the president to discuss drug policy. Jason was evaluated at three different points in time regarding his competence to stand trial in this case.

Competency Evaluation #1

One month after the alleged offense, Jason was seen in the jail, where he was refusing psychotropic medication. He attributed his recent civil commitment to a conspiracy by his parents and the Mafia. He reported that he was hearing the voice of God. His thoughts were disjointed and illogical. He reported bizarre physical symptoms that he attributed to psychotropic medication administered to him in the past. He was agitated and hypervigilant, constantly scanning his environment in a threat-sensitive manner. He was preoccupied with the president and high government officials who were somehow involved in his predicament. He was insistent that he did not have a mental illness and stated that doctors exaggerate because they are desperate for a job.

Jason gave an account of the alleged offense that was factually consistent with the reports of witnesses and investigating officers. He accurately named the charge he faces and the approximate sentence he would receive if convicted. He stated that he could also be sent to a psychiatric hospital. When asked if he had an attorney, he produced his attorney's card. He did not know when he returned to court or the next step in the proceedings. When asked if anyone was against him in court, he initially named the victim, whom he referred to as "one of the prosecuting people." He then stated that "the whole court" is against him: "all the Mafia." He stated that his attorney should defend him based on the drugs he was given, which made him appear mentally ill. When asked about plea options, he became increasingly agitated and his speech became incoherent. It was not possible to administer any formal assessment instruments.

Although Jason had some understanding of the charge he faces and the factual basis for the charge, his thinking about court proceedings and the way his attorney could defend him was based on his delusional system. He quickly became agitated and irrational when attempts to discuss plea options and defense strategies were made. He is likely to become similarly agitated when his attorney attempts to counsel with him and when he is confronted with information in court that is inconsistent with his delusional beliefs. His disordered thinking would prevent him from testifying relevantly and from responding in a realistic, rational manner when evidence is presented against him. The examiner gave the opinion that Jason lacked the capacity to appreciate the nature and objectives of the proceedings against him, to assist his attorney in his defense, and to make decisions about his case in a knowing and intelligent manner, due to symptoms of his untreated mental illness. Jason was found incompetent to stand trial and committed to a hospital, with a court order for involuntary administration of medication.

Competency Evaluation #2

After a period of treatment with antipsychotic medication and didactic groups about court proceedings, the hospital notified the court of the opinion that Jason was now competent to stand trial. A second competency evaluation was ordered at the request of the defense attorney. The attorney expressed the concern that "Jason knows who sits where and what they do" in court, but that she could not reason with him about defense strategy. During this second evaluation, Jason entered the interview room with a Bible, a stack of newspaper clippings, and writings of biblical verses that he described as "evidence." He spoke in a pressured manner about his beliefs that he had been hospitalized by a number of people who wished to discredit him so that he could not be a potential witness against them in drug cases. He produced newspaper clippings about surveys of gang activity and prosecution of drug dealers that he said supported his position.

Jason was administered an intellectual screening measure, on which he scored in the low-average range of intelligence. He was administered the MMPI-2 as an objective measure of response set to the evaluation and of psychopathology. He attended well to the lengthy inventory a few items at a time, but he often interrupted testing to talk excitedly about the "evidence" he had gathered for his case. He insisted on finishing the test, but he took twice as long as the average person to do so. The results indicate that the defendant was able to understand the item content and respond in a consistent fashion. The validity profile is not consistent with overreporting or exaggeration of symptoms, and this data, considered in light of the history of his symptomatology, provide a basis to rule out malingering to avoid prosecution. Elevations on the clinical scales are consistent with persecutory thinking, suspiciousness, feelings of alienation from others, aggressiveness, hypersensitivity, and hypervigilance. Contrary to the defendant's insistence that his beliefs are true and that he is not mentally ill, the MMPI-2 results are consistent with psychopathology of a paranoid nature.

Although Jason knew the charge he faces, his account of events at the time of the offense was delusional and tangential. He proposed that his attorney argue self-defense at trial, based on the "evidence" from newspaper clippings that others had been charged with drug activity and had him hospitalized to discredit him as a potential witness against them. With some difficulty, the examiner was able to refocus Jason to discuss the seriousness of the charge, and he reported the maximum sentence correctly before stating, "I should be able to not go to jail. Somebody should investigate my case. A lot of police are crooked." He could define plea options, although he did not have a thorough understanding of their ramifications. He had a good understanding of the adversarial nature of court proceedings and the roles of court participants in general. However, he frequently became irrational as he discussed his own case and his theory of defense.

The MacCAT-CA was administered to Jason. On the Understanding and Reasoning sections, he earned scores indicative of minimal to no impairment. However, on the Appreciation section, based on his own legal situation, his score was indicative of clinically significant impairment. He felt that he would be less likely to be treated fairly by the legal system "because of what I know about what's going on," and more likely to be found guilty "because somebody wants me out of the way—because I'm a crimp in someone's game." He refused to discuss the question about his likelihood of plea bargaining with anyone other than his attorney.

However, his attorney had expressed concerns about the inability of the defendant to reason about defense strategy.

It was the opinion of the examiner that Jason understood the seriousness of the charge and the allegations underlying it. He was aware of the adversarial nature of court proceedings and the plea options available to a defendant. However, he could not articulate the benefits and disadvantages of various plea options. In responding to questions about a hypothetical defendant, he could make decisions in a rational manner. In discussing his own case, he felt that he would be treated less fairly than the average defendant. He proposed an irrational defense strategy based on his long-standing delusions, and he had difficulty focusing on relevant aspects of the case due to disordered thinking and agitation. His attorney reported that she could not reason with him in making decisions about defense strategy. It was the opinion of the examiner that he had some understanding of the nature and objective of the proceedings against him, but that he lacked the capacity to assist in his defense and to make necessary decisions in a knowing and intelligent manner.

Competency Evaluation #3

After several more months of treatment, the hospital again approached the court with the opinion that Jason was competent to stand trial, and a third evaluation was ordered. Jason was calmer and less overtly delusional. He still did not believe that he is mentally ill, but he expressed an understanding of how others could perceive him this way. He stated that he was willing to continue to take the medication he had been prescribed if it would help him proceed with the case and be discharged from the hospital. He did not become agitated, and his thinking was not tangential and irrelevant as before. He reported that he had been meeting individually with his community case manager, who had explained the likely outcomes of plea alternatives, particularly as they related to his goal of returning to the community and planning a future for himself. He was better informed and displayed the ability to weigh defense options in a self-serving manner. He had ruled out the possibility of pleading not guilty because he had committed the act and "people saw this." He had also abandoned his theory of self-defense. Although he remained interested in having his suspicions about the Mafia and drug dealers investigated, he no longer viewed this as relevant to his case or as the basis for a defense. He was willing to consider the insanity defense because the emotional turmoil he was experiencing at the time of the offense overcame his religious prohibitions against harming another. He identified the advantages of an acquittal by reason of insanity as avoiding a felony conviction, which could limit his employment options and his rights. He stated that he could remain under the jurisdiction of the court longer if found insane than if he pled guilty, but he could avoid a prison sentence and the disadvantages of a felony conviction with an insanity acquittal. Jason expressed confidence in his attorney and an eagerness to discuss his options further with her. The Appreciation scale of the MacCAT-CA was readministered, and he scored in the minimal/no impairment range.

Jason's demeanor was less hypervigilant, anxious, and threat-sensitive on psychotropic medication than it was in his unmedicated state at the time of the offense. The dose of medication he was prescribed did not cause blunted affect or awareness, and it contributed to a considerable improvement in his cognitive capacities. Because he was initially evaluated close in time to the offense, in an untreated state, it is possible to reconstruct for the trier of fact his mental state at that time and to point out the difference between his current demeanor and his condition at the time of the offense.

SUMMARY

Competence to stand trial is a constitutional prerequisite to adjudication of criminal cases and essential to preserving the fairness, accuracy, dignity, and autonomy of criminal proceedings. Psychologists are called on to address the issue of competence more often than any other issue in criminal law. Increasingly, case law developments and psychological formulations of the concept of trial competence have focused on not only the knowledge-based or foundational aspects of competence, but the decisional aspects as well. Competency assessment instruments, multiple sources of data, the relationship between psycholegal impairments and symptoms of psychopathology, and the fluid nature of competency across time and across specific case demands are all aspects of the evaluation of trial competence. Treatment, the needs of special populations, competency assistance strategies, and the problem of the permanently incompetent defendant highlight the complexity of the issue. Psychology makes a significant contribution to the understanding of trial competence through the development of measures, theoretical and empirical research, assessment and treatment, and consultation with courts and attorneys.

REFERENCES

Allard v. Hedgemoe, 572 F.2d 1, 3 (1st Cir. 1978).

Appelbaum, K. L. (1994). Assessing defendants with mental retardation. *Journal of Psychiatry and Law, 22,* 311–327.

Bagby, R., Nicholson, R., Rogers, R., & Nussbaum, D. (1992). Domains of competency to stand trial: A factor analytic study. *Law and Human Behavior, 16,* 491–507.

Barnard, G., Nicholson, R., Hankins, G., Raisani, K., Patel, N., Gies, D., et al. (1992). Itemmetric and scale analysis of a new computer-assisted competency assessment instrument (CADCOMP). *Behavioral Sciences and the Law, 10,* 419–435.

Barnard, G., Thompson, J., Freeman, W., Robbins, L., Gies, D., & Hankins, G. (1991). Competency to stand trial: Description and initial evaluation of a new computer-assisted evaluation tool to stand trial (CADCOMP). *Bulletin of the American Academy of Psychiatry and Law, 19,* 367–381.

Beckham, J., Annis, L., & Bein, M. (1986). Don't pass go: Predicting who returns from court as remaining incompetent to stand trial. *Criminal Justice and Behavior, 13,* 99–109.

Bennett, G., & Kish, G. (1990). Incompetency to stand trial: Treatment unaffected by demographic variables. *Journal of Forensic Sciences, 35,* 403–412.

Berman, L. M., & Osborne, Y. H. (1987). Attorneys' referrals for competency to stand trial evaluations: Comparisons of referred and nonreferred clients. *Behavioral Sciences and the Law, 5,* 373–380.

Bonnie, R. (1990). The competence of criminal defendants with mental retardation to participate in their own defense. *Journal of Criminal Law and Criminology, 81,* 419–446.

Bonnie, R. (1992). The competence of criminal defendants: A theoretical reformulation. *Behavioral Sciences and the Law, 10,* 291–316.

Brown, D. R. (1992). A didactic group program for persons found unfit to stand trial. *Hospital and Community Psychiatry, 43,* 732–733.

Carbonell, J., Heilbrun, K., & Friedman, F. (1992). Predicting who will regain trial competency: Initial promise unfulfilled. *Forensic Reports, 5,* 67–76.

Cochrane, R., Grisso, T., & Frederick, R. (2001). The relationship between criminal charges, diagnoses, and psycholegal opinions among federal pretrial defendants. *Behavioral Sciences and the Law, 19,* 565–582.

Cooper v. Oklahoma, 116 S. Ct. 1373 (1996).

Cooper, D., & Grisso, T. (1997). Five year research update (1991–1995): Evaluations for competence to stand trial. *Behavioral Sciences and the Law, 15,* 347–364.

Cuneo, D., & Brejle, T. (1984). Predicting probability of attaining fitness to stand trial. *Psychological Reports, 55,* 35–39.

Davis, D. L. (1985). Treatment planning for the patient who is incompetent to stand trial. *Hospital and Community Psychiatry, 36,* 268–271.

Drope v. Missouri, 420 U.S. 162, 95 S.Ct. 896 (1975).

Dusky v. United States, 362 U.S. 402, 80 S.Ct. 788 (1960).

Ericson, K., & Perlman, N. (2001). Knowledge of legal terminology and court proceedings in adults with developmental disabilities. *Law and Human Behavior, 25,* 529–545.

Everington, C. (1990). The competence assessment for standing trial for defendants with mental retardation (CAST-MR): A validation study. *Criminal Justice and Behavior, 17,* 147–168.

Everington, C., & Dunn, C. (1995). A second validation study of the competence assessment for standing trial for defendants with mental retardation (CAST-MR). *Criminal Justice and Behavior, 22,* 44–59.

Everington, C., & Luckasson, R. (1992). *Competence assessment to stand trial for defendants with mental retardation (CAST-MR).* Worthington, OH: International Diagnostic Services.

Faretta v. California, 422 U.S., 806 (1975).

Felthous, A. (1994). The right to represent oneself incompetently: Competency to waive counsel and conduct one's own defense before and after Godinez. *Mental and Physical Disability Law Reporter, 18,* 105–112.

Frederick, R. I. (1997). *Validity Indicator Profile test manual.* Minneapolis, MN: National Computer Systems.

Frendak v. United States, 408 A.2d 364 (D.C. 1979).

Frith's Case, 22 How. St. Tr. 307 (1790).

Godinez v. Moran, 61 U.S.L. W. 4749, 113 S. Ct. 2680 (1993).

Golding, S. L. (1992). Studies of incompetent defendants: Research and social policy implications. *Forensic Reports, 5,* 77–83.

Golding, S. L. (1993). *Interdisciplinary Fitness Interview–Revised.* (Training manual and instrument available from the author at the University of Utah, Department of Psychology, Salt Lake City, UT 84112)

Golding, S., Roesch, R., & Schreiber, J. (1984). Assessment and conceptualization of competency to stand trial: Preliminary data on the Interdisciplinary Fitness Interview. *Law and Human Behavior, 8,* 321–334.

Goldstein, A. M., & Burd, M. (1990). Role of delusions in trial competency evaluations: Case law and implications for forensic practice. *Forensic Reports, 3,* 361–386.

Gothard, S., Rogers, R., & Sewell, K. (1995). Feigning incompetency to stand trial: An investigation of the Georgia Court Competency Test. *Law and Human Behavior, 19,* 363–372.

Gothard, S., Viglione, D. J., Jr., Meloy, J. R., & Sherman, M. (1995). Detection or malingering in competency to stand trial evaluations. *Law and Human Behavior, 19,* 493–505.

Grisso, T. (1986). *Evaluating competencies: Forensic assessments and instruments.* New York: Plenum.

Grisso, T. (1988). *Competency to stand trial evaluations: A manual for practice.* Sarasota, FL: Professional Resource Exchange.

Grisso, T., & Appelbaum, P. (1995). The MacArthur Treatment Competence Study (I, II, & III). *Law and Human Behavior, 19,* 105–174.

Grisso, T., Cocozza, J., Steadman, H., Fisher, W., & Greer, A. (1994). The organization of pretrial forensic services. *Law and Human Behavior, 18,* 377–393.

Hoge, S. K., Bonnie, R. J., Poythress, N., & Monahan, J. (1992). Attorney-client decision-making in criminal cases: Client competence and participation as perceived by their attorneys. *Behavioral Sciences and the Law, 10,* 385–394.

Hoge, S. K., Bonnie, R. J., Poythress, N., Monahan, J., Eisenberg, M., & Feucht-Haviar, T. (1997). The MacArthur Adjudicative Competence Study: Development of a research instrument. *Law and Human Behavior, 21,* 141–179.

Jackson v. Indiana, 406 U.S. 715, 92 S. Ct. 1845 (1972).

Keilitz, I., Monahan, B., Keilitz, S., & Dillon, C. (1987). *Criminal defendants with trial disabilities: The theory and practice of competency assistance.* Williamsburg, VA: Institute on Mental Disability and the Law, National Center for State Courts.

Laboratory of Community Psychiatry. (1974). *Competency to stand trial and mental illness.* New York: Aronson.

Ladds, B., Convit, A., Zito, J., & Vitrai, J. (1993). The disposition of criminal charges after involuntary medication to restore competency to stand trial. *Journal of Forensic Sciences, 38,* 1442–1459.

LaFortune, K., & Nicholson, R. (1995). How adequate are Oklahoma's mental health evaluations for determining competency in criminal proceedings? The bench and the bar respond. *Journal of Psychiatry and Law, 23,* 231–262.

Linhorst, D., & Dirks-Linhorst, P. A. (1997). The impact of insanity acquittees on Missouri's public mental health system. *Law and Human Behavior, 21,* 327–338.

Lipsitt, P., Lelos, D., & McGarry, A. L. (1971). Competency for trial: A screening instrument. *American Journal of Psychiatry, 128,* 105–109.

McDonald, A., Nussbaum, D., & Bagby, R. (1991). Reliability, validity and utility of the Fitness Interview Test. *Canadian Journal of Psychiatry, 36,* 480–484.

Melton, G., Petrila, J., Poythress, N., & Slobogin, C. (1997). *Psychological evaluations for the courts* (2nd ed.). New York: Guilford Press.

Morris, G. H., & Meloy, J. R. (1993). Out of mind? Out of sight: The uncivil commitment of permanently incompetent criminal defendants. *U.C.-Davis Law Review, 27,* 1–96.

National Center for Law and Deafness. (1992). *Legal rights: The guide for deaf and hard of hearing people* (4th ed). Washington, DC: Gallaudet University Press.

Nestor, P. G., Daggett, D., Haycock, J., & Price, M. (1999). Competence to stand trial: A neuropsychological inquiry. *Law and Human Behavior, 23,* 397–412.

Nicholson, R., Barnard, G., Robbins, L., & Hankins, G. (1994). Predicting treatment outcome for incompetent defendants. *Bulletin of the American Academy of Psychiatry and the Law, 22,* 367–377.

Nicholson, R., & Johnson, W. (1991). Prediction of competency to stand trial: Contribution of demographics, type of offense, clinical characteristics psycholegal ability. *International Journal of Law and Psychiatry, 14,* 287–297.

Nicholson, R., & McNulty, J. (1992). Outcome of hospitalization for defendants found incompetent to stand trial. *Behavioral Sciences and the Law, 10,* 371–383.

Nicholson, R., Robertson, H., Johnson, W., & Jensen, G. (1988). A comparison of instruments for assessing competency to stand trial. *Law and Human Behavior, 2,* 313–321.

Nicholson, R. A., & Kugler, K. E. (1991). Competent and incompetent criminal defendants: A quantitative review of comparative research. *Psychological Bulletin, 109,* 355–370.

North Carolina v. Alford, 400 U.S. 25, 91 S.Ct. 160 (1970).

Otto, R. K., Poythress, N., Nicholson, R., Edens, R., Monahan, J., Bonnie, R., et al. (1998). Psychometric properties of the MacArthur Competence Assessment Tool-Criminal Adjudication. *Psychological Assessment, 10,* 435–443.

Pate v. Robinson, 383 U.S. 375 (1966).

Pope, K. S., Butcher, J. N., & Seelen, J. (2000). *The MMPI, MMPI-2 and MMPI-A in court* (2nd ed.). Washington, DC: American Psychological Association.

Poythress, N., Bonnie, R., Hoge, S., Monahan, J., & Oberlander, L. (1994). Client abilities to assist counsel and make decisions in criminal cases: Findings from three studies. *Law and Human Behavior, 18,* 437–452.

Pride v. Estelle, 649 F.2d 324 (1981).

Rees, L. M., Tombaugh, T., Gansler, D. A., & Moczynski, N. P. (1998). Five validation experiments of the Test of Memory Malingering (TOMM). *Psychological Assessment, 10,* 10–20.

Riggins v. Nevada, 112 S. Ct. 1810 (1992).

Rodenhauser, R., & Khamis, H. (1988). Predictors of improvement in maximum security forensic hospital patients. *Behavioral Sciences and the Law, 6,* 531–542.

Roesch, R., & Golding, S. (1980). *Competency to stand trial.* Urbana-Champaign: University of Illinois Press.

Roesch, R., Webster, C. D., & Eaves, D. (1984). *The Fitness Interview Test: A method for examining fitness to stand trial.* Toronto, Ontario, Canada: University of Toronto Centre of Criminology.

Rogers, R., Bagby, M., & Dickens, S. (1992). *Structured Interview of Reported Symptoms and professional manual.* Odessa, FL: Psychological Assessment Resources.

Rogers, R., Grandjean, N., Tillbrook, C., Vitacco, M., & Sewell, K. (2001). Recent interview-based measures of competency to stand trial: A critical review augmented with research data. *Behavioral Sciences and the Law, 19,* 503–518.

Schreiber, J. (1978). Assessing competency to stand trial: A case study of technology diffusion in four states. *Bulletin of the American Academy of Psychiatry and the Law, 6,* 439–457.

Siegel, A., & Elwork, A. (1990). Treating incompetence to stand trial. *Law and Human Behavior, 14,* 57–65.

Sieling v. Eyman, 478 F.2d 211 (9th Cir. Ariz. 1973).

Skeem, J., & Golding, S. (1998). Community examiners' evaluations of competence to stand trial: Common problems and suggestions for improvement. *Professional Psychology: Research and Practice, 29,* 357–367.

Skeem, J., Golding, S., Cohn, N., & Berge, G. (1998). Logic and reliability of evaluations of competence to stand trial. *Law and Human Behavior, 22,* 519–547.

State v. Champagne, 497 A.2d 1242 (1985).

State v. Hahn, 707 P.2d. 699 (1985).

Steadman, H., Monahan, J., Hartstone, E., Davis, S., & Robbins, P. (1982). Mentally disordered offenders: A national survey of patients and facilities. *Law and Human Behavior, 6,* 31–38.

Stone, A. (1975). *Mental health and law: A system in transition.* Rockville, MD: National Institute of Mental Health.

Teplin, L. (1994). Psychiatric and substance abuse disorders among male jail detainees. *American Journal of Public Health, 84,* 290–293.

United States v. Charters, 829 F.2d 479 (1987).

United States v. Charters, 863 F.2d 302 (1988).

United States v. Duhon, 104 F. Supp. 2d 663 (W.D. La. 2000).

United States v. Marble, 940 F.2d 1543 (D.C. Cir. 1991).

Vernon, M., Steinberg, A., & Montoya, L. (1999). Deaf murderers: Clinical and forensic issues. *Behavioral Sciences and the Law, 17,* 495–516.

Warren, J., Rosenfeld, B., Fitch, W. L., & Hawk, G. (1997). Forensic mental health clinical evaluation: An analysis of interstate and intersystemic differences. *Law and Human Behavior, 21,* 377–390.

Warrington, E. K. (1984). *Recognition Memory Test manual.* Los Angeles: Western Psychological Services.

Washington v. Harper, 494 U.S. 210 (1990).

Westbrook v. Arizona, 384 U.S. 150 (1966).

Whalem v. United States, 346 F.2d. 812 (1965).

Whittemore, D., Ogloff, J., & Roesch, R. (1997). An investigation of competency to participate in legal proceedings in Canada. *Canadian Journal of Psychiatry, 42,* 869–875.

Wieter v. Settle, 193 F.Supp. 318 (W.D. Mo., 1961).

Wildman, R. W., II, Batchelor, E. S., Thompson, L., Nelson, F. R., Moore, J. T., Patterson, M. E., et al. (1978). *The Georgia Court Competency Test: An attempt to develop a rapid, quantitative measure of fitness for trial.* Unpublished manuscript, Milledgeville, GA.

Wilson v. United States, 129 U.S. App. D.C. 107, 391 F.2d 460 (1968).

Wood, J. B. (1984). Protecting deaf suspects' right to understand criminal proceedings. *Journal of Criminal Law and Criminology, 75,* 166–197.

Wulach, J. S. (1980). The incompetency plea: Abuses and reforms. *Journal of Psychiatry and Law, 8,* 317–328.

Youtsey v. United States, 97 F. 937 (1899).

Zapf, P., & Roesch, R. (1997). Assessing fitness to stand trial: A comparison of institution-based evaluations and a brief screening interview. *Canadian Journal of Community Mental Health, 16,* 53–66.

CHAPTER 20

Evaluation of Criminal Responsibility

ALAN M. GOLDSTEIN, STEPHEN J. MORSE, AND DAVID L. SHAPIRO

Peter Gordon was 4 years old when his parents returned from the hospital with his newborn sister, Karen. Highly sensitive to issues of "sibling rivalry," his parents had carefully prepared Peter for his new role as "big brother." He was included in the process of choosing her name and buying furniture for her room and had accompanied his mother to the obstetrician on several occasions to watch his sister's development on ultrasound. Within days of her arrival at home, Peter had accepted her presence and spent much of his time watching her asleep in her crib. Apparently, Peter had no difficulty adjusting to this major change in his life, showing no signs of resentment, rivalry, or anger toward Karen. For more than five months, he helped his parents care for her (as much as a child his age could assist). He was a warm, caring, sensitive brother. He accepted Karen as part of the family and was clearly proud of his sister.

One night, Peter's father rented a videotape of *Peter Pan.* He and his parents watched the movie and Peter seemed engrossed in the film, no doubt because of its content and because of the shared name with the central character. When it was over, Peter went to sleep. Shortly thereafter, his parents retired for the evening. Two hours later, Peter entered their bedroom in a highly agitated, anxious state. Through his tears, he explained to his parents that he had awoken, entered Karen's room, opened the window, and had taken her out of her crib. Influenced by *Peter Pan,* Peter decided that his sister could fly and, acting on this belief, he carried Karen to the window, held her outside, and then let her go. Her parents found Karen dead in the bushes beneath her window. The police arrived, conducted a preliminary investigation, and left. Peter was never charged with the homicide of his sister.

Peter had purposefully opened the window and let go of his sister, causing her to fall three stories to her death. In this hypothetical case, law enforcement and Peter's parents concluded that because of his age, Peter's state of mind was such that he had not intended to cause her death. Rather, he actually believed that his sister would take flight as he had just seen in the movie. Moreover, there is good empirical evidence to suggest that 4-year-olds do not cognitively understand the concept of death as the complete biological termination of life. Thus, there is a question concerning whether any child of 4 can genuinely intend to cause death.

Undoubtedly, most people reading this chapter would agree that although Peter's action resulted in his sister's death and that Karen was both wronged and harmed, Peter was *not* a morally responsible agent. Causal and moral responsibility are clearly distinct. As former U.S. Supreme Court Justice Oliver Wendell Holmes famously said, even a dog knows the difference between being stumbled over and being kicked, although the resulting injury may be the same. Moral responsibility depends crucially on the mental state with which a person acts. The evaluation of mental states is therefore central to culpability assessment in the criminal law.

Defenses focusing on a defendant's mental state when he or she committed a crime are retrospective in nature. Unlike traditional clinical assessments, which usually are concerned with present functioning, forensic evaluations focus on a defendant's alleged actions and mental states (cognitive and/or volitional) that may have occurred days, weeks, months, and, in some instances, years earlier. The forensic expert must "reconstruct" a past mental state to assist the trier of fact's assessment of criminal culpability and, consequently, the ultimate disposition of the case.

In this chapter, we first consider the basic doctrines of criminal liability, with special attention to mental state issues that are relevant to culpability, such as the negation of *mens rea,* provocation/passion, extreme mental or emotional disturbance, voluntary and involuntary intoxication, imperfect self-defense, and duress. We emphasize the history of the insanity defense, including its development, changes, and recent reforms. Next, we review ethical issues and conflicts that arise when clinicians conduct retrospective forensic mental state evaluations. We then describe a generic model for conducting forensic assessments, with specific application to evaluating defendants' mental states at the time of the offense.

DOCTRINES OF CRIMINAL LIABILITY

There is a lively debate about whether forensic assessments require evaluators to understand the legal questions a case raises, including issues concerning criminal liability that prompted the evaluation. Nonetheless, the vast majority of lawyers and forensic psychologists and psychiatrists believe that the expert's knowledge of the legal questions will help the evaluator provide the fullest possible relevant evidence.

In brief, criminal guilt is established if the prosecution can prove all the definitional criteria of the crime charged—the so-called elements of the crime, including any requisite mental state element. A defendant will be found not guilty of a crime if either the prosecution is unable to prove all the elements beyond a reasonable doubt or an affirmative defense is established. The state may, in its discretion, place the burden of persuasion for affirmative defenses on either the prosecution or the defense. (The most accessible one-volume treatise that covers the substantive and procedural issues is Dressler, 2001.) Forensic evaluations may provide relevant, probative evidence concerning claims that a mental abnormality

negated a mental state element of crime or if the abnormality helps establish an affirmative defense. The evaluator must understand the meaning of mental state elements and excuses and the effect mental abnormality may have on claims about both. Let us therefore consider the requirements for criminal guilt in detail.

A typical criminal statute includes a conduct element (the prohibited act) and a mental state element, the *mens rea,* such as purpose or knowledge, with which the defendant must have acted. Some crimes are defined also to require further elements, such as the presence of a specific circumstance or a result. Consider, for example, the following crime: the intentional killing of a federal officer in the pursuit of her official duties. The conduct element is killing behavior of any type (e.g., shooting, knifing, poisoning, bludgeoning). The circumstance elements are that the victim must be a human being, a federal officer, and in the pursuit of official duties. The mental state elements are that the person must *intentionally* engage in killing conduct toward a person, with at least *knowledge* that the person being killed is a federal officer in pursuit of her official duties. The result element is that the person is actually killed (otherwise, conviction for attempted homicide only is possible). If the prosecution is able to prove all these elements beyond a reasonable doubt, criminal liability is established *prima facie.*

Even if all the elements of the crime are proved beyond a reasonable doubt, the defendant can still avoid liability by raising a partial or complete affirmative defense. In essence, an affirmative defense is a claim that the reason the defendant violated the criminal law and is *prima facie* guilty should, nonetheless, exonerate him or her. Affirmative defenses can be either justifications or excuses. A justification obtains if the otherwise wrongful conduct was objectively right, or at least permissible, under the specific circumstances. The defendant is a fully responsible agent in such cases, but is exonerated because he or she did the right thing in this situation. Self-defense against a wrongful aggressor is the classic example. Intentional harming is right, or at least permissible, if it is done by an innocent agent defending against what he or she reasonably believes to be imminent, wrongful aggression.

An excuse obtains if the defendant's conduct was objectively wrongful, but the defendant was not a responsible moral agent and, therefore, not blameworthy. Briefly put, the excuses identify situations in which (a) the agent lacked the general capacity for rationality, to be guided by reason; or (b) the agent acted under compulsion, such as a threat of death. Legal insanity and duress are classic examples of excuses. Suppose, for example, that a citizen suffering from a severe mental disorder has the delusional belief that a federal officer, apparently in pursuit of her official duties, is, in fact, part of a homicidal conspiracy to kill her. She kills the officer in the delusional belief that she needs to do so to save her own life. In such a case, the defendant's conduct is wrong—there is no justification for killing the officer—but her nonculpable irrationality marks her as a nonresponsible agent who does not deserve blame and punishment. The border between justification and excuse is not always so clear, but the distinction is very useful. With few exceptions, forensic evaluations will be more useful to assess excuse claims.

The term *mens rea* is often used in discussions of criminal liability, but the term has different meanings that may confuse forensic evaluators. Most specifically and traditionally conceived, *mens rea* refers to the specific mental state element that the definition of a crime requires. For example, one traditional definition of murder is the intentional killing of a human being. In this definition of murder, the intent to kill is the *mens rea* required. To be convicted of this offense, the prosecution must prove beyond a reasonable doubt that the defendant intended to cause death. A defendant who kills another person intentionally because he or she delusionally believes that he or she is threatened with death, surely kills with intent and thus acts with the requisite *mens rea* for murder. Sometimes, however, the term *mens rea* is used more broadly and loosely as a synonym for blameworthiness in general. Used this way, any legal claim concerning culpability or blameworthiness by definition concerns *mens rea*. Thus, for example, claims about required elements other than mental state elements and about affirmative defense claims are also relevant to *mens rea* in the broad sense. Thus, in the case of the hypothetical delusional self-defender, she may be exculpated because she is legally insane, even though she did intend to kill. Because she was not culpable, she may be said to lack *mens rea* in the broader sense. It is crucial to keep the two meanings of *mens rea* distinct and not to confuse the broader meaning with any specific legal doctrine.

The Act Requirement and Automatism

All crimes include a conduct element, an act that the defendant performs. This is often referred to as a "voluntary" act, which means simply that the defendant's bodily movement that caused the social harm was intentional and not performed in a state of significant dissociation. For example, if a stronger person pushes the hand of another person who is carrying a knife toward a vital organ of a victim who is killed by the knife wound, or if a person carrying a knife suffers from an unforeseen movement of his or her hand produced by a neurological disorder and thereby kills a victim, the person carrying the knife has not acted at all. His or her bodily movement in each case caused a death, but the bodily movement was not an intentional act and the person will not be guilty of homicide. In addition, conduct committed in a state of substantial dissociation, such as somnambulism, does not satisfy the act requirement. Such conduct is more "actish" than the previous examples. That is, it appears more intentional and goal-directed, but the law does not consider dissociated conduct as "voluntary" for the purpose of satisfying the act requirement. Such cases of dissociation often are categorized under the rubric "automatism." Some jurisdictions treat claims arising from automatism as affirmative defenses, but they are more commonly considered denials of the act requirement that is part of the definition of every crime. Forensic psychological evaluations may be helpful in assessing whether a defendant acted in a state of substantial dissociation.

Mens Rea and Mens Rea Defenses

The agent's fault is a necessary precondition for criminal blame and punishment. The mental state with which an act is performed is a crucial criterion by which morality and the criminal law identify an agent's fault for causing a social harm because mental states indicate an agent's attitude toward the harm and the rights and interests of fellow citizens. For example, violating another's rights by harming the victim intentionally is morally far more blameworthy than causing the same harm accidentally.

Over the centuries, criminal law has developed a large and often bewildering number of *mens rea* terms. Most, however, are encompassed by one of the four *mens reas* the *Model Penal Code* uses (American Law Institute [ALI], 1962): purpose, knowledge, recklessness, and negligence. A prohibited act or result is done with *purpose* if the act or result is the agent's conscious object. *Knowledge* means that the agent is actually aware of some prohibited circumstance, such as that the substance he or she possesses is controlled, or is practically certain that some prohibited result will occur as a result of his or her action. *Recklessness* means that the agent is consciously aware of a great and unjustifiable risk of a social harm that the agent has created. *Negligence* means that the agent is not aware of a substantial and unjustifiable risk that he or she created, but that the agent reasonably should be aware of the risk.

The *Model Penal Code*'s specific *mens rea* terms and the common law specific *mens rea* terms such as "intent" virtually always have ordinary language, commonsense, narrow meanings. To intend to do an act or to achieve a result, for example, means only that it is the defendant's purpose, his or her conscious object, to do that act or to achieve that result. These terms assume that the agent has reasonably intact consciousness, but that is a narrow, implicit limitation on ordinary language meanings. *Mens rea* terms do *not* include broader requirements, such as the ability to act rationally or the ability to comprehend the duty to obey the law. When they are morally and legally relevant, these broader considerations are raised by the affirmative defenses, to be discussed below.

Even if the defendant is suffering from a major mental disorder and acts for entirely bizarre reasons, *mens rea* will be present if the defendant performed the prohibited act or achieved the prohibited result intentionally or with any other *mens rea* properly understood. Thus, a delusional defendant who kills in response to the psychotic and mistaken but honest belief that his or her life is in danger kills intentionally and is *prima facie* guilty of murder. There are various doctrinal means to avoid *prima facie* guilt by denying that *mens rea* existed, such as mistake of fact, but claims that mental abnormality or intoxication negated *mens rea* are the primary contexts in which a forensic psychological evaluation concerning *mens rea* may be helpful.

Mental Abnormality and Mens Rea

A defendant may claim that he or she lacked a required mental state element because the agent suffered from a mental abnormality at the time of the crime. The use of mental abnormality evidence to cast reasonable doubt on the presence of *mens rea* is often referred to as "diminished capacity." Forensic evaluators should be aware, however, that such use of mental abnormality evidence is indistinguishable from the use of any other type of relevant, probative evidence admitted to cast doubt on the prosecution's *prima facie* case. This form of diminished capacity evidence is not an independent defense that requires a special name and it is certainly not an affirmative defense. About half the states in the United States and U.S. federal law permit the defendant to introduce evidence of mental abnormality to negate *mens rea,* but for various reasons, most jurisdictions place substantial limitations on the admissibility of such evidence. There is reason to believe that such limitations are unfair, but the U.S. Supreme Court has never held that criminal defendants have an unlimited right to introduce relevant evidence of mental abnormality to cast reasonable doubt on the presence of a required *mens rea.*

The term diminished *capacity* often leads to confusion when it is used to refer to claims about the negation of *mens rea.* The prosecution must prove that a *mens rea* is formed in fact, not that the defendant had the capacity to form the *mens rea.* The capacity to form *mens rea* and actual formation of *mens rea* are logically related because the latter cannot exist

without the former. But evaluators must remember that the precise legal question is whether *mens rea* was formed in fact, and they should not claim that the defendant lacked the capacity to form a *mens rea* when it is apparent that *mens rea* was formed in fact. In addition, the term often creates confusion between the use of mental abnormality evidence to negate *mens rea* and the use of such evidence to establish a genuine partial or complete excusing condition. These two entirely different types of claims must be kept distinct.

Experienced clinicians will recognize that mental disorders may give defendants bizarre reasons to act or to form beliefs, but even severe mental disorder is seldom inconsistent with a person's ability to act with intent or knowledge narrowly conceived. On occasion, of course, mental abnormality may negate some *mens reas.* Perhaps the most common example is the requirement of premeditation necessary in some jurisdictions to convict a defendant who kills intentionally of first-degree murder. Premeditation roughly means that the defendant has actually thought about the intentional killing in advance. For example, if a defendant acts on the spur of the moment in response to a command hallucination or a delusion, the defendant simply does not premeditate on that occasion. Note, however, that there may be no reason to believe that the defendant lacked the general ability to premeditate and that such psychotic reasons to kill are entirely consistent with the formation of intent to kill.

For another example, suppose a person with a severe mental disorder becomes disoriented on a cold night, cannot find his way home, and breaks into a building simply to keep warm. If the police capture our hapless wanderer, he might be charged with burglary, which requires the intent to commit a felony inside the building, such as theft, in addition to the intent to break in. In this case, evidence of mental disorder will reinforce the credibility of the defendant's claim that he never meant to steal, but entered the home only to keep warm. Note that in this case, the defendant does not lack the capacity to form the intent to steal; he simply did not form that intent on this occasion. Rather, he acted for a perfectly rational reason under the circumstances: to avoid exposure. But evidence of his mental disorder and consequent disorientation surely will support his claim that he never formed the intent to steal.

Intoxication and Mens Rea

Evidence of intoxication may be used to negate *mens rea.* If the defendant was voluntarily intoxicated at the time of the crime, most jurisdictions will allow the defendant to admit evidence of such intoxication. "Voluntary" intoxication means that the defendant intentionally introduced into his or her body a substance the defendant knew or ought to have known was an intoxicant. Virtually all jurisdictions that permit the introduction of voluntary intoxication evidence for the purpose of negating *mens rea* also place substantial and often technical limitations on admission. Moreover, acting wrongly while intoxicated is per se unreasonable, so voluntary intoxication evidence can never be used to negate the *mens rea* of negligence. The U.S. Supreme Court has upheld the constitutionality of a state statute that totally excluded evidence of voluntary intoxication to negate *mens rea,* even in cases in which the evidence is clearly relevant and probative (*Montana v. Egelhoff,* 1996). Although the fairness and wisdom of total exclusion is debatable, a minority of jurisdictions exclude voluntary intoxication altogether.

The rules for admitting evidence of so-called involuntary intoxication to negate *mens rea* are somewhat more permissive because, in contrast to cases of voluntary intoxication, the defendant is not responsible for becoming intoxicated. In general, involuntary intoxication occurs if the defendant (a) was forced to become intoxicated; (b) innocently and unknowingly consumed an intoxicant; (c) consumed an intoxicant pursuant to medical advice; or (d) became vastly more intoxicated than was reasonably predictable, given the amount of intoxicant consumed and the defendant's known susceptibility. Although cases of involuntary intoxication are relatively infrequent, it appears that defendants may use evidence of such intoxication to negate any *mens rea* except negligence. Involuntary intoxication can sometimes support a complete excuse, which is discussed next.

Once again, experienced clinicians will recognize that most intoxication does not prevent a defendant from acting with *mens rea.* Intoxicants may impair judgment, increase impulsivity, and the like, but in the vast majority of cases, they do not prevent an agent from acting intentionally or with other *mens reas.* On occasion, intoxication may be sufficiently extreme to cause unconsciousness or blackout. Although the defendant may appear to act purposefully, *mens rea* is not present in fact because consciousness is grossly impaired. Assuming that evidence of such intoxication is admissible at all, negation of some *mens rea* may therefore result. On other occasions, intoxication may not impair the general ability to form *mens rea,* but evidence of intoxication may support the credibility of a claim that *mens rea* was not present. For example, consider again the case of the mentally disordered and disoriented agent who breaks in to another's home to get warm. Now assume that intoxication produces the disorientation. Evidence of intoxication increases the credibility of the defendant's claim that he broke in to keep warm and not with the intent to commit a felony in the home. If this claim is believed, the defendant may be convicted of criminal trespass (if the jurisdiction has such a crime), but may not be convicted of burglary because the *mens rea* for the more serious crime—the intent to commit a felony in the home—is lacking.

Affirmative Defenses: Excuses

We have seen that the theoretical basis for excusing a defendant is either that the defendant lacked the capacity for rationality or that the defendant was compelled to act. Doctrinally, the criminal law applicable to adults and older juveniles accepts only two full, clear excuses that exonerate because the defendant is not blameworthy: legal insanity and duress. Other excuses, such as infancy, mistake, entrapment, and the statute of limitations, either do not apply to adults (or older minors), deny *prima facie* guilt rather than general blameworthiness, are not clearly an excuse, or do not exonerate because the defendant is blameless. There are a few other excuses, but they are either so archaic or so rare that they do not warrant discussion here.

Legal Insanity

The common law tests or statutes that define legal insanity vary across jurisdictions. Expert evidence is usually crucial in insanity defense cases, but strictly speaking, it is not required. Most insanity defense statutes require that, at the time of the crime, the defendant must have suffered from a mental disorder or defect *and* that, as a result of the mental abnormality, the defendant also suffered from a defect of cognition, a defect of reasoning. Some tests also excuse a defendant who suffers from a defect of control capacity, the ability to control one's conduct, even if cognition is relatively intact. The ALI's (1962) *Model Penal Code* test for legal insanity is a useful example because it includes all the features just described. The test provides: "A person is not responsible for criminal conduct if at the time of such conduct as a result of mental disease or defect he lacks substantial capacity either to appreciate the criminality [wrongfulness] of his conduct or to conform his conduct to the requirements of law" (Model Penal Code, Sec. 4.01(1), 1962).

Note that mental abnormality *alone* does *not* excuse according to any standard of legal insanity. It must also cause the further condition of incapacity to appreciate the wrongfulness of one's actions or to control one's conduct, which are the genuine excusing conditions. The requirement of mental abnormality is included as a relatively gross and verifiable condition that supports the claim that the requisite incapacity was also present. The terms of the test are not self-defining. How much capacity must be lacking is a legal, normative standard that can vary from jurisdiction to jurisdiction and intertemporally within a jurisdiction according to social, political, and legal conditions. In recent years, the control or volitional standard has been attacked on the ground that it is difficult and perhaps impossible validly to assess control capacity independent of cognitive or rationality defects. As a result, only a minority of U.S. jurisdictions include a control or volitional test. A comprehensive consideration of the insanity defense follows in the next section of this chapter.

Involuntary Intoxication

The rules permitting an involuntarily intoxicated defendant to be excused are strict. In effect, the intoxication must cause a mental abnormality that creates a condition that meets the standard for legal insanity. Indeed, in most jurisdictions, the language for the involuntary intoxication excuse test is the same as the language used to define legal insanity, except that the cause is intoxication rather than mental disorder or defect. Thus, even if the involuntarily intoxicated defendant would not have committed the crime but for the intoxication, the defendant will be excused only if he or she is in effect legally insane.

Although this rule may seem harsh, reflection shows that it is sensible. Many nonculpably caused conditions, such as stress or fatigue, may compromise a person's rationality and predispose him or her to criminal conduct that the agent would not otherwise do. Nevertheless, no excusing condition obtains unless the diminution in rationality meets the standard for full excuse exemplified by the insanity defense. People with diminished rationality are still expected to use their reason to avoid criminal conduct, even if it is harder for them to do so than for those without diminished rationality. The same reasoning applies when the cause of diminished rationality is involuntary intoxication. Any mitigation of responsibility in such cases must occur at sentencing, discussed below, because no jurisdiction in the United States has a doctrinal generic partial excuse or specific partial excuse for involuntary intoxication.

Duress

Duress as an excuse obtains if another person threatens the defendant with death or serious bodily harm unless the defendant does something even worse. So, for example, if a desperado threatens to kill an agent unless that person kills two innocent people, duress will obtain if a person of reasonable firmness would have yielded to the threat (ALI, 1962, Model Penal Code, Sec. 2.09(1)). The crucial reasonable firmness criterion is a moral, objective standard. The law is not concerned with the particular defendant's subjective psychological reaction. Duress will obtain whether the defendant was terrified or "cool" when acceding to the threat, as long as a person of reasonable firmness would have done so under the circumstances. Note that a threat of death or grievous bodily harm is usually required. The law assumes that a person of "reasonable firmness" will *not* yield to lesser physical threats or to psychological threats. Because the duress standard is largely objective, forensic evaluations usually have less relevance in cases raising this excuse.

Partial Excuse Defenses

Irrationality and compulsion are matters of degree. Therefore, in principle, some abnormal or threatened defendants may appear to deserve a partial excuse, even if all the elements can be proven and no full excuse can be established. Nonetheless, the criminal law has not adopted, in any jurisdiction, a generic partial excuse that applies to all offenses, that reduces the defendant's degree of culpability, and that is adjudicated at trial. No U.S. jurisdiction has a partial affirmative defense based on mental abnormality that may be termed "diminished capacity." The criminal law has adopted some specific mitigating doctrines that operate in effect as "partial" excuses, but these have limited scope. The most important is a set of doctrines that reduce a homicide that would otherwise be deemed murder to the lesser crime of manslaughter.

Provocation/Passion

The common law's provocation/passion doctrine is used in most jurisdictions. An intentional killing that would otherwise be murder is reduced to voluntary manslaughter if the defendant killed while subjectively in the "heat of passion" as the result of a provocation that would have caused a reasonable person to be in such a state. So, for example, a person engaged in mutual combat who was inflamed and intentionally killed his or her opponent would be guilty only of voluntary manslaughter. Although the rationale for the mitigation is contested, the most convincing explanation is that the defendant's rationality is compromised (but not entirely disabled) by the passion, and the passion is not fully the defendant's fault because it was aroused by a provocation that would have inflamed an objectively reasonable person. Thus, the defendant is partially excused through a doctrinal formula that reduces the degree of crime.

Although provocation/passion operates as a partial excuse and appears to be an affirmative defense, the U.S. Supreme Court has held that if provocation/passion is part of the *prima facie* definition of voluntary manslaughter, the prosecution must prove the absence of provocation/passion beyond a reasonable doubt in cases in which the issue is raised (*Mullaney v. Wilbur,* 1975). Forensic evaluations seldom are necessary in provocation/passion cases because provocation is a moral, objective standard and thus not a matter of psychological expertise. Assessing whether a defendant was inflamed is a commonsense factual determination that is well within the ken of laypeople. In recent years, some jurisdictions have softened the reasonable person standard, allowing the hypothetical reasonable person to be endowed with some of the characteristics of the accused, such as sex. To date, however, no American jurisdiction has been willing to endow the reasonable person with a mental abnormality.

Extreme Mental or Emotional Disturbance

The provocation/passion doctrine arguably is too narrow, providing mitigation to too few deserving defendants charged with murder. Consequently, a minority of jurisdictions have adopted the *Model Penal Code*'s similar but broader "extreme mental or emotional disturbance" doctrine to reduce murder to manslaughter. The Code provides that criminal homicide constitutes manslaughter when

> a homicide that would otherwise be murder is committed under the influence of extreme mental or emotional disturbance for which there is reasonable explanation or excuse. The reasonableness of such explanation or excuse shall be determined from the viewpoint of a person in the actor's situation under the circumstances as he believes them to be. (ALI, 1962, Model Penal Code, Sec. 210.3(1)(b).)

Extreme emotional disturbance is a legal concept rather than a psychiatric diagnosis. It is even more clearly a partial excuse than provocation/passion because defendants who satisfy the criteria clearly have diminished rationality. Once again, because there is reasonable explanation or excuse for the disturbance, it is not fully the defendant's fault that he or she is in such a state. In recognition that this doctrine is really a partial excuse, some jurisdictions formally treat extreme emotional disturbance as a partial affirmative defense and place the burden of persuasion on this issue on the defense, a practice the Supreme Court has declared constitutional (*Patterson v. New York,* 1977). In some of the jurisdictions that have adopted extreme emotional disturbance, evidence of mental abnormality may constitute a reasonable explanation or excuse. For example, this doctrine may apply in murder prosecutions in which the defendant suffers from a stressful condition such as "battered woman syndrome" that does not create sufficient abnormality to satisfy a complete insanity defense (see the chapter by Follingstad in this vol-

ume). In some jurisdictions, such as Kentucky, the court has identified specific requirements for the "triggering events" and "controllable" reactions (Drogin, 1999). Forensic psychological evaluations may be helpful in assessing extreme emotional disturbance when mental abnormality may have produced the disturbance.

A Digression Concerning "Twinkies"

In an infamous case, a defendant who intentionally killed the popular mayor of San Francisco and an also popular city supervisor was charged with murder. He was convicted only of manslaughter, however, even though there had been no objectively adequate provocation and the homicides were intentional and carefully planned. The means used to reduce the degree of conviction was a highly unusual doctrine adopted by the California Supreme Court that allowed reduction from murder to manslaughter if an intentional, unprovoked killer was unable to comprehend his duty to govern his conduct according to the law. At trial, the defendant introduced evidence that he was suffering from depression at the time of the homicides and that his mood disorder was potentiated by the ingestion of large amounts of sugary junk food. The defendant was then making a routine extreme emotional disturbance-like claim in California and there was no independent Twinkies defense. The California legislature later abolished the doctrine the defendant used.

"Imperfect" Self-Defense

Some jurisdictions reduce the degree of homicide liability from murder to manslaughter if the defendant acted in so-called imperfect self-defense; that is, if a defendant honestly (subjectively) but *unreasonably* believes that he or she is in deadly danger and kills. The defendant is not justified, because the belief in the need to use deadly force is unreasonable. The defendant is not excused for the same reason: The ethical lapse in forming and acting on an unreasonable belief, albeit an honest one, is sufficient to hold the defendant criminally responsible. Because his or her belief is honest, however, some jurisdictions are unwilling to hold the defendant fully responsible for murder. In those jurisdictions that do adopt "imperfect" self-defense, the unreasonable but honest mistake appears to operate as a partially excusing condition.

New syndromes may explain why a defendant formed an honest but unreasonable belief. Forensic evaluation may be helpful to assess the honesty of a defendant's belief if mental abnormality is the reason the defendant formed the belief, but whether the belief is reasonable is a moral and legal, objective standard.

Sentencing Practices

Mitigating excusing conditions are routinely taken into account, either formally or informally, at the time of sentencing. For example, capital punishment statutes commonly incorporate the presence of mental disorder at the time of the crime as a mitigating factor and the U.S. Constitution compels the admission at capital punishment proceedings of *any* possible mitigating evidence, even in the absence of statutory authorization (*Lockett v. Ohio,* 1978; see the chapter by Cunningham & Goldstein in this volume).

In jurisdictions that do not have explicit sentencing guidelines, presentencing reports contain and sentencing judges frequently consider a wide range of factors that may bear on the convicted defendant's degree of responsibility and appropriate punishment. For example, although federal sentencing guidelines call for fixed or determinate sentences, judges are sometimes permitted to make downward departures from the guidelines based on factors related to diminished rationality that suggest reduced culpability. For example, a federal judge may consider at sentencing for a nonviolent crime a defendant's mild mental retardation because low intelligence may affect the defendant's judgment, decision making, and acquiescent role in the offense. Forensic psychological evaluations clearly will be helpful in assessing for sentencing whether a mitigating factor, such as mental abnormality or mental retardation, was present at the time of the crime.

An Illustrative Extreme Emotional Disturbance Case

When he retired from the Smithtown Police Department after 33 years of service, Harry D'Amato looked forward to traveling with his wife of 40 years and enjoying time with his grandchildren. As a police officer, he had an undistinguished career, never rising above the rank of patrol officer. He had earned no commendations, nor had he ever been the subject of civilian complaints or lawsuits. Mr. D'Amato was a quiet, shy man who rarely expressed his feelings or thoughts. Soon after his retirement, he found that he had too much time on his hands and took a job as an armed security guard for an armored car company. Shortly thereafter, his plans for the future began to unravel.

His wife experienced shortness of breath and chest pains and refused to see a physician. One night, she suffered a stroke, leaving her partially paralyzed, her speech slurred, and, for the most part, confined to a wheelchair. However, the D'Amatos continued with their tradition of weekly bus trips to a casino to gamble, finding it a relief as well as a distraction. Approximately one month after his wife's stroke, Mr. D'Amato's armored car was held up at gunpoint while parked outside a bank. One robber pointed a gun at the head of one of the guards and another demanded that Mr. D'Amato open the door to the truck. When he hesitated, he was pistol-whipped across the shoulder, causing injuries that later required surgery. Claiming that he feared for his partner's life, Mr. D'Amato complied with the demand that he open the truck door, and the robbers escaped with over $400,000. They were never captured.

Mr. D'Amato was fired because the company insisted that the policy was *never* to open the door and that Mr. D'Amato should have driven away, despite the threat by the robbers that they would kill the other guard. Mr. D'Amato felt betrayed and depressed and never sought employment again. He began psychiatric treatment and remained in therapy and on antidepressant medication until three weeks before the crime he was soon to commit. His diagnosis was posttraumatic stress disorder.

Around the same time he was fired, Mr. D'Amato's oldest son separated from his wife. The former daughter-in-law received custody of the D'Amatos' grandchildren and began to withhold visitation from the D'Amatos whenever child support payments were missed—a frequent occurrence. To see their grandchildren, Mr. D'Amato made the past due payments for his son. When his son was arrested for possession of a controlled substance with intent to sell, Mr. D'Amato retained the services of an attorney, remortgaging their home. When a gambler threatened his son because of a failure to pay for his gambling debts, Mr. D'Amato again came to the financial rescue.

Approximately two months later, an FBI agent appeared at the D'Amatos' door to question him about his involvement in the armored car robbery. Mr. D'Amato was shocked that he was a suspect because he had been a police officer for most of his life and he vehemently denied involvement. For the next four years, investigators returned repeatedly to question him. Through others, he learned that his bank records had been examined and neighbors and friends had been interviewed to learn if there were changes in his spending habits.

Neighbors noticed that the D'Amatos had increased their consumption of alcohol. Friends observed changes in Ms. D'Amato, including becoming more irritable and constantly criticizing and humiliating her husband in front of others. She refused to continue the weekly trips to the casino and her husband remained home to care for her. They purchased a new, motorized wheelchair, but it arrived damaged and, after a two-month wait, the replacement part arrived defective. Consequently, Mr. D'Amato had to push her wheelchair, a task made more difficult by his worsening emphysema.

On the day of the crime, Mr. D'Amato awoke and did the laundry (typically, there were at least two a day because of his wife's incontinence), brought her coffee (which she complained was too weak, "Just like you"), and read the newspaper. At 10 A.M., he left to buy beer and wine at the liquor store. Upon returning to his car, he found a young police officer writing a parking ticket. He explained that he was a retired police officer and showed his honorary badge, expecting that the ticket would be invalidated. Instead, the police officer said, "Too bad, old man," turned his back, and walked away.

Upon returning home, he told his wife what had happened. She berated him for "being such a loser. You can't do anything right; you can't even get out of a parking ticket." About this time, his eldest son entered the house. Ms. D'Amato had called him, complaining that his father was "a lousy drunkard who had abused her." To avoid a confrontation, Mr. D'Amato walked outside, but his son followed him. Mr. D'Amato reentered the house to get away, but his son followed behind him. Mr. D'Amato retreated to his bedroom and locked the door. He sat on his bed. Ten minutes later, he left the room with his two service weapons, walked down the stairs into the living room, a gun in each hand. He pointed the guns at his wife and son and pulled the triggers, killing both. He then called the police, told them what had happened, and waited for them to arrive.

Mr. D'Amato's defense attorney asked that he be evaluated regarding his mental state at the time of the crime. She provided employment records from the Smithtown Police Department, police and FBI reports regarding the armored car robbery, medical and mental health records for both D'Amatos, a copy of Mr. D'Amato's call to the police reporting the homicide, and other documents. During three evaluation sessions, the forensic psychologist interviewed Mr. D'Amato and administered a battery of psychological tests. He also interviewed neighbors and the D'Amatos' daughter.

Mr. D'Amato's daughter recalled that her father had stopped taking his antidepressant medication one month before the crime "to save money." Neighbors indicated that his wife had acted in increasingly degrading ways toward him in recent months, but that he would remain silent and not argue back. Other records confirmed that in his 33 years as a police officer, no charges or complaints had been filed against him. The details of the armored car robbery also were consistent with his recollections.

When arrested, Mr. D'Amato had told the police, "I shot both of them. I watched them bleed to death. I am a man and I did what I had to do. I put my wife out of her misery and my son was no good. I don't have the nerve to shoot myself." A police investigation report indicated that when he returned home from the liquor store, his son "wanted him out of the house because he was not taking care of his wife. He went

upstairs to get his guns and shot both in the head." He reported, "My wife was going to give him all of the money. I don't know why I snapped."

When interviewed, Mr. D'Amato presented details to the forensic psychologist similar to those he reported to the police. He recalled the police officer's reaction of "disrespect" and his wife's response: "She mutilated me. It just got under my skin and I walked away." According to Mr. D'Amato, when his son entered the house, "He took my beer and told me he was taking the house from me." When he walked upstairs "to get away from all of this," he reported "thinking and thinking. I can't take this anymore. I thought I'm going to kill myself because of all the abuse and my son. I'm shaking. I get the guns and I'm sitting there and I don't know—I just snapped. I was in tears, shaking. I walk in and shot my wife and son. I don't know why I'm doing it."

Testing demonstrated that Mr. D'Amato's was preoccupied with his physical illness and suffered from both fatigue and underlying depression. Depression affected his lack of purpose and his precarious sense of identity, his actions at the time of the crime, and his realistic concerns about the future. He was found to be a passive, dependent person, seeking support and encouragement from others. He was preoccupied with what others thought about him and vulnerable to fears of desertion and separation. Prone to episodes of distress, anxiety, and depression, he tended to deny rather than to face conflicts and difficulties. Feelings of self-pity and complaining occasionally broke through, but, in general, his need to maintain a "stiff upper lip" dominated his day-to-day emotional functioning. He was extremely vulnerable to psychological stress, and he lacked the coping skills necessary to appropriately handle emotional situations and crises as they arose in his life. He did not exhibit tendencies toward exaggerated or malingered symptoms of emotional disturbance.

The evaluator concluded that Mr. D'Amato's physical and emotional condition markedly deteriorated following the armored car robbery. He had been physically attacked and humiliated by the perpetrators and, of greater significance, he felt further humiliated and degraded when he found himself to be a suspect in this crime. Following this incident, he relied increasingly on alcohol to block feelings of depression, anxiety, and resentment. Feelings of worthlessness and the perception that he was no longer a person to be respected became constant. He perceived his wife as unsupportive, critical and unsympathetic, withholding of her love, and controlling in her refusal to travel. His intense needs for approval, appreciation, and respect went unanswered.

The evaluator identified three precipitating emotional "triggers" for the crime. Any of these may have been sufficient to stir up feelings that substantially compromised

Mr. D'Amato's judgment, rational thinking, and behavioral controls. The parking summons he received from a "fellow" police officer the morning of the crime reinforced his feelings of inadequacy, worthlessness, and lack of respect. His wife's reaction to this event further increased his feelings of humiliation, frustration, and lack of status. His son's lack of gratitude and his behavior (taking his beer, accusing him of not caring for his wife, and threatening to take away his home) represent the culminating precipitant of the homicides. The opinion was that Mr. D'Amato had acted on a wide array of feelings at the moment of the crime: resentment, humiliation, depression, degradation, hopelessness, and rage. As a result of his underlying personality structure, his past experiences, and the identified precipitating factors, his emotions seriously compromised his reasoning ability.

The prosecutor received a copy of the results of this evaluation. Based on plea negotiations, Mr. D'Amato agreed to enter pleas of guilty to two counts of manslaughter. In essence, this outcome is the same as if he had stood trial and had been found to have committed the crimes while under the influence of extreme emotional disturbance.

THE INSANITY DEFENSE

Although state and federal standards for legal insanity vary among jurisdictions and over time, *all* standards require a mental disease (mental illness) or a mental defect (e.g., mental retardation, organic brain impairment) as a prerequisite for an insanity defense. This condition must, in turn, create a genuine excusing condition that was operative at the time of the offense. A finding of not guilty by reason of insanity (NGRI) relieves the defendant of all culpability for his or her criminal conduct, but in all jurisdictions, the acquitted defendant may be committed to a hospital for evaluation and further detention and treatment if the defendant remains dangerous.

In general, the public tends to overestimate the frequency with which the insanity defense is invoked. Although estimates vary, Silver, Cirincione, and Steadman (1994) found that fewer than 1% of jury trials in the eight states they surveyed involved this defense. Of those cases in which an insanity defense was invoked, approximately 25% ended with a finding of NGRI (Golding, Skeem, Roesch, & Zapf, 1999). Over 70% of insanity acquittals have resulted from plea bargaining or similar arrangements rather than through jury trials (Melton, Petrila, Poythress, & Slobogin, 1997). A large proportion of those persons found NGRI have been under some form of mental health supervision, including involuntary commitment, prior to the crime. In a retrospective study of NGRI acquitees in British Columbia, 78.7% had at least one prior psychiatric hospitalization (Golding, Eaves, & Kowaz, 1989). Golding and his colleagues found that over half of those charged with the crime for which they were found to be NGRI had been discharged from a mental hospital within one year of the crime.

Historical Overview

The insanity defense is ancient. There are indications of different forms of insanity defenses, albeit somewhat crude, extending back to the thirteenth century in England. One of the early concepts involved the so-called wild beast test, based on the belief that individuals who had no more control over their behavior than a wild beast should not be held responsible for their behavior. By the eighteenth century, however, the early tests for legal insanity focused on the defendant's reason and knowledge of right and wrong (Walker, 1968).

The modern approach to legal insanity began in 1843 in England with *M'Naghten's Case*. (Although there are numerous spellings cited in the legal and psychological literature about M'Naghten, we use the one that appears in the original case report.) Misunderstanding of the factual and legal background is common, but the following description is taken from the case itself and from the leading historical account (Moran, 1981). Daniel M'Naghten had an extensive delusional system that included the belief that members of the governing Tory Party were persecuting him and wished to murder him. He traveled to London and attempted to kill the Tory Prime Minister, Sir Robert Peele, but instead mistakenly killed Peele's secretary, Edward Drummond. M'Naghten had the resources to pay for an excellent defense and raised the issue of legal insanity. The standard under which he was tried was quite similar to the famous test for legal insanity—whether the defendant knew right from wrong—that bears his name. M'Naghten was found NGRI. A public outcry followed because many thought the verdict represented a threat to public safety. Queen Victoria herself was concerned because she had been the victim of assassination attempts and in one case, her attacker had been acquitted by reason of insanity. As a result of the reaction to M'Naghten's acquittal, the House of Lords met to debate the case and the insanity defense in general. The English judiciary was invited to attend to answer questions the Lords put to them concerning legal insanity. The so-called *M'Naghten rule* was an answer by the Lord Chief Justice to two of the questions.

The *M'Naghten* standard holds

that to establish a defense on the ground of insanity, it must be clearly proved that, at the time of the committing of the act, the party accused was labouring under such a defect of reason, from disease of the mind, as not to know the nature and quality of the act he was doing; or, if he did know it, he did not know he was doing what was wrong.

This test follows the general format described above, which requires that a mental abnormality be present, which creates a further excusing condition. Thus, *M'Naghten* speaks first of a defect of reason resulting from a mental disease that causes the defendant not to know either the nature and quality of the act or its wrongfulness. Knowledge of the nature and quality of the act is not a self-defining standard; it requires interpretation. It could be understood narrowly or broadly. Extreme cases that meet the standard on even the narrowest reading may be clear, but they are also infrequent. For example, a defendant who strangled a victim to death but genuinely believed that he or she was squeezing a lemon did not know the nature and quality of the act according to any standard of knowledge. Similarly, a defendant who beheaded someone because the defendant thought that it would be humorous to watch that person awaken the next morning and search for her head also does not know the nature and quality of the act.

Many cases are not so clear, however. Assume that a defendant delusionally believes that killing a public figure will produce peace on earth and assassinates the public figure. In one sense, the defendant does know what he or she is doing: The defendant intentionally kills a human being by knowingly using a deadly weapon and fully appreciates the meaning of biological death. On the other hand, the reasons for action are grossly out of contact with reality and, consequently, in a broader sense, the defendant does not know what he or she is doing. How knowledge of the nature and quality of the act should be interpreted is a social, moral, and ultimately legal question.

The second prong of *M'Naghten* refers to the inability to appreciate the wrongfulness of the action. There is continuing debate about whether this refers to legal or moral wrongfulness. For example, suppose a defendant knew that the act was *legally* wrong, that is, legally prohibited, but also believed that the act was morally justified because of some delusional belief. Should such a defendant be considered legally insane or not? The more common interpretation is moral wrongfulness, the inability to understand that the act offended the mores of society.

M'Naghten is an almost exclusively cognitive standard. It does not consider broader variables, such as impulse control. The *M'Naghten* rule was rapidly and widely adopted in the United States after its adoption in English law.

Toward the end of the nineteenth century, questions arose regarding a volitional or control component. Several states in the United States adopted a so-called irresistible impulse test

in addition to the *M'Naghten* test. No jurisdiction adopted solely a control or volitional test. So-called irresistible impulse tests addressed the strength of an impulse or desire to do a particular act, even if the defendant knew that it was wrong. Control tests address criminal behavior influenced by disorders of impulse control, and apparently, actions that were based on delusional beliefs but that did not meet the *M'Naghten* standard.

For example, suppose a defendant had a history of command auditory hallucinations and complied reluctantly with voices he heard that urged him to cut his throat and, later, to chop off his penis. Assume that three years later, the voices urged him to kill his mother. He resisted these command hallucinations for hours, but finally complied. He reveals that he knew at the time he fired his weapon that taking his mother's life was wrong, both legally and morally. When he pulled the rifle's trigger, he was aware that he was taking her life, and he intended to do so. Yet, he claims that he could not stop himself from following these very powerful command auditory hallucinations. Under the irresistible impulse test, legal consideration would be given to his alleged inability to resist the demands of the command hallucinations. Notice, too, that the reason he takes his mother's life—compliance with voices telling him to do so—is also grossly out of touch with reality. Thus, the defendant might be legally insane under a broad reading of the *M'Naghten* test.

The difficulty with the irresistible impulse test is that there has been little attempt to define exactly how strong an impulse or desire must be to be considered irresistible. What, in fact, is the difference between an irresistible impulse and an unresisted impulse, between one that a person could not control and one that the person simply did not control, and how do we know which it was? Indeed, no reliable and valid test exists to assess this question.

A number of states informally adopted the concept of the "policeman at the elbow test," using as the criterion whether someone would have committed this act had there been a police officer standing next to him or her. Although the test appears to be a commonsense means to evaluate the strength of a desire, the question is, how could this be determined? A valid answer is unlikely to result from merely asking a defendant during the course of the evaluation whether the presence of a police officer would have deterred the offense. Moreover, if an agent would commit a crime with a police officer at his or her side, there may very well be some deeply irrational motivation for the action that might satisfy a cognitive standard for legal insanity.

The irresistible impulse standard did not gain great popularity, most likely because it was difficult to evaluate. Most states were left with a rather strict cognitive standard, that is, with a test for legal insanity that defines knowledge narrowly rather than broadly. Some critics believe that this standard will unfairly convict a large number of defendants with mental disorders who commit criminal acts that they narrowly know are wrong and, yet, believe that they need to commit based on a delusional belief. Many agree with this criticism, but claim that the proper response is not adoption of a control test, but rather an expansive reading of the cognitive standard. Furthermore, empirical evidence suggests that defendants grossly out of touch with reality are likely to be found NGRI, even if the cognitive test is formally narrow.

With the advent of psychoanalytic thinking and the expansion of psychoanalytic theories from the consulting room into the courtroom in the 1940s and 1950s, a number of important jurists became convinced of the need for a new, more flexible standard for criminal responsibility. In 1954, the influential Chief Judge of the U.S. Court of Appeals for the District of Columbia, David Bazelon, authored the opinion in *Durham v. United States*. Judge Bazelon wrote that there was a need to extend the widest possible latitude to expert evaluation and to expert testimony. The following broad standard for legal insanity was adopted: "An accused is not criminally responsible [legally insane] if his unlawful act was the product of a mental disease or defect." This test was similar to the rule in only one other jurisdiction, New Hampshire, and it applied only in federal trials in the District of Columbia. Nevertheless, the *Durham* rule was fashioned by an influential court and it had an enormous impact on insanity defense theorizing and scholarship.

Initially, the *Durham* rule appeared to be sound innovation because it seemed to expand the range of mental health input in insanity defense cases. But the standard was based on a number of implicit, incorrect assumptions. For example, it inaccurately assumes that mental health professionals will agree concerning what constitutes a mental disease or defect. There is also little agreement on whether a criminal act is a "product" of mental illness. That is, the implicit assumption that experts could agree about when there was a direct causal link between a particular mental disorder and a specific criminal action was erroneous. In fact, expert disagreement was common.

Different experts use different criteria for determining whether a particular act is "caused by" a particular mental disorder. In actual practice, experts' concept of "product" ranged from considering a person's entire life history as a possible motivator for the crime to a narrow "but for" definition, which is simply whether the crime would have been committed if the mental disorder had not been present. Under the *Durham* standard, large numbers of people were being found NGRI based on loose conceptions of an underlying mental illness and an even looser conception of product.

In *McDonald v. United States* (1962), the federal District Court for the District of Columbia tried to ameliorate such difficulties. *McDonald* attempted to restrict the definition of mental disease or defect to "any abnormal condition of the mind which substantially impairs mental or emotional processes and substantially impairs behavioral controls." Under the *McDonald* definition, only those mental illnesses that "substantially impaired behavioral controls" could be considered the basis for an insanity defense. Such impairment could be demonstrated either by the general definition of the defendant's illness or from the specific manifestations of that illness. *McDonald* tightened the definition of mental disorder, but it did not further clarify the concept of product, and the courts were never able to clarify product successfully.

In the decade following *Durham,* courts were dissatisfied with the influence of mental health professionals in insanity defense cases. For example, a psychiatrist would render an opinion that a defendant's crime was the product of a mental illness, and the trier of fact (the judge or jury) would merely rubber-stamp that conclusion. There was growing concern on the part of many judges that experts were usurping the role of the trier of fact. Therefore, in *Washington v. United States* (1967), the U.S. District Court held that mental health professionals would no longer be permitted to render opinions regarding the causal connection between the mental illness and the specific criminal behavior. They could describe only the development of the mental illness and the adaptation of the individual to that illness, and they could state whether the person was suffering from that mental illness at the time of the offense. Thus, mental health professionals were not allowed to address the so-called ultimate issue, namely, whether the behavior in question was "caused" by the mental illness. This is a legal question, and the role of answering it was reserved solely for the judge or jury.

Even with the restrictions imposed on the *Durham* standard by both *McDonald* and *Washington,* there was still dissatisfaction with the operation of the product test. In *United States v. Brawner* (1972) the Federal Court of Appeals in the District of Columbia overruled *Durham* and substituted the ALI's *Model Penal Code* rule in the federal courts for the District of Columbia. *Brawner* also adopted the rule that evidence of mental abnormality could be used to negate the *mens rea* required by the definition of the offense, but it placed a highly technical restriction on the introduction of such evidence.

The *Model Penal Code* rule, like all other insanity defense tests, requires the presence of a mental disease or defect and contains both a cognitive and a control component. *M'Naghten* and previous control tests treated the disability resulting from mental abnormality as an all-or-none, absolute matter. The *Model Penal Code* test, however, requires only that the disease cause a "*lack of substantial capacity* to appreciate the criminality [wrongfulness] of one's conduct or to conform one's conduct to law" (italics added). This change responded to arguments that the effect of mental abnormality is a matter of degree and that all-or-none language hampered the usefulness of expert testimony. In the cognitive component, the ALI used the word "appreciate" rather than "know" to signal that legal sanity required more than simply abstract knowledge of legal rules or moral standards. The defendant also had to understand the significance and consequence of his or her actions to be found legally sane. The ALI offered jurisdictions alternative terms to characterize the object of the defendant's required appreciation: "wrongfulness" and "criminality." The ALI was responding to differences among the jurisdictions with extant cognitive tests concerning whether substantial lack of appreciation of criminality or of wrongfulness should be required. The ALI recognized that, in most cases, which term was used might not make a difference, but in some it would, and the ALI left this open.

In a subsection of the mental responsibility section (4.01(2)), the ALI standard provides that mental disease or defect does *not* include an "abnormality manifested only by repeated criminal or otherwise antisocial conduct." The purpose of this language was to exclude psychopathy as a disorder that might support a valid insanity defense because many thought this condition not valid and many others thought that it was not a condition suitable for hospital treatment. As experienced clinicians know, however, psychopathy (as defined by Cleckley, 1941, and operationalized by Hare, 1998) is different from antisocial personality disorder (APD; see Chapter 6). The latter had not been defined in 1962 when the *Model Penal Code* test was published, and many APD sufferers are not psychopaths. Nonetheless, most current observers and commentators believe that APD fits within the exclusion originally applied to psychopathy.

The ALI standard was extremely influential. Prior to the trial of John Hinckley Jr. for the attempted assassination of President Reagan and others (*United States v. Hinkley,* 1982), the majority of states that had reformed their insanity defense test since the publication of the ALI test and all but one U.S. Courts of Appeals had adopted the ALI rule. But, after Hinckley was found NGRI under an ALI test, there was a near universal reversal of the trend to adopt that test.

Many believed that Hinkley's deeply unpopular acquittal resulted from the application of the control prong of the ALI test. Consequently, there was a legal backlash against control tests, but the test used may have played a lesser role in Hinckley's acquittal than did a procedural rule concerning the burden of persuasion. Hinckley was charged with attempted homicide under both federal law and the local law of the District of Columbia. Although Hinkley could have been tried in both jurisdictions, the cases were consolidated and tried only in the federal court, which applied the substantive and procedural rules then applicable in the federal courts in the District of Columbia. Although the U.S. Constitution requires the prosecution to prove all the elements of a crime beyond a reasonable doubt, jurisdictions can constitutionally place the burden of persuasion for affirmative defenses such as legal insanity on either the prosecution or the defense. The then applicable rule in the federal courts in the District of Columbia was that the prosecution had to prove that the defendant was legally *sane* beyond a reasonable doubt.

The prosecution put on a strong case, but Hinckley was defended by excellent lawyers and retained fine expert witnesses. As a result, he was able to introduce substantial credible testimony that was consistent with legal insanity. Even if the jury believed that it was more likely than not or even highly likely that Hinckley was legally sane, confronted with such substantial evidence consistent with insanity, it would have been nearly impossible for the prosecution to prove "beyond a reasonable doubt" that Hinckley was sane. For this reason, Hinckley would probably have been found NGRI according to any test for legal insanity. Nonetheless, the control prong of the test was "blamed." (A summary of the trial transcript and an analysis of the Hinckley case can be found in Low, Jeffries, & Bonnie, 1986.)

Insanity Defense Reform

The ensuing debate about legal insanity in the wake of *Hinckley* led to hearings about reform of the insanity defense in many state legislatures and the U.S. Congress. Many professional organizations took specific positions: The American Medical Association urged abolition of the insanity defense; the American Bar Association and the American Psychiatric Association proposed retention, but deletion of a control test. The ABA also recommended placing the burden of persuasion on the defendant. The American Psychological Association did not take an official position, but contended that necessary empirical data were lacking and that more research was needed.

The American Psychiatric Association recommended abolition of a control test because, it claimed, there was insufficient clinical and scientific knowledge to permit accurate evaluation and consequent informed expert opinion about whether defendants could control themselves. Critics claimed, in response, that there was equally insufficient clinical and scientific knowledge to accurately identify the inability to appreciate the wrongfulness of conduct. This criticism was apt, but failed to recognize a crucial distinction. The assessment of another's understanding, intentions, and reasons for action is a commonsense skill that virtually all people have to some degree because successful human interaction is impossible without it. Furthermore, trained clinicians are particularly skillful at discovering a person's reasons for action. Then, the jury can decide if sufficient lack of appreciation of wrongfulness was present. In contrast, assessing whether people can control themselves is a much less developed skill and we know much less about this. Thus, there is reason to make the distinction. The American Psychiatric Association also recommended that mental illness must refer to a *severe* mental illness, further defined as one that substantially and demonstrably impairs perception and judgment.

Most legislatures, including the U.S. Congress, that considered insanity defense reform in the wake of *Hinckley,* abolished the control test. The federal Insanity Defense Reform Act, 18 U.S.C. Sec. 17 (1984), now applicable in all criminal trials in federal courts, is representative. It provides that it is

> an affirmative defense to a prosecution under any Federal statute that, at the time of the commission of the acts constituting the offense, the defendant, as a result of severe mental disease or defect, was unable to appreciate the nature and quality or the wrongfulness of his acts. Mental disease or defect does not otherwise constitute a defense.

The Act also placed the burden of persuasion on the defendant to prove legal insanity by clear and convincing evidence, a standard more rigorous than the civil law "preponderance of the evidence" standard, but less rigorous than proof beyond a reasonable doubt.

The federal test is strictly cognitive and modifies the traditional *M'Naghten* rule in two ways. The mental abnormality must be severe. This is a more restrictive requirement than the wording of *M'Naghten,* but in practice, it will not be restrictive because defendants without severe mental disorder seldom succeed with the insanity defense. Second, the test substitutes the broader term "appreciate" for "know." In sum, the federal test eliminates a control standard, but its cognitive standard is a bit more forgiving than *M'Naghten.*

There were other noteworthy features of the Act. It prohibits mental health professionals from rendering an opinion on the ultimate legal issue. That is, professionals may provide a complete clinical and scientific evaluation of the defendant's mental state, but the professional may not offer a conclusion about whether the defendant is legally insane. This is a legal question that is reserved for the trier of fact. The Act also establishes parity between psychologists and psychiatrists in conducting mental state evaluations. Finally, the Act excludes any partial affirmative defense based on mental abnormality, but all federal courts that have interpreted the Act have also concluded that it does not prohibit the introduction of evidence of mental abnormality to negate *mens rea* (e.g., *United States v. Pohlot,* 1987).

In addition to those jurisdictions that limited their insanity defense tests by eliminating a control standard, five states—Idaho, Kansas, Montana, Nevada, and Utah—abolished the insanity defense and now permit introduction of evidence of mental disorder solely for the purpose of negating *mens rea.* (The Nevada Supreme Court held later that abolition of the insanity defense was unconstitutional.) Because even severe mental disorder rarely negates *mens rea,* in such jurisdictions, a defendant will be convicted even if the defendant was grossly out of touch with reality and committed the crime as a result of psychotic perceptions and beliefs.

Prior and subsequent to *Hinckley,* some jurisdictions attempted to take account of a defendant's mental disorder at the time of the crime by providing for a further verdict, "guilty but mentally ill" (GBMI). A substantial minority of states have now adopted this verdict in addition to, and not as a substitute for, the insanity defense. A defendant will be found GBMI if the defendant was criminally responsible for the crime but suffered from a mental disorder. GBMI defendants are fully culpable and may be sentenced to prison for the full term for the crime charged. That is, unlike the insanity defense, the GBMI bears no relationship to a defendant's blameworthiness for the crime. Indeed, a GBMI defendant may be put to death according to two jurisdictions that addressed this question (*People v. Crews,* 1988; *State v. Wilson,* 1992). At the sentencing judge's discretion, the GBMI convict may be sent to a hospital for treatment, but judges can order this disposition in appropriate cases without a GBMI verdict and prisons can transfer to hospitals disordered inmates who cannot be treated adequately in prison. Thus, the verdict is unnecessary to guarantee that convicts with mental disorders receive treatment. In fact, there is typically no requirement that a GBMI prisoner receive any psychiatric or psychological treatment at all (beyond that treatment that must be provided to any disordered inmate). If the GBMI convict is hospitalized and is treated successfully or hospitalization is not useful or necessary, the convict will be returned to prison to complete the balance of the prison sentence.

Virtually all commentary concerning the GBMI verdict has been scathingly negative for the reasons suggested: The verdict is unrelated to criminal responsibility, and it does not guarantee any special psychiatric treatment. In other words, it is of dubious value. In addition, it may confuse juries or offer them an illegitimate compromise in cases in which they believe the defendant is legally insane but they fear the consequences of an insanity acquittal.

Effects of the Reforms

There have been many reforms in the wake of *Hinckley,* but what has been their actual effect in insanity defense trials? Fulero and Finkel (1991) examined whether the prohibition on ultimate opinion testimony accounted for any variance in the outcomes of trials in which insanity was raised as a defense. They examined diagnosis-only testimony, penultimate testimony (the elements that define the ultimate issue), and ultimate issue testimony (the legal decision to be made by the sentencer: insane or not insane). Results indicated that a negligible percentage of the variance in outcome was accounted for by prohibition on rendering ultimate issues.

Finkel and his colleagues also studied the effects of different insanity standards on mock jurors. Finkel, Shaw, Bercaw, and Koch (1985) presented mock jurors with a scenario and asked them to render a verdict based on *M'Naghten, M'Naghten* plus irresistible impulse, ALI, *Durham,* and wild beast tests. There were no significant differences in the rates of acquittal based on which legal standard was used. Finkel (1989) also studied the effects of the Insanity Defense Reform Act and found that the application of this standard did not affect acquittal rates either.

These studies tend to suggest that the actual legal standard appears to have little effect on the outcome of jury deliberations. Jurors tend to proceed on their "commonsense notions" of what constitutes insanity and how the defendant should act. On the other hand, Steadman et al. (1993) found that some reforms produced significant change. For example, shifting the burden of persuasion on legal insanity from the state to the defendant reduced the rate of successful insanity pleas.

There has been continuing controversy about the length of time a defendant found NGRI can be committed. Most jurisdictions either limit the permissible commitment term to the maximum prison term the defendant might have received if convicted of the crime, or provide for indefinite commitment with periodic review. In 1983, in *Jones v. United States,* a person found NGRI challenged indefinite commitment as unconstitutional. *Jones* held that indefinite commitment was constitutional because the NGRI acquitee was not culpable, and thus the length of commitment bore no rational relationship to the potential prison term for the crime charged. The Court wrote that it was reasonable to presume that both dangerousness and mental illness continued because the crime charged had been proven beyond a reasonable doubt and sufficient mental illness to support an insanity acquittal had been established by a preponderance of the evidence.

In *Foucha v. Louisiana* (1992), the Court addressed the criteria for continued commitment of an individual who had been found NGRI. Foucha continued to suffer from a personality disorder but no longer had symptoms of the mental illness (schizophrenia) that served as the diagnostic basis for his insanity acquittal. He continued to be regarded as dangerous by virtue of his severe personality disorder. The Court ruled that because Foucha no longer suffered from a sufficient mental disorder, he could *not* be held in a mental hospital as an insanity acquitee and would have to be released even though he was still potentially dangerous. Although there was a strong dissent, the holding makes sense. The justification for commitment after an insanity acquittal is that the defendant is both not responsible because mental disorder continues and still dangerous. If the defendant is not dangerous, there is no need for preventive detention. If the defendant is no longer substantially disordered, the defendant is no longer not responsible, and this justification for preventive detention also ends.

ETHICAL ISSUES IN EVALUATION OF MENTAL STATE AT THE TIME OF THE OFFENSE

Informed Consent

The "Ethics Principles of Psychologists and Code of Conduct" (American Psychological Association [APA], 1992) requires those providing psychological services to offer the client "appropriate information beforehand about the nature of such services and appropriate information later about results and conclusions" (p. 1600). Obtaining informed consent is particularly important before performing mental state evaluations in criminal cases because the purpose of the evaluation is legal, not therapeutic. Thus, at a minimum, the evaluator should inform the defendant in a criminal responsibility evaluation of the nature of the evaluation, the lack of confidentiality in the assessment, to whom the results of the evaluation will be revealed, and how the results may be used. In essence, interviewing a defendant regarding the circumstances and details of a crime often provides a more thorough and potentially damaging statement than confessions obtained by police investigators.

In some states, if an expert is retained by a defense attorney and reaches a conclusion that is not helpful to that defense attorney, the negative opinion is shielded by attorney-client privilege and need not be revealed to the prosecution (e.g., *State vs. Pratt, 1979; United States vs. Alvarez, 1975*). On the other hand, several states have ruled that once a psychiatric issue is raised, then the defendant has, in essence, waived attorney-client privilege and the results of an evaluation are available to the government (e.g., *Edney vs. State,* 1977; *Noggle vs. Marshall,* 1983). If the government has retained the expert, on the other hand, any material that would be of material assistance to the defense must be revealed. Finally, if the evaluation is court-ordered, no privilege exists, and the results of the evaluation must be available to all concerned parties (i.e., the prosecution, the defense, and the judge).

The "Specialty Guidelines for Forensic Psychologists" (Committee on Ethical Guidelines for Forensic Psychologists, 1991) expands on the need to obtain informed consent. Once it is obtained, "The psychologist may not use the evaluation work product for other purposes without explicit waiver to do so by the client or the client's legal representative" (pp. 659–660). For example, if the expert is retained to evaluate a defendant's trial competence, that psychologist may not use the data from that assessment to address issues related to the validity of a *Miranda* rights waiver, an insanity defense, or the risk of future dangerousness. In *Estelle v. Smith* (1981), the U.S. Supreme Court held that the findings or data from forensic evaluations performed to determine trial competence could be used *only* for that purpose. To use such findings to address other legal issues, such as whether a defendant should be executed, would represent a violation of the defendant's 5th and 6th Amendment rights, unless he or she competently waived those rights. The scope of informed consent is a complex issue and the clinician doing a forensic assessment must know the law in the state or federal jurisdiction in which he or she is practicing.

Although written informed consent is an ideal in criminal cases involving assessment of insanity or other mental state issues, many defendants are too guarded, suspicious, and mistrustful to sign such a document. In such cases, discussion of the consent issues should be included in the body of the final report, including consideration of the reasons why the examiner believed that the defendant was competent to give the informed consent, despite the refusal to sign the form.

Obtaining informed consent from criminal defendants is good forensic practice, and several recent court decisions are critical of mental health professionals who do not do so. For example, in *Department of Youth Services v. a Juvenile* (1986), the court ruled that it was reversible error to permit testimony by a psychiatrist who had interviewed a juvenile without warning the youth in advance that their conversations were not confidential and could be used against him in a commitment extension proceeding. Even though no actual communications from the juvenile were disclosed at trial, the doctor rendered a diagnosis based partially on conversations with the youth that were not preceded by any warnings. The court granted a new trial, citing "a substantial risk of a miscarriage of justice."

Evaluation, Diagnosis, and Intervention

The provision of the APA "Ethical Principles" (1992) that deals with evaluation, diagnosis, and intervention in a professional context states that the information and techniques used should be "sufficient to provide appropriate substantiation for findings" (p. 1603). This section is applicable to forensic evaluations concerning a criminal defendant's mental state. Forensic evaluators must therefore be careful to include all materially relevant sources of data before reaching an opinion. For example, ethical questions about the sufficiency of the foundation for the opinion would be raised in most cases of criminal responsibility evaluations if a psychologist were to base his or her findings solely on a clinical interview rather than relying on multiple sources of data. At the least, such a skimpy foundation would be a fertile ground for cross-examination of the expert.

The "Specialty Guidelines for Forensic Psychologists" (Committee on Ethical Guidelines for Forensic Psychologists, 1991) urges psychologists to be cautious regarding the reporting of statements and conclusions that may not be relevant to the issue at hand. If, for example, a defendant, in the course of such an examination, tells the expert about other crimes he or she has committed, the psychologist, under most circumstances, should not include that material in a report. The psychologist often is not in a position to judge what may be legally admissible and therefore needs to exercise great caution in the reporting of statements made by the defendant.

Professionalism

The APA "Ethical Principles" (1992) provision concerning professionalism, which states that psychologists working in a given area should have "appropriate knowledge of and competence in the areas underlying such work" (p. 1610), also applies in forensic cases. For example, an examining psychologist who believes that organic impairment may be of relevance in a case should not perform a comprehensive neuropsychological assessment unless he or she has been properly trained in this type of evaluation. Several recent appellate decisions have required such specialized knowledge as the basis for expert opinion in appropriate cases. In *Frederick v. Oklahoma* (1995), a conviction was reversed on appeal because the trial court had failed to appoint an expert with *specific* experience in multiple personality disorder. *Doe v. Superior Court* (1995) reversed a conviction because the expert witness did not have expertise concerning battered spouse syndrome and posttraumatic stress disorder. Locating experts who have been evaluated by peer review and oral examination may be facilitated by consulting such sources as the American Board of Professional Psychology directory of ABPP Board Certified Psychologists (www.abpp.com).

Multiple Sources of Data

The "Specialty Guidelines for Forensic Psychologists" (Committee on Ethical Guidelines for Forensic Psychologists, 1991) urges the forensic psychologist to use a variety of independent data sources. This is usually necessary to perform a valid retrospective mental state examination in criminal cases. The only direct source of the defendant's mental state at the time of the crime is the defendant's self-report. However, the validity of such reports can be compromised by errors in memory, rationalization and other defense mechanisms, malingering, and exaggeration, as well as numerous other factors. Therefore, when it is feasible to do so, the expert should attempt to corroborate the defendant's self-report by examining police, hospital, and jail records and obtaining the observations of family members, friends, neighbors, coworkers, or other observers who may have had the opportunity to observe the defendant at or near the time of the crime.

The "Specialty Guidelines for Forensic Psychologists" (Committee on Ethical Guidelines for Forensic Psychologists, 1991) states, "When forensic psychologists seek data from third parties, prior records, or other sources, they do so only with the prior approval of the relevant legal party or as a consequence of an order of a court to conduct the forensic evaluation" (p. 662). Clearly, then, one does not seek such third-party information without the knowledge of the defendant or the defendant's legal representative, unless the evaluation is being conducted under court order.

The Ultimate Issue

There is considerable debate about whether a testifying mental health professional should offer an opinion on the ultimate legal issue, such as whether a defendant was legally insane or whether a particular *mens rea* was formed in fact. As lawyers and most forensic psychologists and psychiatrists recognize, these are not psychological or psychiatric issues, but in most jurisdictions, experts are allowed to offer such opinions. Nonetheless, some jurisdictions do not permit such testimony—reserving such questions purely for the trier of fact— and some experts believe that they should not offer such opinions, even if the law of the jurisdiction permits them to

do so. Some suggest that in forensic cases, mental health professionals should do no more than describe, in the richest possible detail, the behavior that has been observed or inferred from the evaluation, including what the defendant perceived and believed. They take the position that testimony on the ultimate issue exceeds the professional's expertise and tends to confuse jurors and to usurp the jury's function (Morse, 1999). Others contend that such a position is flawed for two reasons.

First, in many cases, the exclusion of ultimate opinion testimony is useless because the ultimate legal conclusion may be logically entailed by a full behavioral description. For example, consider a jurisdiction that employs a cognitive "appreciation of wrongfulness" test for legal insanity and that permits an insanity defense in cases of so-called deific decree, that is, cases in which the defendant claims that God commanded the defendant to do the deed. In such a case, if the evaluator testifies that the delusional defendant believed that God commanded the deed, this is tantamount to the conclusion that the defendant could not appreciate the wrongfulness of his or her conduct. Therefore, why prevent the expert from drawing the obvious inference? There is much force to this argument, but if the inference is sufficiently obvious, indeed, if it is logically entailed (assuming that the evidence is credible), why does the trier of fact need the expert's help? Moreover, many cases will not be so clear, either because the facts are more contested or because the legal conclusion to be drawn from those facts is not obvious.

A second, possibly more troubling objection to the exclusion of ultimate issue testimony is the potential practical outcome when a mental health professional refuses to address an ultimate issue such as legal insanity. What if the expert states that it is unethical or goes beyond the bounds of his or her competence to offer an opinion on this issue? Some courts may then turn to less competent, less ethical experts, who may offer an opinion on this issue without adequate empirical verification. Whether this happens frequently or rarely is an empirical issue for which the data are lacking.

In the best of all possible worlds, perhaps mental health professionals should not address ultimate legal issues. Legislators, judges, and attorneys should be persuaded to this position through a process of ongoing education. For the present, however, experts are allowed to offer such testimony in virtually all jurisdictions and lawyers and judges expect them to do so. When doing so however, they should be confident that there is an ample empirical basis for those opinions. The next section of this chapter considers the procedures that should be used when conducting evaluations of a defendant's mental state at the time of a crime.

FORENSIC ASSESSMENT PROCEDURES TO EVALUATE MENTAL STATE AT THE TIME OF THE OFFENSE

A Model for Evaluating Mental State at the Time of the Offense

We propose a hypothesis-generating and testing model in which multiple sources of data ordinarily should be used to evaluate a defendant's mental state at the time of the offense (MSO). A given source of data (e.g., clinical interview, history taking, psychological testing, review of prior psychiatric/psychological records) gives rise to a hypothesis or series of hypotheses. Confirmation by numerous sources of data will strengthen confidence in the validity of a hypothesis, and only those hypotheses verified across data sources should be the basis for the final assessment and opinion. Heilbrun (2001) presents a detailed description of the process of data collection from multiple sources.

The evaluator should note inconsistencies across data sources and should appropriately qualify any conclusions for which there are inconsistent or missing data. Such procedures result in more credible opinions, indicate the evaluator's integrity, and are required by APA's 1992 "Ethical Principles." If inconsistency is found across different sources of data, however, this should be noted in the conclusion, so that the conclusion will be appropriately qualified in terms of the data that are missing or inconsistent. Not only will this result in opinions with far more credibility and integrity for the forensic psychologist conducting such forensic assessments, it is a requirement of the "Ethical Principles" (APA, 1992). For example, suppose a defendant charged with assault with a deadly weapon has an extensive history of psychiatric hospitalization, which the expert has reviewed prior to the assessment. A hypothesis the history raises is whether the past mental disorder appears relevant to the MSO. The examiner would first have to review those behaviors documented in the psychiatric records to determine the typical behavior of the defendant when he or she demonstrated signs of the mental disorder. Do the hospital records and history reveal that the person was agitated, withdrawn, assaultive, fearful, delusional, or hallucinating when he or she was acutely ill? Once a coherent picture of this individual's behavior while overtly mentally ill is gained, the evaluation would use these impressions as a basis for interviews with family, friends, witnesses, and arresting police officers. A focus of the interview is to ascertain whether the behaviors typically associated with the defendant's mental disorder were present or absent at the time of the offense.

For example, a defendant is charged with assault with a deadly weapon. He has had an extensive history of psychiatric hospitalization. A hypothesis to be examined is whether the mental disorder with which the defendant had been diagnosed *prior* to the crime bears any causal relationship to the offense. The examiner should first review psychiatric records to determine the range of symptoms the defendant demonstrated during acute phases of his mental illness. As another example, suppose that a defendant has an established history of severe mental disorder, characterized by his huddling in a corner, preoccupied, withdrawn, and fearful. Suppose, further, that his behavior at the time of the offense was described by a number of witnesses as highly intentional, purposeful, and goal-directed. In this circumstance, the examiner would have to question whether the signs and symptoms of the previous mental disorder were consistent with the criminal behavior. In the case described, the examiner might conclude, if this inconsistency existed, that although the defendant had a history of mental disorder, the behavior demonstrated at the time of the offense did not appear to be consistent with the manifestations of that disorder in this particular defendant. This could result in findings suggesting that the defendant was, despite the mental disorder, criminally responsible or that there were not enough data available to render an opinion on criminal responsibility.

For a final example, assume that a defendant is charged with having defaced a church and having attempted to sacrifice her son by placing him in a hot oven. Assume further that the defendant has a psychiatric history characterized by a persistent history of delusions and hallucinations that cause her to believe that she has a specific mission to destroy certain established religions and to make sacrifices as evidence of her commitment to her own religious beliefs. The relationship between her irrational thinking and the criminal conduct is clearer than in the prior case. If the same defendant attempted to rob an individual at gunpoint, however, it is unlikely that her delusional religious beliefs were related to armed robbery. It must be emphasized that the presence of an active mental illness does *not* necessarily mean that irrational beliefs or feelings symptomatic of mental illness motivated the criminal behavior.

The "multiple data source approach" implies that forensic evaluations usually should not overgeneralize from a single data source, but should integrate findings from multiple sources. Failure to integrate sources of data frequently occurs when psychologists who do not have forensic training administer a battery of psychological tests, observe a particular degree of impairment on testing, and conclude without further information that the impairment must have been present at the time of the alleged offense. Valid forensic opinions rarely can be based solely on interviews and psychological test results.

In light of recent court decisions, forensic examiners should adopt what might be described as a standard of care in conducting an assessment of criminal responsibility. Several courts, in fact, have recognized what appropriate forensic evaluation entails. They have noted that traditional clinical psychiatric and psychological evaluations often do not meet the requirements of valid forensic assessments and have criticized experts who depend exclusively on clinical assessment to form forensic opinions (e.g., *Illinois v. Smith* (1984); *Strozier v. Georgia* (1985)).

Opinions based on consistent data sources also protect the forensic expert from potentially harmful cross-examination in which opposing counsel confronts the witness with procedures or activities that the examiner "didn't do but should have done." Ziskin and Faust (1988) provide a compelling series of questions that an aggressive attorney may use to undercut expert testimony. Though Ziskin's material renders many experts quite fearful of testifying, the consistency across data approach, in which psychological observations and inferences are confirmed by other behavioral data, may effectively defuse such an attack. Faust (1990) concedes that integrating multiple sources of data and qualifying conclusions in light of inconsistent data would significantly reduce the criticisms of expert testimony as described by Ziskin and Faust (1988).

Structure of the Examination of Mental State at the Time of the Offense

Both the questions asked by the expert and the answers given by the defendant should be memorialized. Defendants' actual words take on additional significance when they are asked about details of the offense and their state of mind at the time of the crime. Paraphrasing or summarizing the defendant's responses may lead to an opinion, report, and testimony that does not accurately reflect the defendant's actual state of mind at the time of the offense. When the trier of fact evaluates the defendant's mental state according to the legal criteria in question, the trier should consider, insofar as it is possible, the defendant's own words. Indeed, to ensure optimal accuracy and to permit the trier of fact to make an independent judgment, some forensic clinicians recommend audiotaping or videotaping all interviews with the defendant. Reviewing collateral information will serve not only to confirm information obtained by interview, but also to provide some sense of the defendant's veracity regarding "facts" that can be easily confirmed (e.g., prior arrest and convictions).

Any disparity between the defendant's present behavior and behavior claimed to have been evidenced at the time of the crime must be explored. The following factors, among others, may contribute to such differences: (a) spontaneous change in clinical condition; (b) psychotropic medication; (c) significant alterations in the defendant's level of stress; (d) distortion, whether conscious or unconscious, of the defendant's memory and perceptions of the incident; and (e) education by others about possible criminal defenses and how to present a picture of those mental states in which culpability might be reduced or avoided.

Because a defendant's condition can change substantially between the time of the crime and the time of the evaluation, the evaluation should be done as soon as possible after the alleged crime. Memory is likely to be better and the opportunity for distortion is reduced. In addition, the defendant is less likely to have been educated by attorneys or fellow inmates about how to present himself or herself to the forensic psychologist. Unfortunately, the timing of the evaluation is seldom under the expert's control, and all too often substantial time elapses between the crime and the evaluation.

Demographic Data

A comprehensive criminal responsibility assessment and the resulting report should consider demographic information. The defendant's date of birth, age, birth order, place of birth, religion, marital status, occupation, race, and present living arrangement need to be obtained during the interview and confirmed. In the report, a listing of the charges should be included.

Material Reviewed

The documents reviewed (e.g., school, employment, military, hospital), the people interviewed. (e.g., family, friends, employers, police officers), and all the records related to the crime (e.g., police reports, witness statements, jail records) should be listed and considered.

Informed Consent

The confidentiality/privilege waiver is essential on ethical grounds and to avoid judicial limitation of expert testimony. In the absence of a written waiver, the examiner's notes and the final report should contain a detailed description of the waiver procedure, preferably using the defendant's own words. The description should include documentation of the defendant's understanding of the lack of confidentiality in the examination, to whom the results of the examination will be disclosed, and under what circumstances.

Statement of Facts

The records and the interviews with third parties need to be summarized. Such data put in context observations of the defendant's behavior made by others and may provide documentation about whether bizarre behavior, if observed, might be attributed to drug or alcohol intoxication. Interviewing third parties frequently provides information requiring follow-up questions of the defendant. (See the chapter by Heilbrun, Warren, & Picarello in this volume for more information on the use of third parties in forensic evaluations.)

Defendant's Version of Offense

The defendant's own words are critical accurately to describe his or her MSO. Sensitive questions regarding the crime itself should usually be asked only after sufficient rapport and trust are established and thus are generally best deferred until the second or third evaluation session, after nonthreatening information has been obtained. As discussed in the introduction to this section, the defendant's own words should be carefully memorialized and should serve as the basis for addressing this issue in the report and in testimony.

The examiner usually should ask open-ended questions. The defendant should initially be encouraged to provide an uninterrupted account of the events leading up to and including the crime. The expert can then ask the defendant to repeat his or her recollection of the events and other necessary and appropriate clarifying questions. To provide a valid, persuasive report and testimony, the expert should try to resolve any vagueness or lack of clarity in the defendant's version. The examiner must investigate especially carefully discrepancies between various versions provided by the defendant, including statements made by him or her to the police or to other third parties.

In the most general sense, the crucial issue in all mental defense cases is why the defendant committed the criminal offense. Therefore, special attention should be given to the defendant's thoughts, feelings, and perceptions at the time of the offense, and any attempts the defendant made to refrain from the criminal act. Questions such as the following may elicit such data: "You said that you had felt this way before but never did anything like what you're accused of. What was there about *this* situation that was different? Why did you kill him now?" Rogers (1984) also suggests that the expert should gather information from the defendant regarding his or her behavior in the week preceding the offense and immediately following the crime. Information concerning a person's mental state at times close to the time in question is typically more valid evidence of the MSO than behavior more temporally distant.

Behavior in Jail

The defendant's behavior in jail should be considered because it may provide evidence concerning mental state at the time of the crime. For example, a review of jail records may disclose that the defendant decompensated in jail, suggesting that perhaps the defendant was not psychotic prior to arrest. The examiner should consider whether the defendant requested psychiatric consultation, whether the defendant's behavior came to the attention of the medical or psychiatric personnel in the jail, whether a forensic placement was made, whether psychotropic medication or other treatment was provided, and whether a diagnosis was made. Perhaps most important, the examiner should evaluate and report whether the defendant's behavior in jail is consistent with the behavior documented in the previous section, taking into account the effect of the jail environment.

Description of the Defendant's Mental Status at the Time of the Evaluation

This should include such dimensions as appearance, behavior, orientation, attention, perception, memory, affect, speech, and the presence of delusions, hallucinations, and homicidal and suicidal ideation. The forensic psychologist should evaluate the defendant's present judgment, indications of toxicity, insight, and impulse control.

Social and Medical History

The social history can be obtained from the defendant. The expert should note consistencies or inconsistencies between the defendant's self-report and history obtained from interviews with family and friends. When considering the defendant's early childhood, the nature of family interactions, punishment for misbehavior (including child abuse of all types), intactness of the family, major events, illnesses, and injuries, and school performance should be documented.

A consideration of the defendant's adolescent years may include academic performance and behavior in school, sexual development, identity issues, drug and alcohol use, nature of peer interactions, and jobs held. A section on young adulthood might describe the nature of the defendant's interpersonal relationships, employment history, and military service, if any.

A section on adulthood should include marital history, further education, vocational, military and religious history, and any history of drug and alcohol dependence or abuse. The examiner should document the defendant's criminal and medical history, with special attention to medical conditions that might affect psychological functioning. The preceding recommendations are rather general, but deciding on which areas to focus in taking a medical and social history should be made on a case-by-case basis.

Psychological Testing

Psychological testing with traditional clinical tests (e.g., Minnesota Multiphasic Personality Inventory 2 [MMPI-2], Wechsler Adult Intelligence Scale III [WAIS-III]), with forensic assessment instruments (e.g., Rogers Criminal Responsibility Assessment Inventory, Rogers, 1984) and forensically related tests (e.g., Structured Interview of Reported Symptoms, Rogers, 1992; Validity Indicator Profile, Frederick, 1997, and see the chapter by Rogers & Bender in this volume; Hare Psychopathy Checklist Revised, Hare, 1991, and see Chapter 6) frequently provide valuable information. (One of the coauthors of this chapter, Morse, believes that psychological tests of any kind are rarely if ever valid for legal purposes and that using them for these purposes is a waste of resources and potentially a source of confusion. However, he recognizes that this is a minority view among forensic psychologists. Most experts, including Goldstein and Shapiro, believe that when used judiciously and when inferences from test data are conservatively made and are verified by corroborative, real-life data, they can be of significant value as part of the overall assessment process.)

It must be emphasized that psychological tests provide information about the defendant's functioning at the time the tests were administered. They do *not* directly provide information regarding the defendant's behavior at the time of the crime. Testing may, nonetheless, suggest enduring intellectual, neurological, and psychological traits, characteristics, and behavior patterns that are relevant to an understanding of the defendant in general and to those factors that may be relevant to the defendant's MSO. The choice of tests to administer depends on the specific characteristics of the defendant and the specific case, but any test employed should conform to *Standards for Educational and Psychological Testing* (American Educational Research Association, American Psychological Association, & National Council on Measurement in Education, 1999).

Malingering is always a possibility in forensic practice and, in addition to reviewing collateral information, the examiner may want to administer objective, forensically related instruments designed to assess malingering. For example, the Structured Interview of Reported Symptoms (SIRS; Rogers, 1992) may help disclose malingering if the defendant claims or demonstrates symptoms of schizophrenia. The Validity Indicator Profile (Fredrick, 1997) may be appropriate if the defendant claims to have cognitive impairment, including symptoms of mental retardation and memory disturbances. (See Chapter 7 for a discussion of these and other instruments designed to evaluated malingering and exaggeration in a range of psycholegal contexts.)

Malingering falls on a continuum (Resnick, 1997; Rogers, Sewell, & Goldstein, 1994) from purely feigned symptoms of mental defects or mental illnesses to the exaggeration of actual symptoms of an underlying mental disorder. A determination that the defendant may be malingering or exaggerating symptoms should not terminate the evaluation. Malingering and the presence of an authentic mental disorder are not mutually exclusive (Otto, 2001). Defendants with actual mental illness may exaggerate their claimed symptoms to avoid or lessen criminal responsibility (Braginsky & Braginsky, 1967; Resnick, 1997). In a forensic context, malingering is most frequently interpreted by forensic psychologists as an attempt to cope with a threatening, negative situation, not necessarily as an aspect of an antisocial personality (Rogers, Sewell, & Goldstein, 1994; Rogers, Salekin, Sewell, Goldstein, & Leonard, 1998). As such, the presence of signs of malingered or exaggerated symptoms of a mental disorder by itself, does not necessarily exclude the possibility that the defendant was mentally ill at the time of the crime.

The expert should consider using the Rogers Criminal Responsibility Assessment Scales (R-CRAS; Rogers, 1984). It contains 25 "variables" on which the clinician rates the reliability of the defendant's presentation and possible malingering, the presence or absence of organic impairment, mental retardation, and various symptoms of mental illness, and whether there is evidence of either cognitive impairment or loss of behavioral control at the time of the alleged offense—all relevant factors in considering insanity as defined in the ALI statute. Four additional "variables" are provided for the GBMI standard and one other for the *M'Naghten* standard, for use in jurisdictions employing those statutes. The variables of the R-CRAS are rated on a 4 to 6-point scale. Rogers emphasizes that third-party sources of data should be consulted or considered in using the R-CRAS. Rogers then provides criteria-based decision models that the clinician completes to address the issue of criminal responsibility for the ALI, GBMI, and *M'Naghten* standards. Each criterion must be answered yes, no (to a reasonable degree of medical or scientific certainty) or no opinion. If all of the specified criteria are fulfilled, the conclusion is reached that the legal standard is met.

The R-CRAS was subjected to a series of tests of both interrater and test-retest reliability. There was moderate test-retest reliability for individual variables. In a sample of 25 cases, Rogers, Dollmetsch, and Cavanaugh (1981) found a correlation coefficient of .82. Rogers, Wasyliw, and Cavanaugh (1984), in the same size sample, found a kappa of .93; and, in a 30-case study, Rogers, Seman, and Wasyliw (1983) found perfect agreement, a kappa of 1.00. However, Phillips, Wolf, and Coons (1988), in 66 cases, found a significantly lower kappa of .45. It should be noted that the studies by Rogers and his colleagues cited here involved experienced clinicians; no such information is reported on the experience of those clinicians that competed the R-CRAS in the Phillips et al. survey. As Melton et al. (1997) suggest, "the reliability of insanity opinions may be quite respectable under certain conditions—namely, among clinicians with forensic training, working in a hospital or clinic setting where similar concepts and approaches may be shared, with no *a priori* allegiance to either party" (p. 230).

Rogers and his colleagues (Rogers, Wasyliw, et al., 1984) investigated both construct and criterion-related validity using seven different research sites. With skilled forensic examiners in a two-stage discriminant analysis, Rogers found extremely divergent symptom patterns between insane and sane defendants. Rogers, Cavanaugh, Seman, and Harris (1984) found 97% agreement between the conclusions reached as to sanity on the R-CRAS completed by trained examiners and the same finding reached by triers of fact; agreement regarding insanity was somewhat lower, at 70%.

More recent work by Rogers and Sewell (1999) considered two questions: whether R-CRAS variables accurately classified decision variables, and whether predicted relationships between individual variables and the resulting discriminant function were observed. In reference to the first issue, few errors were observed when the discriminant models were implemented; for the second issue, correlations were consistent with the predicted relationships.

Although Rogers developed the R-CRAS to provide an empirically based, quantifiable approach to evaluating insanity in MSO assessments, the degree to which this instrument has succeeded in accomplishing this goal has been debated. A detailed critique of the R-CRAS can be found in Golding, Skeem, Roesch, and Zapf (1999) and Melton et al. (1997). However, the use of this tool requires evaluators to consider multiple data sources, to include relevant behavioral *and* legal criteria, and to address the issue of malingering—all in a systematic fashion. As such, when used as part of an overall assessment of the issue of insanity, the R-CRAS can provide additional information for the mental health professional to consider in forming an opinion.

An Illustrative Insanity Case

Maria Lopez, a 34-year-old immigrant from Brazil, killed her four children by stabbing them to death. The referral question was whether she was legally insane when she killed them.

Ms. Lopez's husband, parents, and neighbors described her as a loving, caring parent. Deeply religious, she attended church regularly. Although many people thought she was somewhat overprotective of her four children, she was an undoubtedly responsible parent. She worked the night shift as a housekeeper for a large hotel, and her husband was employed during the day. The children, ages 11, 9, 8, and 6, were thus rarely left home without parental supervision.

Ms. Lopez's behavior began to change approximately two years before her arrest. She became increasingly withdrawn, depressed, and even more concerned about her children's well-being. She sent her oldest daughter, then age 9, to a summer day camp program in her neighborhood. After two weeks of the program, she reported to the police her suspicions that her daughter's 21-year-old male counselor had repeatedly sexually molested her daughter at the camp. But her daughter, Mary, denied abuse of any kind by anyone at any time. The child's pediatrician found no signs of sexual abuse. A thorough investigation, including interviews of other children, their parents, camp employees, and Mary's counselor, led police detectives to conclude that this was a groundless accusation and charges were never filed. Nonetheless, Ms. Lopez held firmly to her belief that her daughter had been sexually violated. Her concern for her daughter increased along with additional worries for the general safety of all of her children. She withdrew Mary from the program and, throughout the summer, kept her close to her at all times.

When school began in late August, Ms. Lopez appeared to be somewhat less anxious and preoccupied. But the change in her condition lasted for only a month. She became concerned that Mary was abusing drugs. Although she neither witnessed Mary's use of drugs nor found drugs in the home, Ms. Lopez became increasingly more watchful of her daughter. Mary was forbidden to leave the home unaccompanied by a parent or by her aunt, and friends were not allowed into their home. Mr. Lopez believed that his wife's suspicions were ludicrous in light of Mary's age, personality, and Ms. Lopez's constant presence when Mary was not attending school.

At this point, her parents and husband believed that Ms. Lopez required psychiatric help. She agreed to be seen at a local mental health clinic. After an evaluation by the staff, she was placed on antidepressants and antipsychotic medications and was scheduled for weekly psychotherapy sessions. Although she continued to maintain the belief that her daughter had been abused and that all of her children were in potential danger of becoming addicted to drugs, her mood improved modestly. Eventually, she started to voice concerns that her husband no longer cared for her, that he was having an affair, and that his lack of "morality" would affect the children. Despite changes in medication, her delusions remained unaltered. For the next nine months, she attended sessions regularly, sometimes with her husband, and she took her medication as prescribed.

During the last week of May, Ms. Lopez began to believe that Mary had been giving drugs to the youngest child, Paul, then age 8. In addition, she told relatives, teachers, and neighbors about her concern that all her children would eventually become addicted and that her two daughters would turn to prostitution to support their habit. Her depression deepened and she became withdrawn and frightened again. Two weeks later, her husband found empty prescription bottles in the medicine cabinet and realized that his wife had stopped taking her medications. He arranged for her to be seen by the psychiatrist the next morning.

Mr. Lopez left for work at 6 A.M.; his wife and children were sleeping in their bedrooms. He reminded her of her appointment that morning at the clinic and she assured him that she would call him at work on returning home. When he did not hear from her by 11:30 A.M., he became concerned. By 1 P.M., he left work to drive home to check on his wife. He discovered her in bed, unconscious but still alive. She had cut both her wrists and had burn marks on her lips and chin. Mr. Lopez immediately called for an ambulance, and then discovered all four children dead, each in their beds with their throats cut.

Following surgery, Ms. Lopez spoke with the police about what happened after her husband had left for work. In a 15-page statement, she admitted cutting each child's throat and then cutting her wrists in a suicide attempt. When the cuts failed to bleed as heavily as she had hoped, she went to the kitchen, removed a bottle of lye drain opener from under the sink, and drank half of its contents. According to her statement, she took her children's lives so that all five of them could be safely in heaven together.

At the request of her attorney, a forensic psychologist evaluated Ms. Lopez three days after her arrest at a forensic unit at a county medical center. She had difficulty speaking because of permanent damage to her vocal cords and esophagus from the lye. She was severely depressed, begging constantly that her restraints be removed so that she could kill herself and be reunited with her children.

The retained forensic expert evaluated Ms. Lopez on three separate occasions. A general background history was taken and her current mental status was assessed. She was interviewed in detail regarding her recollection of the events leading up to the crime as well as her memories of the crime itself. The *M'Naghten* statutory definition of insanity employed in the state in which the crime occurred determined the focus of the evaluation. A central concern of the evaluation was therefore her thoughts at the time of the crime, particularly as they related to her ability to comprehend and appreciate the nature and consequences of her actions and her awareness of the wrongfulness of taking her children's lives.

A battery of psychological tests was administered, including the WAIS-III, MMPI-2, and SIRS. The WAIS-III was chosen to assess her overall cognitive abilities and especially to determine if the presence of psychiatric symptoms might have impaired her judgment and reasoning as well as her ability to concentrate and focus her attention. To evaluate her personality dynamics and for general diagnostic purposes, the MMPI-2 was selected. The SIRS was administered to evaluate the genuineness of the symptoms of schizophrenia she demonstrated.

Interviews were conducted with her parents, her husband and sister, and with one of her children's teachers. Police reports of her earlier suspicions of sexual abuse of her daughter and the subsequent police investigation were examined, as were all treatment records from the mental health clinic where she had been seen. Records from her pharmacy were also reviewed.

When interviewed, Ms. Lopez tearfully explained that she knew that her children were in danger from all those around them. She believed that her older daughter was a drug-addicted prostitute who had forced her younger siblings to try drugs and that they, too, would soon become addicted. She felt helpless to protect them from this terrible fate. In addition, she thought her husband was an immoral, irresponsible person who would not look after her children if she committed suicide. She understood that no one believed her claims, including the staff at the clinic, the police, the pediatrician, the teachers, and the summer camp personnel. She believed the children were still in a condition of "grace in the eyes of God" because they were so young. She also believed that if she took their lives and then her own, the children would be saved and all five would be reunited in heaven. Her children would be in a state of eternal bliss, free from contamination by the living world, and she would be forever free of her depression and constant worry.

Prior to the crime, the clinic had diagnosed Ms. Lopez as demonstrating symptoms consistent with major depression with psychotic features. Treatment records were replete with her claims that her children were in danger of being "corrupted," and all people interviewed reported that she had expressed similar concerns to them. Her recollections of the crime were consistent with police investigative reports and with the statement she gave to investigators. The psychological tests disclosed that she had psychotic symptoms reflecting underlying delusions, numerous phobias, and severe depression accompanied by suicidal ideation. Moreover, the tests also indicated that she distrusted others, seeing herself as weak and a victim. No indications of malingering or exaggeration appeared on the SIRS.

Based on the entire assessment, the examiner concluded that at the time of the crime, Ms. Lopez was actively psychotic—depressed and delusional—and that the homicides were motivated by her confused, psychotic thinking. She genuinely believed that she was saving each of them from corruption and sin, thereby protecting them and ensuring them a continuous state of safety and bliss. Her serious mental illness prevented her from rationally evaluating her beliefs and considering alternative actions. She did not appreciate the wrongfulness of her behavior at the moment she killed her four children. Her actions were motivated by delusional reasons because she saw their deaths as the only way of ensuring their physical and moral safety, guaranteeing them entry into heaven. For Ms. Lopez, death was equated with heaven and God's wishes rather than an end of life. Rather than killing her children, she believed she was saving each of them from further abuse so that they would be together forever under the protection of God in a world without evil. She was unable to consider the legal prohibitions against homicide and thought that her actions were the moral thing to do.

An evaluation the prosecutor requested yielded similar conclusions concerning Ms. Lopez's mental state at the time of the crime. Consequently, the prosecution and defense agreed that Ms. Lopez was not criminally culpable for the deaths of her children. The prosecution therefore did not contest her plea of Not Responsible by Reason of Mental Disease or Defect, which is the equivalent of being found legally insane by a judge or jury.

SUMMARY

It has been written, "Great dissatisfaction regarding . . . the issue of insanity in criminal cases and the results thereof is being expressed on all sides. The layman claims that sane men are escaping responsibility for their crimes on the plea of insanity by reason of the venality of experts." This viewpoint appeared in a journal in 1912 (Keedy), but remains a popular one today. We have attempted to address this and the broader issue of all mental states from historical, ethical, and practice perspectives. This chapter described the theory and doctrines of mental state defenses to criminal liability. We considered a range of *mens rea* defenses, including extreme mental or emotional disturbance and so-called diminished capacity, and legal insanity. A judge or jury may conclude that a defendant is legally *totally* lacking in culpability for his or her actions (e.g., legal insanity), that the defendant was *partially* responsible for his or her actions (e.g., finding a homicide defendant guilty of a lesser charge because the defendant killed in a state of extreme emotional disturbance for which there is a reasonable explanation or excuse), or that a defendant is fully guilty of a lesser crime (e.g., because the *mens rea* required by the definition of a more serious offense was lacking).

To assist the judge or jury in cases that raise mental state defenses, forensic psychologists should do careful evaluations and present evidence that is persuasive, well-documented, and thorough, and meets the standard of care in the field. Ethical, competent forensic psychological assessments may provide the trier of fact with relevant, probative information that would not otherwise be available and that may assist the trier of fact in determining whether and to what degree the defendant deserves punishment.

Our society and legal system are based on the principle of fairness, including the moral foundational belief that people should be legally punished only if they deserve punishment because they are blameworthy. Mental state defenses are complete or partial denials of blameworthiness. When defendants raise such defenses in bizarre cases or when the victim is a public figure, acquittal by reason of insanity or conviction for less serious offenses often leads to public outcry against such defenses. The acquittal of John Hinckley Jr. for the attempted murder of President Reagan and the conviction of Dan White only for manslaughter for killing San Francisco mayor George Moscone and Supervisor Harvey Milk—the infamous "Twinkies" case—are examples of cases that lead to public hostility and calls for abolition or reform, as was true in 1912. Desert is so fundamental to punishment, however, that a just society cannot fairly abolish mental state defenses.

REFERENCES

American Educational Research Association, American Psychological Association, & National Council on Measurement in Education. (1999). *Standards for educational and psychological testing* (3rd ed.). Washington, DC: American Educational Research Association.

American Law Institute. (1962). *Model penal code*. Washington, DC: American Law Institute.

American Psychological Association. (1992). Ethical principles of psychologists and code of conduct. *American Psychologist, 47,* 1597–1611.

Braginsky, B. M., & Braginsky, D. D. (1967). Schizophrenic patients in the psychiatric interview: An experimental study of their effectiveness at manipulation. *Journal of Consulting Psychology, 31,* 543–547.

Cleckley, H. (1941). *The mask of sanity.* St. Louis, MO: Mosby.

Committee on Ethical Guidelines for Forensic Psychologists. (1991). Specialty guidelines for forensic psychologists. *Law and Human Behavior, 15,* 655–665.

Department of Youth Services v. a Juvenile, 499 N.E.2d 812 (Mass. Sup. Jud. Ct. 1986).

Doe v. Superior Court, 39 Cal. App. 4th 538, 45 Cal. Rptr. 2d 288 (1995).

Dressler, J. (2001). *Understanding criminal law* (3rd ed). New York: Matthew Bender.

Drogin, E. Y. (1999). On the brink of insanity: "Extreme emotional disturbance" in Kentucky law. *Northern Kentucky Law Review, 26,* 99–132.

Durham v. United States, 214 F.2d 962 (D.C. Cir. 1954).

Edney v. State, 556 F.2d 556 (2nd Cir. 1977).

Estelle v. Smith, 451 U.S. 454, 101 S. Ct. 1866 (1981).

Faust, D. (1990, August 11). Expert testimony of mental health professionals: Response to Faust and Ziskin. Symposium presented at annual convention of American Psychological Association. Boston, MA.

Finkel, N. J. (1989). The Insanity Defense Reform Act of 1984: Much ado about nothing. *Behavioral Sciences and the Law, 7,* 403–419.

Finkel, N. J., Shaw, R., Bercaw, S., & Koch, J. (1985). Insanity defenses: From the jurors' perspective. *Law and Psychology Review, 9,* 77–92.

Foucha v. Louisiana, 112 S. Ct. 1780 (1992).

Frederick v. Oklahoma, 902 P.2d 1092 (Okla. Crim. App. 1995).

Frederick, R. (1997). *Validity Indicator Profile.* Minneapolis, MN: National Computer Systems.

Fulero, S. M., & Finkel, N. J. (1991). Barring ultimate issue testimony: An "insane" rule? *Law and Human Behavior, 15,* 495–507.

Golding, S. L., Eaves, D., & Kowaz, A. (1989). The assessment, treatment and community outcome of insanity acquittees: Forensic history and response to treatment. *International Journal of Law and Psychiatry, 12,* 149–179.

Golding, S. L., Skeem, J. L., Roesch, R., & Zapf, P. A. (1999). The assessment of criminal responsibility: Current controversies. In A. K. Hess & I. B. Weiner (Eds.), *The handbook of forensic psychology* (2nd ed., pp. 379–408). New York: Wiley.

Hare, R. D. (1991). *The Hare Psychopathy Checklist–Revised.* Toronto, Ontario, Canada: Multi-Health Systems.

Hare, R. D. (1998). Psychopaths and their nature: Implications for the mental health and criminal justice systems. In T. Millon, E. Simonsen, M. Birket-Smith, & R. D. Davis (Eds.), *Psychopathy: Antisocial, criminal, and violent behavior* (pp. 188–212). New York: Guilford Press.

Heilbrun, K. (2001). *Principles of Forensic Mental Health Assessment.* New York: Kluwer Academic/Plenum.

Illinois v. Smith, 464 N.E.2d 685, (Ill. Ct. of App. 1984).

Insanity Defense Reform Act. (1984). Pub. L. 98-473, 18 U.S.C. §§ 401–406.

Jones v. United States, 103 S. Ct. 3043 (1983).

Keedy, E. R. (1912). Insanity and criminal responsibility. *Journal of the American Institute of Criminal Law and Criminology, 2,* 521–539.

Lockett v. Ohio, 438 U.S. 586 (1978).

Low, P. W., Jeffries, J. C., & Bonnie, R. J. (1986). *The trial of John W. Hinkley Jr: A case study in the insanity defense.* Mineola, NY: Foundation Press.

McDonald v. United States, 312 F.2d 844 (D.C. Cir. 1962).

Melton, G. B., Petrila, J., Poythress, N. G., & Slobogin, C. (1997). *Psychological evaluations for the courts: A handbook for mental health professionals and lawyers* (2nd ed.). New York: Guilford Press.

M'Naghten's Case, 10 Cl.&F. 200, 8 Eng. Rep. 718 (H.L. 1843).

Montana v. Egelhoff, 518 U.S. 37 (1996).

Moran, R. (1981). *Knowing Right from Wrong: The Insanity Defense of Daniel McNaughten.* New York: The Free Press.

Morse, S. J. (1999). Crazy reasons. *Journal of Contemporary Legal Issues, 10,* 189–226.

Mullaney v. Wilbur, 421 U.S. 684 (1975).

Noggle v. Marshall, 706 F.2d 1408 (6th Cir. 1983).

Otto, R. K. (2001, February 15). Assessing malingering and deception. Seminar presented at American Academy of Forensic Psychology Workshop, San Antonio, TX.

Patterson v. New York, 432 U.S. 197 (1977).

People v. Crews, 522 N.E.2d 1167 (1988).

Phillips, M. R., Wolf, A. S., & Coons, D. J. (1988). Psychiatry and the criminal justice system: Testing the myths. *American Journal of Psychiatry, 145,* 605–610.

Resnick, P. J. (1997). Malingered psychosis. In R. Rogers (Ed.), Clinical Assessment of Malingering and Deception. New York: Guilford Press.

Rogers, R. (1984). *Rogers Criminal Responsibility Assessment Scales (R-CRAS) and test manual.* Odessa, FL: Psychological Assessment Resources.

Rogers, R. (1992). *Structured Interview of Reported Symptoms and test manual.* Odessa, FL: Psychological Assessment Resources.

Rogers, R., Cavanaugh, J. L., Seman, W., & Harris, M. (1984). Legal outcome and clinical findings: A study of insanity evaluations. *Bulletin of the American Academy of Psychiatry and the Law, 12,* 75–83.

Rogers, R., Dollmetsch, R., & Cavanaugh, J. L. (1981). An empirical approach to insanity Evaluations. *Journal of Clinical Psychology, 37,* 683–687.

Rogers, R., Salekin, R. T., Sewell, R. W., Goldstein, A. M., & Leonard, K. (1998). A comparison of forensic and nonforensic malingerers: A prototypical analysis of explanatory models. *Law and Human Behavior, 22,* 353–368.

Rogers, R., Seman, W., & Wasyliw, O. E. (1983). The R-CRAS and legal insanity: A cross-validated study. *Journal of Clinical Psychology, 39,* 544–559.

Rogers, R., & Sewell, K. W. (1999). The R-CRAS and insanity evaluations: A re-examination of construct validity. *Behavioral Sciences and the Law, 17,* 181–194.

Rogers, R., Sewell, W., & Goldstein, A. M. (1994). Explanatory models of malingering: A prototypical analysis. *Law and Human Behavior, 18,* 543–552.

Rogers, R., Wasyliw, O. E., & Cavanaugh, J. L. (1984). Evaluating insanity: A study of construct validity. *Law and Human Behavior, 8,* 293–303.

Silver, E., Cirincione, C., & Steadman, H. J. (1994). Demythologizing inaccurate perceptions of the insanity defense: Legal standards and clinical assessment. *Applied and Preventive Psychology, 2,* 163–178.

State v. Pratt, 398 N.E.2d 421 (Md. Ct. App. 1979).

State v. Wilson, 413 S.E.2d 19 (1992).

Steadman, H. J., McGreevy, M. A., Morrissey, J. P., Callahan, L. A., Robbins, P. C., & Cirincione, C. (1993). *Before and after Hinkley: Evaluating insanity defense reform.* New York: Guilford Press.

Strozier v. Georgia, 334 S.E.2d 181 (Ga. S. Ct. 1985).

United States v. Alvarez, 519 F.2d 1036 (3d Cir. 1975).

United States v. Brawner, 471 F.2d 969 (D.C. Cir. 1972).

United States v. Hinkley, 525 F. Supp. 1342 (D. D.C. 1981).

United States v. Pohlot, 827 F.2d 889 (3d Cir. 1987).

Walker, N. (1968). *Crime and insanity in England. Volume 1: The historical perspective.* Edinburgh, Scotland: Edinburgh University Press.

Washington v. United States, 129 U.S. App. D.C. 29 (1967).

Ziskin, J., & Faust, D. (1988). *Coping with psychiatric and psychological testimony* (5th ed.). Los Angeles: Law and Psychology Press.

CHAPTER 21

Sentencing Determinations in Death Penalty Cases

MARK D. CUNNINGHAM AND ALAN M. GOLDSTEIN

The death penalty is an ultimate and irrevocable sanction. For this reason, the U.S. Supreme Court has determined that "death is qualitatively different from a sentence of imprisonment, however long" (*Woodson v. North Carolina,* 1976), and warrants a "greater degree of reliability" (*Lockett v. Ohio,* 1978) in its application. The clinical skills and empirical expertise of forensic psychologists may be sought at a number of junctures in capital litigation. These include the forensically familiar functions of pretrial and guilt phase evaluations regarding various competencies (e.g., ability to waive *Miranda* rights, fitness for trial), as well as mental state at the time of the offense. More unique to capital cases, however, forensic psychological evaluations often address sentencing issues. That is, they focus on those factors that may

assist the trier of fact in determining whether the defendant is to live or die.

Forensic psychologists may be consulted posttrial as well. Years following a death penalty sentence, psychologists may be called on at postconviction proceedings or federal *habeas* review to examine the sufficiency of the pretrial mental health evaluations and trial testimony. When a death row inmate elects to waive appeals, psychological consultation may be sought regarding the inmate's competency to make this determination. Finally, forensic psychologists may be asked to evaluate a death row inmate's competency to be executed.

In capital cases, experts frequently testify regarding the presence of mitigating and aggravating factors that may provide information about the defendant's background or circumstances of the crime that would influence the sentence the defendant is to receive. Frequently included in such evaluations is an assessment of the risk of future violence should the defendant receive a sentence less than death. These sentencing determinations constitute the major focus of this chapter. We consider the nature and structure of capital trials, facts about the death penalty, landmark U.S. Supreme Court decisions relevant to the capital cases, ethical issues, the nature of assessments in capital cases including violence risk assessment, and testimony in such cases.

THE NATURE AND STRUCTURE OF CAPITAL TRIALS

A homicide is committed. At the time of the crime, the defendant is 20 years of age and living in a halfway house for those recently discharged from a mental hospital. He had stopped taking his medication weeks before the crime and others report that he had returned to drug use, abusing crack and marijuana on a daily basis. He is charged with having murdered a 9-year-old girl, a next-door neighbor, by strangling her. It is alleged that prior to killing the girl, he had raped her and burned her body with cigarettes. It is believed that he took her life so that she could not report the crime.

Because of the horrific facts surrounding this crime, the prosecutor is weighing the possibility of declaring this to be a capital case. In each of the 38 states that have death penalty statutes, as well as in federal and military jurisdictions, there is a list of "special circumstances" that, if established by the judgment of the trier of fact (the judge or jury), might result in the defendant being sentenced to death. In a sense, the presence of one or more of these *aggravating factors,* which vary from jurisdiction to jurisdiction, would make the defendant more blameworthy than he might otherwise be in a "simple" homicide.

In this hypothetical case, the prosecutor may claim that a number of aggravating factors exist. Among those that might be alleged are the age of the victim; the depraved indifference shown by the defendant by burning her body with cigarettes and purposefully causing her pain incremental to death; that the murder took place in the commission of another felony (i.e., rape); that the murder was committed to prevent the victim from testifying against him; and a high likelihood of future violent behavior should the defendant receive a sentence other than death. Depending on the jurisdiction, the prosecutor has a specific period of time to reach a decision as to whether to formally pursue the death penalty. Prosecutors are granted considerable "guided" discretion as to whether a murder under special circumstances becomes a capital case.

At this stage in the process, the defense attorney has the job of convincing the prosecutor that death is not an appropriate punishment in this case. Experts may submit preliminary reports at the request of the defense attorney, who will, in turn, meet with the prosecutor to either dissuade him or her from seeking the death penalty or to reach a plea bargain prior to trial, thus avoiding a capital trial in which the defendant's life is at stake. Again, each jurisdiction has its own set of specific circumstances (defined by legislators in each state and by Congress on the federal level) that, if found by the trier of fact to be present, might result in a verdict other than death. These factors, designed to encourage jurors to grant leniency, are referred to as *statutory mitigating factors.* In this case, a number of such mitigators may be claimed to exist: The defendant was mentally ill at the time of the crime (but not rising to the level of a defense against the charges); the defendant's use of drugs at the time of the crime impaired his judgment and impulse control (but not rising to the level of a defense against the charges); and the defendant has no prior record of violence and does not present a risk of future dangerousness. In addition, every jurisdiction allows the defense to present *any* evidence related to the defendant's background and circumstances of the offense that may be considered by the trier of fact as mitigation in reaching the verdict. The *nonstatutory mitigating factors* in this case might include the defendant's history of mental illness; his history of both physical and sexual abuse as a child; that, weeks before the crime, he discontinued use of the psychotropic medications prescribed for him; and that the halfway house staff failed to recognize and treat his decompensation over the two weeks preceding the crime.

Assuming that the prosecutor decides to actively pursue the death penalty, experts will be retained by the defense to evaluate the defendant for the presence of possible statutory and nonstatutory factors. If there is a trial, it is bifurcated; that is, there are essentially two trials. First, a guilt-innocence trial occurs to determine if the defendant is guilty of a capital offense. The defense attorney may use an emotional disturbance defense such as insanity or extreme emotional disturbance (see the chapter by Goldstein, Morse, & Shapiro in this volume). Only if the defendant has pled guilty or is found guilty of a capital offense does a sentencing proceeding take place. In part, a bifurcated trial permits evidence to be admitted during the sentencing phase that, if admitted during the guilt phase of the trial, might be found to be prejudicial or irrelevant. Depending on the jurisdiction, this sentencing trial may continue before the guilt phase jury or may be heard by the trial judge or a panel of judges who determine whether the defendant is sentenced to death or a capital life prison term.

At the sentencing phase of the trial, the defense introduces evidence, often by way of expert testimony, that one or more mitigating factors exist. The prosecutor introduces evidence as to presence of one or more aggravating factors and may call rebuttal experts to respond to the testimony of the defense witnesses. Assuming there is a jury, they are then instructed as to how to weigh the aggravating against the mitigating factors. The consideration of how these factors are balanced varies across jurisdictions.

In *federal* death penalty cases, for example, each juror must find (beyond a reasonable doubt) that one or more aggravating factors exist. A finding with respect to any aggravating factor must be unanimous. If none is found, the defendant receives a sentence other than death. If found, the jury must then decide whether one or more mitigating factors exist. Unanimity is not required to establish the presence of mitigating factors, which are established by a preponderance of the information. If only one juror believes a mitigator exists, it is considered to be present. The Federal Criminal Code and Rules then instructs:

> The jury, or if there is no jury, the court, shall consider whether all the aggravating factor or factors found to exist sufficiently outweigh all the mitigating factor or factors found to exist to justify a sentence of death, or, in the absence of a mitigating factor, whether the aggravating factor or factors alone are sufficient to justify a sentence of death. Based upon this consideration, the jury by unanimous vote, or if there is no jury, the court, shall recommend whether the defendant should be sentenced to death, to life imprisonment without the possibility of release or some other lesser sentence. (18 § 3593 (e))

In federal court, and in some states, a "hung jury" is equivalent to a finding of a sentence other than death. There are numerous variations in this across the states. In some, not all jurors must agree on the death penalty; in others, a hung jury leaves the decision of sentencing to the judge. In some states, if the aggravating factors outweigh the mitigating factors, the jury must impose a sentence of death. In some states, a judge may overrule a jury's verdict and impose a sentence of death over their recommendation of a life sentence. A recent U.S. Supreme Court decision, *Ring v. Arizona* (2002), declared death penalties imposed by judges rather than juries unconstitutional. Citing *Apprendi v. New Jersey* (2000), the Court reasoned that a judge may not make a finding that is higher than a defendant's sentence beyond the maximum as this would amount to an additional conviction. A death sentence imposed by a judge violates the Constitutional right to a trial by jury according to *Ring*.

When fully litigated, death sentences in state courts are followed by state and federal direct appeals, and subsequently by state postconviction petitions and federal *habeas* review. The state appellate process at both the direct appeal and postconviction stages is critically important, as injustices not raised in state petitions likely will be forfeited in federal court. To further explain, the direct appeal process raises and considers legal errors that may have occurred during trial. Postconviction proceedings also examine these issues but, in addition, investigate ineffective assistance of counsel, prosecutorial misconduct, juror misconduct claims, and other matters that may have come to light after the trial. Postconviction and *habeas* review are important protections against miscarriage of justice in capital litigation, as demonstrated by federal *habeas* courts finding uncorrected error and subsequently vacating the death sentences in a substantial proportion of capital cases (Justice Stevens, dissent, *Murray v. Giarratano,* 1989, at p. 13).

FACTS AND FIGURES

Because statistics regarding those on death row and those executed change frequently, it is not possible to present the most up-to-date figures in this chapter. The reader is referred to the Death Penalty Information Center Web site (www.deathpenaltyinfo.org) for the most recent statistics on this topic. Also at that site are state-by-state policies on the death penalty.

As of December 2001, 38 states have capital punishment statutes. In addition, the death penalty is applicable in U.S. Federal Court as well as in U.S. Military Court. Thirteen jurisdictions do not have capital punishment statutes: Alaska, District of Columbia, Hawaii, Iowa, Maine, Massachusetts, Michigan, Minnesota, North Dakota, Rhode Island, Vermont, West Virginia, and Wisconsin (Death Penalty Information Center, 2001).

Death Row Population

There are currently a large number of capital cases in various stages of litigation, including over 3,700 inmates on death row nationwide (NAACP Legal Defense Fund, 2001). Over 98% of this death row group are male. Two percent of those awaiting execution were juveniles at the time they committed their capital offense. Since 1986, there has been a 208% increase in the number of inmates on death row (Death Penalty Information Center, 2001). Of course, death row inmates do not represent the universe of capital cases. Many capital cases are pled out prior to trial, and others may conclude with an acquittal, a finding of guilt to a lesser charge, or a sentence to a capital life term in prison rather than death.

This total also does not include capitally charged defendants who are awaiting trial.

Executions

Since 1976, when the death penalty was found to be constitutional and reinstated, 749 individuals have been executed (all figures are as of December 16, 2001). By far the most common means of execution is by lethal injection (36 states, U.S. Military, U.S. Government), followed by electrocution (10 states), gas chamber (5 states), hanging (3 states), and firing squad (2 states). Only two states using other execution methods do not provide lethal injection as an alternative. Texas has had the most executions (256), followed by Virginia (83), Florida (51), Missouri (53), and Oklahoma (48). Eighteen states have conducted fewer than 10 executions. Most executions have occurred in the South (609), followed by the West (58), Midwest (79), and Northeast (3; Death Penalty Information Center, 2001). Lifton and Mitchell (2000) present a detailed review of the history of methods of execution, including problems associated with each, as well as detailing the history of the death penalty from its appearance in the Code of Hammurabi, Mosaic law, and the Draconion Code to the present time.

Since the first U.S. execution in 1790, 340 federal inmates have been put to death. In the twentieth century, approximately 6% of federal executions have been of minority defendants (Death Penalty Information Center, 2001).

Race and the Death Penalty

Of those executed since 1976 (as of October 2001), 55% were White, 36% were Black, 7% were Latino/Latina, and 2% were Native American or Asian. It is notable that of those executed for interracial murders, 169 involved Black defendant and White victim, and 11 involved White defendant and Black victim. Related to this statistic is the finding that 81% of capital cases involve White victims, although nationally, 50% of murder victims are White (Death Penalty Information Center, 2001; NAACP Legal Defense Fund, 2001).

Women and the Death Penalty

As of April 1, 2001, 56 women are on death row, awaiting execution, representing fewer than 2% of the total death row population. Since 1976, it is reported that seven women have been put to death for capital murder (Death Penalty Information Center, 2001).

Juveniles and the Death Penalty

At present, 23 states allow the death penalty for those who committed capital murder when they were *less* than 18 years of age. As of December 2001, 82 inmates who are awaiting execution were sentenced to death as juveniles, approximately 2% of the death row population. All of them are male and 66% are minority group members (NAACP Legal Defense Fund, 2001). Since 1976, 18 men have been executed for crimes they committed as juveniles (Death Penalty Information Center, 2001).

The Mentally Retarded and the Death Penalty

As we discuss in the next section, the U.S. Supreme Court (*Atkins v. Virginia*, 2002) ruled that it is a violation of the Constitution to execute the mentally retarded. The Court indicated that each state legislature has the "task of developing appropriate ways to enforce the restriction upon the execution of sentences." Prior to this decision, two states and the federal government had prohibited the execution of those with mental retardation. It is estimated that since 1976, 35 mentally retarded inmates were executed (Death Penalty Information Center, 2001). When this decision was made, approximately 200 or more defendants with mental retardation were on death row awaiting execution (*The New York Times*, June 21, 2002).

CASE LAW AND THE DEATH PENALTY

Most challenges as to the constitutionality of the death penalty focus on issues related to the 8th Amendment to the U.S. Constitution, specifically, the "cruel and unusual punishments" clause. U.S. Supreme Court cases frequently address questions of whether the death penalty itself violates this cause, whether a specific provision of a state's statute on capital punishment is unconstitutional, and whether the method or procedures used in executing the condemned violates this clause. According to Latzer (1998), this clause was adopted from the English Bill of Rights of 1689, developed as a response to the torture, cruelty, and brutality directed against rebels revolting against King James II.

To prohibit such practices in the United States, the authors of the Constitution included the cruel and unusual punishments clause. Although Latzer (1998), an 8th Amendment scholar, argues that this clause "was *not* intended to abolish capital punishment" (p. 2), at least two late-twentieth century Justices (Brennan and Marshall) disagree. Latzer cites the 5th Amendment's language: "No person shall be held for a *capital* or otherwise infamous crime, unless on a presentation or indictment of a Grand Jury." He also refers to the use of the phrases "*life* or limb" and "*life,* liberty or property" contained in the 5th Amendment to support his position. He believes that the 8th Amendment was intended, in part, "to forbid the infliction of more pain than was necessary to extinguish life." Latzer reports that in the 1800s, the few cases decided by the Court on the death penalty addressed how it was to be carried out, rather than whether capital punishment itself was constitutional. Specifically, the first case on the cruel and unusual punishments clause (*Wilkerson v. Utah,* 1879) unanimously ruled that a sentence of death by public shooting was constitutional. In 1890, the Court again unanimously held that the use of the electric chair by New York was not a violation of the 8th Amendment (*In re Kemmler*), stating, "Punishments are cruel when they involve torture or a lingering death" (cited by Latzer, 1998, p. 2).

Furman v. Georgia

The first U.S. Supreme Court case to hold that capital punishment was a violation of the cruel and unusual punishments clause was *Furman v. Georgia* (1972), decided by a 5 to 4 vote. (At the same time, the Court struck down the Texas death penalty procedure statute in a companion case, *Branch v. Texas,* 1972.) In *Furman,* each Justice wrote an opinion. The opinion for the Court (*per curriam* opinion) was unsigned. In concurring opinions, two Justices, Brennan and Marshall, held that capital punishment, per se, represents cruel and unusual punishment. Justice Marshall wrote that it "violates the Eighth Amendment because it is morally unacceptable to the people of the United States at this time in their history." However, seven Justices did not object to the death penalty itself as unconstitutional, but rather, in concurring and dissenting opinions, indicated their disapproval of the lack of specific guidelines for indicating when a judge or jury should impose the death penalty and, consequently, its arbitrariness. Justice Douglas wrote that the current system granted "uncontrolled discretion" to judges and juries as to whether a defendant is to live or die: "People live or die, dependent on the whim of one man or of 12."

The death penalty statutes of Georgia and Texas were described as "capricious" (Brennan) and compared to a "lottery system" and to "being struck by lightening" (Stewart). Justice Douglas described it as discriminatory, "[applied] selectively to minorities . . . , who are outcasts of society, who are unpopular, but whom society is willing to see suffer," and as imposed upon those who are "poor and despised, and lacking in political clout, or if he is a member of a suspect or unpopular minority, and saving those who by social position may be

in a more protected position." A deeply divided court left room for future, rewritten capital statutes that would eventually satisfy all but two of the Justices as to their constitutionality. But, as of 1972, the Court found capital punishment to be unconstitutional.

Woodson v. North Carolina

In an effort to overcome the objections of arbitrariness stated in *Furman,* 35 states rewrote their death penalty statutes (Latzer, 1998). One such attempt was that of North Carolina. To avoid the issue of prejudice in capital sentencing, their revised statute made *all* first-degree murder convictions punishable by death. No discretion was granted to the judge or jury in such cases. The Court rejected this sentencing scheme by a 5 to 4 vote in *Woodson v. North Carolina* (1976). It viewed North Carolina's statute as having "simply papered over the problem of unguided and unchecked jury discretion" raised in *Furman.*

North Carolina had defined murder in the first degree as murder "which shall be perpetuated by means of poison, lying in wait, imprisonment, starving, torture, or by any other kind of willful, deliberate and premeditated killing" or murder committed during the commission of a felony. For anyone found guilty of such a crime, the death sentence was to be mandatory. The Court cited "the rejection of the common-law practice of inexorably imposing a death sentence upon every person convicted of a specified offense." The opinion, authored by Justice Stewart, emphasized the failure to permit a sentencing process that would individualize those factors that should be considered before "fixing the ultimate punishment of death." In *Woodson,* it was clear that the Court would be satisfied only by a sentencing scheme that would permit consideration of "relevant facets of the character and record of the individual offender or the circumstances of the particular offense."

Gregg v. Georgia

Georgia's revised capital sentencing statute met a more positive fate than did North Carolina's. Both cases were decided on the same day (Latzer, 1998). By a 7 to 2 vote (Justices Brennan and Marshall dissenting), the Court accepted Georgia's capital sentencing scheme, which called for established procedures as a method to prevent the arbitrariness and capriciousness cited in *Furman.* In *Gregg v. Georgia* (1976), the Court accepted as constitutional that state's requirement that at least one aggravating factor must be established beyond a reasonable doubt before a defendant could be sentenced to death. It permitted the defense to introduce mitigating "facts or circumstances" to be considered by the jury prior to sentencing. Finally, the Court accepted the structure of Georgia's capital trial, a bifurcated one, in which the sentencing phase follows only if the defendant is convicted of capital murder.

According to the decision authored by Justice Stewart, at the sentencing phase, "The defendant is accorded substantial latitude as to the types of evidence that he may introduce." The judge is to consider or instruct the jury that attention must be given to "any mitigating circumstances or aggravating circumstances otherwise authorized by law and any of [10] statutory aggravating circumstances which may be supported by the evidence." In this way, the trier of fact was "given adequate information and guidance" to reach an appropriate, fair sentence. In addition, the statute called for an appellate review process designed to focus on the appropriateness of the death penalty as punishment in each specific case. Specifically, in each death sentence case, the Supreme Court of Georgia would consider "Whether the sentence of death is excessive or disproportionate to the penalty imposed in similar cases, considering both the crime and the defendant." This concept eventually became known as a proportionality review.

In *Gregg,* a concurring opinion authored by Justice White (joined by Justices Burger and Rehnquist) acknowledged that "Imposition of the death penalty is surely an awesome responsibility for any system of justice and those who participate in it. Mistakes will be made and discriminations will occur which will be difficult to explain." *Gregg* served as the model statue for other states seeking to write constitutionally acceptable death penalty legislation.

Coker v. Georgia

Ehrlich Anthony Coker escaped from a correctional institution where he was serving a sentence for murder, rape, kidnapping, and aggravated assault. He broke into a home, threatened a married couple with a "board" and a knife, took the husband's money and car keys, and then raped the wife. He took the rape victim with him in the car; she escaped and notified police. When arrested, Coker was charged with a number of crimes, including rape. He was tried, found guilty of the charges, and under the provisions of *Gregg,* a jury sentenced him to death for rape (after considering his prior conviction for murder as well as whether the rape was committed while in the course of committing another felony).

In *Coker v. Georgia* (1977), the Court concluded that "a sentence of death is grossly disproportionate and excessive punishment for the crime of rape and is thereby forbidden by the Eighth Amendment as cruel and unusual punishment." In this opinion, authored by Justice White (in a 7 to 2 vote), the Court indicated that it "did not discount the seriousness of

rape as a crime," acknowledging that "Short of homicide . . . [rape] is the 'ultimate violation of self.' " However, the Court opined that "rape does not involve the taking of a life," and "Life is over for the victim of the murderer; for the rape victim, life may not be nearly so happy as it was, but it is not over and normally is not beyond repair."

Lockett v. Ohio

Sandra Lockett was found guilty of capital murder in Ohio, a state in which she was limited in her ability to introduce mitigating evidence during the sentencing phase of her trial to those factors specifically described in Ohio's death penalty statute. She challenged the constitutionality of this limitation, in part, arguing that she was deprived of the opportunity to fully inform the jury as to those factors that they may have considered that would have returned a penalty other than death.

In *Lockett v. Ohio* (1978), by a 6 to 2 vote, the Court held that the sentencer could "not be precluded from considering *as a mitigating factor,* any aspect of the defendant's character or record and any circumstances of the offense that the defendant offers as a basis for a sentence of less than death." In the opinion, authored by Chief Justice Burger, *Woodson*'s requirement for "individualized sentencing" was cited. He wrote, "We are satisfied that this qualitative difference between death and other penalties calls for a greater degree of reliability when the sentence of death is imposed."

Consequently, a defendant in a capital case cannot be limited in the type of mitigation he or she offers during the penalty phase of the trial. *Any* information regarding the defendant's background, as a child or as an adult, could be considered relevant. Thus, factors such as a history of childhood trauma (e.g., physical or sexual abuse), verbal abuse, exposure to drugs and alcohol, neglect and abandonment, undiagnosed or misdiagnosed conditions (e.g., mental retardation, emotional disturbance, learning disability, attention deficit/ hyperactivity disorder), gang or cult membership, or witnessing a death of a family member or friend could be considered nonstatutory mitigation. In addition, any circumstances related to the crime could be considered mitigating. Such nonstatutory factors as the minor role played by the defendant in the crime, his or her suggestibility or acquiescence to authority, perceived coercion, a sense of desperation based on real or imaginary beliefs, or a need for self-perceived moral retribution could be introduced as nonstatutory mitigators. *Lockett* requires defense attorneys and forensic psychological and psychiatric experts to explore *all* avenues of mitigation because the factors that can be introduced are not limited to those specifically delineated by statute.

Eddings v. Oklahoma

At the time of the crime, Monty Lee Eddings was 16 years of age and had run away from home with several younger companions in his brother's car. The youths were stopped by Officer Crabtree of the Oklahoma Highway Patrol. As the officer approached the car, Eddings shot him to death. Eddings was tried as an adult and convicted of capital murder. During the penalty phase of this trial, he offered evidence of "a turbulent family history, of beatings by a harsh father, and of serious emotional disturbance." The judge "as a mater of law" refused to consider this evidence. Eddings challenged this ruling as a violation of his 8th and 14th Amendment rights.

In a 5 to 4 decision, the Court held that Eddings's death sentence had been imposed without "individualized consideration of mitigating factors." Justice Powell, writing for the Court in *Eddings v. Oklahoma* (1982), opined that although the sentencer can decide how much weight to give a mitigating factor, if any, a judge cannot exclude a mitigating factor from consideration: "The evidence of a difficult family history and of emotional disturbance . . . should have been duly considered in sentencing." *Eddings* permits the introduction of any evidence regarding a capital defendant's family history and background as mitigation. Consequently, experts must make detailed inquiries into a defendant's past history, considering any and all potential areas of focus.

Barefoot v. Estelle

Thomas Barefoot was convicted of the murder of a police officer in Texas. During the sentencing phase of his capital trial, the jury considered, as required under Texas statute, "whether there is a probability that the defendant would commit criminal acts of violence that would constitute a continuing threat to society," an aggravating factor, which if established, might result in the imposition of death. Two psychiatrists testified, in response to a series of hypothetical questions, that such a probability did exist. Neither psychiatrist had personally examined the defendant, nor had they requested an opportunity to do so. Barefoot petitioned the Court, challenging the testimony of these experts on a number of grounds, including the lack of scientific basis to their opinions.

In *Barefoot v. Estelle* (1983), a 6 to 3 decision, the Court opined, "The suggestion that no psychiatrist's testimony may be presented with respect to a defendant's future dangerousness is somewhat like asking us to disinvent the wheel." Although acknowledging that such predictions may lack a sense of specificity, Justice White wrote that through cross-examination and rebuttal testimony of other experts, such opinions can be "countered not only as erroneous in a partic-

ular case, but also as generally so unreliable that it should be ignored." In addressing an *amicus* brief submitted by the American Psychiatric Association (1983) questioning the validity of opinions on future dangerousness, the Court again questioned whether "the factfinder and the adversarial system will not be competent to uncover, recognize, and take due account of its shortcomings." Also, the Court opined that there are psychiatrists with opposing views on this issue other than those presented in the *amicus* brief.

No fault was found with the experts' responses to hypothetical questions in this capital case, though this practice has been criticized in the forensic literature (Appelbaum, 1984; Davis, 1978; Green, 1984; Leong, Weinstock, Silva, & Eth, 1993). One psychiatrist, James Grigson, described Barefoot, to whom he had never spoken, as falling "within the 'most severe category' of sociopaths (on a scale of one to ten, Barefoot was 'above ten')." Dr. Grigson testified that "whether Barefoot was in society at large or in a prison society there was a 'one hundred percent and absolute' chance that Barefoot would commit future acts of violence that would constitute a continuing threat to society" (Justice Blackmun, dissent, at 1121). Dr. Grigson further testified that he was unfamiliar with studies demonstrating the inherent unreliability of psychiatric predictions of future dangerousness, but stated that those holding such opinions represented a "small minority group" of psychiatrists. Although a plurality of the Court apparently accepted Dr. Grigson's methodology, in July 1995, Dr. Grigson was expelled from the American Psychiatric Association for a pattern of similar conduct in death penalty cases (as described by J. Beck, 1996).

Justice Blackmun's dissenting opinion is of interest to forensic psychologists and psychiatrists involved in and familiar with the field of risk assessment research. He wrote that research demonstrates that "Psychiatric predictions of future dangerousness are not accurate; wrong two times out of three," citing the work of John Monahan (see the chapter by Monahan in this volume) and the writings of Stephen Morse (see Chapter 20). In addition, he opined: "In a capital case, the specious testimony of a psychiatrist, colored in the eyes of an impressionable jury by the inevitable untouchability of a medical specialist's words, equates with death itself." Justices Marshall and Brennan also authored a dissent in this case.

The Court held that testimony on the issue of future risk of violence was constitutional. Consequently, forensic psychologists and psychiatrists are permitted to testify on this issue both for defense and prosecution attorneys, as well as be called as rebuttal witnesses to examine the opinions reached by opposing experts and place such testimony in a more scientific context.

Skipper v. South Carolina

Ronald Skipper was convicted of capital murder and rape. During his sentencing hearing, the state introduced evidence of prior aggressive acts, including sexually assaultive behavior. In mitigation, the defendant presented testimony from his grandmother, mother, former wife, and sister. The defendant testified that during a prior period of incarceration, he had obtained his high school diploma and, if given a life sentence, he intended to work to contribute money to his family. Skipper attempted to introduce testimony from two prison guards and a regular visitor that he had "made a good adjustment" in jail during the seven and a half months between the time of his arrest and trial. The trial judge precluded him from doing so, ruling that such testimony would be irrelevant and inadmissible, stating, "'Whether [petitioner] can adapt or not adapt' was 'not an issue in this case.'" Skipper challenged the decision to exclude such mitigating testimony as a constitutional error.

In *Skipper v. South Carolina* (1986), the Court unanimously held that the exclusion of the testimony of the jailer and visitor denied Skipper the right to inform the sentencer of "all relevant evidence in mitigation of punishment." Justice White wrote that there was little dispute that testimony regarding the defendant's ability to adapt to incarceration might serve "as a basis for a sentence less than death." The role of the forensic expert in evaluating the adaptability of a defendant to a sentence of less than death may be a significant focus of a sentencing assessment. As the Court held, "Consideration of a defendant's past conduct as indicative of his probable future behavior is an inevitable and not undesirable element of criminal sentencing."

Ford v. Wainwright

Following the imposition of the death penalty, defendants are typically placed on an ultrasecure unit of a prison (i.e., death row) while awaiting the results of state and federal appeals (if they were filed). The conditions of confinement on such units can be highly stressful. The defendant is usually single-celled and permitted out of the cell for only short periods of time each day. The stress associated with waiting for the outcome of appeals, and eventually one's own impending execution (with the uncertainty of last-minute stays and commutations of sentence) adds to the underlying stress experienced by those who may have been emotionally damaged and disturbed before sentencing. Some death row inmates become psychotic or exhibit an exacerbation of psychotic symptoms during their tenure on death row. Consequently, it is not surprising that challenges have been filed as to the constitution-

ality of executing defendants who may demonstrate severe thought disorders.

Alvin Bernard Ford had been convicted of capital murder in Florida. Although no evidence of a mental illness or incompetence was noted at the time of the offense, at trial, or at sentencing, he began to "manifest changes in behavior" while awaiting execution. Experts reported his "pervasive delusion that he has become the target of a complex conspiracy, involving the Klan . . . designed to force him to commit suicide." He integrated the prison guards into his delusional system, believing that they were "killing people and putting the bodies in concrete enclosures used for beds." With regard to his death sentence, Ford acknowledged, "I know there is some sort of death penalty, but I'm free to go whenever I want, because it would be illegal and the executioner would be executed." Further, he believed, "I can't be executed because of the landmark case." Ford petitioned the Court that it would be a violation of the cruel and unusual punishments clause to execute him because of his incompetence.

In *Ford v. Wainwright* (1986), the Court (by a 5 to 4 vote) addressed this issue. Citing British common law, Justice Marshall, noted that "executing a prisoner who last lost his sanity . . . has been branded 'savage and inhuman.'" Although the reasons underlying this principle were unclear, Justice Marshall proposed religious, humane, general deterrence, and the belief that "madness is its own punishment" as factors contributing to this long-held belief. In addition, the Court noted that of the states having death penalty legislation at the time, 26 statutes explicitly barred the execution of the "insane." (The Court's use of the term "insane" connotes a condition related to incompetence to be executed rather than the traditional meaning, related to mental state at the time of the offense defense, as described in the chapter by Goldstein, Morse, & Shapiro in this volume.) No clear standard is stated by the Court to define those criteria associated with competence to be executed. Justice Powell, in a concurring opinion, wrote "that the Eighth Amendment forbids the execution only of those who are unaware of the punishment they are about to suffer and why they are to suffer it." As a result of this ruling, mental health experts may be called on to evaluate whether a death row inmate is competent to be executed.

Stanford v. Kentucky

Kevin Stanford, a 17-year-4-month-old defendant, and his accomplice raped and sodomized 20-year-old Barbel Pool. Stanford then shot Pool in the face and head. He was found guilty of capital murder. (In a companion case, Heath Wilkins was 16 years 6 months of age when he and an accomplice murdered a clerk in a store during a robbery, and was also convicted of capital murder.) Stanford argued that it was a violation of the cruel and unusual punishments clause of the 8th Amendment to impose the death penalty on those who were juveniles when they committed their murders.

In a 5 to 4 vote, the Court held that it was not a constitutional violation to impose death on juveniles. The Court's opinion in *Stanford v. Kentucky* (1989), written by Justice Scalia, denied the petitioners' arguments that the execution of juveniles was contrary to the "evolving standard of decency that marks the progress of a maturing society." As evidence that such a standard was not clearly established, the Court cited the 19 states at the time that had set no minimum age in their capital statutes. Arguments that focused on the minimum age (i.e., 18 or more) established for voting and drinking were rejected as well. The Court stated, "It is . . . absurd to think that one must be mature enough to drive carefully, to drink responsibly or to vote intelligently, in order to be mature enough to understand that murdering another human being is profoundly wrong." In addition, the Court opined that these minimum age requirements serve merely to reflect the belief that *most* people who are underage are insufficiently responsible to drive, drink and vote, without "individualized maturity tests" for each driver, drinker, or voter. The criminal justice system, and capital sentencing specifically, though, provides "individualized testing . . . [as] a constitutional requirement." *Stanford,* therefore, established the minimum age of death penalty eligibility as 16, although states can elect to set a higher age standard.

Atkins v. Virginia

Over the last decade, there has been a marked shift in public sentiment regarding execution of the mentally retarded; the majority of those surveyed no longer favors execution of those with mental retardation. In two landmark cases the U.S. Supreme Court addressed this issue, and reached differing majority opinions in each (*Atkins v. Virginia,* 2002; *Penry v. Lynaugh,* 1989).

Justice O'Connor, writing for the Court in *Penry v. Lynaugh* (1989), rejected the notion of a national consensus against execution of the mentally retarded, in part, stating that only two state statutes authorizing capital punishment forbade the execution of those with mental retardation. The Court, in a 5 to 4 vote, reasoned that if defendants were "profoundly or severely retarded and wholly lacking the capacity to appreciate the wrongfulness of their actions," they would most likely avoid conviction by the protection afforded by the insanity defense. Although there were no constitutional barriers to executing those with mental retardation, Justice

O'Connor wrote: "The sentencing body must be allowed to consider mental retardation as a mitigating circumstance in making individual determination whether death is appropriate in a particular case."

Because Penry's sentencing jury did not have an instruction to consider nor a mechanism to give effect to his mental retardation and history of abuse as mitigating factors in making a sentencing determination, he was granted a second penalty trial. He was again sentenced to death, but the U.S. Supreme Court issued a stay of execution, agreeing to examine whether in the second penalty phase, the new jury instructions permitted fair consideration of Penry's mental retardation. In *Penry v. Johnson* (2001), Justice O'Connor wrote, in a 6 to 3 decision, that the instructions provided to the jury were flawed such that a "reasoned moral response" to the mitigating evidence could not be made. A third penalty phase was ordered.

In *Atkins v. Virginia* (2002), the Court reversed itself, forbidding the execution of the mentally retarded, declaring it to be a violation of the Constitution. The petitioner, Daryl Renard Atkins, armed with a semiautomatic handgun, abducted Eric Nesbitt, robbed him, drove him to an automatic teller machine and forced him to withdraw additional funds. He took him to an isolated location, shot him eight times, killing him. Atkins was convicted of abduction, armed robbery, and capital murder and was sentenced to death. A forensic psychologist testified that Atkins had a Full Scale IQ of 59 and was "mildly mentally retarded," based on interviews with third parties and on school and court records.

Writing for the majority in a 6 to 3 decision, Justice Stevens referred to the "dramatic shift in state legislature landscape" since the initial *Penry* decision. When *Penry* was decided in 1989, two states prohibited the execution of the mentally retarded. Since then, 16 additional states have enacted such legislation. Justice Stevens wrote, "It is not so much the number of these states that is significant, but the consistency of the direction of change." In an environment supportive of anticrime legislation, the action of these states "provides powerful evidence that today our society views mentally retarded offenders as categorically less culpable than the average criminal." The Court reasoned, "Mentally retarded defendants in the aggregate face a special risk of wrongful execution," raising questions of "reliability and fairness of capital proceedings . . ." in such cases. States were given the task of establishing "ways to enforce the constitutional restriction upon its execution of sentences." In a dissenting opinion, Justice Scalia questioned whether 18 of the 38 states (47%) barring execution of the mentally retarded represents a national consensus. In addition, he opined that symptoms associated with mental retardation "can be readily feigned."

The implications of *Atkins v. Virginia* for forensic practice are clear. Defendants in capital cases are likely to raise questions regarding sub-average intellectual functioning, requiring objective evaluations of their intellectual functioning. Post-conviction assessments will be required to assist courts on ruling on the validity of claims of mental retardation for those on death rows awaiting execution.

ETHICAL ISSUES IN DEATH PENALTY ASSESSMENT

The U.S. Supreme Court stated in *Woodson v. North Carolina* (1976) that death is different. It is irrevocable. Mental health professionals retained to participate in *any* phase of a capital case (whether pretrial, guilt, or penalty phase, appeals process, or assessments of competence to be executed), face profound professional, ethical, and moral choices and responsibilities. Although the American Psychological Association's (APA) "Ethical Principles of Psychologists and Code of Conduct" (1992) guide psychologists' conduct in *all* professional relationships and activities, its import takes on additional significance in capital cases. Similarly, the expert in a capital case may be faced with legal-ethical conflicts not unlike those encountered in other forensic activities. In capital cases, however, the choices made by the forensic psychologist or psychiatrist literally may have life-or-death implications. Following the professional code of ethics in both letter and spirit (and consulting with informed colleagues) in capital cases is the only way to serve all parties: the defendant, the retaining attorney, the sentencer, your profession, and yourself.

Of particular ethical concern in capital cases are issues related to competence, whether psychologists should conduct assessments for the prosecutor, heightened implications of informed consent, and whether psychologists should be involved in assessing and restoring competence for execution. The limitations and problems with testimony related to future dangerousness are addressed in the risk assessment section later in the chapter.

Competence

In their chapter on forensic ethics in this volume, Weissman and DeBow eloquently advance an essential point: Following the ethical code and guidelines of the profession promotes the highest levels of professional competence. In no situation is professional competence more important than in death penalty cases. Some time ago, one of the present authors

(A. M. Goldstein) received a call from a psychologist who had recently been retained in a capital case. The psychologist wanted to view a tape of an expert offering trial testimony before she began her assessment. When asked what the aggravating factors were in this specific case, the psychologist did not recognize that concept. The psychologist then readily admitted that she had never performed any forensic work before, nor had she taken postdoctoral training in forensic psychology. Most troubling were her beliefs that "I'm a licensed clinical psychologist, so that's not a problem," and "I don't see any ethical issues in taking on this case." Simply stated, capital defendants are not guinea pigs for those without extensive training and experience in forensic psychology. When working in the criminal legal arena, experts need to be familiar with the need to obtain informed consent; the nature of special populations (often minorities); the legal standards controlling the focus of the assessment, the content of report, and the nature of expert testimony; specialized methodology, including forensic assessment instruments and forensically relevant instruments; limitations of tests and expert opinions; the requirement for sufficient data on which to base an opinion; and the imperative to present findings in a thorough, objective fashion. These prerequisites are described in general terms in APA's code of ethics and somewhat more specifically in the "Specialty Guidelines for Forensic Psychologists" (Committee on Ethical Guidelines for Forensic Psychologists, 1991).

Should Experts Offer Sentencing Testimony for Prosecutors in Capital Cases?

When retained by the prosecution in the guilt phase of a capital case, a forensic psychologist is most likely to be a potential rebuttal witness regarding the defendant's mental state at the time of the offense. It is difficult to make a case for any ethical prohibitions regarding testifying to a defendant's failure to meet the criteria of insanity in a capital trial. Although the stakes are higher (making the defendant eligible for capital sentencing), experts frequently appear as rebuttal witness in such cases without criticism of having violated the code of ethics.

Alternatively, the forensic psychologist may be retained by the state to potentially testify as to the presence of aggravating factors and absence of mitigating factors during the sentencing phase. It is equally as difficult to raise ethical objections regarding this role. (We distinguish between *ethical standards,* a professional code of conduct, and *moral positions,* attitudes based on personal beliefs and ideals). As stated by Bonnie (1990), "It would seem that clinical participation in capital cases [in general] is, in principle, no more or less problematic than forensic participation in any criminal cases" (p. 76). If experts refuse to conduct such assessments for the prosecutor, "the legal system would be deprived of evidence that is often essential to fair and reasonable administration of the law in capital cases" (p. 68). In addition, we contend that declining to participate may implicate a lack of objectivity on the part of the expert. Opinions are *not* based on the "side" retaining the expert, but rather, rely on the data, objectively considered. Objectivity is as important in capital cases as it is in any forensic assessment (Goldstein, 2001). In refusing to conduct an assessment, the defendant may be deprived of an objective, fair evaluation that could establish mitigating factors as well. The court, in turn, would be deprived of balanced testimony. Bonnie believes that although there is no ethical prohibition against being retained by the state, experts should decline to do so if "moral scruples" interfere with objectivity, tainting the fairness of the assessment process. Goldstein (2002) describes circumstances in which an expert may decline to participate in a forensic evaluation. Most involve situations in which the expert's objectivity may become clouded for personal or moral reasons.

The Team Approach

Virtually all forensic consultations that are "retained" by a party to the litigation present special ethical challenges (see the chapter by Weissman & DeBow in this volume). Notable among these are overidentifying with and subsequently advocating for the retaining party's desired outcome, rather than simply for the data. The group activity of a death penalty case creates a particularly fertile ground for this overidentification. To explain, the complexity of death penalty cases requires the participation of a group of professionals. At least two attorneys are appointed to represent the defendant, and the state also employs a panel of prosecutors. Both guilt-phase and sentencing-phase investigators routinely are involved, as well as support staff. Additionally, experts in various disciplines may contribute to the case analysis. The necessary joint involvement and interaction of this group, though, can contribute to group identification and group conformance. The defense or prosecuting attorneys may foster these group processes by referring to their own respective collection of investigators, support staff, and experts as a "team." When combined with the intense advocacy that characterizes the stances of both defense and prosecution litigators, "team" psychology can represent a hazard to the professional integrity of any who are involved in the case (Goldstein, 2001). Psychologists must be continuously vigilant of these influences—and draw clear boundaries for themselves as independent and objective professionals who may incorporate the information generated by the team, but are not team members.

Informed Consent

In *Estelle v. Smith* (1981), a Texas judge had requested that a psychiatrist (the same individual referred to previously in *Barefoot v. Estelle,* 1983) evaluate a capital defendant's competence for trial. Following a 90-minute evaluation, the psychiatrist testified that the defendant was competent; the guilt phase concluded with a finding of guilt and the trial proceeded to the penalty phase. Without additional contact with the defendant, the psychiatrist was called by the prosecutor and testified at sentencing as to defendant's lack of "regard for another human being's property or their life" and that as a "very severe sociopath," the defendant was not amenable to treatment. The jury found that the defendant was a future danger, an aggravating factor in Texas capital cases, and imposed a sentence of death. The U.S. Supreme Court reversed, holding that the defendant should have been informed that the results of the initial assessment for trial competence might be used against him during the sentencing phase of his trial (and that his attorney must be notified as well). The Court reasoned that a capital defendant has a right to exercise his 5th Amendment privilege and decline to participate. This decision serves to emphasize the ethical principle for psychologists that "clients" must be informed of the nature and purpose of the assessment, as well as the lack of confidentiality that will apply should the defendant agree to participate. This warning is consistent with the principle that psychologists also consider the rights of those with whom they work. Appelbaum (1981) discussed the implication of *Estelle* for the ethical practice of psychiatrists.

Issues of informed consent in death penalty cases extend beyond simple warnings, though. Even an interview of a defendant by a defense-retained mental health expert as part of a capital sentencing evaluation may have significant impact on the defendant's 5th and 6th Amendment rights. Depending on the jurisdiction, such an interview of the defendant may trigger access to the defendant by a state-retained expert who would not otherwise have been allowed this access (for an analysis of applicable federal statutes and case law, see *U.S. v. Beckford,* 1997). Similarly, if the defense-retained psychologist interviews the defendant regarding the capital offense or prior unadjudicated conduct, this may open the door to a state-retained expert inquiring about the same matters. Forensic psychologists have an obligation to be aware of how their activities may impact on the civil rights of those they evaluate, and direct their own conduct so that these rights are not diminished (Committee on Ethical Guidelines for Forensic Psychologists, 1991). Thus, it is critically important to discuss with defense counsel the implications of evaluating the defendant, and the content of such an interview.

These discussions should educate defense counsel regarding how the presence or absence of evaluation access or data may impact on the expert's role or conclusions. For example, should the defense determine not to make the defendant available for evaluation by the State, the defense-retained psychologist may function as a teaching rather than evaluating witness. (See discussion of roles of expert witnesses later in chapter.) In discussions regarding interview content, defense counsel should be appraised that the defendant's account of thoughts, feelings, and actions at the time of the capital offense are likely to be of fundamental importance in asserting diminished capacity, extreme emotional disturbance, or other grossly aberrant "mental state" as a mitigating factor at sentencing. If such assertions are not contemplated, however, the defendant's description of the capital offense may have little bearing on the sentencing evaluation findings. Specifically, the defendant's account of the crime provides little to no information, beyond what can already by gleaned from offense reports, regarding the adverse developmental factors and experiences that typically comprise the large portion of mitigating evidence at sentencing. (See discussion of mitigation later in chapter.) In most instances, the violence risk assessment at capital sentencing is also not compromised by the absence of the defendant's "confession" to the evaluator—particularly since the context of the assessment is prison or old age parole. (See discussion of risk assessment later in chapter.)

State-retained experts have additional obligations beyond notifying the defendant of their state-retained role and the intended purpose of the evaluation. A state-retained expert must verify that defense counsel is aware of the pending evaluation, the agreed-on parameters of any interview regarding the capital offense or unadjudicated conduct, and how the evaluation will be memorialized. State-retained experts should take care in building rapport and using empathy in capital sentencing evaluations, as the combination of these techniques and the expert's professional identification as a psychologist may contribute to a misplaced anticipation of benevolence and a setting-aside of the initial interview warnings (Showalter, 1990).

As a result of restricted access to the defendant, limitations on interview content, or a "teaching" rather than "examining" witness role (see discussion of roles later in this chapter), the psychologist may lack complete evaluation findings specific to the defendant. Although some opinions may be presented with an "incomplete data set," ethical standards limit testimony to what is supported by the data, and

further require that the trier of fact be informed regarding the limitations of opinions.

Should Experts Offer Testimony Regarding Competence to Be Executed?

Ford v. Wainwright (1986) requires that a defendant be competent as a prerequisite to execution, and experts may be asked to conduct forensic assessment focusing on this psycholegal issue. If a finding of competence is made, the consequence will be the execution of the defendant. Questions are raised as to whether participation in these evaluations is ethical. As stated by Leong et al. (1993), "When evaluating an inmate's competence to be executed, is the finding of the elements of competence tantamount to active participation in the actual death penalty process?" (p. 43).

Bonnie (1990), in addressing this issue, finds no easy answer. Consistent with his position on conducting *any* forensic capital assessment, a major factor for him is the moral scruples of the expert, making this a personal rather than an ethical question. However, Bonnie reasoned that if one's personal beliefs are such that they might interfere with conducting an objective assessment, then the issue becomes an ethical one. Under such circumstances, declining to participate in the evaluation would be the ethical response. In addition, Bonnie argued that if the expert conducts execution competency evaluations, the findings may "promote informed legal decision making and therefore seem more analogous to participation in the trial process than to administration of a lethal inject" (p. 80). He opined that participation in such assessments is not ethically prohibited.

Brodsky (1990) commented on the vagueness of the criteria used to assess competence for execution and the lack of objective instruments or tools to include in the evaluation process. He stated, "The vaguer the goals and criteria are for any given task, the more likely the clinician is to utilize her or his own values" (p. 92). Under such conditions, refusing to conduct these evaluations is neither an act of petulance, nor does it represent avoidance of a societal responsibility: "Rather, it is in part a respect for their own diminished *objectivity*" (p. 92, emphasis added).

Leong and colleagues (1993) found no ethical consensus on this topic, but pointed out that if experts refrain from conducting these evaluations, "an 'insane' prisoner could face execution illegally" (p. 43). Ferris (1997) differentiated that although the participation of psychiatrists in these assessments is not considered unethical, it is ethically unacceptable to provide treatment to restore competence when the sole purpose to do so is to permit an execution to proceed. A. Freedman and Halpern (1999) offered another view.

Disagreeing with the position adopted by the American Medical Association (1995), they argued that participation in competence to be executed evaluations "is unethical because it gives the medical profession a decisive role with respect to the final legal obstacle to execution" (p. 630).

In a study of psychiatrists' attitudes toward participating in a range of death penalty assessments, Leong, Silva, Weinstock, and Ganzini (2000) reported, "There was little agreement among forensic psychiatrists about the acceptability of capital punishment or the role of psychiatrists in capital cases" (p. 428). Only 8.5% believed that is unethical to participate in *any* phase of a capital case. They reported that "22.3 percent felt that pretrial or trial competence evaluations were ethically permissible, but competence for execution evaluations were not" (p. 428). The views of forensic psychiatrists on the ethicality of involvement in various phases of capital cases were associated with their attitudes on the ethical permissibility of capital punishment, but were not totally determinative.

Should Experts Provide Treatment to Those Found Incompetent to Be Executed?

As stated by Leong et al. (1993), "If a condemned prisoner is determined to be incompetent to be executed, is treating the mental disorder in an attempt to restore that person's competence actively participating in the death penalty process?" (p. 43). Ferris (1997) answered this question in the affirmative. He cited the American Medical Association's (1995) statement that providing such treatment is ethically unacceptable (unless "to relieve extreme suffering"; p. 747). He argued, "Almost without exception, treatment that restores or maintains competence to be executed clearly assists the executioner at the condemned patient's expense . . . [and] it should be ethically proscribed" (p. 747). Despite ethical prohibitions against doing so, it is interesting to note that Leong et al. (2000) found that 46.4% of the forensic psychiatrists they surveyed believed that the condemned should receive treatment to restore competence.

Bonnie (1990) viewed this question as a complex one, with no single answer. Those who believe that it is *never* permissible to provide such treatment base their opinion on the assumption "that death is *always* the greater harm, and that treatment to restore competence therefore offends the clinician's ethical duty to avoid harm *in all cases*" (p. 83). In some cases, the condemned may have indicated, in a living will, a desire to have competence restored, preferring death to a life of untreated mental illness. Under such circumstances, Bonnie argued that it may be ethical to treat those who have made it known that they want to be treated. If no preference is known, Bonnie asserted that it is permissible to assume that

no treatment would be wanted by the condemned under the circumstances. In light of a prisoner's "unequivocal preference for life, I see no way to justify treating the patient on the ground that it is beneficial to him" (p. 85).

Even if a defendant indicates a preference for death in accepting treatment to restore competency to be executed, this election may not represent a rational choice—given that the defendant is mentally ill. Further, such an election may be a reaction to the arduous conditions of confinement on death row—and thus be less than fully voluntary (Brodsky, 1990). These complicating factors, related to informed consent, further add to the dilemmas faced by experts in addressing this issue.

THE NATURE OF FORENSIC ASSESSMENTS IN CAPITAL CASES

Pretrial Evaluations

Although detailed discussion of evaluations of various competencies and mental state at time of offense is beyond the scope of this chapter, several issues have particular implications in death penalty cases. (For a comprehensive discussion of these topics, see the chapters by Oberland, Goldstein, & Goldstein; Stafford; and Goldstein, Morse, & Shapiro all in this volume). First, the complexity and issues integral to capital cases may call for the defendant to possess greater capacity to understand and assist than is required in other criminal prosecutions. Adequate assessment of trial competency then requires consideration of the intersection of the abilities of the defendant in the face of the situational demands of the specific context (Grisso, 1986). In addition, a period of weeks and even months of jury selection precedes some capital trials. The entire process of a bifurcated trial may take additional weeks or months, during which time the defendant is expected to be present and attentive to courtroom proceedings and tolerate the stress of having his or her life hanging in the balance. These factors must be considered in conducting fitness-for-trial assessments in capital cases.

Second, a finding of competency to stand trial in a capital case may ultimately have more profound applications than is superficially apparent. A defendant's waiver of counsel, refusal to cooperate with a psychological evaluation, guilty plea in the absence of a sentencing agreement, election of whether to testify, acceptance of trial strategy, failure to disclose mitigating history, courtroom behavior, and other important decisions are likely ultimately to be viewed through the lens of the competency findings.

Third, inquiry into mental state at time of the offense may be determined to have effectively waived the defendant's 5th

Amendment rights. There is thus the potential that this information may be introduced at sentencing regarding the defendant's risk of future violence or to address other aggravating assertions. For this reason, forensic psychologists generally should avoid assessment of both guilt-phase and sentencing-phase psycholegal issues in the same capital case, and should thoroughly discuss with defense counsel the implications of dual assessments before they are undertaken.

Evaluation Parameters

Either the defense or the prosecution may request psychological evaluations for capital sentencing. Regardless of who is requesting the consultation, the assessment is likely to involve one or both of the two primary psycholegal issues at this stage:

1. What factors are present that may be relevant to mitigation and aggravation?
2. What is the likelihood that the defendant will commit acts of serious violence in the future?

Conceptualizations and research integral to these two primary psycholegal issues at capital sentencing are briefly reviewed in the sections that follow. Before that discussion, it is acknowledged that mitigation and violence risk assessment do not encompass the entirety of considerations before the court at capital sentencing. The nature and circumstances of the offense, as well as various aggravating factors, are also aspects of death penalty determinations. The features of the offense, criminal history of the defendant, and the presence of any aggravators, however, typically represent factual determinations or social values—where psychologists possess no special expertise (Melton, Petrila, Poythress, & Slobogin, 1997). Mitigation and violence risk assessment, in contrast, represent arenas where important empirical findings can be brought to bear to assist the court in making more scientifically informed determinations.

Evaluation of Mental State at the Time of the Offense

Capital murder trials often involve heinous behavior on the part of the defendant. The violence of the crime, how the murder occurred, and other "special circumstances" were likely among the factors considered by the prosecutor in determining to track a case as a murder for which the death penalty is sought. Typically, the prosecutor has a high degree of confidence that the defendant will be found guilty, justifying the outlay of time and money necessary to prosecute such

a case. The evidence against the defendant is often close to irrefutable. Consequently, it is not surprising that defense attorneys often functionally stipulate to their client's guilt, in part to avoid inflaming a jury by presenting an argument for innocence that cannot be supported. The hope is that the sentencer's perceptions of the attorneys' candor and goodwill may carry over into the penalty phase, thereby increasing the likelihood of a sentence of less than death. As one death penalty defense attorney aptly phrased: "A death penalty case involves a crime that deserves severe punishment and a person who merits mercy" (Popkin, 2000).

At times, however, the evidence may not be so ironclad and the attorney may attempt to offer a defense during the trial phase. In some cases, there may be questions regarding the defendant's mental state at the time of the offense (MSO). In these cases, the attorney may raise the defenses of diminished capacity or extreme emotional disturbance (if they exist in that jurisdiction) or may raise an insanity defense, as described in the chapter by Goldstein, Morse, and Shapiro in this volume. The same methodology would be used in capital MSO cases as are employed in noncapital cases where the *mens rea* of a defendant is at question.

Mitigation in Capital Cases

The U.S. Supreme Court in *Lockett v. Ohio* (1978) described mitigation at capital sentencing as including: "any aspect of a defendant's character or record, or any of the circumstances of the offense that the defendant proffered as a basis for a sentence less than death." What may be considered mitigating, then, is extraordinarily broad and multifaceted.

Central to many of these potential mitigating factors is the concept of moral culpability, or what the U.S. Supreme Court in *Woodson v. North Carolina* (1976) characterized as "the diverse frailties of humankind." The concept of moral culpability begins with a recognition that is fundamental to psychology as a science: that human beings and their choices are shaped and influenced by their genetic, neurological, intellectual, developmental, psychological, interpersonal, educational, cultural, and community histories (Cunningham & Reidy, 2001). It follows that the degree of "blameworthiness" of an individual for criminal or even murderous conduct may vary depending on what factors and experiences shaped, influenced, and compromised that choice. In other words, although equally *criminally* responsible, capital defendants may vary in their *moral* culpability and, ultimately, in their blameworthiness.

The distinction between criminal responsibility and moral culpability is an important one. As a psycholegal issue, criminal responsibility involves guilt-phase considerations of wrongful awareness, purposeful behavior, and volition. In contrast, moral culpability implicates sentencing-phase issues of formative and situational influences and associated risk factors for adverse outcomes (e.g., *Eddings v. Oklahoma,* 1982; *Penry v. Lynaugh,* 1989). Unless carefully attuned to these subtle but important differences, the forensic psychologist may answer the wrong psycholegal issue at capital sentencing (Cunningham & Reidy, 2001).

An obvious tension is present at capital sentencing between the perspective of the defense and that of the prosecution regarding moral culpability. The defense theory at sentencing is typically deterministic, embracing the view that biopsychosocial factors underlie violent criminal behavior, and applying associated risk factors present in the defendant's life to the analysis of his or her moral culpability. In contrast, the perspective advanced by the prosecution emphasizes the operation of willful choice, asserting that "a defendant's crime stems entirely from his evil makeup and that he therefore deserves to be judged and punished exclusively on the basis of his presumably free, morally blameworthy choices" (Haney, 1997, p. 1459).

It is not surprising, in light of the divergent sentencing theories of the defense and prosecution, that a psychologist is more likely to be called by the defense to testify regarding both the defendant's history and the empirical research relevant to the impact of these factors. The role of a psychologist retained by the state is more likely to entail potential rebuttal testimony regarding the observations or conclusions of the defense-retained expert.

How Empirical Findings Illuminate Mitigation

The importance of investigating a wide range of factors in evaluations of mitigation at capital sentencing is supported by a number of lines of research: (a) investigations of the relationship of risk and protective factors to criminal violence in the community; (b) reports on death row samples; (c) studies reporting the effects of various adverse developmental experiences and contexts; and (d) research on the relationship of mental disorders to disrupted development and criminal outcome. The factors identified in these areas of research can be employed as an outline of factors to explore in a comprehensive mental health evaluation of mitigation at capital sentencing (see Cunningham & Reidy, 2001). These each are summarized briefly below.

First, the U.S. Department of Justice (DOJ) has sponsored research on risk and protective factors associated with chronic delinquency and serious violence in the community. A 1995 DOJ summary details these risk factors by developmental age (see Table 21.1). Consistent with the conceptual-

TABLE 21.1 U.S. Department of Justice Model: Risk Factors for Violence and Delinquency in the Community

Conception to Age 6	Age 6 through Adolescence
• Perinatal difficulties. • Family history of criminal behavior and substance abuse. • Parental attitudes favorable toward, and parental involvement in, crime and substance abuse. • Minor physical abnormalities. • Family management problems. • Family conflict. • Brain damage.	• Extreme economic deprivation. • Community disorganization and low neighborhood attachment. • Parental attitudes favorable toward, and parental involvement in, crime and substance abuse. • Availability of firearms. • Media portrayals of violence. • Family management problems. • Family conflict. • Early and persistent antisocial behavior. • Academic failure. • Lack of commitment to school. • Alienation and rebelliousness. • Association with peers who engage in delinquency and violence. • Favorable attitudes toward delinquent and violent behavior. • Constitutional factors (e.g., low intelligence, hyperactivity, attention-deficit disorders).

Source: Adapted from "Guidelines for Implementing the Comprehensive Strategy for Serious, Violent, and Chronic Juvenile Offenders" by U.S. Department of Justice, Office of Justice Programs, Office of Juvenile Justice and Delinquency Prevention (June 1995).

izations of Masten and Garmezy (1985), DOJ researchers assert that the outcomes of adolescents and young adults reflect the interaction or balancing of risk and protective factors.

Research findings regarding risk factors for youth violence in the community are expanded by Hawkins et al. (2000), who report on the analysis of longitudinal data, research reports, and 66 published studies. Table 21.2 summarizes the individual, family, school, peer-related, and community/ neighborhood categories of risk factors identified in this DOJ-sponsored report. These risk factors are described as having a cumulative impact on the likelihood of violence by early adulthood.

Other DOJ-sponsored longitudinal studies have found a disproportionate incidence of arrest and violence among teens and young adults who suffered maltreatment during childhood (Kelley, Thornberry, & Smith, 1997; Widom, 2000). Similarly, Thornberry (1994) found that hostility, observed violence, and personal violent victimization within the family had a cumulative risk impact on violence rates. Other prestigious governmental publications (e.g., U.S. Department of Health and Human Services, 1999), also detail ways that neglect and traumatic experience may deflect the developmental trajectory.

TABLE 21.2 U.S. Department of Justice Model: Predictors of Youth Violence

Individual Psychological Factors	*School Factors*
• Hyperactivity, concentration problems, restlessness, and risk taking. • Aggressiveness. • Early initiation of violent behavior. • Involvement in other forms of antisocial behavior. • Beliefs and attitudes favorable to deviant or antisocial behavior.	• Academic failure. • Low bonding to school. • Truancy and dropping out of school. • Frequent school transitions. *Peer-Related Factors* • Delinquent siblings. • Delinquent peers. • Gang membership.
Family Factors	*Community and Neighborhood Factors*
• Parental criminality. • Child maltreatment. • Poor family management practices. • Low levels of parental involvement. • Poor family bonding and family conflict. • Parental attitudes favorable to substance use and violence. • Parent-child separation.	• Poverty. • Community disorganization. • Availability of drugs and firearms. • Neighborhood adults involved in crime. • Exposure to violence and racial prejudice.

Source: From "Predictors of Youth Violence" by J. D. Hawkins, T. I. Herrenkohl, D. P. Farrington, D. Brewer, R. F. Catalano, T. W. Harachi, and L. Cothern. U.S. Department of Justice, Office of Justice Programs, Office of Juvenile Justice and Delinquency Prevention (April 2000).

Government-sponsored research and publications relevant to mitigation conceptualizations are emphasized for two reasons. First, these research summaries are quite comprehensive and reflect the involvement of researchers of substantial stature. Second, the origins of the research almost entirely insulate the findings from being ridiculed as an "abuse excuse."

A second source of empirical guidance in capital sentencing mitigation evaluations is provided by descriptions of death row samples. This research has been critically reviewed and summarized by Cunningham and Vigen (in press). As reflected in Table 21.3, clinical evaluations of death row inmate samples have revealed a significant incidence of intellectual limitations, poor academic achievement, psychological disorders, neurological insult and neuropsychological findings, family-of-origin histories of child maltreatment and abuse, parental substance dependence, and preincarceration substance dependence. These represent factors that adversely affect development and may be of mitigating significance to the court.

Third, comprehensive capital sentencing evaluations are supported by empirical literature on the broadly disruptive effects and resultant vulnerabilities associated with numerous adverse developmental factors. For example, the likelihood that a young male will engage in criminal activity doubles if he is raised without a father and triples if he lives in a neighborhood with a high concentration of single-mother households (Hill & O'Neil, 1993). Further, it is notable that 72% of adolescent murderers grew up without fathers (Cornell, Benedek, & Benedek, 1987), and 70% of juveniles in state reform institutions grew up in a single or no-parent context (Beck, Kline, & Greenfield, 1988). Other adverse developmental factors include having a teenage mother, receiving inadequate parental supervision and limit setting, being estranged from peers, observing community violence, modeling on corruptive family members, and being personally victimized (Cunningham & Reidy, 2001). Goldstein and Goldstein (in press) discuss the role of various childhood traumas as mitigating factors in capital cases.

Fourth, the presence of a mental disorder can be relevant as a risk factor for a defendant's involvement in violent behavior in the community (Showalter, 1990; Swanson, Holzer, Granju, & Jono, 1990). Detailing the vulnerabilities, such as substance dependence and inadequate social supports, which are associated with many psychological disorders can be important in explaining the psychological and behavioral progression that culminated in the capital offense (Haney, 1995).

Practical Components of Mitigation Assessments

The range of biopsychosocial factors that should be considered in a capital mitigation evaluation is arguably broader than in any other type of forensic assessment (Cunningham & Reidy, 2001; Liebert & Foster, 1994; Norton, 1992; Stetler, 1999). Indeed, the U.S. Supreme Court in *Eddings v. Oklahoma* (1982) held that at capital sentencing, the trial court cannot refuse to consider *any* mitigating information. Thus, forensic psychologists conducting mitigation evaluations are screening for *any* factors that might adversely affect physical, cognitive, neuropsychological, psychological, interpersonal, social, academic, vocational, civic, and moral development, as well as for positive behavior contributions that might be viewed as having some balancing value in the weighing of moral blameworthiness. Accordingly, the evaluation components are unusually comprehensive and thorough.

Assuming that the defendant submits to evaluation, direct interviews should elicit a comprehensive and highly detailed anecdotal multigenerational biopsychosocial history. Descriptions of specific events, particularly traumatic experiences, can assist the court in understanding the emotional realities of the defendant's childhood. Obtaining a history in this comprehensive detail routinely requires 8 to 20 hours of interview with the defendant, exclusive of any psychological testing. Not infrequently, a collateral benefit of extended and repeated interviewing is increased disclosure—an important counter to the tendency of defendants and their families to minimize or conceal mitigating information (Cunningham & Reidy, 2001; Dekleva, 2001).

TABLE 21.3 Clinical Studies of Death Row Inmates

Study	State	Sample	IQ Score	Education	Psychological Symptoms	Neurological Findings	History
Bluestone & McGahee (1962)	NY	N = 19	37% ≤ IQ 79 74% ≤ IQ 89	63% < 6th grade 100% < h.s. grad	32% delusional. Pervasive maladaptive defenses.		95% father absent. Most reared in foster/institu.
Gallemore & Panton (1972)	NC	N = 8	M = IQ 95.6 (Beta) IQ range = 76–118	M = 9.5 (schooling) Range = 6–12th M = 5.6 (achievement) Range = 1.9–8th	37% poor death row adjustment. All elevated MMPI depression scale		All poverty/psych problems in family. 50% not reared by both par. 87% heavy etoh abuse.
Panton (1976)	NC	N = 34	M = IQ 90.7 IQ range = 74–125	M = 9.4 (schooling) Range = 4–14	Higher MMPI Pa and Sc scales than general population inmates.		
Panton (1978)	NC	N = 55	M = IQ 96.5 (SD = 12.2)	M = 9.8 (SD = 2.2)	Higher MMPI Pa and Sc scales. Symptoms subsided if commuted.		
Lewis (1979)	FL	N = 83	Reported as similar to community distribution	M = 9.7 (schooling) 9.6% < 6th grade	41% diagnosed psych. disorder.		42% not reared by both par. 81% intoxicated at offense.
Johnson (1979)	AL	N = 35			Pervasive depression, mood lability, reduced mental acuity.		
Smith & Felix (1986)	NC	N = 34	Estimated average IQ from brief mental status	58% < h.s. grad Range = 9–12th	Use of denial, suppression, undoing.		Divorce & separation freq. Unsupportive families freq.
Lewis et al. (1986)	5 states	N = 15	M = 86.5 (WAIS-R) IQ range = 50–100	1–12th (achievement) All had islands of poor literacy	40% chronic psychosis. 20% episodic psychosis. 13% bipolar.	33% major impairments. 47% minor neuro. signs. 100% head injuries.	60% child/adol. psych dis. 27% attempted suicide in child/adolescence.
Lewis et al. (1988) (<18 yrs at offense)	4 states	N = 14	M = 83.9 (WAIS-R) SD = 14.3 IQ range = 64–121	M = 7.6 reading comp. M = 6.2 concept form. W-J range = 1–19.9	50% current or past psychosis. 29% severe mood disorders. 21% periodic paranoia.	64% maj. neuro. abnorm. 57% head injury req hosp and/or indenting cranium.	86% phys abused. 36% sex abuse by male rel. Fam. viol/etoh depend. freq.
Evans (1997)		N = 11					
Frierson et al. (1998)	SC	N = 18	M = IQ 90.3 IQ range = 50–122 28% ≤ borderline or MR			24% LOC head injury. Half had abnormal EEG, MRI, neurological exam.	78% sub. abuse disorder. Half intoxicated at offense.
Cunningham & Vigen (1999)	MS	N = 39	M = VIQ 81.5 (WAIS-R) SD = 10.7 IQ range = 58–103 27% ≤ IQ 74	M = 9th (schooling) SD = 2.3 M = 5.1 reading comp. SD = 2.87 WIAT range = 1.2–12+	50% mod-extreme depress (R-BDI). 71% mult PAI scale elevations > T70. 43% reported depression. 30% reported anxiety. 5% psychotic.	46% neurological insults.	57% sub. abusing parent. 73% sub. abuse/depend.
Freedman & Hemenway (2000)	CA	N = 16	69% ≤ borderline or MR	38% illiterate	56% psychosis with hallucinations. 81% severe depression. 88% posttraumatic stress disorder.	12 traumatic brain injury. 12 devel. or cog. impaired. 3 fetal etoh syn./effects.	81% polysub abusers. 88% abused phys/sex. 94% wit. family violence. 94% institutional failure.

MMPI = Minnesota Multiphasic Personality Inventory (Hathaway & McKinley, 1982); PAI = Personality Assessment Inventory (Morey, 1991); R-BDI = Revised–Beck Depression Inventory (Beck & Steer, 1988); WAIS-R = Wechsler Adult Intelligence Scale–Revised (Wechsler, 1981); WIAT = Wechsler Individual Achievement Test (Psychological Corporation, 1992); W-J = Woodcock-Johnson Psycho-Educational Battery (Woodcock & Johnson, 1977).

Source: From "Death Row Inmate Characteristics, Adjustment, and Confinement: A Critical Review of the Literature" by M. D. Cunningham and M. P. Vigen. *Behavioral Sciences and the Law* (in press).

The history provided by the defendant should be confirmed, whenever possible, by third parties and records (see the chapter by Heilbrun, Warren, & Picarello in this volume). Additionally, there may be important history that the defendant does not recall or has failed to report. For this reason, it is customary in capital mitigation evaluations for extensive interviewing of family, teachers, health-care providers, and other third parties to occur. These may be directly obtained by the psychologist; alternatively, the psychologist may rely on interview summaries detailed by social workers, investigators, or mitigation specialists.

The extent of record retrieval and review is uniquely comprehensive in capital mitigation evaluations. Not uncommonly, efforts are made to recover virtually *all* records associated with a defendant's life (i.e., medical, mental health, social service, academic, juvenile, military, criminal).

Neuropsychological and neurological consultations are indicated in most capital cases. This recommendation is based on two primary rationales. First, should neuropsychological deficits or neurological disorder be identified, this brain dysfunction and its potential association with violent acts may be a significant mitigating factor in a jury's deliberation. Second, there is a growing body of research that identifies brain dysfunction as a risk factor for serious violence. For example, a disproportionate incidence of neurological abnormalities has been found among murderers and violent felons (Blake, Pincus, & Buckner, 1995; Langevin, Ben-Aron, Wortzman, Dickey, & Handy, 1987; Martell, 1992). Six studies of death row samples reported a notable incidence of neurologically significant histories among these condemned inmates (Cunningham & Vigen, 1999; Evans, 1997; Freedman & Hemenway, 2000; Frierson, Schwartz-Watts, Morgan, & Malone, 1998; Lewis et al., 1986, 1988).

As the expert gathers a comprehensive biopsychosocial history, other factors or potential disorders may be identified that warrant referral for more specialized consultation. Consultations may be indicated in neuroradiology, endocrinology, mental retardation, psychobiology, toxicology, psychopharmacology, genetics, learning disabilities, addiction medicine, community violence, and other highly specialized areas of expertise.

Personality testing in capital sentencing evaluations remains controversial (Cunningham & Reidy, 2001). Proponents of personality testing note that these techniques often increase the richness of the evaluation, illuminate the defendant's response style, allow for systematic comparisons with norm groups (imparting objectivity to the process), and aid in diagnostic and psychodynamic formulations. Additionally, the incidence of psychological disorders among murderer defendants (Blake et al., 1995; Yarvis, 1990) as well as death

row inmates (Cunningham & Vigen, in press) suggests that careful screening for major psychological disorders could be important to mitigation considerations.

Opponents to routine personality assessment in capital sentencing evaluations express concerns that these tests (a) have not been well-normed on a prison or capital defendant population; (b) generate profiles that routinely change over time (Clements, 1996; Craig, 1996); (c) are only inferentially related to mental state at time of offense; (d) are likely to reveal maladaptive personality traits but without providing information on etiology or formative developmental experiences; (e) are not predictive of long-range prison violence (Cunningham & Reidy, 1998a, 1998b, 1999; Kennedy, 1986; Reidy, Cunningham, & Sorensen, 2001; Zager, 1988); and (f) are subject to mischaracterization and ridicule in the adversarial climate of a capital trial. Forensic psychologists are encouraged to carefully consider these contrasting positions and how these intersect with the referral questions and defendant history in a specific case. Arguably, these issues are germane to informed consent as well.

VIOLENCE RISK ASSESSMENT IN CAPITAL CASES

Formal and widespread consideration of the future violence risk of a capital defendant in assessing the death penalty was initiated in the aftermath of *Furman v. Georgia,* as previously described. This 1972 Supreme Court decision held that the death penalty as it was then being practiced in the United States was unconstitutional. As state death penalty statutes were narrowed and particularized to comply with *Furman,* the Texas legislature crafted a special issue: "Is there is a probability that the defendant will commit criminal acts of violence that would constitute a continuing threat to society?" (Texas Code of Criminal Procedure 37.071.2). This statute was affirmed by the U.S. Supreme Court in *Jurek v. Texas* (1976) and subsequently adopted by Oregon. Rather than a necessary jury finding in returning a death verdict, most jurisdictions (21 states) allow for future dangerousness to be considered as a statutory aggravator at capital sentencing (McPherson, 1996). Future dangerousness has come to be a routine allegation as a nonstatutory aggravator in federal capital prosecutions. Between January 1, 1995, and May 10, 2001, future dangerousness was alleged against 129 of 154 (84%) federal capital defendants in notices of aggravating circumstances (M. O'Donnell, personal communication, May 17, 2001).

Interest in the likelihood that a capital defendant will exhibit serious violence is not restricted to the prosecution. The defense may introduce evidence that the defendant will make a positive adjustment to prison for the jury's consideration as a mitigating factor, as provided by *Skipper v. South Carolina* (1986).

Even when not overtly argued by the state or the defense, the future dangerousness of capital offenders appears to be a primary concern to capital jurors (Blume, Garvey, & Johnson, 2001; Bowers & Steiner, 1999; Costanzo & Costanzo, 1992; Geimer & Amsterdam, 1988; Sandys, 1991). In fact, jurors tend to overestimate the likelihood of future violence of those inmates they have sentenced to death, as well as for sentences other than death (Marquart, Ekland-Olson, & Sorensen, 1989; Sorensen & Pilgrim, 2000).

Common Errors in Violence Risk Assessment at Capital Sentencing

The involvement of mental health professionals in predictions of future dangerousness in capital sentencing has been among the most controversial in the arena of risk assessment (Cunningham & Reidy, 1998b, 1999; Ewing, 1983; Leong et al., 1993; Worrell, 1987). Too commonly, this participation has been accompanied by notoriously defective risk assessment methodology and testimony that grossly overestimated both the likelihood of serious prison violence and the accuracy of the prediction (*Barefoot v. Estelle*, 1983; Cunningham & Reidy, 1999; *Estelle v. Smith*, 1981). Cunningham and Reidy described common errors in violence risk assessment and associated mental health expert testimony at capital sentencing (see Table 21.4). Of these common errors, three are particularly noteworthy.

First, mental health experts continue to neglect the dominance of context in their capital violence risk assessments, using factors from community-based literature that are either

TABLE 21.4   Common Errors in Violence Risk Assessment at Capital Sentencing

- Inadequate reliance on base rates.
- Failure to consider context.
- Susceptibility to illusory correlation.
- Failure to define severity of violence.
- Overreliance on clinical interview.
- Misapplication of psychological testing.
- Faulty implications of antisocial personality disorder and psychopathy.
- Ignoring the effects of aging.
- Misuse of patterns of behavior.
- Neglect of preventive measures.
- Insufficient data.
- Failure to express risk estimate in probabilistic terms.

Source: From "Don't Confuse Me With the Facts: Common Errors in Violence Risk Assessment at Capital Sentencing" by M. D. Cunningham and T. J. Reidy. *Criminal Justice and Behavior, 26,* 20–43 (1999).

pervasively present in an incarcerated population or have not been demonstrated to be predictive in a prison context. This neglect of context persists even though multiple authorities (Hall, 1987; Monahan, 1981; Shah, 1978) have concluded that risk is always a function of context. Further, factors that are associated with violence in the community do not demonstrate the same relationship with prison violence (Alexander & Austin, 1992; Cunningham & Reidy, 1998a, 1998b, 1999, in press; National Institute of Corrections, 1992; Reidy et al., 2001).

Second, many psychologists remain ignorant of or fail to rely on base rate data regarding the frequency of serious violence in prison in making violence risk assessment regarding particular defendants. Shah (1978) described this problem over 20 years ago, noting that even forensic clinicians tend to ignore base rates in the face of specific information or when confronted with a specific individual.

Third, many mental health experts continue to attach unsubstantiated violence risk implications to antisocial personality disorder (APD) or related diagnostic formulations, concluding that such conditions create a high probability that the defendant will seriously assault or kill someone in prison. Such assertions are not supported by empirical data—hardly surprising given the 49% to 80% prevalence rate of APD among American prison inmates (Cunningham & Reidy, 1998a; Meloy, 1988; Widiger & Corbitt, 1995). Additionally, the weaknesses of APD as a diagnostic construct are quite problematic in a life-or-death determination (Cunningham & Reidy, 1998a). Concerns regarding applications of APD to capital risk assessment are not a recent development. The 1984 *Report of the Task Force on the Role of Psychiatry in the Sentencing Process* (Halleck, Applebaum, Rappeport, & Dix, 1984) concluded: "Given our uncertainty about the implications of the finding, the diagnosis of sociopathy or antisocial personality disorder should not be used to justify or to support predictions of future conduct" (p. 25).

In the more recent versions of this type of testimony, the Psychopathy Checklist–Revised (PCL-R; Hare, 1991) have been used to identify the defendant as a "psychopath," again with an explanation that this condition is predictive of *serious prison violence.* Such terminology, even apart from the unsubstantiated institutional risk predictions, has grave implications (see the chapter by Hemphill & Hart in this volume). Introduction of the profoundly pejorative label psychopath into a death penalty sentencing consideration may equate with a sentence of death (*Barefoot v. Estelle,* 1983 [dissent at 916]; *U.S. v. Barnette,* 2000). Balancing the considerable potential of this label to confuse and mislead the court would seem to require a substantial body of empirical research demonstrating the predictive validity of psychopathy specific to the gender and ethnicity of the defendant, as well as the institutional context of American prisons. Such empirical support does not exist.

The PCL-R has *not* been demonstrated to reliably predict serious violence in American prisons, among minorities and women, and or on old-age parole (Cunningham & Reidy, 1998a, 1999; Edens, 2001; Edens, Petrila, & Buffington-Vollum, in press; Freedman, 2001; Reidy et al., 2001). The Violence Risk Appraisal Guide (Quinsey, Harris, Rice, & Cormier, 1998), Sex Offender Appraisal Guide (Quinsey et al., 1998), and HCR-20 (Webster, Douglas, Eaves, & Hart, 1997) suffer from a similar lack of empirical support for their ability to reliably assess the risk of serious violence in American prisons (see the chapter by Monahan in this volume). Particularly in the capital sentencing arena, there is a clear ethical imperative to bridle the enthusiasm of embracing the PCL-R (or other risk assessment instruments) with scrutiny of the empirical support for its application in a specific context with a particular population.

Current Methodology of Capital Risk Assessments

The methodology and empirical data that can be applied in performing reliable violence risk assessments on capital defendants have been extensively described (Cunningham & Reidy, 1998b, 1999, 2001, in press; Reidy et al., 2001). Cunningham and Reidy (2001) summarized that long-range assessment of the probability of future serious violence is most reliable when:

- The risk estimate relies on the past pattern of conduct displayed by the individual in a *similar* context (Morris & Miller, 1985).

- The risk assessment is anchored to the base rate of violence for the group to which the individual most closely corresponds, and is then conservatively individualized (Hall, 1987; Monahan, 1981; Morris & Miller, 1985).

- The final risk estimate is adjusted for risk management or violence prevention/reduction procedures that could be applied (Heilbrun, 1997; Serin & Amos, 1995).

These three fundamental tenets are described below.

Past Pattern

A past pattern of behavior can be reliably predictive of future behavior, assuming that sufficient behavior has been exhibited to form a pattern and the context of prediction is sufficiently similar (Morris & Miller, 1985). In a violence risk

assessment at capital sentencing, then, detailed information regarding the defendant's history of serious violence during his pretrial confinement as well as past incarcerations can be quite important. The presence or absence of a record of serious violence during any past prison sentences is particularly relevant, as this context most closely approximates that of the pending capital life term. The circumstances and context of past institutional violence also may be illuminating. Specific descriptions of prior confinements (i.e., security level and celling arrangement; disciplinary write-ups; any prison gang affiliation; out-of-cell activities; involvement in work, academic, treatment, or religious programming; visitation contacts; and inmate and staff interactions) often provide additional perspectives regarding both the defendant's adjustment to confinement and the correctional staff's appraisal of whether the defendant was disproportionately at risk for serious violence.

Base Rate Anchors

In the absence of a prior history of prison incarceration or serious violence in jail pretrial, the most reliable anchor for a violence risk assessment at capital sentencing involves the application of relevant base rates. This methodology of applying group data to individual risk assessment has well-established empirical support. Group statistical data have repeatedly been demonstrated to enhance the reliability of violence risk assessments (Hall, 1987; Monahan, 1981, 1996; Morris & Miller, 1985; Serin & Amos, 1995), including the violence risk of capital offenders (Cunningham & Reidy, 1998b, 1999, 2001; in press; Reidy et al., 2001). Monahan (1981, 1996) concluded that knowledge of the violence rate in the respective group is the single most important piece of information necessary to make an accurate risk assessment of a particular individual.

Many of the studies that provide base rate anchors for capital risk assessments (see Table 21.5) have used "natural experiments" involving capital inmates who were removed from death row by commutation, retrial, or plea agreement. As Table 21.5 reflects, the overwhelming majority of capital offenders do not have records of serious prison violence. This finding is broadly consistent—despite differences in the decade of follow-up, applicable capital statute, and/or geographic location. Cumulative incidence of violent prison misconduct in the general prison population for former death row inmates across follow-up periods of 2 to 53 years varied from 0% to 31%. This range, however, obscures the striking similarity in number of outcome frequencies. For example, approximately two-thirds of former death row inmates were never confined in administrative segregation in samples from

TABLE 21.5   Assaultive Rule Violations of Former Death Row Inmates and Comparison Inmates

Study	Sample	Follow-Up Interval	Assault Rate	
			Former Death Row Inmates	Comparison Inmates
Marquart, Ekland-Olson, & Sorensen, 1994	N = 100 FDR, Texas	1924–72 (avg. 12 yrs)	.20 cumulative	
Marquart et al., 1994	N = 47 FDR, Texas	1973–88 (avg. 10 yrs)	.07 cumulative	
	N = 156 LS, Texas (128 murderers/28 rapists)	1973–88 (avg. 11 yrs)		.10 cumulative
Marquart, Ekland-Olson, & Sorensen, 1989	N = 90 FDR Texas	1974–88 (avg. 6.3 yrs)	.016 annual .10 ≥ cumulative	
	N = 107 CLS murderers, Texas	1974–88 (avg. 7.2 yrs)		.026 annual .19 ≥ cumulative
	N = 38,246 TDC systemwide	1986		.12 annual
	N = 1,712 TDC high-security unit	1986		.20 annual
Marquart & Sorensen, 1989	N = 533 nationwide (453 murderers/80 rapists)	1972–87 (15 yrs)	.31 cumulative	
Akman, 1966	N = 67 FDR Canada	1964–65 (2 yrs)	0 cumulative	
	N = 7,285, systemwide, Canada	1964–65 (2 yrs)		.007 annual
Bedau, 1964	N = 55 New Jersey	1907–60 (53 yrs)	0 cumulative*	
Sorensen & Wrinkle, 1996	N = 648 murderers, Missouri 93 death row/323 LWOP/232 LWP	1977–92		.218 cumulative
Reidy et al., 2001	N = 39 FDR, Indiana	1972–99 (avg. 9.3 yrs)	.028 annual .205 cumulative	
Sorensen & Pilgrim, 2000	N = 6,390 murderers, Texas	1990–99 (avg. 4.5 yrs)		.024 annual .084 cumulative

*Assault history sufficient to affect parole eligibility.
FDR = Former death row inmates; LS = Life sentence; CLS = Capital life sentence; TDC = Texas Dept. of Corrections; LWOP = Life without parole; LWP = Life with parole.
Source: From "Risk Assessment at Federal Capital Sentencing: Individualization, Generalization, Relevance, and Scientific Standards" by M. D. Cunningham and T. J. Reidy (in press). Originally adapted from Reidy et al. (2001).

both Texas (Marquart et al., 1989) and Indiana (Reidy et al., 2001). Similarly, just over two-thirds of the nationwide sample of Furman commutees were never written up for assaultive conduct. Twenty percent of former death row inmates in Indiana had no disciplinary write-ups of any sort during follow-up in the general prison population that averaged 9 years (Reidy et al.), compared to 27% of former death row inmates and 22% of life-sentenced capital offenders during follow-up in Texas that averaged 7 years (Marquart et al.).

Having the sobering experience of being sentenced to death does not represent a satisfactory explanation of the low rate of serious prison violence among former death row inmates. The frequency of prison violence among capital offenders who were sentenced at trial to a life prison term is quite similar to that of former death row inmates (Marquart et al., 1989, 1994). Similarly, rates of prison violence among convicted murderers sentenced to death, life-without-parole, and life-with-parole have been found to be remarkably consistent (Sorensen & Wrinkle, 1996).

Sorensen and Pilgrim (2000) have recently substantially augmented the statistical support for these base rate estimates

in their report of the rate of serious prison violence among 6,390 murderers in the Texas prison system (see Table 21.6). From this data, Sorensen and Pilgrim extrapolated the probability of serious institutional violence across a 40-year prison term, predicting a prevalence rate of .164. Violence rates among the capital murderers in this sample were lower (not

TABLE 21.6   Violent Acts Committed by 6,390 Incarcerated Murderers, January 1990 through March 1999

Violent Acts	Yearly Rate per 1,000 Inmates	Percentage of Inmates Involved
Against guards		
Aggravated assault	1.1	.5
Against inmates		
Homicide	0.2	.1
Assault with a weapon	12.1	4.4
Fight with a weapon	10.6	4.2
Other violence	0.4	0.2
Total Rate/Percentage	24.4	8.4
Total Frequency	711	536

Source: From "An Actuarial Risk Assessment of Violence Posed by Capital Murder Defendants" by J. R. Sorensen and R. L. Pilgrim, *Journal of Criminal Law and Criminology, 90,* p. 1262 (2000).

significantly) than in the noncapital murderer sample. The extraordinary number of inmates followed in this study allowed for identification of a limited number of variables that served to raise or lower the risk of serious prison violence relative to the overall group risk (see Table 21.7). Depending on the specific predictive factors in a given case, the probability of serious violence across a 40-year prison term could range from .02 to over .50. Consistent with other findings regarding prison violence (Cunningham & Reidy, 1998b, 1999; Harer, 1992), Sorensen and Pilgrim found that the probabilities decreased as the severity of the violence increased. For example, they estimate that the likelihood of an aggravated assault on a correctional officer by an incarcerated murderer is .01, and an inmate killing another inmate is .002 across a capital life term.

Base rates of the incidence of institutional violence among capital offenders and murderers in the general population of maximum-security prisons represent important anchoring points in performing a violence risk assessment of a capital defendant. Other relevant base rates include (a) the frequency of serious violence in specific correctional settings; (b) inmate and staff homicide nationally and in the particular department of correction; (c) disciplinary infraction rates of long-term inmates; and (d) prison disciplinary infractions as a function of age of the inmate (Cunningham & Reidy, in press).

Conservative individualization of base rates examines various factors that might serve to modestly raise or lower the risk as compared to the relevant group anchor such as age of inmate, continuing availability of community supports and visitation, history of employment in the community, prior responses to structured environments, and psychological disorder. In a similar vein, Rogers (2000) described the need for mental health experts conducting fair and balanced risk assessments to describe both risk and protective factors, as well as mediator or moderator effects in a particular context. It is cautioned that before identifying a particularizing factor as operative, the incidence of that factor in the inmate group providing the anchoring base rate of violence risk must be considered. As described above, APD as well as a number of other factors that might be related to risk of violence in the community are so pervasively represented among prison inmates that they lose any predictive value in that setting.

Risk Management

As risk of violence is always a function of context (Hall, 1987; Monahan, 1981; Quay, 1984), consideration of what modifications in context or risk management procedures might be brought to bear to reduce the likelihood of violence is a critically important step in violence risk assessments at capital sentencing (Cunningham & Reidy, 1999, in press; Heilbrun, 1997; Serin & Amos, 1995). Such risk management procedures may include psychotropic medications; counseling or other treatment of psychological disorders; programming and psychoeducational services, such as anger management; academic/work activities; classification and celling procedures; and modifications in confinement, including both psychiatric and supermaximum units.

The availability of supermaximum confinement in virtually all prison systems is a particularly critical variable to consider in violence risk assessment at capital sentencing. These ultra-high-security units are typically characterized by intensive staffing, increased inmate observation, single-celling, in-cell meals, controlled movement, and shackling of inmates when outside of the cell. Under such conditions, opportunities for serious violence toward others are profoundly limited. Consequently, inmates who are viewed as being a disproportionate risk of serious violence toward staff or other inmates can be confined in a context that minimizes that risk (Cunningham & Reidy, 1999, in press).

Challenges to Group Statistical Data

Challenges to the application of group base rates to the violence risk assessment of a specific capital defendant have primarily involved assertions that such "group" data is insufficiently individualized—as compared to "individualized" assessments that rely on clinical factors or testing (Cunningham & Reidy, in press). Cunningham and Reidy asserted that the distinction between individualized as opposed to group methods is a false dichotomy, reflecting a fundamental misunderstanding of the nature of risk assessment and, more broadly, of psychology as a science. They explained: "Simply stated,

TABLE 21.7   **Predicted Probability of Serious Violence among Incarcerated Murderers across a 40-Year Prison Term**

Predictor Variable	Predicted Probability	Predicted Proportional Change
All factors held constant	.164	
Capital offense characteristics		
Robbery or burglary		.074
Multiple murder victims		.056
Attempted murder		.040
Prison gang membership		.104
Prior prison term		.053
Age		
Less than 21		.055
26–30		.072
Over 35		−.144

Source: Adapted from "An Actuarial Risk Assessment of Violence Posed by Capital Murder Defendants" by J. R. Sorensen and R. L. Pilgrim, *Journal of Criminal Law and Criminology, 90,* p. 1262 (2000).

there is no *individualized* assessment of a particular person that does not rest on group data of one sort or another. . . . Psychology exists as a science because it provides a database regarding the behavior of groups of individuals, that is systematically and reliably obtained using the scientific method." Subjective experience and informal case study have a role in professional expertise, yet the vast body of scientifically derived expert knowledge in psychology consists of published observations and research on various groups of animals and individuals. Scientific expertise in psychology, then, consists principally of knowledge about this group-derived data. Sound evaluation, treatment, or behavioral prediction regarding a specific defendant relies on these collective observations and research data from a specified context. Even though there are always ways in which the individual varies from the group, the group experience remains relevant because important characteristics are shared.

Violence risk assessment also fundamentally relies on the accumulation of group data that are then applied to a given individual. Cunningham and Reidy (in press) explained that at the point that group data are applied to a particular person, the methodology becomes individualized. Regardless of whether the violence risk assessment method is clinical (interview/testing), past behavioral pattern, or actuarial (group statistical), conclusions offered by an expert about a particular individual are purported to be reasonably and reliably inferred from group data. The various risk assessment methods simply group individuals in different ways (i.e., personality characteristics, diagnosis, historical variables, test scores, behavior patterns, or incarcerating offense). As Cunningham and Reidy framed it: "The question then is not whether individualized risk assessment will be based on group data, whether applied by an uninformed jury or expert testimony. Instead the issue is whether the grouping provides empirically sound group data regarding the likelihood of prison violence." At this stage of capital violence risk assessment research, no interview-based personality variable, personality testing profile, or risk assessment instrument has been demonstrated to reliably predict serious prison violence. Thus, reliance on these methods is without empirical support and does not represent a meaningful method of grouping capital offenders for capital risk assessment purposes. By contrast, there are consistent group data from both capital samples and general inmate populations that can be meaningfully brought to bear in estimating the probabilities of violence of varying severity for a particular capital inmate.

A second challenge to the application of group statistical data at capital sentencing, as described by Cunningham and Reidy (in press), involves an assertion that the defendant does not match the reference group in some fashion. The appropri-ateness of generalizing from a given group statistical finding to an individual case is always an important consideration in applying this methodology. Operationally, this consideration involves weighing whether the common characteristics are sufficiently similar to provide meaningful inference, despite the inevitable unique features of the individual case. Cunningham and Reidy explained: "The critical issue is not the presence of some *unique* features in the instant appraisal, rather whether there is sufficient *commonality* in the characteristic of interest for the general research to accurately generalize to the specific case. All applications of scientific data involve this generalizing from broader research to the specific case." There is reason to believe that group data on the institutional violence frequencies of capital offenders generalize well to most capitally charged defendants. Base rates of violence among capital offenders in a general prison population have reflected remarkable consistency across varying correctional settings, capital statutes, and periods of the past century—indicative of a very robust finding with broad generalization to current correctional experiences.

EXPERT TESTIMONY IN CAPITAL CASES

Evaluating or Teaching Witness Testimony

Most commonly, capital sentencing assessments and testimony are based on extensive interview of the defendant, interviews of third parties, and review of extensive records. These methods and the associated testimony obviously are highly individualized to the specific defendant. This role we characterize as an *evaluating witness*. There are instances, however, when the defendant does not submit to interview or when the referral question is restricted to describing research findings on the risks associated with various adverse experiences. Alternatively, the forensic psychologist might be asked to describe reliable capital risk assessment methodology and the associated group statistical findings so that the jury can undertake this function in a more fully informed fashion. These latter roles we identify as *teaching witnesses*. Teaching witnesses may not operate entirely insulated from case-specific information, but instead, may offer limited particularization on the basis of records review, interviews of third parties, review of investigation summaries or chronologies, trial testimony of lay witnesses, and/or hypotheticals. In the absence of direct interview, application of research findings to the defendant is necessarily more tentative. At the same time, defendants need not waive their 5th Amendment rights before psychology can illuminate important aspects of the court's considerations.

An Example of Evaluating Witness Testimony

The defendant was 20 years of age at the time of the crime. He was charged with the gangland-style execution of the owner of a pizzeria. He confessed that he shot the victim to death at the request of an older man, someone who had befriended him while he was serving time in prison for auto theft. He described this man as a member of organized crime who would "look out for him." The defendant consistently denied any knowledge as to why his "friend" wanted the victim dead.

The defendant was cooperative with the forensic expert. He was interviewed on several occasions regarding his background, history, and the circumstances of the crime. A comprehensive battery of tests was administered, including tests of cognitive functioning, neuropsychological screening instruments, personality measures, and tests to evaluate malingering. (Based on his performance on the Wechsler Adult Intelligence Scale-III (Wechsler, 1997) and on neuropsychological screening tests, a neuropsychologist was retained by defense counsel.) School records, prior psychological and psychiatric assessments, prison and current jail records, and documents related to this case were reviewed. In addition, interviews were conducted with his former girlfriend, his brother, mother, father, stepmother, and half-sister.

Based on this evaluation, it was opined that his relationship with this older man (who was never charged with this crime) was related to his father's neglect and coldness throughout his childhood and adolescent years. The father had abandoned the family, and was both emotionally detached from his son and highly critical of him. As a result, his need to please and gain his father's acceptance became paramount. His father was or pretended to be a mobster, low-level at best, dropping the names of organized crime figures in an effort to impress those around him. His son began to idolize both his father and those associated with organized crime. His mother became deeply depressed, blaming the father for all of the family's difficulties. Neither she nor his father made any meaningful attempts to control or seek treatment for their son, who, shortly after their separation, began to miss school, regularly abuse marijuana (soon graduating to more serious drugs), and act out. The defendant's older brother died from a drug overdose; an older sister became highly promiscuous (bringing male friends home and taking the defendant with her on "dates"); and another older brother became addicted to drugs as well. The defendant had an undiagnosed severe learning disability and attention-deficit/hyperactivity disorder. At the time of the crime, data suggest that the defendant was high on alcohol and heroin, further impairing his judgment and decision-making abilities. He feared for his own life, as well as the lives of his mother and sister. This and similar evaluating witness testimony may provide both detailed historical information and psychological insights to assist the considerations of the sentencer. Although not an excuse for the crime, such testimony may provide perspectives and/or explanations as to how forces other than pure "evil" shaped the defendant's behavior.

An Example of Teaching Witness Testimony

The defendant, age 32, was accused of murdering a competing drug dealer. He was charged in federal court with conducting a continuous criminal enterprise, a special circumstance qualifying a homicide for capital consideration. This individual had a long history of incarceration, beginning approximately four months after his mother's death (he was 19 years of age at the time of her death). Consistent with his past refusal to cooperate with mental health professionals while in prison, he refused to participate in *any* psychological or psychiatric assessment or interview related to the penalty phase of his capital trial.

His mother was a long-term heroin addict. She developed chronic kidney failure when the defendant was 4 years old. Her contact with social service and public assistance agencies, as well as hospital records documented her role as a mother. As a child, he and his older brother were neglected, physically and verbally abused, and exposed to violence on a regular basis. They witnessed their mother inject heroin and overdose on a number of occasions. Once, the defendant found her syringe taped under a sink, and to protect her, he discarded it. When she discovered it missing, she injected him with water as punishment. Records documented these and other incidents of a continuous, highly traumatic nature. (It was unclear why he was never removed from the home.) On another occasion, his mother did not return home for four days after receiving her social service check. The defendant and his brother were left unattended, locked in their apartment (they were squatters, without electricity). The 6-year-old brother mixed flour with water in an attempt to make pancakes. For syrup, he found a discarded jelly jar in the garbage and mixed it with water. When the mother returned home, she beat both children for using the flour without her permission.

The expert interviewed aunts and cousins. They corroborated the records and supplied other examples of the traumatic events the defendant and his brother experienced as children (the older brother was serving a life sentence for murder). Testimony focused on the effects of these traumas on adult development, citing the professional literature extensively. No connection was made with the circumstances of the offense, and the limits of the testimony were discussed. This testimony had, as its major objective, educated the jury as to how a child can be affected by these incidents such that moral development, judgment, empathy, and impulse control may be significantly impaired.

OTHER CAPITAL CASE ASSESSMENTS

State Postconviction and Federal Habeas Cases

The involvement of psychologists at state postconviction or federal *habeas* is most often part of a claim of ineffectiveness of counsel. In such cases, the defense may have failed to comprehensively investigate the capital defendant's biopsychosocial history and/or neglected to obtain scientifically sound risk assessment consultation. The assistance of a psychologist may be sought to analyze the mitigation and risk assessment evidence that was presented at the capital sentencing trial in light of research perspectives available at the time of trial, as well as records, third-party interviews, and defendant evaluations generated prior to or since sentencing. These consultations and the associated analysis may range from review of transcripts, records, and investigation summaries to a full mitigation and risk assessment workup. On the basis of these findings, the psychologist may be asked to opine on the adequacy and accuracy of the sentencing phase evidence and arguments, as well as detail history and research that could have been presented at sentencing and discuss its relevance. These findings and conclusions typically are initially presented in the form of a detailed affidavit, but may be followed by testimony at an evidentiary hearing.

Competence to Waive Appeals

Appellate review acts to delay imposition of the death penalty and can result in retrial of the guilt and/or sentencing phase or other relief. A waiver of appeals in this context effectively represents volunteering for execution—and thus an abandonment of the self-preservation motivation exhibited by most rational human beings. This phenomenon has a disturbing incidence among death row inmates. As many as 89 of 707 (12.5%) executions in the United States between 1977 and April 2001 involved "volunteers" who had dropped their appeals (Amnesty International, 2001). Many of these volunteers were described as having a history of mental illness. Although an election to waive appeals may ultimately be found to be rational (see *Gilmore v. Utah,* 1976), it is likely to be subjected to some scrutiny. As Richards (1995) described:

Because a lack of information and misinformation may have such grave consequences in the capital context, because capital defendants are likely to be suffering from mental health problems, because they must make their decisions in a coercive atmosphere, and because they may vacillate in their decisions to seek death, lawyers should take protective measures against accepting a decision to seek death made in error. (p. 155)

One such protective measure is a referral for psychological evaluation of competency to waive an appeal. In any waiver evaluation, psycholegal elements of knowing, intelligent, and voluntary should be explored. In a death row context, however, two influences have particular potential to adversely impact on a waiver election.

First, the potential for mental disorder to influence a decision to forgo appeals must be carefully assessed. A number of clinical studies on death row samples have demonstrated significant rates of psychological disorder among this population (see Table 21.3). The implications for a diagnosis of depression in competency to waive appeals are obvious. The depressive experience of feelings of hopelessness and futility may result in the death row inmate not accurately perceiving the chances of eventually securing relief from a death sentence. Conscious and unconscious suicidal ideation can be expressed through volunteering for death via waiver of appeals. Reduced efficiency of thought and impaired problem solving also have the potential to adversely impact waiver decision making.

Second, it is important to explore the conditions of death row confinement, which are often extraordinarily adverse in terms of social isolation, severely restricted activity, and security procedures. To illustrate from survey data summarized by *Corrections Compendium* ("Death Row," 1999), in 35 of 37 jurisdictions, death row inmates are housed in individual cells. In 18 of these jurisdictions, death row inmates average less than an hour of activity outside of their cells each day, and in five other jurisdictions, daily out-of-cell time is less than three hours. Noncontact visitation is the norm for death row in 21 of 37 jurisdictions. Although there is some variability in policy from state to state, death row conditions nationally are characterized by "rigid security, isolation, limited movement, and austere conditions" (Lombardi, Sluder, & Wallace, 1997, p. 3). Not surprisingly, there is evidence that these bleak confinement conditions impact the psychological adjustment of death row inmates, most of whom spend many years in this status (Cunningham & Vigen, in press). Some inmates may find the sustained isolation and chronic deprivation of years of solitary confinement to be so psychologically painful that the escape of death appears preferable. Under these conditions, a waiver of appeals may reflect some degree of environmental coercion, rendering the waiver less than voluntary. As discussed by Brodsky (1990), inmates may not recognize that if an appeal is successful and the death sentence is reversed, a life sentence spent in general population affords more "freedom" than their current status on death row.

Competence to Be Executed

As previously described, evaluations of competency to be executed remain ambiguous, controversial, and ethically complex (Bonnie, 1990; Brodsky, 1990; Deitchman, Kennedy, & Beckham, 1991; Mossman, 1992; Salguero, 1986). *Ford v. Wainwright* (1986) did not articulate a singular standard for the assessment of this competency, although Justice Powell, in a concurring opinion, asserted that the essential construct was whether the inmate was aware of the impending execution and the reasons for this execution.

In the absence of clear standards by the Court, states vary in statutes and degree of guidance regarding how competency to be executed is defined and practically expressed. This creates a context of ambiguity for forensic psychologists undertaking these examinations. Some additional guidance, though, is provided by the majority opinion in *Ford,* which identified a number of miscarriages of justice that are triggered when a prisoner is unaware of the nature of or reason for a pending execution. These include an absence of retribution value, an inability of the inmate to prepare for death in coming to terms with conscience or deity, the experience of fear and pain without understanding, and the diminished dignity of society.

The underlying rationales provided by the majority point to "awareness" being more than rote assent, and instead, extending to the ability to act on that understanding. An aspect of this ability to act arguably involves a capacity to assist appellate counsel, to "recognize or understand any fact which might exist which would make the punishment unjust or unlawful, . . . [and] the ability to convey such information to counsel or the court" (American Bar Association, 1986, p. 290).

Heilbrun (1987) summarized these competency prongs as "understand," "assist," and "prepare." Subsequently, three tasks have been proposed as components of competency for execution: "(1) understanding the nature of capital punishment and the reasons for its imposition, (2) assisting counsel in ongoing collateral appeals, and (3) spiritually and psychologically preparing for death" (Heilbrun, Radelet, & Dvoskin, 1992, p. 599).

Heilbrun (1987) and others (Heilbrun & McClaren, 1988; Small & Otto, 1991; Winick, 1992) have proposed essential components of competency to be executed evaluations. These include (a) disclosure of the purpose of the evaluation;

(b) multiple evaluation contacts with the inmate; (c) specific inquiry regarding the pending execution, including any preparations made by the inmate; (d) comprehensive assessment of psychopathology, cognitive functioning, personality, and symptom exaggeration/minimization; (e) third-party interviews to obtain historical and descriptive information; and (f) a conducive assessment context.

SUMMARY

Forensic psychologists can contribute at many junctures to a higher degree of reliability than currently is being realized in capital litigation. This aspiration, however, is dependent on experts bringing the highest standards of professionalism to bear in this complex and demanding arena of practice. In practical terms, professionalism in capital evaluations involves the same four components that are present in any forensic psychology consultation. However, they take on a special imperative when death is at stake:

1. Clear recognition of the relevant psycholegal issues, including the implications of the evaluation methods and findings.
2. Unwavering adherence to ethical standards, including informed consent, objectivity, and advocating for the data.
3. Assessment methods that are both relevant to the issue in question and comprehensive in application.
4. Familiarity and reliance on the best empirical data and research perspectives.

This chapter has attempted to provide both a broad orientation and specific direction to more expert, more ethical, and more scientifically informed practice in forensic psychology contributions to death penalty litigation.

REFERENCES

Akman, D. D. (1966). Homicides and assaults in Canadian penitentiaries. *Canadian Journal of Corrections, 8,* 284–299.

Alexander, J., & Austin, J. (1992). *Handbook for evaluating objective prison classification systems.* San Francisco: National Council on Crime and Delinquency.

American Bar Association. (1986). *ABA criminal justice mental health standards* (Standard 7–5.6). ABA Criminal Justice Standards Committee.

American Medical Association Council on Ethical and Judicial Affairs. (1995). Physician participation in capital punishment: Evaluation of prisoner competence to be executed: Treatment to restore competence to be executed. *CEJA Report 1995,* Section 6-A-95.

American Psychiatric Association. (1983). *Amicus curiae* brief, *Barefoot v. Estelle.* Washington, DC: Author.

American Psychological Association. (1992). Ethical principles of psychologists and code of conduct. *American Psychologist, 47,* 1597–1611.

Amnesty International. (2001, April). *The illusion of control.* Retrieved May 16, 2001, from www.aiusa.org/abolish/reports/amr510532001.html.

Appelbaum, P. S. (1981). Psychiatrists' role in the death penalty. *Hospital and Community Psychiatry, 32,* 761–762.

Appelbaum, P. S. (1984). Hypotheticals, psychiatric testimony, and the death sentence. *Bulletin of the American Academy of Psychiatry and the Law, 12,* 169–177.

Apprendi v. New Jersey, 500 U.S. 466 (2000).

Atkins v. Virginia, 260 Va. 375, 534 S.E. 2d 312, reversed and remanded (U.S. Supreme Court, No. 00-8452, decided July 21, 2002).

Barefoot v. Estelle, 463 U.S. 880 (1983).

Beck, A., Kline, S., & Greenfield, L. (1988, September). *Survey of youth in custody, 1987.* Washington, DC: Bureau of Justice Statistics.

Beck, A. T., & Steer, R. A. (1988). *Revised–Beck Depression Inventory.* San Antonio, TX: Psychological Corporation.

Beck, J. C. (1996). Psychiatry and the death penalty. *Harvard Review of Psychiatry, 4,* 225–229.

Bedau, H. A. (1964). Death sentences in New Jersey, 1907–1960. *Rutgers Law Review, 19,* 1–64.

Blake, P., Pincus, J., & Buckner, C. (1995). Neurologic abnormalities in murderers. *Neurology, 45,* 1641–1647.

Bluestone, H., & McGahee, C. L. (1962). Reaction to extreme stress: Impending death by execution. *American Journal of Psychiatry, 119,* 393–396.

Blume, J. H., Garvey, S. P., & Johnson, S. L. (2001). Future dangerousness in capital cases: Always "At Issue," *Cornell Law Review, 86,* 397–410.

Bonnie, R. J. (1990). Dilemmas in administering the death penalty: Conscientious abstention, professional ethics, and the needs of the legal system. *Law and Human Behavior, 14,* 67–90.

Bowers, W. J., & Steiner, B. D. (1999). Death by default: An empirical demonstration of false and forced choices in capital sentencing. *Texas Law Review, 77,* 605–717.

Branch v. Texas, 490 S.W.2d 893 (1972).

Brodsky, S. (1990). Professional ethics and professional morality in the assessment of competence for execution: A response to Bonnie. *Law and Human Behavior, 14,* 91–97.

Clements, C. (1996). Offender classification: Two decades of progress. *Criminal Justice and Behavior, 23,* 121–143.

Coker v. Georgia, 433 U.S. 584 (1977).

Committee on Ethical Guidelines for Forensic Psychologists. (1991). Specialty guidelines for forensic psychologists. *Law and Human Behavior, 15,* 655–665.

Cornell, D. G., Benedek, E. P., & Benedek, D. M. (1987). Characteristics of adolescents charged with homicide. *Behavioral Sciences and the Law, 5,* 11–23.

Costanzo, M., & Costanzo, S. (1992). Jury decision making in the capital penalty phase. *Law and Human Behavior, 16,* 185–201.

Craig, R. (1996). MMPI-Based psychological assessment of lethal violence. In H. Hall (Ed.), *Lethal violence 2000: A sourcebook on fatal domestic, acquaintance and stranger aggression* (pp. 505–526). Kamuela, HI: Pacific Institute for the Study of Conflict and Aggression.

Cunningham, M. D., & Reidy, T. J. (1998a). Antisocial personality disorder and psychopathy: Diagnostic dilemmas in classifying patterns of antisocial behavior in sentencing evaluations. *Behavioral Sciences and the Law, 16,* 331–351.

Cunningham, M. D., & Reidy, T. J. (1998b). Integrating base rate data in violence risk assessments at capital sentencing. *Behavioral Sciences and the Law, 16,* 71–95.

Cunningham, M. D., & Reidy, T. J. (1999). Don't confuse me with the facts: Common errors in violence risk assessment at capital sentencing. *Criminal Justice and Behavior, 26,* 20–43.

Cunningham, M. D., & Reidy, T. J. (2001). A matter of life or death: Special considerations and heightened practice standards in capital sentencing evaluations. *Behavioral Sciences and the Law, 19,* 473–490.

Cunningham, M. D., & Reidy, T. J. (in press). Violence risk assessment at federal capital sentencing: Individualization, generalization, relevance, and scientific standards. *Criminal Justice and Behavior.*

Cunningham, M. D., & Vigen, M. P. (1999). Without appointed counsel in capital postconviction proceedings: The self-representation competency of Mississippi death row inmates. *Criminal Justice and Behavior, 26,* 293–321.

Cunningham, M. D., & Vigen, M. P. (in press). Death row inmate characteristics, adjustment, and confinement: A critical review of the literature. *Behavioral Sciences and the Law.*

Davis, P. (1978). Texas capital sentencing procedures: The role of the jury and the restraining hand of the expert. *Journal of Criminal Law and Criminology, 69,* 300–310.

Death Penalty Information Center. (2001, June). Available from www.deathpenaltyinfo.org.

Death row and the death penalty. (1999). *Corrections Compendium, 24,* 6–18.

Dekleva, K. B. (2001). Psychiatric expertise in the sentencing phase of capital murder cases. *Journal of the American Academy of Psychiatry and the Law, 29,* 58–67.

Deitchman, M., Kennedy, W., & Beckham, J. (1991). Self-selection factors in the participation of mental health professionals in competency for execution evaluation. *Law and Human Behavior, 15,* 287–303.

Eddings v. Oklahoma, 455 U.S. 104 (1982).

Edens, J. F. (2001). Misuses of the Hare Psychopathy Checklist–Revised in court: Two case examples. *Journal of Interpersonal Violence, 16,* 1082–1093.

Edens, J. F., Petrila, J., & Buffington-Vollum, J. K. (in press). Psychopathy and the death penalty: Can the Psychopathy Checklist–Revised identify offenders who represent "a continuing threat to society?" *Journal of Psychology and Law.*

Estelle v. Smith 451 U.S. 454 101 S. Ct. 1866 (1981).

Evans, J. R. (1997). Quantitative EEG findings in a group of death row inmates. *Archives of Clinical Neurology, 12,* 315–316.

Ewing, C. P. (1983). "Dr. Death" and the case for an ethical ban on psychiatric and psychological predictions of dangerousness in capital sentencing proceedings. *American Journal of Law and Medicine, 8,* 408–428.

Ferris, R. (1997). Psychiatry and the death penalty. *Psychiatric Bulletin, 21,* 746–748.

Ford v. Wainwright, 106 S. Ct. 2595 (1986).

Freedman, A. M., & Halpern, A. L. (1999). The psychiatrist's dilemma: A conflict of roles in legal executions. *Australian and New Zealand Journal of Psychiatry, 33,* 629–635.

Freedman, D. (2001). False prediction of future dangerousness: Error rates and Psychopathy Checklist–Revised. *Journal of the American Academy of Psychiatry and the Law, 29,* 89–95.

Freedman, D., & Hemenway, D. (2000). Precursors of lethal violence: A death row sample. *Social Science and Medicine, 50,* 1757–1770.

Frierson, R. L., Schwartz-Watts, D. M., Morgan, D. W., & Malone, T. D. (1998). Capital versus noncapital murderers. *Journal of the American Academy of Psychiatry and Law, 26,* 403–410.

Furman v. Georgia, 408 U.S. 238 (1972).

Gallemore, J. L., & Panton, M. A. (1972). Inmate responses to lengthy death row confinement. *American Journal of Psychiatry, 129,* 167–172.

Geimer, W., & Amsterdam, J. (1988). Why jurors vote life or death: Operative factors in ten Florida death cases. *American Journal of Criminal Law, 15,* 1–54.

Gilmore v. Utah, 429 U.S. 1012 (1976).

Goldstein, A. M. (2001). Objectivity in capital cases. *American Psychology-Law Society Newsletter, 21,* 8–9, 14.

Goldstein, A. M. (2002). Death penalty assessments. In K. Heilbrun, G. Marczyk, & D. DeMatteo (Eds.), *Forensic mental health assessment: A Casebook.* New York: Oxford University Press.

Goldstein, A. M., & Goldstein N. E. (in press). Childhood trauma as mitigation in death penalty cases. In S. Sparta & G. Koocher (Eds.), *Forensic assessment of childhood and adolescence: Issues and applications.* New York: Oxford University Press.

Green, W. (1984). Capital punishment, psychiatric experts, and predictions of dangerousness. *Capital University Law Review, 13,* 533–553.

Gregg v. Georgia, 428 U.S. 153 (1976).

Grisso, T. (1986). *Evaluating competencies: Forensic assessments and instruments,* New York: Plenum Press.

Hall, H. V. (1987). *Violence prediction: Guidelines for the forensic practitioner.* Springfield, IL: Charles C. Thomas.

Halleck, S. L., Applebaum, P., Rappeport, J., & Dix, G. E. (1984). *Report of the task force on the role of psychiatry in the sentencing process.* Washington, DC: American Psychiatric Press.

Haney, C. (1995). The social context of capital murder: Social histories and the logic of mitigation [Symposium]. *Santa Clara Law Review, 35,* 547–609.

Haney, C. (1997). Violence and capital law. *Stanford Law Review, 49,* 1447–1486.

Hare, R. D. (1991). *The Hare Psychopathy Checklist–Revised.* Toronto, Ontario, Canada: Multi-Health Systems.

Harer, M. (1992). Assaults on BOP staff and inmates: Where and when they occur. *Research Forum, 2,* 1–19.

Hathaway, S. R., & McKinley, J. C. (1982). *Minnesota Multiphasic Personality Inventory.* Minneapolis, MN: University of Minnesota Press.

Hawkins, J. D., Herrenkohl, T. I., Farrington, D. P., Brewer, D., Catalano, R. F., Harachi, T. W., et al. (2000, April). *Predictors of youth violence.* Washington, DC: U.S. Department of Justice.

Heilbrun, K. (1987). The assessment of competency for execution: An overview. *Behavioral Sciences and the Law, 5,* 383–396.

Heilbrun, K. (1997). Prediction versus management models relevant to risk assessment: The importance of legal decision-making context. *Law and Human Behavior, 21,* 347–359.

Heilbrun, K., & McClaren, H. (1988). Assessment of competency for execution? A guide for mental health professionals. *Bulletin of the American Academy of Psychiatry and the Law, 16,* 205–216.

Heilbrun, K., Radelet, M., & Dvoskin, J. (1992). The debate of treating individuals incompetent for execution. *American Journal of Psychiatry, 149,* 596–604.

Hill, M. A., & O'Neil, J. (1993). *Underclass behaviors in the United States: Measurement and analysis of determinants.* New York: City University of New York, Baruch College.

In re Kemmler, 136 U.S. 436, 10 S. Ct. 930, 34 L. Ed. 519 (1890).

Johnson, R. (1979). Under sentence of death: The psychology of death row confinement. *Law and Psychology Review, 5,* 141–192.

Jurek v. Texas, 428 U.S. 153, 96 S. Ct. 2950 (1976).

Kelley, B. T., Thornberry, T. P., & Smith, C. A. (1997, August). In the wake of childhood maltreatment. *Juvenile Justice Bulletin.* Washington, DC: U.S. Department of Justice, Office of Juvenile Justice and Delinquency Prevention.

Kennedy, T. D. (1986). Trends in inmate classification: A status report of two computerized psychometric approaches. *Criminal Justice and Behavior, 13,* 165–184.

Langevin, R., Ben-Aron, M., Wortzman, G., Dickey R., & Handy, L. (1987). Brain damage, diagnosis, and substance abuse among violent offenders. *Behavioral Sciences and the Law, 5,* 77–94.

Latzer, B. (1998). *Death penalty cases: Leading U.S. Supreme Court cases on capital punishment.* Boston, MA: Butterworth-Heinemann.

Leong, G. B., Silva, J. A., Weinstock, R., & Ganzini, L. (2000). Survey of forensic psychiatrists on evaluation and treatment of prisoners on death row. *Journal of the American Academy of Psychiatry and the Law, 28,* 427–432.

Leong, G. B., Weinstock, R., Silva, J. A., & Eth, S. (1993). Psychiatry and the death penalty: The past decade. *Psychiatric Annals, 23,* 41–47.

Lewis, P. W. (1979). Killing the killers: A post-Furman profile of Florida's condemned. *Crime and Delinquency, 25,* 200–218.

Lewis, D., Pincus, J., Feldman, M., Jackson, L., & Bard, B. (1986). Psychiatric, neurological, and psychoeducational characteristics of 15 death row inmates in the United States. *American Journal of Psychiatry, 143,* 838–845.

Lewis, D. O., Pincus, J. H., Bard, B., Richardson, E., Prichep, L. S., Feldman, M., et al. (1988). Neuropsychiatric, psychoeducational, and family characteristics of 14 juveniles condemned to death in the United States. *American Journal of Psychiatry, 145,* 584–589.

Liebert, D. S., & Foster, M. D. (1994). The mental health evaluation in capital cases: Standards of practice. *American Journal of Forensic Psychiatry, 15,* 43–64.

Lifton, R. J., & Mitchell, G. (2000). *Who owns death? Capital punishment, the American conscience, and the end of executions.* New York: HarperCollins.

Lockett v. Ohio, 438 U.S. 586, 604 (1978).

Lombardi, G., Sluder, R. D., & Wallace, D. (1997). Mainstreaming death-sentenced inmates: The Missouri experience and its legal significance. *Federal Probation, 61,* 3–11.

Marquart, J. W., Ekland-Olson, S., & Sorensen, J. R. (1989). Gazing into the crystal ball: Can jurors accurately predict dangerousness in capital cases? *Law and Society Review, 23,* 449–468.

Marquart, J. W., Ekland-Olson, S., & Sorensen, J. R. (1994). *The rope, the chair, and the needle: Capital punishment in Texas, 1923–1990.* Austin: University of Texas Press.

Marquart, J. W., & Sorensen, J. R. (1989). A national study of the *Furman*-commuted inmates: Assessing the threat to society from capital offenders. *Loyola of Los Angeles Law Review, 23,* 5–28.

Martell, D. (1992). Estimating the prevalence of organic brain dysfunction in maximum-security forensic psychiatric patients. *Journal of Forensic Sciences, 37,* 878–893.

Masten, A. S., & Garmezy, N. (1985). Risk, vulnerability, and protective factors in developmental psychopathology. In *Advances in clinical child psychology* (Vol. 8, pp. 1–52). New York: Plenum Press.

McPherson, S. B. (1996). *Psychological aspects of mitigation in capital cases.* Unpublished manuscript.

Meloy, J. R. (1988). *Psychopathic mind: Origin, dynamics, and treatment.* Northvale, NJ: Aronson.

Melton, G. B., Petrila, J., Poythress, N. G., & Slobogin, C. (1997). *Psychological evaluations for the courts: A handbook for mental health professionals and lawyers* (2nd ed.). New York: Guilford Press.

Monahan, J. (1981). *Predicting violent behavior: An assessment of clinical techniques.* Beverly Hills, CA: Sage.

Monahan, J. (1996). Violence prediction: The past twenty years. *Criminal Justice and Behavior, 23,* 107–120.

Morey, L. C. (1991). *Personality Assessment Inventory.* Odessa, FL: Psychological Assessment Resources.

Morris, N., & Miller, M. (1985). Predictions of dangerousness. In M. Tonry & N. Morris (Eds.), *Crime and justice: An annual review of research* (pp. 1–50). Chicago: University of Chicago Press.

Mossman, D. (1992). The psychiatrist and execution competency: Fording murky ethical waters. *Case Western Reserve Law Review, 43,* 1–95.

Murray v. Giarratano, 492 U.S. 1, S. Ct. 2765 (1989), U.S. LEXIS 3134, 106 L. Ed. 2d 1, 57 U.S.L.W. 4889.

NAACP Legal Defense and Education Fund. (2001, October). *Death row USA: October 2001.* New York: Author. Retrieved June 29, 2001, from www.deathpenaltyinfo.org/DeathRowUSA1.html.

National Institute of Corrections, U.S. Department of Justice. (1992). *Jail classification system development: A review of the literature* (Rev. ed.). Washington, DC: Author.

Norton, L. (1992, May). Capital cases: Mitigation investigations. *Champion,* 43–45.

Panton, J. H. (1976). Personality characteristics of death-row prison inmates. *Journal of Clinical Psychology, 32,* 306–309.

Panton, J. H. (1978). Pre- and post-personality test responses of prison inmates who have had their death sentences commuted to life imprisonment. *Research Communications in Psychology, Psychiatry and Behavior, 3,* 143–156.

Penry v. Johnson, 121 S. Ct. 1910 (2001).

Penry v. Lynaugh, 492 U.S. 1 (1989).

Popkin, A. (2000). Personal communication with A. M. Goldstein.

Quay, H. (1984). Managing adult inmates: Classification for housing and program assignments. *Adult Internal Management System (AIMS) classification manual.* College Park, MD: American Correctional Association.

Quinsey, V. L., Harris, G. T., Rice, M. E., & Cormier, C. A. (1998). *Violent offenders: Appraising and managing risk.* Washington, DC: American Psychological Association.

Reidy, T. J., Cunningham, M. D., & Sorensen, J. R. (2001). From death to life: Prison behavior of former death row inmates in Indiana. *Criminal Justice and Behavior, 28,* 62–82.

Richards, J. L. (1995). A lawyer's ethical considerations when her client elects death: The model rules in the capital context. *San Diego Justice Journal, 3,* 127–175.

Ring v. Arizona, U.S. Supreme Court No. 01-488, decided June 24, 2002.

Rogers, R. (2000). The uncritical acceptance of risk assessment in forensic practice. *Law and Human Behavior, 24,* 595–605.

Salguero, R. G. (1986). Medical ethics and competency to be executed. *Yale Law Journal, 96,* 167–186.

Sandys, M. (1991, November). *Life or death decisions of capital jurors: Preliminary findings from Kentucky.* Paper presented at the annual meeting of the American Society of Criminology, San Francisco.

Serin, R. C., & Amos, N. L. (1995). The role of psychopathy in the assessment of dangerousness. *International Journal of Law and Psychiatry, 18,* 231–238.

Shah, S. (1978). Dangerousness: A paradigm for exploring some issues in law and psychology. *American Psychologist, 33,* 224–238.

Showalter, C. R. (1990). Psychiatric participation in capital sentencing procedures: Ethical considerations. *International Journal of Law and Psychiatry, 13,* 261–280.

Skipper v. South Carolina, 461 U.S. 1 (1986).

Small, M., & Otto, R. (1991). Evaluations of competency to be executed. *Criminal Justice and Behavior, 18,* 146–158.

Smith, C. E., & Felix, R. R. (1986). Beyond deterrence. A study of defense on death row. *Federal Probation, 50,* 55–59.

Sorensen, J. R., & Pilgrim, R. L. (2000). An actuarial risk assessment of violence posed by capital murder defendants. *Journal of Criminal Law and Criminology, 90,* 1251–1270.

Sorensen, J., & Wrinkle, R. D. (1996). No hope for parole: Disciplinary infractions among death-sentenced and life-without-parole inmates. *Criminal Justice and Behavior, 23,* 542–552.

Stanford v. Kentucky, 492 U.S. 361 (1989).

Stetler, R. (1999, January/February). Capital cases. *Champion,* 35–40.

Swanson, J. W., Holzer, C. E., III, Granju, V. K., & Jono, R. T. (1990). Violence and psychiatric disorder in the community: Evidence from the epidemiologic catchment area surveys. *Hospital and Community Psychiatry, 41,* 761–770.

Texas Code of Criminal Procedure. (1996). Article 37.071. Procedure in Capital Case.

Thornberry, T. P. (1994, December). *Violent families and youth violence* (Fact sheet No. 21). Washington, DC: U.S. Department of Justice, National Criminal Justice Resources and Statistics.

U.S. v. Barnette, 211 F.3d 803 (4th Cir. 2000).

U.S. v. Beckford, 962 F. Supp. 748 (E.D. Va., Richmond Division, 1997).

U.S. Department of Health and Human Services. (1999). *Mental health: A report of the surgeon general.* Rockville, MD: U.S. Department of Health and Human Services.

U.S. Department of Justice. (1995). *Guide for implementing the comprehensive strategy for serious, violent, and chronic juvenile offenders* (Juvenile Justice Bulletin: OJJDP Update on Programs, NCJ 153571). Washington, DC: Office of Justice Programs, Office of Juvenile Justice and Delinquency Prevention.

Webster, C. D., Douglas, K., Eaves, D., & Hart, S. (1997). *The HCR-20: Assessing risk for violence* (Version 2). Burnaby, BC, Canada: Simon Fraser University.

Wechsler, D. (1981). *Wechsler Adult Intelligence Scale–Revised.* San Antonio, TX: Psychological Corporation.

Wechsler, D. (1997). *Wechsler Adult Intelligence Scale–Third Edition.* San Antonio, TX: Psychological Corporation.

Wechsler Individual Achievement Test (1992). San Antonio, TX: Psychological Corporation.

Widiger, T. A., & Corbitt, E. (1995). Antisocial personality disorder. In W. J. Livesley (Ed.), *The DSM-IV personality disorders* (pp. 103–134). New York: Guilford Press.

Widom, C. S. (2000, January). Childhood victimization: Early adversity, later psychopathology. *National Institute of Justice Journal* (NCJ 180077) 3–9.

Wilkerson v. Utah, 99 U.S. 130, 25 L. Ed., 345 (1879).

Winick, B. J. (1992). Competency to be executed: A therapeutic jurisprudence perspective. *Behavioral Science and the Law, 10,* 317–337.

Woodcock, R. W., & Johnson, M. B. (1977). *Woodcock-Johnson Psycho-Educational Battery.* Hingham, MA: Teaching Resources Corporation.

Woodson v. North Carolina, 428 U.S. 280, 305 (1976).

Worrell, C. M. (1987). Psychiatric prediction of dangerousness in capital sentencing: The quest for innocent authority. *Behavioral Sciences and the Law, 5,* 433–446.

Yarvis, R. M. (1990). Axis I and Axis II diagnostic parameters of homicide. *Bulletin of the American Academy of Psychiatry and Law, 18*(3), 249–289.

Zager, L. (1988). The MMPI-based criminal classification system: A review, current status, and future directions. *Criminal Justice and Behavior, 15,* 39–57.

CHAPTER 22

Child Sexual Abuse Evaluations

KATHRYN KUEHNLE

SCOPE OF THE PROBLEM

The determination of whether sexual abuse of a child has occurred is a complex problem. Accurate estimates on true and false cases of child sexual abuse evade researchers. The child victim is typically the only witness to the crime, medical evidence usually is absent, behavioral symptoms can result from other events or causes, and admission by the perpetrator is unusual (Myers, 1998). The research community has been polarized over whether child victims of sexual abuse or nonvictims are grossly misidentified, to what degree children are suggestible, and which type of error (i.e., false-positive or -negative) creates the greatest harm (Ceci & Friedman, 2000; Lyon, 1999).

The scientific and clinical communities are in agreement that professionals who assess allegations of child sexual abuse should not assume cause-and-effect associations between a *single* aspect of behavior (e.g., behavioral or emotional symptoms, interactions with anatomically detailed dolls, drawings with genitalia, one statement) and the occurrence or nonoccurrence of a sexual abuse event (Kuehnle, 1998c), nor rely solely on their subjective observations (Ceci, Loftus, Leichtman, & Bruck, 1994; Leichtman & Ceci, 1995). To meet the challenge presented by these complex cases, the scientist-practitioner model has been proposed by Kuehnle (1998b) for evaluating child sexual abuse allegations. This model bases conclusions regarding the issue of child sexual abuse on empirically established relationships between data and the behavior of interest, rather than on subjective opinions. Using empirically derived information, the scientist-practitioner defines child sexual abuse as a life event rather than as a clinical syndrome, relies on base rates of behavior for distinguishing and understanding differences between nonsexually abused and sexually abused children, and considers issues of instrument sensitivity and specificity when using assessment protocols and tools. To address the critical issues in child sexual abuse evaluations, this chapter looks to two sources for information: published research and the law.

Definition of Child Sexual Abuse

Across states, there is great diversity in definitions of child abuse and neglect. There also is sufficient vagueness in many of the child maltreatment definitions in state statutes to raise constitutional questions regarding violations of due process (see Melton, Petrila, Poythress, & Slobogin, 1997). Legal and research definitions of child sexual abuse generally require two elements: sexual activities involving a child and an abusive situation (see Finkelhor, 1994, for comprehensive review). Definition of family, the role of the culture, intentionality of the acts, and discrepancy in age/power are factors that complicate attempts to define child sexual abuse, as well as all forms of child maltreatment (National Research Council, 1998). All states identify children as incompetent to consent to sexual activity with adults; the majority of states identify the age of consent as 18 (Myers, 1997a). Illegal sexual interactions, for which children do not have the maturity to provide consent, include activities of contact and noncontact, such as fondling of genital areas, oral sex, intercourse, exposure to indecent acts, sexual rituals, or involvement in child pornography.

Although some states define the term sexual abuse in their criminal statutes, other states do not but, instead, define sexual abuse by reference to their penal code sections dealing with rape, incest, and sexual battery. Child-on-child sex is not defined as sexual abuse in the majority of state statutes. The professional literature defines child-on-child sexual abuse as sex forced on one child by another, regardless of age difference, and any sexual activity between children who differ by a minimum of three to five years in age.

Incidence and Prevalence

An analysis of maltreatment cases from 1991 to 1998 found child sexual abuse reports declined 26% and substantiated cases declined 31% (Jones & Finkelhor, 2001). Because other forms of child maltreatment do not match the decline in sexual abuse cases, the reasons for this trend are unclear. Jones and Finkelhor conclude that it cannot be determined at this time whether the change is because of an actual decrease in the incidence of child sexual abuse, a change in reporters' behavior, or policy and program changes in child protection agencies.

Currently, there are over 3 million children in the United States reported to state child protection services as alleged victims of physical, sexual, and emotional abuse, and neglect (U.S. Department of Health and Human Services, 2000; Wang & Harding, 1999). Approximately 1 million of these reports are substantiated; 12% of the substantiated cases involve child sexual abuse. There is wide agreement that these incidence figures do not represent accurate estimates. Based on a comparison with retrospective research figures, some studies suggest that national incidence figures may represent fewer than one-third of all occurring cases of maltreated children in the United States (Finkelhor, 1994; Kalichman, 1993).

Factors that suggest national incidence figures represent an underestimate of child sexual abuse victims include the exclusion of child-on-child sexual abuse data, as well as victims' and professionals' underreporting. For example, professionals who were legally mandated to report known cases or suspicions of abuse and neglect failed to report approximately 40% of the alleged child sexual abuse cases they encountered (Sedlak, 1991). In another study, approximately 33% of the licensed psychologists surveyed believed that safeguarding the process of therapy was an important factor in deciding whether they would report abuse, despite mandatory reporting laws (Kalichman & Craig, 1991). Affecting child victims' disclosures are factors such as the child's relationship with the perpetrator, the characteristics of the sexual abuse, and the reaction of his or her mother. In several studies, in over half of the cases in which there was strong evidence of sexual abuse and no disclosure by a child to state investigators, the child had a disbelieving mother (Chaffin, Lawson, Selby, & Wherry, 1997; Elliott & Briere, 1994; Lawson & Chaffin, 1992). Other studies showed that the more closely related the child was to the perpetrator, the more intrusive the sexual acts, and the longer the child experienced the abuse, the less likely the child was to disclose (Arata, 1998; Gomes-Schwartz, Horowitz, & Cardarelli, 1990).

Reports that are determined to be false allegations compose an undetermined percentage of the 2 million unsubstantiated cases reported to state child protection services. Some research findings suggest that the rate of false sexual abuse allegations ranges from approximately 6% to 8% (Faller, 1991; Jones & McGraw, 1987), but experts have argued that this estimate is misleadingly low (Ceci & Bruck, 1995), and a more accurate estimate is 23% to 35% when other comprehensive criteria is included in the approximation (Poole & Lindsay, 1997). Lower estimates of false allegations are based on intentional lying as the sole criterion, whereas the higher estimates are based on both intentional lying and suggestive questioning. Poole and Lindsay proposed that a more appropriate label for these higher estimates would be false "suspicions" rather than false "allegations."

Risk Factors for Child Sexual Abuse

Children are at increased vulnerability to be entrapped by sexual abusers when they live in a home where parents' abilities to nurture and supervise are substantially compromised by violence, substance abuse, poverty, and single-parent status (Sedlak & Broadhurst, 1996). Child maltreatment and parental substance abuse are strongly associated (Emery & Laumann-Billings, 1998; Hawley, Halle, Drasin, & Thomas, 1995), as are child maltreatment and poor family or peer relationships (Fergusson, Lynskey, & Horwood, 1996; Fleming, Mullen, & Bammer, 1997). In a retrospective study conducted by Fleming et al., the variables significantly associated with intra- and extrafamilial child sexual abuse were co-occurring intrafamilial physical abuse, social isolation, absence of someone to confide in, mother's death, and parent alcoholism. In one analysis, physical or sexual child abuse was found to occur concurrently in 30% to 70% of two-parent families in which there was spouse abuse (Straus, Gelles, & Steinmetz, 1980). In another study of a centralized Army database, the risk of child abuse was twice as great in families with a report of spouse abuse, compared to other families (Rumm, Cummings, Krauss, Bell, & Rivara, 2000).

Risk factors associated with increased vulnerability for child sexual abuse also include early sexual maturation in girls (Fergusson & Mullen, 1999), and emotional and physical disabilities (Sobsey, Randall, & Parrila, 1997; Sullivan & Knutson, 1998). The peak in abuse reports occurs at ages 10 and 11 (Anderson, Martin, Mullen, Romans, & Herbison, 1993; Finkelhor & Baron, 1986). However, it is likely that incidents of abuse during the preschool years are most likely to be underreported (Fergusson & Mullen, 1999).

Legal Aspects

Currently, child maltreatment reporting laws are in effect in all 50 states and, in most states, criminal penalties for failure to report known or suspected cases of child maltreatment have been established (Finlayson & Koocher, 1991). Although in all states, professionals have a duty to report suspicions of child maltreatment, the U.S. Supreme Court has determined that states do not have a duty to rescue a child from maltreatment. In *DeShaney v. Winnebago County* (1989), Chief Justice Rehnquist's majority opinion stated that the purpose of the 14th Amendment's due process clause "was to protect people from the State, not to insure that the State protected them from each other."

Child sexual abuse cases may be litigated across a variety of legal venues, including criminal and civil courts. Civil court proceedings may involve dependency, termination of parental rights, child custody, and civil proceedings litigated by victims for monetary damages. The courts' motivations for determining guilt or innocence differ, as do their standards for burden of proof. For example, the criminal court's motivation is to punish the guilty and requires the highest standard (i.e., "beyond reasonable doubt"). Civil courts' motivations are variable (e.g., best interests, protection, damages) and require a lesser burden of proof.

THE MEANING OF SYMPTOMS

Child sexual abuse is an event or a series of events, not a psychiatric disorder. The view of sexual abuse as a trigger that sets off an internal process in the child that surfaces as predictable behavioral and emotional symptoms does not have an empirically based foundation. When sexual abuse is conceptualized as a discrete clinical syndrome, evaluators may inappropriately identify test data and symptoms to support their identification and placement of a child in a fictional homogeneous group labeled "sexually abused children" (Kuehnle, 1998b). Unlike symptom patterns of psychiatric disorders, the potential symptoms that sexually abused children may exhibit vary significantly (Kendall-Tackett, Williams, & Finkelhor, 1993; Kuehnle, 1998a). The broad range of behaviors exhibited by child victims is associated with personality differences, personal interpretation of the event, identity of the perpetrator, characteristics of the sexual acts, co-occurring forms of family violence, family stability, and the parents' response following disclosure.

Patterns of Normative Behavior

If the manifestation of specific behaviors is to be addressed in the identification of children who have experienced sexual abuse, the rate at which these specific behaviors appear in a nonsexually abused group also must be considered. One information source is Achenbach's (1991) Child Behavior Checklist normative data on 1,300 children from the general population. These data indicate that behavior problems are a part of normal children's development, with high percentages of preschool- and elementary school-age children in the general population exhibiting problems such as nightmares, sudden changes in mood, poor concentration, fearfulness, disobedience, and temper tantrums. Throughout children's development, major types of anxieties arise, including fears of injury, parental separation, being alone, robbers, and imaginary creatures (Reed, Carter, & Miller, 1992).

A range of sexual behaviors is demonstrated by children within the general population, including (a) penile and clitoral erections by fetuses in utero; (b) masturbation to orgasm by children 8 months of age and older; (c) frequent massaging of genitals and rubbing bodies against furniture, toys, and other objects by infants and toddlers (see Kelley & Byrne,

1992); (d) comparing one's body and touching other children's bodies by preschoolers; and (e) playing games that involve sexual exposure by school-age children (Freidrich, 1998). The most commonly occurring sexual behaviors observed by preschool teachers include limited looking at and touching by preschoolers of each other's genitals, simulated sexual intercourse, and drawing genitalia (Davies, Glaser, & Kossoff, 2000). Conversely, children inserting anything into another child or engaging in oral-genital contact is rarely observed. Retrospective research conducted by Ryan and her colleagues suggests that presumably nonsexually abused prepubescent children engage in a wide range of sexual behaviors with peers (Ryan, Miyoshi, & Krugman, 1988, cited in Ryan, 2000). Prior to age 12 years, these behaviors rarely (fewer than 5%) involve more intrusive sexual acts (i.e., oral/genital contact, penetration during mutual masturbation, vaginal penetration, and anal penetration). Other research, using parent observation compared to teacher observation indicates a lower occurrence of all types of sexual behaviors in presumably nonsexually abused children under the age of 12 years (Fitzpatrick, Deehan, & Jennings, 1995; Friedrich et al., 1992).

Symptoms Demonstrated by Sexually Abused Children

A review of 45 studies by Kendall-Tackett et al. (1993) found that sexually abused children show more emotional and behavioral symptoms than nonsexually abused children, with abuse accounting for 15% to 45% of the variance. However, sexually abused children do not show a higher symptom pattern or occurrence of Posttraumatic Stress Disorder (PTSD) than physically abused and nonmaltreated psychiatrically hospitalized children (Deblinger, McLeer, Atkins, Ralphe, & Foa, 1989). Children who experience multiple types of maltreatment (e.g., physical and sexual abuse) demonstrate increased risk for long-term psychological problems compared to children who have experienced only one type of abuse (Shipman, Rossman, & West, 1999). Consistent with research findings on the biological effects of prolonged stress, children experiencing multiple forms of maltreatment show psychobiological effects, including dysregulated cortisol, elevated catecholamine levels, and indications of immunilogical problems (see Trickett & Putnam, 1998). Interestingly, children victimized by other children manifest emotional and behavioral problems that are not significantly different from those symptoms exhibited by children sexually abused by adults (Shaw, Lewis, Loeb, Rosado, & Rodriguez, 2000).

Over the past decade, researchers have started to shift the focus from a view that all child sexual abuse victims manifest adjustment problems, to the identification of factors that may vary the experience of sexual abuse. Because a substantial percentage of sexually abused children (21% to 49%) are asymptomatic, with only 10% to 25% showing increased symptoms over a two-year postabuse period (Kendall-Tackett et al., 1993), factors that may ameliorate or exacerbate the impact of abuse on the child are under investigation (Mannarino & Cohen, 1996; Masten, Best, & Garmezy, 1990). Preliminary evidence indicates that sexually abused children's postabuse functioning is related to external and internal factors, such as the manner in which the abuse is disclosed, the abuse experience, social supports, and coping strategies. Nagel and her colleagues found that children who intentionally disclosed their abuse, compared to those whose disclosure was unintentional, reported more anxiety and coping problems at a one-year follow-up (Nagel, Putnam, Noll, & Trickett, 1997). Other researchers have found that children who are abused by fathers and experience abuse that includes intercourse and physical violence have the poorest long-term outcome (Browne & Finkelhor, 1986; Wyatt & Newcomb, 1990).

Further research has shown that only a modest amount of outcome variability appears to be directly attributable to characteristics of the specific abuse incidents because other intervening variables are powerful mediators of outcome. The strongest of these mediators are social support and coping strategies (Everson, Hunter, Runyan, Edelsohn, & Coulter, 1989; Runtz & Schallow, 1997; Spaccarelli, 1994). Preliminary findings support a mediational model in which coping strategies play a role in the transition from abuse and abuse-related stresses to symptomatic outcomes (Chaffin, Wherry, & Dykman, 1997). There is robust evidence showing that the more self-blaming the attributions and negative perceptions held by the child, the greater the risk of long-term negative outcomes (Mannarino, Cohen, & Berman, 1994). Chaffin and his colleagues found each of four identified coping strategies (i.e., avoidant, internalized, angry, and active/social) had a unique set of abuse characteristics, abuse-related environmental characteristics, and behavioral symptoms associated with it. Fewer behavioral problems but greater sexual anxieties were associated with the use of avoidant coping strategies; increased guilt and PTSD hyperarousal symptoms were linked with internalized strategies; and a wide range of behavior and emotional problems were associated with anger strategies. The active/social coping was the only strategy not associated with symptoms; however, neither was it associated with measured benefits.

Psychosexual problems are considered the strongest and most specific effects and one of the most treatment-resistant sequelae of sexual abuse (Cosentino, Meyer-Bahlburg, Alpert, Weinberg, & Gaines, 1995; Finkelhor & Berliner, 1995; Friedrich, 1998). In a normative study of over 2,000 subjects, Friedrich (1998) found sexual abuse was the best predictor of sexual acting-out and sexually precocious behavior. Family sexuality, involving the child's recurrent visual exposure to sexual material and activity, was the second best predictor. Some studies report low maternal support associated with higher levels of female victims' sexually inappropriate behaviors (Leifer, Shapiro, & Kassem, 1993). There also may be a "dose" effect, with unusually high levels of sexualized behaviors in children linked to more intrusive sexual abuse, force or threats of harm, and a greater number of abusers (Friedrich et al., 1992; Friedrich, Urquiza, & Beilke, 1986).

Preliminary findings also show links among different types of deviant sexual behaviors, factors within the family, and factors embedded within the abuse. Hall, Mathews, and Pearce (1998) found four variables to emerge as the most predictive of whether a sexually abused child would sexually act out with others: (a) sexual arousal during the sexual abuse, (b) the perpetrator's use of sadism during the abuse, (c) a history of physical abuse, and (d) a history of emotional abuse. Other abuse-specific variables related to children's sexual behavior problems were (a) being groomed by the perpetrator, (b) watching the perpetrator in sexual acts, and (c) being actively involved in the sexual abuse. However, in contrast to previous research (Browne & Finkelhor, 1986; Wyatt & Newcomb, 1990), physical intrusiveness of the sexual acts, the duration of the abuse, and the child's relationship to the offender were not related to victim's psychosexual problems. Furthermore, whereas sexual arousal during abuse was associated both with children whose sexually deviant behavior was solely self-focused and children whose sexualized behavior was directed toward others, experience of sexual sadism was associated only with the latter group of children. Although significant variability (i.e., 7% to 90%) in numbers of children exhibiting aberrant sexualized behaviors are found in the literature (Kendall-Tackett et al., 1993), this variability may be partially accounted for by the methodological weaknesses impacting this research, including confounded variables and inconsistency in the definitions of sexual behavior problems (see Briere, 1992).

Child Sexual Abuse Accommodation Syndrome

Based on his clinical observations, Summitt (1983) suggested that sexual exploitation of children has consistent, predictable, and deleterious effects, purporting that a set of five symptoms and behaviors consistently occur together (i.e., secrecy, helplessness, accommodation, delayed unconvincing disclosure, and retraction) following the sexual abuse of a child. He coined the term "child sexual abuse accommodation syndrome" (CSAAS) to describe this pattern of symptoms. Although Summitt (1992) never intended CSAAS to be

used as a diagnostic tool, some professionals have used it to argue that when an alleged child victim exhibits these symptoms, the occurrence of sexual abuse can be determined. The CSAAS symptom pattern has not been supported by research, however. As noted by Chaffin et al. (1997), sexual abuse is not an experience leading in some simple and direct manner to a single symptom or syndrome.

Legal Aspects

In child sexual abuse cases, behavioral syndrome testimony is highly controversial, and appellate court decisions on its admissibility have been contradictory. Mason's (1998) review of 122 appellate court decisions between 1980 and 1990 revealed that the characteristics specified as indicators of child sexual abuse by expert witnesses in these cases varied widely, demonstrated a number of critical contradictions, and produced an imprecise behavioral profile. Although some courts have allowed testimony on various permeations of child sexual abuse syndrome, other courts have disallowed such testimony. Courts have been divided on whether to specifically allow testimony on CSAAS (Levine & Battistoni, 1991; Mason, 1995; Richardson, Ginsburg, Gatowski, & Dobbin, 1995). A number of cases involving CSAAS testimony have been overturned (e.g., *Hadden v. State*, 1997; *State v. Michaels*, 1993).

As reported by Myers (1997a) CSAAS testimony primarily has been admitted in criminal cases as rebuttal testimony when the child's behavior has been portrayed by the defense as unrepresentative of an experience of sexual abuse (e.g., *Davenport v. State*, 1991). The most frequent use of this type of CSAAS testimony is to explain factors such as delayed disclosure (e.g., *State v. Gokey*, 1990), a child's recantation (e.g., *People v. Gallow*, 1991), or other behaviors exhibited by the child that might lead a jury to doubt the evidence presented by the prosecutor (e.g., *State v. Reser*, 1989). This type of testimony is most likely to be allowed if the expert indicates that such behaviors are consistent with and could indicate sexual abuse, while also acknowledging other possible causes (e.g., *State v. Roenfeldt*, 1992). However, courts generally have not allowed CSAAS testimony to be introduced by prosecutors to suggest that a child who displays these symptoms is a victim of sexual abuse.

MEMORY

The survival of memories through long-term storage, the influence of traumatic memories on later behavior, and the recollection or repression of memories continue to be investigated. As noted by Howe (2000), within these three areas there exist science and pseudoscience, both of which may be presented as fact in the legal arena.

Early Memory

Although scientific investigation indicates that some form of immature memory is present in utero (DeCasper, Lecanuet, Busnel, Granier-Deferre, & Maugeais, 1994), without current technology to conduct more sophisticated research on fetus memory, one cannot surmise that infants' retention of prenatally exposed auditory stimuli for several hours after birth "is equivalent to remembering one's life events in utero" (Howe & Courage, 1997a). Whereas 2-month-old infants demonstrate little retention after three days (Greco, Rovee-Collier, Hayne, Griesler, & Early, 1986), some meaningful (i.e., causally organized) compared to nonmeaningful (i.e., randomly organized) event sequences can be remembered by 11- and 12-month-old infants for up to three months (Howe & Courage, 1997b; Mandler & McDonough, 1995) and by 13- to 21-month-old toddlers for over eight months (Bauer, 1996; Bauer, Hertsgaard, & Dow, 1994). Emerging research indicates that unique, distinctive, and personally consequential experiences, in contrast to whether the experiences were positive or negative, are well remembered for periods of up to six years during childhood (Conway, 1996; Fivush & Schwartzmueller, 1998; Howe, 1997).

Impact of Stress on Memory

Current research findings are inconsistent regarding the impact of stress on children's memory (see Davies, 1993, for review). Physiological and psychological stress trigger integrated activity of the neural and neuroendocrine systems, which may either create a failure to remember or enhance memory (Gold & McCarty, 1995). Researchers continue to argue over whether memories for traumatically stressful events are processed in a substantially different way than for nontraumatic stressful events (Alpert, 1995; Hembrooke & Ceci, 1995; Howe, Courage, & Peterson, 1994; Whitfield, 1995). According to Howe (2000), memories for traumatic events appear to adhere to the same principles as memories for less salient events, and will endure to the extent that they remain unique and distinctive against a background of other experiences. Quas et al. (1999) also conclude that their results, in conjunction with other findings, "suggest that stressful and traumatic memories tend to be governed by similar, general age-related mechanisms that dictate whether early childhood experiences will be remembered in the long term" (p. 258). Van der Kolk and his colleagues propose a different model, suggesting that when children are confronted with trauma, they (a) are unable to process the information, (b) employ the defense mechanism of dissociation, and (c) compartmentalize the unintegrated memory, which consists mainly of sensory perceptions and affective states (van der Kolk & Fisler, 1995; van der Kolk & van der Hart, 1991).

Other models suggest physiological components associated with traumatic stress and memory problems (Bremner, Krystal, Southwick, & Charney, 1995). Bremner and his colleagues propose that traumatic stress creates abnormalities in the functioning of brain regions involved in memory, which is revealed in lower left hippocampal volume in survivors of child physical and sexual abuse. Currently, researchers continue to search for a clear understanding between stress and memory and note that intensity and chronicity may not be solely responsible for the impact of stress on memory processes. Rather, these factors may interact with individual differences (Cicchetti, Rogosch, Lynch, & Holt, 1993; Goodman & Quas, 1997).

Development of Autobiographical Memory

Several theories exist regarding the development of autobiographical memory (i.e., memory accessible to conscious recollection) and the discontinuation of infantile amnesia. Sociolinguistic theory views autobiographical memory as based on the development of sophisticated language-based representational skills, which allow memories to be retained and organized around a chronological life history (Fivush & Schwartzmueller, 1998; Nelson, 1993). The language skills necessary for autobiographical memory are thought to be incomplete until the late preschool years. Conversely, other theorists (Howe & Courage, 1997a) posit that a sense of self is fundamental to the development of autobiographical memory and serves as a referent around which personally experienced events can be organized in memory. Howe and Courage note that what appears to assist memory is the change in the personalization of the event: There is a shift from a memory of an event that happened to an event that happened to oneself. Although the cognitive self begins to appear around 18 to 24 months of age, it may not be sufficiently developed to support autobiographical encoding until later.

There is little scientific support that memories from the first two years of life can be consciously recollected later in child- or adulthood as experiences that happened to oneself. Although currently, there is no consensus about why early memories are not recalled later in development, researchers are generally suspicious of memories reported by older children and adults that predate an individual's third birthday. Although there is preliminary evidence that children's memories, compared to adults' memories, may fade more quickly, if events are personally significant and repeatedly rehearsed through questioning and cuing, such memories are less likely to be lost (Hudson, 1990; see Melton et al., 1995).

Legal Aspects

The courts have been skeptical about whether young children when testifying can be truthful and have the cognitive and mental skills necessary to give reliable, trustworthy testimony. Some state laws presume a child above a certain age is competent and only require an inquiry into competency when the child is under the specified age. However, many states have now moved to eliminate the need for special procedures to qualify a child witness. They have adopted the approach of the *Federal Rules of Evidence 601*, according children the same presumptive competence as other witnesses; proper understanding rather than age is the basis of competency (*State v. Allen*, 1994; *State v. Stewart*, 1994; *State v. Pham*, 1994). The legal test of a child's competency in most jurisdictions derives from *Wheeler v. United States* (1895), where the U.S. Supreme Court upheld the testimonial competence of a 5-year-old in a murder case. Based on this case, a child of *any* age who possesses the following capacities may testify: (a) appreciate the difference between truth and falsehoods; (b) understand the obligation to tell the truth; (c) accurately perceive and recall the events witnessed; and (d) relate facts accurately (see Myers, 1997a). Thus, determining whether a child is competent to testify must be based on objective facts, rather than on the believability of the child's allegation.

To justify a competency hearing, the Federal Victims of Child Abuse Act (1990) requires a written motion and affidavit from the defense setting forth the reasons, apart from the age of the child, for the hearing. The defense must use age-appropriate questions, and questions must be related solely to competency and not trial issues. The U.S. Supreme Court, in *Kentucky v. Stincer* (1987), upheld the decision that a defendant does not have a constitutional right to be present at a competency hearing.

SUGGESTIBILITY

Because memory for experience is reconstructive, with autobiographical recall filtered through one's current beliefs, knowledge, expectations, and motivations (see Howe, 2000), memory is subject to suggestibility and the construction of inaccurate recollections (see Brainerd & Reyna, 1996; Bruck & Ceci, 1995). Although true memories survive longer than fictitious memories that are based on misinformation, false

memories survive across extended time intervals (Poole & White, 1993). These findings have been obtained for preschoolers as well as for older children (see Bruck, Ceci, & Hembrooke, 1998).

Suggestibility generally refers to errors that arise when children are exposed to information that is false or to social pressures that encourage particular types of answers (Ceci & Bruck, 1993). There is strong disagreement over the degree to which young children are suggestible and the extent to which their suggestibility may lead to false allegations of sexual abuse. However, researchers are in agreement that if adults do not do anything to usurp the memories of children or pressure children for certain answers, even very young preschool children can provide highly accurate accounts of their prior experiences.

Children's exposure to false information can interfere with their source monitoring (i.e., the process of identifying the origin of one's knowledge). Source monitoring deficiencies entail difficulty in distinguishing between events that happened and events one merely thought about or heard discussed. Young children are more likely than older children and adults to have difficulty determining whether they have obtained information from their own experiences or from other sources (Poole & Lindsay, 1995). Children's source monitoring scores are found to predict suggestibility even after individual differences in recall and acquiescence are statistically partialled out (Poole & Lindsay, 1997). Several researchers have focused their efforts on the development of a suggestibility scale to find a standardized tool to measure individual differences in suggestibility of preschool children (Endres, Poggenpohl, & Erben, 1999; Scullin & Ceci, 2000). Validation research continues to progress on these new tools.

Accuracy of Memories

Research on children's disclosures of sexual abuse during interviewing supports two competing perspectives: recounting past events is *enhanced* by adult questions; and recounting past events is *interfered with* by adult questions, especially if the questioning introduces suggestive false information (Snyder, Nathanson, & Saywitz, 1993). Research findings consistently show that when certain conditions are met (e.g., neutral interviewer, open-ended questioning, absence of repeated suggestive interviewing, and no induction of a motive for the child to make a false report), even very young preschool-age children's recall is highly accurate, although limited in the number of details (Baker-Ward, Gordon, Ornstein, Larus, & Clubb, 1993; Parker, Bahrick, Lundy, Fivush, & Levitt, 1999). Research has consistently demonstrated that although preschoolers generally recall less information than older children, the proportion of accurate statements in the free recall reports of children does not vary with age (Goodman, Hirschman, Hepps, & Rudy, 1991). When children are asked open-ended questions, the information narrated is usually accurate because their memory is most likely to be based on their own experiences. However, open-ended questions can elicit inaccurate reports if a child has incorporated repeated misinformation into his or her memory (Leichtman & Ceci, 1995).

External and Internal Variables

External interview factors, such as repetitious questioning (see Fivush & Schwarzmueller, 1995; Poole & White, 1995), the interviewer's style (Carter, Bottoms, & Levine, 1996; Goodman, Bottoms, Schwartz-Kenney, & Rudy, 1991; Lepore & Sesco, 1994; Tobey & Goodman, 1992), and bias (see Ceci & Bruck, 1995) are important factors that may increase children's suggestibility. When interviewers ask numerous specific questions, and the format involves yes-no question pairs (i.e., a yes-no question followed by a request to describe the event: "Did Uncle Joe . . . ?"; "Tell me about that"), children's performance can be compromised (Peterson & Bell, 1996; Peterson & Briggs, 1997; Poole & Lindsay, 1995). Repeating closed-ended or specific questions also tends to elicit inconsistency and speculation by children (Poole & White, 1991, 1993). Further complicating the evaluation of children's statements is the inaccuracy of interviewers' recollection of how information has been elicited from the child. For example, mothers who interviewed their 4-year-old children about a structured play activity, which the mothers did not observe, had difficulty recalling whether their children's statements were prompted or spontaneous and whether specific utterances were spoken by themselves or their children (Bruck, Ceci, & Francoeur, 1999).

Although researchers have made progress in identifying external interview variables that are associated with children's suggestibility, less is understood about other external factors and internal characteristics of children that create individual differences in children's susceptibility to suggestibility (Bruck, Ceci, & Melnyk, 1997; Eisen, Goodman, Qin, & Davis, 1998). These less understood variables are thought to include constitutional (e.g., temperament), social (e.g., attachment), emotional (e.g., self-confidence), and cognitive (e.g., language) factors. Significant correlations between measurements of temperament (i.e., approach-withdrawal and adaptability) and children's memory for stressful medical procedures have been found (Ornstein, Sharpiro, Clubb, Follmer, & Baker-Ward, 1997). Preliminary research further suggests a link between children's secure

attachment (Elicker, Egland, & Sroufe, 1992) and good parent-child communication (Clarke-Stewart, Thompson, & Lepore, 1989) with resistance to suggestibility. Children of parents characterized by a more dismissing avoidant attachment style show heightened suggestibility and make more commission errors to specific and misleading questions (Goodman, Quas, Batterman-Faunce, Riddlesberger, & Kuhn, 1997; Quas et al., 1999). Further, children's self-confidence is inversely related to suggestibility, with high-confidence children showing greater resistance to suggestibility (Vrij & Bush, 1998).

The most robust internal factor associated with suggestibility is the age and developmental level of the child. Young preschoolers (i.e., ages 3 and 4) are most vulnerable to suggestive interviewing, while 6- and 7-year-old children show significant increases in resistance to misinformation (Ceci & Bruck, 1993). The age at which children reach adult levels of resistance is debated, with some studies finding children as young as 10 showing this level of resistance (Saywitz & Dorado, 1998) and other research finding early adolescence as the marker (Warren & Lane, 1995).

Areas of Research and Issues of Ecological Validity

Researchers have attempted to address the question of children's suggestibility through three primary classes of research on children's memories and vulnerabilities to misleading information (see Ceci, Crossman, Gilstrap, & Scullin, 1998). The primary areas of study on children's memories, which are identified as having ecological validity, involve (a) real or imagined personal experiences not involving body contact by another person, (b) events involving nongenital body contact, and (c) events involving genital and other body contact.

Research on children's memories for real or imagined personal experiences involves repeated presentations of misinformation about events that have never occurred; this misinformation is repeated across multiple interviews. The fictitious events in these studies do not involve the child's physical contact by an adult. Findings suggest that when children are repeatedly provided inaccurate information about the occurrence of a fictitious event and instructed to think about whether the event occurred, children are at increased risk to report occurrence. For example, children ages 4 to 6 years were repeatedly presented with several real and fictitious events and asked to think about whether the events had occurred. The false events included experiences such as whether the children had ever gotten their "finger caught in a mousetrap and had to go to the hospital to get the trap off." Interviewer directions to the children were: "Think real hard, and tell me whether this ever happened to you." False narratives for at least one fictitious event were provided by more than half of the children; one-fourth produced false accounts for the majority of the fictitious events; and over one-fourth of the false narrators refused to acknowledge that the fictitious events had not really happened after they were debriefed (Ceci, Crotteau, Smith, & Loftus, 1994). In another study, rather than simply directed to think about whether they had ever experienced an event, children were told real and fictitious events *had* happened to them. They were instructed: "Make a picture of it in your head and think real hard about each thing for a minute" (Ceci, Loftus, et al., 1994). The percentage of fictitious events that the children narrated remembering increased from 29% at the first session to 43% at the twelfth session.

Further investigations show that prior to misleading interviews, when children are presented misinformation that negatively stereotypes an adult or offers a negative opinion, they are at heightened risk to provide inaccurate information to misleading questioning about the identified individual. For example, 46% of the 3- and 4-year-old children who were presented negative information about an individual named Sam Stone provided inaccurate negative information about this individual after four misleading interviews over a 10-week period (Leichtman & Ceci, 1995). In the combined stereotyped information and suggestive interview group, 21% of the 3- and 4-year-olds and 11% of the 5- and 6-year-olds continued to maintain that they saw Sam Stone do the fictitious misdeeds even after their statements were challenged. In all experimental groups, the error rates of younger children were significantly higher than the error rates of older children. Further, the children who were not provided the pre- or postevent misleading information were highly accurate in their recounts of the identified event. In another study, when the interviewer asked 4- to 6-year-old children several misleading questions followed by accusatory statements (e.g., "He wasn't supposed to do that . . . that was bad"), the children's errors increased and they endorsed more biased interviewer interpretations of the events (Lepore & Sesco, 1994).

Researchers have studied the effects of combining suggestive questions with social pressures identified from interviews, such as those used in the McMartin Preschool case (Garven, Wood, Malpass, & Shaw, 1998). These social pressures include (a) other people (e.g., informing the child that other children had already told); (b) positive consequences (e.g., giving praise or approval); (c) negative consequences (e.g., criticizing a child's statement); (d) already answered (e.g., repeating a question the child had already answered); and (e) inviting speculation (e.g., telling the child to speculate on what might have happened). Fifty-eight percent of the 3- to 6-year-old children who experienced misleading questions combined with social pressures made one or more false reports. However, only 17% of the children who solely experienced misleading questions (designed to induce false allegations about an observed adult) made false reports after a single interview occurring one week after the event. In a follow-up article, Garven and her colleagues found a 35% and 52% false claims rate for children who experienced misleading questions combined with social pressures, in contrast to 13% to 15% when only misleading questions were used (Garven, Wood, Malpass, & Shaw, 2000). False claims included that the adult had kissed the child on the nose or tickled the child's tummy.

Researchers posit that children may be more resistant to misleading information about an event if the event involves the child's own body (e.g., pediatric examinations). Research on children's memories for events involving body touch entails repeated presentations of misinformation about events that have involved the child's physical contact by an adult. When children are repeatedly provided misinformation about who touched them, how they were touched, and what their reaction to the touching had been, the length of delay between the actual event and the misleading interview increases children's risk to provide inaccurate information. For example, 3- and 6-year-old children were interviewed immediately after a pediatric examination, one week postexam, and three weeks postexam (Baker-Ward et al., 1993). The younger the child, the higher the number of omissions for factual details to open-ended questions and the poorer the resistance to misleading questions after a short time delay. At the three weeks postexam interview, the number of errors (i.e., commissions and omissions) increased for both age groups. However, both age groups were resistant to misleading information about the identity of the individual who performed their physical examination.

In another study, incorporating a longer time delay, 5-year-old children were examined by a male pediatrician and given a polio vaccine and a Diphtheria-Pertussis-Tetanus inoculation (Bruck, Ceci, Francoeur, & Barr, 1995). The children were immediately presented misleading information and then interviewed one week later. Results indicated that children's reports were not significantly influenced by one suggestive feedback intervention. However, following four misleading interviews at one-year postvisit, 40% of the children given misleading information made errors in their narrations, including errors in the identity of the person who gave them the shot (i.e., doctor or research assistant). In another study, 3- to 7-year-old children were presented misleading information and immediately interviewed after their visit to a pediatric nurse for inoculations (Goodman, Hirschman, et al., 1991). The children were reinterviewed one year later. When immediately interviewed, older children were more accurate than the younger children, and they made fewer omission and commission errors. During the course of the year following the visit, the amount of accurate information in the children's free recall declined for all ages. In the delayed interview, children's inaccuracy increased when they were asked specific questions and when presented with suggestions embedded in misleading questions. These findings suggest that when older preschool children actually experience a salient event (pediatric examination) and are questioned a short time after the event, even if provided one session of misleading information, they can be very accurate in their recall. However, the younger the child or the longer the length of delay between the event and the suggestive questioning, the higher the risk for providing inaccurate information.

Because children may be more resistant to being misled about negative experiences related to sexual abuse activities, researchers have sought out medical procedures that provide the greatest ecological validity for addressing this question. A number of researchers have attempted to address ecological validity by studying children's suggestibility following examinations involving genital contact. For example, Eisen et al. (1998) studied 3- to 5-year-olds, 6- to 10-year-olds, and 11- to 15-year-olds hospitalized for a five-day abuse assessment. All children received a medical checkup; an anogenital examination and swab for culture; and, on day 5, an interview, which included misleading and other suggestive questioning. Results showed that 3- to 4-year-olds made commission errors when answering 40% of the misleading abuse-related questions (e.g., "The doctor did not have any clothes on, did he?"); however, these errors were made by only 21% of the children. Six- to 10-year-old children made errors in answering 16% of the misleading abuse-related questions, and 11- to 15-year-olds erred on 9% of the abuse-related questions. These findings support previous results, which show that the younger the child, the greater his or her susceptibility to misleading information. Unfortunately, this research fails to demonstrate whether the sexual abuse experience increases or decreases suggestibility to misleading abuse-related questions because the researchers' results did not distinguish among physically abused, sexually abused, and neglected children.

The examination of memory following a stressful and painful medical procedure, voiding cystourethrogram fluoroscopy (VCUG), has been the focus of several studies. This procedure involves the child lying on an examination table (some children must be strapped or held down), being catheterized through the urethra, having the bladder filled with a contrast medium, and the child instructed to void. X-rays are taken throughout the VCUG. In one study, 3- and 6-year-old children administered a VCUG were interviewed after one-, three-, and six-week delays (Merritt, Ornstein, & Spicker, 1994). During the interviews, the children demonstrated low omission and commission errors in the identification of event features, suggesting that the salience of the target event has an important impact on memory. However, younger age was again inversely related to increased suggestibility. Goodman, Quas, et al. (1997) found similar results in a study using the VCUG procedure, with 20% of the 3- to 4-year-old children assenting to misleading abuse-related questions (e.g., "Did the doctor kiss you?").

In one unique study, the long-term memory of 3- to 13-year-old children was investigated for their earlier VCUG experience (Quas et al., 1999). The memory interview was divided into four sections: free recall, anatomically detailed doll and props demonstration, direct questions, and false-event questions. Interview delays of less than 36 months were categorized as short delays (M = 24 months) and delays of 36 months or longer were categorized as long delays (M = 51 months). During the interview, none of the nine children who were 2 years old at the time of the VCUG provided information that showed a clear memory of the procedure. Half of the 3-year-old children provided information that indicated they had a clear memory of the procedure. By age 5, the majority of children remembered their VCUG experience. Age at VCUG predicted whether children remembered the procedure and how much information they provided but not the accuracy of their answers to direct questions. Compared to children interviewed after delays of three years or more, children interviewed after shorter delays provided a greater amount of correct information. However, longer delays were not associated with greater inaccuracies in children's memories or with heightened suggestibility. Results on the association between children's stress (e.g., fear and upset) and accuracy of reports were mixed. The type of memory question (e.g., free recall, misleading) and the point of measurement of children's emotional reactions (e.g., before, during, after) may have different implications for memory. Regarding suggestibility, almost half of the 40 children questioned made some type of false affirmation that a fictitious event (i.e., nose test) had occurred. Three- to 5-year-old children scored significantly higher on the false report measures compared to children over age 6.

Legal Aspects

Over the past decade, research on children's memories has been driven by issues raised in a number of legal cases receiving high media attention (e.g., *State v. Fuster,* 1985 [Country Walk]; *State v. Kelly,* 1991–1992 [Little Rascals]; *State v. Michaels,* 1988, 1993, 1994 [Wee Care]; *State v. Buckey,* 1990 [McMartin]) regarding the accuracy and reliability of children's allegations of sexual abuse (see Ceci & Bruck, 1995). Within the past decade, appellate courts have overturned the convictions of a number of individuals accused of child sexual abuse (*Commonwealth v. LeFave,* 1998; *State v. Michaels,* 1993) because evidence was largely based on the testimony of children whose reliability was determined to be compromised by suggestive interviewing techniques and improper expert testimony admitted at trial. Submitted in the Michaels appeal was an *amicus* brief on suggestibility (Bruck & Ceci, 1995) written by the Committee of Concerned Social Scientists and signed by 43 memory researchers. In addition to the decision to reverse Michaels's conviction, the appellate court ruled that if the state decided to retry Michaels, the trial judge should hold a pretrial hearing to determine if the interviewing had so seriously tainted the children's memories that their out-of-court statements and in-court testimony should be inadmissible at trial (*State v. Michaels,* 1994). An appeal to the New Jersey Supreme Court was filed and the appellate court decision was upheld in favor of pretrial taint hearings (see Myers, 1997a, for a review).

STRUCTURING THE INTERVIEW

The informativeness of interviews with child victims is strongly influenced by the skill and expertise of the interviewers and . . . skillful interviewers can make children into reliable and invaluable informants. (Lamb, Sternberg, & Esplin, 1998, p. 815)

When structuring an interview, the evaluator must consider a range of hypotheses (see Kuehnle, 1996) and base his or her interview strategies on an empirical foundation. The failure to remain open to alternative hypotheses can pose serious risks to producing scientifically sound conclusions (Dawes, 1991). For example, if the interviewer holds only one hypothesis about an event, and the hypothesis is correct, it can lead to high levels of accurate recall by young children; however, if the hypothesis is incorrect, it can lead to high levels of inaccurate recall. In designing a sound interview, the evaluator must consider five central factors that are found to strongly affect children's capacity as witnesses: (a) children's tendency to be reticent and generally uncommunicative with unfamiliar adults; (b) children's familiarity with being tested by adults (e.g., "What is the name of this animal?") but lack of familiarity with adults treating them as sources of

information that are unknown by the adult; and, compared to adults, children's (c) poorer linguistic skills, (d) poorer memory for events, and (e) tendency to forget information more quickly (Lamb, Sternberg, & Esplin, 1994). Furthermore, the passage of time must also be considered, in that time can affect both memory and suggestibility (Lamb et al., 1998).

There is consensus among researchers that audiotaping or videotaping the interview is the most accurate method of recording the specific questions and answers. Most research-based guidelines and recommendations for interviewing alleged sexually abused children also form a consensus for the structure and sequence of interview steps (American Professional Society on the Abuse of Children, 1996; Kuehnle, 1996; Lamb et al., 1994, 1996; Poole & Lamb, 1998; Raskin & Yuille, 1989). These steps include: (a) development of rapport, (b) assessment of the child's ability to answer questions and provide details, (c) identification of ground rules for the interview, (d) interview practice on non-abuse-related questions, (e) introduction of the sexual abuse topic beginning with open-ended questions, and (f) interview closure. Despite these recommendations, many interviewers do an inadequate job of building rapport or addressing the interview ground rules (Lamb et al., 1996). Many also progress prematurely to specific questions and rely heavily on specific and yes-no questions (Warren, Woodall, Hunt, & Perry, 1996; Wood, McClure, & Birch, 1996).

Building Rapport

When interviewing children, physical surroundings should not be distracting or confusing. In developing rapport, the goal is to build a comfortable and safe atmosphere that will allow the child to talk openly and without fear of judgment or criticism (Sattler, 1998). Although there is an absence of research on the specific linkage of rapport to more complete and accurate free recall, studies on interviewer style indicate that condescending or disinterested interviewers obtain increased inaccurate information from the children interviewed (Geiselman, Saywitz, & Bornstein, 1991).

Development of rapport begins with introducing oneself to the child and discussing neutral topics that are appropriate for the child's age. Interviewers should be relaxed, convey interest in what the child has to say, and not dominate the conversation with questions (see Poole & Lamb, 1998). Specific techniques for personalizing the interview and communicating empathy without suggesting to the child that the alleged event has occurred include using the child's name, giving the child undivided attention, timing questions and comments appropriately, and repeating the child's last comment when moving to a follow-up question (Fisher & Geiselman, 1992).

In light of the problems with interviewers not fully developing or prematurely terminating this phase, Sternberg and her colleagues (1997) developed a specific script for the rapport-building phase of their interviews.

The presentation of treats or gifts to children preceding or following a sexual abuse interview is controversial. Interviewers who engage in this practice may be criticized and accused of manipulating children's responses to questioning. However, empirical data are not available to establish whether providing children with candy, cookies, or toys enhances, interferes with, or has no effect on the accuracy or completeness of their narrations. Empirical data are also absent on the facilitating or interfering effect of manipulatives (e.g., paper, crayons, clay) used to assist the interviewer in maintaining children's alertness and attention to the forensic interview.

Assessment of the Child's Ability to Answer Questions and Provide Details

To acquire the most accurate and developmentally detailed information and to minimize the chance that the child will impeach himself or herself, the evaluator must determine the linguistic competency of the child. This determination rests on developmental information obtained about the child, observation of the child, and knowledge of child development research. It is generally accepted practice to acquire a developmental history before the interview rather than conduct a blind interview (Hewitt, 1999). A developmental history is helpful for the selection of appropriate interview procedures and placement of the child's answers in a developmental context (Saywitz & Camparo, 1998). Knowledge of the child's developmental level may allow the evaluator to plan ahead and structure some preliminary nonleading questions. Because misinformation provided to interviewers prior to an interview can influence their questions and lead to increased errors of commission by some children (White, Leichtman, & Ceci, 1997), interviewers must be cautious in formulating their questions.

There is little research to support that blind interviewing eliminates leading questions. Although an interviewer may be blind to the variables associated with the child and alleged abuse, the interviewer may still ask inappropriate questions due to a limited knowledge of the child's developmental needs and limitations. However, a thorough knowledge of child development does not ensure that the evaluator, whether blind or informed, will conduct an adequate interview.

Regardless of the court's need for specific facts, children should not be asked questions during the substantive interview requiring answers of specific facts unless the child is developmentally competent to do so. For example, young children may provide inconsistent and inaccurate answers to questions regarding frequency or point in time of an event because they lack the capacity to answer these questions. Prior to 6- or 7-years of age, children cannot count events that are abstract and do not have discrete boundaries (e.g., "How many pieces of candy did you eat yesterday?" versus "How many pieces of candy is this?"), and cannot determine that something happened before or after something else (Saywitz, 1995). The evaluator needs to assess not only linguistic competency but also the child's linguistic style to frame questions that match each child's idiosyncratic use of language (e.g., penis, dick, pee pee) and to determine the child's names for the important people in his or her life. Prior to the age of 8, children may confuse unfamiliar words with words that sound familiar; prior to the age of 10, children have difficulty reporting events in chronological order (Saywitz, 1995). To assess whether children possess the skills necessary to answer specific forensic interview questions such as dates, times, locations, and physical descriptions, the evaluator can ask the child to identify the current season, date, and time; city and state where the child lives; and race, age, and height of the evaluator (Saywitz & Camparo, 1998).

Although the use of anatomical drawings to prompt the labeling of body parts provides the interviewer with the child's words for these parts and functions, the timing of this inquiry is debated. Interviewers who ask for genital labels early in the interview can be criticized for suggesting sexual themes (Poole & Lamb, 1998). It is argued that the use of sexual words may direct the child's conversation, and therefore, drawings should be presented to the child only after a disclosure. Currently, there is little research to show how risk of false reports may increase with the use of these anatomical props when children have been exposed to misinformation in earlier interviews. One preliminary investigation found that 12% of 3- to 6-year-old child subjects falsely reported touching on their buttock, and 7.5% falsely reported touching of their genitals when the interviewer pointed to the body part and asked specifically about touching (Steward & Steward, 1996). However, none of the children falsely reported touching of their buttock or genitals when simply shown an anatomical drawing and not verbally queried about touching.

To document legal competence at the time of the interview and to aid the court in future determinations of admissibility of the interview evidence, children's understanding of truth and falsehood may be directly addressed during this phase of the interview (Myers, 1998). To establish this competency, children must demonstrate their understanding of truth and lies through identification or definition of these concepts.

Although it is not until the age of 10 that most children can explain the difference between truth and lies, by age 4, children can identify if a statement is truthful. Although most 4-year-olds know that a lie is wrong, they have more difficulty identifying if a statement is a lie. It is not until age 7 that most children can define the term "truth" (Lyon & Saywitz, 1999). Based on these developmental findings, the evaluator should use identification questions (e.g., present interviewee with a picture depicting two children with a car on the table between them; one child says the object is a car, the other child says the object is a horse, and the interviewee is asked which child is telling the truth) rather than definition questions ("What does it mean to tell the truth?") with children under the age of 8.

Unfortunately, researchers have shown that children who correctly answer truth/lie questions are not more accurate or less suggestible than same-age peers who are unable to do so (Huffman, Warren, & Frazier, 1997; Pipe & Wilson, 1994). Therefore, truth/lie discussions may have limited value because children's provision of inaccurate information is often based on a misunderstanding of the questions or a failure in their ability to grasp the source of their knowledge. Current competency procedures do not address some of these primary reasons why children misreport events (Poole & Lamb, 1998).

Establishment of the Ground Rules for the Interview

Because the forensic interview setting and tasks are complex and unfamiliar, children may display comprehension problems based on the following assumptions and social behaviors: (a) Children assume that adults' dialogue is sincere and reliable; (b) children perceive adults to be trustworthy conversational partners who would not intentionally deceive them; (c) children consider adults to be highly credible sources of information who know more than they know; and (d) children acquiesce to adults' leading questions to please, avoid anger, or protect themselves from humiliation (Saywitz & Moan-Hardie, 1994). Prior to beginning the substantive segment of the interview, school-age children benefit from instructions on ground rules that address these assumptions and social tendencies, including instructions to (a) tell only what happened; (b) admit lack of knowledge rather than guess; (c) remember that the interviewer was not present during the event of focus; (d) correct the interviewer when he or she misstates the facts; (e) not think they made a mistake if the interviewer asks a question more than once; and (f) tell all the details they can remember, even the ones that they think are unimportant (Reed, 1996). Strategies for enhancing children's resistance to suggestibility are less effective with preschool-age children, especially with children under the age of 5 (Saywitz, Geiselman, & Bornstein, 1992).

Practice Interview on Non-Abuse-Related Questions

The purpose of the practice interview is to encourage the child to volunteer elaborated narratives so that the interviewer can minimize the use of specific queries when questioning the child about the alleged abuse (Sternberg et al., 1997). There are a number of experimentally derived protocols that assist the interviewer in training children to elaborate their narratives (Lamb et al., 1994; Saywitz & Snyder, 1996; Saywitz, Snyder, & Lamphear, 1996; Saywitz, Snyder, & Nathanson, 1999). The core components of these protocols include instructing the interviewer to identify a recent event that the child experienced and ask a sequence of questions that probe for details, such as (a) "Think hard and tell me what happened from the time you got up that morning until [some incident that occurred that same day]"; (b) "Then what happened?"; (c) "Tell me everything that happened after [another event that occurred that same day]"; (d) "Tell me more about [another incident mentioned by the child occurring on that same day]." Children typically are instructed to tell the interviewer details regarding everything they remember and to include things that they think may be unimportant (Poole & Lamb, 1998).

A mnemonic device developed by Saywitz (1995; Saywitz & Geiselman, 1998) in her protocol (narrative elaboration technique) involves presenting children with five cards showing simple drawings representing categories of participant, setting, action, conversation, and affective state. With the cards as reminders, the child practices narrating details from each category when describing routine activities. After practicing on nonabuse events, the child is asked to describe the event under investigation while using the cards as mnemonic aides. Saywitz and Goodman (1996) found that school-age children trained in this technique provided 53% more accurate information in a free recall narrative of a past nontraumatic event compared to children in the control group, who received no training.

Introduction of the Sexual Abuse Topic through Open-Ended Questions

The substantive part of the interview begins when the interviewer transitions to the target topic. Poole and Lamb (1998) suggest using a transition statement, such as "Now that I know you a little better, it's time to talk about the reason that you are here today. Tell me the reason you came to talk to me today" (p. 134). The goal is to introduce the subject of abuse without verbalizing the allegation to the child, naming a particular suspect, projecting adult judgments onto the alleged event, or implying that the child has been harmed (Pence & Wilson, 1994). In a study by Sternberg et al. (1997), 96% of alleged victims of child sexual abuse who had previously disclosed their abuse to someone other than a child protection investigator disclosed their abuse to an investigator when asked the following prompt: "Now that we know each other a little better I want to talk about the reason you are here today. I understand that something may have happened to you. Please tell me everything that happened, every detail from the very beginning to the very end" (p. 1146). These children had been previously trained in answering open-ended questions to non-abuse-related questions.

When asked open-ended questions, children's accounts may be very brief and not produce sufficient information on which the evaluator can draw conclusions regarding the allegation of sexual abuse. As a result, the interviewer may introduce more focused questions. However, as noted by Poole and Lindsay (1998), children's accuracy declines as questioning moves from free recall (e.g., "Please tell me everything that happened, every detail from the very beginning to the very end") to more focused questions (e.g., "Tell me what the room looked like"), to questions about a specific detail (e.g., "What color was the bedspread?"), or to questions that offer the child limited options (e.g., yes-no, multiple choice).

Lamb, Hershkowitz, Sternberg, Epslin, et al. (1996) found that child protection investigators who were not trained in the open-ended interview methods yielded an average of six details to the investigator's first invitation for substantive information. After training, these same child protection investigators' first substantive question yielded an average of 91 details from the children in the open-ended introduction condition (Sternberg et al., 1997). However, Sternberg and her colleagues also found that after the trained interviewers posed their first open-ended substantive question, they reverted back to more focused questions, suggesting the need for the trainers to script further open-ended questions. These findings are consistent with previous research showing that interviewers seldom use the open-ended invitations recommended (Lamb, Hershkowitz, Sternberg, Boat, & Everson, 1996; Warren et al., 1996).

Currently undergoing field-testing is a scripted interview protocol developed by researchers at the National Institute of Child Health and Human Development, which includes a sequence of nine nonsubstantive and substantive phases. This protocol uses the widely accepted funnel approach, in which interviewers begin with open-ended questions, proceed to more direct questions with caution, and then move the interview back to open-ended probes that again elicit narrative information. Preliminary findings indicate that child protection interviewers using the detailed protocol to assist them, compared to investigators who improvise, retrieve more information using open-ended questions, conduct better-organized interviews, follow focused questions with open-ended probes (pairings), and avoid more potentially dangerous interview practices (Lamb et al., 1998).

Legal Decisions

Expert testimony on the credibility of the child victim has been found to be reversible error by many state courts (e.g., *State v. Harris,* 1991; *State v. Batangan,* 1990) and the U.S. Supreme Court (*United States v. Azure,* 1986). Testimony has been disallowed because mental health professionals have no specialized training in detecting the truthfulness of children. However, in limited circumstances, when the defense opens the door by questioning the credibility of the victim's testimony, credibility presented by the prosecution may be admitted as rebuttal testimony in some jurisdictions (e.g., *State v. Bellotti,* 1986).

The courts' responses to whether the interviewer should be blind as to the variables associated with the alleged victim and the abuse event have been mixed. In one case (*Idaho v. Wright,* 1990), a sexual abuse conviction was overturned on the grounds that the physician who testified was provided information that created a "preconceived idea" of what the child would disclose to him. In *Idaho v. Wright,* the U.S. Supreme Court also engaged in its most extensive analysis of factors to consider when evaluating whether hearsay statements of an alleged child victim bear adequate indicators of reliability to justify admission. Acceptable criteria of reliability for hearsay exceptions are based on factors related to the alleged victim, the disclosure, and the interview (cited in National Center for the Prosecution of Child Abuse, 1993). The alleged victim factors have included (a) child's statements were spontaneous (e.g., *United States v. Ellis,* 1991); (b) legal competency of the child (e.g., *State v. Oliver,* 1991); (c) mental state of the declarant (e.g., *George v. State,* 1991); (d) motives of the declarant and witness to speak truthfully (e.g., *State v. Lanam,* 1990); (e) no motive of the declarant or witness to fabricate (e.g., *Idaho v. Wright,* 1990); (f) relationship between the victim and the declarant (e.g., *State v. Oliver,* 1991); and (g) victim was reluctant to speak to men about the incident (e.g., *State v. Bellotti,* 1986). Factors related to disclosure include (a) statements were made immediately after the incident (e.g., *State v. Gill,* 1990); and (b) the story was unique and plausible and would not have been in the experience of the young victim (e.g., *George v. State,* 1991). Factors related to the interview and the child's behavior during the interview include (a) children were interviewed separately (e.g., *State v. Carver,* 1986); (b) statements were not the products of extensive interrogation with leading questions (e.g., *State v. Gill,* 1990); (c) victim used age-appropriate terminology (e.g., *State v. Denning,* 1991); (d) victim did not agree with everything the questioner asked (e.g., *United States v. Ellis,* 1991); and (e) victim's testimony was consistent, or any inconsistencies can be easily explained (e.g., *Idaho v. Wright,* 1990). As noted by Myers (1998), there are problems inherent to applying lists of criteria to children who vary in cognitive ability, personality, coping style, and personal experience (see Kuehnle, 1996, for review of an indicator criteria approach to evaluating allegations of sexual abuse).

Although the testimony of a sexual abuse victim is sufficient to support conviction (e.g., *Davis v. State,* 1996), children's in-court testimony is an area of further concern for the courts. Child hearsay statutes frequently require that the child either testify at trial or be found to be "unavailable" to testify before nontraditional hearsay evidence may be introduced. Reasons for "unavailability" include (a) refusal to testify, (b) lack of memory, (c) incapacity, (d) mental disability, (e) physical illness, and (f) death (Myers, 1998). Some courts have ruled unavailability to include the child's inability to communicate to a jury (e.g., *State v. Giles,* 1989) or experiencing trauma from testifying that would result in substantial, long-term emotional or psychological harm (e.g., *People v. Newbrough,* 1986; *Thomas v. People,* 1990).

There is concern about inflicting further psychological harm on the child by subjecting him or her to the stress of repeating the experience of abuse in a courtroom with the alleged abuser present (Berliner & Barbieri, 1984). Several strategies have been developed by different states to prevent having a child testify in open court. One strategy developed by the state courts and approved by the U.S. Supreme Court is to introduce evidence through hearsay testimony by a mental health professional, teacher, police officer, or child protection investigator who repeats the out-of-court statements. Certain hearsay statements made for purposes of obtaining treatment or a diagnosis have been ruled to be sufficiently reliable to be admitted into evidence (e.g., *People v. Meeboer,* 1992; see Myers, 1997b). Although most court decisions have involved patient-physician communication, children's statements to other mental health professionals have been admitted if the basis supporting the exception (i.e., statement pertinent to diagnosis or treatment) is present (e.g., *Morgan v. Foretich,* 1988; *McClain v. State,* 1996). A child's videotaped statements may also be admissible under exceptions to the hearsay rule (see Myers, 1997a).

A second strategy to protect the child from testifying in criminal court is to allow the closed-circuit testimony of the child, with only the judge, defense attorney, and prosecuting attorney present. This strategy was upheld in a 1990 U.S. Supreme Court ruling that found closed-circuit testimony of a child witness in a sexual abuse case did not deprive the defendant of his 6th Amendment right to confront witnesses against him (*Craig v. Maryland,* 1990). A third strategy is the placement of a one-way screen in front of the defendant so that the child cannot see the defendant while testifying. However, the U.S. Supreme Court overturned a guilty verdict in an Iowa case using this strategy, ruling that the necessity of protecting the victims of sexual abuse did not outweigh a defendant's 6th Amendment constitutional right to confront his accusers face-to-face (*Coy v. Iowa,* 1988).

ASSESSMENT TOOLS

If assessment tools are used in the evaluation of sexual abuse, a specific instrument should be used only if it can provide validity that adds to the predictive accuracy of existing methods. This section covers the research on three of the most frequently used tools: anatomical dolls, projective instruments, and drawings.

Anatomical Dolls

Anatomical dolls have been widely used as an assessment tool by professionals who evaluate child sexual abuse allegations, despite the absence of uniform guidelines and standardized procedures for their use (Conte, Sorenson, Fogarty, & Rosa, 1991; Kendall-Tackett & Watson, 1992). Normative and comparative research that has focused on nonsexually abused and sexually abused children's play with anatomical dolls has been plagued with methodological problems and produced inconsistent findings (Ceci & Bruck, 1993; Koocher et al., 1995). When differences have been found in the doll play of nonabused and sexually abused children, it is undetermined whether they reflect abuse status, exposure to previous questioning about sexual activity, or other family circumstances (Poole & Lamb, 1998). For example, in one study, 50% of the mothers of presumably nonsexually abused children perceived their child to be more sexually focused after a single interview with the anatomical dolls (Boat, Everson, & Holland, 1990). There is robust data that children's play with anatomical dolls cannot be validly used as a component in a sexual abuse evaluation because it does not provide validity that adds to the predictive accuracy of existing methods (Wolfner, Faust, & Dawes, 1993).

There is disagreement among researchers regarding the use of anatomical dolls to assist children in their narration of sexually abusive events. Some findings indicate that the anatomical dolls do not enhance the narrations of children and may even diminish the number of details reported (Lamb, Hershkowitz, Sternberg, Boat, et al., 1996) or increase the number of false statements elicited during children's interviews (Bruck, Ceci, Francoeur, & Renick, 1995; DeLoache & Marzolf, 1995; Steward & Steward, 1996). For example, Bruck and her colleagues (1995) studied 3-year-old children's memory for a physical examination, with half of the children also experiencing a genital examination. Errors of omission were high, with 50% of the genitally examined children failing to indicate they were touched on their genitals when interviewed. Although use of anatomical dolls did not reduce errors of omission, it appeared to increase errors of commission, with 60% of children in both genital exam and nongenital exam groups falsely indicating genital insertions and using the dolls in a sexualized manner. In contrast, anatomical dolls paired with a directed question appeared to assist disclosures of genital touching during a physical examination in slightly older children (Saywitz, Goodman, Nicholas, & Moan, 1991). Saywitz and her colleagues studied 5- and 7-year-old girls who were either given a scoliosis examination or a medical examination, including an examination of the child's genitals. Results showed that to the free recall question "What did the doctor do?", only 22% of the genitally examined girls disclosed that they were touched on their vagina and 11% disclosed that they were touched on their anus. Of the nongenitally examined girls, none falsely claimed to have been touched in the genital area when asked free recall questions. However, when the interviewer pointed to the vagina or anus on the doll, 86% of genitally examined girls disclosed vaginal touching to the interviewer's direction question "Did the doctor touch you here?" and 3% of the nongenitally examined girls falsely claimed vaginal touch. Additionally, 69% of genitally examined girls disclosed anal touching to the interviewer's direct question, and 6% of the nongenitally examined girls falsely claimed anal touch. These research results suggest that children who are touched on their genitals are at heightened risk not to disclose these events unless asked directly. Moreover, although dolls may assist older children, younger preschool-age children are at increased risk of making errors of commission when asked to use anatomical dolls to describe the genital touching they experienced. Poole and Lamb (1998) caution interviewers to be aware that the gains they achieve by using the dolls can easily be outweighed by questions regarding the reliability of the children's reports.

Projective Tests

Although some forensic evaluators maintain that projective techniques are useful for detecting child sexual abuse (Oberlander, 1995), the validity of these techniques for distinguishing sexually abused from nonsexually abused children has not been established (Lilienfeld, Wood, & Garb, 2000). As would be expected, based on the symptom heterogeneity and variability of individual personalities within the population of sexually abused children, comparison research using the Rorschach Comprehensive System or children's drawings (e.g., House-Tree-Person, Human Figure Drawing) to differentiate sexually abused and nonsexually abused children have reported inconsistent differences between these two groups (Friedrich et al., 1992; Hibbard, Roghmann, & Hoekelman, 1987; Leifer, Shapiro, Martone, & Kassem, 1991; Palmer et al., 2000; Shapiro, Leifer, Martone, & Kassem, 1990; Sidun & Rosenthal, 1987; Zivney, Nash, & Hulsey, 1988).

Although West (1998) concluded from her meta-analysis of 12 studies that projective techniques have the ability to discriminate between sexually abused and nonsexually abused children, there were major flaws in West's analysis and conclusions (Garb, Wood, & Nezworski, 2000a, 2000b). In contrast to West's findings, a meta-analysis of 47 studies found the use of projective techniques for detecting child sexual abuse to have little support (Lilienfeld et al., 2000).

Genitalia on Human Figures

The use of children's drawings depicting humans with genitalia is endorsed by some professionals as having utility in the identification of child sexual abuse victims (American Academy of Child and Adolescent Psychiatry, 1997; Burgess & Hartman, 1993). However, research indicates that genitalia drawn on human figures is a low-frequency behavior and is not found to be sensitive or specific to sexually abused children (see Kuehnle, 1996, for a review). With the absence of normative data, it is unknown what nonsexually abused and sexually abused children generally draw when given these drawing tasks. Furthermore, it is undetermined how questioning children about sexual abuse may influence their drawings. Because allegations of sexual abuse prompt questions about sexuality, this type of questioning may influence the content of both nonabused and abused children's drawings (Poole & Lamb, 1998).

Focused Drawings

The use of focused drawings has also been investigated as a source of eliciting further details from children during their interview. For example, following a verbal statement disclosing sexual abuse, the child is asked to draw a picture of his or her abuse. Psychometric properties (e.g., reliability, validity) are not pertinent because the evaluator does not interpret the symbolic meaning of the drawing; rather, the child describes the drawing. Several studies have found that when nonsexually abused children are asked to draw an event they have recently experienced and to narrate their drawings, older children (i.e., 5- to 10-year-olds) narrate significantly more information when they draw compared to their peers who do not draw (Butler, Gross, & Hayne, 1995; Gross & Hayne, 1998, 1999). The error rates are also comparable for both drawers and nondrawers. However, the drawing advantage is smaller for 3- and 4-year-olds, and in another study, the advantage for 5- and 6-year-olds was not replicated over a one year time delay (Salmon & Pipe, 2000). Further research is needed to determine whether there is a greater benefit in using drawings of the event as prompts for a narrative in comparison to nonsuggestive questioning. Also unknown is the risk for increases in omission or commission errors.

Legal Aspects

Current accepted practice in conducting evaluations of child sexual abuse allegations is to avoid using the dolls or drawings as a "test" for "diagnosing" sexual abuse (American Professional Society on the Abuse of Children, 1996; Koocher et al., 1995; Kuehnle, 1996). However, the courts have been largely unwilling to use ethical norms when addressing the threshold reliability requirements for expert testimony (see Shuman & Greenberg, 1998). The legal and professional disputes regarding the types of testimony that may be offered on direct and cross examination continue to be addressed by numerous scholars (Berliner, 1998; Kovera & Borgida, 1998; Myers, 1996).

SUMMARY

Academic and clinical professionals have yet to agree on exactly what factors should be considered and how they should be weighed when forming an opinion in a specific child sexual abuse case. The event of sexual abuse interacts with a complex matrix of personality and family factors, which elicits a wide variety of reactions rather than a syndrome or group of predictable symptoms. Research is robust in showing an association between children's aberrant sexualized behavior and experiences of sexual abuse or exposure to a highly sexualized environment; however, all other symptoms and behaviors are nonspecific and consistent with a variety of other disturbing life experiences and stressors.

Reliance on the presence or absence of specific statement components to confirm or negate whether a child is a victim of sexual abuse is also problematic. Developmental limitations, personality factors, family and cultural contexts,

characteristics of the abuse, interviewing techniques, and other factors may affect children's narration of the abuse allegation. Furthermore, some children, especially those who are very young, are susceptible to pre- and postevent suggestions and misinformation. External variables, including repetitive questioning and interviewer's style and bias, may increase children's suggestibility, and internal factors such as children's temperament, attachment, and self-confidence also appear to influence suggestibility.

Although there does not exist a single standardized interview protocol consistently used by experts, there is agreement regarding the components of a soundly structured interview. The scientific community continues to work on the development of interview protocols to increase the quantity and quality of children's narration of events when sexual abuse is alleged.

The search for ways to accurately distinguish sexually abused from nonsexually abused children has included examining the diagnostic potential of anatomical doll play, projective tests, and children's drawings. Research has not found these instruments or techniques to show specificity to sexual abuse. Projective tools, including projective tests, drawing tasks, and doll play, do not discriminate sexually abused from nonsexually abused children. Children's drawing of genitalia has shown sensitivity to sexual abuse trauma, but these drawings are not specific to trauma caused by sexual abuse.

When providing information to the legal system, the evaluator must be cautious and make statements that can be supported by scientific data. In writing an evaluation or testifying to whether abuse has occurred, experts may want to take the approach of addressing the various possible explanations for and the weight to be accorded to a child's statements and behaviors. This can be accomplished through the generation of multiple hypotheses (see Kuehnle, 1996), with factors presented that both support and weaken a given hypothesis. Using this approach, professionals are able to provide education to the court about the complexity regarding the current state of knowledge and each individual case.

REFERENCES

Achenbach, T. M. (1991). *Manual for the Child Behavior Checklist/4–18 and 1991 profile.* Burlington: University of Vermont, Department of Psychiatry.

Alpert, J. L. (1995). Trauma, dissociation, and clinical study as a responsible beginning. *Consciousness and Cognition, 4,* 125–129.

American Academy of Child and Adolescent Psychiatry. (1997). Practice parameters for the forensic evaluation of children and adolescents who may have been physically or sexually abused. *Journal of the American Academy of Child and Adolescent Psychiatry, 36,* 423–444.

American Professional Society on the Abuse of Children. (1996). *Guidelines for psychosocial evaluation of suspected sexual abuse in young children* (2nd ed.). Chicago: Author.

Anderson, J. C., Martin, J. L., Mullen, P. E., Romans, S. E., & Herbison, P. (1993). The prevalence of childhood sexual abuse experiences in a community sample of women. *Journal of the American Academy of Child and Adolescent Psychiatry, 32,* 911–919.

Arata, C. M. (1998). To tell or not to tell: Current functioning of child sexual abuse survivors who disclosed their victimization. *Child Maltreatment, 3,* 63–71.

Baker-Ward, L., Gordon, B., Ornstein, P. A., Larus, D., & Clubb, P. (1993). Young children's long term retention of a pediatric examination. *Child Development, 64,* 1519–1533.

Bauer, P. J. (1996). What do infants recall of their lives? *American Psychologist, 51,* 29–41.

Bauer, P. J., Hertsgaard, L. A., & Dow, G. A. (1994). After 8 months have passed: Long-term recall of events by 1- and 2-year old children. *Memory, 2,* 353–382.

Berliner, L. (1998). The use of expert testimony in child sexual abuse cases. In S. J. Ceci & H. Hembrooke (Eds.), *Expert witnesses in child abuse cases* (pp. 11–27). Washington, DC: American Psychological Association.

Berliner, L., & Barbieri, M. K. (1984). The testimony of the child victim of sexual assault. *Journal of Social Issues, 40,* 125–137.

Boat, B. W., Everson, M. D., & Holland, J. (1990). Maternal perceptions of non-abused young children's behaviors after the children's exposure to anatomical dolls. *Child Welfare, 69,* 389–400.

Brainerd, C. J., & Reyna, V. F. (1996). Mere memory testing creates false memories in children. *Developmental Psychology, 32,* 467–478.

Bremner, J. D., Krystal, J. H., Southwick, S. M., & Charney, D. S. (1995). Functional neuroanatomical correlates of the effects of stress on memory. *Journal of Traumatic Stress, 8,* 527–553.

Briere, J. (1992). Methodological issues in the study of sexual abuse effects. *Journal of Consulting and Clinical Psychology, 60,* 196–203.

Browne, A., & Finkelhor, D. (1986). Impact of child sexual abuse: A review of the research. *Psychological Bulletin, 99,* 66–77.

Bruck, M., & Ceci, S. J. (1995). *Amicus* brief for the case of *State of NJ v. Michaels* presented by Committee on Concerned Social Scientists. *Psychology, Public Policy, and Law, 1,* 272–322.

Bruck, M., Ceci, S. J., & Francoeur, E. (1999). The accuracy of mothers' memories of conversations with their preschool children. *Journal of Experimental Psychology: Applied, 5,* 89–106.

Bruck, M., Ceci, S. J., Francoeur, E., & Barr, R. (1995). "I hardly cried when I got my shot?" Influencing children's reports about a visit to their pediatrician. *Child Development, 66,* 193–208.

Bruck, M., Ceci, S. J., Francoeur, E., & Renick, A. (1995). Anatomically detailed dolls do not facilitate preschoolers' reports of a pediatric examination involving genital touching. *Journal of Experimental Psychology: Applied, 1,* 95–109.

Bruck, M., Ceci, S. J., & Hembrooke, H. (1998). Reliability and credibility of young children's reports. *American Psychologist, 53,* 136–151.

Bruck, M., Ceci, S. J., & Melnyk, L. (1997). External and internal sources of variation in the creation of false reports in children. *Learning and Individual Differences, 9,* 289–316.

Burgess, A. W., & Hartman, C. R. (1993). Children's drawings. *Child Abuse and Neglect, 17,* 161–168.

Butler, S. G., Gross, J., & Hayne, H. (1995). The effect of drawing on memory performance in young children. *Developmental Psychology, 31,* 597–608.

Carter, C., Bottoms, B., & Levine, M. (1996). Linguistic and socioemotional influences on the accuracy of children's reports. *Law and Human Behavior, 20,* 335–358.

Ceci, S. J., & Bruck, M. (1993). Suggestibility of the child witness: A historical review and synthesis. *Psychological Bulletin, 113*(3), 403–439.

Ceci, S. J., & Bruck, M. (1995). *Jeopardy in the courtroom: A scientific analysis of children's testimony.* Washington, DC: American Psychological Association.

Ceci, S. J., Crossman, A. M., Gilstrap, L. L., & Scullin, M. H. (1998). Social and cognitive factors in children's testimony. In C. P. Thompson, D. J. Herrmann, J. D. Read, D. Bruce, D. G. Payne, & M. P. Toglia (Eds.), *Eyewitness memory: Theoretical and applied perspectives* (pp. 15–30). Mahwah, NJ: Erlbaum.

Ceci, S. J., Crotteau, M. L., Smith, E., & Loftus, E. F. (1994). Repeatedly thinking about non-events: Source misattributions among preschoolers. *Consciousness and Cognition, 3,* 388–407.

Ceci, S. J., & Friedman, R. D. (2000). The suggestibility of children: Scientific research and legal implications. *Cornell Law Review, 86,* 33–108.

Ceci, S. J., Loftus, E. F., Leichtman, M. D., & Bruck, M. (1994). The possible role of source misattributions in the creation of false beliefs among preschoolers. *International Journal of Clinical and Experimental Hypnosis, 42*(4), 304–320.

Chaffin, M., Lawson, L., Selby, A., & Wherry, J. N. (1997). False negatives in sexual abuse interviews: Preliminary investigation of a relationship to dissociation. *Journal of Child Sexual Abuse, 6,* 15–29.

Chaffin, M., Wherry, J. N., & Dykman, R. (1997). School age children's coping with sexual abuse: Abuse stresses and symptoms associated with four coping strategies. *Child Abuse and Neglect, 21,* 227–240.

Cicchetti, D., Rogosch, F. A., Lynch, M., & Holt, K. D. (1993). Resilience in maltreated children: Processes leading to adaptive outcome. *Developmental Psychopathology, 5,* 629–647.

Clarke-Stewart, A., Thompson, J., & Lepore, S. (1989, April). Manipulating children's interpretations through interrogation. In G. Goodman (Chair), *Can children provide accurate eyewitness reports?* Symposium presented at Society for Research on Child Development Meetings, Kansas City, MO.

Conte, J. R., Sorenson, E., Fogarty, L., & Rosa, J. D. (1991). Evaluating children's reports of sexual abuse: Results from a survey of professionals. *American Journal of Orthopsychiatry, 61,* 428–437.

Conway, M. A. (1996). Autobiographical knowledge and autobiographical memory. In D. Rubin (Ed.), *Remembering our past: Studies in autobiographical memory* (pp. 67–93). New York: Cambridge University Press.

Cosentino, C. E., Meyer-Bahlburg, H. F., Alpert, J. L., Weinberg, S. L., & Gaines, R. (1995). Sexual behavior problems and psychopathology symptoms in sexually abused girls. *Journal of the American Academy of Child and Adolescent Psychiatry, 34,* 1033–1042.

Coy v. Iowa, 108 S. Ct. 2798 (1988).

Craig v. Maryland, 110 S. Ct. 3157 (1990).

Davenport v. State, 806 P.2d 655 (Okla. Crim. App. 1991).

Davies, G. M. (1993). Children's memory for other people: An intergrative review. In C. A. Nelson (Ed.), *Memory and affect in development* (pp. 123–157). Hillsdale, NJ: Erlbaum.

Davies, S., Glaser, D., & Kossoff, R. (2000). Children's sexual play and behavior in pre-school settings: Staff's perceptions, reports, and responses. *Child Abuse and Neglect, 24,* 1329–1343.

Davis v. State, 470 S. E.2d 520, 522 (Ga. Ct. App. 1996).

Deblinger, E., McLeer, S. V., Atkins, M. S., Ralphe, D., & Foa, E. (1989). Post-traumatic stress in sexually abused, physically abused and nonabused children. *Child Abuse and Neglect, 13,* 403–408.

DeCasper, A., Lecanuet, J., Busnel, M., Granier-Deferre, C., & Maugeais, R. (1994). Fetal reactions to recurrent maternal speech. *Infant Behavior and Development, 17,* 159–164.

DeLoache, J. S., & Marzolf, D. P. (1995). The use of dolls to interview young children: Issues of symbolic representation. *Journal of Experimental Child Psychology, 60,* 155–173.

DeShaney v. Winnebago County, 109 S. Ct. 998 (1989).

Eisen, M. L., Goodman, G. S., Qin, J., & Davis, S. (1998). Memory and suggestibility in maltreated children: New research relevant to evaluating allegations of abuse. In S. L. Lynn & K. McConkey (Eds.), *Trauma and memory* (pp. 163–189). New York: Guilford Press.

Elicker, J., Egland, B., & Sroufe, L. A. (1992). Predicting peer competence and peer relationships in childhood from early parent-child relationships. In R. Parke & G. Ladd (Eds.), *Family-peer relations: Modes of linkage* (pp. 77–106). Hillsdale, NJ: Erlbaum.

Elliot, D., & Briere, J. (1994). Forensic sexual abuse evaluations of older children: Disclosures and symptomatology. *Behavioral Science and the Law, 12,* 261–277.

Emery, R., & Laumann-Billings, L. (1998). An overview of the nature, causes, and consequences of abusive family relationships: Toward differentiating maltreatment and violence. *American Psychologist, 53,* 121–135.

Endres, J., Poggenpohl, C., & Erben, C. (1999). Repetitions, warnings, and video: Cognitive and motivational components in preschool children's suggestibility. *Legal and Criminological Psychology, 4,* 129–146.

Everson, M., Hunter, W., Runyan, D., Edelsohn, G., & Coulter, M. (1989). Maternal support following disclosure of incest. *American Journal of Orthopsychiatry, 59,* 197–207.

Faller, K. (1991). Possible explanations for child sexual abuse allegations in divorce. *American Journal of Orthopsychiatry, 61,* 86–91.

Federal Rules of Evidence, Rule 601. General Rule of Competency.

Federal Victims of Child Abuse Act, 18 U.S.C., 3509(c) (1990).

Fergusson, D. M., Lynskey, M. T., & Horwood, L. J. (1996). Childhood sexual abuse and psychiatric disorders in young adulthood. Part I: The prevalence of sexual abuse and factors associated with sexual abuse. *Journal of the American Academy of Child and Adolescent Psychiatry, 35,* 1355–1365.

Fergusson, D. M., & Mullen, P. E. (1999). *Child sexual abuse: An evidenced based perspective.* Newbury Park, CA: Sage.

Finkelhor, D. (1994). Current information on the scope and nature of child sexual abuse. *Future of Children, 4,* 31–53.

Finkelhor, D., & Baron, L. (1986). High risk children. In D. Finkelhor (Ed.), *A sourcebook on child sexual abuse* (pp. 60–88). Beverly Hills, CA: Sage.

Finkelhor, D., & Berliner, L. (1995). Research on the treatment of sexually abused children: A review and recommendations. *Journal of the American Academy of Child and Adolescent Psychiatry, 34,* 1408–1423.

Finlayson, L. M., & Koocher, G. P. (1991). Professional judgment and child abuse reporting in sexual abuse cases. *Professional Psychology: Research and Practice, 22,* 464–472.

Fisher, R. P., & Geiselman, R. E. (1992). *Memory-enhancing techniques for investigative interviewing: The cognitive interview.* Springfield, IL: Charles C. Thomas.

Fitzpatrick, C., Deehan, A., & Jennings, S. (1995). Children's sexual behavior and knowledge: A community study. *Irish Journal of Psychological Medicine, 12,* 87–91.

Fivush, R., & Schwartzmueller, A. (1995). Say it once again: Effects of repeated questions on children's event recall. *Journal of Traumatic Stress, 8,* 555–580.

Fivush, R., & Schwartzmueller, A. (1998). Children remember childhood: Implications for childhood amnesia. *Applied Cognitive Psychology, 12,* 455–473.

Fleming, J., Mullen, P. E., & Bammer, G. (1997). A study of potential risk factors for sexual abuse in childhood. *Child Abuse and Neglect, 21,* 49–58.

Friedrich, W. N. (1998). *Child sexual behavior inventory manual.* Odessa, FL: Psychological Assessment Resources.

Friedrich, W. N., Grambsch, P., Damon, L., Hewitt, S. K., Koverola, C., Lang, R. A., et al. (1992). Child Sexual Behavior Inventory: Normative and clinical contrasts. *Psychological Assessment, 4,* 303–311.

Friedrich, W. N., Urquiza, A. J., & Beilke, R. L. (1986). Behavior problems in sexually abused young children. *Journal of Pediatric Psychology, 11,* 47–57.

Garb, H. N., Wood, J. M., & Nezworski, M. T. (2000a). Projective techniques and the detection of child sexual abuse. *Child Maltreatment, 5,* 161–168.

Garb, H. N., Wood, J. M., & Nezworski, M. T. (2000b). Projective techniques and the detection of child sexual abuse. *Child Abuse and Neglect, 24,* 437–438.

Garven, S., Wood, J. M., Malpass, R. S., & Shaw, J. S. (1998). More than suggestion: The effect of interviewing techniques from the McMartin Preschool case. *Journal of Applied Psychology, 83,* 347–356.

Garven, S., Wood, J. M., Malpass, R. S., & Shaw, J. S. (2000). Allegations of wrongdoing: The effects of reinforcement on children's mundane and fantastic claims. *Journal of Applied Psychology, 85,* 38–49.

Geiselman, R. E., Saywitz, K. J., & Bornstein, G. K. (1991). *Effects of cognitive interviewing, practice and interviewing style on children's recall performance* (Rep. No. NI-IJ-CX-003). Washington, DC: National Institute of Justice.

George v. State, 813 S. W.2d 792 (Ark. 1991).

Gold, P. E., & McCarty, R. C. (1995). Stress regulation of memory processes: Role of peripheral catecholamines and glucose. In M. J. Friedman, D. S. Charney, & A. Y. Deutch (Eds.), *Neurobiological and clinical consequences of stress* (pp. 151–162). Philadelphia: Lippincott-Raven.

Goldberg, L. R., Faust, O., Kleinmuntz, B., Dawes, R. M. (1991). Clinical versus statistical prediction. In D. Cicchetti & W. M. Grove (Eds.), *Thinking clearly about psychology: Essays in honor of Paul E. Meehl* (Vol. 1, pp. 173–264). Minneapolis: University of Minnesota Press.

Gomes-Schwartz, B., Horowitz, J. M., & Cardarelli, A. P. (1990). *Child sexual abuse: The initial effects.* Newbury Park, CA: Sage.

Goodman, G. S., Bottoms, B. L., Schwartz-Kenney, B., & Rudy, L. (1991). Children's testimony about a stressful event: Improving children's reports. *Journal of Narrative & Life History, 1,* 69–99.

Goodman, G. S., Hirschman, J. E., Hepps, D., & Rudy, L. (1991). Children's memory for stressful events. *Merrill-Palmer Quarterly, 37,* 109–158.

Goodman, G. S., & Quas, J. A. (1997). Trauma and memory: Individual differences in children's recounting of a stressful event. In N. L. Stein, P. A. Ornstein, B. Tversky, & C. Brainerd (Eds.), *Memory of everyday and emotional events* (pp. 267–294). Mahwah, NJ: Erlbaum.

Goodman, G. S., Quas, J. A., Batterman-Faunce, J. M., Riddlesberger, M. M., & Kuhn, G. (1997). Children's reactions to and memory for a stressful event: Influences of age, anatomical dolls, knowledge, and parental attachment. *Applied Developmental Science, 1,* 54–75.

Greco, C., Rovee-Collier, C., Hayne, H., Griesler, P., & Early, L. A. (1986). Ontogeny of early event memory. I: Forgetting and retrieval by 2- and 3-month-olds. *Infant Behavior and Development, 9,* 441–460.

Gross, J., & Hayne, H. (1998). Drawing facilitates children's verbal reports of emotionally laden events. *Journal of Experimental Psychology: Applied, 4,* 163–179.

Gross, J., & Hayne, H. (1999). Drawing facilitates children's verbal reports after long delays. *Journal of Experimental Psychology: Applied, 5,* 265–283.

Hadden v. State of Florida, 690 So. 2nd 573 (1997).

Hall, D. K., Mathews, F., & Pearce, J. (1998). Factors associated with sexual behavior problems in young sexually abused children. *Child Abuse and Neglect, 22,* 1045–1063.

Hawley, T., Halle, T., Drasin, R., & Thomas, N. (1995). Children of addicted mothers: Effects of the "crack" epidemic on the caregiving environment and the development of preschoolers. *American Journal of Orthopsychiatry, 65,* 364–379.

Hembrooke, H., & Ceci, S. J. (1995). Traumatic memories: Do we need to invoke special mechanisms? *Consciousness and Cognition, 4,* 75–82.

Hewitt, S. (1999). *Assessing allegations of sexual abuse in preschool children.* Newbury, CA: Sage.

Hibbard, R. A., Roghmann, K., & Hoekelman, R. A. (1987). Genitals in children's drawings: An association with sexual abuse. *Pediatrics, 79,* 129–137.

Howe, M. (1997). Children's memory for traumatic experiences. *Learning and Individual Differences, 9,* 153–174.

Howe, M. (2000). *Fate of early memories.* Washington, DC: American Psychological Association.

Howe, M., & Courage, M. L. (1997a). The emergence and early development of autobiographical memory. *Psychological Review, 104,* 499–523.

Howe, M., & Courage, M. L. (1997b). Independent paths in the development of infant learning and forgetting. *Journal of Experimental Child Psychology, 67,* 131–163.

Howe, M., Courage, M. L., & Peterson, C. (1994). How can I remember when "I" wasn't there: Long-term retention of traumatic experiences of the cognitive self. *Consciousness and Cognition, 3,* 327–355.

Hudson, J. A. (1990). The emergence of autobiographical memory in mother-child conversation. In R. Fivush & J. A. Hudson (Eds.), *Knowing and remembering in young children* (pp. 166–196). New York: Cambridge University Press.

Huffman, M. L., Warren, A. R., & Frazier, S. (1997, November). *The effect of a truth/lie discussion on children's accuracy and competence.* Paper presented at the 23rd annual conference of the Association for Moral Education, Atlanta, GA.

Idaho v. Wright, 497 U.S. 805 (1990).

Jones, D., & McGraw, J. M. (1987). Reliable and fictitious accounts of sexual abuse in children. *Journal of Interpersonal Violence, 2,* 27–45.

Jones, L., & Finkelhor, D. (2001). *The decline in child sexual abuse cases.* Washington, DC: U.S. Department of Justice, Office of Juvenile Justice and Delinquency Prevention.

Kalichman, S. C. (1993). *Mandated reporting of suspected child abuse: Ethics, law, and policy.* Washington, DC: American Psychological Association.

Kalichman, S. C., & Craig, M. E. (1991). Professional psychologists' decisions to report suspected child abuse: Clinician and situation influences. *Professional Psychology: Research and Practice, 22,* 84–89.

Kelley, K., & Byrne, D. (1992). *Exploring human sexuality.* Englewood Cliffs, NJ: Prentice-Hall.

Kendall-Tackett, K. A., & Watson, M. W. (1992). Use of anatomical dolls by Boston-area professionals. *Child Abuse and Neglect, 16,* 423–428.

Kendall-Tackett, K. A., Williams, L. M., & Finkelhor, D. (1993). Impact of sexual abuse on children: A review and synthesis of recent empirical studies. *Psychological Bulletin, 113,* 164–180.

Kentucky v. Stincer, 482 U.S. 730 (1987).

Koocher, G. P., Goodman, G. S., White, C. S., Friedrich, W. N., Sivan, A. B., & Reynolds, C. R. (1995). Psychological science and the use of anatomically detailed dolls in child sexual-abuse assessments. *Psychological Bulletin, 118,* 199–222.

Kovera, M. B., & Borgida, E. (1998). Expert scientific testimony on child witnesses in the age of Daubert. In S. J. Ceci & H. Hembrooke (Eds.), *Expert witnesses in child abuse cases* (pp. 185–215). Washington, DC: American Psychological Association.

Kuehnle, K. (1996). *Assessing allegations of child sexual abuse.* Sarasota, FL: Professional Resource Press.

Kuehnle, K. (1998a). Child sexual abuse: Treatment issues. In G. P. Koocher, J. C. Norcross, & S. S. Hill, III (Eds.), *The psychologist's desk reference* (pp. 252–256). Boston: Oxford University Press.

Kuehnle, K. (1998b). Child sexual abuse evaluations: The scientist-practitioner model. *Behavioral Sciences and the Law, 16,* 5–20.

Kuehnle, K. (1998c). Ethics and the forensic expert: A case study of child custody involving allegations of child sexual abuse. *Ethics and Behavior, 8,* 1–18.

Lamb, M., Sternberg, K., & Esplin, P. (1994). Factors influencing the reliability and validity of statements made by young victims of sexual maltreatment. *Journal of Applied Developmental Psychology, 15,* 255–280.

Lamb, M., Sternberg, K., & Esplin, P. (1998). Conducting investigative interviews of alleged sexual abuse victims. *Child Abuse and Neglect, 22,* 813–823.

Lamb, M. E., Hershkowitz, I., Sternberg, K. J., Boat, B., & Everson, M. D. (1996). Investigative interviews of alleged sexual abuse victims with and without anatomical dolls. *Child Abuse and Neglect, 20,* 1239–1247.

Lamb, M. E., Hershkowitz, I., Sternberg, K. J., Esplin, P. W., Hovav, M., Manor, T., et al. (1996). Effects of investigative utterance types on Israeli children's responses. *International Journal of Behavioral Development, 19,* 627–637.

Lawson, L., & Chaffin, M. (1992). False negatives in sexual abuse disclosure interviews. *Journal of Interpersonal Violence, 7,* 532–542.

Leichtman, M. D., & Ceci, S. J. (1995). The effects of stereotypes and suggestions on preschoolers reports. *Developmental Psychology, 31,* 568–578.

Leifer, M., Shapiro, J. P., & Kassem, L. (1993). The impact of maternal history and behavior upon foster placement and adjustment in sexually abused girls. *Child Abuse and Neglect, 17,* 755–766.

Leifer, M., Shapiro, J. P., Martone, M., & Kassem, L. (1991). Rorschach assessment of psychological functioning in sexually abused girls. *Journal of Personality Assessment, 56,* 14–28.

Lepore, S., & Sesco, B. (1994). Distorting children's reports and interpretations of events through suggestion. *Journal of Applied Psychology, 79,* 108–120.

Levine, M., & Battistoni, L. (1991). Corroboration requirement in child sex abuse cases. *Behavioral Sciences and the Law, 9,* 21–32.

Lilienfeld, S. O., Wood, J. M., & Garb, H. N. (2000). The scientific status of projective techniques. *Psychological Science, 1,* 27–66.

Lyon, T. D. (1999). The new wave in children's suggestibility research: A critique. *Cornell Law Review, 84,* 1004–1084.

Lyon, T. D., & Saywitz, K. J. (1999). Young maltreated children's competence to take the oath. *Applied Developmental Science, 3,* 16–27.

Mandler, J. M., & McDonough, L. (1995). Long-term recall of event sequences in infancy. *Journal of Experimental Child Psychology, 59,* 457–474.

Mannarino, A. P., & Cohen, J. A. (1996). A follow-up study of factors that mediate the development of psychological symptomatology in sexually abused girls. *Child Maltreatment, 1,* 246–260.

Mannarino, A. P., Cohen, J. A., & Berman, S. R. (1994). The Children's Attributions and Perceptions Scale: A new measure of sexual abuse-related factors. *Journal of Clinical Child Psychology, 23,* 204–211.

Mason, M. A. (1995). The child sex abuse syndrome: The other major issue in *State of NJ v. Margaret Kelly Michaels. Psychology, Public Policy, and Law, 1,* 399–410.

Mason, M. A. (1998). Expert testimony regarding the characteristics of sexually abused children: A controversy on both sides of the bench. In S. J. Ceci & H. Hembrooke (Eds.), *Expert witnesses in child abuse cases* (pp. 217–247). Washington, DC: American Psychological Association.

Masten, A. S., Best, K. M., & Garmezy, N. (1990). Resilience and development: Contributions from the study of children who overcome adversity. *Development and Psychopathology, 2,* 425–444.

McClain v. State, 675 N.E.2d 329, 331 (Ind. 1996).

Melton, G. B., Goodman, G. S., Kalichman, S. C., Levine, M., Saywitz, K. J., & Koocher, G. P. (1995). Empirical research on child maltreatment and the law. *Journal of Clinical Child Psychology, 24,* 47–77.

Melton, G. B., Petrila, J., Poythress, N., & Slobogin, C. (1997). *Psychological evaluations for the courts: A handbook for mental health professionals and lawyers* (2nd ed.). New York: Guilford Press.

Merritt, K. A., Ornstein, P. A., & Spicker, B. (1994). Children's memory for a salient medical procedure: Implications for testimony. *Pediatrics, 94,* 17–23.

Morgan v. Foretich, 846 F.2d 941, 949 n. 17 (4th Cir. 1988).

Myers, J. E. B. (1996). Expert testimony. In J. Briere & L. Berliner (Eds.), *The APSAC handbook on child maltreatment* (pp. 319–340). Thousand Oaks, CA: Sage.

Myers, J. E. B. (1997a). *Evidence in child abuse and neglect cases* (Vol. 1, 3rd ed.). New York: Wiley.

Myers, J. E. B. (1997b). *Evidence in child abuse and neglect cases* (Vol. 2, 3rd ed.). New York: Wiley.

Myers, J. E. B. (1998). *Legal issues in child abuse and neglect* (2nd ed.). Newbury Park, CA: Sage.

Nagel, D. E., Putnam, F. W., Noll, J. G., & Trickett, P. K. (1997). Disclosure patterns of sexual abuse and psychological functioning at a 1-year follow-up. *Child Abuse and Neglect, 21,* 137–47.

National Center for the Prosecution of Child Abuse. (1993). *Investigation and prosecution of child abuse* (2nd ed.). Alexandria, VA: American Prosecutors Research Institute.

National Research Council. (1998). *Violence in families.* Washington, DC: National Academy Press.

Nelson, K. (1993). The psychological and social origins of autobiographical memory. *Psychological Science, 4,* 7–14.

Oberlander, L. (1995). Psychological issues in child sexual abuse evaluation: A survey of forensic mental health professionals. *Child Abuse and Neglect, 19,* 475–490.

Ornstein, P. A., Sharpiro, L. B., Clubb, P. A., Follmer, A., & Baker-Ward, L. (1997). The influence of prior knowledge on children's memory for salient medical experiences. In N. L. Stein, P. A. Ornstein, B. Tversky, & C. Brainerd (Eds.), *Memory for everyday and emotional events* (pp. 83–111). Mahwah, NJ: Erlbaum.

Palmer, L., Farrar, A., Valle, M., Ghahary, N., Panella, M., & DeGraw, D. (2000). An investigation of the clinical use of the House-Tree-Person projective drawings in the psychological evaluation of child sexual abuse. *Child Maltreatment, 5,* 169–175.

Parker, J., Bahrick, L., Lundy, B., Fivush, R., & Levitt, M. (1999). Effects of stress on children's memory for a natural disaster. In C. P. Thompson, D. J. Herrmann, J. D. Read, D. Bruce, D. G. Payne, & M. P. Toglia (Eds.), *Eyewitness memory: Theoretical and applied perspectives* (pp. 31–54). Mahwah, NJ: Erlbaum.

Pence, D., & Wilson, C. (1994). *Team investigation of child sexual abuse.* Thousand Oaks, CA: Sage.

Peterson, C., & Bell, M. (1996). Children's memory for traumatic injury. *Child Development, 67,* 3045–3070.

Peterson, C., & Briggs, M. (1997). Interviewing children about trauma: Problems with "specific" questions. *Journal of Traumatic Stress, 10,* 279–290.

People v. Gallow, 569 N.Y.S.2d 530 (App. Div. 1991).

People v. Lewis, 569 N.E.2d 1225 (Ill. Ct. App. 1991).

People v. Meeboer, 181 Mich. App. 365 (1992).

People v. Newbrough, 803 P.2d 155 (Colo. 1990).

Pipe, M. E., & Wilson, J. C. (1994). Cues and secrets: Influences on children's event reports. *Developmental Psychology, 30,* 515–525.

Poole, D. A., & Lamb, M. E. (1998). *Investigative interviews of children: A guide for helping professionals.* Washington, DC: American Psychological Association.

Poole, D. A., & Lindsay, D. S. (1995). Interviewing preschoolers: Effects of nonsuggestive techniques, parental coaching, and leading questions on reports of nonexperienced events. *Journal of Experimental Child Psychology, 60,* 129–154.

Poole, D. A., & Lindsay, D. S. (1997, April). Misinformation from parents and children's source monitoring: Implications for testimony. In K. P. Roberts (Chair), *Children's source monitoring and eye witness testimony.* Symposium conducted at the meeting of the Society for Research in Child Development, Washington, DC.

Poole, D. A., & Lindsay, D. S. (1998). Assessing the accuracy of young children's reports: Lessons from the investigation of child sexual abuse. *Applied and Preventive Psychology, 7,* 1–26.

Poole, D. A., & White, L. T. (1991). Effects of question repetition on the eyewitness testimony of children and adults. *Developmental Psychology, 27,* 975–986.

Poole, D. A., & White, L. T. (1993). Two years later: Effects of question repetition and retention interval on the eyewitness testimony of children and adults. *Developmental Psychology, 29,* 844–853.

Poole, D. A., & White, L. T. (1995). Tell me again and again: Stability and change in the repeated testimonies of children and adults. In M. S. Zaragoza, J. R. Graham, G. C. N. Hall, R. Hirschman, & Y. S. Ben-Porath (Eds.), *Memory and testimony in the child witness* (pp. 24–43). Thousand Oaks, CA: Sage.

Quas, J. A., Goodman, G. S., Bidrose, S., Pipe, M. E., Craw, S., & Ablin, D. S. (1999). Emotion and memory: Children's long-term remembering, forgetting, and suggestibility. *Journal of Experimental Child Psychology, 72,* 235–270.

Randall v. State, 803 S.W.2d 489 (Tex. Ct. App. 1991).

Raskin, D. C., & Yuille, J. C. (1989). Problems in evaluating interviews of children in sexual abuse cases. In S. J. Ceci, D. F. Ross, & M. P. Toglia (Eds.), *Perspectives on children's testimony* (pp. 184–207). New York: Springer-Verlag.

Reed, L. J. (1996). Findings from research on children's suggestibility and implications for conducting child interviews. *Child Maltreatment, 1,* 105–120.

Reed, L. J., Carter, B. D., & Miller, L. C. (1992). Fear and anxiety in children. In C. E. Walker & R. C. Roberts (Eds.), *Handbook of clinical child psychology* (2nd ed., pp. 237–260). New York: Wiley.

Richardson, J. T., Ginsburg, G. P., Gatowski, S., & Dobbin, S. (1995). The problems in applying *Daubert* to psychological syndrome evidence. *Judicature, 79,* 10–16.

Rumm, P. D., Cummings, P., Krauss, M. R., Bell, M. A., & Rivara, F. P. (2000). Identified spouse abuse as a risk factor for child abuse. *Child Abuse and Neglect, 24,* 1375–1381.

Runtz, M. G., & Schallow, J. R. (1997). Social support and coping strategies as mediators of adult adjustment following childhood maltreatment. *Child Abuse and Neglect, 21,* 211–226.

Ryan, G. (2000). Childhood sexuality: A decade of study. Part I: Research and curriculum development. *Child Abuse and Neglect, 24,* 33–48.

Ryan, G., Miyoshi, T., & Krugman, R. (1988). *Early childhood experience of professionals working in child abuse.* Paper presented at the seventeenth annual Symposium on Child Abuse and Neglect, Keystone, CO.

Salmon, K., & Pipe, M. E. (2000). Recalling an event one year later: The impact of props, drawing and a prior interview. *Applied Cognitive Psychology, 14,* 99–120.

Sattler, J. M. (1998). *Clinical and forensic interviewing of children and families.* San Diego, CA: Author.

Saywitz, K. J. (1995). Improving children's testimony: The question, the answer, and the environment. In M. Zaragoza, J. Graham, G. Hall, R. Hirschman, & Y. Ben-Porath (Eds.), *Memory and testimony in the child witness* (pp. 113–140). Thousand Oaks, CA: Sage.

Saywitz, K. J., & Camparo, L. (1998). Interviewing the child witnesses: A developmental perspective. *Child Abuse and Neglect, 22,* 825–843.

Saywitz, K. J., & Dorado, J. S. (1998). Interviewing children when sexual abuse is suspected. In G. P. Koocher, J. C. Norcross, & S. S. Hill (Eds.), *The psychologist's desk reference* (pp. 503–509). New York: Oxford University Press.

Saywitz, K. J., & Geiselman, R. E. (1998). Interviewing the child witness: Maximizing completeness and minimizing error. In S. J. Lynn & K. M. McConkey (Eds.), *Truth in memory* (pp. 190–226). New York: Guilford Press.

Saywitz, K. J., Geiselman, R. E., & Bornstein, G. K. (1992). Effects of cognitive interviewing and practice on children's recall performance. *Journal of Applied Psychology, 77,* 744–756.

Saywitz, K. J., & Goodman, G. S. (1996). Interviewing children in and out of court: Current research and practical implications. In L. Berliner, J. Briere, & J. Bulkley (Eds.), *APSAC handbook on child maltreatments* (pp. 297–318). Newbury Park, CA: Sage.

Saywitz, K. J., Goodman, G. S., Nicholas, G., & Moan, S. (1991). Children's memories of physical examinations that involve genital touch: Implications for reports of child sexual abuse. *Journal of Consulting and Clinical Psychology, 59,* 682–691.

Saywitz, K. J., & Moan-Hardie, S. (1994). Reducing the potential for distortion of childhood memories. *Consciousness and Cognition, 3,* 408–425.

Saywitz, K. J., & Snyder, L. (1996). Narrative elaboration technique: Test of a new procedure for interviewing children. *Journal of Consulting and Clinical Psychology, 64,* 1347–1357.

Saywitz, K. J., Snyder, L., & Lamphear, V. (1996). Helping children tell what happened: A follow-up of the narrative elaboration procedure. *Child Maltreatment, 1,* 200–212.

Saywitz, K. J., Snyder, L., & Nathanson, R. (1999). Facilitating the communicative competence of the child witness. *Applied Developmental Sciences, 3*(1), 58–68.

Scullin, M. H., & Ceci, S. J. (2001). A suggestibility scale for children. *Personality & Individual Differences, 30,* 843–856.

Sedlak, A. J. (1991). *National incidence and prevalence of child abuse and neglect: 1988-revised report.* Rockville, MD: Westat.

Sedlak, A. J., & Broadhurst, D. D. (1996). *The third national incidence study of child abuse and neglect.* Washington, DC: U.S. Department of Health and Human Services.

Shapiro, J. P., Leifer, M., Martone, M. W., & Kassem, L. (1990). Multimethod assessment of depression in sexually abused girls. *Journal of Personality Assessment, 55,* 234–248.

Shaw, J. A., Lewis, J. E., Loeb, A., Rosado, J., & Rodriguez, M. (2000). Child on child sexual abuse: Psychological perspectives. *Child Abuse and Neglect, 24,* 1591–1600.

Shipman, K. L., Rossman, B. B. R., & West, J. C. (1999). Co-occurrence of spousal violence and child abuse: Conceptual implications. *Child Maltreatment, 4,* 93–102.

Shuman, D. W., & Greenberg, S. A. (1998). The role of ethical norms in the admissibility of expert testimony. *Judges' Journal: A Quarterly of the Judicial Division, 37,* 1–10.

Sidun, N. M., & Rosenthal, R. H. (1987). Graphic indicators of sexual abuse in Draw-a-Person tests of psychiatrically hospitalized adolescents. *Arts in Psychotherapy, 14,* 25–33.

Snyder, L. S., Nathanson, R., & Saywitz, K. J. (1993). Children in court: The role of discourse processing and production. *Topics in Language Disorders, 13,* 39–58.

Sobsey, D., Randall, W., & Parrila, R. K. (1997). Gender differences in abused children with and without disabilities. *Child Abuse and Neglect, 21,* 707–720.

Spaccarelli, S. (1994). Stress, appraisal, and coping in child sexual abuse: A theoretical and empirical view. *Psychological Bulletin, 116,* 1–23.

State v. Allen, 647 So. 2d 428 (La. Ct. App. 1994).

State v. Batangan, 799 P.2d 48 (Haw. 1990).

State v. Bellotti, 383 N.W.2d 308 (Minn. Ct. App. 1986).

State v. Buckey, Sup. Ct. of L.A. County, Ca. No. a750900 (1990).

State v. Carver, 380 N.W.2d 821 (Minn. Ct. App. 1986).

State v. Denning, 579 N. E.2d 943 (Ill. App. Ct. 1991).

State v. Fuster, Dade Cty., Fla., No. 84-19728 (11th Jud. Cir. 1985).

State v. Giles, 772 P.2d 191 (Idaho 1989).

State v. Gill, 806 S.W.2d 40 (Mo. Ct. App. 1991).

State v. Gokey, 574 A.2d 766 (Vt. 1990).

State v. Harris, 808 P.2d 453 (Mont. 1991).

State v. Kelly, Jr., Sup. Crim. Ct., Pitt Cty., N.C., No. 91-CRS-4250-4363 (1991–1992).

State v. Lanam, 459 N.W.2d 656 (Minn. 1990).

State v. Michaels, Sup. Ct., Essex Cty., N.J. (1988).

State v. Michaels, 264 N.J. Super 579, 642 A.2d 489 (N.J. Super Ad. 1993).

State v. Michaels, 136 N.J. 299, 642 A.2d 1372 (N.J. 1994).

State v. Moore, 404 S.E.2d 695 (N.C. Ct. App. 1991).

State v. Oliver, 467 N.W.2d 211 (Wis. Ct. App. 1991).

State v. Pham, 75 Wash. App. 626, 879 P.2d 321 (1994).

State v. Reser, 767 P.2d. 1277 (Kan. 1989).

State v. Roenfeldt, 486 N.W.2d 197 (Neb. 1992).

State v. Stewart, 641 So. 2d 1086, 1088 (La. Ct. App. 1994).

Sternberg, K. J., Lamb, M. E., Hershkowitz, I., Yudilevitch, L., Orbach, Y., Esplin, P. W., et al. (1997). Effects of introductory style on children's abilities to describe experiences of sexual abuse. *Child Abuse and Neglect, 21,* 1133–1146.

Steward, M. S., & Steward, D. S. (1996). Interviewing young children about body touch and handling. *Monograph of the Society for Research in Child Development, 61*(4–5, Serial No. 248).

Straus, M. A., Gelles, R. J., & Steinmetz, S. K. (1980). *Behind closed doors: Violence in the American family.* Garden City, NY: Doubleday.

Sullivan, P. M., & Knutson, J. F. (1998). The association between child maltreatment and disabilities in a hospital-based epidemiological study. *Child Abuse and Neglect, 22,* 271–288.

Summitt, R. C. (1983). The child sexual abuse accommodation syndrome. *Child Abuse and Neglect, 7,* 177–193.

Summitt, R. C. (1992). Abuse of the child sexual abuse accommodation syndrome. *Journal of Child Sexual Abuse, 4,* 153–163.

Thomas v. People, 803 P.2d 144 (Colo. 1990).

Tobey, A., & Goodman, G. S. (1992). Children's eyewitness memory: Effects of participation and forensic context. *Child Abuse and Neglect, 16,* 779–796.

Trickett, P. K., & Putnam, F. W. (1998). Developmental consequences of child sexual abuse. In P. K. Trickett & C. J. Schellenbach (Eds.), *Violence against children in the family and the community* (pp. 11–38). Washington, DC: American Psychological Association.

United States v. Azure, 801 F.2d 336 (8th Cir. 1986).

United States v. Ellis, 935 F.2d 385 (1st Cir.), *cert. denied,* 112 S. Ct. 201 (1991).

U.S. Department of Health and Human Services, National Center on Child Abuse and Neglect. (2000). *Child maltreatment 1998: Reports from the states to the national child abuse and neglect data system.* Washington, DC: U.S. Government Printing Office.

van der Kolk, B. A., & Fisler, R. E. (1995). Dissociation and the fragmentary nature of the traumatic memories: Overview and exploratory study. *Journal of Traumatic Stress, 8,* 505–525.

van der Kolk, B. A., & van der Hart, O. (1991). The intrusive past: The flexibility of memory and the engraving of trauma. *American Imago, 48,* 425–454.

Vrij, A., & Bush, N. (1998, April). *Differences in suggestibility between 5–6 and 10–11 year olds: A matter of differences in self confidence?* Paper presented at the meeting of the American Psychology-Law Society, Redondo Beach, CA.

Wang, C. T., & Harding, K. (1999). *Current trends in child abuse reporting and fatalities: The results of the 1998 annual fifty state survey.* Chicago: Prevent Child Abuse America.

Warren, A. R., & Lane, P. (1995). Effects of timing and type of questioning on eyewitness accuracy and suggestibility. In M. S. Zaragoza, J. R. Graham, G. C. N. Hall, R. Hirschman, & Y. S. Ben-Porath (Eds.), *Memory and testimony in the child witness* (pp. 44–60). Thousand Oaks, CA: Sage.

Warren, A. R., Woodall, C. E., Hunt, J. S., & Perry, N. W. (1996). "It sounds good in theory, but . . .": Do investigative interviewers follow guidelines based on memory research? *Child Maltreatment, 1,* 231–245.

West, M. M. (1998). Meta-analysis of studies assessing the efficacy of projective techniques in discriminating child sexual abuse. *Child Abuse and Neglect, 22,* 1151–1166.

Wheeler v. United States, 159 U.S. 523 (1895).

White, T. L., Leichtman, M. D., & Ceci, S. J. (1997). The good, the bad, and the ugly: Accuracy, inaccuracy, and elaboration in preschoolers' reports about a past event [Special issue]. *Applied Cognitive Psychology, 11,* S37–S54.

Whitfield, C. L. (1995). The forgotten difference: Ordinary memory versus tramatic memory. *Consciousness and Cognition, 4,* 88–94.

Wolfner, G., Faust, D., & Dawes, R. (1993). The use of anatomically detailed dolls in sexual abuse evaluations: The state of the science. *Applied and Preventive Psychology, 2,* 1–11.

Wood, J. M., McClure, K. A., & Birch, R. A. (1996). Suggestions for improving interviews in child protection agencies, *Child Maltreatment, 1,* 223–230.

Wyatt, G. E., & Newcomb, M. (1990). Internal and external mediators of women's sexual abuse in childhood. *Journal of Consulting and Clinical Psychology, 58,* 758–767.

Zivney, O. A., Nash, M. R., & Hulsey, T. L. (1988). Sexual abuse in early versus late childhood: Differing patterns of pathology as revealed on the Rorschach. *Psychotherapy, 25,* 99–106.

PART SIX

FORENSIC ASSESSMENT OF SPECIAL POPULATIONS

CHAPTER 23

Evaluation of Sexual Predators

MARY ALICE CONROY

Throughout much of the twentieth century, legal and mental health professionals have been searching for ways of dealing with individuals who repeatedly commit sexual offenses. In particular, those who offend against children have been among the most feared, and often most despised, of predators. Their crimes are viewed as aberrant in the extreme, and society has vacillated between treating them as criminals and treating them as mental patients. In recent decades, intense scrutiny has been focused on the adjudication and treatment of sex offenders. During the 1990s, the sex offender population increased faster than any other contingent of violent criminals, with the exception of drug offenders (La Fond, 1998). This spurred legislatures in many jurisdictions to authorize unique combinations of procedures under both criminal and civil law. These included lengthy, mandatory sentences for sex-related crimes, requirements that sex offenders register with authorities following release from incarceration, community notification when a sex offender moves into a neighborhood, the imposition of lifelong periods of probation, and the pursuit of civil commitment after prison terms have expired (Bumby & Maddox, 1999).

Forensic psychologists are increasingly being called on to evaluate sex offenders in both the civil and criminal arenas. Evaluations typically focus on understanding the offender's psychopathology, establishing treatment and management needs, and/or predicting the likelihood that the individual will reoffend. This chapter begins by providing a legal and historical context for these evaluations and proceeds to discuss issues of evaluating the sex offender's mental abnormality and assessing and managing the risk for recidivism. It concludes with some special attention to the pragmatic and ethical issues of providing testimony about evaluation results as well as future directions for psychologists involved in this area of forensic assessment.

SEX OFFENDER STATUTES

Sexual Psychopath Laws

Early in the twentieth century, sex offenders were primarily the object of blame and punishment rather than treatment (Brakel & Cavanaugh, 2000). During the 1930s, society began turning increasingly to the medical community in search of explanations for criminality. In 1936, Dr. James Pritchard coined the term "moral insanity" to refer to those individuals who appeared to lack any well-formed conscience, although otherwise seeming perfectly normal. If sexually deviant behavior was, in fact, a type of mental illness, it surely could be treated. In a rare show of consensus, the medical community, the news media, and the anxious public optimistically converged on the idea that these aberrations could be diagnosed and treated by psychiatrists (Lieb, Quinsey, & Berliner, 1998).

The first of the sexual psychopath laws, allowing for the commitment of sexual offenders to treatment facilities, was passed in Michigan in 1937. Although that particular Michigan law was ultimately ruled unconstitutional by the Michigan Supreme Court, it was followed quickly by similar legislation in Illinois in 1938 and both California and Minnesota in 1939. The Minnesota statute soon reached the U.S. Supreme Court, where it was deemed constitutional. The Justices ruled that the Minnesota law sufficiently narrowed the class of persons to whom it could be applied to those who demonstrated "an utter lack of power to control their sexual impulses and . . . are likely to attack or otherwise inflict injury, loss, pain, or other evil on the objects of their uncontrolled or uncontrollable desires" (*Minnesota ex rel Pearson,* 1940, p. 273).

Sexual psychopath statutes were considered to be enlightened, scientific, and humane, and spread quickly throughout the country. By the mid-1960s, 26 states had enacted such legislation (Lieb et al., 1998). Jurisdictions varied widely in regard to persons included in the scope of the statutes, some limiting the law to the most violent rapists, others covering nonviolent, noncontact offenders such as voyeurs. A few states enacted laws aimed at postconviction commitments and/or indeterminate sentences; however, most mandated treatment programs in lieu of criminal incarceration. Many statutes included some mechanism for transferring unsuitable treatment candidates to prison settings. However, sex offenders committed for treatment were usually released much sooner than if they had received prison time (La Fond, 1998). By the mid-1960s, California was sending the largest number to treatment of any jurisdiction, committing approximately 800 per year (Brakel & Cavanaugh, 2000). Minnesota also had an active program, committing about 15% of their potentially eligible offenders from 1939 until 1969 (Janus, 2000).

By the late 1970s, the pendulum of public opinion was clearly swinging. Citizens began losing faith in the efficacy and inherent humanitarianism of psychiatric treatments for offenders generally and for sex offenders in particular. By the mid-1980s, opposition to the sexual psychopath statutes had been voiced by the American Bar Association, the Group for the Advancement of Psychiatry, and the President's Commission on Mental Health (Brakel & Cavanaugh, 2000). Only five states (Massachusetts, Nebraska, New Jersey, Oregon,

and Washington) were still applying these laws with any frequency by 1985.

Registration and Community Notification

Along with the enactment of sexual psychopath laws, the 1930s saw the initiation of statutes requiring released sex offenders to register with community law enforcement authorities. Over the years, courts found this to be a reasonable measure in the interest of protecting the public at the very small expense to civil liberties (Lieb et al., 1998). In 1994, the U.S. Congress passed the Jacob Wetterling Crimes Against Children and Sexually Violent Offender Registration Program, under which states were required to create a system of registries for released sex offenders or risk forfeiting 10% of their federal crime prevention funding. The law further strengthened the registration program by mandating that registration continue for life, with addresses to be verified every 90 days. By the mid-1990s, all states had sex offender registration programs in place, with approximately 185,000 sex offenders registered nationally (Lieb et al., 1998).

An additional step was taken by the state of Washington in 1990 with the enactment of the first community notification statute. However, this practice was not widely used or publicized until July 1994, when 7-year-old Megan Kanka was brutally raped and murdered in her quiet New Jersey neighborhood. Following the tragedy, it became known that the perpetrator was a twice-convicted sex offender, living with two other convicted sex offenders, across the street from the Kanka family, unbeknownst to anyone in the neighborhood. Approximately three months later, the New Jersey legislature passed a community notification statute, which has become known as "Megan's Law." In 1996, Congress amended the Jacob Wetterling Act to include the major provisions of "Megan's Law." This amendment mandated the states to release information relative to a released sex offender as deemed necessary to protect the public.

Community notification acts have withstood legal challenges in both Washington and New Jersey with relatively minor alterations. Studies to date of the effectiveness of these laws are primarily composed of surveys of law enforcement agencies and policymakers who generally report great satisfaction but provide only anecdotal evidence as to results (Zevitz, Crim, & Farkas, 2000). As yet, no hard data exist demonstrating the effectiveness of community notification laws in reducing recidivism (Quinsey, Harris, Rice, & Cormier, 1998).

Critics of the notification laws decry the weakening of civil liberties protections, arguing that the laws discourage sex offenders from seeking rehabilitation, create a false sense of community security, waste funds that might otherwise be devoted to treatment and prevention programs, and may lead to vigilantism (Lieb et al., 1998). In one survey in which offenders subject to notification were interviewed, Zevitz et al. (2000) found that over half reported problems with exclusion from residence, ostracism by neighbors and acquaintances, threats and harassment, emotional harm to family members, and loss of employment. However, a very small percentage reported actual physical attacks. Verification with law enforcement agencies in Wisconsin, Washington, Oregon, and New Jersey revealed that fewer than 1% of sex offenders subject to community notification reported subsequent physical attack or property damage.

Sexually Violent Predator Statutes

In 1989, a particularly horrendous sex crime in the state of Washington breathed new life into the idea of committing violent sex offenders to treatment programs. Earl Shriner, a repeat violent sex offender who had failed to qualify for commitment under Washington's sexual psychopath law, raped a 7-year-old boy, cut off his penis, and left him to die. Although amazingly, the child survived, broad publicity regarding the brutality of the crime incensed the community and motivated legislators to immediate action.

The next year, the state of Washington enacted the first of a second generation of sex offender civil commitment statutes. Known as sexually violent predator (SVP) statutes, these laws differed from the earlier version in that commitment was generally applied *after* a term of incarceration was completed rather than in lieu of imprisonment. They also differed from more traditional civil commitment statutes in that neither a serious mental illness nor a recent dangerous act was a prerequisite. Whereas the usual civil commitment of the mentally ill was short term and reviewed frequently, SVP commitments were envisioned as long-term containment. In many instances, nothing recognizable as treatment was in place at the time of commitment (La Fond, 1998).

By the turn of the twenty-first century, 16 states had enacted SVP laws and 16 more had proposed legislation toward this end (Janus & Walbek, 2000). Criteria for commitment typically included a past course of harmful conduct, some current "disorder" or "abnormality," and a finding that future risk is connected to that disorder or abnormality (Janus, 2000). Procedures for implementing the laws varied from jurisdiction to jurisdiction. For example, Pennsylvania established a Sexual Offender Assessment Board to decide which cases would be pursued for commitment. Oregon and Texas

constructed their own Sex Offender Risk Assessment scales, and Minnesota developed an actuarial device to measure and compare levels of risk, the Minnesota Sex Offender Screening Tool–Revised (MnSOST-R) (Epperson, Kaul, & Hasselton, 1998), widely adopted in other areas of the country. The Texas statute specifically requires testing for psychopathy, and Texas enacted a law allowing for only outpatient commitment.

Jurisdictions generally limited their commitments to a small percentage of sexual offenders released from custody. Statutes were intended to apply to the highest-risk offenders, due in part to the high cost of these programs. Minnesota, for example, estimated it cost approximately $100,000 per offender simply to complete the court process. Figures from various states on the cost of maintaining one offender in an inpatient setting ranged from $60,000 to $128,000 per year (Janus & Walbek, 2000). The vast majority of jurisdictions screen out over 90% of their sex offender population from consideration for commitment. Nonetheless, figures from the fall of 1999 indicated that 630 sex offenders in the United States resided in treatment facilities under SVP statutes (Brakel & Cavanaugh, 2000).

In addition to civil commitment, states pursued other avenues to contain high-risk sex offenders. Arizona, for example, developed a system of lifetime probation, covering a much larger percentage of offenders than would qualify for civil commitment. In 1997, California was the first state to enact legislation requiring the administration of antiandrogen medications to probated sex offenders, and several other states followed (Lieb et al., 1998).

Kansas v. Hendricks

Early in the 1990s, constitutional challenges to SVP laws began to mount, and those involved knew it was only a matter of time until one of them reached the U.S. Supreme Court. In 1996, the Supreme Court granted *certiorari* in the case of *Kansas v. Hendricks* and subsequently issued a final ruling in June of 1997.

The Kansas act under challenge allowed for the postincarceration civil commitment of "any person who has been convicted of or charged with a sexually violent offense and who suffers from a mental abnormality or personality disorder which makes the person likely to engage in the predatory acts of sexual violence" (*Kansas v. Hendricks,* 1997, p. 2077). Leroy Hendricks, the defendant, had a lengthy history of brutally molesting children. He testified in court that he agreed with his diagnosis of pedophilia and admitted that he continued to harbor sexual desires for children.

The Court ruled on a number of legal issues relevant to SVP statutes generally. They were persuaded that the statute was, in fact, civil and not criminal and, therefore, did not violate defendants' due process rights. They also concluded that it violated neither the double jeopardy nor ex post facto clauses of the federal Constitution.

Of greatest significance to the forensic evaluator were positions taken by the Court regarding diagnoses and treatment requirements. The ruling denied Hendricks's contention that some mental illness was a necessary prerequisite for civil commitment and accepted, as sufficient, the Kansas requirement for a "mental abnormality" or "personality disorder." Writing for the majority, Justice Thomas stated:

> Contrary to Hendricks' assertion, the term "mental illness" is devoid of any talismanic significance. Not only do "psychiatrists disagree widely and frequently on what constitutes mental illness," *Ake v. Oklahoma,* 470 U.S. 68 (1985), but the Court itself has used a variety of expressions to describe the mental condition of those properly subject to civil confinement. (*Kansas v. Hendricks,* 1997, p. 2080)

The Court went on to refute Hendricks's contention that treatment was an essential element in any civil commitment. Justice Thomas wrote:

> Accordingly, the Kansas court's determination that the Act's "overriding concern" was the continued "segregation of sexually violent offenders" is consistent with our conclusion that the Act establishes civil proceedings, . . . especially when that concern is coupled with the State's ancillary goal of providing treatment to those offenders, if such is possible. While we have upheld civil commitment statutes that aim both to incapacitate and to treat, . . . we have never held that the Constitution prevents the State from civilly detaining those for whom no treatment is available, but who nevertheless pose a danger to others. (p. 2084)

THE ISSUE OF DIAGNOSIS

Who Can Be Civilly Committed?

For the past two centuries, our government has allowed persons to be involuntarily committed to treatment facilities either under *parens patriae* authority or under the auspices of police power. *Parens patriae* commitments were generally limited to those who were unable to make decisions for themselves or otherwise unable to care for their own basic needs. Historically, such hospitalizations usually required some combination of mental illness and treatment need. However, the *parens patriae* model is rarely, if ever, applicable to repeat sexual offenders.

The second type of commitment, that conducted under police power, also requires the presence of a mental disorder and cannot be used simply as preventive detention (La Fond, 1998). Mental disorder is considered to be an essential limiting and justifying factor (Janus, 2000). Over the past 50 years, courts often have sought some abnormality that would result in the individual having impaired control over his or her behavior. However, the nature of the disorder involved in a police power commitment often is defined more in terms of the danger posed than the precise nature of the mental incapacity.

Legal versus Clinical Mental Disorder

Both legal and clinical scholars have noted that terminology describing mental conditions means different things to legal authorities than to mental health professionals (E. Campbell, 1990; Datz & MacCarthy, 1989; Gerard, 1987; A. Greenberg & Bailey, 1994; Moore, 1984; Prentky & Burgess, 2000; Schopp & Quattrocchi, 1995; Schopp & Sturgis, 1995; Slovenko, 1984). When appearing in legal treatises, appellations such as "mental disease" and "personality disorder" become more statutory categories than clinical diagnoses. Some mental health professionals contend that, when applied to sex offenders, the term mental abnormality should simply refer to one of the paraphilias outlined in the *Diagnostic and Statistical Manual of Mental Disorders* (DSM-IV; American Psychiatric Association, 1994; see Becker & Murphy, 1998). Others argue that it is the prerogative of the trier of fact and not the clinician to determine which conditions will form an adequate basis for commitment (Melton, Petrila, Poythress, & Slobogin, 1997).

Some evaluators have attempted to tell the court directly how a diagnostic term translates into a legal one, as in a recent Kansas case regarding a sexual predator. Specifically, the psychologist testified that exhibitionism alone would not be enough to find an individual is a sexual predator under the statute. However, in the psychologist's opinion, the defendant should be classified as a sexual predator due to his combination of Antisocial Personality Disorder and exhibitionism (*In the Matter of the Care and Treatment of Michael T. Crane,* 2000).

Although most forensic psychologists are careful to allow the courts to define statutory terms for themselves, courts nonetheless rely heavily on mental health testimony in doing so (Conroy, 2000), leading to conflicting results. One court may rule that Antisocial Personality Disorder is not a mental disease or defect (*U.S. v. Bilyk,* 1994); another may reach the opposite conclusion (*Parrish v. Colorado,* 1996). In lieu of reviewing testimony, courts may review documents published by professional organizations, most notably the *DSM-IV* or *DSM-IV-TR* (American Psychiatric Association, 2000), in their search for explanations. In the case of *U.S. v. Murdoch* (1996), one of the justices of the U.S. Ninth Circuit consulted the *DSM-IV* directly and concluded that Personality Disorder Not Otherwise Specified "comports with the general connotation of a 'disease or defect' in that it is neither a temporary condition nor a chosen way of responding but rather a systemic, impairing psychiatric abnormality" (p. 480). Perhaps, as Friedland (1999) noted, "removing the anchor of psychiatry in determining legal meaning all too often leaves no viable alternative meaning" (p. 139).

Mental Abnormality or Personality Disorder

With the exception of a paraphilia or substance abuse disorder, a serious Axis I diagnosis in a sex offender is rare (Barbaree & Marshall, 1998; Hanson & Bussiere, 1998). The most common diagnoses are substance abuse, a paraphilia, or a personality disorder. These diagnoses are based almost entirely on observable, quantifiable behavior. For example, someone who is at least 16 years of age, has molested a child on more than one occasion over a six-month period, and has experienced a resulting dysfunction or impairment (e.g., incarceration) qualifies for the diagnosis of pedophilia. It has been suggested that diagnoses such as this are more psychosocial than biomedical (Winick, 1998). Harris, Rice, and Quinsey (1998) contend that Antisocial Personality Disorder is most accurately described as neither a mental illness nor a mental disorder, but rather as a pattern of aberrant behavior. The Kansas statute, upheld by the Supreme Court in *Hendricks,* specifically recognized that most SVPs have Antisocial Personality Disorder and are not amenable to the treatment modalities used to treat mental illness (Cornwell, 1998). During the court proceedings, the state admitted that the defendant did not have any mental illness.

Courts historically have had difficulty grappling with the concept of personality disorder as presented by the mental health community (Conroy, 2000). In the highly publicized case of *Foucha v. Louisiana* (1992), the U.S. Supreme Court appeared to decide that Antisocial Personality Disorder was not a mental illness; however, the opinion was somewhat murky and lacked extensive explanation. Subsequent decisions, such as *Hendricks,* appear to reach differing conclusions. Although much mental health testimony has been recorded explaining the personality disorder construct, it has generally failed to clarify the issue and, in some cases, has obfuscated it.

A major part of the difficulty may arise from the propensity to confuse a discriminative with a causative category (Schopp, Scalora, & Pearce, 1999). A discriminative category is merely a group of people who evidence a particular behavior, whereas a causative category is a group of people evidencing a behavior caused by a common factor. Simply including personality disorders under the large umbrella of mental disorders—the same umbrella that shades schizophrenia, bipolar disorder, and dementia—may imply that there is some definable entity, distinct from the behaviors themselves, causing the individual to have symptoms (as in certain viruses causing flu symptoms). However, to date, science has identified no such entity.

Hendricks and the Issue of Control

Leading authorities in the field of risk assessment have questioned the necessity of considering psychopathology as central to an evaluation of risk (Lieb et al., 1998). However, the legal community has long relied on some type of "control incapacity" as the legitimizing principle in civil commitments or other nonpunitive restrictions on individual liberties (Janus, 2000). Specifically, in *Kansas v. Hendricks* (1997), Justice Thomas wrote: "A finding of dangerousness, standing alone, is ordinarily not a sufficient ground upon which to justify indefinite involuntary commitment" (p. 2080).

The U.S. Supreme Court found the Kansas SVP statute constitutional precisely because of what they judged to be its narrow focus. Commitment required some "factor," beyond simply the sexual offenses, that served to define and limit the class of persons who may be committed and to justify dealing with their behavior as something other than a criminal justice matter. The Court went on to describe the obligatory "factor" as an entity that must significantly impair the individual's ability to exercise control over his or her behavior in some domain:

> The Kansas Act is plainly of a kind with other civil commitment statutes: It requires a finding of future dangerousness, and then links that finding to the existence of a "mental abnormality" or "personality disorder" that makes it difficult, if not impossible, for the person to control his dangerous behavior. The precommitment requirement of a "mental abnormality" or "personality disorder" is consistent with the requirements of these other statutes that we upheld in that it narrows the class of person eligible for confinement to those who are unable to control their dangerousness. (*Kansas v. Hendricks,* 1997, p. 2080)

Even the dissenting Justices conceded: "Hendricks' abnormality does not consist simply of a long course of antisocial behavior, but rather it includes a specific, serious, and highly unusual inability to control his actions" (pp. 2088–2089). No less than 17 times in *Hendricks* does the Court reiterate the central importance of some factor that impairs volition. No alternative paradigm is suggested.

In a subsequent test of the Kansas SVP statute, the Kansas Supreme Court reinforced the requirement that volitional impairment be proven. During an SVP commitment hearing, a lower court judge had instructed the jury that the prosecution need not prove the defendant could not control his behavior, but only that his mental abnormality or personality disorder made it more likely that he would reoffend. The Kansas Supreme Court reversed and remanded, saying, "A commitment under the Sexually Violent Predator Act is unconstitutional absent a finding that a defendant suffers from a volitional impairment rendering him or her dangerous beyond his or her control" (*In the Matter of the Care and Treatment of Michael T. Crane*, 2000, p. 286). The following year, the Arizona Court of Appeals ruled the Arizona Sexually Violent Persons Act to be unconstitutional because it did not require volitional impairment as mandated by Hendricks (In re Leon G., 2001). The U.S. Supreme Court heard the Crane case on appeal and ruled that proof of some "lack of control" was necessary for a civil commitment (*Kansas v. Crane*, 2002). However, many questions were left open, including a definition of "control" and the degree to which control must be impaired. Given the continued controversy on interpreting the role of. volition, it is unlikely this ruling will put the issue to rest.

The concern over impaired volitional abilities is not new; in fact, it has been central to court rulings on the exercise of police power in civil commitment hearings for the past 50 years (Janus, 1998). Beyond insisting on its importance, however, courts have provided little guidance as to what constitutes volitional impairment. Nonetheless, attorneys seeking testimony regarding a personality disorder in relation to sexually violent predators clearly are seeking testimony about some factor that would impair control (Schopp et al., 1999).

Given the vagueness of the legal conceptualization of impaired volition and the paucity of scientific evidence regarding entities that would so impair an individual, it is doubtful a forensic psychologist should or could testify with any degree of clinical certainty that a diagnosis of personality disorder or paraphilia or even substance abuse would make it impossible or nearly impossible for an individual to control his or her behavior. Even the authors of the *DSM-IV-TR* (2000) include the following caveat:

> The fact that an individual's presentation meets the criteria for a *DSM-IV* diagnosis does not carry any necessary implication regarding the individual's degree of control over the behaviors that

may be associated with the disorder. Even when diminished control over one's behavior is a feature of the disorder, having the diagnosis in itself does not demonstrate that a particular individual is (or was) unable to control his or her behavior at a particular time. (p. xxxiii)

Perhaps a decision as to the impact of any mental abnormality or personality disorder on a person's capacity to exercise free will should rightfully be left to the trier of fact.

RISK ASSESSMENT OF SEX OFFENDERS

The assessment of risk and the prediction as to whether a specific individual is apt to reoffend have been areas fraught with controversy for many years. High rates of "false-positive" predictions have been recorded even when evaluators were attempting only to predict *any* criminal offense and not that it be specifically violent or specifically sexual. In 1983, the American Psychiatric Association submitted an *amicus curiae* brief to the U.S. Supreme Court in the case of *Barefoot v. Estelle,* acknowledging that when members of their organization made predictions about future dangerousness, they were likely wrong two out of three times. Not withstanding the evidence presented, the Justices ruled that psychiatrists could continue to testify in this regard because they were not always wrong, they were only wrong most of the time.

Since the *Barefoot* case, a whole new generation of risk assessment research has emerged, providing additional tools to improve the accuracy of predictions. However, the advent of SVP statutes has increased the difficulty faced by evaluators. Most sex offender commitment laws focus only on repeat sexual offenses and not on criminal offenses in general (Janus, 1997). Variables that predict general recidivism or violent recidivism may not be applicable to prediction of exclusively sexual reoffending (Hanson & Bussiere, 1998; Hanson, Scott, & Steffy, 1995; Rice & Harris, 1997). Therefore, the task becomes exceedingly complex and requires a highly sophisticated knowledge of the research literature.

The Problems Associated with Clinical Prediction

The term "clinical prediction" is generally applied to an evaluation in which the clinician relies exclusively on very traditional methods combined with his or her own anecdotal experience and clinical wisdom. This method may include interviews, an assessment of clinical presentation, a review of case files, and the application of broad testing batteries, not specifically designed for the purpose at hand.

As early as 1954, Meehl compared this type of prediction with predictions made using actuarial methods and found it to, be inferior. More recent studies, including large meta-analyses, have confirmed his conclusion that actuarial approaches are generally more accurate than clinical judgment (Grove & Meehl, 1996; Hanson & Bussiere, 1998; Janus & Meehl, 1997; Mossman, 1994). Karl Hanson (1998) described a meta-analysis of 10 studies (N = 1,453) in which the predictive accuracy of clinical judgments regarding sex offender recidivism yielded a correlation of r = .10. This was small compared to even a single item from the record (prior sexual offenses), which yielded a correlation of r = .19. One of the problems identified by Hanson was clinicians' reliance on certain factors that research indicates are not predictive. For example, commonly used clinical factors such as general psychological maladjustment, low self-esteem, a history of being sexually abused as a child, and denial of one's offense all yielded a correlation close to zero in regard to recidivism (Hanson, 1998).

Despite evidence of its flaws, courts have largely continued to admit testimony from mental health professionals about risk assessments based solely on clinical judgment. (For a comprehensive discussion of this issue, see the chapter by Meloy in this volume.) As a result, courts have been schooled in numerous beliefs that do not stand up to scientific scrutiny. For example, in surveying the judiciary, Bumby and Maddox (1999) found that over two-thirds of judges believed that one of the main reasons sex offenders abuse others is because they were sexually abused as children. Because the courts have not always acted as effective gatekeepers in this area, it becomes incumbent on the profession to carefully scrutinize its own practices and to educate the court regarding the science in the field.

The Use and Abuse of Sex Offender Profiles

Another belief commonly held in the community is the existence of a sex offender profile, that is, a set of clearly identifiable characteristics of persons who commit sex crimes. Of the judges surveyed by Bumby and Maddox (1999), 47.6% believed mental health professionals had the ability to present such a profile to the court.

It is not unusual for attorneys to ask whether the Minnesota Multiphasic Personality Inventory-2 (MMPI-2) profile of a specific defendant demonstrates that the person is or is not a sex offender. In fact, research has not yielded a profile specific to sex offenders, nor to any particular category of such offenders. MMPI-2 profiles do not successfully differentiate sex offenders from other criminal or mental health populations (Becker & Murphy, 1998; Levin & Stava, 1987;

Murphy & Peters, 1992). Edens (2001) described a case in which the PCL-R was used to support expert opinion that the defendant was not a sex offender.

Data based on profiles of identified groups may prove useful in researching personality constructs and in determining whether an individual exhibits the symptoms of a certain psychopathology. However, it is misleading to use such data to establish that a particular individual has engaged in a specific type of behavior. It is one thing to consider a defendant's state of mind at the time of a crime and quite another to establish whether the person actually committed the crime in question. The case of *New Jersey v. Cavallo* (1982) is illustrative of this point. Two defendants were indicted for abduction, sodomy, private lewdness, and rape. The defense proffered the testimony of a psychiatrist, who proposed to testify that defendant Cavallo simply did not have the traits of a rapist. The testimony was excluded by the trial judge as more prejudicial than probative. On appeal, the Supreme Court of New Jersey affirmed, stating:

> that defendants have not met their burden of showing that the scientific community generally accepts the existence of identifiable character traits common to rapists. They also have not demonstrated that psychiatrists possess any special ability to discern whether an individual is likely to be a rapist. Until scientific reliability of this type of evidence is established, it is not admissible. (Monahan & Walker, 1998, p. 444)

In the intervening years, no sex offender classification systems or psychometric instruments for profiling sex offenders have been developed (Prentky & Burgess, 2000). Federal courts have continued to reaffirm that mental health experts are not allowed to testify as to whether a defendant could or could not have committed the crime at issue (*U.S. v. Robinson,* 2000). Thus, it is incumbent on the forensic psychologist to take great care not to imply that any personality characteristics found are probative in establishing whether any individual committed or did not commit a specific offense or types of offenses.

The Rise of Actuarial Prediction

A growing awareness in the scientific community of the inadequacy of much information being given to the courts regarding risk spurred a plethora of studies in recent decades aimed at establishing solid actuarial predictors of recidivism. Research specifically directed toward sex offenders generated one of the largest bodies of data (Quinsey & Lalumiere, 1996). In addition to the investigation of individual risk factors, a number of instruments were developed that have shown promise on cross-validation (Rice & Harris, 1997). Some prominent researchers argue that the science is sufficiently developed to form the basis for social policy:

> The quantitative information necessary to inform the debate about civil commitment laws is thus readily available. We need not be satisfied with an unsatisfactory answer to a primitive question such as whether prediction "works" but, rather, what ratio of hits to false alarms is desirable. The accuracy that actuarial instruments can achieve in predicting violent and sexual recidivism is comparable to many other areas in which predictions are commonly made, such as predicting hurricanes, and is more than sufficient to make a large contribution to public safety. (Lieb et al., 1998, p. 95)

The Highest Correlates of Sex Offender Recidivism

A number of individual factors have proven to correlate with recidivism in sexual offenders across studies and over time, and these have been especially helpful in identifying the highest-risk offenders. Researchers have generally found that variables predictive of sex offender recidivism are not identical to those predictive of other types of criminal reoffending (Hanson & Bussiere, 1998; Rice & Harris, 1997).

History. One of the most consistent and robust predictors of the propensity to reoffend is a history of criminal offenses generally and sexual offenses in particular (Boer, Wilson, Gauthier, & Hart, 1997; Epperson et al., 1998; Hanson, 1998; Harris et al., 1998; Prentky, Knight, & Lee, 1997). If one's predictions are to be limited to future sexual crimes, a history of these specific crimes is most predictive (Quinsey, Rice, & Harris, 1995). Within that history, an identifiable pattern of sexually deviant interests has been found to be specifically related to sexual reoffending. Such interests may be assessed using phallometric devices (Barbaree & Marshall, 1989; Freund & Watson, 1991) or by examining social histories for evidence of a wide array of victims, deviant victim choices, and unusually deviant activities (Hanson, 1998; Lieb et al., 1998). In terms of victim choice, evidence of deviance is generally defined as victims who are extrafamilial or complete strangers, victims much younger than the perpetrator, and male victims (Hanson, 1998; Hanson & Bussiere, 1998; Harris et al., 1998; Quinsey & Maguire, 1986; Prentky et al., 1997).

Treatment Compliance. A failure to cooperate with law enforcement authorities or treatment providers may be indicative of reoffense potential. For example, a history of conditional release violation is included in four of the more widely used actuarial instruments (Boer et al., 1997;

Epperson et al., 1998; Quinsey, Harris, et al., 1998). A history of treatment refusal or withdrawal from treatment also correlates with recidivism in a number of studies (Epperson et al., 1998; Hanson, 1998; Hanson & Bussiere, 1998; Hanson & Harris, 1998). This should not, however, be interpreted simply as not receiving treatment increases risk; nor should the conclusion be drawn that the treatment itself is effectively curtailing further offenses. Rather, the data focus on refusal to accept or withdrawing from treatment that is made available.

Substance Abuse. The abuse of drugs or alcohol has been found to be highly predictive of criminal recidivism in general (Gendreau, Little, & Goggin, 1996). It has been included in a number of actuarial instruments designed to assess sex offender risk (Boer et al., 1997; Epperson et al., 1998; Quinsey, Harris, et al., 1998). However, in what is probably the largest meta-analysis of recidivism predictors in sex offenders conducted to date, substance abuse was not among the highest correlates (Hanson & Bussiere, 1998). To determine whether substance abuse is a significant risk factor in an individual case may require a careful examination of the individual's offenses. If the person's pattern of aberrant behavior is somehow triggered by drugs or alcohol, such usage would elevate risk. On the other hand, there are offenders who commit sex crimes only when sober, despite a history of alcoholism or drug abuse. In such cases, it would be difficult to opine that the history of substance abuse in itself raises their level of risk.

Psychopathology. In general, neither personality variables nor the major psychopathologies have been found to predict risk in sex offenders. One exception is psychopathy, that is, psychopathy as conceptualized by Cleckley (1941) and Hare (1993), *not* what the *DSM-IV-TR* outlines as Antisocial Personality Disorder (APD). APD is a much broader construct, one that can be applied to the majority of individuals with a substantial criminal history. APD is primarily defined in behavioral terms; psychopathy also requires an array of personality traits, such as grandiosity, superficial charm, egocentricity, insincerity, shallow affect, a lack of empathy, and a propensity to manipulate other people.

As measured by the Psychopathy Checklist–Revised (PCL-R; Hare, 1991), psychopathy has proven to be a particularly robust predictor of future violent behavior (Hart, 1998; Hemphill, Hare, & Wong, 1998; Salekin, Rogers, & Sewell, 1996). In addition to general criminal behavior, it has also been effective in predicting future sexual violence (Hanson, 1998; Hanson & Bussiere, 1998; Prentky et al., 1997). Some states (e.g., Texas) formally require testing for psychopathy under their SVP commitment laws. One difficulty in using psychopathy as a predictor of violence (sexual or otherwise) is a misunderstanding on the part of the courts that it can be equated with APD. Expert witnesses have on numerous occasions reinforced this thinking by applying the empirical data on psychopathy and risk to anyone who met the *DSM-IV* criteria for APD (Hare, 1998; Ogloff & Lyon, 1998). This would be an egregious error resulting in serious overprediction of risk. In the prison system alone, up to 80% of the population may qualify for a diagnosis of APD, but less than a third of these individuals would meet the criteria for psychopathy (Cunningham & Reidy, 1998).

Offense Type.   Some differences have been found in prediction of recidivism for child molesters versus rapists. These have been significant enough for some authorities to suggest developing different actuarial instruments for the two groups (Lieb et al., 1998). In general, rapists are more criminally versatile. Although they may be at high risk for criminal recidivism, it is difficult to predict whether their crime will be sexual in nature (Quinsey, 1984). Child molesters, on the other hand (particularly those with male victims), may be totally focused on a single type of offense (Hanson & Bussiere, 1998). Even in the area of psychopathy, elevated PCL-R scores are much more predictive for rapists than for child molesters (Rice & Harris, 1997). In evaluations of chronic child molesters who have no other criminal record, it is relatively rare to encounter PCL-R scores in the psychopathic range. However, this does not mean that the offender does not present a high risk to this very specific population.

Although significant and consistent across numerous studies, the actual predictive value of each indicator alone is relatively small. Hanson (1998) noted that correlation coefficients of the strongest single variables range from r = .11 to r = .32. For such analysis to be of value, the psychologist needs to examine an array of factors.

Static versus Dynamic Predictor Variables

Researchers have generally divided variables thought to be predictive of future risk into two categories: static and dynamic (Bonta, Law, & Hanson, 1998; Hanson & Harris, 1998; Quinsey et al., 1995). Static variables are fixed and unchanging (e.g., number of past offenses, age at first offense), whereas dynamic variables may fluctuate or be amenable to intervention (e.g., anger, availability of social support systems). Dynamic predictors are then further subdivided into stable and acute. The more stable dynamic variables are those that may change over time (e.g., deviant sexual preferences, substance abuse), whereas acute dynamic variables may

change from day to day or moment to moment (e.g., sexual arousal, drunkenness). To date, much of the research on sex offender recidivism has focused primarily on static predictors. The major scales developed for this purpose are composed almost entirely of static variables. Those dynamic variables that have been investigated have been mainly very stable ones, such as personality disorders and deviant sexual preferences (Hanson & Harris, 1998).

Although the well-researched static variables (such as number and type of victims and prior conditional release violations) can be very helpful in predicting long-term recidivism potential, they tell us little about the imminence of risk, nor are they useful in the measurement of change. Research on static factors provides no guidance to the probation staff attempting to predict when an offender is at greatest risk and may warrant additional restrictions. Rather, clinicians are seeking information about dynamic changes that may occur during treatment that can be demonstrated to correlate with reduced recidivism. Symptoms of traditional psychopathology or limited ability to cope with stress may not predict long-term risk, but it is entirely possible they may contribute to an increased level of risk in the immediate future (Bonta et al., 1998). A better understanding of these issues could assist those monitoring offenders on an ongoing basis. Suggestions for dynamic variables to be explored have included intimacy deficits, attitudes tolerant of sexual offending, general self-regulation, negative social influences, negative mood, current substance abuse, anger control problems, and victim access (Hanson & Harris, 1998; Seidman, Marshall, Hudson, & Robertson, 1994).

Hanson and Harris (2000) have published preliminary findings on a scale designed specifically to measure dynamic variables and assess their relationship to risk of recidivism. The Sex Offender Need Assessment Rating (SONAR) has yielded some early positive results. It is composed of five stable dynamic variables (intimacy deficits, negative social influences, attitudes tolerant of sexual offending, sexual self-regulation, and general self-regulation) and four more acute markers (current substance abuse, negative mood, anger, and victim access). Research thus far suggests that general self-regulation (e.g., impulsivity, poor behavioral controls) may be the strongest predictor, followed by sexual self-regulation, attitudes tolerant of sexual offending, and negative social influences. Further analysis found the overall SONAR score to be moderately accurate in distinguishing recidivists from non-recidivists (Hanson & Harris, 2001).

Overall, sufficient data on static variables have been collected and studies replicated to provide a solid basis on which to formulate predictions of long-term risk. Dynamic variables clearly play a crucial role in prediction and are particularly valuable in the day-to-day management of risk. However, much more research in this area is needed before definitive conclusions can be drawn.

Adjusting Actuarial Predictions

Given the poor track record of using clinical judgment alone to conduct risk assessment, no authority in the field is likely to recommend using it as the primary predictive tool. Some suggest eliminating it altogether and relying solely on actuarial formulas. Quinsey and his colleagues (Quinsey, Harris, et al., 1998) have adamantly defended pure actuarial prediction, saying that currently available actuarial methods are too good to risk contaminating them with clinical judgments. (See the chapter by Meloy in this volume for additional discussion of this topic.)

Others, however, have taken a more moderate position, believing that applying clinical judgment to some degree is unavoidable (Grove & Meehl, 1996; Hanson, 1998). They argue that factors found to be empirically validated predictors still account for only less than half the variance in most risk assessments. Dynamic variables have not been well researched, yet few would argue they are not significant. Issues unique to a specific case may merit attention (e.g., a physical disability, a direct threat, a unique social circumstance, a major mental illness clearly related to past offenses). From this perspective, actuarial predictions could act as screening devices and serve to anchor the risk assessment. However, in making adjustments, the clinician should establish compelling reasons to do so and avoid the use of factors that have been demonstrated insignificant as predictors.

Problems Establishing Base Rates

Most risk assessments begin by establishing a base rate against which to compare the particular offender. If one is to conclude that the individual is at low, moderate, high, or extremely high risk to reoffend, it is generally in comparison to the base rates for reoffending in the particular category. However, this becomes a daunting task when considering sex offenders. In a landmark review of the literature, Furby, Weinrott, and Blackshaw (1989) found reported base rates for sexual reoffending ranging from 0% to 50%. The general public commonly believes that recidivism for sex offenders approaches 100%. However, a review of Bureau of Justice statistics from 1992, 1993, and 1995 indicates no higher rate of parole violations than among other offenders (Heilbrun, Nezu, Keeney, Chung, & Wasserman, 1998). Conservative estimates, based on reconvictions over a five-year period, indicate an overall recidivism rate for sex offenders of 13.4%,

with an 18.9% rate for rapists and 12.7% for child molesters (Hanson & Bussiere, 1998).

The reasons for the wide range of base rates recorded in the literature are complex and need to be kept in mind while reviewing that literature (Prentky & Burgess, 2000). The very term "sex offense" is imprecise, often used to refer only to offenses with stranger victims (Lieb et al., 1998). However, when incest offenses are included, the overall rate of reoffending is lower (Barbaree & Marshall, 1988). Some data include any reoffense by a sex offender in the recidivism rate; others count only those offenses that are sexual. If only offenses of a sexual nature are included, the rate is significantly reduced, particularly for rapists, who are apt to be more criminally versatile (Harris et al., 1998). Other statistics refer only to violent offenses or only to contact offenses. A significant number of offenses that involve sexual violations are subsequently plea-bargained down to charges that make no mention of sexual offending. The problem comes when attempting to compare the various data sets.

Base rates for sexual offense recidivism may be predicated on conviction for a new sexual offense, conviction for any new offense, arrest for one or both, parole or probation violation, or other reason to believe a reoffense has occurred. Some argue that a conviction is the most solid event on which to base the analysis. However, it is generally agreed that sex offenses are grossly underreported (Furby et al., 1989). Past research has demonstrated that chronic sex offenders fail to be apprehended for a sizable proportion of their crimes (Abel, Becker, Mittelman, Cunningham-Rathner, Rouleau, & Murphy, 1987; Doren, 1998). Barbaree and Marshall (1988) estimate that the recidivism rate for sexual offenders is 2.5 times higher if unofficial sources of information are included.

The time frame on which a recidivism rate is based is especially critical when studying sex offenders. Most studies are based on research that is time limited, resulting in the majority of follow-up periods being five years or less. However, sex offenders tend to spread their aberrant activities over longer periods of time than other offenders (Harris et al., 1998). Sex offenders have been known to receive their first new conviction 20 to 28 years after the original offense, and a significant number reoffend after their first five years in the community (Hanson, Steffey, & Gauthier, 1993). Rapists reoffend more in the earlier years, resulting in a higher base rate for rape if studies of five years or less are used (Doren, 1998). Prentky et al. (1997) suggest that, if long-term projections were made, the rate of recidivism for child molesters would surpass that for rapists and be as high as 52%.

Finally, in examining the literature on base rates, it is important to consider whether the investigator relied on cumulative frequencies or survival analysis. Cumulative frequencies simply count the number of offenders who have or have not recidivated as of a specific time. Survival analysis, however, allows the researcher to consider the actual time at risk or exposure time (Doren, 1998; Hanson, 1998; Prentky et al., 1997). Given that some offenders will be reincarcerated shortly after release and others will remain in the community for a considerable period of time, survival analysis will yield different base rates than will the more traditional cumulative frequencies, and the two methods will not yield comparable data.

Perhaps, then, it is impossible to agree on a base rate for sexual reoffending, even if rapists, child molesters, and incest offenders are considered separately. Even if a number were established, it would be difficult to come to agreement on its meaning. Therefore, great caution should be exercised in quoting such base rates in the legal forum.

The Use of Forensic Specialty Instruments

Traditional psychological tests and test batteries often have limited value in the forensic arena. They are not designed to answer the specific questions posed by most courts and, thus, may tempt the evaluator to overinterpret the profiles. They also may yield a plethora of information not relevant to the question at hand and risk unnecessary invasion of privacy. Over the past decade, a number of forensic specialty instruments (also called forensic assessment instruments or FAIs) have been designed specifically to answer commonly posed psycholegal questions. An array of measuring devices is now available to address a variety of civil and criminal competencies, criminal responsibility, and malingering. Instruments have been developed to measure both violence risk generally and sexual offense risk in particular.

The Development of Instruments to Assess Risk

Early efforts by the mental health community to scientifically assess risk generally took the form of establishing base rates for various diagnostic groups (Grisso & Appelbaum, 1992; Swanson, Holzer, Ganju, & Jono, 1990). This was quickly refined to looking at specific symptoms rather than broad categories (Monahan & Steadman, 1994). Researchers recognized that to make the most accurate predictions, it would be necessary to examine variables outside the clinical arena. A Canadian team began to examine data amassed over many years at a secure facility housing violent, chronic offenders (Harris, Rice, & Quinsey, 1993). The researchers considered a wide variety of variables gleaned from the literature and from personal experience and applied stepwise discriminant analysis to determine which variables possessed the greatest

predictive power. The 12 variables that contributed most to the equation were then weighted and formed into the original Violence Prediction Scheme (Webster, Harris, Rice, Cormier, & Quinsey, 1994). Although factors from the offenders' criminal histories were included, predictions made from the instrument proved superior to predictions made from history alone (Quinsey, Harris, et al., 1998).

Further refinements came in targeting *specific* groups of offenders for prediction. Sex offenders were among the first to inspire the development of separate instruments. Not all of these were designed to be administered by clinicians. Rather, several were constructed to be completed by case managers and probation officers from information readily available in most correctional files.

With more actuarial tools becoming available, it became important to have an easily understood method of comparing the various instruments for particular purposes. One of the most valuable statistical tools for this purpose is the Receiver Operating Characteristic curve (ROC; Mossman, 1994). Put simply, the ROC of a specific predictor may range from 0.50 (indicating it is equivalent to chance) to 1.00 (indicating perfect prediction). The ROCs of the more valid instruments currently in use are often in the 0.70 range, indicating that use of the tool would result in a prediction significantly better than chance but less than perfect. The ROC provides a simple method of comparing one instrument with another. It is also possible for a single instrument to have different ROCs for different populations. For example, it might predict general violent recidivism better than it predicts sexual reoffending in particular. Finally, ROCs are particularly useful in domains where accurate base rates are not available.

Specific Instruments for Use with Sex Offenders

As reviewed by Salekin et al. (1996), the instrument currently demonstrating the strongest positive predictive power for violent recidivism in general is the PCL-R. In the arena of sexual offenses, it is a much stronger predictor of reoffending for rapists than for child molesters (Rice & Harris, 1997). Its use, however, requires not only clinical skill, but specialized training. Many of the items on their surface appear very subjective, and the developer emphasizes that all reliability data were gathered with specially trained examiners (Hare, 1991). Untrained examiners take the risk of presenting inaccurate data to the court.

The Violence Risk Appraisal Guide (VRAG), the final version of the Violence Prediction Scheme, was designed by researchers in Ontario to assess violent offenders in an effort to predict future risk (Quinsey, Harris, et al., 1998). It is composed of 12 static variables, the single, most heavily weighted, being the PCL-R score. It should be emphasized that the instrument was normed on a population of inmates with a significant history of violence. Although it has been used with sex offenders, it is a better predictor of violent recidivism in general (ROC = .76) than of sexual reoffending in particular (ROC = .62; Harris et al., 1998).

Based on studies applying the VRAG to sexual offenders, the developers concluded that the sex offender population required a more specific instrument. Sexual deviance has been demonstrated to be predictive of sexual reoffending (Hanson & Bussiere, 1998), a factor not included on the VRAG. The penile plethysmograph is designed to measure physiological responses to deviant and nondeviant sexual stimuli. A number of studies support its usefulness in identifying high-risk pedophiles (Barbaree & Marshall, 1988; Freund & Watson, 1991; Lalumiere & Harris, 1998). Evidence suggests plethysmographic data can be particularly strong predictors when combined with psychopathy (Rice, Harris, & Quinsey, 1991; Serin, Mailloux, & Malcolm, 2001). With these factors in mind, the research group developed the Sex Offender Risk Appraisal Guide (SORAG). This is a 14-variable actuarial device, which includes most of the VRAG factors, but adds a plethysmographic assessment (Quinsey, Harris, et al., 1998). Initial results appeared promising. However, on cross-validation, the SORAG performed only marginally better that the VRAG in predicting sexual offender recidivism (Rice & Harris, 1997). Work is still being done to refine the instrument.

One additional clinical tool in the armamentarium is the Sexual Violence Risk-20 (SVR-20; Boer et al., 1997). It is best characterized as a set of guidelines or a checklist rather than an actuarial instrument. Although it is possible to calculate an additive score, the number does not correspond to any specific level of risk. The instrument encompasses 20 factors in three domains: psychosocial adjustment, sexual offending, and future plans. Rather than an application of statistical equations, it is derived from a broad review of the professional literature and includes some dynamic as well as static factors. A formal test manual is commercially available. A number of the factors are consistent with those found on other instruments and have strong support in the empirical literature (e.g., psychopathy, sexual deviance, past supervision failures). However, others on the list (e.g., being the victim of child abuse, denial/minimization of one's offense) have not been found to correlate strongly with recidivism (Hanson & Bussiere, 1998).

Two of the most widely used sex offender risk assessment measures are not clinical, do not require interviewing the defendant, and are designed to be completed by case management personnel. The Static 99, developed by Hanson and Thornton (2000), is actually a refinement and combining of two previous instruments, the Rapid Risk Assessment for Sex Offense Recidivism (RRASOR) (Hanson, 1998) and the Structured Anchored Clinical Judgment (SACJ-Min) (Grubin, 1998). It is designed to measure long-term risk potential and, true to its name, is composed of ten static variables, including items such as number of prior sexual offenses, contacts with male victims, and prior nonsexual assaults. The Minnesota Sex Offender Screening Tool– Revised (MnSOST-R) is a similar device (Epperson et al., 1998), although it does include four variables the developers describe as institutional/dynamic. These are institutional disciplinary record, substance abuse treatment, sex offender treatment, and age at time of release. Users should note that the MnSOST-R is very different from the original MnSOST and has much greater empirical support.

Opinions as to the utility of these instruments and the wisdom of their use in clinical settings vary. Some consider them to be only experimental, with such limited reliability and validity data as to meet neither ethical nor legal standards for use in court (T. Campbell, 2000). Others argue that risk assessments must be done and practitioners should contribute the best information they have to assist the trier of fact (Boer et al., 1997). While not unequivocal, on-going research has continued to demonstrate that the VRAG, SORAG, RRASOR, Static 99, and MnSOST-R provide data valuable to the conduct of risk assessment both for sex offenders and general violent recidivists (Barbaree, Seto, Langston, & Peacock, 2001). Surely, caution and careful explanation are always the rule of thumb.

One important function of the currently available techniques might be screening offenders into risk groups for further assessment. Most states with active SVP programs are invested in selecting the offenders who present the very highest level of risk to the community. No state currently commits more than 15% of those potentially eligible (Epperson et al., 1998). To accomplish the triaging task, most states use some tiered level of risk rather than identifying specific crimes or types of offenders. Current actuarial instruments can provide a scientific foundation to this ranking process. Evidence suggests they are most accurate at the very highest and lowest levels of risk. For example, developers of the VRAG have demonstrated that scores are linearly related to the likelihood of recidivism (Quinsey, Harris, et al., 1998; Rice & Harris, 1997). They did this by dividing their sample of offenders into nine groups based on VRAG scores (each group divided by eight points). The overall ROC for prediction of violent recidivism was .76. However, in a seven-year study, all of those in the highest-scoring group reoffended and no one in the lowest group did, suggesting that at the extreme ends predictions can be very accurate.

Collateral Information Databases

Whether the evaluator is relying on a specific instrument or examining individual risk factors, a solid base of collateral information is essential to valid assessment. Offenders in general, and sex offenders in particular (Barbaree, 1991), often deny and minimize their offense conduct and should not be relied on as the primary or sole source of information. The PCL-R manual is extremely clear that ratings "*should NOT be made in the absence of adequate collateral information*" (Hare, 1991, p. 6). Some jurisdictions (e.g., Colorado, Tennessee) have standards/guidelines to be followed by evaluators that may mandate examining specific pieces of collateral information.

Sex offenders constitute a very heterogeneous group. An adequate database needs to be broad in scope and multidisciplinary in nature. It must include general criminal history, in addition to sexual offenses. It should extend to a variety of functional domains, including sexual deviance, interpersonal relationships, past treatment, and biological functioning (e.g., the possibility of neurological damage). It is not unusual for attorneys, courts, and correctional agencies to misunderstand what collateral information is needed and provide only mental health records.

A starting point for record review is often the correctional files. However, as many familiar with such documents can attest, their quality and accuracy is quite variable. Details contained in such files should be cross-referenced. It is also possible that, unless otherwise specified, information provided in a case management report or progress report is simply derived from an interview with the offender. Preincarceration information is also essential. Sources for such data may include pre/postsentence investigations (PSIs), police reports, victim statements, and reports from probation/parole officers. Mental health records should include any treatment or evaluation received, whether in an institution or in the community. Given sufficient time and availability, interviews with sources familiar with the offender can be enlightening.

Special Populations

Women

The population that is the focus of sexual predator evaluations is primarily adult males, and research described in this chapter deals almost exclusively with this group of offenders. Females who perpetrate against children constitute a very small percentage of the sex offender population (Green & Kaplan, 1994). Only recently has the research community considered women who perpetrate sexual abuse on children, and, to date, only a handful of uncontrolled studies and case descriptions

have been produced (Grayston & DeLuca, 1999; Wakefield & Underwager, 1991). Available data do suggest that female perpetrators victimize children with whom they have an ongoing relationship and for whom they are often a primary caregiver (Rudin, Zalewski, & Bodmer-Turner, 1995). In contrast to males, female sex offenders generally have an accomplice, most commonly a male (Grayston & DeLuca, 1999; Solomon, 1992). In this relationship, they often take the role of passive partner, observing and failing to intervene, as opposed to actively participating (Green & Kaplan, 1994). To date, no specific instruments have been validated to assess this population and much more research is needed.

Juveniles

Recent studies have demonstrated that juvenile sex offenders differ in significant ways from adults, and much of the research on assessment of adults may not apply. It is difficult to predict the potential for recidivism in this group, particularly if one is trying to make a prediction stretching into adulthood. More so than with adults, sexual offending among juveniles may be part of a more pervasive pattern of delinquency. Juvenile sex offenses may be more predictive of nonsexual reoffending than of future sex crimes (Rasmussen, 1999). Recent years have seen the development of an extensive literature on the etiology, assessment, and treatment of sexual offending among adolescents (Becker & Hunter, 1997; Bourke & Donohue, 1996; Marshall, 1996; Pithers & Gray, 1998). The Joseph J. Peters Institute (JJPI)-Maine Juvenile Sex Offender Assessment Protocol (JSOAP) is an actuarial instrument currently under development to assess risk in juvenile sex offenders prior to treatment and at the time of discharge (Prentky, Harris, Frizzell, & Righthand, 2000). Initial studies using the youth version of the PCL-R (PCL-YV) indicate that psychopathy may have much the same implications for juvenile sex offenders as it does for adults (Gretton, McBride, Hare, O'Shaughnessy, & Kumka, 2001). This can be particularly significant when PCL-YV scores are used in conjunction with results from testing with the penile plethysmograph.

The issues surrounding sexual offending among juveniles are complex and merit discussion well beyond the scope of the present chapter. The national Office of Juvenile Justice and Delinquency Prevention maintains a Web site (www.ojjdp.ncjrs.org) that includes an extensive, and frequently updated, bibliography of resources in this area.

Ethnic Minorities

There is always a concern about applying test instruments or predictor variables across cultures without careful validation.

In the case of specialty instruments to assess risk among sex offenders, the majority (e.g., PCL-R, VRAG, SORAG, Static 99) were originally developed in Canada, using populations primarily White and male (Salekin et al., 1996). The PCL-R is probably the most well-established of these instruments, with a research base in Europe as well as North America. Yet the database for African American and Hispanic populations remains small. Cross-cultural research has uncovered cultural differences in mean PCL-R scores as well as prevalence rates (Cooke, 1996, 1998). However, on the key variable of prediction of violent recidivism, the instrument appears to predict across cultures, although the magnitude of the prediction may vary (Hemphill et al., 1998; Kosson, Smith, & Newman, 1990). Less research is available on the newer instruments specifically designed for the assessment of sex offenders. Therefore, there is general agreement that clinicians need to carefully access the relevant database before selecting assessment strategies for minority populations.

RISK MANAGEMENT WITH SEX OFFENDERS

Managing and reducing risk in any clinical population generally means assessing treatment needs. The lay public tends to believe that providing some kind of therapy to a sex offender will reduce the risk to the community, a belief shared by many judges (Bumby & Maddox, 1999). Few comprehensive studies have been conducted evaluating the actual impact of sex offender treatment programs on subsequent recidivism. The data that were collected and analyzed over the past 20 years tended to support the premise that treatment had a modest, but positive effect (Hall, 1995). However, further analysis of these data raised serious questions as to the validity of this conclusion (McConaghy, 1999; Rice & Harris, 1997). It is currently the general consensus among prominent researchers that there is no solid evidence that any particular treatment is effective in reducing overall sex offender recidivism (Barbaree, 1999; Furby et al., 1989; Hanson & Bussiere, 1998; Harris et al., 1998). As Prentky and Burgess (2000) noted, "At the present time, the most informed and dispassionate conclusion must be that we simply do not know what percentage of the aggregated (highly heterogeneous) population of sex offenders can return to a nonoffending lifestyle through treatment" (p. 217).

Methodological Problems in Evaluating Treatment

One of the primary problems in demonstrating treatment effectiveness is *poor controls* in those studies conducted. It would be ethically questionable to randomly deny potentially effective treatment to sex offenders who request it and then release them to the community. Therefore, individuals who refuse to participate or drop out of treatment programs often are used as controls. However, such studies may do little more than separate the more motivated, prosocial offenders from their less motivated counterparts and say little about the effectiveness of the program being evaluated. Researchers at Atascadero State Hospital in Atascadero, California are in the process of conducting one of the more carefully controlled longitudinal evaluations of a treatment program. Preliminary results suggested that specific treatment effects may ultimately be demonstrated (Marques, Day, Nelson, & West, 1994). However, it is still too early to draw conclusions.

A second methodological issue limiting many program evaluations is *sample selection*. Past research has tended to confirm the risk principle of offender treatment; that is, treatment is much more apt to be effective in reducing recidivism in higher-risk offenders (Bonta, Wallace-Capretta, & Rooney, 2000). Among offenders in general, some studies indicate that intensive services for those in a low-risk group may actually increase the potential for recidivism (Andrews, Bonta, & Hoge, 1990). However, the public is often hesitant to put high-risk offenders in less restrictive programs (Lieb et al., 1998). Well-funded treatment programs with research components are often very selective, admitting only those who are nonviolent, motivated, and evidencing no additional problems such as mental illness or substance abuse.

Another issue to be considered is the *criteria used to measure recidivism*. The Atascadero study seeks to combine actual convictions with carefully defined charges and accusations (Marques, 1999); however, this approach requires very broad record acquisition and review. One criterion clearly demonstrated to be ineffective as a predictor of recidivism is program behavior and the achievement of within-program goals (Barbaree & Marshall, 1998; Rice et al., 1991). In fact, several studies suggest that ratings of success by program clinicians may actually be inversely related to avoidance of reoffending (Quinsey, Khanna, & Malcolm, 1998; Seto & Barbaree, 1999).

Perhaps one of the most frustrating aspects of sex offender treatment evaluation is the tendency of researchers to lump all sex offenders together. Perhaps a more appropriate question than What works? is What works for which offenders? For example, data obtained thus far in the Atascadero study suggest a number of differences in program response between rapists and child molesters (Marques, 1999). An important personality variable to consider in measuring treatment outcome is psychopathy. Up to now, no one has demonstrated a treatment modality effective in reducing violence potential in this group. At least one study would suggest that incorporating them into the traditional therapeutic community may actually exacerbate this potential (Rice, 1997). Yet sex offender programs are only now beginning to analyze outcome data for psychopathic offenders separately. In short, it is essential that anyone planning to testify regarding research on sex offender treatment outcome examine carefully the methods used in research that forms the basis for that testimony.

Specific Treatment Modalities

Given currently available research results, it would be accurate to say that there is no evidence that any particular treatment modality will reduce the probability of sex offender recidivism. However, given the plethora of methodological difficulties with outcome research on sex offender treatment, it would be inaccurate to say that treatment has been proven ineffective with this population. Clinicians cannot simply ignore treatment needs until more is known, so it is important for anyone working in the field as evaluator or treatment provider to be familiar with what is known about the various modalities.

Organic Interventions

Although psychosurgery and physical castration have been considered to curb sexual reoffending, it is unlikely either will be widely used in our society. Therefore, this discussion concentrates on medications. Beginning with California in 1997, a number of states have chosen to require probated sex offenders to accept such treatment.

As early as the 1940s, researchers were experimenting with progesteronal hormone compounds to reduce sexual drives. In 1960, experiments began in Europe with cyproterone acetate (CPA) and were followed in the 1970s by studies of medroxyprogesterone (MPA) at Johns Hopkins. MPA has since been approved for use in the United States.

The concept behind hormonal treatments for sex offenders is to reduce levels of circulating progesterone to control serum levels of testosterone, thereby reducing the sexual drive. Evidence has emerged that such treatment can effectively reduce overall sexual behavior (Bradford, 1990; Marshall, 1993). There is even some support for a reduction in recidivism among child molesters who comply with treatment (Harris et al., 1998). However, it must be remembered that hormonal treatment does nothing to change the object of one's attraction, only the intensity of the drive. There is little evidence that the majority of sex offenders have exaggerated sexual drives (Rosler & Witztum, 2000).

A major problem with hormonal treatments developed thus far is that compliance is relatively rare. The drugs have numerous unpleasant side effects, including weight gain, fatigue, headaches, reduction in body hair, depression, and gastrointestinal problems (Miller, 1998). Less common, but more serious side effects reported have been diabetes (Bradford, 1985; Emory, Cole, & Meyer, 1992), infertility, and feminization (Kravitz et al., 1995). Effectiveness of treatment can also be reversed by the ingestion of testosterone or anabolic steroids.

Some recent research has focused on the gonadotropin-releasing hormone. In rare cases, it can induce severe hypogonadism and some reduction in normal sex drive is often noted. It is considered promising by some, but still in the early research stage (Rosler & Witztum, 2000).

Finally, selective serotonin reuptake inhibitors (SSRIs) have been used in treating sex offenders. Serotonin, a neurotransmitter, has been associated with depression and obsessive-compulsive thinking. There is some evidence that it may function to reduce excessive sexual fantasies, which may curb reoffending (Federoff, 1993). However, research has been limited, and studies to date are primarily retrospective (D. Greenberg & Bradford, 1997).

The Penile Plethysmograph

The plethysmograph provides a mechanical measurement of penile tumescence in response to deviant and nondeviant sexual stimuli. Proponents of its use as a treatment adjunct believe the therapist needs to know the reality of a sex offender's deviant thinking, and some objective measure is essential due to the denial and underreporting common among sex offenders (Dutton & Emerick, 1996). It may further be useful in monitoring changes in sexual preference over time. Its inclusion in therapy was endorsed by the Association for the Treatment of Sexual Abusers (ATSA, 1993), the primary national organization for those engaged in the treatment of sex offenders. In 1995, the guidelines were revised to exclude the use of visual stimuli. ATSA does caution, however, that the plethysmograph should not be used in place of other treatment techniques and is not infallible and can be faked (Quinsey & Carrigan, 1978). More recent research indicates greater potential for faking with repeated use (Harris et al., 1998). Data on its actual effectiveness as an adjunct to treatment remain primarily anecdotal. The critics of plethysmography point out the lack of standardization of stimuli and procedures, the lack of uniform training requirements for plethysmographers, the variability in data interpretation, and the lack of norms for subgroups of sexual offenders (Prentky & Burgess, 2000).

The Polygraph

Commonly known as the lie detector, the polygraph is another mechanical device recommended by ATSA (1993) as an adjunct to treatment. It serves a purpose similar to the plethysmograph: to encourage historical disclosure, validate self-report, monitor progress, and break down denial. In a survey of 732 probation and parole offices throughout the country, English (1998) found that approximately 10% require regular polygraphs for sex offenders under supervision. However, here again, evidence as to its actual effectiveness in reducing recidivism is primarily anecdotal.

If the polygraph is to be used in treatment, some arrangement must be made to safeguard 5th Amendment rights. In some jurisdictions, limited immunity agreements are employed. However, prosecutors often oppose this approach due to potential impact on future prosecutions.

Cognitive-Behavioral Therapy (CBT)

Clinicians engaged in the treatment of sexual offenders have generally abandoned the more humanistic, psychodynamic, and insight-oriented approaches. Behavioral therapy (classical and operant conditioning techniques) alone has not proven effective either. In recent years, cognitive-behavioral therapy (CBT) has become the preferred modality (ATSA, 1993). In 1987, Gendreau and Ross reviewed a number of studies and early meta-analyses regarding the effectiveness of specific treatment modalities for offenders generally. With reduction in recidivism as the criterion, they found the largest effect sizes for behavioral and cognitive-behavioral approaches both with juveniles and adults.

For all the reasons noted in the discussion of methodological problems, a solid demonstration of treatment effectiveness with sex offenders has proven elusive. Initial studies using CBT in an effort to reduce recidivism showed promising treatment effects, particularly when the relapse prevention model was used (Hall, 1995; Hildebran & Pithers, 1992). However, later studies and data analyses called these results into question (Marshall & Anderson, 1996; McConaghy, 1999). Individual program evaluations often yielded positive but confusing results. For example, the Vermont Treatment Program for Sexual Aggressors found that rapists provided CBT had lower rates of reoffense (Freeman-Longo & Knopp, 1992). However, Marshall, Jones, Ward, Johnston, and Barbaree (1991) found the modality more effective for child molesters.

Marques (1999) remains actively engaged in collecting and analyzing longitudinal follow-up data on the CBT sex offender program at Atascadero. Results may provide additional data. Until then, it may be best to say that CBT is effective for some sex offenders some of the time.

The Containment Approach

As defined and investigated by English (1998), the containment approach involves using all available resources, both clinical and correctional, to assure the safety of the community and hold the sex offender fully accountable while in the community. It is interdisciplinary and interagency by nature. It involves specially trained case managers and treatment providers coordinating myriad conditions placed on the offender. These may include such requirements as counseling, approved employment, residency restrictions, curfews, polygraphs, random searches, and electronic monitors. Conditions are enforced by a broad array of short-term and intermediate sanctions. Confidentiality among those enforcing the conditions, including treatment providers, is commonly waived.

Advocates of the containment model are generally enthusiastic. Parole/probation departments using it report positive results. However, hard data demonstrating those results are still lacking.

PRESENTING EXPERT TESTIMONY

A forensic psychologist might be called to appear in court either because he or she has evaluated a specific sex offender or because the court simply wants to know what scientific findings might be helpful in reaching a decision in some related matter. In either case, the expert is there to lend expertise needed to assist the trier of fact. That assistance should take the form of the most valid, most reliable, most relevant scientific data or techniques the field has to offer. That is the criterion that should distinguish an expert, professional opinion from the personal opinion of an individual with numerous degrees and licenses.

Many jurisdictions now rely on criteria developed in *Daubert v. Merrell Dow Pharmaceuticals* (1993) to determine the admissibility of evidence to be offered by an expert. Under *Daubert*, evidence should be evaluated as to whether (a) the theory or technique on which it is based has been tested; (b) the data have been peer-reviewed and published; (c) there is a known or potential error rate; and (d) there is evidence of acceptance in the relevant scientific community. It has become increasingly common for formal *Daubert* hearings to be conducted prior to the actual sex offender commitment proceedings to determine which experts will be allowed to testify and what specific data will be admitted into evidence. For example, in the *U.S. v. Robinson* (2000), the court subpoenaed Dr. Gene Abel to testify regarding how the Abel Assessment for Sexual Interest met each of the four *Daubert* criteria before allowing the expert witness to present results to the jury.

In the arena of sexual predator assessment, a number of variables have been heavily researched and are consistently predictive across studies. Data have clearly been published and peer-reviewed. An actuarial instrument would also have the advantage of an established error rate. Of course, it would be incumbent on any expert to make certain the variables or instrument selected truly matched the individual or situation involved. There is also the ethical obligation to honestly and clearly acknowledge the limits of the data and our expertise. Although research has advanced by leaps and bounds in recent years and our predictive ability is well beyond chance and better than a simple historical review, we are nowhere near the 95% certainty mark some jurisdictions now seek.

The professional literature in the field of sex offender evaluation is vast and changing rapidly. Errors in earlier studies are being uncovered and prominent experts are adjusting their views to accommodate the new knowledge. Any psychologist proffering himself or herself as an expert to the court owes it to the trier of fact to have the most current information available. What is published in books and journals often is outdated before the presses are cold. To feel secure in one's expertise, it is good practice to visit the Internet and bookmark key Web sites. Establishing contact/correspondence with important researchers can serve as an additional aid.

SPECIAL ETHICAL CONCERNS

A psychologist performing forensic services needs to be familiar with the general code of ethics established for practice by the American Psychological Association (APA, 1992), as well as the "Specialty Guidelines for Forensic Psychologists" (Committee for Ethical Guidelines for Forensic Psychologists, 1991). However, the area of sexual offenders presents several recurrent dilemmas for the evaluator and for the treating professional.

Ethical Issues for the Evaluator

Three areas of ethical concern commonly arise in the assessment of risk in the case of a sex offender. The first revolves around *records,* as an adequate, well-verified record is essential to the endeavor. Truly complete, consistent documents are rarely available. It is incumbent on each evaluator to decide when documentation is totally inadequate and the task should be declined, absent further information. Even when reasonably extensive information is provided, the evaluator must carefully assess its accuracy and reliability and not assume that what is contained in an official document is truth. The evaluator must then decide whether only convictions for sexual offenses will be taken into account in reaching conclusions, or whether arrests, charges later reduced, or accusations will also be weighed in the equation. If uncertain, but very important information is relied on, the evaluator must make this clear in all reports and testimony.

A second critical issue involves *adequate notice* to the person being evaluated. Unlike many other forensic evaluations, sexual predator assessments often are conducted to assist a facility in the process of deciding whether to file a commitment petition or to go forward with some type of conditional release. In such instances, when no formal proceedings have been initiated, it is unlikely the offender will have an attorney appointed. Nonetheless, ethical guidelines indicate that the individual is entitled to seek legal counsel prior to the evaluation. Therefore, it is essential that the person be notified of the pending evaluation and its potential consequences well in advance. Such notice should be negotiated with the institutional contractor before the clinician agrees to the evaluation.

A final ethical consideration is *disclosure of information.* In some circumstances (e.g., court order or statutory requirement), the person being evaluated is not required to consent to the evaluation. However, he or she nonetheless is entitled to full disclosure regarding the purpose of the evaluation, its possible consequences, and what parties will have access to any information gleaned by the evaluator. Those evaluated should also be informed if the assessment is to be completed solely from the record should they decline to participate.

Ethical Issues for the Treatment Provider

If a psychologist is to function as a treatment provider for a sex offender released on some condition, several issues need to be clarified prior to initiating treatment. The first regards the boundaries of confidentiality—if any, in fact, exists. Under a containment model, the expectation may be that the therapist have complete, open communication with other members of the interdisciplinary team, including probation officers and representatives of the district attorney's office. Other arrangements may leave intact some confidentiality, but require the therapist to report any number of undesirable behaviors, ranging from an additional offense to drinking a beer.

Treatment providers need to know if they are expected to play a dual role as therapist and ongoing risk assessor. Will they be expected to return to court at some time and report not only whether the individual has attended counseling sessions and completed assignments, but what progress has been made in terms of a reduced level of risk? The latter role is best avoided, not only because of the conflict of interest, but because the field currently lacks the appropriate scientific tools to measure change in level of risk.

Finally, treatment providers should know whether there is an expectation that therapy will be continued indefinitely regardless of outcome. If the clinician determines further therapy will be nonproductive or even counterproductive, it is important to know the consequences of terminating it.

FUTURE DIRECTIONS

Research in the field needs to investigate the additional dynamic variables that may predict reoffending on a more immediate basis. More longitudinal data need to be gathered on effectiveness of various interventions over the long term and with more clearly defined and circumscribed populations. No treatment approaches have yet been devised to successfully rehabilitate the psychopathic offender. Collaboration among practitioners serving a diversity of populations is critical both for instrument development and program evaluation. To accomplish these tasks requires participation not only of large research institutions but of individual practitioners who are evaluating the work they do.

To facilitate productive communication between the legal and mental health communities, interdisciplinary training will be essential. Clinicians cannot continue to assume that terms they use with colleagues on a daily basis (e.g., mental illness) carry the same connotation in a court of law. In providing reports and testimony, psychologists must become more mindful of their educative function, conveying an understanding of psychology as a science rather than an art. The APA/ABA conference in Washington, D.C. held in the fall of 1999 laid the foundations for ongoing productive dialogue. It is hoped that this dialogue will continue in national, regional, and local forums.

Forensic psychologists need to become involved on the policymaking level. Most clinicians with expertise in dealing with sex offenders are at least somewhat dismayed by current statutes and recent court decisions. These experts often have knowledge and experience that could contribute to better solutions, if provided early in the policymaking process. For this to happen it will become increasingly important for psychologists engaged in therapeutic jurisprudence to organize and communicate on a local as well as national level, increasing awareness and developing agendas for the twenty-first century.

REFERENCES

Abel, G. G., Becker, J. V., Mittelman, M. S., Cunningham-Rathner, J., Rouleau, J. L., & Murphy, W. D. (1987). Self-reported sex crimes of nonincarcerated paraphiliacs. *Journal of Interpersonal Violence, 2*, 3–25.

Ake v. Oklahoma, 470 U.S. 68 (1985).

American Psychiatric Association. (1994). *Diagnostic and statistical manual of mental disorders* (4th ed.). Washington, DC: Author.

American Psychiatric Association. (2000). *Diagnostic and statistical manual of mental disorders* (4th ed., text rev.). Washington, DC: Author.

American Psychological Association. (1992). Ethical principles of psychologists and code of conduct. *American Psychologist, 47*, 1597–1611.

Andrews, D. A., Bonta, J., & Hoge, R. D. (1990). Classification for effective rehabilitation: Rediscovering psychology. *Criminal Justice and Behavior, 17*, 19–52.

Association for the Treatment of Sexual Abusers. (1993). *The ATSA practitioner's handbook*. Lake Oswego, OR: ATSA.

Barbaree, H. E. (1991). Denial and minimization among sex offenders: Assessment and treatment outcome. *Forum on Corrections Research, 3*, 30–33.

Barbaree, H. E. (1999). The effect of treatment on risk of recidivism in sex offenders. In American Psychological Association (Ed.), *Psychological Expertise and Criminal Justice: A Conference for Psychologists and Lawyers* (pp. 217–220). Washington, DC: American Psychological Association.

Barbaree, H. E., & Marshall, W. L. (1988). Deviant sexual arousal, demographic features, and offense history variables as predictors of reoffense among untreated child molesters and incest offenders. *Behavioral Sciences and the Law, 6*, 257–280.

Barbaree, H. E., & Marshall, W. L. (1989). Erectile responses among heterosexual child molesters, father-daughter incest offenders, and matched non-offenders: Five distinct age preference profiles. *Canadian Journal of Behavioural Science, 21*, 70–82.

Barbaree, H. E., & Marshall, W. L. (1998). Treatment of the sexual offender. In R. M. Wettstein (Ed.), *Treatment of offenders with mental disorders* (pp. 265–328). New York: Guilford Press.

Barbaree, H. E., Seto, M. C., Langston, C. M., & Peacock, E. J. (2001). Evaluating the predictive accuracy of six risk assessment instruments for adult sex offenders. *Criminal Justice and Behavior, 28*, 490–521.

Barefoot v. Estelle, 463 U.S. 880 (1983).

Becker, J. V., & Hunter, J. A. (1997). Understanding and treating child and adolescent sexual offenders. *Advances in Clinical Child Psychology, 19*, 177–197.

Becker, J. V., & Murphy, W. D. (1998). What we know and do not know about assessing and treating sex offenders. *Psychology, Public Policy, and Law, 4*, 116–137.

Boer, D. P., Wilson, R. J., Gauthier, C. M., & Hart, S. D. (1997). Assessing risk of sexual violence: Guidelines for clinical practice. In C. D. Webster & M. A. Jackson (Eds.), *Impulsivity: Theory, assessment and treatment* (pp. 326–342). New York: Guilford Press.

Bonta, J., Law, M., & Hanson, R. K. (1998). The prediction of criminal and violent recidivism among mentally disordered offenders: A meta-analysis. *Psychological Bulletin, 123,* 123–142.

Bonta, J., Wallace-Capretta, S., & Rooney, J. (2000). A quasi-experimental evaluation of an intensive rehabilitation supervision program. *Criminal Justice and Behavior, 27,* 312–329.

Bourke, M. L., & Donohue, B. (1996). Assessment and treatment of juvenile sex offenders: An empirical review. *Journal of Child Sexual Abuse, 5,* 47–70.

Bradford, J. M. W. (1985). Organic treatments for the male sexual offender. *Behavioral Sciences and the Law, 3,* 355–375.

Bradford, J. M. W. (1990). The antiandrogen and hormonal treatment of sex offenders. In W. L. Marshall, D. R. Laws, & H. E. Barbaree (Eds.), *Handbook of sexual assault: Issues, theory, and treatment of the offender* (pp. 297–310). New York: Plenum Press.

Brakel, S. J., & Cavanaugh, J. L. (2000). Of psychopaths and pendulums: Legal and psychiatric treatment of sex offenders in the United States. *New Mexico Law Review, 30,* 69–94.

Bumby, K. M., & Maddox, M. C. (1999). Judges' knowledge about sexual offenders, difficulties presiding over sexual offense cases, and opinions on sentencing, treatment, and legislation. *Sexual Abuse: A Journal of Research and Treatment, 11,* 305–315.

Campbell, E. (1990). The psychopath and the definition of "mental disease or defect" under the Model Penal Code Test of Insanity: A question of psychology or a question of law? *Nebraska Law Review, 69,* 190–229.

Campbell, T. (2000). Sexual predator evaluations and phrenology: Considering issues of evidentiary reliability. *Behavioral Sciences and the Law, 18,* 111–130.

Cleckley, H. (1941). *The mask of sanity.* St. Louis, MO: Mosby.

Committee on Ethical Guidelines for Forensic Psychologists. (1991). Specialty guidelines for forensic psychologists. *Law and Human Behavior, 15,* 655–665.

Conroy, M. A. (2000, August). *Improving testimony regarding psychological characteristics of persons with personality disorders.* Paper presented during a symposium at the American Psychological Association Convention, Washington, DC.

Cooke, D. J. (1996). Psychopathic personality in different cultures: What do we know? What do we need to find out? *Journal of Personality Disorders, 10,* 23–40.

Cooke, D. J. (1998). Psychopathy across cultures. In D. J. Cooke, A. E. Forth, & R. D. Hare (Eds.), *Psychopathy: Theory, research and implications for society* (pp. 13–45). Boston: Kluwer Academic/Plenum.

Cornwell, J. K. (1998). Understanding the role of the police and *parens patriae* powers in involuntary civil commitment before and after *Hendricks. Psychology, Public Policy, and Law, 4,* 377–413.

Cunningham, M. D., & Reidy, T. J. (1998). Antisocial Personality Disorder and psychopathy: Diagnostic dilemmas in classifying patterns of antisocial behavior in sentencing evaluations. *Behavioral Sciences and the Law, 16,* 333–351.

Datz, A. T., & MacCarthy, T. F. (1989). *ABA criminal justice and mental health standards.* Washington, DC: American Bar Association.

Daubert v. Merrell Dow Pharmaceuticals, Inc., 509 U.S. 579, 113 S. Ct. 2786 (1993).

Doren, D. M. (1998). Recidivism base rates, predictions of sex offender recidivism, and the "sexual predator" commitment laws. *Behavioral Sciences and the Law, 16,* 97–114.

Dutton, W. A., & Emerick, R. L. (1996). Plethysmograph assessment. In K. English, S. Pullen, & L. Jones (Eds.), *Managing adult sex offenders: A containment approach* (pp. 14-1–14-13). Lexington, KY: American Probation and Parole Association.

Edens, J. F. (2001). Misuses of the Hare Psychopathy Checklist–Revised in court: Two case examples. *Journal of Interpersonal Violence, 16,* 1082–1093.

Emory, L. E., Cole, C. M., & Meyer, W. J. (1992). The Texas experience with depoprovera: 1980–1990. *Journal of Offender Rehabilitation, 18,* 89–108.

English, K. (1998). The containment approach: An aggressive strategy for community management of adult sex offenders. *Psychology, Public Policy, and Law, 4,* 218–235.

Epperson, D. L., Kaul, J. D., & Hasselton, D. (1998, October). *Final report of the development of the Minnesota Sex Offender Screening Tool–Revised (MnSOST-R).* Presentation at the 17th annual Research and Treatment Conference of the Association for the Treatment of Sexual Abusers, Vancouver, British Columbia, Canada.

Federoff, J. P. (1993). Serotonergic drug treatment of deviant sexual interests. *Annals of Sex Research, 6,* 105–121.

Foucha v. Louisiana, 112 S. Ct. 1780 (1992).

Freeman-Longo, R. E., & Knopp, F. H. (1992). State-of-the-art sex offender treatment: Outcomes and issues. *Annals of Sex Research, 5,* 141–160.

Freund, K., & Watson, R. J. (1991). Assessment of the sensitivity and specificity of a phallometric test: An update of phallometric diagnosis of pedophilia. *Psychological Assessment, 3,* 147–155.

Friedland, S. I. (1999). On treatment, punishment, and the commitment of sex offenders. *University of Colorado Law Review, 70,* 73–155.

Furby, L., Weinrott, M. R., & Blackshaw, L. (1989). Sex offender recidivism: A review. *Psychological Bulletin, 105,* 3–30.

Gendreau, P., Little, T., & Goggin, C. (1996). A meta-analysis of the predictors of adult recidivism: What works! *Criminology, 34,* 575–607.

Gendreau, P., & Ross, R. R. (1987). Revivication of rehabilitation: Evidence from the 1980s. *Justice Quarterly, 4,* 349–408.

Gerard, J. B. (1987). The usefulness of the medical model to the legal system. *Rutgers Law Review, 39,* 377–423.

Grayston, A. D., & DeLuca, R. V. (1999). Female perpetrators of child sexual abuse: A review of the clinical and empirical literature. *Aggression and Violent Behavior, 4,* 93–106.

Green, A. H., & Kaplan, M. S. (1994). Psychiatric impairment and childhood victimization experiences in female child molesters. *Journal of the American Academy of Child and Adolescent Psychiatry, 33,* 954–961.

Greenberg, A. S., & Bailey, J. M. (1994). The irrelevance of the medical model of mental illness to law and ethics. *International Journal of Law and Psychiatry, 17,* 153–173.

Greenberg, D. M., & Bradford, J. M. W. (1997). Treatment of the paraphilic disorders: A review of the role of the selective serotonin reuptake inhibitors. *Sexual Abuse: A Journal of Research and Treatment, 9,* 349–360.

Gretton, H. M., McBride, M., Hare, R. D., O'Shaughnessy, R., & Kumka, G. (2001). Psychopathy and recidivism in adolescent sex offenders. *Criminal Justice and Behavior, 28,* 427–449.

Grisso, T., & Appelbaum, P. S. (1992). Is it unethical to offer predictions of future violence? *Law and Human Behavior, 16,* 621–633.

Grove, W. M., & Meehl, P. E. (1996). Comparative efficiency of informal (subjective impressionistic) and formal (mechanical, algorithmic) prediction procedures: The clinical–statistical controversy. *Psychology, Public Policy, and Law, 2,* 293–323.

Grubin, D. (1998). *Sex offending against children: Understanding the risk* [Police Series Research Paper]. London: Home Office.

Hall, G. C. N. (1995). Sexual offender recidivism revisited: A meta-analysis of recent treatment studies. *Journal of Consulting and Clinical Psychology, 63,* 802–809.

Hanson, R. K. (1998). What do we know about sex offender risk assessment? *Psychology, Public Policy, and Law, 4,* 50–72.

Hanson, R. K., & Bussiere, M. T. (1998). Predicting relapse: A meta-analysis of sex offender recidivism studies. *Journal of Consulting and Clinical Psychology, 66,* 348–362.

Hanson, R. K., & Harris, A. H. (2000). *The Sex Offender Need Assessment Rating (SONAR): A method for measuring change in risk levels.* (User Report 2000–1). Ottawa: Department of Solicitor General of Canada.

Hanson, R. K., & Harris, A. J. R. (1998). *Dynamic predictors of sexual recidivism* (User Report 97–04). Ottawa: Department of Solicitor General of Canada.

Hanson, R. K., & Harris, A. J. R. (2001). A structured approach to evaluating change among sexual offenders. *Sexual Abuse: Journal of Research and Treatment, 13,* 105–122.

Hanson, R. K., Scott, H., & Steffy, R. A. (1995). A comparison of child molesters and non-sexual criminals: Risk predictors and long-term recidivism. *Journal of Research in Crime and Delinquency, 32,* 325–337.

Hanson, R. K., Steffy, R. A., & Gauthier, R. (1993). Long-term recidivism of child molesters. *Journal of Consulting and Clinical Psychology, 61,* 646–652.

Hanson, R. K., & Thornton, D. (2000). Improving risk assessments for sex offenders: A comparison of three actuarial scales. *Law and Human Behavior, 24,* 119–136.

Hare, R. D. (1991). *The Hare Psychopathy Checklist–Revised.* Toronto, Ontario, Canada: Multi-Health Systems.

Hare, R. D. (1993). *Without conscience: The disturbing world of the psychopaths among us.* New York: Pocket Books.

Hare, R. D. (1998). The Hare PCL-R: Some issues concerning its use and misuse. *Legal and Criminological Psychology, 3,* 99–119.

Harris, G. T., Rice, M. E., & Quinsey, V. L. (1993). Violent recidivism of mentally disordered offenders: The development of a statistical prediction instrument. *Criminal Justice and Behavior, 20,* 315–335.

Harris, G. T., Rice, M. E., & Quinsey, V. L. (1998). Appraisal and management of risk in sexual aggressors: Implications for criminal justice policy. *Psychology, Public Policy, and Law, 4,* 73–115.

Hart, S. D. (1998). The role of psychopathy in assessing risk for violence: Conceptual and methodological issues. *Legal and Criminological Psychology, 3,* 121–137.

Heilbrun, K., Nezu, C. M., Keeney, M., Chung, S., & Wasserman, A. L. (1998). Sexual offending: Linking assessment, intervention, and decision making. *Psychology, Public Policy, and Law, 4,* 138–174.

Hemphill, J. F., Hare, R. D., & Wong, S. (1998). Psychopathy and recidivism: A review. *Legal and Criminological Psychology, 3,* 139–170.

Hildebran, D. D., & Pithers, W. D. (1992). Relapse prevention: Application and outcome. In W. O'Donohue & J. H. Greer (Eds.), *The sexual abuse of children: Clinical issues* (Vol. 2, pp. 365–393). Hillsdale, NJ: Erlbaum.

In re Care and Treatment of Michael T. Crane, 7 P.3d 285 (2000).

In re Leon G., 18 P.3d 169 (2001).

Janus, E. S. (1997). The use of social science and medicine in sex offender commitment. *Criminal and Civil Confinement, 23,* 347–386.

Janus, E. S. (1998). *Hendricks* and the moral terrain of police power commitment. *Psychology, Public Policy, and Law, 4,* 297–322.

Janus, E. S. (2000). Sexual predator commitment laws: Lessons for law and the behavioral sciences. *Behavioral Sciences and the Law, 18,* 5–21.

Janus, E. S., & Meehl, P. E. (1997). Assessing the legal standard for predictions of dangerousness in sex offender commitment proceedings. *Psychology, Public Policy, and Law, 3,* 33–64.

Janus, E. S., & Walbek, N. H. (2000). Sex offender commitments in Minnesota: A descriptive study of second generation commitments. *Behavioral Sciences and the Law, 18,* 343–374.

Kansas v. Crane, 122 S. Ct. 867 (2002).

Kansas v. Hendricks, 117 S. Ct. 2072 (1997).

Kosson, D. S., Smith, S. S., & Newman, J. P. (1990). Evaluating the construct validity of psychopathy in Black and White male inmates: Three preliminary studies. *Journal of Abnormal Psychology, 99,* 250–259.

Kravitz, H. M., Haywood, T. W., Kelly, J., Wahlstrom, C., Liles, S., & Cavanaugh, J. L., Jr. (1995). Medroxyprogesterone treatment for paraphilics. *Bulletin of the American Academy of Psychiatry and the Law, 23,* 19–33.

La Fond, J. Q. (1998). The cost of enacting a sexual predator law. *Psychology, Public Policy, and Law, 4,* 468–504.

Lalumiere, M. L., & Harris, G. T. (1998). Common questions regarding the use of phallometric testing with sexual offenders. *Sexual Abuse: A Journal of Research and Treatment, 10,* 227–237.

Levin, S. M., & Stava, L. (1987). Personality characteristics of sex offenders: A review. *Archives of Sexual Behavior, 16,* 57–79.

Lieb, R., Quinsey, V. L., & Berliner, L. (1998). Sexual predators and social policy. In M. Tonry (Ed.), *Crime and justice: A review of research* (Vol. 23, pp. 42–114). Chicago: University of Chicago Press.

Marques, J. K. (1999). How to answer the question: "Does sex offender treatment work?" *Journal of Interpersonal Violence, 14,* 437–451.

Marques, J. K., Day, D. M., Nelson, C., & West, M. A. (1994). Effects of cognitive-behavioral treatment on sex offender recidivism: Preliminary results of a longitudinal study. *Criminal Justice and Behavior, 21,* 28–54.

Marshall, W. L. (1993). A revised approach to the treatment of men who sexually assault adult females. In G. C. Hall, R. Hirschman, J. R. Graham, & M. S. Zaragoza (Eds.), *Sexual aggression: Issues in etiology, assessment, and treatment* (pp. 143–165). Washington, DC: Taylor & Francis.

Marshall, W. L. (1996). Assessment, treatment, and theorizing about sex offenders: Developments during the past twenty years and future directions. *Criminal Justice and Behavior, 23,* 162–199.

Marshall, W. L., & Anderson, D. (1996). An evaluation of the benefits of relapse prevention programs with sex offenders. *Sexual Abuse: A Journal of Research and Treatment, 3,* 499–511.

Marshall, W. L., Jones, R., Ward, T., Johnston, P., & Barbaree, H. E. (1991). Treatment outcome with sex offenders. *Clinical Psychology Review, 11,* 465–485.

McConaghy, N. (1999). Methodological issues concerning evaluation of treatment for sexual offenders: Randomization, treatment dropouts, untreated controls, and within-treatment studies. *Sexual Abuse: A Journal of Research and Treatment, 11,* 183–194.

Meehl, P. E. (1954). *Clinical versus statistical prediction: A theoretical analysis and a review of the evidence.* Minneapolis: University of Minnesota Press.

Melton, G. B., Petrila, J., Poythress, N. G., & Slobogin, C. (1997). *Psychological evaluations for the courts: A handbook for mental health professionals and lawyers* (2nd ed.). New York: Guilford Press.

Miller, R. D. (1998). Forced administration of sex drive reducing medication to sex offenders: Treatment or punishment? *Psychology, Public Policy, and Law, 4,* 175–199.

Minnesota ex rel. Pearson v. Probate Court, 309 U.S. 270, 60 S. Ct. 523, 84 L. Ed. 744 (1940).

Monahan, J., & Steadman, H. J. (Eds.). (1994). *Violence and mental disorder: Developments in risk assessment.* Chicago: University of Chicago Press.

Monahan, J., & Walker, L. (1998). *Social science in law: Cases and materials* (4th ed.). Westbury, NY: Foundation Press.

Moore, M. S. (1984). *Law and psychiatry: Rethinking the relationship.* Cambridge, England: Cambridge University Press.

Mossman, D. (1994). Assessing predictions of violence: Being accurate about accuracy. *Journal of Consulting and Clinical Psychology, 62,* 783–792.

Murphy, W. D., & Peters, J. M. (1992). Profiling child sexual abusers: Psychological considerations. *Criminal Justice and Behavior, 19,* 24–37.

New Jersey v. Cavallo, N.J. 508, 443, A. 2d 1020 (1982).

Ogloff, J. P., & Lyon, D. R. (1998). Legal issues associated with the concept of psychopathy. In D. J. Cooke, A. E. Forth, & R. D. Hare (Eds.), *Psychopathy: Theory, research, and implications for society* (pp. 399–422). Boston: Kluwer Academic Press.

Parrish v. Colorado, 78 F. 3d 1473 (1996).

Pithers, W. D., & Gray, A. (1998). The other half of the story: Children with sexual behavior problems. *Psychology, Public Policy, and Law, 4,* 200–217.

Prentky, R. A., & Burgess, A. W. (2000). *Forensic management of sexual offenders.* New York: Kluwer Academic/Plenum.

Prentky, R. A., Harris, B., Frizzell, K., & Righthand, S. (2000). An actuarial procedure for assessing risk with juvenile sex offenders. *Sexual Abuse: A Journal of Research and Treatment, 12,* 71–93.

Prentky, R. A., Knight, R. A., & Lee, A. F. S. (1997). Risk factors associated with recidivism among extrafamilial child molesters. *Journal of Consulting and Clinical Psychology, 65,* 141–149.

Quinsey, V. L. (1984). Sexual aggression: Studies of offenders against women. In D. N. Weisstub (Ed.), *Law and mental health: International perspectives* (Vol. 1). New York: Pergamon Press.

Quinsey, V. L., & Carrigan, W. F. (1978). Penile responses to visual stimuli: Instructional control with and without auditory sexual fantasy correlates. *Criminal Justice and Behavior, 5,* 141–149.

Quinsey, V. L., Harris, G. T., Rice, M. E., & Cormier, C. A. (1998). *Violent offenders: Appraising and managing risk.* Washington, DC: American Psychological Association.

Quinsey, V. L., Khanna, A., & Malcolm, B. (1998). A retrospective evaluation of the Regional Treatment Centre Sex Offender Treatment Program. *Journal of Interpersonal Violence, 13,* 621–644.

Quinsey, V. L., & Lalumiere, M. L. (1996). *Assessment of sexual offenders against children.* Thousand Oaks, CA: Sage.

Quinsey, V. L., & Maguire, A. (1986). Maximum security psychiatric patients: Actuarial and clinical prediction of dangerousness. *Journal of Interpersonal Violence, 1*, 143–171.

Quinsey, V. L., Rice, M. E., & Harris, G. T. (1995). Actuarial prediction of sexual recidivism. *Journal of Interpersonal Violence, 10*, 85–105.

Rasmussen, L. A. (1999). Factors related to recidivism among juvenile sexual offenders. *Sexual Abuse: A Journal of Research and Treatment, 11*, 69–86.

Rice, M. E. (1997). Violent offender research and implications for the criminal justice system. *American Psychologist, 52*, 414–423.

Rice, M. E., & Harris, G. T. (1997). Cross validation and extension of the Violence Risk Appraisal Guide for child molesters and rapists. *Law and Human Behavior, 21*, 231–241.

Rice, M. E., Harris, G. T., & Quinsey, V. L. (1991). Sexual recidivism among child molesters released from a maximum security psychiatric institution. *Journal of Consulting and Clinical Psychology, 59*, 381–386.

Rosler, A., & Witztum, E. (2000). Pharmacology of paraphilias in the next millennium. *Behavioral Sciences and the Law, 18*, 43–56.

Rudin, M. M., Zalewski, C., & Bodmer-Turner, J. (1995). Characteristics of child sexual abuse victims according to perpetrator gender. *Child Abuse and Neglect, 19*, 963–973.

Salekin, R. T., Rogers, R., & Sewell, K. W. (1996). A review and meta-analysis of the Psychopathy Checklist and Psychopathy Checklist–Revised: Predictive validity of dangerousness. *Clinical Psychology: Science and Practice, 3*, 203–215.

Schopp, R. F., & Quattrocchi, M. R. (1995). Predicting the present: Expert testimony and civil commitment. *Behavioral Sciences and the Law, 13*, 159–181.

Schopp, R. F., Scalora, M. J., & Pearce, M. (1999). Expert testimony and professional judgment: Psychological expertise and commitment as a sexual predator after *Hendricks. Psychology, Public Policy, and Law, 5*, 120–174.

Schopp, R. F., & Sturgis, B. J. (1995). Sexual predators and legal mental illness for civil commitment. *Behavioral Sciences and the Law, 13*, 437–558.

Seidman, B. T., Marshall, W. L., Hudson, S. M., & Robertson, P. J. (1994). An examination of intimacy and loneliness in sex offenders. *Journal of Interpersonal Violence, 9*, 518–534.

Serin, R. C., Mailloux, D. L., & Malcolm, P. B. (2001). Psychopathy, deviant sexual arousal and recidivism among sexual offenders: A psycho-culturally determined group defense. *Journal of Interpersonal Violence, 16*, 234–246.

Seto, M. C., & Barbaree, H. E. (1999). Psychopathy, treatment behavior, and sex offender recidivism. *Journal of Interpersonal Violence, 14*, 1235–1248.

Slovenko, R. (1984). The meaning of mental illness in criminal responsibility. *Journal of Legal Medicine, 5*, 1–61.

Solomon, J. C. (1992). Child sexual abuse by family members: A radical feminist perspective. *Sex Roles, 27*, 473–485.

Swanson, J., Holzer, C., Ganju, V., & Jono, R. (1990). Violence and Psychiatric Disorder: Evidence from the Epidemiological Catchment Area surveys. *Hospital and Community Psychiatry, 41*, 761–770.

United States v. Bilyk, 29 F. 3d 459 (1994).

United States v. Murdoch, 98 F. 3d 472 (1996).

United States v. Robinson, 94 F. Supp. 2d 751 (2000).

Wakefield, H., & Underwager, R. (1991). Female child sexual abusers: A critical review of the literature. *American Journal of Forensic Psychology, 9*, 43–69.

Webster, C. D., Harris, G. T., Rice, M. E., Cormier, C., & Quinsey, V. L. (1994). *The violence prediction scheme: Assessing dangerousness in high risk men.* Toronto, Ontario, Canada: University of Toronto, Centre of Criminology.

Winick, B. J. (1998). Sex offender law in the 1990s: A therapeutic jurisprudence analysis. *Psychology, Public Policy, and Law, 4*, 505–570.

Zevitz, R. G., Crim, D., & Farkas, M. A. (2000). Sex offender community notification: Managing high risk criminals or exacting further vengeance? *Behavioral Sciences and the Law, 18*, 375–391.

CHAPTER 24

Battered Woman Syndrome in the Courts

DIANE R. FOLLINGSTAD

The serious social problem of wife battering too often culminates with the killing of one of the partners in the relationship. Although the person killed often is the wife, abusive men also are killed at times by the women, who claim that they were defending themselves at the time of the death. These cases very frequently result in murder charges against the women, who must provide evidence that they killed in self-defense. Professionals in both mental health and legal arenas have tried to determine why so many of these cases result in charges against the battered women who, on the face of it, seem to be the "victims." Because the facts of these cases often appear to deviate from traditional conceptions of self-defense, the cases are not dismissed. At the trials, the legal strategy for the defense often has been to provide social science evidence to explain how the experience of battered women actually fits within the standards for self-defense.

Twenty years after the first writings about battered women, there is a vast amount of literature on this topic. However, when information about battered women was first applied to criminal cases, the field was in its infancy. Thus, it was the initial conceptualization of battered women's experiences, labeled the battered woman syndrome (Walker, 1979, 1984), that shaped the criteria by which judges determined

admissibility and that provided the "scientific evidence" about battered women that informed appellate court review of these decisions. Unfortunately, almost all court decisions and legal commentary have centered around this one formulation of battered women's experiences, which has greatly limited the applicability of social science research to this issue. This is especially important in light of that fact that serious problems have been raised with regard to the validity of the battered woman syndrome, even though it has experienced widespread acceptance by the courts.

The battered woman syndrome has taken a linear path in the extent of its usage and the frequency of its admissibility in forensic settings, but a curvilinear path in terms of legal and psychological scholars' views of the appropriateness of its use. When evidence about a phenomenon called the battered woman syndrome, said to be present in women who were abused by intimate men in their lives, first appeared in court cases in which the woman had killed or injured the man, U.S. courts were reluctant to admit such testimony. Once a small number of jurisdictions allowed experts to supply information about battered woman syndrome and, at times, apply the syndrome to specific cases, there was a relatively quick reversal of sentiment in courts around the country. The courts began to embrace such testimony as enlightened. Thus, the trajectory of the admissibility of battered woman syndrome has been steep, as seen by the concept's rise from obscurity to broad-scale acceptance across most jurisdictions.

The use of the battered woman syndrome has been propelled by legal practitioners and mental health professionals who, in contrast to many legal scholars, believe "The body of relevant scientific and clinical knowledge in the scholarly literature strongly supports the validity of considering battering as a factor in the reactions and behavior of victims of domestic abuse" (Gordon, 1998, p. 312). Mental health professionals tend to view testimony about battering and its effects as relevant in trials of battered women who are defendants. However, exactly how the battered woman syndrome, a clinical-psychological construct, fits within legal theories and concepts is often poorly understood and explicated by mental health practitioners.

Although certain jurisdictions historically have held that the battered woman syndrome did not fulfill various rules of evidence, and although there have been occasional dissenting voices amid the enthusiasm for battered woman syndrome testimony, only in more recent years has dissatisfaction regarding the use of battered woman syndrome evidence in court cases been voiced more strongly and more frequently. This dissatisfaction has come not only from legal analysts, who have been concerned about the use of syndrome defenses in general and the scientific validity of the concept in particular, but also from some advocates for battered women. Many of these advocates have come to believe that the battered woman syndrome has not been as effective in securing desired outcomes as had been expected. In addition, they currently fear that there have been ironic consequences of promoting the use of this type of evidence, in that some women, in subsequent criminal and civil court cases, have had features of the battered woman syndrome used against them. Thus, while the use of battered woman syndrome evidence was initially greeted with applause by advocates for battered women and at least neutral acceptance by the courts, the efficacy, validity, and appropriateness of introducing this syndrome into court cases have now come to be seriously questioned.

Although legal commentators have been more accepting of certain uses of battered woman syndrome than other, more exotic syndromes that have found their way into the legal arena, many legal scholars (e.g., Faigman, 1996; Mosteller, 1996) are concerned that syndrome evidence has influenced outcomes in controversial cases in a way that "displays the [law's] wishful desire to come to the correct political outcome" (Faigman, 1996, p. 821) rather than holding to well-established evidentiary rules. Echoing this concern, Slobogin (1998) warned that this trend could lead to mental health professionals, rather than time-proven legal principles, dictating legal policy.

Before developing the numerous issues that need to be addressed regarding testimony about battered woman syndrome, it is important to state that the task of representing battered women in criminal and civil cases is, and will remain, a difficult, challenging, and important one. Even those commentators who criticize the use of battered woman syndrome in court recognize the serious social problem of domestic violence and the need for the most appropriate representation of battered women who come into contact with the legal system. Therefore, the concerns and critiques discussed in this chapter focus on the uses and validity of the battered woman syndrome specifically and do *not* question the need for the vigorous defense of battered women who have killed their partners or vigorous representation of battered women in divorce and custody cases. Over and over again, legal analysts and mental health professionals acknowledge that information about the nature and existence of domestic violence often needs to be part of the context of a case. No debate exists over recognizing the need for full knowledge of a case to inform those who represent the community in making judgments about personal responsibility and culpability. However, at issue is whether making such judgments is best, or more appropriately, or most accurately, or most validly accomplished through the use of battered woman syndrome evidence in the courtroom. If the battered woman syndrome is not explicitly used as a concept, there needs to be further discussion as to what information about battered women should be admissible and where it might be relevant to legal issues.

HISTORY OF THE USE OF BATTERED WOMAN SYNDROME IN FORENSIC CASES

While the use of the battered woman syndrome has been far-reaching since its introduction, most testimony about the syndrome has been heard in criminal courts. Most typically, this evidence has been proffered to support some aspect of the defense of a woman who has been charged with harming (often killing) her abusive partner. In fact, Downs (1996) stated that introduction of the battered woman syndrome in these cases has become the predominant method of defending battered women who have killed or assaulted their partners or committed other crimes, and that the battered woman syndrome is considered the most successful syndrome in the history of the courts in terms of its acceptance as evidence.

At the same time that the social problem of wife abuse began filtering into the general public's awareness, there was a concomitant recognition within the legal profession that battered women might not have been represented appropriately in criminal cases, in that the defense of these women often did not take into account their experience at the hands of their abusers. Especially compelling was the notion that the battered woman's ultimate aggressive action toward the man may have been precipitated by his physical aggression at the time of the incident or even by his prior aggression, setting the stage for her to expect serious harm at the time she killed or injured him.

Because the plight of battered women was horrifying to many, early defense strategies often were geared toward making the woman a sympathetic character. As a way to accomplish this, while also trying to relieve the woman from culpability for her actions, early strategies of defense presented the woman as insane, or at least as temporarily insane, at the time she killed him and attributed this mental state to the terrifying experiences she suffered at her abuser's hands. A few of these defenses resulted in acquittals, probably because of the jury's desire to demonstrate that they empathized with the battered woman's circumstances, rather than because the woman's case clearly fit the legal requirements of the insanity defense. A successful insanity defense in the 1970s and 1980s typically involved meeting a stringent standard wherein the person needed to have a cognitive impairment due to a mental disease or defect such that the person either literally would not have known what he or she was doing, or would not have known that what he or she did was wrong. Few battered women would have been able to fully meet this level of required mental impairment then, and few would meet this stringent cognitive impairment standard today.

The main reason defense attorneys did not immediately embrace the seemingly more plausible strategy of self-defense over the insanity defense in battered women's cases was that the facts of the cases often did not fit easily into the traditional concept of self-defense. (See Gillespie, 1989, for a discussion of the development of self-defense law as arising from a model of confrontation between two males, either from the standpoint of sudden attack, e.g., robbery, or a fight between strangers that takes on serious and/or deadly overtones.) Across states, the requirements for a killing to be considered justifiable due to self-defense typically include (a) a reasonable perception that the person was faced with a situation likely to result in death or grievous bodily injury; (b) a reasonable perception that the threatened harm was immediate or imminent; (c) that the person engaging in self-defense was not responsible for provoking the confrontation;

and (d) that the person used only force necessary to end the attack and used force comparable to that which was directed at the person. A number of states include some variation of the requirement that, to claim self-defense, the person considered avenues to escape but perceived no opportunities for retreating from the dangerous situation without using force. Slobogin's (1998) analysis of the courts' change in attitudes toward admissibility of the battered woman syndrome concluded that the initial resistance was due to the apparent discrepancy between the requirement in self-defense that the killing was necessary to prevent death or grievous bodily injury and the facts surrounding numerous battered women's cases. In many, the killings occurred at times other than when the batterer was directly assaulting her.

Many writers have suggested that a high proportion of these cases have been "nonconfrontational," meaning that the now deceased abuser was *not* engaging in the act of physically assaulting the woman at the time she killed him. For example, the specific facts might show that (a) the woman killed him around the time of an assault but not when he was in the act of assaulting her; (b) she was responding and reacting to his *threats* of harm; (c) she seemed to use force far beyond what would be required to disable a person from attacking further; or (d) she reported believing that her life was in imminent danger at the time, although, objectively to strangers, this belief may not seem to be clearly supported from the overt facts of the situation.

Maguigan (1991) has challenged the view that many battered women have killed during nonconfrontational situations. She reviewed hundreds of appellate court decisions and determined that approximately 75% of the cases more closely fit the description of confrontational situations. She also extrapolated from appellate-level decisions that cases that are appealed are likely to contain proportionally more nonconfrontational cases due to their controversial nature and increased likelihood of resulting in a guilty verdict. Thus, Maguigan suggested that cases that are not appealed are even more likely to involve situations that fit a self-defense context in which the woman reacts to a confrontation/attack by her partner, potentially fitting well within the requirements for claiming self-defense.

Even in cases in which the battered woman responded with force to a direct attack by the abuser, the contextual knowledge about her experience of abuse at the man's hands is still typically considered necessary to enhance jurors' understanding that the woman's response was reasonable. For example, information about a battered woman's experiences might clarify why the woman interpreted the abuser's actions as implying imminent danger or a particular level of danger, or how her history with him would explain her perception that she had no means of escape or retreat, or how her perception of the man's dangerousness would seem reasonable based on her history with him. Over time, support for and advocacy of battered women appears to have influenced the courts to consider self-defense in these cases in a more subjective light (Mosteller, 1996), making testimony about their experience of being physically abused, and their expectations that such experiences give rise to, more relevant.

The first time battered woman syndrome evidence was presented in an actual case appears to be Lenore Walker's testimony in a criminal trial in Montana in 1977 (as reported by Walker, 1989). This case took place before she had published her major thesis about battered woman syndrome in her 1979 and 1984 books. In ensuing cases, other advocates for battered women, whether legal practitioners or mental health professionals, believed that the purpose of introducing battered woman syndrome testimony was to supplement the justifiability of the self-defense claim. Faigman (1986) described the inclination to use battered woman syndrome evidence as an effort to "use social science research on battered woman syndrome to bring [the women] within the bounds of self-defense doctrine" (p. 335). This was especially pertinent in those cases where battered women's ultimate aggressive reactions toward their abusive partners did not clearly fit the traditional elements of self-defense.

Walker's (1979, 1984) introduction of the new concept of battered woman syndrome suggested that battered women, as a result of physical abuse, experience specific psychological sequelae. Subsequently, Walker and other mental health professionals have used the proposed psychological reactions to abuse as a way to explain a range of ensuing behaviors by these women. These behaviors include the battered women's perception of danger, their decision to remain with their abusing partners, their belief that they are trapped with no alternative but to kill the partner, and the killing of the partner during what appears to be a nonconfrontational period rather than during a direct confrontation. To this day, the direct causal connections between particular psychological features of battered woman syndrome and particular behaviors of battered women have never been empirically established, but instead remain theoretical and conceptual in nature.

The major elements of the battered woman syndrome that Walker (1979, 1984) proposed were the cycle of violence theory and learned helplessness (although she did postulate the existence of other psychological reactions, such as depression and low self-esteem). The theory of the cycle of violence purports that physical aggression follows a predictable pattern. Initially, tension in the batterer mounts over time, which is evident to the man's partner. (The theory does not, however, specify a period of time for the buildup in tension.)

Following the increase in tension, the theory proposes, an acute aggressive incident occurs that serves to discharge the buildup of tension. The acute aggressive incident is thought to be followed by a period of tension reduction, with possibly a "honeymoon" phase of loving contrition as an accompaniment. Walker believes the importance of this cycle is that battered women remain in constant fear during the period of mounting tension due to their expectation that violence will recur.

Based on Seligman's (1975) theory of learned helplessness, Walker (1984) proposed that the psychological experience of helplessness was present in battered women after they had been in aggressive environments that they could neither control nor easily predict. This experience of helplessness was predicted to render them passive and unable to initiate escape attempts from the situation. Walker believes learned helplessness explains why battered women may be incapable psychologically of leaving the abusive relationship. Thus, Walker's proposed battered woman syndrome would have implications for the reasonableness of battered women's perception of danger and for promoting jurors' understanding of why battered women remain in the abusive relationship.

ADMISSIBILITY OF BATTERED WOMAN SYNDROME AS RELATED TO SELF-DEFENSE IN COURT CASES

The first case in which higher courts debated whether the battered woman syndrome met evidentiary requirements for admissibility was the criminal case of *Ibn-Tamas v. United States* in 1979. This attempt to introduce the battered woman syndrome as evidence was unsuccessful, even through two appellate-level reviews. (The first appeal was an effort to overturn the trial judge's ruling that the expert was not qualified; the second appeal attempted to overturn the ruling that there was no evidence to show that the methodology of the information was generally accepted by the scientific community, i.e., that the battered woman syndrome did not meet the *Frye* standard.) A Washington case (*State v. Wanrow,* 1977) two years earlier addressed the standard by which jurors should judge whether a battered woman acted reasonably, although no battered woman syndrome testimony was introduced. The Supreme Court of Washington ruled that a battered woman was entitled to have the jury determine whether her actions were reasonable from a subjective standpoint, (i.e., based on her own perceptions of the situation, which would be influenced by her prior experiences with the abuser). That is, a subjective viewpoint was employed rather than the traditional objective viewpoint of whether the average reasonable person would have perceived the situation as imminently dangerous, thus justifying the self-defensive aggressive response.

Blowers and Bjerregaard (1994) reported that battered woman syndrome evidence was initially rejected for a number of evidentiary reasons, including: (a) that it was not relevant to the case (*People v. White*, 1980; *State v. Thomas*, 1981); (b) that it was not sufficiently reliable as scientific information (*Ibn-Tamas v. United States*, 1983); and (c) that it was not beyond the ken of the average juror's knowledge (*Mullis v. State*, 1981; *State v. Thomas*, 1981). However, the courts were more likely to rule that battered woman syndrome was inapplicable to a particular case, rather than concluding that battered woman syndrome evidence did not meet other evidentiary requirements (Blowers & Bjerregaard, 1994). Surprisingly, only in 15 of 72 cases reviewed by Blowers and Bjerregaard did the courts consider the scientific methodology of battered woman syndrome or its acceptance in the general scientific community. And only in some early cases did the courts rule that scientific acceptance of the battered woman syndrome was not established or that the syndrome was still controversial (e.g., *Burhle v. State*, 1981). "After 1985, only one court ruled that the state of the art was not sufficiently developed" (Blowers & Bjerregaard, 1994, p. 551).

Blowers and Bjerregaard's (1994) review suggested that although battered woman syndrome evidence has been steadily admitted through case law and appellate review, the *type* of testimony that the different jurisdictions have allowed varies widely and the criteria for determining the admissibility of battered woman syndrome testimony have lacked uniformity. The relevance of battered woman syndrome evidence has usually been assessed in light of whether the information will help the trier of the fact assess the reasonableness of the battered woman's actions. A few rulings have allowed the relevance of battered woman syndrome testimony to be extended to the woman's actions after the killing or to the credibility of the battered woman's testimony.

Once the battered woman syndrome passes the relevance requirement for evidence by the courts, the role and scope of expert witness testimony appears to vary. There have been few cases in which the appellate review determined that jurors did *not* need an expert to help them understand the battered woman syndrome to make the requisite judgments facing them (e.g., whether the defendant felt remorse, whether the defendant was experiencing reasonable fear, and whether the defendant killed in self-defense). Experts' qualifications were rarely the evidentiary issue around which admissibility of battered woman syndrome testimony centered.

Blowers and Bjerregaard (1994) reported that the allowed scope of testimony ranged significantly across jurisdictions to include: characteristics of battered women, typical patterns of abuse, myths regarding battering relationships, "diagnosis" of the defendant as a battered woman, and opinion as to the defendant's state of mind at the time of the killing. However, testimony as to the defendant's state of mind has been limited in some jurisdictions because those courts viewed an expert's opinion that the battered woman syndrome influenced a defendant's state of mind as tantamount to giving the ultimate opinion (which the courts viewed as the province of the trier of the fact). In addition, some courts have determined that battered woman syndrome testimony may *not* be used (a) to give an opinion on whether the woman was justified in killing the man (*State v. Kelly*, 1984); (b) to support the notion that the shooting was a direct result of experiencing the battered woman syndrome (*Commonwealth v. Craig*, 1990); nor (c) to give an opinion that the woman's responses were reasonable (*Commonwealth v. Miller*, 1993; *Motes v. State*, 1989; *State v. Koss*, 1990).

Today, despite the concerns of a number of legal scholars, most jurisdictions permit testimony in criminal court about battered woman syndrome and "a number actually guarantee its legitimacy through legislation" (Slobogin, 1998). Twelve states provide for battered woman syndrome testimony by statutory law. In 1992, President George Bush signed the Battered Women's Testimony Act, which specifically authorized a study of this type of testimony and required training materials to be developed to assist the courts (Posch, 1998). This Act also strongly encouraged state officials to accept battered woman syndrome testimony based on a recognition that many women are victims of physical violence.

ADDITIONAL USES OF BATTERED WOMAN SYNDROME IN COURT CASES

The battered woman syndrome has been used for purposes beyond supporting the claim of self-defense. This syndrome testimony has been admitted as relevant evidence into a broad range of criminal cases (Coughlin, 1994): fraud (*State v. Lambert*, 1984); drug running (*United States v. Johnson*, 1992); child abuse (Loggins, 1992); child homicide (*State v. Bordis*, 1992); and homicide of an adult other than the batterer (*Neeley v. State*, 1985). As part of the defense in these criminal cases, battered woman syndrome testimony has been offered to accomplish one of three things: (a) to bolster the woman's claim that she engaged in a criminal act under the duress/coercion of her abusive partner; (b) to support the notion of mitigation for the woman at the time she pleads guilty; or (c) to bolster a claim of diminished capacity in the sentencing phase of a case.

A review of cases in which battered woman syndrome testimony has been offered suggests that legal practitioners have creatively used this evidence even when general acceptance for using battered woman syndrome testimony in these ways has not existed. In addition, the specific links between this evidence and the function of the testimony have not always been clearly spelled out. For example, the syndrome has been introduced to support an insanity plea (e.g., *State v. Felton,* 1983), even though this evidence was initially conceptualized as a way to explain that the battered woman's action was *not* the product of insanity at the time she killed her partner, but rather a response born out of terror, helplessness, and fear.

Battered woman syndrome evidence has been used in postconviction relief hearings to support the contention that a battered woman received ineffective assistance of counsel. This applied specifically for cases in which the woman's history of being physically abused would have been relevant to her criminal trial, but the attorney of record did not pursue this aspect of the case or introduce evidence concerning the impact of the battering on the woman. Battered woman syndrome documentation has also been presented to parole boards and governors to request mitigation or clemency of battered women's sentences in light of their experiences as victims. In addition, battered woman syndrome testimony is finding its way more frequently into family court, where it has been deemed to have applicability to some divorce and custody cases. (However, as will be discussed below, the introduction of battered woman syndrome evidence in these cases often has been to the detriment of battered women.) Most recently, there have been some examples of personal injury claims by battered women against their former partners (Kohler, 1992).

In an unusual turnaround, battered woman syndrome evidence has been introduced into prosecutors' cases against men who have physically abused their wives, although, in these instances, it is usually directed toward explaining some inconsistency in the woman's behavior, such as a retraction of an earlier statement in which she claimed she was harmed by her partner.

MAJOR LEGAL ISSUES IN THE USE OF BATTERED WOMAN SYNDROME

Although there has been widespread admission of battered woman syndrome evidence in state courts and the uses of the syndrome continue to expand, many problems exist with respect to the actual validity of this syndrome as it has been historically defined and used in court. The major legal issues discussed below are aimed at the battered woman syndrome as currently conceptualized rather than at the general realm of knowledge about domestic violence that may prove to be relevant for and applicable to battered women's cases.

Problem in Defining and Designating Who Is a Battered Woman

Several years ago, while preparing to conduct a workshop on the use of the battered woman syndrome in criminal cases, I noticed that both legal and mental health writings used the terms "battering" and "battered woman" as if there were consensus about their meanings. However, my review of the literature revealed no specific research standards or empirical threshold markers that defined these terms. The lack of definition makes it difficult to know at what point interpersonal aggression becomes "abuse," when abuse becomes "battering," how much battering one has to endure to be considered a "battered woman," and when and how being a battered woman results in battered woman syndrome.

Typically, the literature on battering offers vague descriptions of interpersonal experiences that include, but are not confined to, repeated physical aggression on the woman by her partner. This literature entirely skirts the question of how much and what type of physical aggression is necessary to warrant labels of abuse or battering. Some authors, such as Walker (1979), dealt with the definitional problem by arguing that *any* physical aggression constitutes battering, which would mean that a woman whose husband grabbed her arm two times and a woman who is repeatedly beaten and terrorized would both be considered "battered." (Walker considers a woman to be battered who has been through the battering cycle at least twice.) Egregious cases would be easy to identify, but physical abuse can range widely. Remarkably, given the history and prevalence of these concepts, there is no empirical or conceptual consensus about what types and frequencies of physical aggression constitute abuse and battering.

Adding to the definitional murkiness, some descriptions in the literature define abuse as consisting of psychological maltreatment as well, implying that the presence of psychological abuse *alone* might qualify a woman as battered. Walker's (1979) definition of a battered woman, for example, specifically includes nonphysical types of abuse: "A battered woman is a woman who is repeatedly subjected to any forceful physical or psychological behavior by a man in order to coerce her to do something he wants her to do without any concern for her rights" (p. xv). Thus, Walker's definition left open the possibility that battered woman syndrome could result from psychological abuse without accompanying physical violence (Walker, 1983). The broadening of the concept of abuse to include psychological forms and the stretching of the concept of battering to include low-frequency, mild aggression might have value from a political, therapeutic, or advocacy standpoint, but has undermined attempts to precisely define core terms in the field, which is necessary if this information is presented as scientifically credible in other arenas.

Many writers in the field have argued that the very attempt to define aggression, abuse, battering, and the battered woman syndrome from an objective-empirical perspective is misguided and an affront to the subjectivity of the battered woman's experience, which they argue should be the standard by which abuse is judged and defined. Walker (1979), for one, has stated that battered women themselves are the best judge of whether or not they are being battered. From this subjective point of view, each individual determines when she believes aggression becomes abuse, abuse becomes battering, and battering turns her into a battered woman. Although the sensibility of a psychotherapist and woman's advocate shines through this viewpoint, neither the sensibility of a researcher seeking conceptual clarity nor that of a forensic expert seeking to offer well-defined constructs to assist the court in its decision making is advanced.

Leaving aside the self-serving reasons for which some women might define themselves as battered, or contrarily, the many reasons for which truly battered women would define themselves otherwise, trusting the definition of core constructs to the frailties of personal, idiosyncratic interpretation has yielded only conceptual chaos. Now, more than 20 years after the birth of these concepts, the question of who is a battered woman has never been resolved or even seriously considered in terms of empirically based definitions. Research studies cited in court have included women with strikingly varied abuse histories. Remarkably, Walker's (1979) subjective definition is "the most widely accepted definition of a battered woman" (Archer, 1989), even though there is no empirical basis for it.

Problem with Conceptualization of the Battered Woman Syndrome

Most references addressing the battered woman syndrome, whether psychological or legal, cite Walker (1979, 1984) as the source for the conceptualization of the syndrome. This is unfortunate, because although Walker's pioneering efforts were important for focusing attention on the plight of battered women, there has been extensive research since then that has rarely been acknowledged or applied to legal cases.

Rather, the desire to have a "defined" syndrome as a way of conceptualizing battered women's experiences seems to have fueled the reliance on the earliest ideas proposed by Walker.

Based on her clinical observations, Walker (1979) described the characteristics and psychological sequelae she perceived as evident in battered women. Anecdotally, she listed the common characteristics as follows: low self-esteem; a tendency to underestimate her abilities; traditionalist attitudes about sex roles; acceptance of responsibility for the batterer's actions; guilt, but denial of the terror and anger she feels; a passive approach presented to the world, but having the strength to manipulate her environment enough to prevent further violence and being killed; severe stress reactions with psychophysiological complaints; use of sex as a way to establish intimacy; and a belief that no one will be able to help her resolve her predicament. Walker also applied the concept of learned helplessness to battered women at this time, but concluded that the small sample of women did not allow for a conclusion that the women were depressed. Walker also reported that the women exhibited less anxiety than she had expected to find. This first treatise was also the source for Walker's introduction of the cycle theory of violence, wherein she postulated a tension-building stage, followed by an acute battering incident, and ending with a phase consisting of contrite and/or loving behavior. The stages or phases were hypothesized to repeat themselves over the length of the relationship.

Walker's (1984) next book, *The Battered Woman Syndrome,* furthered her original ideas and included some data. She attempted to differentiate which characteristics previously attributed to battered women could be potential susceptibility factors (i.e., those that would interfere with a woman's ability to stop the batterer's abuse) from those characteristics that were likely to be psychological sequelae of the physical abuse. Walker suggested that susceptibility factors for experiencing abuse were traditional sex-role socialization; repeated sexual molestation and assault as a child; being a member of a violent family; and experiencing "critical or uncontrollable" events in childhood. What needed to be distinguished further, however, was whether the potential psychological sequelae of the susceptibility factors could explain the current psychological symptoms that Walker was hypothesizing to be the *results* of being a victim of physical abuse. Unfortunately, the data Walker presented in this book did not provide adequate support for her suggested syndrome (see Downs, 1996, and Faigman, 1986, for critiques of Walker's investigations).

Walker's (1984) data indicated that battered women's scores on measures showed that they were *less* traditional in their sex-role socialization than college females; they believed they had a great deal of control over what happened to them; they did not strongly believe that their lives were chiefly controlled by powerful others; they possessed stronger and more positive self-perceptions than other women or men in general; and they did not espouse a consistently pessimistic view of the world. Walker's comparison of women still in a battering relationship with women who were out of an abusive relationship ironically found that women *out* of the relationship often showed more negative symptoms than the women still being abused (e.g., more depression, more problems with learned helplessness in the present, more likely to see themselves as controlled). Although the overall group had scores above a normative cutoff score for high risk for depression, a number of factors other than abuse appeared to be affecting depression (e.g., employment status, marital status), and there were no community control groups to help clarify the findings.

Walker's (1984) sample also did not provide good support for the idea that battering is a cyclical phenomenon, as only 65% of the women reported a tension-building phase and only 58% reported a contrition phase. Extrapolation of this data suggests that only a minority of cases would report the three phases suggested by Walker (1979). The lack of confirming data is important because it is from the cycle of violence that the "psychological sequelae that constituted a large part of battered woman syndrome" are hypothesized to arise (McMahon, 1999, p. 27). In forensic cases, the cycle of violence has served to explain the woman's reactions when a time gap existed between the aggressive actions or threats of the batterer and the battered woman killing her partner (McMahon, 1999). The cycle of violence was advanced by Walker as "the 'psychological link' for the battered woman between the two temporally distinct events" (McMahon, 1999, p. 27).

Because admissible testimony in the courtroom about battered women has almost exclusively relied on the battered woman syndrome as conceptualized by Walker (1979, 1984), the cycle of violence and learned helplessness have been the two aspects of the syndrome most often put forth as links between battered women's experience of abuse and their subsequent actions. Thus, when researchers or legal commentators have addressed battered woman syndrome evidence, Walker's conceptualization is the one that has been analyzed, whereas the greater field of information about battered women is rarely tapped. Also, the battered woman syndrome has rarely been analyzed for its reliability or applicability in appellate reviews beyond the factors of the cycle of violence and learned helplessness.

Schuller and Vidmar (1992) investigated the bases on which judicial decisions have admitted battered woman syndrome testimony into evidence. They concluded that there was no evidence to suggest that all abusing relationships go through the proposed cycle of violence and that the lack of a time frame for the proposed cycle makes it fairly impossible to either stringently assess this proposed phenomenon or identify its existence. In reviewing the literature regarding the characteristics of the battered woman syndrome, Schuller and Vidmar also reported that there was no empirical verification of the reliability of the hypothesized psychological symptoms as existing across all victims of battering or reliably occurring as a result of the battering. Regarding learned helplessness, McMahon (1999) observed that Walker's own conceptualization of it has changed several times, such that it is difficult to know the current definition of learned helplessness as applied to battered women's cases and as applied to the syndrome itself. Even so, most references to battered women's learned helplessness in criminal trials emphasize Walker's (1979, 1984) earliest references to extreme passivity on the part of battered women, a phenomenon that has not been well supported in the ensuing research literature (see below).

Aside from Walker's descriptions, the only other conceptual attempts to define what might constitute a battered woman syndrome were by an author, writing as Douglas in 1987 and later as M. Dutton (1992). It is interesting to note that, although these sources are at times given nodding reference in legal sources, these more fully developed and organized pictures of the battered woman syndrome are mentioned only infrequently. Douglas's (1987) chapter on the battered woman syndrome proposed a more specific definition of particular characteristics and effects of abuse on battered women. She included the following aspects: (a) traumatic effects of victimization by violence, (b) learned helplessness deficits from violence and others' reactions to it, and (c) self-destructive coping responses to the violence. The self-destructive coping responses were reported as an idealization of the abuser, denial of danger, and suppression of anger. M. Dutton (1992) later pooled her ideas on battered women in a book but did not use the term battered woman syndrome. Rather, she presented a systematic view of proposed psychological effects of abuse. Dutton organized the effects of battering as: (a) changes in cognition, such as cognitive schemas, self-esteem, expectations, self-efficacy, attributions, perceptions; (b) psychological distress and/or dysfunction, such as fear, anger, depression, alcohol or drug abuse; and (c) disturbances in relationships above and beyond the abusive relationship, such as difficulty trusting or fear of intimacy.

M. Dutton (1992) was clear to state that not all battered women experience the same psychological effects of abuse and do not all react similarly to the abuse experience. In addition to the vast number of symptoms she proposed battered women could develop, Dutton recognized that there were many potential *mediators* of psychological effects from battering, which could include vulnerability factors, personal resources, institutional responses, social support, other aspects of the abusive relationship, the presence of concurrent stressors, and the severity of the abuse. Dutton's opinion that battered women do not develop the same symptoms in response to physical abuse implies that developing a syndrome that reliably classifies battered women is a daunting task.

Because the focus unfortunately has been to identify a particular syndrome associated with battering, the considerable research investigating the effects of battering has never been cited in court cases, commentaries, or appellate reviews. However, for the mass of research to be usable, a systematic approach to understanding the quality of individual studies, to reconciling conflicting results, and to organizing the findings into a coherent body of knowledge may be necessary. Additionally, the available research is not without problems. One of the difficulties plaguing the field is that the research often has been conducted in a piecemeal fashion. Researchers may investigate only one or a limited number of factors, rendering an understanding of the relationship among these variables impossible to know. If these relationships were known, we might have a comprehensive picture identifying correlational as well as causal factors. Conducting sophisticated, well-validated research also has been difficult to accomplish due to the problems inherent in this type of research. Difficulties include identifying the most appropriate and representative sample; finding appropriate control samples; partialling out confounding factors (e.g., prior victimization, marital distress, socioeconomic status); having confidence that the variable assessed was validly measured; and using the most appropriate methodology for understanding the interrelationships of the myriad factors along with potential mediating and moderating factors.

Due to these impediments, no single investigation or series of investigations has been able to thoroughly and competently answer the question of whether empirical support exists for the battered woman syndrome as conceptualized by Walker (1979, 1984). However, the study that came closest to assessing the validity of some of the major proposed sequelae for battered women (as garnered from a wider sampling of research) was conducted by D. Dutton and Painter (1993). These researchers assessed the presence of trauma symptoms over time, deficits in self-esteem, and traumatic bonding, and claimed that they identified the three targeted sequelae as coexisting for at least six months in their participants. Because the characteristics appeared to be related to each other, the authors believed the interrelationships suggested a syndrome.

More typically, articles about battered women assess whether particular elements of Walker's proposed syndrome appear to be accurate representations of the battered woman's experience. Researchers' expansions or modifications of Walker's early conceptualization have also contributed to the evolving body of knowledge about women's reactions and responses to physical abuse.

The literature review below has been organized to aid the reader in determining whether support exists for major categories of proposed psychological sequelae for women who have been battered. Overall, studies typically found that an investigated variable was present in *some* portion of the battered women who made up the sample, although not unanimously. Some studies even found that a higher proportion of battered women exhibited the psychological variable or exhibited the symptom at a higher level than did women in a control or comparison group. More important, a consistent finding was that many of the proposed psychological symptoms and effects were more likely to be found in women who had experienced the most severe and most frequent physical abuse. (This finding might be useful for narrowing the definition of battered women to those with more severe types of force and more frequent abusive incidents directed toward them.)

Cycle of Violence

There is a paucity of support for the cycle of violence theory. Walker's (1984) data did not provide convincing evidence for this factor as a consistent pattern in abusive relationships. The only study to investigate this more closely was conducted by D. Dutton and Painter (1993). They claimed that *intermittency* of the abuse was the most significant factor for predicting distress and psychological symptoms in the women, rather than the predictability or cycling of abusive incidents. Hence, it may be the intermittency of the abuse that should be investigated further.

Posttraumatic Stress Disorder

Numerous researchers have assessed whether battered women in their samples qualified for posttraumatic stress disorder (PTSD; Astin, Lawrence, & Foy, 1993; Houskamp & Foy, 1991; Kemp, Green, Horvanitz, & Rawlings, 1995; Khan, Welch, & Zillmer, 1993; Vitanza, Vogel, & Marshall, 1995). Estimates have varied from 45% to 84%, and PTSD in battered women has most often been identified in women who had experienced more severe abuse, who had perceived that their lives were threatened, and who had experienced sexual abuse in the physically abusive relationship. Other researchers have documented the presence of specific criteria of PTSD in the women (e.g., reexperiencing the trauma; Finkelhor & Yllo, 1985; Hilberman & Munson, 1977–1978). Some researchers have advocated using PTSD as the clinical framework for understanding battered women's psychological aftereffects (e.g., Roth & Coles, 1995); others have argued that PTSD is inadequate as a framework for conceptualizing the long-term sequelae of interpersonal violence (e.g., Herman, 1992b). Researchers have pointed to a broader range of symptoms than those accounted for by PTSD that appear to be associated with interpersonal violence (e.g., Pelcovitz et al., 1997). Herman (1992a) also suggested that the psychological sequelae involve more characterological disturbances and include the following range of symptoms: somatization, dissociation, affect disturbance, relationship changes, impact on identity, and repetition of harm. Even so, battered women who are more severely abused appear to be at greater risk for developing PTSD.

Learned Helplessness

The data on the existence of learned helplessness in battered women have been contradictory. Learned helplessness was *not* present in battered women in the vast majority of studies investigating some form of this variable, although the way it was defined in particular studies appeared to potentially influence whether researchers believed that their findings corroborated the idea that battered women exhibit learned helplessness. The way learned helplessness has been introduced in court cases as relevant to battered women's cases appears to be negated by the following studies (representing a range of the ways learned helplessness has been defined): Bowker (1983) reported that battered women sought a wide range of helping sources that *increased* as the abuse became more intense and prolonged; Gondolf and Fisher (1988) found that help seeking *increased* as abuse increased in severity; Khan et al.'s (1993) analysis of Minnesota Multiphasic Personality Inventory (MMPI) data did *not* support the model of dependent, passive women; and Campbell, Miller, Cardwell, and Belknap (1994) found that battered women generated *more* potential solutions to relationship problems than nonbattered women.

Low Self-Esteem

The initial conceptualization of battered women as exhibiting low self-esteem has resulted in some variable findings, but the concept is mostly supported. Aguilar and Nightingale (1994), Cascardi and O'Leary (1992), Dutton and Painter (1993), Frisch and MacKenzie (1991), and Mitchell and Hodson (1983) all found lower levels of self-esteem in abused women than in nonabused women, although whether this is a direct result of being abused is unknown.

Depression

The presence of depression in battered women seems well supported (Cascardi & O'Leary, 1992; D. Dutton & Painter, 1993; Gleason, 1993; Mitchell & Hodson, 1983), but the findings are not universal. Where physical violence is frequent, severe, and results in serious consequences, depression is more likely to occur (Cascardi & O'Leary, 1992; Kemp, Rawlings, & Green, 1991; Shields & Hanneke, 1983). However, other factors also appear to influence whether battered women experience depression, including a history of depression, deficient self-reinforcement, loss of sources of reinforcement, and realistic assessments of the relationship (Sato & Heiby, 1992). Unfortunately, this research has not partialled out many potentially confounding factors for depression in battered women.

Self-Blame

The presence of self-blame in battered women is *not* well supported by research findings. Studies typically indicate that only a small percentage of battered women blame themselves for the violence in the relationship (Cascardi & O'Leary, 1992; Holtzworth-Munroe, 1988). And women are even *less* likely to blame themselves as physical abuse increases in frequency and severity (Frieze, 1979).

Psychopathology

General distress and psychopathology are found in battered women samples. For example, more severely battered women had increased rates of suicidal behavior (Vitanza et al., 1995) as well as psychopathology as defined by standard diagnostic classifications (e.g., Gleason, 1993; Kemp et al., 1991). However, some studies suggesting that psychopathology was widespread among battered women lacked appropriate control groups. Kemp et al. (1991) and Khan et al. (1993) supported their contention of increased psychopathology in battered women by citing elevations on the MMPI as evidence of psychopathology. However, Rosewater (1988) has cautioned clinicians in their interpretations of battered women's MMPIs due to the difficulty of determining whether elevations suggest psychopathology predating abuse, psychopathology resulting from abuse, or posttraumatic effects of the battering that would not support a diagnosis of psychopathology. McMahon (1999) viewed Gleason's (1993) evidence of a higher prevalence of mental disorders in battered women as partial support for the existence of the battered woman syndrome. The knowledge that battered women seem to have more mental disorders, however, still leaves us uncertain as to what this fact actually means for the existence of the battered woman syndrome due to the lack of specificity of the proposed effects of battering and the lack of causal connections between the disorders and being battered.

Interpersonal Disturbance

Interpersonal disturbance due to battering (Dutton, 1992) or trauma (Herman, 1992a) was *not* well supported by the research data (Kemp et al., 1995); rather, research results tended to find no results or opposite results with periodic exceptions. Sato and Heiby (1992) concluded that their sample of battered women had adequate social support, even for those women experiencing fairly high levels of violence. Warren and Lanning (1992) did not find differences between battered women and others seeking services at a mental health center in terms of desire to make social contact or to have others initiate contact with them, although neither group was highly social. Finn (1985) and Star (1978) found that battered women were *more* social than their control group. However, Star, Clark, Goetz, and O'Malia (1979) reported that battered women had a greater tendency to withdraw and avoid interpersonal contact.

Cognitive Disturbances

Some cognitive disturbances (e.g., memory difficulties) have been identified in some battered women and have been cited as criteria for PTSD. However, no study has established how cognitive disturbances are related to or result from battering. In contrast, Vitanza et al.'s (1995) study found that "cognitive failure" had no relationship or only a modest relationship with intrusive thought and avoidance scores, which are criteria for PTSD.

Traumatic Bonding

Only one well-conducted study examined the concept of traumatic bonding (Dutton & Painter, 1993). The authors found high rates of heightened paradoxical attachment (i.e., increased attachment in the face of negative treatment) in their sample, but whether this finding is a direct result of the battering has not been conclusively established.

Other Variables

There are insufficient data on the following variables to suggest any conclusions as to whether they develop as a result of battering: shame, dependency, psychological stress, self-destructive coping responses, panic attacks, emotional lability, and dissociation.

As can be seen by this brief review, not only is there no clear conceptualization of which variables/characteristics/effects specifically constitute the battered woman syndrome, but the research to date does not consistently support the psychological effects originally conceptualized.

Problem with Determining Whether the Psychological Sequelae of the Battered Woman Syndrome Actually Constitute a Syndrome

The question at hand is whether there is enough support for the battered woman syndrome to be established as a bona fide syndrome. Morse (1998) stated, "A syndrome, in medical terminology, is the collection or configuration of objective signs (e.g., fever) and subjective symptoms (e.g., pain) that together constitute the description of a recognizable pathological condition" (p. 364). When used in relation to behavioral conditions, the term syndrome implies that there is a pathological entity that comprises psychological phenomena that co-occur, that can be validly demonstrated to jointly comprise this entity, and that arise from a particular etiological cause. Schopp, Sturgis, and Sullivan (1994) stated that "a psychological syndrome is a clinically significant pattern of impaired psychological functioning" (p. 93). A number of Morse's points regarding syndromes in general will be used for this discussion.

Defining a syndrome by noting a number of symptoms that occur simultaneously and lead to the designation of a pathological condition is the first step. In designating *behavioral* syndromes, the process has usually occurred backwards from the medical precedents for defining syndromes. Rather, a common experience is identified and an investigation determines whether similar symptoms or effects are present in those who experienced the event(s). That is, individuals are noted to have undergone a similar experience (e.g., battering, sexual abuse as a child, participation in the Gulf War), and ensuing investigations determine post hoc whether the individuals exhibit similar psychological characteristics. This post hoc research strategy has certainly been the predominant mode of collecting data on battered women, mostly due to their identification as they require medical, psychological, and legal services, but also because longitudinal studies investigating the psychological well-being of vast numbers of the general population do not exist to allow for pre- and post-battering data to be compared.

If there is strong evidence to descriptively support concurring psychological phenomena as constituting a syndrome, the next step is to determine whether the syndrome is valid (Morse, 1998). Individuals with battered woman syndrome should be qualitatively and quantitatively different on a cluster of relevant psychological variables to demonstrate that this entity is uniquely different from other psychological entities. This type of validity has not been investigated or established for the battered woman syndrome (Schopp et al., 1994). Psychological results of battering have not been demonstrated to be uniquely different from the psychological results arising from other severe stressors or traumas. PTSD or even Herman's (1992a) more inclusive complex PTSD in battered women parallel the psychological symptoms resulting from a wide variety of other traumatic experiences (e.g., childhood sexual abuse).

By definition, a syndrome is pathological (Morse, 1998). The battered woman syndrome has never been designated as a diagnostic category as defined by the *Diagnostic and Statistical Manual of Mental Disorders,* fourth edition, text revision (*DSM-IV-TR;* American Psychiatric Association, 2000), although some authors (e.g., Regehr, 1995) have suggested that certain characteristics of the syndrome could be subsumed under the diagnostic category of PTSD. The ambivalence of professionals and advocates has been evident in deciding whether to label battered women as pathological as a result of the abuse. On one hand, advocates for battered women believe professionals and laypersons need to understand the serious impact of battering in terms of the significant psychological and physical injuries to them. On the other hand, advocates do not want battered women to be viewed as impaired and dysfunctional, but rather as individuals responding as best they can to a terrorizing life experience. The debate on whether battered women are normal and just experiencing pathological but transitory reactions to horrible life conditions or are psychologically impaired as a result of experiencing these horrible conditions remains undecided. As will be discussed later, whether the battered woman syndrome results in or rises to the level of a pathological psychological state that can impact/impair/affect the woman's actions at the time she commits an unlawful act has been debated vigorously.

Once the validity of a syndrome is established, classification rules are required for determining when an individual possesses a particular syndrome (Morse, 1998). The discussions surrounding battered woman syndrome have not clarified whether all battered women should exhibit all of the proposed effects or whether battered women have battered woman syndrome by virtue of exhibiting *some* of the characteristics. Also at issue is whether battered women, as a group, can be said to have battered woman syndrome on the basis of some of the women exhibiting all of the symptoms, or even when *some* of the battered women exhibit *some* of the symptoms. No studies to date have assessed whether professionals could reliably "diagnose" a sample of women as suffering from battered woman syndrome. Mosteller (1996) spoke to the importance of this issue, stating that "consistent, stable, and well-defined group behavior—perhaps not a 'syndrome' but at least 'group character'—must exist in response to a set of conditions assumed or proven to be present in the case" (p. 473).

Courts have wrestled with this classification issue. Jurisdictions have differed as to whether an expert is allowed to conclude that a defendant belongs to the class of persons exhibiting battered woman syndrome (e.g., the court in *State v. Hennum,* 1989, ruled that the expert was not allowed to classify the woman in this way, the court in *State v. Steel,* 1987, ruled that this was acceptable). Some jurisdictions have allowed an expert to testify only *in general* about battered women; some have only allowed testimony specific to the particular battered woman. Others have allowed a combination, in which the expert is permitted to determine whether the woman actually appears to fit the characteristics or has the history that allows her to be classified as a battered woman.

Problems with Syndrome Evidence in General

Once a syndrome is reliably and validly established, how this information is applied to legal issues becomes the next step to consider. Mosteller (1996) has grappled with the issues of introducing evidence about syndromes into criminal trials and, more specifically, discussed these issues in relation to the battered woman syndrome.

There are three major ways in which evidence about syndromes or "group character" have been used in criminal cases to date (Mosteller, 1996). First, the existence of a constellation of symptoms has been used to support the contention that certain actions (crimes) have occurred. Examples of this would be the introduction of rape trauma syndrome or child sexual abuse accommodation syndrome as evidence that a rape or sexual abuse of a child had occurred. Proving that certain behaviors occurred from the presence of psychological symptoms in a person makes the verifiability of this conclusion a paramount issue. Whether a conclusion of this type could or should actually be derived from this type of data, no matter how extraordinarily carefully derived, is highly questionable. Used in this manner, a constellation of symptoms/characteristics would have to be an exceedingly reliable and accurate indicator that a specific action, *and no other,* could be the cause of the symptoms. The many postulated effects of being battered and the many hypothesized characteristics of the women postbattering have been too amorphous and potentially multidetermined to allow for a reliable conclusion that certain symptoms in women are evidence of battering. Only some of the specific content of certain symptoms might possibly suggest a link between the symptoms and battering (e.g., intrusive thoughts regarding battering incidents, content of nightmares). Mosteller argued that syndrome evidence that is used to argue backwards that a criminal action was committed "must be of the highest quality and should satisfy the standard set out in *Daubert v. Merrell Dow Pharmaceuticals, Inc.* Here the difficulty of the scientific task is the greatest, and the impact of misguided expert evidence, in terms of potential prejudice, can be the most devastating" (p. 468). A cluster of symptoms that have not reliably discriminated diagnostically between groups should be viewed as dangerous and biasing if the syndrome evidence was presented to establish that a particular etiology/event was the only possible reason for the symptoms to exist.

The second way that group character evidence (i.e., syndrome evidence) has been used is for the purpose of establishing credibility or rebutting attacks on credibility (Mosteller, 1996). When the courts determine that the introduction of particular testimony for correction or bolstering is advisable, they assume that, without this evidence, misperceptions could prejudice the decision making of the jury/judge and, thus, result in an unfair outcome. An example of admitting syndrome testimony to rebut an attack on a witness's credibility is testimony about rape trauma syndrome explaining why a woman might have delayed reporting a rape or why she was not hysterical in the emergency room. This testimony would be introduced after the lawyer for a defendant highlighted these facts to imply that the woman's claim of rape was a lie.

Although testimony regarding the battered woman syndrome has definitely been introduced for corrective and rehabilitative functions, it has also been introduced proactively to address (i.e., correct) preestablished erroneous attitudes and beliefs that the trier of the fact is *presumed* to hold. A number of research studies have demonstrated that the knowledge and attitudes of laypersons are, at times, significantly different from those of experts/advocates in the field of domestic violence (e.g., Dodge & Greene, 1991; Greene, Raitz, & Lindblad, 1989). Because these discrepancies imply that certain information about battered women is not common knowledge for laypersons (i.e., beyond the ken of the jurors), some courts have allowed testimony about the battered woman syndrome or about research pertaining to battered women to prevent jurors from basing their decisions on misconceptions. For example, the court in *State v. Koss* (1990) *did* allow battered woman syndrome testimony for this reason, but the court in *Commonwealth v. Dillon* (1989) did not. Specifically, testimony as to why a battered woman does not

leave an abusive relationship falls into the category of correcting myths or misinformation that may be common among jurors. When experts address specific issues regarding battered women, such as why they remain in the violent relationship, information about group behavior of battered women is often available and applicable to a case without requiring the expert to establish that the defendant exhibits battered woman syndrome.

Establishing the reasonableness of a person's actions or perceptions in light of a particular legal standard is a third use of group character testimony (Mosteller, 1996). There have been cases involving battered women in which the evidentiary testimony consisted of a combination of data about battered women in general to address myths, as well as an analysis of the woman's unique battering history to address the reasonableness of her perceptions. An analysis of the individual woman's *overall* experience in the battering relationship by an experienced clinician might provide evidence, for example, to support the reasonableness of her perception of danger in the *particular* incident in which she killed the man. A historical perspective of the violent relationship might establish that the violence escalated in recent months such that woman began to fear for her life.

Mosteller (1996) believes that battered women's cases that require restoration of credibility or proactive use of evidence often do *not* require the establishment of the battered woman syndrome to do so. Mosteller also believes that the courts would not require an exceptionally high standard of scientific exactitude before admitting testimony into evidence that addresses the woman's credibility regarding the reasonableness of her actions. On the other hand, he argues that expert testimony on whether the woman believed she faced imminent danger is testimony about the ultimate question, which is typically the province of the jury or judge. If testimony suggests that the woman, by virtue of experiencing battered woman syndrome, had particular perceptions or reactions bearing on the reasonableness of her conduct at the time of the killing, Mosteller believes that more stringent tests of science should be placed on the admissibility of this type of testimony. When the ultimate question of the reasonableness of the woman's actions is viewed through the filter of battered woman syndrome, the necessity for the concept to be scientifically valid and predictive becomes paramount. Mosteller lists the following questions as the crux of the issue:

> First, what are the precise, rather than the general, dimensions of that social reality, that syndrome? Is there a precisely defined syndrome that establishes a causal relationship between the pattern of abuse suffered by the defendant, her psychological

reactions, and her perceptions or subsequent conduct? Second, to what degree are experts able to diagnose a woman as "suffering from" or fitting within the precisely defined syndrome? (p. 481)

Mosteller (1996) perceives several biases inherent in expert testimony of the battered woman syndrome, thus increasing the salience that this syndrome be scientifically verifiable. An expert testifying that a woman is similar to other battered women may enhance her credibility as a defendant while simultaneously, and possibly unfairly, labeling the deceased man as a villain, even in circumstances where the expert is unable to independently establish the accuracy of the reported history. Credibility may be automatically enhanced for a defendant if jurors conclude that her experience must be believable if others have experienced similar phenomena. Another potential bias may occur when a judge allows an expert to testify on the reasonableness of a defendant's conduct as a jury is exposed to an expert essentially casting a "not guilty" vote, which could, in turn, influence their own decision making.

Problem with Placing the Battered Woman Syndrome within the Context of Legal Defenses of Justification versus Excuse

Whether battered woman syndrome evidence provides a *justification* or an *excuse* for the actions of the defendant has provoked much controversy among legal commentators, even when the woman claims that she acted in self-defense or under duress. The rationale for putting forth such affirmative defenses is to claim that the *reason* the defendant violated the criminal law exonerates her, because the woman is not disputing that she engaged in the action (Morse, 1998). Thus, in the eyes of justice, her actions will need to be justified or excused for her to avoid punishment.

The distinction of justification versus excuse is an important one for the appropriateness of introducing evidence. Justification for an action indicates that the person was fully responsible (i.e., mentally competent) when committing the actions for which he or she has been charged with a criminal offense. However, the person deserves to be exonerated because the conduct, typically considered wrongful, was permissible under the circumstances or was appropriate for the particular situation (e.g., killing when one's life is threatened; Morse, 1998). In contrast, an excuse for a person's conduct indicates that the person is not responsible for his or her actions because the person cannot be considered a responsible moral agent at the time of the action (e.g., being an infant or being legally insane; Morse, 1998). Therefore, the question to be considered is whether battered woman syndrome evidence is intended to support the contention that the woman's actions were *permissible* or the contention that the experience of being a battered woman rendered her *incapable* of being a responsible moral agent. (See Morse, 1998.)

The courts have chosen to confine evidence about the battered woman syndrome within a justification scenario (i.e., claims of self-defense). No courts have knowingly or intentionally established a battered woman syndrome defense creating an excuse for a woman to engage in deadly force toward her partner, acting in response to the psychological reactions to battering, irrespective of whether she perceived herself to be in danger at the time. Based on the appellate court decisions to date, consensus exists that evidence that a woman was battered or that she exhibited the battered woman syndrome may not provide an "excuse" for her actions. In addition, evidence of this type must be linked to the elements of self-defense.

Even though the courts have limited battered woman syndrome evidence within a justification framework, Morse (1998) has suggested that some of the more controversial cases (usually involving nonconfrontational killings where even imminence requirements have been loosened) have pushed the use of the syndrome into the realm of excuse defenses. Strong opinions have been voiced on both sides of the legal argument as to whether there should be an expansion of battered woman syndrome evidence beyond how it has been currently allowed. Advocates for battered women (e.g., Bradfield, 1998; Cipparone, 1987; Kaser-Boyd & Balash, 1993; Rosen, 1986) believe that expanding the use of the syndrome to incorporate the concept of excuse for these women would reflect our awareness of their dilemmas and realities. In contrast, many legal scholars (Faigman, 1986; McMahon, 1999; Morse, 1998, Mosteller, 1996) are concerned that our concepts of responsibility for upholding certain social standards will be eroded.

Coughlin (1994) fears that allowing excuse defenses for women, unique from those permitted for men, will perpetrate the view that women are deficient persons incapable of regulating their own behavior when placed in difficult circumstances. Coughlin views using the battered woman syndrome in defenses providing an excuse as paralleling the "marital coercion doctrine," which historically viewed a woman as blameless for crimes committed (a) under the coercion of her husband, (b) at his request, or (c) merely in his presence. This prior doctrine perceived women as not acting as free agents and as not having the capacity for rational choice. Coughlin writes, "Criminal law has been content to excuse women for criminal misconduct on the ground that they cannot be expected to, and, indeed, should not, resist the influence exerted by their husbands" (p. 5). Coughlin believes that under the old doctrine of marital coercion, women were viewed as deserving of sympathy rather than condemnation and that the decision to excuse, rather than punish, followed from that orientation. As a parallel, she suggests that the current conceptualization of the battered woman syndrome presents women as psychologically disabled and impaired, thus implying that their behavior should be excused. The danger, Coughlin argues, lies in continuing the view that women are not self-reliant and not self-determined, which is likely to influence courts to impose restraints and special (negative) conditions on women in family or civil court.

Problem with Clarifying the Uses of and Purposes for the Battered Woman Syndrome in the Courtroom

Reviewing literature that is both supportive of and antagonistic toward the use of battered woman syndrome evidence can only result in the conclusion that there is no consistency in the way commentators, analysts, professionals, and advocates believe this syndrome should most appropriately be applied. First of all, confusion is evident as to what is allowable or appropriate courtroom evidence of battered woman syndrome. Almost any information about battered women and their plight (e.g., why battered women do not leave the abusive relationship, reasonableness of the woman's actions) has variously been placed under the label of battered woman syndrome.

Second, commentators, analysts, and advocates writing about battered woman syndrome may differ markedly in their views from practitioners dealing with the actualities of defending a battered woman. A strict analysis of legal principles applied to this syndrome may seem alien to the defendant's attorney piecing together relevant evidence for the case. On the other hand, however, advocates who support a fairly unlimited expansion of this evidence may be unaware of, or at least less concerned about, the legal constraints and limitations that courts impose and the historical and noteworthy principles on which evidence laws have been founded.

Third, the battered woman syndrome's introduction into specific cases has been accomplished for such a variety of purposes that the exact purpose for using this evidence is unclear. Is the evidence intended to specifically support elements of self-defense, or to explain aspects of the defendant's life to make her seem more sympathetic to the jury, or to bolster the woman's credibility by having an expert support her perceptions? Schopp et al. (1994) presented a cogent argument to suggest that the cited aspects of battered

woman syndrome (e.g., cycle of violence, learned helplessness, depression, lowered self-esteem) are most likely to create a picture of a woman in distress rather than to produce a coherent causal link between the syndrome and the elements of self-defense. These same authors argued that the extended history of abuse a woman experienced, in and of itself, goes much further to support the reasonableness of her belief that she reacted to perceived immediacy of a threat from her partner when killing him than does testimony about the battered woman syndrome per se. (See Follingstad, 1996, for a detailed discussion of the aspects of a battered woman's experience that may be relevant to elements of self-defense.)

Fourth, the courts create confusion as to the purpose of battered woman syndrome evidence when they differ in their rulings on the content about which experts can testify. For example, courts that permit an expert to testify about battered woman syndrome only in general may unintentionally grant credence to the defendant's testimony as to her "battered woman" status without any outside confirmation or requirement of a demonstration that this classification fits the defendant. Courts have come down on different sides of evidentiary rules for allowing the testimony to be introduced and for the purpose for the testimony (e.g., to address reasonableness of the actions, credibility, why the woman remained in the violent relationship).

Evidence about battered woman syndrome has sometimes been used as a backdoor route for introducing evidence about past abusive incidents other than what happened specifically at the time of the killing. This legal strategy has been used when direct introduction of violent behavior historically committed by the deceased (whether directed toward the woman or toward other individuals) has not been permitted due to the court's determination that such testimony is prejudicial and biasing. However, some commentators (e.g., Faigman, 1986) believe that the man's violent history, especially in relation to the woman, would provide a more understandable picture of the woman's experience and her perception of danger. Faigman believes that the man's violent history would be the crucial information on which jurors could, in turn, base their decision as to the reasonableness of the woman's actions, rather than trying to make an indirect link between battered woman syndrome and the woman's ensuing behavior. Because some new federal evidence rules designed specifically to address sex offenses (which are frequently characterized as private incidents occurring in an ongoing relationship where the person has some control over the victim) have allowed evidence of prior behavior to be introduced (Fingar, 1996), Posch (1998) recommended that similar rules allowing evidence of past instances of physical violence should be admitted into evidence, thus eliminating the need to use battered woman syndrome testimony in these cases.

Potential Negative Effects of Introducing Evidence on the Battered Woman Syndrome

Initial criticisms of the use of battered woman syndrome in court cases were leveled by legal commentators. Some recent critiques have been written by feminist scholars (e.g., Posch, 1998). Because testimony about battered woman syndrome has typically portrayed the woman as suffering from a psychological condition/impairment that has had an impact on her final act of killing or her inability to leave the abusive relationship, numerous writers have expressed concern that the women are portrayed as weak, helpless, and pathological (e.g., Browne, 1987; Posch, 1998). Coughlin (1994) states, "The defense itself defines the woman as a collection of mental symptoms, motivational deficits, and behavioral abnormalities; indeed, the fundamental premise of the defense is that women lack the psychological capacity to choose lawful means to extricate themselves from abusive mates" (p. 7). For example, postulating that battered women exhibit learned helplessness pathologizes battered women by determining that they are incapable of engaging in actions to help themselves. This concept has been used to conclude that, as a result of the battering experience, these women are "unable to think clearly," suffer "emotional paralysis," and possess the "delusion that things will improve" (Schopp et al., 1994, p. 70).

Attempting to establish the *reasonableness* of the defendant's actions based on the man's abusive experiences may backfire because of the portrayal of battered women's mental state as defined by the battered woman syndrome: "Expert testimony regarding depression, decreased self-esteem, learned helplessness, or other psychological characteristics of the defendant does not show the defendant's 'reasonableness'" (Schopp et al., 1994, p. 87). The portrait of the woman as psychologically impaired appears incompatible with establishing her as capable of making reasoned and reasonable decisions regarding the imminence and potential severity of an attack.

The uses of the battered woman syndrome in court have spanned over a number of apparent purposes that have intended to (a) engender sympathy for the woman based on the psychological sequelae she experiences as a result of the abuse; (b) aid the trier of fact in understanding how the resulting psychological sequelae from the syndrome distort and impair the woman's perceptions, abilities, and volition (e.g., to leave the abusive relationship); and yet (c) have the judge

or jury *not* view the syndrome and its effects as a disorder that interferes with her ability to make a reasonable decision about the need to defend herself. Those making judgments about a battered woman's case are likely to find it difficult to believe that the woman, by definition, is impaired and experiences distortion in very specific and particular areas but is unaffected in parallel cognitive mechanisms that govern other specific and particular areas. Rather than demonstrating that the woman made reasonable interpretations and decisions, using battered woman syndrome evidence usually requires that "the defense concedes that the woman's conduct was unreasonable, but then excuses her from criminal liability if she can prove that she was a passive, obedient wife whose choices were determined not by her own exercise of will, but by the superior will of her husband" (Coughlin, 1994, p. 50).

Cornia (1997) raised the concern that the portrayal of battered women in criminal cases as irrational and/or mentally defective to suggest their behavior should be excused will be carried over into family and civil courts. This portrayal may be useful in criminal court to engender sympathy for the woman and to suggest that her behavior should be excused; however, the same portrayal has been used in other legal contexts to the detriment of battered women (e.g., child custody battles, child abuse cases; Cornia, 1997). If the battered woman syndrome paints women as irrational and/or lacking in self-control, their credibility in family court proceedings, after their status as battered women has been established, is automatically reduced.

Because battered women have been known to recant prior statements regarding the batterer's violence toward them, battered women have been portrayed as incapable of telling the truth (*Carnahan v. State*, 1997; *Hawks v. State*, 1996; *State v. Griffin*, 1988). Women who have been abused may be at a serious disadvantage in having to prove their fitness as parents, rather than having fitness assumed unless proven otherwise. For example, one court already decided that the existence of battering in a household where children live constitutes child neglect (*In re Heather*, 1996). Parental unfitness may be assumed by the court due to testimony that a woman who was battered in the past would be likely to choose an abusive partner in the future (*In re John V.*, 1992; *In re Ranker*, 1996). One court even allowed general testimony regarding battered woman syndrome that alleged that some battered women have been known to abuse their children (*State v. Stevens*, 1997). Thus, the portrayal of battered women as not responsible for their behavior or behaving in unreasonable ways due to debilitating effects of the battering has not only been questioned as an accurate portrayal for self-defense cases, but poses dangers due to a backlash in other legal arenas where battered women are perceived as possessing a permanent disabling psychological condition.

ASSESSMENT ISSUES FOR BATTERED WOMEN'S LEGAL CASES

Clinicians involved in battered women's court cases must first determine the specific legal question to be answered. In criminal cases, the legal question may be to determine the woman's mental status at the time of the offense (MSO), when she killed or injured her partner, similar to a determination of criminal responsibility. If the MSO evaluation is specific to a claim of self-defense, then information must be collected in line with elements of self-defense. An insanity defense requires a different approach, addressing the elements of insanity for the particular statute of each state. When diminished capacity is being claimed or the defendant's attorney believes the concept of duress might apply to her case, the legal question becomes the determination of the woman's intent or ability to form a particular intent to commit a crime. Other legal questions for criminal cases could involve the defendant's credibility or require information to be gathered to address myths or misconceptions regarding battered women so that these issues do not cloud the factual picture of the case. In civil cases, the likely assessment questions focus either on a determination of how a woman's experiences as a victim of abuse have affected her (e.g., establishing psychological damages for a civil tort case or demonstrating the impact of abuse on a woman in a divorce and/or custody case) or a determination of how battering experiences did *not* affect a battered woman (e.g., why she is not automatically deemed unfit as a parent).

Because many of the legal questions are familiar to forensic practitioners, the issue to address becomes how these evaluations might be different from typical evaluations for forensic purposes. Thus, these ideas for assessment are specifically geared for determining how a history of being battered affects these particular evaluations. For those unfamiliar with evaluations of criminal responsibility, MSO, diminished capacity, duress, psychological damages in tort cases, and divorce/custody cases, the reader is advised to consult sources specific to these forensic topics as well as corresponding chapters in this volume.

As a general rule, clinicians venturing into these cases should be thoroughly familiar with the vast body of literature regarding battering, rather than relying on the narrow and now controversial battered woman syndrome. The body of literature is useful for understanding what psychological factors are consistently related to battering experiences,

remaining in abusive relationships, motivations for using physical force, and psychological coercion. However, familiarity with this literature should be cautiously translated into general testimony about battered women, as this chapter has noted the difficulty of proving that all battered women respond in one way to battering.

The most important methodology for approaching battered women's cases is likely to be a *thorough* and *informed individual* evaluation. The informed clinician, aware of the literature to date, is able to ask more pertinent questions, probe more effectively, and bring aspects to light that the woman might not have known to raise as significant. The thorough evaluation implies that the woman is interviewed, observed, and given appropriate psychological testing at the same time that pertinent records (e.g., medical, police) are reviewed, other relevant persons are interviewed as to their knowledge, and clinical information is assessed for consistency and credibility of the information. The individual evaluation allows for an understanding of the specific battered woman's experience, which informs her perceptions, decisions, choices, and beliefs. And *this* type of evaluation is most likely to produce information that is usable for battered women's cases.

Studies that have investigated psychological testing of battered women have cautioned clinicians in making interpretations (e.g., Rosewater, 1988; Strauss, 1996). In the absence of any comparison psychological testing prior to the woman being battered, the appropriate meaning of elevations on general measures of psychopathology may be difficult to ascertain (e.g., Rosewater, 1988). The unanswered question is often whether the woman exhibited the particular psychological symptoms or disturbances prior to the battering, whether pathology developed over time while the woman was in the abusive relationship, or whether symptoms developed directly as a result of the battering. However, deducing the woman's responses to a standard objective measure of psychopathology is often necessary for understanding the extent of her psychological distress, and in the case of the MMPI-2, there is a PTSD scale that can be used (the Keane PTSD Scale; Keane, Malloy, & Fairbank, 1984; Schlenger & Kukla, 1987), although it was normed on Vietnam veterans. The Personality Assessment Inventory (PAI), a general measure of psychopathology, also has a unique scale measuring PTSD. A number of measures of trauma symptoms (e.g., Trauma Symptom Inventory [TSI], Briere, Elliott, Harris, & Cotman, 1995; Modified Fear Survey III, Resick, Veronen, Calhoun, & Kilpatrick, 1986; Crime-Related PTSD, Saunders, Arata, & Kilpatrick, 1990) could be administered twice to the woman, asking for her best recollection of whether she exhibited particular symptoms prior to being abused as well as her current state of functioning. Although this method is suspect due to the ease with which a person can manipulate data if there is a motivation to do so, a report of the woman's general functioning and even information about specific symptoms can be obtained through independent collateral interviews with individuals who knew the woman well before the abusive relationship. The comparison of women's responses and collateral interview information can be used as one means of determining general credibility of the woman's report of symptoms. Also, more obvious measures of trauma symptoms can be compared with the PTSD scale on the MMPI-2, which consists of more subtle items. The TSI has three validity scales that assess consistency and overreporting of unlikely symptoms for assessing credibility of the data.

Although normed measures may be useful to suggest psychological effects due to battering, much of the information needed to answer legal questions requires development through an interview. For example, Follingstad (1996) detailed the types of information a clinician needs to elicit from a battered woman that would be useful to support various elements of self-defense. To obtain evidence that a battered woman was under duress at the time she committed a crime, both a general propensity to be dominated in addition to a very careful enumeration via interview of her thought processes, actions, and beliefs at the time of the crime are necessary.

A careful and thorough compilation of the abuse history is necessary for any case. Most commentators who have questioned using the battered woman syndrome for battered women's cases have endorsed the inclusion of the woman's history of abuse in the facts introduced in court cases. The full explication of the battered woman's experience should be included when it appears relevant to understanding her perceptions regarding imminent danger at the time she killed her partner, the reasons she remained in the abusive relationship, her attempts to escape or use other resources, and her lack of alternatives to the actions in which she engaged. The abuse history can be elicited through a combination of interviewing and measures, such as Dutton's (1992) Abusive Behavior Observation Checklist, Attribution Questionnaire, Appraisal of Violent Situation measure, and Response to Violence Inventory. However, measures of this type provide restricted information and invariably are incomplete, thus necessitating a thorough interview. Further probing and clarification could occur as follow-up to these questionnaires. Tolman's (1989) Psychological Maltreatment of Women Inventory is a beginning step regarding assessment of psychological aggression, although this measure needs to be viewed as self-report subject to interpretation and bias with obvious face content like

any others requiring a person to report on an intimate's behavior toward him or her. The physical abuse history possibly can be corroborated by medical and police records as well as by independent interviews with family and/or friends.

CONCLUSIONS AND FUTURE DIRECTIONS

The focus of this chapter has been to review the validity and applicability of the battered woman syndrome to legal cases with the purposes of determining the current state of the art and of ascertaining directions for the future. Commentators and analysts of this syndrome's use in court have not been unsympathetic to the plight of battered women, nor have they argued that battered women do not experience effects, whether physical, psychological, or social, from the abuse. Rather, an important issue for this chapter has been whether there is a specific and distinct syndrome that consistently reflects the psychological sequelae of battered women's experience, and, if so, whether the syndrome has specific application to forensic cases. This critique did not apply to other potentially relevant and valid research about battered women and their experience that could inform certain aspects of their court cases. In fact, Gordon (1998) pointed out that the term battered woman syndrome does not adequately reflect the breadth or nature of current knowledge concerning battering and its effects. But before considering whether there are other ways to use social science research regarding battering in valid and appropriate ways, the confusion surrounding the use of the battered woman syndrome needs to be confronted and decisions regarding its use need to be made.

The careful analyses of the problems surrounding the battered woman syndrome as a concept, irrespective of whether it is a useful explanatory mechanism for court cases, have shown that it is difficult to conclude anything other than that the syndrome is virtually unsupportable as a well-defined and valid concept. The definition of who might be liable to develop this syndrome is still not clarified, leaving advocates as well as analysts uncertain as to when to define a woman as a battered woman. The criteria that would be required to be present in a battered woman before she could be said to be experiencing battered woman syndrome have neither been clearly specified nor have they received clear empirical support. Attempts to define battered woman syndrome have had different foci, including abuse patterns, hypothesized psychological sequelae, and susceptibility factors. It is also unclear whether factors influencing the development of this particular syndrome as well as the effects of those factors *equally* constitute the syndrome.

The battered woman syndrome appears to fail all tests of a true syndrome: specific criteria are lacking; the required etiology is unclear; the syndrome does not explain why some women develop symptoms and others do not; it is unclear whether all women with the syndrome would exhibit all of the suggested characteristics; it is difficult for the syndrome to prove that the present symptoms are uniquely different from related entities (i.e., would not have been produced by other sources); and it has not been established that professionals can reliably "diagnose" women as suffering from battered woman syndrome.

In addition to definitional problems, the validity of various purported aspects/characteristics/symptoms of the battered woman syndrome varies in the research literature from unsupportable to probable. Walker's (1979, 1984) research on the battered woman syndrome, on which most legal cases have relied, has been criticized as not only consisting of questionable methodology (thus calling any results into question), but also as not supporting her own hypothesized syndrome. My review of the effects hypothesized by Walker, as well as by Dutton (as Douglas in 1987; M. Dutton, 1992), as comprising the effects of battering shows that a number of factors are unsupported by current research, some have contradictory findings, and some have more promising results. However, even among the effects that appear better supported by the data, the results are not consistent or unanimously found among research participants labeled as battered women, who actually vary greatly in their abuse histories. The relationship between greater severity and higher frequency of violence with a greater likelihood of psychological symptoms seems to be the important relationship for predicting effects of battering such as PTSD and depression. This illustrates that the way battering is defined in a research study may influence whether psychological sequelae are identified.

It may, in fact, be naïve, or even futile, to attempt to establish a single pattern of responses and symptoms subsequent to the experience of battering. Battering itself can range widely in terms of patterns, frequency, and severity, and expecting that the responses and reactions of a battered woman can be clearly, directly, and consistently predicted is likely to result in disappointment. But even more important, it is highly unlikely that the same pattern of symptoms lead to the same specific behaviors in *all* battered women. Even if the psychological sequelae of being battered could be succinctly described and ensuing research subsequently verified the existence of these symptoms, we still would be hard pressed to demonstrate that the psychological symptoms inevitably lead to specific behaviors by the women. As Faigman (1986) stated, "Researchers have not . . . convincingly demonstrated that the battering experience gives rise to a single distinctive

behavior pattern" (p. 644). Thus, even psychological symptoms that have been noted in a high proportion of women who have been severely and frequently abused (e.g., PTSD and depression) are unlikely to specifically predict how the woman will behave in relation to the battering man. No one has ever suggested that exhibiting trauma symptoms, for example, will result in all women using force against the abuser when they feel threatened.

The two factors cited as important by Walker (1979, 1984) for understanding the battered woman defendant's behavior were the cycle of violence and learned helplessness, both of which have not been well supported empirically. In addition, the cycle of violence has been considered by numerous commentators to be so flexible and limitless (i.e., no time intervals are ever specified) as to be useless for predicting behavior. Because of these increasing criticisms of the battered woman syndrome, many legal commentators now take the stance that this syndrome, especially in its current poorly conceptualized and validated state, is not relevant to rigorous application of the self-defense claim (e.g., Schopp et al., 1994). Rather, Maguigan (1991), in her analysis of appellate court decisions, concluded that "existing substantive law and related evidentiary and procedural rules are defined in a way consistent with the self-defense claims of battered women who kill" (p. 458) without needing the battered woman syndrome as a mechanism for explaining their behavior.

The positive news is that most analysts who eschew the use of battered woman syndrome do not see it, or its hypothesized elements, as necessary components for defending a battered woman. If an attorney is working to establish that a battered woman acted in self-defense, her history of abuse by the man may be more convincing evidence to increase the jury's understanding of the woman's fear of him than an expert's representation of the cycle of violence, which may or may not fit well with the woman's experience. The woman's unique experiences, explicated in detail to the jurors, may provide the link between certain cues at the time of the killing and her perception of imminent danger.

If diminished capacity or insanity are the issues at stake rather than self-defense, then a clinical assessment of the woman, her psychological symptoms, and the impact of these symptoms on her behavior would be relevant to her defense. It is more important to demonstrate which symptoms *each* woman exhibits and how these *specific* symptoms influenced her behavior, rather than introducing general information about battered women that may or may not apply.

Those who believe that the experience of being battered should rise to the level of an excuse for a battered woman's behavior might wish to reconsider this idea. Advocates present mixed views as to whether they endorse the idea that a history of battering creates psychological impairment that affects the woman's perceptions, beliefs, and actions when she kills the abuser. Even more controversy is apparent regarding whether the battered woman's existence in an egregious situation should, in and of itself, be taken into consideration in a criminal case if it does not directly apply to a particular claim of defense. It is understandable that sympathy for battered women's plight has influenced some to take the stance that an aggressive act in response to a long-term and brutal history of aggression should not be severely punished. However, the courts are unlikely to broaden the use of evidence in this way uniquely for battered women, as precedents over time indicate that our system of law consistently supports the premise that persons must employ mechanisms other than reciprocal or retaliatory aggression to handle maltreatment by others.

Numerous legal analysts, as well as some advocates, now believe that moving away from using battered woman syndrome represents a positive step both for battered women's cases and for a view of women as competent, rational beings. Initially, the shift from the defense of insanity/diminished capacity to self-defense for battered women was guided by the perception that these women were acting "reasonably" by responding with force in situations they accurately perceived as dangerous. However, battered woman syndrome implied that the women, due to helplessness, terrorized states, and depression, were incapable of employing reason, which seemed to conflict with the idea that the women reasonably defended themselves against life-threatening violence. Thus, those currently recommending the elimination of battered woman syndrome as the structure around which information about battered women is introduced contend that their stance is in line with viewing these women as exercising reason and responsibility.

If we move away from using battered woman syndrome as a mechanism for organizing information and addressing legal issues regarding battered women, what remains? Most commentators believe that certain data about battered women are still applicable in ways that inform aspects of battered women's cases without requiring the use of battered woman syndrome, with its conceptual, definitional, and validity problems. Myths and misconceptions about battered women (as documented by Dodge & Greene, 1991; Greene et al., 1989; and noted by many other authors) continue to require "correction" by experts who can cite relevant research. Research findings that enlighten misperceptions and are pertinent to elements of legal defenses should still be admitted into battered women's cases. As a guideline, Faigman (1986) offered a standard for this type of evidence: "In battered woman cases, the court should at a minimum ensure that the evidence is genuinely relevant to a material aspect of the self-defense claim and that the researcher offering to testify has correctly applied the methodology of the general field of clinical psychology" (p. 350).

Support from commentators (e.g., Schopp et al., 1994) is fairly unanimous regarding introduction of the pattern of abuse the woman endured as directly relevant to these cases. Faigman (1986) made a convincing case for working toward an expansion of the evidence allowed into battered women's cases. He purported that to "understand the context in which the woman acted is essential to understanding the reasonableness of her act" (p. 644). Downs (1996) echoed this sentiment, stating his belief that judges and juries need to understand that battered women experience life circumstances and pressures that are out of the ordinary. Maguigan (1991) also thought that admitting evidence regarding the abuse history would maximize information for jurors about the "social context of the act of the defendant whose case they must decide" (p. 459). Thus, evidence of the man's violent disposition when he was alive, the narrowing of the woman's perceived and/or realistic alternatives over time, and corroboration of information regarding the man's dangerousness would all be relevant as to the woman's reasonableness of expected harm.

All of the suggested directions—moving away from using battered woman syndrome testimony, promoting admissibility of evidence of the violence history, allowing testimony as to valid research on relevant aspects of battered women's cases—would be likely to influence the courts to consider this issue on a case-by-case basis. Although some might fear that this would represent a step backward as to how these cases are tried, this does not have to be the case and, in fact, parallels the process of all court cases. Where specific relevant and valid research was applicable, the court could admit testimony it considered necessary for the jury to understand the context of the woman's perceptions and decision making. There would no longer be generic assumptions of battered women's psychological impairments and incapability applied to *all* battered women; this may prevent those assumptions from being generalized to family and civil court. Additionally, the expert testimony given in these cases would appear more credible, because it would not be coming from a perceived advocacy position based on a shaky conceptualization and data, but would be derived from relevant and sound psychological information.

REFERENCES

Aguilar, R. J., & Nightingale, N. N. (1994). The impact of specific battering experiences on the self-esteem of abused women. *Journal of Family Violence, 9,* 35–45.

American Psychiatric Association. (2000). *Diagnostic and statistical manual of mental disorders* (4th ed., text rev.). Washington, DC: Author.

Archer, N. H. (1989). Battered women and the legal system: Past, present and future. *Law and Psychology Review, 13,* 145–163.

Astin, M. C., Lawrence, K. J., & Foy, D. W. (1993). Posttraumatic stress disorder among battered women: Risk and resiliency factors. *Violence and Victims, 8,* 17–28.

Blowers, A. N., & Bjerregaard, B. (1994). The admissibility of expert testimony on the battered woman syndrome in homicide cases. *Journal of Psychiatry and Law, 22,* 527–560.

Bowker, L. H. (1983). *Beating wife beating.* Lexington, MA: Lexington Books.

Bradfield, R. (1998). Is near enough good enough? Why isn't self-defence appropriate for the battered woman? *Psychiatry, Psychology and Law, 5,* 71–85.

Briere, J., Elliott, D. M., Harris, K., & Cotman, A. (1995). Trauma Symptom Inventory: Psychometrics and association with childhood and adult victimization in clinical samples. *Journal of Interpersonal Violence, 10*(4), 387–401.

Browne, A. (1987). *When battered women kill.* New York: Free Press.

Burhle v. State, 627 P.2d 1374 (Wyo. 1981).

Campbell, J. C., Miller, P., Cardwell, M. M., & Belknap, R. A. (1994). Relationship status of battered women over time. *Journal of Family Violence, 9,* 99–111.

Carnahan v. State, 681 N.E.2d 1164 (Ind. Ct. App. 1997).

Cascardi, M., & O'Leary, K. D. (1992). Depressive symptomatology, self-esteem, and self-blame in battered women. *Journal of Family Violence, 7,* 249–259.

Cipparone, R. C. (1987). The defense of battered women who kill. *University of Pennsylvania Law Review, 135,* 427–452.

Commonwealth v. Craig, 783 S. W.2d 387 (Ky. 1990).

Commonwealth v. Dillon, 562 A.2d 885 (Pa. Super. 1989).

Commonwealth v. Miller, 634 A.2d 614 (Pa. Super. 1993).

Cornia, R. D. (1997). Current use of battered woman syndrome: Institutionalization of negative stereotypes about women. *UCLA Women's Law Journal, 8,* 99–123.

Coughlin, A. M. (1994). Excusing women. *California Law Review, 82,* 1–93.

Daubert v. Merrell Dow Pharmaceuticals, Inc., 509 U.S 579, 113 S. Ct. 2786 (1993).

Dodge, M., & Greene, E. (1991). Juror and expert conceptions of battered women. *Violence and Victims, 6,* 271–282.

Douglas, M. A. (1987). The battered woman syndrome. In D. J. Sonkin (Ed.), *Domestic violence on trial* (pp. 39–54). New York: Springer.

Downs, D. A. (1996). *More than victims: Battered women, the syndrome society, and the law.* Chicago: University of Chicago Press.

Dutton, D. G., & Painter, S. (1993). The battered woman syndrome: Effects of severity and intermittency of abuse. *American Journal of Orthopsychiatry, 63,* 614–622.

Dutton, M. A. (1992). *Empowering and healing the battered woman.* New York: Springer.

Faigman, D. L. (1986). The battered woman syndrome and self-defense: A legal and empirical dissent. *Virginia Law Review, 72,* 619–647.

Fingar, K. M. (1996). And justice for all: The admissibility of uncharged sexual misconduct evidence under the recent amendment to the Federal Rules of Evidence. *Southern California Review of Law and Women's Studies, 5,* 501–548.

Finkelhor, D., & Yllo, K. (1985). *License to rape: Sexual abuse of wives.* New York: Holt, Rinehart, and Winston.

Finn, J. (1985). The stresses and coping behavior of battered women. *Social Casework, 66,* 341–349.

Follingstad, D. R. (1996). Forensic evaluations of battered women defendants: Relevant data to be applied to elements of self-defense. *Applied and Preventive Psychology, 5,* 165–178.

Frieze, I. R. (1979). Perceptions of battered women. In I. R. Frieze, D. Bar-Tal, & V. S. Carroll (Eds.), *New approaches to social problems* (pp. 79–108). San Francisco: Jossey-Bass.

Frisch, M. B., & MacKenzie, C. J. (1991). A comparison of formerly and chronically battered women on cognitive and situational dimensions. *Psychotherapy, 28,* 339–344.

Frye v. United States, 293 F. 1013 (D.C. Cir. 1923).

Gillespie, C. K. (1989). *Justifiable homicide: Battered women, self-defense, and the law.* Columbus: Ohio State University Press.

Gleason, W. J. (1993). Mental disorders in battered women: An empirical study. *Violence and Victims, 8,* 53–68.

Gondolf, E. W. (with Fisher, E. R.). (1988). *Battered women as survivors: An alternative to treating learned helplessness.* Lexington, MA: Lexington Books.

Gordon, M. (1998). *Validity of "battered woman syndrome" in criminal cases involving battered women* (Edited version of review paper by M. A. Dutton). Rockville, MD: National Institute of Mental Health.

Greene, E., Raitz, A., & Lindblad, H. (1989). Jurors' knowledge of battered women. *Journal of Family Violence, 4,* 105–125.

Hawks v. State, 479 S.E.2d 186 (Ga. Ct. App. 1996).

Herman, J. L. (1992a). *Trauma and recovery.* New York: Basic Books.

Herman, J. L. (1992b). Complex PTSD: A syndrome in survivors of prolonged and repeated trauma. *Journal of Traumatic Stress, 5,* 377–391.

Hilberman, E., & Munson, K. (1977–1978). Sixty battered women. *Victimology: An International Journal, 2,* 460–470.

Holtzworth-Munroe, A. (1988). Causal attributions in marital violence: Theoretical and methodological issues. *Clinical Psychology Review, 8,* 331–344.

Houskamp, B. M., & Foy, D. W. (1991). The assessment of post-traumatic stress disorder in battered women. *Journal of Interpersonal Violence, 6,* 367–375.

Ibn-Tamas v. U.S., 407 A.2d 626 (D.C. 1979).

Ibn-Tamas v. U.S., 455 A.2d 893 (D.C. 1983, 2nd app.).

In re Heather, 60 Cal. Rptr. 2d 315, 321 (Ct. App. 1996).

In re John V., 7 Cal. Rptr. 2d 629 (Ct. App. 1992).

In re Ranker, 1996 WL 761159 (Ohio Ct. App. 1996).

Kaser-Boyd, N., & Balash, S. R. (1993). Battered woman syndrome in the courtroom. In M. Conte & L. L. Ammons (Eds.), *Defending battered women in criminal cases.* Chicago: American Bar Association.

Keane, T. M., Malloy, P. E., & Fairbank, J. A. (1984). Empirical development of an MMPI subscale for the assessment of combat-related posttraumatic stress disorder. *Journal of Consulting and Clinical Psychology, 52,* 888–891.

Kemp, A., Green, B. L., Hovanitz, C., & Rawlings, E. I. (1995). Incidence and correlates of posttraumatic stress disorder in battered women: Shelter and community samples. *Journal of Interpersonal Violence, 10,* 43–55.

Kemp, A., Rawlings, E. I., & Green, B. L. (1991). Post-traumatic stress disorder (PTSD) in battered women: A shelter sample. *Journal of Traumatic Stress, 4,* 137–148.

Khan, F. I., Welch, T. L., & Zillmer, E. A. (1993). MMPI-2 profiles of battered women in transition. *Journal of Personality Assessment, 60,* 100–111.

Kohler, R. L. (1992). The battered woman and tort law: A new approach to fighting domestic violence. *Loyola of Los Angeles Law Review, 25,* 1025–1072.

Loggins, K. (1992, July 9). Mother gets 15 years for not protecting sons. *Tennessean,* 5B.

Maguigan, H. (1991). Battered women and self-defense: Myths and misconceptions in current reform proposals. *University of Pennsylvania Law Review, 140,* 379–486.

McMahon, M. (1999). Battered women and bad science: The limited validity and utility of battered woman syndrome. *Psychiatry, Psychology and Law, 6,* 23–49.

Mitchell, R. E., & Hodson, C. A. (1983). Coping with domestic violence: Social support and psychological health among battered women. *American Journal of Community Psychology, 11,* 629–654.

Morse, S. J. (1998). Excusing and the new excuse defenses: A legal and conceptual review. *Crime and Justice, 23,* 329–403.

Mosteller, R. (1996). Syndromes and politics in criminal trials and evidence law. *Duke Law Journal, 46,* 461–516.

Motes v. State, 384 S. E.2d 463 (Ga. App. 1989).

Mullis v. State, 282 S. E.2d 334 (Ga. 1981).

Neeley v. State, 494 So.2d 669 (Ala. Crim. App. 1985), *aff'd,* 494 So. 2d 697 (Ala. 1986), *cert. denied,* 480 U.S. 926 (1987), *cert. denied,* 488 U.S. 1020 (1989).

Pelcovitz, D., van der Kolk, B., Roth, S., Mandel, F., Kaplan, S., & Resick, P. (1997). Development of a criteria set and a structured interview for disorders of extreme stress. *Journal of Traumatic Stress, 10,* 3–16.

People v. White, 414 N. E.2d 196 (1980).

Posch, P. (1998). The negative effects of expert testimony on the battered women's syndrome. *American Journal of Gender and the Law, 6,* 485–503.

Regehr, C. (1995). Battered woman syndrome defense in Canadian courts. *Canadian Journal of Psychiatry, 40,* 130–135.

Resick, P. A., Veronen, L. J., Calhoun, K. S., & Kilpatrick, D. G. (1986). Assessment of fear reactions in sexual assault victims: A factor analytic study of the Veronen–Kilpatrick Modified Fear Survey. *Behavioral Assessment, 8*(3), 271–283.

Rosen, C. J. (1986). The excuse of self-defense: Correcting a historical accident on behalf of battered women who kill. *American University Law Review, 36,* 11–56.

Rosewater, L. B. (1988). Battered or schizophrenic? Psychological tests can't tell. In K. Ylloe & M. Bograd (Eds.), *Feminist perspectives on wife abuse* (pp. 200–216). Thousand Oaks, CA: Sage.

Roth, D. L., & Coles, E. M. (1995). Battered woman syndrome: A conceptual analysis of its status vis-à-vis *DSM-IV* mental disorders. *Medicine and Law, 14,* 641–658.

Sato, R. A., & Heiby, E. M. (1992). Correlates of depressive symptoms among battered women. *Journal of Family Violence, 7,* 229–245.

Saunders, B. E., Arata, C. M., & Kilpatrick, D. G. (1990). Development of a crime-related post-traumatic stress disorder scale for women within the Symptom Checklist-90–Revised. *Journal of Traumatic Stress, 3*(3), 439–448.

Schlenger, W. E., & Kukla, R. A. (1987, August). *Performance of the Keane-Fairbank MMPI scale and other self-report measures in identifying post-traumatic stress disorder.* Paper presented at the 95th annual convention of the American Psychological Association, New York.

Schopp, R. F., Sturgis, B. J., & Sullivan, M. (1994). Battered woman syndrome, expert testimony, and the distinctions between justification and excuse. *University of Illinois Law Review, 1994,* 45–113.

Schuller, R., & Vidmar, N. (1992). Battered woman syndrome evidence in the courtroom: A review of the literature. *Law and Human Behavior, 16,* 273–291.

Seligman, M. E. P. (1975). *Helplessness: On depression, development and death.* San Francisco: Freeman.

Shields, N. M., & Hanneke, C. R. (1983). Attribution processes in violent relationships: Perceptions of violent husbands and their wives. *Journal of Applied Social Psychology, 13,* 515–527.

Slobogin, C. (1998). Psychiatric evidence in criminal trials: To junk or not to junk? *William and Mary Law Review, 40,* 1–56.

Star, B. (1978). Comparing battered and non-battered women. *Victimology: An International Journal, 3,* 32–44.

Star, B., Clark, C. G., Goetz, K. M., & O'Malia, L. (1979). Psychosocial aspects of wife battering. *Social Casework: Journal of Contemporary Social Work, 60,* 479–487.

State v. Bordis, No. 91-C-1441 (Tenn. Crim. Ct. 1992).

State v. Felton, 329 N.W.2d 161, 172–174 (Wis. 1983).

State v. Griffin, 749 P.2d 246 (Wyo. 1988).

State v. Hennum, 441 N.W.2d 793 (Minn. 1989).

State v. Kelly, 478 A.2d 364 (N.J. 1984).

State v. Koss, 551 N.E.2d 970 (Ohio 1990).

State v. Lambert, 312 S.E.2d 31 (W.Va. 1984).

State v. Steel, 359 S.E.2d 558 (W.Va. 1987).

State v. Stevens, 938 P.2d 780 (Or. 1997).

State v. Thomas, 423 N.E.2d 137, 66 Ohio St.2d 578 (Ohio 1981).

State v. Wanrow, 549 P.2d 548, 88 Wash. 2d 221 (Wash. 1977).

Strauss, K. L. (1996). Differential diagnosis of battered women through psychological testing: Personality disorder or posttraumatic stress disorder? *Dissertation Abstracts International: Section B: The Sciences and Engineering, 57*(3-B), 2166.

Tolman, R. (1989). The development of a measure of psychological maltreatment of women by their male partners. *Violence and Victims, 4,* 159–177.

United States v. Johnson, 956 F.2d 894 (9th Cir. 1992).

Vitanza, S., Vogel, L. C. M., & Marshall, L. L. (1995). Distress and symptoms of posttraumatic stress disorder in abused women. *Violence and Victims, 10,* 23–34.

Walker, L. E. (1979). *The battered woman.* New York: Harper & Row.

Walker, L. E. (1983). Victimology and the psychological perspectives of battered women. *Victimology: An International Journal, 8,* 82–104.

Walker, L. E. (1984). *The battered woman syndrome.* New York: Springer.

Walker, L. E. (1989). *Terrifying love.* New York: Harper Perennial.

Warren, J., & Lanning, W. (1992). Sex role beliefs, control, and social isolation of battered women. *Journal of Family Violence, 7,* 1–8.

CHAPTER 25

Pathologies of Attachment, Violence, and Criminality

J. REID MELOY

One of the great paradoxes of human existence is that most interpersonal violence occurs between people who are attached or bonded to each other. Proximity seeking toward another and acute distress when unpredictably or permanently separated, the empirical components of attachment, appear to be the most fertile territory for physical combat. This is an association filled with irony, reminding one that the tendency to "debasement in the sphere of love" (Freud, 1912, p. 177) is a widely observed phenomenon.

Violent attachments (Meloy, 1992) are not lost in the commonsense behavior of those professionals charged with risk managing violent individuals: Judges are most likely to issue protection or restraining orders to prevent domestic violence; homicide detectives first suspect sexually or affectionately intimate members of the victim's kinship network when investigating a murder; and child abuse as a form of interpersonal violence has received an enormous amount of publicly funded legal, clinical, and research attention during the past quarter-century.

The clinical and forensic investigation of the relationship among attachment, violence, and criminality is quite recent and very promising. In this chapter, I summarize and highlight this situation, argue for its relevance on the basis of

clinical and empirical evidence in two emerging areas of criminality, develop theoretical links to other areas of forensic knowledge, and suggest directions for both future forensic research and practical applications.

THE ORIGINS OF ATTACHMENT THEORY AND RESEARCH

Attachment is a biologically rooted, species-specific behavioral system that, when activated, maintains close proximity between a child and his or her caretaker. It was first proposed and investigated by John Bowlby, James Robertson, and Mary Ainsworth at the Tavistock Clinic in London following World War II (Ainsworth & Bowlby, 1954; Bowlby, 1953; Robertson & Bowlby, 1952). Attachment behaviors are evident in both birds and mammals, but are generally absent in reptiles. Individuals with reptiles as pets often misinterpret their thermotropic (heat-seeking) behavior as an emotion related to attachment or bonding and project on the animal their own affectionate feelings.

John Bowlby was the fourth child born to a London surgeon and a country parson's daughter. He was trained as a child psychiatrist and joined the British Psychoanalytic Society at a time when there was great turmoil between the followers of Melanie Klein and those of Anna Freud. Bowlby's personal analyst was Joan Riviere, and one of his

This chapter was supported by a grant from Forensis, Inc. (www.forensis.org).

supervisors was Klein. Troubled by the dogmatism of psychoanalysis at the time, its extrapolations from the couch to the crib, and its dismissive attitude toward empirical investigation of normal development, Bowlby's long-standing interests in Darwinism led him to the new science of ethology. This provided him with a truly scientific framework within which to reformulate his psychoanalytic knowledge. Attachment theory began (Holmes, 1995).

The origins of attachment theory are found in three psychoanalytic papers (Bowlby, 1958, 1960, 1961) which were later expanded into Bowlby's trilogy of books: *Attachment* (1969), *Separation* (1973), and *Loss* (1980). The early papers emphasized three findings: (a) There is a primary attachment between mother and child that is "hard-wired" and whose evolutionary purpose is to protect the infant from predators; (b) anxiety is an affective response to either separation from a loved one or external threat; and (c) infants and children experience grief when they experience loss. Although these postulates are accepted by most contemporary psychologists, they were revolutionary during their time because they challenged the primacy of sexuality in development and emphasized the impact of evolution and biology on personality. Attachment theory was an interpersonal theory of mind that stressed an essential harmony between mother and child unless it was disturbed. Bowlby unified the psychoanalytic world against him for nearly 20 years; he began to achieve a rapprochement only after his appointment as Freud Memorial Professor of Psychoanalysis at University College in London, an appointment now held by his heir-apparent, Peter Fonagy.

Mary Salter Ainsworth, a Canadian psychologist who studied at the University of Toronto, accompanied her husband to London in 1950 and answered a job advertisement in the London *Times* for a research position investigating the impact of maternal separation on personality development. This serendipitous event changed her life, and she collaborated with Bowlby for many years to come. She left for Africa with her husband in 1953 and conducted the first empirical study of normal attachment among 26 families with unweaned babies in Uganda. It was here that she began to validate Bowlby's ethological theory of attachment and also the importance of maternal sensitivity in attachment quality. The genesis of secure and insecure attachment can be found in the "Ganda data" (Ainsworth, 1967).

While mulling over the findings from Africa, Ainsworth began a second observational study with 26 families after she relocated to Baltimore in 1963. She collected 72 hours of data during home visits that spanned the first year of the newborns' lives. These meticulous narratives documented the difficulties some mothers had responding to their baby's cues, and the interactions in the first quarter of observation

predicted the nature of the mother-infant relationship in the last quarter. The Baltimore work also led to the formulation of the "Strange Situation," a 20-minute contrived naturalistic experiment that examined attachment and exploration under minimal and maximal stress. Mother and baby would play, a stranger would enter the room, mother would leave briefly and then return. The various stages of this experiment allowed Ainsworth to discern differences in the infants' reunion behavior with their mother. Most of the infants were immediately soothed by their mother's return and quickly responded to her nurturing. A few, however, were very angry, cried and wanted contact, but would not cuddle and accept the nurturing. They were markedly ambivalent. Others would dismiss and ignore the mother even if they searched for her until she returned. They were avoidant. Robertson (1953) had documented similar behaviors in his film, *A Two Year Old Goes to Hospital,* and Harlow (1961) had noticed similar patterns in some monkeys. The Baltimore studies are remembered for the development of the Strange Situation classification system, which identified three attachment styles: secure, avoidant, and ambivalent/resistant (Ainsworth, Blehar, Waters, & Wall, 1978).

THE PSYCHOBIOLOGY OF ATTACHMENT

Secure or normal attachment assures proximity of the child to the attachment figure, usually the mother. Smiling, vocalizing, and approaching are signaling behaviors that communicate a desire on the part of the child for interaction; other behaviors, most notably crying, are aversive events for the mother and bring her close to the child to terminate them, a negative reinforcement for both caregiver and child through the alleviation of their mutual distress.

From an evolutionary perspective, attachment behavior ensures the survival of the child by protecting him or her from predators. Although Bowlby (1969) originally emphasized survival of the species as the goal of attachment, contemporary evolutionary thinking has refocused on the reproductive fitness of the child if he or she grows up, thus increasing the probability that the genes of the individual will survive into the next generation. If the child is eaten, a seemingly universal and unconscious fear that has sparked both intellectual curiosity (Freud, 1919) and enormous cinematic success (*Jaws*), there will be no future children.

Attachment as a Behavioral System

Attachment is a species-specific system of behaviors that leads to certain predictable outcomes through *organization*. It can "goal-correct," depending on the behavior of the caregiver. My dog Rubin shows this very clearly. If I call him from a distance, he begins running toward me; if I move from my original location, he will adjust the vector of his approach to most efficiently arrive next to me. His goal—proximity to his caretaker—does not change but his adaptation is fluid. This is theory based on a control-systems perspective (Ashby, 1956). Bowlby (1969) emphasized that the goal is not the object, but rather behavioral homeostasis: optimal distance from the caregiver. The attachment system is activated in many contexts, two of which are danger and stress. If the child is hungry, in pain, or ill, he or she will approach the caretaker; if the child is threatened by a stranger, he or she will also approach the caretaker.

Biology and Attachment

There is a growing body of research indicating that attachment behavior is influenced by and causes changes in various biological mechanisms. Hofer (1995; Polan & Hofer, 1999) has made significant contributions in his study of rat pups in his laboratory. For example, milk and other nutrients reduce the rate of calling behavior of the pups for their mother due to the stimulation of intraoral sensory receptors, an effect that is mediated by endogenous opioids. This connects attachment behaviors organized around suckling to less vocalization during comforting, and strengthens the association between oral ingestive behavior and the formation of a bond. In other research, human infants who appear stressed during Ainsworth's Strange Situation are likely to exhibit increases in measurable cortisol levels in saliva (Nachmias, Gunnar, Mangelsdorf, Parritz, & Buss, 1996). Individual differences in infant temperament, a largely heritable characteristic, show distinct physiological markers when the infant is distressed in the Strange Situation, which likely influence attachment behavior and attachment classification (Fox & Card, 1999). Based on a growing body of empirical evidence, Fisher (1998) theorized that the primary neuroregulators of attachment in humans are the hormones oxytocin and vasso-pressin, what she has termed the "cuddly chemicals." She has developed a model of three relatively independent, evolutionarily evolved psychobiological systems that regulate behaviors related to lust, attraction, and attachment.

Emotion and Cognition

Bowlby (1979) was very clear on the importance of emotions in relation to attachment. He observed that the most intense emotions arise during the formation, maintenance, disruption, and renewal of attached relationships: "Threat of loss arouses anxiety and actual loss gives rise to sorrow; whilst each of these situations is likely to arouse anger. The unchallenged maintenance of a bond is experienced as a source of joy" (p. 130). The evolutionary purpose of emotion in relation to attachment is that humans actively work to maintain a bond to another due to the pleasure it brings, which, in turn, enhances their reproductive fitness or success: their likelihood of mating. Emotions serve as conscious regulators of attachment behavior, and when conditioned in a secure context as an infant, provide a template for approach and avoidance behavior in adulthood.

Cognitions have played an increasingly complex role in the development of attachment theory and research. Bowlby (1969) originally proposed that cognitions, which he referred to as "internal working models" or "representational models," were derived from actual experience of the self, the caretaker, and the environment. They also serve a regulatory function, and are active motivational schematas that internally represent the external world, more or less accurately, and predict future interpersonal experience. When the child is operating from a secure base, internal working models can be adaptively updated with new experience. "Defensive exclusion," however, may be used to ward off perceptions, feelings, and thoughts that provoke anxiety or suffering. Bowlby's rethinking of the psychoanalytic term "defense" is broader and more active than the Freudian construct; it postulates that children, because of the frequency and intensity of their attachment arousal, are especially vulnerable to defensive exclusion. A consequence is that different and incompatible sets of internal working models may begin to operate that, in themselves, may cause contradictory behavior and maladaptation later in life: for example, the conscious idealization of a mother by a criminal, who was, in fact, severely neglected by her, and subsequently as an adult has become a serial rapist. As Bowlby wrote in 1979:

> The more details one comes to know about the events in a child's life, and about what he has been told, what he has overheard and what he has observed but is not supposed to know, the more clearly can his ideas about the world and what may happen in the future be seen as perfectly reasonable constructions. (p. 23)

Bowlby's work on cognitions drew from his psychoanalytic training and is somewhat convergent with contemporary object-relations theory (Fonagy, 1999c). It was also heavily influenced by George Herbert Mead's (1934) symbolic interactionism and the social psychologists Kurt Lewin (1933) and Fritz Heider (1958). Fonagy's (1999b) work on "mentalizing" and the reflective capacity is an important extension of the role of thought and feeling in attachment. He has been able to empirically measure the parent's capacity to mentally represent the child as a whole, real, and meaningful human being, and has shown its causative impact on the child's secure or insecure attachment behavior.

Attachment and Exploration

There is an exploratory behavioral system that is biologically based and complements attachment. When a child feels secure, what Ainsworth (1963) called a secure base from which to explore, the attachment system is not activated and the child can go forth and gather new information about how the world works. This dynamic equilibrium is mutually inhibiting; when there is a threat or a potential hazard, exploratory behavior will diminish or cease altogether as the attachment system activates. Empirical research has demonstrated that the infant's belief that the mother will be available when needed enhances exploration (Sorce & Emde, 1981). In several studies (Ainsworth & Wittig, 1969; Carr, Dabbs, & Carr, 1975), the mother's physical or psychological presence was experimentally manipulated, producing data that strongly supported the theoretical association between maternal availability and infant exploration, what Ainsworth referred to as an "attachment-exploration balance" (Ainsworth, Bell, & Stayton, 1971).

Attachment and Fear

Although fear is evoked when there is a real threat, there appears to be a fear behavioral system that initiates attachment seeking when danger is *likely*. Bowlby (1973) called the stimuli that trigger this system "natural clues to danger." He included such things as high places, darkness, loud noises, aloneness, and sudden looming movements. These clues are not inherently dangerous, but provoke attachment behaviors that, in turn, diminish fear if the caretaker is accessible. These clues are distinguishable from other objects that provoke fear that are inherently dangerous to infants, such as poisonous and predatory creatures (some spiders, snakes, and large mammals). The infant's capacity to experience fear in all of these situations is an evolutionarily adaptive trait that contributes to its survival and eventual reproductive success.

Attachment and Socialization

Individuals in the company of others are much less likely to be killed by predators (Eisenberg, 1966). In addition, there are other important survival advantages to spending time with people, including food gathering, building shelters, learning, and finding a mate. Affiliative or social behavior,

however, is *not* attachment, although it does appear to be a behavioral system that is activated under certain circumstances. Children, for example, engage in more playful activity with their peers when their attachment to a primary caretaker is secure (Bowlby, 1969). Harlow (1969) showed, moreover, that monkeys reared with their mother but without peers were subsequently impaired in their adult social, mating, and parenting behavior. Bowlby understood affiliation as a broader concept than attachment, the former covering all "friendliness and goodwill, of the desire to do things in the company of others," but without the object specificity of attachment (p. 229).

Attachment and Caregiving

There also appears to be a biologically based caregiving system that protects the child and works in concert with attachment. When caregiving is activated by the parent, the child's attachment seeking is unnecessary and deactivated. When the child is an infant, the chief caregiving behavior is retrieval. Exploratory behavior is also enhanced if caregiving is activated. Cassidy (1999) noted that a child exploring a park will cover much more territory if the mother actively follows. Caregiving is activated by a variety of internal (hormones, beliefs, fatigue states, emotions, and attachment style of the mother) and external clues (familiarity of the environment, presence of danger, and behavior of the infant). Cassidy proposed that soothing also facilitates caregiving by ensuring the monitoring of potential or real dangers to the child; for instance, continued holding of the child after his or her distress subsides may reveal a splinter in the child's finger.

Attachment Behavior and the Attachment Bond

Attachment behavior is not the same as a bond to another person. Empirical research has substantiated that attachment behavior exists throughout the human life cycle, and early attachment experiences predict to a certain degree later attachment expectancies and behaviors (Cassidy & Shaver, 1999). Crowell, Fraley, and Shaver (1999) caution, however, that measurement of attachment across methods (interview versus self-report) and domains (parent versus romantic partner) produces different correlations, averaging $r = .39$ and $r = .31$, respectively. Ainsworth (1989) described six criteria for an attachment bond: (a) it is persistent; (b) it involves a specific person; (c) it is emotionally significant; (d) proximity with the person is wished for and sought; (e) distress is felt when there is involuntary separation; and (f) the relationship brings security and comfort. Although activation of the attachment behavioral system is situational, and often initiated by an internal or external threat, an attachment bond exists over time and can be inferred, but not observed.

The importance of this distinction is clear if we assume, for a moment, that there is no distinction. Then we would wrongly conclude that a child who fearfully clings to his or her mother is securely bonded to her; a child who has lost his or her mother and temporarily seeks comfort from a stranger is bonded to the stranger; and a child who confidently plays with another child in the presence of his or her mother, but does not seek her comfort, is not bonded to her. The difference is even more apparent when we turn to abnormal or pathological attachments. Paradoxically, the absence of a secure bond activates the attachment behavioral system in unusual, strange, and sometimes dangerous ways.

PATHOLOGIES OF ATTACHMENT

Two pathological forms of attachment were first discovered by Ainsworth et al. (1978) in the Strange Situation. The avoidant infants (Type A) were exploratory without paying attention to mother's location, were minimally distressed when she left, and largely ignored her when she returned. The secure infants (Type B) competently expressed their needs and accepted maternal care. The ambivalent/resistant infants (Type C) had difficulty separating from their mother and exploring or playing in the environment, were also very distressed when mother left, but could not "settle in" with her when she returned. Separation distress did not distinguish secure from insecure (avoidant or ambivalent) infants; all three groups evidenced such distress to one degree or another. The reunion behaviors most clearly demarcated the groups.

These three forms of attachment behavior worked well in research for many years and were used to successfully test the hypothesis that attachment types were generally stable from childhood to adulthood (Goldberg, Muir, & Kerr, 1995). There were always some subjects, however, who could not be classified, especially in research with clinical samples. Main and Solomon (1986, 1990) subsequently developed criteria for a fourth type: disorganized/disoriented attachment (Type D). These infants had no organized strategy for managing arousal during the activation of their attachment behavioral system while seeking comfort and security. Behaviors included apprehensiveness, helplessness, depression, unexpected alterations in approach or avoidance toward mother, prolonged "freezing," and psychomotor slowing. Cortisol levels remained significantly elevated and higher than other, more organized attachment types, whether secure or insecure (Spangler & Grossman, 1993).

Disorganized attachment in infants has been associated with severe maternal psychosocial problems, including depression, history of violence or abuse, inpatient psychiatric history, and the mother's own abuse of the infant (Lyons-Ruth, Repacholi, McLeod, & Silva, 1991). By 6 years of age, disorganized attachment often becomes controlling behavior toward the mother, either caregiving or coercive, and this role reversal is often accompanied by childhood aggression and a disparity between verbal and performance IQ (Lyons-Ruth et al., 1991). It appears strongly related to diagnoses of oppositional defiant disorder, conduct disorder, and other externalizing problems in childhood (Lyons-Ruth, 1996). Most interestingly, disorganized attachment in infants is reliably predicted by the mother's lack of resolution of a previous loss or trauma, measured before the birth of the child (van Ijzendoorn, 1995). For example, a mother who suffered from posttraumatic stress disorder due to chronic physical abuse by her ex-boyfriend is at great risk to raise a child who evidences disorganized attachment within the first few years of life. Main and Hesse (1990) theorized that this intergenerational transmission of attachment is related to frightening or frightened parental behavior and may be a product of dissociation in the parent. Other psychiatric disorders in parents may also be strongly related to risk of disorganized attachment in infants (Lyons-Ruth, 1996).

Models of adult attachment have been developed by Hazan and Shaver (1987), Main, Kaplan, and Cassidy (1985), and Bartholomew (1990, 1994, 1997). The latter's work is most promising because it is consistent with earlier infant and childhood theories of attachment, further delineates avoidant strategies, and incorporates an object- and self-representational perspective. It contains three pathological types:

1. *Preoccupied* individuals have a negative perception of self and a positive perception of others. Attachment behaviors and internal regulation of arousal have been conditioned by inconsistent parenting in childhood. They blame themselves for a lack of love and appear to be very dependent in their attempts to gain others' approval and acceptance.

2. *Fearful* individuals have a negative perception of both self and others and avoid close contact, usually due to a history of rejecting or unresponsive parents. Others are viewed as uncaring due to the fearful individual's unlovable nature. Although they desire acceptance, they fear rejection.

3. *Dismissing* individuals have a positive perception of self and a negative perception of others. They have managed rejecting or unresponsive parents by distancing and becoming self-reliant, inoculating themselves against the devaluation they have learned to expect.

Bartholomew has used a circumplex model of interpersonal behavior to validate her attachment prototypes along dimensions of control and affiliation (Bartholomew & Horowitz, 1991). There has also been substantial research on both concurrent and predictive validity of her model (Bartholomew, 1997). The fourth type of adult attachment pathology, which is not included in her model, is the *disorganized* individual. Although research with such adults is limited, it appears closely associated with severely disturbed clinical and forensic samples of individuals (Fonagy, 1999b).

These four adult attachment pathologies—preoccupied, fearful, dismissing, and disorganized—are becoming keys to unlocking the raison d'être for violent attachments.

ATTACHMENT AND VIOLENCE

Although there have been many models proposed for classifying violence, converging lines of theory and empirical research have divided violence into two modes: predatory (instrumental, premeditated, attack) and affective (impulsive, reactive, defensive). Labels have varied, but the underlying characteristics have been similarly described and, in some cases, measured by different research groups (Barratt, Stanford, Felthous, & Kent, 1997; Cornell et al., 1996; Meloy, 1988, 1997; Raine et al., 1998). *Predatory violence* is planned, purposeful, and emotionless, with absent autonomic arousal. *Affective violence* is a reaction to a threat, accompanied by anger and fear, and involves high levels of autonomic (sympathetic) arousal. The evolutionary basis of predatory violence is hunting; affective violence is rooted in a protective and defensive response to an imminent threat. Both serve reproductive success and genetic viability. In other words, our ancestors thousands of years ago were adept at both predatory and affective violence (more so than their neighbors who did not survive to reproduce and raise their young).

Research on attachment and violence during the past decade has largely focused on intimate partner, or domestic, violence. There has been limited research on attachment and violent criminality. The discoveries are new and very promising.

Intimate Partner Violence

In July 2000, the U.S. Department of Justice published findings from the National Violence Against Women Survey concerning the extent, nature, and consequences of intimate partner violence (Tjaden & Thoennes, 2000). Risk factors associated with intimate partner violence were discerned using logistic regression on separate samples of women (N = 4,896) and men (N = 5,056). The strongest predictor of victimization by an intimate partner for both men and women was physical assault as a child by a caretaker. Other predictors included unmarried (but cohabitating) status, African American race, verbal abuse by the partner, jealousy or possessiveness, and educational or racial disparities between the partners. The authors wrote, "Violence perpetrated against women by male partners is part of a systematic pattern of dominance and control, or what some researchers have called 'patriarchal terrorism'" (p. 34). Despite the merit of these empirical findings, attachment theory, even the word attachment, was never used throughout this study. Instead, the authors chose to interpret their findings in a narrower feminist sense, which begs the question: If American society is suffused with "patriarchal terrorism," why is it that most men do not assault their intimate partner?

I think the psychosocially deeper and more comprehensive answer to this question is that most men form secure attachments. The ones who are not capable of forming such attachments are at greatest risk for intimate partner violence. Research continues to accumulate that empirically supports the general hypothesis that insecure attachments are significantly associated with, and in some cases intergenerationally predict (Adamson, 1998), intimate partner violence (Holtzworth-Munroe, Stuart, & Hutchison, 1997). Most studies have focused on the male's attachment pathology (Dutton, 1995a), but some recent studies indicate that securely attached individuals are more likely to form sexual pair bonds, devoid of violence, with each other. The sexual intimates of insecurely attached individuals, on the other hand, are also likely to have a history of insecure attachment, thus embarking on a pathogenic dance that is at greater risk of violence (Babcock, Jacobson, Gottman, & Yerington, 2000; Irwin, 1999). Birds of a feather appear to flock together. Tjaden and Thoennes (2000) also found that intimate partner violence was highest among homosexual males and lowest among homosexual females, an important point of reference that underscores the biological propensity of men to be more violent than women regardless of their target. Such findings also contradict the argument that any psychopathology, including attachment, in the (usually) female victim of domestic violence is irrelevant to understanding the violence, and is nothing more than "blaming the victim." Attachment pathology in the male perpetrator of domestic violence also appears to be a more stable correlate than any one specific personality disorder (Tweed & Dutton, 1998; Waltz, Babcock, Jacobson, & Gottman, 2000).

Several researchers and their colleagues dominate the work in this area, and despite different foci, each has shaped scientific thinking about intimate partner violence and attachment.

Kesner conducted two studies (Kesner, Julian, & McKenry, 1997; Kesner & McKenry, 1998) drawing on Bowlby's (1984) notion that intimate violence may be a product of maladaptive anger to keep the partner from separating. In his first study of violent male spouses (Kesner et al., 1997), he found that attachment variables served as unique predictors of male intimate violence: (a) the male's recollection of his relationship with his mother (a perceived deficiency in love and caring), and (b) his perceived relationship support from his spouse. In his second study (Kesner & McKenry, 1998) of heterosexual couples, he found that attachment factors of both the male and female partners were unique predictors of male violence; specifically, the males were more fearfully attached and less secure, and their female partner had more of a dismissing attachment and were less secure. He wrote, "The anger that acts to communicate fear of separation in the secure relationship intensifies into violent behavior by the fearful individual in a gross escalation of this anger" (p. 429). Concurrent life stressors failed to predict violence. Kesner's work empirically supports the importance of a negative maternal transference in male batterers and the contribution to the violence of the victim's insecure attachment, and also emphasizes the affective, rather than predatory, mode of violence in the couples whom he has studied.

Downey and her colleagues have made similarly important contributions. In two recent papers (Downey & Feldman, 1996; Downey, Feldman, & Ayduk, 2000), she has studied "rejection sensitivity" as predictive of male violence toward romantic partners. Defining her construct as "the disposition to anxiously expect, readily perceive, and intensely react to rejection by significant others" (p. 45), Downey has shown that it is a vulnerability factor for two maladaptive styles of coping with intimacy: fearful avoidance of such an intimate, and a preoccupied search for an unconditionally supportive intimate. The latter style predicted relationship violence, usually affective, in a large nonclinical sample of college males (Downey et al., 2000). Rejection sensitivity (what Gabbard, 1989, termed "hypervigilant narcissism") may be an important personality trait that is a product of insecure attachment. In a related study, Oderberg (1995) found in a sample of college undergraduates that witnessing parental violence as a child was positively associated with insecure attachment as a young adult.

Dutton (1995a, 1998) and his colleagues have made enormous contributions to our understanding of domestic violence. Their discoveries have emerged along three lines of research: the etiology of intimate violence; the perpetuation of intimate violence (in particular, the reasons why a victim stays in the abusive relationship); and typologies of intimately violent men.

Dutton's work is unique among these researchers because he has used both attachment and object-relations theories to propose hypotheses concerning batterers, developed instruments when needed to measure his hypotheses, and then tested them on various samples of batterers in treatment programs and in prisons around Vancouver, Canada. He has shown that the etiology of battering is not simply child abuse of the batterer when he was a young boy. Instead, shaming of a child by a caretaker, witnessing violence directed toward the self or mother, and insecure attachment (fearful or preoccupied) form a triad that predicts battering as a adult (Dutton, 1999). All contribute to the formation of a borderline personality organization (Kernberg, 1984) that stimulates an "intimacy anger" when in a relationship. This largely impulsive group of batterers are prone to experience rejection anxiety, which is quickly converted into abandonment rage when loss is imminent and is then violently expressed to diminish tension (Dutton, 1994, 1995a, 1995b, 1995c). His empirical findings using various predictive statistical models have validated his etiological theories (Dutton, 1998).

The continuation of violence by the batterer, largely through the inability of the victim to leave the relationship, led Dutton and his colleagues to apply the theory of traumatic bonding to such phenomena. Drawing on the social psychology hypothesis of a traumatic bond that forms between hostage and hostage taker, the so-called Stockholm Syndrome, he and his student (Painter & Dutton, 1985) posited that reinforcement mechanisms interact with extreme power differentials to constitute traumatic bonding. For example, both intermittent punishment (the onset of violence) and negative reinforcement (the termination of violence) can further cement the relationship. In a subsequent study (Dutton & Painter, 1993), their hypothesis was empirically tested and demonstrated that 55% of the variance in their attachment measure of female victims six months after separation was accounted for by the traumatic bonding variables. They emphasized the prolonged effects of abuse and dismissed other, more static, theories of female victimization, such as masochism.

Another area in which Dutton has made important contributions is the development of a typology for batterers. Drawing on the earlier work of Hamberger and Hastings (1986) and Holtzworth-Munroe and Stuart (1994), which identified three subgroups of batterers—the generally violent/antisocial, dysphoric/borderline, and family only/overcontrolled—his work has refined our understanding of the first two groups. Dutton (1998) has referred to the dysphoric/borderline group of batterers as the "abusive personality." Characteristics of this subgroup include a fearful attachment style, borderline personality organization, chronic anger, and impulsivity. They are withdrawn, asocial, moody, hypersensitive to slights, volatile, reactive, and oscillate rapidly between indifference and rage. The modal *Diagnostic and Statistical Manual of Mental Disorders* (*DSM-IV;* American Psychiatric Association, 1994) diagnosis appears to be borderline personality disorder. Saunders (1992) referred to them as the Type 3, Emotionally Volatile group. I earlier described the etiology of this group, which appear to make up 25% of batterers in treatment. Their violence is affective rather than predatory.

The generally violent/antisocial group is the most psychopathic of the batterers. Although psychopathy has yet to be directly measured in a study of spousal batterers, this group tends to elevate on the Antisocial, Narcissistic, and Aggressive-Sadistic scales of the Millon Clinical Multiaxial Inventory II (MCMI-II; Millon, 1981). They are also more severely physically violent, are narcissistically entitled, and manipulative. In contrast to the dysphoric/borderline group, they exhibit low levels of depression and anger. Their abuse of drugs and alcohol is frequent, and they are more violent outside the home than other groups. They also represent approximately 25% of batterers (Holtzworth-Munroe & Stuart, 1994). They have moderate marital satisfaction, but fail to achieve any sense of relationship reciprocity or whole-object relatedness to their partner (in analytic terms, she remains a selfobject or part-object). Most interestingly, their violence is predatory (instrumental): planned, purposeful, and emotionless. Their attachment pathology, however, appears to be preoccupied, but not fearful. Although at first blush, this appears contradictory, and one would expect a dismissive attachment style, Tweed and Dutton (1998) note that such an attachment pattern would not motivate a high investment in a troubled relationship nor an ongoing effort to use violence to control a partner. What appears to be present is, instead, a preoccupation with attaining a relationship in which the psychopathic batterer dominates and controls his partner. Measurement of psychopathy in a future study of batterers will clarify this issue. The severe psychopath—individuals that score ≥30 on the Psychopathy Checklist–Revised (PCL-R; Hare, 1991)—may be relatively infrequent among spousal batterers because all of his relationships are generally fleeting. Without any capacity to attach or bond, he moves on to another sexual object, engaging in a pattern of search polygyny (Meloy, 1992, 2000b) that precludes any sustained effort to control a noncompliant mate. The batterers in Dutton's instrumental group are likely to be significantly more psychopathic than his impulsive group, but may not be severe psychopaths.

Gottman and Jacobson (Gottman et al., 1995) have directed their research efforts toward understanding and treating marital violence for a number of years, and have likewise made enormous contributions. Most recently, they have validated the three types of batterers, which they call generally violent, pathological, and family only (Waltz et al., 2000), the typology originally proposed by Holtzworth-Munroe and Stuart (1994). Although the first two groups did not differ on personality disorder—both elevated on the borderline and antisocial scales of the MCMI-II—the types differed as predicted on the frequency of their emotionally abusive behavior, their history of witnessing parental violence, attachment pathologies, jealousy, and presence of chemical abuse. (The authors also noted the high overlap between these scales on the MCMI-II and their correlation of 0.64. The MCMI-III, however, shares only 18% of items between these two scales, suggesting further research may benefit by using the latter measure.) The generally violent men were dismissing and avoidant, whereas the pathological men were preoccupied and ambivalent. The "family-only" batterers showed a "compulsive care-seeking" attachment style.

Their most compelling work, moreover, has been in the area of physiology, emotional regulation, and marital violence. In an earlier study which received considerable attention, Gottman et al. (1995) recruited a sample of couples with maritally violent histories and measured their physiology in the laboratory while the pair engaged in conversations about highly conflicted issues in their relationship. They identified two groups: Type I batterers (<20% of their sample) demonstrated heart rate decreases during intimate conflict; Type II batterers demonstrated heart rate increases. They referred to the former as "vagal reactors," in reference to the vagus nerve, which, when activated, reduces autonomic arousal. This group was also more likely to be generally violent and antisocial, and had scale elevations on the MCMI-II for Antisocial and Aggressive-Sadistic behavior. Although they did not measure psychopathy, nor discuss it in this study, their findings were highly consistent with the autonomic hyporeactivity that has been documented in psychopaths for decades, particularly in aversive circumstances (Meloy, 1988). Low resting heart rate is also one of the most replicated physiological findings among adolescent delinquents, and is a measurable aspect of the chronic cortical underarousal seen in habitual criminals (Raine, 1993). Most interestingly, during long-term followup, none of the women married to these men had left them.

Babcock et al. (2000) further advanced their work in a study that integrated attachment pathology as an "index of emotional regulation" (p. 392) and the function of violence in marital relationships. They viewed insecure attachment along a dimension of deactivation (dismissing) versus hyperactivation (preoccupied) attentional systems that serve to regulate affect during stress. They showed, first of all, that violence was most likely to occur in an insecure attachment according to the Adult Attachment Interview (AAI; Main & Goldwyn, 1984).

The AAI is a semistructured interview about childhood attachment experiences that has been refined and expanded over the past 15 years (Main & Goldwyn, 1994) but has yet to be published. Extensive training is required to use the instrument. The narrative of the interview is transcribed and scored according to three criteria: (a) the coder's assessment of the subject's childhood experiences; (b) the language used by the subject during the interview; and (c) the individual's ability to give an integrated and credible account of his or her experiences as a child. Two sets of scales, Parental Behavior and State of Mind, result in the assignment of the subject to one of three major classifications: secure, dismissing, or preoccupied. Individuals may also be classified as "unresolved" (what I have termed "disorganized" in this chapter) and "cannot classify." The AAI is the gold standard for assessment of attachment (Crowell et al., 1999).

Babcock et al. (2000) further demonstrated two functional patterns of intimate partner violence that were tied to both attachment pathology in the male and triggering behavior in the female. The dismissing batterers were most likely to use violence instrumentally (a predatory mode) to control the behavior of their spouse. This subgroup also had the most extensive antisocial traits and were likely the most psychopathic of their types; although, once again, psychopathy was not directly measured. They were also most likely to be violent when the spouse became defensive during an argument. The preoccupied batters were most likely to use violence expressively (an affective mode) to regulate affect in their interaction with their spouse. They were most likely to be violent when she attempted to withdraw during an argument. Both attachment pathologies tended to be more domineering than the secure husbands. The researchers hypothesized that the dismissing batterers used a controlling and distancing style of interaction to get what they wanted, whereas the preoccupied batterers were remarkable for their inability to use distancing and disengage from conflict: When their spouse withdrew, they perceived imminent abandonment, and their anger escalated into dysregulated fury and violence.

Holtzworth-Munroe and her colleagues (Holtzworth-Munroe & Stuart, 1994) have been the undisputed leaders in the formulation of a reliable and valid overall batterer typology. Their theory is an intrapersonal one, focusing on the predisposing and precipitating factors *within the batterer* that contribute to his violence.

Following a review of the existing research, Holtzworth-Munroe and Stuart (1994) theorized that batterers could be categorized along three descriptive dimensions: (a) the severity and frequency of marital violence, (b) the generality of violence, and (c) the batterer's psychopathology or personality disorder. This dimensional approach yielded three types previously mentioned: the family-only batterers, the dysphoric-borderline batterers, and the generally violent-antisocial batterers. They further proposed a developmental course for the three types, which included both historical (e.g., genetic and prenatal factors, violence in the family of origin) and proximal correlates (e.g., attachment style, dependency, hostility toward women, social skills). They built predictions for their model based on their proposed types and risk factors.

One hundred and two men were recruited from the community to test their model (Holtzworth-Munroe, Meehan, Herron, Rehman, & Stuart, in press), selected on the basis of a wide range of violence toward their spouse. Two nonviolent comparison samples were also recruited (distressed and not distressed). When they completed their analyses of both their dependent and independent variables, their three predicted subgroups emerged, along with a fourth group. The subgroups generally differed along their three descriptive dimensions and their proposed developmental risk factors. One independent research group has also found three subgroups that closely fit the Holtzworth-Munroe and Stuart typology (Hamberger, Lohr, Bonge, & Tolin, 1996).

The fourth unpredicted cluster was labeled the "low-level antisocial" group. These men appear to fall within an intermediate range on a number of variables between the family-only and the generally violent-antisocial groups. Holtzworth-Munroe (2000) argued that the family-only group in their community sample probably represents the young, newlywed couples where low levels of aggression are almost normative (O'Leary et al., 1989). These men, however, did not differ on measures of attachment or psychopathology from the nonviolent but distressed comparison group. It may be that their violence is socioculturally based, rather than rooted in any psychological abnormalities.

Holtzworth-Munroe (2000) also proposed a condensing of her three descriptive dimensions into two: an antisocial continuum (measurement of psychopathy would work best here) and a borderline continuum (perhaps a measure of borderline personality organization) to account for the severity of violence and the degree of attachment pathology, respectively. She also emphasized the dynamic, rather than static, nature of spousal violence, and endorsed, at least in theory, the application of predatory versus affective modes of violence in demarcating the behavior of the generally violent-antisocial from the borderline-dysphoric batterer.

Fonagy (1999c) and his colleagues have charted exciting new territory in our understanding of violent attachments and the psychology of the self. Approaching attachment theory from the perspective of psychoanalysis, their theoretical and empirical work has focused on the "mentalizing" function and the reflective self, the capacity of an individual to recognize subjective states and the subjectivity, or inner states, of others. This is the experience of oneself and others as having wishes, feelings, thoughts, desires, beliefs, and expectations—in short, an "intentionality" that is motivated by an internal psychology. Fonagy's work is a deepening and broadening of Bowlby's (1961) early theory on internal working models that, in essence, posits that the absence of a theory of mind (a theory of self) is a fundamental cause of insecurity of attachment and, in certain cases, intimate violence. As Fonagy (1999a) wrote:

> The child finds himself in the caregiver's mind as an intentional being motivated by mental states, beliefs, and desires. This representation is internalized as the core of the psychological self. Thus, the realization of subjectivity might be more accurately stated: "My caregiver thinks of me as thinking, therefore I exist as a thinker." (pp. 12–13)

Fonagy has empirically tested his theory in a number of ways. Fonagy, Steele, Moran, Steele, and Higgitt (1991) found that the capacity for caregivers to reflect on mental states in themselves and others when describing their own childhood predicted their children's security of attachment. Reflective self ratings were reliable (r > .80) and provided a good prenatal prediction of their child's behavior in the Strange Situation experiment. Highly reflective parents were three or four times more likely to have secure children than low-reflective parents. In another study, Fonagy, Steele, Steele, Higgitt, and Target (1994) factored in social deprivation of the mother (single parent, living in overcrowded conditions, unemployed father, low income, etc.) to see if it would affect the impact of the reflective self on secure attachment. It did not. The deprived mothers with a capacity to fully represent and reflect on themselves and others all had securely attached infants, and virtually all of the deprived mothers who could not reflect had insecure infants. In a third study, children securely attached in infancy were more likely to cognitively understand the affective states in others at 5 years of age when compared to insecurely attached children (Fonagy, Redfern, & Charman, 1997).

The psychoanalytic basis of Fonagy's work is that children find themselves in the mind of their caretaker, and the psychobiological vehicle for this discovery is a loving and secure attachment. When this is not available, when, for instance, the parent is constantly angry at or even hates the children, the children's contemplation of the parent's feelings toward them is intolerable. Therefore, they do not think of themselves; rather, they internalize the hateful, perhaps persecutory mental representations of the parent. These hateful introjects then become a source of emotional volatility and turmoil in subsequent attachments throughout their life, as they continuously project them onto their intimates as a means of evacuating and controlling them. These individuals are clinically observed as impulsive, emotionally unstable, and prone to violence toward self and others; the diagnosis is often borderline personality disorder. Fonagy (1999a) has emphasized the importance of trauma and disorganized attachment in the genesis of such a personality disorder.

Although Fonagy's (1999b) theory of male violence toward female intimates has yet to be empirically tested, it is an elegant conceptual extension of his other work. The frequent childhood abuse and shaming of the male (Dutton, 1998) when he is little is managed by refusing to acknowledge his caretaker's thoughts about him and his wish to harm him. The lack of safety with his caretaker continuously triggers his attachment behavioral system, which is responded to with neglect or abuse. The nascent mentalizing stance in the child is disavowed, and under the combined pressure of needing comfort and escaping abuse from the same person, he disrupts his capacity to represent the mental states of himself and others. People become objects or bodies, rather than whole, real, and meaningful individuals. A failure of mentalizing also causes a moral disengagement for four reasons: (a) Individuals without a well-established sense of themselves have no sense of personal agency; (b) they cannot anticipate the psychological consequences of their actions on others; (c) others are treated as objects; and (d) rationalization and minimization (plausible but false fluidities of thinking) are more prominent (Fonagy, 1999a). Violence toward the intimate results from a maladaptive escalation of anger to keep the partner from neglecting or abandoning, as well as an overwhelming need to control the other so that intolerable self states can be projected (or projectively identified) into her. One 26-year-old male who killed his estranged wife told me, "I didn't know what to feel. I was in a rage and also numb. I needed to shoot the pain . . . I killed the woman I loved." A 38-year-old male who sexually assaulted and killed a 12-year-old girl told me that his father would always say to him, "The best part of you got spilled on your mother's bedsheets." These devaluing and hateful self and other representations constantly oscillate between two insecurely attached partners who attempt to manage, often unsuccessfully, a volatile interpersonal space.

Violence and Criminality

The research on attachment and other forms of criminal violence is much more limited than the intimate partner research. Antisocial personality disorder (*DSM-IV*), or conduct disorder in adolescence, appears to be associated with dismissing or disorganized attachment pathology. Allen, Hauser, and Borman-Spurrell (1996) found that both pathologies predicted criminality in a sample of adolescents 10 years after their attachment was measured. This prospective study compared adolescents who were psychiatric inpatients with a group of high school students. Derogation of attachment (dismissing) and lack of resolution of trauma (disorganized) were the best predictors, and did so when psychiatric hospitalization was controlled as a confounding variable. Likewise, Rosenstein and Horowitz (1996) found in a small sample of conduct disordered adolescents ($N = 7$) that most were classified as dismissing and none were classified as unresolved (disorganized). Fonagy et al. (1996) found that most paranoid and antisocial personality disordered adults in a nonrandom sample were classified as disorganized, with clearly unresolved trauma, when a four-category system of attachment classification was used.

The most compelling theory and supportive empirical findings concerning pathological attachment as a risk factor for violence and criminality have been advanced by Fonagy (1999a; Fonagy et al., 1997). In a small study comparing prison inmates, psychiatric patients, and controls (Levinson & Fonagy, cited in Fonagy, 1999a) using the AAI, the vast majority of the prisoners were classified as either dismissing (36%) or preoccupied (45%). Although 82% of psychiatric patients were disorganized, only a minority of prisoners were disorganized (36%). However, most of the prisoners had been physically or sexually abused, and neglect was also prevalent. Anger was highest among the prisoners, and their reflective function was lowest among the three groups. Reflective function among the violent prisoners, as measured by index offense, was significantly lower than among the nonviolent prisoners.

Fonagy (1999a) argued that these findings, although only a pilot study, support the theory that weak bonding and the dismissal of objects is a risk factor for violent criminality, a relatively consistent finding over the past 50 years (Bowlby, 1958; Meloy, 1992); more important, "criminal behavior may be seen as a socially maladaptive form of resolving trauma and abuse. Violent acts are committed in place of experienced anger concerning neglect, rejection, and maltreatment. Committing antisocial acts is facilitated by a nonreflective stance toward the victim" (Fonagy, 1999a, p. 64).

This thinking is in accord with other work concerning disorganized, traumagenic attachment in infants and the emergence of coercive and aggressive behavior in later childhood (Lyons-Ruth, 1996). It usefully extends it into the object representations of the violent criminal. But it does not account for the prominence of dismissing attachment pathology among criminals, likely related to the construct of psychopathy, that may instead have its roots in a temperament-environmental misfit that leads to avoidant strategies by both mother and child (Shaw & Bell, 1993). It also does not leave room for the possibility that a constitutional defect in the capacity to bond may exist in the child, and despite heroic efforts by the securely attached parents to stimulate a bond, nothing works.

In the domain of attachment and violent criminality we are left with intriguing theory, very little research, and some tentative findings: (a) Insecure attachment is a risk factor for violent criminality; (b) secure attachment may be a protective factor against violent criminality, particularly when the child is raised in a deprived economic or social environment (Klevens & Roca, 1999; Marcus & Gray, 1998); (c) the reflective function may be an important mediating variable for understanding affective violence in particular; and (d) dismissing and disorganized pathologies of attachment may correlate with constitutional and traumagenic pathways to violent criminality, respectively.

NEW AVENUES OF FORENSIC RESEARCH AND APPLICATION

If we conceptualize attachment pathologies as lying on a continuum between hyperarousal (the preoccupied type) and hypoarousal (the dismissive type), and see this autonomic activation or deactivation (whether acquired or inherited) as being related to both attention and emotion (Babcock et al., 2000), two intriguing new areas of forensic research and application become apparent: understanding the nature and dynamics of stalking and psychopathy.

Stalking: The Preoccupied Crime

Stalking is an old behavior but a new crime (Meloy, 1999). First codified in California in 1990, stalking laws now exist throughout the United States, Canada, Great Britain, Australia, and New Zealand. Typically defined as "the willful, malicious, and repeated following and harassing of another that threatens his or her safety" (Meloy & Gothard, 1995, p. 259), stalking victimization affects a large proportion of both the adult and adolescent populations.

Stalking laws typically have three elements: a pattern of unwanted pursuit, a credible threat, and the induction of reasonable fear in the victim. In California, the current stalking law reads as follows (Penal Code Section 646.9):

> Any person who willfully, maliciously, and repeatedly follows or harasses another person and who makes a credible threat with the

intent to place that person in reasonable fear for his or her safety, or the safety of his or her immediate family, is guilty of the crime of stalking.

Although the law is new, Mullen, Pathé, and Purcell (2000) note that the first attempt to prosecute stalking behavior was brought before the English court in *Dennis v. Lane* in 1704. Dr. Lane, a physician, engaged in an unwanted pursuit of Miss Dennis. During the course of his stalking, he assaulted two parties, a man accompanying Miss Dennis on a trip and a barrister who had escorted her to London. He was eventually ordered to pay 400 pounds as security to ensure the peace. The eventual outcome of the case is unknown.

At the end of the twentieth century in the United States, it appears that 8% of adult women and 2% of adult men will be stalked some time in their life (Tjaden & Thoennes, 1997); approximately 25% of college-age students will be victimized by stalking behaviors, although most incidents do not arise to the level of criminal activity (McCann, 2001).

Stalking and violence are closely allied. Rates of violence are disturbingly high, usually directed toward the target of the stalking. They range from 25% to 40%, but they typically exceed 50% when there has been a prior sexual intimacy between the stalker and his or her victim (Meloy, in press). The nature of the stalking violence is also being studied. In most cases of "private" stalking in which there has been a previous known relationship, the violence is affective: Victims are pushed, shoved, grabbed, choked, slapped, punched, fondled, or their hair is pulled. There is typically no weapon used. In cases of "public" stalking, in which the target is a public figure such as a celebrity or politician, the violence is predatory: Victims are attacked with a weapon, usually a firearm, after a lengthy period of obsessive thought, dysphoric rumination, planning, and approach (Fein & Vossekuil, 1999; Meloy, 1999; 2001). Mark David Chapman, the assassin of John Lennon, traveled from Hawaii, where he was living, to New York City and back, only to return again in December 1980 to carry out his killing. He made himself known to the doormen at the Dakota Building as a fan of Lennon over the course of a number of days and actually got Lennon's autograph on a compact disk before he murdered him later that evening by shooting him in the back using a .38 caliber revolver (Jones, 1992).

Meloy (1989, 1992) first proposed that stalking may be a pathology of attachment in relation to unrequited love and the wish to kill. His clinical and theoretical assertion was largely based on the obsessive nature of the cognitions and the lability and intensity of the affect apparent in the rejected (either in fantasy or reality) individual. Kienlen, Birmingham, Solberg, O'Regan, and Meloy (1997) were the first to

observe and document two empirical findings that strongly suggested attachment pathology in stalking cases. In a small sample of incarcerated stalkers in a Missouri prison, the majority had lost a primary caretaker in childhood and had had a major loss, usually a personal relationship, in the six months preceding the onset of stalking. The researchers proposed that these two findings respectively predisposed and precipitated the criminal behavior. Although Meloy (1996, 1999) focused on a preoccupied attachment style among stalkers in subsequent writings, Kienlen (1998) reported case examples and theory consistent with a variety of attachment pathologies among stalkers.

The preoccupied, hyperaroused nature of stalkers has been supported by several negative findings. Most individuals who stalk are not antisocial personality disordered (Meloy et al., 2000), and the psychopathic stalker is a rare event (Meloy, 1999). These empirical findings are consistent with the hypothesis that chronically emotionally detached individuals who evidence a "dismissing" attachment would not waste their time stalking someone; they do not form an enduring, meaningful emotional bond with another. Instead, they manipulate, exploit, and then dispose of their objects. It is also consistent with findings I described concerning the surprisingly preoccupied attachment pathology among some antisocial batterers (Tweed & Dutton, 1998); they are probably not psychopaths.

More recent studies continue to verify the hyperaroused, preoccupied pathology of individuals who stalk prior sexual intimates. Mechanic, Weaver, and Resick (2000) found in a large sample of battered women that emotional and psychological abuse in the relationship were strong predictors of postrelationship stalking, even when the effects of physical violence were controlled. They wrote, "It appears that one function of pursuit-oriented behaviors, of which stalking is a particularly virulent form, is to regulate attachment and proximity seeking via coercive control strategies" (p. 70). Others have found that attachment disturbances (preoccupied and fearful) are related to jealousy, following, surveillance, and separation behaviors (Dutton, Saunders, Starzomski, & Bartholomew, 1994; Guerrero, 1998; Holtsworth-Munroe et al., 1997). Research among college students is promising. Langhinrichsen-Rohling, Palarea, Cohen, and Rohling (2000) found in a large sample of undergraduates that unwanted pursuit behaviors were significantly predicted by an ex-partner who was anxiously and insecurely attached and evidenced higher levels of "possessive" and "dependent" love. These latter terms concerning "love styles" have recently played a role in the research of Cupach and Spitzberg (1998), who have made important contributions to our understanding of "obsessive relational intrusion," a typically nonviolent and less severe form of stalking, among college students.

Love styles were first proposed by Lee (1976) and measured by Hendrick and Hendrick (1986). A secondary style, called "mania," blends *eros* (passion and romance) and *ludus* (game playing and exploitation); it is possessive, dependent, and addictive. In a large study of undergraduates, Spitzberg (2001) found that both a preoccupied attachment pattern and manic love had small but significant associations with some of the obsessively intrusive tactics of relational pursuit, specifically, physical threats and hyperintimacy (unwanted messages, intruding on interactions with others, monitoring, exaggerated affection).

This new area of forensic research—stalking as a preoccupied crime—is important because of the high rates of violence associated with it, its prevalence in society, its relationship to domestic violence, and accumulating evidence that it is a chronic behavior for which a hyperaroused, preoccupied attachment pathology may be central. Empirical studies, however, that directly measure the attachment pathologies of samples of convicted stalkers, both men and women, have yet to be done.

Psychopathy: The Dismissive Criminal

At the other end of a hypothetical attachment continuum is the underaroused, affectively avoidant, chronically emotionally detached individual. This dismissing attachment pathology, in its most extreme and virulent form, is likely found in the psychopath. A plethora of research during the past 20 years has shown the construct of psychopathy—a constellation of behaviors and traits (Hare, 1991)—to be both reliable and valid, particularly as a predictor of violent criminality (Millon, 1998). Psychopaths, when compared to other nonpsychopathic criminals, are more frequently and severely violent, are more likely to target strangers, engage in both affective and predatory violence, perpetuate violent criminal acts for a longer period of time across their life span, and are often found among the most feared and unpredictable offenders: those who commit sexually sadistic acts and serial sexual homicides (Meloy, 2000a, 2000b).

Curiously, there are no published studies that have directly measured psychopathy (Hare, 1991) and attachment (using the AAI or other direct self-report measures) in samples of male inmates, despite the work cited earlier concerning the externalizing, disruptive, and controlling behavior found in children and adolescents with various attachment pathologies, and the chronic cortical underarousal found in habitual criminals (Raine, 1993). There has, however, been work in two related areas. Gacono and Meloy (1994) found in a

number of antisocial samples—including children, adolescents, and adults—that a Rorschach measure of attachment, the texture response, was significantly less frequent than in normal samples. As degree of psychopathy increased across these subjects, the frequency of the texture response decreased. Meloy (1988) described this measure, which involves the perception of a tactile quality to the inkblot, as a somatosensory analog for early skin contact with the mother, the primary vehicle of affectional relatedness for the infant and perhaps the corporal genesis of secure attachment.

Attachment and psychopathy have been measured among female inmates. Both Strachan (1993) and Taylor (1997) found that a dismissive attachment pathology, inferred by the voluntary relinquishment of their children, significantly correlated with psychopathy in samples of incarcerated women, even when other confounding variables, such as drug abuse and prostitution, were controlled. On the other side of this coin is the finding by Raine, Brennan, and Mednick (1997) that birth complications and maternal abandonment during the first year of life were significant predictors of early-onset violent criminality in their adult male offspring.

This new area of forensic research, the psychopath as a dismissive criminal, is important because of his high rates of violence and the chronic, nonviolent destruction he causes through dominance, manipulation, and exploitation of others—despite his apparent conscious disavowal of any need for affectional relatedness, a striking paradox. Attachment theory also can bring to the psychopathy research an empirically based, psychobiologically informed construct that may help complete the unfinished patchwork quilt that best describes the current findings within the neurobiology of the psychopath (Millon, 1998). For example, I would hypothesize that a dismissing attachment pathology may be inherited in some cases, rather than acquired through parental abuse, neglect, or an unreflective parent, a possibility heretofore unacknowledged among attachment researchers. Testing of this hypothesis may contribute to our fuller understanding of the exact nature of heritability of psychopathy. Another intriguing area of investigation is the role that deficiencies in vasopressin and oxytocin, two hormones apparently related to attachment (Fisher, 1998), may play in the biology of psychopathy, two biochemicals unexplored by psychopathy researchers. This might help us understand the psychopath's lack of empathy and enormous capacity for cruel aggression.

CONCLUSION

It may become an empirically grounded truism, years from now, that attachment pathology is a centrally necessary, but alone insufficient, component to explain violence: whether it is the hyperaroused, preoccupied attachment pathology of stalking behavior that often results in affective violence, or the hypoaroused, dismissive attachment pathology of the psychopath that often results in predatory violence. In a more applied context, violent attachments and their measurement through the use of reliable, valid, and normed forensic instruments, none of which currently exist, may become *de rigueur*, a standard of practice requirement, for the forensic psychologist of the future. Current research is certainly lighting the way.

REFERENCES

Adamson, J. L. (1998). *Predicting attachment and violence in relationships: An investigation across three generations* (Order No. AAM9805493). Unpublished doctoral dissertation, University of Nebraska-Lincoln.

Ainsworth, M. (1963). The development of infant-mother interaction among the Ganda. In B. Foss (Ed.), *Determinants of infant behavior* (Vol. 2, pp. 67–112). New York: Wiley.

Ainsworth, M. (1967). *Infancy in Uganda.* Baltimore: Johns Hopkins University Press.

Ainsworth, M. (1989). Attachments beyond infancy. *American Psychologist, 44,* 709–716.

Ainsworth, M., Bell, S., & Stayton, D. (1971). Individual differences in strange situation behavior of one-year-olds. In H. R. Schaffer (Ed.), *The origins of human social relations* (pp. 17–52). New York: Academic Press.

Ainsworth, M., Blehar, M., Waters, E., & Wall, S. (1978). *Patterns of attachment.* Hillsdale, NJ: Erlbaum.

Ainsworth, M., & Bowlby, J. (1954). Research strategy in the study of mother-child separation. *Courr. Cent. Int. Enf, 4,* 105.

Ainsworth, M., & Wittig, B. (1969). Attachment and exploratory behavior of one-year-olds in a strange situation. In B. M. Foss (Ed.), *Determinants of infant behavior* (Vol. 4, pp. 113–136). London: Methuen.

Allen, J., Hauser, S., & Borman-Spurrell, E. (1996). Attachment theory as a framework for understanding sequelae of severe adolescent psychopathology: An 11-year followup study. *Journal of Consulting and Clinical Psychology, 64,* 254–263.

American Psychiatric Assoc. (1994). *DSM-IV.* Washington: author.

Ashby, W. R. (1956). *An introduction to cybernetics.* New York: Wiley.

Babcock, J., Jacobson, N., Gottman, J., & Yerington, T. (2000). Attachment, emotional regulation, and the function of marital violence: Differences between secure, preoccupied, and dismissing violent and nonviolent husbands. *Journal of Family Violence, 15,* 391–409.

Barratt, E., Stanford, M., Felthous, A., & Kent, T. (1997). The effects of phenytoin on impulsive and premeditated aggression: A controlled study. *Journal of Clinical Pharmacology, 17,* 341–49.

Bartholomew, K. (1990). Avoidance of intimacy: An attachment perspective. *Journal of Social and Personal Relationships, 7,* 147–178.

Bartholomew, K. (1994). The assessment of individual differences in adult attachment. *Psychological Inquiry, 5,* 23–27.

Bartholomew, K. (1997). Adult attachment processes: Individual and couple perspectives. *British Journal of Medical Psychology, 70,* 249–263.

Bartholomew, K., & Horowitz, L. (1991). Attachment styles among young adults: A test of a four-category model. *Journal of Personality and Social Psychology, 61,* 226–244.

Bowlby, J. (1953). Some pathological processes set in train by early mother-child separation. *Journal of Mental Science, 99,* 265–272.

Bowlby, J. (1958). The nature of the child's tie to his mother. *International Journal of Psychoanalysis, 39,* 350–373.

Bowlby, J. (1960). Separation anxiety. *International Journal of Psychoanalysis, 41,* 89–113.

Bowlby, J. (1961). Processes of mourning. *International Journal of Psychoanalysis, 42,* 317–340.

Bowlby, J. (1969). *Attachment and loss. Volume I: Attachment.* New York: Basic Books.

Bowlby, J. (1973). *Attachment and loss. Volume II: Separation: Anxiety and anger.* New York: Basic Books.

Bowlby, J. (1979). *The making and breaking of affectional bonds.* London: Tavistock.

Bowlby, J. (1980). *Attachment and loss. Volume III: Loss: Sadness and depression.* New York: Basic Books.

Bowlby, J. (1984). Violence in the family as a disorder of the attachment and caregiving systems. *American Journal of Psychoanalysis, 44,* 9–27.

Carr, S., Dabbs, J., & Carr, T. (1975). Mother-infant attachment: The importance of the mother's visual field. *Child Development, 46,* 331–338.

Cassidy, J. (1999). The nature of the child's ties. In J. Cassidy & P. Shaver (Eds.), *Handbook of attachment* (pp. 3–20). New York: Guilford Press.

Cassidy, J., & Shaver, P. (Eds.). (1999). *Handbook of attachment.* New York: Guilford Press.

Cornell, D., Warren, J., Hawk, G., Stafford, E., Oram, G., & Pine, D. (1996). Psychopathy in instrumental and reactive violent offenders. *Journal of Consulting and Clinical Psychology, 64,* 783–790.

Crowell, J., Fraley, R. C., & Shaver, P. (1999). Measurement of individual differences in adolescent and adult attachment. In J. Cassidy & P. Shaver (Eds.), *Handbook of attachment* (pp. 434–465). New York: Guilford Press.

Cupach, W., & Spitzberg, B. (1998). *The dark side of close relationships.* Hillsdale, NJ: Erlbaum.

Dennis v. Lane (1704). 87 English Reports (Queens Bench), 887–888.

Downey, G., & Feldman, S. (1996). Implications of rejection sensitivity for intimate relationships. *Journal of Social and Personality Psychology, 70,* 1327–1343.

Downey, G., Feldman, S., & Ayduk, O. (2000). Rejection sensitivity and male violence in romantic relationships. *Personal Relationships, 7,* 45–61.

Dutton, D. (1994). Behavioral and affective correlates of borderline personality organization in wife assaulters. *International Journal of Law and Psychiatry, 17,* 26–38.

Dutton, D. (1995a). *The domestic assault of women.* Vancouver, Canada: University of British Columbia Press.

Dutton, D. (1995b). Intimate abusiveness. *Clinical Psychology: Science and Practice, 2,* 207–224.

Dutton, D. (1995c). Male abusiveness in intimate relationships. *Clinical Psychology Review, 15,* 567–581.

Dutton, D. (1998). *The abusive personality.* New York: Guilford Press.

Dutton, D. (1999). Traumatic origins of intimate rage. *Aggression and Violent Behavior, 4,* 431–447.

Dutton, D., & Painter, S. (1993). Emotional attachments in abusive relationships: A test of traumatic bonding theory. *Violence and Victims, 8,* 105–120.

Dutton, D., Saunders, K., Starzomski, A., & Bartholomew, K. (1994). Intimacy-anger and insecure attachment as precursors of abuse in intimate relationships. *Journal of Applied Social Psychology, 24,* 1367–1386.

Eisenberg, J. (1966). The social organization of mammals. *Handbuch Zoologie, 8,* 1–92.

Fein, R., & Vossekuil, B. (1999). Assassination in the United States: An operational study of recent assassins, attackers, and near-lethal approachers. *Journal of Forensic Sciences, 44,* 321–333.

Fisher, H. (1998). Lust, attraction, and attachment in mammalian reproduction. *Human Nature, 9,* 23–52.

Fonagy, P. (1999a). Attachment, the development of the self, and its pathology in personality disorders. In Derksen et al. (Eds.), *Treatment of personality disorders* (pp. 53–68). New York: Kluwer Academic/Plenum.

Fonagy, P. (1999b). Male perpetrators of violence against women: An attachment theory perspective. *Journal of Applied Psychoanalytic Studies, 1,* 7–27.

Fonagy, P. (1999c). Psychoanalytic theory from the viewpoint of attachment theory and research. In J. Cassidy & P. Shaver (Eds.), *Handbook of attachment* (pp. 595–624). New York: Guilford Press.

Fonagy, P., Leigh, T., Steele, M., Steele, H., Kennedy, R., Mattoon, G., et al. (1996). The relation of attachment status, psychiatric classification, and response to psychotherapy. *Journal of Consulting and Clinical Psychology, 64,* 22–31.

Fonagy, P., Redfern, S., & Charman, T. (1997). The relationship between belief-desire reasoning and a projective measure of attachment security (SAT). *British Journal of Developmental Psychology, 15,* 51–61.

Fonagy, P., Steele, M., Moran, G., Steele, H., & Higgitt, A. (1991). The capacity for understanding mental states: The reflective self in parent and child and its significance for security of attachment. *Infant Mental Health Journal, 13,* 200–216.

Fonagy, P., Steele, M., Steele, H., Higgitt, A., & Target, M. (1994). Theory and practice of resilience. *Journal of Child Psychology and Psychiatry, 35,* 231–257.

Fox, N., & Card, J. (1999). Psychophysiological measures in the study of attachment. In J. Cassidy & P. Shaver (Eds.), *Handbook of attachment* (pp. 226–248). New York: Guilford Press.

Freud, S. (1912). On the universal tendency of debasement in the sphere of love (contributions to the psychology of love II). *The standard edition of the complete psychological works of Sigmund Freud* (Vol. 11, pp. 177–190). London: Hogarth Press.

Freud, S. (1919). A child is being beaten. *The standard edition of the complete psychological works of Sigmund Freud* (Vol. 17, pp. 179–204). London: Hogarth Press.

Gabbard, G. (1989). Two substypes of narcissistic personality disorder. *Bulletin of the Menninger Clinic, 53,* 527–532.

Gacono, C., & Meloy, J. R. (1994). *The Rorschach assessment of aggressive and psychopathic personalities.* Hillsdale, NJ: Erlbaum.

Goldberg, S., Muir, R., & Kerr, J. (1995). *Attachment theory: Social, developmental, and clinical perspectives.* Hillsdale, NJ: Analytic Press.

Gottman, J., Jacobson, N., Rushe, R., Shortt, J., Babcock, J., LaTaillade, J., et al. (1995). The relationship between heart rate reactivity, emotionally aggressive behavior, and general violence in batterers. *Journal of Family Psychology, 9,* 227–248.

Guerrero, L. (1998). Attachment-style differences in the experience and expression of romantic jealousy. *Personal Relationships, 5,* 273–291.

Hamberger, L., & Hastings, J. (1986). Personality correlates of men who abuse their partners: A cross-validation study. *Journal of Family Violence, 1,* 323–341.

Hamberger, L., Lohr, J., Bonge, D., & Tolin, D. (1996). A large sample empirical typology of male spouse abusers and its relationship to dimensions of abuse. *Violence and Victims, 11,* 277–292.

Hare, R. D. (1991). *Manual for the Psychopathy Checklist–Revised.* Toronto, Ontario, Canada: Multi-Health Systems.

Harlow, H. (1961). The development of affectional patterns in infant monkeys. In B. M. Foss (Ed.), *Determinants of infant behavior* (pp. 75–97). London: Methuen.

Harlow, H. (1969). Age-mate or affectional system. In D. Lehrman, R. Hinde, & E. Shaw (Eds.), *Advances in the study of behavior* (Vol. 2, pp. 334–383). New York: Academic Press.

Hazan, C., & Shaver, P. (1987). Romantic love conceptualized as an attachment process. *Journal of Personality and Social Psychology, 52,* 511–524.

Heider, F. (1958). *The psychology of interpersonal relations.* New York: Wiley.

Hendrick, C., & Hendrick, S. (1986). A theory and method of love. *Journal of Personality and Social Psychology, 50,* 392–402.

Hofer, M. (1995). Hidden regulators: Implications for a new understanding of attachment, separation, and loss. In S. Goldberg, R. Muir, & J. Kerr (Eds.), *Attachment theory: Social, developmental, and clinical perspectives* (pp. 203–230). Hillsdale, NJ: Analytic Press.

Holmes, J. (1995). "Something there is that doesn't love a wall": John Bowlby, attachment theory, and psychoanalysis. In S. Goldberg, R. Muir, & J. Kerr (Eds.), *Attachment theory: Social, developmental, and clinical perspectives* (pp. 19–44). Hillsdale, NJ: Analytic Press.

Holtzworth-Munroe, A. (2000). A typology of men who are violent toward their female partners: Making sense of the heterogeneity in husband violence. *Current Directions in Psychological Science, 9,* 140–143.

Holtzworth-Munroe, A., Meehan, J., Herron, K., Rehman, U., & Stuart, G. (in press). Testing the Holtzworth-Munroe and Stuart batterer typology. *Journal of Consulting and Clinical Psychology.*

Holtzworth-Munroe, A., & Stuart, G. (1994). Typologies of male batterers: Three subtypes and the differences among them. *Psychological Bulletin, 116,* 476–497.

Holtzworth-Munroe, A., Stuart, G., & Hutchinson, G. (1997). Violent versus nonviolent husbands: Differences in attachment patterns, dependency, and jealousy. *Journal of Family Psychology, 11,* 314–331.

Irwin, H. (1999). Violent and nonviolent revictimization of women abused in childhood. *Journal of Interpersonal Violence, 14,* 1095–1110.

Jones, J. (1992). *Let me take you down.* New York: St. Martin's Press.

Kernberg, O. (1984). *Severe personality disorders.* New Haven, CT: Yale University Press.

Kesner, J., Julian, T., & McKenry, P. (1997). Application of attachment theory to male violence toward female intimates. *Journal of Family Violence, 12,* 211–228.

Kesner, J., & McKenry, P. (1998). The role of childhood attachment factors in predicting male violence toward female intimates. *Journal of Family Violence, 13,* 417–432.

Kienlen, K. (1998). The social antecedents of stalking. In J. R. Meloy (Ed.), *The psychology of stalking: Clinical and forensic perspectives* (pp. 52–67). San Diego, CA: Academic Press.

Kienlen, K., Birmingham, D., Solberg, K., O'Regan, J., & Meloy, J. R. (1997). A comparative study of psychotic and nonpsychotic stalking. *Journal of the American Academy of Psychiatry Law, 25,* 317–334.

Klevens, J., & Roca, J. (1999). Nonviolent youth in a violent society: Resilience and vulnerability in the country of Colombia. *Violence and Victims, 14,* 311–322.

Langhinrichsen-Rohling, J., Palarea, R., Cohen, J., & Rohling, M. (2000). Breaking up is hard to do: Unwanted pursuit behaviors following the dissolution of a romantic relationship. *Violence and Victims, 15,* 73–90.

Lee, J. (1976). *The colors of love.* Englewood Cliffs, NJ: Prentice-Hall.

Lewin, K. (1933). Environmental forces. In C. Murchison (Ed.), *A handbook of child psychology* (2nd ed., pp. 590–625). Worcester, MA: Clark University Press.

Lyons-Ruth, K. (1996). Attachment relationships among children with aggressive behavior problems: The role of disorganized early attachment patterns. *Journal of Consulting and Clinical Psychology, 64,* 64–73.

Lyons-Ruth, K., Repacholi, B., McLeod, S., & Silva, E. (1991). Disorganized attachment behavior in infancy: Short-term stability, maternal and infant correlates, and risk-related subtypes. *Development and Psychopathology, 3,* 377–396.

Main, M. & Goldwyn, J. (1984). Adult attachment scoring and classification system. Unpublished manuscript. University of California at Berkeley.

Main, M., & Hesse, E. (1990). Parents' unresolved traumatic experiences are related to infant disorganized attachment status: Is frightened and/or frightening parental behavior the linking mechanism? In M. Greenberg, D. Cicchetti & E. Cummings (Eds.), *Attachment in the preschool years* (pp. 161–184). Chicago: University of Chicago Press.

Main, M., Kaplan, N., & Cassidy, J. (1985). Security in infancy, childhood, and adulthood: A move to the level of representation. *Monographs of the Society for Research in Child Development, 50,* 66–104.

Main, M., & Solomon, J. (1986). Discovery of an insecure-disorganized/disoriented attachment pattern. In T. B. Brazelton & M. W. Yogman (Eds.), *Affective development in infancy* (pp. 95–124). Norwood, NJ: Ablex.

Main, M., & Solomon, J. (1990). Procedures for identifying infants as disorganized/disoriented during the Ainsworth Strange Situation. In M. Greenberg, D. Cicchetti & E. Cummings (Eds.), *Attachment in the preschool years* (pp. 121–160). Chicago: University of Chicago Press.

Marcus, R., & Gray, L. (1998). Close relationships of violent and nonviolent African American delinquents. *Violence and Victims, 13,* 31–46.

McCann, J. (2001). *Stalking of children and adolescents: The primitive bond.* Washington, DC: American Psychological Association.

Mead, G. H. (1934). *Mind, self, and society*. Chicago: University of Chicago Press.

Mechanic, M., Weaver, T., & Resick, P. (2000). Intimate partner violence and stalking behavior: Exploration of patterns and correlates in a sample of acutely battered women. *Violence and Victims, 15*, 55–72.

Meloy, J. R. (1988). *The psychopathic mind: Origins, dynamics, and treatment*. Northvale, NJ: Aronson.

Meloy, J. R. (1989). Unrequited love and the wish to kill: The diagnosis and treatment of borderline erotomania. *Bulletin of the Menninger Clinic, 53*, 477–492.

Meloy, J. R. (1992). *Violent attachments*. Northvale, NJ: Aronson.

Meloy, J. R. (1996). Stalking (obsessional following): A review of some preliminary studies. *Aggression and Violent Behavior, 1*, 147–162.

Meloy, J. R. (1997). Predatory violence during mass murder. *Journal of Forensic Sciences, 42*, 326–329.

Meloy, J. R. (1999). Stalking: An old behavior, a new crime. *Psychiatric Clinics of North America, 22*, 85–99.

Meloy, J. R. (2000a). The nature and dynamics of sexual homicide: An integrative review. *Aggression and Violent Behavior, 5*, 1–22.

Meloy, J. R. (2000b). *Violence risk and threat assessment*. San Diego, CA: Specialized Training Services.

Meloy, J. R. (2001). Communicated threats toward public and private targets: Discerning differences among those who stalk and attack. *Journal of Forensic Sciences, 46*.

Meloy, J. R. (in press). Stalking and violence. In J. Boon & L. Sheridan (Eds.), *Stalking and psychosexual obsession*. London: Wiley.

Meloy, J. R., & Gothard, S. (1995). Demographic and clinical comparison of obsessional followers and offenders with mental disorders. *American Journal of Psychiatry, 152*, 258–263.

Meloy, J. R., Rivers, L., Siegel, L., Gothard, S., Naimark, D., & Nicolini, R. (2000). A replication study of obsessional followers and offenders with mental disorders. *Journal of Forensic Sciences, 45*, 189–194.

Millon, T. (1981). *Disorders of Personality DSM-III: Axis II*. New York: Wiley.

Millon, T. (1998). *Psychopathy: Criminal, violent, and antisocial behaviors*. New York: Guilford Press.

Mullen, P., Pathe, M., & Purcell, R. (2000). *Stalkers and their victims*. New York: Cambridge University Press.

Nachmias, M., Gunnar, M., Mangelsdorf, S., Parritz, R., & Buss, K. (1996). Behavioral inhibition and stress reactivation: The moderating role of attachment security. *Child Development, 67*, 508–522.

Oderberg, N. (1995). *History of family violence, adult attachment, and child abuse potential: Interrelationships in a sample of college students* (Order No. AAM9506364). Unpublished doctoral dissertation, University of Colorado, Boulder.

O'Leary, K., Barling, J., Arias, I., Rosenbaum, A., Malone, J., & Tyree, A. (1989). Prevalence and stability of physical aggression between spouses. *Journal of Consulting and Clinical Psychology, 37*, 263–268.

Painter, S., & Dutton, D. (1985). Patterns of emotional bonding in battered women: Traumatic bonding. *International Journal of Women's Studies, 8*, 363–375.

Polan, H. J., & Hofer, M. (1999). Psychobiological origins of infant attachment and separation responses. In J. Cassidy & P. Shaver (Eds.), *Handbook of attachment* (pp. 162–180). New York: Guilford Press.

Raine, A. (1993). *The psychopathology of crime*. San Diego, CA: Academic Press.

Raine, A., Brennan, P., & Mednick, S. (1997). Interaction between birth complications and early maternal rejection in predisposing individuals to adult violence: Specificity to serious, early-onset violence. *American Journal of Psychiatry, 154*, 1265–1271.

Raine, A., Meloy, J. R., Bihrie, S., Stoddard, J., LaCasse, L., & Buchsbaum, M. (1998). Reduced prefrontal and increased subcortical brain functioning assessed during positron emission tomography in predatory and affective murderers. *Behavioral Sciences and Law, 16*, 319–332.

Robertson, J. (1953). *A two year old goes to hospital* [Film]. London: Tavistock Child Development Research Unit. (Available from Penn State Audiovisual Services, University Park, PA).

Robertson, J., & Bowlby, J. (1952). Responses of young children to separation from their mothers. *Courr. Cent. Int. Enf, 2*, 131–142.

Rosenstein, D., & Horowitz, H. (1996). Adolescent attachment and psychopathology. *Journal of Consulting Clinical Psychology, 64*, 244–253.

Saunders, D. (1992). A typology of men who batter women: Three types. *American Journal of Orthopsychiatry, 62*, 264–275.

Shaw, D., & Bell, R. (1993). Chronic family adversity and infant attachment security. *Journal of Child Psychology and Psychiatry, 34*, 1205–1215.

Sorce, J., & Emde, R. (1981). Mother's presence is not enough: Effect of emotional availability on infant explorations. *Developmental Psychology, 17*, 737–745.

Spangler, G., & Grossman, K. (1993). Biobehavioral organization in securely and insecurely attached infants. *Child Development, 64*, 1439–1450.

Spitzberg, B. (2001). *Forlorn love: Attachment styles, love styles, loneliness, and obsessive thinking as predictors of obsessive relational intrusion*. Unpublished manuscript. San Diego State University.

Strachan, C. (1993). *The assessment of psychopathy in female offenders*. Unpublished doctoral dissertation, University of British Columbia, Vancouver, Canada.

Taylor, C. (1997). *Psychopathy and attachment in a group of incarcerated females*. Unpublished doctoral dissertation, California School of Professional Psychology, San Diego.

Tjaden, P., & Thoennes, N. (1997). *Stalking in America: Findings from the National Violence Against Women survey*. Denver, CO: Center for Policy Research.

Tjaden, P., & Thoennes, N. (2000). *Extent, nature, and consequences of intimate partner violence* (NCJ 181867). Washington, DC: U.S. Department of Justice.

Tweed, R., & Dutton, D. (1998). A comparison of impulsive and instrumental subgroups of batterers. *Violence and Victims, 13,* 217–230.

van Ijzendoorn, M. (1995). Adult attachment representations, parental responsiveness, and infant attachment: A meta-analysis on the predictive validity of the Adult Attachment Interview. *Psychological Bulletin, 117,* 387–403.

Waltz, J., Babcock, J., Jacobson, N., & Gottman, J. (2000). Testing a typology of batterers. *Journal of Consulting and Clinical Psychology, 68,* 658–669.

CHAPTER 26

Violence Risk Assessment

JOHN MONAHAN

In this chapter, I consider first why and in what ways law is concerned with anticipating violence and how evidence in the form of violence risk assessment is legally evaluated. I then contrast clinical and actuarial methods of risk assessment and address key issues and controversies pertinent to each. Finally, I survey ways in which clinical or actuarial estimates of violence risk are best communicated to legal decision makers.

VIOLENCE RISK ASSESSMENT: LAW AND POLICY

Substantive Issues

Concerns about whether violence risk assessments offered by psychologists and other mental health professionals were "good enough" to incorporate into mental health law and policy, once a staple of commentary in the field (e.g., Ennis & Litwack, 1974), now seem quaintly dated. Courts across the country and, in particular, the U.S. Supreme Court, answered with a resounding no the question Does a reliance on clinical predictions of violence invalidate an otherwise valid law? Consider just two of the many cases relevant to this point.

In 1978, Thomas Barefoot was convicted of the capital murder of a police officer. At a separate sentencing hearing, the same jury considered the two questions put to it under the Texas death penalty statute, namely, (a) whether the conduct causing the death was "committed deliberately and with reasonable expectation that the death of the deceased or another would result" and (b) whether "there is a probability that the defendant would commit criminal acts of violence that would constitute a continuing threat to society." The jury's affirmative answer to both questions required the imposition of the death penalty. In *Barefoot v. Estelle* (1983), the Supreme Court considered the constitutionality of using clinical predictions of violence for the purpose of determining whom to execute. In an opinion upholding the Texas statute, Justice White wrote:

> It is urged that psychiatrists, individually and as a group, are incompetent to predict with an acceptable degree of reliability that a particular criminal will commit other crimes in the future and so represent a danger to the community. . . . The suggestion that no psychiatrist's testimony may be presented with respect to a defendant's future dangerousness is somewhat like asking us to disinvent the wheel. In the first place, it is contrary to our cases . . . and if it is not impossible for even a lay person sensibly to arrive at that conclusion, it makes little sense, if any, to submit that psychiatrists, out of the entire universe of persons who might have an opinion on the issue, would know so little about the subject that they should not be permitted to testify. (pp. 896–897)

The next year, in *Schall v. Martin* (1984), the Supreme Court upheld a New York statute that authorized pretrial detention, without probable cause, of an accused juvenile delinquent based on a finding that there was a "serious risk"

527

that the juvenile "may before the return date commit an act which if committed by an adult would constitute a crime." The district court had invalidated the statute after reviewing the research literature and concluded that "no diagnostic tools have as yet been devised which enable even the most highly trained criminologists to predict reliably which juveniles will engage in violent crime," and the Second Circuit had affirmed. In reversing the Second Circuit, Justice Rehnquist, writing for six members of the court, stated:

> Appellees claim, and the district court agreed, that it is virtually impossible to predict future criminal conduct with any degree of accuracy. . . . The procedural protections are thus, in their view, unavailing because the ultimate decision is intrinsically arbitrary and uncontrolled. Our cases indicate, however, that from a legal point of view there is nothing inherently unattainable about a prediction of future criminal conduct. Such a judgment forms an important element in many decisions, and we have specifically rejected the contention, based on the same sort of sociological data relied upon by appellees and the district court, "that it is impossible to predict future behavior and that the question is so vague as to be meaningless." (pp. 278–279)

Little has changed since *Barefoot* and *Schall*. In *Kansas v. Hendricks* (1997), the Supreme Court upheld a civil means of lengthening the detention of certain criminal offenders scheduled for release from prison. Kansas's Sexually Violent Predator Act established procedures for the civil commitment to mental hospitals of persons who may not have a major mental disorder, but who have a "mental abnormality or personality disorder" (in Hendricks's case, pedophilia) that makes them "likely to engage in predatory acts of sexual violence" (p. 350). A mental abnormality was defined in the Act as a "congenital or acquired condition affecting the emotional or volitional capacity which predisposes the person to commit sexually violent offenses in a degree constituting such person a menace to the health and safety of others" (p. 352). The language of the Act implies the need for a violence risk assessment to determine which individuals meet the defined standards. In upholding Hendricks's civil commitment under the Act, the Supreme Court emphasized two specific facts of the case: Hendricks's own admission of his uncontrollable urges and a risk assessment predicting high risk. The Court noted:

> Hendricks even conceded that, when he becomes "stressed out," he cannot "control the urge" to molest children. This admitted lack of volitional control, coupled with a prediction of future dangerousness, adequately distinguishes Hendricks from other dangerous persons who are perhaps more properly dealt with exclusively through criminal proceedings. (p. 360)

Not only courts, but also professional organizations have concluded that predictions of violence are here to stay. For example, the American Bar Association's Criminal Justice Mental Health Standards (1989) recommended that a person acquitted of a violent crime by reason of insanity be committed to a mental hospital if found to be currently mentally ill and to present "a substantial risk of serious bodily harm to others" (Standard 7-7.4). The American Psychiatric Association's (1983) model state law on civil commitment included the involuntary hospitalization of persons with mental disorder who are "likely to cause harm to others" (p. 672). Likewise, the guidelines for involuntary civil commitment of the National Center for State Courts (1986) urged that

> Particularly close attention be paid to predictions of future behavior, especially predictions of violence and assessments of dangerousness. Such predictions have been the bane of clinicians who admit limited competence to offer estimates of the future yet are mandated legally to do so. [However,] such predictions will continue to provide a basis for involuntary civil commitment, even amid controversy about the scientific and technological shortcomings and the ethical dilemmas that surround them. (p. 493)

Now that the Supreme Court clearly has rejected constitutional challenges to risk assessment, tort law frames the legal questions asked of violence prediction (Monahan, 1993). *Tarasoff v. Regents of the University of California* (1976) is the landmark case in this area. Initially the subject of vilification by mental health professionals, the California Supreme Court's holding in *Tarasoff,* that psychotherapists who know or should know of their patient's likelihood of inflicting injury on identifiable third parties have an obligation to take reasonable steps to protect the potential victim, has become a familiar part of the clinical landscape. Although a few state courts have rejected *Tarasoff* and others have limited its scope, most courts addressing the issue have accepted the essence of the "duty to protect," and several have expanded that duty to include nonidentifiable victims (Appelbaum, 1988). The duty to protect, in short, is now a fact of professional life for nearly all American clinicians and, potentially, for clinical researchers as well (Appelbaum & Rosenbaum, 1989; Monahan, Appelbaum, Mulvey, Robbins, & Lidz, 1994).

Evidentiary Issues

The evidentiary test for the admissibility at trial of expert psychological testimony on violence risk assessment was given by the U.S. Supreme Court in *Daubert v. Merrell Dow*

Pharmaceuticals (1993). Many American state courts, where the vast majority of psychological and psychiatric testimony is offered, have adopted the *Daubert* standard (although not all state courts have done so, California, Florida, and New York being notable exceptions). For illustrative purposes, I rely on one representative case from a state that has adopted the *Daubert* standard, *E.I. du Pont de Nemours & Co. v. Robinson* (Tex. 1995) to frame the discussion. In *Robinson,* the Supreme Court of Texas specified six factors "that a trial court may consider in making the threshold determination of admissibility" (p. 557). My evaluation of the points at issue follow these six factors (see also Monahan, 2000).

The Extent to Which the Theory Has Been Tested

As described below, at least seven empirical studies conducted since the 1970s have tested the proposition that psychologists and psychiatrists have greater-than-chance accuracy at predicting violent behavior toward others in the open community. Many additional studies have tested the proposition that psychologists and psychiatrists have greater-than-chance accuracy at predicting violence toward others within closed institutions (e.g., McNiel, Sandberg, & Binder, 1998).

Reliance on the Subjective Interpretation of the Expert

The American Bar Association published the *National Benchbook on Psychiatric and Psychological Evidence and Testimony* (1998). The *Benchbook* is directed to state and federal judges and explicitly "designed to aid decision-making . . . regarding admissibility of evidence" (p. iii). While acknowledging that subjective clinical interpretations often play a role in predictions of violence, the *Benchbook* concludes:

> Despite recent commentary indicating that clinicians are better at addressing possible risk factors and probabilities than providing definitive predictions of dangerousness, courts have remained reluctant to totally exclude such [clinical] evidence, in part, perhaps, because courts are ultimately responsible for making these decisions and though the information may remain open to challenge, it is the best information available. The alternative is to deprive fact finders, judges and jurors of the guidance and understanding that psychiatrists and psychologists can provide. (p. 49)

Subject to Peer Review and Publication

All seven empirical tests of the ability of psychologists and psychiatrists to clinically assess risk of violence in the community have been published. Five have been published in peer-reviewed scientific journals rather than in books or student-edited law reviews, including the most methodologically sophisticated study (Lidz, Mulvey, & Gardner, 1993), which was published in the *Journal of the American Medical Association.*

Potential Rate of Error

No one questions that the state of the science is such that the prediction of violence is subject to a considerable margin of error. But in acknowledging this error rate, the American Bar Association's *National Benchbook on Psychiatric and Psychological Evidence and Testimony* (1998) nonetheless stated:

> While the frustration with psychiatry and psychology from a legal standpoint centers on the certainty or lack thereof with which mental health experts speak to the ultimate issues in a case (for example, dangerousness . . .), this frustration should not lead courts to reject all such input, but rather should encourage courts to recognize the proper role and limitations of expert evidence and testimony in the courtroom. (pp. 47–48)

General Acceptance in the Relevant Scientific Community

The best-known recent study of the validity of clinical predictions of violence, Lidz et al. (1993), concluded: "What this study [shows] is that clinical judgment has been undervalued in previous research. Not only did the clinicians pick out a statistically more violent group, but the violence that the predicted group committed was more serious than the acts of the comparison group" (p. 1010). Likewise, a critical analysis of existing risk assessment research (Mossman, 1994) reached this measured judgment: "This article's reevaluation of representative data from the past 2 decades suggests that clinicians are able to distinguish violent from nonviolent patients with a modest, better-than-chance level of accuracy" (p. 790).

Nonjudicial Uses of the Theory or Technique

Violence risk assessment not only permeates the legal system but is a significant component of general clinical practice in the mental health fields. As McNiel (1998) stated, "Clinical assessment of violence potential and management of aggressive behavior are routine components of contemporary practice in psychiatric emergency rooms and inpatient units" (p. 95).

There are no post-*Daubert* U.S. Supreme Court cases on the admissibility of clinical violence risk assessment. There has however, been much post-*Daubert* commentary on this issue in the legal and scientific literatures. Virtually all of this commentary suggests that testimony by a qualified expert regarding a properly conducted clinical violence risk assessment will remain admissible as evidence. For example, the American Bar Association's *National Benchbook on Psychiatric and Psychological Evidence and Testimony* (1998) concluded:

> Even given the underlying uncertainties and discrepancies within the psychiatric and psychological communities, psychiatrists and psychologists—through their education and experiences—acquire special information and skills that are beyond that of the lay community to better understand and interpret human behavior (normal and abnormal). Thus, in many instances the knowledge of psychiatrists and psychologists can assist factfinders in understanding and interpreting human behavior within a legal context. (p. 47)

Likewise, a leading professional work in this area (Melton, Petrila, Poythress, & Slobogin, 1997) stated:

> Some critics might argue that much of the empirical and clinical analysis [of violence prediction] relies on "face valid" factors that lay decisionmakers, applying common sense, could use to reach the same judgments. We disagree. Although the implications of some factors are evident on their face . . . laypersons will not be as familiar with or be able to interpret as well other types of factors. . . . Such informed testimony can help prevent the courts from reaching inappropriate conclusions based on stereotypical views of "psychopaths" or "schizophrenics" and may thus facilitate more disciplined and humane dispositions by judges and juries. (pp. 292–293)

THE PROCESS OF CLINICAL RISK ASSESSMENT

Mulvey and Lidz (1985) have argued that to study the *outcome* of clinical prediction before studying the *process* of clinical prediction is to "put the cart before the horse" (p. 213). They stated:

> It is only by knowing "how" the process occurs that we can determine . . . the strategy for improvement in the prediction of dangerousness. Addressing this question requires systematic investigation of the possible facets of the judgement process that could be contributing to the observed low predictive accuracy. (p. 215)

Along these lines, Segal, Watson, Goldfinger, and Averbuck (1988a, 1988b) observed clinicians evaluating over 200 cases at several psychiatric emergency rooms. Observers coded each case on an 88-item index referred to as Three Ratings of Involuntary Admissibility (TRIAD). Global ratings of patient "dangerousness" were completed by each clinician. TRIAD scores correlated highly with overall clinical ratings of dangerousness:

> Symptoms most strongly related to [clinical judgments of] danger to others in our sample were irritability and impulsivity, but there were also consistent moderate associations with formal thought disorder, thought content disorder, and expansiveness as well as weaker but consistent significant correlations with impaired judgment and behavior and inappropriate affect. (1988b, p. 757)

Similarly, Menzies and Webster (1995) studied the clinical decision-making process regarding risk for a large group of Canadian mentally disordered offenders. They concluded that "previous violence, alcohol use, presentation of anger and rage, lack of agreeability, and tension during the interviews were the main contributors to the resulting decisions" (p. 775).

In the research program of Mulvey and Lidz (1985; Lidz, Mulvey, Apperson, Evanczuk, & Shea, 1992), observers trained in speedwriting recorded interviews between clinicians and patients admitted to a hospital's psychiatric emergency room. Clinicians later completed ratings of current and chronic dangerousness in the community. A patient's history of violence was the best single predictor of clinician ratings; patient hostility and the presence of serious disorder also correlated highly with clinical ratings of current dangerousness. In addition, explicit judgments of the likelihood of future violence were rarely found in actual practice, with this conclusion instead embedded in other decisions about clinical care.

THE OUTCOMES OF CLINICAL RISK ASSESSMENT

Early research on the accuracy of clinicians at predicting violent behavior toward others was reviewed by Monahan (1981). Five studies (Cocozza & Steadman, 1976; Kozol, Boucher, & Garofalo, 1972; Steadman, 1977; Steadman & Cocozza, 1974; Thornberry & Jacoby, 1979) were available as of the late 1970s. The conclusion of that review was:

> Psychiatrists and psychologists are accurate in no more than one out of three predictions of violent behavior over a several-year period among institutionalized populations that had both committed violence in the past (and thus had high base rates for it) and who were diagnosed as mentally ill. (pp. 47–49)

Only two studies of the validity of clinicians' predictions of violence in the community have been published since that time (for reviews, see Blumenthal & Lavender, 2000; Monahan, 2001). Sepejak, Menzies, Webster, and Jensen (1983) studied court-ordered pretrial risk assessments and found that 39% of the defendants rated by clinicians as having a medium or high likelihood of being violent to others were reported to have committed a violent act during a two-year follow-up, compared to 26% of the defendants predicted to have a low likelihood of violence (p. 181, note 12), a statistically significant difference, but not a large one in absolute terms.

More recently, researchers have shown a renewed interest in the topic of clinical prediction. For example, Lidz et al. (1993), in what is surely the most sophisticated study published on the clinical prediction of violence, took as their subjects male and female patients being examined in the acute psychiatric emergency room of a large civil hospital. Psychiatrists and nurses were asked to assess potential patient violence toward others over the next six-month period. Violence was measured by official records, patient self-report, and the report of a collateral informant in the community (e.g., a family member). Patients who elicited professional concern regarding future violence were found to be significantly more likely to be violent after release (53%) than were patients who had not elicited such concern (36%). The accuracy of clinical prediction did not vary as a function of the patient's age or race. The accuracy of clinicians' predictions of male violence substantially exceeded chance levels, both for patients with and without a prior history of violent behavior. In contrast, the accuracy of clinicians' predictions of female violence did not differ from chance. Although the actual rate of violent incidents among discharged female patients (46%) was higher than the rate among discharged male patients (42%), the clinicians had predicted that only 22% of the women would be violent, compared with predicting that 45% of the men would commit a violent act. The inaccuracy of clinicians at predicting violence among women appeared to be a function of the clinicians' serious underestimation of the base rate of violence among mentally disordered women (perhaps due to an inappropriate extrapolation from the great sex differences in rates of violence among persons without mental disorder).

McNiel and Binder (1991) report research predicting inpatient violence (rather than violence in the community). They studied clinical predictions that patients would be violent during the first week of hospitalization. Of the patients whom nurses had estimated had a 0% to 33% probability of being violent on the ward, 10% were later rated by the nurses as having committed a violent act; of the patients whom nurses had estimated had a 34% to 66% chance of being violent, 24% were later rated as having committed a violent act;

and of the patients whom nurses had estimated had a 67% to 100% chance of being violent, 40% were later rated as having acted violently.

ACTUARIAL RISK ASSESSMENT

The general superiority of statistical over clinical risk assessment in the behavioral sciences has been known for almost half a century (Grove, Zald, Lebow, Snitz, & Nelson, 2000; Meehl, 1954; Swets, Dawes, & Monahan, 2000). Despite this, and despite a long and successful history of actuarial risk assessment in bail and parole decision making in criminology (Champion, 1994), there have been only a few attempts to develop actuarial tools for the specific task of assessing risk of violence to others among people with mental disorder (for reviews, see Borum, 1996; Douglas & Webster, 1999; Monahan & Steadman, 1994). For example, Steadman and Cocozza (1974), in an early study of mentally disordered offenders, developed a Legal Dangerousness Scale based on the presence or absence of a juvenile record and a conviction for a violent crime, the number of previous incarcerations, and the severity of the current offense. This scale, along with the patient's age, was significantly associated with subsequent violent behavior. Likewise, Klassen and O'Connor (1988) found that the combination of a diagnosis of substance abuse, prior arrests for violent crime, and young age were significantly associated with arrests for violent crime among male civil patients discharged into the community. (A discussion of risk assessment of sexually violent "predators" can be found in the chapter by Conroy in this volume.)

The Violence Risk Appraisal Guide

More recently, the Violence Risk Appraisal Guide (VRAG; Harris, Rice, & Quinsey, 1993; Quinsey, Harris, Rice, & Cormier, 1998; Rice & Harris, 1995) was developed on a sample of over 600 men from a maximum-security hospital in Canada, all charged with a serious criminal offense. Approximately 50 predictor variables were coded from institutional files. The criterion was any new criminal charge for a violent offense, or return to the institution for a similar act, over a time at risk in the community that averaged approximately seven years after discharge. A series of regression models identified 12 variables for inclusion in the VRAG, including the Hare Psychopathy Checklist–Revised (PCL-R; Hare, 1991), elementary school maladjustment, and age at the time of the offense (which had a negative weight). When the scores on this actuarial instrument were dichotomized into high and low, the results were that 55% of the group scoring high committed a new violent offense, compared with 19% of the group scoring low.

The HCR-20

Douglas and Webster (1999) reviewed ongoing research on a structured clinical guide that can be scored in an actuarial manner to assess violence risk, the "HCR-20," which consists of 20 ratings addressing *h*istorical, *c*linical, and *r*isk management variables (Webster, Douglas, Eaves, & Hart, 1995). Douglas and Webster also reported data from a retrospective study with prisoners, finding that scores above the median on the HCR-20 increased the odds of past violence and antisocial behavior by an average of four times. In another study with civilly committed patients, Douglas, Ogloff, Nicholls, and Grant (1999) found that during a follow-up of approximately two years after discharge into the community, patients scoring above the HCR-20 median were 6 to 13 times more likely to be violent than those scoring below the median.

The MacArthur Violence Risk Assessment Study

As a final illustration of the use of actuarial approaches to improve the prediction of violence, the MacArthur Violence Risk Assessment Study (Monahan et al., 2001) assessed a large sample of male and female acute civil patients at several facilities on a wide variety of variables believed to be related to the occurrence of violence. The risk factors fall into four domains. One domain, *dispositional* variables, refers to the demographic factors of age, race, sex, and social class, as well as to personality variables (e.g., impulsivity and anger control) and neurological factors (e.g., head injury). A second domain, *historical* variables, includes significant events experienced by subjects in the past, such as family history, work history, mental hospitalization history, history of violence, and criminal and juvenile justice history. A third domain, *contextual* variables, refers to indices of current social supports, social networks, and stress, as well as to physical aspects of the environment, such as the presence of weapons. The final domain, *clinical* variables, includes types and symptoms of mental disorder, personality disorder, drug and alcohol abuse, and level of functioning. Community violence is measured during interviews with the patients and with a collateral conducted postdischarge in the community, as well as from a review of official records. Data are available for two time periods: the first 20 weeks after discharge and the first year after discharge.

Because this is the largest study of its kind yet undertaken, I consider it in some detail. First, I address a number of risk factors for violence (Kraemer et al., 1997) on their own merits, and then consider the risk factors in combination.

Variables are highlighted here based on their clinical and theoretical prominence in the field of violence risk assessment. Variables considered include both those that have long been considered in the criminological literature to be prime risk factors for violence, as well as those whose status as important risk factors for violence has been advanced by clinicians.

Sex

Findings from the MacArthur research that men are no more likely to be violent than women over the course of the one-year follow-up differ dramatically from results generally found in the criminological literature, but not from findings of other studies of men and women with a mental disorder. Although the overall prevalence rates are similar for women and men, there are some substantial sex differences in the quality and context of the violence committed. Men are more likely to have been drinking or using street drugs and less likely to have been adhering to prescribed psychotropic medication prior to committing violence. Women are more likely to target family members and to be violent in the home. The violence committed by men is more likely to result in serious injury (requiring treatment by a physician) than the violence committed by women.

Prior Violence and Criminality

The MacArthur data suggest quite clearly that, regardless of how the measure is obtained, prior violence and criminality are strongly associated with the postdischarge violent behavior of psychiatric patients.

Childhood Experiences and Violence

Although prior *physical* abuse as a child was associated with postdischarge violence, prior *sexual* abuse was not. Patients' reports of deviant behaviors by fathers and mothers, such as excessive alcohol and drug use, were associated with increased rates of postdischarge violence; having lived with either the father or the mother prior to age 15 was associated with a decreased rate of violence.

Neighborhood Context

The MacArthur findings suggest that research efforts aimed at assessing violence risk among discharged psychiatric patients may benefit from specifying a role for the neighborhood contexts into which patients are discharged, in addition to measuring their individual characteristics. That is, violence by persons with mental disorders may be, in part, a function of the high-crime neighborhoods in which they typically reside. The association between race and violence, for example, was rendered insignificant when statistical controls were applied to the crime rate of the neighborhoods in which the patients resided.

Diagnosis

The presence of a co-occurring diagnosis of substance abuse or dependence was found to be a key factor in the occurrence of violence. A diagnosis of a major mental disorder was associated with a lower rate of violence than a diagnosis of an "other" mental disorder, primarily a personality or adjustment disorder. Further, within the major mental disorders, a diagnosis of schizophrenia was associated with lower rates of violence than a diagnosis of depression or of bipolar disorder, as several other studies have found (e.g., Gardner, Lidz, Mulvey, & Shaw, 1996; Quinsey et al., 1998).

Psychopathy

Despite the low base rate of psychopathy per se, as measured by scores on the Hare Psychopathy Checklist: Screening Version (PCL-SV; Hart, Cox, & Hare, 1995) among the civil psychiatric patients studied, limited traits of psychopathy and antisocial behavior were predictive of future violence. The PCL-SV added incremental validity to a host of covariates in predicting violence, including recent violence, criminal history, substance abuse, and other personality disorders. However, most of the PCL-SV's basic *and* unique predictive power is based on its "antisocial behavior" factor, rather than the "emotional detachment" factor.

Delusions

The MacArthur data suggest that the presence of delusions does not predict higher rates of violence among recently discharged psychiatric patients. This conclusion remains accurate even when the type of delusions and their content (including violent content) is taken into account. In particular, the much discussed findings of a relationship between threat/control-override delusions and violence (Link & Stueve, 1994) were not confirmed in the MacArthur study. On the other hand, nondelusional suspiciousness—perhaps involving a tendency toward misperception of others' behavior as indicating hostile intent—does appear to be linked with subsequent violence and may account for the findings of previous studies.

Hallucinations

Although command hallucinations per se did not elevate violence risk, if the voices commanded violent acts, the likelihood of their occurrence over the subsequent year was significantly increased. These results should reinforce the tendency toward caution that clinicians have always had when dealing with patients who report voices commanding them to be violent.

Violent Thoughts

The MacArthur results indicate that when patients report violent thoughts during hospitalization, there is indeed a greater likelihood that they will engage in violent acts during the first 20 weeks and during the year following discharge. It was especially increased for patients who continued to report imagined violence after discharge.

Anger

Patients with high scores on the Novaco Anger Scale (Novaco, 1994) at hospitalization were twice as likely as those with low anger scores to engage in violent acts after discharge. The effect, although neither highly predictive nor large in absolute terms, was statistically significant.

A few of the variables from the MacArthur Study examined here were quite predictive of violence, as expected (e.g., prior violence). Contrary to expectations, other variables were found not to be risk factors for violence at all in our sample (e.g., delusions, schizophrenia). Most criminological and clinical variables we examined, however, had a complex relationship to violence. The complexity of the findings reported here underscores the difficulty of identifying *main effect* or *univariate* predictors of violence: variables that are across-the-board risk factors for violence in all populations. This complexity is no doubt one of the principal reasons why clinicians, relying on a fixed set of individual risk factors, have had such difficulty making accurate risk assessments. It suggests the need to take an *interactional* approach to violence risk assessment, such that the same variable could be a positive risk factor for violence in one group, unrelated to violence in another group, and a protective factor against violence in a third group. Such an interactional strategy for violence risk assessment is the one adopted in the MacArthur Study.

Risk Factors in Combination

The MacArthur Study developed what the researchers called an iterative classification tree, or ICT. A classification tree approach to violence risk assessment is predicated on an interactive and contingent model of violence, one that allows many different combinations of risk factors to classify a person as high or low risk. Whether a particular question is asked in any clinical assessment grounded in this approach depends on the answers given to each prior question by the person being evaluated. Based on a sequence established by the classification tree, a first question is asked of all persons being assessed. Contingent on the answer to that question, one or another second question is posed, and so on, until each person is classified into a category on the basis of violence risk. This contrasts with the usual approach to actuarial risk assessment, in which a common set of questions is asked of everyone being assessed and every answer is weighted and summed to produce a score that can be used for purposes of categorization.

The first test of the ICT method (Steadman et al., 2000) focused on how well the method performed in making violence risk assessments under ideal conditions (i.e., with few constraints on the time or resources necessary to gather risk factors). For example, the risk factor that most clearly differentiated high-risk from low-risk groups was the PCL-SV (Cox, Hart, & Hare, 1995). Given that the full Hare PCL-R requires several hours for data gathering and administration (the Screening Version alone takes over 1 hour to administer), resource constraints in many nonforensic clinical settings will preclude its use. Monahan et al. (2001) sought to increase the utility of this actuarial method for real-world clinical decision making by applying the method to a set of violence risk factors commonly available in clinical records or capable of being routinely assessed in clinical practice. Results showed that the ICT partitioned three-quarters of a sample of psychiatric patients into one of two categories with regard to their risk of violence toward others during the first 20 weeks after discharge. One category consisted of groups whose rates of violence were *no more than half* the base rate of the total patient sample (i.e., equal to or less than 9% violent). The other category consisted of groups whose rates of violence were *at least twice* the base rate of the total patient sample (i.e., equal to or greater than 37% violent). The actual prevalence of violence within individual risk groups varied from 3% to 53%.

Finally, rather than pitting different risk assessment models against one another and choosing the one model that appears "best," Monahan et al. (2001) adopted an approach that integrates the predictions of many different risk assessment models, each of which may capture a different but important facet of the interactive relationship between the measured risk factors and violence. Using this multiple models approach, these researchers ultimately combined the results of five prediction models generated by the ICT methodology. By combining the predictions of several risk assessment models, the multiple models approach minimizes the problem of data overfitting that can result when a single "best" prediction model is used. As important, this combination of models produced results not only superior to those of any of its constituent models, but superior to any other actuarial violence risk assessment procedure reported in the literature to date. Monahan et al. (2001) were able to place all patients into one of five risk classes for which the prevalence of violence during the first 20 weeks following discharge into the community varied between 1% and 76%, with an area under the Receiver Operating Characteristic curve (Swets et al., 2000) of .88.

THE CLINICAL ADJUSTMENT OF ACTUARIAL ESTIMATES

Should the kinds of actuarial risk assessment described be used *to supplant* clinical judgment of violence risk? Or is actuarial risk assessment best considered a tool, a very powerful tool, *to support* the exercise of clinical judgment regarding violence risk? The question is not easily or unambiguously answered.

The group that developed the VRAG addressed the issue of whether, and to what extent, the results produced by such an instrument should be subject to "adjustment" by clinicians. Interestingly, their answer has evolved over time. In 1994, Webster, Harris, Rice, Cormier, and Quinsey stated:

> If adjustments are made conservatively and *only* when a clinician believes, on good evidence, that a factor is related to the likelihood of violent recidivism in an individual case, predictive accuracy may be improved. (p. xx; emphasis in original)

Four years later, however, Quinsey et al. (1998) had a change of heart:

> What we are advising is not the addition of actuarial methods to existing practice, but rather the complete replacement of existing practice with actuarial methods. This is a different view than we expressed in Webster et al. (1994), where we advised the practice of adjusting actuarial estimates of risk by up to 10% when there were compelling circumstances to do so. . . . We no longer think this practice is justifiable. Actuarial methods are too good and clinical judgment too poor to risk contaminating the former with the latter. (p. 171)

Others in this field, although strongly approving of the use of actuarial instruments in violence risk assessment, have taken a more sanguine view of allowing clinicians to review and, if they believe necessary, to revise actuarial risk estimates. Hanson (1998), for example, has stated that "it would be imprudent for a clinical judge to automatically defer to an actuarial risk assessment" (p. 53), and Hart (1998) has written, "Reliance—at least complete reliance—on actuarial decision making by professionals is unacceptable" (p. 126).

Two primary reasons are given in support of allowing clinicians the option to use their judgment to revise actuarial violence risk assessment estimates. The first reason can be termed *questionable validity generalization* and the second *rare risk or protective factors*.

Questionable Validity Generalization

The VRAG was constructed and cross-validated on a sample that consisted entirely of male forensic patients who were predominantly White Canadians. The instrument has impressive validity in predicting violence among people with these attributes. But does that validity generalize—at least, does it generalize as impressively—when the instrument is used to assess the violence risk of women, or of civil psychiatric patients, or of people of African ancestry, or of people (of either sex and whatever race and legal status) from the United States? This is a question of validity generalization (Cook & Campbell, 1979). Likewise, the ICT generated by the MacArthur Violence Risk Assessment Study was constructed and bootstrapped on a sample that consisted of White, African American, and Hispanic civilly hospitalized patients from the United States, who were between 18 and 40 years old. Is the considerable predictive validity of the ICT generalizable to people of Asian ancestry, or to forensic patients, or to people in Canada, or to people who are less than 18 or more than 40 years old, or to the emergency room assessments of persons who have not recently been hospitalized? The predictive validity of these two instruments may well generalize widely. Yet, there comes a point at which the sample to which an actuarial instrument is being applied appears so fundamentally dissimilar to the sample on which it was constructed and originally validated (e.g., using the VRAG on the kinds of patients studied in the MacArthur research, or using the ICT on the kinds of offenders studied in the VRAG research) that one would be hard pressed to castigate the evaluator who took the actuarial estimate as advisory rather than conclusive.

Rare Risk or Protective Factors

The second reason often given in defense of allowing a clinician the option to review and revise actuarial risk estimates is that the clinician may note the presence of rare risk or protective factors in a given case, and that these factors—precisely because they are rare—will not have been properly taken into account in the construction of the actuarial instrument. This issue has been termed *broken leg countervailings* by Grove and Meehl (1996, following Meehl, 1954). The story is simple: A researcher has developed an actuarial instrument that predicts with great accuracy when people will go to the movies, and the instrument yields an estimate of .80 that a given individual, Professor Smith, will go to the movies tomorrow. But the researcher then learns that Professor Smith has just broken his leg and is immobilized in a hip cast. "Obviously, it would be absurd to rely on the actuarial prediction in the face of this overwhelmingly prepotent fact" (p. 307). Grove and Meehl call the countervailing of actuarial risk estimates by rare events "one of the few intellectually interesting concerns of the antistatistical clinicians" (p. 307), but they are skeptical about its applicability to areas such as violence risk assessment. In the broken leg story, they state, there is "an almost perfectly reliable ascertainment of a fact [a broken leg] and an almost perfect correlation between that fact and the kind of fact being predicted [going to the movies]. Neither one of these delightful conditions obtains in the usual kind of social science prediction of behavior from probabilistic inferences" (p. 308).

In the context of actuarial instruments for assessing violence risk, the most frequently mentioned "broken leg" is a direct threat, that is, an apparently serious statement of intention to do violence to a named victim. Assuming that most minimally rational people who do not want to be in a hospital can consciously suppress the verbalization of such intentions while they are being evaluated, direct threats are presumably rare, and for that reason will not emerge as items on an actuarial instrument. Yet, as Hart (1998) states, "Does it matter at all what an offender's total score is on the VRAG, how many risk factors are present or whether he scores above a specific cut-off, if he also expresses genuine homicidal intent?" (p. 126). Similarly, Hanson (1998), in the context of predicting violence among sex offenders, has taken this position: "Although I am aware of no study that has examined the relationship between behavioral intentions and sexual offense recidivism, it would be foolish for an evaluator to dismiss an offender's stated intention to reoffend" (p. 61).

Grove and Meehl (1996) no doubt would respond that the "genuineness" of homicidal intent, or whether an offender has actually "stated" his or her intention to reoffend, cannot be determined with anything like the reliability of assessing whether a leg is broken. Even if it could, the relationship between stated intention to be violent and violent behavior is much more tenuous than the relationship between being put in a body cast and going out to the movies.

Consider the example of delusions. The MacArthur Study found that the presence of delusions was not generally a risk factor for violence (see previous text). Yet, Appelbaum, Robbins, and Monahan (2000) have cautioned against ignoring delusions in a given case:

> Even on their face, [these data] do not disprove the clinical wisdom that holds that persons who have acted violently in the past on the basis of their delusions may well do so again. Nor do they provide support for neglecting the potential threat of an acutely destabilized, delusional person in an emergency setting, in which the person's past history of violence and community supports are unknown. (p. 571)

It may be instructive in thinking about this difficult issue, as it has been in thinking about other topics in this area (Monahan & Steadman, 1996), to analogize violence prediction to weather prediction. The National Weather Service (NWS) routinely collects data on risk factors (e.g., barometric pressure) known to be predictors of one or another type of weather. This information is analyzed by computer programs that yield what the NWS refers to as "objective" (what would here be called actuarial) predictions of various weather events. These predictions are given at regular intervals to meteorologists in local areas. The local meteorologists, who refer to the actuarial estimates as "guidance, not gospel," then review and, if they believe necessary, revise them. For example, a local meteorologist might temper an objective prediction of "sunny and dry" for the forecast area if he or she looked out the window and saw threatening clouds approaching. A "subjective" (what would here be called clinical) prediction is then issued to the media.

Weather forecasting is one area in which the clinical review and revision of actuarial risk estimates has been empirically studied (for others, see Grove & Meehl, 1996; Quinsey et al., 1998). Clinical involvement actually increases, rather than decreases, predictive accuracy in the meteorological context. The clinically revised predictions of temperature and precipitation are consistently more valid than the unrevised actuarial ones (Carter & Polger, 1986).

Will clinical review and revision increase the validity of actuarial predictions of violence, as it increases the validity of actuarial predictions of the weather? Reasonable people will differ on the aptness of the weather analogy. As with validity generalization, the advisability of allowing clinicians to take into account rare risk or protective factors is ultimately an empirical question. It would be invaluable to make a careful study of (a) *how often,* when they review actuarial risk estimates, clinicians feel it necessary to revise those estimates; (b) *why* clinicians feel it necessary to revise the actuarial estimates (e.g., the specific reason that the validity of the

actuarial instrument is believed not to generalize, or the specific rare risk or protective factor that is believed to be present); and (c) *how much* clinicians want to revise actuarial risk estimates. Pending such research, I believe that actuarial instruments (including, among others, the multiple ICT presented here) are best viewed as "tools" for clinical assessment (cf. Grisso & Appelbaum, 1998)—tools that support, rather than replace, the exercise of clinical judgment. This reliance on clinical judgment, aided by an empirical understanding of risk factors for violence and their interactions, reflects, and in my view should reflect, the standard of care at this juncture in the field's development.

RISK COMMUNICATION

Risk communication as an essential adjunct to risk assessment is an issue that will become increasingly salient in the future (Monahan & Steadman, 1996). After a clinician—perhaps with the assistance of an actuarial risk device—has made an estimate of the likelihood of harm that a person represents, how is the clinician to communicate this information to decision makers? "Risk communication" has been defined by the National Research Council (1989) as:

> an interactive process of exchange of information and opinion among individuals, groups, and institutions; often involves multiple messages about the nature of risk or expressing concerns, opinions, or reactions to risk messages or to legal and institutional arrangements for risk management. (p. 322)

For example, in the United States, most states have adopted the language of the California "dangerousness standard": that to be admitted to a mental hospital against his or her will, a person must be mentally disordered and "dangerous to self or others." But some states refer to the "likelihood" that the individual will cause "serious harm." The National Center for State Courts (1986) spoke of "predictions of violence," and the American Bar Association (1989) made reference to "a substantial risk of serious bodily harm to others." Finally, one influential court decision phrased the issue in terms of a "probability" of future harm (*Cross v. Harris,* 1969).

Dangerousness, likelihood, risk, and probability, therefore, often have been used fungibly to refer to the level of uncertainty of undesirable outcomes that may occur if some persons with mental disorder are left at liberty. However, the extensive literature in the area of risk perception and behavioral decision theory has uncovered many subtle and anomalous effects that suggest that these various terms may not be fungible. They may, in fact, have differential effects on the judgments that are rendered by clinicians and courts.

Although there is a great deal of research on the communication of some risks (e.g., risk of disease or environmental damage; National Research Council, 1989), research on the communication of violence risk is in its infancy. Two recent studies by Heilbrun and colleagues addressed clinicians' practices and preferences in this area. Heilbrun, Philipson, Berman, and Warren (1999) found that clinicians were reluctant to employ numerical probabilities in communicating risk estimates. Clinicians stated a number of reasons for this reluctance, ranging from their view that "the state of the research literature doesn't justify using specific numbers" to "I don't want to be held accountable for being that precise." Heilbrun, O'Neill, Strohman, Bowman, and Philipson (2000) presented experienced psychologists and psychiatrists with vignettes that varied in their method of risk communication. There were virtually no significant differences between the disciplinary groups. Clinicians tended to prefer categorical risk communication (high/moderate/low-violence risk) and risk communication that had explicit implications for risk management. In this regard, McNiel and Binder (1998) compared how clinicians' categorical assessments of the violence risk presented by newly admitted psychiatric patients compared with their probabilistic assessments. They found that clinical designations of low, medium, and high risk that the patient would be violent in the next week (if not admitted to the hospital) corresponded to mean clinical probability estimates of 29%, 64%, and 76%, respectively.

In a study by Slovic and Monahan (1995), adults were shown hypothetical stimulus vignettes describing mental patients and were asked to judge (a) the probability that the patient would harm someone else; (b) whether the patient should be categorized as "dangerous"; and (c) whether coercion should be used to ensure treatment. Probability and dangerousness judgments were systematically related and were predictive of the judged necessity for coercion. However, judged probability was strongly dependent on the form of the response scale, suggesting that probability was not represented consistently and quantitatively in the subjects' minds. For example, one response scale for expressing the probability of harm went from 0% to 100% in 10% increments. Another response scale went from "less than 1 chance in 1,000" to "greater than 40%." Judgments about the probability of violence were much higher using the first response scale than using the second. In a second study, Slovic and Monahan (1995) replicated these findings with experienced forensic clinicians as subjects.

· Slovic, Monahan, and MacGregor (2000) continued this line of research. Forensic psychologists and psychiatrists were shown case summaries of patients hospitalized with mental disorder and were asked to judge the likelihood that the patient would harm someone within six months after discharge from the hospital. They also judged whether the patient posed a high risk, medium risk, or low risk of harming someone after discharge. This studies replicated, with real case summaries as stimuli, the response-scale effects found by Slovic and Monahan (1995). Providing clinicians with response scales allowing more discriminability among smaller probabilities led patients to be judged as posing lower probabilities of committing harmful acts. This format effect was not eliminated by having clinicians judge relative frequencies rather than probabilities or by providing them with instruction in how to make these types of judgments. In addition, frequency scales led to lower mean likelihood judgments than did probability scales. But, at any given level of likelihood, a patient was judged as posing higher risk if that likelihood was derived from a frequency scale (e.g., 10 out of 100) than if it was derived from a probability scale (e.g., 10%). Similarly, communicating a patient's dangerousness as a relative frequency (e.g., 2 out of 10) led to much higher perceived risk than did communicating a comparable probability (e.g., 20%). The different reactions to probability and frequency formats appear to be attributable to the more frightening images evoked by frequencies.

Clearly, it makes no clinical or policy sense to keep twice as many people in the hospital when their risk of violence is characterized as "20 out of 100" than when it is characterized as "20%." If the individual communicating information about violence risk believes that patients "should" be hospitalized for longer periods of time, our data suggest that one way to accomplish this goal is to communicate violence risk in terms of frequencies rather than in terms of probabilities. Indeed, an intuitive grasp of this finding may explain why advocates for longer hospital stays frame their arguments in terms of frequencies rather than probabilities. For example, Torrey and Zdanowicz (1998) write that "approximately 1,000 homicides a year are committed nationwide by seriously mentally ill individuals who are not taking their medication," and not that the annual likelihood of being killed by such an individual is approximately .0000036 (i.e., 1,000 out of 273 million Americans will die in this manner each year). These advocates are quite open about their motivation: They *want* to frighten the general public about violence by people with mental disorder, in the hope that this fear will translate into increased funding for mental health services (Satel & Jaffe, 1998). The use of frequencies rather than probabilities may promote the desired fear arousal.

Can we give any advice to the risk communicator who is not an advocate for one outcome or action over another, but rather desires to present the decision maker with an "objective" or "unbiased" estimate of violence risk? I offer two possibilities. Our findings suggest that probabilities and frequencies each come with a complex set of advantages and disadvantages as formats for communicating violence risk. Neither is inherently superior to or less susceptible of bias than the other. One option, therefore, is that clinicians employ *multiple* formats for communicating violence risk. For example, a risk communication might read: "Of every 100 patients similar to Mr. Jones, 20 are expected to be violent to others. In other words, Mr. Jones is estimated to have a 20% likelihood of violence." If multiple formats were used in violence risk communication, the biases associated with any given risk communication format might, at least to some (unknown) extent, cancel each other out. In addition, the possibility of strategic behavior in choosing a risk communication format that promoted a favored policy outcome would be reduced if the risk communicator was instructed to use multiple formats rather than to select a single one.

A second option was suggested by Monahan and Steadman (1996). They analogized violence prediction to weather prediction, as practiced by the NWS. Whereas the risk of some common meteorological events, such as precipitation, is communicated using a probabilistic format (e.g., 40% chance of rain), the risk of rarer and more severe events, such as tornadoes and hurricanes, is communicated using a *categorical* format (e.g., a hurricane "watch" or a tornado "warning"). Monahan and Steadman give illustrative examples of categorical violence risk communications, ranging from *low violence risk* ("Few risk factors are present. No further inquiry into violence risk or special preventive actions are indicated") to *very high violence risk* ("Many key risk factors are present. Enough information is available to make a decision. Take preventive action now; e.g., intensive case management or treatment, voluntary or involuntary treatment, and warning the potential victim"). Of course, the decision maker who received such a categorical communication would also have to be informed about what behaviors constituted violence, what time period was at issue, what specific risk factors were present, and what cutoff scores were used to generate the risk categories. Note that Heilbrun, Philipson, et al. (1999) found that both psychologists and psychiatrists preferred a categorical format for communicating risk, especially when the risk communication was coupled with prescriptions for risk management (as in the above examples from Monahan & Steadman).

CONCLUSION

The future of violence risk assessment is likely to see more precise depictions of which specific risk factors are associated with violence in which specific types of people. Violence risk assessment is likely to continue to move strongly in an actuarial direction, including the introduction of the first violence risk assessment software (Monahan et al., 2001). Increased attention is likely to be given to how estimates of risk are best communicated to those who have to make decisions based on them, and to how risk, once communicated, is clinically managed (Monahan & Appelbaum, 2000).

REFERENCES

American Bar Association. (1989). *ABA Criminal Justice Mental Health Standards*. Chicago: Author.

American Bar Association. (1998). *National benchbook on psychiatric and psychological evidence and testimony*. Washington, DC: Author.

American Psychiatric Association. (1983). Guidelines for legislation on the psychiatric hospitalization of adults. *American Journal of Psychiatry, 140*, 672–679.

Appelbaum, P. (1988). The new preventive detention: Psychiatry's problematic responsibility for the control of violence. *American Journal of Psychiatry, 145*, 779–785.

Appelbaum, P., Robbins, P., & Monahan, J. (2000). Violence and delusions: Data from the MacArthur Violence Risk Assessment Study. *American Journal of Psychiatry, 157*, 566–572.

Appelbaum, P., & Rosenbaum, A. (1989). *Tarasoff* and the researcher: Does the duty to protect apply in the research setting? *American Psychologist, 44*, 885–894.

Barefoot v. Estelle, 463 U.S. 880 (1983).

Blumenthal, S., & Lavender, T. (2000). *Violence and mental disorder*. Hereford, England: Zito Trust.

Borum, R. (1996). Improving the clinical practice of violence risk assessment: Technology, guidelines, and training. *American Psychologist, 51*, 945, 948.

Carter, G., & Polger, P. (1986). *A 20-year summary of National Weather Service verification results for temperature and precipitation* (Technical Memorandum NWS FCST 31). Washington, DC: National Oceanic and Atmospheric Administration.

Champion, D. (1994). *Measuring offender risk: A criminal justice sourcebook*. Westport, CT: Greenwood Press.

Cocozza, J., & Steadman, H. (1976). The failure of psychiatric predictions of dangerousness: Clear and convincing evidence. *Rutgers Law Review, 29*, 1084–1101.

Cook, T., & Campbell, D. (1979). *Quasi-experimentation: Design and analysis issues for field settings*. Skokie, IL: Rand McNally.

Cross v. Harris, 418 F.2d 1095 (1969).

Daubert v. Merrell Dow Pharmaceutical, Inc., 509 U.S. 579, 113 S. Ct. 2786 (1993).

Douglas, K., Ogloff, J., Nicholls, T., & Grant, I. (1999). Assessing risk for violence among psychiatric patients: The HCR-20 Violence Risk Assessment Scheme and the Psychopathy Checklist:

Screening version. *Journal of Consulting and Clinical Psychology, 67,* 917–930.

Douglas, K., & Webster, C. (1999). The HCR-20 Violence Risk Assessment Scheme: Concurrent validity in a sample of incarcerated offenders. *Criminal Justice and Behavior, 26,* 3–19.

E.I. du Pont de Nemours & Co. v. Robinson, 923 S.W.2d 549 (Tex. 1995).

Ennis, B., & Litwack, T. (1974). Psychiatry and the presumption of expertise: Flipping coins in the courtroom. *California Law Review, 62,* 693–752.

Gardner, W., Lidz, C., Mulvey, E., & Shaw, E. (1996). A comparison of actuarial methods for identifying repetitively violent patients with mental illness. *Law and Human Behavior, 20,* 35–48.

Grisso, T., & Appelbaum, P. (1998). *Assessing competence to consent to treatment: A guide for physicians and other health professionals.* New York: Oxford University Press.

Grove, W., & Meehl, P. (1996). Comparative efficacy of informal (subjective, impressionistic) and formal (mechanical, algorithmic) prediction procedures: The clinical-statistical controversy. *Psychology, Public Policy, and Law, 2,* 293–323.

Grove, W., Zald, D., Lebow, B., Snitz, B., & Nelson, C. (2000). Clinical versus mechanical prediction: A meta-analysis. *Psychological Assessment, 12,* 19–30.

Hanson, R. (1998). What do we know about sex offender risk assessment? *Psychology, Public Policy, and Law, 4,* 50–72.

Hare, R. (1991). *The Hare Psychopathy Checklist–Revised.* Toronto: Multi-Health Systems.

Harris, G., Rice, M., & Quinsey, V. L. (1993). Violent recidivism of mentally disordered offenders: The development of a statistical prediction instrument. *Criminal Justice and Behavior, 20,* 315.

Hart, S. (1998). The role of psychopathy in assessing risk for violence: Conceptual and methodological issues. *Legal and Criminological Psychology, 3,* 121–137.

Hart, S., Cox, D., & Hare, R. (1995). *The Hare Psychopathy Checklist: Screening version.* Niagara, NY: Multi-Health Systems.

Heilbrun, K., Dvoskin, J., Hart, S., & McNiel, D. (1999). Violence risk communication: Implications for research, policy, and practice. *Health, Risk and Society, 1,* 91–106.

Heilbrun, K., O'Neill, M., Strohman, L., Bowman, Q., & Philipson, J. (2000). Expert approaches to communicating violence risk. *Law and Human Behavior, 24,* 137–148.

Heilbrun, K., Philipson, J., Berman, L., & Warren, J. (1999). Risk communication: Clinicians' reported approaches and perceived values. *Journal of American Academy of Psychiatry and Law, 27,* 397–406.

Kansas v. Hendricks, 521 U.S. 346 (1997).

Klassen, D., & O'Connor, W. (1988). A prospective study of predictors of violence in adult male mental patients. *Law and Human Behavior, 12,* 143–158.

Kozol, H., Boucher, R., & Garofalo, R. (1972). The diagnosis and treatment of dangerousness. *Crime and Delinquency, 18,* 371–392.

Kraemer, H., Kazdin, A., Offord, D., Kessler, R., Jensen, P., & Kupfer, D. (1997). Coming to terms with the terms of risk. *Archives of General Psychiatry, 54,* 337.

Lidz, C., Mulvey, E., Apperson, L., Evanczuk, K., & Shea, S. (1992). Sources of disagreement among clinicians' assessments of dangerousness in a psychiatric emergency room. *International Journal of Law and Psychiatry, 15,* 237–250.

Lidz, C., Mulvey, E., & Gardner, W. (1993). The accuracy of predictions of violence to others. *Journal of the American Medical Association, 269,* 1007–1011.

Link, B., & Stueve, A. (1994). Psychotic symptoms and the violent/illegal behavior of mental patients compared to community controls. In J. Monahan & H. Steadman (Eds.), *Violence and mental disorder: Developments in risk assessment* (pp. 137–159). Chicago: University of Chicago Press.

McNiel, D. (1998). Empirically based clinical evaluation and management of the potentially violent patient. In P. Kleespies (Ed.), *Emergencies in mental health practice: Evaluation and management* (pp. 95–116). New York: Guilford Press.

McNiel, D., & Binder, R. (1991). Clinical assessment of the risk of violence among psychiatric inpatients. *American Journal of Psychiatry, 148,* 1317–1321.

McNiel, D., & Binder, R. (1998, March). *Comparison of categorical and probabilistic approaches to communication about psychiatric patients' risk of violence in clinical practice.* Paper presented at the biennial conference of the American Psychology-Law Society, Redondo Beach, CA.

McNiel, D., Sandberg, D., & Binder, R. (1998). The relationship between confidence and accuracy in clinical assessment of psychiatric patients' potential for violence. *Law and Human Behavior, 22,* 655–669.

Meehl, P. (1954). *Clinical versus statistical prediction: A theoretical analysis and a review of the evidence.* Minneapolis: University of Minnesota.

Melton, G., Petrila, J., Poythress, N., & Slobogin, C. (1997). *Psychological evaluations for the courts: A handbook for mental health professionals and lawyers* (2nd ed.). New York: Guilford Press.

Menzies, R., & Webster, C. (1995). Construction and validation of risk-assessments in a six-year follow-up of forensic patients: A tridimensional analysis. *Journal of Consulting and Clinical Psychology, 63,* 766–778.

Monahan, J. (1981). *The clinical prediction of violent behavior.* Washington, DC: U.S. Government Printing Office.

Monahan, J. (1993). Limiting therapist exposure to *Tarasoff* liability: Guidelines for risk containment. *American Psychologist, 48,* 242–250.

Monahan, J. (2000). Violence risk assessment: Scientific validity and evidentiary admissibility. *Washington and Lee Law Review, 57,* 901–918.

Monahan, J. (2002). The scientific status of research on clinical and actuarial predictions of violence. In D. Faigman, D. Kaye,

M. Saks, & J. Sanders (Eds.), *Modern scientific evidence: The law and science of expert testimony* (2nd ed., pp. 423–445). St. Paul, MN: West.

Monahan, J., & Appelbaum, P. (2000). Reducing violence risk: Diagnostically based clues from the MacArthur Violence Risk Assessment Study. In S. Hodgins (Ed.), *Effective prevention of crime and violence among the mentally ill* (pp. 19–34). Dordrecht, The Netherlands: Kluwer Press.

Monahan, J., Appelbaum, P., Mulvey, E., Robbins, P., & Lidz, C. (1994). Ethical and legal duties in conducting research on violence: Lessons from the MacArthur Risk Assessment Study. *Violence and Victims, 8,* 380–390.

Monahan, J., & Steadman, H. (Eds.). (1994). *Violence and mental disorder: Developments in risk assessment.* Chicago: University of Chicago Press.

Monahan, J., & Steadman, H. (1996). Violent storms and violent people: How meteorology can inform risk communication in mental health law. *American Psychologist, 51,* 931–938.

Monahan, J., Steadman, H., Silver, E., Appelbaum, A., Robbins, P., Mulvey, E., et al. (2001). *Rethinking risk assessment: The MacArthur Study of Mental Disorder and Violence.* New York: Oxford University Press.

Mossman, D. (1994). Assessing predictions of violence: Being accurate about accuracy. *Journal of Consulting and Clinical Psychology, 62,* 783–792.

Mulvey, E., & Lidz, C. (1985). Back to basics: A critical analysis of dangerousness research in a new legal environment. *Law and Human Behavior, 9,* 209–218.

National Center for State Courts. (1986). Guidelines for involuntary commitment. *Mental and Physical Disability Law Reporter, 10,* 409–514.

National Research Council. (1989). *Improving risk communication.* Washington, DC: National Research Press.

Novaco, R. (1994). Anger as a risk factor for violence among the mentally disordered. In J. Monahan & H. Steadman (Eds.), *Violence and mental disorder: Developments in risk assessment* (pp. 21–59). Chicago: University of Chicago Press.

Quinsey, V., Harris, G., Rice, M., & Cormier, C. (1998). *Violent offenders: Appraising and managing risk.* Washington, DC: American Psychological Association.

Rice, M., & Harris, G. (1995). Violent recidivism: Assessing predictive validity. *Journal of Consulting and Clinical Psychology, 63,* 737–748.

Satel, S., & Jaffe, D. (1998). Violent fantasies. *National Review, L,* 36–37.

Schall v. Martin, 467 U.S. 253 (1984).

Segal, S., Watson, M., Goldfinger, S., & Averbuck, D. (1988a). Civil commitment in the psychiatric emergency room. I: The assessment of dangerousness by emergency room clinicians. *Archives of General Psychiatry, 45,* 748–752.

Segal, S., Watson, M., Goldfinger, S., & Averbuck, D. (1988b). Civil commitment in the psychiatric emergency room. II: Mental disorder indicators and three dangerousness criteria. *Archives of General Psychiatry, 45,* 753–758.

Sepejak, D., Menzies, R., Webster, C., & Jensen, F. (1983). Clinical predictions of dangerousness: Two-year follow-up of 408 pretrial forensic cases. *Bulletin of the American Academy of Psychiatry and the Law, 11,* 171–181.

Slovic, P., & Monahan, J. (1995). Danger and coercion: A study of risk perception and decision making in mental health law. *Law and Human Behavior, 19,* 49–65.

Slovic, P., Monahan, J., & MacGregor, D. (2000). Violence risk assessment and risk communication: The effects of using actual cases, providing instruction, and employing probability versus frequency formats. *Law and Human Behavior, 24,* 271–296.

Steadman, H. (1977). A new look at recidivism among Patuxent inmates. *Bulletin of the American Academy of Psychiatry and the Law, 5,* 200–209.

Steadman, H., & Cocozza, J. (1974). *Careers of the criminally insane.* Lexington, MA: Lexington Books.

Steadman, H., Silver, E., Monahan, J., Appelbaum, P., Robbins, P., Mulvey, E., et al. (2000). A classification tree approach to the development of actuarial violence risk assessment tools. *Law and Human Behavior, 24,* 83–100.

Swets, J., Dawes, R., & Monahan, J. (2000). Psychological science can improve diagnostic decisions. *Psychological Science in the Public Interest, 1,* 1–26.

Tarasoff v. Regents of the University of California, 17 Cal 3d 425, 551 P. 2d 334 (1976).

Thornberry, T., & Jacoby, J. (1979). *The criminally insane: A community follow-up of mentally ill offenders.* Chicago: University of Chicago Press.

Torrey, E., & Zdanowicz, M. (1998, August 4). Why deinstitutionalization turned deadly. *Wall Street Journal,* A18.

Webster, C., Douglas, K., Eaves, D., & Hart, S. (1995). *HCR-20: Assessing Risk for Violence* (version 2). Vancouver: Simon Fraser University.

Webster, C., Harris, G., Rice, M., Cormier, C., & Quinsey, V. (1994). The violence prediction scheme: Assessing dangerousness in high risk men. Toronto: Centre of Criminology, University of Toronto.

PART SEVEN

EMERGING DIRECTIONS

CHAPTER 27

Forensic Psychology, Public Policy, and the Law

DANIEL A. KRAUSS AND BRUCE D. SALES

For many years, clinical practitioners have been involved in forensic services without the benefit of specialized training or expertise. Not surprisingly, forensic specialists criticize their work, pointing to their lack of specialized knowledge about forensic populations, legal issues, and forensic techniques. This same complaint can be leveled against forensic specialists who are untrained in the laws that directly affect their practice and the ways in which those laws are intended to influence forensic services. Unfortunately, it is fairly common to hear from forensic practitioners that they never studied law as part of their graduate training and still do not consider it critical to their work. This chapter makes the case that a knowledge of law and policy is critical to forensic work and explains how that knowledge can positively affect forensic practice and research.

Because of the breadth of activities subsumed under forensic practice (e.g., consultation, assessment, testimony, treatment, administration, and policy drafting), this chapter focuses on the two most visible of these activities: forensic assessment and testimony, using them as examples for larger

points about the importance of law and policy to forensic psychology. The main body of the chapter considers the critical points in the interaction between law, policy, and forensic assessment and testimony. The conclusion to the chapter discusses the implications of these interactions for forensic clinical practice and policy.

CRITICAL POINTS IN THE INTERACTION BETWEEN LAW, POLICY, AND FORENSIC PRACTICE

The most basic interaction of law and policy with forensic practice is that of defining what the law, the legal system, and legal actors expect from forensic practitioners. This involves policy choices within the legal system. When legislators create laws such as one allowing for the commitment of violent sexual persons, lawmakers are making a policy decision about how to handle persons who suffer from a mental abnormality, what professionals may be involved in that legal process, and what specific roles forensic practitioners must and may play. Such policy decisions are also made at other points in the legal system. For example, the federal and state judiciaries, which are responsible for developing, approving, and implementing the rules of evidence in their respective jurisdictions, are responsible for

---

Some of the examples used to support the arguments made in this chapter have been drawn from our prior writings (Krauss & Sales, 1999, 2000, 2001; Shuman & Sales, 1998, 1999a, 1999b; Tor & Sales, 1994).

deciding what evidentiary standards and thresholds will have to be met for a psychologist to be permitted to provide expert testimony in a case. We will return later in this chapter to a detailed consideration of the implications of the particular rules chosen for the admissibility of proffered forensic testimony.

Assigned Role as a Forensic Expert

Perhaps the most important and basic policy decision the law has made regarding the use of forensic psychologists in court cases is to allow them to serve current or prospective litigants or courts in one of four roles:

1. Consultant.
2. Expert witness providing adjudicative testimony.
3. Expert witness providing educational testimony.
4. Expert witness providing legislative testimony.

Understanding these roles is critical because the assigned role can affect the validity and/or the appropriateness of the forensic service. Understanding policy is critical because it affects the ability of forensic psychologists to provide their services and circumscribes the way in which those services can be utilized. Ironically, research on psychologists abilities to influence policy and the best means to create such influence is still in its infancy (Wursten & Sales, 1992).

In a consulting role, forensic practitioners are asked to inform clients about how specific psychological knowledge, experience, and information that may be beneficial to the client's interaction with the legal system. For example, a forensic practitioner in a consulting role to an attorney might be asked by the client how to select a jury favorable to their case or what questions the attorney may want to ask an opposing psychological expert during depositions or trial. Legal policies have allowed for the use of psychologists as jury consultants, who can sit at the attorney's table in the courtroom, provide questions for the attorney to ask of prospective jurors, and/or offer insights for the attorney to use to accept or reject prospective jurors. But such policies can change and have changed in some courts with an attorney's right to question jurors (and hence effectively use jury consultants) being severely limited or eliminated (Suggs & Sales, 1981).

In contrast, forensic experts retained to offer adjudicative testimony will focus their attention on providing expert testimony concerning a specific individual or fact to aid the jury (if there is one) or the judge (when no jury is empanelled). For example, such testimony might focus on the defendant's mental state at the time of the crime, whether the defendant is competent to stand trial, or the most appropriate custody arrangement in a contested child custody proceeding. The role of expert proffering adjudicative testimony is likely the one with which forensic practitioners are most familiar, and it will serve as the main focus of the rest of this chapter. In such a role, the court will be judging the admissibility of the proffered testimony, which places preparatory obligations on the expert that differ from those imposed on the consulting expert. Legal policy in this role, and in the next two roles, focuses on whether and under what standards will forensic psychologists be allowed to present such testimony. As noted earlier, we will consider these legal policies in greater detail later in this chapter.

Forensic practitioners also provide educational testimony to courts. Such testimony is typically offered to educate the jury so that they can improve their decision making on a particular issue in the trial. For example, an educational witness on the fallibility of eyewitness identifications would help the jury understand the scientific reasons why any eyewitness' testimony should not be automatically accepted, while the same witness serving in an adjudicative role would testify as to whether a particular eyewitness in a case was likely to have been accurate in his or her identification. The law has adopted a policy of allowing such testimony to aid the jury in its task, with a specific limitation that such testimony cannot invade the province of jury. Stated another way, educational experts cannot tell the jury that which jurors already should know or are likely to know. But it is not a great leap for some jurisdictions to rule that certain kinds of educational expert testimony, for example on the ability of eyewitnesses, would be barred. Indeed, this has occurred in a number of states. The import for this discussion should be obvious: Change the legal policy and specific wording of the law, and you change the ability to use psychological expertise, or the shape of the expert's services within the legal context.

Finally, forensic experts asked to provide legislative testimony in court cases are typically being requested to address the social facts that will influence whether a particular law is constitutional. For example, when the U.S. Supreme Court in *Brown v. Board of Education* (1954) was asked to determine whether separate public education was unequal for the races and violated the U.S. Constitution, the Court turned to psychological experts to provide testimony about the impact that educational segregation had on children. In this case, Kenneth Clark, a social psychologist, offered expert testimony detailing the harmful effects of segregation based on studies he performed on segregated and desegregated elementary school students.

If the expert provides legislative testimony, the use of nomothetic science (i.e., based on group data) would be appropriate to answer the court's questions, while the provision of adjudicative testimony based on nomothetic data without idiographic information (i.e., based on individual data) would more likely be ruled inadmissible. Thus, the role that the forensic expert is assigned affects the forensic services being requested, and the approach and information that the expert should offer to fulfill their role obligations. Other legal and policy issues and lessons here are very similar to those discussed under adjudicative testimony and will not be repeated.

LEGAL QUESTIONS AND DEFINITIONS

Once the role of the expert is determined, law and policy affects specific aspects of the forensic service being requested. This presents unique problems for forensic practitioners who do not understand the dependence of forensic practice on law. When psychologists are asked to provide psychological assessments and testimony in court, their services must often address legal questions and constructs that are defined in the law, but which do not directly correspond to psychological constructs, assessment instruments, and nomenclature (Anderer, 1990; Grisso, 1986; Marson, Schmitt, Ingram, & Harrel, 1994; Melton, Petrila, Poythress, & Slobogin, 1997). For example, in the criminal context, the legal definition of "insanity" does not reflect any particular mental illness or diagnosis. The current federal statute defines legal insanity as: "At the time of the commission of the acts constituting the offense, the defendant, as a result of severe mental illness or defect, was unable to appreciate the nature and quality or the wrongfulness of his acts. Mental disease or defect does not otherwise constitute a defense" (18 USC 4242).

Under the federal formulation, there is no specification about the type of mental disorder that the defendant must be suffering from other than it must be "severe." Does "severe" refer to solely Axis I conditions? To solely psychotic conditions? Does it include personality disorders? Or, will any disorder that is significantly impairing qualify? Similarly, the exact level of relationship between the mental disorder and the defendant's inability to "appreciate the nature and quality or the wrongfulness of his acts" is also not specified in the statute. Does the mental illness have to be the sole cause of the defendant's inability "to appreciate his acts," the primary cause, or a major cause? Likewise, definitions of "appreciate," "nature and quality," and "wrongfulness" are not contained within the statute or within the code, and are subject to a variety of different interpretations by practitioners and by the courts. Consequently, diagnosing a defendant as "psychotic," "paranoid schizophrenic," or as a "borderline" does not answer the question of whether the defendant is legally insane (see the chapter by Stafford in this volume).

Analogously, the determination of mental illness does not directly substitute for a decision about legal competency or incompetency (Appelbaum & Grisso, 1995a; Grisso, 1986; Marson et al., 1994; Melton et al., 1997). In Appelbaum's and Grisso's (1995a, 1995b, 1995c) study of the competency of the mentally ill to make treatment decisions, for instance, they found that over 50% of schizophrenics and 76% of those considered to be clinically depressed were judged legally competent to make hypothetical treatment decisions.

The broader lesson to be learned from this discussion is that as the explicit wording of the law changes, forensic practitioners are required to change their forensic practice. It is understandable then why forensic practitioners who are untrained in the law have ignored the importance of subtle shifts in legal language over the years. Not surprisingly, the majority of psychological diagnoses and assessment instruments were not designed to address legal questions because if they were so intended they would have to be constantly reconceptualized and revalidated based on the policy decisions of the legislature and judiciary.

In addition to the lack of legal training, there are two other possible explanations that could account for this dilemma. First, the disjuncture between law and forensic practice may occur because forensic practitioners are not engaging in the development of appropriate forensic assessment approaches. But this potential problem can only occur if the law is clear about what it expects in its legal standard, and what it wants from the expert, which leads us to the second explanation. Legal standards often offer very limited guidance in defining the appropriate testable components of a standard and what a specific forensic assessment should entail. We refer to this as the problem of operationalization.

Operationalizing the Legal Question and Rule into Psychological Constructs and Methods

For example, how should we operationalize a forensic assessment for a child custody hearing? The legal standard in all states is "what is in the best interests of the child" (BIC). The Uniform Marriage and Divorce Act (Uniform Marriage & Divorce Act 402, amended 1973) suggests that in determining the BIC, the court should consider: (a) the wishes of the child's parent or parents with respect to custody; (b) the wishes of the child as to his or her custody; (c) the interaction and interrelationship of the child with his or her parents, his or her siblings, and any other person who may significantly affect the child's best interest; (d) the child's adjustment to home, school, and community; and (e) the mental and physical health of all individuals involved. Although the UMDA has not been adopted by most jurisdictions in unaltered form (Schneider, 1991), its factors are used by a majority of jurisdictions explicitly in their child custody statutes and implicitly in their judicial determinations (Melton et al., 1997; Rohman, Sales, & Lou, 1990). Many jurisdictions have added a number of other factors to some or all of the UMDA requirements, such as the identification of the primary caretaker or the psychological parent, the moral fitness of the parents, and the parent's ability to provide food and clothing (Miller, 1993; see the chapter by Kovera, Dickinson, & Cutler in this volume).

As a consequence of the widespread variations in the BIC standard from jurisdiction to jurisdiction, there is a multitude of different BIC standards. It is not clear, for example, if the BIC standard is referring to a child's short-term or long-term psychological adjustment, a child's emotional adjustment, a child's school performance, a child's self-report of happiness, the stability of the child's family, the quality of a child's interaction with his parents or other significant individuals, all of these things, or some combination of these factors (Bricklin & Elliot, 1995; Kelly, 1993; Rohman et al., 1990; Sales, Manber, & Rohman, 1992). We return to the importance of this observation later in this chapter.

Furthermore, in each jurisdiction, final custody decisions are made by some implicit, unspecified judicial weighing and balancing of that jurisdiction's particular statutory criteria. This inexact judicial balancing between and within jurisdictions has led to wide variance in the factors that judges use to make child custody decisions. It has also resulted in wide variance in final adjudications (Grisso, 1986; Melton et al., 1997; Reidy, Silver, & Carson, 1989; Rohman et al., 1990; Sales et al., 1992). Thus, despite the frequency with which psychologists perform these evaluations and testify in court, standardized procedures for conducting these evaluations can be problematic when the same procedure is used in different jurisdictions.

Without definitional specificity, it is not possible to effectively measure and study the legal construct using psychological techniques. In other words, the lack of an operational definition prevents forensic evaluators and forensic researchers from developing valid measurement techniques, valid standardized assessment instruments, and valid summaries of the existing research in the field (see Krauss & Sales, 2000 for a extensive examination of this issue with regard to the BIC).

Moreover, many scholars argue that a complete translation and operationalization of legal concepts into psychological constructs may not be possible, because legal decisions necessarily involve a value and normative judgment by the court, which no mechanical psychological formulation can ever approximate (Grisso, 1986). Following this logic, a standardized assessment instrument can never replace the traditional

hearing process because the judge, not the forensic practitioner, must decide at what level a psychological state or set of behaviors becomes sufficiently impaired to warrant a certain legal outcome. This does not mean, however, that the attempted operationalization and objective measurement of legal standards is useless. Rather, it means that this measurement process should be viewed as a way to enhance and inform judicial decision making in most cases, rather than as a substitute for the judicial or jury decision. Ironically, the law allows for such "ultimate issue" testimony by psychologists in all cases but insanity. For example, Federal Rules of Evidence 704(b) states: "No expert witness testifying with respect to the mental state or condition of a defendant in a criminal case may state an opinion or inference as to whether the defendant did or did not have the mental state or condition constituting an element of the crime charged or of a defense thereto. Such ultimate issues are for matters for the trier of fact alone."

Returning to our first explanation of why a disjuncture exists between law and forensic psychological practice (apart from a lack of legal education on the part of the psychologists): It can occur because forensic practitioners are not engaging in the development of appropriate forensic assessment approaches. Why do we see this as an important forensic psychology law and policy issue? The answer is that even if a more operationalized legal standard, such as the best interest of the child standard, could be formulated, it is not clear that psychologists would be able to overcome a number of technical assessment problems associated with performing such evaluations and providing valid expert clinical opinion testimony. For example, a substantial difficulty associated with child custody evaluations is that such assessments necessarily involve a future prediction. Consequently, psychologists are commonly called on to forecast how a particular child is likely to be psychologically adjusted several years post-divorce based on many complex factors and interactions.

A variety of research suggests that psychologists as a group may be particularly inaccurate in making future behavioral predictions and may even be more inaccurate than lay persons (Grisso, 1986; Melton et al., 1997). For instance, clinical opinion predictions of an individual's future dangerousness have been demonstrated to be inaccurate a substantial percentage of the time (Monahan & Steadman, 1994). Further exacerbating this problem, is the fact that psychological research also demonstrates that psychologists are not generally perceived by the court or by judges as being inaccurate in making these judgments (Krauss & Sales, 2001). As a result, the potentially inaccurate and unscientific predictions offered by psychologists in this context as well as in other forensic contexts are likely to have a substantial effect on the final decisions of judges and juries without improving their accuracy (see the chapter by Meloy in this volume).

This example exemplifies many of the policy decisions that lawmakers engage in when dealing with forensic practitioners. Lawmakers presume the expertise of forensic practitioners in all forensic topics. They assume that the forensic practitioners will provide information that is directly appropriate to the legal question in issue. They believe that the information will allow the trier of fact to make better decisions, and that it is better to allow in forensic information for consideration and subsequent evaluation by the trier of fact than to exclude it. Such simplistic policy assumptions rarely aid decision making, society, or forensic professionals, nor do they promote the development of rigorous and better forensic practice. Without programmatic input from forensic practitioners and scientists to the policy process, laws will continue to be written and used in a manner that is unlikely to help promote improved forensic practices.

Despite this pessimistic perspective, there are some appropriate guideposts for improving the quality of forensic service to the law. The initial step must be to identify the legal question or questions that the forensic expert is asked to evaluate and to define the terms that the law is using in its question. For example, in the area of guardianship (a legal mechanism whereby the court can impose a substitute decision maker, known as the "guardian," on a person, known as the "ward," who is incapacitated to make personal or financial decisions), a growing number of states have adopted statutes that emphasize a ward's actual behavioral or functional inabilities or incapacities. Functional guardianship statutes, therefore, focus on what actions and behaviors a ward may not be able to perform, rather than solely on what conditions a potential ward suffers from or the potential ward's capacity to make "reasonable" decisions. Functional statutes list crucial, specific activities of daily living and financial management in their statutory definitions (Nolan, 1984; Tor & Sales, 1994). A typical guardianship statute of this type would specify that individuals not able to meet essential requirements for physical health and safety are those individuals who are incapable of undertaking actions necessary to provide health care, food, shelter, clothing, personal hygiene, and other care without risk of serious physical injury (DC code 21-2011 (16)).

This type of law is asking a forensic evaluator to determine how effectively a proposed ward performs concrete, everyday skills in his or her actual environment (Tor, 1993; Tor & Sales, 1994). Functional skills are the manifest abilities or inabilities that underlie the need for a legal guardian. Mental illness and physical disability might increase the probability that individuals cannot perform important life activities, but these conditions, by themselves, do not necessitate that these tasks and activities cannot be adequately accomplished. Thus, an appropriate evaluation would have to consider both the proposed ward's decision-making behaviors for specific tasks and the potential causes for those behaviors. It is possible and likely, therefore, that a proposed ward could be found to be incapable of performing some specific tasks, but not others. For example, a proposed ward could be unable to obtain adequate health care, but could be able to provide for his or her shelter, clothing, and hygiene (Krauss & Sales, 1997).

Explicitly identifying and defining the legal question to be assessed and understanding the specific components of the question will allow forensic practitioners to offer more focused, pragmatic, and empirically valid opinions about a potential ward's abilities. Such functional guardianship criteria could and should also lead to the development of specific assessment instruments that are designed to incorporate the skills contained within guardianship statute, and these new assessment instruments should more reliably and validly measure these legal criteria. This, in turn, should lead to more accurate expert opinions that are at least partially based on an objective instrument rather than a practitioner's subjective beliefs about incapacitation. (We will return to the distinction between subjective clinical opinion and objective scientifically derived information later.) Scores that signify a statistically significant deviation from the norm for an age group—cut-off scores—could potentially be calculated for the different skills pertinent to guardianship. This information could be used to aid in determining both the severity of a deficit and at what levels a deficit might warrant guardianship (Krauss & Sales, 1997).

The danger of not seeking to achieve this level of precision in the forensic task is that the practitioner, as an expert, can provide the attorney and the court with clinically inappropriate or legally irrelevant information. Returning to BIC standard, for example, some commentators have noted that there exists some statutory child custody criteria that a psychologist has no expertise in evaluating. Consider a state that includes the moral fitness of the parents or financial capability in its child custody statutes. Some have argued that a psychologist should not offer expert opinions regarding these factors (Grisso, 1986; Otto & Butcher, 1995). As to the latter, the majority of statutory child custody criteria (i.e., the mental health of the parents and child; the child's wishes; the child's adjustment to home, school, and community; and the relationship between the child, the parents, and siblings), all seem to highlight areas in which psychological assessment might be useful (Clark, 1995; Gindes, 1995; Oberlander, 1995). Unfortunately, the various child custody statutes, the courts, forensic practitioners, and psychological science, have not been able to specify *how* these different factors should be assessed and weighed by psychologists or on which of these specific factors psychologists have expertise to offer opinions. To pretend before the court that experts have expertise relevant to a legal question when they do not denigrates both the forensic profession and the legal process.

JUDICIAL SCRUTINY OF, AND GATEKEEPING FOR, SUFFICIENT QUALITY IN FORENSIC TESTIMONY

The law and legal policy have a complex interaction with forensic practice. Each of these layers of interaction provide important lessons and challenges for forensic practice. To fully unpack each of these interactions requires that we ask and answer questions such as why did the legal decision makers choose to consider this a question that requires expert input? If expert input is allowed, then why did legal decision makers select to use certain approach and standards that determine who is an acceptable expert and what is the acceptable scope of testimony? Is the policymaker searching for some independent verification of the wisdom of their selection of an approach and rules? If so, what is the verification procedure?

In this section of the chapter, we address these concerns by presenting an example of a policy decision by the federal judiciary with regard to the standards for admitting expert testimony into the federal courts. We limit our discussion to forensic practice and law concerns, leaving the legal policy implications for the concluding section of this chapter.

Even if the appropriate forensic assessment procedures were used, it is one of the primary legal actors, the judge, who must, according to the rules of evidence, decide whether to admit the proffered forensic testimony (i.e., testimony that is offered). Indeed, it is important to recognize that the courts (i.e., judges) are not supposed to rely on the forensic evaluators self-assessment as to the quality of their testimony.

Federal and state law has adopted complex rules that the judge is supposed to apply to proffered testimony to ensure that it has sufficient evidentiary reliability to be considered by the trier of fact. If the judge determines during the evidentiary admissibility hearing for this testimony that the forensic evaluator's proposed testimony is not sufficiently reliable, the court will preclude it from being entered into evidence. Thus, when considering the relationship of forensic assessment and testimony to law and policy, it is critical that forensic practitioners know what criteria the court will use in judging their work. Not to do so can lead to

their proffered testimony being excluded, and their forensic work being of little to no value to their clients (e.g., attorney, litigant).

The Federal Rules of Evidence (FRE) govern the admissibility of evidence, expert testimony, and scientific evidence in the federal courts and in many state courts, with 38 states having crafted their own state evidentiary requirements based on these rules (Imwinkelreid, 1994). Under the FRE, scientific or nonscientific evidence is admissible if it is relevant and not prejudicial (FRE 401 & 403). Relevant evidence is any evidence that makes a fact in issue more or less probable while nonprejudicial evidence is evidence which is more probative than it is prejudicial. For example, overly gruesome pictures of a murder victim are not generally allowed into evidence when the brutality of the crime is not an issue. Courts have assumed that the admission of such evidence will cause the trier of fact to place undue weight on this evidence in determining a verdict or a sentence rather than basing its judgment on other more relevant evidence.

Under the FRE, individuals presenting expert testimony and scientific evidence have been granted broader leeway in presenting their testimony than fact witnesses. Experts are allowed to offer opinions concerning behavior they have not directly observed and to offer opinions not based on otherwise admissible evidence (see FRE 702 & 703). For example, experts may incorporate inadmissible hearsay evidence. Hearsay evidence is a statement in court by a party about the statement of an out-of-court party that is introduced to prove the truth of the out-of-court statement. Such proffered testimony is generally inadmissible in court due to its unreliability because the originator of the statement is not available for questioning or cross-examination.

The FRE and the courts, however, have placed additional evidentiary constraints on the admission of expert testimony because it is believed that jurors lack the requisite ability to make an intelligent evaluation of the credibility of this evidence and, as a result, may place excessive weight on it regardless of its veracity (Strong, 1995; *Daubert v. Merrell Dow Pharm. Inc.,* 1993). Prior to 1993, a wide variety of standards were used to adjudicate the admissibility of expert testimony presenting scientific evidence (Strong, 1995). The most commonly used of these tests was the *Frye* test, which was based on a 1923 Washington District of Columbia Circuit Court case concerning the admission of an interpretation of an early polygraph test (*Frye v. United States,* 1923). The *Frye* court ruled that expert testimony on novel scientific evidence is admissible if it is "sufficiently established to have gained general acceptance in the particular field to which it belongs." Under this standard, mainstream scientific theories, evidence, and information was deemed admissible, while new or novel evidence would be judged inadmissible unless the field as a whole had generally accepted it.

In *Daubert v. Merrell Dow Pharmaceutical Inc.* (1993), the U.S. Supreme Court based on their interpretation of Federal Rule of Evidence 702, held that "evidentiary reliability" was the major concern in determining the admissibility of expert, scientific testimony and that this standard, not *Frye*'s "a general acceptance within its field" standard, controlled the admissibility of scientific testimony. The Court also concluded that the explicit language and history of FRE 702 suggested specific relevancy and reliability determinations as prerequisites to the admission of expert scientific testimony. The Court explained that under the FRE the trial judge is responsible for acting as a gatekeeper in deciding whether to admit scientific evidence. Note that under the *Frye* general acceptance test the trial judge is also responsible for determining whether novel scientific evidence is admissible at trial. Yet unlike *Daubert,* under the *Frye* standard, the scientific community more accurately acts as the gatekeeper of the admissibility of scientific evidence because general acceptance test is commonly met by testimony from members of the appropriate scientific community. As a consequence, *Frye* allows greater discretion to the scientific community to determine what science is admissible in the courtroom, when compared to *Daubert*.

Through FRE 104(a), the trial judge is required to make a two-prong preliminary admissibility determination prior to the presentation of the expert testimony at trial. The judge must determine whether the *reasoning or methodology* underlying the expert testimony is scientifically valid (i.e., evidentiary reliable) and whether that *reasoning or methodology* can be applied to the facts of the case (i.e., relevant).

This admissibility decision is not a simple one. To meet the implicit evidentiary reliability requirements of FRE 702, the U.S. Supreme Court in *Daubert* explained that the trial judge must examine the scientific basis and the scientific validity of the proffered evidence, and evaluate whether it "assists the trier of fact" to "understand or determine a fact in issue." The Court suggested that these requirements are only met when: (a) the proffered expert scientific testimony has bearing on a factual dispute in the case, and (b) the expert testimony effectively links the scientific evidence to the facts in the case in such a way that it aids the jury in its decision making. The former of these two requirements appears to be a general relevancy concern (i.e., is the expert testimony on the scientific evidence related to an important fact in the case?), while the latter requirement is a more specific aspect of relevancy that is best described as an issue of *fit* between the scientific evidence and specific facts of the case (i.e., will the expert testimony on scientific evidence help the jurors to resolve or understand specific facts of the case?). The Court referred to this latter requirement as the helpfulness standard.

Many lower courts have ignored this linking or *fit* requirement, and appear to treat relevance and reliability as discrete constructs and standards or subsume fit under relevance (see generally, *Moore v. Ashland,* 1998). The Supreme Court's discussion of the helpfulness standard in *Daubert* suggests that the lower courts' interpretation is suspect. The Supreme Court stated that FRE 702's "helpfulness standard requires a valid scientific connection to the pertinent inquiry as a precondition to admissibility" (*Daubert,* p. 2796). This language implies that reliability must be determined in specific reference to the legal question that the proffered expert testimony is going to address. As the Court noted: "The consideration has been aptly described as one of 'fit' " (*Daubert,* p. 2796) between the science and the legal question. Only if the fit exists can the judge be certain that the proffered testimony will "assist the trier of fact" as FRE 702 demands. The importance of this interpretation cannot be overemphasized. Science that is only generally within the broad area of legal concern in the trial would be irrelevant because it would not meet the helpfulness standard's requirement of fit. As the court noted: ". . . scientific validity for one purpose is not necessarily scientific validity for other, unrelated purposes" (p. 2796).

Evidentiary Reliability, Relevance, and Fit in Forensic Practice

How would the *Daubert* scientific admissibility standard apply to the psychological research underlying experts' testimony on the best interest of the child standard? Different research findings related to children and parenting would fare differently under *Daubert*'s reliability, relevancy, and helpfulness framework. For instance, expert testimony on the best interest of a particular child based on psychological research might meet the reliability requirements of the *Daubert* standard but fail its relevancy considerations and consequently be determined inadmissible. For example, research has consistently demonstrated that the physical abuse of children by their parents leads to poor post-divorce adjustment for these children. More specifically, continued contact with the abusing parent has been linked to poor post-divorce adjustment for the children (Buchanan, Maccoby, & Dornsbusch, 1991; Camera & Resnick, 1988; Johnston, 1996; Johnston, Kline, & Tschann, 1989; Peterson & Zill, 1986). This robust finding, however, would be irrelevant in a case in which there are no substantiated allegations of abuse. Expert testimony detailing this research would not be relevant or helpful to the trier of fact because this testimony would not aid the judge in determining the best custodial arrangement for a child who has not suffered physical abuse. Consequently, even if this type of testimony is offered, the judge would be likely to rule it inadmissible under the *Daubert* standard.

This example is an easy case for determining the irrelevancy and unhelpfulness of expert testimony based on the scientific research. A more difficult *Daubert* analysis is presented by expert testimony based on most psychological research on post-divorce adjustment of children. This research highlights what *might not be* in a particular child's best interest, but rarely suggests which of several custodial arrangements *would be* in a child's best interest. The pathology or poor adjustment focus of child custody research does little to answer the question of what type of arrangement would maximize a child's positive post-divorce adjustment. A strict *Daubert* relevancy and helpfulness (fit) analysis might find almost all expert testimony relying on this research as inadmissible even though it is reliable, because the testimony does not aid the trier of fact to determine what would be in the *best* interest of a particular child. For further discussion of this issue and other problems with the present BIC standard, see Krauss and Sales (2000).

The *Daubert* opinion suggests that the relevancy of expert testimony on scientific evidence is only determined if it is first found to be reliable, but for purposes of analytic precision we assume that research and testimony may appear relevant while being unreliable. Other expert testimony based on research findings on the post-divorce adjustment of children would likely meet the relevancy requirement of the *Daubert* standard, but would likely fail the reliability considerations of this standard. An example of relevant but unreliable research relating to the best interest of the child standard are experiments demonstrating the superiority of joint legal custody arrangements (i.e., those in which both parents share the ability to make important legal decisions for their children, usually accompanied by visitation with both parents) over all other custodial possibilities for children of divorce. Many early research studies on post-divorce adjustment of children found that joint legal custody arrangements led to better outcomes for these children (Bricklin, 1995; Sales et al., 1992). Consequently, this finding would be relevant to any decision based on the best interest of the child standard. If almost all children have better adjustment in joint legal custody arrangements it would be useful for the trier of fact to use this information to determine the best custodial arrangement for a particular child. Judges would likely use this expert testimony to lean toward joint legal custody in most cases. In fact, because of this research, many states made joint legal custody the presumptive arrangement in child custody determinations, and in these states judges are only allowed to deviate from this de facto arrangement when one party makes an adequate

showing that joint custody will be ineffective (Bricklin, 1995; Kelly, 1993). However, the superiority of joint legal custody arrangements over other custodial arrangements has not been demonstrated to be a reliable research finding. Studies, using more varied populations, have not demonstrated similar results to the earlier studies (Bricklin & Elliot, 1995; Buchanan et al., 1991; Kline, Tschann, Johnston, & Wallerstein, 1989; Maccoby, Buchanan, Mnookin, & Dornsbusch, 1993; Sales et al., 1992). It turns out that the early studies used populations that were highly educated, had high socioeconomic status, and chose (rather than had the court award) a joint legal custody arrangement. As a consequence, expert testimony suggesting that joint legal custody is superior to other custodial arrangements in all or most cases would likely fail the reliability component of *Daubert,* and therefore be inadmissible.

In contrast, some research results concerning the post-divorce adjustment of children appear, at first glance, to meet the relevancy, reliability, and helpfulness aspects of the *Daubert*'s standard, and therefore, expert testimony based on this research would be admissible. For instance, a number of different studies have demonstrated that children with high-conflict parents who are placed in joint legal custody arrangements and believe that they are caught between the parents have poorer post-divorce adjustment than others (Buchanan et al., 1991; Johnston, 1996; Johnston et al., 1989; Maccoby et al., 1993). It is theorized that the continued contact between the high-conflict parents, necessitated by joint legal custody arrangements, causes the children to continually act as mediators between the two parents. This continued mediation is extremely stressful for the child and leads to adjustment difficulties. Several different researchers using large samples and variable population groups have reported similar results. This research would be relevant in a situation in which an expert was proffering expert testimony concerning an appropriate custodial arrangement for a child with high-conflict parents. It would aid the trier of fact in assessing what custodial arrangement would be in this child's best interest, and in this case would suggest that a joint custody arrangement might not be appropriate. The research on this finding also appears to be fairly reliable or scientifically valid (Krauss & Sales, 2000; but see Kelly, 1993).

PROBLEMS WITH TRYING TO USE THE LAW TO GUIDE FORENSIC EVALUATIONS AND TESTIMONY

Although knowledge of the law can be critical to planning for one's forensic service to a client, the law, including the opinion in *Daubert,* can often leave forensic practitioners frustrated and uncertain how their work and testimony will fare in court. We address a number of these problems in this section.

Vagaries in Applying *Daubert*'s Pragmatic Considerations

When is proffered scientific expert testimony reliable (i.e., valid) for the legal purpose it was intended? The U.S. Supreme Court in *Daubert* suggested criteria to aid the trial judge in determining both the evidentiary reliability (or scientific validity) of expert scientific testimony and the admissibility of expert scientific testimony (see the chapter by DeBow in this volume). The pragmatic considerations include: (a) whether the proffered scientific evidence is testable and has been tested; (b) whether the proffered scientific evidence has been published and subject to peer review; (c) whether the proffered scientific evidence is generally accepted within the appropriate scientific community (which is similar to the "general acceptance" test that was originally announced in *Frye* to determine the admissibility of novel scientific evidence); (d) whether the proffered scientific evidence has a known error rate and whether there is a probability that using the evidence will result in an error; and (e) whether the court should include any other factors in its assessment of the proffered scientific evidence that might indicate the evidentiary reliability of the scientific information. Unfortunately, the Court did not provide guidelines on how these criteria should be used by a trial judge to determine admissibility of scientific evidence, how many of these considerations need to be met for scientific evidence to be admitted, how these considerations should be weighted in reaching a decision, nor how these considerations should be applied to the evidence presented in the original *Daubert* case (*Moore v. Ashland Chemical*, 1998).

Not surprisingly, the application and use of *Daubert*'s pragmatic considerations might lead to varying admissibility decisions even when applied to research judged to be reliable, relevant, and helpful in the previous section. When these considerations are applied to expert testimony based on psychological research on the best interest of the child standard, for example, it is clear that the admissibility of the testimony under *Daubert* is wholly dependent on which reliability concerns are applied by the judge, how they are weighted by the judge, and how strictly judges adjudicate the fit of the evidence to the legal question.

To illustrate this point, if only two of *Daubert*'s pragmatic considerations (whether the proffered information has been tested and whether the proffered information has been published or subject to peer review) are applied by trial court judges to expert testimony documenting that joint custody in

high-conflict families may cause poor adjustment for the children post-divorce, it is not readily apparent if this expert testimony should be admitted or excluded under these considerations. On one level, the psychological research on the relationship between joint custody and high-conflict families meets the requirements of both reliability considerations. This research conclusion has been empirically tested and has been subject to peer review. Research on multiple populations samples has demonstrated similar results, and different research groups have published this finding in peer review journals (Buchanan et al., 1991; Johnston, 1996; Johnston et al., 1989; Maccoby et al., 1993). Consequently, a trial court judge might admit this expert testimony as meeting the *Daubert* standard. More generally, a similar level of judicial analysis might lead to the admission of expert testimony on a variety of different forensic topics, such as clinical predictions of future dangerousness, competency to execute a will, competency to be executed, and so on.

Yet, under a more strict analysis by trial court judges, expert testimony based on this research may not satisfy reliability or helpfulness concerns. Expert testimony on the best interest of a particular child is rarely limited to presenting the research on the relationship between high conflict and joint custody. Rather, the expert testimony usually offered in these cases concerns placement opinions in specific cases. The ability of forensic experts to: (a) assess in specific cases the level of conflict between two parents; (b) assess in specific cases how "caught between their parents a child or children feel"; (c) predict accurately in specific cases which children would be better served by custody arrangement other than joint custody; and (d) predict accurately in specific cases which alternative of several custody arrangements would maximize a child's best interest or children's best interest, is unknown. Expert testimony on the best interest of the child standard rarely suggests that one type of custodial arrangement (i.e., joint custody) would not be good for a particular child. The expert testimony commonly proffered in these cases goes on to propose which particular type of custodial placement would be in the child's best interest. To date, no empirical research has been performed nor has any study been published that scientifically evaluates any of the four concerns noted previously. Under this more exacting examination, expert testimony concerning specific placements for a child based on research showing a relationship between joint custody and high-conflict parents would be inadmissible because it failed to meet these two *Daubert* reliability concerns.

Furthermore, if the *Daubert* pragmatic reliability consideration (d), (i.e., whether there is a known error rate to the proffered information and whether there is a probability that using the proffered information will result in an error), is added to the judicial *Daubert* assessment, the appropriate admissibility decision becomes even more variable. Assume for the sake of argument that the expert testimony on the relationship between joint custody and high-conflict parents passes the first two *Daubert* pragmatic considerations (i.e., a less stringent analysis by the trial court judge of the empirical testing concern and the peer review concern). The exact error rate associated with making best interest decisions based on the relationship between joint custody, high-conflict parents, feeling "caught in the middle," and poor post-divorce adjustment is unknown and likely variable. The error rate will depend on three criteria:

1. The research sample chosen. Although the research documenting this relationship has been completed on a variety of different population samples, it is safe to surmise that while all the research found a statistically significant link between these factors the exact numerical correlation varied widely.

2. Whether the decision is an individual or group prediction. An error rate associated with a group prediction is likely to be much smaller than the error rate associated with trying to make a prediction in a single case. For example, the error rate associated with a prediction of the mean score on administration of the SATs is considerably smaller than the error rate associated with the prediction of one individual's score during that same administration.

3. The exact definition of error rate. In scientific writing and research, error rate has no uniform definition. It can mean false positive rate, which is the percentage of false positives (the percentage of individuals who were predicted to have a certain outcome who failed to have that outcome) divided by the combination of true negatives (the percentage of individuals who were predicted not to have an outcome and who did not have that outcome) and false positives; percent false positives, which is the percentage of false positives divided by the combination of true positives (the percentage of individuals predicted to have an outcome who actually did have that outcome) and false positives; or any number of different possibilities that may vary greatly even within one research sample (Hart, Webster, & Menzies, 1993).

Even if a consistent error rate for decisions based on this research could be calculated and accepted, it would not end the problems inherent for trial court judges in making appropriate *Daubert* admissibility decisions, nor would it provide sufficient guidance to forensic experts on what they should do to help their client and the court most. Assume that the

error rate for decisions based on this psychological testimony and research was 27 percent. The *Daubert* standard offers no guidance to trial court judges at what point an error rate exceeds what is acceptable for this pragmatic reliability consideration. Some trial court judges might decide that a 27% error rate is too high while other trial court judges might find that the 27% error rate is acceptable. Additionally, even if a trial court judge finds the 27% error too high, the *Daubert* standard gives no indication how trial court judges should balance this finding against pragmatic reliability considerations (a) and (b). On the one hand, some trial court judges might decide that since the expert testimony on the relationship between joint custody and high-conflict families passed (a) testability and (b) peer review, that these considerations overshadow the failure of the expert testimony to pass (d) error rate, and therefore, the testimony should be admitted. On the other hand, other trial court judges might adjudicate that the failure of the expert testimony concerning joint custody and high-conflict parents to meet consideration (d), error rate, necessitates that the expert testimony be inadmissible even though it met the requirements of (a) and (b).

As can be seen from this example, the *Daubert* relevance, reliability, and helpfulness framework offers no guidance to forensic practitioners or judges on how to apply its components. Even if trial court judges apply only a few of the pragmatic reliability considerations to what appears to be relevant, reliable, and helpful expert testimony on the best interest of the child standard, there will be immense variation among judges in final admissibility decisions on this testimony. Under the present conceptualization of the *Daubert* standard, eventual admissibility decisions will be a product of the what scientific information the forensic expert offers during the testimony, the pragmatic reliability considerations chosen by the judge to evaluate that testimony, the manner in which the judge weighs the different chosen reliability considerations, and the level at which the judge attempts to fit the science to the legal question.

Liberal Admissibility Thrust of the Federal Rules of Evidence

One reason that the law may not provide adequate guidance to forensic experts can be traced to the "liberal admissibility thrust" of FRE 702. In *Daubert,* the Court explicitly acknowledged that the FRE ". . . allow district courts to admit a somewhat broader range of scientific testimony than would be admissible under *Frye.* . . ." (p. 2795). Yet, a careful reading of the case can appropriately lead to the opposite conclusion and confusion on the part of forensic experts and trial judges about how to correctly apply FRE 702. If FRE 702 is more liberal than *Frye* then should not more expert testimony be admissible? If yes, then forensic experts should not have to be concerned with scientific validity if there is a general acceptance by other forensic scholars of the forensic clinical approach they are using. Yet, if that is the case, then why is the *Frye* standard only one of a number of pragmatic considerations that the Court listed? A resolution of this apparent inconsistency is that the drafters of the FRE only intended FRE to be more liberal in the case where good science could be admitted into court, even though it was not yet generally known to the relevant scientific community, and therefore, was not yet generally accepted by it.

This explanation does not suggest that the rules governing the admissibility of expert scientific testimony will allow more testimony to be admitted into court. Specifically, the framework for analyzing and admitting scientific evidence announced in *Daubert,* using reliability (i.e., scientific validity of the proffered expert testimony), relevancy (i.e., does the proffered expert testimony speak to the legal question being addressed), and helpfulness (i.e., how well does the science fit the question being addressed) also introduces the possibility that a *Daubert* analysis by the trial court judge might easily lead to the exclusion of expert scientific testimony that would have been admitted under *Frye*. Thus, depending on the science presented in a case, and the trial judge's selection and weighting of pragmatic considerations to this science, the *Daubert* scientific admissibility standard might be a more or less strict admission rule than the previously used "general acceptance" standard, despite the Court's assertion of the rule's more liberal thrust. Once again, the forensic expert and the judge are left without a clear *a priori* set of guidelines to direct their professional behavior.

Further complicating this already confusing situation is the relationship between *Daubert's* expert testimony adjudication framework, state rules of evidence, and these frameworks' relationship to all forms of expert testimony. Although a majority of states have relied on the FRE in drafting their evidence code and laws, no state courts are bound by the Daubert decision because it involves the interpretation of evidentiary rule and not a constitutional issue (Shuman & Sales, 1999b). Because of these discrepancies, it is imperative that psychologists working in the court system know which rule applies in their own jurisdiction, and how that rule has been interpreted and implemented with respect to psychological expert opinion testimony. Knowing the appropriate jurisdictional rule will allow the forensic expert to more accurately gauge how his or her testimony will be evaluated by the court, and whether it is likely to be admitted in a particular case.

Applying *Daubert* to Nonscientific Clinical Testimony

Prior to and post-*Daubert,* some courts made a distinction between expert clinical opinion testimony and expert testimony based on scientific evidence. For example, in both *State v. Flanagan* (Fla. 1993) and *People v. McDonald* (Cal. 1984), the state courts have explicitly held that expert clinical opinion testimony does not have to meet scientific evidence admissibility standards to be admitted at trial (e.g., *Frye* or *Daubert*). These courts have assumed that jurors will accord expert clinical opinion less deference than that given to expert testimony based on scientific evidence in reaching decisions, and thus there is not the need for a judge to scrutinize the proffered clinical testimony as rigorously. The jurors will do that when assessing the credibility of the expert testimony.

Immediately following *Daubert,* other state courts adopted an intermediate position in applying *Daubert* to expert testimony (see *Moore v. Ashland,* 1998, for a review of different jurisdictions policies). These courts applied a modified *Daubert* standard to both clinical opinion testimony and 'softer' scientific testimony, by applying some but not all of the *Daubert* criteria to determine the admissibility of the proffered evidence or by creating new criteria to assess the reliability of the proffered information (*Moore v. Ashland,* 1998). For example, under the Texas scientific evidence admissibility standard, the appropriate *Daubert* questions for clinical opinion testimony are: (a) whether the field of expertise is a legitimate one; (b) whether the subject matter of the expert's testimony is within the scope of that field; and (c) whether the expert's testimony properly relies upon and/or utilizes the principles involved in the field (*State v. Nenno,* 1998).

In 1999, the U.S. Supreme Court in *Kumho v. Carmichael* (1999) weighed in on this issue, ruling that the reliability standard announced in *Daubert* applies to all expert testimony regardless of whether it is scientific expert testimony or clinical opinion expert testimony. The Court clarified that the trial judge must find that the expert testimony reliable and relevant to admit the expert testimony at trial, and that some, all, or none of the factors mentioned in the *Daubert* case may be relevant in making this adjudication. The broad discretion allowed to federal trial court judges to admit expert testimony still leaves the admissibility of clinical opinion expert testimony unclear even after *Kumho.*

A trial court judge, following *Kumho,* could weakly apply the *Daubert* admissibility standard by not applying any of the reliability factors mentioned in the *Daubert* case to the proffered testimony, and admit clinical opinion expert testimony simply because other experts in the field commonly offer similar testimony. In contrast, a trial court judge could more stringently apply the *Daubert* admissibility standard by applying one or more of the factors mentioned in *Daubert* to the proffered testimony, and conclude that clinical opinion expert testimony is too unreliable to be admitted.

Part of the reason that *Daubert* and *Kumho* has not helped to predict admissibility for clinical testimony is that it is difficult to nearly impossible to directly translate some of the *Daubert* pragmatic considerations to clinical testimony. For example, *Kumho* does not answer the question of how to assess the evidentiary reliability of expert information when there is no science to support it. If anything, *Kumho* confounds the question in two ways. First, it encourages forensic experts to use *Daubert*'s pragmatic considerations, developed to assess scientific information, to assess which nonscientific information they will offer to the court. Second, it requires the court to judge that nonscientific information according to criteria that cannot be logically applied. How can the courts apply *Daubert*'s concern with judging the error rate of the proffered science to clinically-based testimony? Simply stated they cannot. And what does peer review mean for more clinically based writings or case studies? In science, peer review suggests a level of agreement on the validity of the science, but what does this mean with respect to more clinically based writings or case studies? Peer review may suggest that it presents an interesting idea, but not necessarily a valid one. It may mean that the ideas agree with those of the journal's consulting reviewers and the editor, which at best is a judgment about the writing's reliability and consistency with the views of other practitioners, and not a judgment about its scientific validity. Moreover, because *Daubert*'s concerns with testability, publication, and error rates have little relevance beyond science, courts assessing nonscientific clinical experts are left with little guidance on how to evaluate such testimony other than the *Frye* standard, "general acceptance" test. This lack of guidance for judges may result in the admissibility of testimony that is professionally reliable but invalid. Or, courts could exclude the proffered information because it could not meet the threshold set by *Daubert*'s pragmatic considerations, and lose information that represents "best clinical practices."

Deference to Trial Court Admissibility Decisions

The problem is further compounded by the U.S. Supreme Court's decision in *General Electric v. Joiner* (1997). *Joiner* opines that absent an "abuse of discretion," appellate courts should not second guess the admissibility decisions of trial courts, and that trial courts do *not* have to use the *Daubert* pragmatic considerations in their admissibility decision making. The result is likely to be wide variability in admissibility decisions for some time to come, which will result in "forum shopping" by attorneys for the best place to bring cases and little guidance for the forensic expert. Forum shopping is likely to be encouraged, at least in some cases, because litigants and attorneys will seek to bring lawsuits in jurisdictions that have previously admitted expert testimony similar to that which they would likely proffer, and avoid bringing lawsuits in jurisdictions in which such expert testimony has previously been adjudicated inadmissible.

Combining Nonscientific Clinical and Scientific Testimony

A final conundrum facing forensic experts is whether and how much to use scientific information in their presentation. Forensic experts can present: (a) opinions based on clinical judgments because there is no scientific research available on the issue; (b) opinions based on clinical judgments, even though there is scientific research available on the issue; (c) the results of scientific research, coupled with opinions based on clinical judgments when asked for opinions that go beyond the actual results of that research; and (d) the results of scientific research. These scenarios present interesting challenges for both the expert trying to decide how to frame their testimony and to courts trying to decide whether to admit the proffered testimony.

Scenarios (a) and (b) place the forensic experts at risk of not being able to testify in the federal courts and most state courts because the lack of science could be used to prove a lack of evidentiary reliability in their proffered testimony. Only two states have explicitly rejected this approach, opting for an admissibility rule that favors the use of pure clinical opinion (*Logerquist v. McVey* (Ariz. 2000); *Kuhn v. Sandoz Pharmaceuticals* (Kan. 2000)). Scenarios (c) and (d) present equal problems for forensic experts. This is because of dilemmas posed by research on nomothetic data being used for idiographic explanations and predictions, and because of the problems posed by the current state of development of forensic assessment instruments. We will use the best interest of the child standard to explore these latter two issues.

Even if an assessment instrument could be developed that effectively predicted an agreed upon definition of best interest of the child standard, or accurately predicted one or more of a jurisdiction's best interest of the child standard's factors, it is not clear that this assessment instrument would greatly improve child custody decision making in a particular case. The scientific basis of both actuarial prediction and standardized assessment instruments is nomothetic or group data.

Both of these methods' reliance on group data cause them to be ineffective or subject to large degrees of bias and error when they are used to determine the behavior of an individual, even if the instruments were able to achieve a high level of scientific reliability and validity. For example, an extremely good psychological assessment instrument might obtain a .50 correlation with a specified outcome variable. This only indicates that the assessment instrument is capable of explaining 25% of the variance associated with the outcome. Another way of saying this is that the scientist is unable to determine what relates to changes more than half the time in the outcome variables. Any individual prediction based on this instrument is likely to be extremely inaccurate (i.e., the child's adjustment could be affected by the 75% of variance not explained by the assessment instrument). Furthermore, in any individual prediction, there is also a significant chance that some attribute specific to the case (e.g., a supportive school teacher who the child identifies with will greatly improve a child's functioning) will not be included in or measured by the assessment instrument, and consequently, the results of instrument will be faulty.

Given the importance of child custody decisions, the complexity of the factors that are likely to contribute to a successful custody prediction, and the low probability that an assessment instrument or actuarial prediction will be able to accurately determine outcomes in individual cases, indicates that these instruments should play a very limited role in the custody decision-making process. If the forensic expert attempts to use such an instrument in his or her evaluation, the proffered testimony could be rejected for failing to pass the *Daubert* pragmatic criterion of helpfulness (fit).

This hypothetical discussion of an effective actuarial assessment is somewhat inaccurate. Not only is it unlikely that an assessment instrument that achieves a 0.50 correlation with positive child postdivorce adjustment will be developed, but it is also unlikely that such an instrument, if developed, would be used exclusively to determine custodial arrangements. The actuarial assessment would probably also be combined with other forms of data (interviews, observations, and other collateral data) to reach a decision concerning custodial placement. It has not been determined if a mixed actuarial assessment evaluation would achieve greater or lesser predictive accuracy than an exclusively actuarial-based prediction. But these observations do not change the importance or accuracy of our prior point.

Even if a valid assessment instrument existed, would practicing clinicians actually use it? Practitioners have shown an amazing propensity to ignore research findings that might improve the quality of their child custody assessments. The widespread use of both the MMPI-2 and the Rorschach,

which have little identifiable relationship to the most central of child custody issues, highlights the lack of knowledge of many practicing clinicians in this regard.

A multitude of different instruments have been used to assess aspects of parents, children, and their interactions thought to be pertinent to child custody evaluations, but these instruments were not intended to lead the practitioner to a final opinion nor were they designed to specifically address statutory child custody criteria. For a recent review of these various instruments, see Hyjulien, Wood, and Benjamin (1994) and the chapter by Kovera, Dickinson, and Cutler in this volume. Partly as a result of the limitations of these instruments and the existing psychological research, two forensic assessment instruments have been created exclusively for use in child custody evaluations. These instruments are: (a) the Bricklin Scales (Bricklin Perceptual Scale, Parent Perception of Child Profile, Perception of Relations Test, and Parent Awareness Skills Survey), which assess various behaviors and attitudes of parents and children that are relevant to child custody decisions; and, (b) the Ackerman-Schoendorf Scales for Parent Evaluation of Custody (ASPECT) which is a rating scale designed to assess parental fitness in custody evaluations (Ackerman & Schoendorf, 1982; Bricklin, 1995; Otto & Butcher, 1995). In addition to assessment instruments, a number of different interview techniques have been suggested by MHPs for use in child custody dispute resolution. For instance, Schultz, Dixon, Lindenberger, and Ruther (1989) have proposed a semistructured interview. At present, there is no evidence that such interviews improve the quality of child custody evaluations.

Even though the Bricklin Scales and the Ackerman-Schoendorf Scales were explicitly designed for use in the child custody context, recent surveys of practicing clinicians have indicated that these instruments are not often used in child custody evaluations (Ackerman & Ackerman, 1997; Bricklin, 1995). In fact, clinicians most commonly administer the MMPI-2 and the Rorschach to parents for child custody evaluations (Ackerman & Ackerman, 1997; Keilin & Bloom, 1986; Reidy et al., 1989).

Although the Bricklin scales and the ASPECT were created to assess child custody issues, they have been criticized for their lack of validity (i.e., their ability to measure what they purport to measure) (Otto & Butcher, 1995; and see the chapter by Kovera, Dickinson, & Cutler in this volume). This criticism is not surprising considering that there is no legally clear definition of the best interest of the child standard nor any standardized custody criteria from jurisdiction to jurisdiction. Without the development of one or several explicit outcome variables based on the BIC, it is not possible to create an assessment instrument that has scientific validity. In other words, it is impossible for psychologists to accurately and validly measure or assess an idea (i.e., the child's best interest) that has no clear definition or functionally specific outcome.

The result is that the forensic expert can be challenged on the validity of the forensic assessment instrument used and the proffered testimony likely will be rejected under the *Daubert* test in most jurisdictions.

CONCLUSION

What are overarching lessons to be learned about forensic psychology's interdependence with law and policy? The most important lesson is that forensic psychologists have the potential to significantly influence the legal process and legal outcomes. For example, in regard to litigation, empirical research on expert testimony and juror and mock juror decision making has demonstrated that psychological expert testimony strongly affects final outcomes when it is presented on: (1) the fallibility of eyewitness identifications (e.g., Cutler, Penrod, & Dexter, 1989; Fox & Walters, 1986; Hosch, Beck, & McIntrye, 1980; Loftus, 1986; Wells, 1986; Wells, Lindsay, & Tousignant, 1980; and see the chapter by Borum, Super, & Rand in this volume); (2) clinical syndromes (i.e., battered wife, rape trauma, child sexual abuse, and repressed memory) (Brekke & Borgida, 1988; Brekke, Enko, Clavet, & Seelau, 1991; Ewing, 1987; Gaboras, Spanos, & Joab, 1993; Kovera, Gresham, Borgida, Gray, & Regan, 1997; Schuller & Vidmar, 1992; Walker, 1990; and see the chapter by Conroy in this volume but see Finkel, Meister, & Lightfoot, 1991; Follingstad et al., 1989, for evidence of an indirect effect of expert testimony on juror decisions); (3) insanity (Greenberg & Wursten, 1988; Rogers, Bagby, & Chow, 1992; Rogers, Bagby, Crouch, & Cutler, 1990); and (4) future dangerousness of a defendant (e.g., Krauss & Sales, 2001; Morier, 1987; and see the chapter by Meloy in this volume). The potential for such influence carries a special ethical and moral burden for forensic practitioners to provide quality service that represents the state of the field. To do less comprises and denigrates both the profession and the legal process.

Forensic practitioners need to carefully scrutinize, and in some cases modify, their professional behavior. Initially, they must understand their role in the eyes of the law (e.g., consulting to an attorney or the court, providing adjudicative testimony, providing educational testimony). Different roles bring different responsibilities, which can translate into different tasks to be performed at different levels of confidence. Once the role is identified and understood, the forensic expert must understand the legal questions and definitions that he or she will be asked to address. These questions influence how experts operationalize their task and should lead to clear boundaries for what they tell their client they can do for them both outside and inside the courtroom.

This work requires a sophisticated analysis of the subtleties of legal analysis. There are numerous jurisdictional differences in the law affecting forensic services as well as in the law admitting expert testimony (Sales & Miller, 2001). Forensic experts need to evaluate what information they intend to proffer to the court in light of the specific jurisdiction's rules. They must critically evaluate the appropriateness of their proposed forensic work to the legal questions they are being brought in to address (i.e., relevance and fit in proffered expert testimony), or to the forensic services that prompted the referral. Experts must also critically evaluate any science that they propose to use in their testimonial work because the courts are likely to carefully scrutinize the validity (evidentiary reliability) of this information. This admonition is less relevant from the law's side for forensic services provided outside of the courtroom. For example, in court-mandated therapy provided to offenders, the law has not yet required the use of empirically validated treatments. Even in these situations, forensic psychologists should strive to provide those services that reflect the best of psychological science and practice (Schopp, Scalora, & Pearce, 1999). Part of this evaluative process requires forensic psychologists to understand the limits of psychological knowledge for specific forensic services. Returning to an example noted earlier in regard to forensic testimony, using nomothetic data to address idiographic questions carries special responsibilities to explain to the attorney and the court the limits of this information and how other parts of the forensic clinical assessment allow the expert to ethically reach conclusions about a specific person. Use of forensic assessment instruments can be part of this forensic clinical process, but these instruments must be carefully selected and evaluated because they often lack validation data to support their use to address specific legal questions.

Ultimately, forensic psychologists must acknowledge exactly what they can legitimately provide in legal settings and the limits of those services. For example, in regard to forensic testimony, although forensic experts can testify as to the ultimate legal issue on most forensic issues (e.g., need for a guardianship, whether the testator was competent at the time he signed the will) in most jurisdictions (federal and state), they should avoid doing so unless they can be confident in their conclusion. If forensic experts were willing to limit themselves to the role of specialized investigator and expert factual witness for the court, they might well improve the validity of forensic service and testimony. Outside of the courtroom, this admonition suggests that forensic psychologists should clearly inform legal actors of the clinical implications of their services for the law. For example, forensic therapists who provide court-mandated therapy to juvenile offenders should clearly inform the court of the outcomes likely to ensue from such dispositions (e.g., recidivism rates for different subpopulations with different presenting problems undergoing different therapeutic regimens). Not to do so encourages or at least allows the law to inappropriately evolve based on false assumptions by legal decision makers. Thus, it is important to understand the distinction the law draws between science and clinical art and opinion, and the ways this distinction plays out in different jurisdictions for different types of forensic services. When integrating information for forensic clinical decisions, experts must be able to identify and differentiate the psychological *facts*, psychological *inferences*, and psychological *opinions* that they are drawing upon and making.

As to forensic psychology's interdependence with policy, there are five major policy lessons that ensue from the previous discussion:

1. Although the law is partially based on normative legal concerns and considerations (e.g., adhering to the U.S. Constitution), empirical, political, social, and moral concerns and considerations also greatly affect the direction and form policy will take in our country. Part of the reason for this is that normative legal constraints on policy formation and revision are relatively small. Whenever policymakers create a law to address the concerns of forensic psychologists (e.g., guardianship for mentally incapacitated adults; provision of treatment services to delinquent juveniles), constitutional (i.e., normative) issues rarely arise, and where they do (e.g., the constitutionality of civilly committing sexual predators after release from prison) the courts often determine that these policy initiatives do not run afoul of the legal norms (e.g., see *Kansas v. Hendricks,* 1997). Thus, one of the essential lessons that forensic psychologists must keep in mind in regard to forensic psychology's interdependence on policy is that policymakers have enormous latitude in crafting societal responses to many mental health problems. If forensic psychologists as experts do not attempt to influence and shape this policy development, it can result in inappropriate policy formation with such policies forcing forensic psychologists to participate in the legal system in ways for which they are not well trained or suited (e.g., performing order maintenance rather than therapeutic functions in institutions) (Sales & Shah, 1996).

2. Policymaker discretion extends beyond creating laws to address myriad psychologically related topics. It also includes deciding who should be involved in implementing the policy reflected by the law. We have already witnessed the fight for inclusion of psychologists in health insurance (Dorken, 1983). A similar issue is still of concern in the forensic arena today. Policymakers in the legislatures and administrative agencies (e.g., states' departments of mental health; states' departments of corrections) have the latitude to select which forensic mental health professionals must and may fill, or may not fill, particular roles in the legal process and the specific responsibilities these professionals will have when filling a role. Where policy choices are made based on the training and expertise of the forensic professional, rather than on the turf battles between disciplines (e.g., psychiatry versus psychology), clients typically win. It is important that forensic psychologists recognize the extent to which their participation in the forensic arena will partially depend on decisions made by policymakers who may be unaware of the skills that forensic psychologists can bring to the legal setting. It is up to the forensic community to educate policymakers about the appropriate fit between forensic services, forensic practitioners, and the legal system's needs.

3. Even where forensic psychologists are recognized as potentially appropriate service providers under a specific law, these psychologists are still dependent on policy because policy makers select the standards the law will use for gatekeeping which particular professionals within the larger disciplinary group can provide the particular forensic service in the given circumstance. We discussed an example of this earlier in our consideration of *Daubert* and *Kumho,* and how these cases can affect whether a forensic expert is admitted to testify in the federal courts and the majority of state courts. The choice of the particular standard selected by the U.S. Supreme Court to guide the federal courts is to some extent arbitrary and reflects a policy decision. Indeed, a number of states have opted away from these standards, applying different ones to decisions of admissibility of expert testimony in their states (e.g., *Logerquist v. McVey,* 2000, applying to the Arizona state courts). Thus, even where forensic psychologists are empowered to participate under the law, individual forensic practitioners may not be able to meet the threshold standards for participation because of lack of specific training or other criteria imposed by the policymakers who created the law. The policy lesson here is that the forensic community either needs to influence the policymaker's gatekeeping standards; or provide sufficient education, training, or experiential opportunities to help forensic practitioners have the requisite skills to meet the gatekeeping standards.

4. Policymakers also create standards that can circumscribe what services can be offered and how they can be applied. The example given in our earlier discussion of forensic assessment and testimony is the legal standard for child custody determinations. By setting the standard for these determinations, the policymaker dictates how relevant particular types of forensic psychological services will be to the law. Beyond specifying the particular questions forensic services must address, policy also specifies the practice context in which that service will occur. For example, policymakers can specify how much confidentiality is due to the patient; who must be notified of certain client behaviors; and whether certain therapies are permissible and under what conditions (e.g., aversive therapies) (Sales & Miller, 2001). Moreover, policy and policymakers have an enormous range of power over forensic practice, and thus the interdependence of forensic psychological services with policy should not be ignored. Knowing the law can help one practice competently, and ultimately improve the administration of the law and the delivery of services to individuals who are involved in the legal system. Understanding policy also can help forensic psychologists intercede in the policy-making arena so that forensic services are utilized more effectively.

5. Not all policy is legally created. Forensic psychologists also are responsible for the creation of both de facto (by custom) and de jure (by rule) policies. For example, the decision to rely on intuitive judgments without scientific validation is a de facto policy underlying forensic clinical practice for decades. Today, however, such practices are being seriously scrutinized by the law, at least in regard to the admissibility of expert testimony, and some scholars argue for the extension of that scrutiny to other forensic clinical services (Schopp et al., 1999). Conversely, rigorous forensic clinical science and thinking can offer to the law possible solutions to some vexing and protracted legal problems (e.g., Ashford, Sales, & Reid, 2001; Boeschen, Sales, & Koss, 1998). The goal, therefore, should not be for forensic psychology to be dependent on law and policy, but for each side to be interdependent with the other.

REFERENCES

Ackerman, M., & Ackerman, M. (1997). Custody evaluation practices: A survey of experienced professionals (Revisited). *Professional Psychology: Research and Practice, 28,* 137–145.

Ackerman, M., & Schoendorf, K. (1982). *The Ackerman–Schoendorf Parent Evaluations for Custody Tests (ASPECT).* Los Angeles: Western Psychological Services.

Anderer, S. J. (1990). A model for determining competency in guardianship proceedings. *Mental and Physical Disability Law Reporter, 14,* 107–114.

Appelbaum, P., & Grisso, T. (1995a). The MacArthur treatment study I. *Law and Human Behavior, 19,* 105–126.

Appelbaum, P., & Grisso, T. (1995b). The MacArthur treatment study II. *Law and Human Behavior, 19,* 127–148.

Appelbaum, P., & Grisso, T. (1995c). The MacArthur treatment study III. *Law and Human Behavior, 19,* 149–174.

Ashford, J. B., Sales, B. D., & Reid, W. H. (Eds.). (2001). *Treating adult and juvenile offenders with special needs.* Washington, DC: American Psychological Association.

Boeschen, L. E., Sales, B. D., & Koss, M. P. (1998). Rape trauma experts in the courtroom. *Psychology, Public Policy, and Law, 4,* 414–432.

Brekke, N., & Borgida, E. (1988). Expert psychological testimony in rape trials: A social-cognitive analysis. *Journal of Personality and Social Psychology, 55,* 372–386.

Brekke, N., Enko, P., Clavet, G., & Seelau, E. (1991). Of juries and court appointed experts: The impact of nonadversarial versus adversarial expert testimony. *Law and Human Behavior, 15,* 451–475.

Bricklin, B. (1995). *The child custody evaluation handbook: Research-based solutions and applications.* New York: Brunner/Mazel.

Bricklin, B., & Elliot, G. (1995). Postdivorce issues and relevant research. In B. Bricklin (Ed.), *The custody evaluation handbook: Research-based solutions and applications* (pp. 27–62). New York: Brunner/Mazel.

Brown v. Board of Education of Topeka, 74 S. Ct. 686 (1954).

Buchanan, C., Maccoby, E., & Dornsbusch, S. (1991). Caught between parents: Asolscentsí experience in divorced homes. *Child Development, 62,* 1008–1029.

Camera, K., & Resnick, G. (1988). Intraparental conflict and cooperation: Factors moderating childrenís post-divorce adjustment. In E. M. Hetherington & J. D. Arasteh (Eds.), *Impact of divorce, single parenting, and stepparenting on children* (pp. 169–177). Hillsdale, NJ: Erlbaum.

Clark, B. (1995). Acting in the best interest of the child: Essential components of a child custody evaluation. *Family Law Quarterly, 29,* 19–37.

Cutler, B., Penrod, S., & Dexter, H. (1989). The eyewitness, the expert psychologist, and the jury. *Law and Human Behavior, 13,* 311–332.

Daubert v. Merrell Dow Pharmaceuticals Inc., 509 U.S. 579, 113 S. Ct. 2786 (1993).

Dorken, H. (1983). Health insurance and third-party reimbursement. In B. D. Sales (Ed.), *The professional psychologist's handbook* (pp. 249–284). New York: Plenum Press.

Ewing, P. (1987). *Battered women who kill: Psychological self-defense as a legal justification.* Lexington, MA: Heath.

Federal Rules of Evidence, Rules 104a, 401–403, 702–706 (2001).

Finkel, N., Meister, K., & Lightfoot, D. (1991). The self-defense and community sentiment. *Law and Human Behavior, 15,* 585–602.

Follingstad, D., Polek, D., Hause, E., Deaton, L., Bugler, M., & Conway, Z. (1989). Factors predicting verdicts in cases where battered women kill their husbands. *Law and Human Behavior,* *13,* 253–269.

Fox, S., & Walters, H. (1986). The impact of general versus specific expert testimony and eyewitness identification confidence upon mock juror judgment. *Law and Human Behavior, 10,* 215–228.

Frye v. United States, 293 F. 1013 (D.C. Cir. 1923).

Gaboras, N., Spanos, N., & Joab, A. (1993). The effects of complaint age and expert psychological testimony in a simulated child sexual abuse trial. *Law and Human Behavior, 17,* 103–119.

General Electric v. Joiner, 118 U.S. 512 (1997).

Gindes, M. (1995). Guidelines for child custody evaluations for psychologists: An overview and commentary. *Family Law Quarterly, 29,* 37–62.

Greenberg, J., & Wursten, A. (1988). The psychologist and psychiatrist as expert witnesses: Perceived credibility and influence. *Professional Psychology: Research and practice, 19,* 373–378.

Grisso, T. (1986). *Evaluating competencies: Forensic assessments and instruments.* New York: Plenum Press.

Hart, S., Webster, C., & Menzies, R. (1993). A note on portraying the accuracy of violence predictions. *Law and Human Behavior, 17,* 695–700.

Hosch, H., Beck, E., & McIntyre, P. (1980). Influence of expert testimony regarding eyewitness accuracy on jury decisions. *Law and Human Behavior, 4,* 287–296.

Hysjulien, C., Wood, B., & Benjamin, G. (1994). Child custody evaluations: A review of methods used in litigation and alternative dispute resolution. *Family and Concilliation Courts Review, 32,* 466–489.

Imwinkelreid, E. (1994). The next step after *Daubert:* Developing a similarity epistemological approach to ensuring reliability of nonscientific expert testimony. *Cardozo Law Review, 15,* 2271–2294.

Johnston, J. (1996). Childrenís adjustment in sole custody compared to joint custody families and principles for custody decision making. *Family and Concilliation Courts Review, 33,* 415–425.

Johnston, J., Kline, M., & Tschann, J. (1989). Ongoing post-divorce conflict: Effects on children of joint custody and frequent access. *American Journal of Orthiopsychiatry, 59,* 576–592.

Kansas v. Hendricks, 521 U.S. 346 (1997).

Keilin, G., & Bloom, L. (1986). Child custody evaluation practices: A survey of experienced professions. *Professional Psychology: Research and Practice, 17,* 338–346.

Kelly, J. (1993). Current research on children's post-divorce adjustment: No simple answers. *Family and Conciliation Court Review, 31,* 29–49.

Kline, M., Tschann, J., Johnston, J., & Wallerstein, J. (1989). Children's adjustment in joint and sole physical custody families. *Developmental Psychology, 25,* 430–438.

Kovera, M., Gresham, A., Borgida, E., Gray, E., & Regan, P. (1997). Does expert psychological testimony inform or influence juror decision making? A social cognitive analysis. *Journal of Applied Psychology, 82,* 178–191.

Krauss, D. A., & Sales, B. D. (1997). Guardianship and the elderly. In P. D. Nussbaum (Ed.), *Handbook of neuropsychology and aging* (pp. 528–540). New York: Plenum Press.

Krauss, D. A., & Sales, B. D. (1999). The problem of "helpfulness" in applying *Daubert* to expert testimony: Child custody determinations in family law as an exemplar. *Psychology, Public Policy and Law, 5,* 78–99.

Krauss, D. A., & Sales, B. D. (2000). Legal standards, expertise, and experts in child custody decision-making. *Psychology, Public Policy, and Law, 6*(4), 843–879.

Krauss, D. A., & Sales, B. D. (2001). The effects of clinical and scientific expert testimony on juror decision-making in capital sentencing. *Psychology, Public Policy, and Law, 2,* 267–310.

Kuhn v. Sandoz Pharmaceuticals, 14 P.3d 1170 (Kan. 2000).

Kumho Tire Company Ltd. et al. v. Carmichael, 526 U.S. 137 (1999).

Lilienfeld, S. O., Woods, J. M., & Garb, H. N. (2000). The scientific status of projective tests. *Psychological Science in the Public Interest, 2,* 27–66.

Loftus, E. (1986). Ten years in the life of an expert witness. *Law and Human Behavior, 10,* 241–263.

Logerquist v. McVey, 2000 W.L. 419980 (Ariz. 2000).

Maccoby, E., Buchanan, C., Mnookin, R., & Dornsbusch, S. (1993). Postdivorce roles of mother and father in the lives of their children. *Journal of Family Psychology, 1,* 24–38.

Marson, D. C., Schmitt, F., Ingram, K., & Harrel, L. (1994). Determining the competency of Alzheimerís patients to consent to treatment and research. *Alzheimerís Diseases and Associated Disorders* (Suppl. *8*), 5–18.

Melton, G., Petrila, J., Poythress, N., & Slobogin, C. (1997). *Psychological evaluations for the courts: A handbook for mental health professionals and lawyers* (2nd ed.). New York: Guildford Press.

Miller, G. (1993). The psychological best interest of the child. *Journal of Divorce and Remarriage, 19,* 21–35.

Monahan, S., & Steadman, H. (1994). *Violence and mental disorder: Developments in risk assessment.* Chicago: University of Chicago Press.

Moore v. Ashland Chemicals Inc., 151 F.3d 269 (5th Cir. 1998).

Morier, D. (1987). *The role of expert psychiatric predictions of dangerousness in a capital murder trial: A mulitmethod investigation.* Unpublished dissertation. University of Minnesota.

Nolan, B. S. (1984). Functional evaluations of the elderly in guardianship evaluations. *Law, Medicine, and Health Care, 12,* 210–217.

Oberlander, L. (1995). Ethical responsibilities in child custody evaluations: Implications for evaluation methodology. *Ethics and Behavior, 5,* 311–332.

Otto, R., & Butcher, J. (1995). Computer assisted psychological assessment in child custody evaluations. *Family Law Quarterly, 29,* 79–96.

People v. McDonald, 37 Cal.3d 351 (Cal. 1984).

Perlin, M. L. (1994). *The law and mental disability*. Charlottesville, VA: Michie.

Peterson, J., & Zill, N. (1986). Marital disruptions, parent-child relationships, and behavior problems in children. *Journal of Marriage and Family, 48*, 295–407.

Reidy, C., Silver, L., & Carson, R. (1989). Child custody decisions: A survey of judges. *Family Law Quarterly, 23*, 75–90.

Rohman, L., Sales, B., & Lou, M. (1990). The best interest standard in child custody decisions. In D. Weisstub (Ed.), *Law and mental health: International perspectives* (Vol. 5, pp. 40–90). New York: Pergamon Press.

Rogers, R., Bagby, R., & Chow, M. (1992). Psychiatrists and the parameter of expert testimony. *International Journal of Law and Psychiatry, 15*, 387–396.

Rogers, R., Bagby, R., Crouch, M., & Cutler, B. (1990). Effects of ultimate opinions on juror perceptions of insanity. *International Journal of Law and Psychiatry, 13*, 225–232.

Sales, B., Manber, R., & Rohman, L. (1992). Social science research and child custody decision-making. *Applied and Preventive Psychology, 1*, 23–40.

Sales, B. D., & Miller, M. O. (Series Eds.). (2001). *Law and mental health professionals*. Washington, DC: American Psychological Association. A series of approximately 60 volumes that comprehensively reviews and integrates the law that affects mental health professionals (*e.g.*, psychologists, psychiatrists, social workers, counselors) in each jurisdiction. http://www.apa.org/books/lmhptest.html.

Sales, B. D., & Shah, S. A. (1996). Definition and perspective in mental health and law interactions. In B. D. Sales & S. A. Shah (Eds.), *Mental health and law: Research, policy and services* (pp. 1–16). Durham, NC: Carolina Academic Press.

Schneider, C. (1991). Discretion, rules, and law: Child custody and the UMDA best interest standard. *Michigan Law Review, 89*, 215–246.

Schopp, R. F., Scalora, M. J., & Pearce, M. (1999). Expert testimony and professional judgment: Psychological expertise and commitment as a sexual predator after *Hendricks*. *Psychology, Public Policy, and Law, 5*, 120–174.

Schuller, R., & Vidmar, N. (1992). Battered wife syndrome evidence in the courtroom: A review of the literature. *Law and Human Behavior, 16*, 273–291.

Schultz, B., Dixon, E., Lindeberger, J., & Ruther, N. (1989). *Solomon's sword*. San Francisco: Josey Bass.

Shuman, D., & Sales, B. (1998). The admissibility of expert testimony based upon clinical judgment and scientific research. *Psychology, Public Policy, and Law, 4*, 1226–1252.

Shuman, D. W., & Sales, B. D. (Eds.). (1999a). *Daubert's* meaning for the admissibility of behavioral and social science evidence. [Special issue] *Psychology, Public Policy, and Law, 5*(1), 3–15.

Shuman, D. W., & Sales, B. D. (1999b). The impact of *Daubert* and its progeny on the admissibility of behavioral and social science evidence. *Psychology, Public Policy, and Law, 5*, 3–15.

State v. Flanagan, 625 So.2d 826 (Fla. 1993).

State v. Nenno, 970 S.W.2d 549 (Ct. Crim. App. 1998).

Strong, J. (1995). *Evidence law: Cases and materials* (5th ed.). St. Paul, MN: West.

Suggs, D., & Sales, B. D. (1981). Juror self-disclosure during the voir dire: A social science analysis. *Indiana Law Journal, 56*, 245–272.

Tor, P. B. (1993). Finding incompetency in guardianship: Standardizing the process. *Arizona Law Review, 35*, 739–764.

Tor, P. B., & Sales, B. D. (1994). A social science perspective on the law of guardianship: Directions for improving the process and practice. *Law and Psychology Review, 18*, 1–41.

Uniform Marriage and Divorce Act, 402 9a U.C.A. 197–198 (1975), amended (1973).

United State Code 18 U.S.C. 4242 (2001).

Walker, L. (1990). *Terrified love: Why battered women kill and how society responds*. New York: Harper & Row.

Wells, G. (1986). Expert psychological testimony: Empirical and conceptual analyses of effects. *Law and Human Behavior, 10*, 83–95.

Wells, G., Lindsay, R., & Tousignant, J. (1980). Effects of expert psychological advice on human performance in judging the validity of eyewitness testimony. *Law and Human Behavior, 4*, 275–285.

Wursten, A., & Sales, B. (1992). Utilization of psychologists and psychological research in legislative decision making on public interest matters. In D. K. Kagehiro & W. S. Laufer (Eds.), *Handbook of psychology and law* (pp. 119–138). New York: Springer-Verlag.

CHAPTER 28

Therapeutic Jurisprudence

SUSAN DAICOFF AND DAVID B. WEXLER

Therapeutic jurisprudence is an innovative, interdisciplinary field that brings together law and the social sciences by studying the role of law as a therapeutic agent. Therapeutic jurisprudence (TJ) acknowledges that law is a social force with inevitable effects on the mental health and psychological functioning of the people it affects (Stolle, Wexler, Winick, & Dauer, 1997). Slobogin (1995) defined TJ well when he wrote that it uses social science to "study the extent to which a legal rule or practice promotes the psychological and physical well-being of the people it affects" (Slobogin, 1995, p. 767).

Therapeutic jurisprudence recognizes that legal rules, procedures, and actors are social forces that intentionally or unintentionally often produce therapeutic or antitherapeutic consequences. Its explicit goals are to maximize these therapeutic consequences and minimize any antitherapeutic effects. It therefore focuses on individuals' psychological and emotional well being and welfare. This focus frequently results in suggestions for applying or reforming laws and legal procedures in ways that achieve more therapeutic outcomes (Stolle et al., 1997). TJ focuses not only on the effects of substantive legal rules but also on the effects of legal procedures. It also evaluates the behavior of legal actors, including attorneys, judges, probation officers, and police officers (Ramirez, 1998).

The term *therapeutic outcome* is used somewhat broadly and is purposefully vague, to allow for further discussion and research. However, it usually refers to psychological well-being and may encompass the reduction of stress, anxiety, or agitation. Laws, legal procedures, and legal actors can be therapeutic for individuals when they encourage or foster certain functional behavior or attitudes. The most dramatic example may occur when the legal system provides an incentive structure to induce a drug-addicted person to pursue a course of substance abuse treatment and the individual thereafter achieves a successful treatment outcome. Other examples, however, may include empowering formerly victimized individuals or helping other individuals become more responsible. For example, the law and lawyers can help domestic violence victims abandon learned helplessness and gain greater voice and autonomy, can assist in reframing an individual's overly negative, dysfunctional cognitive beliefs (about self) through proper attribution of blame and responsibility (to someone else), and can encourage criminal offenders to accept appropriate responsibility for their actions and develop genuine remorse and a desire to reform.

When it emerged, around 1990, TJ originally focused on using its unique perspective and insights solely to propose changes to existing laws (Stolle, 2000). However, its approach was quickly expanded and it began to be used to evaluate ways in which existing laws and procedures might be more therapeutically applied or administered (Stolle et al., 1997; Wexler, 1996). TJ has been applied to suggest more therapeutic ways in which lawyers can interact with their clients (Winick, 1998, 1999, 2000). While some TJ scholarship has focused on trial courts (Schma, 2000), recent publications have also applied it to appellate courts (Des Rosiers, 2000) and the role of judges in dealing with litigants and criminal defendants (Chase & Hora, 2000; Merrigan, 2000). It is now equally relevant to legal reform; legislative efforts; appellate courts' opinions; methods and strategies; and the work of judges, police officers, and probation officers. Thus, the insights of therapeutic jurisprudence can lead to proposals for new laws, for changes in the way judges, lawyers, and other legal actors interact with others; and for changes in the processes by which existing laws are administered, applied, and enforced.

Schopp (1999) outlined the history of the development of TJ. The concept appeared in the late 1980s to identify common features of a small but emerging approach to mental health law. At the time, it was becoming obvious that legal institutions dramatically influenced the psychological well-being of the people they affected. Mental health law was relatively stable. Mental health law experts had balkanized into several groups of clinicians, academics, and lawyers working toward different agendas. Against this backdrop, TJ emerged with the goal of integrating and reinvigorating mental health law and providing a truly interdisciplinary approach to mental health law issues.

Because the TJ perspective originated in the area of mental health law, its first applications focused on traditional mental health topics: the insanity plea, civil commitment, the right to refuse mental health treatment, and competence to stand trial. However, its scope rapidly broadened to include "quasi" mental health law. Thus, it was applied to evaluate laws involving individuals with mental health issues, including sex offender notification statutes and outpatient civil commitment laws for pregnant substance abusers. Subsequently, it was applied to many substantive areas of the law: correctional law, criminal law, family law, juvenile law, disability law, labor and employment law, health law, evidence law, personal injury law, contract law, commercial law, and probate law (Wexler & Winick, 1996). It has also been applied to the legal profession (Elwork & Benjamin, 1995), mediation, and alternative dispute resolution (Schneider, 2000). Therefore, TJ is no longer simply a new way to evaluate law applicable to mentally disabled or mentally disordered individuals; it is equally relevant to the legal problems of psychologically "normal" individuals and to numerous legal matters in which emotional or psychological concerns may not be initially apparent.

TJ relies on empirical and clinical social science research to determine what may be, and what may not be, therapeutic.

Thus, it builds on existing empirical research (e.g., McGuire, 1995; Tyler, 1992) and, in some cases, calls for additional empirical work to be conducted to assess whether its proposed reforms are, indeed, therapeutic or antitherapeutic. Finally, it requires empirical research in those areas of law that are devoid of empirical data regarding their psychological consequences on individuals.

TJ has become international in scope. It has been employed to evaluate laws and legal processes in Canada (Des Rosiers, 2000), the United Kingdom (Carson, 1995; Carson & Wexler, 1994; Ferencz & McGuire, 2000), Australia (Birgden & Vincent, 2000; Magner, 1998), South Africa (Allan & Allan, 2000), and New Zealand (Levine, 2000). Finally, because it signals a shift from an exclusive focus on legal rights, autonomy, separation, argument, and competition (Wexler, 1999c, 2000) to therapeutic concerns, preventing legal difficulties, and solving legal problems creatively (Daicoff, 2000), TJ has been hailed as a philosophically significant development in law.

This chapter first examines how laws can be applied and legal practice conducted in a more therapeutic manner. Then, it discusses therapeutic aspects of judges' actions and judicial opinions. It then explores common philosophical and ethical issues raised by the practice of therapeutic jurisprudence. Finally, it asserts the leadership role of therapeutic jurisprudence in a larger movement viewing law as a healing profession.

APPLYING THE LAW THERAPEUTICALLY

The application of therapeutic jurisprudence to substantive law has primarily taken two forms. First, TJ suggests changes to the lawyer-client relationship that produce more therapeutic outcomes for clients. This is discussed next as "therapeutic lawyering." Second, TJ suggests ways in which laws might be changed, administered, or applied differently to enhance their therapeutic consequences. Specific applications of therapeutic jurisprudence to various types of legal cases are discussed.

Therapeutic Lawyering

In Litigation

Winick (2000), one of the founders of therapeutic jurisprudence, has considered how lawyers can interact with clients in ways that are more therapeutic. For example, he explains that attorneys can ameliorate the stress of litigation for clients by coaching clients through the trial process, role playing, formulating responses to potential questions, raising objections, slowing down or accelerating the pace of the trial process, being present when a decision is reached, explaining the results of a decision, being a good listener, ensuring that the client's story is told during the process, and generally monitoring the emotional state of the participants during the process. He describes a number of specific actions a lawyer can take to provide emotional support and prevent antitherapeutic consequences for a client, during difficult portions of litigation. For example, during a deposition in which the client is being questioned, the client may receive cues from the lawyer if the lawyer sits closer to the client than would normally be comfortable. In addition, such action may reduce the client's perception that the interactions are limited to the client and opposing counsel and enhance the perception that the lawyer is more involved and visible. Instead of having the client wait alone for the judge's or jury's decision, the lawyer may reduce the emotional stress of this process for the client by remaining with the client. It may also be therapeutic for the lawyer to be present with the client when the decision is presented to explain what it means, frame it positively, and assist with any strong emotional responses.

The Integration with Preventive Law

In a series of articles, a number of authors explored the integration of therapeutic jurisprudence with the longstanding approach to lawyering known as *preventive law* (Patry, Wexler, Stolle, & Tomkins, 1998; Stolle, 1996, 1997; Stolle & Wexler, 1997; Stolle et al., 1997; Stolle, Wexler, & Winick, 2000). Preventive law focuses on predicting legal disputes and avoiding, preventing, or minimizing them before they occur (Hardaway, 1997). Stolle and his colleagues (1997) argued that traditional techniques of preventive law, such as having clients undergo "legal check-ups" to diagnose and intervene early in potential legal problems, could be enhanced if they were implemented with a therapeutic eye. In turn, they argued that TJ, as a primarily theoretical and philosophical endeavor, could benefit from the practical, concrete, and skills-oriented tools of preventive law.

The integration of these two disciplines resulted in a number of specific suggestions for therapeutic lawyering. For example, a therapeutically oriented preventive lawyer would consider, when working with an elderly couple, that certain aspects of the clients' situation contain therapeutic dimensions. In particular, being labeled "elderly" can have a negative impact on their self-image. Health maintenance is likely to become a future concern. The couple's need to direct the distribution of their assets upon their deaths may raise therapeutic issues. If the couple is currently caring for the wife's mother because she has Alzheimer's disease, then they will

need resources to care for her in the future. There is a distinct possibility that the wife has an increased risk of developing this disease, and the couple may need resources to care for the wife in the future. The lawyer would raise these concerns in a sensitive and respectful manner, being aware of how psychologically difficult it may be for the couple to acknowledge and plan for them (Stolle et al., 1997).

A therapeutically oriented preventive lawyer, working with this same elderly couple, would also point out concerns raised by the couple's intentions regarding their wills. Suppose the couple wants to leave their assets to their children, but think that their third child, who has a severe alcohol and drug problem, will spend his inheritance less wisely than will their two other children. Most lawyers would simply suggest putting the third child's share in trust. If the clients agree, there would be no further discussion. However, the TJ/preventive lawyer would take legal consultation a step further. The attorney would discuss the potentially negative psychological and emotional consequences of treating the children differently. Such an arrangement can foster resentment between the children and erode their relationships, or it may result in the third child feeling less loved by the parents than the others (Patry et al., 1998; Stolle et al., 1997). In some cases, such disparate arrangements might result in the third child bringing legal action to contest the will (Patry et al., 1998). The lawyer would openly discuss the psychological impact of such legal action with the clients. The couple could then consider ways of ameliorating the negative emotional consequences of their decisions or, at least, make truly informed decisions about what legal action to take (Stolle et al., 1997). For example, the clients might discuss their wills with their children, or might draft a letter to their children explaining the disparate treatment of them in their wills, a statement that would be read after their parents' deaths.

A therapeutically oriented preventive planning approach can minimize antitherapeutic consequences of legal documents and legal actions for clients with HIV/AIDS, who often have significant psychological concerns (Stolle et al., 1997; Winick, 1998). The lawyer would be sensitive to the client's own grief process and the possibility that the client has strained or alienated relationships with family members. The attorney would consider that such a client might benefit psychologically from the sense of control that can result from legal planning for death. The lawyer would also consider that individuals close to the client who can serve as surrogate health-care decision makers may also be experiencing grief, suggesting the need to identify secondary or tertiary decision makers. In cases like this, the lawyer's sensitivity to and ability to discuss psychological concerns specific to the client's situation would be invaluable (Winick, 1998).

Psycholegal Soft Spots

Winick (1999) explained that the therapeutically oriented preventive lawyer should be able to identify the client's psychological and emotional needs, the effects of lawyer-client interactions on the client's well-being, and "psycholegal soft spots"—areas "in which certain legal issues, procedures, or interventions may produce or reduce anxiety, distress, anger, depression, hard or hurt feelings, and other dimensions of [emotional] . . . well-being" (Winick, 1999, p. 252). Psycholegal soft spots often represent potential difficulties. They challenge the attorney to devise means to reduce the unintended antitherapeutic effects of legal action. For example, leaving an inheritance to one child outright and to the other child in trust, no matter how legally appropriate, is likely to foster resentment and alienation between the two heirs. The TJ oriented lawyer might take steps to reduce or minimize such unintended negative emotional consequences (Stolle et al., 1997). On the other hand, psycholegal soft spots may present the attorney with an opportunity to serve a therapeutic function. Lawyers frequently have opportunities to make statements to clients or litigants that promote the individual's psychological or emotional well-being. This latter type of psycholegal soft spot is optional, while the former type of psycholegal soft spot represents an issue that the lawyer should not ignore. To practice TJ/preventive law, lawyers must educate themselves regarding potential psycholegal soft spots presented by various clients and/or legal problems.

For example, elderly clients may present developmental, end-of-life concerns, health concerns, and delicate extended family relationships. Clients with cancer or HIV/AIDS are likely to have needs relating to the dying process, the emotional stages of grief, and family relationships. Personal injury clients are likely to present anger, depression, a desire for revenge, and a need for the opportunity to "tell their story" and be "heard." Domestic violence victims are likely to need understanding, support, and improved, self-esteem, and may have ambivalent feelings toward the offender. Alcohol or drug dependent clients are likely to engage in denial, rationalization, and resistance and may be likely to relapse. These potential emotional or therapeutic issues constitute psycholegal soft spots relevant to the lawyer's representation of the client. They suggest that different courses of legal action may have vastly different therapeutic or antitherapeutic potential. After consideration and discussion of these issues, the lawyer and client can then choose the course of action that is most likely to have the desired therapeutic outcome.

The TJ/preventive lawyer considers not only legal and economic issues presented by clients and legal matters, but also the personal goals, values, relationships, and psychological states of the individuals involved. A consideration of these issues allows the lawyer to better assess and evaluate the desirability of various legal actions. Stolle and his colleagues argue that this allows the lawyer to render superior legal advice. They also assert that the result of such an integrated approach is a superior set of legal documents (e.g., wills, trusts, health care directives, living wills) or legal strategies for action minimizing the potential for antitherapeutic outcomes for the client (Stolle et al., 1997).

Emphasis on Human Relationships or Development

TJ recognizes and emphasizes the continuity of relationships between parties to litigation and the desirability of the litigant's continued personal development after the court process (Des Rosiers, 2000). A therapeutically oriented lawyer is likely to discuss with a client the consequences of various alternative courses of action upon his or her relationships with others. The lawyer is likely to explicitly recognize that the client's well-being may be affected by the condition of his or her relationships. Thus, the lawyer and client together may seek to avoid legal actions that vindicate the client's legal rights but simultaneously decimate the client's important relationships.

The lawyer may formulate plans for action that foster the client's personal development and well-being. For example, a conditional release (or probationary) plan that is developed by the criminal defendant and lawyer together is likely to be more effective and more often adhered to by the client, than a plan that is devised by the lawyer alone or judge and imposed on the client by the court (Wexler, 1993, relying on Meichenbaum & Turk, 1987). This is due to the importance of the client's "active involvement in negotiating and designing the . . . program," which is an insight gained from a TJ approach applying social science research findings regarding medical treatment compliance to criminal sentencing (Wexler, 1993, p. 165). Involving the client in designing the plan also maximizes the client's sense of autonomy and personal investment in the plan. This not only increases the likelihood of compliance with the plan, but may foster the development of the client's personal responsibility and maturity as well.

Similarly, Winick (1995) has criticized the application of the label of "mentally incompetent," to individuals who are found legally incompetent to stand trial. He considers this determination to be potentially detrimental to their personal development. He asserted that the label has antitherapeutic effects in that it can stigmatize individuals, damage their self-concept, erode their sense of internal control, diminish their intrinsic motivation, increase their tendency to "self-handicap," and result in a self-fulfilling prophecy effect (p. 31).

Psychological Sophistication of the Therapeutic Lawyer

Consideration of the emotional and psychological dimensions of legal matters raises a question as to whether formal training in psychology is necessary to practice law therapeutically. Winick (1999) asserted that a therapeutically oriented lawyer need not be trained in psychology to be effective. However, he asserted that such a lawyer must possess sufficient psychological sophistication and understanding of basic interpersonal and intrapersonal dynamics to identify psycholegal soft spots and other emotional concerns inherent in legal matters.

In addition, Winick observed that lawyers practicing TJ or therapeutically oriented preventive law must "have a heightened sensitivity to the psychological dimensions of the attorney-client relationship" (Winick, 1998, p. 330). Silver (1999) noted that they must be aware of and able to handle transference and antitransference dynamics in the attorney-client relationship. Winick (1998) also asserted that they must be able to convey empathy to their clients. Empathy is central in creating the therapeutically oriented lawyer-client relationship. Empathy is critical if a client is exhibiting denial of or resistance to a particular situation (e.g., his or her own death, or dependence on drugs or alcohol).

Winick (1998) has extensively examined the lawyering issues inherent in working with clients who are nearing death. Services frequently include preparing advance directive instruments, such as living wills, health-care proxies, mental health-care and hospitalization proxies, and nursing home admission proxies. He noted that such clients are particularly likely to experience denial and resistance regarding the dying process. As a result, they are likely to resist or avoid preparing these important and valuable legal documents. He references clinical wisdom from Tomb (1995) and Othmer (1994) when working with such clients. Specifically, he advises the lawyer to be "supportive, empathic, warm, and attentive" (Winick, 1998, p. 335, citing Tomb, 1995, pp. 102–105) and noted the possible efficacy of clinical management techniques for handling denial, including "bypassing, reassurance, distraction, confrontation, and interpretation" (Winick, 1998, p. 335, citing Othmer, 1994, pp. 83–88). While recognizing that attorneys may not be trained to utilize all of these techniques, he argued that at least some of these measures could be employed without sophisticated psychological training.

Specific Applications of Therapeutic Jurisprudence in Criminal, Personal Injury, Employment, and Family Law

The following section describes selected applications of TJ to various areas of criminal and civil law. Within civil law, TJ as applied to tort law, employment law, and family law is emphasized. Therapeutic jurisprudence has also been applied to other civil areas, including law relating to the psychotherapist-patient relationship (Levine, 1993; Shuman, 1993), the right to refuse mental health treatment (Winick, 1996), contract and commercial law (Harrison, 1994), nursing law (Kjervik, 1999), and law relating to sexual abuse or battery (Feldthusen, 1993).

Criminal Law

Therapeutic jurisprudence has been applied to many areas of criminal law. It has been useful in proposing laws and legal processes designed to reduce recidivism (Wexler, 1999b) and in assessing the therapeutic and antitherapeutic potential of sex offender laws (Birgden & Vincent, 2000; Gould, 1998; Kaden, 1998; Klotz, 1996; Klotz, Wexler, Sales, & Becker, 1992; Schopp, 1995), the federal sentencing guidelines (Gould, 1993), victims' rights (Wiebe, 1996), the role of the criminal defense attorney (Winick, 1999), the insanity defense (Perlin, 1996), and law relating to the competency to stand trial (Barnum & Grisso, 1994; Winick, 1996).

Wexler (1999b), one of the founders of therapeutic jurisprudence, applied a TJ approach to criminal law by proposing that criminal sentencing incorporate psychological principles relating to relapse prevention and treatment compliance. Previously, Wexler (1993) had noted that Meichenbaum and Turk's (1987) research in the health-care area indicates that patients are more likely to comply with medical treatment plans when they are engaged in a "respectful dialogue," family and friends are involved in the plan, a behavioral contract is signed, a public commitment is made by the patient, and the patient is presented with "mild anti-arguments" regarding his or her probable compliance (Wexler, 1999b, p. 1031, citing Meichenbaum & Turk, 1987, p. 176). He also argued that these compliance-enhancing techniques could be applied to the probation setting in order to improve criminal defendants' rate of compliance with the terms of probation (Wexler, 1993).

Second, Wexler examined recent research on "what works" in rehabilitation programs for criminals, which found that cognitive-behavioral programs are the most successful (McGuire, 1995). Cognitive-behavioral programs contain concrete, behavioral or skills-oriented components, including the development of abilities designed to increase offenders' cognitive self-awareness (Wexler, 1999b, citing McGuire, 1995). They also resemble relapse prevention programs designed to increase self-control and reduce impulsive behavior. Offenders are taught to develop awareness of their problem, identify alternative courses of action, plan a course of action, and anticipate the consequences of that proposed course of action upon themselves and upon others. Wexler argued that the psychological research demonstrating the efficacy of such programs suggested their explicit incorporation into criminal sentencing and probation conditions in order to reduce criminal recidivism.

Wexler also noted that the Vermont correctional system uses similar, cognitive-behavioral programs and that courts in south Wales order probationers to engage in similar programs. However, Wexler (1999b) suggested that the psychological principles found in Meichenbaum and Turk's (1987) and McGuire's (1995) work should be more universally applied, by courts sentencing offenders or establishing conditions of probation. For example, courts could require offenders to prepare and submit a relapse prevention plan and incorporate the plan into the terms of their probation; family, friends, and other community members could be involved in the plan preparation process; a community conference with the offender and the offender's family, friends, and other community members could be held; and the court could engage the offender in a dialogue about the proposed plan (including presenting mild antiarguments to the plan and allowing the offender to respond to them). This approach incorporates the need for the offender to have a "voice" during the plan development process and to develop a sense of authorship of that plan. It also respects and incorporates the other psychological principles described by Wexler earlier.

As described, the integrated practice of preventive law and TJ requires the lawyer to identify and deal effectively with psycholegal soft spots. For example, psycholegal soft spots arise when a criminal defense attorney's client is a chronic substance abuser whose criminal difficulties stem from his or her addiction. Because of the addiction underlying the criminal problems, the criminal defense attorney should attempt to facilitate the defendant's recovery from the underlying addictive problem. This defendant has specific needs or concerns, including the possibility of relapse, the need for addiction relapse planning, denial of the addiction, resistance to giving up the addiction, and psychological distress resulting from having been arrested. The psychologically minded criminal defense attorney can be more effective in plea bargaining and in the sentencing process because he or she will incorporate advance planning for these psycholegal soft spots (Winick, 1999).

Further, the client is likely to have developed a relationship of greater trust with a therapeutically oriented preventive lawyer because of his or her understanding of the emotional aspects of the client's problem. Because of this greater level of trust in the attorney, the client may be more likely to communicate and cooperate with the attorney, follow the attorney's advice, focus on his or her psychological well-being, and ultimately resolve his or her problem. In addition to the psychological benefits of a therapeutic approach to the client, there may be legal advantages as well. For example, many courts are allowing reduced sentences (i.e., downward departures from federal sentencing guidelines) for criminal defendants when there is evidence of true postoffense rehabilitation of the offenders (Winick, 1999).

Schopp (1999) applied therapeutic jurisprudence to the proper treatment of sex offenders. Current legal interventions for sex offenders include enhanced criminal sentences, voluntary and involuntary treatment programs, community notification programs, surgical and chemical castration, and civil commitment. The common goal is to prevent recidivism. Schopp asserted that a therapeutic analysis of sex crimes would have multiple goals. In particular, a TJ approach would seek to promote victim well-being by reducing offender recidivism, promoting offender well-being, avoiding undermining other aspects of the law that tend to deter or prevent sex crimes, and respecting principles of justice.

Schopp also asserted that a TJ approach would produce a research agenda for empirical work. In the context of sex offenders, future research should assess: the effect of various current legal interventions on offenders' recidivism; whether these interventions are more successful if voluntary or involuntary; the effect of these interventions on other crimes such as assault and homicide; the effect of these interventions on the victim's recovery process; and how these interventions affect the efficacy of concurrent empathic or cognitive-behavioral modes of psychological treatment of the offenders (Schopp, 1999). Future empirical research in this area would then identify variables that affect the answers to these questions, such as "diagnosis, age, intelligence, substance abuse, type of prior offense, . . . [and] social structure" (p. 602). Using this empirically derived information, the therapeutically oriented lawyer could then choose the psychologically optimal legal intervention for the specific sex offender at hand.

Personal Injury Law

TJ has been applied to tort law to assess the therapeutic value of an apology (Shuman, 1994, 2000), to evaluate the therapeutic effect of various legal tests for liability (Shuman, 1992), and to evaluate the therapeutic potential of the United States' system of compensating individuals for personal injuries (Shuman, 1994). For example, it has been used to criticize no-fault insurance laws relating to personal injury losses (Shuman, 1994). Because no-fault systems separate responsibility for compensation from responsibility for harm and eliminate decisions about responsibility for the accident, the wrongdoer is never adjudicated to be "at fault." The party who ultimately pays for the plaintiff's loss is an impersonal third party, the defendant's insurance company. As a result, this law deprives plaintiffs of a sense of satisfaction and deprives wrongdoers of an opportunity to accept personal responsibility for their actions.

Shuman also investigated the therapeutic or antitherapeutic effects of bringing a personal injury claim. Although he noted the antitherapeutic effects of prolonged litigation, he argued that litigation might actually be neutral or therapeutic for tort claimants, rather than antitherapeutic, because he asserted that pursuing litigation against the wrongdoer does not necessarily prolong the plaintiff's illness or injury. In addition, he observed that blame might actually be therapeutic for some plaintiffs; in some cases, plaintiffs benefit from legally establishing another's fault for or contribution to their injury. For example, blaming yourself for injuries from *in utero* exposure to DES is antitherapeutic for the injured person. It may foster low self-esteem, harsh self-criticism, and depressive thinking in the injured person. In contrast, bringing a lawsuit and legally establishing another's fault for these injuries may be beneficial for such a plaintiff (Shuman, 1994).

Shuman also explored the effects of litigation on grief resolution. Litigation may facilitate or suspend the plaintiff's process of resolving the loss caused by the personal injury. For example, in wrongful death actions, litigation can interrupt or stall the process of grieving if it focuses too long on the cause of or responsibility for the death. On the other hand, litigation may facilitate the grief process if it assists the survivors in understanding the events leading to the death, or fulfills their sense of duty to the deceased person, and is begun and concluded shortly after the death (Shuman, 1994).

Finally, the importance of an apology in tort law has been recognized (Keeva, 1999; Shuman, 2000). This emerging focus on apology is consistent with a TJ approach to tort law (Shuman, 2000). Shuman (1994, p. 460) asserted, "a meaningful apology may advance the plaintiff's emotional healing more effectively than an award of damages for the intangible portion of the loss." The plaintiff receiving an apology from the defendant may experience vindication, satisfaction, and a reduction in negative emotions. These effects may assist the plaintiff in resolving his or her feelings about the injury. The

defendant may undergo personal development as a result of apologizing if he or she experiences genuine shame and remorse (Scheff, 1998). The defendant may also develop a greater capacity for empathy through apologizing. The relationship between the parties (if ongoing) may, furthermore, improve as a result of the apology.

Schma (2000) noted that, in medical malpractice cases, some insurance companies prohibit the insured physicians from contacting the plaintiffs, because an apology by the defendant physician could be admissible in court and viewed as an admission of fault. However, Schma (2000, p. 4) observed that this practice deprives the plaintiffs of what they "may want most" and denies the physician the opportunity to resolve the incident in his or her mind and "return to productive work." Schma concluded that, because the law forces the physician "into a position of denial" (p. 4) more malpractice suits are likely to be filed against the doctor in the future. In this situation, an apology can have positive psychological effects on both defendant and plaintiff.

Empirical research on lawyers suggests that attorneys may tend to underestimate the value of a sincere apology in a civil lawsuit. According to one empirical study, lawyers tend to assess various legal outcomes on the basis of the economic value received by the plaintiff (Korobkin & Guthrie, 1997). In contrast, nonlawyers are more influenced by noneconomic, psychological factors, such as the degree of remorse and public apology demonstrated by the defendant. Thus, the therapeutically oriented lawyer should be alert to his or her possible predisposition to seek monetary damages rather than an apology.

Employment Law

Therapeutic jurisprudence has been applied to employment law in many areas, including the Americans with Disabilities Act (Daly-Rooney, 1994; Dorfman, 1993–1994; Perlin, 1993–1994), sexual harassment and discrimination (Daicoff, 1999), the military's policy towards homosexuality (Kavanagh, 1995), labor arbitration law (Abrams, Abrams, & Nolan, 1994), and workers' compensation law (Lippel, 1999). For example, Daly-Rooney explored the antitherapeutic aspects of the Americans with Disabilities Act's provision permitting confidentiality of employee claims made pursuant to the Act. She argued that confidentiality deprives the employee's coworkers of an opportunity to assist in designing and implementing reasonable accommodations for the employee's disability. She observed that coworker assistance and participation in accommodation plans reduces resentment toward the accommodated employee and increases social support for the accommodation and the accommodated employee (Daly-Rooney, 1994). Therefore, she argued, it could be most therapeutic for a disabled employee to waive confidentiality and include his or her coworkers in the process of fashioning his or her accommodations.

TJ has also been applied to the U.S. military's policy on homosexuality of "Don't ask, don't tell" (Kavanagh, 1995). Kavanagh analyzed this policy and concluded that its effect was to isolate gay service members from their coworkers and indirectly decrease their emotional well-being. This policy is often referred to as "Don't ask, don't tell, and don't pursue." First, the armed services no longer require applicants to disclose whether they are homosexual or bisexual (Don't ask). Second, the military will not discharge homosexual members unless homosexual conduct is engaged in, but making a statement that one is homosexual or bisexual is deemed to be "homosexual conduct." Thus, a member of the armed forces who states that he or she is gay or bisexual can be discharged from military service (Don't tell). Third, no investigations or inquiries will be conducted solely to determine a member's sexual orientation (Don't pursue). Kavanagh asserted that this policy is antitherapeutic for gay service members because it requires them to avoid disclosing their sexual orientation. To avoid such disclosure, they must constantly engage in deception. They cannot discuss any activities that would suggest that they are engaging in homosexual acts. For example, they cannot discuss with whom they spent the weekend, from whom they are receiving a phone call, and so on. This sets them apart from their colleagues. It forces them to remain emotionally distant, isolated from their coworkers. This reduces the social support available to gay service members, results in constant strain and tension, and lowers their self-esteem because they must be deceptive (Kavanagh, 1995).

Family Law

Family law, including divorce and child custody law, is particularly appropriate for a therapeutic jurisprudence analysis. A TJ analysis has been applied to family law generally (Anderer & Glass, 2000; Armstrong, 1999; Babb, 1997; Maxwell, 1998), unified family courts (Babb, 1998), child welfare proceedings (Brooks, 1999), divorce (Bryan, 1999; Tesler, 1999a, 1999b), domestic violence (Paradine, 2000; Simon, 1995), domestic violence courts (Fritzler & Simon, 2000a), teen court (Shiff & Wexler, 1996), and legal planning for unmarried committed individuals (Robbennolt & Johnson, 1999).

For example, Maxwell reviewed empirical research regarding the effects of divorce on children. She asserted that this research revealed that children of divorced parents suffer significantly more emotional, behavioral, and academic problems than do children of married parents. These difficulties included: greater depression and anxiety; lower self-confidence; lower grades and standardized test scores; and more antisocial and self-destructive behavior (e.g., drug abuse, aggression, delinquency, and promiscuity). She also asserted that previous empirical research pointed to three factors as the most important predictors of problems for post-divorce children: "instability in the child's life, interparental conflict, and an absence, at least temporarily, of effective parenting" (Maxwell, 1998, pp. 163–164). She explored whether a TJ/preventive law approach could ameliorate or minimize these factors.

Maxwell evaluated three recent changes to divorce law, which were designed to mitigate the negative consequences of divorce on children: (a) an emphasis on the best interests of the child; (b) joint custody; and (c) divorce mediation. According to Maxwell (1998), joint custody and divorce mediation did have some therapeutic effects, but in some ways all three legal reforms fell short of their intended goals. For example, the "best interests" standard, which was intended to focus on the effects of divorce on children, is too vague to provide meaningful guidance to judges. Joint custody, which was in part designed to increase the noncustodial parent's (e.g., usually the father's) involvement with the children, did not necessarily do so. Because it was not linked to physical custody, it became simply a legal label that did not necessarily increase the amount of time fathers spent with their children. Finally, divorce mediation, which was expected to prevent postdivorce interparental conflict and promote parental cooperation, did not necessarily do so.

However, because it gave both parents equal decision-making power over their children's lives, joint custody did prevent fathers from dropping out of their children's lives entirely. With joint custody, fathers were less likely to stop visiting or providing financial support for their children. This fostered fewer feelings of rejection and abandonment in the children and maintained the children's economic standard of living, improving their postdivorce emotional and financial stability (Maxwell, 1998).

Divorce mediation did afford fathers greater participation in, control over, and satisfaction with the divorce process. Because of this, they were more likely to comply with the terms of the custody and support agreements. Also, mothers were more likely to receive the child support awards they wanted. Therefore, according to Maxwell (1998), divorce mediation and joint custody had certain therapeutic effects on the children of divorced parents.

Maxwell theorized that therapeutically oriented preventive lawyers could educate clients about the negative effects of instability, interparental conflict, and ineffective parenting. She also stated that lawyers could craft divorce agreements that attempt to minimize these three conditions. For example, if the divorce agreement mandates interparental conferences about the children twice a week, without the child's presence, the child should suffer less from interparental conflict (Maxwell, 1998).

Anderer and Glass based a therapeutic approach to family law on a stage theory of the development of relationships. They observed that the law might have salutary or detrimental effects at each stage of the relationship. First, they asserted that all relationships proceed through several stages, from "Pre-Relationship," through "Relationship," to "Post-Resolution." Troubled relationships undergo a "Problem" stage during which lawyers and mental health professionals are consulted. The troubled relationship then moves into a "Break" stage and proceeds into a period of formal "Legal Involvement." "Resolution" follows and is accompanied by an agreement or court order. Issues of implementation raised in "Post-Resolution" ensue (Anderer & Glass, 2000).

These authors argued that lawyers, judges, and mental health professionals could prevent problems in all of these stages. For example, in the Pre-Relationship stage, prenuptial agreements, parenting classes, conflict resolution skills training, and premarital counseling can serve a preventive and therapeutic function. In the Legal Involvement stage, psychological evaluations can have therapeutic or antitherapeutic effects on the family. On the positive side, psychological testing and evaluations of the parents prepared for court use can provide a "reality check" that helps the parents realistically assess their own and the other's strengths and weaknesses, sometimes for the first time. Other aspects of the process can be less therapeutic. For example, the process of obtaining a court order and appealing it may be unavoidably adversarial, which in turn might be antitherapeutic (Anderer & Glass, 2000).

During the Legal Involvement stage, the ability of the parties to resolve conflicts dictates which issues must be decided by a third-party decision maker (e.g., a judge) and which can be mediated between the parties. For example, one couple who lived in different states could not agree on custody, but once the judge decided custody, they could mediate the rest of their concerns. Some couples may be negotiating issues themselves reasonably well, and thus the lawyers should draft a brief settlement agreement. Such an agreement would leave the details to be worked out between the parties, encouraging the development of a cooperative partnership between them. Others may have such an inability to agree that every detail must be spelled out in a formal, highly structured settlement agreement (Anderer & Glass, 2000).

Finally, a therapeutic jurisprudence analysis of the contractual terms used in settlement agreements can enhance the effectiveness of such agreements. For example, the custody language used in a settlement agreement can have a dramatic emotional impact on divorcing spouses. Some may respond favorably to "shared" and very unfavorably to the words "primary" or "sole." Others may object to the term "shared" and thus it is best omitted (Anderer & Glass, 2000). Finally, Anderer and Glass identified a need for future empirical research to determine whether a TJ approach results in better legal and emotional outcomes for divorcing spouses.

An innovative therapeutic jurisprudence approach to family and divorce law is embodied in several recent developments in family law, including unified family courts (Anderer & Glass, 2000; Babb, 1998) and collaborative divorce (Tesler, 1999a, 1999b). Unified family courts attempt to coordinate the resolution of different legal issues related to the same family (Chase & Hora, 2000). These courts attempt to consolidate matters such as juvenile delinquency, child abuse or neglect, guardianship of children, divorce, paternity, child support, and domestic violence, that otherwise would be handled by different courts. This unified approach is intended to provide a more positive psychological outcome for the family as a whole.

In a series of articles, Tesler (1999a, 1999b, 1999c) introduced collaborative divorce as a method of resolving divorce and child custody disputes without the necessity of litigation and the courts. According to Tesler, this approach "was the inspiration of a single disgusted family lawyer (Stuart Webb) practicing in Minneapolis" (Tesler, 1999b, p. 199). It was quickly adopted by practicing family lawyers who were seeking a better, more economic way for their clients to resolve their differences. Tesler (1999a) explained that the linchpin of the collaborative model is that both lawyers are contractually bound to withdraw from representing their respective clients if the collaborative process breaks down and the parties resort to litigation. This contrasts with the usual model, where the attorneys collect a fee whether the parties settle their differences outside of court or litigate. Attorneys in this position often have the attitude that they "win either way" because they collect their fee regardless of how the legal problem is resolved. In contrast, the collaborative model aligns the self-interest of the attorneys and the clients. By doing so, it dramatically improves the incentive of the lawyers to reach a settlement (Tesler, 1999a, 1999b).

In a collaborative divorce process, the lawyer first assesses, with the client, the appropriateness of the client for a collaborative process. Tesler (1999a) asserts that the client must be able to identify his or her negative emotions (what Tesler refers to as the client's "shadow self"), effectively manage them, and negotiate with honesty and in good faith with his or her spouse. Second, the process occurs through a series of four-way meetings between the lawyers and the spouses, in which the lawyers create a collaborative atmosphere through ground rules, guidelines for interaction, and consequences of inappropriate behavior by a participant (which can include halting the process temporarily, calling a recess, or even terminating the process) (Tesler, 1999a). These four-way meetings are combined with other, two-way meetings between each lawyer and client and between the two lawyers to discuss the progress of the process (Tesler, 1999a).

According to Tesler (1999b), the advantages of collaborative divorce law are that it is often quicker and less costly for the parties (Kelly, 1990), but most importantly, it facilitates a collaborative process, encouraging each party to interact with others in a cooperative manner. This can foster the beginning of a better, collaborative, problem-solving relationship between the spouses. Tesler explained, "Collaborative Law melds vigorous attorney advocacy and advice with a very sophisticated dispute resolution process that, at its best, engages the highest intentions and creativity of the participants" (Tesler, 1999b, pp. 203–204). It has on occasion resulted in acts of spontaneous generosity or reconciliation on the part of divorcing spouses. Its reduction of the vengeful behavior, aggression, unproductive blaming, posturing, and intense conflict that is often found in traditional divorces is certainly therapeutic for children of the marriage and may be therapeutic for the spouses themselves.

THERAPEUTIC JUDGING

Judges have studied therapeutic jurisprudence enthusiastically (Schma, 2000). At the 1996 meeting of the National Association for Court Management, the need for judges to become "more therapeutic" in outcome was cited as one of the top 10 issues facing courts (p. 5). Schma observed that courts are moving toward a problem-solving approach to judging. Therapeutic jurisprudence is being formally recognized as relevant for judging. For example, a Trial Court Performance Standard explicitly charges trial courts with responding to "realities that cause [their] . . . orders to be ignored" (p. 5, citing Trial Court Performance Standard 3.5 of the Commission on Trial Court Performance Standards). The Conference of Chief Justices (Resolution 22) and the Conference of State Court Administrators (Resolution 4) jointly adopted a resolution in August 2000 that specifically labeled courts utilizing therapeutic jurisprudence principles (such as drug treatment courts) as "problem solving courts

and calendars." This resolution also clearly encouraged the expansion of the principles and methods of such TJ courts into other courts in the state court systems. Therapeutic judging involves a greater focus on the process rather than the outcome, endorses different roles and functions for judges, and suggests different judicial tools than those traditionally used by the courts in disposing of cases.

Emphasis on Judicial Process Rather than Outcome

TJ places a greater emphasis on the process of adjudication than on its outcome (Des Rosiers, 2000). This emphasis on process results from its focus on the psychological consequences of litigation for participants. In particular, TJ utilizes insights gained from "procedural justice" research, which found that litigants value the opportunity to participate in decision-making processes (Tyler, 1992). Procedural justice discovered, through empirical research of litigants' satisfaction with the litigation process, that participants' satisfaction with and assessment of the fairness of lawsuits depended less on the win/lose outcome. It depended more on three intangible factors: (a) being given the opportunity to be heard; (b) being treated with respect and dignity; and (c) perceiving the authority figures as being trustworthy. Trustworthiness, which may be the strongest factor contributing to litigants' perception of fairness, is enhanced when the judge explains the reasons for his or her decision and appears to be concerned about the litigants' welfare (Tyler, 1992). However, having the judge simply listen to the litigants tell their story is likely to be therapeutic and is likely to enhance the litigants' perception of the fairness of the judicial process (Des Rosiers, 2000; Tyler, 1992).

Consistent with procedural justice findings, Paradine found that female domestic violence victims measured success of a legal intervention on the basis of "how they were treated as people, what was said to them, how it was said, . . . how carefully they were listened to, . . . [and] whether the law helped them to feel safer" (Paradine, 2000, p. 45). Legal actors who appeared cold and distant or who ignored, ridiculed, dismissed, or misunderstood the victims were perceived negatively, even when the legal outcome was objectively successful. Therefore, a TJ analysis suggests that the litigation process and the listening abilities of judges are critically important to litigants.

Therapeutic jurisprudence may also be relevant to the outcome of litigation, however. It has been applied to constitutional law to argue that the Canadian Supreme Court's 1998 appellate opinion on the majority/minority dispute between Canada and Quebec had a therapeutic effect (Des Rosiers, 2000). Des Rosiers asserted that this legal outcome was therapeutic because both sides applauded the decision and a sense of "relief and peace" (p. 54) emerged afterward. Specifically, the court used a TJ approach, first by viewing the dispute as one between two parties with a continuous, long-standing relationship rather than a one-time legal decision. Second, the court acknowledged the complexity and ambiguity of the problem before it, gave a voice to the minority losing party, suggested a creative solution for an ongoing negotiation between the parties, and refrained from casting the losing party as blameworthy.

Wexler (2000) expanded this concept. He argued that courts could utilize therapeutic jurisprudence to fashion remedies and issue opinions that lessen contentiousness and promote harmony and dialogue. He suggested that, through the careful drafting of legal doctrine, appellate opinions, and legal remedies, courts can be more sensitive to the emotional consequences of their actions on the parties and thereby foster the development of better outcomes and legal rules.

Different Role for Judges and Other Legal Actors

Therapeutic jurisprudence's greater emphasis on process places a greater emphasis on the role of judges, lawyers, and other legal personnel as listeners. Des Rosiers (2000, p. 54) asserted that therapeutically oriented judges function less as evaluators and more as "process-oriented listeners, translators, educators, and . . . facilitators." For example, the judicial role of drug treatment court judges (whose work is intended to be explicitly therapeutic) changed from that of a "detached, neutral arbiter to the central figure in [a] . . . team, which is focused on the participants' sobriety and accountability" (Chase & Hora, 2000, p. 12). The judge in this setting is "both a cheerleader and stern parent" who rewards compliance and metes out consequences for noncompliance (p. 12). Rottman (2000, p. 25) described a therapeutically-oriented judge's role as that of a "sensitive, empathic counselor" rather than a "dispassionate, disinterested magistrate."

Therapeutic jurisprudence also investigates the therapeutic potential of the particular "words, attitudes, and personal responses" of legal actors in legal procedures (Paradine, 2000, p. 40). Paradine applied a therapeutic approach to domestic violence cases. First, she noted that victims' feelings and decisions undergo a complex series of changes before a permanent solution to the violence is found. As a result, she argued that legal actors may need to be sensitive to victims' emotions and coping strategies, which may include denial, love for the perpetrator, hope for the relationship, and love of children and home. She asserted that empathy, which includes "the process of meeting a survivor where she is rather than where we might wish her to be" (pp. 45–46), can have

a therapeutic effect on survivors of domestic violence. Paradine repeatedly makes the point that a lawyer's demonstrated understanding of the complexity of a victim's emotions and decisions facilitates the victim's resolution process. In contrast, a lawyer's or judge's insistence that the victim be completely finished with the relationship, or (at the other extreme) their agreement with the victim's denial and justification, can be antitherapeutic. For example, one lawyer told a victim that the perpetrator was behaving poorly because he "still loves you," at a time when she said she most needed to hear, "You don't have to put up with that behavior" (p. 44).

Broader Range of Judicial Tools: Specialized Courts

The most well-known application of therapeutic jurisprudence to judging is found in the specialized court movement. Specialized courts were established specifically to deal with psychology-laden issues, such as domestic violence, drug and alcohol addiction, and mental health issues (Rottman, 2000). Their goal is to provide improved outcomes for individuals with "underlying social and emotional problems" (p. 22). Instead of meting out traditional justice in the form of fines or sentences, these courts employ an interdisciplinary, problem-solving approach, utilizing knowledge gained from psychology and mental health.

For example, one specialized court dealing with domestic violence cases was explicitly founded on the principles of therapeutic jurisprudence, restorative justice, and preventive law (Fritzler & Simon, 2000a, 2000b). Its goals are to hold the offender accountable, ensure the safety of victims and children, and improve victim satisfaction with the judicial process (Fritzler & Simon, 2000a). This is accomplished by coordinating the work of the courts, police, corrections officers, probation officers, and victims' advocates.

Hora and Schma have written at length about the success of drug treatment courts (Hora & Schma, 1998; Hora, Schma, & Rosenthal, 1999). Disenchanted with the existing mechanisms for dealing with drug and alcohol addicted criminal defendants, judges conceived of a specialized, interdisciplinary court for defendants with an alcohol or other substance abuse problem (Hora et al., 1999). The first such court was established in Miami, Florida, in 1989. Hora and her colleagues explained that, in these courts, the judge functions as an involved person in the defendant's recovery program. There is accountability of the defendant to the judge (via regular, frequent court appearances), mandated substance abuse treatment and therapy, and judicial understanding of and use of the empirical and clinical knowledge about alcoholism and substance abuse. The judge functions as part of an interdisciplinary team, including treatment providers, to create a plan for the defendant. The approach is nonadversarial and explicitly focused on the biopsychosocial aspects of the defendant's condition.

The results of these courts have been dramatic. Hora and her colleagues reported that: "From 1989 to 1993, Miami's drug court placed over 4,500 offenders into court-supervised treatment. By 1993, two-thirds had remained in treatment (1,270) or graduated (1,700). Among graduates, the re-arrest rate one year later was less than 3 percent, compared to 30 percent for similar drug offenders who did not go through drug court" (Hora et al., 1999, p. 456). Hora also observed that drug treatment court judges have greater interest in judging and greater satisfaction with their work because of its positive, beneficial effect on defendants (Chase & Hora, 2000).

PHILOSOPHICAL AND ETHICAL ISSUES

The TJ approach to law has raised a number of issues. First, we must define what constitutes a "therapeutic" effect. Second, the lawyer must assess how to present therapeutic concerns to the client. Third, we must determine how to resolve conflicts where a particular legal action might be therapeutic to one individual but antitherapeutic to another. Fourth, one must make the difficult determination of the relative importance of therapeutic concerns compared to legal rights or individuals' autonomy, particularly when they conflict. Each of these concerns has generated a lively debate and discussion, which continues to be refined (Kress, 1999; Schopp, 1999; Slobogin, 1995). Not all lawyers may be prepared to practice law therapeutically. Finally, the role of psychologists in the practice of therapeutic jurisprudence should be explored. Each of these concerns is discussed.

Defining What Is "Therapeutic"

Slobogin (1995) and Schopp (1999) observe that what constitutes a "therapeutic" consequence can be defined differently. For example, one could seek psychological contentment, the absence of distress or psychopathology, social adjustment, occupational health, fulfillment of one's goals, autonomy, maximal insight, or self-actualization. Therapeutic jurisprudence itself does not define what is therapeutic (Schopp, 1999), thus allowing individualized definitions to develop. Kress (1999) recommends, however, that a therapeutic jurisprudent should be explicit about his or her concept of what is therapeutic. At the least, a therapeutically oriented lawyer should discuss with his or her client their respective definitions of therapeutic effect, to avoid misunderstandings.

Therapeutic Jurisprudence and Zealous Advocacy

Some lawyers are convinced that their duty to be a "zealous advocate" for their client requires them to pursue the client's wishes or goals, rather than suggesting different courses of action. This approach has been described as a neutral partisan, hired gun, zealous advocate, or objective approach to lawyering (Daicoff, 1998). The lawyer functions as a means to accomplish the client's ends. Because of this approach, some attorneys assert that it is inappropriate for them to raise therapeutic issues with their clients (Stolle et al., 1997). However, some versions of the lawyers' ethics codes strongly encourage lawyers to raise extra-legal concerns, such as therapeutic outcomes, with clients. Thus, there is support in the formal codes of legal ethics for attorneys who wish to include therapeutic concerns in their representation of clients.

Further, adopting an exclusive, zealous advocate approach can actually have antitherapeutic consequences. For example, Anderer and Glass (2000) observed that, often, clients seeking a divorce enter the lawyer's office with an aggressive, adversarial attitude toward their spouse. The lawyer who simply agrees with the client and becomes invested in vanquishing the other party may disserve the client and others. Maintaining and fostering the client's anger toward his or her spouse in this way may have emotional costs for the client. Further, interparental aggression and conflict are associated with negative effects on children's well-being (Maxwell, 1998). Certainly, if the client insists on such a course of action *after* an open discussion with the lawyer of its potential emotional costs, then the lawyer should respect the client's wishes. But, according to Stolle and his colleagues, the lawyer should not accept the client's wishes without first offering professional guidance, even when that guidance includes an analysis of the emotional consequences of the client's proposed course of action. In fact, the lawyer may have a duty to provide such guidance (Stolle et al., 1997).

Therapeutic to Whom?

Another important issue raised by Slobogin is: To whom does TJ seek to be therapeutic? He noted that a rule might be therapeutic for some and potentially antitherapeutic for others (he refers to this as "external balancing," Slobogin, 1995, p. 789). Certainly, when a lawyer is representing an individual client in a particular legal matter, such as defending a criminal action or bringing a civil lawsuit, the lawyer may initially seek therapeutic consequences for that client alone. However, when other individuals will be affected by the attorney's work (such as drafting a will, representing the client in a child custody and divorce action, or assisting the client to solve a dispute with his or her employer), the lawyer and client might well consider the effects of the legal representation on others. For example, they might mutually agree to seek the most therapeutic consequences for the client's family, children, or employment relationship, rather than simply for the client alone.

The dilemma of external balancing is likely to arise most often in what can be thought of as areas of law that involve relationships, or "relationship law." Relationship law includes contract law, family law, employment law, partnership law, trusts and estates, and some forms of small business law.

An example is found in child custody law. In a child custody dispute, traditional lawyers are likely to focus on the client's demands. This may or may not coincide with what is most therapeutic for the children. For example, both parents may desire joint custody, and joint custody may be most therapeutic for them, but such an arrangement may be antitherapeutic for the children, due to the instability of the arrangement (having two homes). In other situations, one legal action may be therapeutic for all individuals involved. For example, if there is domestic interspousal violence in the home, the action of removing the abusive parent from the home may be the most therapeutic action for both the parents and the children. In cases of conflicts, the lawyer and client may have a variety of choices for the ultimate goal of the legal representation (e.g., what the client wants or what is most therapeutic for the client, his or her children, or his or her ex-spouse).

Employment law and other civil litigation may raise the issue of whether therapeutic outcomes should be sought for the client alone, or for both the client and the opposing party. Doing the latter can be complex. For example, it may indeed be therapeutic for a plaintiff in a sexual harassment lawsuit against his or her employer to prevail in the legal action. It may represent empowerment of the plaintiff or appropriate assertiveness on his or her part. It may not be the most positive or pleasant outcome for the employer, but there may be long-term therapeutic consequences for the employer who loses the lawsuit, becomes educated about legal and appropriate workplace behavior, and reforms (Daicoff, 1999). On the other hand, there can be antitherapeutic consequences if the plaintiff prevails. If the plaintiff wins, then the plaintiff may feel self-satisfied and ignore real needs to change himself or herself because he or she believes the employer was entirely at fault.

Again, TJ does not attempt to resolve the question of external balancing. Rather, it simply suggests that legal actors consider the various therapeutic and antitherapeutic consequences of particular legal actions on all individuals involved, when making decisions about what legal action to take.

Conflicts between Therapeutic Values and Other Values

Perhaps the most well-explored challenge for therapeutic jurisprudence is the criticism that TJ does not provide a method for "choosing among competing values or of balancing other values [such as legal rights and duties] against therapeutic values" (Behnke & Saks, 1998, pp. 980–981). It does not dictate whether to promote therapeutic values or recognize legal rights (e.g., constitutional rights), when to do both would be impossible and the values are in conflict. However, Wexler and Winick consistently assert that therapeutic considerations should not trump other considerations, such as justice, legal rights, due process, individual autonomy, integrity of the fact-finding process, community safety, efficiency, and economy (Stolle et al., 1997; Wexler & Winick, 1996).

Slobogin's example of the conflict between therapeutic values and traditional legal rights involves an individual diagnosed with schizophrenia. Suppose that empirical research shows that an adversarial civil commitment process will be antitherapeutic for this individual. However, the individual is entitled to constitutional rights to counsel, rights to confront witnesses, and other quasicriminal setting rights that tend to make the process adversarial. Slobogin (1995) noted that TJ fails to decide whether the therapeutically oriented lawyer should promote a therapeutic process for the client or protect the client's entitlement to these constitutional rights, due process rights, and autonomy (even though to do so may be antitherapeutic). Another example is found in the context of divorce and child custody law. One spouse may choose to relinquish some of his or her legal rights (e.g., forego a claim for alimony or child support) and avoid a bitterly litigated fight, in order to facilitate compromise, settlement, and an improved emotional climate of cooperation between the parents. Such an improved, cooperative climate may be therapeutic for the spouses and the children (Maxwell, 1998), but does not maximize the client's legal rights and financial entitlements.

Kress (1999) responded to this criticism by concluding that TJ alone cannot resolve such conflicts, nor should it. Instead, Wexler and Winick (1996) explain that it simply proposes first that legal actors be sensitive to the therapeutic or antitherapeutic consequences of various legal actions. Second, it seeks to minimize antitherapeutic consequences and enhance therapeutic consequences, without subordinating due process and other justice values. Third, it recommends that when legal rights and therapeutic consequences can be harmonized, they should be (Wexler & Winick, 1996).

Kress (1999) observed that one method for resolving such conflicts between constitutional rights and therapeutic goals is to view therapeutic aims as being the ultimate purpose of all law. Under this perception, law's purpose is to improve the mental health of those subject to it. Thus, where legal (e.g., constitutional) rights would be antitherapeutic, such rights should not be afforded. Kress observed that another method for resolving the conflict is by referring to one's own personal belief system. Each individual may make an individual, moralistic, ethical decision as to which of these two competing values is most important. However, this latter mode of resolving the conflict depends on one's own personal morality, or "normative theory" (p. 588). Kress asserts that TJ alone cannot resolve conflicts between therapeutic values and other values, but TJ combined with a normative theory (such as an individual's belief system, ethics system, or morality) can adequately resolve this conflict. Further, for clients who can make competent decisions, the ultimate answer to these concerns lies in the client's right to make an informed decision, after being presented with the various options, possible legal outcomes, and their potential therapeutic and antitherapeutic consequences. This client can be the final decision maker as to the appropriate course of legal action. The therapeutically oriented lawyer simply provides the client with information as to his or her legal entitlements as well as the emotional consequences or impact of different options. With this information, the client should be able to make an independent, informed decision as to how to proceed.

In conclusion, therapeutic jurisprudence's position that therapeutic concerns should not outweigh other concerns, such as justice, is important. It responds directly to criticisms that it embodies an unwanted form of paternalism (Slobogin, 1995) that tramples on individuals' legal rights or that it "seduce[s] . . ." one "into slighting autonomy values" (p. 788). However, where therapeutic aims and legal rights collide, other theories (such as personal morals and beliefs) must be employed to resolve the resulting conflict.

Philosophical Analyses of Therapeutic Jurisprudence

Kress extensively analyzed the criticism that TJ is simply "old wine in new bottles," because it is a form of utilitarianism, or "consequentialism" (Kress, 1999, p. 558). In this view, therapeutic jurisprudence's goal is to create the most good by maximizing mental health. It may seek the most good for one client, for the client and his or her family, friends, and community, or for the greatest number of people. However, because TJ does not elevate therapeutic outcomes over legal rights, Kress argued that it is not truly utilitarian (i.e., consequentialist) but is really a hybrid theory that inte-

grates therapeutic concerns with more rights-based (i.e., deontological) concerns. Finally, he noted that, unlike traditional utilitarianism, TJ defines mental health as an intrinsic good or an end in itself.

Schopp (1999) also addressed several criticisms leveled at therapeutic jurisprudence. He concluded that TJ does not concern itself with whether therapeutic outcomes are desirable in legal matters. Instead, TJ assumes that we are motivated to provide therapeutic outcomes for individuals interfacing with the law. It then focuses on identifying ways that laws, legal processes, and legal actors can be more therapeutic, on finding empirical research that sheds light on the emotional consequences of law, and on proposing agendas for empirical research on the therapeutic or antitherapeutic effects of various legal measures. In Schopp's words, TJ generates instrumental prescriptions or hypothetical imperatives (e.g., if one values therapeutic outcomes, then this is how one should behave); it is normatively neutral and thus does not generate principled prescriptions (e.g., it does not advocate that we must value therapeutic outcomes). Freed of the debate over whether or not law should promote psychological well-being, TJ focuses squarely on its greatest contribution to the field: a research program that promotes "increasingly interdisciplinary analyses integrating subtle legal analysis with sophisticated empirical inquiry" (Schopp, 1999, p. 601).

Finally, Schopp (1999) concluded that, through the empirical questions it raises and explores, TJ would require society to resolve certain conflicts. For example, in the sex offender context, suppose that a TJ approach leads to empirical studies demonstrating that sex crime recidivism can be reduced and victim well-being promoted by severe punishment and cruel treatment of offenders. Then, society will be forced to decide explicitly which is most important (e.g., whether it wants to maximize victim well-being at the expense of offenders' constitutional rights). Schopp predicted that such societal decisions would become more evident as TJ becomes more widespread.

Therapeutic Jurisprudence and Lawyer Personality

Therapeutic jurisprudence acknowledges that it may not be the appropriate approach for all legal matters, all clients, or all lawyers. There are certainly clients who, when presented with therapeutic considerations, will choose to ignore them. Some legal matters may not lend themselves to a TJ analysis (e.g., regulatory compliance matters such as the calculation of federal income taxes owed on the sale of real estate or the proper method of federal income tax depreciation on an item of depreciable property). Finally, empirical research on the personality characteristics of lawyers indicates that many attorneys may be ill-suited to practice law therapeutically because of an insensitivity to emotional concerns (Daicoff, 1997, 1999).

Empirical data on the "lawyer personality" revealed that most lawyers had a low interest in interpersonal and emotional concerns as children. As prelaw students they preferred interpersonal dominance and avoided abasement and deference to others, and as law students and lawyers they preferred styles of decision making that emphasized rational, logical analysis over emotional and relational concerns (Daicoff, 1997). One of these decision-making styles is Gilligan's (1982) "rights orientation," which focuses on "rights, rules, independence, objectivity, fairness, and freedom from others' interference" (Daicoff, 1997, p. 1400). The opposite dimension, the "ethic of care," focuses on relationships, interpersonal harmony, emotions and needs, and preventing harm. Compared to a rights orientation, the ethic of care was less often endorsed by lawyers (Jack & Jack, 1989; Weissman, 1994) and was discouraged or extinguished in law school (Janoff, 1991).

Another decision-making style is the Thinking/Feeling dimension of the Myers-Briggs Type Indicator (Richard, 1994). There is an extremely consistent finding that male and female law students (Natter, 1981) and lawyers (Richard, 1993, 1994) overwhelmingly preferred "Thinking" to "Feeling" as a decision-making style on the Myers-Briggs Type Indicator. These results suggest that a subset of attorneys, specifically those with an ethic of care, a Feeling preference, or other interpersonally oriented traits, will be particularly adept at practicing TJ. They may more readily identify therapeutic concerns, acquire interpersonal sensitivity and skills, and learn to act therapeutically (Daicoff, 1999). Further, it suggests that nonlawyers may be best suited to teach attorneys these important interpersonal and psychological skills (Daicoff, 1998). Finally, research suggesting a link between psychological distress among lawyers and the atypical traits of an ethic of care (Weissman, 1994) and a Feeling preference (Richard, 1994) further underscores the importance of TJ practice for those in the legal profession with these humanistic traits (Daicoff, 1999).

The Role of Psychologists in TJ Practice

Certainly lawyers are neither well-suited nor trained to practice psychology. Therefore, to practice therapeutic jurisprudence effectively, most lawyers rely on the research, insights, and skills of psychologists and other mental health professionals. Psychologists may have several roles in the practice of therapeutic jurisprudence. First, lawyers need social science research and knowledge to learn more about the psychological concerns that may be involved in the legal problems that their clients present. Second, lawyers may need psychologists to function as consultants in various cases to assist the lawyer in identifying the therapeutic and nontherapeutic aspects of various legal outcomes and processes, to identify psycholegal soft spots, and to assess the psychological impact of various strategies. Third, lawyers and psychologists may form a collaborative team to assist the client as legal representation proceeds. Some lawyers routinely refer their clients to psychologists for therapy as an adjunct to legal representation, particularly in divorce and substance-abuse-related criminal cases. However, this is done simply as a referral or suggestion; whether or not to enter therapy and the choice of therapists remain the client's decision. In sum, psychologists should have a greater level of involvement in TJ-managed cases, as compared to more traditional approaches to legal representation.

If the interdisciplinary team approach is taken in a case, it may be beneficial to ask the client to execute limited waivers of confidentiality for the lawyer and psychologist. This allows the lawyer and psychologist to collaborate and agree on the most appropriate (i.e., therapeutic) legal actions to take in the client's case. The client may or may not be involved in all of these team discussions; however, the ultimate decisions as to what legal actions to take belong to the client.

THERAPEUTIC JURISPRUDENCE AND RELATED PERSPECTIVES

TJ is one of the largest and most important parts of an emerging trend toward a more humanistic or therapeutic form of law. This trend, or movement, is evident in legal scholarship, in judges seeking more satisfactory outcomes for adjudicated cases, in practicing lawyers seeking more effective ways to serve clients, in police forces, in social scientists' work, and in legal education (Daicoff, 2000). Examples of this movement are found in the United States, Canada, the United Kingdom, Australia, New Zealand, Austria, and in a variety of legal areas, including corporate law, estate planning, AIDS law, criminal law, juvenile justice, domestic violence, drug and alcohol offenses, divorce law, medical malpractice, constitutional law, appellate practice, police practices, tort law, employment law, and mental health law.

This approach has garnered various names, including therapeutic jurisprudence, creative problem solving (Barton, 1998; Cooper, 1998), "theralaw" (Stempel, 1999, p. 853), holistic justice, and the "comprehensive law movement" (Daicoff, 2000, p. 467). Despite different names for this broad movement toward law as a healing or helping profession, the concept is the same. It consists of a family of related approaches, including therapeutic jurisprudence, preventive law, therapeutically oriented preventive law (Stolle et al., 1997), restorative justice (Umbreit, 1988), specialized "problem solving" (TJ) courts (e.g., drug treatment courts [Hora et al., 1999], domestic violence courts [Fritzler & Simon, 2000a], and mental health courts), creative problem solving (Barton, 1998; Cooper, 1998), collaborative (divorce) law (Tesler, 1999a), holistic justice (Katz, 2000), procedural justice (Tyler, 1992), transformative mediation (Bush & Folger, 1994), law and socioeconomics (Harrison, 1999), and affective lawyering (Mills, 2000). In lectures, Winick has suggested that the subdisciplines of the movement are as alike as the members of a large family and yet are as distinctive and individual as brothers, sisters, fathers, mothers, aunts, uncles, grandparents, and cousins. Certainly, the subdisciplines qualitatively differ. Specifically, some of the subdisciplines are broad, philosophical approaches to law and lawyering, or "lenses" through which legal tools and processes can be evaluated. Others are tools of the trade, or concrete legal processes that can be used to achieve specific outcomes.

Bridges or links between many of the subdisciplines of the greater movement have formed. For example, the similarities and relationships between TJ and restorative justice; TJ and preventive law; TJ and collaborative law; creative problem solving and preventive law; TJ and specialized courts; and TJ, restorative justice, and preventive law are well-known (Daicoff, 2000; Fritzler & Simon, 2000a; Scheff, 1998; Schopp, 1998; Stolle et al., 1997). Notably perhaps, TJ appears to be a unifying discipline, facilitating the collaboration and synthesis of the subdisciplines of the movement.

The subdisciplines intersect at two points. First, all of these developments seek to improve, restore, or maintain the psychological or mental well-being of the individuals involved, while solving the legal problem at hand. Each explicitly focuses on the emotional, psychological, or mental consequences of various legal actions on people, relationships, and communities. For example, restorative justice principles focus on the emotional needs of the individuals involved in domestic violence. It recommends that victims have input into the legal proceedings, that the state restore victims to their former condition through compensation and economic and social support, and that victims receive varied support to become independent. To improve offenders' well-being, restorative justice proposes that offenders be held accountable, required to make amends, required to participate in rehabilitation programs, and reintegrated into the community. Finally, restorative justice involves and relies on the community in assisting the victim, the offender, and their family through the process of solving the problem (Fritzler & Simon, 2000a).

Second, all of these approaches explicitly consider concerns in addition to the parties' strict legal rights and entitlements. In informal conversation, Tesler has called this characteristic a "rights plus" approach. Relevant extralegal concerns include the parties' emotional states, resources, needs, strengths, weaknesses, values, beliefs, morals, relationships, and priorities. These may not override the parties' legal rights, but they are included in the analysis of the legal problem.

Because of this extralegal focus and therapeutic goal, these approaches are frequently collaborative, nonadversarial, and nongladiatorial. Interactions between judges, lawyers, and nonlawyers are also often less hierarchical and reflect a more equal division of power. For example, the lawyer and client are more likely to work as equal partners together toward a mutually agreed-upon outcome. The attorney or judge is less likely to act as an ultimate adjudicator or detached, authoritative professional with greater power, wisdom, status, and knowledge than the client. However, where aggressive litigation is appropriate, such as in domestic violence cases where the abuser is intractable, most of these approaches would continue to employ a traditional, adversarial stance.

The breadth of and popular interest in this burgeoning movement are growing. It remains to be seen whether therapeutic jurisprudence will become the overarching, "umbrella" theory for the broader movement, but it is certainly poised at its epicenter. As the movement coalesces and gains visibility, TJ will continue to be one of its elder statesmen. In large part thanks to therapeutic jurisprudence, the twenty-first century promises to be an exciting, dynamic, and transformative time for law, lawyering, judging, and the legal profession in general.

REFERENCES

Abrams, R. I., Abrams, F. E., & Nolan, D. R. (1994). Arbitral therapy. *Rutgers Law Review, 46,* 1751–1785.

Allan, A., & Allan, M. (2000). The South African truth and reconciliation commission as a therapeutic tool. *Behavioral Sciences and the Law, 18,* 459–478.

Anderer, S. J., & Glass, D. J. (2000). A therapeutic jurisprudence and preventive law approach to family law. In D. P. Stolle, D. B. Wexler, & B. J. Winick (Eds.), *Practicing therapeutic jurisprudence: Law as a helping profession* (pp. 207–234). Durham, NC: Carolina Academic Press.

Armstrong, M. W. (1999, July). Therapeutic justice: An interdisciplinary approach to family law cases. *Maricopa Lawyer, 1,* 3.

Babb, B. (1997). An interdisciplinary approach to family law jurisprudence: Application of an ecological and therapeutic perspective. *Indiana Law Journal, 72,* 775–808.

Babb, B. (1998). Fashioning an interdisciplinary framework for court reform in family law: A blueprint to construct a unified family court. *Southern California Law Review, 71,* 469–528.

Barnum, R., & Grisso, T. (1994). Competence to stand trial in juvenile court in Massachusetts: Issues of therapeutic jurisprudence. *New England Journal on Criminal and Civil Confinement, 20,* 321–344.

Barton, T. D. (1998). Creative problem solving: Purpose, meaning and values. *California Western Law Review, 34,* 273–296.

Behnke, S. H., & Saks, E. R. (1998). Therapeutic jurisprudence: Informed consent as a clinical indication for the chronically suicidal patient with borderline personality disorder. *Loyola Los Angeles Law Review, 31,* 945–982.

Birgden, A., & Vincent, F. (2000). Maximizing therapeutic effects in training sexual offenders in an Australian correctional system. *Behavioral Sciences and the Law, 18,* 479–488.

Brooks, S. L. (1999). Therapeutic jurisprudence and preventive law in child welfare proceedings: A family systems approach. *Psychology, Public Policy, and Law, 5,* 951–966.

Bryan, P. E. (1999). Collaborative divorce: Meaningful reform or another quick fix? *Psychology, Public Policy, and Law, 5,* 1001–1017.

Bush, R. A. B., & Folger, J. P. (1994). *The promise of mediation.* San Francisco: Jossey-Bass.

Carson, D. (1995). Therapeutic jurisprudence for the United Kingdom? *Journal of Forensic Psychiatry, 6,* 463.

Carson, D., & Wexler, D. B. (1994). New approaches to mental health law: Will the U.K. follow the U.S. lead, again? *Journal of Social Welfare and Family Law, 1,* 79–96.

Chase, D. J., & Hora, P. F. (2000). The implications of therapeutic jurisprudence for judicial satisfaction. *Court Review, 37,* 12–20.

Cooper, J. M. (1998). Towards a new architecture: Creative problem solving and the evolution of law. *California Western Law Review, 34,* 297–323.

Daicoff, S. (1997). Lawyer, know thyself: A review of empirical research on attorney attributes bearing on professionalism. *American University Law Review, 46,* 1337–1427.

Daicoff, S. (1998). Asking leopards to change their spots: Should lawyers change? A critique of solutions to problems with professionalism by reference to empirically-derived attorney personality attributes. *Georgetown Journal of Legal Ethics, 11,* 547–595.

Daicoff, S. (1999). Making law therapeutic for lawyers: Therapeutic jurisprudence, preventive law, and the psychology of lawyers. *Psychology, Public Policy, and Law, 5,* 811–848.

Daicoff, S. (2000). Afterword: The role of therapeutic jurisprudence within the comprehensive law movement I. In D. P. Stolle, D. B. Wexler, & B. J. Winick (Eds.), *Practicing therapeutic jurisprudence: Law as a helping profession* (pp. 465–492). Durham, NC: Carolina Academic Press.

Daly-Rooney, R. (1994). Designing reasonable accommodations through co-worker participation: Therapeutic jurisprudence and the confidentiality provision of the Americans with Disabilities Act. *Journal of Law and Health, 8,* 89–104.

Des Rosiers, N. (2000). From telling to listening: A therapeutic analysis of the role of courts in minority-majority conflicts. *Court Review, 37,* 54–62.

Dorfman, D. A. (1993–1994). Effectively implementing Title I of the Americans with Disabilities Act for mentally disabled persons: A therapeutic jurisprudence analysis. *Journal of Law and Health, 8,* 105–121.

Elwork, A., & Benjamin, G. A. H. (1995). Lawyers in distress. *Journal of Psychology and Law, 23,* 205–229.

Feldthusen, B. (1993). The civil action for sexual battery: Therapeutic jurisprudence? *Ottawa Law Review, 25,* 205–234.

Ferencz, N., & McGuire, J. (2000). Mental health review tribunals in the U.K.: Applying a therapeutic jurisprudence perspective. *Court Review, 37,* 48–52.

Fritzler, R. B., & Simon, L. M. J. (2000a). Creating a domestic violence court: Combat in the trenches. *Court Review, 37,* 28–39.

Fritzler, R. B., & Simon, L. M. J. (2000b). Principles of an effective domestic violence court. *Court Review, 37,* 31.

Gilligan, C. (1982). *In a different voice: Psychological theory and women's development.* Cambridge, MA: Harvard University Press.

Gould, K. A. (1993). Turning rat and doing time for uncharged, dismissed, or acquitted crimes: Do the federal sentencing guidelines promote respect for the law? *New York Law School Journal of Human Rights, 10,* 835–875.

Gould, K. A. (1998). If it's a duck and dangerous–permanently clip its wings or treat it till it can fly? A therapeutic perspective on difficult decisions, short-sighted solutions and violent sexual predators after *Kansas v. Hendricks. Loyola Los Angeles Law Review, 31,* 859–882.

Hardaway, R. M. (1997). *Preventive law: Materials on a nonadversarial legal process.* Cincinnati, OH: Anderson Publishing Company.

Harrison, J. L. (1994). Class, personality, contract, and unconscionability. *William and Mary Law Review, 35,* 445–501.

Harrison, J. L. (1999). Law and socioeconomics. *Journal of Legal Education, 49,* 224–236.

Hora, P. F., & Schma, W. G. (1998). Drug treatment courts: Therapeutic jurisprudence in practice. *Judicature, 82,* 9–12.

Hora, P. F., Schma, W. G., & Rosenthal, J. T. A. (1999). Therapeutic jurisprudence and the drug treatment court movement: Revolutionizing the criminal justice system's response to drug abuse and crime in America. *Notre Dame Law Review, 74,* 439–540.

Jack, R., & Jack, D. C. (1989). *Moral vision and professional decisions.* Cambridge England: Cambridge University Press.

Janoff, S. (1991). The influence of legal education on moral reasoning. *Minnesota Law Review, 76,* 193–238.

Kaden, J. (1998). Therapy for convicted sex offenders: Pursuing rehabilitation without incrimination. *Journal of Criminal Law and Criminology, 89,* 347–391.

Katz, B. E. (2000). Putting the counsel back in counselor. *Student Lawyer, 28,* 32–36.

Kavanagh, K. (1995). Don't ask, don't tell: Deception required, disclosure denied. *Psychology, Public Policy, and Law, 1,* 142–160.

Keeva, S. (1999). Does the law mean never having to say you're sorry? *American Bar Association Journal, 85,* 64–68, 95.

Kelly, J. B. (1990). Is mediation less expensive? Comparison of mediated and adversarial divorce costs. *Mediation Quarterly, 8,* 15–26.

Kjervik, D. (1999). Therapeutic jurisprudence and nursing law. *Journal of Nursing Law, 6,* 5.

Klotz, J. A. (1996). Sex offenders and the law: New directions. In B. D. Sales & S. A. Shah (Eds.), *Mental health and law: Research, policy, and services* (pp. 257–282). Durham, NC: Carolina Academic Press.

Klotz, J. A., Wexler, D. B., Sales, B. D., & Becker, J. V. (1992). Cognitive restructuring through law: A therapeutic jurisprudence approach to sex offenders and the plea process. *University of Puget Sound Law Review, 15,* 579–595.

Korobkin, R., & Guthrie, C. (1997). Psychology, economics, and settlement: A new look at the role of the lawyer. *Texas Law Review, 76,* 77–141.

Kress, K. (1999). Therapeutic jurisprudence and the resolution of value conflicts: What we can realistically expect, in practice, from theory. *Behavioral Sciences and the Law, 17,* 555–588.

Levine, M. (1993). A therapeutic jurisprudence analysis of mandated reporting of child maltreatment by psychotherapists. *New York Law School Journal of Human Rights, 10,* 711–738. (Reprinted in *Law in a therapeutic key,* pp. 323–341 by D. B. Wexler & B. J. Winick, Eds., 1996, Durham, NC: Carolina Academic Press.)

Levine, M. (2000). The family group conference in the New Zealand Children, Young Persons and Their Families Act of 1989 (CYP&F): Review and evaluation. *Behavioral Sciences and the Law, 18,* 517–556.

Lippel, K. (1999). Therapeutic and anti-therapeutic consequences of workers compensation. *International Journal of Law and Psychiatry, 22,* 521–546.

Magner, E. S. (1998). Therapeutic jurisprudence: Its potential in Australia. *Revista Juridica Universidad de Puerto Rico, 67,* 119–133.

Maxwell, K. E. (1998). Preventive lawyering strategies to mitigate the detrimental effects of client's divorces on their children. *Revista Juridica Universidad de Puerto Rico, 67,* 135–162.

McGuire, J. (1995). *What works: Reducing reoffending.* Chicester, England: Wiley.

Meichenbaum, D., & Turk, D. C. (1987). *Facilitating treatment adherence: A practitioner's guidebook.* New York: Plenum Press.

Merrigan, T. T. (2000). Law in a therapeutic key: A resource for judges [Book review]. *Court Review, 37,* 8–10.

Mills, L. G. (2000). Affective lawyering: The emotional dimensions of the lawyer-client relation. In D. P. Stolle, D. B. Wexler, & B. J. Winick (Eds.), *Practicing therapeutic jurisprudence: Law as a helping profession* (pp. 419–446). Durham, NC: Carolina Academic Press.

Natter, F. L. (1981). The human factor: Psychological type in legal education. *Research on Psychological Type, 3,* 55–67.

Othmer, E. (1994). *The clinical interview using DSM-IV.* Washington, DC: American Psychiatric Press.

Paradine, K. (2000). The importance of understanding love and other feelings in survivors' experiences of domestic violence. *Court Review, 37,* 40–47.

Patry, M. W., Wexler, D. B., Stolle, D. P., & Tomkins, A. J. (1998). Better legal counseling through empirical research. *California Western Law Review, 34,* 439–455.

Perlin, M. L. (1993–1994). The ADA and persons with mental disabilities: Can sanest attitudes be undone? *Journal of Law and Health, 8,* 15–45.

Perlin, M. L. (1996). The insanity defense: Deconstructing the myths and reconstructing the jurisprudence. In B. D. Sales & D. W. Shuman (Eds.), *Law, mental health and mental disorder* (pp. 341–359). Pacific Grove: Brooks/Cole.

Ramirez, J. D. (1998). Inauguration therapeutic jurisprudence forum of the international network on therapeutic jurisprudence. *Revista Juridica Universidad de Puerto Rico, 67,* 95–96.

Richard, L. R. (1993). How your personality affects your practice: The lawyer types. *American Bar Association Journal, 79,* 74–78.

Richard, L. R. (1994). *Psychological type and job satisfaction among practicing lawyers in the United States.* Unpublished doctoral dissertation, Temple University, Philadelphia.

Robbennolt, J. K., & Johnson, M. K. (1999). Legal planning for unmarried committed partners: Empirical lessons for a preventive and therapeutic approach. *Arizona Law Review, 41–2,* 417–457.

Rottman, D. (2000). Does effective therapeutic jurisprudence require specialized courts (and do specialized courts imply specialist judges? *Court Review, 37,* 22–27.

Scheff, T. J. (1998). Response to comments. *Revista Juridica Universidad de Puerto Rico, 67,* 677–683.

Schma, W. G. (2000). Special issue overview: Judging for the new millennium. *Court Review, 37,* 4–6.

Schneider, A. K. (2000). Building a pedagogy of problem-solving: Learning to choose among ADR processes. *Harvard Negotiation Law Review, 5,* 113–135.

Schopp, R. F. (1995). Sexual predators and the structure of the mental health system: Expanding the normative focus of therapeutic jurisprudence. *Psychology, Public Policy, and Law, 1,* 161–192.

Schopp, R. F. (1998). Integrating restorative justice and therapeutic jurisprudence. *Revista Juridica Universidad de Puerto Rico, 67,* 665–669.

Schopp, R. F. (1999). Therapeutic jurisprudence: Integrated inquiry and instrumental prescriptions. *Behavioral Sciences and the Law, 17,* 589–605.

Shiff, A. R., & Wexler, D. B. (1996). Teen court: A therapeutic jurisprudence perspective. *Criminal Law Bulletin, 32,* 342–357.

Shuman, D. W. (1992). Therapeutic jurisprudence and tort law: A limited subjective standard of care. *Southern Methodist Law Review, 46,* 409–432.

Shuman, D. W. (1993). The duty of the state to rescue the vulnerable in the United States. In M. A. Menlowe & A. M. Smith (Eds.), *The duty to rescue: The jurisprudence of aid* (pp. 131–158). Aldershot, Hantz, England: Dartmouth.

Shuman, D. W. (1994). The psychology of compensation in tort law. *University of Kansas Law Review, 43,* 39–77.

Shuman, D. W. (2000). The role of apology in tort law. *Judicature, 83,* 180–189.

Silver, M. A. (1999). Love, hate, and other emotional interference in the lawyer/client relationship. In D. P. Stolle, D. B. Wexler, & B. J. Winick (Eds.), *Practicing therapeutic jurisprudence: Law as a helping profession* (pp. 357–417). Durham, NC: Carolina Academic Press.

Simon, L. M. J. (1995). A therapeutic jurisprudence approach to the legal processing of domestic violence cases. *Psychology, Public Policy, and Law, 1,* 43–79.

Slobogin, C. (1995). Therapeutic jurisprudence: Five dilemmas to ponder. *Psychology, Public Policy, and Law, 1,* 193–219. (Reprinted in *Law in a therapeutic key,* pp. 763–793 by D. B. Wexler & B. J. Winick, Eds., 1996, Durham, NC: Carolina Academic Press)

Stempel, J. W. (1999). Theralaw and the law-business paradigm debate. *Psychology, Public Policy, and Law, 5,* 849–908.

Stolle, D. P. (1996). Professional responsibility in elder law: A synthesis of preventive law and therapeutic jurisprudence. *Behavioral Sciences and the Law, 15,* 459–478.

Stolle, D. P. (1997). Preventive law and therapeutic jurisprudence: A symbiotic relationship. *Preventive Law Reporter, 16,* 4–7.

Stolle, D. P. (2000). Introduction. In D. P. Stolle, D. B. Wexler, & B. J. Winick (Eds.), *Practicing therapeutic jurisprudence: Law as a helping profession* (pp. xv–xvii). Durham, NC: Carolina Academic Press.

Stolle, D. P., & Wexler, D. B. (1997). Therapeutic jurisprudence and preventive law: A combined concentration to invigorate the everyday practice of law. *Arizona Law Review, 39,* 25–33.

Stolle, D. P., Wexler, D. B., & Winick, B. J. (Eds.). (2000). *Practicing therapeutic jurisprudence: Law as a helping profession.* Durham, NC: Carolina Academic Press.

Stolle, D. P., Wexler, D. B., Winick, B. J., & Dauer, E. A. (1997). Integrating preventive law and therapeutic jurisprudence: A law

and psychology based approach to lawyering. *California West Law Review, 34*(1), 15–51. (Reprinted in *Practicing therapeutic jurisprudence: Law as a helping profession,* pp. 5–44 by D. P. Stolle, D. B. Wexler, & B. J. Winick, Eds., 2000, Durham, NC: Carolina Academic Press.)

Tesler, P. H. (1999a). Collaborative law: A new paradigm for divorce lawyers. *Psychology, Public Policy, and Law, 5,* 967–1000.

Tesler, P. H. (1999b). Collaborative law: What it is and why lawyers need to know about it. *American Journal of Family Law, 13,* 215–225. In D. P. Stolle, D. B. Wexler, & B. J. Winick (Eds.), *Practicing therapeutic jurisprudence: Law as a helping profession* (pp. 187–205). Durham, NC: Carolina Academic Press.

Tesler, P. H. (1999c). The believing game, the doubting game, and collaborative law: A reply to Penelope Bryan. *Psychology, Public Policy, and Law, 5,* 1018–1027.

Tomb, D. (1995). *Psychiatry* (5th ed.). Baltimore: Wilkins & Wilkins.

Tyler, T. R. (1992). The psychological consequences of judicial procedures: Implications for civil commitment hearings. *Southern Methodist University Law Review, 46,* 433–445. (Reprinted in *Law in a therapeutic key,* pp. 3–15 by D. B. Wexler & B. J. Winick, Eds., 1996, Durham, NC: Carolina Academic Press.)

Umbreit, M. S. (1988). Mediation of victim/offender conflict. *Missouri Journal of Dispute Resolution, 31,* 85–105.

Weissman, E. S. (1994). *Gender-role issues in attorney career satisfaction.* Unpublished doctoral dissertation, Yeshiva University, New York.

Wexler, D. B. (1993). Therapeutic jurisprudence and the criminal courts. *William and Mary Law Review, 35,* 279–299. (Reprinted in *Law in a therapeutic key,* pp. 157–170 by D. B. Wexler & B. J. Winick, Eds., 1996, Durham, NC: Carolina Academic Press.)

Wexler, D. B. (1996). Applying the law therapeutically. *Applied and Preventive Psychology, 4,* 179–187.

Wexler, D. B. (1999a). The development of therapeutic jurisprudence: From theory to practice. *Revista Juridica Universidad de Puerto Rico, 68,* 691–705.

Wexler, D. B. (1999b). Relapse prevention planning principles for criminal law practice. *Psychology, Public Policy, and Law, 5,* 1028–1033.

Wexler, D. B. (1999c). Therapeutic jurisprudence and the culture of critique. *Journal of Contemporary Legal Issues, 10,* 263–271. (Reprinted in *Practicing therapeutic jurisprudence: Law as a helping profession,* pp. 449–464 by D. P. Stolle, D. B. Wexler, & B. J. Winick, Eds., 2000, Durham, NC: Carolina Academic Press.)

Wexler, D. B. (2000). *Lowering the volume through legal doctrine: A promising path for therapeutic jurisprudence scholarship.* Unpublished manuscript. University of Arizona, Tucson, AZ.

Wexler, D. B., & Winick, B. J. (Eds.). (1996). *Law in a therapeutic key.* Durham, NC: Carolina Academic Press.

Wiebe, R. P. (1996). The mental health implications of crime victims' rights. In B. D. Sales & D. W. Shuman (Eds.), *Law, mental health, and mental disorders* (pp. 414–438). Pacific Grove, CA: Brooks/Cole.

Winick, B. J. (1995). The side effects of incompetency labeling and the implications for mental health law. *Psychology, Public Policy, and Law, 1,* 6–42. (Reprinted in *Law in a therapeutic key,* pp. 17–58 by D. B. Wexler & B. J. Winick, Eds., 1996, Durham, NC: Carolina Academic Press.)

Winick, B. J. (1996). *The right to refuse mental health treatment.* Washington, DC: American Psychological Association.

Winick, B. J. (1998). Client denial and resistance in the advance directive context: Reflections on how attorneys can identify and deal with a psycho-legal soft spot. *Psychology, Public Policy, and Law, 4,* 901–923. (Reprinted in *Practicing therapeutic jurisprudence: Law as a helping profession,* pp. 327–355 by D. P. Stolle, D. B. Wexler, & B. J. Winick, Eds., 2000, Durham, NC: Carolina Academic Press.)

Winick, B. J. (1999). Redefining the role of the criminal defense lawyer at plea bargaining and sentencing: A therapeutic jurisprudence/preventive law model. *Psychology, Public Policy and Law,* 5. (Reprinted in *Practicing therapeutic jurisprudence: Law as a helping profession,* pp. 245–305 by D. P. Stolle, D. B. Wexler, & B. J. Winick, Eds., 2000, Durham, NC: Carolina Academic Press.)

Winick, B. J. (2000). Therapeutic Jurisprudence and the Role of Counsel in Litigation. *California Western Law Review,* 37. (Reprinted in *Practicing therapeutic jurisprudence: Law as a helping profession,* pp. 309–324 by D. P. Stolle, D. B. Wexler, & B. J. Winick, Eds., 2000, Durham, NC: Carolina Academic Press.)

Author Index

Subject Index